Richard Cook's Jazz Encyclopedia

# Richard Cook's Jazz Encyclopedia

## Richard Cook

PENGUIN BOOKS

PENGUIN BOOKS

Published by the Penguin Group
Penguin Books Ltd, 80 Strand, London WC2R 0RL, England
Penguin Group (USA) Inc., 375 Hudson Street, New York, New York 10014, USA
Penguin Group (Canada), 90 Eglinton Avenue East, Suite 700, Toronto, Ontario, Canada M4P 2Y3
(a division of Pearson Penguin Canada Inc.)
Penguin Ireland, 25 St Stephen's Green, Dublin 2, Ireland (a division of Penguin Books Ltd)
Penguin Group (Australia), 250 Camberwell Road, Camberwell, Victoria 3124, Australia
(a division of Pearson Australia Group Pty Ltd)
Penguin Books India Pvt Ltd, 11 Community Centre, Panchsheel Park, New Delhi – 110 017, India
Penguin Group (NZ), cnr Airborne and Rosedale Roads, Albany, Auckland 1310, New Zealand
(a division of Pearson New Zealand Ltd)
Penguin Books (South Africa) (Pty) Ltd, 24 Sturdee Avenue, Rosebank 2196, South Africa

Penguin Books Ltd, Registered Offices: 80 Strand, London WC2R 0RL, England

www.penguin.com

First published 2005
1

Set in TheAntiqua and TheSans
Typeset by Rowland Phototypesetting Ltd, Bury St Edmunds, Suffolk
Printed in England by Clays Ltd, St Ives plc

For Lee Ellen
with love

# Contents

# Illustrations

# Introduction

Considering that, for a large part of its existence, jazz was the popular music of choice in Western society, it's surprising what a complicated, obscure and often plain bewildering matter it is. Like most British people under 50, I grew up with the sounds of pop ringing helplessly in my ears, and while there was some jazz mixed in with it – my cousin had a 45 by The Temperance Seven early on – it was hardly a pressing part of the culture by the middle 60s. I had to make my own way into the music, and it was a long and difficult journey. Because I started collecting records from an early age, going to jumble sales looking for 78s, I inevitably began finding discs by musicians such as Jelly Roll Morton, whose 'Dr Jazz Stomp' was one of my early favourites, and from there I embarked on a precipitous voyage of discovery. In my early teens, I didn't know anyone else who liked jazz, and I didn't know how to find out about it. The few accessible books on the subject seemed to talk in code, fascinating though it was. There was no jazz on television that I could find, and not much on the radio, although I thank Humphrey Lyttelton, Charles Fox, Brian Priestley, Peter Clayton and Steve Race for their efforts. I couldn't really understand how what Morton played had somehow turned into what musicians such as Albert Ayler were playing.

Many years later, that progression seems straightforward enough to me now. But it's not hard to understand how most find jazz a very awkward conundrum. The evangelist in me feels infuriated when I hear someone saying, if only facetiously, 'Why can't they play the tune?' The pragmatist just smiles and shrugs. Most of us just want to be entertained by music. But jazz *is* entertaining, whether it's Louis Armstrong scatting his way through 'Heebie Jeebies' or Charlie Parker hurtling around the curves of 'Ornithology'. As listeners, we can linger over Billie Holiday's mythopoeic pain or be drenched by Cecil Taylor's marathon improvisations, but they are just a small part of what is a jostling and superbly crowded idiom. Whether one is in search of timeless, immortal art or the high spirits of a musician simply having fun, jazz has it both ways. I might even suggest that it is unrivalled at delivering both of those extremes within the same piece of music.

Making sense of it all is a challenge for any listener, no doubt of that. Like the grand history of Western classical music, jazz has its own genealogies, and its onward march can be studied by any willing student. But one curiosity of the music is the way its various stylistic schools have all remained current, at least since earlier approaches began to be 'revived' in the 40s: jazz is as subject to the whims of fashion as any other kind of music, yet if you live in a major city, it won't be hard to find musicians playing in the style of traditional or swing or bebop or free jazz somewhere on the same evening. Once upon a time, these various styles created warring factions of fans, but today the jazz audience is much more of a United Nations. Since the music has, since the end of the big-band era at least, prospered far away from mass audiences, there is an unspoken bond within the jazz listenership which has always tended to foster an us-and-them feeling. We treasure our elitism, while grumbling about jazz's marginalization within an increasingly unsophisticated culture.

But if you want to join in the fun, all you really need is a sympathetic pair of ears. Many popular jazz musicians – such as Louis Armstrong, Ella Fitzgerald, David Sanborn, Billie Holiday, Herbie Hancock, George Benson – aren't even regarded as 'jazz' by many of their admirers. There's no point in pretending that jazz is simple and undemanding: it isn't. Absorbing the music of Parker or Taylor can be the greatest challenge a listener can set him- or herself. But, to return to the top of the page, jazz was, during the swing era at least, a music admired and danced to and listened to by an audience in the tens of millions. The principles which fired that music – for more detail, you might like to turn to the entry on 'Jazz', under the letter J – remain good for everything which came before it, and most of what has come after. Jazz spread around the world very quickly – there are recordings from almost every territory on earth which was able to make records and which, by the 30s and 40s at least, showed some trace of jazz in their popular music – and its stature as an international musical practice continues to evolve. American players far from home often had the complaint that, away from the US, they couldn't find a swinging rhythm section to work with; but that old sore has been largely healed. I won't perpetrate the familiar nonsense about music being a 'universal language', but, as a musical procedure at least, jazz is more universal than most.

The convenience of an A to Z format doesn't hurt in the task of trying to sift through something which has a cast of thousands and far, far more foot soldiers than generals. An enduring fascination of this music is the way it can accommodate so many individuals, even within relatively strict parameters (another clichéd idea, that jazz is mainly about 'breaking down barriers', is a further nonsense. If it were, all the barriers would have disappeared long ago). Jazz has a modest genius count: you might like to use the fingers of each hand to count them, but that's probably as many as you'll need. That doesn't prevent every instrument in every style from throwing up musicians who can be identified with just a few bars of their playing. Perhaps the classical aficionado can pass a blindfold test and spot different interpreters of Beethoven's *Appassionata*. They surely cannot have the jazz fan's legerdemain in hearing and enjoying the dramatic differences between Earl Hines, Hampton Hawes, André Previn, Tommy Flanagan, Willie 'The Lion' Smith, Diana Krall and Oscar Peterson, all of whom recorded piano versions of 'Between The Devil And The Deep Blue Sea', and all of whom (well, Previn might give a few problems, and Diana sings too, so that's a slight cheat) are easily identified.

This book celebrates as many of these players as I felt it was sensible to include. Inevitably, some will ask why X was included

when Y is absent. It is entirely my choice, and I am sure there have been unfair and neglectful omissions. American musicians necessarily dominate, and since I have grown up in the environment of British jazz, there are probably more UK musicians included than are justified by their overall eminence. There should probably be more from Italy, France, Australia, Denmark and other jazz-loving countries with healthy communities of players. But I drew the line where I did, and there it is for now. It is, perhaps, the individuality discussed above which has largely been the deciding factor in including a musician or not.

Which is not to say that every musician herein receives unstinting praise. I've attempted to be as honest as I can in writing each entry. Jazz writers are often (despite what some musicians think) afraid to be critical, because of a saintly belief that the benighted jazz player has it so tough that words of dissent are somehow dishonourable. This ignores the point that a jazz writer's first responsibility is to the jazz *audience* – the people who buy CDs and pay for concert tickets – rather than jazz musicians. To read some reference works on the music, you'd think that jazz is stuffed with godlike figures who never played a bad gig or made a dull record in their lives. I've done my level best to avoid both that starting point, and what I would call the one-of-the-finest school of jazz writing. This is where so-and-so is 'one of the finest bassists/trumpeters/bandleaders/composers in Britain/the world/Dixieland/jazz' (delete as applicable), and can recur so frequently that the reader starts wondering just who *isn't* one-of-the-finest. Whoever they are, good for them: jazz is and should be full of vulnerable, inconsistent and unpredictable human beings, and that's another thing that makes it fascinating.

Along with the artist entries are those which cover musical terminology, jazz jargon, venues, festivals, writers, record labels, and whatever other matters seemed appropriate in an A to Z of jazz. I've often discussed a musician's career on record, because jazz has been documented by gramophone recordings for almost its entire history, to an amazingly comprehensive degree, and we can only guess at the abilities of those musicians who, through their own choice or the intercession of fate, chose not to make records. Most of the artist entries conclude with the listing of a single CD (in a few rare instances, a vinyl LP) which seems to me to be especially characteristic of the artist in question – although that doesn't necessarily mean it's either their very finest work or, in some cases, even a good record. If you wish for more information, I would point you in the direction of the rather useful *Penguin Guide To Jazz On CD*.

I've tried to avoid making the artist entries slavishly biographical, since such an approach is rarely fun to read: if you must know exactly who played with whom and for how long, consult *The New Grove Dictionary Of Jazz*, a peerless factual resource which I am happy to acknowledge. Instead, I've attempted either a lightning sketch or a more detailed and considered portrait. At the same time, please excuse me if there are any errors of fact.

Finally, I hope that the contents herein will also raise an occasional smile as well as offering some measure of enlightenment. For a music which is so full of laughter and sheer joy, it's surprising how so many jazz reference works aspire to being solemn, worthy and unswinging.

R D Cook

# Acknowledgements

As with recordings, it's surprising how extensively jazz has been documented in book form via commentaries, biographies and histories. Necessarily, I can only mention a few particularly valuable resources. *The New Grove Dictionary Of Jazz* (Grove, ed Barry Kernfeld) is these days probably every jazz scholar's first port of call in checking a fact or a date of birth. *The Rough Guide To Jazz* (Rough Guides/Penguin, Carr/Fairweather/Priestley) should be acknowledged too. Among many, many other sources, some remembered and some forgotten over decades, I would particularly mention *Preservation Hall* (Cassell, William Carter), *Jazz And Ragtime Records 1897–1942* (Mainspring, Brian Rust), *We Called It Music* (JBC, Eddie Condon), and *Jazz On Record* (Hanover, Harrison/Morgan/Oliver/McCarthy). Jazz magazines such as *Down Beat*, *Jazz Journal International*, *The Wire* and *Jazz Review* all provided material of some sort, and the numerous Q&A interviews published in *Cadence* magazine over many years have offered valuable oral histories.

I always rely on 'good ideas' people. In this case, Penguin's esteemed reference editor Nigel Wilcockson should take the lion's share of the credit for the book coming into being, even though at the last minute he handed over the project to Georgina Laycock (had I originally finished it on time, poor Georgina would have been spared). My agent Anthony Goff doesn't quite believe that I've finished it, either, but he's a good lad. My co-author on *The Penguin Guide To Jazz On CD*, Brian Morton, has given me plenty of bright and constructive ideas in amongst a number of peculiar ones and I thank him for all of them. My friend Guy Barker has offered much insight into how a jazz musician's life really works.

In addition, there are many other people whose verbal input, often unwitting and sometimes unwanted, can claim to have influenced the contents. They would include: Fiona Alexander, Ronald Atkins, Karen Bennett, Chris Bohn, Philip Clark, Jack Cooke, Tony Danaher, Francis Davis, Derek Day, Wendy Day, John Fordham, Garry Giddins, Derek Gorman, Andy Hamilton, Max Harrison, Tony Herrington, Paul Johns, Graham Lock, Alan Luff, Angus Mackinnon, Leonard Newman, Chris Parker, Alan Parsons, Steve Sanderson, Bill Shoemaker, Roger Spence, Becky Stevenson, the late Eric Thacker, Roger Thomas, Liam Toner, Ben Watson, Philip Watson, Eddie Wilkinson and Barry Witherden. My gratitude goes to them, and also to the hundreds of musicians who have given up some of their time to speak to me over the past three decades.

Finally, thanks always to my gracious and understanding wife, to whom this book is dedicated.

RC

# Juhani Aaltonen

SAXOPHONES
*born* 12 December 1935

Born in Kuovala, 'Junnu' Aaltonen is one of the foremost Finnish modernists. He didn't start on the saxophone until he was 18, and although he began associations with Edward Vesala and Heikki Sarmanto in the 60s, he was mostly hidden in studio settings until a featured slot with the Arild Andersen groups of the 70s, which recorded for ECM. He helped found the UMO Jazz Orchestra in 1975, but otherwise had few recording opportunities outside his native scene, and in 1986 he was given a 15-year state grant, although at the same time he became more interested in sacred music. A terse player whose severe tone and plangent delivery let him fit into situations ranging from pastoral modes to harsh free playing, Aaltonen is rather poorly represented on CD, although a recent burst of activity has seen some new material arrive. 'I think like an engineer, yet act according to my own instincts. For me, life is an ongoing school and I am an enigma even to myself.'
**Arild Andersen,** *Green Shading Into Blue* (ECM)

# Ahmed Abdul-Malik

BASS, OUD
*born* 30 January 1927; *died* 2 October 1993

Born plain Sam Gill in New York, Abdul-Malik (he adopted his Muslim name during the 50s) was a solid bass man who worked with several important leaders – Randy Weston and Thelonious Monk among them – from the late 40s onwards. Like Weston, he was interested in the African survivals in American jazz, and attempted a more explicit synthesis between the two currents in his own work on record than even Weston, at least at first. The albums *East Meets West*, *Jazz Sahara* and *Sounds Of Africa* were among the results, and John Coltrane was sufficiently intrigued to engage Abdul-Malik for one of his dates. Frankly, though, the music suggests African and American sources running in parallel rather than intermingling, and the use of oud and other instruments feels more like tacked-on exotica than a genuine fusion. After 1970 Abdul-Malik largely disappeared into music education, but the records have returned on

CD and still hint at stirrings which other hands would make more meaningful.
**Sounds Of Africa** (New Jazz)

# Kaoru Abe

SAXOPHONES, HARMONICA, GUITAR
*born* 3 May 1949; *died* 9 September 1978

Born in Kawasaki, Abe worked primarily on the alto saxophone, although by the time of the music made on the marathon series of *Solo Live At Gaya* sessions in 1977 he had also taken up sopranino sax, harmonica, guitar and piano. He played full-on free jazz with an untutored ferocity and commitment which is still startling. He first recorded in 1970 (a duo with Masayuki Takayanagi) and thereafter worked both by himself and in other groups; there was at least one memorable meeting with Derek Bailey. On his solo records, cold silences are sundered by ear-splitting outbursts on the alto, while he approaches the other instruments as if they've just been invented and he is the first to play them. His death at 29 sent him into legend.
**Solo Live At Gaya** (DIW)

# John Abercrombie

GUITAR
*born* 16 December 1944

Abercrombie played in rock bands while at school and studied at Berklee in the early 60s, but like so many guitarists of his generation his jazz education came in the format of the organ combo, in his case with Johnny 'Hammond' Smith. His first name gig was with the Brecker Brothers in Dreams (1969), but real international attention came with Billy Cobham's Spectrum in 1974, when Abercrombie threatened to become a leading force in fusion. The same year, though, he started making records for Manfred Eicher's ECM, and Eicher encouraged the blossoming of Abercrombie's pastoral side. His early records *Timeless* (1974) and *Gateway* (1975) explored the two sides of the guitarist's art, the latter a power-packed trio with Dave Holland and Jack DeJohnette, the former mollified by such gorgeous originals as 'Timeless', 'Ralph's Piano Waltz' and 'Remembering'. Abercrombie thereafter recorded mostly for ECM in the 70s and early

80s, but he has subsequently turned up elsewhere as a sideman in numerous though carefully chosen situations: with Richie Beirach, Andy LaVerne, Marc Copland, Hein Van de Geyn and others. He tinkered with the guitar synthesizer in the 80s but finally gave it up as miscreant technology and he now prefers a meticulously organized set of effects pedals. His trio with Dan Wall (organ) and Adam Nussbaum (drums) is a beautifully characterized revision of that classic three-way sound, and the Gateway trio has also been occasionally reunited. Though sometimes suggested as a player for all seasons and weathers, Abercrombie is a little more conservative than that: his 'free' playing has more to do with thoughtful impressionism than any sort of rootless searching, and he has bypassed such options as blues licks and Bill Frisell's kind of down-home delivery in favour of a universal lyricism which is just slightly more ornery than mere chamber-jazz. He rarely delivers a record which is less than special, but the fresh beauty of those first ECMs perhaps remains unique.
**Timeless** (ECM)

# Brian Abrahams
DRUMS
*born* 26 June 1947

Born in Cape Town, Abrahams was part of the second wave of South African jazz players who gravitated to London, arriving there in 1975. While he was soon busy as a sideman, it was the formation of his own group, District Six (named after a sector of his home city), which settled his ideas into a proper focus, and the group's live performances were usually exhilarating affairs. On record, though, the group never enjoyed much success, and the albums were poorly produced and failed to capture the spark in the live music. Abrahams subsequently taught and worked with Abdullah Ibrahim, but he has been much less in evidence in recent years.
**To Be Free** (Editions EG)

# Muhal Richard Abrams
PIANO, COMPOSER
*born* 19 September 1930

A panel of judges (including the author) once picked Abrams as the first recipient of an international jazz prize; and they were dismayed when so many at the subsequent press conference asked who Richard Abrams was. A Chicagoan whose work has been based almost entirely around that city's musical community (even though he actually moved to New York as long ago as 1976), Abrams is the paterfamilias to more than one generation of black players. His Experimental Band (1961) was one of the first workshop situations for the budding free-jazz movement, and its evolution into the Association for the Advancement of Creative Musicians (AACM) set the way in which the city's contemporary jazz would run, providing resources and rehearsal and teaching facilities, and building the climate which enabled groups such as Art Ensemble Of Chicago and Air to come into existence. While questioning much received wisdom about jazz and musical performance, Abrams remains something of a classicist, and the tension in his work is a characteristic result of the contrary forces of form and freedom. Early records such as *Levels And Degrees Of Light* (1967) and *Young At Heart/Wise In Time* (1968) have the feel of history in the making about them, with such players as Leo Smith and Henry Threadgill involved, but they are not much listened to now and are largely unknown except to scholars of the period. Abrams hasn't been especially lucky with records, and his sequence of albums for Black Saint in the 80s is extraordinarily hit and miss, fine sets such as *The Hearinga Suite* (1989) mixing with insubstantial failures. He has recorded only occasionally in recent years and seems more interested in large-scale composition for orchestral and chamber groups. If jazz musicians are to be judged by the recordings they leave behind, he will probably not quite get his due.
**One Line, Two Views** (New World)

# Acid jazz

A term probably coined by the British DJ Gilles Peterson, reputedly as a flippant response to a query about the kind of jazz he was listening to at that moment. It then came into use to describe a broad swathe of American black music made between the late 60s and the early 80s, the deciding factor being a rhythmical allegiance to funk rather than jazz, yet with jazz elements – usually a horn section of some sort – stirred in. Unlike acid house or acid rock, hallucinogenic drugs were not necessarily involved. The style was then taken up by such British groups as Raw Stylus, who were attempting to duplicate the style in live performance with a few more contemporary touches grafted on. 'Acid jazz' has also been mistakenly used to denote the entire Jazz Revival movement, spearheaded by club DJs and London players such as Courtney Pine and Steve Williamson in the mid-to-late 80s. It was merely a subtext in that much more expansive milieu. By 2000, the term and the style were both seen as decidedly retro. Even uncool.

## George Adams

TENOR SAXOPHONE, FLUTE
born 29 April 1940; died 14 November 1992

Adams heard plenty of gospel, blues and R&B in his childhood (in Covington, Georgia) and he was working with no less than Sam Cooke as far back as 1961. But he spent most of the 60s as an obscure figure in organ combos and his real breakthrough came with his association with Charles Mingus, starting in 1973 and ending with the bassist's final illness. Subsequently he worked as a leader himself, and the quartet he co-led with pianist Don Pullen was one of the great touring bands of the 80s, even though their records were sometimes disappointing. Gil Evans called on him for many of his orchestral gigs and George took a major role in the staging of Mingus's *Epitaph* in 1989, but his health was already failing. A rumbustious soloist of fierce energy, with a sound that could break into a bluesy, vocalized cry, Adams will be fondly remembered by many gig-goers of the 70s and 80s.
*Live At The Village Vanguard* (Soul Note)

## Pepper Adams

BARITONE SAXOPHONE
born 8 October 1930; died 10 September 1986

After starting on piano and then other saxophones, Park Adams (the 'Pepper' came from his resemblance to baseball star Pepper Martin) switched to baritone, a choice inspired by Harry Carney's example. Based in Detroit, he played extensively with many of the leading black musicians in the city, and after turning pro following his army service in 1953, he remained in that community rather than following many of his contemporaries and seeking commercial studio work. Adams was the one baritone exponent to commit himself entirely to the hard-bop vocabulary, and his signature sound was rough, fast and aggressive (he disliked the sort of timbre represented by both Gerry Mulligan and Serge Chaloff). There were memorable dates as a sideman with Lee Morgan (*The Cooker*) and Charles Mingus (*Blues And Roots*) among countless record sessions, but the albums under his own leadership were comparatively few and unremarkable. There was a group with Donald Byrd that lasted for three years from 1959, and based by now in New York he did a lot of the baritonist's inevitable spacefiller, big-band section-work, eventually holding down a chair in the Thad Jones–Mel Lewis orchestra for many years. Like many of his generation he started visiting Europe as a solo in the 70s. Feisty to the end – lung cancer killed him in 1986 – he was still playing only months before his death, and *Conjuration*, a 1983 live date with an unlikely front-line partner in Kenny Wheeler, made a nice farewell.
*10 To 4 At The Five Spot* (Prestige)

## Julian 'Cannonball' Adderley

ALTO SAXOPHONE
born 15 September 1928; died 8 August 1975

Julian and Nat Adderley enjoyed a comfortable time of it in their home base of Tampa, Florida: the elder brother taught music in schools, sold cars (his gift of the gab later helped him win over audiences too) and enjoyed the lovely climate. But both were eventually persuaded to move North and try their luck in New York, and 'Them Adderleys' (as an early album for Savoy christened them) were soon a club sensation in the city: 'He was the baddest thing we'd ever heard,' Phil Woods later remembered. The Adderleys toured as a quintet before Cannonball joined the Miles Davis group, staying for such key records as *Milestones*

and *Kind Of Blue*. In 1959 he re-formed the quintet with Nat, and the combo became one of the most durable groups in jazz, lasting in one form or another until Cannonball's death from a stroke in 1975. During that time, such musicians as Victor Feldman, Yusef Lateef and Joe Zawinul served time in the ranks, and the superb rhythm team of Sam Jones and Louis Hayes were in the engine room. Cannon led his team with a genial authority, and his bonhomie often led critics to accuse him of shallowness or mere populism: it is more accurate to hear him as a generous musician whose commitment to communicating the universal lessons of bop and the blues has endured, many years after his tragically early death. His swaggering sound and delivery were not so much influential as a personification of many virtues in the music, and his updating of Bird's vocabulary for a world which had expanded to allow entry to Ornette Coleman and Albert Ayler is still entirely plausible. He liked to help younger musicians and he gave every opportunity to the likes of Zawinul, who contributed such catchy pieces as 'Sticks' and 'Mercy Mercy Mercy' to the band's book. The quintet's funky, pressure-cooker style exemplified the new trend in soul-jazz, and they made many records for Riverside and Capitol; unlike many other outfits, though, their music still stands out for its passionate enjoyment of what might have been mere routine in other hands.
*At The Lighthouse* (Riverside)

## Nat Adderley
CORNET
*born* 25 November 1931; *died* 2 January 2000

The younger Adderley spent much of his career in Cannonball's shadow (literally: Nat was a much smaller man), but they were a terrific team, the bursting, bluesy sound of the saxophonist tempered by Nat's more lyrical style. While he started out on trumpet, Nat found that he preferred the less plangent sound of the cornet, and he was never tempted to go back. After Julian left Miles Davis in 1959, the two of them worked together continuously until the saxophonist's death, although Nat led a handful of record dates of his own: *That's Right!* (Riverside, 1960) might be the pick of them,

although nothing he did away from the brothers' group surpassed his work there. He wrote some of the best pieces in the band's book, including the irresistibly catchy 'Work Song' and 'Jive Samba', and after Cannon died Nat began leading groups of his own which followed in much the same footsteps, using alto men such as Sonny Fortune, Antonio Hart and Vincent Herring, all of whom could 'do' Cannon just fine. Nat also toured Europe with the Paris Reunion Band in the 8os. He was still playing at the end of the century, but diabetes was troubling him and he eventually lost a leg to the disease. Like his brother, Nat was an affable man who lived the jazz life and was a loyal friend to his many colleagues.
**Cannonball Adderley Quintet,** *At The Lighthouse* (Riverside)

## Jamey Aebersold
EDUCATOR
*born* 21 July 1939

Aebersold had an unremarkable career as a player, in and around Indiana and Kentucky, but he has become the most influential of all jazz educators. He began a week-long 'jazz camp' in the early 70s, a workshop practice which has since spread to many other countries and is still held on a regular basis. In addition, there are his 'method books' (first produced in 1967), which have expanded into a vast library covering history, theory and jazz styles, and *A New Approach To Jazz Improvisation*, a series of play-along recordings where students can be accompanied by master players (at least on record). Some might say that jazz can't be taught, but Aebersold has done very well out of disproving that idea.

## Ron Affif
GUITAR
*born* 30 December 1965

The son of a Pittsburgh middleweight boxer, Affif says that 'I think of tempos as my father used to think of his punch combinations. Sticking to the same old tempo can get you in trouble after a while.' Nevertheless, he is basically a fast, conservative swing-to-bop guitarist whose debt to George Benson is obvious – although since Benson

is a far less ubiquitous influence than he once was, this is no demeaning thing. He won the attention of Pablo Records in the 90s and made a sequence of strong and likeable records for the label. Since then, he appears to have done little to excite much interest. Unlikely to graduate from the middleweight ranks.
**52nd Street** (Pablo)

## Mervyn Afrika
PIANO
*born* 18 October 1950

Along with Brian Abrahams, Afrika was one of the second-generation South African jazzmen who resettled in London, in 1979. He worked with Julian Bahula and with Abrahams in District Six, and latterly led groups of his own, although with little notable success. It's possible that, with his style so close in timbre to that of Abdullah Ibrahim, Afrika hasn't been able to persuade audiences that there is enough of himself in the music to warrant their attention.
**District Six, Azuzwakale** (D6)

## Air
GROUP

See under HENRY THREADGILL.

## Airshot

A recording made from a broadcasting source, usually a commercial radio station, and subsequently circulated among fans and collectors. Airshots (or airchecks) eventually came to be collected on LPs and commercially issued: huge tracts of music by bands of the swing era have survived this way, as well as precious survivals of the bebop masters. By the 60s, when bootlegging became big business, people were taking their own recording machines to concerts, and the radio became a less essential source.

## Toshiko Akiyoshi
PIANO
*born* 12 December 1929

The pianist's background is a rare one in jazz: born to Japanese parents in Manchuria, she was expelled from the area, with her family, in 1946 and began learning piano in Tokyo. Moonlighting from classical studies in dance bands, she began performing jazz, and was heard by a number of visiting Americans, although she stayed in Japan until winning a Berklee scholarship in 1956. She played in Boston and New York in the late 50s, often in heavy company, and she formed a group with her new husband, Charlie Mariano, in 1959: their sole album for Candid, *Toshiko–Mariano Quartet*, is a collectors' favourite. But she was sighted less often in the 60s, and her marriage broke up in 1967. She subsequently married saxophonist Lew Tabackin, and together they formed what was at first a rehearsal big band: as it gathered momentum, it became a leading modern jazz orchestra, with a string of admirable records to its credit, most of them revolving around Toshiko's compositions. The group broke up and re-formed a number of times, and was for a long period in the 90s as familiar to New York audiences as the Thad Jones–Mel Lewis Band (to which it bore a strong resemblance) had been. A sequence of excellent albums has been mysteriously neglected in the CD era, and in her 70s the pianist is seen rather less often now. Her Bud Powell influence, mollified a little by the pianist who first brought her to jazz, Teddy Wilson, is the obvious touchstone in her small-group work. Her best legacy, though, is surely the big-band music, where elegant melodies and a penchant for certain section sonorities (especially Tabackin's flute) set her music apart.
**Road Time** (RCA)

## Pheeroan akLaff
DRUMS
*born* 27 January 1955

Born Paul Maddox in Detroit, akLaff was in love with percussion from an early age and has taken it very seriously, studying with African drummers and investigating drumming traditions from around the world. He has only rarely been highlighted as a leader, but since the mid-70s he has been involved in free playing and post-bop and most shades in between. Among notable associations have been those with Jay Hoggard, Oliver Lake, Anthony Davis, Don Byron, Yosuke Yamashita and Andrew Hill.

**Yosuke Yamashita,** *Dazzling Days* (Verve)

# Mannie Albam
ARRANGER
*born* 24 June 1922

Although he worked on the New York scene playing baritone sax in various orchestras during the 40s, Albam's gift was for composing charts, and by 1950 he had more or less stopped playing to write full time. Along with such contemporaries as Johnny Richards, Albam mopped up many of the studio chores available during the 50s and early 60s, writing for big bands (Basie, Kenton), singers (Sarah Vaughan, Carmen McRae) and small groups (Stan Getz, Terry Gibbs). Although he had several opportunities to write and release albums under his own name, most of them are along the lines of *Jazz Goes To The Movies* (1962) and novelty outings such as *Drum Feast* (1959), and there is nothing to compete with the best work of Gil Evans or Eddie Sauter. He subsequently went into film and TV scoring, and was still working in the 90s.

*Jazz Workshop* (RCA)

# Joe Albany
PIANO
*born* 24 January 1924; *died* 11 January 1988

Albany is a ghostly figure in the bebop story. He was one of the young men who fell under the spell of bop in its first phase, and he befriended Charlie Parker and the other new stars of the moment, having already worked on the West Coast in Benny Carter's band. But he had no luck in recording, and a bad narcotics habit shadowed his progress. There was a glimpse of his mastery in the 1958 date for Riverside with Warne Marsh, *The Right Combination*, but it was a solitary pronouncement which collectors had to muse on for many years – until Albany's sudden reappearance in the later 70s. Nils Winther recorded him for his Steeplechase label, and a film was made about his strange existence, *Joe Albany – A Jazz Life*. The comeback records were, though, often sad suggestions of a talent which had simply drifted into neglect and disrepair, and when Joe died in 1988, he was practically forgotten again.

*The Right Combination* (Riverside)

# Alvin Alcorn
TRUMPET
*born* 7 September 1912

Alcorn's unflashy and steady manner might have told against his being better known. He was a solid New Orleans trumpeter, working with such leaders as Armand Piron and Papa Celestin in the 30s and 40s. In the following decade he did some of his best work on record with Kid Ory and Paul Barbarin, and also partnered George Lewis for a time. Subsequently he worked as a guest or led his own group in the city, although he was still to be seen in Europe from time to time. A stint at Commander's Palace saw him still playing into the 80s. Never too keen to be the soloist, his firm lead and capable mid-register playing allowed him to keep his chops intact over a long career. He was also the only jazz musician to appear in both *The Benny Goodman Story* and a James Bond film (*Live And Let Die*).

*Sounds Of New Orleans Vol 6* (Storyville)

# Howard Alden
GUITAR
*born* 17 October 1958

Raised in Newport Beach, California, Alden began on banjo and then moved on to guitar, getting local jobs and working at Disneyland. As a teenager, he was a bit out of step with his peers: 'I'd mention people like Barney Kessel and my friends in high school would look at me like I was from another planet.' He moved East in 1982 and soon fell in with the other young mainstreamers who were working in the city at that point, recording extensively for Concord, and eventually going on to play duets with the veteran George Van Eps. He subsequently switched to a seven-string electric guitar, 'which gives you almost the entire range of the string bass'. The best of his Concords, which don't rely solely on

mainsteam staples and have tunes from all over the jazz spectrum, are superb repertory records. He has a basically plain-spoken, straight-ahead style and abjures anything but a clean open tone, but he can get all over the guitar as well as anybody. He taught the instrument to Sean Penn for the actor's role in Woody Allen's *Sweet And Lowdown*. His wife Terrie is a decent singer.
**Take Your Pick** (Concord)

# Eric Alexander
TENOR SAXOPHONE
*born* 4 August 1968

Alexander is heir apparent to the school of East Coast tough tenors exemplified by such as Lockjaw Davis and Johnny Griffin. He studied in Indiana and New Jersey but subsequently relocated to Chicago to work with the likes of Charles Earland and Harold Mabern. In the past ten years, he has divided his time between Chicago, New York and Philadelphia, and recorded extensively as both sideman and leader, working with bands such as One For All and setting down a series of albums for Criss Cross, Delmark and Milestone. There isn't much to choose between them for quality: Eric looks at the tune and takes off, whether it be a choice as unlikely as 'Matchmaker Matchmaker' or a simple blowing vehicle. So far, his enthusiasm, gumption and concern to keep the music honest have sustained him through a lot of records and gigs. Where it goes on from here is hard to tell.
**The First Milestone** (Milestone)

# Monty Alexander
PIANO
*born* 6 June 1944

One of only a handful of Jamaicans to make any significant impact on jazz, Alexander played with local eminence Ernest Ranglin in Kingston in the early 60s before going to the US and making some waves in Miami and New York. He has now been making records under his own name for 40 years and the discography is fairly vast. While he also worked under other leaders – notably Milt Jackson and Ray Brown, both of whom liked the Jamaican's barnstorming kind of swing playing – his own groups have made Monty's mark on jazz. Although he originally tried to transplant himself directly into the American idiom, he discovered that a little authenticity would help him stand out from the crowd of post-Peterson pianists, and his groups Ivory And Steel (with steel-pan percussionists) and Yard Movement (which is a direct attempt to jazz up reggae material) have both brought him a mix of notoriety and popular success. The latter direction in particular smacks a bit of a canny opportunism, and the blending in question is scarcely profound; but Alexander can fairly claim his roots, and he's entitled to make the most of them.
**Stir It Up** (Telarc)

# Rashied Ali
DRUMS
*born* 1 July 1935

Ali will always be known as the man who took over from Elvin Jones in the John Coltrane group. He already had a long period as a professional behind him, working with R&B bands in his home town of Philadelphia before arriving in New York in 1963 and quickly finding himself in the thick of the New Thing. He joined Coltrane in 1965, working in tandem with Jones, and remained until Coltrane's death. Their record of duets, *Interstellar Space*, is one of the final glories in the Coltrane discography. At this point, Ali still sounded much in thrall to Elvin's own discoveries, but he was an ounce less beholden to the bop tradition and Coltrane felt that his elegant kind of 'freedom' was the way he wanted his rhythmic base to go. Ali has never quite enjoyed the same stature since, but he was an important force in aiding musicians to achieve a better degree of self-help, forming his own label and running his own performance space (Ali's Alley) throughout the 70s. In the 80s and 90s he was an acknowledged godfather in his scene, and worked with many senior spirits. *Touchin' On Trane* (1991), a trio record with Charles Gayle and William Parker, is a powerful and moving collaboration that finds Ali exulting in the memory of his old mentor.
**John Coltrane, *Interstellar Space*** (Impulse!)

# Jan Allan

TRUMPET
*born* 7 November 1934

Born in Falun, Sweden, Allan played both trumpet and piano in his teens and was a founding member of the groundbreaking quartet The Modern Swedes, who backed Lars Gullin during the middle 50s. That association with Gullin continued, but Allan also ran a small group with Rolf Billberg in the early 60s (curtailed only by Billberg's sudden death) and thereafter led a larger ensemble which wavered between jazz and light music. The composer-arranger Nils Lindberg got some of the best out of the trumpeter, featuring him as soloist on some of his orchestral projects, and Allan's finest hour came with the little masterpiece *Jan Allan – 70* (1970), where Lindberg's scores (including a beautiful requiem for Billberg) elicit Jan's finest work. Since then he has continued to play in his own style, much in debt to the cooler hard-bop trumpeters of the 50s – Art Farmer, Kenny Dorham – yet long since personalized to his own ends.
**Jan Allan – 70** (Phono Suecia)

# Ed Allen

CORNET
*born* 15 December 1897; *died* 28 January 1974

Forgotten except by collectors of pre-war jazz, Allen was an unfailingly appealing trumpeter in the traditional style. Although born in Nashville, he grew up in St Louis and worked in New Orleans from 1923. But his longest association by far was with Clarence Williams, whom he started working with on arriving in New York in 1925. He is on scores of Williams's records right up until 1937, always playing in an agreeably sweet-to-hot style, with a touch of Joe Oliver when he had the mute in. Allen was an old-school stylist, and the swing era wasn't very kind to players of his ilk: he performed in anonymous dance-hall groups until illness made him give up playing in the early 60s.
**Clarence Williams, *Dreaming The Hours Away*** (Frog)

# Geri Allen

PIANO
*born* 12 June 1957

Allen has been a prolific presence in American jazz for some 20 years, without quite suggesting that she has something to offer which will keep her in the front rank of jazz performers. Early studies with Marcus Belgrave, Kenny Barron and Nathan Davis gave her a broad range of sympathies, and when she began working under her own leadership in New York in the middle 80s, she was soon moving in heavy company: Oliver Lake and James Newton used her in their bands, and she was involved in the first stirrings of the M-Base movement with Steve Coleman and Greg Osby. Trios with Charlie Haden and Paul Motian, and Dave Holland and Jack DeJohnette (the latter formed to accompany Betty Carter on a European tour), cemented the impression that she was a leader on her instrument. She dabbled in electronic keyboards, an approach she has tried at various points on her own records, and in the more fusion-directed band of her husband, Wallace Roney. She also won the JAZZPAR Prize in 1996. On record, Allen has been stylistically evasive: drawing from free jazz and the bop vocabulary in an even-handed way, she arrived at a synthesis which was lyrical, even charming, yet with a dark and sometimes turbulent undertow also present. Her compositions suggest a characterful but rather private thinker. Problematically for her career on record, she has been taken up by several major labels – Columbia, Blue Note, Verve – only for them all to let her go after disappointing sales, and her discography is unwontedly scattered. A fresh start with Telarc in 2004 may help.
**The Nurturer** (Blue Note)

# Harry Allen

TENOR SAXOPHONE
*born* 12 October 1966

The baby-faced Allen is a terrifically swinging tenor player in the Gonsalves–Webster manner. He emerged from Rutgers with a huge sound and a rock-solid delivery already in place and he was soon lionized by the audience keen to see mainstream jazz still breathing as a live attraction, working with

such peers as Keith Ingham, Michael Moore and the Concord set. He was signed by the Japanese arm of BMG–RCA in the 90s and made a string of fine albums, but they received scant promotion in most of the places where Allen might have been expected to do well. He is an uncomplicated and perhaps slightly glib stylist – almost in a Tubby Hayes tradition – but being on the receiving end of one of his full-tilt solos is undeniably exhilarating. In 2004, he appeared in a two-tenor date with Scott Hamilton, which has a ring of inevitability about it.
*Day Dream* (RCA)

## Henry 'Red' Allen
TRUMPET, VOCAL
*born* 7 January 1908; *died* 17 April 1967

Red Allen was the last great trumpet stylist to emerge from New Orleans until Wynton Marsalis revived his city's venerable tradition. He was signed by Victor as a possible rival to Louis Armstrong, and when he moved to New York and joined Luis Russell in 1929 (there were some other New Orleans homeboys in the ranks then) he fitted right in to the city's musical elite. His sessions for Victor feature magnificent playing on the likes of 'Funny Feathers Blues' and 'Swing Out', suggesting that while Allen followed Armstrong like everyone else, he had his own style under control: brassy rips and slurs and growls suggesting a sometimes surreal humour to go with ferociously hot phrasing. His singing was equally individual: try the frantic version of 'Ol' Man River' which he recorded when he joined Fletcher Henderson in 1933. He went back to the Russell band in 1937 and acted as a warm-up act for Armstrong during the period when the Russell group backed Pops, but he also recorded prolifically under his own name for Vocalion, even though the records were mostly not a patch on the earlier sides for Victor. From 1940 onwards he led his own groups, often with favourite partners – Coleman Hawkins and Edmond Hall were two, although his most congenial comrade was the trombonist J C Higginbotham – and while he survived the 50s respectably enough, in the 60s he found himself unexpectedly in fashion again, in part owing to a famous assertion by Don

Ellis that 'Red Allen is the most avant-garde trumpet player in New York'. He wasn't, but he was still the unmistakeably individual Red. He recorded with Kid Ory and (for Prestige) with only a rhythm section, and he toured England with the Alex Welsh Band, who adored him. His approval of a solo ('That's nice!') and fondness for English bitter endeared him to audiences too, but the Welsh-men were shocked on his final tour to see how illness had suddenly reduced him: his once capacious clothes were hanging off his frame. Allen died of cancer in 1967.
*Henry 'Red' Allen 1929–1933* (Classics)

## Marshall Allen
ALTO SAXOPHONE
*born* 25 May 1924

Allen was in Europe with military bands before moving to Chicago in 1951, and there he met Sun Ra and began a lifelong dedication to his bandleader's music, although he didn't join Ra's Arkestra full time until 1957. There is scarcely a single Sun Ra record which doesn't prominently feature Allen's bluesy, trenchant alto playing, which would come to the fore in furious setpiece duels with fellow saxophonist Danny Davis, a cosmic version of the old saxophone battles of the bebop era. In addition, Allen played oboe, flute, piccolo and even a wind synthesizer. He embraced Ra's concepts and musical directions fully and seemingly without question, and probably influenced many of Ra's own directions: his flute playing, for instance, has a quasi-Middle Eastern feel which evokes the music of the pyramids Ra attempted to conjure. His loyalty extended into his 70s, and beyond the end of Ra's own life: Allen took over the Arkestra on his leader's demise, and carried on in his memory.
**Sun Ra, *The Heliocentric Worlds Of Sun Ra Vol II*** (ESP-Disk)

## Steve Allen
PIANIST, PRESENTER
*born* 16 December 1921; *died* 30 October 2000

Steve Allen was a good friend to jazz. He was a disc jockey in the 40s and then moved to television: he was the founding host of *The*

*Tonight Show* in 1951, and subsequently moved to *The Steve Allen Show*. Even though rock'n'roll was becoming the youth music of choice in this period, Allen – a decent pianist himself – had many jazz performers on his shows and sponsored some recording sessions too. It was largely thanks to him that the house-band music on *The Tonight Show* is still, more than 50 years later, jazz-rather than rock-orientated.

## Mose Allison
PIANO, TRUMPET, VOCAL
*born* 11 November 1927

One of his early albums was called *Young Man Mose*, and even though he now qualifies as a senior citizen (and can't stop writing about it), there is something ageless about the piano man from Tippo, Mississippi. He played piano and trumpet while doing military service, and by the early 50s was playing clubs with a trio. This was mostly in the South, but in 1956 he went to New York and played piano for some illustrious horn players, including Zoot Sims and Al Cohn, Stan Getz and – of all people – Steve Lacy. He began recording as a leader for Prestige in 1957, and after the trio records became successful, he stuck with the format, which he still works with to this day. Steeped in the blues and boogie woogie, Allison took what he wanted from these idioms and made up his own style – a gentle, tough-tender approach which could sound bucolic and rural one moment and snappily metropolitan the next. His singing – bluesy, faintly sarcastic, but freighted with that most rare commodity, American irony – is another unique matter (and a style which some say Georgie Fame appropriated wholesale). He should be further recognized as one of the better 20th-century American songwriters: a brief list of masterpieces would have to include 'Parchman Farm', 'Don't Forget To Smile', 'I'm Not Talking', 'Certified Senior Citizen' and 'It Didn't Turn Out That Way'. Luckily, he has been extensively recorded over the years, with Atlantic and Columbia looking after the 60s and 70s and Blue Note taking over in the 80s and 90s.
*The Word From Mose* (Atlantic)

## Karrin Allyson
VOCAL, PIANO
*born* 1964

Allyson grew up in Nebraska and studied classical piano, before moving to Minneapolis and working in piano bars in the 80s. After putting out one self-made album she was signed to Concord and began releasing records regularly, starting with *I Didn't Know About You*. She continued to work in Minneapolis and Kansas City ('Kansas has a certain swing thing going on') and while her records sold respectably, she didn't have any kind of hit until *Ballads: Remembering John Coltrane* (2000), a very adept and convincing rethink of Coltrane's *Ballads* album spun around her vocals. She has a particular timbre – not quite husky, not too sweet – which gives her vocals a distinctive edge at a time when too many soundalike singers are working on standards, and she is young enough to tackle rock material without making it seem modish.
***Ballads: Remembering John Coltrane*** (Concord)

## Mikhail (Misha) Alperin
PIANO
*born* 1956

Alperin is a Moldavian (although he was actually born in the Ukraine, he grew up in Bessarabia), who found himself involved in the local jazz scene, such as it was, after years of piano study and playing in folk bands. By 1983, when he moved to Moscow, he was literate in all the post-bop styles, but on the evidence of his records – mostly with brass player Arkady Shilkloper, with whom he has worked for many years – he sublimated this into a brooding, parsimonious manner which has at least as much folk and classical breeding in it as any jazz leanings. It seems inevitable that he ended up on ECM, where he recorded *North Story* (1995) and *First Impression* (1997), albums which fit easily into the label's musing manner. In live performance with Shilkloper the pair can create some breathtakingly poignant music, although both there and on record there can be discouragingly little joy in the delivery.
***North Story*** (ECM)

# Maarten Altena
BASS
*born* 22 January 1943

Altena played a significant role in the Dutch free-music scene of the 70s and 80s. He began making solo albums for ICP in 1973 (the memorable *Handicaps*, where, suffering from a broken hand, he also put his bass in a cast) and was present at the first Company Week in London in 1977. Hat Hut and his own label Claxon subsequently documented his larger-scale music and he formed an octet in 1981: the music is a characteristic Dutch blend of composition, free playing, a whiff of theatricality and a slick of faintly macabre humour. A skilful synthesizer of received ideas, he has not been heard from enough in the past ten years or so.
*Cities And Streets* (hatOLOGY)

# Barry Altschul
DRUMS, PERCUSSION
*born* 6 January 1943

Altschul's career and influence have perhaps never quite fulfilled early promise. Bronx-born, he was hired by Paul Bley in 1963 and worked with the pianist for the rest of the decade, although he also visited Europe and the West Coast and worked with other leaders. Bley's rigorous kind of freedom was a useful barometer for Altschul's own proclivities and his work with Chick Corea and Anthony Braxton in Circle carried on in a similar vein. He continued to work with Braxton and then with Sam Rivers until leading his own small groups from around 1980. There were a few worthwhile albums for Soul Note, but Altschul has never suggested that he has a classic record in him, at least under his own leadership. While he has studied and absorbed drumming styles from many disciplines outside jazz, his natural *métier* is in a relatively conservative freebop manner, and occasional reunions with Bley and Rivers have found him at his most settled and persuasive.
**Paul Bley,** *Copenhagen And Haarlem* (Freedom)

# Ari Ambrose
TENOR SAXOPHONE
*born* 3 October 1973

Ambrose, who grew up in Washington DC, has a rumbustiously huge tenor sound in the Sonny Rollins tradition, and his sequence of albums for Nils Winther's Steeplechase label posit him as a saxophonist whose progress may prove to be compelling. He moved to New York in 1991 and has since then taken numerous sideman gigs on the local scene, without seemingly coming to the attention of any American labels. Despite the Rollins feel, he prefers to name Coltrane and players in the Don Byas–Coleman Hawkins axis as his principal influence, and the swagger and heftiness of his delivery have so far been nicely countered by relatively light and swinging frameworks on his studio records.
*Cyclic Episode* (Steeplechase)

# Franco Ambrosetti
TRUMPET
*born* 10 December 1941

The Swiss trumpeter came to prominence via a long association with George Gruntz, which began in the 60s and has endured through the various incarnations of Gruntz's Concert Jazz Band. He is a characteristic European hard bopper, obviously in hock to American models but playing with a clean and bright sound and articulation which allows him to hold his own in most situations. Until recently, he also ran a parallel career in his family's industrial firm, enjoying the two sides of a busy professional life. His albums are enjoyable while rarely asking for more than an occasional spin. His father, Flavio, is a veteran alto player who often worked with Franco, and who likewise divided his time between engineering and music.
*Light Breeze* (Enja)

# American Music
RECORD COMPANY

Established by the doyen of New Orleans scholars, Bill Russell, this label started issuing recordings by hardcore New Orleans traditionalists – Bunk Johnson, George Lewis,

Wooden Joe Nicholas – in 1944, and continued until 1957, also reissuing some rare early material drawn from Paramount. In the CD era it has been revived as part of the George Buck group of labels (GHB) and most of the original holdings are available again.

# AMM
GROUP

Founded by Lou Gare (alto saxophone), Edwin Prévost (drums) and Keith Rowe (guitar) in 1965, this British group is one of the most durable in modern music. Cornelius Cardew (piano) also worked with the group, until 1973, which then subsequently existed as the duo of Prévost and Gare, and then the pairing of Prévost and Rowe. John Tilbury (piano) joined in 1982, and Rohan de Saram (cello) appeared with the group on and off during the 80s. Their themeless and seemingly timeless music exists as improvisation in, possibly, its purest form, less fettered to conventional musical principle than any comparable outfit. Early links with 'free jazz' were soon discarded, and with an increasing use of electronics (via Rowe), the sound of AMM drifts in a netherworld of acoustic/electric soundmaking which might equally be held as jazz or chamber music, even as it obstinately refuses to admit idiom or even any sense of personal expression. In its neutral and unasked-for way, the group has been enormously influential, particularly on recent generations of European improvisers. However, an increasing rift between Prévost and Rowe may have terminated their collective activity. Nobody knows what the name AMM means, if anything.
*The Inexhaustible Document* (Matchless)

# Albert Ammons
PIANO
*born* 23 September 1907; *died* 3 December 1949

Ammons was part of the triumvirate of boogie-woogie players who rode the crest of a fad for the music at the end of the 30s. He had already known Meade Lux Lewis for many years (they worked together at a Chicago taxi company and tried out ideas at the piano between shifts) when the two of them joined up with the Kansan Pete

Johnson as the godfathers of their idiom, creating a sensation at the 1938 From Spirituals To Swing concert at Carnegie Hall. Thereafter Ammons remained in New York, although he toured extensively and remained a successful performer throughout the 40s, sometimes working with the blues singer Joe Turner, and overcoming a brief period when his hands suffered a paralysing condition. But his health failed rapidly at the end of the decade. His great records were cut for Decca, Blue Note and Commodore. 'Shout For Joy' is typical of his zesty playing, but 'Chicago In Mind' shows up his other, contemplative side, and is just as effective.
*Albert Ammons 1936–1939* (Classics)

# Gene Ammons
TENOR SAXOPHONE
*born* 14 April 1925; *died* 23 July 1974

Son of Albert – they worked together for a time in the 40s – Gene was old enough to be a first-generation bopper, yet took more of his style from an even earlier mould: it's possible to hear much of both Hawkins and Young in his playing. He worked for both Billy Eckstine and Woody Herman before going out on his own, and enjoyed jousting with Sonny Stitt in a small group convened at the start of the 50s, an association which continued to the end of Ammons's life. He was an early signing to the Prestige label and as the 50s progressed they recorded him at a bewildering pace – in jam sessions and tenor-and-rhythm sets alike. They were still recording him in the 70s, and by the end of his life he had made dozens of albums for the company. He might have made even more had his career not been disastrously interrupted by drugs problems, which led to two separate periods in jail (1958–60 and 1962–9) – hence the title of *The Boss Is Back!* (1970). 'Jug' Ammons (the epithet was bequeathed by Billy Eckstine, a comment on Gene's hat-size) was a hard man who played tough, yet he found that many admirers liked him best when he played pretty, on such dates as the one listed below. He was utterly reliable as a licks-man in the many jamming situations he played in, and the basic simplicity of his approach was a building-block in the soul-jazz idiom and, perhaps, pointed the way towards the smoother delivery of the 70s, as picked up by younger men such as Stanley Turrentine and Grover Washington. Like his father, Jug died young, although he left a voluminous legacy on record.

**The Soulful Moods Of Gene Ammons** (Prestige)

## Curtis Amy
TENOR AND SOPRANO SAXOPHONES
*born* 11 October 1927

Amy was part of the fabric of Los Angeles musical life for decades, but he actually grew up in Texas, going West only in the mid-50s. Some of his first appearances there were with the R&B leader Amos Milburn, but Amy branched out on his own and led his own bands all through the early and middle 60s, although his seven albums for Pacific Jazz suggested a reluctance to claim sole responsibility, since Paul Bryant, Dupree Bolton, Vic Feldman and Frank Butler were given equal billing. Amy's cheerfully bluesy delivery was very likeable if not especially distinctive, and though he subsequently spent much of his time teaching, it wasn't surprising to find him in demand for touring dates with Ray Charles and numerous studio pop sessions. When a writer asked him in the 80s where he'd been, the smiling reply was, 'Making money!' The title track off a 1967 Verve album, *Mustang*, is Curtis at his grooviest, but the Pacific Jazz records should be better regarded. He made what might be a valedictory record in 1994, *Peace For Love*, which has a vocal by his wife of many years, the soul singer Merry Clayton.

**Mustang** (Verve)

## Arild Andersen
BASS
*born* 27 October 1945

Andersen was in the thick of Norway's new jazz at the end of the 60s, playing with Jan Garbarek and studying with George Russell. He went to America for a brief spell in the early 70s but has otherwise worked primarily at home and on the European circuit ever since. His small-group work has involved the likes of Juhani Aaltonen, Jon Balke and Nils Petter Molvaer, and with Jon Christensen he co-led Masqualero in the

80s. Manfred Eicher's ECM operation has been responsible for recording most of his albums as leader, and they are an interesting and sometimes prescient lot: the likes of *Green Shading Into Blue* (1978) hint at some of the folk-jazz currents later explored by others. While some of his music lingers in this pastoral idiom, Andersen himself is quite an aggressive and loud player, and it is a little surprising to realize that he has also worked extensively with singers, including Karin Krog, Radka Toneff and Sheila Jordan.

**Hyperborean** (ECM)

## Cat Anderson
TRUMPET
*born* 12 September 1916; *died* 29 April 1981

The first of the high-note trumpet specialists, although Maynard Ferguson wasn't far behind, William Alonzo Anderson (the nickname came after a fight in the orphanage where he grew up) spent much of his professional life with Duke Ellington, first joining in 1944 and staying on and off until 1971. Cootie Williams had originally suggested Anderson as his replacement (although Duke first took on Ray Nance), and it was ironic that there would be some friction between the two men in later years. Duke loved Anderson's fearsome abilities at hitting freakishly high notes and features such as 'El Gatto' were fashioned around that ability; although Anderson was also a proper and accomplished section-leader and could solo in an ebullient 'normal' style. After Ellington's death, Cat worked in guest-star roles and spent some time in Lionel Hampton's touring band, with whom he had once worked before joining Ellington.

**Duke Ellington, Afro-Bossa** (Reprise)

## Chris Anderson
PIANO
*born* 26 February 1926

Anderson has had a difficult, in-and-out career, complicated by the crippling condition osteogenesis imperfecta, which left him blind at 18. He grew up in Chicago and played club gigs there, with Von Freeman and others, and he made a single, exceedingly rare LP for Jazzland in 1961, *Inverted Images*. But he has only occasionally been

heard from on a wider basis, which made his lyrical album of duets with Charlie Haden, *None But The Lonely Heart* (1997), even more of a surprise, since it shows a crafted and immaculate style with a harmonic approach that is markedly individual.
**None But The Lonely Heart** (Naim)

## Ernestine Anderson
VOCAL
*born* 11 November 1928

Born in Houston, Anderson had a heavy family background in gospel music, and they weren't too happy about Ernestine's teenage singing, although when they moved to Seattle things got even worse – she began singing with Ray Charles and finally (at 18) joined the Johnny Otis revue. She worked with Lionel Hampton in 1952 and went to Europe with Gigi Gryce, eventually making a record (*Hot Cargo*) in Sweden in 1956 with the Harry Arnold band. It was released on Mercury in the US, and there were four follow-ups, but her career never really got started in America and from around 1966 she left music altogether. Anderson's singing on her early records is clean and confident, but her timbre seems pitched self-consciously between cool and hot and too many of the interpretations sound unremarkable. Carl Jefferson induced a comeback in the mid-70s and made a string of albums with her for Concord: there's no masterpiece among them, but there's little to dislike in her mature style. Her voice was rougher, but less mannered, and she could sing 'Stormy Monday' alongside 'Days Of Wine And Roses'. By the 90s, though, she was slipping back into the margins again.
**Live From Concord To London** (Concord)

## Fred Anderson
TENOR SAXOPHONE
*born* 22 March 1929

Along with Von Freeman, Fred Anderson is the grand old man of Chicago's avant-garde. He was one of the first spirits in the AACM in 1965, but despite moving in the same circles as some of the starrier names involved, he was less lucky with recording and made only a few dates prior to the 80s. He has been a fixture on his home turf via running two clubs of his own: The Birdhouse (1977–8) and The Velvet Lounge, which has been operating since 1982. The past ten years have seen him getting on to record in a much bigger way. His original Parker–Hawkins methodology has been strengthened by subsequent developments in sax language, but his earthy, thunderous delivery remains rooted in an older style, and he often sounds like his local forebear (and near-contemporary) Gene Ammons.
**Birdhouse** (Okkadisk)

## Ivie Anderson
VOCAL
*born* 10 July 1905; *died* 28 December 1949

Duke Ellington's singers were a largely unimpressive lot. Ivie Anderson was the great exception. She had been singing in Los Angeles from her middle teens and actually had a spell at the Cotton Club in 1925, prior to Ellington's arrival; but after a stint with Earl Hines in Chicago, she joined Duke for a four-week trial in 1931 and stayed until 1942. 'Ivie was our good-luck charm,' said Ellington, and photographs of the graceful singer speak eloquently of the elegance which she lent to the band. She can be seen in the Marx Brothers' *A Day At The Races*, and though it is a typically unflattering role for a black performer, she brightens her scene. As Ellington's principal singer, she had a considerable range, from the famous original version of 'It Don't Mean A Thing If It Ain't Got That Swing' to the pastel musing of 'Solitude', and even lesser pieces such as 'Me And You' are lifted by her input. Since her peak years just predated the unstoppable rise of the band singer, she is far less remembered than she should be: perhaps only Billie Holiday and Mildred Bailey matched her among swing-era female vocalists. But asthma ruined her career, and she left Ellington in 1942, singing less often after opening a restaurant, and dying much too young.

## Ray Anderson
TROMBONE, VOCAL
*born* 16 October 1952

Anderson vies with Gary Valente for the role of class clown of the trombone, but like Valente, he's more serious than that. A

Chicagoan, he started early on the horn, studied, but also took a keen interest in both the AACM movement and the city's blues clubs. By 1970 he was playing in funk bands, and two years later he went to New York, where he gradually slipped over to the avant-garde side of things, recording with Anthony Braxton and leading his own small groups. In the 80s, he began trying a more fusion-oriented direction, seeing if a trombone-led avant-funk outfit could pay the bills: Slickaphonics, The Alligatory Band, Lapis Lazuli, BassDrumBone, Pocket Brass Band and the four-'bone SlideRide have been among the results, usually mixed, but always with some compensating improvisational savvy in the music. In between times, Ray has done sideman work from Barbara Dennerlein to Karl Berger. He sometimes picks up the trumpet and likes to sing the blues, too. Anderson never plays a clean line when a blowsy, cracked, apoplectic one will do, and he has a rare command of the horn's top register, which he can sustain over the course of lip-busting solos with no apparent fatigue. This can get a bit tiresome at length, but in most contexts Anderson is usually a tonic.
**Wishbone** (Gramavision)

## Ray Anthony
TRUMPET
*born* 20 January 1922

Not quite a jazzman himself, Anthony worked with Glenn Miller and Jimmy Dorsey and had an unlikely hit of his own with a dance record, 'Bunny Hop', in 1946. After this he ran a big band which cut dozens of albums for Capitol in the 50s and 60s, mostly in a sweetly dreamy style which updated the Miller effect for the LP-era audience. The word 'dream' does, indeed, come up in quite a few of the album titles, especially in connection with 'Dream Dancing'. He was a decent soloist in the manner of Bobby Hackett or Harry James and he had the nous to realize that jazzmen would give his band a lift even when they weren't playing hot, and he gave work to many. Though he slimmed down to a sextet in the 60s, Anthony was back with an orchestra in the 70s and started his own record label, Aerospace, which has reissued much of his old catalogue.
**Jam Session At The Tower** (Capitol)

## Charly Antolini
DRUMS
*born* 24 May 1937

One of the few Swiss musicians to make much international impact on jazz, Antolini began early on drums (in marching bands) and was playing Dixieland when still in his teens. His group The Tremble Kids was formed at the end of the 50s, but like many others he moved on to a more boppish outlook and while accompanying visiting Americans he was able to move between most jazz styles without much trouble. While he spent some time in Cologne in studio bands at the beginning of the 70s, Charly's native Zurich remains his base, and from the mid-70s onwards he has led his own group under the name Jazz Power. A little surprisingly, it has often had a core group of Brits in the line-up, including Brian Lemon, Dick Morrissey and Danny Moss. As a drummer, he likes to boot the band along as strongly as possible: two of his albums were called *Knock-Out* and *Crash*.
**Jazz Power In London** (Bellaphon)

## Tatsu Aoki
BASS
*born* 19 September 1957

Aoki took up the bass in his teens and was working in his native Tokyo by the middle 70s. He left Japan for America in 1976 and has since been largely based in and around Chicago. Like many young musicians of the period, he found himself torn between the lively rock and jazz scenes of the time, but since the late 80s he has been largely involved in jazz. Aoki has worked extensively with such Chicago elders as Von Freeman and Fred Anderson as well as involving himself in the Asian-American circle of Glenn Horiuchi and Jon Jang, and he founded the Chicago Asian-American Jazz Festival. As an instrumentalist, he has a typically strong and supple technique which allows him to move easily between styles, but as is common for many 'regional' American players, he has had almost no impact outside his own patch. The record listed shows off an inventive solo style.
**Needless To Say** (Sound Aspects)

## Peter Apfelbaum
SAXOPHONES
*born* 21 August 1960

Apfelbaum's Hieroglyphics Ensemble was one of the more exciting groups in American jazz in its heyday, which lasted from the late 80s through the early 90s. Born in Berkeley, Apfelbaum founded the first edition of the Ensemble while still in his teens, as an oversized big band, but it settled down into a large-small combo in the early 80s while he was living in San Francisco. They made two prescient records for Antilles which mixed up jazz, West Coast rock and world-music strains into a prodigious and entertaining jumble, but the albums hardly sold and the leader has only made a single subsequent disc, *Luminous Charms*, although he relocated to New York and began the usual round of working in numerous set-ups. Too big to tour and isolated from the usual centres of jazz attention, the Ensemble was probably doomed from the start, but its best moments remain vivid and surprising. Apfelbaum himself impressed more as a leader-organizer than a soloist.

**Signs Of Life** (Antilles)

## A&R Men

While rock A&R (Artist & Repertoire) men are seen as a cool breed of instinctive talent-spotters, geniuses at finding and nurturing new blood, their jazz equivalents are generally despised as agents of misfortune who seek to smother and commercialize a jazz musician's ambitions. In the past, when the industry was a good deal less honest than it was obliged to become, the A&R man was more of a technician, assisting in studio work. His modern equivalent spends much more time on devising concepts for players who might otherwise be making plain documentations of work in progress. That said, few labels can afford to hire full-time jazz A&R men anyway. There is virtually no female equivalent of the species.

## Jimmy Archey
TROMBONE
*born* 12 October 1902; *died* 16 November 1967

The diminutive, dapper Archey became known as a revivalist player, but at heart he was an impeccable big-band performer, who worked and recorded with Fletcher Henderson and King Oliver in the 20s: his solos stand out for their punch and accuracy, and he could give a blues chorus some beautiful inflections. In the 30s he spent much time with Luis Russell, and his other credits were with such demanding leaders as Claude Hopkins, Benny Carter and – as a dep for Joe Nanton – Ellington. But from the 40s onwards he was a small-group player, including a long stint with Earl Hines from 1955, and he gradually turned into a Dixieland/New Orleans yeoman. On one of his last records, with his Crescent City Delegates Of Pleasure (February 1967), he stands alongside Punch Miller and Albert Burbank.

**Earl Hines, *A Monday Date*** (Prestige)

## Neil Ardley
KEYBOARDS, COMPOSER
*born* 26 May 1937; *died* 23 February 2004

Ardley came to prominence in the British scene of the later 60s as a bandleader with plenty of compositional study behind him. He had already been leading the New Jazz Orchestra for some time, but it wasn't until the pair of albums *Le Déjeuner Sur L'Herbe* (1968) and *The Greek Variations* (1969) that he attracted wider attention. Even so, these were hardly best-sellers (and are now, predictably, sought-after by collectors), and Ardley's scholarly mix of Gil Evans, Ellington, and bits and bobs from the European tradition could sound a bit four-square and worthy (perhaps unsurprisingly, his next project, *A Symphony Of Amaranths*, won an Arts Council Award). In 1975 he put together *Kaleidoscope Of Rainbows*, with an all-star British band of the period: fondly regarded by some, it still sounds like a boring and ponderous record which might almost sum up why British jazz was losing so much of its audience at the time. Ardley was, though, never a career jazz musician, working and writing prolifically in other areas of the arts and sciences. A subsequent band called Zyklus, a mix of electronic form

and acoustic improvisation, has been rapidly overtaken by the furious pace at which electronic music-making has developed.
*Kaleidoscope Of Rainbows* (Line)

## Argo
RECORD COMPANY

This was Chess Records' attempt at breaking into the jazz market. The hottest of all the blues labels must have figured that they could do well in the jazz area too, but their Chicago-based operation never quite had the gravitas of the New York or Californian labels. Early signings included Ahmad Jamal and Ramsey Lewis, both very successful, although both typified the label's attempts to cross jazzmen over into a more jukebox-orientated market. Argo became Cadet in 1965, after the British classical label objected, somewhat belatedly, to the use of its name. When Leonard Chess sold out in 1969, the label went into a period of confusion and there was all kinds of litigation to follow. Today, it is part of the vast Universal holdings. LP collectors regard Argo with interest but little passion: too many of its productions look cheap and poorly designed, and compared to Blue Note and Prestige it is way down the pecking order.

## Julian Arguëlles
SAXOPHONES
*born* 28 January 1966

The younger Arguëlles brother is another graduate of the Loose Tubes big band and is – along with Django Bates and Iain Ballamy – one of its few participants whose star hasn't much faded since the group's heyday. Julian was still in his teens when he began playing with that group, and since then his playing has settled into a capacious style which finds him at home with most of the saxophone family and able to move rapidly between contemplative balladry and fast, acerbic improvising which owes little to the book of post-bop licks. The octet record *Skull View* is a strong showcase for both his writing and his playing. He has since tried his hand at a with-strings record, and though he likes to be the boss, he's also been a very impressive sideman in the Colin Steele

group, which he joined after moving north to Edinburgh.
*Skull View* (Babel)

## Steve Arguëlles
DRUMS, ETC
*born* 16 November 1963

Arguëlles was one of the stars of the Loose Tubes collective and the cheerful irreverence of that group has carried over into his subsequent work: with Human Chain, Arguëlles, Ambitronique and The Recyclers. At the end of the 80s he was one of the brightest talents in London's jazz scene, but since decamping for Paris he has been much less visible and his appearances on record have declined. The comic bent of recordings such as *Busy Listening* (1993) is tempered by a sometimes rustic-sounding lyricism, and Steve's trademark hustle-and-bustle delivery is sufficiently unfettered to make his music slot into plenty of other categories besides jazz.
*Busy Listening* (Babel)

## Lil Armstrong
PIANO, VOCAL
*born* 4 August 1898; *died* 27 August 1971

Lillian Hardin was, along with Lovie Austin, one of two female pianists who made a surprising impact on the Chicago jazz of the early 20s. She worked for the second and third kings of New Orleans trumpet, Freddie Keppard and Joe Oliver, and it was in Oliver's Creole Jazz Band that she met Louis Armstrong, three years her junior: they married in 1924, and she proved to be a driving force behind his sometimes reluctant ascendancy. From 1925, the trumpeter even worked in his wife's own group, and she plays sometimes effortful piano on the first series of Hot Five recordings. Although Lil was the better-schooled musician – she secured a teacher's diploma in Chicago and a postgraduate degree in New York in the later 20s – it was Louis who had the epochal talent, and relations between them grew strained, culminating in their separation in 1931. Ever after, they had a curious relationship, where lawsuits – and Lil constantly billing herself as 'Mrs Louis Armstrong' – never quite sundered their affection for each other. Lil had

an unremarkable subsequent career, in Chicago, New York and Paris, and the small-band swing style heard in her group sessions of the late 30s makes for unde-manding fun: she sings as often as she plays piano. A 1961 date in Prestige's *Chicago: The Living Legends* series shows that she could still lead a band with teeth-rattling energy. She died only a few weeks after her beloved former husband, taken ill while playing at a concert in his memory.
***Chicago: The Living Legends*** (OJC)

## Louis Armstrong
TRUMPET, VOCAL
*born* 4 August 1901; *died* 6 July 1971

Armstrong never knew his real birthday: he always claimed 4 July 1900. The little boy with the gaping mouth (the 'Satch', short for 'Satchelmouth', was bestowed on him from an early age) lived in the characteristically abject conditions of many New Orleans blacks, working at menial jobs to earn a dollar and living largely as a street urchin. He bought a cornet from a pawnshop but was detained after setting off a pistol on New Year's Eve, 1912, and sent to a waifs' home, where the bandmaster gave him lessons and soon had him leading the band. On his release, he delivered coal and played in local bands before coming under the wing of Joe Oliver, whom he idolized. Soon enough he was playing second cornet to Oliver's lead in Chicago, having previously worked in Kid Ory's band and on riverboats with Fate Marable. Their two-cornet breaks were a sensation, and if only a modest part of the band's power comes through on their 1923 records, it's still impressive enough. Armstrong married their pianist, Lil Hardin, and left Oliver to join Fletcher Henderson in New York, where his hick manners caused amusement, although his playing electrified Henderson's then somewhat stately orches-tra. 'I Miss My Swiss' (1925), which turns from a quaint dance performance to a blaz-ing jazz record when Armstrong takes a solo, is characteristic: for the first time, we can hear jazz in terms of swing, the indefinable rhythmic propulsion which, when heard, seems to ripple through the human frame.

But he grew dissatisfied with Henderson's group and returned to Chicago in November 1925, where over the course of three years he set down the sessions for local label OKeh listed as Louis Armstrong & His Hot Five/Seven. Although the band was basically a studio group – initially Armstrong with Hardin, Johnny Dodds, Kid Ory and Johnny St Cyr – the players knew each other well. But Armstrong entirely dominates what would otherwise have been a merely inter-esting small group. Clear of distractions, he sets down on record after record chorus-length solos which became a clarion call to jazz soloists everywhere, unleashing all the possibilities of improvisation in the idiom. Played in an extravagantly rich, open tone, their virtuosity is stunning, their range unprecedented: Armstrong switched from cornet to trumpet around this time, and it appeared to encourage his venturing still further. Rhythmically and harmonically, he seems to be a light year ahead of every other player, and daring as the trumpet play-ing is, it has a poise and high finish to go with the risk-taking. Even the experienced Dodds and Ory seem overwhelmed, although Dodds sounds much better on the Seven sides. Besides the trumpet, Armstrong also began singing: the scat chorus he takes on 'Heebie Jeebies' (1925), perhaps the first of its kind on record, is musically almost as smart as his trumpet work, and everywhere he swings the lines and makes his gravelly timbre into something bewitchingly new. By the time of the 1927–8 sides, he is Olympian: 'Potato Head Blues', 'Wild Man Blues', 'West End Blues' and 'Tight Like This' offer music which is still undimmed in its splendour and excitement. For the later sessions, Earl Hines came in as pianist, and their shared brilliance is well caught on 'Weather Bird' (1928).

Away from the studios, Armstrong was being featured as a star soloist with various bands, including those of Erskine Tate, Carroll Dickerson and Clarence Jones, and eventually this became a touring position, working with Dickerson or Luis Russell-led aggregations in many cities. His records began to feature similar orchestral back-drops, and in 1933 he signed with Victor, where he made records which often amounted to mini-concertos, a vocal chorus of a popular song followed by a majestic trumpet improvisation. The best of them, such as 'I've Gotta Right To Sing The Blues' (1933), still assert his magnificence. He trav-elled to Europe in 1933–4, where he received a king's welcome in many cities, his records having already gone round the world. Back home, he engaged Joe Glaser as his manager, a position which the latter held for the rest of Armstrong's life: manipulative and devious Glaser may often have been, but he made sure Louis was always looked after and protected. Armstrong moved to Decca from RCA, and while the records became more formulaic, given the right circumstances Armstrong still made delightful music. He made films and became more of a showbiz personality under Glaser's stewardship. As the big-band era declined and costs mounted, the orchestra was taken off the road and – following some very successful Town Hall (New York) concerts in May 1947 – a new group (Louis Armstrong And His All Stars) became the trumpeter's performing vehicle, initially a sextet with Barney Bigard, Jack Teagarden and eventually Earl Hines at the piano. Their earlier music was by far the best: both Hines and Teagarden soon became bored or disgruntled, and the eventual reliance on Dixieland staples as their core repertoire blunted any sense of adventure which might have remained in Armstrong's work.

Yet he seemed oblivious to shortcomings, always loving to entertain crowds, and the bravado of his early work was steadily displaced by an economy of delivery which assumed a monolithic majesty. Although his voice grew ever more scarred, his delivery was unimpaired, and as a recording artist his progress through the early LP era is fascinating: his Decca albums are an engaging mix of pop and jazz material, and the sets he made for George Avakian at Columbia include some beautiful reshapings of his jazz past, including *Plays W C Handy* (1954). He also partnered Oscar Peterson and Ella Fitzgerald at Verve, and in 1961 made exquisite and long-undervalued records with Duke Ellington. By the 60s, 'Ambassador Satch' had visited many countries and was all but an unofficial representative of the State Department: some regarded his mugging in these situations as offensive, but Billie Holiday summed up the feeling of many when she said that 'Sure Pops Toms, but he Toms with class.' Armstrong had never bothered too much about hurtful opinion, even when boppers derided him as a bygone, but he didn't sleep on his principles either: this generous man, who always had a

roll of dollars for friends down on their luck, angrily admonished his government during the Little Rock integration crisis of 1957 and cancelled one of his tours in protest. Later in the 60s, he became a pop star once again: 'Hello Dolly' (1964) bested The Beatles in the charts, and 'What A Wonderful World' (1967) became such an enduring success that many who knew nothing of his jazz work thought Armstrong was an elderly pop singer. By this time the All Stars had become a tiring routine and at the end Armstrong had little left to give: his final records feature only vocals.

Although a beloved showbiz figure, he lived quietly in a Queens suburb, in a house which has now been opened as an Armstrong museum, often tapping away at his typewriter and chatting with friends. Since his death in 1971, his star has been in the ascendant again: his records are readily available, from the Hot Fives onwards, and contemporary jazz celebrities such as Wynton Marsalis have insisted on the primacy not only of the universally acknowledged early work but the rest of Armstrong's oeuvre as a potent and powerful legacy. If the world's music still swings today, it is in large part because of what he was first doing, eight decades ago.

*The Complete Hot Five And Hot Seven Recordings* (Columbia)

# Harry Arnold
BANDLEADER
*born* 7 August 1920; *died* 11 February 1971

While he was a competent saxophonist, Arnold's *métier* was as a bandleader. He was already leading bands in Malmö in the 40s before moving on to work in Stockholm as part of Thore Ehrling's group, but his principal success came as leader of the Swedish Radio Big Band, called Radiobandet, from 1956. The orchestra used many of the leading local musicians – including Bengt Hallberg, Bjarne Nerem and Arne Domnérus – as well as engaging the best arrangers. A session by the band was issued in America on Jazztone as *The Jazztone Mystery Band*, which was strong enough to convince local critics that it was an American group, and Arnold had five other albums issued in the US as a consequence, including a 'meeting' with Quincy Jones, who wrote several charts

for the band's book. Arnold stepped down from Radiobandet in 1965 and died prematurely in 1971.
*Studio Sessions* (Dragon)

# Kenneth Arnström
CLARINET, SAXOPHONES
*born* 11 May 1946

Arnström exemplifies the kind of unassuming skill which many northern Europeans display in rekindling the flame of older jazz styles. He grew up in Stockholm and began playing clarinet and saxophone in a style which was a throwback to the sounds of swing and traditional jazz. By the time he was 15 he had already helped to found the Kunstbandet orchestra, a gig which he held (in spite of the interruption of military service) until 1977. Two years later he left music altogether and worked as a carpenter in northern Sweden, before returning to semi-regular playing, a career which he finally went full time with in 1995. Besides the reed family, all of which he plays with a cultivated gusto that forces the sound into modern times, he also plays piano, guitar, bass, banjo, tuba and violin. His records are rare in number. He dominates them with a sound and delivery that seem careless of whether the idiom is traditional, swing or whatever.
*Rhythm King* (Opus3)

# Sidney Arodin
CLARINET
*born* 29 March 1901; *died* 6 February 1948

A very fine player in the New Orleans tradition, Arodin is still little recognized. He played locally before going to New York in 1922 and joining the Original New Orleans Jazz Band, but returned three years later and jobbed around the city. He is on some of the rare recording sessions which took place in New Orleans prior to the 40s, and it's interesting to hear him on Johnnie Miller's 1928 version of 'Dipper Mouth Blues': rather than follow the Johnny Dodds solo, he comes up with an entirely fresh one. In the 30s he tried his luck in Kansas City and back in New York, working with Louis Prima and Wingy Manone, but by 1940 he was back in New Orleans again and illness curtailed his

playing. As scattered as his best playing is, any record which offers him a few bars is worth hearing.

# Arrangement
A basis for a single musical performance, achieved either through a written score or a procedure worked out by one or more of the musicians and thereafter memorized (the latter is usually called a 'head arrangement'). The arrangement might be conceived around an entirely original composition, or be something imposed as a fresh orchestration of a standard song or some other source. Arrangements might be sufficiently open-ended to allow much improvisation, or tightly marshalled to reflect the character of the band or the arranger over individuals. Arrangers and composers are usually one and the same, although most writers arrange other people's tunes as hired hands rather than freely creative souls. While aspects of this may seem antithetical to the freedoms and individualities in jazz, it's hard to imagine the music without such great arrangers as Gil Evans, Fletcher Henderson, Jimmy Mundy or Billy May.

# Lynne Arriale
PIANO
*born* 29 May 1957

The gamine Arriale is an exceptionally strong voice among contemporary pianists. She graduated with a masters in classical music from Wisconsin Conservatory, but fell into jazz almost by accident and was won over by its inherent capacity for improvisation. She won the 1993 Great American Jazz Piano Competition, and since then has worked steadily, most often in a trio context: her working book includes many arrangements for trio, and she prefers to see what can be wrought from a chart rather than simply calling up tunes on the stand. Her approach is notably adroit at avoiding licks-playing: 'I tend to work with shapes and with singing, and I also practise rhythms a lot, playing a simple rhythm over and over.' Her trio (like so many others) is often compared to the Bill Evans group, but she insists that they sound nothing like them and prefers to cite the Jarrett

Standards group as an influence. Her records have emerged on the obscure European TCB label, and it's surprising that there's been little apparent interest from American companies in her work.
*Melody* (TCB)

# Art Ensemble Of Chicago
GROUP

The Ensemble grew out of one of Roscoe Mitchell's groups, convened under the broad auspices of Chicago's Association For The Advancement Of Creative Musicians, and in its original form it was the quartet of Mitchell, Lester Bowie, Joseph Jarman and Malachi Favors. Although they began recording on home turf as far back as 1967, the AEOC didn't come into 'official' being until a relocation to Paris in 1969, where they embarked on a burst of recording. Besides their basic instruments, the members doubled on numerous percussion devices, and when drummer Don Moye joined in 1970 it was the sole natural progression in the Ensemble's life. The music was fashioned around long, open-ended improvisations on whoever's composition was currently in play, and while there was plenty drawn from the freakout end of free jazz, there was an equal emphasis on lyrical and contemplative playing, and formal ingredients such as solo and ensemble patterns were submerged in what seemed like a genuinely instinctive and generously sensitive group identity. Political-art ingredients came in the form of costume, make-up and occasional spoken-word contributions. Their performance spaces were crowded with woodwinds and percussion, as if readied for an exotic bargain sale. As lavish as the Ensemble later became, there's a case for their earliest recordings being their best, and it's possible to suggest that their most original energies had been spent by the time Moye arrived. In the 70s and 80s, as pillars of revolutionary art, they toured the world as a concert attraction and recorded for upmarket labels such as ECM and DIW. The content of the records thinned, and the concerts became more like routine, but at their best they were hard to forget: Jarman and Favors bedecked in paint and costume, the leering Bowie usually attired in a lab-technician's white coat, Moye thundering along at the drums and the sober, imperturbable Mitchell often providing the most furious instrumental passages. They are sometimes deemed pioneers of world-jazz and were feted for their African borrowings, but their meetings with the likes of the African chorus Amabutho were disappointing: the Ensemble was a very American creation, and, like Ellington, they outlived their time. Jarman took a long sabbatical in 1993 and Bowie died in 1999; after that, there were a couple of reunion records, but Favors's death in 2003 finally closed their chapter.
*People In Sorrow* (Nessa)

# Georges Arvanitas
PIANO
*born* 13 June 1931

Arvanitas grew up in Marseilles but was in Paris by the early 50s, working on the club circuit and backing visiting Americans. His own first recording was made with Doug Watkins and Art Taylor in 1958, and was quickly followed by several more, although he actually did very little under his own name in the 60s. He married Barbara Belgrave, an American singer, and worked in the US for a time, but back home formed a long-standing trio with Jacky Samson and Charles Saudrais. In the 80s and 90s, like many of his generation, he became an honoured elder (awarded a coveted Chevalier in 1985) and recorded rather more frequently, sometimes turning up in unexpected company – David Murray was one duo partner. His style tends towards a gentlemanly kind of bebop, which often makes more impact in accompaniment than as a soloist, and he has surprised more than one distinguished horn player by the vigour in both hands.
*Rencontre* (Columbia)

# Vic Ash
CLARINET, TENOR SAXOPHONE
*born* 9 March 1930

Ash should have been a part of the last generation of British dance-band musicians, but he actually worked in a more jazz-orientated context than most, as a sideman with Kenny Baker and Vic Lewis, as well as leading his own small groups during the 50s. He also played at least as much clarinet as tenor saxophone, and did more than anyone to keep it credible as a sound in the British bop of the day. The Jazz Five, which he co-led with baritonist Harry Klein in the early 60s, was perhaps his finest band, and *The Hooter* is one of the very few British albums of the period to gain an American release. After the group disbanded, though, Ash gradually slipped away into session-work and touring in orchestras that backed singers – a career which, perhaps, worked in reverse.

**The Jazz Five, *The Hooter*** (Riverside)

## Dorothy Ashby
HARP
*born* 6 August 1932; *died* 13 April 1986

The fact that Ashby managed to work convincingly in the bop and post-bop music of the 50s and 60s alone earns her place in jazz history. Although she also played piano, she performed and recorded primarily as a harpist, and in some heavy company: Frank Wess (on flute, a piquant and complementary voice), Roy Haynes, Richard Davis and Jimmy Cobb were among her sidemen on record. She worked primarily in and around her home town of Detroit (where she also had her own radio programme for a time), and her husband John was a drummer who sometimes worked with her. She was still making the occasional record after relocating to the West Coast in the mid-60s (one of them is called *Afro-Harping*!), but despite finding a way to make her instrument occupy a plausible middle ground somewhere between the piano and the guitar, at the time of her early death she was almost forgotten.

***In A Minor Groove*** (New Jazz)

## Harold Ashby
TENOR SAXOPHONE
*born* 21 March 1925

A Kansas City tenorman, Ashby has a scouring, pugnacious tone which sat well with the R&B bands he started playing with in Chicago in the early 50s. He went to try his luck in New York later in the decade, and began subbing with Duke Ellington and others; but it wasn't until Duke hired him

full time in 1968 that he began enjoying any real limelight. He took over Jimmy Hamilton's chair, but seldom took out the clarinet, and most prefer to regard him as Ben Webster's real successor with Ellington. They certainly shared the same grouchy sound at a quicker tempo, and lush way with a pretty tune, but Ashby was a much more mobile and adventurous improviser than the indolent Webster. He stayed until after Duke's death, then freelanced as a solo, and in the late 80s and early 90s enjoyed a brief Indian summer as a leader in the studios. There is always an Ellington tune somewhere in the setlist.

***What Am I Here For?*** (Criss Cross)

## Bill Ashton
SAXOPHONE, LEADER AND ADMINISTRATOR
*born* 6 December 1936

British jazz would certainly be a different place without Ashton, though it's hard to say *how* it would be different. While he played sax in various graduate bands, it wasn't until he started teaching in London that he really became involved in jazz organization. He was so impressed by the talent of the young Frank Ricotti – and so unimpressed by the kind of schooling available to young players of Ricotti's type – that he decided to establish a schools orchestra based around jazz repertory, rather than any kind of classical idiom. The London Schools' Jazz Orchestra/London Youth Jazz Orchestra was the result, first formed in 1965, although by 1970 it was the National Youth Jazz Orchestra and has ever since been called by its acronym, NYJO. Ashton overcame obstacles of indifference and mistrust by countering them with sheer bloody-minded determination, and it is entirely through his energy and persistence that the Orchestra has thrived ever since, going through countless changes of personnel and almost as many sources of sponsorship. There are many records, and Ashton's insistence on a book of originals means that NYJO has most likely got one of the biggest catalogues of compositions in the music. Ex-players include many of the brighter lights in the music of the past 30-something years. Critics can point to a basically unadventurous style in the somewhat homely tradition of British dance orchestras, as if Ted

Heath were still the *sine qua non* of big-band music. But the facts of Ashton's achievement – keeping a profoundly unfashionable entity prospering through every kind of cultural fad since its inception – remain extraordinary.

**National Youth Jazz Orchestra,** *Maltese Cross* (NYJO)

# Svend Asmussen
VIOLIN
*born* 28 February 1916

He might have become a sculptor, a dentist or an attorney – all of which he studied for, in his native Copenhagen – but Svend Asmussen preferred showbiz, and he began professional music-making in 1933. He has always liked being an entertainer as much as being a jazzman: he was involved in act-ing and revues during the 40s, and worked with Alice Babs as part of The Swe-Danes in the late 50s and 60s. But jazz violin is surely his forte. He was particularly affected early on by hearing Stuff Smith, and his style musters a nice mix of earthiness and conservatory elegance: not quite the Copenhagen blues, but there's nothing overly sweet in his sound. There have been occasional appearances outside Scandinavia, including a violin summit with Stéphane Grappelli, Jean-Luc Ponty and Ray Nance at the 1967 Monterey Festival, but for the most part Asmussen, now active well into his 80s, has remained a paterfamilias to Danish jazz and entertainment. John Lewis especially admired him, and remembered their *Euro-pean Encounter* (1963) with particular affec-tion. The CD era has not been outstandingly kind to him and there is a lot of music await-ing reissue, but the record cited below dates from 1999 and still finds the old man in fine form.

**Still Fiddling** (Storyville)

# Association For The Advancement Of Creative Musicians
ORGANIZATION

Founded on 8 May 1965, the AACM grew out of one of Richard Abrams's Experimental Bands, a sprawling ensemble which at one

time or another had gathered in most of the more adventurous spirits in black Chicagoan jazz in the early 60s. It imposed a sense of order on the scene by enabling rehearsals and public performances, as well as offering instruction to younger players and offering resources for composition. With such forma-tive players as Abrams, Anthony Braxton and Roscoe Mitchell, the AACM was soon right in the vanguard of America's new jazz, sponsoring recordings and presenting con-certs in the city. It has endured through nearly 40 years of activity, receiving spon-sorships and continuing to affirm the prin-ciples of dissemination (as well as moral practice) which it set out to follow.

# Gilad Atzmon
ALTO AND SOPRANO SAXOPHONES
*born* 9 June 1963

Born in Israel, Atzmon studied in Jerusalem before beginning to tour Europe with his own groups. Dismayed at his country's atti-tude towards Palestine, he exiled himself to first Germany and then London in the mid-90s, working with rock musicians such as Ian Dury as well as leading his own bands. Atzmon's combustible views – he is a dedi-cated anti-Zionist whose polemics in inter-views can be scathingly uncompromising – are to some extent mirrored in his playing, which is ferociously full-on, although his records thus far have to some extent tamed what is in performance a much wilder approach. There is as much Turkish influ-ence as anything Jewish in his musical make-up, and recent work has uneasily intro-duced pop elements into what is at root a power-packed improvisational stance from a fine saxophonist. He has also published two scurrilously hilarious novels.

*Exile* (Enja)

# Georgie Auld
TENOR AND ALTO SAXOPHONES
*born* 19 May 1919; *died* 7 January 1990

Although his early experience was with swing big bands – Bunny Berigan, Artie Shaw, Benny Goodman and then Shaw again – when Auld formed his own band in 1943 he showed his progressive intentions by hir-ing the likes of Dizzy Gillespie and Erroll

Garner. He ran a club of his own, The Troubador, on 52nd Street and even took one of the saxophone chairs in the legendary Billy Eckstine big band. If he liked the style of bebop, though, he remained – like Charlie Ventura – more like a swing stylist, and in the 50s, following a move to California to assist his health, he became a studio regular, and cut albums with titles such as *Georgie Auld Plays For Melancholy Babies* (1958). Although he went back to New York at the end of the decade, the 60s saw him in Las Vegas lounges and the lure of steady work in Californian studios took him back there again. He became suddenly successful in Japan in the 70s, where he toured and made many records, and he took a role in Martin Scorsese's *New York, New York* (and also dubbed in Robert De Niro's saxophone parts). A much-respected pro, Auld's American records are a rather motley lot, but he should be remembered as a distinctive and likeable swing stylist.
**Georgie Auld Plays To The Winners** (Philips)

# Lovie Austin
PIANO
*born* 19 September 1887; *died* 10 July 1972

Originally from Chattanooga, Tennessee, Austin (born Cora Calhoun) led a series of sessions for the black record label Paramount – by Lovie Austin & Her Blues Serenaders – which are comparatively little-known cornerstones in Chicago's jazz heritage. College-trained, she was skilled enough to win the position as house pianist at Paramount, where she accompanied some of the best women singers, as well as leading her own sessions with such formidable sidemen as Tommy Ladnier and Johnny Dodds. The Blues Serenaders sessions use a carefully varied series of devices based around the blues, some of which – especially a penchant for going into a startling double-time – lend the music real individuality. She rarely took a solo role herself and, like Lil Hardin, she mostly executed a steady-rolling comp which nevertheless bossed the band. She then led the house band at Chicago's Monogram Theater for many years, before eventually working as pianist in a dance school. Like several of her surviving contemporaries, she was rediscovered for a farewell date in 1961, when she backed Alberta Hunter, as she had done for Paramount some 40 years earlier. Her best legacy is the Blues Serenaders sessions, which deserve to be more celebrated than they are.
**Lovie Austin 1922–1926** (Classics)

# Herman Autrey
TRUMPET, VOCAL
*born* 4 December 1904; *died* 14 June 1980

Although he only played with Fats Waller for seven years out of a career that stretched from the 20s to the 70s, Autrey will always be remembered as a Waller acolyte: they shared a taste for excess, and the trumpeter would often accompany Fats on one of his many binges. He was discovered by the pianist while working with the Charlie Johnson band in New York, although he'd already spent many years in the South, Washington and Philadelphia. Waller hired him when he formed his Rhythm group for Victor recording dates, and in between times Autrey found work in numerous different New York trumpet sections. After Waller's death, Autrey then led his own group at a long-lived residency in Philadelphia, but he was badly injured in a car crash in 1954, and thereafter had a lower profile until he joined the swing-revivalist group The Saints And Sinners in 1960, a gig which he clearly relished, working alongside the likes of Vic Dickenson, and which lasted through the 60s. In later years, he sang as often as he played trumpet, in a style which owed plenty to his old boss. Although he had to endure Waller shouting over many of his best solos, Autrey is a powerful presence on many of the Waller Rhythm sessions; and though in the end he might be accounted as a minor Louis Armstrong disciple, many of Waller's records would have been much poorer without him.
**Fats Waller, *The Middle Years*** (Bluebird)

# George Avakian
PRODUCER
*born* 15 March 1919

Avakian was one of the first jazz producers. He was writing jazz criticism while still in college at Yale, and after putting together an album of Chicago jazz for Decca he joined Columbia in 1940, where he worked on reissue programmes of some of their classic material, from Armstrong's Hot Fives onwards. He was there until 1958, producing both original and reissue albums, and then worked for Warners and RCA; in the 90s, although in supposed retirement, Avakian was still doing consultancy work for Columbia as they once again trawled their vintage archives in the CD era.

## Avant-garde

The term used to collectivize those individuals who are ahead of the pack and pushing at artistic barriers has been as much used in jazz as it has in every other kind of 20th-century art. Mostly, though, it refers to the free players of the 60s and after. It is nevertheless possible to describe outlaw figures in other areas in the same way, as in, 'Wow, that cat plays really avant-garde Dixieland!'

## Bent Axen
PIANO
*born* 12 August 1925

Axen worked in what were effectively light-music bands in his native Copenhagen, but he loved Charlie Parker's playing and wanted to have his own bop group. He formed Jazz Quintet '60 in 1959, with Allan Botschinsky and Bent Jaedig, and then recorded with his own trio and backed various visitors to the Danish capital. After 1967 he played mostly for TV and in theatre orchestras, and reluctantly left jazz behind: 'if you want to tackle it, you must be out there every night sharpening your talent and your powers'. The available recorded legacy isn't large, but what there is sounds remarkably fresh and lively and unbeholden to hard-bop clichés. A 1961 trio session included on the disc cited also offers the opportunity to hear Niels-Henning Ørsted Pedersen on his very first date.
*Axen* (Steeplechase)

## Roy Ayers
VIBES, VOCAL
*born* 10 September 1940

Ayers is a supreme example of a minor talent which has succeeded far beyond its relatively modest means. Raised in Los Angeles, he tried out various instruments before settling on the vibraphone, and in the early 60s became a fixture on the city's club scene with numerous leaders. In the second half of the decade he worked regularly with Herbie Mann, who produced several of Ayers's albums. *Virgo Vibes*, made for Atlantic in 1967, is a characteristic record, the music coming out of a settled hard-bop territory, with just enough catchiness to soften the tone. But *Stoned Soul Picnic*, made a year later, shows where Ayers would ultimately head – straight for the pop-soul audience. His band Ubiquity, formed at the start of the 70s, helped him thrive in what would have been hard times for a hard bopper: mixing ingredients from every kind of popular idiom, the group's sound was both prescient and often a bit muddled, yet Ayers's natural cheerfulness kept it likeable, and he often spent as much time singing as using his mallets. He recorded a long string of albums for Polydor, several of which – especially *Everybody Loves The Sunshine* (1976), *Vibrations* (1977) and *Let's Do It* (1978) – are central texts in the lightweight jazzing of soul music, and nobody who went clubbing during the era will have forgotten hits such as 'Running Away'. Perhaps no jazz musician adapted to disco – and survived its decline – as capably as Ayers. His appeal as a recording artist waned a little in the 90s but he continues to perform tirelessly on the touring circuit. As a vibes player he has been neither influential nor individually memorable, but his real talents – as a bandleader and popularizer – demanded no instrumental virtuosity anyway.
*Vibrations* (Polydor)

## Albert Ayler
TENOR SAXOPHONE
*born* 13 July 1936; *died* November 1970

The opening moments of Ayler's *Spiritual Unity* (1964) are still shocking and extraordinary (the recording engineer reputedly fled the studio as the music continued), and it is a measure of Ayler's continuing mystique that in 2004 the appearance of *Holy Ghost*, an extravagant archive of largely unheard material, was greeted with worldwide fascination on its first release. Born in Cleveland, he began working in blues bands on alto sax, touring with Little Walter at 16, before going into the army. On his discharge (he had been stationed in France until 1961), by now playing tenor, he was luckless in finding gigs, and went to Scandinavia, recording for the first time in Stockholm: the contrast between a boppish rhythm section and his braying, tempestuous saxophone is already bizarre. He carried on playing in Stockholm and Copenhagen (where he played with Don Cherry and Cecil Taylor) and went to New York in 1963. His 1964 group with Cherry, Gary Peacock and Sunny Murray was seminal, and it was this band (minus Cherry) that recorded *Spiritual Unity*. His themes were utterly simple, sometimes no more than a bugle-call motif, something which he might have remembered from the army: yet that contrasted with collective improvisations (there were few 'solos' in Ayler's music) which were furious, seemingly inchoate, yet played with shredding virtuosity by all hands – Peacock and Murray seem lit up by Ayler's playing. His brawling tenor sound, full of overtones, multiphonics, a juddering vibrato and passages which appear as close to screaming as any saxophonist has come, can seem like mere madness at first, yet the music coheres soon enough into a thrilling exposition. But it was never popular in Ayler's lifetime: in 1965, which might have been his greatest year as a performing artist, he played fewer than a dozen concerts. He put together new groups with his brother Donald (b 1942) on trumpet, and other players such as Call Cobbs, Charles Tyler, Henry Grimes and Milford Graves. Ayler made four albums for ESP-Disk, and a further four for Impulse! were issued in his lifetime, but in 1968, perhaps demoralized by years of poverty and inattention, Ayler went from excoriating free playing to a kind of hippified R&B, with the disastrous *New Grass*, a decline which included mundane singing and material of – in comparison with what came before – unfathomable banality.Yet this apparent sellout had a troubling undertow, for Ayler claimed to see visions and he said that 'We had the right seal of God almighty on our forehead', in an open letter which hinted at a kind of religious mania. Two further records followed, while surviving live recordings from the last months of his life suggest that Ayler was moving back to the strength and substance of his earlier music. On 5 November 1970 he went missing in New York, and his body was recovered from the East River three weeks later, an apparent suicide. All the so-called energy players who came after him are in Ayler's lineage, but few indeed approach the kind of intensity which this sharp-dressed, soft-spoken man left as his gift to jazz expression.

*Spiritual Unity* (ESP-Disk)

# Ab Baars

TENOR SAXOPHONE, CLARINET
*born* 21 November 1955

Baars sometimes gives the impression that he's the severest of improvisers, but his discography has gradually revealed a warmer player. He studied in Rotterdam and spent many years in the 70s and 80s both with the De Volharding orchestra and with Theo Lovendie, and then formed a trio with Wilbert de Joode and Martin van Duynhoven which continues to this day. Two mirthless solo records have presented grim listening, but his trio music is a lot more engaging, suggesting debts to such as Rollins, and his clarinet playing reflects a period of study with John Carter. The recent *Party At The Bimhuis* is the most approachable of the lot, with several guest players.

*Party At The Bimhuis* (Wig)

# Harry Babasin

BASS, CELLO
*born* 19 March 1921; *died* 21 May 1988

Babasin grew up in Dallas and played in Midwestern territory bands before fetching up first in New York and then (1945) California, where he remained. He was playing both cello (pretty rare in a bebop context, where he recorded with Dodo Marmarosa) and bass, and toured with Woody Herman before getting involved in studio work. In 1953 he recorded with Oscar Pettiford in a quintet, both men playing cello, and a year later Babasin founded Nocturne, a label which didn't last long but

put out a single ten-inch LP of his own quartet. In 1956 he started another chamber-jazz outfit, The Jazzpickers, which made three albums, one of which was the delightful *For Moderns Only* (1957). He was still working in the 60s and 70s although there appear to be no further records. From 1974 he also curated the Los Angeles Theaseum, which chronicled the story of West Coast jazz. In the brief story of jazz cello, he deserves at least a chapter or so.
*For Moderns Only* (Emarcy)

## Alice Babs
VOCAL
*born* 26 January 1924

Alice Nilsson became a star on Swedish radio and film even when she was a teenager, taking Babs as a suitable stage-name, and in wartime Sweden she was the nation's sweetheart. Working with swing-styled groups came easily to her and she had a gift for a lightly swinging delivery. Many of her records are more middle-of-the-road than jazz, but Duke Ellington regarded her fondly and she worked with him quite often from 1963; she sang at his funeral, too. In the new century she has recorded again. Like Monica Zetterlund, Babs has a modest voice which, with its inimitable accent, has offered her a small but unique part of jazz vocal history.
*Swing It!* (Phontastic)

## Gérard Badini
TENOR SAXOPHONE, PIANO
*born* 16 April 1931

Badini's rollicking tenor playing was a fixture in the Paris scene since he came to prominence in the middle 50s. He was a regular sideman with Claude Bolling and as a solo, earning the nickname 'Mr Swing'. In 1973 he founded Swing Machine, which included at one time or another three separate expat American drummers: Bobby Durham, Sam Woodyard and Sonny Payne. This was eventually succeeded by Super Swing Orchestra, which nodded towards the Basie idiom. Poor health eventually obliged him to keep to the piano and put down the horn, but his fat sound and Lockjaw-like exuberance is captured

on numerous sessions from the 60s and 70s.
*A Night At The Popcorn* (Black & Blue)

## Bad Plus
GROUP

Formed by Ethan Iverson (piano), Reid Anderson (bass) and David King (drums) in 2000, each of whom had played with the others in various combinations for some years, The Bad Plus became one of the first American groups in the new century to attract what some see as jazz 'hype'. They play a fierce version of acoustic piano-trio music, emboldened by a fine book of originals from all hands, and enlivened by unexpected choices of covers from the rock and pop canon, which have included Black Sabbath's 'Iron Man', Blondie's 'Heart Of Glass' and Abba's 'Knowing Me Knowing You' (Iverson, who claims almost no knowledge of rock music, usually has to be taught these by his companions). They made a single album for Jordi Pujol's Fresh Sounds label (for whom Iverson and Anderson have also made fine solo projects) but were then signed to Columbia, hence the hype. There was a somewhat absurd controversy in the US over whether their attention emanated from their being white and playing rock material; actually, their two Columbia albums to date have featured demanding and strikingly original playing.
*Give* (Columbia)

## Benny Bailey
TRUMPET
*born* 13 August 1925; *died* 14 April 2005

Emerging from Cleveland in the mid-40s, Bailey worked with Jay McShann, Dizzy Gillespie and Lionel Hampton, remaining with the latter until 1953, when he stayed behind in Europe following one of Hamp's overseas jaunts. He found the Old World much to his taste and worked there more or less for the rest of his life, in numberless studio situations, and with such straight-ahead groups as the Clarke–Boland big band. A Quincy Jones chart called 'Meet Benny Bailey' has been used as a headline on practically every article printed about him. An ideal man to lead a section, he was also a very smart soloist, boppishly quick and agile but thinking out his solos along long-form lines. There's relatively little under his own nominal leadership on record, but the Candid album listed below is a cracker.

**Big Brass** (Candid)

## Buster Bailey

CLARINET
*born* 19 July 1902; *died* 12 April 1967

Bailey was working on the Chicago scene as early as 1919. He was on some of the King Oliver Jazz Band sessions, and he joined fellow sideman Louis Armstrong in New York when both enlisted with the Fletcher Henderson orchestra, Bailey himself staying until 1929. A terror at cutting contests (even Benny Goodman wouldn't go up against him), Bailey could get all over the clarinet with insouciant ease: his bizarre record of 'Man With A Horn Goes Berserk' (1938) is an almost frightening display of virtuosity. Bailey didn't find much of a niche as any kind of leader and he was back with Henderson soon enough, staying until 1937, and then joining the John Kirby group, whose polite dissertations on small-group swing seemed to suit the clarinettist's most detached style. After the war he worked with Sidney De Paris and then, in particular, Henry Allen, a happy association which lasted for many years. At the very end of a contented and professionally successful life, he worked with Louis Armstrong's All Stars. Bailey is one of the great figures of jazz clarinet, yet like so many important performers of the pre-LP era his reputation has suffered neglect simply because he is not closely associated with a single group of famous sessions. Although many of his records suggest a buttoned-up performer, he was more a distinguished professional who was happy to fit in. There are many brief, exciting solos in his Henderson years, and the cultivated style of the Kirby sessions shows his other side to good advantage.

**Fletcher Henderson, *A Study In Frustration*** (Columbia)

## Dave Bailey

DRUMS
*born* 22 February 1926

Originally a minor figure on the New York hard-bop scene, Bailey did some of his most renowned work behind Gerry Mulligan and in the Clark Terry–Bob Brookmeyer groups of the 60s, although his three records as a leader – *One Foot In The Gutter*, *Gettin' Into Something* (both 1960) and *Bash!* (1961) – are collectors' favourites. He gave up music for a spell to go into aviation at the end of the 60s, but came back as more of a teacher-administrator and has been involved as director of the Jazzmobile, which runs performance programmes in New York.

**One Foot In the Gutter** (Epic)

## Derek Bailey

GUITAR
*born* 29 January 1932

Bailey is a Yorkshireman whose relationship with jazz has been, to say the least, tenuous, since he regards himself as an improviser and guitarist first. He worked in commercial music-making, often accompanying singers, in the 50s and early 60s, but on moving to London in 1966 he found himself fascinated by the free playing centred around the John Stevens circle, and he worked in both the Spontaneous Music Ensemble and with Tony Oxley's group, as well as in a trio, Joseph Holbrooke, with Oxley and Gavin Byers. Two subsequent bands were Music Improvisation Company and Iskra 1903 (with Barry Guy and Paul Rutherford), but Bailey eventually became disenchanted with fixed groupings of musicians and in 1976 formed the floating ensemble Company, convened only occasionally and consisting of a different group of improvisers each time. His own playing had by this time moved from its popular-music origins – Bailey never appears to have sounded much like any jazz guitarist one could name – to an entirely original vocabulary of improvising, on both the electric (for many years played through a tiny and beaten-up-looking amplifier) and acoustic instrument, the music played without recognizable pitch or meter, the phrasing splintery and spidery but driven by its own, often ruthless logic. For a number of years he was closely associated with Evan

Parker, with whom he co-founded the Incus label, but that association foundered in the 80s after disagreements and they have not performed together since. In the 90s, Bailey became more eminent than ever before, an association with John Zorn yielding numerous American connections and recording opportunities, and his long-standing appreciation by the Japanese audience continuing. He recorded with Pat Metheny, The Ruins, Bill Laswell, Tony Williams and Min Tanaka (a dancer) among many others, and was persuaded into making exploratory forays into drum'n'bass music, an album of feedback and eventually – and this was once unthinkable – a record of ballads, although done as only Bailey can. His book *Improvisation: Its Nature And Practice In Music* (1980) is an absorbing treatise, even if he has seemed to subsequently go back on many of the principles he establishes therein. As bluffly cantankerous as any Yorkshireman can be, Bailey has recently decamped from his world-renowned Hackney address to live in Spain.
*Playing* (Incus)

# Mildred Bailey
VOCAL
*born* 27 February 1907; *died* 12 December 1951

Bailey's life rivals Billie Holiday's for tragedy, and the two women were, along with Connee Boswell and Ella Fitzgerald, the leading female jazz singers of their day (Bailey admired Holiday's singing but disliked the person). She was born Mildred Rinker in Tekoa, Washington, and began singing on local radio stations. Her brother Al was one of Paul Whiteman's Rhythm Boys, and Whiteman hired Mildred too in 1929. She stayed four years, long enough to make the hit version of 'Rockin' Chair' which landed her with the unwelcome sobriquet 'The Rockin' Chair Lady'. It didn't help that she was hugely overweight. She married Red Norvo in 1933 and he featured her on many of his records. By the end of the decade she was an established star, cutting scores of records and a regular on the radio, using her girlish voice to gently swing through a comprehensive book of the day's better popular songs; but her marriage began to fail and her dreadful mood swings started to sour her reputation. Her V-Disc recordings of the

40s show that her artistry was still on a high, even though she had to sing some awful tunes (one, 'Scrap Your Fat', about losing weight to help the war effort, must have wounded her). But she had health problems which slowed her career down, and at the end of the decade she barely survived a spell in hospital. Still greatly admired by other singers and musicians who had worked with her, she was working again a year later but her health finally collapsed at the end of 1951 and she died broke. Where Holiday's records have endured, Bailey, who never made it to the LP era, is by comparison practically forgotten. The best of her records – 'Weekend Of A Private Secretary', 'These Foolish Things', 'Harlem Lullaby' – are unique in their blending of charm and impeccable musicianship.
*The Rockin' Chair Lady* (Proper)

# Chet Baker
TRUMPET, FLUGELHORN, VOCAL
*born* 23 December 1929; *died* 13 May 1988

Baker's picaresque life and overpowering legend sum up the romantic myth of the jazzman as a doomed young man, although inconveniently enough for that he lived to a late middle age and devastated several lives besides his own. Born in Yale, Oklahoma, he grew up around Los Angeles in the late 40s and – with Bix Beiderbecke a suitable inspiration – began playing trumpet at 13. After working in army bands he worked for a brief spell with Charlie Parker (back East, Bird is reputed to have warned Miles Davis about 'a little white cat who's going to eat you up'). But his great association remains the one with Gerry Mulligan, which began in 1952 in the baritonist's pianoless quartet. They played in little clubs such as The Haig and created a jazz sensation, Baker's movie-star looks combining with a delicate trumpet tone that was, nevertheless, fleet and skilful, his solos often measured within a single octave and at a smoothly even dynamic (latter-day suggestions that Baker was a technical incompetent are never borne out by the records). Matched with Mulligan's gruffly good-natured timbre, it was an irresistible combination which seemed to personify a new West Coast sound. But the group only stayed together a year or so, and Baker was soon out on his own, leading quartets with

Russ Freeman and Dick Twardzik and seemingly with the jazz world at his feet. He began singing, in a pale, almost asexual style which broke at least as many hearts as his trumpet playing. But when Twardzik died of a heroin overdose while on tour with Baker in Paris, it hinted at a darkening horizon. When Baker himself became addicted, he never got off junk, and the rest of his life was spent in a twilight world of playing and fixing. He wandered through Europe and the US, often busted (he spent a period in an Italian jail in 1960–61), but making as many gigs as he could and still recording – for Jazzland, Riverside and, in a burst of recording in a group with George Coleman, for Prestige. He endured a terrible beating in 1968 which ruined his teeth (and brass players depend for their embouchure on their teeth staying strong), but eventually he rebuilt his style and by the mid-70s was playing regularly again, although more frequently in Europe than the US. In the later 70s and all through the 80s he was recorded almost obsessively by admiring labels, and his latter discography is huge and almost indiscriminate. His playing lost some of its fluency, but much of it still had real intelligence, and his singing stayed musical even as his looks declined, his face a mask of sunken tragedy. Despised by many fellow musicians and blindly revered by others, he retained an eerie retinue of lovers and admirers despite a catalogue of exploitative relationships, chronicled in the painful memoir *Deep In A Dream*. He died after a fall from a hotel window: whether self-induced, accident or homicide, nobody is quite sure.

*Chet Baker Sings* (Pacific Jazz)

# Harold 'Shorty' Baker
TRUMPET
*born* 26 May 1914; *died* 8 November 1966

It's a little unfair if inescapable to remember Shorty Baker as a minor Ellingtonian. He grew up in St Louis and started out on drums, but in his brother Winfield's band he played lead cornet. He worked in several big bands during the 30s – including Ellington's, briefly, in 1938 – and also in a small group with Mary Lou Williams, who was his first wife. But after joining Ellington in 1942 he stayed ten years (with a brief interruption

for army service), went freelance for a while in the middle 50s and then went back to the Ducal fold in 1957. He didn't take that many solos – Ellington was never short of star trumpeters – but he was a studious and dedicated section-man, and when he did take a solo (usually on a ballad such as 'Stardust') his sweetness and unshowy elegance were a delight. 'He had no bad notes at all,' remembered Ellington. Shorty finally left for good in 1964 and led his own small group for a time, but he was eventually hospitalized with cancer.

**Duke Ellington, *Masterpieces*** (Columbia)

# Kenny Baker
TRUMPET, FLUGELHORN
*born* 1 March 1921; *died* 7 December 1999

A tough little Yorkshireman with an avuncular smile, Baker was the consummate professional and a fixture in British jazz for 60 years. He had learned his craft in local brass bands, and by his early 20s he was surprising listeners in London jam sessions with his superb command of the trumpet. He joined Ted Heath as lead trumpet in 1945 after working in RAF orchestras, and besides his instrumental work he turned in some of the more jazz-orientated charts for the band. After leaving Heath, he turned his hand to small-group work, and studio music for radio, TV and films, all of which took up the rest of his busy life. He led an octet early in the 50s, and then Kenny Baker's Dozen, the latter broadcasting on a weekly basis for the remainder of the decade. Thereafter he was always on call as a star soloist, and began to specialize in swing-era re-creations: he was a regular in revivals of the Heath Orchestra, and was even asked by the Harry James estate to take over that band after James's death. One project he saw through later in life was to re-create the earlier music of Louis Armstrong, with Armstrong's voice overdubbed on to Baker's revisions. Kenny was still working with such old friends as Don Lusher and Laurie Johnson in the last year of his life, still master of the brass instruments which had kept his diary full for more than half a century.

*A Date With The Dozen* (Lake)

# Burt Bales
PIANO
*born* 20 March 1916; *died* 26 October 1989

Although born in a town in Montana, Bales made his name in San Francisco, where he began working professionally in 1939, soon joining the Lu Watters–Turk Murphy–Bob Scobey group of traditionalists (and working with all three leaders). Bales was a strong player in the Jelly Roll Morton tradition, offering little of his own in his perform-ances but keeping the flame of 20s jazz piano very much alive. He recorded as a solo-ist for Good Time Jazz and was a regular in many San Francisco clubs; and though he left music for some time and worked as an electrician, he returned to regularly playing in his old haunts in 1975 and was still per-forming within weeks of his death.
***New Orleans Joys*** (Good Time Jazz)

# Jon Balke
PIANO
*born* 7 June 1955

Balke hasn't secured the attention accorded to some Norwegian modernists but he is a quietly pivotal figure in his country's music. He grew up in Oslo and began playing in jazz-rock groups while in his teens. But his first important association was with Arild Andersen, recording for ECM, and he then spent some years as an accompanist to Radka Toneff. In the 80s his principal associ-ation was with the group Masqualero, which he co-led, before working with the larger group Oslo 13. He recorded only sparely in the 90s, and recent years have yielded only two records, *Kyanos* and *Diverted Travels*, which have renewed his association with ECM. These are credited to the Magnetic North Orchestra (named for a piece com-missioned by the 1994 Winter Olympics), and feature curious instrumentations through which Balke's keyboards wind like the meanders of a river. Very much music of texture and open harmonies, but in person the Orchestra also has great rhythmic power: if Balke could tour more widely, he would surely be much better known and appreciated.
***Kyanos*** (ECM)

# Kenny Ball
TRUMPET, VOCAL
*born* 22 May 1930

Ball was a dominant part of the trad boom. He started out in big bands under such leaders as Eric Delaney, and formed his own Dixieland outfit in 1958, with John Bennett (trombone, and still there) and others. It was a smart, polished outfit almost from the start, and recording for Pye, Ball soon had hits: 'I Love You Samantha', 'Sukiyaki' and above all his 'Midnight In Moscow', a classic of British jazz (Ball finally played in the USSR in 1985). The band's early records are their best, with Kenny's own playing a typi-cally forceful mix of Louis Armstrong and a more modern outlook, but like Acker Bilk and others he realized that when the beat groups took over his future would be in cab-aret. Regulars on television in the 70s and 80s, the Ball Jazzmen have never stopped touring. The leader has had a hard and unfair time of it with critics, even though a lot of his later material amounted to ordi-nary British showbiz: all he ever says is he wants to play trumpet the best he can. It was sad to hear that, in the new century, he has had to stop playing the horn, but he is still fronting the band and singing.
***The Pye Jazz Albums*** (Castle)

# Ronnie Ball
PIANO
*born* 22 December 1927; *died* October 1984

Ball had very few featured roles on record but he was a skilful and compelling player who deserved better. Born in Birmingham, he was one of the lucky British players who heard some American jazz first-hand after working on the ocean liners, and back in London he put lessons with Lennie Tristano to good use in bands with Ronnie Scott and others. But he moved to New York for good in 1952. His highlighted appearances on record are with Warne Marsh, Lee Konitz and Art Pepper, although it's his sole American leadership date, the admirable *All About Ronnie* (Savoy, 1956) with superb work from Ball and Ted Brown, which finds him at his best – much indebted to Tristano, but full of fresh and vital playing. There-after, though, he played in less conspicuous settings and while he was still playing in the

70s he worked more regularly as a music copyist.

**All About Ronnie** (Savoy)

## Ballad

The ballad form in jazz is basically a love song played at a slow tempo: anything from the American popular songbook is fair game for this treatment, and many musicians have their favourite ballads to improvise on as a breather or a change of pace in a set which might otherwise be dominated by faster music. It is often used as a feature for one of the horn players in a hard-bop band. Actually, almost any piece of music played at a slowish tempo can be described as 'a ballad'.

## Iain Ballamy

TENOR, ALTO AND SOPRANO SAXOPHONES
*born* 20 February 1964

Self-taught on the saxophone, Ballamy fell in with such young talents as Django Bates (his most frequent collaborator), Mick Hutton and Steve Arguëlles on the London scene of the early 80s, and was one of the principals in the Loose Tubes big band, an association which helped him to get major-label backing for his *Balloon Man* set (1988). Since then he has enjoyed various associations – with Bates's Human Chain band, Bill Bruford's Earthworks and with singers Claire Martin and Ian Shaw – as well as leading various projects of his own, including an acclaimed Anglo-Norwegian venture, Food. Ballamy mostly plays tenor and has an interestingly idiosyncratic sound and manner, which avoids licks and obvious saxophone role models and is an odd mix of assertion and a kind of twinkling lyricism. A garrulous fellow who thinks nothing of ringing up a writer to complain about an 'unsupportive' review, he is perhaps waiting for some kind of breakthrough project that will take his career up another level.

**Food** (Feral)

## Whitney Balliett

WRITER
*born* 17 April 1926

Balliett is arguably the pre-eminent American jazz journalist. He wrote for the *Saturday Review* in the early 50s and for *The New Yorker* from 1957, contributing what amounted to a regular essay on contemporary happenings in New York jazz, most often based around a profile of a single musician, occasionally a record release. He has received extravagant praise over the years, and regarding his impressionist style, 'I have been told that I come closer to delineating the music than any notator,' doubtless to his own satisfaction. Yet even a cursory reading of Balliett makes it clear that he has a significant technical knowledge too. All of his books are collections of his journalism. Some of his finest pieces – on Pee Wee Russell, Henry Allen and others – are little masterpieces.

## Rudy Balliu

CLARINET
*born* 3 August 1941

Born in Ghent, Balliu began playing trumpet on the Belgian trad scene, notably with the Cotton City Jazz Band, but switched to clarinet in 1965. He has since often recorded with some of his American inspirations, such as Louis Nelson, Alton Purnbell and Kid Thomas Valentine, and his later group The Society Serenaders makes fair claim to being one of the leading European groups playing in the traditional style, recording for Stomp Off and others. He has also played in New Orleans.

**New Orleans Trio** (GHB)

## Dave Ballou

TRUMPET
*born* 22 April 1963

Ballou has been active on the New York scene since the early 90s. He might be accounted as typical of his time: a strong player with a clear cool tone, he has worked in a broad variety of settings and has managed to make four albums of his own as leader, which mix excellence with original writing that often sounds more like some-

one trying out ideas in public than presenting something finished and satisfying. That said, there's an unpretentious finesse to much of his playing and the record cited gives a good picture of his circle of playing as it stood in 1999.
***The Floating World*** (Steeplechase)

## Band

While jazz has its solo tradition via, in particular, the piano, it is at heart a group music, where a 'band' of musicians – at least three in number, although the more players there are, the more it is a band – will work cooperatively on a musical performance. It is fair to say that every kind of jazz band is an evolution from the variety of ensembles which worked in New Orleans from around the turn of the 20th century. These would include the marching bands, involved in street parades, funerals and other such functions, derived from a military model; the rough-and-ready small groups that worked in brothels and saloon parlours and which might have been made up of a variety of melody and rhythm instruments (piano, guitar, horns, drums, etc); the smarter dance or society orchestras, which worked at the upmarket end of New Orleans entertainment (often for white audiences), playing a more schooled kind of music; and the bands which played at dances and picnics, where the likes of Bunk Johnson and Buddy Bolden probably did most of their professional playing. While any number of musical tributaries fed into these bands, they in turn disseminated the music out into the wider world of American entertainment; and when the Original Dixieland Jazz (Jass) Band set out to conquer the world, they established jazz in the public mind as a band music.

## Billy Bang
VIOLIN
*born* 20 September 1947

William Walker Vincent studied classical violin in his youth, yet left it alone, disliking the idiom, until he came back from a tour of duty in Vietnam in 1968. In the middle 70s he began drawing attention on the New York loft scene, and joined the String Trio Of New York in 1977, a line-up which lasted for ten

years, and which settled the differences between Bang's bluesy, roughened sound and his instinctive grasp of the violin's formal heritage. While he has made some interesting records since, touring for a time in partnership with Frank Lowe under the name The Jazz Doctors (they wore white surgical gowns on stage), Bang has never quite recaptured the finer passions of his earlier music, and perhaps he is best in a cooperative like the STNY. His most striking project of recent times, though, has been *Vietnam: The Aftermath* (2001), an often disquieting evocation of Bang's military experience, with kindred spirits such as Lowe, Ted Daniel and Sonny Fortune in the ensemble.
***Valve No 10*** (Soul Note)

## Danny Bank
BARITONE SAXOPHONE, FLUTE, ETC
*born* 17 July 1922

Danny Bank has made an uncountable number of records, even though many fans are scarcely aware of his existence: 'there must be over ten thousand albums that have my name on them. That doesn't mean much except you can up the scale!' Born in Brooklyn, he grew up in a Jewish family where music was revered, and he learned violin, although polio ruined his legs and he could never take a stage job that meant standing up. In the 40s he worked regularly with Charlie Barnet, having taken up the baritone, and then with many leaders – Goodman, Shaw and both Dorseys – before going the studio route in the 50s, which took him towards that extraordinary number of records. Bank scarcely ever took a solo, and never wanted to: content as a master craftsman on baritone, flute, piccolo or whatever, he became a familiar part of the studio wallpaper. He sold Serge Chaloff his first baritone, and got Gerry Mulligan his first important gig (having got the impecunious Mulligan's horn out of the hock shop for him). Teddy Reig once offered him his own date ('We'll call it *Danny's Bank Account*') but 'it was too much work and I had too much to do'. At the time of Harry Carney's death, Ellington's baritone maestro was taking flute lessons – from Danny Bank.

# Denys Baptiste
TENOR AND SOPRANO SAXOPHONES
*born* 14 September 1969

Baptiste's big, vociferous tenor sound has been a fixture on the London scene of the last few years. Inspired by Courtney Pine's example, he switched from clarinet to tenor and took a Guildhall course, subsequently hooking up with Gary Crosby and working in the bassist's Nu Troop and Jazz Jamaica groups. His own quartet has been the main focus of his recent playing (and is recorded by Dune, Crosby's label). Like so many younger players, Baptiste has sought to find a context for his playing which stands out from the pack on record, and he seemed to have found it on the acclaimed *Let Freedom Ring!*, a festival commission which uses Martin Luther King's famous 1963 speech as the basis for a suite.
*Let Freedom Ring!* (Dune)

# Amiri Baraka
WRITER
*born* 7 October 1934

Born Everett LeRoi Jones, Baraka studied on various instruments, but it is as a journalist and commentator that he is significant. One of the few blacks to make a significant impact in an otherwise overwhelmingly white critical establishment in the 60s, he was active equally as a poet, playwright and critical commentator in that period, his most prolific decade from a jazz point of view. The groundbreaking works *Blues People* (1963) and *Black Music* (1967), the latter a compilation of his journalism, are his most important, in particular the former, where for the first time a black writer offered a full-scale study of how jazz was obliged to function within other people's parameters: 'Negro music is *always* radical in the context of formal American culture.' Subsequently, though, Baraka's involvement waned as he addressed himself to other cultural areas, even though he remains a potent influence through the force of his original vision.

# Paul Barbarin
DRUMS
*born* 5 May 1899; *died* 10 February 1969

Barbarin packed a huge amount of music into his 70 years, which began and ended with New Orleans brass bands. His father Isidore (1872–1960) was an alto horn veteran, and his brother Louis (1902–97) also played drums. As a boy, Paul loved banging on whatever percussive devices he could find, and in that connection had to go to court to answer to a charge of public disturbance: when the judge heard him play, he offered him 50 cents for his trouble and threw out the case. Barbarin played (with Jimmie Noone) in Buddy Petit's Young Olympia Band before trying his luck in Chicago in 1917, arriving in time to play with King Oliver, Freddie Keppard and Sidney Bechet. He went back home to play in other brass bands, but then rejoined Oliver in Chicago and eventually went to play drums for Luis Russell in New York. He was with Russell for most of the period when they backed Louis Armstrong, who always seemed lit up by his New Orleans-styled beat, but in the end Barbarin was sacked in 1938 and returned home. Aside from occasional spells in Chicago, Los Angeles and New York, there he basically remained. In the 50s he recorded regularly as a leader and formed his own Onward Brass Band. Barbarin was an old-fashioned player, in that he drew much of his playing from the unshakeable momentum of the parade bands, used the simplest of kits, and even went back to two-beat rhythms if he felt that the dancers in the audience weren't responding to the band. His Onward Brass Band was the closest to his heart, and his last act as a musician was to lead it at the 1969 Proteus parade, which is the curtain-raiser to Mardi Gras. At this moment of triumph, he died while the band played.
*Jazz At Preservation Hall* (Atlantic)

# Chris Barber
TROMBONE, BASS
*born* 17 April 1930

Barber is a key figure not just in British jazz but in the whole field of popular music as it developed in Britain in the 50s and 60s. He started on trombone in 1948 and formed his first band a year later, studying at the Guildhall in the early 50s. His first five-piece group – with Monty Sunshine, Jim Bray, Lonnie Donegan and Ron Bowden – was joined by Ken Colyer in 1953, and although 'We all knew Ken had a better instinct about jazz than any of us', Colyer's temperament split up the band and Pat Halcox joined instead. With this line-up, Barber began to assert himself as perhaps the major force in British traditional jazz. Even on their earliest sessions for Decca, the mix of skill, feel and enthusiasm for their material is infectious and powerful. Donegan stayed until 1956, when 'Rock Island Line', actually recorded for a Barber album, became a hit for him (Barber played bass on that track – his best-selling appearance on record by far, somewhat to his chagrin). If Barber helped initiate the skiffle boom, he also got round the British MU ban on American artists playing in the UK by bringing in singers (who were exempt), such as Big Bill Broonzy and Sister Rosetta Tharpe: 'We were trying to be part of the real thing. The idea was to play this music and let it go. Wherever it went didn't matter.' Besides the tradition, Barber also liked Charlie Parker and Ornette Coleman (whom he heard at the Village Vanguard), and as the trad boom began to die away at the beginning of the 60s, he regrouped as the Chris Barber Jazz & Blues Band, bringing in guitarist John Slaughter (who had been rejected by John Mayall). Albums such as *Folk Barber Style* and *Battersea Rain Dance* (1968) expanded his audience without losing his diehards: the Barber band remained hugely popular in Germany and the Eastern bloc. By the 70s, Barber had expanded his associations further and worked with John Lewis, Louis Jordan, Trummy Young, Wild Bill Davis and Dr John among others. But he never quite went down the mainstream road followed by Humphrey Lyttelton: the rough edge of trad persisted, to his satisfaction. In the 80s and 90s he premiered some large-scale works, including a trombone concerto, and in the new century he created a Big Chris Barber Band, which adds extra horns and plays Ellington material in an attempt to revive some of the inimitable Ducal voicings. In 2004, he celebrated 50 years of continuous bandleading. Barber's impact on trad, skiffle, British R&B and practically every other kind of US-derived 'roots music', as it has been

played in Britain, is huge and profound, and he has put his name on one of the most consistently appealing bodies of work to come out of British popular music.
*The Decca Sessions* (Lake)

## Patricia Barber
PIANO, VOCAL
*born* 8 November 1955

Barber's father played in Glenn Miller's reed section, but he died an alcoholic, and for a long time she tried to keep away from music: 'It's only been very recently that I haven't almost hated what I was doing.' Born in Lisle, Illinois, she moved to Chicago at the beginning of the 80s and began playing piano in clubs, holding down long residencies at the Gold Star Sardine and the Green Mill Inn. She made a single album in 1991 for Antilles and toured Europe, but a perpetual stagefright kept her away from wider success, and only when she began recording for Blue Note (via a separate imprint, Premonition) did she begin to gather in a bigger reputation. Barber admires the standard repertory but finds it frustratingly old-fashioned, and her albums are full of startling original material – sung in a husky contralto – and unexpected covers, such as Sonny & Cher's 'The Beat Goes On'. She works with a small group which puts her flinty piano playing at its heart. Still based in Chicago, Barber has put together a sequence of records which have 'cult following' written all over them, although she is as original and stylish a performer as any in what is currently a very oversubscribed field.
*Modern Cool* (Premonition)

## Gato Barbieri
TENOR SAXOPHONE, FLUTE
*born* 28 November 1934

An Argentinian, Barbieri was a late starter: though he played clarinet early on, he didn't even pick up the tenor until he was 20, and didn't leave his native country until the 60s. He went to live in Rome in 1962 and began an association with Don Cherry, who used him on some of his Blue Note dates. Carla Bley used him brilliantly on her *Escalator Over The Hill* (1968 71): his astounding solo passage in the 'Overture' is a defining moment for him. Yet a reputation as a great saxophone screamer was eventually dissipated by a sometimes self-conscious return to 'my roots', and a mix of jazz with Latin American musics that started out virile and ended almost as Muzak. Barbieri scored a big break when he was the saxophone voice on the soundtrack to *Last Tango In Paris* in 1972, a date that made his fortune. His own albums for Flying Dutchman and A&M were often heftily orchestrated and nigglingly mixed and it is frequently hard to recognize Barbieri's distinctive voice in amongst the percussion and whatnot. In the 90s, he came back from illness to start recording again for Columbia, with mixed results. He often seems like a potentially major voice that never quite found its right timbre.

**Last Tango In Paris** (Rykodisc)

## Eddie Barefield
ALTO AND TENOR SAXOPHONES, CLARINET
*born* 12 December 1909; *died* 4 January 1991

Barefield worked quietly in various territory bands before joining Bennie Moten's reed section in 1932 and going to New York. Thereafter he had separate spells in many of the best bands in the city, including those of Cab Calloway, Fletcher Henderson and Don Redman, before moving on to mostly studio work in the 40s. Barefield directed pit bands on Broadway, went back with his old boss Calloway for some years as MD, toured Europe in various groups and eventually worked in a circus orchestra for much of the 70s. In the 80s, he turned up in numerous touring and festival bands, having lived through several jazz eras with the ability to authenticate whichever music was before him with genuine swing-era craft and *joie de vivre*. He left little to remember him by except a career marked by unflashy professionalism.

**Bennie Moten, Band Box Shuffle** (Hep)

## Dave Bargeron
TROMBONE, EUPHONIUM, TUBA
*born* 6 September 1942

A specialist in low brass, Bargeron was an accomplished technician at an early age and held down chairs in the Clark Terry and Doc

Severinsen bands before joining Blood Sweat & Tears in 1970, staying long enough to make eleven albums with them. This lent him the mantle of a man who could move easily between jazz situations and horn chores for rock stars, and, ever since, he has turned up in all sorts of settings, from Gerry Mulligan to David Sanborn to Howard Johnson's Gravity. Like many such performers he seems to have little to say as an individual beyond a display of top chops, but he has had few opportunities to be out front in any case. One thing he has worked on is a valve which goes into the mouthpiece of a slide-trombone to give it more fluency.

**Blood Sweat & Tears, Live** (Columbia)

## Danny Barker
GUITAR
*born* 13 January 1909; *died* 13 March 1994

A great stalwart of New Orleans jazz on several levels, Barker worked around Mississippi and the South in the later 20s and by 1930 he had arrived in New York, having made the inevitable switch from banjo to guitar. He toiled through the Depression years but was recording widely, with everyone from Henry Allen to Cab Calloway, who especially liked his playing and hired him for seven years from 1939. He also worked behind his wife, the vocalist Blue Lu Barker. He went back to the banjo in time for the revivalist movement, although he also struck up an unlikely friendship with pianist Herbie Nichols. Barker worked on New York's Dixieland circuit through the 50s but eventually went back to New Orleans. He became concerned to see the city's marching-band tradition maintained, founded the Fairview Baptist Church Brass Band, and found time to be assistant curator at the New Orleans Jazz Museum, as well as lecturing on the music's history. A gifted talespinner and eloquent historian, he set down three volumes of sometimes fanciful memoirs. A fine rhythm player on both banjo and guitar, towards the end of his long and busy life he was lionized by the likes of Wynton Marsalis and found himself to be a bit of a legend. There are certainly few players who can claim to have played with musicians as distant from each other as Little Brother Montgomery, Herbie

Nichols, Billie Holiday, Bunk Johnson and Marsalis.
**Blue Lu Barker, *1938–1946*** (Classics)

## Guy Barker
TRUMPET
*born* 26 December 1957

Born in Chiswick, west London, Barker joined the NYJO at 13 and became one of its most eminent graduates. In the 80s he was one of the top sessionmen in London, playing on countless studio dates in every kind of music, the star player of a generation which also included Chris Hunter and Clark Tracey – though they had less profile than the Jazz Warriors–Loose Tubes players, they were just as significant in maintaining the impetus of British jazz at a time when it generated little media interest. Barker worked in Tracey's quintet as well as in Tracey senior's small groups, but he was shy of group leadership himself until the 90s, when he began gigging with his own, international quintet, the players drawn from associations he had made from working around the world. At various times this has included the saxophonists Sigi Flosason, Perico Sambeat, Rosario Giuliani and Denys Baptiste and pianists Bernardo Sassetti and Jim Watson. His own playing has grown into a mature style which reflects an abiding love for Dizzy Gillespie and Clark Terry, while dwelling securely in modern jazz times. He made three albums for Verve/Emarcy during this period and has since made another for Colin Towns's Provocateur label. His work on soundtracks (he appears briefly in Anthony Minghella's *The Talented Mr Ripley*) has become an important adjunct to his other work, as composer and musician. These days he plays a Monette trumpet, custom-made by an American brass designer, of the same sort used by his friend Wynton Marsalis. There is no more committed and accomplished jazz musician in the UK.
***What Love Is*** (Emarcy)

## Everett Barksdale
GUITAR
*born* 28 April 1907; *died* 29 January 1986

Born in Detroit, Barksdale played several instruments but settled on guitar when he began working in Chicago at the start of the 30s. For most of his career he played in small groups, including those of Eddie South, Zutty Singleton, Herman Chittison and Cliff Jackson, and he plays some notable music on several sessions with Sidney Bechet. But his most famous work came with Art Tatum; he joined the pianist in 1949 and remained in his trio until Tatum's death. He had few pretensions to virtuosity and while he played electric guitar like everyone else, the origins of his style were in the louder and more percussive method he had developed on the acoustic instrument. In the 60s, he disappeared into TV work.
**Art Tatum, *The Complete Capitol Recordings*** (Capitol)

## Dale Barlow
SAXOPHONES
*born* 25 December 1959

A Sydneysider, Barlow is one of the few contemporary Australian players to have made any impact outside his local scene, principally because he has made an effort to seek out the wider jazz world. He studied in New York at the end of the 80s and spent time both there and in London, eventually working as a late-period Jazz Messenger (1989–91) and in Guy Barker's international quintet (1994–5). He still spends most of his time in Sydney, though. His group Wizards Of Oz has sought some kind of fusion between jazz and native Australian music, yet it tends to crowd Dale's own style of playing, which has terrific force and intensity when he's on. The record cited may be a plain post-bop setting, but the saxophone sounds huge and powered by a fine imagination.
***Live*** (Jazzhead)

## Bob Barnard
TRUMPET
*born* 24 November 1933

Barnard was caught up in the Australian trad boom of the 50s, playing with Graeme Bell and in his drummer brother Len's band. While he did much work as a sideman, he began leading his own groups in the 70s, and his elegant mainstream style has endured to the point where he is widely known, touring the UK, Europe and America as a guest star and inviting the likes of Ralph Sutton and Ruby Braff over to his regular 'Jazz Parties', held in Melbourne (his home town) during the 90s. He is a carefully reconstructed Armstrong man at heart, tempering the Pops influence with the lyrical shadings of Braff and Hackett.

**The Joint Is Jumpin'** (La Brava)

## Alan Barnes
ALTO AND BARITONE SAXOPHONES, CLARINET
*born* 23 July 1959

Britain's leading mainstreamer was actually first inspired by hearing Acker Bilk play clarinet, whereupon he 'started buying records with saxophones on the cover – you stumble through it, and I find that the exciting bit'. He studied at Leeds College and then joined the Pasadena Roof Orchestra, playing dance-band music, before being hired by Tommy Chase for his hard-bop combo. He then spent four years in the Humphrey Lyttelton band (1988–92) before freelancing as leader himself. He made 14 albums for John Bune's Zephyr label, in various combinations, and has recently established his own imprint, Woodville. Although alto and clarinet are his first instruments, he has also taken up the baritone to great effect. A plangent and superbly resourceful improviser, Barnes has become perhaps the most popular of a younger generation of British players, primarily through a perceived adherence to traditional values – a respect for melody, and 'I'll always stay with chord sequences I think' – even though he thinks Evan Parker is 'magnificent' and is versatile enough to stand his ground in almost any jazz company.

**Swingin' The Samba** (Woodville)

## George Barnes
GUITAR
*born* 17 July 1921; *died* 5 September 1977

Even by the standards of studio guitarists, Barnes played with a remarkably diverse group of names. He was working in his own trio as a teenager before taking an NBC staff job, where he worked behind the likes of Washboard Sam and Jazz Gillum. After war service he ran an octet and moved from Chicago to New York, still in demand for studio jobs and recording with, among others, both Bobby Hackett and Louis Armstrong. Although still playing sessions (Decca had him under a long contract in this respect), he went on to form a guitar duo with Carl Kress and, after Kress's death in 1965, another with Bucky Pizzarelli. Barnes was a quick-tempered man and he and Pizzarelli eventually fell out, only for the former to solder a new partnership with the equally fiery Ruby Braff. Inevitably, this didn't last either, but for a while in the early 70s the Braff–Barnes quartet was among the most lyrical and swinging of jazz groups. Barnes's style might seem conservative now, but in his time he was quite a revolutionary: one of the first on the electric guitar, and one of the few who could knock off the clipped, simple urgencies of rock phrasing while still maintaining swing-styled thinking as his premier turf. He died suddenly of a heart attack.

**The Ruby Braff/George Barnes Quartet** (Chiaroscuro)

## John Barnes
SAXOPHONES, CLARINET
*born* 15 May 1932

A Mancunian, Barnes worked with the local Zenith Six in the early 50s before joining Mike Daniels, and then finally turning pro with Alan Elsdon at the beginning of the 60s. By this time he had moved on from a New Orleans-styled clarinet vocabulary to a wider delivery of swing saxophone styles, taking in alto, tenor and particularly baritone. He became a potent force in the Alex Welsh band, enlisting in 1964 and staying ten years, and in 1979 he joined Humphrey Lyttelton, staying there for a dozen busy years of gigs and records. In the 90s he picked gigs as he pleased, on top of his game, and often working with his old Welsh sideman Roy Williams.

**Alex Welsh, *Classic Concert*** (Black Lion)

## Paul 'Polo' Barnes
CLARINET, SOPRANO AND ALTO SAXOPHONES
*born* 22 November 1901; *died* 13 April 1981

Like his brother Emile, Paul Barnes played classic New Orleans clarinet. In 1923, he joined Papa Celestin's Original Tuxedo Jazz

Orchestra and did some fine work on their few records, but he also played with both King Oliver and Jelly Roll Morton, his solo on the latter's 'Deep Creek Blues' standing as a notable example of the soprano sax getting a beneficial early airing. He performed with Oliver again in the early 30s and was on the King's disastrous last tour, where some nights the band only mustered cents in door money. Barnes played in numerous New Orleans outfits until 1950, when he went to California and all but quit playing. But he returned to New Orleans in 1959 and went back with the likes of Paul Barbarin and Kid Thomas Valentine. Thereafter he was a regular at Preservation Hall, and even went to Europe in the 70s, finally retiring in 1977. Where Emile (1892–1970) was a rougher, bluesier player, Paul preferred shapely phrases and a fine line. The session below pairs him with John Handy on three tracks, and their sound together is wonderful.

***Paul Barnes And His Polo Players*** (American Music)

## Walter Barnes
CLARINET AND SAXOPHONES
*born* 8 July 1905; *died* 23 April 1940

Barnes was fatally unlucky. Born in Vicksburg, he studied in Chicago and formed an orchestra, The Royal Creolians, which was good enough to work regularly on the competitive local scene and even win a residency at New York's Savoy Ballroom. They made only eight issued sides in 1928–9 and they're fast and hot enough to make one wish that there were many more. But Barnes chose eminence as a touring attraction in the 30s, working steadily around the Midwest and the South, and was out of the limelight as far as record making went. He was back in Chicago by 1939 but a few months later he and nine members of his band perished in a terrible fire at the Rhythm Club in Natchez.

***Walter Barnes & His Royal Creolians*** (Retrieval)

## Charlie Barnet
ALTO AND SOPRANO SAXOPHONES
*born* 26 October 1913; *died* 4 September 1991

The most-married man in jazz and one of the richest, Barnet breezed cheerfully through the music for decades, turning out scores of records, although very few have survived as jazz classics. The music was irresistibly attractive to a wealthy New York boy who liked to hang out in Harlem, and he began bandleading for himself as early as 1933 (a year later, Barnet's band were playing at the Apollo). He had a shot at the movie world but never landed a part, yet bandleading kept calling him back: there was another band in 1936, and another in 1938, and when Barnet's crew lost all their instruments and arrangements in a ballroom fire, Basie and Ellington helped out with gratis charts. Barnet had always hired mixed bands, and when he at last had a hit with 'Cherokee', he played all over the black circuit too. Charlie's bands included stellar jazz talent all through the 40s – Howard McGhee, Roy Eldridge, Buddy DeFranco, Clark Terry, Barney Kessel and Oscar Pettiford were just some of the names, as well as singer Lena Horne – and his own saxophone playing, while heavily in hock to Johnny Hodges, wasn't without interest. He was also among the few to make a go of the soprano sax in the big-band era. 'Skyliner' (1944), an arrangement which seems to sum up the swing era in its mix of dance-band catchiness and jazz feel, was one of his greatest moments. On his own admission, he held out against bop, but as he lost players to the draft, that influence finally crept in. In any case, as the big-band era went into a tailspin, Barnet, like almost everyone else, was obliged to disband, at the end of 1949. He made a handful of records for Verve, Clef and Capitol in the 50s and still led bands for dancing as and when he pleased, but hotel management took up more of his time – as well as dealing with nine or ten wives.

***Swingsation*** (GRP)

## Joey Baron
DRUMS
*born* 26 June 1955

Baron is an eminence in what used to be called New York's Downtown circles, but he had plenty of straight-ahead jazz experience before that. After Berklee studies he moved to Los Angeles, where he drummed for singers Carmen McRae and Al Jarreau in the later 70s as well as freelancing for numerous horn players. In 1982 he decided to go East, settled in New York, and began associations with both Toshiko Akiyoshi (small group and big band) and Bill Frisell, the latter an alliance which persists to this day. This led to gigs with John Zorn (another repeated collaborator), Herb Robertson, Dave Douglas and others, although at the same time Baron has continued his playing in more sober modern contexts, as with pianists Enrico Pieranunzi and Steve Kuhn. He hasn't had time, seemingly, to do much bandleading himself, though Baron Down and The Down Home Band were two such efforts. Baron's a chameleonic drummer, adaptable to any of the situations described, and though some of his outside work has at times sounded fussy, he swings the band, whoever it belongs to.

**Bill Frisell,** *Before We Were Born* (Elektra Musician)

## Barrelhouse

More a blues than a jazz term by origin, 'barrelhouse' piano may have come out of the saloons and bars set up in Southern logging camps. It is a steady, stomping style of playing, using regular left-hand figures although cast in a standard 4/4 beat, rather than the eight-beats-to-the-bar of boogie woogie. In the 20s, it depicted the kind of music being played in nascent urban blues areas such as Chicago, expanded to a small group and taking in New Orleans elements too. This rough-and-ready, banging style is best heard in the music of Jimmy Blythe, Jimmy O'Bryant, Natty Dominique, Buddy Burton and other Chicago-based players, whose output for Paramount and other labels typified barrelhouse jazz. The style was smoothed away by the middle 30s, with the new medium of R&B taking precedence, although a group such as The Harlem Hamfats still had plenty of barrelhouse in them.

## Dan Barrett
TROMBONE, CORNET
*born* 14 December 1955

Barrett is one of the new mainstreamers who've made a plangent case for swing-styled jazz holding its relevance. One thing that helps is his catholic taste: on *Melody In Swing* (1997), he plays everything from 'My Mother's Eyes' to 'Besame Mucho', with just a rhythm section for company. He began as a high-school player, working with different and mostly revivalist groups in and around southern California. Associating with this movement enabled Barrett to play alongside New Orleans and Chicagoan old-timers who'd been playing since the 30s, and gave him a strong grounding in the material, the style and the delivery of older jazz. But it wasn't until a move to New York in 1982, at the suggestion of Howard Alden, that he won any real attention. He worked briefly with Woody Herman and Benny Goodman, and then with Buck Clayton's big band, but his real impact has been as a sideman and leader in new-mainstream situations, recording extensively for Arbors (for whom he is a kind of MD) and Nagel Heyer. He is fluent on cornet but the trombone is perhaps his signature horn. He also likes the phrase 'You never know when Jazz will strike' – meaning that one can be playing a routine gig with a routine band, and even then some unexpected spark will turn the whole thing into a magical occasion.

*Melody In Swing* (Arbors)

## Sweet Emma Barrett
PIANO, VOCAL
*born* 25 March 1897; *died* 28 January 1983

Sweet Emma was playing piano in New Orleans dance halls for 60 years. She started in some serious company – Papa Celestin's Original Tuxedo Orchestra, in 1923 (Baby Dodds remembered that 'She had big eyes – we used to call her "Eyes". Very thin but oh my God, she could play nice piano'). Afterwards she worked with various local leaders before leading her own groups at Happy Landing and Preservation Hall. Her trademark was a set of bells attached to her red stocking-garters, which jingled merrily while she played and earned her the nickname 'The Bell Gal'. She worked continuously into the 60s and 70s, though she grew famously cranky: one musician who sat in with the band one night went over to say how much he'd enjoyed it, and she snapped back, 'The feeling's not mutual! Who *are* you?' A stroke put her in a wheelchair in 1967, but she carried on performing using only her right hand and was still playing in the 80s.

***Sweet Emma The Bell Gal*** (Riverside)

# Ray Barretto

PERCUSSION
*born* 29 April 1929

The sideman-veteran of probably hundreds of record dates in the 50s and 60s, Barretto grew up in New York's Puerto Rican community, although he didn't take up playing professionally until he came out of the army in the late 40s. He joined Eddie Bonnemare's Latin Jazz Combo before moving into Tito Puente's band in 1957, and then leading his own groups into the 60s, all the time doing sideman work (on congas) on albums for Prestige and other labels. From the 70s he was involved more in salsa and Latin groups which had rather less jazz about them, although bop has its inevitable part in the playing of many of his horn players.

***Acid*** (Fania)

# Bill Barron

TENOR SAXOPHONE
*born* 27 March 1927; *died* 21 September 1989

The Barron family lived in Philadelphia, where Bill took up the saxophone in his teens and played in army bands (beginning in 1943) before performing back home in local groups. In 1958 he moved to New York, where he recorded – somewhat surprisingly – with Cecil Taylor, and then co-led a band with his much younger brother Kenny. Bill made a handful of records under his own name and spent a period working in Europe, but returned home in 1967 and began working in jazz education at Columbia University and Wesleyan University as much as performing himself. Barron's rather spotty discography does something of a disservice to a player who was an interesting amalgam of hard bop and freer methods.

***Modern Windows Suite*** (Savoy)

# Kenny Barron

PIANO
*born* 9 June 1943

Aided by his brother Bill, Barron got off to a fast start: he was working with the likes of Philly Joe Jones and Yusef Lateef when only 16. Two years later he was in New York, and in 1962 he was hired by Dizzy Gillespie as his pianist, staying four years. Subsequently, he enjoyed long associations with Freddie Hubbard, Lateef, Ron Carter and the Monk tribute band Sphere, besides freelancing with any number of other leaders both on record dates and in live performance: Barron is probably one of the most recorded pianists of the past 30 years. He struck up a notable association with Stan Getz towards the end of the saxophonist's life and is his duo partner on several valedictory recordings. He has recorded as a leader with increasing regularity since the middle 80s, and while some of the results have seemed more like a record company's idea of putting him into an interesting context than anything which has come from inside himself, Barron's musicality usually makes the most of whatever opportunity's been put in front of him. There is little in his style which is distinctively his own: he's more a vessel that calmly articulates and lays out a fat-free distillation of post-bop piano jazz.

***Wanton Spirit*** (Verve)

# Gary Bartz

ALTO AND SOPRANO SAXOPHONES, FLUTE
*born* 26 September 1940

Bartz's authority and fierce sound mark him out as a major saxophonist, although his combative relationship with the business of jazz has sometimes made it difficult to follow the progress of his work. He studied at both Juilliard and Peabody (the latter in his home town of Baltimore) and worked in a hard-bop context in the 60s, spending time under Max Roach and Art Blakey among other leaders. He was one of the saxophonists who spent time in an electric Miles Davis group, during 1970–71, and that helped his star ascend; he had also been signed by Milestone, and he made a sequence of albums for them before switching to Prestige in the middle 70s. Opinion is sharply divided about this period: after he had set down some ferocious music for Milestone, his Prestige work seems like a disastrous decline towards pop-funk, although others have excused it as a symptom of changing times in black music. Two soft albums for Capitol made matters even more difficult, but in the 80s Bartz regrouped and returned to a mature hard-bop idiom: a pair of Candid albums showcase magnificent alto playing. But a later signing to Warners soured an already sceptical attitude towards major labels, and Bartz has gone the solo route since in determining his own recording career. An eloquent man with a radical intelligence, and a gifted actor as well as saxophonist, Bartz has lately taken to working for a variety of leaders besides himself, and is perhaps settling into a grandmasterly seniority: whether he will ever again be documented as truthfully as his talents deserve remains to be seen.

*West 42nd Street* (Candid)

# Count Basie

PIANO

*born* 21 August 1904; *died* 26 April 1984

William Basie was almost the same age as Fats Waller, and when a teenager he took advice from his fellow pianist. As a result, his early intrigues established him as a performer in the stride style, which he took with him into New York and New Jersey clubs at the beginning of the 20s. Then he toured on the vaudeville circuit, accompanying singers, before settling in Kansas City in 1927, having acquired his aristocratic nickname (his business cards offered the legend, 'Beware the Count is here'). He joined the highly rated Walter Page's Blue Devils the following year, and eventually switched to the Bennie Moten band (along with several other Devils, including Page himself), staying through the early 30s.

Moten's band had by this time grown into one of the strongest outfits in its territory, and the records make space for Basie's stride playing; when Moten died during surgery in 1935, Basie reorganized a new nine-piece band, The Barons Of Rhythm, which took up a residency in KC and began broadcasting, a move that led to a signing to Decca. Lester Young and Jo Jones were already with him; when Basie expanded to a 13-piece, Buck Clayton and Jimmy Rushing joined too. At the end of 1936, the band went to New York on tour, and while it was an institution which was destined to be almost permanently on the road, they never returned home to Kansas and remained based in New York. By the middle of 1938, Basie had recruited Harry Edison, Freddie Green, Benny Morton, Dicky Wells and Helen Humes, and the band had entered the top divison of swing-era orchestras. Green's arrival had particularized Basie's rhythm section like no other. With Green, Walter Page and Jones behind him, Basie established a new standard: the old two-beat music of the 20s had already gone, but this group smoothed and settled four-beats-to-the-bar, abetted by Page's walking-bass buoyancy, Green's imperturbable chording (he scarcely took a single-string solo in 50 years with the band), Jones's lithe rhythms with the bass drum diminished and the hi-hat cymbal taking over much of the beat, and Basie's own Morse-code approach, small bluesy phrases dropped on to the beat, accenting and commenting and prodding. The band's material was grown out of their native fondness for riffs and head arrangements, which often developed out of rehearsal ideas: 'One O'Clock Jump', a vintage example, was reputedly titled thus when an announcer asked for its name and Basie looked at the clock and christened it then and there. This gave his peerless team of soloists – Clayton, Edison, Wells, Young, Herschel Evans, Morton – the simple ground they needed to give of their best. The band's blues performances were amplified by the presence of Rushing, perhaps the greatest big-band singer of that time.

For their freshness and swinging exuberance, the Basie records of 1937–9 are definitive. But eventually the band's book had to change, and commissioned arrangements (from Eddie Durham, Buster Harding and others) began to arrive. Basie lost some key soloists (Evans, Young), but new men came in too, including Buddy Tate, Don Byas and Tab Smith. By the middle 40s the band's style had begun to ossify a little, and by 1950 the touring situation had declined to the point where Basie was forced to disband, although his fondness for playing the horses didn't always help finances. He led a small group for a couple of years, but in 1952 Basie's big band came back, and thereafter stayed busy until its leader's demise. In the

50s he began touring Europe and Japan for the first time, and new contracts with Verve and Roulette gave rise to hit records such as *April In Paris* (1955) and *The Atomic Basie* (1958). By now, the band had matured into a sleek, luxurious, failsafe machine – lacking in feel and passion to its critics but delighting admirers with the purring power of its delivery, and still boasting top-drawer soloists such as Thad Jones, Frank Foster, Eddie 'Lockjaw' Davis and Frank Wess. The band's book grew larger with smart commissioned pieces by the likes of Neal Hefti, Quincy Jones, Benny Carter and Ernie Wilkins. It rode out the 60s, a terrible period for this kind of jazz, with an almost careless aplomb: Basie recorded 'Green Onions' and a couple of Beatles collections, but if it paid a few bills, he didn't seem to mind.

In the 70s, Norman Granz revitalized Basie's recording career by signing him to his new Pablo label, and a vast sequence of fresh recordings appeared, by both the big band and Basie in small-group contexts, or trading licks with Oscar Peterson. The touring never stopped: even when the leader had to come on stage in a motorized wheelchair, he quipped to the audience, 'How do you like my new limo?' After his death, Thad Jones, Frank Foster and Grover Mitchell in turn kept the Basie band alive, still touring under its old name and still working through what had evolved into a timeless book. Basie's orchestra had by this time became the blueprint for thousands of aspiring mainstream big bands, although matching the original in its deceptively effortless class and clout is something which has eluded most of them.

*The Original American Decca Recordings* (MCA)

## Gianni Basso
CLARINET, TENOR SAXOPHONE
*born* 24 May 1931

An early Italian modernist, Basso played in dance orchestras before joining Gil Cuppini's quartet and then his own Sestetto Italiano, which changed to a quintet, a format he played in regularly until the 70s. It has been a little difficult to follow his music since he has been recorded only seldom (and then only for small Italian labels), and has always preferred to work in a live context, but the evidence suggests that the lighter,

Lester Young style he played in early on has gradually thickened and deepened into more of a classic hard-bop approach. Guido Manusardi and Franco D'Andrea have been favourite partners through the years, and the duo set listed is a good example of both men at their best.

**With Guido Manusardi,** *Maestro + Maestro = Exciting Duo* (Splasc(h))

## Django Bates
KEYBOARDS, TENOR HORN
*born* 2 October 1960

Bates studied music in London during the 70s (he gave up a Royal College of Music course after two weeks) and formed his band Human Chain in 1979: originally a trio, then a quartet when Iain Ballamy joined, it has been his signature vehicle over the years. During the 80s he also worked in several other groups, primarily the big-band collective Loose Tubes, for which he was one of the principal writers. When that foundered, expectations were high for Bates to embark on some kind of starry solo career, yet ever since he has seemed to merely drift from one project to another. He has performed in a duo with the concert pianist Joanna MacGregor, garnered commissions for his occasional big band Delightful Precipice, worked as a sideman with Tim Berne (a very unlikely pairing), and worked at least as much in Europe as at home; he won the Danish JAZZPAR Prize in 1997. Bates's music all but defines jazz as a post-modernist lark: influences are cheekily stirred into a multicultural mix which tends to be instantly attractive but often lacks staying power. Appreciation of what he does often depends on a taste for a certain strain of laddish humour, but it would have helped if he had had the support of a record company able to accommodate the range of his composing and playing, and present it in a coherent way: his discography is exceptionally scattered. His perennially babyfaced looks still get him referred to as part of the wave of 'young British jazz', even though he's now nearer 50 than 40.

*Winter Truce (And Homes Blaze)* (JMT)

## Alvin Batiste
CLARINET
*born* 7 November 1932

Batiste is an unfortunately excellent example of a major musician whose lack of recordings means that he is all but unknown to the wider jazz audience. Born in New Orleans, after he came out of the army he made friends with Ornette Coleman in Los Angeles and played with him on numerous occasions; he returned to New Orleans, taking with him Ellis Marsalis, Harold Battiste and Ed Blackwell, and they became the American Jazz Quintet. Batiste then freelanced before more or less disappearing into academia: he taught at Southern University in Baton Rouge for most of the 70s and 80s, although he occasionally appeared as part of John Carter's Clarinet Summit. In 1987 he resumed his playing career and led a band called The Jazzstronauts. Yet he has hardly made any records: a single album for Columbia, *Late* (1993) – which most likely came about via the Marsalis connection with the label – and an even more obscure one for India Navigation, *Bayou Magic* (1988), include much compelling clarinet playing, going all the way back to the founding fathers and blossoming out towards the free language which he and Coleman had toyed with in the middle 50s.
***Bayou Magic*** (India Navigation)

## Stefano Battaglia
PIANO
*born* 31 August 1965

Classically trained, Battaglia performed in that role initially but turned to jazz in the later 80s, a student of Enrico Pieranunzi. Since then he has worked prolifically in Italy in the trio format and has recorded extensively for Splasc(h). Taking a Tristano influence and adding some Paul Bley to it, he has arrived at a spare but considered style which nevertheless has great vitality: 'I'm more interested in voices under the melody – counterpoint – not voicings or harmony', perhaps a surprising point of view for a pianist.
***Confession*** (Splasc(h))

## Ray Bauduc
DRUMS
*born* 18 June 1909; *died* 8 January 1988

Bauduc grew up in a musical New Orleans family (his brother Jules led bands in the city) and worked in a group called the Scranton Sirens which fetched up in New York in 1926. Thereafter he played dance music with Freddie Rich and Ben Pollack, taking freelance recording gigs, until the Pollack band turned into the Bob Crosby Orchestra in 1935. With Crosby, Bauduc set the style for Dixieland drumming, performing with a precision which might seem almost military if it wasn't for his flair and intuitive swinging, accompanying soloists with chattering woodblocks and rimshots. While these were his glory years, after the band's demise he still found plenty to do, leading a quintet, working for Jimmy Dorsey and Jack Teagarden, and eventually leading a small group with his old friend from the Sirens, Nappy Lamare. He was on the West Coast for much of the 60s but eventually moved to Texas, where he played only rarely. The record cited includes his Crosby signature feature, 'The Big Noise From Winnetka'.
**Bob Crosby,** ***The Big Noise*** (Halcyon)

## Billy Bauer
GUITAR
*born* 14 November 1915

Bauer played without much incident in big bands before joining Woody Herman in 1945, and from there becoming closely associated with Lennie Tristano – 'Lennie was only a couple of years of my life, even though working with him was what gave me a reputation.' He is on several of the important Tristano sessions, his tight tone and phrasing mirroring precisely the difficult Tristano theme statements, and his improvising cast in a coolly interrogative bop style. After 1950, Bauer went more into studio work, and was a regular staffer with NBC, although he also recorded with Lee Konitz and Warne Marsh and made a single date of his own, *Plectrist* (1956), for Norman Granz. From the 60s onwards he became more heavily involved in teaching, and he has produced various instructional books and a voluminous autobiography, *Sideman*.
**Lee Konitz,** ***Inside Hi-Fi*** (Atlantic)

# Conrad Bauer
TROMBONE
*born* 4 July 1943

The elder of the Bauer brothers jumped straight into free music, working with Ernst-Ludwig Petrowsky at the end of the 60s and then leading his own bands. He has been a regular sighting in numerous European free-music events and with many different playing partners, although one of his best vehicles has been the two-trombone/two-guitar quartet Doppelmoppel, a funny and surprising ensemble. Less of a 'radical' than the likes of Gunter Christmann and Paul Rutherford, Conny Bauer's prodigious technique (including circular breathing) is nevertheless put at the service of a thoughtful and personal vision.
**Doppelmoppel, *Aventure Québécoise*** (Victo)

# Johannes Bauer
TROMBONE
*born* 22 July 1954

The younger of the Bauer brothers spent a long period in classical studies and performed in a band playing medieval and baroque wind music during the 70s. He also worked in soul bands and eventually joined his brother in the East German free-music movement, making the usual list of associations as he went, although he has often performed in rather more aggressive environments than Conny and is a somewhat more in-your-face kind of improviser, which has let him hold his own in environments such as the free-rock band Slawterhaus, although he has recorded rather less often than his brother.
***Organo Pleno*** (FMP)

# Mario Bauza
TRUMPET, ALTO SAXOPHONE
*born* 28 April 1911; *died* 11 July 1993

Bauza was a classical musician, playing both oboe and clarinet with the Havana Philharmonic, who moved to New York in 1930 and began working for the black bands in the city. He switched to trumpet and joined Chick Webb in 1933, staying five years, before moving first to Don Redman's band and then to the Cab Calloway orches-

tra. An authority figure in all of his groups, Bauza brought Dizzy Gillespie into the Calloway band (and a decade later introduced him to Chano Pozo). But he more or less left jazz in 1941, when he became MD of Machito's band, a position he held until 1975, when the two fell out after 35 years of continuous work. While Bauza's jazz experience had an impact on this ensemble, it was basically an Afro-Cuban dance band, and after leaving Machito, Bauza went on to lead groups of his own. He found himself revered as the godfather of his music and he worked right up until his death, as both a concert and a recording artist.
***Afro-Cuban Jazz*** (Caiman)

# Jim Beard
KEYBOARDS
*born* 26 August 1960

After various music studies, Beard arrived in New York in 1985 and worked with several high-profile leaders in touring groups: Wayne Shorter, John McLaughlin, John Scofield, Pat Metheny. But his real forte proved to be as a studio man, scoring charts, programming keyboards and eventually producing entire albums for numerous stars of the fusion universe, including Dennis Chambers, Mike Stern and the Breckers. A shrewd and imaginative pro, Beard understands the seductiveness of smooth jazz and has employed some of the genre's procedures in his work, but fortunately he prefers a tougher and more surreal result, and the handful of discs under his own name offer plentiful and surprising twists on the standard moves in the field.
***Truly*** (Escapade)

# Beat

This has at least three jazz meanings. In strict musical terms, it refers to the number of pulses within a single measure of music: the standard 4/4 denotes four beats in a bar. In a wider sense, 'the beat' – also much used in discussing rock and pop – describes the overall rhythmic character of a musical performance. 'This has a great beat' might be one instance of its typically rather vague use. The truth is that most jazz performances are made up of the interplay of numerous beats and pulses, and there is no one beat to listen for, even if the time-signature is absolutely clear. 'Beat' is also the name given to the group of poets and bohemians which sprang up and thrived briefly in America in the 50s, claiming jazz as their musical soundtrack. The immortal phrase 'Dig that crazy beat', a mix of metaphor and oxymoron, could therefore be applied to appreciating either a fine piece of jazz or (admittedly less likely these days) a coffeehouse poetry reading.

## Bebop/bop

Bop was the next stage in jazz evolution after the swing era (the term is itself a shorthand for either 'bebop' or, less commonly, 'rebop', a phonetic word drawn from the loose vocabulary of scat singing). While pre-echoes of bop can be heard in the music of several players and groups thought of as swing-era fixtures – Charlie Christian, Coleman Hawkins, John Kirby's sextet – bop is unusual in that its origins can be traced to almost a specific time and place: the after-hours club Minton's in New York, where in the early 40s the likes of Dizzy Gillespie, Thelonious Monk and Kenny Clarke would gather to play at jam sessions and explore advanced musical ideas away from the increasingly formularized environment of the big bands where most earned their daily bread (allegedly, bop's complexity arose partly out of a desire to play difficult ideas which would keep lesser players off the stand).

Its significant characteristics include a much wider harmonic vocabulary; angular and seemingly 'abstract' melodies used almost as an offhand motif, since it was the underlying chord sequence which mattered to the soloists; and above all a much greater rhythmic variety. The swing era's fundamentalism (a four-beat approach insisted on by the drums) was displaced by the bop drummer's elaborate language, shifting the beat from the drums to the ride cymbals and hi-hat, and conversing with the other players via snare and bass drum punctuations, the latter often described as 'dropping bombs' because of the booming surprise of their arrival. Meanwhile, the bassist was obliged to be much more 'rhythmical'. This loosening led to the bop group becoming a notably fluid, conversational ensemble, although bop convention still obliged the soloists to have the major say in the music: once the melodic line was out of the way, it set up a horn player to create an improvisation which reflected what was usually a state of nervous, jittery exhilaration, perhaps the emotional acme of the original bop idiom. While Gillespie, Clarke and Monk were bop's premier theoreticians, it was the arrival of Charlie Parker, whose virtuosity and creative genius emboldened and personified the idiom, which sealed its significance.

It took the small independent labels such as Savoy, Dial and Blue Note to actually set down bop on record, but the music created such an electrifying impact among younger players and listeners that it quickly took over as the next jazz insurrection. Many older players were mystified or even openly hostile – 'We drink our fifths, not flatten them,' remarked Eddie Condon, referring to bop's appropriation of the flatted-fifth interval – but by the end of the 40s bop had travelled the world and settled down. The jangled nerves which created the likes of 'Anthropology', 'Shaw 'Nuff', 'Ornithology' and other early bop anthems were cooled by simpler themes, and the assimilation of bop musicians into the surviving big bands, such as those of Woody Herman and Stan Kenton, mainstreamed the style for good. While bop had effectively run its course as a new thing, its matter and methods have remained as a central part of all jazz development since. While it shifted the emphasis away from orchestral to small-group music (the bop-orientated big bands of Billy Eckstine and Dizzy Gillespie were unsustainable commercial failures), it also lifted jazz into the realms of art music and arguably banished its popular audience for ever, since for every person who can hum the line to 'Groovin' High' there are a hundred who would prefer to whistle 'In The Mood'. 'Bop' also has a vernacular meaning referring to dancing ('let's have a bop'), though this has passed far away from belonging to jazz.

## Sidney Bechet
CLARINET, SOPRANO SAXOPHONE
*born* 14 May 1897; *died* 14 May 1959

One of five New Orleans brothers, all of whom played music, Bechet started on clarinet and had a few lessons from Lorenzo Tio, but otherwise went his own way on the instrument. In the teens of the century he worked with Bunk Johnson, Buddy Petit, Freddie Keppard and others, before – always a restless spirit – he left the city in 1916 to tour on the vaudeville circuit of the Midwest. It led him to Chicago, where he played again with Keppard and with Joe Oliver, before he was heard by the impresario and bandleader Will Marion Cook, who took him to Europe with his Southern Syncopated Orchestra in 1919. It was with this group in London that the classical establishment discovered Bechet: the conductor Ernst Ansermet heard him there, and wondered about this 'fat boy . . . who can say nothing of his art save that it follows his "own way", and then one thinks his "own way" is perhaps the highway the world will swing along tomorrow'. Bechet enjoyed himself in Europe and bought a soprano saxophone in London in 1920, but he was eventually deported after an arrest for assault and in 1923 he was back in New York with Clarence Williams. His earliest records date from this time, and it's astonishing how powerful and advanced he sounds, apparently the equal of the young Louis Armstrong on their work together on Williams's 'Cake Walking Babies From Home' (1924).

Bechet opened his own club in Harlem, where he had young Johnny Hodges in his band, but he lost interest in it and returned to Europe at the end of 1925. He played with Josephine Bradley in Paris, got as far east as the Soviet Union, and otherwise worked in Berlin, Rome, Frankfurt and Paris again, although he was once more in trouble with the law and spent 11 months in prison. He was back in New York in 1930, then in Berlin again, but he made a final return to the US in 1931, playing with Noble Sissle's orchestra as a featured soloist. At this point, Bechet might have become little more than an exotic footnote in jazz history, since his old-school playing was suddenly out of favour and he began a tailoring business with Tommy Ladnier. A year later, though, he was back on the road with Sissle, and by the end of the decade Bechet was in prime shape to take advantage of the burgeoning interest in a form of New Orleans revivalism: he was in the From Spirituals To Swing concerts, the jazz press began lauding him, and he made

records for Victor, Blue Note and latterly King Jazz, in a quintet with Mezz Mezzrow. Electrical recording revealed a sound on soprano sax (by now his preferred horn, and since he was almost the only one playing it, his style dominated the instrument) which was huge. At times it was filled with a baleful melancholy, but most often it rippled with an exhilarating, almost headlong momentum, his phrasing taking every opportunity to decorate a line, which his mile-wide vibrato underscored. While he was a difficult man (as his misadventures in Europe suggest), and his presence often overpowered his playing companions, there were many occasions when he secured a thrilling compatibility: with Armstrong ('2.19 Blues', 1940), Muggsy Spanier ('Lazy River', 1940) or the best of the sides with Mezzrow ('Out Of The Gallion', 1945). When he went back to the clarinet, he was just as masterful ('Blue Horizon', 1944). In the 40s he was a Dixieland king in New York, holding court at Nick's and Jimmy Ryan's, although a reunion with Bunk Johnson in Boston in 1945 led to tears. But wanderlust took hold of him again, and in 1949 he returned to Paris, where he was greeted like a prodigal son, and began new associations with the likes of Claude Luter. He returned to the US for a final fling in 1950 but otherwise made his home just outside Paris, an honoured man at last. He recorded and played regularly in the 50s, wrote and performed a ballet, and although his heart never strayed too far from the two-beat music which he had grown up playing, he was at least inquisitive about more recent developments and made some recordings with the contemporary pianist Martial Solal. Since his death, Bechet's star has waned somewhat: although he was a showbiz celebrity in the 20s, that is very long ago now, and his contrary nature helped prevent him from securing the immortality which accrued to more durable entertainment figures such as Armstrong and Ellington (his centenary passed almost unremarked in 1997). But the glorious exuberance of his music remains an inspiration to any who aspire to playing in a traditional style, and he remains perhaps the most immediately identifiable of all jazz musicians.
*Shake 'Em Up* (Avid)

## Gordon Beck
PIANO
*born* 16 September 1928

Beck worked as a draftsman by day and played piano at night during the 50s, and by 1960 he had decided to turn to music full time. He worked with several of the better modern London bands before joining the Tubby Hayes group in 1962: he is outstanding on the pair of albums they recorded that year at Ronnie Scott's. Three years later he led a trio of his own, with Tony Oxley, Jeff Clyne and latterly Ron Mathewson, during which time they often worked as the house rhythm section at the Scott club, and he then joined the Phil Woods Rhythm Machine in 1969. He formed another new band, Gyroscope, in 1972, and then worked for various leaders before carving out a largely solo career in the 80s and 90s. One association occasionally renewed is his work as an accompanist to Helen Merrill. Beck is largely a prophet without honour in his own country – in France, by comparison, he is much liked – and he has never really got himself on to record in a way which would have documented his great gifts in an unequivocal manner.
*Gyroscope* (Art Of Life)

## Joe Beck
GUITAR
*born* 29 July 1945

Beck is a fusion pioneer of sorts. He played with some high-profile leaders – Charles Lloyd, Chico Hamilton, Mike Mainieri – in the 60s, and even had a brief stint as the first electric guitarist to play with Miles Davis, on two 1967 dates (the tracks only showed up later on out-take compilations). His groups Pleasure Principle and Beck took him through the early 70s and had numerous significant players in them, even though he also spent time in the same period working as, of all things, a dairy farmer. Eventually he formed a successful company which makes music for commercials and TV backgrounds.
*Beck!* (Kudu)

## Harry Beckett
TRUMPET, FLUGELHORN
*born* 30 May 1935

A Barbadian, Beckett moved to England in 1954 and worked on the London club scene during the rest of the decade, although he wasn't able to get on record. In the 60s, as the London scene expanded, he began working with the likes of Graham Collier, Mike Gibbs and Neil Ardley, and managed to make a couple of albums of his own for RCA, the fine (and largely forgotten) *Flare Up* and *Warm Smiles* (1970–71). In the 70s and 80s he was likely to be found sharing bandstands with Stan Tracey, John Surman, Dudu Pukwana and Kathy Stobart, and his big-band experience suited him for Pierre Dørge's New Jungle Orchestra and for writing charts for the Jazz Warriors. By the 90s he was a respected senior spirit on a scene which has perhaps not acknowledged him as much as it might. Unlike the more romantically regarded Joe Harriott, Beckett has had little in the way of legend attached to him, and his quite complex style forgoes any kind of sensational appeal. He is a gracious, lyrical player whose adaptability means that he can blow hot and hard in the same way, and he is similarly unafraid of stark settings and open space.
*Images Of Clarity* (Evidence)

## Bix Beiderbecke
CORNET
*born* 10 March 1903; *died* 6 August 1931

Beiderbecke almost helplessly fell into legend. His origins were in a respectable Davenport family, who were unimpressed by his interest in playing the cornet, sending him to Lake Forest Academy in 1921 (he was expelled). His father tried to interest him in working at home, but Chicago's musical life was too tempting and Beiderbecke joined the Wolverine Orchestra: it was accounted one of the best white groups in the city, but the rest of them sound stiff and pallid next to the cornetist on their 1924 sessions for Gennett. Even through the dusty recording, Bix's almost luminous tone and calmly melodious phrasing stand out as something special. He became great pals with Frankie Trumbauer, and after a brief period with one of Jean Goldkette's bands he joined

Trumbauer in St Louis in 1925. They then joined Jean Goldkette's main band in September 1926, where even the somewhat routine arrangements didn't hold Beiderbecke back from creating some lovely solos on their comparatively few records; better still, though, were the small-group studio sessions for OKeh. The 'Bix & His Gang' dates ran to 13 titles during 1927–9, while those under Trumbauer's name were more extensive, and between them they set down the best of Beiderbecke's playing. Although many of the pieces work to comparatively tame arrangements and plenty of the Trumbauer titles in particular come close to mere hot dance music, Bix's contributions lend an almost mystical air to the music. Where Armstrong sounded as if he was bursting with his own creativity, Beiderbecke exemplified restraint, a note of inward contemplation, even as his playing spoke directly and plainly to the listener. His celebrated solo on Trumbauer's 'Singing The Blues' (1927) is a nearly perfect illustration of his art – the musicologist Gunther Schuller expounded at length on a single phrase in the improvisation, an abrupt rip up to a high note which in the context of Bix's approach is almost shocking – but there are many other passages on these dates where his playing is just as powerful. If it seems strange to use such an adjective to describe what's usually seen as a fundamentally fragile delivery, there's no denying the ingenuity of Beiderbecke's placement of emphases, his clever pacing of himself within otherwise orthodox rhythmic settings, and a resilience which is the counter to his supposed vulnerability.

Besides the cornet (he reportedly considered the trumpet to sound 'thin and puny', and never adopted it), Beiderbecke liked to tinker at the piano: his one piano solo record, 'In A Mist', seems like a characteristic invention, and though its upbeat humour is scarcely Debussyan, this and the other pieces he never recorded (including 'Flashes' and 'In The Dark') have at least a sliver of impressionism in them, and stories about him dreamily listening to that school of classical music fit the romantic myth even more. When he and Trumbauer both joined Paul Whiteman in 1928, they were reprising their starring roles with Goldkette, but the oversized Whiteman orchestra tended to cover their tracks and the solo spots were fewer and less engaging. Still, it was regular work for a man who appeared to have few aspirations to lead: yet drink had already ruined Beiderbecke. He was obliged to leave Whiteman in September 1929 and never really returned, although he is on some of their later record dates. He attempted to recuperate, and played with the Dorseys and others of the New York circle, and there was a final session under his own name for Victor in 1930 which produced three titles. But friends kept visiting him with a bottle.

A man of slight character, who perhaps never reconciled the demands of jazz with a background which preferred more genteel aspirations, he is, along with the image of the young Armstrong, the one icon of the original 'Jazz Age' which has endured with the same strength, in spite of 75 intervening years of musical furore. While he can scarcely be accounted a direct influence on any figure from bebop onwards, he established a dialect within the music which remains intact and alive. Pneumonia killed him in New York, and he was buried in Davenport: a photograph of members of his family at the graveside, their faces uncomprehending, seems heartbreakingly poignant.

*Bix And Tram* (JSP)

# Richie Beirach

PIANO
*born* 23 May 1947

Born in Brooklyn, Beirach studied classical music first, then jazz at Berklee, then composition at the Manhattan School Of Music. Armed with a prodigious knowledge, he went out into the world via an association with Dave Liebman, joining the saxophonist's Lookout Farm group in 1974 and often renewing the partnership since. Beirach has a formidable knowledge of harmony, in and out of jazz, and while his music isn't terribly exciting it has a lot of academic appeal. Recent projects on record have seen him attempting to synthesize jazz procedures with material drawn specifically from the European heritage: Scriabin, Kodály, Bartók and even Monteverdi.

*Round About Bartók* (ACT)

## Bob Belden
SAXOPHONES, KEYBOARDS
*born* 31 October 1956

Belden had an uneventful career as a player, working in Woody Herman's sax section and in one of Donald Byrd's undistinguished later groups, before he began working as an arranger and making large-scale records packed with ambitious orchestral charts, starting out at the independent Sunnyside in 1989. He built up a huge book of contacts and by the end of the century had established close working relationships with both Blue Note and Columbia, making 'homage' records for the former (all-star ensembles jazzing the music of Sting, Prince, The Beatles and so on) and producing major Miles Davis reissue projects for the latter. He also produced new sessions by the likes of Cassandra Wilson and Herbie Hancock. A knowledgeable and astute figure, if perhaps not a very interesting musician.
**Black Dahlia** (Blue Note)

## Marcus Belgrave
TRUMPET
*born* 12 June 1936

Belgrave has charted a rather unusual course. He was touring with Ray Charles at the end of the 50s, yet also worked with Max Roach and Charles Mingus. He settled in Detroit in 1963 and built up a sessionman career, but founded the Jazz Development Workshop there in the 70s. Despite a few sideman appearances he was less visible in the following decade, but in the 90s he recorded more extensively, in the Lincoln Center Orchestra and with the likes of Geri Allen, David Murray and Cecil Payne. Maybe his most important work, though, has been in education, and many significant pupils (Allen and Kenny Garrett among them) have studied under him.
**Geri Allen, *The Nurturer*** (Blue Note)

## Graeme Bell
PIANO
*born* 7 September 1914

For many years, Bell was the only Australian jazzman to have any kind of presence outside his home territory. In the early 40s he led a group at the Melbourne venue Leonard's Café, then moved to the Heidelberg Town Hall and helped establish the Uptown Club, perhaps the first significant jazz-dedicated venue in Australia. In 1947 Bell's band went to the UK – a remarkable feat in itself – and his policy of playing for dancers and the less stiff-backed members of any prospective audience sent a modest shockwave through what was a cautious kind of British traditional jazz. Back home, Bell established the Swaggie label in 1949 and on a second visit to Europe in 1951 joined forces with Humphrey Lyttelton on some memorable recordings. He settled in Sydney in 1957 and from there continued as the great eminence of Australian Dixieland jazz, all the way into the 90s. It was a poignant moment when he returned to the UK and played a reunion concert with Lyttelton in 1993.
**Graeme Bell Jazz** (Jazzology)

## Louie Bellson
DRUMS
*born* 6 July 1924

Born Luigi Paolino Bassaloni, Bellson joined Benny Goodman at 18 and then worked with Tommy Dorsey and Harry James before his most starring early role, in Duke Ellington's orchestra: he replaced Sonny Greer in 1951 and his great feature, 'Skin Deep', was the only real drum showcase Ellington ever had. He married Pearl Bailey in 1952 and acted as her MD for some years, while otherwise doing more big-band work and Jazz At The Philharmonic concerts, which he loved ('You played in the best theaters and the concerts were two and a half hours long – but two and a half hours of these guys was worth more than five hours of most others'). From the 60s on he did a lot of educational work but has also led big bands of his own, and he was still busy in the new century. Perhaps too many of the albums under his own name have been saddled with inconsequential material and faintly pointless contexts for his undoubted virtuosity: at his best, Bellson can swing a big band as powerfully as any of his generation, and he is the last of the great swing-era drummers.
**Inferno** (Concord)

# Joe Benjamin

BASS

*born* 4 November 1919; *died* 26 January 1974

'Crazy Joe Benjamin', as Sarah Vaughan characterized him on her great 'Shulie A Bop', was a solid professional as both bassman and music copyist: he worked in the latter capacity for Jimmie Lunceford, and he covered the same duties for Ellington on and off between 1950 and the end of the band's life. He backed Vaughan in the early 50s, then worked in Gerry Mulligan's small group and subsequently in the Concert Jazz Band. In the 60s he was basically a studio player, and he turns up on many mainstream-modern dates.

**Sarah Vaughan, *No Count Sarah*** (Emarcy)

# Lou Bennett

ORGAN

*born* 18 May 1926; *died* 10 February 1997

Bennett was from Philadelphia, originally a pianist, then taking to the organ after Wild Bill Davis had shown the way, and subsequently following the Jimmy Smith style. But he had little luck at home, and found the reception much more welcoming when he went to Paris in 1960: he became a regular at the Blue Note there, and made only a single further visit home to play, at Newport in 1964. Eventually he opened his own club in Paris, and developed a synthesizer-organ, the Bennett Machine. He recorded only seldom but a handful of albums were made and Universal has reissued one, *Pentecostal Feeling*, in the last few years.

***Pentecostal Feeling*** (Emarcy)

# Han Bennink

DRUMS, OTHER INSTRUMENTS

*born* 17 April 1942

At first, Bennink's course was much like that of many other European players, working on his local scene in Holland and playing behind numerous American visitors in the early 60s, from Ben Webster to Eric Dolphy (he is on Dolphy's valedictory *Last Date*). But his alliance with Willem Breuker and Misha Mengelberg led to the formation of the ICP (Instant Composers Pool), and ever since he has been linked with the supposedly theatri-cal end of free playing, where every performance is a performance and music can at times play a subsidiary role to the antics of the event. Actually, Bennink is as capable a timekeeper as any in Europe, and his reputation as a comedian – while justified, since he is a peerless entertainer – has obscured his outstanding musicianship. He has worked with Mengelberg in a partnership which has outlasted almost any comparable dialogue in modern jazz, and he has also struck creative sparks with improvisers of numerous generations and backgrounds, including Cecil Taylor, Ellery Eskelin, Curtis Clark, Dexter Gordon, Steve Lacy, Derek Bailey, Matthew Shipp and many more. If anything, these days he plays in a more straight-ahead style than he used to in the 70s heyday of improvisation, when he would often play banjo, clarinet and 'home-made junk', especially in his records with Peter Brötzmann. Equally at home in a trio, an octet or an orchestra, Bennink loves to swing the band as much as he likes subverting and distracting its players. He is one of the tallest as well as the most energetic of drummers.

**Bennink/Mengelberg, *Eine Partietischtennis*** (ICP)

# George Benson

GUITAR, VOCAL

*born* 22 March 1943

A master among jazz guitarists, Benson is also one of the more exasperating musicians of recent times. In the 60s he worked out of his native Pittsburgh, playing with the likes of Jack McDuff, and eventually he made enough waves to enable Columbia to bill his debut for them as *The Most Exciting New Guitarist On The Jazz Scene Today: It's Uptown With George Benson* (1966). Benson's combination of speed, attack and lyricism suggested a step forward from the then-dominant Wes Montgomery approach, and the likes of Miles Davis and Lee Morgan soon had him on their records. Creed Taylor got him signed to CTI and began making records which were a halfway-house between jazz and pop, but the pop sound took over when he signed to Warners and delivered *Breezin'* (1976), one of the biggest-selling jazz records ever, even if the jazz content was under strict supervision. Thereafter

Benson turned increasingly to singing (to be fair, he had been singing on gigs since he was in his teens), and the music moved towards upmarket soul as its basic ground. By the end of the 80s Benson's pop success had declined and he looked to be heading back towards jazz again, but the records since have been a hopeless stylistic mish-mash and one wonders if Benson will ever again give himself clear space to simply play jazz guitar. At his 80s concerts, he would usually start the show with a couple of instrumentals which showed his chops unimpaired and still dazzling. Maybe they still are.

*Breezin'* (Warner Bros)

## Bob Berg
TENOR SAXOPHONE
*born* 7 April 1951; *died* 5 December 2002

Berg had something of a stop-start career. He switched from piano to tenor sax when he heard John Coltrane's music, and he was touring with Jack McDuff while still in his teens. He joined Horace Silver in 1973 and then had a long association with Cedar Walton, but his career was turned around when he was hired by Miles Davis in 1984, sharing the front line with Davis and John Scofield in one of the strongest of the trumpeter's latter-day groups. He left in 1987 and worked in a fusion band with Mike Stern, as well as making some rather dreary records for Denon. A later association with Chick Corea steered him back towards more straight-ahead playing, although a tour with a new edition of Steps Ahead suggested that Berg was never really going to shake off fusion. His career on record now seems muddled and unresolved – many great moments scattered under many flags – and while such contemporaries as Michael Brecker ascended to a kind of summit in their work, Berg's power-packed playing, a steely successor to the innovations of Coltrane and Wayne Shorter, never seems to go anywhere much. The New York jazz community was shocked by his death in a car accident at the end of 2002.

**Miles Davis, *You're Under Arrest*** (Columbia)

## Anders Bergcrantz
TRUMPET
*born* 5 December 1961

Born in Malmö, Sweden, Bergcrantz followed in the family business (his father was a jazz pianist) and he took up the trumpet in his teens. He studied at Berklee and made some useful associations in the US, subsequently leading a quartet with Richie Beirach, Adam Nussbaum and Ron McClure, as well as playing with Scandinavian groups. Bergcrantz exemplifies the European approach to the post-bop repertory: he is completely in the tradition set up by Lee Morgan and Freddie Hubbard, yet seeks to wring something of his own out of music remote from the kind of setting he grew up in. At his best he is a resourceful and often sparkling improviser, a pleasure to listen to.

*C* (Dragon)

## Karl Berger
VIBES
*born* 30 March 1935

Berger is one of the few to try and do something – anything – with the vibraphone which takes it away from its pretty self. His answer was to play in dry, atonal settings where the music dallies in abstraction. Born in Heidelberg, he spent most of the 50s in academia. He worked in Paris with fellow vibesman Michel Hausser, then played with Don Cherry and Steve Lacy during 1965–6, moving over to New York in the process. He founded the Creative Music Studio in Woodstock in 1972. Since then he has involved himself largely in education, in both Germany and the US, and has returned to the piano, his original instrument. As a vibes player, Berger hasn't been remotely influential, and his modest oeuvre on record is all but unknown except to dedicated enthusiasts. Unlike Gunter Hampel, who has at least pitched himself into demanding situations, Berger seems to have been picky about recordings, and there is very little to go on in assessing his contribution.

*Conversations* (In & Out)

## Borah Bergman
PIANO
*born* 13 December 1926

Bergman wasn't so much a late starter as someone who worked for many years and was hardly noticed at all. He studied music (and taught English) in New York, playing his first gigs in 1954 and carrying on almost unnoticed for a further 20 years. Then he began making records, to surprising acclaim: years of woodshedding, and intense practice on his left hand in particular, had forged a style of overwhelming virtuosity, enabling two-fisted demonstrations which rival Taylor and Tatum in their intensity. Stylistically, he seems to cover the range from Tristano to Taylor and beyond, and it is significant that a large part of his discography is now made up of duo peformances with horn players (Evan Parker, Roscoe Mitchell, Anthony Braxton, Oliver Lake, Peter Brötzmann – not exactly easy company), since Bergman's delivery can take the Hines 'trumpet' style to its natural limits. Marathon solo performances mix high-voltage explosions with soliloquies of tranquil pensiveness. Perhaps he is in a great North American keyboard tradition – Harry Partch, Glenn Gould – of one-off mavericks.
*The River Of Sounds* (Boxholder)

## Jerry Bergonzi
TENOR SAXOPHONE
*born* 21 October 1947

Bergonzi is a Bostonian whose scholarly yet impassioned approach to the saxophone personifies that city's mix of detachment and intense commitment. He went the Berklee route until he was 25, whereupon he moved to New York and played in a variety of situations, taking the saxophone role in the Dave Brubeck quartet for a spell. But he went back to Boston in 1981 and has based himself there since. He plays in a style which sounds like a rough yet carefully chosen path through the mixed language of Coltrane and Rollins, controlled yet absorbingly powerful. Numerous records attest to his strengths, although he has perhaps yet to make one which really focuses and concentrates his undoubted gifts.
*Lost In The Shuffle* (Double Time)

## Gunnar Bergsten
BARITONE SAXOPHONE
*born* 1945

Bergsten continues the Swedish baritone tradition of Lars Gullin in handsome style. He started on trumpet but gave up on that because his teeth weren't strong enough, and he bought his first baritone in 1965 (he still has it). He studied in Stockholm and worked in Rolf Ericson's big band before starting a closer association with Bernt Rosengren. He didn't, though, make a record under his own name until 1995. Three gorgeous albums have, however, attested to his craft: a light-bodied sound which lets him get around the big horn with ease, and a style which has nothing revolutionary about it but which seems personal to its progenitor. The record of Gullin interpretations is, inevitably, definitive.
**With Peter Bergsten, *Play Lars Gullin*** (Proprius)

## Bunny Berigan
TRUMPET
*born* 2 November 1908; *died* 2 June 1942

Rowland Berigan took up trumpet when he played in a boys' brass band, and by the time he moved to New York in 1929 he was already a commanding player. Throughout the early 30s he freelanced as a trumpet section-player with some of the better dance bands playing in New York, and collectors still seek out his many uncredited appearances – with the likes of the Dorsey Brothers, The Boswell Sisters, Hal Kemp and Paul Whiteman – where he takes eight or 16 bars and lights up the record. He began making records under his own name in 1935, and became an early star of the Benny Goodman band, and then with Tommy Dorsey; but he had leadership aspirations of his own and from 1937 ran his own big band. Berigan was a soft touch and no businessman, and after a long period of struggle he had to give it up. It didn't help that he had taken on a chronic addiction to alcohol. His great hit under his own name was a version of 'I Can't Get Started', where he both sang the wistful vocal and played an epic trumpet solo, and it became one of the great hits of the swing era. As a soloist, Berigan stood at a point almost exactly between Armstrong and

Beiderbecke: his playing has the fire and natural virtuosity of the former, and the sweet tone and mellifluous cadences of the latter, as well as an unusually ripe lower register. When his band fell apart (he was declared bankrupt in 1940), Tommy Dorsey gave him his old job back, but drink had already ruined him and his attendances became erratic. Berigan tried again on his own, but he was too far gone, and he died in a New York hospital the day after a scheduled concert. Fans (including the author) still treasure surviving airshots of the Berigan band: as remote as he now is, Berigan seems an irreplaceable part of jazz, and he was quietly mourned by a community of musicians who knew they would never see his like again.
*Portrait* (ASV)

## Berklee College Of Music
INSTITUTION

Of all the American music colleges, Berklee is the premier location. Founded in Boston by the composer Lawrence Berk in 1945, it offers undergraduate degrees in a formidably wide range of studies connected with the business of playing music, with jazz a particular area of interest, and there is a master's programme conceived in the same spirit. Besides the recognized areas of study, Berklee is renowned as a seedbed for jazz talent via its extracurricular opportunities in terms of meeting, working and playing together in informal situations. Countless jazz musicians have passed through its portals.

## David Berkman
PIANO

Berkman grew up in Cleveland and has been playing classical and jazz piano from an early age, though he studied fiction at Michigan College. He spent some time at Berklee and has been in New York since the mid-80s, although only recently has he come to prominence with records under his own name. There is some brilliant and original writing on all of them, which suggests that Berkman has thought hard about how to individualize his work and how to take it

aside from the usual forms: 'Every tune of mine is supposed to put the band into some space, some zone, some kind of mood. I think jazz is a really creative field but it's not always the most imaginative.' He also worked regularly with the Mel Lewis Vanguard Orchestra and has accompanied Jane Monheit.
*Communication Theory* (Palmetto)

## Sonny Berman
TRUMPET
*born* 21 April 1925; *died* 16 January 1947

Only remembered by connoisseurs of the period, Berman's brief stay in jazz was tantalizing and bittersweet. He was working as a teenager with Louis Prima and had already been through at least a half-dozen big-band jobs before joining Woody Herman early in 1945. He and Pete Candoli took the trumpet solos in the First Herd, and Berman's fiery mix of swing and bebop gleams through some of the better Herman sides of the time, including a curiously affecting 'Let It Snow! Let It Snow! Let It Snow!' He was still with Herman when the First Herd broke up at the end of 1946 but was killed by a heart attack only weeks later while playing at a jam session. His work on four privately recorded titles made at a friend's apartment in January 1946 suggests that he might have turned out to be on a par with the likes of Fats Navarro.
**Woody Herman,** *Blowing Up A Storm!* (Columbia)

## Tim Berne
ALTO AND BARITONE SAXOPHONES
*born* 16 October 1954

Berne's period of study with Julius Hemphill in New York (1974–8) was the formative influence on his career. He made records for Empire, his own label, starting in 1979, and had a brief spell on Columbia during one of their occasional avant-garde flings. By the end of the 80s he was one of the masters of New York's avant-garde and was also making records for the independent JMT. A fierce player whose free thinking is saturated with blues elements and a penchant for appropriating some of the visceral elements of rock-

derived noise, Berne likes to perform in small, combative groupings which play long, open-ended pieces that are worked to the point of exhaustion. The names of some of his latter-day bands – Caos Totale, Loose Cannon, Bloodcount, Big Satan – give the flavour. In 1996 he started another company of his own, Screwgun, which has been busy issuing multidisc sets of live and studio work, although it has also reissued some of Hemphill's old music.
*Visitation Rights* (Screwgun)

# Milt Bernhart

TROMBONE
*born* 25 May 1926

A minor West Coast player, Bernhart nevertheless enlivened almost every date he played on. He worked with Boyd Raeburn in his teens, then with Stan Kenton, but his great moments came when he was part of the West Coast studio gang centred around Shorty Rogers in the 50s. There, and with Kenton, he played what were rarely more than eight- or 16-bar solos with a crisp aplomb, getting a sound which had a mellow, rounded tone yet was delivered with a contrarily punchy attack. He carried on working into the 70s, although only rarely did he get a noticeable role. His only starring albums, *Modern Brass* (1955) and *The Sounds Of Bernhart* (1959), are rare and engaging.
*Modern Brass* (RCA)

# Peter Bernstein

GUITAR
*born* 3 September 1967

Early impressions of Bernstein were that he was just another bop-orientated guitarist ready to play licks in the neoclassic style of organ-combo jazz, part of the generally retrospective jazz movement which grew up around New York in the late 80s. But he has inhabited the style with enough personality to move a step on from there. He has worked with such inquisitive contemporaries as Bill Stewart, Larry Goldings, Joshua Redman and Brian Lynch (as well as authentic old masters of the order of Lou Donaldson and Trudy Pitts), and his albums as leader for Criss Cross have lately reached

a fine pitch of individuality and assertiveness.
*Heart's Content* (Criss Cross)

# Bill Berry

TRUMPET
*born* 14 September 1930; *died* 13 November 2002

Like many lesser figures in the music, Berry will most likely be remembered for his one famous job, as a member of the Ellington trumpet section (1961–4). In fact, he had worked all down the East Coast, with Maynard Ferguson, Woody Herman and others, and went on to play in numerous other big bands, forming his own New York Big Band in 1970, and latterly working on the West Coast. British audiences saw him quite often in the 80s as a touring guest.
**Duke Ellington,** *My People* (Columbia)

# Chu Berry

TENOR SAXOPHONE
*born* 13 September 1908; *died* 20 October 1941

Berry's early death, in a car accident, was a particularly unhappy loss, since he may have had his best music ahead of him. He was certainly one of the tenor's leading stylists in the late 30s, coming out of West Virginia as a Coleman Hawkins fan, playing in Chicago with Sammy Stewart's band and settling in New York in 1930. He played in numerous bands and began gathering attention which, while he was with Fletcher Henderson, snowballed and led to him becoming in the highest demand for record dates. He has beautiful moments on record with Billie Holiday, Lionel Hampton, Teddy Wilson and Count Basie, and there are some fine sides under his own name too. When he joined Cab Calloway in 1937 he helped set new standards for the band, both in his own playing and in advising the leader on new sidemen: Dizzy Gillespie was one recommendation. Berry played with a lithe but heftily powerful momentum, a point somewhere between Hawkins and Young, and while he might never have quite equalled their best moments listeners were spellbound by his accuracy and fondness for plaintive high notes. His nickname (his real name was Leon) either came from Chu-Chin-Chow, after the goatee he affected, or from a

chewing habit; either way, he was held in loving esteem by his fellow musicians, and Calloway and his men were devastated by his sudden death, leaving his chair empty on the stand for weeks afterwards.
*Blowing Up A Breeze* (Topaz)

# Emmett Berry
TRUMPET
*born* 23 July 1915; *died* 22 June 1993

Berry grew up in Cleveland and moved to New York in 1933. His most eminent job was with Fletcher Henderson (and latterly brother Horace), holding down the principal trumpet soloist's chair in the later 30s. He then worked with Teddy Wilson and Raymond Scott, and found his most comfortable niche with the Count Basie orchestra of the later 40s, a natural successor to Buck Clayton who played very much in Buck's style. He racked up countless sideman credits all through the 50s and 60s, but his health began to fail and he retired and went home to Cleveland in 1970. Little was heard of him subsequently. Comfortable in any trumpet player's job, he left behind a vast number of appearances, hardly any of which stand out – the price of being a modest professional.
**Count Basie, *1948–49*** (Classics)

# Eddie Bert
TROMBONE
*born* 16 May 1922

A jazz everyman who's played in countless situations, Bert was in the Sam Donahue band at 18 and joined Red Norvo a year later, working in both his small group and his big band. Following army service he was with Kenton and Goodman and took part in the rehearsals for the Miles Davis nonet sessions. In the 50s he was on call for both big-band and small-group work, with every kind of leader; he even joined the first edition of Charles Mingus's Jazz Workshop, but only stayed a month. His only LPs as leader were made during this period, small-group sessions for Discovery, Jazztone, Savoy and Trans World, all of which showcase a quick, agile stylist with a sonorous sound. In the 60s he was involved more with pit bands and TV work but he has latterly returned to

more jazz-orientated music and was again a prolific campaigner in such outfits as the American Jazz Orchestra, Gene Harris's Superband and the New York Jazz Repertory Company. A fine photographer and teacher, Bert is one of those musicians who have made up the backbone of jazz playing in the past 50 years.
*Musician Of The Year* (Savoy)

# Bob Bertles
SAXOPHONES
*born* 6 March 1939

Bertles played saxophone in Australian rock'n'roll bands and led a jazz quintet with, variously, Bryce Rohde or Mike Nock on piano. While touring with a rock group he arrived in England and joined Ian Carr's Nucleus in 1970, staying for six years, although he then returned to Australia. On his home turf Bertles is a rock-solid hard bopper and his albums for Rufus display an enjoyably no-nonsense approach to the idiom. He has recently turned up in the Australian all-star group Ten Part Invention, and he fits right in.
*Cool Beans* (Rufus)

# Vic Berton
DRUMS
*born* 6 May 1896; *died* 26 December 1951

Berton played in Sousa's band during the First World War and studied classical percussion before – being somewhat older than the others – taking over the drum role in The Wolverines in Chicago, where he befriended Bix Beiderbecke. Later he appeared with some of the superior New York dance bands as well as working in the Red Nichols circle of players and featuring on many of their small-group dates. Berton was a dedicated musician who constantly tried to better both his playing and his equipment: he thought up the idea of placing his cymbal on a vertical rod, which soon became part of the standard drum kit, and he may even have invented the hi-hat, which he called a sock cymbal. A hot-tempered man with a major ego, he got the sack from the Paul Whiteman orchestra after getting into a punch-up with the leader. When the Depression took hold he

left for Hollywood and worked as a studio percussion man and director on soundtracks. He comes through vividly in his brother Ralph's memoir *Remembering Bix*, and is said to have had an unhealthy interest in the occult.
**Red Nichols, *1925–1927*** (Classics)

## Gene Bertoncini
GUITAR
*born* 6 April 1937

A prolific presence on the recent New York scene. He played mostly in mainstream situations in the 60s and 70s but his duo with Michael Moore was more boppish in nature, and he has since made something of a speciality of the duo format. While he played mostly electric guitar earlier in his career, he has latterly preferred to use an amplified acoustic, and he gets a distinctively warm and full-bodied sound out of it.
***O Grande Amor*** (Stash)

## Jimmy Bertrand
DRUMS, PERCUSSION
*born* 24 February 1900; *died* August 1960

Busy on the Chicago scene from 1918, Bertrand worked and recorded with such local stalwarts as Jimmy Blythe and Tiny Parham, but his great moment was as leader of a 1927 session which included a moonlighting Louis Armstrong and Johnny Dodds. He plays xylophone on some records (including one with Blind Blake!) and he taught the young Lionel Hampton for a spell. He carried on bandleading until the 40s but then vanished from sight. Bertrand is a pivotal figure in the fascinating circle of Jazz Age Chicago's lesser lights, though as a drummer he was hardly in the Zutty Singleton class.
**Various, *Jazz Of The 20s, Hot And Rare*** (Verve)

## Denzil Best
DRUMS
*born* 27 April 1917; *died* 24 May 1965

Best was unlucky in his career and should be more frequently remembered than he is. He came rather late to the drums – in the early 40s, after previously playing piano, bass and trumpet. He worked behind various leaders, including Coleman Hawkins and Chubby Jackson, but came to wider prominence as the first drummer in George Shearing's popular quintet, working with them until 1952, when an injury in a car crash took him out of circulation for a while. Among musicians, though, Best was already known as a capable composer, placing 'Move', 'Wee' and 'Dee Dee's Dance' in the bebop repertory, although he was happy to work with swing-styled players. On his return he played with Artie Shaw and, in particular, Erroll Garner, but a starring role eluded him and his arms were increasingly handicapped by a progressively worsening bone condition. Best was one of the most elegant drummers in New York's bop and hard-bop heyday, often preferring to play with brushes rather than sticks, and he was an ideal member of a piano trio, musically deft without drawing the attention. He had all but stopped playing again when he died after falling down a flight of steps.
**Erroll Garner, *Concert By The Sea*** (Columbia)

## Bethlehem
RECORD COMPANY

For a time, Bethlehem could call itself one of the premier jazz independents. It was founded by Gus Wildi in 1953, and issued some 40 albums in the ten-inch vinyl format before changing over to 12-inchers in 1955. The catalogue grew steadily, and by the late 50s, the label's peak period, they had material by a broad range of players and singers, including Chris Connor, Mel Tormé, Booker Ervin, Zoot Sims, Jack Teagarden, Dexter Gordon and Art Blakey. But they appeared to have no exclusive contracts with any artists, and a haphazardness often intruded into recording quality and sleeve design. It was sold to King in the early 60s, who gave up on any new jazz recording, and the rights appear to have drifted from one hand to another ever since: it was up for sale again early in 2004.

# Ed Bickert
GUITAR
*born* 29 November 1932

One of the best-known Canadian main-streamers, Bickert worked in Toronto as a studio musician in the 50s and 60s, and via an association with Paul Desmond he began to travel more widely. In the 80s he signed with Concord and led several dates of his own, as well as acting as the sideman guitarist on many of their other sessions. He has a deceptively soft tone, which masks quite a plangent attack, and while he is basically working in the mainstream, bop tempos hold no fears for him.

***Third Floor Richard*** (Concord)

# Barney Bigard
CLARINET, TENOR SAXOPHONE
*born* 3 March 1906; *died* 27 June 1980

Although Bigard was tutored in New Orleans by Lorenzo Tio, perhaps the most distinguished clarinet man in the city, he subsequently began working in a novelty duo with Albert Nicholas, where Bigard played tenor sax. King Oliver, though, hired him as a clarinet player, and after three years of good work Bigard joined Duke Ellington at the start of the Cotton Club residency. Bigard stayed with Ellington right up until 1942, enjoying numerous features and tossing countless ideas Duke's way – the subsidiary themes of 'Mood Indigo' and 'C Jam Blues' were just two of them. He then tried several groups and leaders for a time before joining up with Louis Armstrong's All Stars in 1947, the second of the two great associations in his career. Life on the road almost wore him out and he left in 1955, but rejoined Armstrong for a brief spell in 1960. Thereafter he hovered between a stately retirement and picking and choosing dates which appealed. Bigard's big, woodsy sound, his rustic yet impeccable technique and bursts of sheer invention as a soloist had a huge impact on clarinet players of several generations: never as invincible as such counterparts as Goodman and Shaw, he still sounded closer to the heart of jazz clarinet, a bridge between Johnny Dodds and the cooler virtuosos of the swing era.

**Duke Ellington,** *Never No Lament* (RCA Bluebird)

# Big bands

Swing was the era of the big bands, a heyday which lasted some ten years or so from 1935, to the point where this is still often referred to as the 'Big Band Era'. The large swing bands grew out of the somewhat smaller dance bands of the 20s, where brass, reeds and a rhythm section combined to create a credible popular counterpart to the symphony orchestra. A band of 13 pieces was not untypical, but by the 40s this was growing further: the likes of Artie Shaw and Harry James added string sections too. Yet this often resulted in the big bands becoming too sluggish and overweighted to allow the music to develop much, and the jazz initiative passed back to the small groups of bebop. By the 50s, the number of touring big bands in America and Europe had dramatically declined, and by the 60s the frequently encountered question 'Will the big bands ever come back?' was a notable cliché soon enough. In fact, leaders such as Woody Herman, Count Basie, Duke Ellington and Stan Kenton never went away (and the Basie and Ellington bands carried on after their founders' deaths). While it is economically hardly possible to keep a big band on the road on any regular basis, they are still convened as vehicles for college players, local semi-professionals and festival-season attractions. A few shrewd operators, such as George Gruntz or Matthias Ruegg of the Vienna Art Orchestra, have elicited formidable sponsorships to keep their bands going. But often a modern big band will grow up out of the musicians' shared pleasure in playing together and making a big sound – a jazz imperishable which can be understood by any open-eared listener, once heard.

# Acker Bilk
CLARINET
*born* 28 January 1929

Born Bernard Stanley Bilk in Pensford, Somerset, he took up the piano first and learned clarinet while doing army service. His own first band was uneventful but he then joined Ken Colyer in 1954 and won wider attention before starting out with another group, the Paramount Jazz Band. While this was at first a local (Bristol)

phenomenon, Bilk began making waves as the trad boom gathered pace and by the end of the 50s they were among the leading units in the style, touring widely in the UK and Europe and playing in a bluff New Orleans vernacular which will surprise those who know the smoother side of Acker. It was the latter, though, which won him pop stardom. Two huge chart hits in the form of 'Summer Set' (1960) and the immortal 'Stranger On The Shore' (1961), written for his daughter Jenny and in the charts for an astonishing 55 weeks, established a very successful formula. Acker and his group also dressed in bowlers and waistcoats and their album sleeves were written in a pseudo-Edwardian dialect. There were 'Big Build-Up Boys Behind Bilk' according to a 1961 *Melody Maker* headline, but The Beatles intervened, and subsequently Bilk's group moved towards cabaret and the albums (usually with the Leon Young String Chorale) went to the middle of the road. Still, in perform-ance Bilk still played solid mainstream jazz, the rough edges having been polished down, and he even had another top-ten hit with 'Aria' in 1976. In the 80s he was still as likely to be found on a German bill with James Last as playing in an English jazz venue, but by the 90s a few health prob-lems caused him to slow down a little. His clarinet sound became as personal and immediately identifiable as Pee Wee Russell's, and scattered through his many records are numerous small gems of writ-ing from his own pen. He is very likely the most affectionately regarded of all British jazzmen.
*Stranger On The Shore* (Redial)

## Rolf Billberg
ALTO SAXOPHONE
*born* 22 August 1930; *died* 17 August 1966

Billberg started on tenor, playing in dance orchestras in Gothenburg and Stockholm, but switched to alto when he began working with his close friend Lars Gullin, and his archetypally cool and pointed playing is a precious survival on the handful of featured records he left behind. He formed a quintet with Jan Allan which was cast in the Tristano mould, and he does some fine sideman work on record with Gullin and Nils Lindberg; but a heart attack ended his life three days before his 36th birthday.
*Rolf Billberg* (Dragon)

## Chris Biscoe
SAXOPHONES, CLARINET
*born* 5 February 1947

Biscoe is an utterly dependable second banana. He taught himself to play the alto and was one of the early stars of the NYJO, joining them in 1970. He worked through various associations in the 70s but found his ideal boss in 1979 in the shape of Mike Westbrook, who has used Biscoe's virtuosity on virtually the entire saxophone and reed family to fine effect on almost all of his sub-sequent projects. Biscoe has led various groups of his own, and is the horn player in Full Monte and Mingus Moves, one close to free playing and the other a repertory band. Biscoe's reticent appearance and unassum-ing command has perhaps worked against his securing any kind of wider recognition; that, and the fact that no album with his name above the title has really demanded attention. He is nevertheless regarded by his peers as a master.
**Mike Westbrook, *London Bridge Is Broken Down*** (Virgin)

## Walter Bishop Jr
PIANO
*born* 10 April 1927; *died* 24 January 1998

Bishop was in on bebop soon enough, hav-ing ended his military service in 1947 and begun sitting in on New York jam sessions. Charlie Parker and Miles Davis both liked him as an accompanist and he is on a number of significant sessions from the late 40s and early 50s. Then a drug problem almost ruined him: he lost his cabaret card and did time in jail. But from 1960 onwards he revitalized his career, touring, visiting Europe and working with a diverse clan of players that stretched from Tubby Hayes to Terry Gibbs, as well as leading his own groups. Bishop moved to the West Coast in 1969 but returned East six years later, and though he recorded occasionally and toured regularly enough, he never seemed to win much attention. He was still playing in the 90s and a handful of fine late records attest

to his powers – still a diehard bopper, but his style broadened by Garneresque touches and a feel for the blues. Too little of his LP work has made it to CD so far. His father was a songwriter who befriended Art Tatum.
*Coral Keys* (Black Jazz)

# Black Artists Group
COLLECTIVE

Inspired by Chicago's AACM, the St Louis-based BAG never had the same kind of success or influence. The group sponsored performances and had its 'house band' in the shape of Charles 'Bobo' Shaw's Human Arts Ensemble; but while some illustrious names were involved (Joseph Bowie, Hamiet Bluiett, Oliver Lake, Julius Hemphill) there was no real commitment to long-term achievement, and when funding money was lost in 1972 the Group petered out.

# Black Lion
RECORD COMPANY

One of the imprints used by the British producer/entrepreneur Alan Bates, this came into being in 1968 and followed a prolific programme of issues: one strand was devoted to new releases by international artists, one to British traditional and mainstream jazz, and another to reissues of licensed material, from such sources as V-Disc and Sunset. While the label always seemed like a hotch-potch that mixed outstanding material with mere potboiler records, the astute Bates built a formidably large catalogue, which contained outstanding music by Earl Hines, Thelonious Monk, Ben Webster and other American leaders alongside some fine homegrown releases, particularly by Humphrey Lyttelton and Chris Barber. Bates subsequently sold his interest in the label and its availability in the CD era has been erratic.

# Cindy Blackman
DRUMS
*born* 18 November 1959

Blackman studied in Hartford before moving to New York in 1982. She slowly built a reputation and began getting profile gigs with such leaders as Freddie Hubbard and Wallace Roney, the latter a particular mentor for her. She began leading bands and record dates of her own, starting in 1987, but none of them has had any special impact, and while she is a powerful drummer in the modern tradition, as a composer she seems nothing special. Lenny Kravitz has used her as a touring drummer and rock seems as likely to be her preferred idiom as jazz.
*The Oracle* (Muse)

# Black Saint
RECORD LABEL

In the 70s and 80s the Black Saint operation (which has a sister label called Soul Note) was unrivalled in documenting the American jazz avant-garde. It was founded in Milan in 1975 by Giacomo Pellicciotti but is much more closely associated with Giovanni Bonandrini, who took over and began growing the catalogue in 1978. Every month during the decade 1978–88 seemed to produce remarkable new records, and the roster of names involved included David Murray, Cecil Taylor, Steve Lacy, Anthony Braxton, World Saxophone Quartet, Muhal Richard Abrams and many more. When Bonandrini severed ties with his chief distributor, Polygram, in 1988 the pace slackened, and in recent times the label has looked more towards its 'local' players, recording the likes of Furio Di Castri and Giorgio Gaslini, although there have still been American records by Glenn Spearman, Larry Ochs and other less starry US names. It's some comment on the poor state of affairs at home that so many American leaders had to look to Italy for recording sponsorship at this point.

# Ed Blackwell
DRUMS
*born* 10 October 1929; *died* 7 October 1992

A New Orleans man, Blackwell is for ever associated with Ornette Coleman's music, but he was playing in local R&B bands as far back as 1948. Still, he worked with Coleman for the first time only a year later, and then on and off all through the 50s. In 1960 he moved to New York, where he took over from Billy Higgins in the Coleman quartet, and he is on several of the major Atlantic sessions by Coleman. But he went on to work with other seniors in the new avant-garde too: Don Cherry, Eric Dolphy, Archie Shepp. In 1973, he suffered kidney failure, which obliged him to spend the rest of his life with a dialysis machine in close attendance, although it didn't really slow him down. He taught and played all through the 70s and 80s and the year before he died he was playing with Joe Lovano and Steve Coleman. Blackwell was the most melodious of drummers, getting a resonant, almost singing sound out of the toms in particular, and his natural swing helped keep Coleman's music honest and more integrated with jazz 'tradition' than many thought at the time.

**Ornette Coleman, *This Is Our Music*** (Atlantic)

## Brian Blade

DRUMS
*born* 25 July 1970

Born in Shreveport, Louisiana, Blade studied in New Orleans and worked locally, although his reputation soon spread far enough for him to be touring England with Courtney Pine in 1990. Since then he has steadily grown in stature and in his associations, initially with high-profile groups led by Kenny Garrett and Joshua Redman, then as a gun for hire in supergroups, as well as with several New Orleans confederates. Blade's dexterity, polyrhythmic control and power are often breathtaking. He is also interested in other traditions of American drumming, and explored them more specifically on his first record, *Fellowship* (1997), although both this and its successor were unsuccessful in terms of sales and he has apparently been dropped by Blue Note. He is a thinker about the drums – 'the strike of the cymbal is almost mystical to me' – and has, unusually, worked with some significant rock figures too, such as Bob Dylan and Joni Mitchell. How far he goes may depend on whether he pursues leadership ambitions.

**Fellowship** (Blue Note)

## Eubie Blake

*born* 7 February 1883; *died* 12 February 1983

Jazz's most famous centenarian was a natural wonder, who played before the music even existed and lived long enough to perform through a time when many claimed that jazz was already dead. Born in Baltimore, the son of a couple who had been slaves, he learned to play the organ and began working in nightclubs when he was 15, delighted to be part of a bustling scene of exciting new music. His first piece, 'Sounds Of Africa' (later 'Charleston Rag') was composed in 1899. His career turning point, though, didn't come until 1915, when he joined forces with a singer, dancer and budding songwriter, Noble Sissle. One of their first efforts, 'It's All Your Fault', was a major hit, and encouraged them to relocate to New York, where they worked with the orchestra of James Reese Europe for a spell. They worked in vaudeville as a duo and produced a musical, *Shuffle Along*, which opened on Broadway in 1921 and was still going strong a year later. The duo wrote other stage pieces and toured Europe, making a particular success in London. Blake had recorded piano rolls back in the teens and cut the likes of 'Jazzing Around' on disc in 1917, but otherwise he set down very little of his instrumental music in the 20s (there are two disappointing sides made in 1921 by his Shuffle Along Orchestra); mostly, he simply accompanies Sissle on many records. Four 1931 sessions by an orchestra are similarly only modestly interesting. Blake mainly wrote for the stage in the 30s, and toured as an MD for military shows during the war, but retired in 1946. Eventually he was rediscovered, although it wasn't until 1969, when he made the celebrated *The Eighty-Six Years Of Eubie Blake* for John Hammond, that Blake's seemingly ageless exuberance was widely heard again. A small, bald, sinewy man, he seemed to remember everything about his early days and his playing was unimpaired – vigorous, correct in the classic ragtime manner which he helped create, but the form enlivened by improvised breaks and a momentous kind of swing. By the middle 70s he was firmly ensconced as a living legend, and a 1978 Broadway show, *Eubie*, gathered together some of the details of his life. Honours were showered on him, and he took it all in his brisk stride· when

Earl Hines tried to help him offstage at one festival, Blake brushed his assistance aside and pointed out that he was old enough to be his father. Everyone in jazz was convinced he would see 100, and in the end, he just made it.

*The Eighty-Six Years Of Eubie Blake* (Columbia)

# John Blake
VIOLIN
*born* 3 July 1947

The Philadelphian has gathered a considerable list of playing partners but has never made that much impact on the music himself. He studied the literature of his instrument in great depth (including Indian classical techniques) but played in the rather simpler settings of the Grover Washington group (1976–9) and McCoy Tyner's band (1979–84). While he has subsequently led numerous small groups of his own, he hasn't been lucky in recording and there is very little under his own name. A long-standing association with Avery Sharpe (formed during their work together with Tyner) has at least resulted in a duo recording (1997), cited below.

*Ebony Epic Journey* (JKNM)

# Ran Blake
PIANO
*born* 20 April 1935

Blake worked in comparative obscurity until he was in his 40s. Raised in Springfield, Massachusetts, he has always seemed more of a ruralist than any kind of metropolitan jazz player, heavily influenced by black church music as well as the diverse streams of 20th-century composition. He struck up a long-standing association with the singer Jeanne Lee while both were at Bard College in the late 50s, and although he made a single album for ESP in 1965 – the stark, startling *Ran Blake Plays Solo Piano*, which had all the working parts of his style already in place – he remained largely out of sight to the jazz audience, and aside from a single (and unsuccessful) album for Milestone in 1969 he didn't make any further records until some work for European labels in the mid-70s. He doesn't see himself in any jazz-piano tradition, and he has done more work

as a scholar and teacher than as a gigging player: in 1973, he began heading the New England Conservatory's third-stream department. He has a special affinity with singers, and claims to be more influenced by the likes of Mahalia Jackson and Chris Connor than Bud Powell. All of this informs a style which tends to be dark, slow, exactingly dissonant, but lyrical in its chill, skeletal way. Of his subsequent records, *The Short Life Of Barbara Monk*, with Ricky Ford (a comparatively frequent collaborator), Ed Felson and Jon Hazilla, is an eerie masterpiece much concerned with reflections on death. His modest accounting of his own place in jazz disguises a deep thinker and a genuine original.

*The Short Life Of Barbara Monk* (Soul Note)

# Seamus Blake
TENOR SAXOPHONE
*born* 8 December 1970

Although he was actually born in London, Blake grew up in Canada, went to Berklee in 1988 (staying four years) and then arrived in New York. One of his highest-profile gigs was with John Scofield in 1996, but since then he hasn't done much to put him lastingly in the spotlight. He is, though, a saxophonist of fine command whose interests look broad enough to sustain him in any likely context: he has a Scofield-like combo called the Bloomdaddies, and one or two of his own-name records have moved through some queer terrain that might suggest an introverted progressive rock. In a straightforward post-bop band, though, he has plenty to say. He won the saxophone prize in the 2002 Thelonious Monk competition (at the advanced age of 31) and seemed bemused: 'probably some gigs will fall at my doorstep – great, because I haven't been much of a hustler'.

*Four Track Mind* (Criss Cross)

# Rob Blakeslee
TRUMPET
*born* 9 December 1952

Blakeslee's music advertises that the 'regional' jazz of America is well worth hearing, even if it's fostered in places remote from the more fashionable and intense

areas of music-making. Born in Portland, Oregon, Blakeslee first worked in West Coast groups in the 70s, then moved to Dallas and became a close confidant of Dennis Gonzalez. In 1988 he returned to Portland, and since then has worked in the creative axis which involves himself, Vinny Golia, Rich Halley, Ken Filiano and Tad Weed. He is also a member of the Northwest Creative Music Orchestra. A classically trained trumpeter, he has technical skills which allow him to perform difficult scored music as well as working on a completely free canvas, and his best music – documented mostly via Golia's Nine Winds label – is powerful if sometimes introverted.
*Long Narrows* (Nine Winds)

# Art Blakey
DRUMS, BANDLEADER
*born* 11 October 1919; *died* 16 October 1990

Blakey began as a pianist, getting lessons in his native Pittsburgh, and by his mid-teens he was already leading a local band. But he moved to the drums, after being shown up by Erroll Garner at the piano, and began modelling himself on Chick Webb and Sidney Catlett (who once told him: 'Son, when you're in trouble, roll'). In 1942 he arrived in New York and worked with Fletcher Henderson, before leading his own big band and then joining Billy Eckstine's orchestra in St Louis in 1944, where he stayed for three years. Blakey began leading a group called Jazz Messengers when Eckstine disbanded, and was in on some major record dates with Thelonious Monk and Fats Navarro, before travelling through Africa for a year. Here he took his Islamic name of Abdullah ibn Buhaina, and though he always denied any African influence on his drumming, his rimshot-rapping does seem to have been introduced into his style after this period.

Back in America, he worked for several leaders before forming an alliance with Horace Silver in 1953: this was the real beginning of Art Blakey's Jazz Messengers, the small-group format – usually two or three horns and rhythm section – which the drummer led for the rest of his career. Blakey turned the group into a dynasty: 'Yes, sir,' he says on his Birdland recording of 1954 with Clifford Brown and Lou Donaldson, 'I'm

going to stay with the youngsters – when these get too old, I'm going to get some younger ones.' Scores of musicians passed through the Blakey academy thereafter: Jackie McLean, Johnny Griffin, Lee Morgan, Wayne Shorter, Freddie Hubbard, Bobby Timmons, Cedar Walton, Keith Jarrett, Chick Corea, Joanne Brackeen, Gary Bartz, Woody Shaw, Bobby Watson, Wynton and Branford Marsalis, Mulgrew Miller and Terence Blanchard are only some of the most significant. The band's book was expanded with each new compositional talent that joined the band: Blanchard, one of the last MDs of the group, remembers playing an entire week of two sets a night and only repeating a single tune once during the engagement (once too often, the club owner complained). Luckily, Blakey was seldom out of a recording contract, and there are dozens of albums by the different editions of the Messengers, many classics emerging on Blue Note, Atlantic and (latterly) Concord in particular. Blakey managed to work through jazz's leanest commercial periods without being obliged to change his format or go electric, and when the Marsalis brothers joined the group in 1980, it heralded a revival of interest in the hard-bop vernacular and Art found himself acclaimed as a godfather-figure all over again. His own drumming is among the most forceful and distinctive in jazz: trademarks include the chomping hi-hat on two and four, the volcanic press roll (which Sid Catlett had suggested), the huge cymbal-sound with its very slow decay and the cross-rhythms which he delighted in. Besides his Messengers dates, there are several records which he made in the company of African and Latin American drummers, each a tremendous percussive noise. If he felt a soloist was going wrong, or going on too long, an ominous rattling would come from the kit that basically said, time's up. In his white-haired old age, he loved to talk to audiences and would never miss a chance to beat the drum for jazz and how music should be respected: 'It washes away the dust of everyday life.' He somehow found the time to raise seven children, too.
*Buhaina's Delight* (Blue Note)

## Terence Blanchard
TRUMPET
*born* 13 March 1962

Blanchard emerged as a young New Orleans contender straight after Wynton Marsalis. He first studied at the city's Center For The Creative Arts, where he met saxophonist Donald Harrison, then went to Rutgers (and played in the Lionel Hampton band). In 1982 he linked up with Harrison again and the two replaced the Marsalis brothers as Art Blakey's front line. They stayed two years before co-leading a quintet, then went back to the Messengers for a further spell. In 1988, Blanchard began scoring films for Spike Lee, an undertaking which has continued to this day, and though he took some time off playing to deal with an embouchure problem, the trumpeter has continued working as leader of his own small groups too. His work for Lee has yielded perhaps the most significant sequence of jazz-orientated soundtracks of recent times, from the ambitious *Malcolm X* to the modest *She Hate Me*, but his small-group records have been even more impressive: *Jazz In Film* and *Wandering Moon* are full of superbly realized music. A peerless craftsman, Blanchard is as impressive a technician as his contemporary Marsalis, but if anything he is a more profound and affecting ballad player, which gives even his slowest music a special radiance. In 2002 he moved from Columbia/Sony (his home for many years) to Blue Note and opened with an auspicious debut.
***Wandering Moon*** (Sony Classics)

## Jimmy Blanton
BASS
*born* October 1918; *died* 30 July 1942

It's curious to find that the great revolutionary of the bass spent his summer vacations (from Tennessee State College) playing in the old-time riverboat bands of Fate Marable. Duke Ellington discovered Blanton in 1939 and hired him straight away. From his very first session (14 October, where he replaced Billy Taylor) he changed the sound and pulse of the Ellington orchestra. He had a fluency, sonority, intonation and buoyancy of swing which, added together, put him on a different level to every other bass-man of his day. Soloists could follow him almost as a duet partner, since he added passing notes which hinted at a turn of phrasing which might have eluded them, but it was the almost levitational quality of his musicianship which made the difference to the band as a whole, and that comes through even on records made in an era when the bass was never well recorded. Ellington gave him a classic feature – 'Jack The Bear' (1940) – and within weeks had recorded the first of several piano/bass duets with him, an unprecedented departure. When soloing, Blanton stood aside from the usual walking-bass figures and was as inventive as he was in his ensemble playing. All this from a man barely 21 years old. He was also involved in some of the Minton's jam sessions which pointed the way towards bop. But tragedy intervened: in 1941, Blanton's health began to give Ellington cause for concern, and eventually he was hospitalized with what turned out to be tuberculosis. When Ellington visited him for the last time, he could see that Jimmy was already gone.
**Duke Ellington,** ***Never No Lament*** (RCA)

## Rudi Blesh
AUTHOR, BROADCASTER
*born* 21 January 1899; *died* 25 August 1985

Blesh was an industrial and architectural designer by trade, but he was a jazz lover who started covering the music for the *San Francisco Chronicle* in the early 40s, and then promoted some concerts himself. He moved to New York and continued writing there, although he provoked trouble by getting into debates on the authenticity of different strands of the music, contending that the 20s were good and the 30s bad. Eventually, there was some relenting, and in an amusing about-face he put Wild Bill Davison on the same bill as Charlie Parker in 1947. He founded a small label, Circle, in 1946, and some of the best things he did were in the *This Is Jazz* broadcasts of 1947, which left precious survivals of Sidney Bechet and others. His great work was *They All Played Ragtime* (1950), written with Harriet Janis, which was the first real scholarship done on that music and led to the rediscovery of Eubie Blake and others. He later taught in New York. Blesh was perhaps no great writer, but his pioneering work did a lot for many musicians.

## Carla Bley
PIANO, COMPOSER, BANDLEADER
*born* 11 May 1938

Karen Borg was born in Oakland and moved to New York when she was 17, sometimes playing piano in public. She married Paul Bley in 1957, and he encouraged her to write: Bley, Jimmy Giuffre and others recorded some of the results, such as 'Ida Lupino', 'Jesus Maria' and 'Ictus'. In 1964 she helped to form the Jazz Composers' Orchestra, and subsequently an association connected with it, which aided the dissemination of much avant-garde jazz and contemporary composition (mostly via its New Music Distribution Service). By now partnered by trumpeter Michael Mantler (she divorced Bley in 1967), Bley eventually won wider attention with her music for Gary Burton's *A Genuine Tong Funeral* (1967) and Charlie Haden's *Liberation Music Orchestra* (1969), although it wasn't until the release of her three-record 'chronotransduction' *Escalator Over The Hill* (1971) that Bley herself got on to record in a significant way. She sings, plays keyboards and otherwise directs this famously sprawling work, part jazz score, part operetta and extended avant-garde satire, which remains very fine in parts. The JCOA came to an end in 1975 and from 1985 Bley has led her own largeish band, usually around ten pieces or so, for tours and records (she co-founded a label, WATT, with Mantler in 1973). After she divorced Mantler in 1992, Steve Swallow became her partner, and they have toured as a duo and as a trio with saxophonist Andy Sheppard.

Bley's discography isn't very large, considering she has been working on it for 40 years, and a lot of her latter-day music circles around the same themes and ideas. She likes The Beatles, Robert Wyatt, Albert Ayler and Bruckner, and one can hear all those sources in what she does; but her gift is for coming up with original melodies, and one often regrets that the boisterous music of her later years has largely bowdlerized and devalued the gentler ingenuities of her early work. Very few of her later records seem like much more than echoes of the older, more original scores, although this is

necessarily true of many composers. Interestingly, when given an 'outside' project to work on, such as Charlie Haden's *Ballad Of The Fallen* (1982), she sheds some of the self-indulgence and turns in stronger music. The Bley ensemble has at least provided regular exposure for many maverick players, especially Gary Valente, Sheppard, Frank Lacy, Vincent Chancey and Steve Slagle.
*Escalator Over The Hill* (JCOA)

## Paul Bley
PIANO
*born* 10 November 1932

Though virtually unknown outside the jazz audience, Bley ranks among the real masters of the music in its modern era. Born in Montreal, he began piano lessons at eight and went on to study composition at Juilliard. He recorded at 19 with Oscar Pettiford, was playing behind Charlie Parker a year later and made *Introducing Paul Bley* the year after that, with Charles Mingus and Art Blakey behind him. But he chose to relocate to the West Coast in 1957, working a steady gig at the Hillcrest Club, where the likes of Don Cherry and Ornette Coleman would play as sidemen: Bley has joked since that you could always tell when that band was on stage because the audience would be out in the street. Back in New York, where he was also encouraging his wife Carla to compose, Bley was offered the piano seat in the George Russell group but chose to work instead with Sonny Rollins (1963–4). He was deeply involved in the 'October Revolution' and helped co-found the Jazz Composers' Guild; his albums *Footloose* (Savoy) and *Barrage* (ESP) set an agenda for the piano in free jazz which was a countering voice to Cecil Taylor's, spare and lyrical at times but also darkly turbulent in its way. He worked in the trio format with several players but took an abrupt move into electronics in 1969, with the assistance of his second wife Annette Peacock (the group was called the Bley–Peacock Synthesizer Show). Yet within three years he had made a permanent return to the acoustic piano. He founded the Improvising Artists label in 1974, primarily for his own work but also sponsoring Sam Rivers, Ran Blake and others; it eventually foundered as a going concern, although the sessions have surfaced on CD from time to time.

In the 80s he embarked on a prolific campaign of record-making which has continued to this day, taking advantage of seemingly every opportunity to document his music. Solo, duo, trio and quartet sessions have resulted, although he shies away from anything larger than a small combo. His style grew more directly lyrical and less agitated, though not necessarily warmer. While his own writing was at first parsimoniously distributed among his records – he often preferred to play the music of Carla Bley and Annette Peacock, and his interpretations of their finest compositions are an invaluable archive in themselves – he has latterly been more generous in airing his own work: aphoristic, delicately nuanced but with an iron backbone of carefully distilled musical thinking. Sometimes, as in a solo treatment of Eric Dolphy's 'Music Matador', he has brought a wholly unexpected piece to the piano and worked a breathtaking transformation. Despite his lack of 'outside' recognition, he is as influential as any modern pianist, and to judge from his own book *Stopping Time: Paul Bley And The Transformation Of Jazz* he is strongly conscious of his own importance. Still, it goes along with a nice dry humour, as when he was asked if he listens to his own records: 'I *only* listen to my own records. That's why I make so many – that way, I have more things to listen to.'
**Paul *Plays Carla Bley*** (Steeplechase)

## Urs Blöchlinger

ALTO, SOPRANINO AND BASS SAXOPHONES
*born* 4 June 1954; *died* 4 March 1995

Blöchlinger was a Swiss saxophonist of marvellous energy and inventiveness. He didn't start on the saxophone until he was 18, but soon mastered the alto and in the middle 70s played in a curious jazz-comedy troupe, the Jerry Denal Kollekdoof. His best work was done in small groups such as his trio with Thomas Dürst and Thomas Hiestand, and the group which he named Legfek and which varied between three and 14 in number. As with many European bands, the music offered was an unlikely mix of meticulously structured passages blended with meteoric free music. Blöchlinger him-

self liked both the high and low ends of the saxophone and was one of the few free players to make some sense of the bass sax. Alas, his suicide concluded an only occasionally documented career on a tragic low note.
**Aesthetik *Als Widerstand*** (Plainisphare)

## Jane Ira Bloom

SOPRANO SAXOPHONE
*born* 12 January 1954

Bloom is one of the lonely few who play only the soprano saxophone. She studied at Berklee and Yale and was in New York by the end of the 70s. At this point she was still playing some alto, but she dropped the lower horn after 1980, and began leading groups of her own, often with notably heavy company: Charlie Haden, Fred Hersch, Bobby Previte, Rufus Reid. She toured and recorded with a David Friedman group but otherwise has resisted working under other leaders and almost all of her appearances on record have been on projects of her own. Surprisingly, she was signed to Columbia for a spell in the middle 80s, but the records soon disappeared and she has otherwise recorded for independents, as well as writing a lot of commissioned music for film, dance and theatre situations. She has an abiding interest in aviation and space flight and was the first to receive an arts commission from NASA. Her records are a mixed bag but the best of them showcase a cool, even chilly lyricism which her vibratoless sound and patient delivery personify. She also likes to incorporate electronics, which sometimes hang over her music like a glittering night sky.
**The *Red Quartets*** (Arabesque)

## Blue note

Often characterized as 'the cracks between the piano keys', blue notes are a primary characteristic of jazz's musical language – an inflection more than a specific point on the diatonic scale. A blue note will emerge from the lowering or flattening of the third or seventh or (less often) fifth of the scale. How it sounds, how much impact and intensity it carries, depends entirely on the performer's use and expression of that note, as well as the context they are using it in. Indeed, rather than a simple lowering of a point on the scale, it might move between several points, within a microscopic range of pitches. The attack, decay, placement and resonance of a single blue note, or of a combination of blue notes, are characteristics which individualize any and every jazz performance, on any instrument (bar the fixed-pitch piano – hence the truism mentioned above). Given the inexhaustibility of range of such expression, it underlines how jazz improvisation itself is probably limitless in its capacity to find new expressions in even the most familiar material. Where the blue note originates from is a subject which has engaged scholars for many years, but it certainly predates the blues idiom itself. To pick a single example from known recorded evidence, hear Pete Hampton's cylinder recording of 'The Mouth Organ Coon', recorded by Edison in 1904.

## Blue Note Records
RECORD COMPANY

Arguably the greatest of the independent jazz labels, Blue Note was founded by a German expatriate and enthusiastic jazz fan, Alfred Lion, in 1939. Fired by attending the From Spirituals To Swing concert at Carnegie Hall and inspired by the example of Milt Gabler at Commodore, Lion, who had no previous experience, hired several musicians to record some sessions in the city (he was so engrossed in the music that he let the players – pianists Meade Lux Lewis and Pete Johnson – overrun, and the results had to be issued on 12-inch discs, rather than the customary ten-inch size). Joined by a partner, Frank Wolff, Lion saw through the early 40s and two recording bans, recording mostly small-group swing; but when he was introduced by Ike Quebec to Thelonious Monk, the label abruptly switched direction and began recording bebop. Blue Note made painstaking progress through the 50s, employing the best engineer in the city (Rudy Van Gelder) and hiring a fashion-magazine designer, Reid Miles, to do the covers for their LPs, mostly using Frank Wolff's session photography. The label captured some of the best hard bop of the era on record after record, much of it from the label's principal musician, Horace Silver, who remained with Blue Note

until the 70s. Other discoveries included Jimmy Smith and The Three Sounds, and the albums were impeccably turned out and packaged, setting a rare standard for LPs of any origin. But on finally scoring a countrywide hit with Lee Morgan's *The Sidewinder* in 1963, the business – operated all through on a tight shoestring – couldn't cope with the pressure, and Lion eventually sold out to Capitol. Artistically, the label fell away and was effectively closed in the 70s, but in the following decade Michael Cuscuna organized a major reissue programme and the label was revived under the tutelage of veteran executive (and long-time fan) Bruce Lundvall. Twenty years on, it is the most successful jazz arm of a major label (now part of EMI) and balances serious jazz releases with crossover moneyspinners such as the unprecedentedly successful Norah Jones. Lion, always a canny businessman, would probably have been pleased.

## Blues

1. Blues is primarily a vocal music, developed by African-Americans in the first quarter of the 20th century. Its uniqueness lies in the fact that, although it has continuously evolved through many stages of both instrumental and vocal development, it has remained essentially and recognizably the same. In its 'purest' form, it consists of a musical chorus structure of 12 bars across a three-line stanza, in which the words of the second line repeat those of the first; although it is also open to constant variation through the performer's improvisation. A vocal blues may have been performed without any instrumental accompaniment at all, although many of the first blues singers were itinerant country musicians, travelling from town to town and accompanying themselves on an acoustic guitar or banjo. Some of the earlier performers to record, such as Henry Thomas, had in their repertoire many pre-blues folk songs; they were often termed 'songsters' rather than bluesmen. Blues as an idiom, though, is distinct from jazz, even where the two have interacted: rhythm and blues (and consequently rock and roll) is at heart an amalgam of vocal blues bands and the instrumental licks and solos of swing-era jazz horn players. Such jazz traditions as the

New Orleans brass bands have had little or no relevance to blues. The emotional content of the blues, though, is as ambiguous as any jazz performance: while it is stereotypically an expression of melancholy, this does not take into account such emotions as anger, jealousy, bewilderment, resignation, exuberance or affection, all of which can be routinely found in a blues.
2. *A* blues, in jazz terms, has a more formal identity. It is a purely musical structure, which borrows the chorus format of 12 bars continually repeated, most likely with no vocal input. This simplicity makes it open to both the most direct interpretation – a plain blues in B flat, which even the greenest beginner can make a fist of improvising on – or something more complex, via an unusual key or a variation in chorus length. More usually, though, a blues is used by jazz musicians as a convenient meeting point, often between unfamiliar players. If someone wants to sit in with a band and jam, a blues could be called up as a common ground for everyone to settle on.

## Hamiet Bluiett
BARITONE SAXOPHONE, CLARINET
*born* 16 September 1940

Bluiett's sometimes bewildering range of approach is symptomatic of a notably restless jazz character. He played in navy bands before moving to St Louis in the middle 60s, where he quickly fell in with the city's avant-garde spirits and became a member of the Black Artists Group. He went to New York in 1969 and then worked with Charles Mingus, before becoming a formidable presence on the loft scene of the middle 70s: *Birthright* (1977), recorded at a typical concert during the period, is one of the very rare examples of a solo baritone saxophone record. With Julius Hemphill, Oliver Lake and David Murray he formed the World Saxophone Quartet in 1976, and his huge sound has anchored and flavoured all of their records. Under his own name his discography has been rambling and unpredictable, though never dull. He made *The Clarinet Family* (1984) for Black Saint, which involved himself and seven other reed players; he essayed sets which suggested a pan-African, multikulti kind of music; he issued a *Libation For The Baritone*

*Saxophone Nation*, which set him alongside James Carter, Alex Harding and Patience Higgins in a four-person bari band. While acting as a producer for the Mapleshade label, he has also made tributes to Nat Cole, an organ-trio date and straightforward blowing vehicles. Bluiett's cavernous lower register is enough to rattle anyone's floor, and it's odd that he seems to have an almost perverse liking for going up into a skinny, squealing high register on the horn too.
**Libation For The Baritone Saxophone Nation** (Justin Time)

## Arthur Blythe
ALTO AND SOPRANO SAXOPHONES
*born* 5 July 1940

Born in Los Angeles, Blythe played in R&B bands until jazz turned him around, and he worked as part of the community of musicians based around Horace Tapscott in the 60s, as well as with a group called Black Music Infinity. Nicknamed Black Arthur by some of his friends after bending their ears about achievements in black cultural history, he moved to New York in 1974 and played on the then-burgeoning loft scene, although like many others involved he looks back on it with mixed feelings – 'the business side of it was so raggedy'. After a few appearances on independent labels he was signed by Columbia in 1979 and made a series of records which apotheosize some of the jazz developments of that time: surprising instrumentations (tuba, cello, organ) and a worldly outreach blended with a profound investment in the traditional roots of gospel and blues, a vivid synthesis of ancient and modern. His own alto sound – with an oboe-like rotundity and a bursting high register – was ecstatic and monumental. Yet sales of the albums petered out, as the Marsalises began to influence the label's direction, and Blythe ended the sequence with a disastrous funk record. After that he worked with The Leaders and continued recording as a leader for independent labels, although the music became more settled and conventional. While his music is still a pleasure to hear, one looks back to that sequence of classics (many of them still awaited on CD) and regrets that Arthur became, somehow, becalmed.
**Lenox Avenue Breakdown** (Columbia/Koch)

## Jimmy Blythe
PIANO
*born* 1901; *died* 21 June 1931

Very little is known about Blythe. He came from Louisville and arrived in Chicago in his teens, and in 1924 he made his first records, piano solos for Paramount. From then until his death he was a busy man in the Chicago studios, recording primarily for Paramount, but also turning up on such labels as Gennett, Vocalion and Champion. Blythe was, indeed, involved in so many of Paramount's sessions – as leader, sideman or accompanist, with Johnny Dodds, Jimmy O'Bryant and many others – that it is assumed that he was under tenure as the house pianist there. A thumping player who nevertheless could finesse a part when it was appropriate, he contributed to a host of enjoyably rough-and-ready sessions which give a vivid picture of the blues and barrelhouse music of 20s Chicago.
*Jimmy Blythe* (Document)

## Peter Bocage
CORNET, VIOLIN
*born* 31 July 1887; *died* 3 December 1967

Bocage worked in New Orleans music from around 1900, and the names of some of the groups he played with evoke a long-gone era: The Eagle Band, The Superior Orchestra and 'Bab' Frank's Peerless Orchestra. In the teens he was working in some of the city's brass bands, but in 1915 he joined A J Piron and stayed with him as lead trumpet until 1928, recording with him on Piron's 1923–4 sessions for Columbia. He subsequently formed the Creole Serenaders (with some of his friends from the Piron band), which lasted until the 40s, although they made no records. Bocage didn't travel much and he was a respected and looked-up-to member of the New Orleans community, leading his own groups, and working with both the Love–Jiles Ragtime Orchestra and the Eureka Brass Band. He was a regular at Preservation Hall in the 60s. A neat, slight man, Bocage played in a sweetly hot style, but since he'd been around as long as he had, he was entitled to be old-fashioned. His entry in the Riverside *New Orleans Living Legends* series was unfortunately disappointing, and a set he made a year later for Mono is better.
*Peter Bocage* (Mono)

## Francy Boland
PIANO
*born* 6 November 1929

Francis Boland was born in Namur, Belgium, and he wrote charts for some of the better French bandleaders in the early 50s. He then went out as a pianist, spending time in New York for a season, and in 1959 he struck up a relationship with Kenny Clarke which resulted in the formation of a big band. The Clarke–Boland group may have had the drummer's name in front, but it was very much Boland's vehicle: he wrote all the charts, and most of the band's book was made up of his originals, several of them extended into suite length. Their records for Polydor, some recently restored to CD, sometimes strain after immortality: for many, the attraction of the group was its star soloists (Johnny Griffin, Benny Bailey, Ronnie Scott, Tony Coe and others), and while Boland's settings found a secure balance between individuals and the group sound, the original material was sometimes fussy and overworked. That said, at its best it was the equal of any contemporary big band in executing the best of its book. After it disbanded in 1973, Boland settled in Geneva, where he has continued to write for other orchestras and does occasional small-group dates, without recapturing the attention his old orchestra engendered.
*Off Limits* (Polydor)

## Buddy Bolden
CORNET
*born* 6 September 1877; *died* 4 November 1931

The unrivalled legend of early New Orleans jazz. Nobody today has any real idea of what Bolden sounded like, and contradictory accounts about him have settled a mythopoeic mist around his name. He seems to have started playing the cornet comparatively late, around 1894, taught by one Manuel Hall, and he began working in a group that played for dances (rather than one of the city's brass bands), led by Charlie Galloway. Within a couple of years he was leading the group, which included Frank Lewis on clarinet. At the turn of the century, Bolden's band had grown into a six-piece unit, and it is this line-up which is shown in one of the two surviving photographs of

Bolden. He had grown enormously popular: compared to other, similar bands, Bolden led his group with an aggressive power which led to the circulation of one legend that his sound could be heard 'fourteen miles on a clear night'. Jelly Roll Morton remembered him as the 'great ragtime trumpet man', and whatever jazz or blues there was in Bolden's playing must have been intuitive. He was apparently a capable player when it came to ornamenting a melody, but it's unlikely there was any real improvising in what he did, more a natural dependence on what would have been crowd-pleasing licks. 'King' Bolden – the first New Orleans man to be have that title bestowed on him – was busier than ever by 1905, but a year later drink and overwork had begun to take a toll on him, and his behaviour grew strange and erratic. At the Labor Day parade in 1906 he was arrested in a state of apparent dementia; on release, he moved to a new district with his family. But alleged domestic violence led to him being incarcerated the following year, and he spent the final 24 years of his life in the Jackson Mental Institute, oblivious to where the music would travel to: at the time of his death, two other trumpet kings of New Orleans (Keppard and Oliver) had already come and gone, and Louis Armstrong ruled the jazz world. Another great legend surrounds Bolden's only recording: a member of his band insisted that they had cut a cylinder before the turn of the century, but it has never been otherwise documented or traced. His music is entirely lost to us.

## Claude Bolling

PIANO
*born* 10 April 1930

Born in Cannes, Bolling was already leading his own jazz group in Paris by the time he was 15, and he subsequently played piano behind many American visitors, from Rex Stewart to Lionel Hampton. In 1955 he formed his own orchestra, which he has basically led ever since. He has largely modelled the big band on American influences, primarily Ellington: as a composer he has an ingenious flair for soundalike compositions in the style of other hands, and his numerous good-natured Ellington take-offs have enlivened many of his records. At the same time, he took the trouble to record the first completely unabridged version of Ellington's own *Black, Brown And Beige* in 1989, and made a very good fist of it. Through the years his orchestras have included many of the best French mainstreamers, including Gérard Badini and Claude Tissendier, and his own piano style is bouncily extrovert – he likes to play ragtime, and is again skilled at counterfeiting other players. While his music has rarely travelled very far, he is a great jazz hero in his own country – his band played at the 1994 memorial concert for D-Day, which exists as a DVD release – and not many days go by in France without a Bolling record being played on the radio.
***Rolling With Bolling*** (Frémeaux)

## Dupree Bolton

TRUMPET
*born* 3 March 1929; *died* 5 June 1994

Bolton's jazz career was brief and embattled. He was born in Oklahoma and turned up in Buddy Johnson's orchestra in 1945, playing trumpet in New York. After a brief spell with Benny Carter he vanished, seemingly with a bad drugs problem, and didn't reappear until playing with Harold Land, on his Contemporary album *The Fox* (1959) – a brilliant cameo. But he was abruptly jailed following a further narcotics offence, and subsequently made another fleeting but stylish appearance, on Curtis Amy's *Katanga* (1963). He was later in more trouble with the law, and aside from an album made by a prison band in the 70s, nothing else was heard from him, at least on record. He seems to have disappeared somewhere in California, although other reports suggest he was living on the streets in New York. His tiny body of recorded work is, though, good enough to make you wonder what else he might have achieved.
**Harold Land**, ***The Fox*** (Contemporary)

## Sharkey Bonano

TRUMPET, VOCAL
*born* 9 April 1902; *died* 27 March 1972

Joseph Gustaf Bonano was working in New Orleans from around 1920, and despite occasional forays elsewhere he remained

based in the South until the mid-30s. He was sometimes recorded in the 20s (with Johnnie Miller and Monk Hazel) and these glimpses suggest a good if not exceptional hot lead man. In the New Orleans revival of the 40s Bonano found himself much in demand, and he led new groups which emphasized his singing and showmanship. They made some entertaining records in the LP era, two of the Capitols shared with Lizzie Miles, and Sharkey carried on with his people's Dixieland until failing health caused him to step down in 1971.
**Midnight On Bourbon Street** (Capitol)

## Boogie woogie

In its purest form, this is a variation of piano blues, the left hand playing a repetitive bass figure, most often a walking bass in broken octaves, while the right hand plays a rhythmical, percussive commentary. Although the walking bass has a likely origin in ragtime piano, the boogie woogie developed out of a dance: pianists would have been playing this music for dancers at rent parties and in honky-tonks, and the cornerstone record of the style, Pinetop Smith's 'Pinetop's Boogie Woogie' (1928), features Smith's vocal instructions on how to perform the dance. At first it was just another part of the blues style, but its popular moment arrived in 1938, when the boogie specialists Albert Ammons, Meade Lux Lewis and Pete Johnson were the sensation of the Carnegie Hall From Spirituals To Swing concert, and were recorded (separately and together) by both major labels and new independents such as Blue Note. Swing bandleaders sorted out their own boogie specialities (Count Basie's 'Basie Boogie' from 1941 is one such) and even the likes of The Andrews Sisters had a boogie-woogie song. But the fad passed, and eventually the boogie method reverted to becoming part of the broader idiom of blues playing, although occasional novelties such as Humphrey Lyttelton's 'Bad Penny Blues' (1956) sometimes got boogie back in the charts. In the hands of the masters – besides those listed, the list would include such as Big Maceo, Jimmy Yancey and Professor Longhair – it is as open to endless variation as any blues procedure. The idea that it was all a bit naughty also lifted boogie's appeal: that

great pianist Chico Marx admonishes some young piano students in one of his films thus: 'No woogie-boogie!'

## Bossa nova

While other musical forms from South America have had only a limited impact on jazz and a wider listenership, the bossa nova's soothing and peaceable feel was insidious enough to make it still influential nearly 50 years after its arrival. Essentially a sweet, easygoing melody settled on the gentlest kind of samba beat, its practitioners were musicians such as Antonio Carlos Jobim and João Gilberto, and when Charlie Byrd heard it on a tour of Brazil he found it a perfect medium for his own playing. The album he made with Stan Getz, *Jazz Samba* (1962), kicked off the bossa nova craze which was for a while a dominant part of popular music, and made fortunes for both Getz and Byrd. 'Desafinado' was the first big hit, but this was surpassed by 'The Girl From Ipanema', a Jobim tune which is still the number one jazz choice in wine bars everywhere. But while musicians such as Getz and Jobim put enough of themselves into the music to make it endure, most other musicians have learned that the bossa nova is a dangerously tranquillizing style.

## Earl Bostic
ALTO SAXOPHONE
*born* 25 April 1913; *died* 28 October 1965

Bostic might be called the first crossover star. He had a fairly anonymous big-band section career in the later 30s, but then led groups of his own and had a more prominent role with Lionel Hampton. In 1946 he was recording with a septet, a big-small format which he liked, and while he was very much the star soloist, he had a shrewd ear and eye for a good sideman: John Coltrane, Jaki Byard, Benny Golson and Stanley Turrentine were some of the young players who passed through the Bostic ranks. His big sound and slurping way with a melody – a simplification of what had previously been an eccentric deconstruction of a line – began to win wide appeal, and by 1951, when he scored his huge hit with 'Flamingo', Bostic was a jukebox star whose records became regulars on the best-seller lists. Soulful and mannered in equal weights, it was a sound which nodded towards jazz and R&B without losing appeal to a more pop-orientated audience, and Bostic kept the saxophone in vogue at a time when Charlie Parker had all but driven the uncommitted away. The records were samey but it was, after all, a successful formula. Bostic carried on touring through the 50s but a heart problem slowed him down.

*Flamingo* (Proper)

## Boswell Sisters
VOCAL GROUP

The three Boswell Sisters were the hippest white singers of their day, along with Bing Crosby – who made some delightful duet records with Connee (1907–76), the principal voice of the group. They grew up in New Orleans and all three played various instruments, but they began working as a close-harmony group and started broadcasting from Los Angeles in the late 20s. In 1931 they more or less took New York by storm and were the top American entertainers for some five years. They recorded as a trio for Brunswick, Connee taking the lead and lower range while Martha (1908–58) and Vet (1909–88) sang harmony which was beautifully registered and always swinging – their best records, with the likes of the Dorseys and Bunny Berigan offering hot fills, are as fine as any jazz singing of the 30s. Connee carried on latterly as a solo, worked in film and television and recorded a classic final set in 1956 with some old friends including Miff Mole. Because of the way studio photographs had been ingeniously manipulated, few realized that she had been crippled by polio when young and spent most of her life in a wheelchair.

*It's The Girls* (ASV)

## Allan Botschinsky
TRUMPET, FLUGELHORN
*born* 23 September 1940

Botschinsky's father played classical bassoon and the young man was soon studying at Copenhagen Royal Conservatory, but he also worked in big-band music and was soon part of the Danish Radiojazzgruppen. He went on

to lead bands of his own, many of them fusion-styled, and with more work coming in from the rest of Europe he eventually resettled in Hamburg, although he has often guested in groups from other territories. His records on MA Music, a label he co-founded, show a skilful if clinical player whose Miles Davis penchant is often cleverly directed.

*The Night* (MA Music)

## Ralph Bowen
TENOR AND SOPRANO SAXOPHONES
*born* 23 December 1961

A Canadian, Bowen played in local bands in and around Toronto in the early 80s and then studied at Rutgers (where he has subsequently taught). He was a member of the group OTB and also worked with Michel Camilo and Renee Rosnes. Bowen is regarded as a senior spirit of great authority by many of the younger New York players and his work as both leader and sideman on Criss Cross in particular has been outstanding for its strength and thoughtful virtuosity.

*Soul Proprietor* (Criss Cross)

## Joseph Bowie
TROMBONE
*born* 17 October 1953

One of three brothers, Joe Bowie looked for a time as if he would put together a more significant career than trumpeter Lester. Inspired, indeed, by Lester's work in Chicago, the younger Joseph followed a similar tack in St Louis, where he joined up to the Black Artists Group with Oliver Lake. He moved through various *outré* groups of one sort or another during the rest of the 70s, but stardom seemed to beckon when he formed a band called Defunkt, which briefly won crossover success with its mix of jazz licks for the horns over a metropolitan funk bottom. But the band actually sold few records and broke up in 1983, and Joe went into a period of recuperation from personal problems. A new Defunkt emerged in the later 80s and Bowie has kept it on a low simmer ever since, securing a New York audience and another in Japan, where they have long memories. Besides this, he's recorded regularly with Kahil El'Zabar's Ethnic Heritage Ensemble. As a trombone player,

Joe is more a useful man in a context than a particularly notable soloist.
*Defunkt* (1981)

## Lester Bowie
TRUMPET
*born* 11 October 1941; *died* 8 November 1999

The great maverick of the trumpet was born in Frederick, Maryland, but grew up in Little Rock and St Louis. He had already been on the road with R&B bands before moving to Chicago in 1965 and quickly getting involved with the nascent AACM. His alliance with Roscoe Mitchell took the two of them to Paris and from there they formed the Art Ensemble Of Chicago, which Bowie worked with regularly for the rest of his life. In addition, though, he formed his own bands: a quintet with Arthur Blythe and Amina Claudine Myers; a gospel-jazz unit, From The Root To The Source, which featured singers David Peaston and Fontella Bass (Bowie's first wife); the 50-strong Sho' Nuff Orchestra, which never recorded; and the New York Hot Trumpet Repertory Company, which originally featured a quintet of trumpeters by themselves. This last group was later augmented by other brass players and a rhythm section and became Brass Fantasy, Bowie's most successful band, which made several records and toured regularly. He was also in the all-star touring group The Leaders and in 1990 briefly led the New York Organ Ensemble, with Myers and James Carter. Bowie's playing in all of these ensembles was a model of originality, employing every kind of trumpet effect and distortion and somehow creating a logical and expressive style out of it. He saw his path as the real marker for jazz progress and was openly hostile to the stance adopted by Wynton Marsalis: 'He has been used to thwart the development of the music.' Ironically, Marsalis had been a member of the Trumpet Repertory Company, and some of his latter-day playing has a lot of Bowie in it. Brass Fantasy's repertoire encompassed pop standards old and new and was a canny bridge between high art and carnival entertainment, a tack which personified Bowie's whole approach. He loved a good cigar and was an unfailingly entertaining interviewee, but an unpublished biography reveals a darker and more troubled personality with a notably contemptible attitude to women in particular.
**Brass Fantasy,** *The Great Pretender* (ECM)

## Charles Brackeen
TENOR AND SOPRANO SAXOPHONES
*born* 13 March 1940

Originally from Oklahoma, Brackeen lived in Texas, New York and Los Angeles as a teenager and played in R&B groups as well as falling in with Ornette Coleman's circle on the West Coast. Settled back in New York in 1964, Brackeen made rather rare appearances on the scene and recorded only little: there was one date with Don Cherry in 1968, and also one for him in 1973, and then only a couple of albums for the independent Silkheart in the 80s. The highest profile he's enjoyed was as a member of the Paul Motian trio which made a pair of excellent albums for ECM, *Dance* (1977) and *Le Voyage* (1979). Like Coleman, Brackeen has a bluesy edge in his playing which can sound either rough or oddly cultivated, and he bridges free playing and a more formal vocabulary in sometimes intriguing ways. But he has had no real luck in a career which seems to have gone precisely nowhere, since nothing has now been heard from him for many years. He was married to the pianist Joanne Brackeen but they divorced in 1983.
**Paul Motian,** *Le Voyage* (ECM)

## Joanne Brackeen
PIANO
*born* 26 July 1938

Born in Ventura, California, Joanne Grogan was playing in West Coast clubs by the time she was 19. She married saxophonist Charles Brackeen and gave up music while she raised a family, but in 1966 she was in New York and starting to go back to the piano. She was in Art Blakey's Jazz Messengers for two years from 1969 and then joined first Joe Henderson and then Stan Getz, both of whom brought her to much wider attention. Since the middle 80s she has worked mostly as a leader herself, although she has had a rather mixed time of it on record: two albums for Columbia are rare and haven't been reissued, and other sessions for Timeless and Concord have come and gone.

Her most recent affiliation, with Bob Karcy's Arkadia label, has produced some of her best work. A surprisingly tall figure with a gentle, laughing voice, Brackeen has worked at the highest levels and is a tough-minded, adventurous player who tackles her music with gusto and intensity. Her composing touches classical and Latin as well as jazz bases and she likes her bands to brim with players who prefer to hang on for dear life.

*Pink Elephant Magic* (Arkadia)

## Don Braden
TENOR SAXOPHONE
*born* 20 November 1963

Braden emerged as a characteristic young turk of the 80s hard-bop movement, when he worked with the Harper Brothers, Betty Carter and Tony Williams in the latter part of that decade. Since then he has freelanced extensively and has done his best to pursue a leadership career, but a promising relationship with RCA sputtered out and albums for several independent labels have suggested that Braden is a fine executant but a player who struggles to really assert himself on a record date.

*After Dark* (Criss Cross)

## Bobby Bradford
TRUMPET
*born* 19 July 1934

Bradford grew up in Texas and studied in Austin before moving to Los Angeles in 1953, where he linked up with Ornette Coleman at an early stage. When he moved to New York in 1961 he briefly replaced Don Cherry in Coleman's quartet, but by 1964 he was back in Los Angeles, where he established his most significant working relationship, with the clarinettist John Carter. Their New Art Jazz Ensemble continued the work suggested by Coleman's quartet, although away on the West Coast they had considerably less exposure. Bradford taught in elementary schools and in the 70s and 80s was largely involved in education, although he continued his work with Carter and actually spent a period in London – where he built an association with John Stevens – in 1971. His relationship with Carter was often pared back to the duo format, and the author will

always remember one of the concerts they played in England in the 80s, a pure flow of melody which was enchanting. After Carter's death, Bradford worked with David Murray and others, although his sightings have become more infrequent.

*Tandem* (Emanem)

## Ruby Braff
CORNET, TRUMPET
*born* 16 March 1927; *died* 9 February 2003

Nobody in jazz was saltier or more pugnacious than the diminutive Braff, but he was able to back everything up with playing of the highest order. He arrived at exactly the wrong time, from a career point of view: a trumpet man from Boston who played in an impeccable Armstrong style was hardly the hottest property in the early 50s, but Braff nevertheless found audiences when he moved to New York and in 1954 he and Vic Dickenson set down some of the recording dates for Vanguard which would solidify the idea of a swing-styled jazz mainstream. Although he later complained about a lack of work, he recorded regularly enough in the later 50s (and for major labels such as Epic and RCA), and in the 60s he partnered George Wein in some of his all-star groupings as well as visiting Europe as a touring solo. In the 70s he formed a superb small group with George Barnes, although their quarrelling brought it to an early and inevitable end, and when he signed to Concord Records later in the decade he was given a platform to set down a long sequence of albums which showcased his lovely tone – singingly lyrical at the top end and with a fat, blowsy lower register – and fleet solo construction, setting him up with such amenable companions as Dick Hyman, Ellis Larkins (a particularly apposite duet partner) and Scott Hamilton. In the 90s he switched affiliations to Arbors and carried on at the same imperturbable pace, which only came to an end with his hospitalization early in 2003. The more Ruby groused and grumbled, the greater affection he was held in by an adoring mainstream audience, and he never let them down with his playing.

**With Ellis Larkins,** *Calling Berlin* (Arbors)

# Wellman Braud

BASS

born 25 January 1891; *died* 27 October 1966

The oldest member of the early Duke Ellington orchestra, Braud has been neglected in the light of the attention focused on one of his successors, Jimmy Blanton. A New Orleans man, he was with Ellington between 1927 and 1935, and while his playing was beginning to sound old-fashioned by the end of that period (Ellington eased him out by hiring a second bassist, Billy Taylor), he drove the band with enormous power, which comes through on most of their early records in particular, his fingers slapping the fingerboard with bruising intensity. Yet he also used the bow more often than many of his contemporaries. After leaving Ellington he never had much limelight again, although he worked with numerous other leaders and was still playing until shortly before his death.

**Duke Ellington,** *1929* (Classics)

# Anthony Braxton

SAXOPHONES, CLARINETS, PIANO

born 4 June 1935

The most ambitious of musicians, Braxton is an unprecedented figure in the music. He grew up in Chicago and took up clarinet and alto in his teens, joining in with the early days of the AACM and forming the trio Creative Construction Company with Leroy Jenkins and Leo Smith. They followed the Art Ensemble Of Chicago to Paris, but the music was perceived as too academic and unyielding, at least next to that of the Ensemble. Braxton went to New York in 1970 and did as much chess playing as music-making, but he joined Chick Corea in the group Circle, an unlikely alliance which foundered when Corea decided that he needed to find a more communicative idiom. Meanwhile, a double-album of Braxton's alto saxophone solos, recorded in 1968, belatedly emerged on Delmark and caused a small sensation, winning him real attention at last (and setting a trend for solo horn records). Braxton set his face against prevailing (electronic) trends and formed new groups with Dave Holland, Kenny Wheeler and others, winning a contract with Arista records, where Michael Cuscuna man-

aged to produce and release some of Braxton's increasingly grandiose projects: besides more solo music, there was the bulging three-disc *For Four Orchestras* (1973) amongst other pieces of enjoyable hubris. As well as the alto, he played every other member of the clarinet and saxophone family, including the elephantine contrabass instruments.

Braxton played duets with Derek Bailey and maintained a never-broken link with Europe; critics suggested that his music was increasingly beholden to European tradition anyway. He paid his bills with teaching and in 1985 established a new quartet (Marilyn Crispell, Mark Dresser, Gerry Hemingway) which was his principal performing vehicle until the middle 90s. In 1994, Braxton received a MacArthur Award which financed his Tri-centric Foundation, to facilitate the performance of his works, and he set up his own label, Braxton House, although this seems to have ground to a halt after a dozen releases or so. Meanwhile, he continues to make records for other labels at a prodigious rate: solos, duos, quartets where he plays piano, octets, orchestral pieces, and the importing of everyone from a stand-up comic to a bagpiper into his otherwise familiar agglomerations of instrumentalists. A series known as 'Ghost Trance Music' has preoccupied his composing in recent times. Individual compositions have been routinely titled by numbers or Braxton's own system of mathematical symbols, and his performers have often found that his methods of musical notation have been just as unique and private. His detractors hear a music stuffed with a calculating artiness, driven by procedure and dry of emotion; his supporters, and there are many, see him as a visionary whose every musical utterance is an important link in his composer's chain. It seems sadly unlikely that the intended apogee of his work, a piece for 100 orchestras, will ever be either completed or performed.

*For Alto* (Delmark)

# Break

Essentially, this is an improvised solo in miniature. The rest of the band, or perhaps just the rhythm section, plays the first beat of the bar as a marker, and then the soloist fills the rest, perhaps continuing on for a few more measures. When the rhythm returns, the tension is released as the solo ends. Jazz of the 20s was full of this kind of thing – for Jelly Roll Morton, solos should be deliberately contained, into the form of breaks – and it was an essential ingredient of hot dance music too. A stop-time solo is made up of a series of breaks, a classic instance being Louis Armstrong's climactic effort on 'Potato Head Blues'. Charlie Parker's sensational outburst on 'A Night In Tunisia' was even banded on an early LP as 'The Famous Alto Break'. As jazz rhythms loosened, the break all but disappeared.

## Lenny Breau
GUITAR
*born* 5 August 1941; *died* 12 August 1984

Breau was a connoisseur's guitarist, not a particularly secure position in a field where crowd pleasers tend to hold sway. His Canadian parents were country singers and Breau played in this style in Canada, but a pair of RCA albums from 1969 were a real surprise, showing an advanced solo style which seemed to weave together strands from bop, rock and even flamenco and Indian music to some striking ends. Heroin addiction ruined his career, though, and he died young with little else to his name, although some tapes of live performances were also posthumously released.
*The Guitar Sounds Of Lenny Breau* (RCA)

## Michael Brecker
TENOR SAXOPHONE
*born* 29 March 1949

Brecker has set formidable standards in saxophone playing. Four years younger than his brother – a considerable gap in popular-music terms – Michael's early interests were in rock and R&B. He moved to New York in 1970 and was soon crossing between two sides, jazz with Horace Silver, rock as a sessionman with the likes of James Taylor, and fusion with Billy Cobham's Dreams. A nonpareil technician on the saxophone, he formed The Brecker Brothers with Randy and enjoyed crossover success under his own name: the records were catchy enough to make the R&B charts, while satisfying musos with their displays of prowess. In

1979, he joined Steps (later Steps Ahead), Mike Mainieri's group, which was effectively another bridging point between jazz, rock and fusion, although this was at least more acoustically orientated. Thereafter he worked more as a solo, and as a very high-price sessionman. He also took up the EWI (electronic wind instrument), effectively a saxophone-synthesizer, although latterly he has preferred to play the acoustic horn. Tours with the likes of Paul Simon have brought him some of his biggest exposure, although he is not much of a showman, content to let the horn do the talking. He finally made a full-fledged jazz album under his own name in 1987, for MCA, and has since recorded regularly for Verve. Brecker's iron-clad tone, his steely poise and absolute certainty of delivery have electrified other saxophone players and have engendered whatever superstar status there is for a jazz player these days. In a curious way, though, he is not very influential: he sets a standard for other players to aspire to, but a certain neutrality of style makes him difficult to emulate on any level other than technical expertise. A recent tour where he played in an entirely solo context seemed to illustrate his difficulty: remote from Coltrane's spiritual questing or Rollins's humorous urbanity, the soul of his music is deeply protected and perhaps untouchable.
*Michael Brecker* (Impulse!)

## Randy Brecker
TRUMPET, FLUGELHORN
*born* 27 November 1945

The older Brecker brother learned to play classical trumpet in his home town of Philadelphia before jazz came into the picture, although he bought a copy of Charles Mingus's *Blues And Roots* in 1959 and 'it just completely turned my life around'. He toured Europe with a college band and arrived in New York in 1967, where he spent time with Blood Sweat & Tears and then joined Horace Silver's group. Already superb technicians, he and his brother found themselves in high demand for sessions and live work, at a time when there were far fewer outstanding achievers among the younger players. They formed Dreams with Billy Cobham in 1969, an association which lasted into the 70s, and in 1974 The Brecker

Brothers was formed as a three-horn band with David Sanborn. For their first records they double-tracked all the horn parts, which gave the sound tremendous strength, and with R&B chart hits such as 'Sneakin' Up On You' coming out of the sessions, the band became a surprise commercial success, eventually making six albums for Arista. In the same period, Randy was still in demand as a sessionman: he plays the memorable trumpet part on Bruce Springsteen's 'Meeting Across The River'. In the 80s, though, he diversified between the Latin feel of a new group with his then wife Eliane Elias, fusion work with Jaco Pastorius and (to tie in with the revival of interest in the medium) straight-ahead hard bop. In the 90s, by now a somewhat older statesman, Randy worked where he chose, sometimes as a star soloist, and sometimes in bally-hooed reunions of the Brothers. He has recorded as a leader comparatively rarely, though, and hasn't found the major-label affiliation which Michael has enjoyed. He probably still likes the looseness and chops-manship of R&B fusion best, but the dignity and calibre of his classical playing has never deserted him, and even when he doesn't sound as if he's trying all that hard, the lovely sound breaks through.
*The Brecker Brothers* (Arista)

# John Wolf Brennan
PIANO
*born* 13 February 1954

Born in Dublin, of Irish-Swiss parentage, Brennan is a prolific composer in many idioms – theatre music, classical compo-sition, dance, installation. He also plays jazz piano. In the 70s he was in the thick of the Swiss jazz- and prog-rock scene – not, admit-tedly, a major international phenomenon – as well as studying music formally. Over the years he has been variously based in Lucerne, Dublin, London, New York and Berlin, and he has formed numerous groups along the way: Impetus, Triumbajo, Pago Libre, Esa, the Creative Works Orchestra and his ten-piece Sinfonietta are among them. It's difficult to even try and pin down a stylist such as Brennan, who surely belongs in this book – as a solo pianist Brennan is a markedly thoughtful improviser – yet whose music deliberately resists idiom. The

record cited finds him with major impro-visers such as Paul Rutherford and Evan Parker and involves poetry settings for Julie Tippetts, the kind of mixed-media assem-blage which Brennan has made his own.
*... Through The Ear Of A Raindrop* (Leo)

# Willem Breuker
SAXOPHONES, CLARINET
*born* 4 November 1944

In the 60s, Breuker was at the centre of the Dutch avant-garde. He co-founded the ICP (Instant Composers Pool), with Misha Mengelberg and Han Bennink, which acted as both record label and sponsor of live performance, much of it based around Amsterdam's BimHuis venue. A self-taught saxophonist, Breuker was as uncompromis-ing as any of the other players in the European scene, but by the end of the decade he was already starting to become more interested in formal organization: one ICP release, *Lunchconcert For Three Barrelorgans* (1969), suggested ambitions very different to those of many of his con-temporaries. In 1973 he began his own label, BVHaast, and founded the Breuker Kollektief a year later, an 11-piece ensemble which persists to this day as the main per-forming vehicle for his music. The Kollektief has had many long-standing members, and while it has middle-aged a little, at their fier-iest they create a hugely entertaining colli-sion of genres during the course of a single performance, blusteringly irreverent, savag-ing whatever musical form comes their way, but playing with an often martial precision too. Breuker loves theatre, and his band are the most theatrical in jazz, although this comes – unusually – without sacrificing musical content too. BVHaast has assidu-ously documented the Breuker canon, which now runs to a fat discography, and while the records are often an inadequate substitute for seeing the Kollektief in person, the underlying strength of the leader's inven-tion shines through their progress on record. While Breuker himself has long since given up on free playing, glimmers of his original inspirations regularly peer through his meticulous arrangements. If the Kollektief has a sideways relationship with any jazz tradition, they have melded 'European' borrowings with swinging

big-band music better than perhaps any other group. Breuker himself received a Dutch knighthood in 1998.
*Parade* (BVHaast)

# Dee Dee Bridgewater
VOCAL
*born* 27 May 1950

The unquenchable spirit of a born performer lights up Bridgewater's music. Denise Eileen Garrett was born in Memphis but grew up in Michigan. She married trumpeter Cecil Bridgewater in 1970 and went to New York (although the marriage lasted only five years), and she sang with the Jones–Lewis Jazz Orchestra for two years before taking a leading role in the Broadway musical *The Wiz* in 1974, winning a Tony award for her work. Then she went to Los Angeles to try her luck in the pop-soul business, although her Atlantic albums in this style weren't too successful and haven't worn well. In 1983, she joined the touring revue *Sophisticated Ladies* and settled in France, where she began working with a European trio, which has been her preferred setting since. At the same time, she appeared in a play in London and Paris, *Lady Day*, where she took the Holiday role. Signed to Verve in 1990, she finally broke through as a jazz recording artist, with a sequence of strong records structured around various concepts – Horace Silver's music and Ella Fitzgerald, for two. As a touring act, she wowed audiences with performances of stunning exuberance, scatting and improvising around songs with tigerish aggression, and she admits that 'the closest to catching what I'm like is *Live At Yoshi's*' (1996). Somehow, though, she has found herself bypassed by the gentler, less archetypally soulful vocalists of the Diana Krall type, and with her records enjoying little in the way of serious promotion her career may again be on a downturn. There's surely no other singer who's ever brought Broadway hoofing and jazz-vocal virtuosity so closely together.
*Live At Yoshi's* (Verve)

# Nick Brignola
BARITONE SAXOPHONE
*born* 17 July 1936; *died* 8 February 2002

Brignola played in New York and Boston in the late 50s, was with Woody Herman in the early 60s and then formed a small group with Ted Curson which visited Europe. In the 70s he tried his hand at jazz-rock but went back to acoustic music with Curson and they continued to work together into the 80s. He maintained a catholic approach all through a busy career: besides those associations mentioned, he also played at one time or another with Muggsy Spanier, Dewey Redman and Barney Bigard. In the 80s and 90s he came into his own as a leader with a series of albums for Reservoir, which showcased his authoritative swing and command of the big saxophone (he also played flute and the rest of the saxophone family, but the baritone was his main horn). The final one in the sequence was released just as he died from cancer.
*The Flight Of The Eagle* (Reservoir)

# Alan Broadbent
PIANO
*born* 23 April 1947

Broadbent is all class. A New Zealander, born in Auckland, he went to study in Berklee in 1966 and had some lessons with Lennie Tristano. In 1969 he joined Woody Herman as pianist and chief arranger, staying as a band member until 1972 but continuing to write charts for the band's book. Basing himself in California, he spent the rest of the decade in a variety of small-group situations: backing Irene Kral, playing behind John Klemmer and Bud Shank, and taking a long stint as the house pianist at a Malibu club named Pasquale's. He went back to New Zealand for a brief spell at the beginning of the 80s but soon returned to Los Angeles, and eventually took the piano role in Charlie Haden's Quartet West, perhaps the major West Coast group of the past 20 years. He remained in demand as an arranger, especially in writing string charts for singers, and found time to make some exquisite trio dates for Concord. A witty man who is excellent company, Broadbent's interest in chamber music, his deft way with forces of varying sizes and his abiding love for

Charlie Parker's playing go together to make a jazz sensibility which is inventively lyrical without falling into cloying sweetness. His touch at the piano is extraordinarily fine. Some of the singers who've benefited from his arranging hand include Natalie Cole, Sue Raney, Sheila Jordan and, most recently, Jane Monheit.

*Personal Standards* (Concord)

# Bosse Broberg
TRUMPET
*born* 6 September 1937

Broberg will never be much known outside Sweden, but he is a skilful exponent of his favourite jazz language, which is unadorned hard bop. He was already playing in the style while at music college in Uppsala, and thereafter he struck up several long-term playing relationships, with Gugge Hedrenius and Arne Domnérus among others. He was an influential force at Swedish radio for a while and helped get the Radiojazzgruppen off the ground. In the 80s he enjoyed a camaraderie with Christer Boustedt in the Contemporary Bebop Quintet, which Broberg carried on after Boustedt's early death. His records are nothing special, just satisfying, humid examples of bop as a repertory resource.

*Circles And Triplets* (Dragon)

# Till Brönner
TRUMPET
*born* 6 May 1971

Brönner was somewhat bewilderingly groomed in Germany as a young jazz idol with matinée looks. He went through the classical system and followed many of his contemporaries into the RIAS Big Band in Berlin, but was eventually signed by Polygram as a possible star in the Chet Baker mould. Much of his playing does, indeed, sound as if it's been swiped directly from Baker's healthiest period. So far he hasn't really broken through internationally, and, in his mid-30s, time may be running out.

*My Secret Love* (BMG)

# Bob Brookmeyer
VALVE-TROMBONE, PIANO
*born* 19 December 1929

Brookmeyer grew up in Kansas City and worked mainly as a pianist with a number of big bands during the early 50s. He returned to the valve-trombone, which he had studied in high school, and joined Stan Getz's group at the end of 1952. It was a good time to be in a starry 'West Coast' kind of group, and Brookmeyer went on to replace Chet Baker with Gerry Mulligan (1953–7) and play in Jimmy Giuffre's trio. In every context, his droll, deceptively drowsy playing was entirely apposite, a perfect foil for the energetic Getz and Mulligan and a clever counterpart to the rustic-sounding Giuffre. His occasional piano features here and elsewhere (he went on to cut a piano-duo record with Bill Evans in 1959) kept his hand in on that instrument, and he proceeded to write charts for Mulligan's Concert Jazz Band, while also working in a two-horn quintet with Clark Terry which lasted through the early 60s. On his own admission a heroic drinker – 'I pretty well had drunk myself out of New York' – he moved to the West Coast in 1968, shed his booze problem and left music alone for a while. But friends like Bill Holman urged him back, and he toured Europe with Stan Getz in 1978. He became MD for the Jones–Lewis big band before dividing his time between Cologne, Denmark and New York: his European alliances continue to this day, and he has done some magnificent work with the New Art Orchestra of Cologne. Brookmeyer has led a modestly tempestuous life but in his autumnal years, settled with a fourth wife, he enjoys a jazz reputation which, while remote from any wider 'stardom', is copper-bottomed. On both valve-trombone and piano – on which he has a percussive, oddball style – he is all but unique, and both his records and his arrangements make up a vivid, funny, ingenious body of work. The Dutch Challenge label has made a point of recording him regularly in recent years, a responsibility which the American industry has shamefully neglected.

*The Blues Hot And Cool* (Verve)

## Cecil Brooks III

DRUMS, PRODUCER
*born* 16 August 1959

The son of a drummer, Brooks grew up in Pittsburgh and worked on the scene there until the middle 80s, when he moved to New York. Since then, he has been busy as a freelance, but has also built a secondary career as a record producer, and currently does a lot of work in that capacity for the Savant label, for which he also records himself. Perhaps as a result it's given him an extra gravitas as a group leader, and recent records assert a powerful hard-bop style.
*Live At Sweet Basil* (Savant)

## Tina Brooks

TENOR SAXOPHONE
*born* 7 June 1932; *died* 13 August 1974

A great favourite among Blue Note collectors, Harold Brooks (the nickname came from his modest stature) had some ten years in jazz, but only four as a visible artist, and his career seemed to vanish in an eyeblink. He moved with his family from North Carolina to New York when he was 12, and began working in R&B bands before befriending some of the hard boppers in the city. Benny Harris recommended him to Blue Note and Alfred Lion began using him on dates in 1958. In all, Brooks appeared on 12 albums for the label, four of them under his own leadership: at his best he was a wholly individual and compelling improviser, with a middleweight tone which was nevertheless surprisingly expressive, and a formidable ability to get around the horn. As with Hank Mobley, perhaps his best qualities were simply too oblique to win a wider audience, even though his masterful *True Blue* (1960) was one of the great Blue Notes of its year (he also wrote all of the original material on the date). Some of his other dates were never issued in his lifetime and it wasn't until the 90s that everything was made available in one place. This was far too late to offer Brooks any satisfaction, since he never recorded again after 1961 and died after years of illness brought on by drug abuse. His brother Bubba (b 1922) is a much less interesting player, although he has worked and recorded frequently in a leathery soul-jazz style.
*True Blue* (Blue Note)

## Brotherhood Of Breath

GROUP

Chris McGregor's group is among the most fondly remembered bands Britain ever fostered. Starting in 1970, McGregor built it around the handful of South African expatriates who had settled in London – himself, Dudu Pukwana, Johnny Dyani, Louis Moholo and Mongezi Feza – and added important locals of the calibre of Evan Parker, Harry Beckett, Mike Osborne and others. The result was a jostling, often joyful big band that stirred up African and European sources into a brew that sounded like an Ellington band clothed in post-bop and free-jazz garments. When McGregor decamped for France later in the decade, the BOB – never an easy group to keep intact with its participants often on call elsewhere – fell into disrepair, but it was still convened from time to time, usually as a festival attraction. After McGregor's death, Louis Moholo kept its spirit alive via The Dedication Orchestra. Little of the BOB survived on record and what there is sounds unvarnished and sometimes shambling: it's a band that lives best in people's memories.
*Brotherhood Of Breath* (RCA Neon)

## Peter Brötzmann

SAXOPHONES, TARAGATO
*born* 6 March 1941

Although born in Remscheid, Brötzmann is always associated with Wuppertal, where he attended the Art Academy. While he began as a Dixielander with local groups, he soon switched to the freest kind of jazz playing, and by the time of his first recording, *For Adolphe Sax* (1966), he was as forthright and uncompromising a saxophonist as any in jazz. Whether Albert Ayler had influenced him or not, his was the sound of a European, with no blues roots, fighting to create a significant voice by playing as loudly and furiously as possible. *Machine Gun* (1968) is a signature document of its time, an octet performance recorded in the basement of a disused munitions factory, where the players seem to be firing off round after round of ecstatic aggression. Brötzmann co-founded Free Music Production, to record and present free music, at the end of the decade, a period of which he has said, 'that was heavy

times, and you had to find your way and fight all sides'. While some of the older German players were at first suspicious, Brötzmann received support from many American players (including Don Cherry and Lee Konitz) and also worked with Dutchmen Han Bennink and Fred Van Hove. He worked steadily through the 70s and 80s, as free music became more institutionalized, and recorded frequently for FMP. His solo records are beautiful distillations of his blustering group work, tempered by a sometimes stark poignancy. In the later 80s he worked with the improvising supergroup Last Exit, and flirted, with no apparent bemusement, with the fringes of avant-garde rock (his son Caspar is a thrash guitarist). In the 90s, he was being hailed as a Founding Father, and a new generation of improvisers – led by the Chicago-based saxophonist Ken Vandermark – paid homage by placing him as the central voice in many new projects. Whatever the context, Brötzmann always seems ready to give his all, and how his lungs have held up all these years remains a wonder. While he remains primarily a tenor saxophonist, he also likes the squally taragato and once made an entire album (*Low Life*, with Bill Laswell) on bass sax.
*Machine Gun* (FMP)

## Cameron Brown
BASS
*born* 21 December 1945

Brown has created a strong presence in what's been a surprising variety of bands and settings, even for a modern bassist. He was in Europe in the 60s, playing with George Russell and Don Cherry, but was in New York by the end of the decade, where he became the house-band bassist at the St James Infirmary club. He was in the Don Pullen–George Adams quartet for its lifetime, forming an intimate team with drummer Dannie Richmond, and has latterly formed long-lasting partnerships with Dewey Redman and Sheila Jordan, who sings in Brown's band Hear And Now. Moving from in to out and back again seems to come as easily to him as breathing.
*Here And How!* (Omnitone)

## Cleo Brown
PIANO, VOCAL
*born* 8 December 1909; *died* 16 April 1995

The daughter of a minister, Brown learned piano in Chicago and was a regular in the city's clubs from the late 20s. When she took over Fats Waller's radio show in 1935, her popularity grew further, and she was busy all through the rest of the 30s and 40s. But she retired from music altogether in 1953 to take up nursing. Her discography is rather meagre, most of it done in the mid-30s, and while many of the tracks are little more than novelty tunes, two piano features – 'Pinetop's Boogie Woogie' and 'Pelican Stomp', issued on Decca and Brunswick – have real power and authority. She was rediscovered by Marian McPartland in the 80s and appeared on the PBS *Piano Jazz* series, though by this time she was playing and singing gospel music.
*Cleo Brown 1935–1951* (Classics)

## Clifford Brown
TRUMPET
*born* 30 October 1930; *died* 26 June 1956

While other figures of the bop era had drugs as their tragedy, it was left to a car accident to terminate Brown's wonderful contribution to jazz, a cruelty which a half-century later still seems devastating. Born in Wilmington, Delaware, he began on trumpet at 13 and quickly developed a breathtaking facility on the horn. In Philadelphia jam sessions he was a sensation: Fats Navarro especially liked him. He was in a first car crash in 1950, which took him off the scene for a while, but was back in action by 1952 and began making records (with an R&B group led by Chris Powell). He joined Lionel Hampton's touring band in 1953 and went with them to Europe, where he made some informal recordings (away from Hamp's watchful eye). In February 1954 he was back in New York and with Art Blakey's new Jazz Messengers: their Birdland recordings on Blue Note are enthralling, as were the results of Brown's next and as it turned out final association, a quintet co-led with Max Roach, based in California. What Brown did was sew together the best qualities of the bop players who had preceded him – Gillespie's full-tilt ebullience, Navarro's big

sound, Miles Davis's melodious appeal – and intensify them, in one forthright style. He could get all over the horn with incomparable fluency, his high range as easily covered as his middle and low, but this was amplified by his voluptuous sound and vibrato and the joyful assurance he seemed able to switch on without any warming-up passages. As a ballad player he might have been the best the trumpet could muster at that time, making even the promising Davis seem like a beginner, and Emarcy recorded him with strings and as an accompanist to Sarah Vaughan. Following his work through – luckily, he was extensively set down both in the studios and in live recordings in his brief heyday – he seems to get better and better as he goes on, his later live recordings almost unbelievably skilled and exciting. The final icing was his composing, which again had the marks of natural greatness: 'Joy Spring', 'Daahoud', 'Blues Walk' and others have the easy stride of a writer who had music spilling out of him. But it all came to an abrupt end in June 1956, in a crash on a rainy Pennsylvania night, which also killed pianist Richie Powell and robbed jazz of one of its golden princes. Who can tell what he might have gone on to achieve?
*At Basin Street* (Emarcy)

## Donald Brown
PIANO
*born* 28 March 1954

Brown came out of Memphis to join the Jazz Messengers in 1981, but a year later arthritis – which has handicapped all of his career – obliged him to quit, and since then he has done more work in education than on the bandstand. He has, though, recorded occasionally, for Muse in the 80s and 90s and more recently on his own Spacetime label, although the latter sets are difficult to find. Unusually, Brown is a contemporary composer whose pieces have often been picked up for performance by other jazz musicians, and tunes such as 'Insane Asylum', 'Booker T', 'The Biscuit Man' and 'Theme For Malcolm' have substance and melodic nourishment to spare.
*Send One Your Love* (Muse)

## Jeri Brown
VOCAL
*born* 1952

The St Louis singer was busy in the field of classical music and studies before working as a jazz singer on the local scene in the 70s. She was then involved in education more than performing, but her career took an upswing after she moved to Montreal in 1989 and began recording for the Canadian label Justin Time. While she hasn't really broken though internationally, a series of nine albums (to date) for the label have presented a considerable and mature body of work which, with proper promotional opportunities, should have made her much better known than she is: challenging programmes of material presented with a skilful and passionate singer's best concentration.
*A Timeless Place* ( Justin Time)

## Lawrence Brown
TROMBONE
*born* 3 August 1907; *died* 5 September 1988

Brown grew up on the West Coast and tried various instruments before settling on trombone. He had featured roles in Paul Howard's Quality Serenaders and in the Les Hite band which acted as a backdrop to Louis Armstrong, but his career found its mark when he joined Duke Ellington in 1932. Next to the expressionist Joe Nanton, Brown was a conservative, but his impeccably sonorous delivery gave the trombone section a rare richness and – like many of Ellington's main characters – he was a two-sided coin, the mellifluous balladeer paired with the tougher, bluesy soloist, even though it is the former role which Brown is best remembered for. He worked with Ellington all through the 30s and 40s before leaving in 1951 to work with a Johnny Hodges group, but he eventually went back to the Ducal field in 1960 and remained until he quit playing in 1970. Brown was a serious-minded man – his friends nicknamed him Deacon, acknowledging a lugubrious bent – who never pushed himself ahead of the demands of the musical job in hand; yet he surely stands, along with the likes of Teagarden, Dorsey and Higginbotham, among the premier trombonists of the swing era, a player whose standards and concentration never faltered.

**Duke Ellington,** *Never No Lament* (Bluebird)

# Les Brown

BANDLEADER

*born* 14 March 1912; *died* 4 January 2001

Les Brown 'And His Band Of Renown' bridged the gap between orchestral dance music and swing-styled jazz for decades. Brown himself was an unremarkable reed player who was bandleading as far back as 1936 but enjoyed his greatest success in the late 40s and 50s, with hits such as 'Sentimental Journey' (sung by one of his best vocalists, the young Doris Day). Latterly he had featured TV-show residencies with Dean Martin and Steve Allen. Brown typified the group of American bandleaders who basically catered to dancers and an easy-listening crowd who weren't averse to leaving space for jazz soloists or a brisker, more swinging chart. He never really retired and was still working occasional dates into the 21st century. Out of scores of albums, the one cited has perhaps the most to offer to a jazz listener.

*Jazz Song Book* (Coral)

# Marion Brown

ALTO SAXOPHONE

*born* 8 September 1935

Born in Atlanta, Brown studied both music and law in the 50s but his military service more or less decided him on a musical course after he played in various army bands. He arrived in New York at a crucial moment, taking advice from Ornette Coleman, playing on John Coltrane's *Ascension* and recording *Three For Shepp* for Impulse!, as well as cutting a couple of powerful sets for ESP. But none of it had much significant or lasting impact. As an alto player, Brown shied away from the powerhouse free playing represented by Archie Shepp, Coltrane and Albert Ayler, and his own recordings have a more conservative, even mournful bent. Ever since, his career has had the trajectory of a man on the verge of great things which have never quite come to fruition. He recorded for ECM, lived in Europe and the US, and formed occasional

partnerships with Mal Waldron, Gunter Hampel and Stanley Cowell; unlike Jimmy Lyons, though, a player whose sound he has a strong kinship with, he never formed the kind of bond with another musician of the sort which Lyons enjoyed with Cecil Taylor, which might have kept him more firmly in the public eye, and he has done relatively little in the past two decades.

*Three For Shepp* (Impulse!)

# Marshall Brown

VALVE-TROMBONE

*born* 21 December 1920; *died* 13 December 1983

Brown had a curious career. He was more involved in education than in any kind of musical career of his own, yet mostly he's remembered as a sideman alongside Pee Wee Russell, Ruby Braff and Lee Konitz. He was directing high-school bands through the early 50s and one group scored an unlikely hit at the 1957 Newport Festival: thereafter he organized a Newport Youth Band, which played there and at other festivals at the end of the decade and made two now-forgotten records (the line-ups featured such future notables as Eddie Gomez, Ronnie Cuber and Mike Abene). In the 60s he began his association with Russell and Konitz. He was a limber, clean-toned soloist on the valve-trombone, but left little that could be called memorable in that regard.

**Pee Wee Russell,** *New Groove* (Columbia)

# Oscar Brown Jr

VOCAL

*born* 10 October 1926

Brown came from a Chicago family that was full of lawyers, but despite attending a whole string of colleges in the 40s and early 50s he had no aspirations in the law. He began working as a singer after coming out of the army and was on Max Roach's *We Insist! Freedom Now Suite* (1960) before recording a sequence of albums for Columbia, which pitched him somewhere between jazzman, soul singer, hipster and politician. One of his trademarks was bringing new lyrics to soul-jazz hits such as Nat Adderley's 'Work Song'. His career mostly revolved around club work but he was a man of the streets in Chicago, where he brought members of the local gangs into some of his theatrical work. He was on television in the 70s, and in the 80s began working with his bassist son Oscar Beau Brown III in a duo; this came to a sad end when the younger Brown was killed in a car accident in 1996. He has never been quite as cool as some more touted crossover figures, but Brown deserves recognition for what became a very long career in the end.

**Oscar Brown Jr Tells It Like It Is** (Columbia)

## Pete Brown

ALTO SAXOPHONE
*born* 9 November 1906; *died* 20 September 1963

Although Brown is ostensibly an uncomplicated swing-era alto man, his music has excited surprisingly diverse opinions. He grew up in Baltimore, where he played piano in local bands, but he moved to New York in 1927 and freelanced in anonymous jobs before forming a partnership with Frankie Newton, appearing on his early sessions as a leader. He made no records under his own name until a session for Decca in 1942 (with Dizzy Gillespie), yet his gritty sound and almost staccato phrasing have been credited as a central plank in the creation of the style of 'jump' saxophone. He remained loyal to the small-group format and seemed troubled by the advent of bebop, his later records losing some of the brazen confidence of his earlier sound. A great session with Joe Turner, *Boss Of The Blues* (1956), reasserted his strengths, but his time was gone.

**Joe Turner, *Boss Of The Blues*** (Atlantic)

## Ray Brown

BASS
*born* 13 October 1926; *died* 2 July 2002

The most ubiquitous and versatile bassist jazz has known. Born in Pittsburgh, Brown moved past an early affection for the trombone to take up the acoustic bass, and began working with local groups before arriving in New York just as bebop was starting to be documented. Although he worked with Parker, Gillespie (especially – Ray worked with Gillespie's small groups and big bands in the middle 40s) and Milt Jackson, he was perhaps most at home in the piano/bass/

drums trio format, and a long spell with Hank Jones from 1947 cemented his original mastery of that idiom. He married Ella Fitzgerald while with Jones, although they divorced after only a few years. The bassist had already done time in various Jazz At The Philharmonic packages, and it was probably inevitable that he hooked up with Norman Granz's great protégé, Oscar Peterson. They first worked together as a duo in 1950, and then as a trio with guitarist Herb Ellis. Brown matched Peterson's virtuosity by playing rock-steady but quietly creative lines which fit handsomely into the group's momentum, and it helped settle and make the pianist's music more communicative. He picked up the cello, like Oscar Pettiford, but made use of it only infrequently. Brown left the Peterson group in 1966 and thereafter became a fixture on the Californian session scene. He was one of the founder members of The L.A.4 (with Bud Shank, Laurindo Almeida and Jeff Hamilton) and their Concord albums are coolly pleasant if mostly forgettable situations. There were numerous other dates for Concord, but for a time in the 80s he tried his hand at music management, although it went sour when his relationship with the Modern Jazz Quartet ended in litigation between the two sides. In the 90s he was busier than ever, leading trios with Benny Green and recording a string of dates for Telarc under the general rubric *Some Of My Best Friends Are . . .*, where guest stars on a particular instrument would join in the fun. Brown might have amassed a greater fortune out of a very lucrative career, but he was exceptionally fond of visiting the casino in whichever town he was playing in. At the Verve 50th Anniversary Concert in 1994, where Ray was an inevitable participant, Herbie Hancock quipped that 'Ray Brown was born in a tuxedo.' Christian McBride called him 'Dad'. He died during an afternoon nap on tour in Japan.

**Some Of My Best Friends Are . . . Guitarists** (Telarc)

## Reuben Brown

PIANO
*born* 1 December 1939

One peculiarity of jazz documentation is the way certain American players from unfashionable locations have been set down for posterity by European admirers. Nils Winther, who bosses the Danish label Steeplechase, is a past master at this, and if it weren't for him, the Washington-based pianist Reuben Brown might never have had any kind of attention beyond his immediate circle. Aside from a couple of tours with Joe Henderson and Buck Hill, another local man, he has scarcely played outside his home town. Winther recorded two sessions with him in 1994, one trio and one solo, and they show a surprising, original thinker, who draws on the masters but makes his own matter out of even familiar material: his remarkable version of 'Mack The Knife' is the signature example. But not long after the date, Brown suffered a stroke and apparently has been obliged to curtail his playing. *Ice Scape* (Steeplechase)

## Sandy Brown

CLARINET
*born* 25 February 1929; *died* 15 March 1975

Brown's brief jazz career touched some surprising bases. He was born in India but came home to Edinburgh when a child and taught himself the clarinet, playing in his own trad group in the late 40s. He moved to London in 1954 and quickly got himself involved in the music there, joining up with trumpeter Al Fairweather to form an exceptional group whose records were a bold mix of trad staples and more mainstream colours, with Brown's interest in African high-life music adding a final quirk. His own playing exuded a taciturn authority on the blues and a sweeter, more melodious drive on the faster pieces. In the 60s he mixed playing with a business which designed and installed sound studios, and in 1968 he made *Hair At Its Hairiest*, a record of jazzed tunes from the *Hair* musical played by the mystifying line-up of Brown, George Chisholm, Kenny Wheeler and John McLaughlin. Thereafter his health began to fail: a 1971 quartet date found him still in top fettle, but he died only four years later, a much-mourned one-off in his community. *McJazz And Friends* (Lake)

## Dave Brubeck

PIANO
*born* 6 December 1920

Brubeck was studying to be a vet (his father was a California stockman), but he had already been won over by playing jazz on the piano, and he quit those ambitions to lead a band before serving in the army. In 1946 he began studying with Milhaud, and founded an octet which made its first records in 1948, an interesting mix of bop, swing and neoclassical styles. Brubeck then set out to do trio work before adding Paul Desmond (who had previously stolen some of Brubeck's sidemen) to make up the quartet which, almost from the word go, was a success on the American college circuit: a record such as *Jazz At Oberlin* (1953) shows how much enthusiasm the band generated in concert. Columbia poached him away fom Fantasy and Brubeck even turned up on the cover of *Time*. By 1957, when the quartet included Gene Wright on bass and Joe Morello on drums, they were arguably the most popular jazz small group in America, namechecked by Mort Sahl and marketed as the first thing in modern music. The contrast between Desmond's airy, thin-lipped sound and Brubeck's bouncing attack was one draw; the other was the sense of composerly adventure which the leader seemed set on, with his oddball time-signatures and snippets from classical procedure. Some critics were unimpressed by what they saw as unswinging art, but time has softened such hostility, and there is surprisingly little rote music in any of Brubeck's stack of Columbia albums (many of which, inexplicably, have yet to make it to CD reissue). Desmond, who wrote the million-seller 'Take Five', wasn't always pleased at the attention on the leader, although his royalty cheques consoled him. Besides, 'Blue Rondo A La Turk', 'Unsquare Dance' and 'It's A Raggy Waltz' are at least as effective in exploring the group's identity.

By 1967 the group was disbanded, and the leader chose to concentrate more on composition, but he soon founded a new trio and had Gerry Mulligan and, less frequently, the returning Desmond as regular guests. His sons Darius, Chris and Daniel helped make up a family group, and latterly a fourth son, Matthew, has also joined in the fun. By the 80s the quartet was a touring favourite once

again, and Brubeck embarked on new recording contracts for Concord (1979–87) and Telarc (1992 up to the present), the albums emerging at regular intervals and none of them without fresh interest. In his 80s, he has been as prolific as ever: by now his opuses include ballets, oratorios, a mass and some chamber music, in addition to hundreds of jazz compositions. Little of this has been covered by anyone else – 'In Your Own Sweet Way' and 'The Duke' are about the only Brubeck tunes which get much attention elsewhere – but together they make up a profound lifetime in music-making, which has received many honours down the years.
*Time Out* (Columbia)

## Georg Brunis
TROMBONE
*born* 6 February 1902; *died* 19 November 1974

Although the spelling above is the one he most used, he was born George Clarence Brunies, one of five brothers in a New Orleans family, all of whom played music. His career was uneventful until he joined the vaudevillian Ted Lewis, staying ten years and learning many lessons in crowd-pleasing showmanship, many of which he later adopted himself. Brunis only occasionally steps forward on Lewis's records, but his tailgate-Dixieland delivery was heard to better advantage on the great sessions by Muggsy Spanier's Ragtimers (he's the one who exhorts Spanier on 'Big Butter And Egg Man') and with Wild Bill Davison and various Condonite groups in the 40s and 50s. Never much of a soloist, he was, like Kid Ory, an ensemble man, whose lines rattled between trumpet and clarinet with a braying intensity.
**Muggsy Spanier, *The Great Sixteen*** (RCA)

## Ray Bryant
PIANO
*born* 24 December 1931

Many premier musicians have come out of Philadelphia, and Ray Bryant might head the list. He was the regular piano man at the city's Blue Note club from 1953, where he accompanied all the visiting giants, and later in the 50s he performed a similar role at Prestige, taking the piano seat on such sessions as *Worktime* (Sonny Rollins) and several in the great sequence of discs which Coleman Hawkins recorded there. In 1959, though, he settled in New York, establishing his own trio, although he never shied away from playing on his own and – unlike such contemporaries as Red Garland – he has set down a distinctive body of solo work on record. He recorded prolifically for Cadet and Columbia in the 60s (although the latter label wasted his time with pop material) and for Pablo in the 70s, but he saved many of his finest hours for an outstanding sequence of records for Emarcy in the late 80s and early 90s, which have been too quickly deleted and are too little appreciated. Outgoing and capacious in his style, with a great feel for gospel currents and a gracious touch with the blues, Ray is perhaps only fully appreciated in Japan, where he has always had a large and loyal following. His brother Tommy (1930–82) was a bassist.
*Through The Years* (Emarcy)

## Rusty Bryant
TENOR SAXOPHONE
*born* 25 November 1929; *died* 25 March 1991

Bryant was more of a rhythm-and-blues man than a small-group jazz player, playing in Columbus to popular local acclaim in the 50s, but he made a sequence of records for Prestige at the beginning of the 70s which play out as a particularly likeable and simmering take on the soul-jazz formula, especially the one cited. None had any lasting impact, though, and after that he went back home to Columbus.
*Friday Night Funk For Saturday Night Brothers* (Prestige)

## Milt Buckner
ORGAN, PIANO
*born* 10 July 1915; *died* 27 July 1977

Born in St Louis but raised mostly in Detroit, Buckner worked locally as a pianist before joining Lionel Hampton in 1941. He stayed for most of the next ten years, although he had a crack at leading a big band of his own for a spell. At some point during the Hampton years he switched from piano to organ, and this became his main instrument

from then on: he used it to re-create big-band section voicings, and realized that it could stand alone at the centre of a small group. Thereafter he toured and recorded in this capacity. He nearly tapped in to the craze for easy-listening organ in the later 50s, but three albums for Capitol didn't really click and three more for Argo are similarly rather scarce; perhaps Milt was too much of a jazzman. From the late 60s he was a regular in Europe, backing many of the swing-mainstream stars who recorded for Black & Blue. He died while preparing for a gig with Illinois Jacquet.
*Green Onions* (Black & Blue)

## Teddy Buckner
TRUMPET, VOCAL
*born* 16 July 1909; *died* 22 September 1994

Buckner was an Armstrong man through and through. He was born in Texas but went to the West Coast in 1924 and played with sundry Californian outfits, even going to Shanghai on Buck Clayton's Chinese trip in 1934. But for most of his career he stayed in and around California. He took over Lionel Hampton's band in 1936 and worked with other leaders in the 40s before spending five years with Kid Ory, all the time playing in a manner which was often perilously close to copying Louis (he had actually worked as Armstrong's stand-in on the 1936 film *Pennies From Heaven*). Buckner enjoyed working in Hollywood and he is on numerous film soundtracks. But he may be best known for the small groups which he led after leaving Ory, which were akin to a more Dixiefied Armstrong All Stars and which cut several albums for Gene Norman.
*A Salute To Louis Armstrong* (Dixieland Jubilee)

## Dennis Budimir
GUITAR
*born* 20 June 1928

Budimir has done all his work on the West Coast and he is a member of the circle of musicians who recorded the distinctively lean and cool-toned jazz found on the Californian independent Revelation. He did big-band work before joining Chico Hamilton in 1959, and thereafter was a

studio regular right into the 90s, although this largely obscured him from the jazz audience. But his most interesting music is on his four albums for Revelation, which showcase a style which comes out of Tal Farlow but has a neatly idiosyncratic edge to it.
*Second Coming* (Revelation)

## Monty Budwig
BASS
*born* 26 December 1929; *died* 9 March 1992

Another of the honourable clan of bass-playing foot-soldiers, who have powered the music while only rarely taking any notable bows, Budwig was a West Coast fixture for four decades. He was a regular under many leaders for both recording and live work during the 50s and 60s, although perhaps his most consistent partnership was with Shelly Manne. In 1975 he was enlisted as the house bassman for Concord, where he recorded his sole album as leader, *Dig* (1978) – nice, but leading sessions wasn't really Monty's thing. He latterly toured with his pals in the reconstituted Lighthouse All Stars.
**Shelly Manne, *At The Black Hawk Vols 1–4*** (Contemporary)

## John Bunch
PIANO
*born* 1 December 1921

Born in Tipton, Indiana, John Bunch played piano for fun until he was well into his 30s. As soon as he turned pro, though, he was in demand, and worked for big bands (Herman, Goodman, Maynard Ferguson) and small groups (Buddy Rich, Gene Krupa) through the late 50s and early 60s. Tony Bennett engaged him as his first-choice pianist between 1966 and 1972 and he renewed his relationship with Benny Goodman in the same period. From the 80s, this good-natured performer began to be noticed as a leader himself, and he was much liked by the new mainstreamers; but he was adaptable to pretty much any jazz situation, working with Dizzy Gillespie on the trumpeter's 75th birthday tour, as well as with his old friend Bucky Pizzarelli and the quartet New York Swing. A failsafe stylist in the manner of Hank Jones or Teddy Wilson, Bunch divides his time between New York and

Europe; he stays in a cottage in Norfolk in the summer months.
***John Bunch Solo*** (Arbors)

# Larry Bunker
DRUMS
*born* 4 November 1928

Bunker's career is akin to a barometer of Californian popular music from the 50s onwards. He joined Howard Rumsey in 1951 and all through the decade worked with West Coast leaders, as well as vocalists such as Peggy Lee and June Christy. While he worked with Bill Evans and Bud Shank in the 60s, more of his time was spent in studio work and doing film and TV soundtracks. In the 80s and 90s this had moved towards Californian pop dates of various kinds. He also plays vibes and has experience with symphonic music as a classical percussionist.
**Bill Evans,** *Trio '65* (Verve)

# Teddy Bunn
GUITAR
*born* 7 May 1910; *died* 20 July 1978

A journeyman associated with several bands and styles, Bunn is on many records although few count as well-known, and today he is largely overlooked in discussions of jazz guitar. He grew up around New York and worked with calypso singers and washboard groups before recording with Duke Ellington and sometimes depping for Fred Guy. He joined The Spirits Of Rhythm in 1932 (it was the idea of Leo Watson, a longtime friend) and after leaving in 1937 tried various sideman jobs before going back to The Spirits in 1939. Four guitar solos made for Blue Note in 1940 showcased his adeptness, and were his farewell to the acoustic guitar, since he went over to electric shortly afterwards, though he never used a pick. He moved to California with The Spirits that same year. By the 50s he was adapting to R&B and rock and roll, although there was no stardom in it for him and he mostly worked behind the likes of Louis Jordan. He still played in the 60s, but his final years were marred by illness. An elegant soloist and a driving rhythm man, Bunn had few peers, and since The Spirits Of Rhythm

records have enjoyed little in the way of a revival, much of his best work is hidden.
**Spirits Of Rhythm,** *1933–1934* (Classics)

# Jane Bunnett
SOPRANO SAX, FLUTE
*born* 22 October 1956

Toronto-born, Bunnett studied piano but switched to clarinet and flute. On a trip to California she heard the Charles Mingus group at Keystone Korner and that decided her on a jazz career. She talked both Don Pullen and Dewey Redman into playing on her first album, *In Dew Time* (1988), and after that maintained close ties with Pullen in particular. She visited Cuba on a number of occasions and subsequently moved to Paris. In the 90s, she secured a contract with Blue Note, and although the records have not been very widely distributed, they show her making a specific rapprochement with Cuban music, with mixed but often highly entertaining results. Her soprano playing owes something to Steve Lacy, but her flute work may be the particular key to the direction her music has travelled in.
***Ritmo + Soul*** (Blue Note)

# Albert Burbank
CLARINET
*born* 25 March 1902; *died* 15 August 1976

Burbank might be mentioned in the same breath as George Lewis, but he rarely travelled away from New Orleans and all his great work was done in the city. He was playing for dances while still in his teens, but worked only locally and in low-profile groups until the 40s, when he was belatedly discovered by Bill Russell. Thereafter he had rather more distinguished associations, with Billie and De De Pierce, Paul Barbarin, Kid Ory, Kid Thomas Valentine and (finally, in 1973) Percy Humphrey. Burbank was, not surprisingly, not one to draw attention to his playing, but he had a beautiful tone in all registers and he would get all over the horn without seeming to show off.
***Albert Burbank*** (Smoky Mary)

# Raymond Burke

CLARINET

*born* 6 June 1904; *died* 21 March 1986

Ray Burke hardly ever left New Orleans. He took up clarinet at 16 and he was bandleading and playing as a sideman from the 30s onwards. When Preservation Hall opened in 1960 he was one of its earliest regulars, and he remained an amiable presence in the local music right up until the 80s, his last great association being with Kid Thomas Valentine. Though little known or spoken of outside New Orleans circles, he was absolutely characteristic of the sweeter side of the city's music, playing in a warm tone and insidious style which seems to breathe the air of the city. Burke never liked noisy drummers behind him, and there was something almost home-made about his style, rather like the amateur instruments he liked to accumulate; by day he ran a little collectables shop in the city.

**Raymond Burke And Cie Frazier With Butch Thompson In New Orleans** (504)

# Dave Burns

TRUMPET

*born* 5 March 1924

A regular on the New York scene since the early 40s, Burns packed a lot of playing into a career which has been reasonably documented but earned very little attention. He was in Dizzy Gillespie's big band in the late 40s (and sometimes covered for the leader's solos), and spent two years with Duke Ellington and much of the 50s in James Moody's small group. He made two albums of his own for Vanguard in the early 60s, both virtually unknown, but otherwise was busy as a studio player and sideman, latterly much involved in education. He had a particularly bright, fiery tone and was well suited to Latin dates as well as more straight-ahead music.

**Art Taylor, A.T.'s Delight** (Blue Note)

# Ralph Burns

PIANO, ARRANGER

*born* 29 June 1922; *died* 21 November 2001

Burns studied in New England and by 1943 was in New York with Charlie Barnet. But it was his time with Woody Herman (where he eventually left the piano role and concentrated on writing) which sealed his stature as a jazz arranger. Herman's band was poised between swing and bop, and Burns brought a sophistication to the book which let the orchestra work at both the shouting level and in pastels and fine textures. 'Apple Honey' was at the loud end, and the four-part 'Summer Sequence', the kind of extended composition which only Ellington was otherwise investigating, was at the other. Burns eventually went out on his own as an arranger and composer for orchestras and vocal groups, and over the years led a handful of record dates under his own name: *Very Warm For Jazz* (1959) and *Swingin' Down The Lane* (1962) are two of them. He never stopped working, and latterly did some filmscore work, including *New York, New York* for Martin Scorsese.

**Woody Herman, *Blowin' Up A Storm!*** (Columbia)

# Ronnie Burrage

DRUMS

*born* 19 October 1959

Burrage sat in with Duke Ellington (at the age of nine) but has never quite achieved the eminence that start might have prophesied. In the 80s and early 90s he worked in many high-profile situations, with Woody Shaw, Pat Metheny, Joe Locke, Sonny Fortune, World Saxophone Quartet and others, but in the new century he has faded from international view and has few recent credits to his name.

**Four Play** (DIW)

# Dave Burrell

PIANO

*born* 10 September 1944

After Berklee studies, Burrell went to New York and worked for several high-profile leaders of the avant-garde: Archie Shepp, Pharoah Sanders, Marion Brown. His first 'name' group was the 360 Degree Music Experience, with Beaver Harris and Grachan Moncur. He has been intermittently visible since, turning up in various parts of Europe and the US, and working with David Murray, Khan Jamal, Bob Stewart and others. His solo

work has been sometimes documented: a jazz opera, *Windward Passages*, has been a key part of his composing, partly recorded as a series of piano solos (1979), and finally rehearsed for full performance in 1999. His style always seems in transit between past and present: completely free playing mingles with interpretation which goes back to Monk, and even Jelly Roll Morton.
**Windward Passages** (hat Hut)

# Kenny Burrell

GUITAR
*born* 31 July 1931

Burrell is on hundreds of records, many of which are among the more famous jazz sessions of the LP era, yet he has never secured the popularity which a guitarist might have expected in a period when its practitioners became as important as saxophonists and pianists. He grew up in Detroit and worked there until a tour with Oscar Peterson minded him to look further afield, and he moved to New York in 1956. His Christian-derived style helped get him a job with Benny Goodman, but thereafter he played in settings which were in the heartland of hard bop, for Prestige, Blue Note and New Jazz. Less a sideman and more a partner with several small-group leaders – especially Jimmy Smith, who was a favourite collaborator – Burrell's easygoing manner fits so snugly and accommodatingly into any jazz groove that he can almost disappear in a band situation, but his solos and rhythm parts are bluesily effective whatever the prevailing conditions. Gil Evans arranged *Guitar Forms* for him at Verve, which is perhaps the closest Burrell has ever been to a big-time date, but earlier or later records alike are highly enjoyable and only occasionally slip towards noodling. He presided over a wonderful Ellington tribute record, *Ellington Is Forever* (1975), which blends the feel of a jam session with insuperable mainstream values. He sang on some of his early 60s sessions, and lately has taken to doing so again.
**Ellington Is Forever** (Fantasy)

# Gary Burton

VIBES, MARIMBA
*born* 23 January 1943

Burton grew up in Anderson, a small farming community in Indiana, and his parents wanted him to study an instrument: by chance, the only music teacher in town taught marimba. He began playing along to Brubeck and Miles Davis records, and in order to fill in the harmonies more he played with four mallets rather than the customary two. He then went to Berklee to study, toured with George Shearing in 1963, and joined the Stan Getz quartet, staying three years: Getz taught him much about how to reach an audience by just playing a melody. But he had already been making records under his own leadership for RCA (since *New Vibe Man In Town*, 1961), and eventually cut 11 albums for the label – covers of Broadway scores, country-fusion albums and the Carla Bley-composed set *A Genuine Tong Funeral* making up a curious sequence. He worked alongside Larry Coryell, moved to Atlantic for six albums, played with Keith Jarrett and generally set a fresh pace on an instrument which hadn't made much progress since Milt Jackson's bebop moves. Burton's four-mallet virtuosity certainly created a new standard, which has become accepted procedure for vibes players since. He then moved over to Manfred Eicher's ECM for a spell (*Hotel Hello* and *Matchbook* are masterful duet records with Steve Swallow and Ralph Towner respectively) and ran new small groups with the likes of Eberhard Weber and Pat Metheny.

He has been on the staff at Berklee since 1971, a great nurturer of young talent, and can fairly claim credit for a beneficial effect on many nascent careers, including those of Metheny, Danny Gottlieb, Makoto Ozone and Tommy Smith. He has seldom been out of a record contract but in the past two decades has worked mainly for independents, most recently at Concord, with projects such as an Astor Piazzolla tribute and a classical-jazz crossover. A studious thinker with a dry and sometimes invisible humour, Burton has preferred to see the vibes as a kind of keyboard, enjoying every opportunity for chords and multiple lines, and when his music takes off – as it does at least once in every record and concert – it becomes dizzying and intoxicatingly beautiful.
**Hotel Hello** (ECM)

## Garvin Bushell
CLARINET, SAXOPHONES
*born* 25 September 1902; *died* 21 October 1991

Bushell had an indecently long career without troubling too many headline-writers. He was playing in vaudeville in his teens, already having mastered clarinet, sax, oboe, bassoon and flute, and was one of the pioneer members of Mamie Smith's Jazz Hounds in 1921. He toured Europe and the Americas with Sam Wooding before taking numerous theatre and big-band jobs all through the late 20s and 30s. Latterly he played in theatre orchestras and in symphonic music and taught, but was still able to pop up in surprising situations: he is surely the only Mamie Smith sideman to also play with John Coltrane (in 1961!).
**Cab Calloway, *1934–1937*** (Classics)

## Joe Bushkin
PIANO
*born* 7 November 1916; *died* 4 November 2004

Bushkin barrelled his way through jazz. The son of a New York barber, he played with Bunny Berigan, Muggsy Spanier and Joe Marsala in the 30s before Tommy Dorsey snared him. He was a musician in the Air Corps before he worked with Benny Goodman, and later took up a residency at the Embers. Capitol signed him in the middle of the decade and he made a sequence of lush, successful records somewhat akin to the George Shearing easy-listening dates, although they have not been reissued. That helped him get work in Las Vegas besides New York, and he was busy through the 60s (when he spent some time in the UK), before settling in California and leaving music alone until Bing Crosby brought him back as one of his final accompanists. In the 80s and 90s he was again busy on the club and festival circuit, although he also raised thoroughbred horses. A busy, almost hyperactive swing player, he told Whitney Balliett: 'I'm happy 95 per cent of the time, and the other five per cent I'm asleep.'
***Piano After Midnight*** (Epic)

## John Butcher
TENOR AND SOPRANO SAXOPHONES
*born* 25 October 1954

Butcher is a Londoner who has patiently worked his way to the forefront of European improvisation. He 'fumbled his way through things' while working in a duo with pianist Chris Burn at college in the 70s, and while he heard a lot of jazz he determined to try and find his own way at a distance from the prevailing models. He played in the final edition of John Stevens's Spontaneous Music Ensemble and has since then gathered in what is, in this era, the customarily wide range of playing associations in the UK, Europe, America and Japan. His playing adopts a range of extended saxophone techniques which has little to do with any free-jazz archetypes, and he has shown a special interest in solo recording which involves multitracking and sound-altering techniques, the better to find a more personal and individualized aesthetic.
***Fixations (14)*** (Emanem)

## Frank Butler
DRUMS
*born* 18 February 1928; *died* 24 July 1984

Although born in Kansas City, Butler became an exemplar of West Coast drumming, although stylistically he was indebted to the hard-bop school of Roach and Blakey. He moved to San Francisco in 1950 and from there arrived in Los Angeles, where he played behind such local leading lights as Curtis Counce, Art Pepper, Hampton Hawes and Curtis Amy. He was off the scene for a long spell from the mid-60s, but returned to playing in the mid-70s, one of the veterans rediscovered by Don Schlitten: he made his only album as leader for Schlitten's Xanadu label.
**Art Pepper, *Smack Up*** (Contemporary)

## Billy Butterfield
TRUMPET, FLUGELHORN
*born* 14 January 1917; *died* 18 March 1988

Born in Middleton, Ohio, Butterfield worked locally before joining Bob Crosby in 1937. He starred in that trumpet section (along with Yank Lawson) and subsequently went with Artie Shaw and Benny Goodman before

military service. He tried bandleading himself later in the 40s but lost money and went back into studio work. In the 50s, he mixed sessions with live work, where he played with members of the Condon clan. Ray Conniff used him on many dates and it was similar (though more friendly) to the partnership which Bobby Hackett had with Jackie Gleason. He later reunited with Lawson in The World's Greatest Jazz Band and spent his later years touring as a solo, always welcomed in Europe. Butterfield's style sounded rather like his name – large, rich, oleaginous, with a fiery edge to it at times. Like Hackett, he looked after the long melodic line. Most of his own-name American records are in more of an easy-listening mould and are these days difficult to access, but scattered through a sizeable discography is much excellent playing.
**Billy Plays Bix** (Epic)

# Jaki Byard
PIANO, SAXOPHONES
*born* 15 June 1922; *died* 11 February 1999

Byard worked through several jazz eras and maintained a striking individuality, even as he absorbed something from seemingly every musician he ever heard. He worked professionally from his teens, and at the end of the 40s was playing piano behind Earl Bostic; but he was also a capable saxophonist, and he spent much of the 50s in the sax section of the Herb Pomeroy band, basing himself in Boston. In the 60s he ran his own groups – his sidemen included Joe Farrell, Booker Ervin and Jimmy Owens – and spent two spells with Mingus, sometimes even depping for the leader (on bass) when the latter felt like taking a turn at the keyboard. In the 70s and 80s he ran a big band called the Apollo Stompers, and often liked to work in duo with other pianists: in New York it was with Tommy Flanagan, and he also toured the UK with the Yorkshireman Howard Riley. Byard loved to laugh in his music: when playing on Mingus's 'Parkeriana' he used his solo spot to play unaccompanied stride piano, and occasionally he would end a solo performance by dissolving into laughter himself. He knew European music as thoroughly as anyone in jazz, and he liked teaching, and passed on wisdom to many younger pianists: Jason

Moran is one who honours his memory. The jazz community was shocked at the announcement of Jaki's death, from gunshot wounds at his home in New York: the circumstances have remained mysterious.
**Here's Jaki** (Prestige)

# Don Byas
TENOR SAXOPHONE
*born* 21 October 1912; *died* 24 August 1972

Byas always seems like a modernist, but he was playing with Bennie Moten and Walter Page as far back as the late 20s, albeit originally as an alto saxophonist. By the time he moved to New York in 1937, he was a tenorman with touring experience, and he took a chair in several saxophone sections before joining Count Basie in January 1941 as Lester Young's replacement. He left in November 1943 to join a Dizzy Gillespie group, but then worked in a variety of contexts, sometimes as leader, and mixing it with both swing players and boppers. He became one of the most recorded tenormen of that period and was considered at the top of his particular tree: laden with a big-toned delivery (which sometimes told against him in a boppish situation), he sounds like the next stage on from the Hawkins prototype, harmonically more questing, and with the huge timbre nicely suited to romantic ballad set-pieces. He went to Paris in 1946, and settled there, returning only once to the US, in 1970. He was a star on the Paris scene, and later settled in the Netherlands, content to roam European clubs as a solo (although Stan Tracey remembered him as difficult and dislikeable). While he was prolific in the 40s, though, his recorded output thinned dramatically in the LP era.
**Laura** (Dreyfus)

# BYG
RECORD COMPANY

The acronym came from the founders, Jaques Bisceglia, Jean-Luc Young and Jean Georgakarakos, three Parisian jazz fans. Formed in 1969 – a notable year of Parisian upheaval – the label set down a large tranche of work, mostly by visiting Americans such as Don Cherry, Archie Shepp and the Art Ensemble Of Chicago, in its first few months of activity. It carried on, at a slightly lesser pace, into the early 70s, with the likes of Anthony Braxton, Steve Lacy and Sun Ra among the later contributors. Many of the superior BYG albums are free-jazz classics of the period. As with many other labels of the time, rights to the material seem to have regularly passed between different hands, but one way or the other much of it has by now appeared on CD.

## Charlie Byrd
GUITAR
*born* 16 September 1925; *died* 2 December 1999

As an enthusiastic young guitarist Byrd met his hero, Django Reinhardt, in wartime France, and when he returned home he took various low-profile musical jobs; but the guitar's time hadn't really yet come in jazz, and he studied the classical guitar repertoire and thought about a concert career. In the end, though, he applied his studies to jazz playing, working in Washington for much of the 50s, and began recording for Savoy and Riverside. Albums such as *Blues For Night People* (1957) suggest a neatly cultivated swing-to-bop style, but Byrd's career took an upswing when he began investigating Latin rhythms and cut *Jazz Samba* (1962) with Stan Getz (unfortunately, a litigious spat developed over the album's royalties). Thereafter he made dozens more albums and toured regularly, often for the State Department, mostly in a style which offered a deliberately tasteful mix of jazz, Brazilian music and lightweight pop. By the end of the 60s he was making Christmas albums for Columbia, and in the 70s he began a long association with Concord: there was plenty of fluff there too, but an occasional record stands out for Byrd's skill and dedication. He remained committed to finger-playing, and in the age of electric guitars and their endless array of effects he belonged to another time.
*Brazilian Byrd* (Columbia)

## Donald Byrd
TRUMPET, FLUGELHORN
*born* 9 December 1932

Byrd was in some ways the archetypal hard-bop trumpeter: very prolific in the recording studio, adaptable to any set of material, he epitomized reliability, from his first dates with Art Blakey's Jazz Messengers in 1956. The trumpeter worked alongside a huge number of leaders, and was recording for Savoy, Prestige and Riverside alike, but it is his Blue Note dates which are best remembered, mainly as he did most of his leadership records there. He spent some time in Europe (recording in Paris) in 1958, and back in the US he struck up a partnership with Pepper Adams. But his interest turned increasingly towards education, and he has secured several distinguished qualifications, as well as a degree in law. *A New Perspective* (1963) was a hit record for him, but his biggest success came with *Black Byrd* (1972), cleverly produced by Larry Mizell to tap into the funk audience, and thereafter Byrd drifted into poor music (clearly patterned after the thinnest areas of Miles Davis's electric period), where his trumpet playing counted for very little. Perhaps sensibly, he has since then spent most of his time away from actual music-making, and a couple of late-80s albums for Landmark suggested that a comeback of any sort was ill-advised. Fine tone, excellent technique, but even in his glory years Byrd missed out on the token of individuality which could have put him amongst the music's immortals.
*Royal Flush* (Blue Note)

## Don Byron
CLARINET
*born* 8 November 1958

Byron might exemplify the modern musician as resister of pigeonholes, and his exasperation is that if anything he has been more regularly pigeonholed than most. A New Yorker with plenty of formal study behind him, he was a regular in Downtown circles in the 80s before leaping to surprise prominence with a project dedicated to the klezmer-styled music of Mickey Katz, a novelty which has become something of an albatross for him. Since then he has jumped imperturbably between idioms, including chamber music, art song, poetry, funk, 'literate' rap and others, usually making the best fist that a clarinet player can in situations which scarcely seem welcoming to his chosen instrument. His records have been similarly eclectic, with homages to Raymond

Scott and Ellington as well as Schumann and Sondheim, and he has been fortunate in securing major-label patronage from first Elektra Musician and subsequently Blue Note: it's hard to see even adventurous indie companies financing such projects. Byron might be accused of working as a *pasticheur*, but he approaches each musical strand with such intensity and exactitude that such a charge is easily dismissed, even if the overall effect is a little chilly. He might be the Spike Lee of jazz, although his preferred role model is the author Joyce Carol Oates: 'she tackles so many idioms and finds a dark and pathetically weird way of doing everything'. *You Are #6* (Blue Note)

## George Cables
PIANO
*born* 14 November 1944

Although he's played with a long roll-call of leaders, from Art Blakey to Freddie Hubbard, Cables is probably still best known for long-ish associations with both Dexter Gordon and Art Pepper (who called him 'Mr Beautiful'). As far back as 1963, though, when he formed a band with Billy Cobham and Steve Grossman, he was playing at the top level. Although he was born in New York, most of his work has been done in California. Contemporary gave him a few dates as a leader, but like so many American performers of his generation he has more recently had to look to Europe for sponsorship, and the Danish Steeplechase label has recorded him at length in the 90s. An unfussy and unselfish player – which is why horn players have always valued him so highly as an accompanist – Cables likes to respect the material and usually nods to his original masters, Monk, Ellington and Hancock. Either solo or in a trio context, his own records rarely disappoint. *Person To Person* (Steeplechase)

## Ernie Caceres
BARITONE AND ALTO SAXOPHONES, CLARINET
*born* 22 November 1911; *died* 10 January 1971

Caceres was a pioneer soloist on the baritone saxophone, working in and around New York in the later 30s and joining Bobby Hackett (a favourite and often-renewed part-nership) in 1938. Like Harry Carney, Caceres had the patented big sound which would be the norm for baritone players, and he worked with numerous swing bands during the 40s. In the end, though, he moved over to the Dixieland end of things and was a regular in the Eddie Condon circle soon enough. He did TV work for much of the 50s but in the following decade he was working in clubs and doing one-nighters again. Unrecorded as a leader during the LP era, he has been somewhat forgotten, and his work has to be sought out under many other leaders. **Bobby Hackett,** *Gotham City Jazz Scene* (Capitol)

## Cadence Jazz
RECORD LABEL

Founded in 1980 by Bob Rusch, whose company publishes the similarly named *Cadence* magazine, this small but busy and quite prolific independent label works out of Redwood, New York. While Rusch originally produced most of the material to appear on the label, lately it has acted more as a clearing-house for projects brought in from outside which appeal to him. In the meantime, Rusch and his son Marc have turned their energies more to the offshoot label CIMP, which records most of its sessions in 'The Spirit Room', a space where they attempt to record music as 'naturally' as possible without equalization or other 'studio techniques'. Both labels (especially CIMP) are primarily devoted to the American avant-garde and they record very few names perceived as stars by the rest of the jazz media – which suits Rusch, one of the most opinionated men in his field and a fierce champion of what he sees as the independent creative spirit.

## Michael Cain
PIANO
*born* 2 April 1966

Cain's sometimes mercurial progress seems to have been halted lately. A fan of both prog-rock and jazz, he made some waves on arriving in New York in 1990, working with some of the leading M-Basers, and playing regularly in Jack DeJohnette's groups, as well as with Dave Holland and Ravi Coltrane. Some records of his own showcased a clever

style which could sound both urgent and contemplative, but also sometimes pretentious and obscure. In the new century, though, he has been much less documented.
*Circa* (ECM)

## Uri Caine
PIANO
*born* 8 June 1956

Born in Philadelphia and raised on the local scene there, Caine emerged from a steady if unspectacular career as a mainstream-modern sideman – with everyone from Hank Mobley and Terry Gibbs to Annie Ross and Sam Rivers – to almost suddenly come to prominence as a significant player in the New York avant-garde of the early 90s. He was a regular in Don Byron's groups and struck up an important association with record company boss Stefan Winter, who has recorded almost all of Caine's own-name work. The earlier records such as *Toys* offer a lot of engaging and gripping music, Caine's extensive knowledge of jazz piano styles worked into a tough contemporary framework, but he has since become known for a sequence of records which amount to a post-modern jazzing of the classics: Mahler, Wagner and most recently J S Bach and Beethoven. Teetering between reconstructive brilliance and arduous shoe-horning of one style into another, the records have been a difficult though undeniably adventurous proposition. One wonders where he can take it all next.
*Gustav Mahler In Tobach* (Winter & Winter)

## Joey Calderazzo
PIANO
*born* 27 February 1965

Calderazzo was switched on to jazz by his older brother Gene (b 1961), a drummer who has worked in both New York and London. He was hired by Michael Brecker in 1987 and recorded two albums with the saxophonist before being signed as a solo to Blue Note. He has since worked regularly with Branford Marsalis and now records for the independent Marsalis Music label. Calderazzo's earlier work was larded with notes and his Herbie Hancock approach was griddled over a lot of superfluous activity, but the recent

records have been more considered and melodically inventive, even if he often sounds like a very capable *pasticheur* much of the time.
*Haiku* (Marsalis Music)

## California Ramblers
GROUP

Although they scarcely existed outside the recording studios, the California Ramblers were one of the most prolific white groups in the early years of jazz, cutting their first session for Vocalion in 1921 and their last in 1937, although at that point the name was a disguise for the Charlie Barnet orchestra! In between were hundreds of titles made largely in the style of hot dance music rather than jazz, and even then the results were often more tepid than genuinely jazz-directed. Although it was supposedly under the leadership of singer Ed Kirkeby, vocals where taken were just as likely to be by that great bawler Irving Kaufman and others. Core members of the band included Adrian Rollini and pianist Irving Brodsky, but at one time or another the band sported everyone from Red Nichols to the Dorseys – in other words, the better white sessionmen in New York. Other studio bands with such names as The Varsity Eight and the Five Birmingham Babies are little more than the Ramblers going under an alternative name. Early on they did appear in public, but this seems to have been short-lived. Considering their vast output, surprisingly little has been reissued in either the LP or the CD era. A complete edition would certainly run to dozens of CDs.
*California Ramblers With Adrian Rollini* (Village)

## Red Callender
BASS, TUBA
*born* 6 March 1916; *died* 8 March 1992

Although he started working in New York, a tour took Callender to Hollywood, where he recorded with Louis Armstrong in 1936 and played with several local groups, from time to time turning up in films. Red had an extraordinary knack for finding himself in the best bands and the most important sessions: he was with a Lester Young group for three years, and recorded with Erroll Garner, Charlie Parker, Wardell Gray and Dexter Gordon, besides touring with his own small group and getting plenty of television and film recording work. He was in on some of the classic final Art Tatum sessions in 1956 and managed to introduce the tuba into several Californian 'modern' dates (he was still playing it with John Carter in the 80s). One of his last important sessions was with the Satchmo Legacy Band, where he played some of the repertory of the man he'd first recorded with some 50 years earlier. A big, genial man with a long memory of a long career, he put together a very enjoyable autobiography in *Unfinished Dream* (Quartet, 1985). Although rarely credited as a major on his instrument, he was actually one of the few bass players who was as comfortable with the kind of swing playing introduced by Jimmy Blanton as with the more modern manner of bebop.

**Art Tatum, *The Tatum Group Masterpieces Volume Six*** (Pablo)

## Cab Calloway
VOCAL, BANDLEADER
*born* 25 December 1907; *died* 18 November 1994

The Dean of American Jive (he was honoured thus by New York University), Cabell Calloway sang and danced in Chicago cabarets with his sister Blanche before taking over a local band, the Alabamians, in 1929. They were defeated in New York in a battle of the bands by The Missourians, but Calloway promptly took over The Missourians and as Cab Calloway and his Orchestra they held court at The Cotton Club from 1931 until the end of 1940, making scores of records in addition. A supreme showman, he was too little captured on film in his prime: fragments such as 'Minnie The Moocher' (one of his greatest setpieces, caught in the 1932 *The Big Broadcast*) show his mastery of singing, mugging and hoofing. The Betty Boop cartoon setting of *St James Infirmary*, setting his incredible vocal to surreal imagery, shows how extraordinary Calloway's interpretations could be. His huge vocal range and virtuoso scatting (earning him the nickname 'The King Of Hi-De-Ho') blasted his material, but although his band acted often as a mere backdrop for his antics, it remained one of the best in New York, with

Doc Cheatham, Chu Berry, Ben Webster, Cozy Cole, Claude Jones, Dizzy Gillespie and others all in the ranks at various times. Calloway worked through the leaner years of the swing era (and insisted his men be on the best wages), turning up on radio and appearing in *Stormy Weather* (1943) with Lena Horne, but he finally disbanded the band in 1948 and slimmed down to a small group. He took on the part of Sportin' Life in *Porgy And Bess* (which Gershwin had most likely modelled on Calloway anyway) and was in the musical theatre for a number of years. Cab was still working right into his 80s, assembling occasional bands and touring with his own shows as well as taking a cameo in *The Blues Brothers*. His grandson Chris was bequeathed the Calloway book of arrangements, and formed a band to perform them. Cab himself was perhaps too *sui generis* to be really accounted as a great influence, but along with Louis Armstrong he made jazz singing into both high art and deliciously low entertainment.

***Kickin' The Gong Around*** (ASV)

## Michel Camilo
PIANO
*born* 4 April 1954

A Dominican, born in Santo Domingo, Camilo moved to New York in 1954 and gradually built a reputation as a smart and exciting small-group player, somewhat in the almost generic manner of Latin émigrés which became a populous category during the 80s. Fast, accurate and unstintingly exuberant, his manner is exhilarating yet open to the kind of listener-exhaustion which his type of energy playing always flirts with. He looked set for stardom when Columbia began recording him in the late 80s, but the records – which in the end jammed together too many modish touches – had no lasting impact and in recent years little has been heard from him.

***Michel Camilo*** (Portrait/Columbia)

# Roy Campbell

TRUMPET
*born* 29 September 1952

Campbell is a trumpeter whose approach is a carefully considered walk between form and freedom. He grew up in New York and worked on other instruments before taking up the trumpet at 15, then slowly gained a foothold on the competitive scene, preferring the free environs of Jemeel Moondoc's group even though he had played plenty of bop before that. In the 80s he joined the group Other Dimensions In Music, which became a long-standing quartet (with Daniel Carter, Rashid Bakr and William Parker); aside from a period when he lived in Rotterdam, he has spent much of his playing time in this context, although he's also led other groups. Campbell's patient progress shows in music which is both freely spaced and under calm control.

**Other Dimensions In Music, *Now!*** (AUM Fidelity)

# Candid

RECORD COMPANY

In its first incarnation, Candid didn't last long. Nat Hentoff and Archie Bleyer owned and ran it, producing some 40 records during 1960–61, but the quality of the music was astonishingly high: several of the most important discs by Charles Mingus, Eric Dolphy, Cecil Taylor and Booker Little, as well as fine one-offs by the likes of Don Ellis, Richard Williams and the Toshiko–Mariano group. The label then went into abeyance
for some years and was bought by (of all people) the singer Andy Williams, though it wasn't reactivated as far as new material was concerned. Candid LPs drifted in and out of circulation before Britain's Alan Bates acquired the catalogue via the Black Lion group in 1989. He has restored the original material to the CD catalogue but has also embarked on many new recordings, by both established and new names. In recent times, Candid has become something of a singers' label, with Stacey Kent, Jamie Cullum and Claire Teal all releasing Candid albums.

# Conte Candoli

TRUMPET
*born* 12 July 1927; *died* 14 December 2001

Conte joined the Woody Herman band when he was barely 16, then after army service he worked primarily in the Stan Kenton Orchestra, until setting up his own small group in 1954. His playing reflected a lifelong admiration for Dizzy Gillespie ('A magnificent man, in his playing and his personality') but filtered through a style which had a silvery, dancing elegance to it. He worked on the West Coast through the rest of the 50s, often co-leading a band with brother Pete, but also turning up with Terry Gibbs and Stan Levey. In the 60s he was busy with Shelly Manne and on *The Tonight Show* (all the way up to Doc Severinsen's departure in 1992). Thereafter he played regularly with West Coast buddies old and new. He was still playing and performing right up until his death, a voice from a golden age of jazz improvisation who never fell out of love with his music.

***Conte-nuity*** (Fresh Sound)

# Pete Candoli

TRUMPET
*born* 28 June 1923

The elder Candoli brother was more of a high-note specialist than his brother (they loved to tell a story of their formidable mother's disbelieving reaction when told that he could be bested by Maynard Ferguson). He played lead with nine different major bands during the 40s, Tommy Dorsey and Woody Herman among them, then moved over to the West Coast, where he worked with Les Brown and Stan Kenton. The Candoli Brothers' group did good business between 1957 and 1962, but Pete then went out on his own and eventually ran a club act where he worked with his wife, the singer Edie Adams. He was less visible to international jazz audiences than his brother and underwent heart surgery, but he still played at anniversary concerts in the 80s and 90s where he met up with his old colleagues.

***The Brothers Candoli Sextet*** (Mercury)

# Frank Capp

DRUMS
*born* 20 August 1941

He joined Stan Kenton in 1951, and has basically played big-band drums ever since, although there have also been spells with singers, with West Coast small groups, and in every kind of TV and film soundtrack situation. Capp co-led a big band with Nat Pierce from 1975 known as the Capp–Pierce Juggernaut (after Nat's death it became just The Juggernaut), a fiercely drilled and tight ensemble which owes its spirit to the Count Basie legacy. Their several albums for Concord will appeal to those who love the style, although each tends to pall before the end, and sometimes one wonders why one hasn't put on a Basie record instead.
*Play It Again Sam* (Concord)

# Mutt Carey

TRUMPET
*born* 1891; *died* 3 September 1948

'Papa' Mutt Carey was a fine trumpeter who is among the many under-documented voices of the early years in New Orleans. He started, inevitably, in brass bands before joining Kid Ory in 1914, then working in Chicago and California, where he stayed for much of the 20s (when King Oliver visited to play some jobs, local audiences thought he sounded like a Carey impersonator). During the Depression he had to take other work, including a spell as a Pullman porter, but when the New Orleans revival got under way, Carey was well placed to take advantage: he renewed his association with Kid Ory, which by this time stretched back 30 years, and a group of 1947 sessions by Mutt Carey's New Yorkers are important markers in the revival. Unlike many of the New Orleans brassmen, Papa Mutt was a less forthright player, curtailing some of the bitten-off phrasing which many of his contemporaries used for attack, and sometimes giving the impression that he was musing his way through a solo line. It would have been intriguing to hear him in his original prime, but there is very little from the early 20s other than a session with Ory and some blues accompaniments. He was back working in California again at the time of his death.
**Kid Ory,** *Kid Ory's Creole Jazz Band* (GHB)

# John Carisi

TRUMPET, ARRANGER
*born* 23 February 1922; *died* 3 October 1992

Carisi's individual talent was largely wasted in jazz. He played in Glenn Miller's AAF band and was then making a modest living as a freelance arranger when he came up with 'Israel', a polyphonic fantasy on the blues which is one of the highlights of the Miles Davis *Birth Of The Cool* (1949) sessions (he also contributed 'Springsville' to the later *Miles Ahead*, 1957). Carisi was always busy as a composer, yet much of this work crossed into other idioms and his opportunities for jazz projects seem frustratingly few in number: a session for RCA which wasn't even released until the 80s, an album of scores for a guitar 'choir' and a curious album for Marvin Stamm (1968) make up a very modest legacy. Yet his three pieces for a celebrated album sponsored by Gil Evans, *Into The Hot* (1961), are absolutely remarkable, densely scored, yet freely flowing – 'Moon Taj' in particular, an impression of moonlight on the Taj Mahal, is quite ravishing. John Litweiler called them 'an unforgettable advance in the jazz sensibility'. Carisi carried on playing trumpet in, surprisingly enough, a few Dixieland bands, and did some more writing for Max Roach in the 80s, but he never went back to the idiom of those marvellous 1961 recordings.
**Gil Evans,** *Into The Hot* (Impulse!)

# Rüdiger Carl

TENOR SAXOPHONE, CLARINET, ACCORDION
*born* 26 April 1944

Carl began on the accordion, taught by his grandmother, though he soon looked for an alternative as 'it didn't look very sexy having an accordion on your knees'. He began on flute at 18 and alto at 22. Basing himself in Berlin and Wuppertal, he became involved in the German free-music scene and worked with his own bands, as well as with Globe Unity and regularly with pianist Irène Schweizer, and in a duo with guitarist-violinist Hans Reichel. By the 90s he had grown tired of the tenor sax – 'I was somehow fed up with this vocabulary of this old revolutionary and not really renewed and aesthetic shape of the 60s, 70s free jazz shit' – and returned to the accordion, as well as

trying studio projects where the notion of 'improvisation' was put through the conceptual wringer. Carl is only occasionally encountered on record (next to a musician such as Brötzmann he is practically undocumented) but he is an interesting thinker who challenges many free-music stereotypes.
**Book/Virtual COWWS** (FMP)

# Larry Carlton
GUITAR
*born* 2 March 1948

Carlton has spent much of his career in big-ticket rock situations but he is a jazz fan whose playing was soaked in the style. As a teenager he listened obsessively to Joe Pass and John Coltrane, and 'Still to this day on the road in my iTunes there'll be Trane.' That gave him a broader knowledge of harmony than the average rock player, and he was soon in demand as a West Coast sessionman before he was even out of his teens. He joined The Crusaders in 1971 and plays on most of their best albums of the 70s, besides doing star solo work with the likes of Steely Dan. In the 80s he worked more as a leader, trying to find a middle ground between pop and jazz that would keep him interested, but his career suffered a setback when he was injured in a random shooting incident outside his studio in 1988. Some think that the more docile byways of his playing in recent years may have been brought on by that trauma.
**The Crusaders, *Those Southern Knights*** (MCA)

# Harry Carney
BARITONE SAXOPHONE, CLARINET
*born* 1 April 1910; *died* 8 October 1974

Carney was an anonymous young band player in Boston when Duke Ellington hired him for a local job in 1926. After that, their association lasted for a further 48 years, and Carney most likely spent more time in Duke's company than any other person. Although he regularly doubled on clarinet in the early years of the Ellington band, it was the baritone sax which was his preferred instrument – his sonorous and surprisingly mobile way with the horn set the pattern for every baritone man who followed, at least

until the 50s, and as the anchor man in the reed section he became perhaps the key instrumentalist in the orchestra. While he enjoyed plenty of solo space, Ellington offered him fewer star vehicles than he did some of his soloists, as if acknowledging that so much of the music revolved around Carney's sound anyway. He scarcely made any record dates away from Ellington, but Norman Granz did at least feature him on a strings date in 1955. He latterly developed circular-breathing techniques in order to hold very long notes – 'Praise God' from *Third Sacred Concert* is a fine example. As the Ellington era drew to a close, Carney became Duke's driver from one gig to the next, and they remained the closest confidants. On Ellington's death, Carney's response was 'Without Duke, I have nothing to live for', and he passed away later the same year.
**Duke Ellington, *Never No Lament*** (Bluebird)

# Ian Carr
TRUMPET, FLUGELHORN
*born* 21 April 1933

Born in Dumfries, Carr studied literature in Newcastle and hooked up with the small local scene there, playing with the EmCee Five at the beginning of the 60s. He then moved to London and established a quintet with Don Rendell which became one of the premier British bands of its day. The trumpeter went on to form Nucleus in 1969, a jazz-rock hybrid which picked up several cues from the contemporary music of Miles Davis yet had its own, rather British character. They were a great kick to hear live, the front line of Carr and saxophonist Bob Bertles striking many sparks, and in retrospect their records are in comparison a little disappointing. Carr has subsequently received numerous commissions for extended works and is heavily involved in jazz education; but he has re-formed Nucleus from time to time and the group still has its followers. While his own playing remains in debt to Miles Davis (Carr has written grandly ambitious biographies of both Davis and Keith Jarrett), he abjures the pre-ening side of the trumpeter and prefers a tougher approach which still nods to the hard-bop masters. His brother Mike (born 1937) was a sideman with him in the EmCee Five, and has since gone on to work in

numerous groups based around his Hammond organ playing – he probably knows more about the instrument than anyone else, and has a garage full of them.
**Nucleus,** *Elastic Rock/We'll Talk About It Later* (BGO)

# Terri Lyne Carrington
DRUMS
*born* 4 August 1965

Carrington was an extraordinary prodigy, gaining a scholarship to Berklee at the age of 11, and her babyfaced looks do not prepare the listener for the ferocity and virtuosity of her drumming. She was working with such seniors as Kenny Barron and Clark Terry from the early 80s, but soon proved that she could handle virtually any kind of jazz drumming, from funk to mainstream, and an early stint with one of Wayne Shorter's groups brought her particular attention. She made a single album for Verve as a leader, which turned out to be a one-off, and had to wait until 2001 for another go in that capacity when she signed to the German independent ACT. Her writing is interesting rather than striking but she has such a wide circle of musical friends to call on that future projects will surely be worth following. Although Herbie Hancock used her as the drummer on some recent tours, she has no stars in her eyes and will clearly make her own way forward.
*Jazz Is A Spirit* (ACT)

# Baikida Carroll
TRUMPET
*born* 15 January 1947

Carroll looked set to become a prominent voice among those emerging from the left-field St Louis scene in the early 70s, but he never quite found a way to deploy his ideas in a way that would bring him attention and a serious illness in 1987 seems to have devastated his career. He was a close compadre of Oliver Lake in his native city, and a move to New York in the 80s found him moving in various of the city's avant-garde circles, including gigs with Anthony Braxton and Charlie Haden. But no label was much interested in recording him as a leader, and in the 90s he was sighted very infrequently.

Carroll is one of the very few trumpeters to make an all-solo record (*The Spoken Word*, 1977) and both that and a single date for Soul Note (the rather unsatisfactory *Shadows And Reflections*, 1982) show how he intelligently brought a fine tone and an almost classical delivery to bear on outside ideas.
*The Spoken Word* (hat Hut)

# Barbara Carroll
PIANO, VOCAL
*born* 25 January 1925

Carroll's long career has been conducted almost entirely away from critical attention, and she is scarcely mentioned in most reference works. She had a classical piano education but was as interested in the work of Art Tatum, and in the 40s she led a trio which worked in the bop idiom: Chuck Wayne and Charlie Byrd were among her sidemen. In the 50s she made five albums for Victor and three for Verve, but retired to raise a family and didn't restart her career until the 70s. Since then she has played frequently in New York and was for many years a regular at the Carlyle Hotel, latterly singing as well as playing piano. Her style is a placid truce between swing and bop which is undemonstrative and lightly enjoyable.
*Live At The Carlyle* (DRG)

# Bill Carrothers
PIANO
*born* 3 July 1964

Carrothers came out of Minneapolis and arrived in New York in the early 90s, but he has since moved to Michigan. He had lessons from a church organist and has never learned to read music properly – when he did Dave Douglas's *Moving Portrait* (1997) album, he was 'hanging on for dear life'. That hasn't stopped him from recording a small but remarkable body of work, built around slow playing, the rediscovery of forgotten material (Carrothers has unearthed such 20s obscurities as 'I'm Just A Vagabond Lover'), and the patient exploration of standards until they reveal new details. The result is a sequence of 'weird, moody records, filled with Americana', which have received little support or attention and have

obliged Carrothers to earn his main living from fixing computers. His latest project is an audacious recital of songs associated with the First World War, on which his wife Peg sings vocals.
*Ghost Ships* (Sketch)

# Ernie Carson
CORNET, VOCAL
*born* 4 December 1937

Born in Portland, Carson joined the West Coast gang of revivalists in the 50s and has been a fixture there since. He played lead cornet for the Turk Murphy band in the early 60s and subsequently assumed leadership of the Castle Jazz Band. A ferociously brassy player with a snarling lead style, he has recorded a raft of tremendous records for the GHB group of labels, packed with British music hall songs, Dixieland obscurities and oddball Americana of the order of 'When A Peach From Georgia Weds A Rose From Alabam', sometimes taking the vocals too.
*Southern Comfort* (GHB)

# Benny Carter
ALTO SAXOPHONE, TRUMPET
*born* 8 August 1907; *died* 12 July 2003

For all his mastery of almost every part of the jazz lexicon – as technician, improviser, composer, arranger and bandleader – Carter has left a curiously neutral legacy: few of his recordings are indelible, almost none known beyond the core jazz audience. He started on trumpet before moving to the alto, and in the middle 20s he moved between several leaders – Earl Hines, Horace Henderson, Charlie Johnson and eventually Fletcher Henderson, with whom he stayed for a year or so from 1926. He led a band of his own at the Savoy Ballroom but rejoined Henderson in 1930 and began contributing charts to an already imposing book. He spent eight months with McKinney's Cotton Pickers before leading his first important band, which was studded with such future stars as Bill Coleman, Chu Berry and Ben Webster. But it had little commercial success, and in 1935 Carter went to Europe, where he resided in London for a time and wrote many charts for the BBC Dance Orchestra,

besides leading a band based in the Netherlands.

Back in the USA, he ran new bands in New York before settling on the West Coast in 1942. He was still leading a band – again sprinkled with stars of the future, including Miles Davis and Max Roach – but studio work began to take up much of his time. He was one of the first black arranger-composers to have a significant say in Hollywood music, and his acceptance paved the way for more to follow. In the 50s and 60s he performed less – Jazz At The Philharmonic was one of his few regular features – but wrote extensively for singers and bands (Count Basie in particular). Then the 60s ushered in an Indian summer in the studios, where he set down some of his best work as a player for Impulse! on the strangely titled *Further Definitions* (1962) and *Additions To Further Definitions* (1966). His alto sound was singular, yet oddly generic: he used very little vibrato, maintained a groomed, unruffled delivery, and gave the impression that his neatly logical lines started and stopped with an inevitability which felt almost antithetical to the jazz process. Yet this went hand in hand with a compositional ingenuity which never failed him, even as its easy facility prepared his career in Hollywood with the same kind of certainty. From such early works as 'Symphony In Riffs' (1933) to the enduring 'When Lights Are Low' and 'Blues In My Heart', Carter's creativity was full, urbane and consummately tailored.

By the 70s he was an acknowledged elder statesman, yet he still had more than two decades of active duty ahead. He signed to Norman Granz's Pablo and made a few decent records there, but his final flowering was on the Musicmasters label, where *Harlem Renaissance* (1993) and *Elegy In Blue* (1994) were autumnal works of unimpaired elegance. A lesser-known disc with Marian McPartland, *Plays The Benny Carter Songbook* (Concord, 1990), was also very fine. He had long since given up on the trumpet, but the instrument which gave him his start never betrayed him and the comparatively few examples of his trumpet improvising on record show the same shrewd conviction as his alto playing. In the end, a vast body of work in terms of both recordings and arrangements remains neglected, a patrician history which requires a

patient and thorough investigation to reveal itself. One critic complained of Carter's 'Republican tone', but perhaps it was his sheer self-effacement which denied him a larger audience. He seemed indestructible, but finally passed away in his Los Angeles home a few weeks before his 97th birthday.
***Further Definitions*** (Impulse!)

## Betty Carter
VOCAL
*born* 16 May 1929; *died* 26 September 1998

Her real name was Lillie Mae Jones: the 'Carter' came from a chosen stage-name, Lorraine Carter, but when she joined Lionel Hampton in 1948, Hamp started calling her Betty Bebop, and it was 'Betty Carter' which stuck. She grew up in Detroit and studied piano and singing there, while hanging out with the visiting boppers. With Hampton she had a hit version of 'The Hucklebuck', but then went out as a solo in nightclub work, and her next notable association was with Ray Charles in 1961 (their 'Baby It's Cold Outside' is second only to the Carmen McRae–Sammy Davis version). In 1964 she retired to raise her family, but her career had largely failed to gain any impetus up to this point anyway: her preferred method of improvising around lyrics in a bebop-vocal idiom was deemed completely uncommercial, hardly a surprise in an era when even Sarah Vaughan had her most creative work suppressed. In 1969, she returned to live work, formed her own company (Bet-Car records) and generally worked on rebuilding what was really only a modest cult reputation. By the 80s, though, her uniqueness and intensity were paying off, and by the time she'd turned 60 she was acknowledged as the godmother of modern jazz singing. Where Vaughan and Ella Fitzgerald eventually worked solely on the concert circuit, Carter remained a club singer for most of her career. Her backing trio became an institution comparable with the Jazz Messengers as a forcing-ground for young talent, and players from John Hicks to Xavier Davis benefited from her tough-love approach: she made sure they were in awe of her, but there was hardly a player who didn't acknowledge her greatness. No one who saw and heard her in performance will ever forget it: she was brilliant at holding an audi-

ence, and the audacity of her vocal improvisations (seemingly crystallized in her album title *It's Not About The Melody*) seemed to increase with age. Yet there were many doubters, and plenty who felt that her radical departures from a song's original form could become a virtuoso exercise in meaninglessness. She had a rather tempestuous relationship with the label which recorded her final albums, Verve, and the unhappy truth is that no recording came even close to Betty Carter in person: none of her records sold very well. Supremely mannered, sometimes unearthly in her timbres and choice of notes, she was one of the few complete originals in jazz music.
***The Audience With Betty Carter*** (Bet-Car/Verve)

## James Carter
SAXOPHONES, BASS CLARINET
*born* 3 January 1969

Carter seemed to blow into the scene from nowhere. He grew up in Detroit, had a trip to Europe with a student ensemble and worked briefly with Wynton Marsalis before joining Lester Bowie in 1988. After moving to New York in 1990 he opened a wider book of associations and was making albums of his own from 1993, the first for the Japanese label DIW (later released by Columbia). He then had major-label moves with Warners and, currently, Columbia's newest jazz division. From the first, Carter amazed with his dexterity and technical resource on seemingly the whole family of saxophones – Neanderthal and brawling on the baritone, funkily surreal on tenor, a horn which he uses to deliver revisionist treatments of the saxophone lineage, suggesting the likes of Ben Webster and Don Byas while vaulting straight past Coltrane into the avant-garde. As with David Murray's youthful work, the sheer exuberance and impact of Carter's playing can be enthralling, yet he is as likely to descend into showmanship and incoherence as deliver any kind of masterpiece, and while every album has had sensational moments, sensation can often tip over into indulgent nonsense. The recent live record, where the likes of Murray and Johnny Griffin come to join in the fun, is, with all its sometimes tiresome brouhaha, probably the most accurate sketching of Carter to date.
***Live At Baker's Keyboard Lounge*** (Atlantic)

# John Carter

CLARINET

*born* 24 September 1929; *died* 31 March 1991

Carter was playing alongside Ornette Coleman in their shared home town of Fort Worth as far back as the late 40s. But he came to prominence only many years later, after extensive academic study. He settled on the West Coast and in 1965 formed a quartet with trumpeter Bobby Bradford, a partnership which lasted for the rest of Carter's life: a British concert by the duo, with no other instrumental support, remains in the author's memory as a transcendent occasion. Carter, who always looked the professorial part, formed the four-man Clarinet Summit in 1981 and founded the Wind College in Los Angeles in the same period. His recordings with Bradford are a beautiful distillation of the style of the Coleman quartet, taken in an even more rootsy, folkish direction, yet they are hardly known (originally recorded for Revelation and Flying Dutchman) and are now impossible to find. Carter was still playing alto and tenor at this point, but by the 80s he was focusing solely on the clarinet, and his masterpiece is the five-part *Roots And Folklore: Episodes In The Development Of American Folk Music*, which included completely solo playing and superbly refined writing for various ensembles. Again, though, it was recorded for two different labels, and much of it is languishing out of print. John Carter's music would surely be a prime candidate for Wynton Marsalis's advocacy.

*A Suite Of Early American Folk Pieces* (Moers Music)

# Kent Carter

BASS, CELLO

*born* 12 June 1939

Carter studied at Berklee and from 1960 was backing everyone who came into town to play at Lenny's, a Peabody club in the Boston suburbs. Mostly they were hard boppers, but the bassist was more interested in free playing and began visiting Europe, where he hooked up with Paul Bley and Steve Lacy. In the end he settled permanently in France, from where he has formed numerous playing relationships: Trevor

Watts, Carlos Zingaro and Itaru Oki are some of those involved. He was a pioneer solo improviser on his instruments and the quiet elegance of the record cited epitomizes his intelligent approach.

*Beauvais Cathedral* (Emanem)

# Regina Carter

VIOLIN

*born* 6 August 1966

Carter is a violinist who has never seemed sure of which way to go. She grew up in Detroit and did classical studies, while also playing in a funk band called Brainstorm. Then she tried a fusion outfit, Straight Ahead, before moving to New York in 1991 and taking the violin chair in the String Trio Of New York, a setting which still stands as perhaps her most successful vehicle. She left in 1997 and besides working with the likes of Wynton Marsalis and Cassandra Wilson has embarked on a leadership career of her own. On record she has had a mixed time of it. A single album for Warners disappeared quickly, and subsequent sessions for Verve are a mixture of homage, concept album and original material which have left only fleeting impressions. She plays with real dash and ingenuity on an instrument which has never found much of a footing in post-bop jazz, and is in sore need of the right context.

*Rhythms Of The Heart* (Verve)

# Ron Carter

BASS, CELLO

*born* 4 May 1937

Carter started out as a cellist but found that they weren't hiring too many blacks on that instrument in Detroit. He changed to bass around 1954, but still preferred to seek out a classical environment and he was performing symphonic music for much of the 50s. However, everything changed when he went to New York, where he joined Chico Hamilton and then began working as a freelance. When he was hired by Miles Davis in 1963, he found himself on the central stage of small-group jazz, and he responded superbly. Carter's technique was fine enough to cope with any playing situation, but it was his ability to respond quickly and creatively to the high-level dialogues that Davis was instigating which set him apart, mixing and moving between different jazz-bass methods so smoothly that he was able to transcend the obvious roles of timekeeping and harmonic floor. And it was all done so adroitly that he never drew unnecessary attention to himself. Besides the records with Davis, he is marvellous on other key 60s dates, such as Herbie Hancock's *Maiden Voyage* and Wayne Shorter's *Speak No Evil*. He left Davis in 1968 and has ever since chosen whatever context has taken his interest, playing on hundreds of dates in both jazz and popular music. He has brought back the cello when he wished, taken up the piccolo bass in some of his own bands and enlisted a second bassist as timekeeper, and worked in chamberish situations, such as an occasionally convened nonet and duos with the likes of Jim Hall. Inevitably, he has been involved in all-star reunions such as the various VSOP concerts with the likes of Hancock, which have been more to do with business than any musical imperative. Recent records as a leader for the Japanese arm of Blue Note have been interesting rather than compelling: with nothing left to prove, Carter's music has taken on a quiet, almost satisfied demeanour, which his assurance underlines.

*Third Plane* (Milestone)

## Dick Cary
PIANO, ALTO HORN
*born* 10 July 1916; *died* 6 April 1994

A solid pianist but an outstanding arranger, Cary is a backroom talent much admired by other musicians. He held down the piano role with all sorts of mostly traditional groups, including those of Louis Armstrong and Muggsy Spanier, before a residency with Bobby Hackett in New York offered steadier work. He went over to the West Coast in 1959 and worked steadily and quietly as an arranger, only occasionally finding himself in the playing limelight. His most remarkable legacy might be his own Tuesday Night Band, which met on a weekly basis to play new scores he'd come up with. By the time of his death the band's book was enormous, and while the disc listed below is a good sample of his own playing in this context, the posthumous *Got Swing?* (2000) is a rip-roaring celebration of some of the best of his charts.

*Dick Cary And His Tuesday Night Friends* (Arbors)

## Glen Gray And The Casa Loma Orchestra
GROUP

Saxophonist Glen Gray (1906–63) is perhaps not a much-remembered name among bandleaders, but as the effective boss of what was originally a cooperative, the Casa Loma Orchestra, he was among the most successful of his kind. The group came together out of a contract band and was named after a hotel that never actually opened. When they began a residency in New York in 1929, they also picked up a record deal, and cut many sessions throughout the early and middle 30s. The Casa Lomas were a rather curious hybrid of sweet dance orchestra and old-fashioned (as in late 20s) hot band. Several of their discs were great hits in their day, yet the likes of 'Black Jazz' and 'Maniac's Ball' are powerful and fast without really swinging. The only notable soloists in the band were high-note trumpeter Sonny Dunham and trombonist Pee Wee Hunt, who went on to have a successful second career as a Dixie revivalist in the 50s. Arranger Gene Gifford did most of the important scoring. Gray kept the band going until 1950, and even then Capitol hired him to work with a studio version of the orchestra, which by the 60s was churning out 'hi-fi re-creations' of other bandleaders' swing-era hits. Essentially, Gray was a middle-of-the-road pioneer, which helps explain his enduring success when many more jazz-directed leaders slipped away.

*Maniac's Ball* (Hep)

## Al Casey
GUITAR
*born* 15 September 1915

Casey's very long career has been happy and prolific, but he is still most closely associated with Fats Waller. He was a member of Waller's Rhythm group on record beginning in 1934 and continuing until the pianist's death in 1943. He wasn't generously featured as a soloist but his driving rhythm work is a constant on their hundreds of records. After the war he switched to electric guitar and took work wherever he could find it, subsequently featuring behind King Curtis for some years. He nearly left playing altogether in the 70s but he had become a favourite in England and Europe and he was a regular on the British circuit all through the 80s and into the 90s, working also with the Harlem Blues & Jazz Band.

**Fats Waller, *1941–42*** (Classics)

## Lee Castle
TRUMPET
*born* 28 February 1915; *died* 16 November 1990

Born Aniello Castaldo, he worked in several major swing bands during the 30s (at that point still using Castaldo as his surname). As Lee Castle, he did bandleading himself in the 40s, although there were only a handful of records and little in the way of national success. He joined the Dorsey Brothers' final venture in 1953 and took over half the band on Jimmy's death in 1957, making it into a memorial band to the saxophonist. He was still leading such a group into the 80s. Castle was a good, sweet-toned trumpeter and a professional who knew all about playing for an audience and giving them what they wanted.

***Jimmy Dorsey's Greatest Hits*** (Epic)

## Cat

This most likely originated as black slang for any friend of the speaker, but it was largely appropriated by jazz musicians and fans to denote a member of their community, although it wasn't heard so often outside the US. The Coasters' hit 'Three Cool Cats' (1958) is a definitive usage at a time when it was part of the dialect. It's now archaic, but jazz musicians still use it with a kind of ironic affection.

## Dick Cathcart
TRUMPET
*born* 6 November 1924; *died* 8 November 1993

After war service, Cathcart played with Bob Crosby and did studio work, which led him to a gig on Jack Webb's radio series *Pete Kelly's Blues*. When they made a movie out of it, he played in that band too, and went on to lead a Dixieland group named Pete Kelly's Big Seven. Cathcart's style leaned heavily towards that of Bix Beiderbecke, a comparison sealed by a 1958 album which the Seven made in homage to Beiderbecke. He later worked on the festival circuit and in small-band mainstream. Much admired by other trumpeters, Cathcart never really found a larger audience.

***Bix MCMLIX*** (Warner Bros)

## Philip Catherine
GUITAR
*born* 27 October 1942

Though born in London, Catherine grew up in Brussels and was inspired to take up the guitar after hearing Django Reinhardt on record. His style, though, was not in that mould: he played hard bop with Lou Bennett and Dexter Gordon, free-fusion with Jean-Luc Ponty, and rock with Focus. In the 80s he set up associations with other guitarists, including John McLaughlin, Larry Coryell and Biréli Lagrène, and expanded his palette further to include flamenco and, inevitably, a bit of gypsy guitar. Since then he has worked in whichever style seems to please him at any one time. A humorous man with an easygoing attitude to music-making, but his many recordings lack a bona fide masterpiece, and he is best heard as an accomplished journeyman.

***Guitar Groove*** (Dreyfus)

## Sidney Catlett
DRUMS
*born* 17 January 1910; *died* 25 March 1951

With his huge hands, beaming showmanship and concern to raise everyone's game on the stand, Big Sid Catlett might be the great drummer of his era, which was over all too quickly. He began freelancing in New York from 1930 and worked in the bands of Fletcher Henderson, Don Redman and McKinney's Cotton Pickers before taking the drum role in the big band which backed Louis Armstrong, who loved Catlett's style and would always use him if possible. He spent six memorable months in Benny

Goodman's orchestra – airshots from the period show how exciting the band sounded with Catlett behind it – then joined Teddy Wilson's small groups and led a few sessions of his own. He was back with Armstrong in the All Stars (1947–9) but his health suffered and despite gigs with the Condon clan he was clearly ailing. He caught pneumonia, recovered, but was suddenly felled by a heart attack. Catlett liked to do tricks for his audiences but he was never a show-off in the Krupa or Rich mould. He controlled the beat with insouciant assurance, scattered rimshots like pebbles flicked on to a tin roof, and even played solos which sounded musical and free of mere tub-thumping. He was immensely liked by all of his fellow musicians and there was widespread dismay at his early passing. At least Gjon Mili caught some of the essence of Catlett in his short film *Jamming The Blues*.
**Benny Goodman, *Roll 'Em!*** (VJC)

## Oscar 'Papa' Celestin
TRUMPET
*born* 1 January 1884; *died* 15 December 1954

Most of the great New Orleans players up until 1950 played for Papa Celestin at one time or another. He formed his Tuxedo Orchestra for the first time around 1910, but it was the edition known as the Original Tuxedo Orchestra, which he co-led with Bebe Ridgley, which was a great success, beginning in 1917, although the two men led separate bands after 1925. Celestin left music for a time when his group broke up in the early 30s, but in 1946 he returned to bandleading, and his new Tuxedo Jazz Orchestra became a regular on the radio, a boisterous unit led with fine showmanship by its leader.
***The 1950s Radio Broadcasts*** (Arhoolie)

## Henri Chaix
PIANO
*born* 21 February 1925; *died* 11 June 1999

One of the few Swiss-based musicians to make any impact on jazz outside his country, Chaix was actually French, even though he was born and lived in Geneva. He played sound mainstream piano and, inevitably, backed dozens of jazz visitors to

Switzerland: Rex Stewart thought him a superb accompanist, and he was much liked by Sidney Bechet and Bill Coleman too. He kept a swing-styled small group going into the 90s, and a frequent partner was the alto saxophonist Roger Zufferey. His most well-known records are a group he made for the Canadian label Sackville, which offer much pleasure without exactly stirring the blood.
***Jumpin' Punkins*** (Sackville)

## Bill Challis
ARRANGER
*born* 8 July 1904; *died* 4 October 1994

Challis's admirers insist that he is a major figure among jazz arrangers. He sprang to prominence as arranger for Jean Goldkette's Orchestra in 1926, forming a close alliance with the group's star member, Bix Beiderbecke, and it was his charts which helped Goldkette best the Fletcher Henderson Orchestra in a famous battle of the bands at New York's Roseland Ballroom. Challis then moved over to Paul Whiteman, with Beiderbecke, and came up with several settings for the cornetist which were among Bix's finest hours, including 'Lonely Melody' and 'Changes'. In the 30s, though, Challis freelanced for numerous leaders and never found the singularity which he had enjoyed a decade earlier. In his old age, his student Vince Giordano persuaded him to re-create some of his old Goldkette charts. Perhaps he was a transitional figure, between the sweeter dance styles of the 20s and the more liberating swing of the decade to follow.
***The Goldkette Project*** (Circle)

## Serge Chaloff
BARITONE SAXOPHONE
*born* 24 November 1923; *died* 16 July 1957

Some consider Chaloff the most gifted of all baritone players; others find him too much of a sentimentalist. Certainly he created some of the most poignant music the horn has ever offered up. A Bostonite, he played with several big bands in the early and middle 40s before an important association with Woody Herman, playing the baritone part on 'Four Brothers'. Herman found him difficult and argumentative and the sax-

ophonist left in 1949, eventually returning to Boston. He was somewhat off the scene, but managed to front three remarkable sessions: *Boston Blow-Up!*, *The Fable Of Mabel* and the extraordinary *Blue Serge*, a quartet date with Sonny Clark where Chaloff creates some of the most haunting and intensely felt music of his day in the likes of 'Easy Street' and the unforgettable 'Thanks For The Memory'. As a ballad player, he emphasized the big horn's majesty of tone, and through a canny utilization of vibrato (which Pepper Adams found distasteful) he suggested emotional treatments that the baritone had hardly yet touched on in jazz. It was disturbing to realize that Chaloff had contracted spinal paralysis, and had to hobble into the studio on crutches to make the date. His final session was, ironically enough, a Four Brothers reunion early in 1957.
**Blue Serge** (Capitol)

## Dennis Chambers
DRUMS
*born* 9 May 1959

Chambers, a master technician of kit drumming, might never have entered jazz at all: he grew up in Baltimore, played in funk and soul bands, and was eventually enlisted by George Clinton for Funkadelic and its various offshoots. It wasn't until he joined the John Scofield group in 1987 that he really entered the jazz world. Since then he has enthusiastically thrashed the kit behind a vast number of leaders, from John McLaughlin and Bill Evans to Michael Brecker and Mike Stern. He has done very little as a leader himself, but since fusion drummers have an inauspicious track record in this regard, we might be grateful for the respite. Chambers clearly enjoys the working-out aspects of drumming and he can be slightly terrifying to watch, but there's no denying his capabilities, and actually he has been a force for good in several otherwise bland groups. It might be a pointless distinction, but he is really a groove drummer rather than an exponent of swing.
**The Free Spirits, *Tokyo Live*** (Winter & Winter)

## Joe Chambers
DRUMS
*born* 25 June 1942

Chambers is a rare example of a drummer with a singular alter ego as a composer. He arrived in New York in 1963 and was soon taking some important gigs, playing on such albums as Freddie Hubbard's *Breaking Point* (1964) and Andrew Hill's *Compulsion* (1965). Latterly he has played for many other leaders, mostly in a post-bop idiom, and has been heavily involved in music education since 1985; but his work as a composer is at least as interesting, drawing on sophisticated compositional forms, some of which he contributed to projects by Bobby Hutcherson. His recent records *Mirrors* (1998) and *Urban Grooves* (2002) are unpredictable and often enigmatic revisions of standard material as well as his own music.
**Mirrors** (Blue Note)

## Paul Chambers
BASS
*born* 22 April 1935; *died* 4 January 1969

In his unemphatic way, Chambers did much to set the agenda for modern bass players, and it was cruel that he became all but forgotten by the middle of the 60s. He played in Detroit in the early 50s and arrived in New York in 1955, on a tour with Paul Quinichette. Immediately in demand, he joined Miles Davis that same year and enjoyed a long stay, all the while freelancing on a huge number of record dates: he is on Coltrane's *Blue Train* and *Giant Steps* as well as the likes of Sonny Rollins's *Tenor Madness*. But it was his work with Davis which won most attention. Although he played in the already classic walking-bass style, something about his fingerings and note-choices set him apart: he does nothing disruptive, yet nothing sounds routine. As perhaps the first bassist to receive regular solos in the LP era, he again followed logical yet unpredictable paths in his improvising. His heroin addiction sometimes made Davis curse him for nodding out on the stand, but it also made him less combative, and Chambers stayed with the trumpeter for eight years, one of his longest-serving sidemen. Afterwards, though, his career went nowhere, his apparent conservatism suddenly less in favour. Three Blue Note albums, none of them that remarkable, are his main legacy as leader. Ill-health finally took him off the scene altogether.

**Miles Davis,** *Steamin' With The Miles Davis Quintet* (Prestige)

# Eddie Chamblee
TENOR SAXOPHONE
*born* 24 February 1920; *died* 1 May 1999

Chamblee was leading army bands in Chicago in the 40s, and after leaving the military he ran small groups of his own. A spell with Lionel Hampton offered him the chance to show off his blowing chops and he also turns up on some of Dinah Washington's records (he was one of her many husbands). An over-the-top showman in the Illinois Jacquet tradition, Chamblee enjoyed both big bands and the organ-combo format: the Prestige set listed below, from 1964, is a crazed take on the idiom, and in the 70s he was recording with Milt Buckner in Europe, still sounding pretty wild.

**The Rocking Tenor Sax Of Eddie Chamblee** (Prestige)

# Changes
MUSICAL TERM

The series of chords which constitutes the harmonic basis for a particular piece of music. 'The changes' may be simple or complex, but if you don't know what they are, you're not on top of the playing situation. If a jazz group is playing a standard from the American songbook repertoire, piano and bass at least need to assert the changes in their playing in order to create a framework for the other musicians to improvise within.

# Thomas Chapin
ALTO SAXOPHONE, FLUTE
*born* 9 March 1957; *died* 13 February 1998

Chapin is often seen as a part of the New York avant-garde of the 80s and 90s, but he was much more of a mainstreamer than that. He was lead alto in the Lionel Hampton band for five years from 1981, latterly acting as MD, and he was also with one of Chico

Hamilton's small groups. It was, though, his own bands which made his most character-istic music, particularly the trio he formed at the end of the 80s with bassist Mario Pavone and drummer Steve Johns (later, Michael Sarin). Chapin was a smart writer and a clever, often humorous improviser, able to switch easily between licks-playing and more obviously passionate improvising in what might be termed the New York dia-lect of out playing. His alto work was eventu-ally supplemented by much music on the flute, for which he wrote and played in a not-ably intense and graceful manner. This much-liked figure died all too prematurely as a result of leukaemia.

*Night Bird Song* (Knitting Factory)

# Bill Charlap
PIANO
*born* 15 October 1966

The son of composer Moose Charlap and singer Sandy Stewart, Charlap grew up well versed in the Broadway-song tradition and is able to inhabit its possibilities for improvisa-tion much more naturally than many of his contemporaries. Besides, inevitably, accom-panying numerous singers, he was in some of Gerry Mulligan's final groups and has led his own trio since 1990. It was an encourag-ing investment by Blue Note when they signed Charlap as a solo artist: he has since repaid them by recording three exquisite and thoroughly original albums of standard interpretations, culminating (so far) in a superlative set dedicated to the music of a composer covered surprisingly rarely by jazz players, Leonard Bernstein.

*Somewhere: The Songs Of Leonard Bernstein* (Blue Note)

# Dennis Charles
DRUMS
*born* 4 December 1933; *died* 26 March 1998

Charles was born in St Croix in the Virgin Islands, where he started out as a bongo player. He moved to New York in 1945 and played calypso music before shifting towards jazz. Cecil Taylor hired him as his drummer when his group played a famous engagement at New York's Five Spot in 1956, and he is on most of Taylor's earliest recordings, for which he has perhaps not been sufficiently lauded: as Whitney Balliett remarked, 'Charles is uncanny at divining which tortuous rhythmic path his leader is about to explore', and while he is a conservative next to Sunny Murray and Andrew Cyrille, he is still beautifully responsive and swinging. But Charles did comparatively little in the 60s and less in the 70s, with a heroin addiction to deal with, and his reappearance in the 80s – with such as Billy Bang and David Murray – was a surprising comeback. His last appearances on record found him still strong.

**Cecil Taylor,** *Jazz Advance* (Blue Note)

## Teddy Charles
VIBES
*born* 13 April 1928

Charles is perhaps unique in the distinction of combining the roles of jazz performer and running a successful sailing and nautical salvage business. He worked rather anonymously in various big bands before leading small groups of his own, from 1952. He left a tantalizingly brief group of recordings: a trio set for Prestige; a small-group date, *New Directions*, which featured himself and Shorty Rogers improvising in ways which toyed with free settings but resolved back to a chord sequence; and two amazing sessions for Atlantic, *The Word From Bird* and *The Teddy Charles Tentet* (both 1956), which featured his ten-piece group working through a daring group of scores by George Russell, Jimmy Giuffre, Gil Evans and Charles himself. While his own music set up a challenging interface between scored music and improvisation, he also played with Charles Mingus and acted as a producer at Bethlehem, where he was involved in some 40 albums. All this faded disappointingly away, though, when he decided to concentrate on his sailing business, which he eventually shifted to New York, from where he played very occasional gigs. As a performer, Charles was no more than a competent improviser, but his interest in more challenging music and sponsorship of a small gathering of remarkable charts left a tiny, permanent mark on his time.

**The Teddy Charles Tentet** (Atlantic)

## Chase

A sequence in a performance where two or more soloists 'chase' each other through an improvisation, each taking a turn before the other has a rejoinder. It might start with the soloists taking alternate choruses, but as the sequence moves forward the pace may change in order to heighten the excitement and sense of a dialogue, so the exchange comes at the half-chorus mark, and may then be reduced further, perhaps to a single phrase. A 'chase chorus' squeezes the procedure into a single chorus. It was a favourite practice in the bebop era, when chases between tenormen like Dexter Gordon and Wardell Gray set audiences cheering. It can also form part of a big-band arrangement, as in Woody Herman's tumultuous chase for his trumpet section in '23 Red' (*Woody's Winners*, 1963).

## Tommy Chase
DRUMS
*born* 22 March 1947

The notorious hard man of modern British bop is really no more than a particularly zealous jazz fan at heart. He loved the sound of the Clifford Brown–Max Roach group so much that he took up drums himself, playing in cabaret and pier shows before moving to London in the 70s. He had his own hard-bop band from 1975, with Art Themen, Dave Cliff and others, and in the 80s led quartets with younger musicians such as Alan Barnes, which set a steaming pace for bop repertory in the capital and were at the heart of the so-called jazz revival of the period. Chase led a disciplined, well-dressed outfit and was a no-nonsense leader, and the scene has latterly missed some of his peculiar tunnel vision: muscle problems have obliged him to all but give up playing. Every musician who worked with him has a fund of stories, most of them unprintable, but Barnes for one credits him as the one who 'certainly got me into having musical criteria'.

*Rebel Fire* (Mole)

## Adolphus 'Doc' Cheatham

TRUMPET, VOCAL
born 13 June 1905; died 2 June 1997

Others may have lived longer, but surely no other horn player enjoyed such a lengthy and latterly garlanded career as Adolphus Anthony Cheatham. Born in Nashville, he backed the likes of Bessie Smith in vaudeville tent shows before going to Chicago in 1926. He worked for various leaders over the next decade and a half, including Sam Wooding (with whom he visited Europe), Wilbur De Paris, McKinney's Cotton Pickers and Cab Calloway, but his health suffered and the arduous demands of playing shows during the testing big-band era took their toll on a style which was – unlike the prevailing models – nuanced, even wistful, bright rather than shouting. With Calloway, he remembered, 'We played so fast that the musicians didn't have a chance to show what they could do.' Doc returned to duty in the 40s but disliked the new bop scene and worked for a time in the post office. He played more regularly in the 50s, although it was more often in New York Latin bands than on the jazz scene, and then he had a long residency at the International on Broadway. By the 70s he was being rediscovered at every festival and jazz party he was invited to, a link to a jazz age already long gone, and in the last 20 years of his life he enjoyed more attention than he had in the previous 70. His last jazz home was at New York's Sweet Basil club, where he held forth on Sunday afternoons regularly for more than a decade. His later albums defied Father Time, even if the sound had inevitably dried out a little, and they ended with a joyous meeting with the generations-younger Nicholas Payton. Cheatham died following a final gig with Payton at Blues Alley in Chicago.

*Doc Cheatham & Nicholas Payton* (Verve)

## Vladimir Chekasin

SAXOPHONES, KEYBOARDS
born 24 February 1947

Chekasin was a founder member of The Ganelin Trio, the Soviet jazz trio which caused something of a sensation when their records made it to the West in the 80s. Based in Vilnius, Chekasin worked both in the trio setting and as a solo artist and group leader; he recorded with spendthrift carelessness through the 80s and 90s, although many of the records never made it to a wider audience. He resettled in Moscow in 1994. The showman of the Ganelin group, he likes to play two saxes at once, and manages the contrary impression of near-chaotic freedom and a careful sense of organization.

*New Vitality* (Leo)

## Don Cherry

CORNET
born 18 November 1936; died 19 October 1995

One group titled their album *I Can't Imagine This World Without Don Cherry*, and the trumpeter's influence has been an extraordinarily potent one in the jazz of the past five decades. Born in Oklahoma City, he was playing with Ornette Coleman and Billy Higgins in 1956 and became a regular Coleman associate. Their arrival in New York in 1959, and subsequent residency at The Five Spot, remains an epochal jazz moment. Cherry played a tiny member of the brass family, a pocket cornet, which his large fingers seemed to completely surround, and he played in an airy, melodious, sometimes sputtering style which had its line back to the bop masters but which had a uniquely unfettered cast. If anything, he sounds even more free than Coleman does in their great Atlantic albums, and Steve Lacy remembered practice sessions when Cherry would simply say, 'Let's just play.'

After leaving Coleman, Cherry worked with Lacy, Sonny Rollins, and (in the New York Contemporary Five) Archie Shepp and John Tchicai, before going to Europe with Albert Ayler and remaining there. Cherry wandered through the continent for the rest of the 60s, although he also cut three albums for Blue Note in New York. For much of the 70s and 80s he was based in Sweden, where he and his wife Moki taught and raised a family (two of his children, Neneh and Eagle Eye Cherry, have had intermittently successful pop careers). He explored ethnic music with Colin Walcott in the trio Codona, revisited the Coleman legacy in Old And New Dreams, with Charlie Haden, Ed Blackwell and Dewey Redman, and formed a band of his own named Nu. In 1985 he returned to the US and created the Multikulti Orchestra. Cherry's music had by this time grown to be as capacious as any musician's in the jazz field. His interest in music from virtually every part of the world led him to introduce drones, vamps and chordless settings drawn from many non-jazz situations, and he took up the flute, the berimbau and other percussive devices. His composing has never entered the jazz-standard lineage but since his death it has been increasingly re-examined by latter-day Cherry fans such as Ken Vandermark, who have reinterpreted many of the pieces.

There is a considerable discography under his own name, but Don's music was never easy to pin down with microphones and many of the discs are disappointing. In his final years, Cherry's playing seemed to falter, as if he was overwhelmed himself at the world of possibility in music without frontier or discrimination, and in the end his health gave out: he never got away from a narcotics addiction which he had long struggled with. He died in Malaga, Spain, from liver failure.

*Codona* (ECM)

## Cyrus Chestnut
PIANO
*born* 17 January 1963

Chestnut is a great piano entertainer. Born in Baltimore, he took classical studies but learned about jazz in high school and studied composition at Berklee. He worked in the Blanchard–Harrison quintet in the 80s but first came to some prominence as Betty Carter's pianist during 1991–3. Since then he has freelanced with numerous leaders but has run his own trio too, managing to record regularly for Atlantic. Chestnut is a huge man, but his mighty delivery can also be shaded down to a tranquil medi-tation, and he is one of the few contempor-ary pianists who has made a consistent commitment to bringing gospel material into the modern repertoire. Like Benny Green, he loves playing for the people, and feels he's not doing his job if he doesn't communicate to an audience.

*You Are My Sunshine* (Atlantic)

## Chiaroscuro
RECORD COMPANY

Like Carl Jefferson's Concord, which came into being at around the same time, Hank O'Neal's Chiaroscuro was conceived as a home for mainstream American jazz. They managed around 100 releases in the period up until 1977, by the likes of Earl Hines, Joe Venuti and Teddy Wilson, before selling the company in 1978. However, O'Neal bought back the rights in 1987 and has brought the label back to life; the parameters are still largely the same even if a certain amount of bebop (by such veterans as Lou Donaldson) has crept in. A consistent and solid venture.

## Buddy Childers
TRUMPET
*born* 12 February 1926

A principal among lead trumpeters, Childers grew up in St Louis but has been a fixture on the West Coast since the 40s. He was lead trumpet for Stan Kenton for much of the 40s and early 50s, though he also played in other bands, and he then freelanced in Los Angeles and Las Vegas, doing time as a studio man and eventually showing up with Bob Florence and as MD for Frank Sinatra Jr. In the 90s he began recording occasional big-band projects of his own, and in recent years he formed an occasional two-trumpet partnership with his old friend (and fellow Dizzy Gillespie fan) Conte Candoli: 'I spent 50 years being a lead trumpet player, and I've spent the last ten years trying to become a jazz player. I'm practising every day.'

*It's What's Happening Now!* (Candid)

## John Chilton
TRUMPET, WRITER
*born* 16 July 1932

A Londoner, Chilton was a strong if unre-markable swing-styled trumpeter who worked with Bruce Turner in the early 60s and then in groups of his own. He might have settled for footnote status if the researcher and scholar in him had not come to prominence, but after working with Max Jones on a fine Louis Armstrong biography, he has since written meticulously researched biographies of many of the major pre-bop jazz masters, including Billie Holiday, Roy Eldridge, Louis Jordan, Coleman Hawkins, Bob Crosby and – perhaps the finest of them – Sidney Bechet. In addition, his *Who's Who Of Jazz*, covering musicians born before 1920, has become a standard source on the subject. John Chilton's Feetwarmers became a warmly popular collaborative act with singer George Melly, with their annual Christmas season a fixture at Ronnie Scott's Club, but Chilton surprised many with the announcement of his retirement from playing in 2002.

**George Melly, *Nuts/Son Of Nuts*** (Warner Bros)

## George Chisholm
TROMBONE
*born* 29 March 1915; *died* 6 December 1997

A Glaswegian, Chisholm was one of the group of Scots players who moved to London in the mid-30s and took leading roles in the dance-band circuit. He led his own band, The Jive Five, on a few record dates, and played with Fats Waller and other American visitors; but when the war came he went into the RAF dance orchestra, The Squadronaires (along with his pal Tommy McQuater). In the 50s he worked in the BBC Show Band and began turning up on shows such as *The Goons*. Eventually, when he made it to television, Chis became more familiar as a comic turn – in commercials and on the long-running and unspeakably improbable *Black And White Minstrel Show* – than as a jazzman. But as a trombonist he remained a master: a sweeping, melodious tone (he made several albums of near mood-music which Tommy Dorsey would have admired) and a peppery bite at fast tempos that he could slow into a conversational vernacular. He belatedly won some American recognition when he latterly became a surprise hit at a number of US festivals. He was still playing in fine form up until 1990, but his wife's passing hit him hard and he was in a nursing home when he died. Chisholm made many records, but most are hidden on small labels and very few have so far made it to CD.

***In A Mellow Tone*** (Lake)

## Herman Chittison
PIANO
*born* 15 October 1908; *died* 8 March 1967

Born in Flemingsburg, Kentucky, he worked on the Southern circuit in the late 20s before going to New York in 1931. He joined the Willie Lewis orchestra and went to Europe with them in 1934, subsequently settling in Paris. He recorded numerous sides as a soloist and is on some of Louis Armstrong's European discs, but he returned to the US in 1940 and worked on 52nd Street while playing on radio as 'Ernie The Blue Note Pianist'. His profile dimmed in the 50s but he still worked as a soloist in lounges and hotels up until his death. Chittison was quite a virtuoso (he even outshone Armstrong on some of their shows together) and could apply an unwholesome speed to a style which was originally rooted in stride and even ragtime. But he latterly cooled this down to a level which resembles kitsch, and the title of one of his few 50s albums, *Cocktail Time*, hints at where his music more or less ended up.

***Herman Chittison 1933–1941*** (Classics)

## Chops

Originally, the chops were a wind player's facial muscles or their embouchure – 'My chops have had it' suggests playing fatigue. But it can be extended to cover any instrumentalist – a pianist could refer to their fingers in the same way. Latterly, though, it has come to stand for a player's all-round technical ability, as in 'he has fantastic chops'.

## Chorus

The first popular songs in the modern idiom were the 'chorus songs' of music hall culture, but in jazz a chorus is denoted by a single run through the whole tune. The verse-and-chorus format of classic Tin Pan Alley material was usually abbreviated in performances, eliminating the verse – a practice which applies as much to popular singers as to any jazz rendition. A chorus might be of 12, 32 or 64 bars – it's still 'the chorus'. A jazz soloist might take 'a chorus', which would be an improvisation on one such run-through of a tune. Or they might take two choruses (which is, in the language of Lester Young, 'having another helping').

## Jon Christensen
DRUMS
*born* 20 March 1943

Christensen was playing drums in his native Oslo in his teens and went the usual route of backing visiting Americans and locals before striking up a close association with Jan Garbarek, playing in his quartet from 1970. He subsequently took the drum chair in the Keith Jarrett 'European' quartet, Eberhard Weber's Colours, Bobo Stenson's trio, and other multinational groups. Much of his recording has been done for ECM. Christensen has a beautiful touch at the kit, getting a clean and clear sound out of every part of it without sounding fussy or excessively tutored. He can play with rock crunch but is a sensitive accompanist too. A humorous man, he has been on a lot of very serious-sounding records but was very likely smiling his way through most of them.
**Eberhard Weber,** *Yellow Fields* (ECM)

## Charlie Christian
GUITAR
*born* 29 July 1916; *died* 2 March 1942

Christian came from a poor Oklahoma family, and there was always something of the country boy in the city about him. He played with local touring bands and word of his capabilities travelled only slowly, but John Hammond got wind of him and brought him to Los Angeles in 1939 to audition for Benny Goodman, who hired him for his sextet. Christian's decision to play an electric instrument and make himself heard against what had become large, loud bands created a turning point for the jazz guitar; but his capabilities went well beyond what had already been heard on the instrument, swinging hard but playing lines which scrambled through chromatic figures, the emphasis on single-note runs setting him up as competition for the horn players. Goodman's sextet was an almost perfect idiom to showcase his style and the bandleader used Christian only rarely in the context of the full band, both on stage and in

recording dates. But Goodman had back problems in this period and Christian was sometimes left kicking his heels; instead, he spent time jamming at Minton's club, and some surviving recordings provide the clearest evidence that his playing was pointing straight towards bebop. As it turned out, Christian would take no part in that revolution: in the middle of 1941 he contracted tuberculosis, and died the following March after succumbing to pneumonia. He remained a profound influence – on Barney Kessel, Tal Farlow and countless others – whose unfulfilled future progress stands as another of the great what-ifs in jazz.
**Benny Goodman,** *The Rehearsal Sessions* (Jazz Unlimited)

## Jodie Christian
PIANO
*born* 2 February 1932

Christian started playing piano in Chicago clubs as far back as 1948. He was drafted into the air force, and he did some playing with local groups while stationed in Japan, even working with Toshiko Akiyoshi at one point. Back in Chicago he played as a sideman, making very occasional records, although a stint behind Eddie Harris in the late 60s brought him some recognition. He was on hand at the founding of the AACM although he was of a rather more mainstream temperament than most. In the 90s he was finally recorded as a leader for Delmark. A distinctive neighbourhood player, whose presence in Chicago jazz has been a quiet but beneficial resource for decades.
*Rain Or Shine* (Delmark)

## Keith Christie
TROMBONE
*born* 6 January 1931; *died* 16 December 1980

With his brother Ian (b 1927), Christie joined the Humphrey Lyttelton band as far back as 1949, but he had a more modern outlook and went on to work first with John Dankworth, then Tommy Whittle, and ultimately joined the Ted Heath band in 1957. He had a short-lived group with Allan Ganley, The Jazzmakers, which unfortunately didn't record, and figured in several other big bands during the 60s, including those of Tubby Hayes, Stan Tracey and Harry South. His later years were plagued by problems with alcoholism and he died young. Christie's best work is buried away in many corners of the British jazz discography, but his early playing (and Ian's) is well framed by the record cited, which catches British trad at an early and sometimes furious pitch.

**Christie Brothers Stompers** (Cadillac)

# Pete Christlieb
TENOR SAXOPHONE
*born* 16 February 1945

Christlieb is an archetype of the latter-day West Coast jazzman: born in Los Angeles, he has worked there for most of his career, starting in such big-bands-for-dancing as Si Zentner's in 1965, then joining the *Tonight Show* band and freelancing as an occasional member of numerous other big groups, from the Basie band to the Capp-Pierce Juggernaut. He had his own record label for a spell (Bosco), but his featured albums have been few: some of the best-known were sessions where he played in a two-tenor front line with Warne Marsh, an avowed inspiration. An absolutely reliable professional with a suitably big sound.

**Conversations With Warne** (Criss Cross)

# Gunter Christmann
TROMBONE, CELLO
*born* April 1942

Christmann was born in Poland. Like several first-generation free players, he was inspired by trad musicians and actually started as a banjo player. Coltrane turned him on to free playing and his early appearances were in a duo with drummer Detlef Schönenberg and in Peter Kowald's quintet. Christmann was a familiar figure in the free scene of the 70s and early 80s, playing in Globe Unity, recording notably peculiar solo music, trying his hand at mixed-media presentations and organizing a loose-knit improv group named Vario. He gets a variety of inhuman sounds out of the trombone and his work with mutes and mouthpieces takes him to the very edge of abstraction. As a cellist, he's a little more conventional. Not much was

heard from him in the 90s but in the last few years he has recorded more prolifically again.

**Remarks** (FMP)

# June Christy
VOCAL
*born* 20 November 1925

One of the loveliest singers of her era is now largely remembered only by jazz fans. She was singing with the likes of Boyd Raeburn in Chicago when she took over Anita O'Day's slot in the Stan Kenton orchestra in 1945, staying until the 50s and then occasionally going out with the band on tours. Although many of her features with Kenton are on flimsy material, she brought a consistently musical approach to everything, with a smallish voice that had a modern, husky edge and a tight vibrato that could be uniquely affecting. She recorded as a solo for Capitol in the 50s, many of the records ending up as modest best-sellers. Pete Rugolo arranged many of the albums and brought some of his best work to bear: several of the records project a lonely, unforgettable aura which is as mature and grown-up as Sinatra's music of the same era. The most famous is surely *Something Cool*, with its classic title song: curiously, the album was originally completed as a mono issue (1955) and was then re-recorded in stereo in 1960. Christy suffered from stage nerves in the later part of her career and she drifted away from performing in the 60s; there was one late album for Discovery (1977) and a farewell festival tour with Shorty Rogers in 1985, which her husband, Bob Cooper, also took part in. June's best work stands very high in the jazz-singing pantheon, and with singers such as Diana Krall recalling elements of her style, her records now sound like both period pieces and curiously modern statements too.

**Something Cool** (Capitol)

# Mino Cinélu
PERCUSSION
*born* 10 March 1957

Cinélu grew up in Paris, and in his teens he was working with numerous local groups. In 1979 he went to New York and was soon getting plenty of sideman work, but his career really took off when he was hired by Miles Davis. He left Davis in 1984 and then worked (although only briefly) with Weather Report. Like so many others who passed through those ranks, the associations buoyed up his profile enormously, and ever since he has been something of a superstar in his percussion field, hired by everyone from Sting and Pat Metheny to Jan Garbarek and Herbie Hancock. Besides his vast arsenal of percussive devices, he also plays keyboards and guitar, and sings a bit.

**Miles Davis,** *Decoy* (Columbia).

## Sonny Clark

PIANO

*born* 21 July 1931; *died* 13 January 1963

Conrad Yeatis Clark spent his teens in Pittsburgh and moved to Los Angeles when his mother died. There he began making a name for himself on the LA club scene, and by the time he had joined Buddy DeFranco in 1953, his style was in place, a bluesy take on bebop which had strong links to the Horace Silver style. The sessions with DeFranco for Verve are full of understated mastery from both clarinettist and pianist. But Clark already had a heroin habit, and when he went to New York in 1957 (initially as Dinah Washington's pianist) his problems ran his life, even though he managed a prolific career in the recording studios. Alfred Lion of Blue Note especially liked him, and he appeared on 29 different dates for the label. *Sonny Clark Trio* (1957) is a small masterpiece, Clark essaying a version of 'Be-Bop' where he rolls out chorus after chorus of impish, funky invention. A gracious accompanist, he was much liked by several horn players – Dexter Gordon in particular – and admired by fellow pianists, and even when live work became problematical because of both his habit and an increasing dependency on alcohol, he was still offered many record dates. His death was a melancholy finale: ostensibly from a heart attack, his demise was brought on by a drug overdose in the back of the club where he was working, and the owners shifted his body to a nearby apartment to avoid the resulting publicity.

***Sonny Clark Trio*** (Blue Note).

## Kenny Clarke

DRUMS

*born* 2 January 1914; *died* 26 January 1985

Born in Pittsburgh, Clarke worked there in local bands before joining the Edgar Hayes orchestra in New York in 1937. Hayes took him to Europe (where Clarke made the first discs under his own name, in Stockholm) and on his return the drummer led the house band at Minton's Playhouse, one of the hippest haunts for musicians and the fabled seedbed of the bebop revolution: Thelonious Monk was also in the band, and Gillespie and Parker were never far away. After his army service, Clarke joined Dizzy Gillespie's band and went with them to Europe in 1948, remaining to savour the Paris scene for a few months before returning to the US. Klook (the nickname came from his style of stroking the snare on an off-beat) liked Europe and spent more time in Paris, Switzerland and Tunis, but he settled on the East Coast for a spell when he became drummer for the Modern Jazz Quartet in 1951. Disliking the way John Lewis was taking the band, he left in 1955. Life had been hectic – he had also worked on many record sessions and as a talent scout for Savoy – and he decided to settle permanently in France a year later. Inevitably, he was first call for visiting Americans and worked regularly with Bud Powell and Oscar Pettiford. In 1961, he began co-leading an all-star big band with Francy Boland: it lasted until 1972, and though not regularly convened, the personnel (Johnny Griffin, Ronnie Scott, Tony Coe, Art Farmer, Benny Bailey and others) remained remarkably constant.

All through these many years of playing, Clarke's technique remained stylishly trim and fluent. He was most likely the real architect of bop drumming, sending the rhythmic pulse out from the cymbal rather than the bass drum and interjecting every accompaniment with deftly placed rimshots and snare flicks, but even in bop's heyday his style was almost calm in nature, rather than ladling out the neurotic rhythms which the music's agitated rush seemed to insist on. With the MJQ, in other small groups and especially in his big-band work, he set standards of refinement coupled with dash and swing which always made the band sound good. He continued to visit the US and

other parts of Europe, but he was in semi-retirement when he died, spending his last years in a Paris suburb.
***Bohemia After Dark*** (Savoy)

## Stanley Clarke

BASS
*born* 30 June 1951

Clarke's musical promiscuity has told against his holding on to a greater jazz reputation. He played violin, cello and acoustic bass in high school but moved over to the electric bass and playing in rock and R&B groups. He moved to New York in 1970 and was with some major names – Joe Henderson, Pharoah Sanders, Stan Getz – but found budding stardom in the new Chick Corea group, Return To Forever. He was still playing some acoustic bass on their first records but by the time of *Where Have I Known You Before* and his solo debut *Stanley Clarke* (both 1974) it was all about the electric version, slapped, twanged and thumbed with an amazing and then revolutionary dexterity. Ever since, Clarke's prolific output has crossed back and forth between lightweight (and heavyweight) fusion, straight-ahead jazz and the lightest pop music. Frequent collaborators have included George Duke, Lenny White and Al Di Meola (other musicians easily led astray) and he has turned up in all-star groups of varying kinds. Feeble fusion records such as *Rocks, Pebbles And Sand* (1980) have let his talent down, yet even on otherwise dismissable records there is some show of strength which makes one never want to give up on Stanley. In the last decade or so he has played more straight-ahead music than before, but unforgiving jazz writers have never made life easy for him.
***Stanley Clarke*** (Epic)

## Classics

RECORD COMPANY

The label which, perhaps more than any other, has moved to create a comprehensive library of out-of-copyright jazz for anyone who wants to build a wide-ranging jazz collection. With European law allowing any recording more than 50 years of age to be transferred and issued by an independent company, which need not own the original masters, everything in jazz prior to the LP era is now fair game. Classics, based in Paris and beginning in 1990, chose to offer chronological series of the complete works (master takes only) by any musician who had recorded at least enough to fill up one CD. Thus far they have tackled everyone from Duke Ellington and Louis Armstrong to The Three Peppers and Hazel Scott. With the likes of Ellington and Benny Goodman, these have grown into vast sequences which are still ongoing, and the complete catalogue stands at well over 1,000 CDs. Transfer qualities are, however, often inconsistent, and they never credit sources.

## Thomas Clausen

PIANO
*born* 5 October 1949

A capable and likeable musician, Clausen has been around on the Danish scene for many years but has seldom won wider recognition. He was in groups with the likes of Alex Riel and Palle Mikkelborg in the 70s and 80s and Gary Burton engaged him for some work in the 90s. But his own bands have been the best vehicles for him, showing off a neat lyric voice which handles familiar material in ways which take care to offer an original view. He has a Brazilian Quartet (not so hot) and a newish trio with Jesper Lundgaard and Peter Danemo (much hotter).
***My Favorite Things*** (Stunt)

## James Clay

TENOR SAXOPHONE
*born* 8 September 1935; *died* 6 January 1995

Clay's modest reputation came in part via his brief association with Ornette Coleman and Don Cherry, in 1957–8. He was born in Dallas but at 20 he was working on the Los Angeles scene, and he performed with Cherry in Vancouver (playing Coleman tunes, in a band named The Jazz Messiahs) and subsequently with Coleman himself. But Clay returned to Dallas in 1959, and seldom left his native area thereafter: there were a couple of undistinguished albums for Riverside, and occasional tours with the likes of Ray Charles. He was rediscovered after a fashion at the end of the 80s, but again the recordings were relatively light-

weight. Clay mixed swing, bop and R&B flavours into his playing and he was a somewhat untypical Texas tenor: lighter and less swaggering than the norm.
*A Double Dose Of Soul* (Riverside/OJC)

# Buck Clayton
TRUMPET
*born* 12 November 1911; *died* 8 December 1991

Wilbur 'Buck' Clayton came to prominence in the Count Basie Orchestra, joining in 1936 shortly before they left Kansas City for New York. But he had already been all over jazz: working in territory bands of varying degreees of obscurity and even leading his own group in China for two years. Clayton stayed with Basie until getting his draft papers in 1943, and in those seven years he set down a long list of fine performances, his solos on the likes of 'Topsy' and 'Don't You Miss Your Baby' managing to suggest a calm superiority even when his surroundings were heated to excess. That versatility and authority helped him ever afterwards. Following the war, he was a regular at Jazz At The Philharmonic, and in the 50s he drifted from band to band, working with Joe Bushkin, Tony Parenti, Benny Goodman and others. In the studios, George Avakian began recording what became generically grouped as 'Buck Clayton Jam Sessions', where Buck and various buddies from the swing era (plus newcomers such as Ruby Braff) would set down long, joshing workouts on standards and blues, taking advantage of the new freedoms of the LP era. Buck visited England regularly, striking up a notable partnership with long-time admirer Humphrey Lyttelton, and worked in Europe as a solo, but eventually a recurring lip problem became so troublesome that Clayton surrendered his trumpet chops and concentrated on teaching and his own big band, an exuberant aggregation which was a great joy in the old warrior's final years (it still continues, playing Buck's book, as The Buck Clayton Legacy). A tall, handsome man with a countenance that could look noble or rascally, Clayton was a master of muted playing, a sophisticated thinker who could spin new lines on old tunes with deceptive ease, and a blues player who always elevated the dusty old form to fine art.
*The Complete CBS Jam Sessions* (Mosaic)

# Jay Clayton
VOCAL
*born* 28 October 1941

Clayton is a vocalist who challenges her listeners, which hasn't helped her much in an age when audiences want jazz singers to soothe. She studied piano and sang in choirs in her native Youngstown before moving to New York in 1963 and finding herself fascinated by the new free-jazz scene. She sometimes worked in partnership with Jeanne Lee but didn't get on record until the 70s, and then only occasionally. Much of her career has been spent in teaching and she has sometimes worked with groups of her own students. Less an abstract singer than someone who abstracts bop lines into wide-ranging interpretations, her freest music is constantly surprising and often engaging, although her sometimes wayward sense of time and pitch will dismay those who found Betty Carter difficult. Yet she can deliver standards straight with a beguiling candour, as in her duet record with Fred Hersch, *Beautiful Love* (1996). The record cited shows up most sides of her art, to advantage.
*Brooklyn 2000* (Sunnyside)

# Jeff Clayton
SAXOPHONES
*born* 16 February 1955

# John Clayton
BASS
*born* 20 August 1952

The Clayton brothers grew up in Venice, California, and while their careers have taken them elsewhere at times, they have primarily worked out of the West Coast scene. John studied bass and often worked with Jeff Hamilton in the 70s, eventually spending five years in the Netherlands in the Amsterdam Philharmonic, where he made use of his exceptional arco technique. In 1980, though, he had already formed the Clayton Brothers Quartet with Jeff, a saxophonist who'd spent much of the 70s doing pop session work. Jeff also played in the final edition of the Count Basie Orchestra, which was in many ways a blueprint for the Clayton–Hamilton Jazz Orchestra, which involved both brothers and some of the cream of the West Coast players of the past 20 years. Primarily an alto man, Jeff spent a few years in New York in the 90s but has since returned to the Los Angeles area. As their various projects have matured, the mastery of each brother on his respective instrument has come into a clearer focus. Their work carries on the kind of traditions represented by Basie, Jones–Lewis, and other practitioners of a timeless kind of mainstream-modernism.

**Expressions** (Qwest)

# Rodney Cless
CLARINET
*born* 20 May 1907; *died* 8 December 1944

Cless was a brilliant young man – a school star, and gifted on several musical instruments – who was, arguably, ruined by jazz. He was living in Des Moines in 1925 when he heard The Wolverines, and was so captivated he took up clarinet as a jazz horn. He fell in with a Chicago crowd and eked out a living during the Depression, and by the time he joined Muggsy Spanier's Ragtimers in 1938 he was already having problems with alcohol. He is, along with Spanier himself, the star of the 'Great Sixteen' records, turning in gorgeous solos played with a lovely, bluesy tone. Thereafter he worked in and around the Condon circle but died following a fall in the street after a night's drinking.

**Muggsy Spanier, *The Great Sixteen*** (RCA)

# Jimmy Cleveland
TROMBONE
*born* 3 May 1926

Born in Wartrace, Tennessee, Cleveland played locally before joining Lionel Hampton in 1949. He stayed four years and cemented a reputation as an impeccable technician, a fast reader and an even-voiced soloist. Thereafter he worked with many different outfits and was hugely prolific as a studio player, appearing on probably hundreds of dates during the 50s and 60s, although scarcely any under his own leadership (the few he did lead are unremarkable). He befriended Quincy Jones while with Hampton, and Jones used him on many dates. After moving to the West Coast in the 70s he began to drift away from music and

became a landlord, although late in the century he started to play locally again.

**Quincy Jones, *The Great Wide World Of Quincy Jones*** (Mercury)

# Dave Cliff
GUITAR
*born* 25 June 1944

Cliff is from the far north of England, in Hexham, and he taught himself jazz guitar at night, eventually playing gigs in Newcastle and Leeds. At the beginning of the 70s he moved to London, taught and worked as a freelance, eventually touring Europe with Lee Konitz and Warne Marsh, and then with Bob Wilber. Since then he's worked under many flags: with Ken Peplowski, Brian Lemon, Kenny Davern, André Previn, Nina Simone. His sound is clean and melodic, indebted in the main to Pass and Montgomery, and he dislikes anything more than 'just a touch' of electric distortion. At the same time, he knows that 'if you're just playing standards, you end up playing pizza joints for fifty quid'.

**Sippin' At Bells** (Spotlite)

# Alex Cline
DRUMS
*born* 4 January 1956

Like his brother Nels, Alex Cline began in rock groups, but in the mid-70s he started working with reed players, including Oliver Lake, Julius Hemphill and particularly Vinny Golia, who has been an important colleague ever since. His interest in the wider world of percussion has led him to investigate areas such as the Tibetan percussion tradition, although this has tended to take him away from jazz and towards hippieish world-music noodling. Golia's groups remain his best setting.

**Vinny Golia, *Nation Of Laws*** (Nine Winds)

# Nels Cline
GUITAR
*born* 4 January 1956

Nels has pursued a rather tougher course than his twin Alex. Like his sibling, he has worked with Julius Hemphill and various

lights in the West Coast improv axis centred around Vinny Golia's Nine Winds operation, but he has also run small groups of his own which tend towards a rocky, bitingly abstract music. None of this has won a great deal of international attention but Cline seems likely to be a fixture in the global underground which has built up around this kind of playing as an appreciative chorus.
*Chest* (Little Brother)

# Larry Clinton
BANDLEADER, ARRANGER
*born* 17 August 1909; *died* 2 May 1985

Clinton's work has always enjoyed a solid following, even though much of it scarcely has more than a toehold on jazz. He played modest trumpet, but was more notable as an arranger-composer, starting out with some of the sweet-to-hot orchestras working in New York in the early 30s. 'A Study In Brown' (Casa Loma Orchestra), 'Dorsey Dervish' (Jimmy Dorsey) and 'The Dipsy Doodle' (Tommy Dorsey) are characteristic Clinton pieces for other bands, but in the end he started leading his own groups, and he made scores of records for Victor and Bluebird between 1938 and 1941. One trait he enjoyed (and which has always won approval from one end of the big-band audience) was jazzing the classics, and some of his best-known pieces are things like 'My Reverie' (1938, a straight steal from Debussy). Clinton led bands again at the end of the 40s but thereafter he was more involved in music publishing.
*Larry Clinton & His Orchestra 1937–1941* (Sunbeam)

# Rosemary Clooney
VOCAL
*born* 23 May 1928; *died* 29 June 2002

Clooney was a rare example of a popular singer who turned to jazz and got better and better at it. She sang with Tony Pastor's big band at the end of the 40s but Columbia marketed her as a pre-rock pop singer in the 50s, with hits such as 'Come On-A My House' and big movies including *White Christmas*, which she starred in with Bing Crosby, an association which continued on record. When rock took over the market-

place her career fell away, but in the 70s Concord began recording her with their stable of mainstreamers in support, and Rosie (as she preferred to be called) came into her own. There was a superb series of 'songbook' albums, perhaps the best of their kind since the Ella Fitzgerald sequence, and though her voice eventually went into inevitable decline, she remained a gently masterful interpreter of the best lyrics. Even in her earlier days, though, she'd done some fine jazz work: an album of songs with the Ellington orchestra (though Clooney overdubbed all her parts) and a lively collaboration with Nelson Riddle for RCA, *Rosie Solves The Swinging Riddle!* (1961). She had grown to an enormous size by the time of her final live work, but she looked queenly with it.
*Sings The Lyrics Of Johnny Mercer* (Concord)

# Jeff Clyne
BASS
*born* 29 January 1937

Clyne caught the attention early on in the London scene of the late 50s, and after joining The Jazz Couriers in 1958 he remained associated with Tubby Hayes for most of the 60s. At the same time, the nascent free-playing scene piqued his interest and he also performed in the Spontaneous Music Ensemble, perhaps the only member of that circle to also work in much more straight-ahead situations; and he also plays on the British jazz milestone *Under Milk Wood*, by Stan Tracey. By the end of the decade he had begun to turn to fusion and joined Nucleus (playing electric bass) in 1969. He co-led the softer fusion outfit Turning Point later in the next decade, but eventually returned to acoustic playing and gradually drifted more into academia, at both the Guildhall School and the Royal Academy of Music.
*Stan Tracey, Under Milk Wood* (Columbia)

# Arnett Cobb
TENOR SAXOPHONE
*born* 10 August 1918; *died* 24 March 1989

A classic Texas tenor. He worked with local bands in and around Houston before joining Lionel Hampton in 1942, taking over the Illinois Jacquet role and proving himself adept at playing in the same wailing manner. He then led a small group of his own, but suffered misfortunes with his health: he was out of action at the start of the 50s and then had his legs wrecked by a car crash in 1956. Still, Arnett was never away from playing for long. Early Apollo sides such as 'Cobb's Idea' (1947) all but set the agenda for the R&B tenor player, rough-housing around favourite licks and spearing into the high register. He recorded occasionally in the 60s but was more or less rediscovered in the following decade, playing European festivals and sometimes lining up alongside Jacquet and Buddy Tate as one of the Texas Tenors. Although his more straight-ahead records are good enough, his forte was more in that style of jamming.

**Arnett Cobb**, *Sizzlin'* (Prestige)

## Jimmy Cobb
DRUMS
*born* 20 January 1929

Cobb has been a fixture in the music for decades although, unusually for a drummer, he's been closely associated with only a relatively small number of musicians. He worked in his home town of Washington DC until going out on tour with Earl Bostic, and then worked as MD for Dinah Washington until 1955 (he was one of her numerous husbands). He played with Cannonball Adderley and with him joined the Miles Davis band of 1958, staying five years: he is perhaps the least-noticed player on *Kind Of Blue*, but he was a definite asset to the session. He was a regular with Wynton Kelly until the pianist died and then spent a long period in Sarah Vaughan's group. Nat Adderley remained a close friend and Cobb often played in the trumpeter's groups. Lately he has been leading groups of his own under the title Cobb's Mob. A patient timekeeper with little interest in solos, Cobb prefers to push the band, and usually pushes hard.

**Miles Davis**, *Kind Of Blue* (Columbia)

## Billy Cobham
DRUMS
*born* 16 May 1944

Cobham set new standards for jazz – or, at least, fusion – drumming. Born in Panama,

he went to New York as an infant and started on drums early enough to be playing with his father at eight. He joined the army and played for a military band – 'They didn't train me – I ended up rewriting the examination for everyone else that came in' – and afterwards joined Horace Silver, in 1968. Soon enough he was moving in the new crossover circles developing in New York, forming Dreams with the Brecker brothers and playing on several Miles Davis records. He drove the Mahavishnu Orchestra for two years from 1971, creating some of the biggest tumult in the genre at that point, then set up Spectrum, which featured the likes of John Scofield and George Duke. But he turned away from bandleading in the later 70s, lived and worked in Switzerland and Germany, and eventually began leading bands of his own again – including groups named Paradox and Jazz Is Dead – while enjoying occasional high-priced gigs as a superstar-for-hire. A string of records on the Cleopatra label have appeased Cobham-watchers, although with their often strange line-ups and Euro-American alliances they've made little real impact, certainly not in America. In 2003–4 he was touring again with a much more straight-ahead, acoustic line-up. In his youthful pomp, Cobham's speed, dexterity and precision were perfectly in tune with what rock-reared audiences hungered for. Worthwhile as much of his later music is, the fiery braggadocio of that playing has clearly been tempered by age.

**Spectrum** (Atlantic)

## Tony Coe
CLARINET, TENOR, ALTO AND BARITONE SAXOPHONES
*born* 29 November 1934

Coe grew up in Canterbury and had classical clarinet lessons, but he played with a local trad band (and was sacked for being too modern) and with an army band during National Service in the early 50s. He joined Humphrey Lyttelton in 1957, staying five years, then turned down a job with the Count Basie band ('I'm glad it didn't come off – I would have lasted about a fortnight') but kept a chair in both the John Dankworth orchestra and the Clarke–Boland Big Band, the latter until 1973. Ever since, he has

worked in a prodigious variety of settings: free improv with Derek Bailey, composed music with fellow clarinettist Alan Hacker, The Melody Four with Steve Beresford, film-score writing, big commissions and playing on small, vanishing record dates. His is the original tenor sound on Henry Mancini's celebrated *Pink Panther* theme. One of his best deployments in recent years has been his place in various Franz Koglmann groups: Coe brings just the right amount of mil-dewed romanticism to Koglmann's de-manding pieces. His clarinet playing is among the most individual in post-bop jazz, although he credits Alan Hacker as a pro-found influence on this horn. As wide-ranging as his musical interests are, though, he appears to like playing the conservative: 'Pierre Boulez said he couldn't stand more than two bars of improvised music and I can sort of see what he means.'
**Mainly Mancini** (Nato)

# Avishai Cohen
BASS
*born* 20 April 1970

One of a burgeoning wave of Israeli players starting to make their mark on the music, Cohen moved to St Louis from his home town of Naharia in 1984, and played piano in his high-school jazz group. He switched to bass after hearing Jaco Pastorius and Stanley Clarke, went back to Israel for army service, then arrived in New York in 1992. By the end of the century he had experience as both sideman and leader under his belt, had signed to Chick Corea's Stretch imprint and was in the pianist's Origin band. Corea's world is a good fit for Cohen, who likes to work in ultra-busy modal situations, though he goes native by using Amos Hoffman on oud for some of his own music. Nothing immortal has come out of it so far, though Cohen is clearly a talented executant.
**Adama** (Stretch)

# Al Cohn
TENOR SAXOPHONE
*born* 24 November 1925; *died* 15 February 1988

Al Cohn's career was closely aligned with that of his regular tenor partner Zoot Sims, and while Al's gruffer and more heavy-set sound was never a match for Zoot, he was arguably the greater all-round musician. Born in Brooklyn, he was good enough to be working in New York sax sections when still in his teens, and was one of the 'Four Brothers' Woody Herman section in 1948–9. By the 50s he was much in demand as an arranger (after an unhappy spell working in the family textile business), and he could turn in swinging and not too complicated charts on standard material to order: Elliot Lawrence was one leader who used him a lot. In 1956 he began making albums with Sims in a two-tenor pairing that set stan-dards for swinging saxophone dialogue, although four albums made for RCA in the same period are unjustly little known. If Cohn never sounded as skippingly light on his feet as Sims, he made up for it with his burry tone. In the 60s and 70s he worked extensively in show and television scoring and recorded less as an instrumentalist, although when he was persuaded to do so – notably by Don Schlitten, who made several gorgeous Cohn sets for his Xanadu label – the results were hugely enjoyable. His guitar-ist son Joe (b 1956) worked with Cohn senior in small-group settings in the 80s. Al carried on working after Zoot's passing, but less than three years later he was, like Sims, a victim of cancer.
**Play It Now** (Xanadu)

# Dolo Coker
PIANO
*born* 16 November 1927; *died* 13 April 1983

Originally from Hartford, Coker worked in Philadelphia backing many visitors to the city, but he won more attention when he moved west to Los Angeles in 1961. Although he spent much of the next 15 years in rela-tive obscurity, working quietly as a solid professional, he became one of the hard bop-pers rediscovered by record producer Don Schlitten, and in a burst of activity in the middle 70s he recorded more than he had done in the rest of his career. Coker's Xanadu albums showcase an attractive, musical take on the bop language, and he was a particularly sympathetic accompanist.
**Dolo!** (Xanadu)

# Kid Sheik Cola
TRUMPET
*born* 15 September 1908; *died* 7 November 1996

George 'Kid Sheik' Cola was bequeathed his nickname owing to his penchant for wearing 'sheikh' suits, but Shake might have been a more apposite title given his infamous vibrato on the horn. He began bandleading in 1925 and worked in and around the Storyville district in New Orleans for some 20 years. After military duty he returned to New Orleans bandleading, sometimes working with George Lewis and some of the city's brass bands, but usually leading such groups of his own as The Swingsters and the Storyville Ramblers; John Handy was a favourite partner during the 60s. By the 70s he was one of the longest-serving band-leaders in the city and he became a regular at Preservation Hall. He was a regular in front of microphones, although many of the records sound shambling, and Kid Sheik's shortwinded phrasing doesn't always come across too well. He once visited England, where he was recorded at Egham Cricket Club. He married the singer and pianist Sadie Goodson when they were both nearly 80, and they both carried on playing well into the 90s.
*Kid Sheik At The Tudor Arms* (Mono)

# Cozy Cole
DRUMS
*born* 17 October 1906; *died* 29 January 1981

'Topsy' was Cozy's greatest hour, at least commercially speaking: the two-sided rock'n'roll-era novelty was a hit on both sides of the Atlantic in 1958 (and the 'hour' lasted about five minutes). But the former tap-dancer had a jazz career stretching back to Wilbur Sweatman and Jelly Roll Morton in the 20s, and was a regular in New York studios during the 30s: his playing on numerous tracks of the Teddy Wilson–Billie Holiday sessions is where many will have unwittingly heard him, since he is often nearly inaudible. But his virtuosity came to the fore on the records he made with Cab Calloway, studies in big-band swing drumming which set a standard for others in the style between 1938 and 1942. He replaced Sidney Catlett in Louis Armstrong's All Stars in 1949 and stayed four years, before setting up a drum school in New York with Gene Krupa. After 'Topsy', Cole had enough name and impetus to go touring with his own band, and he did so long into the 60s. He was still working as a freelance, with Benny Carter and others, until well into the 70s. His brother Jay (1916–75) was a pianist who was often in Cozy's bands.
*Cab Calloway 1939–1940* (Classics)

# Freddy Cole
VOCAL, PIANO
*born* 15 October 1931

There was something a little desperate in the title of Cole's 'debut' record, *I'm Not My Brother, I'm Me* (1991). Actually, Freddy's point was fair enough, since he has actually been singing and playing piano since the 50s and making the occasional record for almost as long. His style is a close relative, if not quite a complete derivation of Nat's style, and in the 90s he unexpectedly became a much warmer property, taken up by Fantasy and then Telarc, who made a sequence of enjoyable albums where his voice is cushioned by blue-chip jazz players on good behaviour. Recently, though, he has been trying his luck with middle-aged rock material, which sounds like a turn for the worse.
*To The Ends Of The Earth* (Fantasy)

# Nat 'King' Cole
PIANO, VOCAL
*born* 17 March 1917; *died* 15 February 1965

Perhaps the first great crossover musician. Cole's evolution from dazzling pianist to lux-uriant crooner has often caused the wringing of hands in the jazz audience. Yet one also wonders if, by the time he had become a singing star, he had already said everything he had to on the keyboard, during the enormous series of records he made for Capitol in the 40s. The son of a pastor, whose church in Montgomery he often played in, Nathaniel Adams Cole studied the European piano literature in high school but paid as much attention to Art Tatum and Earl Hines, and when he settled in Los Angeles in 1936 he formed a trio (with guitar-ist Oscar Moore and bassist Wesley Prince) which proved to be both musically exciting and historically influential, since the piano trio had yet to find a prominent exponent, and Cole's success led the likes of Art Tatum (and, subsequently, Oscar Peterson) to follow the same style. The King Cole Trio was a big hit on Hollywood turf and recorded extensively for first Decca and then, from 1943, Capitol. While a session with Lester Young from 1942 showed off Cole's dexterity and improvisational flair at the keyboard – he was by now as masterful in his way as Tatum and Hines – it was his singing which won over audiences, starting with the 1943 hit 'Straighten Up And Fly Right'. His sumptuous baritone was poured over lyrics and found favour with white audiences who otherwise had trouble with black diction: like Billy Eckstine, Cole made you hear every word, but where Eckstine's singing was pure oleaginous romance, Cole had more of the hipster about him at this point, which explains such hits as 'Meet Me At No Special Place' and the outrageously titled 'A Trio Grooves In Brooklyn'. Out of hundreds of sides, there are surprisingly few rote performances, and there is much fine piano to go with the singing. Cole mollified some of the rhythmic bravado of Hines, favouring a style which had a slightly cooler timbre for all its crispness and ingenuity, and it fitted perfectly with the mood of hip good humour which the trio purveyed.

Nevertheless, Cole steadily worked less and less in this format in public, and with 'The Christmas Song' (1946), 'Nature Boy' (1948) and 'Mona Lisa' (1950), his transition to vocal superstar was virtually complete. He had his own radio show at the end of the 40s and his own TV series for a season in the 50s, and despite the glittering playing on a single LP session for Capitol where his piano was back in the foreground, *After Midnight* (1956), he had all but left jazz behind. His albums for Capitol were handsome sellers right through the early 60s, although by now the material was more typified by 'Ramblin' Rose' and 'Those Lazy Hazy Crazy Days Of Summer'. A courteous man who loved golfing and watching movie comedies with his children, Nat Cole was also a quiet radical, establishing a home in a white Hollywood neighbourhood and ignoring local complaints, and taking a discreet interest in black politics, even though he was sometimes criticized as an Uncle Tom in some quarters. A lifelong smoker who lit up first thing in the morning and put out his last one along with the bedroom light – cancer killed him when he was only 47.
*Nat King Cole 1944–1945* (Classics)

## Richie Cole
ALTO SAXOPHONE
*born* 29 February 1948

Cole's career has seemingly foundered after a pacy beginning. He studied with Phil Woods in high school and then went to Berklee for two years, before working in big bands in the early 70s. He formed a group with Eddie Jefferson in 1975, which continued until the singer's death, and Jefferson remains a primary inspiration for him. Thereafter he toured with a group he called Alto Madness and worked with musicians of a similarly mercurial temperament to his own, such as Bobby 'Wild Man' Enriquez. His records for Muse and Milestone suggested a man who was in a hurry to make a pact with pop audiences that might be swayed by some bebop alto. But the dreaded 'personal problems' intervened in the later 80s and his recording career came to a virtual halt, along with much of the touring. In person Cole was fun to hear, even if he did come across as little more than a zanier version of Phil Woods, but the records now seem dated and misconceived.
*Popbop* (Milestone)

## Bill Coleman
TRUMPET
*born* 4 August 1904; *died* 24 August 1981

Bill Coleman was one of the first American jazzmen to make a significant mark in Europe. He was born in Paris (Kentucky!) and arrived in New York in 1927, a dedicated Armstrong man. There are American recordings where Coleman shines, but his greatest sides were set down in Paris (France) when he moved there in 1935 and became an honoured member of the jazz community. A trio session which produced masterful readings of 'I'm In The Mood For Love' and 'After You've Gone' shows how well his hot but cultured, almost manicured style thrived in the Paris air. He went back to New York in 1940, but despite some excellent records – Coleman never seemed to play below him-

self, even in sometimes inappropriate sur-roundings – he began to feel out of place in a city that was turning to bebop, and when invited back to Paris for a club opening he decided to stay in France. A popular figure, Coleman turned up in various European cities over the next 30 years, and although rather rarely recorded he was still in fine fettle in his senior years.
**Bill Coleman 1936–1938** (Classics)

# Denardo Coleman
DRUMS
*born* 19 April 1956

It's Denardo's misfortune that many still think of him as the ten-year-old kid engaged by his dad to play on *The Empty Foxhole* (1966), made for Blue Note. He worked on and off with Ornette for some years before joining his Prime Time group full-time in 1979, by now a much more accomplished drummer. He has latterly become his father's business manager, doubtless a com-plex position to hold, and he has played on all Coleman's recent albums.
**Ornette Coleman, *In All Languages*** (Verve/Harmolodic)

# George Coleman
TENOR AND SOPRANO SAXOPHONES
*born* 8 March 1935

Coleman is the saxophonist everyone for-gets when the comparative merits of Miles Davis's horn players are under discussion. He actually played with Davis for only a single season (1963–4); before that, the Memphis-born tenorman had worked in R&B bands before joining first Walter Perkins (Chicago) and then Max Roach and Slide Hampton (New York, 1958–62). With Davis, Coleman was on the face of it miscast, like Hank Mobley in a similar period, yet his playing on *In Europe* and *My Funny Valentine* (both 1963) has a no-nonsense virility and unpretentious intensity which blows serenely past the posturing which Davis's bands were often wont to slip into. He subsequently did a lot more sideman work on New York records of the period, turn-ing up on Herbie Hancock's *Maiden Voyage* (1965) and making a string of albums with Chet Baker as an unlikely front-line partner. In the 70s, he began working in an octet for-

mat, which obliged him to produce some of his best writing, and he has worked on that book ever since; it is a major mishap that very little of that music has ever been recorded, and it took his student and fan Ned Otter to sponsor the appearance of a single CD of some of Coleman's eight-piece charts in 2000 (the record cited). Coleman has, indeed, been recorded surprisingly infrequently over a long career, which has taken in a lot of teach-ing and workmanlike gigs along the way. His grand sound and sense of magisterial calm, even in the heat of a power-packed improvisa-tion, mark him out as a major saxophonist.
**Danger High Voltage** (Two And Four)

# Ornette Coleman
ALTO SAXOPHONE, TRUMPET, VIOLIN
*born* 9 March 1930

It seems strange to look back and regard the outrage which Coleman's music once caused. Born in Fort Worth, Texas, he played tenor in R&B groups, his sound at that time much in the bebop idiom, although he was already hearing things a little differently: at one dance he played at, a particularly off-colour solo caused such disquiet in the audience that he was assaulted and his instrument smashed up. Changing to alto, he fetched up in Los Angeles in 1949, worked as a lift operator and taught himself music theory from books. He had already made friends with the drummer Ed Blackwell, and they subsequently formed the grand-sounding American Jazz Quintet; at the same time, he sometimes worked with Don Cherry and Billy Higgins in the similarly imposingly titled Jazz Messiahs.

In 1958, Paul Bley enlisted both Coleman and Cherry to play in his resident group at the Hillcrest Club, although they weren't kept on for long. The same year, Coleman made his first records for Contemporary. The bassists on the dates, Red Mitchell and Percy Heath, independently remembered asking Coleman about a musical point and being baffled by his answer, a trend which has largely continued ever since. But the records nevertheless showcased an extraordi-nary new sound, which was extended further by Coleman's recordings for Atlantic during 1959–61, and which took New York by storm when Coleman arrived there in 1959, with Cherry, Higgins and Charlie

Haden making up perhaps the definitive edition of his famous quartet. What shocked listeners was Coleman's almost calm delivery of a style which sounded both new and old at once. After years of bebop soloists dominating bandstands, Coleman went back to a group sound, an approach which was akin to that of the first jazz ensembles, yet one which was not fettered by slavish adherance to chord sequences, chorus lengths, tonalities or even symmetrical beats. His themes had the simple inevitability of untutored folksong, and the rhythms which Higgins and Haden played were mobile and freely swinging. Out of this grew improvisations which were like streams of clear melody, an even more unshackled approach than the one Miles Davis was currently following in his modal music, yet one which still referred back to the blues, an inescapable part of Coleman's language.

Listeners such as John Lewis and Leonard Bernstein were astonished and delighted (for every complaint about Coleman's music there was at least one hurrah, and even Miles Davis said, 'I like Ornette, because he doesn't play clichés'); and it was through Lewis's intervention that Coleman made his Atlantic recordings. Besides the magnificent quartet sessions which produced the likes of *The Shape Of Jazz To Come*, *This Is Our Music* and *Change Of The Century*, there was the single 37-minute piece *Free Jazz*, made by a double quartet, and a date where Coleman returned to the tenor saxophone (for almost the only time in his career on record). The music went round the world and everything felt changed. Yet the quartet soon broke up: Cherry went on to work with Albert Ayler and others, and Coleman retired for a spell to teach himself trumpet and violin. On his return, many were dismayed by the sounds he made on the latter instruments (Freddie Hubbard: 'I wish he'd leave the trumpet to me, man!'), but a new trio with David Izenzon and Charles Moffett visited Europe and made some masterful live recordings in Stockholm.

Coleman himself seemed unsure of his own aspirations: having changed jazz perceptions so fundamentally, perhaps he was at a loss for an encore. There were some albums for Blue Note in the late 60s and his son Denardo Coleman (at the age of ten) began playing in his band. But John Coltrane's looming influence and Albert Ayler's more explosive freedoms had eclipsed Coleman, and he did comparatively little until recording *Dancing In Your Head* (1972) with a group of Moroccan musicians. This seemed to pave the way for a fresh rhythmic basis for his work, and in 1975 he founded a new band, Prime Time, which featured multiple electric guitars, basses and drums. They still did little in the way of recording – never shy of justifying his own stature, Coleman has always asked for absolute top dollar for concerts and records alike – but in the 80s he gradually became more visible, recording with Pat Metheny and occasionally getting Prime Time on to record: the 1987 set *In All Languages* offered one disc of Prime Time and one of a reunion of the old quartet with Cherry, Haden and Blackwell. In the meantime, he again foxed musicians and listeners alike with a new theoretical basis for his current music, which he referred to as 'harmolodics': in the 20 or so years since the word came into use, nobody (including its creator) has ever offered a clear and comprehensible explanation of what it means.

In the 90s, the French producer Jean-Philippe Allard realized a dream by signing Coleman to Polygram records, but out of a string of scheduled projects only three records emerged, two by a new quartet (with Geri Allen on piano – almost the only time the keyboard has entered Coleman's music) consisting of alternative versions of the same material. Despite the many changing contexts, though, Coleman's own playing has changed little: his trademark legato wail is perhaps used more frequently as he has to counter ranks of electric instruments, but the familiar melodic fertility in his improvising remains. In his old age, Ornette remains as elusive and enigmatic as ever. He is a kindly man, with a soft speaking voice (and a slight lisp), whose faintly amused demeanour in conversation is very beguiling, as he well knows. As much work as he has done, he has been far less prolific – in terms of issued recordings – than such contemporaries as Coltrane, Davis or Cecil Taylor, and one can only hope that some day the extensive archive he has maintained of his own recordings will be opened to the world at large. In 2004, it was fascinating to hear that Wynton Marsalis had been visiting him in New York, and jamming until the small hours.

*Change Of The Century* (Atlantic)

# Steve Coleman

ALTO SAXOPHONE
*born* 20 September 1956

Born in Chicago, Coleman sat in at local clubs and listened endlessly to Charlie Parker records before moving to New York in 1978. He was hidden in the Thad Jones–Mel Lewis band at first, but gradually moved over to small groups and in 1981 he formed the first edition of Five Elements, a format which has been his primary ensemble since. Here he began developing the concepts which were subsequently (in 1984) crystallized by the term M-Base, formally established as a musicians' cooperative although Coleman is largely seen as its principal architect. Besides Five Elements, Coleman also worked with the Dave Holland Quintet (until 1990 or so) and played alongside fellow M-Basers such as Greg Osby and Graham Haynes. The constant in this activity, and in his larger groups such as The Council Of Balance and Rhythm In Mind, is Coleman's own alto playing: steely in its poise, vibrato-less, chilled by its diffidence but warmed by an interior passion, it is as singular as any saxophone sound of the past 30 years. His music has thickened over the years, moving from the almost mathematical funk of the likes of *Motherland Pulse* (1985) to the orchestral density of *Genesis And The Opening Of The Way* (1997), a progression which has taken him away from most of the familiar currents in the jazz mainstream. The price on this is that he is ignored by the jazz business in his own country: his first records were for a German label, his RCA albums were sponsored by the French rather than the American division, and he is now on another French independent, Label Bleu. There isn't much humour in Steve's music but it is a vivid, pulsing work in progress: every solo he plays seems like a continuation of some hugely extended opus which he picks up and puts down as he chooses.
**Resistance Is Futile** (Label Bleu)

# Johnny Coles

TRUMPET
*born* 3 July 1926; *died* 21 December 1997

'Little Johnny C', as the title of his sole Blue Note album had it, made his first mark in the R&B band run by Eddie 'Cleanhead' Vinson (alongside John Coltrane). He worked for a variety of leaders in the 50s, including Gene Ammons, Earl Bostic and James Moody, but the one who got the best out of him was, surprisingly, Gil Evans: he is on most of Evans's projects of the late 50s and early 60s, and his fragile, bluesy delivery is beautifully suited to a miniature tone poem such as 'Sunken Treasure' from *Out Of The Cool* (1960). He toured Europe with Charles Mingus and was part of Herbie Hancock's 1968 sextet, but he never really found much attention as a soloist and he buried himself in Duke Ellington's Orchestra (1971–4) and, in the 80s, a late edition of the Count Basie band. He was back in Philadelphia, where he had grown up, in 1989, and despite encroaching cancer was still playing up until his death. Though he made four records as a leader, his best music remained his Evans interpretations.
**Gil Evans, *Out Of The Cool*** (Impulse!)

# Buddy Collette

FLUTE, CLARINET, TENOR SAXOPHONE
*born* 6 August 1921

Born in Los Angeles, Collette ran a navy band during the war and found a niche for himself in the LA session scene of the early 50s – one of the very few blacks to make the transition at that time. He was always an important force in crossing the divide, and it was partly through his work that segregation in the American Federation of Musicians came to a close. He co-founded the quintet with Chico Hamilton which recorded for Contemporary, and besides this appeared in numerous studio situations, some of them under his own leadership: one curious example was The Swingin' Shepherds, which consisted of four flutes (Collette, Bud Shank, Paul Horn and Harry Klee) plus rhythm section – the Shepherds dressed in monks' habits for their album covers. Flute and to a somewhat lesser extent clarinet were the instruments which preoccupied Collette for much of his recording work: while they sometimes failed to climb out of the novelty bracket, Collette did as much as anyone to make these sounds swing in a contemporary way. Like many others, after 1960 he did film and TV scoring, but also turned up with Mingus, Kenton and others, as well as leading his own groups. A great teacher, he once numbered both Eric Dolphy and James Newton among his students (he made *Flute Talk* with Newton in 1988). As a saxophonist, Collette plays in a much brawnier style, but it's his flute playing that set him apart from other reed players. A 1996 date, *Big Band In Concert*, found him directing though not playing with a fine orchestra, working through his own book.

*Nice Day* (OJC)

## Max Collie
TROMBONE
*born* 21 February 1931

One of the great diehards of British trad is actually an Australian, who went to England with the Melbourne New Orleans Jazz Band in 1963 and liked it enough to stay. A bluff, hearty player whose brassy punch is straight out of his brass-band background, Collie has led a series of cheerfully irreverent outfits, never seeming to worry too much about authenticity but nevertheless doing very well: he actually won the World Championship of Jazz (whatever that was) in Indianapolis in 1975, and led a New Orleans touring show which the arch-purist Ken Colyer took part in during the early 80s. As jazz entertainers go, Max is entitled to be considered a champ.

*Sensation* (Timeless)

## Graham Collier
BASS, COMPOSER
*born* 21 February 1937

Collier spent six years in army bands before winning a scholarship to Berklee in 1961, subsequently becoming the school's first British graduate. He came home and formed Graham Collier Music, an ensemble of shifting size which lasted through the 60s and 70s, and at one time or another had many of the leading modernists in its ranks. His early music, such as *Deep Dark Blue Centre* (1967) and *Down Another Road* (1969), is based around smallish ensembles and offers some of his most vivid work, a personal take on the composition–improvisation crossing point with fine contributions from the likes of the young Stan Sulzmann. Collier also

played bass in these groups but subsequently concentrated on directing mostly bigger groups. He retired from the Royal Academy in 1999 after many years of teaching and moved to Spain. The later music is unfortunately long-winded and self-important.

*Down Another Road* (Philips)

## James Lincoln Collier
AUTHOR
*born* 27 June 1928

Collier had a huge list of written works behind him – adult and juvenile fiction, social history and more – before he even began writing about jazz, in 1974, following a long acquaintance with the music. But after *The Making Of Jazz* (1978), which was popular enough to be used as a college textbook for some years, in the 80s he published biographies of Louis Armstrong, Duke Ellington and Benny Goodman which attracted as many howls of complaint as cheers of acclaim. Collier's tunnel vision as an interpreter of facts and identity lead him down numerous contentious byways, but at the same time he is good at spotting a phoney opinion and has a strong nose for detecting cant, although he is weak on recent developments in the music. Read with a sceptical eye, his work is a provocative challenge.

## George Colligan
PIANO, TRUMPET
*born* 29 December 1969

Colligan grew up in Columbia, Maryland, but he has been a regular on the New York scene since the middle 90s. Like many of the younger players trying to make their way in a crowded scene, he has taken whatever playing opportunities have come his way, which have included plenty of sideman gigs, although he has also been surprisingly well documented as a leader already, with several albums for both Steeplechase and Fresh Sounds. The best of them have been filled with strikingly imaginative music: Colligan likes to rethink a familiar piece from top to bottom, and might entirely reharmonize it or send it to some remote place. He also sets his small groups some surprising tasks, often leaving blank spaces where a horn player might leap into dangerously clear air. A prodigious talent who started out on trumpet and occasionally plays it on record: he's not bad on this horn, either.

*Agent 99* (Steeplechase)

## John Collins

GUITAR

*born* 20 September 1913

Collins worked alongside many of the most eminent jazz leaders in a very long career, starting with Art Tatum in 1935: after that came Roy Eldridge, Benny Carter, Erroll Garner, Tadd Dameron and Coleman Hawkins. He was with Nat Cole between 1951 and Cole's death in 1965, and latterly settled in Los Angeles. He was still playing all through the 80s and made a single album under his own name, *The Incredible! John Collins*, in 1984. Basically a rhythm man, his occasional solos suggested that he could have done much more in that direction had he been so inclined.

**Benny Carter, *Further Definitions*** (Impulse!)

## Lee Collins

TRUMPET

*born* 17 October 1901; *died* 3 July 1960

A close New Orleans contemporary of Louis Armstrong's, Collins played with many local outfits before going to Chicago in 1924 and succeeding Armstrong in the King Oliver band. But he returned home a year later and didn't leave again until 1930, when he went to New York, and from there to Chicago again. He played there through the 30s and 40s, although often in comparatively low-profile company, and latterly figured a little in the revivalist movement, playing with the likes of Mezz Mezzrow and travelling to Europe. Emphysema cut his career short. Collins's recordings are very scattered: there were four rare sides with Jelly Roll Morton in 1924 ('Fishtail Blues'), and some of his best work is with the Jones And Collins Astoria Hot Eight (four classic sides made in 1929) and various blues accompaniments with such as Chippie Hill and Lil Johnson.

## Colorado Jazz Party

EVENT

Dick Gibson was an investment banker and diehard enthusiast for swing-styled jazz, who decided to use some of his wealth to create his own private jazz party. In 1963, he bussed some 60 musicians into Vail, Colorado, for three days of jam sessions in front of an invited audience of several hundred guests. The musicians were treated in royal fashion, and Gibson was so pleased with the results that he made it into an annual event. By the early 80s it was taking up all of his time, and by the end of that decade he was organizing a dozen other jazz parties around the world. Many of the musicians came back time and again, and eventually the guest list swelled to some 600. Among the regular participants were Teddy Wilson, Zoot Sims, Joe Venuti, Scott Hamilton and Dick Hyman. Gibson himself died in 1998, but the jazz-party culture he created still endures. It sustained careers among many supposedly unfashionable jazz players, and provided a regular helping of live music to an ageing audience which otherwise felt disenfranchised by the way live music culture had gone.

## Alice Coltrane

PIANO, HARP

*born* 27 August 1937

Born Alice McLeod in Detroit, she did some of her first visible work with the Terry Gibbs quartet, and during this period she met John Coltrane; they were married following his divorce in 1966. The year before she took over the piano chair in his group, and remained in that role until Coltrane's death. Thereafter she led groups of her own, often with former Coltrane sidemen, and in 1972 founded the Vedantic Center in California, for the study of Eastern religions. Her records are an idiosyncratic shepherding of the Coltrane legacy: she overdubbed string charts on to some original Coltrane material, and her albums of her own music often come across as soft-headed and incoherent rambling. She is, not unnaturally, regarded with reverence in many quarters and musicians who have worked with her speak warmly of her work; but one wonders if she would have enjoyed any attention at all if she had remained plain Alice McLeod.

*Journey To Satchidananda* (Impulse!)

# John Coltrane

TENOR AND SOPRANO SAXOPHONES
*born* 23 September 1926; *died* 17 July 1967

Coltrane was almost 30 before he did any-thing of jazz significance. Born in Hamlet, North Carolina, he learned alto and clarinet in school, then studied in Philadelphia and played in a navy band. He played alto for Joe Webb and tenor with Cleanhead Vinson, and both horns with Jimmy Heath, Earl Bostic and Dizzy Gillespie (he is hidden in the ensemble on some of Gillespie's 1949 records). In the 50s he was still holding down uneventful roles with Gillespie, and in a Johnny Hodges septet, and had finally joined a Jimmy Smith group in 1955 when the offer came in to enlist with Miles Davis, replacing Sonny Rollins. Coltrane's playing on the Davis quintet sessions is, with this previous history, astonishing: the massive sound, spilling notes which touch on as many points of the bop chord progression as possible, bursts out of the otherwise urbane setting of the quintet with what might have been ridiculous force, had it not been for Coltrane's control and the gun-metal polish of his timbre. This was at medium or fast tempo; on ballads, he can sound almost indolent, unprepared to elab-orate much on the melody, letting the tone of his playing tell the story. It was a startling yet glowing contrast to Davis's own playing, which the leader must have recognized. But many of Coltrane's solos in this period still lacked the centre of a rounded approach, and often at quicker tempos, impetus alone drove the playing. Cannonball Adderley recalled Davis asking Coltrane why his solos went on so long: 'It takes that long to get it all in,' was the mild response.

Drugs (a heroin addiction) and alcohol were, however, plaguing his behaviour; twice in this period Davis fired and reinstated him, and he often fell asleep on the stand when not playing. Meek as a lamb, he hardly responded when Davis slapped and punched him for a typical trans-gression. But he reputedly got himself off heroin at least in 1957, and his career started to go up several gears. He played with

Thelonious Monk for a spell and recorded prolifically as a leader for Prestige, as well as honouring a handshake agreement to make a single album for Blue Note (the fine *Blue Train*, 1957). By 1959, when he made both *Kind Of Blue* with Davis and *Giant Steps* as the start of a brief association with Atlantic, Coltrane had expanded his playing range: the investigation of chords had taken on the form of what Ira Gitler called 'sheets of sound', sixteenth-note trajectories which enabled him, as he played a solo, to slam through as many possibilities in each chord before the next arrived. This was countered by the escape from those strictures which the *Kind Of Blue* music hinted at, by impro-vising around motifs and scales as an alternative.

The formation of his signature quartet in 1960 – with McCoy Tyner, Jimmy Garrison and Elvin Jones – set in place the kind of ongoing workshop which Coltrane felt he needed. In his years with Davis he had hardly even seemed like leadership material, but he was so focused on the act of playing that it inspired his men, who seemed to join in with the feel of something remarkable in the making. Over the next five years, the quartet toured regularly (to Europe and beyond) and startled audiences everywhere: a young Jan Garbarek recalls hearing this group, attired in grimy tuxedos and off-white shirts, playing the hell out of an Oslo bandstand. Coltrane had added soprano saxophone to his armoury (for which Steve Lacy must take the major credit), and played 'My Favorite Things' as his great setpiece on that horn. Otherwise there were endless explorations of the same handful of pieces, including 'Giant Steps', 'Mr P.C.', 'Impressions', 'Naima' and the occasional standard such as 'I Want To Talk About You'. His accompanists follow in his wake as best they can, although the most significant dia-logue is the one with Jones, whose cross-rhythms and mass of sound from both drums and cymbals make him step out from the drummer's usual accompanying role. Tyner, instead, was often left as the time-keeper with chordal vamps.

After seven albums with Atlantic, Coltrane moved to Impulse! in 1961, where Bob Thiele produced the remainder of his records. There were some attempts at marketing him to a wider and more easily accessed audi-ence, via albums of ballads and vocals by

Johnny Hartman, but there were also churning masterpieces such as *Live At The Village Vanguard* (1961), with its marathon performance of 'Chasin' The Trane', *Africa/Brass* (1961) and eventually the four-part epic *A Love Supreme* (1964), a thanksgiving for Coltrane's supposed release from drug dependence, based around a simple four-note motif from which an album-length suite is created. This is *Kind Of Blue*'s only rival as the most famous modern jazz record: a lofty distillation of Coltrane's vision, which has become a spiritual touchstone in the music, even though simply as a performance it is arguably no more or less remarkable than many of his other records of the period.

Coltrane experimented with having Eric Dolphy in the group for a time, and eventually, with the ferment of New York's latest wave as represented by Albert Ayler and Archie Shepp going on around him, he instigated a wholehearted change. Tyner and Jones departed at the end of 1965, and Alice Coltrane (his second wife), Rashied Ali and a second saxophonist, Pharoah Sanders, all joined the group. By this time he was among the highest-paid musicians in jazz, with substantial record royalties accruing and the band as in demand as any in the music, but compared to his old boss Davis there was nothing of the star about Coltrane. He spent his time offstage looking after his family and maintaining his saxophones, not driving fast cars, and his interviews were full of expressions about humility and the need for spiritual growth. In contrast, the music became louder and wilder. Coltrane had already recorded *Ascension* (1965), an extended and often tormented large-scale piece for 11 players, but the new band took even that approach to extremes. Concerts lasted for hours, and solos seemed as though they would never end; Sanders became the screaming alter ego to Trane's plain good man, even though it seemed as though Coltrane wanted to end up that way himself, his concern for tonality gradually obliterated. The duo album with Ali, *Interstellar Space* (1967), is a calmer intercourse, the playing bronzed and athletic even as it boils, and though very late live recordings such as *The Olatunji Concert* are often a bloody mess, Coltrane still returned to playing 'Naima' as a point of repose.

Where might he have gone next? For Coltrane, it seemed as if the journeying was everything: there is no conclusion in his work, and perhaps there never would have been. One popular idea is that he would have gone on to explore other musics from other places, and perhaps leave jazz behind altogether. 'You have to remember, Coltrane was a very greedy man,' said Miles Davis, and for all the aura of spirituality which has been settled on him – and he was, no doubt of it, a generous and thoughtful figure, respectful and concerned to support the work of others – there is something insatiable about his many musical explorations and passions. He might be surprised to find himself still, decades afterwards, the great influence on saxophonists everywhere – in his sound, technical aplomb and sheer dedication to a difficult craft. But he would never be around to see it: increasingly troubled by the legacy of his old addictions, he died in July 1967 from liver failure.

*A Love Supreme* (Impulse!)

# Ravi Coltrane
TENOR AND SOPRANO SAXOPHONES
*born* 6 August 1965

John's son has, on the face of it, something impossible to live up to, and he didn't take much interest in playing jazz until studying in California in the later 80s. In a piquant meeting, his first significant job was with Elvin Jones's Jazz Machine, and he subsequently did other sideman work before finally beginning a leadership career on record in the later 90s. Often sounding more like Sonny Stitt and Dexter Gordon than his father, he is clearly a gifted player, but so far the records have offered little in the way of anything special.

*Moving Pictures* (RCA)

# Ken Colyer
TRUMPET, GUITAR
*born* 18 April 1928; *died* 8 March 1988

Colyer's puritanical insistence on the one true way coloured appreciation of an important and valuable musician. He taught himself to play the cornet and co-founded the Crane River Jazz Band in 1949: rough and ready and sounding like several men pulling in several directions, their early work is

British primitivism at, one supposes, its best. While in the merchant navy, Colyer managed to get to New Orleans and sat in with the likes of George Lewis and Emil Barnes. He was later deported and returned home to a kind of hero's welcome. He formed a new Ken Colyer's Jazzmen with Chris Barber and Monty Sunshine, but disagreements split the band and Barber and Sunshine went their own way. Colyer nevertheless pursued his fundamentalist line, believing that anything later than Bunk Johnson was, stylistically, not the way to play New Orleans jazz. When asked by sideman Acker Bilk if they could do a Hot Five number, the leader told him sharply that he wouldn't try anything that modern. Colyer lost out to Barber in the popularity stakes, but his Decca albums of the 50s are strong and fiercely loyal to his philosophy, and when the trad boom collapsed it made not a whit of difference to someone who had no 'commercial' leanings anyway. He ran his own club, Studio 51, in London and worked through the beat era but had to retire owing to stomach cancer. By the end of the 70s, though, he had returned and was playing with his old intensity, although some of the truculence of his earlier music had been replaced by a more sullen orthodoxy. Further illness finally stopped him playing in the middle 80s. 'The Guv'nor' still inspires an almost fanatical devotion among his remaining faithful: there is a Ken Colyer Trust, with its own band, and scores of available CDs testify to the enduring demand for this strange man's stubborn, British Orleans music.

*Club Session With Colyer* (Lake)

## Alix Combelle

CLARINET, TENOR SAXOPHONE
*born* 15 June 1912; *died* 27 February 1978

Though he began as a drummer, Combelle switched to clarinet and saxophone and worked in Parisian bands. He was good enough to work as a sideman with many visiting Americans, including Coleman Hawkins, Bill Coleman and Benny Carter, and he led groups of his own, particularly Jazz De Paris, which included Django Reinhardt as a sideman. Somehow he managed to keep playing jazz and even toured while France was occupied by the Nazis. In

the 60s he ran his own nightclub and made no more records. Combelle never made many waves outside France and only Reinhardt collectors have kept his recordings familiar: his best sides take all their cues from American models but the mix of US and Gallic material is, in its way, idiosyncratically his own.

*Alix Combelle 1940–1941* (Classics)

## Commodore
RECORD COMPANY

Commodore was perhaps the first of the independent jazz labels. Milt Gabler had a radio and record store on 42nd Street in Manhattan and was himself a jazz fan and record collector. He realized that a collectors' market for hard-to-find jazz records was developing and in 1934 he began leasing old masters from the major labels and reissuing them under the logo 'Commodore Music Shop'. He even organized jam sessions in the shop on Sundays. By 1938, the label was well established and Gabler began recording new music, starting with seven titles by Eddie Condon (who told *Life* magazine, 'It's an important thing, a little record store doing its own recordings. It doesn't like the records that the big companies make'). Commodore lasted until the 50s, although Gabler himself crossed the floor and joined Decca. Their catalogue was a class act, filled with the best in small-group swing, and traditional and vocal jazz (Billie Holiday made some fine sides there), and when Mosaic released a complete set of Commodore sessions in the 90s it filled 128 LP sides. The rights to the catalogue are currently held by Universal, although they have been comparatively neglectful of them in the CD era.

## Company
GROUP

Company never existed as such: it was a convenient banner for an idea of Derek Bailey's, whereby a group of improvisers would come together and perform a series of concerts, the personnel at each 'set' decided on an ad hoc basis, the better to create fresh and changing circumstances for the music. The first Company 'Week' took place at London's ICA in 1977, and it continued (mostly in

London) on a regular basis until 1994, when Bailey – the only musician who took part in every series, bar one – abandoned it. Notoriously resistant to routine, he felt it had run its course as an idea. It certainly involved some strange bedfellows, including Lee Konitz, Peter Brötzmann, Alex Balanescu, Steve Lacy and Buckethead. Numerous live records from different Company Weeks have been issued on Bailey's Incus label.

## Concord
RECORD COMPANY

Concord fostered interest in mainstream and swing-styled jazz at a point when there was effectively no interest from the major record labels. It was founded in 1973 by a wealthy businessman and jazz lover, Carl Jefferson (1919–95), and he recorded scores of established musicians – Ruby Braff, Mel Tormé, Charlie Byrd and Marian McPartland among them – as well as creating discographies for such younger players as Scott Hamilton (perhaps Concord's signature musician), Warren Vaché and Howard Alden. Jefferson expanded into festival activity and sent out Concord All Stars packages; he also went Latin with his Concord Picante subsidiary and recorded some four dozen solo piano recitals in an ongoing series made at Maybeck Recital Hall. Shortly before his death, he sold the company, but it continues to this day, although it has perhaps grown a little more contemporary in feel. In 2004, it took the major step of acquiring the Fantasy group of jazz labels, which has in theory created the biggest 'independent' jazz operation in the world.

## Eddie Condon
GUITAR, BANJO
born 16 November 1905; died 4 August 1973

The principal front-man and raconteur for Chicago jazz was actually born in Goodland, Indiana and spent most of his life in New York. He worked in Midwestern dance bands in the early 20s, where he hung out with Bix Beiderbecke and others, and was part of the Austin High School Gang in Chicago, where the likes of Red McKenzie, the Dorseys, Benny Goodman and Bud Freeman were

part of his circle. Record dates such as those by the McKenzie–Condon Chicagoans helped cement the idea of a new Chicago jazz – young, white and rowdy, fuelled on prohibition liquor – but Condon himself was already on his way to New York, where he began hustling and leading occasional bands. In 1937 he began a long association with Nick's, a club on West 10th Street, where he held forth nightly and expanded his gang of sidemen. Major labels weren't so much interested in his style of jazz, but he began making records for the independent label Commodore, and club audiences were enthusiastic. He made a point of having racially mixed bands and began booking all-star concerts at Town Hall and the Ritz Theater from 1942. After quitting Nick's in 1944 he opened his own place, originally on West 3rd Street.

A regular on radio and even on television – he had his own TV show for a year in 1948–9 – he began recording for major labels again in the 50s, and there are five oustanding sets made for Columbia during this period. Condon's the club endured (it moved to East 56th Street in 1958) but he was often away on tours himself, visiting Europe, Japan and Australia, and, finally tiring of the city, settled into a house in New Jersey. His own playing was rarely showcased in his own groups and he was no soloist, but as a driving rhythm guitarist Condon was up there with the best. He was a stickler for the band finding the right tempo, and would often halt a performance after a few bars if it wasn't right. Despite a general sense of laissez-faire, he knew what he wanted on a bandstand and he usually got the result he looked for. He inspired exceptional loyalty from a seemingly mismatched and often misbegotten band of players, who over the years numbered in the dozens, and out of it came a timeless, swinging, fierce kind of jazz which had its own peculiar lyricism. Dissenters such as Pee Wee Russell at times claimed to be sick of Condon's sort of jazz, yet Russell, like many others, did much of his best work there. Condon's autobiographical *We Called It Music* is one of the best books by a jazz musician, funny and acerbic yet deeply affectionate towards the music he cared about. His drinking was of legendary proportions and to some extent set the tone for his circle; it finally slowed him down, and he died in 1973 after two seri-

ous illnesses. When they bulldozed Condon's after its closure in 1985, his era was long gone.
**Bixieland** (Columbia)

# Harry Connick
PIANO, VOCAL
*born* 11 September 1967

It's hard to say whether that should be 'piano, vocal' or 'vocal, piano'. Since one critic nicknamed him 'Mittens', the keyboard prowess has been called into question, but Connick, a New Orleans man who burst to prodigy-prominence in 1987, is a talented fellow. He was one of the first musicians to be talked up as a fresh star of jazz at a time when it was threatening to breast a new wave of popularity, and when Connick's nightclub act – basically doing Sinatra standards in an outgoing, this-is-showbiz-not-just-jazz kind of way – won him the soundtrack to *When Harry Met Sally*, the big movie hit of 1989, he became a star far beyond the jazz environment. Yet he has never quite caught up to that promise, either as a jazz musician or as an all-round entertainer. He toured with his own big band, and Columbia made solo, orchestral and New Orleans R&B records with him; he also took straight roles in several films. But most still associate him, indelibly, with that original soundtrack. In 2003, he released a straight-ahead album on Branford Marsalis's Marsalis Music label: as fellow New Orleans homeboys, the Marsalis and Connick clans have always been close. Since the hype has died away, it's easier to appreciate Harry's merits: a strong voice, a pushy piano style which enjoyably bowdlerizes Garner and Monk, and a good dollop of insouciant charm.
**20** (Columbia)

# Chris Connor
VOCAL
*born* 8 November 1927

June Christy recommended Chris Connor to Stan Kenton: she had previously worked for Claude Thornhill, but joining Kenton in 1953 was her first real break. Much of her style can be traced back to Anita O'Day, but Connor had a smoother, less daredevil manner, and where O'Day swung her

material hard, Chris found a more poignant and bittersweet delivery. She won a contract with Bethlehem in 1954 and then, in 1956, made a series of albums for Atlantic which should be far more widely acclaimed than they have been: although she was very successful in her prime, her reputation has been guarded only by jazz vocal connoisseurs. Some of her finest performances, such as the heartbreaking 'Ev'rytime' (*Chris Connor*, 1956) or 'Here Lies Love' (*Chris Craft*, 1958), show a mastery of dynamics – and of singing softly – so finely controlled that it's difficult to imagine them being bettered. In 1960 she was a star, but like so many singers of her generation rock cut her audience away, and by the 70s she was all but forgotten. The rehabilitation of the 'classic jazz singer' has brought her back, and she has recently made some new records for High Note, although it would be kinder to suggest that newcomers should acquaint themselves with the old albums as a priority.
**Chris Connor** (Atlantic/Collectables)

# Willis Conover
DISC JOCKEY
*born* 18 December 1920; *died* 17 May 1996

Nobody did more for jazz on the radio than Conover – even though he was seldom heard on the American airwaves after 1955, when he began broadcasting for Voice Of America, which cannot be heard in the US itself. He worked on college radio in the 30s and at a Washington station in the 40s and early 50s. His VOA jazz shows commenced in January 1955, and according to station estimates he may have had as many as 100 million listeners, at a time when the station was being beamed over the Iron Curtain. He also promoted concerts, helped several big bands to get under way (one of them turned into the Thad Jones–Mel Lewis orchestra) and served as MC and announcer at several Newport Festivals.

# Contemporary
RECORD COMPANY

Lester Koenig (1918–77) founded the label in Los Angeles in 1951. Like Alfred Lion of Blue Note, Koenig was a committed fan who felt that the important music of his native scene had to be documented, and although West Coast jazz had an indifferent rep for many years (at least, in comparison to its East Coast counterpart), it is difficult to see why when the breadth of Contemporary's coverage is considered. Besides such archetypal West Coasters as Art Pepper, Howard Rumsey, Chet Baker and Shelly Manne, the label also recorded Hampton Hawes, Harold Land, Howard McGhee and – on his visits West – Sonny Rollins. Koenig also captured the first sessions by Ornette Coleman and even one date by Cecil Taylor. Hit records such as Manne's *My Fair Lady* and the Manne–Barney Kessel–Ray Brown *Poll-winners* series paid for the less commercial efforts, and at the time of his early death Koenig had re-signed and recorded Art Pepper in his comeback period. The label was subsequently bought by the Fantasy group, which has restored most of its greatest records to the catalogue in the CD era.

## Junior Cook

TENOR SAXOPHONE
*born* 22 July 1934; *died* 4 February 1992

Born in Pensacola, Florida, Cook joined Horace Silver's front line in 1958, and then worked with his fellow Silver sideman Blue Mitchell in the latter's quintet until 1969. Those ten years were his peak: a hearty, unambitious player who learned his craft and was content to look no further, he sounded to have come to rest at a point somewhere between Dexter Gordon and Joe Henderson. In the 70s and 80s he taught and worked as a freelance, but it was at first an unfashionable time for a hard bopper, and he wasn't quite old enough to be hailed as an elder statesman when the times came round again. In his final years he often worked with Bill Hardman, who was a similar underachiever on trumpet.
**Horace Silver,** *Horace-Scope* (Blue Note)

## Willie Cook

TRUMPET
*born* 11 November 1923; *died* 22 September 2000

There always seemed to be a regular turnover in Duke Ellington's post-war trumpet section, but Willie Cook joined in 1951 and stayed – aside from a couple of brief

absences – for a dozen years. A distinctive lead man whose early idols were Harry James and Charlie Spivak, Cook was a strong soloist too but had fewer opportunities since there were usually other trumpet stars on hand. He joined for one final spell in 1968, but left in 1970 and stopped working in music for a while. In the 80s he relocated to Scandinavia and was an honoured guest soloist with numerous groups.
**Duke Ellington,** *Historically Speaking The Duke* (Bethlehem)

## Cool

'Cool' supposedly goes all the way back to the 20s, but as a jazz term it came into its own in the early 50s, when 'The Cool School' came to denote those musicians whose art was characterized by reserve, a certain sleekness, and a lack of overt emoting – the opposite, then, of 'hot' playing. On his live recording *At The Shrine* (1954), Stan Getz was introduced by Duke Ellington as one of 'the leading musicians of the cool school'. This came six years after the Miles Davis nonet sessions of 1948, which were dubbed (in their 1956 LP issue) *The Birth Of The Cool*. In truth, neither Davis nor Getz really fitted the cool archetype, which suggested an almost blasé detachment. The West Coast jazz of the 50s was often seen as the vanguard of cool, but with its apparent glibness much of that music brought the term into disrepute. Subsequently, musicians as remote from each other as Bix Beiderbecke and Jimmy Giuffre, and Paul Bley and Lester Young, have all been branded as cool. Gloving the emotions is, inevitably, part of the make-up of many musicians, cool or otherwise. In the new century, 'cool' has become an inescapable part of youth vocabulary. It scarcely belongs to jazz any more.

## Bob Cooper

TENOR SAXOPHONE, OBOE
*born* 6 December 1925; *died* 5 August 1993

Coop was an archetypal West Coast tenorman. His style was already in place when he joined Stan Kenton in 1945, but a six-year stint helped him polish it further, and he also met and married Kenton's band singer June Christy in 1947. Through the 50s he

enjoyed the life of a busy studio pro and member of the Lighthouse All Stars, leading to the occasional album where he was featured as a jazz oboist, although time hasn't dealt especially kindly with the results (usually pairing him with Bud Shank's flute). He had a smoothly discursive style, very much in the Lester Young lineage, although his big sound gave him more authority than many Lesterians at a fast tempo. He joined in the minor West Coast revival of the late 80s and 90s, touring with the re-formed Lighthouse gang, and he was still working when he suffered a fatal heart attack.
*Coop!* (Contemporary)

# Ray Copeland
TRUMPET
*born* 17 July 1926; *died* 18 May 1984

Copeland's handful of featured album appearances don't afford much for him to be remembered by. He worked in various New York bands in the later 50s but found opportunities scarcer in the following decade. Eventually, his career took up a little more momentum, although he took Latin gigs as well as jazz work and was as likely to be hidden in the Lionel Hampton orchestra as with Art Blakey or – the leader who offered him his most creative opportunities – Randy Weston. He toured Africa with Weston and played with him on and off into the 80s, but in the 70s he was more involved in education and composed orchestral music for occasional big-band concerts. His son Keith (b 1946) is a drummer with wide experience himself.
**Randy Weston, *Little Niles*** (United Artists)

# Marc Copland
PIANO
*born* 27 May 1948

It seems a long way from the Marc Cohen of *Friends* (1972), a rough-and-tumble prototype fusion album where he plays electric saxophone with John Abercrombie, to the musing pianist (now named Copland) of more recent albums. He didn't record much for the rest of the 70s and into the 80s and was somewhat off the scene in Washington until returning to New York in 1985. Since then he has played and recorded regularly

with a variety of players – although Abercrombie remains a favourite partner, and they have often worked as a duo or with like-minded souls such as Kenny Wheeler. His piano style is lushly melodic and contemplative, and while some of his records have been a little too quiet, a recent meeting with Greg Osby on *Round And Round* (2003) shows greater mettle.
*Lunar* (hatOLOGY)

# Corky Corcoran
TENOR SAXOPHONE
*born* 28 July 1924; *died* 3 October 1979

Gene Patrick Corcoran started out in Sonny Dunham's band in 1940, but a year later he joined up with the leader who set the agenda for the rest of his career, Harry James. Although he spent occasional periods away from the fold, he worked in the James ranks for the rest of his professional life. He was one of the small regiment of saxophonists who built on the Coleman Hawkins model and took an agreeable solo every time they were asked to step out of the ranks.
**Harry James, *Record Session*** (Hep)

# Chick Corea
PIANO
*born* 12 June 1941

Corea's now long and busy career is protean and wildly erratic in terms of its appeal. His father played trumpet and bass and gave him early encouragement, and the young man listened spellbound to the music of Horace Silver and Bud Powell. But two tries at music college bored him, and instead he went out to play in the Latin groups of Mongo Santamaria and Willie Bobo, which instilled in him an affection for these rhythms that has lasted through all his work. He spent two years with Blue Mitchell (1964–6) and joined Stan Getz a year later. But it was as a writer that he was starting to get real attention, and the compositions premiered on *Now He Sings, Now He Sobs* (1968) in particular took the fancy of many: catchy melodies, Silveresque funk, but also an interest in free space and diverse structural procedures. He joined Miles Davis in 1968, staying two years and playing mostly electric keyboards in Davis's new environment, but he and Dave Holland left to form the group which became Circle, joined by Barry Altschul and Anthony Braxton. In the end this turned into a quartet that was pulling in several directions, and Corea seemed to lose interest in free playing: he made two charming sets of solo piano for ECM, then formed a new group, Return To Forever, with Joe Farrell, Stanley Clarke and Airto Moreira, which grafted some of that charm on to a mix of light hard bop and Latin feel. But that didn't last long, either, and a new Return To Forever went back to full-on electronic jazz-rock. It was a hit with college-rock audiences (much as Davis and Weather Report were), but Corea also pursued a parallel path with acoustic music, doing duets with Herbie Hancock and Gary Burton, and bringing together various all-star trios and quartets.

The common thread in almost all of this work was Corea's puzzling lack of quality control: powerful or surprising music can sit side by side with hopelessly inconsequential noodling, on the same record, in whichever context. In 1985 he formed the Elektric Band, to some the summit of his electric work and to others – at least via the series of records they made for GRP – ear-numbing tedium. The Akoustic Band became a spin-off of the sort suggested by the title. In the 90s he debuted his newest group, a sextet called Origin, and his own imprint Stretch began releasing both his records and some of those of favoured sidemen: among recent collaborators have been John Patitucci, Kenny Garrett, Bobby McFerrin (on a misguided record called *The Mozart Sessions*, 1996), Steve Wilson, Avishai Cohen and Tim Garland. Corea's conversion to Scientology in 1971 has been a motivating force in his life, but it's hard to say how this has been reflected in his music. His best work as a composer – tunes such as 'Spain', 'Tones For Joan's Bones', 'Crystal Silence', '500 Miles High' – mostly dates from early in his career. His later output often sounds as if it's fallen prey to the meaningless eclecticism which has spoiled so many contemporary musicians, and there is a pixilated quality in his playing which can dismay even the gamest listener. As ever, though, picking the best out of his work does offer fine reward, as painstaking as that process has to be.
*Return To Forever* (ECM)

# Larry Coryell
GUITAR
*born* 2 April 1943

Born in Galveston, Texas, Coryell played high-school rock'n'roll before going to New York in 1965, where he joined Chico Hamilton. A year later he co-founded a group called Free Spirits, which might have some claims on the title of First Fusion Band, but more prominent gigs followed with Gary Burton and Herbie Mann. He started leading his own groups and records in 1969, and *Spaces* (1970), which includes John McLaughlin and Miroslav Vitous, sounds like another dry run for the fusion era: spacier and less frenetic than Mahavishnu, rockier than Davis or Weather Report. But Coryell's Eleventh House group subsequently moved towards the formulaic solos of 'purist' jazz-rock. Surprisingly, Larry went acoustic for most of the rest of the 70s, and though he went back to the electric instrument in the 80s, he kept his hand in in numerous areas: there were transcriptions of Ravel and Gershwin, straight-ahead hard-bop dates, near-ambient music and a thorough examination of Brazilian rhythms. It didn't assist his admirers that he seemed to be on a new record label every month. In 1997, he even reconvened the *Spaces* instrumentation for *Spaces Revisited*, and there was a family band involving his two sons. Throughout all this activity, Coryell's impressive command of his instrument is unstinting and undimmed. Though he is sometimes portrayed as a figure of some anguish, that hardly squares with time spent in his company, which is mostly full of anecdotes and a good deal of laughter. In his 60s, he is something of a great survivor.
*Spaces* (Vanguard)

# Eddie Costa
PIANO, VIBES
*born* 14 August 1930; *died* 28 July 1962

After he came out of the army, Costa quickly found himself in high demand: an excellent reader and a twin threat on both piano and vibes, he took all the studio work he could handle, and he stars on sessions with Tal Farlow, Kai Winding, Coleman Hawkins, Shelly Manne, Herbie Mann, Bob Brookmeyer and many others. His percussive touch was strikingly in evidence on both vibes and piano: he managed bop rhythms in both hands and was outstanding at giving a soloist maximum impetus without quite overpowering them. There are only four albums under his own name (and three of those were on minor labels) and his death in a car accident robbed the music of a talent which was undoubtedly going places.

*Guys And Dolls Like Vibes* (Coral)

## Curtis Counce
BASS
*born* 27 January 1926; *died* 31 July 1963

Who can forget the cover of Counce's great Dooto LP, *Exploring The Future* (1958)? It features the bassist-leader decked out in a space suit, toting his instrument with one arm and beckoning the brave new world of interplanetary travel with the other. He was born in Oklahoma but settled in Los Angeles in the late 40s and played under numerous leaders. He was one of the bassists of choice on the West Coast studio scene all through the 50s and eventually (1956–8) ran a quintet which was one of the smartest Californian groups of its day: the sidemen included Carl Perkins, Jack Sheldon, Harold Land and Frank Butler, and their handful of records distil the cool-to-hot music of their scene beautifully. Sadly, Counce never even got to see a man walk on the moon: he died at 37 of a heart attack.

*Exploring The Future* (Dooto)

## Stanley Cowell
PIANO
*born* 5 May 1941

Born in Toledo, Ohio, Cowell fell under the spell of Art Tatum from an early age (eventually, he went on to play a concerto written in Tatum's honour, in 1992). He went to New York after various studies and played in Max Roach's group for three years from 1967, and he then formed an association with Charles Tolliver, which resulted in a band (Music Inc) and a musician-run label (Strata East), although the subsequent history of that venture was notably ill-fated and caused a good deal of bad blood between musicians. He worked in The Heath Brothers' Band for some ten years until 1983,

and then spent much time in education. In the 90s, he became another in the line of Americans neglected at home but recorded extensively by European labels, when Steeplechase put out a series of solo and group records under his name. His style goes some way to negotiating a truce between standard bebop piano and the open complexities of free playing: while not given to brooding as either soloist or group leader, Cowell has mastered a very thick harmonic knowledge which he delivers generously. That makes his better discs a tough but rewarding listen.

*Angel Eyes* (Steeplechase)

## Lol Coxhill
SOPRANO SAXOPHONE
*born* 19 September 1932

Although he has also played alto and tenor, Lowen Coxhill is primarily master of the soprano horn. In the 50s and 60s he played in groups of every kind – R&B, rock'n'roll, Afro-Cuban, beat, bop and free-playing ensembles – a catholicity which left him with a permanent case of anti-snobbery about musical form. He also liked busking on Hungerford Bridge, and tapes of him playing there are included on *Ear Of The Beholder* (1971), his belated debut as a solo artist, made for John Peel's Dandelion label. During the 70s he steadily increased a considerable reputation as a free player, playing at the first Company week in 1977, recording with pianist Steve Miller on two fondly remembered albums for Virgin's budget-priced Caroline label, and appearing on stage with primal punk group The Damned. Other associations have included The Recedents with Mike Cooper and Roger Turner and The Melody Four with Steve Beresford (a regular duo partner) and Tony Coe. Lol's imaginary radio play *Murder In The Air* was a solo *tour de force*, and he also compered several editions of the Crawley Jazz Festival. With his bald head, granny glasses and resonant singing voice (he especially likes 'Embraceable You'), Coxhill is seen as a bit of a comedian by many, but he is a spirited and superbly resourceful improviser, a skilled exponent of the solo recital in particular, whose beautiful sound on the often intractable soprano is always unmistakeable.

*Divers* (Ogun)

# Bob Cranshaw

BASS
*born* 10 December 1932

Cranshaw is among the most-recorded jazz musicians of modern times. His dad played drums and he learned bass in high school, taking gigs as a teenager in Chicago before a regular gig with pianist Walter Perkins. He went to New York in 1960 and began playing with Sonny Rollins, an association which continued on and off into the 2000s. Thereafter he worked in countless musical situations, as ready to back Johnny Griffin and James Moody as to do the bass work on the TV series *Sesame Street*. When he hurt his neck in a car accident in 1965, Cranshaw switched to bass guitar, and was perhaps the first jazz musician to directly translate the traditional qualities of swinging acoustic bass to the electric instrument: he remained a favourite of the likes of Rollins and Milt Jackson – both suspicious of any hint of fusion crossover – for that reason. Yet he doesn't look down on the simple chores of the pop bassman, which no doubt helped him get through 27 years of *Sesame Street*.
**Sonny Rollins,** *The Bridge* (RCA)

# Hank Crawford

ALTO AND BARITONE SAXOPHONES
*born* 21 December 1934

Crawford is a prolific recording artist, and his rootsy background is unimpeachable. He worked on the Memphis blues circuit with B B King and Bobby Bland before finding a niche in the Ray Charles touring band, join-ing in 1958 and staying five years. There he formed associations with the likes of David Newman which have lasted for decades. His other great partnership has been with organ-ist Jimmy McGriff, the two of them working on a long sequence of albums for Milestone which continue to this day. Creed Taylor pro-duced him in a crossover capacity in the 70s but his real forte was in the bluesy, road-house kind of playing which his later records have whittled down to a fine and somewhat gentrified art.
**Groove Master** (Milestone)

# Wilton Crawley

CLARINET
*born* 18 July 1900; *died* 1 November 1967

Though he hardly contributed much to the clarinet literature, Crawley was surely one of a kind. His playing, as captured on various record dates up until 1930 or so, is unmatched for its variety of squawks, honks, gurgles, slap-tongue effects and other depravities which make even Ted Lewis and Boyd Senter seem tame. He toured all over America (and, amazingly, even played in England in 1930), and was an impressive con-tortionist as well as a clarinet tooter. One account has him standing on his head, pro-pelling himself backwards with one hand and playing clarinet with the other. His com-panions on record include, incredibly, Henry Allen, Jelly Roll Morton and Eddie Lang, and something like 'New Crawley Blues' (1930) is an unrepeatable mix of clarinet madness and genuine jazz playing. He disappeared after the 30s and nobody seems to know where he went.
**Various,** *Jazz Of The 20s, Hot And Rare* (Verve)

# Marilyn Crispell

PIANO
*born* 30 March 1947

A late starter in jazz, Crispell studied piano in Boston but left music alone for a spell before being inspired by the work of McCoy Tyner in Coltrane's groups. She went to the Creative Music Studio in Woodstock and was heard there by Anthony Braxton in 1978; he asked her to join his Creative Music Orchestra, and she subsequently became the pianist in one of Braxton's most renowned quartets, from 1983. This brought her atten-tion and the possibilities of a wide circle of work: with Reggie Workman, Billy Bang, Joseph Jarman, Gerry Hemingway, and in her own groups and as a soloist. She has been recorded on a regular basis, and it's possible to follow her development in an unusual amount of close-up. With Braxton and in her earlier music she seemed entirely in thrall to a Europeanized form of free play-ing, atonal, thickly voiced and rather dry of melody; Cecil Taylor was one inevitable (and largely inappropriate) point of comparison. Latterly, though, she has seemed to settle increasingly into a niche where she can mix that style with a more obviously jazz-based repertoire, suggesting lines that go back to Monk and others. Her discography is by now rather bewilderingly large, but her later records for ECM – while they may disenchant some who prefer the more toughly cadenced strains of her earlier playing – find a very pleasing ground which retains space for lush melodizing.

**Nothing Ever Was, Anyway** (ECM)

## Sonny Criss
ALTO SAXOPHONE
*born* 23 October 1927; *died* 19 November 1977

Born in Memphis, Criss was a West Coaster for most of his career. He worked in bop and R&B small groups before making some records of his own as a leader: three 1956 records for Imperial show a stylist who seems a little uncertain whether he's coming out of bebop or swing, but the music's exciting all the same. His later work took him to Europe on occasion and he made a sequence of albums for Prestige in the later 60s which have long been collectors' favourites: *Portrait Of Sonny Criss* (1967) and *Sonny's Dream* (1968) are especially fine, his playing marked by a gripping fluency which seems to get stronger with every release. But he never found much of an audience: he spent much time in the 60s working with young offenders, and in 1977, afflicted with stomach cancer and with a career in the doldrums, he took his own life.

**Sonny's Dream** (Prestige)

## Criss Cross Jazz
RECORD COMPANY

Gerry Teekens, a Dutch schoolteacher and jazz lover, began arranging tours for some of his favourite American musicians in the 70s: Warne Marsh, Jimmy Raney and others. In 1981, he began taking the opportunity to record some of them, and since then his label, Criss Cross, has grown into a formidable focal point for much of the best new jazz being recorded on the American East Coast. Teekens, who retired from his other work in 1991, began making regular recording trips to New York, block-booking studios for a week and setting down as many albums' worth of music as he could in

the time. Having started with established players, he increasingly sought out less familiar names, and can be credited for introducing the likes of Ralph Moore, Benny Green, Don Braden, Chris Potter, Walt Weiskopf, Mark Turner and the groups One For All and Tenor Triangle to international audiences. Teekens makes no bones about the fact that he records only the kind of jazz which appeals to him and to hell with commercial aspirations; in consequence, he has created what is probably the most uncompromised and qualitatively excellent archive of new, acoustic American jazz from the last two decades, a worthy successor to the 'old' Blue Note.

## Tony Crombie
DRUMS
*born* 27 August 1925; *died* 18 October 1999

Crombie was a Londoner who came up in the later years of the dance band era, although he was doing small-group work in the clubs from the early 40s onwards. A regular at Club Eleven and a favourite partner of Ronnie Scott's, he went on to be a contracted player in the Decca studios during the 50s and, with an eye for the way the wind was blowing, had an early crack at rock'n'roll with his band The Rockets (their ten-inch LP *Rockin' With Tony Crombie & The Rockets* is a famously sought-after collector's piece). But he went back to jazz, with his own band Jazz Inc and a stint at the Scott club when he backed many of the visitors. He began writing film and TV music (Miles Davis covered his 'So Near So Far', latterly the title of Joe Henderson's homage to Davis) and he worked in various British groups, although he still liked backing Scott whenever he had the chance. Georgie Fame was another high-profile employer, but Crombie was happy to work with good players of numerous kinds.

**Drums! Drums! Drums!** (Top Rank)

## Bob Crosby
VOCAL, BANDLEADER
*born* 25 August 1913; *died* 9 March 1993

Bing's brother, almost ten years younger than the crooner, sang with dance bands such as Anson Weeks's before he was appointed as a figurehead leader of a cooperative New York band made up partly of players from the disbanded Ben Pollack Orchestra in 1935. What was exceptional about Crosby's orchestra was its commitment to jazz at a time when most of the swing-era big bands were really little more than dance orchestras in disguise. Packed with Dixieland-directed soloists such as Yank Lawson, Irving Fazola and Eddie Miller, and with a great rhythm section in Bob Haggart and Ray Bauduc, the Crosby band – as well as its small-group spin-off, The Bob Cats – stuffed more hot music into its sets than most, as the collections of airshots on *1937–40 Broadcasts* (Soundcraft) suggest. Latterly, the studio sessions rather fell away as the standard of material declined, and the band broke up in 1942. Crosby himself was an amiable singer, a small-scale Bing, and he subsequently presided over reunions of the band or acted as an MC. He was still doing this kind of thing in the 90s.

**You Can Call It Swing** (Halcyon)

## Gary Crosby

BASS
*born* 26 January 1955

Crosby is a strong bassist who was in the thick of the new London jazz of the 80s, powering the rhythm section of the Jazz Warriors and working behind Courtney Pine, Steve Williamson and others. But it is as a bandleader, educator and organizing force that he has made his greatest contribution. His group Jazz Jamaica has pursued the synthesis which its name suggests and is a popular festival attraction, epitomizing the Caribbean influence which Crosby thinks has already been integrated into the vernacular of black British players – 'the Caribbean sound is so similar to that New Orleans vibe'. He established Tomorrow's Warriors in the early 90s as a collective training ground for younger players, and co-founded Dune as a vehicle for putting out records by such musicians. A thoughtful, enthusiastic man with a can-do attitude, Crosby is a very valuable asset to the British scene.

**Jazz Jamaica, *Massive*** (Dune)

## Israel Crosby

BASS
*born* 19 January 1919; *died* 11 August 1962

Crosby was a Chicagoan who spent much of his life working on the city's musical scene. He took up the bass at 15 and within a year was working with Jess Stacy and Teddy Wilson. His work on Gene Krupa's 'Blues Of Israel', made when he was barely 16, shows how gifted and advanced he already was. He worked with Horace Henderson and other leaders and was a regular studio sideman, but it wasn't until 1954, when he joined the Ahmad Jamal trio, that he spent a long time with one leader. He had just joined George Shearing's group when he died suddenly of a heart attack. A close contemporary of Jimmy Blanton, Crosby is less recognized as a pioneer, but his most prominent performances on his better record dates show how easily and fluently he displayed a modern approach to the instrument.

**Ahmad Jamal, *At The Pershing*** (Chess)

## Connie Crothers

PIANO
*born* 2 May 1941

Born in Palo Alto, California, Crothers studied classical piano and composition but took a greater interest in jazz and moved to New York in 1962. She had 12 years of sometimes intermittent study with Lennie Tristano, and since then has become one of the principal exponents of the Tristano-ite style. Her quartet with Lenny Popkin is perhaps the closest thing there is to a modern equivalent of the Konitz–Tristano partnership. If her style of delivery is bound up in her mentor's approach, though, Crothers has imposed much of herself on the idiom: the music is rather warmer, less brittle, and while the coolly complex layers of musical dialogue are familiar in terms of procedure, she and Popkin have characterized it themselves. They founded a label called New Artists to issue this and similar work.

**Jazz Spring** (New Artists)

# Stanley Crouch
DRUMS, WORDS
*born* 14 December 1945

Crouch grew up in Los Angeles and as a
drummer was soon associated with such
local young spirits as Arthur Blythe and
David Murray. In the mid-70s he moved to
New York, began writing about the music,
and took up performance poetry. As a
musician and thinker he was completely
involved in the avant-garde, claiming Albert
Ayler as a primary influence on his drumming. But he completely changed tack in the
80s, all but renouncing free jazz, and becoming sleevenote-writer-in-chief to Wynton
Marsalis, to whom he seemed to become a
mentor. Crouch has often found himself in
hot water, being sacked from more than one
magazine as a contributor, and using his
various platforms for discussions of racism
in jazz and jazz appreciation. The pity is that
he has apparently never finished his biography of Charlie Parker, which took up much
of his time in the 80s: those who have seen
completed chapters have called it very fine.

# Bill Crow
BASS
*born* 27 December 1927

Crow studied drums in an army band but
when he arrived in New York in 1950 he
decided to switch to bass. He played under
numerous leaders during the 50s and
60s: the two most notable were Marian
McPartland (Crow was a regular in her
Hickory House trio) and Gerry Mulligan,
whom he joined in 1955 and stayed with on
and off for the next ten years, working in
both small groups and Mulligan's Concert
Jazz Band. Thereafter he could be seen at
Eddie Condon's as well as doing society-
band gigs and working in theatre orchestras,
which kept him busy into the 90s. Latterly,
though, he has become most well known for
his collection *Jazz Anecdotes*: Crow is a good
storyteller and there is a lot of hilarity as
well as some sadness in this book. He has
also written an autobiography.
**Gerry Mulligan, *What Is There To Say?*** (Columbia)

# Crusaders
GROUP

Founded by Joe Sample (piano), Wilton
Felder (sax) and Stix Hooper (drums), the
group was first called The Swingsters, but
grew to be the Modern Jazz Sextet with the
addition of Hubert Laws (flute), Wayne
Henderson (trombone) and Henry Wilson
(bass). They spent their early years in
Houston, but when four of them moved to
California (Laws and Wilson chose not to)
they eventually became The Jazz Crusaders.
Signed to Richard Bock's Pacific Jazz in 1961,
they began making albums and eventually
built up a large catalogue for the label,
including several live albums recorded at
The Lighthouse. One distinctive element of
their sound was the unison melodies played
on trombone and tenor saxophone, a faintly
lugubrious sound which sounded soulful
enough to lend the band a place in the growing soul-jazz movement. By the end of the
60s they were engaged in studio session-
work as well as their own music. When Larry
Carlton joined on guitar and Sample added
electric keyboards they really began clicking
with crossover audiences, and a new contract with Blue Thumb/ABC resulted in a
series of outstanding albums, with hit tracks
such as 'Put It Where You Want It' among
the material. Max Bennett or Pops Popwell
handled bass chores in live work, but Felder
often saw to it that he played the bass parts
on the records himself. Their 1979 hit 'Street
Life' finally brought them to a pop audience
but they never duplicated that success.
Sample and Felder had solo successes but
relations between the two grew strained and
the group foundered in 1988, although
Felder and Henderson subsequently toured
and made records as a new Crusaders: these
were, however, a shadow of what had been a
terrific band, the other side of the fusion
coin to Weather Report and a naturally progressive group that left a huge legacy of
approaching 100 records.
***Chain Reaction*** (Blue Thumb/ABC)

# CTI
RECORD COMPANY

The initials stand for Creed Taylor
Incorporated, and if ever a record label was
conceived for one man's vision, it was CTI.

Taylor began using it while heading up A&M's jazz division in 1967, and it continued as an independent label when he left in 1969. From the start, Taylor pursued a policy of easy-listening jazz, apparently convinced that it was possible to make records which had plenty of musical meat in them without switching off audiences that didn't want to work at their listening. He made albums by Freddie Hubbard, Milt Jackson, Stanley Turrentine, George Benson and others, and packaged them in arty sleeves which disguised the jazz content. While there were occasional discs which mixed artistic worth with popular appeal (Hubbard's *Red Clay* is one example), most of them are among the worst recordings by the musicians in question. A few second-division talents such as Bob James and Hubert Laws fared better, but in the end the label failed anyway and Taylor filed for bankruptcy in 1978. Columbia won control of the catalogue and they have lately repackaged much of it in new CD editions, in a pathetic attempt to reposition what was a folly from the start.

## Ronnie Cuber
BARITONE SAXOPHONE
*born* 25 December 1941

Already making records at 16 (two albums with the Newport Youth Band – which also featured Eddie Gomez and Michael Abene), Cuber has hardly stopped since. He is the first-choice baritone man in New York session circles, and this Brooklynite has been a force of nature in several big bands, including those of Maynard Ferguson, Woody Herman and Lionel Hampton. He has run what amounts to a parallel career in Latin music, starting with Eddie Palmieri in the early 70s – Cuber likes the explosiveness of Afro-Latin music and he fits right in. He also turns up on numerous expensively budgeted rock records for high-end leaders such as Paul Simon and Steely Dan. Such a prolific output might suggest a facile but faceless technician, yet Cuber remains a short-fuse player who can bring spontaneous excitement to just about any situation. Unsurprisingly, he has had little time to do much as a leader. He picks up tenor and alto on a few recordings, but he's a baritone man at heart.
*The Scene Is Clean* (Milestone)

## Jamie Cullum
VOCAL, PIANO
*born* 20 August 1979

Cullum played in bars and with local pop bands in his teens before studying drama at college and then putting out a self-made CD. He was signed to the British independent Candid but in 2003 was poached by Universal and has since enjoyed a huge crossover success with his debut for the major, *Twentysomething*. Though he sings standards in an oddly gruff midatlantic baritone and plays clattery piano, Cullum is a born showman and a perfectly likely pop idol: while he likes to talk a lot about jazz in interviews, and a few hysterical media pieces have hailed him as the avatar of a new wave of British jazz, he is clearly being marketed as someone who belongs in the pop charts.
*Pointless Nostalgic* (Candid)

## Jim Cullum
CORNET
*born* 20 September 1941

Jim Cullum's Happy Jazz was actually founded by Cullum Senior, a part-time clarinet player, but the younger Jim has built it into a superior traditional-repertory outfit. Based in San Antonio, Texas, Cullum and his men operate at some distance from much of the rest of this style of playing, which these days is strongest on the West Coast of the US, but with a regular base at the Landing Hotel, a record label and a full diary of work, Cullum has carpentered a decent following. His own playing is an energetic take on the familiar revivalist models.
*Super Satch* (Stomp Off)

## Ted Curson
TRUMPET
*born* 3 June 1935

Curson grew up in Philadelphia, where he was a neighbour to the Heath brothers, and in 1956 he went to New York. Little happened for him there until he joined Charles Mingus in 1959: he is excellent on *Charles Mingus Presents Charles Mingus* (1960), a fine foil for Eric Dolphy. In 1962 he left to form a group with Bill Barron, but the group found little in the way of work and he moved to fresh fields in 1965, basing himself in Denmark and appearing regularly in European festivals. He returned to New York in 1976 but retained his European ties, while running jam sessions at the Blue Note in Manhattan, an open house which young players flocked to. Curson has maintained a keen interest in jazz education and he is not shy about passing on his wisdom; it's a pity that his own eloquent playing, in a conservatively free idiom, has never found a truly outstanding documentation on record.

**Tears For Dolphy** (Fontana)

## King Curtis
TENOR SAXOPHONE
*born* 7 February 1934; *died* 14 August 1971

Curtis Ousley grew up in Fort Worth, Texas (and played alongside Ornette Coleman at high school), but went to New York in the middle 50s after touring with Lionel Hampton. There he began playing on rock'n'roll records, sharing with Gil Berne the saxophone solos on sessions by The Coasters, and with his own group he became a hit attraction at the Harlem Apollo. His knack for fitting an appropriate fill on to an R&B record led him into production, and he had hit records of his own – 'Memphis Soul Stew' and the like. As if wary of leaving jazz behind altogether, he cut a handful of straight-ahead sessions too. Life was good and busy for him all through the 60s, in an era before pop saxophone meant Kenny G, but he met an unhappy end when stabbed by a mugger outside his home in New York in 1971.

**Greatest Hits** (Atlantic)

## Michael Cuscuna
PRODUCER, SCHOLAR
*born* 20 September 1948

Cuscuna was a jazz nut who sidled his way into the business when most men his age were much more interested in rock'n'roll. He was writing articles about jazz while still in college and in 1972 he began producing albums for Atlantic. In 1975, a chance conversation with the Blue Note executive Charlie Lourie led him to begin excavating the Blue Note tape library, and he reissued and

brought to light for the first time many of the label's classic sessions. Subsequently he did much the same at Impulse!, as well as producing new music for Arista (including a huge tranche of Anthony Braxton records) and Columbia. In 1982, he and Lourie founded Mosaic, a specialist reissue company which releases deluxe limited editions of vintage jazz material drawn from many different eras of the music. He also assisted in Bruce Lundvall's revitalization of Blue Note as an ongoing label when helping to organize the celebratory concerts of 1985 in New York and Japan, and he continues to act as a creative consultant in reissuing material for Blue Note and other labels. Cuscuna has set unrivalled standards in this field and he was a major force in disseminating awareness of post-war jazz as an important living tradition at a time when rock had all but annexed priorities at American record companies.

## Cutty Cutshall
TROMBONE
*born* 29 December 1911; *died* 16 August 1968

His first name was Robert, but everybody knew him as 'Cutty'. A smart and reliable bone man, he worked in Jan Savitt's dance band before joining Benny Goodman in 1940, forming a great two-man section with Lou McGarity. After the war he drifted into the Eddie Condon circle, which basically sustained him for the rest of his career: although he occasionally worked with other leaders, he stuck with Condon, and he died from a heart attack while working with the Condon group in Toronto. McGarity also remained a close friend and associate, and the two of them were still playing duets in the line-up which became (after Cutty's death) The World's Greatest Jazz Band.

**Eddie Condon, *That Toddlin' Town*** (Warner Bros)

## Cutting contest

A competition between two players on the same instrument, each trying to best the other (usually at a jam session) and affirm their superiority. The winner metaphorically 'cuts' the loser, a relevant comparison in a time when many musicians carried knives as a matter of routine. These events most likely emerged out of such rivalries as those which grew up between the Harlem stride pianists in the teens and 20s, but by the 30s they were more likely to be between horn players (the rhythm men would have to accompany all comers). Coleman Hawkins was famously bested at an all-night session involving Lester Young in Kansas in 1933, and his friend Roy Eldridge would often go out looking for such contests, keen to prove his combative edge over any pretender. Such events honed instrumental skills to a formidable edge, and paved the way for the new virtuosities of bop.

## Leo Cuypers
PIANO
*born* 1 December 1947

Cuypers studied piano at Maastricht conservatory and on meeting Willem Breuker in 1969 joined in with the Dutch improvisation movement and the ICP, eventually joining Breuker's Kollektief in 1973. He brought a lot of creative energy and compositional input to the group but left in 1980 to lead his own groups. Since then he has enjoyed rather less exposure outside Holland and periods of poor health haven't helped. He has, though, asserted himself more regularly as a soloist, and the author finds the recital cited below a particularly haunting meditation on many aspects of 20th-century piano, jazz and otherwise.
*Songbook* (BVhaast)

## Andrew Cyrille
DRUMS
*born* 10 November 1939

Cyrille's most prominent association was with Cecil Taylor, and that is arguably still his benchmark work. He took all kinds of gigs in New York in the early 60s – Nellie Lutcher, Illinois Jacquet, Roland Kirk – but he joined Taylor's trio in 1965 and worked with him for the next ten years. In 1975 he formed his own group, Maono, which included Ted Daniel and David S Ware, but he has had relatively little impact as a leader and since then he has worked on a more ad hoc basis with a wide spread of other players. With Taylor, Cyrille demonstrated –

like Sunny Murray before him – a style based around tremendous propulsion without using excessive force or volume. Although the idea of drummers being 'melodic' seems like a contradictory description, Cyrille's approach to the kit has a measured quality which seems to consider each drum and cymbal as a melodious object. He has often worked in all-percussion ensembles and has much experience as an accompanist to dancers. As a recording artist, he could perhaps benefit from sympathetic time and resources to document some of his more ambitious ideas.
**Cecil Taylor,** *Conquistador* (Blue Note)

## Tony Dagradi
TENOR AND SOPRANO SAXOPHONES
*born* 22 September 1952

Until the Marsalis brothers emerged, it seemed that Dagradi was spearheading a new wave of New Orleans jazz, although he is actually from New York and worked both there and in Boston before going to the Crescent City in 1977. His circle of associates – David Torkanowsky, Steve Masakowski and Johnny Vidacovich – have worked with him on and off since then, and he has also founded a New Orleans Saxophone Ensemble. Dagradi hasn't been too lucky with recording, though: his big sound and swaggering delivery show how easily he's settled into a New Orleans style, but his relatively few records haven't achieved much in the way of general currency.
**Images From The Floating World** (Core)

## Nils-Bertil (Bert) Dahlander
DRUMS
*born* 13 May 1928

Bert Dahlander is a veteran of Swedish modern jazz. He was playing with the likes of Lars Gullin as far back as 1950, and has been leading his own groups since 1952. He spent two periods in America in the 50s and kept up his associations there, working with Teddy Wilson and others, although he has only ever made a handful of records under his own nominal leadership. A mainstream player of benign outlook, he established his own label (Everyday) in the CD era and has belatedly made a series of enjoyable dates on local turf.

*Lady Be Good* (Everyday)

## Albert Dailey

PIANO
*born* 16 June 1938; *died* 26 June 1984

Born in Baltimore, Al Dailey had a workman-like career which veiled a gifted and singular pianist. He worked in some distinguished company over many years – Art Blakey's Jazz Messengers, Sonny Rollins, Milt Jackson and, in his own band of the early 80s, the young Joe Lovano. He was a fine accompanist and Stan Getz especially liked his playing – despite his saying to Getz, 'I never liked saxophone players.' Their duo record *Poetry* (1983), made only a year before Dailey's early death, is a neglected beauty.

*Poetry* (Elektra Musician)

## Dave Dallwitz

PIANO, ARRANGER
*born* 25 October 1914

Dallwitz is an eminence in the somewhat undiscovered field of Australian Dixieland. He bossed the Southern Jazz Group, from Adelaide, from the late 40s until 1961, but then went into composition and light music, not making a jazz comeback until 1972. He then led a variety of bands, including one dedicated to playing ragtime material, the Euphonic Sounds Ensemble. As a composer, perhaps his finest hour came when Earl Hines recorded an entire album of Dallwitz compositions, *Piano Portraits Of Australia* (1974) – which was surely the only time that Fatha performed tunes with titles such as 'Waukaringa Memories'.

*Nostalgia* (Stomp Off)

## Meredith D'Ambrosio

VOCAL
*born* 28 March 1941

D'Ambrosio was born in Boston, where both of her parents were working musicians, but she worked in other occupations before trying out as a singer in the 70s. She began

recording in 1978 and made a long sequence of records for the Sunnyside label; she married the pianist Eddie Higgins in 1988. She is a close-up singer with a careful microphone technique, and the best of D'Ambrosio's records have a quietly grown-up feel which can be persuasively affecting. One technique she likes is to medley a standard with a jazz theme to which she has appended new lyrics.

*South To A Warmer Place* (Sunnyside)

## Tadd Dameron

PIANO
*born* 21 February 1917; *died* 8 March 1965

Dameron's great gifts are hard to evaluate because so much of his career was wasted and his great moments were squeezed into a tiny time-frame. He had an undistinguished career as pianist and arranger before scoring charts for Harlan Leonard, Jimmie Lunceford and Count Basie (who disliked what he was presented with). By the mid-40s he was starting to follow the nascent bebop movement and he wrote for Billy Eckstine and Dizzy Gillespie before recording as a leader himself in 1947. This was his peak period: he had a residency at the Royal Roost, with Fats Navarro in the band, in 1948, and by the following year was leading a ten-piece group with Miles Davis, with whom he went to Europe. But by the time of his return, bop had begun to change, and though he led other groups, a drug problem began to interfere with his professional work. He made two albums for Prestige in 1956 (one with John Coltrane), but he was abruptly imprisoned for drug offences and his career never really recovered. On his release, he did some arranging duties and made one last record, the disappointing *The Magic Touch*, in 1962, but his time was gone, and he died from cancer three years later. Dameron's great music belongs to the bebop era: 'Good Bait', 'Hot House', 'Lady Bird', 'Our Delight', every one a bop anthem, yet couched in terms which are as much derived from swing-era practice – rhythmically, at least – as bebop harmony. Fats Navarro was his great interpreter, and he never found another on the same level. The title track of his 1956 date *Fontainebleau* is a fully scored piece of impressionism which sits as a one-off in his work. In the 90s his work was being rediscovered and enshrined as part of the modern repertory. What would Tadd have thought?

**Fats Navarro Featured With The Tadd Dameron Band** (Prestige)

# Stanley Dance
WRITER, PRODUCER
*born* 15 September 1919; *died* 23 February 1999

Although he was born in Braintree, Essex, Dance became an American by proxy: he was writing about jazz from 1935, and by the 50s was one of its most prolific commentators. He eventually moved to Connnecticut in 1959, having already visited the US many times, and he latterly lived in California. Dance was one of the great champions of Duke Ellington's music, and he subsequently worked almost as a Boswell to Ellington and his entourage, assisting on numerous recordings and working on many biographical writings. In the 50s he became a self-proclaimed guardian of swing-era values and he found post-bop jazz distasteful. Malign or not, his influence endures, particularly in England.

# Dance band

Dance orchestras came into being in the teens of the 20th century. Liberated by the syncopated rhythms of ragtime, the salon orchestra of the Edwardian era gave way, on British bandstands, to a livelier agenda, which revolved around the fox-trot, the most popular dance step of the inter-war years (although they would still play waltzes and quadrilles). American bands had got there first, and their 'dance bands' of a similar era had more jazz in them: but even at the height of the swing era, the most popular of the big bands were playing for dancers as much as for listeners. 'Dance Band', though, remains an archaic term, which suggests an ensemble yet to be ignited by swing.

# Franco D'Andrea
PIANO
*born* 8 March 1941

D'Andrea didn't start on piano until he was 17, having already tried several other instruments. He worked in both the Milanese and Roman jazz communities in the 60s, with such diverse figures as Gato Barbieri, Franco Ambrosetti and Enrico Rava, and formed the Modern Art Trio in 1968. Trio work has been his real speciality over the years, although he has also been a member of Rava's small groups and in the 70s spent several years playing keyboards in a jazz-rock group, Perigeo. In the 80s and 90s he really came into his own as a mature force, one of the Italian players best known to the wider jazz community, forging alliances with the likes of Lee Konitz and Phil Woods. He has been extensively recorded by both Red and Philology, and Paolo Piangiarelli of the latter label took the audacious step of recording ten solo CDs of D'Andrea over the space of a few days in the studio. He is a strong player in both hands, often sounding like a modern descendant of Lennie Tristano, although he takes material from all over the jazz spectrum and masters it in his own thoughtful way.

**Airegin** (Red)

# Putney Dandridge
VOCAL, PIANO
*born* 13 January 1902; *died* 15 February 1946

Dandridge worked in vaudeville from the teens of the century and was in New York by 1934. His great hour came in a series of recording sessions for Vocalion in 1935–6, where his pleasant tenor voice was accompanied by some remarkable line-ups, including Henry Allen, Bobby Stark, Joe Marsala, Teddy Wilson, Buster Bailey, Roy Eldridge, Chu Berry and others. After his final session in December 1936 he disappeared from the music, but the sessions have rarely been out of print and are still available on CD.

**Putney Dandridge 1936** (Classics)

# Eddie Daniels
CLARINET, TENOR SAXOPHONE
*born* 19 October 1941

After various musical-academic studies, Daniels was at Juilliard when he became a founding member of the Jones–Lewis Big Band and cut an album for Prestige, *First Prize!*, in 1966. At this point he was playing as much tenor as clarinet, but he didn't take Tony Scott's advice ('Stick to the tenor, son')

and in the 70s and 80s became one of the few specialists on clarinet in modern-mainstream circles, abandoning tenor altogether in 1986 (although he subsequently went back to it). A series of records for GRP in the 80s and early 90s showed off a prodigious technique; the trouble was, the discs were unspeakably dull. Daniels remains a proficient musician but he has slipped into the margins somewhat.
*This Is Now* (GRP)

## Lars Danielsson
BASS
*born 5 September 1958*

Danielsson came to prominence on the Swedish scene of the 80s, following in the footsteps of his teacher, Anders Jormin. He led groups with such international guests as Dave Liebman and John Abercrombie, as well as doing a voluminous amount of sideman work and, latterly, producing other artists. Two records for Dragon, *New Hands* (1985) and *Poems* (1991), remain exemplary documents of the new European jazz of that time. Subsequently, though, Danielsson's interest in faddish sorts of fusion has been dangerous; a new record for ACT in 2004 was a near disaster.
*Poems* (Dragon)

## Palle Danielsson
BASS
*born 15 October 1946*

Danielsson is from Stockholm, where he studied in the early 60s, and one of his regular early gigs was in the Steve Kuhn trio with Jon Christensen, who has been a regular partner ever since. He co-formed Rena Rama with Bobo Stenson in 1971, and was in both the Garbarek–Stenson quartet and Keith Jarrett's 'European' quartet in the 70s. Although he has evinced few leadership ambitions of his own – a group called Contra Post, which made a single album in 1994, is about it in that regard – Danielsson has been a powerful character in almost every band he's been in, and he counts as one of Europe's few 'stars' on his instrument.
**Jan Garbarek–Bobo Stenson, *Witchi-Tai-To*** (ECM)

## Danish Radio Big Band/ Jazz Orchestra
GROUP

It was first formed in 1964 and over 40 years of almost continuous activity has become an institution among the world's jazz orchestras. Sponsored by an enlightened radio authority, it has always used the better Danish players as well as making room for an occasional distinguished visitor from overseas. Directors over the years make up quite a roll-call by themselves: Ib Glindemann (the first), Thad Jones, Jim McNeely, Palle Mikkelborg and Bob Brookmeyer have been some of those involved. One of their finest hours was backing Miles Davis on his *Aura* record, which was scored by Mikkelborg. It has latterly changed from 'Big Band' to 'Jazz Orchestra'.
*Crackdown* (Hep)

## Harold Danko
PIANO
*born 13 June 1947*

Danko was born in Sharon, Philadelphia; his brothers both played saxophone and he became proficient at the piano. In the 70s he was in big bands (Herman, Jones–Lewis) and small groups (Chet Baker, Lee Konitz), but latterly he has spent much time in education, as well as leading his own small group, often with Rich Perry as the saxophone voice. The glib summary would be that Danko's professorial music suits his occupation, but he is a subtle thinker whose knowledge of harmony has marked his music as absorbing if short on fireworks. Nils Winther of Steeplechase clearly likes him a lot, as he's recorded prolifically for that label.
*Tidal Breeze* (Steeplechase)

## John Dankworth
ALTO AND SOPRANO SAXOPHONES, CLARINET
*born 20 September 1927*

Although he began as a clarinettist in what were the first stirrings of British trad jazz, Dankworth was quickly won over by bebop, and in the late 40s he began working on liners (along with such contemporaries as Ronnie Scott) in order to hear the genuine article. He co-founded London's Club Eleven, the capital's first home of modern jazz, and put a seven-piece group together to play bop tunes and his own material. By 1953 it had turned into a big band; five years later, he married the band's singer, Cleo Laine. The Dankworth Orchestra lasted until 1964, had two hit singles ('Experiments With Mice' still raises a smile), and was (along with Ted Heath's band) one of the few vehicles which took British musicians to America. By the 60s Dankworth was in demand for film and television scores (he wrote the original – though less famous – themes for both *Danger Man* and *The Avengers*), and with Cleo's career also in the ascendant the couple became the leading Mr and Mrs of British jazz. John's orchestral recordings have been insufficiently reissued in the CD era: the likes of *What The Dickens!* (1963), *Zodiac Suite* (1964) and *The $1,000,000 Collection* (1969), the last-named including some ambitious writing in the 12-tone idiom, helped create the British taste for jazz suites (perhaps a dubious advance), and they should be far better known than they are to contemporary audiences. In the 70s, with Cleo's career taking an increasingly middle-of-the-road course, Dankworth cut back on his jazz work, busy as her MD; but since then he has played regularly with a quintet, and has a Dankworth Generation Big Band with his son Alec (b 1960), a gifted bassist. Besides this, he established a music centre at his home in Wavendon, which holds concerts and runs courses and masterclasses. Friends of royalty and the great and good, the Dankworths retain a large following in America and spend much of their year there. John's own playing has moved some way on from his original Parker influence: he has inveigled a notably British outlook into his delivery, which sometimes suggests Noël Coward tackling 'Ornithology'.

**The Best Of John Dankworth** (Redial)

## James Dapogny
PIANO
*born* 3 September 1940

Dapogny is a teacher and scholar who has nevertheless made some entertaining jazz himself. His principal work is the study of Jelly Roll Morton's music, and he has compiled a set of transcriptions of Morton's most important solos. He teaches in Michigan but also plays piano, in his own Chicago Jazz Band, and their CD in dedication to Morton, *Original Jelly Roll Blues*, is an outstanding example of jazz repertory, Dapogny orchestrating seven pieces which the Red Hot Peppers themselves never recorded. Besides Morton, he plays other early repertory, and one can only hope that his work in reconstructing the James P Johnson opera *De Organizer* is actually recorded some day.

**Original Jelly Roll Blues** (Discovery)

## Olu Dara
CORNET, GUITAR, VOCAL
*born* 12 January 1941

Dara has reinvented himself in an extraordinary way. A late starter, he joined Art Blakey's Jazz Messengers in 1971 and then went on to become a significant force on New York's loft scene: he is on several of the major records of the era, but always as a sideman (with David Murray on *Flowers For Albert*, 1976, for instance). While he did some work with Henry Threadgill in the 80s, he then seemed to disappear, until reappearing in the mid-90s with a couple of cameo appearances. Then he made records for Atlantic as a kind of one-man show of black popular music: singing, playing guitar and harmonica, and (in performance) dancing, all skills he learned during his Louisville boyhood in the 40s and 50s. Sourced out of blues, soul and Afro-Caribbean strains, the music has some kinship with Taj Mahal's explorations, although it is less self-consciously 'rural'. While this is all very interesting, it might be regretted that such a fine cornet player as Dara no longer plays in the kind of contexts where he made such an impact 20-something years earlier.

**In The World: From Natchez To New York** (Atlantic)

## Carlo Actis Dato
REEDS
*born* 21 March 1952

A reedsman who plays most of the family, from bass sax to soprano, Dato was busy in the early 70s on the Turin scene, where he co-founded the pioneering Art Studio quar-

tet. In the 80s he settled into various other associations but it's as leader of his own quartet (Piero Ponzo on reeds, Enrico Fazio bass and Fiorenzo Sordini drums) that he has been most busy. The group plays helter-skelter music which borrows from a world of rhythm – anywhere is fair game, although Dato seems to have a particular penchant for North African beats from Tunisia and the like – and creates an entertaining jostle of free playing with the more particular demands of the pulse. He is also in The Atipico Trio and has made a couple of suitably rambunctious all-solo records.
*Delhi Mambo* (YVP)

## Wolfgang Dauner
PIANO, ELECTRONICS
*born* 30 December 1935

Dauner's music has seldom travelled much beyond his German base, but he can claim a fair amount of pioneer work. His trio with Eberhard Weber and Fred Braceful made an album in 1964, *Dream Talk* (for German CBS – and never reissued) which showcased some of the first free playing in a European studio. Later records such as *Free Action* (1967) and *Output* (1970), both of which remain in vinyl limbo, could also stand a revival. Dauner spent much time in commercial work for film and advertisements but went on to found a jazz-rock group (Et Cetera), the Free Sound & Super Brass Big Band, and eventually the long-running United Jazz And Rock Ensemble, which features many veterans of the European free and jazz-rock scenes. Dauner got stuck into art music and *musique concrète* early on, and he has done a lot of composing with synthesizers; but his acoustic piano work remains a very particular mix of freedom, form, lyricism and a sometimes oddball humour, with a dash of Euro-kitsch thrown in. Much of his output eventually appeared on the Mood label, which he co-founded.
*Get Up And Dauner* (MPS)

## Kenny Davern
CLARINET, SOPRANO SAXOPHONE
*born* 7 January 1935

Born in Huntington, NY, Davern was doing gigs while still in high school, and he joined Jack Teagarden before he was 20, having started out on the much more difficult Albert system (he later switched to the Boehm, which has easier fingerings). He then spent the rest of the 50s in the company of such elders as Henry Allen and Pee Wee Erwin ('The problem with younger players is they never had the opportunity to stand next to Coleman Hawkins and Red Allen, the *schtarkers* – they don't know the volume of air those guys put through'), and joined The Dukes Of Dixieland in 1963, although in between he also led groups of his own. A turning point came when he formed Soprano Summit with Bob Wilber in 1974: it lasted five years, but has been occasionally revived (as Soprano Reunion), and its two-horn front line became a favourite with mainstream audiences everywhere. Since then he has worked largely as a solo and star guest, although he has numerous players he especially likes to work with, among them Dick Hyman, Warren Vaché, Marty Grosz and (until his death) Ralph Sutton. He has been prolific in front of microphones, particularly in the 80s and 90s, and has recorded sequences of dates for Musicmasters and Arbors which show off his superior technique, big sound and keen awareness of what the clarinet does best. What he *doesn't* like are live microphones, and he has campaigned to have them removed from wherever he plays (including Carnegie Hall – 'and the whole audience cheered'). Disarmingly, he is a big fan of Albert Ayler, and once made a free record with his Dixieland contemporary Steve Lacy.
*Breezin' Along* (Arbors)

## John R T Davies
TRUMPET, SAXOPHONES, TURNTABLES
*born* 20 March 1927; *died* June 2004

Variously known as John RT or 'Ristic', Davies was in at the start of British trad, playing with the Crane River Jazz Band, Steve Lane, Cy Laurie and Sandy Brown in the 50s, and The Temperance Seven in the 60s. While John loved to play, though, his great contribution was as a remastering expert on old records. Via his own label Ristic, and then Retrieval, Hep, Jazz Oracle, Timeless, Cylidisc and numerous others sensible enough to call on his services, a huge swathe of recordings – from the earliest ragtime sides up to the swing era and beyond – were painstakingly remastered and refitted to appease modern ears through CD reissue. Nothing was too much trouble for John, if it meant bringing a venerable recording back to life. His death early in 2004 was greeted with great sadness by the collecting fraternity the world over.

## Anthony Davis
PIANO
*born* 20 February 1951

Davis took classical studies as a child and graduated in music from Yale. He made some useful associations with like-minded scholars – George Lewis, Leo Smith, James Newton – whose thoughtful approaches to the composition–improvisation dichotomy mirrored his own to some extent. He is also an unstinting admirer of Thelonious Monk, whose music he has studied and transcribed at length. Davis's relatively few recordings were nearly all done in the 70s and 80s, and he has all but disappeared into academia since (currently at the University of California). His opera *X*, based around the life of Malcolm X, was performed in the 80s but not, apparently, since. A composer who prefers to rein in improvising, Davis has had the problem that most of his records suggest a boring, uneventful and long-winded personality, which is probably unfair, although he hasn't gone out of his way to present an alternative case.
**With James Newton, *Hidden Voices* (India Navigation)**

## Art Davis
BASS
*born* 5 December 1934

Davis made a mark for himself via an association with John Coltrane, with whom he played on various occasions between 1958 and 1967; he is on such important dates as *Olé*, *Africa/Brass* and *Ascension*. He was on numerous significant New York records in the same period, and played in studio orchestras for NBC and CBS in the later 60s. But Davis had his career in that sphere soured when he tried to bring a lawsuit aimed at promoting opportunities for blacks to work in symphony orchestras: he was sub-sequently, as he described it, 'whitelisted'. He taught in New York colleges and qualified as a psychologist in the 70s, but the following decade he moved to the West Coast and he has played in various situations there, often in homages to Coltrane's work.
**John Coltrane, *Africa/Brass* (Impulse!)**

## Charles Davis
TENOR AND BARITONE SAXOPHONES
*born* 20 May 1933

Davis studied in Chicago in the late 40s and then worked locally, on both tenor and baritone. In 1956 he played in Sun Ra's Arkestra, and though that remained as only an occasional association, it is the one by which he is largely known. He has been a sideman in countless other situations, although only seldom has he found himself on an important record: one of the best-known to feature his fine supporting work is *The Straight Horn Of Steve Lacy* (1960). He co-led the Baritone Saxophone Retinue with Pat Patrick in 1972, and at the end of the century he made up the Three Baritone Saxophone Band with Gary Smulyan and Ronnie Cuber; but at other times he has preferred to play tenor.
**Steve Lacy, *The Straight Horn Of Steve Lacy* (Candid)**

## Eddie 'Lockjaw' Davis
TENOR SAXOPHONE
*born* 2 March 1921; *died* 3 November 1986

A New Yorker, Davis taught himself to play the saxophone and passed through various orchestras in the early 40s before he began leading his own small groups: at one of his first record dates, for Haven, he cut a piece called 'Lockjaw', and the name stuck, although he was frequently referred to as either 'Jaws' or 'The Fox'. Between then and 1962 he led numerous small groups, interspersed with two brief but memorable spells with Count Basie: he is one of the star soloists on the *Atomic Basie* sessions. Shirley Scott worked with him between 1955 and 1960 and he then formed a two-tenor partnership with Johnny Griffin. After a short time as a booking agent, he rejoined Basie in 1964 and stayed until 1973, thereafter settling in Las Vegas and touring as a solo until his sudden death. Jaws had a huge, apparently temperamental sound, which could tear a blues to pieces, then suddenly turn into a cuddly old bear on a beseeching ballad, where he often sounds like a less exhausted Ben Webster. The organ group with Scott featured some titanic blowing on the blues and standards book, and indeed the Davis discography is littered with great and surprisingly undervalued albums: *The Cookbook* (1958), the four-tenor slugfest *Very Saxy* (1959) and the Oliver Nelson charts for *Trane Whistle* (1960) are all superb, while any of the sets with Griffin – but especially *The Tenor Scene* (1961) – cut the mustard with stunning panache. Some of his later records are comparatively uneventful, although the Davis sound is never less than exhilarating, even when he doesn't have much left to say.

*Trane Whistle* (Prestige/OJC)

# Jesse Davis
ALTO SAXOPHONE
*born* 11 September 1965

New Orleans-born, Davis studied with Ellis Marsalis, who gave him a cassette with Charlie Parker on one side and Sonny Stitt on the other, firing (after some initial discomfort) an intense admiration for four-square bebop alto. He went on to study in New Jersey and New York and made a sequence of admirable records for Concord, walking his music from bop orthodoxy into a resoundingly contemporary feel (his first love was, after all, Grover Washington). Dropped by the label, though, he has lately found himself on the awkward middle ground between youth and middle age as far as a jazz career goes. In the new century he has spent much time in Europe and has been a welcome recent visitor to the UK.

*Young At Art* (Concord)

# Lem Davis
ALTO SAXOPHONE
*born* 22 June 1914; *died* 16 January 1970

Born in Tampa, Davis was a minor swing-era alto man who spent the 40s in such bands as those of Coleman Hawkins, Eddie Heywood and Rex Stewart. In New York during the following decade he turned up on some of Buck Clayton's jam session dates; but the author treasures a few R&B sides which he made later in the 50s, notably the hilarious 'Hot Chocolate' (which is backed with 'Lem Told Beethoven'!). Whoever owns these should ensure their immediate reissue. No great talent, but a character in a Harlem scene which has long since vanished.

**Buck Clayton,** *A Buck Clayton Jam Session* (Columbia)

# Miles Davis
TRUMPET
*born* 25 May 1926; *died* 28 September 1991

Davis set countless questions and dilemmas for listeners, musicians and commentators in a monumental and unprecedented body of work. With a personality which vacillated continuously between devil and angel – he must have enjoyed the sobriquet 'Prince Of Darkness', even though any reference to race, however harmlessly meant, drove him to fury – the emotional tenor of his music is all but impossible to read. But he left a mouthwatering, jostling oeuvre, even though masterpieces sometimes rub shoulders with mere spacefillers. His father was a dentist and the young Davis grew up in a middle-class environment in East St Louis. He took up trumpet at 13 and had some useful early advice from Clark Terry, who advised him to forget about using a vibrato – 'You'll get old and start shaking anyway'. When the Billy Eckstine band visited St Louis he sat in, and he went to New York in 1945, determined to make friends with Charlie Parker. He succeeded, but he didn't work formally with him until April 1947; in between he was with Benny Carter, Eckstine and Dizzy Gillespie.

Davis was in Parker's quintet until December 1948 and is the trumpeter on most of the saxophonist's key sessions for Savoy and Dial. While his playing has often been criticized as the weak link on these recordings, it's fairer to say that he was already working towards an altered state in the bebop language: unequipped to be the kind of virtuoso which Gillespie or Fats Navarro were, he stepped cautiously within the middle register of the horn, repeated figures which he liked while subtly varying their placement, and generally bided his time, content to let Bird take the lead. At the same time, he began rehearsing with other musicians of similar temperament, including Gil Evans and Gerry Mulligan, and these sessions led to a small group of 1949–50 nonet recordings which, when first released in a 12-inch LP format, were named *Birth Of The Cool* (though this wasn't until 1956). The nonet made a few public appearances but didn't find much work, and after a visit to Paris to play with Tadd Dameron, Davis returned to New York and started using heroin, an addiction which badly impeded his progress.

Records for Blue Note and Prestige were at first nothing too special, but in 1954 – when he reportedly overcame his addiction – Davis began to hit his stride. A headline-making appearance at the 1955 Newport Festival put him in the forefront, and with the formation of a fresh quintet (John Coltrane, Red Garland, Paul Chambers, Philly Joe Jones), the sudden demise of Charlie Parker that same year, and the first in a sequence of dazzling records for Prestige by the new band, Davis was set fair to be jazz's premier leader. The quintet's entire output was set down at only a few recording sessions, but the impact of that group – the trumpeter growing ever more concise as a counter to Coltrane's huge outpourings, while the rhythm section set up a feline interplay behind them – rocked a new generation of jazz listeners, and seemed to set the first great standard for the music in the LP era. Davis had also begun using the Harmon mute, which gave his sound a uniquely wounded timbre on ballads in particular. There were some fluctuations in the personnel, in part owing to all four of the sidemen being addicts themselves: at one time Davis had both Coltrane and Sonny Rollins together in the band ('And I have no tapes of that band, damn!').

A larynx operation in 1956 led to Davis spoiling his voice by shouting before his throat had recovered: ever after, he spoke in a cracked whisper. A year later he began the first of several projects where Gil Evans orchestrated backgrounds for Davis as soloist: *Miles Ahead* (1957), *Porgy And Bess* (1958) and *Sketches Of Spain* (1959) were the results, and despite Davis sometimes turning into a preening soliloquist in the gorgeous settings, much of the music is astoundingly beautiful. After a visit to Paris,

where he recorded the music for Louis Malle's *Ascenseur pour l'échafaud*, Davis was back in New York and extending the small group to a sextet, with Cannonball Adderley and, briefly, Bill Evans. Tiring of the way bop-orientated material had gone and complaining that the music had become too thick with chords, Davis sought a fresh direction, which led to the so-called modal playing crystallized in his best-known session, *Kind Of Blue*, surely the most famous jazz record of the LP era. Abandoning a strict timetable of chords, his group edged towards melody as the directing element, with scales and modes, and rhythmic vamps and drones, folding together to create an allusive new feel which felt elliptical and just mysterious enough to captivate even uncommitted audiences. Davis was by now on Columbia, where he would stay for most of his career, and loved the limelight he was enjoying, although there was the occasional sharp reminder that the world hadn't yet changed that much: in August 1959 he was clubbed by a policeman while innocuously standing outside the Village Vanguard.

After the departure of both Adderley and Coleman, though, Davis's group went through a state of flux: he tried several different saxophonists, from Sonny Stitt to Sam Rivers, and didn't seem to care too much for any of them. In 1963, though, the new backdrop he sought finally fell into place, with the recruitment of Herbie Hancock, Ron Carter and the improbably youthful Tony Williams. While Coltrane was achieving stardom by himself, Davis had seemed to tread water since *Kind Of Blue*, but Wayne Shorter's arrival to complete the line-up in 1964 drove the music forward: after a period when Davis had explored the same small group of works over and over, Shorter's writing expanded Davis's book and moved towards a further abstraction, his idiosyncratic melodies suiting his leader's taste for ambiguity. Meanwhile, the rhythm section broke further away from the simplicity of 4/4, Williams in particular devising endless rhythmical variations and subtleties without any lessening of power and momentum. A week's work at The Plugged Nickel in 1965 was recorded, and remains a daringly revealing document of one group's collective creativity.

By 1968, though, Davis began to turn away from acoustic music: the Olympian achievements of the quintet must have seemed impossible to sustain, and in any case the leader was tempted by the popular audience won by Jimi Hendrix. *In A Silent Way* (1969) and *Bitches Brew* (1970) unveiled the new, electric Miles: recruiting young players such as Joe Zawinul, John McLaughlin, Chick Corea and Jack DeJohnette, Davis dived into a fusion of jazz improvisation with what sounded like rock rhythm and viscerality, although it was inevitably a more sophisticated alliance than that. For five years he was prolific as never before, going into the studio more often than ever, and leading groups at such rock-orientated venues as Fillmore West, the once dapper figure now bedecked in all the extravagant robes of rock fashion. It attracted new fans and repelled many older ones, but it was all signature Miles. After the Japanese live recordings of the remarkable *Agharta* (1974), though, the trumpeter's health was again suffering: a likely sickle-cell anaemia condition, plus the effects of a car accident, drove him into semi-retirement, and for the rest of the 70s he did little (Eric Nisenson's depressing memoir outlines some of the habits he got into during this time). But by 1981 he was touring again. Much of the darkness of the 70s music had evaporated, and Davis took to covering recent pop material, including Cyndi Lauper's 'Time After Time' and Michael Jackson's 'Human Nature', which he played over and over, just as he once did with 'Bye Bye Blackbird'. His bands were again filled with young players, including Darryl Jones and a succession of guitarists and saxophonists; the bassist Marcus Miller produced many of his later records, and drummer Al Foster, perhaps his closest latter-day colleague, was on most of them, although a few late waves in the direction of rap and hip-hop suggested that even Miles Davis couldn't adapt to every trend in youth music. There were still many great concerts ahead, and the occasional interesting byway: a Gil Evans-like piece, *Aura*, was scored for him in 1985 by Palle Mikkelborg, and not long before his death he played some of the old Evans orchestrations at a 1991 Montreux Festival show with Quincy Jones. By this time, though, he was clearly ailing, and he died the following year.

'I have to change,' he once said, 'it's like a curse.' This aspect of Davis's art has always been overplayed by his many biographers and followers. Davis certainly went through far more stylistic ground than most, but he was exceptionally shrewd in his choice of collaborators, and it would be wrong to ignore or undervalue the role of such as John Coltrane, Bill Evans, Gil Evans, Wayne Shorter and Joe Zawinul in the development of his many 'innovations'; nor should the role of Teo Macero, his record producer of many years' standing, be overlooked, particularly in regard to the *Bitches Brew* era of recordings: Macero appeared to be the only one who made sense of the hours of wayward noodling which went into such records. As a composer, Davis is similarly hard to evaluate: major pieces with his name on them, such as 'Tune Up', 'Four', 'Blue In Green' and 'Solar', are known to be by other hands, and he increasingly relied on the likes of Shorter in later years to come up with most of the basic material for his music. Perhaps his two great gifts were his ability to lead and focus groups thick with talent but lacking a collective persona; and his charisma as a soloist, employing an uncanny knack of turning a musical situation in the direction he chose and using his own instrumental voice to personify it. As an icon, both in the music and at the high end of popular culture, he has no jazz rivals: even Armstrong and Ellington have to bow to him in that regard. Consumed by the corrosive consequences of racism, which obsessed him, and drugs, which shadowed him for most of his adult life, he could be a despicable character, even to friends and lovers; yet he was equally beloved by most of those who knew him. Either way, he left his audience an incomparable legacy.
*Kind Of Blue* (Columbia)

# Nathan Davis
TENOR AND SOPRANO SAXOPHONES, BASS CLARINET
*born* 15 February 1937

Another collector's favourite, Davis grew up in Kansas City, worked in a band with Carmell Jones while at college there, and while doing army service in Germany played with Benny Bailey. After his discharge he stayed in Europe but returned to the US in 1969 and settled in Pittsburgh. He has hardly recorded at all in the US – two rare albums for Segue and another for a

local Pennysylvania label, Tomorrow, are about it – and most of his 60s sessions are very sought-after, especially *Happy Girl* and *The Hip Walk* (both 1965). Davis plays in a tough straight-ahead style which remains rooted in his Don Byas influence but which takes in Coltrane too. He was greeted with great affection when he toured with the Paris Reunion Band in 1991.
**London By Night** (DIW)

## Richard Davis

BASS
*born* 15 April 1930

At least one generation of music fans know Davis for his contribution to Van Morrison's *Moondance*. He is rather more important as a jazz bassist whose work opened several new doors. He performed locally in his native Chicago in the early 50s, doing classical work as well as small-group dates with Ahmad Jamal, then went to New York and made some important connections. Eric Dolphy (in his quintet with Booker Little) was one of the first to engage him, and Davis plays on such key New York records of the time as *Out To Lunch*, Andrew Hill's *Point Of Departure* and Joe Henderson's *In 'N Out*. Adventurous leaders liked Davis's independence, often challenging the dominance of the underlying beat, double-stopping and interpolating a surprising high note in an otherwise big, subterranean timbre. Besides his small-group work he was in on the early days of the Thad Jones–Mel Lewis Orchestra, and proved as strong in that context as in any other. By the end of the decade he was as eminent as any bassist in jazz, which probably got him sessions like Morrison's, but in the 70s he did less straight-ahead jazz work and eventually moved to Wisconsin, where he holds a teaching position which has taken up much of his time since. His own-name records are no more than a handful in number, although the recent *The Bassist: Homage To Diversity* (2001) is a pleasing summary of many of his musical interests and has a valedictory air about it.
**Eric Dolphy, Out To Lunch** (Blue Note)

## Steve Davis

TROMBONE
*born* 14 April 1967

Trombonists are still relatively few in number in the post-bop field, but Davis has been prominent since he was in his teens, only starting on the horn at 14 but quickly involved with the Charli Persip Superband and, after moving to New York, joining Art Blakey in 1989. In the 90s he freelanced for numerous leaders, and although he moved back out to Hartford, he was still in great demand in Manhattan bands and was a founder member of the One For All collective of modern hard boppers. He has the smooth tone and fast attack which are synonymous with his instrument in this jazz milieu, and has the adaptability which has tended to be a necessary gift for any trombonist seeking a full diary. His own-name dates for Criss Cross have been enjoyably crafted. Steve Davis (1929–87), a bassist who played in John Coltrane's quartet, was no relation, and nor is Steve Davis (b 1958), a fine drummer who works in Lynne Arriale's trio.
**Crossfire** (Criss Cross)

## Wild Bill Davis

ORGAN, PIANO
*born* 24 November 1918; *died* 17 August 1995

Davis was really the first significant player on the electric organ. He was working as an arranger in Chicago when he joined the Louis Jordan band in 1945, playing piano; but he took up the Hammond organ on leaving Jordan in 1949, and quickly found work leading trios of himself, a guitarist or bassist and a drummer. Though he didn't exactly create a genre overnight, he was ahead of the similarly inclined Bill Doggett and inspired Jimmy Smith to follow a similar path. He still worked as an arranger, coming up with one of the classic Count Basie charts, 'April In Paris', and made albums for Epic and Everest which found him moving between jazz, R&B and easy listening. In the 60s he formed a recording partnership with Johnny Hodges, and in 1969 he joined Duke Ellington for a couple of years as a soloist and occasional piano deputy: he has a memorable feature on 'Blue For New Orleans' from the *New Orleans Suite* (1971). Davis was in France for some of the 70s and appears

on many of the Black & Blue albums cut during that period, but he never missed a summer residency he had at Atlantic City's Little Belmont club, which began in the 50s and lasted into the 90s.
*Live At Count Basie's* (RCA)

# Wild Bill Davison
CORNET
*born* 5 January 1906; *died* 14 November 1989

Davison started playing in Ohio bands in the early 20s, and was in Chicago soon enough, quickly into the fast company of the Eddie Condon–Red McKenzie circle. He was a busy and popular musician there, but in 1932 he was at the wheel of a car involved in an accident that killed Frank Teschemacher and suddenly found himself out of favour. He spent the 30s in Milwaukee, leading small groups, but in 1941 he moved to New York (overcoming a lip injury, reputedly the result of being smacked in the mouth by a beer mug) and was leading bands at Nick's. A classic session for Commodore (1943) cemented his reputation, and after army service he was a regular at Condon's and on the Rudi Blesh *This Is Jazz* broadcasts. By this time, Davison's style was fully set, and thriving in the Condon environment. He had a limited but cunningly deployed vocabulary, based around short, ripping phrases, an almost snarling tone, and a contrarily heart-tugging way with a ballad. By the mid-50s he was almost in command of the Condon gang and even made a couple of Columbia albums with strings; by the end of the decade he had decided to work as a solo, and spent the rest of his career wandering the jazz globe, ready to play a one-nighter with anybody and happy to cut a record date for whoever was paying. Though he had an enormous thirst for the hard stuff, his wife Ann (who often acted as his manager) managed his drinking, even if it meant secreting whisky bottles in handbags. Davison carried on playing almost to the end. He remained faithful to the cornet (a period when he played valve-trombone, in the 30s, was never documented on record) and audiences privileged to hear him in the 80s were listening to a giant of a bygone age.
*Lady Of The Evening* (Jazzology)

# Ernest Dawkins
ALTO AND TENOR SAXOPHONES
*born* 2 November 1953

Dawkins has been heavily involved in Chicago's jazz for many years. Hearing a Lester Young record inspired him to take up the sax and he studied at AACM. In the late 70s he formed his New Horizons Ensemble, a small group that rounds up trends in the local music. In the 90s he began taking the band to South Africa, where he helped found an exchange programme between South African and Chicagoan musicians. While his records don't suggest a profoundly original voice, he is clearly a proud standard-bearer for the ongoing dissemination of his city's jazz.
*South Side Street Songs* (Silkheart)

# Alan Dawson
DRUMS
*born* 14 July 1929; *died* 23 February 1996

Dawson played on a lot of record dates, but he will very likely be best remembered as a teacher. He studied both drums and marimba in his teens before working in an army band and then (1953) with Lionel Hampton, with whom he went to Europe. He was on the faculty at Berklee between 1957 and 1975, and guided the hands of such future heavyweights as Tony Williams, Harvey Mason and Joe LaBarbera, but he performed extensively around Boston too: he often worked at Lennie's on the Turnpike with Jaki Byard, and with both Byard and Booker Ervin he made numerous records for Prestige. He enjoyed a long period as the drummer in Dave Brubeck's quartet (1968–76), and though he had left Berklee, he continued to teach privately, still guiding the likes of Terri Lyne Carrington and Vinnie Colaiuta.
*Jaki Byard, Live At Lennie's* (Prestige)

# Elton Dean
ALTO SAXOPHONE, SAXELLO
*born* 28 October 1945

The man who bequeathed his name to the former Reg Dwight (aka Elton John), Dean worked in British R&B groups before joining Soft Machine in 1969, an association which netted him the chance to make his own solo debut for CBS. After 1972 he ran sundry bands of his own – Just Us, Ninesense, El Skid – all warmly remembered by veteran British gig-goers of that time. Since then he has largely worked in more ad hoc situations, and he ran his own label ED for a spell, although more recent albums (including a newer form of his old nonet, named Newsense) have been on George Haslam's SLAM imprint. A fierce, tight-toned altoist who also plays the more rowdy, skirling saxello, Dean's methodology runs the gamut from boppish note-spinning to entirely free meditations, and he is a convincing and unsentimental exponent at whichever base he touches.

*The Vortex Tapes* (SLAM)

## Blossom Dearie

PIANO, VOCAL
*born* 28 April 1928

That is her real name. She first appeared as a singer in The Blue Flames, a group that worked with Woody Herman in the 40s, and was a satellite member of New York bop circles before going to Paris in 1952, where she formed another vocal group, The Blue Stars (this in turn spawned – though without Blossom – The Double Six and The Swingle Singers). She married the saxophonist Bobby Jaspar in 1955, and then returned to the US, where she worked in clubs with a trio, playing piano as well as singing. Norman Granz signed her to Verve and recorded six delightful small-group records, where many of the standards end up in surprising clothes: 'Manhattan', for instance, is played very slowly, and almost becomes a blues. Blossom sings in a very small voice which seems to come from the top of her throat, and while she takes few liberties with phrasing a song, the variety of emphasis she uses during the course of a lyric is completely her own. In the 60s she became known for her own material as well as standards: she is in a classic tradition of American wry, with such songs as 'I'm Hip' ('I even call my girlfriend man'). A favourite at both Ronnie Scott's in London and The Ballroom on West 28th in New York, she dislikes noisy crowds but can easily charm an attentive room. From 1972 she made records for her own label, Daffodil, and she still lives in upstate New York.

*Once Upon A Summertime* (Verve)

## Santi Debriano

BASS
*born* 27 June 1955

Debriano's family moved from Panama to New York when he was three. He studied bass and guitar and in the 80s and 90s played with a broad range of leaders, from Hank Jones to Don Pullen. He seems quite content playing in either in or out contexts, even working with Cecil Taylor at one point, but in the groups he has led himself Debriano appears to be seeking more of a rootsy exercise: The Panamaniacs were a specific nod to his origins, and he has also played with David Sanchez, Danilo Perez and Helio Alves. Little of this work has been recorded, however.

*Soldiers Of Fortune* (Freelance)

## Brian Dee

PIANO
*born* 21 March 1936

Dee exemplifies a solid, reliable and starless generation of British jazz musicians. He actually won *Melody Maker*'s New Star award in 1960, but that has led him nowhere beyond a regular showing in the club circuit, as leader, section-man or accompanist, and his unflashy and dependable work has helped build up the backbone of the music in the UK. A Londoner, he was in at the start of Ronnie Scott's in 1959 (playing there on Mondays) and then joined Vic Ash in The Jazz Five, a British group which even had an album released on Riverside in the US. Mostly, though, he has been in the thick of studio, radio and club work ever since. Producer Tony Williams, never one to neglect a talent simply because it's seldom been noticed, recorded some of Dee's best work on the 1995 date listed below: a superb 'I Should Care' is as flashy as Brian gets.

*Climb Every Mountain* (Spotlite)

# Barrett Deems

DRUMS
*born* 1 March 1915; *died* 15 September 1998

A group leader in the early 30s, Deems had an unremarkable working life, with Joe Venuti and other leaders, before he fetched up in Louis Armstrong's All Stars in 1954, and working with jazz's first superstar – at a time when Pops was on a regular round of world tours – gave him wider visibility for the first time. While Deems had a powerful technique, the All Stars wasn't really the place to hear it, even if Bing Crosby did sing 'Now listen to Mr Barrett Deems!' in *High Society*. The rest of his career was less eventful, at least until his old age: he worked in Jack Teagarden's last band and with The Dukes Of Dixieland, but spent most of his last three decades in Chicago, backing visitors and eventually leading a big band again, which incredibly worked on a weekly basis from 1988 right up until Deems's death at the age of 83. He loved to play, and the Delmark record by the big band has no shortage of excitement.
*How'd You Like It So Far?* (Delmark)

# Volly De Faut

CLARINET
*born* 14 March 1904; *died* 29 May 1973

A veteran of the first Chicago jazz scene, Voltaire De Faut turns up on record at either end of his playing life. He replaced Leon Roppolo in the New Orleans Rhythm Kings when he was only 19, and he is on a handful of famous dates from the 20s: with Muggsy Spanier in The Bucktown Five, on Jelly Roll Morton's session for Autograph and with the Merritt Brunies band that made 'Sugar Foot Stomp' (all 1924–5). Later he played with Jean Goldkette's orchestra but in the 30s he disappeared into radio orchestras before resurfacing at the end of the 40s. A date with Art Hodes in 1953 looked like his farewell, but Hodes persuaded him out of retirement and they made a couple of memorable sessions together for Delmark in 1966 and 1972. An old-school player of bluesy authenticity.
*Up In Volly's Room* (Delmark)

# Joey DeFrancesco

ORGAN, TRUMPET, VOCAL
*born* 4 October 1971

Still only in his early 30s, DeFrancesco already seems to have been around jazz a long time (his dad, Papa John, also plays the Hammond, and got Joey started early). He loves the rough-and-tumble setting of the vintage organ-combo blues, but a surprising association with John McLaughlin (in a trio called Free Spirits) broke him through to a wider and fusion-oriented audience in the middle 90s. Columbia had tried to make him into a star with a string of sessions a few years earlier, but the albums sold modestly and since then Joey has made himself into an all-round jazz entertainer. A recent stint with Concord has served him better, and he has done some jousting with Jimmy Smith and Jack McDuff, as well as trying to emulate Sinatra with the Basie band. As with all showmen, the act only occasionally transfers to record with the right impact.
*Goodfellas* (Concord)

# Buddy DeFranco

CLARINET
*born* 17 February 1923

DeFranco has had to endure almost a lifetime of critical remarks from writers who consider his playing cold, mechanical and tediously perfect. It would be fairer to suggest that the clarinettist, born Boniface Ferdinand Leonardo DeFranco in New Jersey, refuses to conceal perhaps the finest technique developed by a jazz performer on his instrument and prefers a cool, linear delivery to any kind of expressionism. He began as a section saxophonist with various leaders in the 40s (Krupa, Barnet, Tommy Dorsey) and even ran his own big band for a spell, but it was his small-group sessions of the 50s – by this time solely as a clarinettist – that made DeFranco's reputation. Norman Granz recorded him extensively for his labels, but out of some 20 albums very few have been widely available on CD, and even when Mosaic compiled a set of his quartets with pianist Sonny Clark, the edition sold poorly. DeFranco moved to the West Coast in the 60s and while he began to be involved in teaching he also led a version of the Glenn Miller Orchestra from 1966.

Besides visiting Europe as a solo, he also formed a regular partnership with Terry Gibbs, and in his old age he still plays regularly at jazz parties and on cruises, still practising several hours a day. His unblemished tone and faultless articulation let him express ideas at great speed, yet there rarely seems to be much which could be called glib in his playing, and even as the clarinet fell out of favour as a jazz instrument, DeFranco secured a timeless position: he remained a swing-schooled player, who recognized the innovations of bop but preferred to take just the odd fragment of that vocabulary for his own use. His session with Art Tatum – all the more extraordinary since both men were unwell at the time – is one of the great virtuoso meetings in jazz history, and should be heard by everyone who doubts DeFranco's artistry.

**With Art Tatum,** *The Tatum Group Masterpieces* (Pablo)

# Rein De Graaff

PIANO
*born* 24 October 1942

De Graaff worked on the Netherlands scene in the late 50s and early 60s as the piano man in various unexceptional groups, but in 1964 he formed a quartet with the saxophonist Dick Vennik which lasted into the 90s. Besides this, he played behind innumerable visitors from America. A quirky hard-bop man, De Graaff's career in some ways mirrors that of Stan Tracey in England, although he has not been significant (or particularly ambitious) as a composer.

*Chasin' The Bird* (Timeless)

# Harold Dejan

ALTO SAXOPHONE
*born* 4 February 1909

One of the longest-serving players in New Orleans music, Dejan studied clarinet with Lorenzo Tio before working professionally in the middle 20s. He was busy under such leaders as Bebe Ridgley and Sam Jefferson until he went into the navy in 1942, but nothing was set down on record. After military service he was back in New Orleans and busy as a sideman before leading a band of deps which filled in for the Eureka Brass

Band when they were double-booked. This eventually turned into the Olympia Brass Band in 1962, which became a key part of the city's music. Unlike the older brass bands, Dejan saw to it that they began bringing R&B and soul material into their repertoire, and this was the outfit which paved the way for the pop success of the likes of the Dirty Dozen Brass Band. Dejan himself was off the scene through illness for a while in the 80s, but returned to active duty and was still playing into the 90s, an honoured master of New Orleans tradition.

*Dejan's Olympia Brass Band* (77)

# Jack DeJohnette

DRUMS, PIANO
*born* 9 August 1942

DeJohnette could have gone in one of many musical directions as his first choice, and jazz ended up in pole position almost by accident. He studied classical piano for ten years in his native Chicago, and put in as intensive a period of practice on drums. When he arrived in New York in 1966 he was just another drummer on the block, taking unremarkable gigs, but a spell with the Charles Lloyd band drove him to prominence and commenced his long-standing association with the pianist in the group, Keith Jarrett. Miles Davis hired him for the *Bitches Brew* sessions in 1969, and the following year he spent some time in the Davis touring group. Manfred Eicher began recording him as both sideman and leader for ECM, with the groups New Directions and Special Edition, and the association has continued to this day – although the drummer has also had spells with Blue Note and Impulse!. The link with Jarrett continues in the Standards trio, with Gary Peacock, and DeJohnette also has a long-standing musical partnership with the English saxophonist John Surman. He has written many agreeable compositions, some of which – 'Silver Hollow', for instance – would enrich the jazz repertory if some other musicians would pick them up. Jack has tried to synthesize his interests in 'world' music with his jazz directions, but so far the recorded evidence on such as *Music For The Fifth World* (1992) has been somewhat muddled. Although one can hear the powerful influences of Max Roach and Elvin Jones on his technique, he's

not really a swinging drummer in that tradition: polyrhythms and grooves dominate his playing, and one can hear why Davis felt him the right man to power his early electric music. It's likely that many will know him only as Keith Jarrett's drummer, but his own piano playing has been undeservedly neglected on record. John Surman says that he can always spot the drummer by the way he plays his bass drum.
*Special Edition* (ECM)

## Lea DeLaria
VOCAL
*born* 23 May 1958

DeLaria is a smart antidote to a contemporary vocal scene overstuffed with mundane standards singers. Her background is as a stand-up comic, but her father is a jazz pianist and she has taken a nicely irreverent approach to records of show tunes and modern rock material, setting each in the context of a tough, contemporary New York post-bop idiom. While she might do Soundgarden's 'Black Hole Sun', she can also scat her way through 'Jumping With Symphony Sid'.
*Double Standards* (Warner Bros)

## Charles Delaunay
WRITER
*born* 18 January 1911; *died* 16 February 1988

Delaunay pioneered jazz appreciation in France and Europe. The son of celebrated parents, the painters Delaunay, he started out in the same idiom but was soon in love with the new hot music coming over from the US. He was secretary of Hot Club De France, founded the magazine *Jazz Hot* in 1935 and brought out *Hot Discography* in 1936, the first ever catalogue of jazz recordings. A year later he helped Swing, the first French jazz label, get off the ground. Unlike his long-time colleague Hugues Panassié, Delaunay was open-minded about the music and was excited by the advent of bebop (Panassié never forgave him): it was through him that Dizzy Gillespie made the celebrated Salle Pleyel concert in Paris in 1948. A lifelong friend to the music, he brought a draftsman's temperament to the study of jazz and helped cement France's famously hospitable attitude towards jazz and its musicians.

## Delmark
RECORD COMPANY

Although Bob Koester originally established his label in St Louis, where it took its name from Delmar Street, it's Chicago which it is mainly associated with. Koester moved his business there in 1958 and added a K to the name. It recorded both traditional and modern jazz as well as blues: Art Hodes and Albert Nicholas numbered among the traditional players involved, but there was also a major commitment to recording music by the AACM, involving Roscoe Mitchell, Anthony Braxton (the pioneering *For Alto*) and others. New recordings were whittled down in the 70s, but in the CD era much of the older material was reissued and new records by the likes of Harold Mabern, Roscoe Mitchell and Malachi Thompson helped reassert Chicago's place in the jazz mainstream. Koester's legendary Jazz Record Mart was also the place to buy them.

## Barbara Dennerlein
ORGAN
*born* 25 September 1964

Born in Munich, Dennerlein was playing in clubs as a teenager, and began putting out albums on her own BeBab label before recording for Enja (from 1988) and subsequently getting a contract with the German arm of Verve, which has released a sequence of albums. The novelty of a tall young German woman working in the Jimmy Smith tradition hasn't been lost on marketing departments, but before any sense of the big time intruded into her career, she was a familar sight on many local TV shows, almost as a novelty act in the strange culture of German light entertainment. Nevertheless, her playing is a convincing if finally somewhat formulaic blend of organ-combo grooves, funk and the occasional more *outré* setting. She certainly gets many major players on to her albums, which have included Ray Anderson, Andy Sheppard, Bob Berg, Dennis Chambers and others.
*Unhipped* (Verve)

# Willie Dennis
TROMBONE
*born* 10 January 1926; *died* 8 July 1965

Scarcely recognized by the jazz audience, Dennis was a Philadelphian whose invisible professionalism was a decided asset to several big bands (Woody Herman, Claude Thornhill) and particularly to Charles Mingus, who used Dennis on both *Mingus Ah Um* and *Blues And Roots* (both 1959), though he had first worked with the bassist back in 1953. Dennis's clever delivery, relying on the lip rather than a normal tonguing technique, was admired by other trombonists and, inevitably, unknown to everyone else. He was married to Morgana King.
**Charles Mingus, *Blues And Roots*** (Atlantic)

# Sidney De Paris
TRUMPET
*born* 30 May 1905; *died* 13 September 1967

De Paris was one of the best young trumpeters in New York in the early 30s. He had been in the city since 1925, working in Charlie Johnson's band, but from there he went to high-profile record dates with McKinney's Cotton Pickers and then to the Don Redman orchestra, which he stayed with until 1936. As a stylist he was unusual in that he employed growl and mute work which looked back rather than forward, coupled with the more freely swinging delivery of the 30s. Jelly Roll Morton and Sidney Bechet liked him in their front line; Mezz Mezzrow (who sacked him from a session) didn't. His role in the early sessions for Blue Note – with Ed Hall and James P Johnson – was notably effective. But he had few apparent ambitions as a leader, and after the war years he spent most of the time in the company of his brother, playing a firm, expressive lead on their many records for Atlantic. The association only ended with Sidney's death.
**Wilbur De Paris, *& His New New Orleans Jazz*** (Atlantic)

# Wilbur De Paris
TROMBONE
*born* 11 January 1900; *died* 3 January 1973

De Paris had an uneventful time of it as a sideman, but he was an outstanding bandleader. Born in Crawfordsville, Indiana, where his father ran a circus band, he began leading groups of his own in Philadelphia in the 20s before going to New York. Various associations did little to put his name on the map, although he toured Europe with Teddy Hill in 1936 and then performed in the orchestra backing Louis Armstrong between 1937 and 1940. But although he also had a spell in the Ellington orchestra in the middle 40s, Wilbur spent most of his time thereafter as a bandleader. With his brother Sidney he worked at Ryan's in New York from 1951 to 1962, and made a long sequence of records for Atlantic, often using such illustrious names as Omer Simeon and Sonny White as sidemen. The music was based in a New Orleans style, but drew on many surprising areas of repertory – hymns, marches, folk tunes and even modern popular pieces – which were arranged in unpredictable and diverse flavours, much like a Morton Red Hot Peppers group updated to involve swing and post-swing developments. Their nine Atlantics were made available on CD in the new century, and the music still sounds remarkably fresh and unhackneyed, the New Orleans idiom presented in its most generous and flexible spirit. Sidney's death brought the long-standing group to an end, but Wilbur carried on leading groups almost until his own passing.
***Over And Over Again*** (Atlantic)

# Claude Deppa
TRUMPET
*born* 10 May 1958

Deppa is a great favourite among British audiences. Born in Cape Town, he was one of the last South African expatriates to make an impact on the London scene, arriving in the UK in the middle 70s. He has been a valuable sideman in many bands, notably the Jazz Warriors, Viva La Black, District Six and Jazz Jamaica, and has a particular partnership with Andy Sheppard, working in several of the saxophonist's groups in the 80s and 90s. Latterly he began leading groups of

his own, but none of them seems to have lasted or had a significant impact thus far.
**Andy Sheppard, *Rhythm Method*** (Blue Note)

## Paul Desmond
ALTO SAXOPHONE
*born* 25 November 1924; *died* 30 May 1977

Desmond took up clarinet in high school and moved on to alto in 1943. After army service he studied writing and began an occasionally fractious working relationship with Dave Brubeck when he stole half the pianist's band (Brubeck eventually went along as a sideman for a spell). He joined the Brubeck Octet in 1949 and in 1951 became the sole horn in the Brubeck Quartet. It chafed with him that although he contributed so much to their success – he wrote 'Take Five', the biggest hit in the band's book, and his limpid alto tone was as emblematic of their sound as anything the pianist put in – Brubeck himself received most of the attention. After the quartet disbanded in 1967, Desmond played with temperamentally like-minded souls such as Jim Hall, and even when with Brubeck he was making splendid records under his own name for RCA and Warners, although it's a moot point as to whether – as with Milt Jackson and the Modern Jazz Quartet – he was really fettered in any way by Brubeck's contextualizing. The dates pairing him with Gerry Mulligan were outstanding; yet when reunited with Brubeck, on an album of duets made in 1975, the results were exceptionally fine. Desmond had the coolest of tones, rising to a forlorn yet forthright high register, and as a melodist he was the equal of Bobby Hackett when it came to spinning a long line. He was also among the wittiest of commentators on his chosen art form, characterizing himself as 'the slowest alto player in the world' and comparing his sound to a dry martini. Cancer took him at an early age.
**Brubeck And Desmond: Duets 1975** (A&M)

## Ted Des Plantes
PIANO, VOCAL

Des Plantes's groups are a strong advertisement for the new American revivalism. A pianist and scholar of the music of the 20s

and 30s, his band the Washboard Wizards take vintage selections from those respective heydays and give them the kind of affectionate but unsentimental going-over which brings the music into the modern age without too many cobwebs attached. He has made a sequence of excellent records for the Stomp Off label since the late 80s, and also plays piano in other bands of a similar school.
**Midnight Stomp** (Stomp Off)

## Stefano Di Battista
TENOR AND SOPRANO SAXOPHONES
*born* 14 February 1969

Di Battista studied with Massimo Urbani in his teens and although he went on to do horn chores for pop bands, in 1992 he began playing in Paris and eventually settled there when joining the Orchestre National Du Jazz. This has enabled him to gain major-label attention, since he has been signed by the French arm of Blue Note, recording with a quintet which includes another Italian journeyman, Flavio Boltro. A busy-sounding player with exemplary chops, Di Battista brings a bit of Mediterranean sunshine to Blue Note, although the most recent record is an orchestral setting and is a bit too softly sentimental.
**Stefano Di Battista** (Blue Note)

## Furio Di Castri
BASS
*born* 12 September 1955

Di Castri has been active on the Italian scene for many years. He tried trumpet and electric bass before moving over to the acoustic in the early 70s, and was proficient enough to hold down gigs with important names in Milan and Rome all through the 80s. While he has led some interesting groups of his own – a recent one is called Wooden You, a sax/bass/marimba trio which takes an eccentrically folksy approach to Thelonious Monk's music – his most important association is with Paolo Fresu, with whom he has worked and recorded regularly as a duo, using electronics to variegate their fundamentally lyrical conversation.
**Urlo** (YVP)

# Vic Dickenson
TROMBONE
*born* 6 August 1906; *died* 16 November 1984

Dickenson was born in Ohio and worked with territory bands before making a mark with Bennie Moten and Claude Hopkins in the 30s. His essential unobtrusiveness, plus the fact that he played trombone rather than any more attention-grabbing horn, tended to make him more of a musicians' favourite than a star with the public, and one of the few times he gained some limelight was with his Vanguard dates of the early 50s, when he and front-line partner Ruby Braff blueprinted the idea of mainstream swing jazz. He spent many years in both Boston and New York, never quite landing any big-name jobs (Ellington pussy-footed around with him for a time), but always ready to play his brand of humorous, precisely crafted swing playing. He and Bobby Hackett were great pals, and their records together always raise a smile of pleasure. He wrote many songs, most of which were never sung or played by anyone else, and was likely to know every other tune that was called on the stand, too. His tone could go from a conspiratorial mumble to a brassy shout, and even on an ordinary blues he managed to improvise something apparently new every time.
*Gentleman Of The Trombone* (Storyville)

# Walt Dickerson
VIBES
*born* 16 April 1928

Born in Philadelphia, where he still bases himself, Dickerson was working in California at the end of the 50s, where he had a group which included Andrew Hill on piano. He moved to New York in 1960, and his albums for New Jazz attracted considerable attention at the time. In 1965, he made a record for MGM which included Sun Ra as a sideman. Yet at this point he disappeared from the scene altogether, only resurfacing in the middle 70s, playing and recording (for Steeplechase) in Europe. His dry and unsentimental approach to the instrument makes him a somewhat unique figure among vibes players: he prefers a decisive melodic and harmonic approach, almost a Tristano-esque style on his instrument, and his damped-down sound and reluctance to 'play pretty' can make his music a little intimidating to newcomers. Since his return to Philadelphia in the middle 80s not much has been heard from him, and it feels as if the music has passed him by.
*To My Queen* (New Jazz)

# Neville Dickie
PIANO
*born* 1 January 1937

Britain's only real stride-piano player has the ebullience and propriety common to all the masters of this difficult idiom. He began working in his native Durham in his teens and moved to London at the end of the 50s, working in pubs and with trad groups, and even (in 1969) pinching a spot in the pop charts with 'The Robin's Return'. Although he has recorded only rarely in England, recent years have found him cutting a sequence of admirable sets for Bob Erdos's Stomp Off operation, tackling stride and ragtime repertoire and hammering through fine programmes of homage to both King Oliver and Louis Armstrong.
*Don't Forget To Mess Around* (Stomp Off)

# Al Di Meola
GUITAR
*born* 22 July 1954

Di Meola is an excellent example of a musician whose capabilities and sympathies might have settled him in jazz, whereas his ambitions have taken him some distance away. He went to Berklee twice in the early 70s but was each time seduced away, the second time to join Chick Corea's Return To Forever band: flashy and power-packed, his soloing attracted guitar aficionados without suggesting to a wider audience that he had anything much to say. After leaving Corea he embarked on a career which has taken him in several directions: ambient music, speedfreak jazz-rock, and eventually a kind of supercharged world music in the group World Sinfonia. At the same time, he has performed in an acoustic trio with John McLaughlin and Paco de Lucía, which has specialized in what sounds like flamenco on rocket fuel. It is tempting to quote

Shakespeare if asked what all this sound and fury signifies.
**Chick Corea, *Where Have I Known You Before*** (Polydor)

# Danny D'Imperio
DRUMS
*born* 14 March 1945

D'Imperio is a New Yorker who keeps the bebop flame with iron determination. He was playing drums in his dad's band at 12, and then worked in Dixieland outfits before a great deal of big-band and small-group work in the 70s and early 80s. He did a lot of depping for Buddy Rich during the latter's final years and then went out as leader of his own hard-bop small groups, where the book of Blue Note tunes would be ransacked for high-speed heads and truculent solos, musicians such as Greg Gisbert and Ralph Lalama filling the front line. D'Imperio's Metropolitan Bopera House band (he eventually had to change the name after a spat with the 'real' Met) made a superb series of hardcore hard-bop records in the 90s which asserted the repertorial qualities of his kind of jazz better than almost anybody else's.
***Blues For Philly Joe*** (VSOP)

# Gene DiNovi
PIANO
*born* 26 May 1928

A precocious Brooklynite, DiNovi was already on paying gigs in New York at the age of 14, recording with Joe Marsala in 1945. He worked all kinds of swing and bebop gigs in the later 40s but spent most of the next decade as an accompanist to singers, particularly Lena Horne. After doing studio work in Hollywood, he worked regularly with Carmen McRae, and subsequently settled in Canada. A stylish, impeccably fluent player at the songful end of the bop idiom, DiNovi is relatively unfollowed – moving to Canada, whose jazz scene is virtually unknown internationally, probably hasn't helped in that regard – but his few sessions as a leader assert his individuality.
***Renaissance Of A Jazz Master*** (Candid)

# Dirty Dozen Brass Band
GROUP

The DDBB represent the New Orleans marching-band tradition in an updated and frankly bastardized manner. They have been around since the mid-70s, originally a ragtag gang of drummers and horn-blowers, and now an improbably slick outfit with only marginal relevance to the kind of traditions represented by the likes of Paul Barbarin. The mix of brass, saxophones, and bass and snare drummers makes for an exhilarating sound, but it has quickly been dominated by an admittedly old-fashioned (in contemporary terms) soul and R&B mix, which purports to personify the musical mix of the city yet largely leaves behind the stately and sober dialect of the old brass-band music.
***My Feet Can't Fail Me Now*** (Concord)

# Disco

Disco seemed like a disaster for jazz. It emerged in the middle 70s as the principal fad in popular dance music, characterized by a pulse which obliged the drummer to use the bass-drum pedal continuously while accenting this with an opening of the hi-hat cymbal on the first and third beats and the sharp closing of it on those beats following. It became a worldwide phenomenon following the huge success of The Bee Gees and *Saturday Night Fever*, but for jazz players it suggested a further stiffening of the funk beats many had been playing for the first half of the 70s, in order to keep in touch with youth music. Opportunists such as Herbie Hancock and Donald Byrd seemed quite happy to dilute their music even further to accommodate this trend, but like every other dance craze disco didn't last. Any jazz drummer setting up a disco beat today is having a laugh.

# Discography

Charles Delaunay's French classic *Hot Discography* (1936) christened this form of academic study, which is basically the listing of sound recordings in a systematic and comprehensive way, usually chronological, where the recorded work of a group of musicians – defined by their musical vocation, or perhaps by the leader in question – is set down for collectors, historians or the merely curious to consult. Besides Delaunay, there were other pioneering works by Hilton Schleman and Orin Blackstone; but the most important jazz discographer of the 78 era is Brian Rust, whose *Jazz And Ragtime Records 1897–1942* is today and for ever the standard work on its period. The LP era was subsequently covered by a Dane, Jorgen Grunnet Jepsen, and then by competing works from Walter Bruyninckx (Belgium) and Tom Lord (USA). Meanwhile, specialists have attempted to examine the work of individual musician-leaders in almost microscopic detail: one of the most formidable is Chris Sheridan (UK), whose works on Count Basie, Thelonious Monk and Cannonball Adderley have set a prodigious standard of scholarship. In general, this kind of work has to some extent brought the charge of anorakism to bear on jazz followers, although a more sympathetic view is that it honours and elevates the work of musicians whose careers may otherwise have received little recognition by posterity.

## Diz Disley
GUITAR
*born* 27 May 1931

Cartoonist, designer and guitarist, Disley was actually born in Canada but grew up in Wales and Yorkshire and made his debut with the Yorkshire Jazz Band (on banjo) in 1949. He moved to London in 1953, found work as a cartoonist for newspapers, and played with various luminaries of the trad scene and in skiffle; he also had his own group, the Soho String Quintet. As the trad scene declined he moved more towards folk music, but in 1973 he began a fruitful association with Stéphane Grappelli, which lasted until he injured his arm in 1979. On the face of it, it was a very successful alliance, but Disley has subsequently said that 'I deeply regret having anything to do with Grappelli at all, as he turned out to be the most unpleasant character I have ever met.' In the 80s he was back playing folk and other stuff, and he later settled in Spain, opened a club and re-formed his old string quintet, turning up in both the UK and Europe.
**With Stéphane Grappelli,** *I Got Rhythm* (Black Lion)

## DIW
RECORD COMPANY

A division of the Japanese electronics firm Disk Union, DIW (Discs In the World), established in 1983, quickly became a prominent label for recording the new American jazz of that decade. David Murray was one of its first artists and remained an important one for a number of years, and they also recorded James Blood Ulmer, Lester Bowie, David S Ware and John Zorn's Masada. Archive sets by the Japanese saxophonist Kaoru Abe also emerged, and they were the first to record James Carter, the albums subsequently being licensed to Columbia. Sumptuously produced in the accustomed Japanese manner, the records were widely distributed, but in the new century their activities have shown a marked slackening-off, perhaps as a result of the relatively depressed Japanese marketplace.

## Dixieland

Although its historical origin is unfortunate – 'Dixie's Land' referred to the estate of the slave trader Jonathan Dixie, and 'Dixie' came to be a generic nickname for the (Confederate) American South during the Civil War – Dixieland is a term which covers a lot of jazz, both historical and current. While it formed part of the name of the first jazz group to record (the Original Dixieland Jazz Band), it was used to describe the Chicago-styled jazz of the later 20s, rowdy music with featured soloists, a move away from the more classical polyphony of the New Orleans ensemble. Subsequently, though, in the US Dixieland came to mean more or less any kind of traditional jazz, although admirers and exponents of the classic New Orleans idiom found the term distasteful and would use it to denote commercially orientated music for jazz tourists. These days it has about as much definition as the word 'bebop'.

## Bill Dixon
TRUMPET
*born* 5 October 1925

Although Dixon studied in Manhattan and worked as a trumpeter as far back as the late

40s, he didn't make any significant impact until the early 60s, when he began working with Archie Shepp in a quartet which was a dramatic early entry for the avant-garde. They went to Europe, where in Stockholm Albert Ayler deputized for Shepp, and on his return Dixon became involved with Shepp and John Tchicai in the New York Contemporary Five. In 1964 he organized what became known as the 'October Revolution In Jazz', a series of gigs at the Cellar Café in Greenwich Village where some of the leading names in the nascent New Thing were showcased, a breakthrough moment in the presentation of the avant-garde. Dixon also helped organize the Jazz Composers' Guild, although it foundered before long. He began working with the dancer Judith Young in 1965, a groundbreaking mixing of jazz and dance which lasted until Young's death in 1983. After the 60s, though, Dixon never quite regained his old momentum. His own playing, where melodic improvising was subverted by 'extended' trumpet techniques and carved up into small expressionist episodes, has never taken all that well to any group idiom, and much of his later work on and off record was conducted either in duos or in a solo form. Some of his later collaborators have included William Parker and Tony Oxley. A huge six-disc set of his solo material is both absurdly indulgent and, from moment to moment, remarkable.
*Solo Works – Odyssey* (no label)

## Baby Dodds
DRUMS
*born* 24 December 1898; *died* 14 February 1959

Warren Dodds began playing drums in New Orleans at 16, and was soon working with Bunk Johnson, Willie Hightower and Roy Palmer. He spent some three years with Fate Marable, working on riverboats, where his flamboyant style made his reputation. He joined King Oliver (and his brother Johnny) in San Francisco and then Chicago in 1922, and when Oliver's band broke up he stayed in the city, always under the eye of the reproving Johnny, who disliked Baby's wilder tendencies. There were record dates with Jelly Roll Morton and others, but Dodds latterly came into his own in the 40s, in time for the New Orleans revival. He was

back with his original boss, Bunk Johnson, for a time (although Johnson found his playing all too much) and was often heard on Rudi Blesh's *This Is Jazz* broadcasts from New York. Bill Russell recorded him talking at length and demonstrating his techniques, and he also made discs of drum solos for Circle. His short press rolls, insistence on finely tuned tom-toms and varying kinds of accompaniment (rather than a brass band-like regularity) set him apart from all his New Orleans contemporaries, and set techniques which the swing-era drummers would build on. He suffered a stroke in 1949, which was the first of several, and though he carried on playing into the 50s, he was never quite the same.
*Baby Dodds* (American Music)

## Johnny Dodds
CLARINET
*born* 12 April 1892; *died* 8 August 1940

Virtually every clarinettist in British trad wanted to sound like Johnny Dodds. Jimmie Noone was smoother and sweeter, and Sidney Bechet was too godlike, but Dodds's weaving, intensely bluesy lines with their inimitable vibrato were something to aspire to. He began surprisingly late on the horn, at 17 or so, and he worked in New Orleans with Kid Ory's band from 1912, staying with him on and off until leaving for Chicago in 1920, where he joined the King Oliver band in 1922. In 1923 he took over leadership of the house band at Kelly's Stables in the city: a tough disciplinarian, he insisted that his men were on time for work, and sober. He also recorded scores of sides for Paramount, Columbia, Vocalion, OKeh and Victor, from rudimentary barrelhouse sessions with the likes of Jimmy Blythe and Junie Cobb to a central role in the Louis Armstrong Hot Five and Seven sessions (he is mystifyingly average on the earlier records, as if overwhelmed by Armstrong's bursting genius, but his playing on the sides by the Seven is mostly magnificent). Dodds never had Noone's limber technique and he sometimes gargles a line, but the personality of his playing is customarily powerful and he cuts through what were often indifferent recording situations, sometimes in the way that Charlie Parker would, a generation later, on his airshots. Shrewd with his money, he became a landlord and saw through the Depression without too many problems, but his style was eventually deemed archaic for a scene which had turned its attention to Benny Goodman and Artie Shaw. Even so, a late session (1938) with the young Charlie Shavers, on the likes of '29th And Dearborn', shows that he was still playing beautifully, even if work was scarce. He suffered a stroke in 1939 and died the next year, only 48 years old.

**Johnny Dodds 1926** (Classics)

# Jerry Dodgion

ALTO AND SOPRANO SAXOPHONES, FLUTE
*born* 29 August 1932

A great section-man, Dodgion (originally from Richmond, California) worked with Gerald Wilson on the West Coast and toured with Benny Goodman before settling in New York. He was the lead alto with the Thad Jones–Mel Lewis Orchestra from the start, and stayed until 1979; subsequently he has been in the Carnegie Hall Jazz Band, the American Jazz Orchestra and the Lincoln Center Jazz Orchestra. Occasional small-group records, with Marian McPartland and others, have given him a few spotlights. He's a smooth-toned player with, inevitably, great fluency and a good feeling on a blues. His wife Dottie is a sometime drummer and vocalist herself.

**Thad Jones–Mel Lewis, *Live At The Village Vanguard*** (Solid State)

# Niels Lan Doky

PIANO
*born* 3 October 1963

Doky began on guitar (his Vietnamese father is a classical guitarist) but switched to piano at 11 and was playing in public by the time he was 15. He left Copenhagen to study at Berklee and after graduating went to New York. In the 80s and 90s he ran up a sequence of albums for both Storyville and Milestone, and with his brother Christian Minh (bass) he was signed to Blue Note as a double-act: but the records there were insubstantial and frustratingly bitty, and Doky has since turned up on Verve. A capacious talent for sure, but Doky at present looks caught awkwardly between idioms: absorbed by jazz, rock, funk and various

threads of world music, his gathering-in of these interests has so far resulted in an exotic muddle. The straight-ahead records he made for Storyville were, for all their dwelling in convention, much more satisfying.

**Close Encounter** (Storyville)

# Klaus Doldinger

ALTO, TENOR AND SOPRANO SAXOPHONES
*born* 12 May 1936

A Berliner, Doldinger has gone all the way from trad to fusion. He led a group called The Feetwarmers in the 50s and early 60s, playing alto, and performed with them in New York and New Orleans as well as at home. But he was also interested in hard bop, and led a quartet in that style in the 60s. He became best known, though, for a fusion group called Passport, which was formed in 1970 and went on to make best-selling albums for Atco in an undemanding flavour of jazz-rock.

**Cross-Collateral** (Atco)

# Eric Dolphy

ALTO SAXOPHONE, BASS CLARINET, FLUTE
*born* 20 June 1928; *died* 29 June 1964

Dolphy's legacy is an indecently rich jumble of great, fleeting moments. Born in Los Angeles, he started on clarinet at six, and took up alto and oboe in high school. After study at Los Angeles City College he joined Roy Porter's band on alto but then served in the US Navy before returning to Los Angeles. He practised, played at jam sessions and worked in bands led by Gerald Wilson and Buddy Collette, but he didn't get himself any recorded features until joining Chico Hamilton's Quintet in 1958. In 1959 he settled in New York and joined Charles Mingus. For the next five years, his career on record seemed peculiarly at odds with his live work: on almost every album date he played on he created extraordinary music, yet in terms of public appearances he struggled to find a consistent level of work. His music with Mingus includes the remarkable bass and bass clarinet duo 'What Love', on *Charles Mingus Presents Charles Mingus* (1960) – even though Mingus characterized Dolphy's bass clarinet, then scarcely used in jazz, as 'that silly thing – and their European tour of 1960 resulted in a host of semi-official concert recordings of which that on *The Great Concert Of Charles Mingus* (1960) is outstanding. In the same period, he made *Outward Bound*; *Out There* and *Far Cry!* (all 1960) for New Jazz, and after leaving Mingus formed a quintet with the equally star-crossed Booker Little. In each session, he improvised solos which were uniquely par-ticularized as one man's synthesis of bebop, free playing and the taut disciplines of 20th-century art music (Dolphy also played works by Varèse and his ilk in live performance). His alto sound, with its eerie leaping between intervals, can remind the listener equally of human speech and birdsong, vocalized as few saxophones are. On bass clarinet, he all but invented the jazz vocabu-lary, extending his alto approach into a thick, cello-like rotundity. His flute playing was his most conventional, and is some-times charged as technically deficient, but a solo such as that on Oliver Nelson's 'Stolen Moments' (from *Blues And The Abstract Truth*, 1961) is still affecting and exciting.

In 1961 he joined the John Coltrane group, in time to play on *Live At The Village Vanguard* and *Impressions*, and to go to Europe on Trane's autumn tour. In 1962–3 he led his own groups, with Jaki Byard, Woody Shaw, Freddie Hubbard and others, yet gigs were scarce, and he was soon free-lancing with Orchestra USA, Coltrane and Mingus again. His sole date as leader for Blue Note, *Out To Lunch*, emerged at the beginning of 1964 and, flawed though it is, it remains a thrilling document of the new American jazz, the playing and the writing memorable and intensely challenging; for many, it is the greatest record Blue Note ever released. Dolphy's music nudged the borders of free playing, and he is marvellous on Ornette Coleman's *Free Jazz* (1960), avow-edly influenced by that leader; but his music never quite escapes the logic and the trajec-tories of bebop, and how far he might have taken it remains a fascinating and unanswer-able question. As with Coltrane, who in some ways was behind Dolphy in rates of progress, musics from other parts of the world may have played a significant role in shaping a future aesthetic which never had the chance to be fully realized. If nothing else, although his influence can still be felt in many less obvious ways, his multi-instrumentalism set a dynamic example for reed players of generations to come. His dis-cography has always been a bit of a muddle, since there are so many 'unofficial' record-ings emanating from his various European sojourns. The kindest of men, who seemed to do so much in music just for the love of it, Dolphy is remembered with a sort of heartbroken affection by everyone who knew him: 'He was the type of man who could be just as much a friend to a guy he'd met today as he was to one he'd known ten years,' remembered John Coltrane. He made a final trip to Europe with Mingus in April 1964, and left that group shortly afterwards with the intention of settling in Paris: 'If you try to do anything different in this country,' he told A B Spellman shortly before he left the US, in a rare display of bitterness, 'people put you down for it.' He was sud-denly taken ill in Berlin, and died from a heart attack, which was probably hastened by a diabetic condition.
*Out To Lunch* (Blue Note)

## Sophia Domancich
PIANO
*born* 25 January 1957

A distinctive talent, Domancich studied at the Paris Conservatoire but moved into jazz in the 80s and formed some surprising affiliations – with Laurent Cugny's Big Band Lumière, several Pip Pyle groups, Robert Wyatt and John Greaves. Her own small-group records, though, are of particular inter-est, the music teetering between curious, doomy rhapsodizing (one of her records is called *Funerals*) and a stoic lassitude. Her improvising is perhaps rather less interest-ing than her composing and manipulation of group form.
*La Part Des Anges* (Gimini)

## Natty Dominique
TRUMPET
*born* 2 August 1894; *died* 30 August 1982

Anatie Dominique played good, enthusiastic New Orleans trumpet, although on the evi-dence of his records with Johnny Dodds and Jimmie Noone he had a thin though pierc-ing tone and an almost whinnying vibrato. He was working as a porter in Chicago in the

40s (a doctor told him if he wanted to live, he should hide his trumpet) but he began playing again in the 50s and was still making occasional appearances a decade later. In the end, he lived a long time.
**Johnny Dodds,** *New Orleans Stomp* (Frog)

# Arne Domnérus
ALTO SAXOPHONE, CLARINET
*born* 20 December 1924

'Dompan' is the grand old man of Swedish modernism – provided that takes in traditional, mainstream, bop, free and third-stream elements, all of which he has calmly investigated. He came to the fore as a soloist in some of the better Swedish dance-into-swing bands of the 40s, particularly those of Lulle Ellboj and Simon Brehm. He led a group at the Paris Jazz Fair in 1949, sharing the stage with some eminent boppers, and it helped to put Swedish jazz on the map. He led bands at Nalen in Stockholm between 1951 and 1964, which often had the likes of Lars Gullin and Jan Johansson involved, and he was a significant presence in the Harry Arnold Radio Big Band and its successor, Radiojazzgruppen. A veteran of probably hundreds of record dates as leader and sideman, he has been as likely to work with old friends such as Bengt Hallberg and Rune Gustafsson as younger talents such as Jan Lundgren (his regular pianist in the 90s), and he has worked in almost every kind of instrumentation from duos to orchestras and with choirs. Smoothly assertive as an altoist and richly melodious on the clarinet, his sound's sometimes passionless timbre derives from the professionalism he admired in Benny Carter, but to that he has added his own variations on Charlie Parker, and even when he's gliding easily over the face of the music there's usually a cunning melodic twist in there somewhere. Any record with his name on it has something going for it.
*Face To Face* (Dragon)

# Barbara Donald
TRUMPET
*born* 2 September 1942

Born in Minneapolis, Donald began on trumpet early on, and moved with her family to California when still very young. She already had big-band and R&B experience behind her when she married the saxophonst Sonny Simmons in 1964, and they worked together for most of the next ten years. A vigorous if not especially individual player, Donald worked with her own groups in the 80s and 90s but enjoyed very little attention.
**Sonny Simmons,** *Manhattan Egos* (Arhoolie)

# Lou Donaldson
ALTO SAXOPHONE
*born* 1 November 1926

Donaldson has followed the bebop gospel for his entire professional life. After navy service he began working in New York, and was soon in heavy company: his first record dates were with Thelonious Monk and Milt Jackson, and he was with Clifford Brown in an early edition of the Jazz Messengers (1953). Thereafter, though, he was his own leader, and he has never really worked for anyone else. He was one of the first stalwart musicians for the Blue Note label, recording many albums for them between 1954 and 1975: while he was never 'family' at the label the way that Horace Silver was, he was happy to create a sequence of albums which tracked the move from hard bop to soul-jazz to a kind of R&B-funk music. He carried on into the 80s and 90s, still playing in a style extracted primarily from Charlie Parker but with the kind of simple bluesy feel which characterized the R&B saxophonists. Nevertheless, he regards Parker's music as the one true way, and he likes to consider crossover players as 'con-fusion musicians'.
*Alligator Bogaloo* (Blue Note)

# Dorothy Donegan
PIANO
*born* 6 April 1922; *died* 19 May 1998

In her way, Donegan is a unique figure in the music. She grew up in Chicago and was something of a piano prodigy: on her first record date, in 1942, she plays Rachmaninov as well as boogie-woogie piano, and she performed a classical programme at a concert at the city's Orchestra Hall in 1943. But her career centred on club work, first in Chicago and then in New York, where she developed a club act which included virtuoso piano playing alongside singing, comedy and impersonations. She was actually very good at all three, and her gallery of take-offs included a devastatingly accurate (and cruel) treatment of Billie Holiday. She was hidden away on the club circuit for most of the 50s, 60s and 70s, but by the 80s she had been rediscovered and she was latterly extensively recorded and booked for jazz parties and cruises. Donegan never let her technique get rusty, and she was compared by some to Art Tatum.

***The Explosive Dorothy Donegan*** (Progressive)

# Pierre Dørge
GUITAR
*born* 28 February 1946

Born in Copenhagen, Dørge led a relatively undistinguished career in the 60s and 70s, tinkering with rock, free jazz and jazz-rock in sundry combinations, before he formed his New Jungle Orchestra in 1980. This middle-sized ensemble caught the approaching wave of new fusions of jazz with world music with near-perfect timing, and Dørge's guitar was combined with African polyrhythms, cacophonous near-free jazz and a humorous kind of party music which has resulted in some memorable records. It has now lasted for some 25 years, and on the evidence of recent reports shows no sign of any declining voltage. With a world of music there to be ransacked, perhaps Dørge's only limitation is his imagination.

***Music From The Danish Jungle*** (Dacapo)

# Kenny Dorham
TRUMPET
*born* 30 August 1924; *died* 5 December 1972

Dorham was perhaps the lost master of bebop trumpet, and his career was in the end a disappointing and frustrating one. Born in Fairfield, Texas, he began on trumpet in his teens and after army service joined the Russell Jacquet band in 1943. He went to New York and joined the big bands of Billy Eckstine and Dizzy Gillespie, also leading some small groups on record. He joined Charlie Parker as Miles Davis's replacement at the end of 1948 and stayed 18 months, but had a low profile after that

until he joined the first edition of the Blakey–Silver Jazz Messengers: he is on their Café Bohemia sessions (1955), and when he left to form his own Jazz Prophets he made more memorable live dates at the same venue (1956). He then joined Max Roach, but after he left in 1958 his career never quite got back on track. Although he led a quintet with Joe Henderson from 1962, and cut some more fine dates for Blue Note, there were other trumpeters gaining more plaudits and Kenny's own playing began to grow erratic. Aspirations to be a singer, which he had explored as far back as his time with Gillespie, also came to little. He kept heavy company throughout his career on record and his best playing is superbly finished: as crisp and exact as Gillespie on a quick tempo, bluesier than Miles Davis, his most assured improvising is remarkable, even in an era of great trumpeters. It was his misfortune to be around when the likes of Gillespie, Davis and Clifford Brown – and later Freddie Hubbard and Lee Morgan – were taking more of the jazz audience's attention. He died of kidney failure. His real Christian name was McKinley, which became Kinney and was somehow corrupted into Kenny.

***Round Midnight At The Café Bohemia*** (Blue Note)

# Bob Dorough
PIANO, VOCAL
*born* 12 December 1923

Dorough began working in New York clubs at the end of the 40s, first just on piano, later singing too. He moved to Paris in 1954 but came home to the US at the end of the decade, and since then has been a hipster for hire – with Miles Davis in 1962, but mostly as a solo, or in tandem with bassist Bill Takas. Dorough hasn't made many records in a 50-plus-year career, but he has done a few sets of standards (as well as a jazz version of *Oliver!*) and in 1997 made a sort of comeback album for Blue Note. Denied an immortal song or a signature album, he is instead the definitive cult singer.

***Right On My Way Home*** (Blue Note)

# Jimmy Dorsey

CLARINET, ALTO SAXOPHONE
*born* 29 February 1904; *died* 12 June 1957

Dorsey's early career was closely tied in to his brother's: tuition with their father, then dance-band work which led to both of them becoming some of the most in-demand sessionmen in the New York of the later 20s. Dorsey's style was a little prim and not very bluesy, but he could get around the clarinet and any of the saxophones with insouciant ease: 'He was a master saxophonist, Bird knew that too,' according to an admiring Dexter Gordon. The Dorsey Brothers Orchestra existed more as a studio creation in the early 30s, backing the likes of The Boswell Sisters, but after it began touring an argument between the brothers led to Jimmy taking over sole leadership. If his subsequent bands weren't quite as successful as Tommy's, Jimmy still had his share of hits, and he made many records: it was, again, the sweet stuff which was successful, but hidden away among numerous record dates are some fine swinging sides, and Dorsey managed to keep his orchestra active even through the declining years of the big-band era. At the end of the 40s he was working more frequently with a smaller group, the Dorseyland Band, and he finally rejoined his brother in their last venture together in 1953, carrying on after Tommy's death. A gentler man than Tommy, and at heart rather shy, Jimmy was liked by his musicians, and he only outlived his brother by less than a year: cancer took him in 1957.
***Contrasts*** (MCA)

# Tommy Dorsey

TROMBONE
*born* 19 November 1905; *died* 26 November 1956

Dorsey's sobriquet, 'The Sentimental Gentleman Of Swing', derived from his band's theme tune, 'I'm Getting Sentimental Over You'; it certainly didn't match up with his manner, since he was a hot-tempered and feared martinet. Like his brother Jimmy, he studied various instruments with his father before settling on trombone (he plays trumpet capably enough on some of his 20s sessions). Both brothers worked their way through the better dance bands and Tommy is on probably hundreds of dance records from the 20s, often getting eight or 16 bars to himself. The occasionally convened Dorsey Brothers Orchestra kept them busy in the studios, and when they began touring the band in 1934, it lasted only until the quarrelsome siblings went their separate ways. Dorsey formed a new band which went on to become one of the most successful of the swing era: as smoothly melodious as its leader's trombone playing, it was in most of its recordings more of a dance orchestra than a swinging big band, but Dorsey still hired some strong jazz soloists – Bud Freeman, Bunny Berigan, Yank Lawson – and had Buddy Rich at the drums. He also created a spin-off small group, The Clambake Seven, which recorded hotter material in a kind of sweet Dixieland style, and had two of the best swing-era vocalists in Edythe Wright and Frank Sinatra (who later said that he learned much about breath control from watching Dorsey himself, taking a breath through the corner of his mouth while still keeping a perfect timbre). Dorsey's band was recorded incredibly prolifically by Victor – they recorded 78 titles in 21 sessions in 1938 alone – and all through the late 30s and early 40s it was one of the premier bands in America, even though Tommy's black temper often drove sidemen away. The decline of the big bands, though, caused Dorsey to disband in 1947 (the year that his Hollywood biopic *The Fabulous Dorseys* came out). He formed a new band and, reunited with Jimmy, it was the Dorsey Brothers Orchestra from 1953 until the trombonist's death. As an instrumentalist, Dorsey has been critically undervalued: he was not in Teagarden's class during the 20s, but few other trombonists played as well in the hot dance music of the day, and with his own bands Dorsey moulded a style that suited his impeccable technique. Even so, he takes some fine solos on his records: because the band's discography is so huge (and so stuffed with routine dance material) much of his best work is scattered and little known. As ruthless as he was professionally, he could show sudden acts of kindness: he paid Bunny Berigan's hospital bills when his former trumpet star became mortally ill. Dorsey was only 51 when he choked to death in his sleep.
***The Song Is You*** (Bluebird)

# Dave Douglas
TRUMPET
*born* 24 March 1963

Douglas has become a focal point in the marketing of new jazz to an audience sometimes confused by its many directions: he is held up as an exemplar of the questing modern musician. He went a familiar route of study (Berklee and New England Conservatory) and pilgrimage to New York (1984), where he began working with likeminded contemporaries before firming up his straight-ahead chops in one of Horace Silver's groups. In the 90s he began to perform, write and record at a furious pace – running several bands (New And Used, Tiny Bell Trio, a 'string' band, a quintet and an eight-piece group called Sanctuary), working with such high-profile leaders as John Zorn and Don Byron, and eventually signing to RCA as a standard-bearer of out-jazz at a major label. In the interim, he was heavily talked up in the American jazz press and began winning critical polls. He already has some 20 albums under his belt as a leader alone. In the eager hunt for jazz 'stars', Douglas is a rather strange choice for the vacant throne: a lot of his work is inscrutable, and peculiarly rootless. He seems fascinated by so many influences that a record such as *Witness* (RCA, 2000) seems impossibly replete with contributions from all over the place. Since eclecticism is now held up as a necessary virtue, his eminence is unsurprising as a consequence, and he is clearly a very skilful musician; it may just take a long time to assess how important he will turn out to be. To his credit, he is quick to assert that many other musicians deserve at least as much attention as he has received. The record listed below offers some of the clearest space he's had to work in: he does sound very good.
**Songs For Wandering Souls** (Winter And Winter)

# Tommy Douglas
CLARINET, SAXOPHONES
*born* 9 November 1906; *died* 9 March 1955

Douglas spent most of his career in the South and Midwest of the US, and as a result has been largely forgotten. He was playing clarinet and alto in Kansas City for much of the 30s, doing sideman work, arranging and leading numerous outfits too. He was a dazzling technician, whose harmonic thinking was exceptionally adroit and advanced: Jo Jones thought him the equal of Benny Carter, and he is reputed to have influenced the young Charlie Parker. But Douglas never got on record in a big way, and only rarely enjoyed big-name associations: he was with Duke Ellington for a mere three weeks in 1951. There are only twelve 78 sides made under his own name, with an unremarkable Kansas City band in 1949, although 'Hot Sauce' and 'The Killion' hint at how good he must have been, and a few accompaniments to Julia Lee offer some impressive solos.
**Julia Lee, *1938–44*** (Classics)

# Down beat
MUSICAL TERM

Either the first beat in any single performance or the first beat of each bar. *Down Beat* is also the name of one of the leading jazz periodicals, which has been published in America since 1934.

# Dragon
RECORD COMPANY

Founded in Stockholm in 1975 by musician Lars Wallgren and journalist Lars Westin, this is the pre-eminent Swedish label. Westin, who carried on the label with producer Leif Collin after Wallgren's death, has ensured that, in its quiet way, the label is entirely uncompromising: there is no crossover music in its catalogue, and despite a few records which hint at fusion, most of its output consists of acoustic and straight-ahead jazz. The majority of issues are by Swedish artists, though there are some by visitors (Stan Getz, Lee Konitz, Chet Baker), as well as archive editions of rare Swedish jazz.

# Hamid Drake
DRUMS
*born* 3 August 1955

Drake has steadily progressed to the forefront of jazz drumming. Though born in California, he spent his teens in Chicago and played rock music. After joining a collective named the Mandingo Griot Society in 1978, he began playing with Don Cherry, an association which lasted until Cherry's death. But it wasn't until the 90s that Drake really began to net a wider attention. He became a linchpin of Chicago's new-music scene, along with Fred Anderson and Ken Vandermark, and these associations helped him meet and work with the likes of Peter Brötzmann and Georg Gräwe. He has played in reggae bands, has studied tabla techniques and has a notable partnership with bassist William Parker. While he works in some of the freest jazz of this time, he is a musician who bridges time playing with free rhythm and does it better than perhaps any other American drummer of today.

**DKV Trio, *Live In Wels & Chicago 1998*** (Okkadisk)

## Ray Draper

TUBA

*born* 3 August 1940; *died* 1 November 1982

Draper was about the only player to make a go of playing tuba in a bebop situation. He is, rather amazingly, on record with both Jackie McLean and John Coltrane, and is also on Max Roach's *Deeds, Not Words* (1959). In the 60s, though, he didn't fare as well. Although he worked briefly with Don Cherry, he also spent three years in prison and led an unsuccessful jazz-rock group, Red Beans And Rice, before going to (of all places) England in 1969. On his return in 1971, he did at least find a soulmate in Howard Johnson, and was in Johnson's brass-heavy group Gravity, although he didn't live long enough to participate in any of that band's subsequent records. He died of gunshot wounds, murdered in the street by an unknown attacker.

***Tuba Jazz*** (Jubilee)

## Mark Dresser

BASS

*born* 26 November 1952

Dresser's formative decade was the 80s. Previously, he studied at UCLA with Bert Turetzky, who helped him build a formidable proficiency of out techniques on the bass, and played symphonic music and free jazz on the Californian scene in the early 70s. But on moving East he worked extensively with Ray Anderson, Tim Berne and Anthony Braxton, three leaders whose music was between them diverse enough to give Dresser a peerless field of experience in New York's new jazz, the Braxton association (1985–94, where he worked alongside frequent partner Gerry Hemingway) being particularly important. Since then, Dresser has been more of a leader himself and has acquired the stature of an elder in his scene, yet perhaps without quite putting his name on a band or a record which counts as his masterpiece. He has recently worked extensively in duo situations, with the likes of Mark Helias (as The Marks Brothers) and pianist Denman Maroney, and in 2003 he recorded a fine album with his old friend Ray Anderson. Despite the reservation above, he is a musician of great distinction.

***Force Green*** (Soul Note)

## Kenny Drew

PIANO

*born* 28 August 1928; *died* 4 August 1993

A prolific recording pianist and a gracious team-player, Drew perhaps suffered a little from his easygoing manner: nobody could object to finding that he's holding down the piano part, but he never made it into lists of leaders on his instrument. Born in New York, he was engaged by several seniors at the beginning of the 50s, notably Lester Young, Charlie Parker and Coleman Hawkins. He went over to the other coast in 1954 but came back East two years later. Between then and 1961 he was on countless record dates, before a move to Paris, and subsequently Copenhagen. There he remained for most of the rest of his life, running a publishing company and a record label, and becoming a pianist-in-residence both at Café Montmartre and on sessions for Nils Winther's Steeplechase label. It may not have helped his profile in the US, but like many expatriates Drew seemed to care little about that: an honoured figure in Denmark, he inevitably backed many of his old colleagues when they came to visit. He could play either thickly voiced chords or springheeled bop lines in the classic manner. Out of a huge discography, the

judgement must be that one performance is much like another.
**This Is New** (Riverside/OJC)


# Kenny Drew Jr

PIANO
*born* 14 June 1958

Although he is Kenny Drew's son, the pianist was not raised by his father, and he spent his teenage years playing in rock and soul groups. He began to gain attention in the 80s and has since been a regularly sighted sideman, and quite a prolific leader, having been recording at various times for Claves, Antilles, Evidence, Milestone, Concord, TCB and Arkadia. Besides his straight-ahead work, Drew has a career as a classical concert pianist: 'I like a lot of modern things, so every once in a while a little Schoenberg or Messiaen might sneak into my playing.' His music can sometimes feel excessively heavy and improvisations may tend towards the prolix, but at his best and most uncluttered Drew is a fine and eloquent talent.
**At Maybeck** (Concord)


# Martin Drew

DRUMS
*born* 11 February 1944

A native of Northampton, Drew might have been no more than a middleweight (metaphorically speaking) in the British mainstream ranks: he didn't turn pro until he was 29, when he became a regular drummer at Ronnie Scott's in London. But an association with Oscar Peterson brought him to international attention: he began recording with the pianist in 1982, and thereafter Norman Granz also used him on other sessions involving the Granz circle of mainstreamers. Drew has also led bands of his own (John Critchinson is a favourite partner) and many American visitors, from Jimmy Smith to Buddy Childers, like to have his rock-solid time behind them.
**Oscar Peterson, Freedom Song** (Pablo)


# Paquito D'Rivera

ALTO AND SOPRANO SAXOPHONES, CLARINET
*born* 4 June 1948

D'Rivera was in the first wave of post-bop Cuban musicians to make an impact on jazz. His father played tenor and Paquito picked up jazz broadcasts at his home in Havana on Voice Of America, but he was sharp enough to be playing a Weber concerto (on clarinet) at ten. Chucho Valdés became a major influence on his direction, and in the 70s D'Rivera joined Irakere. It was while on a 1980 European tour with the band that he defected, settling soon enough in New York and subsequently gaining US citizenship. He was a key figure in the Dizzy Gillespie United Nation Orchestra, which he eventually took over, and he also put time into the Caribbean Jazz Project, as if the Afro-Cuban blend wasn't enough. As with so much of the music emerging from these fusions, though, D'Rivera's skill and intensity are unanswerable, while the musical value is harder to assess. He made a string of albums for Columbia in the 80s which are spoiled by too much flash-harry exuberance (although there is a decent *Best Of* now available on CD) and later projects such as *100 Years Of Latin Love Songs* (1998) are Latin jazz as showbiz vehicle. Yet D'Rivera has a more cultivated side which seems to be denied to, say, Arturo Sandoval, and the recent *Habanera* (1999) puts his talents into a variety of sometimes chamber-like contexts which work unexpectedly well: his clarinet work in particular is exceptional. However posterity will judge him, he should be seen as one of the important figures in a palpable musical wave.
**Habanera** (Enja)


# Drugs

Narcotics of one sort or another have been around jazz from the beginning, starting with the alcoholism which afflicted many early pioneers. This was the most pernicious part of jazz culture until the early 40s, although the likes of the Eddie Condon circle all but made alcohol their religion: it nevertheless ruined and destroyed Bix Beiderbecke, Dave Tough, Bunny Berigan and many others. Marijuana was also popular, especially from the early 30s, and the reefer references in Cab Calloway's language of jive are manifold. Everyone from Louis Armstrong to Dizzy Gillespie enjoyed a little smoke. But it was the explosion in heroin usage in the 40s which decimated the boppers: if Charlie Parker, the most high-profile drug user in jazz, set a terrible example, it was one which all too many – Fats Navarro, Red Rodney and countless others – paid a price for. Things hadn't improved much in the 50s: the members of Miles Davis's great quintet were all heroin users, even if their boss had eventually cleaned up his own act. It was this kind of dependence above all which sealed jazz's reputation as a music by and for drug takers, one which still lingers in the minds of many. By the time of the chemical revolution of the 60s, when recreational drugs took another leap forward into psychedelics, jazz addicts just seemed sad and remote to popular culture. Heroin, though, remains a temptation which many in jazz succumb to, with its promise of relief from a pressure for artistic creativity which the non-player can perhaps only guess at, and a glamour drug such as cocaine is even harder to escape in affluent, liberal societies. In an age where doctors, policemen and lawyers are at least as likely to be drug users as any jazz player, though, who can sit in judgement any longer?

# Billy Drummond

DRUMS
born 19 June 1959

Drummond's background was in rock and pop and he didn't arrive on the New York jazz scene until he was almost 30, a bit old to be a Young Lion of the 80s. He is one of the gang of regular kit players who are in demand for every kind of post-bop date in the city, and is as reliable as any of them. Although he's led a few dates for Criss Cross, he seems to have little interest in bandleading and none in composing. Drummond is married to pianist Renee Rosnes.
*The Gift* (Criss Cross)

# Ray Drummond

BASS
born 23 November 1946

A huge man, sometimes called 'Bulldog', Drummond exudes authority on bass. Born into an army family (he learned to hum riffs off his father's jazz records to impress friends), he tried various instruments before settling on bass, and in the 70s he became a regular on the San Francisco circuit. He has been in New York since 1977 and has played in countless sideman situations ever since. Drummond can play as supportively and unobtrusively as any bassman, but in solo or leadership situations he seems to double his sound. He has made a sequence of good, varied albums for the independent Arabesque label, though none of them have made much impact.
*Continuum* (Arabesque)

# Gerd Dudek

TENOR AND SOPRANO SAXOPHONES, FLUTE
born 23 September 1938

Dudek is a senior spirit in the European avant-garde, although his modest showing on record has tended to obscure him from a grander reputation. He worked in a big band led by his trumpeter brother Ossi before first joining the Berliner Jazz Quintet (1960) and then playing in Kurt Edelhagen's orchestra (until 1965). The new music in Germany caught his ear, though, and soon enough he was working alongside Manfred Schoof and Alex von Schlippenbach. He has since forged various alliances, including work with Albert Mangelsdorff and, in particular, Ali Haurand's European Jazz Quintet/Ensemble. Mysteriously, he has only ever made a handful of records as a leader, and Evan Parker made a point of recording him for his new label, releasing *Smatter* in 1999. Dudek's Trane-like tenor sound has a hard edge which he mollifies with often surprisingly melodic improvising; he is also one of the few free players to make something of the flute.
*Smatter* (psi)

# Dukes Of Dixieland
GROUP

The Assunto Brothers (trumpeter Frank and trombonist Freddie) formed this unremarkable Dixieland combo in 1949. They began a residency at The Famous Door in New Orleans in 1950 and were a principal force in the formation of Dixieland-for-tourists: the playing was blandly spirited rather than genuinely hot, but it suited the tastes of visitors who didn't want to take their jazz home with them. In 1956, they moved to the even more suitable climes of Las Vegas, and began a series of records for the Audio Fidelity label: as with Al Hirt after them, they were promoted through American audio magazines and sold in the thousands. In all they made 14 albums for that label (including one set with Louis Armstrong) and followed these with two more for Columbia and six for Decca in the 60s. Freddie died in 1966 and Frank followed him in 1974, but the band carried on, returning to New Orleans in the 70s, and it was still active as a sextet in the late 90s. While some superior players passed through the group's ranks – George Wettling, Don Ewell, Tony Parenti – the records never amount to much more than what the band set out to do, play Dixieland in its simplest and least testing form. Outside the US, the Dukes are scarcely known at all.
*The Phenomenal Dukes Of Dixieland* (Audio Fidelity)

# Candy Dulfer
ALTO SAXOPHONE
*born* 19 September 1969

# Hans Dulfer
TENOR SAXOPHONE
*born* 28 May 1940

Hans was an Ike Quebec fan (one of his groups was named Heavy Soul Inc, after the Quebec Blue Note classic) who went on to perform in a rather extraordinary variety of playing situations in his native Amsterdam: free jazz alongside Han Bennink and Frank Wright, straight-ahead music in Tough Tenors, and a strange sort of heavy-metal jazz in a band called Reflud. He split his career between jazz playing and working as a car salesman, but for some he is better known as the father of Candy Dulfer, a glamorous alto player whose Sanborn-styled jazz-funk albums made her something of a star in the 90s (particularly after a hit single shared with the rock musician Dave Stewart). Actually, her records have often been very entertaining, and while her star has waned a bit, at least it allowed her dad to make a few crossover records of his own in the later 90s.
**Candy:** *Sax-A-Go-Go* (BMG Ariola)
**Hans:** *Bohemia* (Nowa)

# Louis Dumaine
CORNET
*born* 1890; *died* 1949

Dumaine was a schooled New Orleans man, and although he only made eight sides for Victor in 1927 his proper lead and fierce attack is very much in an archetypal New Orleans mould, one which many revivalist trumpeters would follow. The four tracks by Dumaine's Jazzola Eight, with excellent clarinet by Willie Joseph, are well worth hearing, especially 'Franklin Street Blues' and 'Pretty Audrey'. Dumaine also accompanied the blues singer Ann Cook in the same month: she sounds surprisingly effective, given that she reputedly came straight to the date from an all-night drinking session. Dumaine continued to play in the city but, like so many first-generation New Orleans jazzmen, he never recorded again.
**Various Artists,** *Sizzling The Blues* (Frog)

# Ted Dunbar
GUITAR
*born* 17 January 1937; *died* 29 May 1998

Born in Port Arthur, Texas, Dunbar played in local jazz and R&B bands in his youth, moving to Dallas (where he worked as a pharmacist) and following a similar course, although he also kept up with his day job. He subsequently went into music education but carried on working as a sideman. He made a single album as a soloist for Don Schlitten's Xanadu label and cut several other records in a more expansive hard-bop context.
*Opening Remarks* (Xanadu)

# Paul Dunmall
SAXOPHONES, CLARINETS
*born* 6 May 1953

Dunmall is a high-energy post-Coltrane sax-ophonist whose playing has been a ubiqui-tous part of the British free scene for many years. He actually studied clarinet for sev-eral years but taught himself the saxo-phone, and he worked on the US club circuit in the 70s with soul groups (as well as Alice Coltrane). When he returned home, he took leading roles in numerous groups formed in the 70s, 80s and 90s, including Spirit Level, Tenor Tonic (with Alan Skidmore), Whatever, The British Saxophone Quartet, and in par-ticular Keith Tippett's group Mujician, an association which is now a long-standing alli-ance. Dunmall has lately been releasing CD-Rs of his own music and it is already a lengthy list.
*Babu* (SLAM)

# Johnny Dunn
TRUMPET
*born* 19 February 1897; *died* 20 August 1937

Dunn was a pioneer on several levels: in early black jazz bands, as a leader himself and as an early visitor to Europe. He grew up in Memphis and played as a solo act in the local theatres before joining W C Handy's orchestra in 1917, which took him to New York. He turns up on the first sessions by Mamie Smith's Jazz Hounds in 1920, then formed his own Jazz Hounds, which recorded the likes of 'Sergeant Dunn's Bugle Call Blues'; and his 'Hawaiian Blues' sold an incredible 700,000 copies in 1922. The Jazz Hounds themselves were an unremarkable group, but Dunn's own playing – big and loud, with a penchant for bugle motifs – tells us much about jazz brass techniques before Armstrong's arrival. He visited Europe in 1923 and 1926 (recording four sides with The Plantation Orchestra in London) and back in New York led a record date in 1928 with Jelly Roll Morton on piano. He went back to Europe for a third time and settled in the Netherlands, but died in Paris when only 40. Dunn had much of the right stuff to be a great jazz trumpeter – a big tone, a taste for quite intricate passage-work, and a basic wa-wa style which may have influenced Bubber Miley – and only the stiff-ness of the early idiom consigns him, just, to the wrong side of the jazz era.
*Cornet Blues* (Frog)

# Dutch Swing College Band
FORMED 1945

The longest-serving jazz group in Europe and one with very few rivals anywhere for longevity, the DSCB was established in 1945 by reed player Peter Schilperoot, who bossed the band until his death in 1990. There have been many long-standing members over the years, including Oscar Klein and Bert de Koort (trumpets), Wout Steinhaus (guitar), Jan Morks (clarinet) and Frits Kaatee (reeds), and current leader Bob Kaper (clarinet) has been with them since 1966. Although they began as diehard traditionalists, the music has expanded to include the small-group swing repertoire and an occasional original. A vast discography includes many live dates, as well as sessions with Sidney Bechet, Jimmy Witherspoon and Teddy Wilson. Although they went through a bit of a dry spell in the 70s, the group came back stronger than ever under Kaper's leadership, and is still touring and recording and 'having a ball' doing it. Kaper suggests that their jazz isn't old but 'aged – like good French cognac'.
*Forty Years At Its Best* (Timeless)

# Honoré Dutrey
TROMBONE
*born* c1887; *died* 21 July 1935

Dutrey was an able member of an early gen-eration of New Orleans jazzmen, whose small but significant contribution should not be forgotten. He worked in several of the city's brass bands before serving time in the navy, and on his return he joined King Oliver's band in Chicago, staying until 1924. Thereafter he freelanced around the Chicago area and made a few records with Louis Armstrong and Johnny Dodds (1927–8). His health obliged him to retire in 1930. Dutrey had little in the way of improvisational capa-bility, but he had a fine rich tone on the trombone and created a dignified style on the horn at a time when it was still basically being played as a kind of vaudeville instrument.

**King Oliver, _The Complete_** (Retrieval)

# Dominic Duval
BASS
_born_ 27 April 1944

Duval grew up in Brooklyn and started on saxophone, then switched to bass in his teens. He worked in relative anonymity in the 70s and eventually took a job in a window-cleaning business in 1980, which lasted until 1993. In recent years, though, he has become a prolific member of the avant-garde team centred on Bob Rusch's CIMP label, and he has recorded numerous dates for that outfit as both leader and sideman, often with drummer Jay Rosen. Years of private woodshedding have given Duval a considerable technique, which he deploys to varying advantage on his records, although it has often led to a private conversation as much as anything which communicates to even a sympathetic listener.

**_The Wedding Band_** (CIMP)

# George Duvivier
BASS
_born_ 17 August 1920; _died_ 11 July 1985

Duvivier joined New York jazz in the late 30s, eventually working as a writer for Jimmie Lunceford in the 40s, before working as bassist with various singers throughout most of the 50s. From 1960, as an unflappable pro, he cut hundreds of record dates, the majority of them away from jazz, although when required to work under leaders as disparate as Eric Dolphy and Terry Gibbs he was always up to whatever the task demanded. Duvivier will be on records in every admirer's collection, but it's hard to remember him for any singularity: a characteristic of the invisible, necessary bass man.

**Bud Powell, _The Amazing Bud Powell Vol 2_** (Blue Note)

# Mbizo Johnny Dyani
BASS
_born_ 30 November 1945; _died_ 25 October 1986

A member of Chris McGregor's Blue Notes, Dyani was a South African who left for Europe in 1965, working in Britain for several years and then decamping to Denmark around 1972. His style and taste were flexible enough to accommodate some of the severest avant-garde settings, as well as the township music of his youth and the freebop material mined by the likes of Don Cherry, John Tchicai and Abdullah Ibrahim, all of whom he worked with. He was a familiar figure at European festivals, and his ebullience could lift a bandstand, as well as quieten an audience with music that could overflow with sorrow as well as joy. Records under his nominal leadership were, though, often rather disappointing. He died suddenly while in Berlin in 1986.

**_Song For Biko_** (Steeplechase)

# Allen Eager
TENOR SAXOPHONE
_born_ 10 January 1927; _died_ 13 April 2003

Handsome, well connected, and a bit of a playboy, Eager was, to say the least, an untypical bebopper. He worked with a string of New York bands while still in his teens and he was recording for Savoy under his own name as early as 1946; at one point he was leading a quintet on 52nd Street with J J Johnson, Bud Powell, Max Roach and Curley Russell. He was in one of the best of Tadd Dameron's small groups and his finest solos on record – in hock to Lester Young, but fully up to speed with which direction bop language was going – are all but unique in their mix of suave confidence and careless urbanity. As soon as he'd got going, though, Eager drifted off the scene: he dallied with narcotics, and his interest in jazz seemed ultimately no more dedicated than his taste for racing cars. He worked spasmodically through the 50s before quitting music altogether, only to suddenly reappear in 1982; and then he disappeared again, not heard from further until the announcement of his death in 2003.

**_Anthropology_** (Spotlite)

# Jon Eardley

TRUMPET
*born* 30 September 1928; *died* 2 April 1991

Unlike Chet Baker before him and Art Farmer afterwards, Eardley's time as a member of the Gerry Mulligan group didn't do him a lot of good. He worked with little prominence in Washington and New York before joining Mulligan in 1954, visiting Europe with him two years later. A heroin habit stopped his career in its tracks, though, and he more or less quit music until the early 60s, when he moved to Europe. At the end of the decade he was in Cologne and doing studio work, as well as working on the club scene there; but American audiences forgot about him. A 1981 club recording where he is featured along with Chet Baker could have had a poignant resonance, but Eardley actually played powerfully and well.
*The Jon Eardley Seven* (Prestige)

# Charles Earland

ORGAN, KEYBOARDS
*born* 24 May 1941; *died* 11 December 1999

Earland was a late developer among organ-combo leaders because he'd actually started out on saxophone. But he immediately struck lucky with his first (1969) set for Prestige, *Black Talk*, which was a big radio hit, this success pushing the album into the jazz best-seller lists. As an organist he was more or less straight out of the Jimmy Smith bag, but he adapted his style to the newer funky rhythms better than many of his peers and he had a good ear for small-group arrangements. Still, the success of *Black Talk* was never quite repeated, even though Earland went on to add synthesizers to his arsenal. He eventually dropped them again when it became apparent that the 'classic' organ-combo instrumentation was going to weather the years better.
*Black Talk* (Prestige/OJC)

# Bill Easley

REEDS
*born* 13 January 1946

Easley started on clarinet but added saxophone in his teens, and after military service he joined George Benson's group in 1968.

The soul-jazz combo suited him fine, and when he settled in Memphis in 1971 his diary was full of work with the likes of Isaac Hayes and Albert King. He was back in New York in 1980, and was again at work with organ-leaders: Jimmy McGriff, Charles Earland, Papa John DeFrancesco and Jimmy Smith all used him, and he was also a reliable section-man in several big bands. He has had a few opportunities to record as his own leader, although the albums have perhaps been nothing special: Easley's forte is to take the occasional, apposite solo, and step back again.
**Jimmy McGriff, *Blue To the Bone*** (Milestone)

# East Coast jazz

A term created more or less as a direct counter to the idea of West Coast jazz – simplifying the notion that everything out West was light, cool and not that profound, whereas everything in the East was tough, bluesy and soulful. Though it came into being in the 50s, it has never been used with much sincerity, and, ever since, dissenters have delighted in pointing out the innumerable exceptions to both stereotypes.

# Peter Ecklund

CORNET, TRUMPET
*born* 27 September 1945

Ecklund had a classical training, but he was a Boston high-school teacher who moonlighted on gigs before finally choosing to turn pro in the early 70s. Since then he has worked steadily but relatively unobtrusively, much of his work coming to light on studio and soundtrack projects, although he has a prominent role in the gang of swing revivalists usually led by Marty Grosz. Ecklund is a scholar of historical styles (he has done analytical tomes on both Armstrong and Beiderbecke) and he is one of those players who is almost unnervingly correct in his solos. The few records under his (reluctant?) leadership are whimsically enjoyable, if slight.
*Gigs* (Arbors)

# Billy Eckstine

VOCAL, TRUMPET
*born* 8 July 1914; *died* 8 March 1993

Eckstine grew up in Pittsburgh and began singing more or less for fun, although by the time Budd Johnson heard him in 1939 – and recommended him to Earl Hines, who was looking for a singer – he had done plenty of club gigs. He stayed four years and enjoyed huge hits with 'Stormy Monday' and 'Jelly, Jelly'. Eckstine had a cavernous baritone voice, which he used in a silky, beguiling way, and that combination of dignity and sexiness was almost unique among black singers of his time. He formed his own big band in 1944; it lasted three years and at one time or another listed many of the major bebop names among its personnel (Dizzy Gillespie, Charlie Parker, Miles Davis, Art Blakey, Sonny Stitt, Dexter Gordon and Gene Ammons among them). But the trouble with the band was that, although 'people still talk today about that legendary Billy Eckstine band, the legendary Billy Eckstine was about to starve with that motherfucker'. He switched to a small group, and by the 50s was recording for MGM and Emarcy, often with sumptuous orchestral backings. A golden period of middle-of-the-road success lay ahead of him, but B (as he was known by musicians) never stood aside from jazz, and even his most commercial records have some fine players on them somewhere. The wonderful *No Cover, No Minimum* (Roulette, 1961) is a valuable record of his club act. Though he was latterly associated with a brand of middle-aged soul, he subsequently went back to jazz clubs, and in the 80s he could still be found at Ronnie Scott's in London. Along with Nat Cole, Eckstine crossed the line which had hitherto denied black crooners their audience, and his best work is an indispensable part of black popular culture.
*No Cover, No Minimum* (Roulette)

# ECM

RECORD COMPANY

The German bassist Manfred Eicher started his label in Cologne in 1969, the first issue a piano album by Mal Waldron, and from there he began recording and issuing sessions on a regular basis, featuring a mix of both European and American musicians (which at the time was an all but unprecedented strategy). Among his key early releases were *Afric Pepperbird* (1970) by Jan Garbarek and *Facing You* (1972) by Keith Jarrett: both artists have remained with ECM to this day, each building a huge discography at the label in the process. All through the 70s Eicher demonstrated a uniquely intuitive touch in finding 'new' artists and placing them in a creative context, and among many discoveries were John Abercrombie, Ralph Towner, Eberhard Weber, Terje Rypdal, Egberto Gismonti, Enrico Rava and Edward Vesala, while established names such as Paul Bley, Jack DeJohnette and Kenny Wheeler have also done some of their best work for the label. Eicher commenced a parallel New Series of records devoted to mainly contemporary composition in 1983. By the new century, Editions of Contemporary Music had swelled to a catalogue approaching 1,000 records in total. It has been controversial along the way: Eicher has had to endure criticism of 'coffee-table music', a production style which seems to bathe the music in reverberant echo (the ECM 'sound') and charges of European aloofness and elitism. On another level, though, his achievement is incredible: no other label has maintained such dramatic independence of spirit and singularity of vision across such a long period of time and with so many releases to its credit. Just as remarkable is that Eicher has produced the majority of these records himself, and still oversees the overall creative direction of the company.

# Harry Edison

TRUMPET
*born* 10 October 1915; *died* 27 July 1999

Though born in Columbus, Ohio, Edison was raised in Kentucky and returned to his home town when he was 12, whereupon he began playing with local bands. He was with the Jeters–Pillar Orchestra in Cleveland and St Louis before joining Lucky Millinder in New York in 1937 and, from there, joining the band he was perennially associated with, the Count Basie group. He stayed with Basie right up until the group's temporary disbandment in 1950. Edison was, alongside the tougher-sounding Buck Clayton, one of

Basie's principal soloists, and he steps out on dozens of sides, of which 'Texas Shuffle' (1938), 'Rock-A-Bye Basie' (1939) and 'Easy Does It' (1940) are characteristic. Lester Young called him 'Sweets', which stuck, and after a comparatively wild early manner he pared back to an immaculate, wasteless delivery – rarely shifting much out of the middle register of the horn – which soon became instantly identifiable. After the Basie years he led his own groups for a spell and strolled into the Jazz At The Philharmonic camp, but he moved over to the West Coast and found that he could make a handsome living in the studios. Frank Sinatra made sure that Harry was present on both his tours and his records, and as Gary Giddins once noted, Sweets basically played three different fill-in solos as required: beep beep beep, beep beeeep beep, and b'beem'm b'beep. In the 60s, there were many reunions with Basie, and he often toured America and Europe as a solo or a guest star, a regimen which he kept up into the 80s and 90s, turning up with the likes of Lockjaw Davis, Lionel Hampton and Woody Herman on small-band visits. Sweets paced himself perfectly over a very long career. He was diagnosed with cancer as far back as 1984, but continued to work up until shortly before his death. Whether playing muted (with the Harmon mute, a device which he helped to define in the music) or open, he took his time, and as a result never seemed to run short of breath or space.

*Gee Baby, Ain't I Good To You?* (Verve)

## Teddy Edwards
TENOR SAXOPHONE
*born* 26 April 1924; *died* 23 April 2003

Originally from Jackson, Mississippi, Edwards eventually fetched up in Los Angeles in 1945, having played in minor territory bands for several years. He remained based there for the rest of his life, one of the great figures in the Central Avenue scene. He played with LA acolytes like Benny Carter and Gerald Wilson in the 40s and early 50s and was the tenorman in the Max Roach–Clifford Brown group in 1954. Thereafter he led combos of his own, while always ready to take a sideman role for an interesting gig: Wilson used him as one of his main soloists in his Pacific Jazz

Sessions of the 60s, and Teddy himself recorded four fine albums for Contemporary, two for Pacific Jazz and two for Prestige. Thereafter he was for a time hard to find on record, but in the late 80s he began turning up as a leader again, travelling to Europe and delighting fans with long memories. His edgeless, muscular sound furred over a little as he grew older, but he never lost his fluency and it is hard to find a record where he sounds anything like below par.
**With Howard McGhee,** *Together Again!* (OJC/Contemporary)

## Marty Ehrlich
REEDS
*born* 31 May 1955

Ehrlich is closly associated with New York's avant-garde of the past 20 years, but he actually comes from St Paul and grew up in St Louis, and even as a teenager he was working with the likes of Oliver Lake and Joe Bowie. He arrived in New York in 1977, and has been busy there virtually ever since, although it has taken the German label Enja to record his most significant work. A list of some of his most significant collaborators would have to include Julius Hemphill, Anthony Braxton, Anthony Davis, Muhal Richard Abrams, Bobby Previte, Andrew Hill and Myra Melford, but Ehrlich has been happy to work in a wide field: one of his most fruitful roles was in the Don Grolnick group which recorded two superb Blue Note albums. As a leader himself, he runs trios (including The Dark Woods Trio, with bass and cello), quartets and quintets of varying personnel: although Michael Cain is sometimes involved, Ehrlich mostly avoids the piano, preferring another reed player to spar with. While he can play as garrulously as any player in the formal-to-free style, he is not a screamer, nor much of an expressionist. A group like The Dark Woods Ensemble has a suitably chamberish feel which he is perfectly comfortable with. Alto and clarinet are his main instruments, but his flute playing can be particularly appealing, graceful without being overly sweet, and his bass clarinet work with Grolnick was outstanding.
*New York Child* (Enja)

# Thore Ehrling

BANDLEADER
*born* 29 December 1912; *died* 21 October 1994

Ehrling was a fine trumpeter and a skilled arranger-composer, and in 1938 he put together a seven-piece band from the best of Stockholm's jazz players which eventually became enlarged into a big band. All through the 40s and 50s it ruled the Swedish popular jazz roost: it was featured more than any other band on Swedish radio (which at that time offered only one station), and Ehrling, a shrewd businessman as well as a creative musician, made sure that he had many of the best soloists and writers under wraps. That said, it was, as with a band such as Ted Heath's, at least as much a commercial dance orchestra as any kind of jazz outfit. Ehrling eventually disbanded in 1957 and concentrated on his music publishing business: the Ehrling Award, which he was involved in up until his death, is an important music prize in Sweden.
*Jazz Highlights 1939–55* (Dragon)

# Roy Eldridge

TRUMPET, VOCAL
*born* 30 January 1911; *died* 26 February 1989

'Little Jazz', a nickname bestowed by Otto Hardwick, started on drums and then moved to trumpet, playing mostly in carnival bands before arriving in New York in 1930. He didn't manage to get on record until 1935, when his solos with the Teddy Hill band won him attention, and he joined Fletcher Henderson for a year in 1935 before working with an eight-piece band in Chicago, which broadcast nightly from The Famous Door. Four titles he cut for Commodore in 1938 with Chu Berry, including their cross-talk on 'Sittin' In', are a vivid picture of the young Eldridge, his style flaring and fizzing, his sound sometimes almost overheated: his admiration for Coleman Hawkins, later a favourite partner, comes through strongly. Other musicians soon regarded Eldridge as Louis Armstrong's successor, with Pops seemingly lost to commerce, but Eldridge was more interested in carving his own path and loved to be out on the town, looking for cutting contests and taking on all-trumpet-comers. In 1941 he

joined Gene Krupa, who placed his black lead trumpeter centre-stage in his otherwise white band, and often featured him alongside Anita O'Day. Eldridge's features with the band were often terrific, but he was worn down by racist incidents while out on the road, and when the same things happened when he joined Artie Shaw in 1944, he had had enough after a year. Eldridge tried his own big band, but it was the wrong time to do it, and it folded soon enough; marginalized by bebop, which he disliked, the great trumpet hope of a few years earlier suddenly seemed out of place.

He was on tour with Benny Goodman when he decided to stay on in Paris, and a year there, lionized at last by an adoring public, revived his spirits. He was back in the US in 1951 and joined the Jazz At The Philharmonic roadshow, worked in small groups with Coleman Hawkins and made some decent albums for Norman Granz: one of them found him making up his differences with Dizzy Gillespie. He didn't record much in the 60s and took on rather desultory roles with Count Basie and Ella Fitzgerald, but Granz's all-star packages of the 70s found a context for him again, and the diminutive, now white-haired titan was still playing fit to burst, even if the old dexterity and assurance had become sometimes muddled. One of the oldest clichés in jazz criticism is that Eldridge was the link between Armstrong and Gillespie: it's a fair enough point, but Eldridge actually took little from Armstrong and never admitted to Gillespie's bebop grammar. As great as he was, his work is disappointingly scattered on record and the LP era wasn't especially kind to him, although his later work with Hawkins could do with a reappraisal. He suffered a stroke in 1980 and that finally took him off the bandstand.
*Heckler's Hop* (Hep)

# Eliane Elias

PIANO, VOCAL
*born* 19 March 1960

Originally from São Paulo, Brazil, Elias moved to New York at the beginning of the 80s, where she joined Steps Ahead (she is on their debut set for Elektra) and subsequently married Randy Brecker, although they later separated. In 1989 she signed to Blue Note

and stayed with the label for a dozen years; in the new century she has now moved to RCA. Her records are on the face of it a lightweight bunch, but she has mined a seam between soft Brazilian pop-jazz and a tougher New York sound with considerable finesse, and the best of the albums include a lot of captivating music. Although she sings from time to time, the accent has been on her piano playing, and she has successfully resisted any temptation to go for a more obvious kind of fusion. However, the RCA debut seems to be pushing her towards more singing and less piano.
**The Three Americas** (Blue Note)

## Fred Elizalde
PIANO
*born* 12 December 1907; *died* 16 January 1979

Although Elizalde created some of the best jazz records ever made in Britain, his name is these days known only to a small contingent of collectors. Born in Manila, he went to Cambridge to study in 1926 and formed a band he named the Quinquaginta Ramblers, although it recorded a solitary pair of titles for HMV as 'Fred Elizalde And His Cambridge Undergraduates'. He was a sensation in the dance-band community, and wrote a suite, *The Heart Of A Nigger*, which was premiered at the London Palladium and recorded for Decca (though not until 1932). His greatest music, though, came when he was hired by the Savoy Hotel and imported (from The California Ramblers) the Americans Adrian Rollini, Bobby Davis and Chelsea Quealey. What a sound it must have made at the Savoy! Their records suggest a remarkable cool-to-hot outfit, but the Savoy patrons were eventually disenchanted and Elizalde left in 1929. He remained in London until 1933, still recording band sides and piano solos, but then moved to Spain, where he went back to classical music; he composed, and conducted symphony orchestras. Like Spike Hughes, he left his dalliance with jazz far behind him in the end.
**Jazz At The Savoy** (Decca)

## Kurt Elling
VOCAL
*born* 2 November 1967

In a sense, it has been Elling's misfortune to come to prominence at a time when the adventurous style of jazz singing which he represents has dropped dramatically out of favour. Born in Chicago, he began working on his local scene at the beginning of the 90s, and he secured the extraordinary coup of signing a contract with Blue Note in 1994 after sending them a demo tape. Although his voice is quite different in style and timbre, Elling is stylistically in deep debt to Mark Murphy: for his microphone technique, phrasing, and kinship to the beat culture which Murphy himself came out of. In performance, he is as likely to sing (and dramatically deconstruct) a familiar standard as he is to recite from a literary text and take it to a startling new place. A mesmerizing live performer, after a mixed start his recent records for Blue Note have been triumphant portrayals of his art, deep and sophisticated documents which have actually received scandalously little attention in the era of Krall. If the precinct of the hipster-artist has any relevance in the contemporary world, Elling is surely its principal guardian.
**Man In The Air** (Blue Note)

## Duke Ellington
PIANO, BANDLEADER
*born* 29 April 1899; *died* 24 May 1974

He may have professed an occasional dislike for the term, but Duke Ellington was and is jazz. His father was a butler and their home life in Washington was comfortable, with the young Edward Kennedy Ellington devoted to his mother. He studied piano from the age of seven and seemed to have an artistic career ahead of him, although it was the ragtime pianists such as Willie 'The Lion' Smith who really took his fancy. He wrote his first tune in 1913 ('Soda Fountain Rag', which he played only a handful of times on record) and was playing on the Washington nightlife scene by 1917: 'Duke' came from his habitually seigneurial manner and appearance. Six years later, by now a big man in this milieu, he tried a move to New York. He ended up broke, but tried again later that year and played piano in Elmer Snowden's Washingtonians, which he eventually took over; Sonny Greer, Otto Hardwick and Artie Whetsol were already among the sidemen. The band became a fixture in some of the smaller New York clubs and gradually added more players, but the key arrival was trumpeter Bubber Miley, with his sensational growl techniques.

Ellington first recorded in 1924, but it wasn't until 1926 that he began making records regularly, at first for a host of different labels: 'East St Louis Toodle-Oo', initially made on 29 November 1926, is perhaps the first characteristic Ellington record. The following year, Duke took his band into The Cotton Club (the engagement which Joe Oliver had turned down), and over the next four years propelled his reputation and orchestra into the front rank of the music. With the arrival of such significant players as Cootie Williams, Johnny Hodges, Harry Carney and Barney Bigard, the Ellington ensemble was now bursting with solo talent, but it was his skill in devising sound-palettes for the orchestra and individual vehicles for his distinctive soloists which set them apart. While at The Cotton Club, a 'jungle' style predominated to fit in with the floor show, with Miley's growl trumpet as the lead voice and Ellington's sly exoticism (exemplified in the likes of 'Jungle Nights In Harlem', 1927) as a framing device, but after hits such as 'Mood Indigo' (1930) his ambitions widened, and with 'Creole Rhapsody' (1931) he tried his hand at extended composition, the piece first recorded across two sides of a 12-inch 78.

All through the 30s, his creativity seemed limitless: scores of compositions exploited the unique gifts of his players and the confines of the three-minute record. Harry Carney's baritone sax gave the reed section an unrivalled sonority, and the various trumpet sections made light of the fundamental differences between each performer when they all played together. Juan Tizol's valve-trombone, often blended with the reeds rather than the brass, added another individual touch. Although the death of his mother was a very black moment for Ellington (he wrote 'Reminiscing In Tempo', 1934, as a requiem), most of the decade found him enjoying a scintillating success, which two European tours in 1933 and 1939 added to. When he hired Jimmy Blanton on bass in 1939, it was another turning point:

Blanton seemed to modernize the band's rhythms at a stroke. With the further arrival of saxophonist Ben Webster and, as Duke's new compositional right-hand man, Billy Strayhorn, the period 1939–44 glittered with genius, from Strayhorn's tune 'Take The "A" Train' (which became the Ellington theme tune ever after) to such miniature masterpieces as 'Harlem Air Shaft', 'Ko Ko', 'Jack The Bear' and countless others: every new record date for Victor seemed to offer fresh riches, and more than any other period of Ellington's music, this is the one scholars agree on as his most consistently inspirational.

Duke began to appear annually at Carnegie Hall, a respectability he hankered after, although the poor reception for another extended work premiered there, 'Black, Brown And Beige' (1943), crushed him. Perhaps that was a turning point: after that, the band's personnel started to shift more often than not. Blanton was dead, Cootie Williams, Ben Webster and others left, and Ellington's compositional zest, while scarcely retarded, seemed to lose some of its invincibility. By 1950 he was becoming seen – as he had surely wished – as a great American composer, even as most of his weekly life was taken up with touring, and playing as many dances as 'concerts'. The long-playing record gave him the chance to explore the extended form as never before, and such works as 'Liberian Suite', 'Harlem' and the Shakespearean delight 'Such Sweet Thunder' were pieces he seemed to reserve his most concentrated thinking for, although critics complained that the beautiful brevity of the older music was being dispersed, and Ellington never again wrote a popular hit on the level of 'Satin Doll', 'Sophisticated Lady' or 'Mood Indigo'.

In the rock'n'roll era Ellington had lost much of his popular audience, like all of the swing bandleaders, but an epochal appearance at the 1956 Newport Jazz Festival – with its flag-waving solo by Paul Gonsalves on 'Diminuendo And Crescendo In Blue' – put him back in the headlines and recharged the band's spirit. He never stopped recording, creating a block of otherwise unreleased works which he referred to as 'the stockpile', much of it of the highest quality, and most of it not issued until after his death; but after a long association with RCA in the 30s and 40s, he subsequently made discs for

Columbia (1950–62), Capitol (1953–8), Reprise (1962–6 – a ballyhooed signing which disappointingly produced little in the way of great work) and then RCA again (1966–8), with his final recordings emerging on Fantasy and Atlantic. In the 60s he began to be showered with honours – doctorates, fellowships, awards of every kind – which he took in his humorous, gracious stride, while always maintaining the mask behind which most of his feelings were usually hidden: interviewing Ellington, as Michael Parkinson would later discover, never led to a revelation of any kind.

The band was still in great shape during the 60s, with Cootie Williams returning to the fold and latter-day soloists such as Gonsalves and Russell Procope joining the ageless Hodges, and there were magisterial late works such as *The Far East Suite* (1967), *And His Mother Called Him Bill* (1967 – a requiem for the recently dead Strayhorn) and *New Orleans Suite* (1971) to savour. By 1970, though, a picture seemed to be emerging of a man who had somehow outlived his own orchestra: the death of Hodges in 1970 seemed a particularly cruel blow, and Ellington had started to withdraw into religious writing, which was eventually recorded as the three *Sacred Concerts*. Duke carried on regardless, as if he didn't know of any other way, and with son Mercer as his road manager, he maintained a punishing schedule which was finally closed by his hospitalization with cancer early in 1974.

'The piano player', as he liked to refer to himself in stage announcements, became inimitable: never one to give himself features, he nevertheless provided links, comped, suggested and directed, much as Count Basie did, although with even more flair and with a wider variety of invention. Studio meetings with the likes of John Coltrane and Charles Mingus in the 60s at least gave him some more expansive space as an instrumentalist than he usually allowed with the orchestra. His solo rendition of Strayhorn's 'Lotus Blossom' became his one later indulgence, beautifully realized on the memorial album to his long-serving partner. Strayhorn's work with Ellington is so *simpatico* that it has been a problem for scholars to figure out who did what in their collaborative work, but 'Monster', as Strayhorn referred to Duke, usually took the credit anyway. He inspired the profoundest loyalty from his men, some of whom – Carney, Hodges, Williams, Gonsalves – stayed with him for decades, even though he would wryly remark that he had 'discovered a gimmick – I give them money'. Whatever his ambitions were as a composer, there is today no more highly regarded figure in American music, and it is the sustained irony of Ellington's life that so much of it was spent in an environment which was considered antithetical to the established cultural hierarchies. The body of work he left behind is so vast – thousands of compositions, tens of thousands of individual recordings in both live and studio conditions – that it is a study which needs a lifetime to comprehend, but the beauty of Ellington's music is that almost any three minutes of it is life-enhancing. Miles Davis's insistence that there should be a day on which every musician gets down on their knees and thanks Duke hardly seems too much of an encomium.

*Never No Lament* (Bluebird)

# Mercer Ellington
TRUMPET, BANDLEADER
*born* 11 March 1919; *died* 8 February 1996

Ellington's difficult relationship with his father became the tonic note in a career which amounted to a long and largely frustrated search for personal recognition. Initially encouraged by Duke as both performer and composer – Mercer wrote some fine pieces for the band's book early on, including 'Things Ain't What They Used To Be' and 'Moon Mist' – he led bands of his own too, but found his father's jealousy and manipulation led to his own career (particularly as a recording artist) being largely stifled. He worked for Ellington as an assistant and copyist, and eventually became his road manager for the final decade of Duke's life, assuming command of the band on his father's death. He directed the Broadway show *Sophisticated Ladies* and wrote a memoir of his father, but leading the Ellington ghost band when it should have passed into history eventually defeated him, and he spent his final years in Denmark. When he latterly spoke of his father, he usually referred to him simply as 'Ellington'.

*Digital Duke* (GRP)

## Don Elliott

TRUMPET, MELLOPHONE, VIBES
*born* 21 October 1926; *died* 5 July 1984

Elliott tried several instruments as a boy, and he rehearsed with Bill Evans when both were in their teens (a private recording of one of their sessions was released a couple of years ago). He played trumpet in an army band and studied vibes in Miami, before playing under a variety of leaders in New York. He also had his own group, which sometimes had Evans at the piano. Playing trumpet, vibes and the rare mellophone, and sometimes singing as well, Elliott somehow found himself popular and made records for 11 different labels, but in the 60s he went into stage, film and TV scoring and despite a brief comeback in the 70s little was heard from him in jazz again. Like many other 50s jazz personalities, his name is hardly recognized at all a half-century later.
***Double Trumpet Doings*** (Riverside)

## Don Ellis

TRUMPET
*born* 25 July 1934; *died* 17 December 1978

Ellis now seems like a creation of the 60s, a child of an era where anything seemed possible and every musical problem was really an opportunity in disguise. He grew up in Los Angeles and studied in Boston, played trumpet with Maynard Ferguson, then moved to New York, where he joined the George Russell group for a spell. His own bands were like workshops of unusual musical ideas, actively put into practice on the albums *How Time Passes, New Ideas* (both 1961) and *Essence* (1962). He formed a Hindustani Jazz Sextet, which unfortunately never recorded, played a contemporary concerto with the New York Philharmonic and eventually formed his own big band. This became something of a sensation on the festival circuit, and its modish trappings made Ellis a hit with the American college audience: he used sitars and multiple percussion, electric keyboards and an amplified string quartet, and he himself played a four-valve trumpet which he could utilize to play quarter-tones (and sometimes he had the rest of his trumpet section use them too). It was a sensation because the music was sensational, too: despite Ellis seeking to take his

theories to seemingly absurd limits in performance – writing pieces in elongated metres, which he would explain to the audience with a kind of zany delight, and taking his interest in the quarter-tone to the point of inventing a 12-pitch quarter-tone scale – all most audiences could hear was brash, exhilarating, mostly thrilling big-band music. *Shock Treatment* and *Electric Bath* (1968) are both definitive portrayals of Ellis's work, and an avenue which jazz has hardly explored since. By the 70s, times had suddenly changed: Ellis became busier with filmscore work (*The French Connection* and others) and composing in more of a contemporary-classical field, but he suffered a serious heart attack in 1975. He came back from it, playing a hybrid trombone he called a 'superbone', but died three years later. Without his own lively presence to speak up for his music, it now feels remote, and belonging only to its own time.
***Electric Bath*** (Columbia)

## Herb Ellis

GUITAR
*born* 4 August 1921

Ellis is from Texas (he studied there along with his contemporary, Jimmy Giuffre) and had a fairly uneventful career in big bands before joining the Oscar Peterson Trio in 1953. Peterson's high profile shed lustre on his sideman, but Ellis was content to stay in an accompanying role with Ella Fitzgerald for some years, and then disappeared into studio work. In the 70s and 80s he joined the Concord stable of mainstreamers and turned out many albums, alone and with the Great Guitars group, sitting alongside Barney Kessel and Charlie Byrd. While not necessarily seen as a speed player, Ellis could match any guitarist's bebop chops: Peterson's set-closer at the 1957 Newport Festival, '52nd Street Theme', is reeled off by Ellis at incredible velocity. He made five albums for Verve, *Nothing But The Blues* (1958) being especially outstanding, but these were largely forgotten and it wasn't until his Concord years that he got back on to record in a big way. Herb's able mix of Charlie Christian, bop and the blues puts him up there with the best guitarists of his generation.
***Nothing But The Blues*** (Verve)

# Ziggy Elman
TRUMPET
*born* 26 May 1914; *died* 26 June 1968

Elman has often been held up as an example of bad taste, but it might be fairer to suggest that his premier trumpet performances – with Benny Goodman (1936–40) and Tommy Dorsey (1940–43) – were too Jewish to find universal acclaim. Elman took every spotlit solo as if he was leading the band at a *fralich*, and signature records such as 'And The Angels Sing' gush with sentiment as much as they swing over the beat. While with Goodman he also recorded as a leader for Victor, which spawned such *ur*-Elman pieces as 'Bublitchki'. His features with Dorsey were a little more tamed, and showed off a more conventional swing approach. He failed as a bandleader himself in the 40s and instead went to radio and television for most of his work. Ziggy was still working in the 60s but a drink problem more or less put an end to his career.
*Ziggy Elman 1938–1939* (Classics)

# Alan Elsdon
TRUMPET
*born* 15 October 1934

Elsdon is an accomplished player whose association with the second division of British trad has perhaps done him few favours. He played with Cy Laurie and Terry Lightfoot in the 50s before leading his own groups, which were usually capable enough without really sounding very exciting. Their relatively polite approach, though, brought Elsdon a lot of cabaret work over the years. Since the late 70s he has often played in groups led by Keith Nichols, and under the astute direction of this canny MD he has turned in some of his best work.
*Jazz Journeymen* (Black Lion)

# Kahil El'Zabar
DRUMS
*born* 11 November 1953

El'Zabar is a notably enthusiastic spirit on the current Chicago scene, acting as performer, leader and entrepreneur. He joined the AACM in 1971 and was later president of the Association for a spell. His groups Ethnic Heritage Ensemble and Ritual have been among the best post-Art Ensemble groups to come out of the scene: while El'Zabar uses both a kit set-up and a broad range of percussion devices from around the world, he makes sure that the music is steeped in the American jazz tradition and there is no wispy world-music filibustering in what he does. Busy also with teaching and other areas of the performing arts, El'Zabar hasn't worked much outside his local area and is known internationally mostly through his records.
*Renaissance Of The Resistance* (Delmark)

# Emanem
RECORD COMPANY

Although Martin Davidson's favourite jazz is probably the early traditional music, his London-based label has been recording the most hardcore improvised music (primarily of British origin) since 1974. While the label began in London, it followed Davidson himself around the world, and was variously based in the UK, America and Australia. In the CD era, Davidson returned to London and began reissuing the catalogue in the later format and issuing new recordings and previously unreleased archive material. There is now a great trove of material by the likes of Spontaneous Music Ensemble, Evan Parker, Paul Rutherford, Derek Bailey, John Butcher, Roger Smith, Lol Coxhill and many others, which lives up to one of Emanem's slogans, 'Unadulterated free music for people who prefer their free music unadulterated'.

# James Emery
GUITAR
*born* 21 December 1951

Emery took up the guitar at ten and studied at Cleveland University. He moved to New York in the early 70s and made various alliances, but the important one was with Billy Bang and John Lindberg, the three of them making up the String Trio Of New York. Emery remains in the line-up, though these days it is only occasionally convened, and he has stepped out as a leader himself more frequently. Emery's signature is to use an acoustic or semi-acoustic instrument, as well as sometimes picking up the tenor or the soprano guitar. The resulting style is an ear-catching mix of free playing in timbres that recall various old worlds of Americana, though Emery's music still has a metropolitan edge to it.

*Standing On A Whale Fishing For Minnows* (Enja)

## Bob Enevoldsen
VALVE-TROMBONE, TENOR SAXOPHONE, BASS
*born* 11 September 1920

Enevoldsen is an intriguing musician whose handful of featured recordings are all but forgotten. Born in Billings, Montana, he studied music at Montana University before his army service and then taught in Salt Lake City, before moving to Los Angeles in 1951 and joining the West Coast movement there. He persisted with the unusual double of tenor sax and valve-trombone and then went on to play bass with Bobby Troup's trio. He went to Las Vegas at the end of the decade, working with Terry Gibbs and eventually becoming staff arranger on the Steve Allen TV show. In the 80s and 90s he re-emerged, after many years away from jazz, playing in Bill Holman's occasional big band and Roger Neumann's Rather Large Band. Enevoldsen always has something of interest to say in the 16-bar paragraphs he was allotted on his many West Coast dates, holding forth in an attractively dusky tone on both tenor and valve-trombone, but his own Liberty date, *Smorgasbord* (1954), is a fascinating record where most of the players are asked to double instruments, there is one blues line arranged for three pianos, and one track features engineer John Neal on feedback (a harbinger of the New Conception Of Jazz to be sure).

*Smorgasbord* (Liberty)

## Enja
RECORD COMPANY

A long-standing European independent, Enja (European New Jazz Association) came out of the shared enthusiasms of Matthias Winckelmann and Horst Weber in 1971. Based in Munich (like that other great independent, ECM) they recorded the likes of Mal Waldron and Terumasa Hino locally before commencing activity in New York and at European festivals. The company expanded quickly, taking in archive material by Eric Dolphy and Charles Mingus and making numerous sets with Abdullah Ibrahim (one of their longest-serving artists), John Scofield, Elvin Jones, Tommy Flanagan and many others. In 1986 the co-founders disagreed over policy and divided their activities; confusingly, productions from both men (though Winckelmann is much more prolific) still appear under the same label name. Winckelmann also started two offshoot labels, Tiptoe (various kinds of fusion) and Blues Beacon (blues). While Enja has never had quite the intense quality control and vision of ECM, it is a worthy contemporary, and there is much treasure in their catalogue.

## Rolf Ericson
TRUMPET
*born* 29 August 1922; *died* 16 June 1997

While many Scandinavians took up the challenge of playing swing and bebop, Ericson was one of the very few who took his talents to America and succeeded there as well as at home. He took up trumpet after hearing Louis Armstrong in Stockholm and worked in Swedish orchestras in the 40s before going to New York in 1947. He did better on the West Coast at first, playing with Charlie Barnet and Woody Herman, but returned to Sweden in 1950 in the extraordinary role of bandleader of a group with Charlie Parker. He returned to the US in 1952 and he turns up on many fine American records of the 50s, particularly some of the Curtis Counce sessions for Contemporary, and he was with Stan Kenton in 1959–60. Thereafter he tended to divide his time between Sweden and the US, enjoying a season with the Duke Ellington orchestra, and settling in Germany in the 70s. In a long and prolific recording career he was rarely out of sorts before microphones, playing in a graceful but lively boppish manner, and one always waits in anticipation for Rolf's solo to come up.

*Stockholm Sweetnin'* (Dragon)

## Peter Erskine
DRUMS
*born* 5 June 1954

Erskine came up through the Stan Kenton academy: he attended Kenton's National Stage Band camps while still not much more than an infant, and by 1972 he was in the Kenton Orchestra itself. The drummer has had a knack for being in the right groups at the right time: he was with Weather Report in its highest-profile period (1978–82), and at the same time began playing with Michael Brecker in Steps. By the mid-80s he was familiar enough to start leading his own groups, and to indulge his writing, which turned out to be a lot more creative and surprising than a typical drummer's composing. He signed to ECM as a leader (having already done memorable session-work there with the likes of John Abercrombie) and has made a sequence of impeccable trio records with John Taylor and Palle Danielsson. He briefly recorded for RCA as a leader at the beginning of the 90s, but that association soon ended, and he has since established his own label, Fuzzy Music: an early, memorable result is the trio album *Live At Rocca* (1999) with Alan Pasqua and Dave Carpenter. Erskine's great gift is an intuitive understanding of what kind of playing will work best for the gig he's on. Since he came up through the system himself, he is very good at educational clinics, and it is both unforgettable and highly entertaining to hear him demonstrating how best to play for Steely Dan one minute and a straight-ahead bop group the next. It seems like a very long way from the kind of polyrhythmic muscle required for the Weather Report music to the mood-painting of the ECM dates, but Erskine seems equally adept in both climes. He has also composed for the theatre, and is a great Shakespeare addict.
*As It Is* (ECM)

## Lars Erstrand
VIBES
*born* 27 September 1936

Born in Uppsala, Erstrand began on piano but, entirely in love with Lionel Hampton's playing, switched to vibes and formed a popular group with the clarinettist Ove Lind, cut very much in the style of the Goodman small groups. He and Lind made numerous albums together and, after Lind's death, Erstrand carried on with the Swedish Swing Society. If he has little original to say in his idiom, he has nevertheless nurtured the peculiarly Scandinavian love for this branch of the swing mainstream, and in 1991 his dream came true when he got to record with Lionel Hampton for Phontastic.
*The Lars Erstrand Sessions* (Opus 3)

## Ahmet Ertegun
EXECUTIVE AND LABEL BOSS
*born* 31 July 1923

## Nesuhi Ertegun
EXECUTIVE AND LABEL BOSS
*born* 27 November 1917; *died* 15 July 1989

The Ertegun brothers came from a diplomatic family in Constantinople and travelled frequently in their youth via their father's various postings. Nesuhi was the real jazz fan of the two, promoting gigs when they settled in Washington in the 40s and starting a label to record Kid Ory (Crescent; later came Jazz Man Records). Meanwhile, in New York, Ahmet co-founded Atlantic records in 1947, with Herb Abramson, recording a mix of R&B, jazz and doo wop. Nesuhi had been lecturing in jazz at UCLA (the first ever such course in an American college) but joined Ahmet in New York in 1955, his input accounting for many new jazz signings, from Ray Charles to John Coltrane. While the brothers sold the company to Warners in 1967, they remained busy there: Nesuhi was still producing jazz reissues right up until his death, and Ahmet, who had a brilliant ear for a possible hit act, was still working regularly for the company in the new century. Two great old-time record men.

## Booker Ervin
TENOR SAXOPHONE
*born* 31 October 1930; *died* 31 August 1970

Ervin had one of the most immediately identifiable sounds of all the many tenormen who've picked up the horn: a puncturing wail, which he may have drawn equally from his homegrown Texas-tenor tradition

and the more limber, beseeching sound of Dexter Gordon. It made his every phrase into something which sounded 'emotional', and Ervin's music is preferred by those who want their hard bop to sound as if it's being sung by a particularly idiosyncratic bluesman. Oddly enough, he started out on trombone, but by the mid-50s he had switched to saxophone and was playing in Boston R&B bands. Charles Mingus hired him in 1958 and he plays an explosive role on records such as *Mingus Ah Um* (1958); although not with him continuously, Ervin played for Mingus on and off between then and 1964. He spent some time in Europe before returning home in 1966, but kidney disease forced him to stop playing and he died only weeks before his 40th birthday. His series of 'Book' albums for Prestige are scorched-earth, warts-and-all documents, sometimes sloppily performed by his accompanists, but Booker himself is constantly daring and unpredictable: the phenomenal solo on 'Eerie Dearie', from *The Blues Book* (1964), is a single example among many. He was also – like Coltrane, though only in this respect – able to handle very long solos without running out of steam or ideas.
*The Blues Book* (OJC/Prestige)

## Pee Wee Erwin
TRUMPET
*born* 30 May 1913; *died* 20 June 1981

New York bandleaders quickly recognized George Erwin's exceptional skills as a sight reader and lead man, and he was working for Benny Goodman, Ray Noble and particularly Tommy Dorsey in the 30s. Thereafter he was, in the main, a studio man, although he did lead combos of his own at Nick's and other New York clubs. He was still working for CBS until well into the 60s, but in the 70s began playing in package tours and jazz parties and became a great favourite of mainstream audiences. A fine teacher – Warren Vaché regards him with particular affection in this regard – and a great natural on the trumpet, even though he never stopped working at it. The handful of records under his own name only cover a fraction of the ground he worked in.
*Dixieland At Grand View Inn* (Cadence)

## Christian Escoudé
GUITAR
*born* 23 September 1947

Escoudé has sometimes been unthinkingly lumped in with the Django Reinhardt school, but while he has a taste or two of the gypsy players in his armoury he is more like a French Wes Montgomery. He arrived in Paris in 1971 and was soon working with Eddy Louiss and leading his own group. By the end of the decade he had recorded in duo with Charlie Haden and in the 80s made a series of records for JMS. In 1989 he was signed to Emarcy/Verve and from that point his records took on a more obviously 'Gallic' touch, as in the guitar gypsy-trio record *Holidays* (1993). These were strong entries, but in a music suddenly crowded with guitarists Escoudé has since found it difficult to sustain the earlier interest in his playing.
*Cookin' In Hell's Kitchen* (Verve)

## Ellery Eskelin
TENOR SAXOPHONE
*born* 16 August 1959

Though born in Wichita, Eskelin grew up in Baltimore in a particularly musical situation: his mother, Bobbi Lee, played Hammond organ on the club circuit and his father did studio work. There are still echoes of tenor-and-organ in his music (he also did a stint with Jack McDuff), but while his early New York gigs were in post-bop situations, he soon ventured into more free-form groups, at first with regular partners Paul Smoker, Phil Haynes and Drew Gress, and then with a trio of himself, Andrea Parkins and Jim Black. This latter band has cut a series of discs for hatOLOGY, which offer the best evidence of Eskelin's work. With Parkins playing a sampler (although it just as often sounds like her accordion) and Black's busy drums, the music has a prodigiously brainy feel, which perhaps springs from compositional ideas and structures that are as taxing on the listener as the players. Eskelin has an oblique, almost furtive way of delivering ideas, which sits curiously with a rather heavy and old-fashioned tenor sound.
*One Great Day* (hatOLOGY)

## ESP-Disk
RECORD COMPANY

The label which documented some of the most important recordings in New York's new jazz of the 60s has suffered from an almost continuous confusion over ownership and distribution ever since. Founded by an attorney, Bernard Stollman, in 1963, it barely lasted into the 70s. Among the artists who made records for Stollman were Albert Ayler, Paul Bley, Ornette Coleman, New York Art Quartet, Pharoah Sanders, Sun Ra and Ornette Coleman; there were also archive live sessions by Billie Holiday and Charlie Parker, though the release of these was curtailed before their proposed completion. Bizarre sleeves and Esperanto liner-notes added to the general air of bohemianism. Various attempts at putting the music on to CD have met with enigmatic distribution complications, although the whole catalogue does drift in and out of availability. Original pressings of the vinyl are prized collectors' pieces these days.

## John Etheridge
GUITAR
born 12 January 1948

John Etheridge followed Allan Holdsworth into Soft Machine in 1975, and one guitar hero was immediately succeeded by another, equally fast and adept. But Etheridge had slightly deeper jazz interests than Holdsworth, and he also toured with Stéphane Grappelli during 1976–81 and later worked with such as Barney Kessel and Biréli Lagrène. More of a harmonic thinker than a vertical, chromatic licks-player, Etheridge has nevertheless won an audience of guitar fetishists and made a lot of noisy music as well as working in more rhapsodic settings. The record cited is a charming homage to Grappelli.
Sweet Chorus (Dyad)

## Kevin Eubanks
GUITAR
born 15 November 1957

American audiences know Eubanks as the bandleader and straight-man for Jay Leno on The Tonight Show, a role he took over when Branford Marsalis left the job in 1995. But he already had a lot of jazz work behind him: he was leading jazz-rock groups while at Berklee in the late 70s, made a single album for Elektra in 1982 (Guitarist), which showcased his range of approaches, and then signed to GRP for what became a dispiritingly ordinary series of jazz-lite-funk records. His sideman work was much more powerful and in 1992 he switched to Blue Note for three better records; but his television duties appear to take up most of his time now. Eubanks has expressed his dismay at the cavalier attitude of the major companies to recording jazz artists, and has attempted to establish an imprint of his own which supports players of his generation – too old to be young lions but not aged enough to be grandmasters.
Live At Bradley's (Blue Note)

## Robin Eubanks
TROMBONE
born 25 October 1955

Kevin's older brother was for a long time the better-known figure. He freelanced in Philadelphia and New York and joined the Dave Holland group in 1986, an association which still continues, and he was a Jazz Messenger for two years from 1987. Then came numerous sideman roles for a broad spectrum of leaders, although his own groups – Mental Images, a sort of brainy fusion band; Mass Line, a large ensemble; and a boppish small group – never made much of an impact, and his own records for JMT were poorly produced and scattershot in their impact. Eubanks has done his best to rehabilitate the trombone's continuing poor reputation in a post-bop environment, but he hasn't been best served by his records and a perhaps important talent has yet to be well documented; his music with Holland still offers his most lucid work.
Dave Holland, Not For Nothin' (ECM)

## Eureka Brass Band
GROUP

One of the most stately and (although this is always a loaded word) authentic of the New

Orleans brass groups. It was founded by trumpeter Willie Wilson in 1920, who stayed, despite periods of ill-health, until 1937. Thereafter it went under the leadership of such local trumpeters as Red Clark and T-Boy Remy before Percy Humphrey assumed command around 1948. Although Humphrey was also busy in other bands – such as Preservation Hall Jazz Band and his own groups – the EBB remained an entity until it was eventually disbanded in 1975. The instrumentation varied, but a typical line-up might be three trumpets, two trombones, three reeds (most likely one clarinet and two saxes), tuba, snare drum and bass drum. They were recorded on a number of occasions, and those sessions reissued by American Music are close to magnificent: the one cited, with Humphrey and George Lewis in the line-up, and actually recorded in an alleyway in the French Quarter rather than on the job, has a ragged poignancy all its own.

*New Orleans Funeral And Parade* (American Music)

## James Reese Europe

BANDLEADER
*born* 22 February 1881; *died* 10 May 1919

Born in Mobile, Alabama, Europe moved to New York early in the century and was directing theatre bands when he took part in a 1905 concert of syncopated music. He then organized an association of black musicians, The Clef Club, and in 1913 Europe's Society Orchestra recorded 'Too Much Mustard' and 'Down Home Rag' for Victor, the first American recordings by a black band. He recorded eight other sides (two were unissued) before leading a military band, the 369th Infantry, during the First World War. Europe was a sensation in Paris in 1918, and the following year cut 24 titles for Pathé as he embarked on a barnstorming tour of the US. Europe's own remarks on his music confirm how it was seen as a proudly eccentric novelty: his players, he said, 'embroider their parts in order to produce new, peculiar sounds'. The records sound stiffer than that yet are a fascinating pre-jazz survival, including such titles as 'Memphis Blues' and 'Clarinet Marmalade'. But it ended suddenly for Europe: he was murdered by another

musician when the band was playing in Boston.

*James Reese Europe Featuring Noble Sissle* (IAJRC)

## Bill Evans

PIANO
*born* 16 August 1929; *died* 15 September 1980

Although he remains one of the most admired and listened-to musicians of the era after bebop, Evans left a difficult and sometimes contradictory legacy. He studied classical piano and violin from an early age but played in bands for dancing in his teens and first performed in New York around 1950. After army service, he began working with a circle of players which included Don Eliott and Tony Scott, and in 1956 made two important recordings, the George Russell *Jazz Workshop* date, with Evans's dazzling feature 'Concerto For Billy The Kid', and his own debut for Riverside, *New Jazz Conceptions* (producer Orrin Keepnews was persuaded into recording him simply through hearing some of his music played down a telephone line). At this point, Evans was already very much his own man as a stylist, although there was also an extra energy in his early music which was, arguably, subsequently dispersed. He was briefly with Charles Mingus (*East Coasting*, 1958), and then made a crucial alliance with Miles Davis: his participation in the *Kind Of Blue* sessions in 1959, to which he contributed much of the musical substance despite receiving no composer credits, helped Davis's movement towards modal jazz – ironically enough, since as a pianist Evans might have been perceived as dependent on chordal sequences.

What Davis admired and drew from was Evans's ability to convey an impressionistic feel, at a time when most pianists played in more of a funky, even an abrasive manner. Evans didn't entirely shy away from that approach – his right hand often sounds like a graft from Horace Silver – but he did voice his harmonies in ways which melted preordained chord sequences and let melodies flow with more freedom. However, his appearance on this date was more like a coda to his work with Davis: he had actually left the working band some months previously because of his drug addiction, a habit he had first picked up in the army and which would blemish the rest of his life. At the end of 1959 he formed a new trio with bassist Scott LaFaro and drummer Paul Motian, and made a series of memorable studio and live (at New York's Village Vanguard) dates with them. Abetted by LaFaro's extraordinary virtuosity, the group reached almost ecstatic heights of collective playing, the polyphonic voicings of piano and bass intermingling over Motian's calmly propulsive work. But it all fell to pieces when LaFaro was killed in 1961, and Evans withdrew from performing altogether for a time. Eventually he put together a new group in 1963, with Larry Bunker and Chuck Israels, and for the rest of his career Evans toured and recorded in the trio format with only a few scarce exceptions to his regimen. His later groups included Eddie Gomez and Marty Morell, Gomez and Eliot Zigmund, Michael Moore and Philly Joe Jones, and finally Marc Johnson and Joe LaBarbera.

While his playing seemed to retreat into a more evasive lyricism after the LaFaro period, he never lost the energy in his performances, and it merely came out in different ways. The oft-repeated idea that Evans's music somehow became becalmed is untrue, especially with such assertive players as Gomez behind him. As a composer, he gradually compiled an impressive book: 'Waltz For Debby', his best-known piece, was there right at the start, and he never stopped playing it, but other significant tunes included 'Turn Out The Stars', 'Very Early', 'Re: Person I Knew' and more. He also had his own favourite setlist of standards, which he added to only slowly and cautiously. There are scores of live and studio albums by his various trios, but only occasional visits to other playing situations: a couple of meetings with Jim Hall are gorgeous, and there are a few solo sets, although *Conversations With Myself* (1963) was a celebrated, multi-tracked solo record. Other meetings with players he might have been expected to do great work with – Stan Getz, Lee Konitz – were disappointing.

His posture at the piano – hands almost flat on the keys, back bent, his face nearly touching the keyboard – added to the sense of Evans as introvert, but it was his narcotics addictions – both heroin and latterly cocaine – which may have fuelled this impression of a man in withdrawal. Despite a final break-down in his health, he worked to the very end. Some multidisc sets exist of music made in the last days of his life: outwardly expansive, they hint at a beauty turning mechanical and sour. His influence, though, remains close to overpowering: there must be hundreds of pianists who came after him whose work has been compared directly with his own example.

***Sunday At The Village Vanguard*** (Riverside)

# Bill Evans
TENOR AND SOPRANO SAXOPHONES
*born* 9 February 1958

Evans was the first latter-day (post-1975) Miles Davis sideman to make a name for himself. Dave Liebman, who taught him, recommended him to the trumpeter and he toured with the Davis group between 1980 and 1984. Like many such musicians, Evans has managed to use this platform to assist in building a career without quite shaking off the tag of 'ex-Miles Davis'. An accomplished saxophonist, he's tried to find his own furrow in the fusion field, running a band called Petite Blonde in the 90s and making several records in a vein that might be considered a meeting point between fusion and post-bop, but little of the music has a pressing need to be heard. Ironically enough, he can play beautifully in a standard, acoustic style, as the meeting with Hank Jones and Red Mitchell, *Moods Unlimited* (1982), demonstrated. An album for Blue Note, though, *The Alternative Man* (1985), is his single most interesting effort: ableep with 80s technology of various kinds, Evans here came up with a fusion one-off.

***The Alternative Man*** (Blue Note)

# Gil Evans
PIANO, ARRANGER
*born* 13 May 1912; *died* 20 March 1988

Ian Ernest Gilmore Green, born in Toronto, came south and west and began bandleading in California around 1933. He was still with the group when it was eventually taken over by Skinnay Ennis in 1938, but Evans moved over when the band's new pianist, Claude Thornhill, decided to form a fresh group of his own in 1941. Evans joined as arranger and contributed a string of surprising charts to the book, turning bop anthems such as 'Donna Lee' and 'Anthropology' into almost sensuous works via use of french horns and the cool-toned, mellifluous section-timbres which Thornhill favoured. When the group eventually disbanded, Evans found a basement apartment in New York and haunted the scene, making friends with Miles Davis and his circle and contributing a couple of scores to the Davis Nonet sessions which were like a slimline version of his Thornhill work. But none of this found him much acclaim or even all that much further work, and he mostly did quite anonymous scores for singers' records until Davis engaged him again to create the settings for what came to be a triumvirate of records, *Miles Ahead* (1957), *Porgy And Bess* (1959) and *Sketches Of Spain* (1960). In their reconciliation of diffidence and forthrightness, their gathering of darkening textures and bursts of melodic and rhythmic fire, their harmonic translucence, they are all remarkable, and Davis was more than fortunate to have such a gifted collaborator. But Evans made some admirable records of his own, such as *Gil Evans And Ten* (1957), the dazzling revisionism of *Great Jazz Standards* (1959) and the brooding, evanescent sounds of *Out Of The Cool* (1960), which arguably surpasses his work with Davis. Yet his attempts at creating a permanent orchestra came to nothing, and during the 60s he was visible only intermittently: a possible collaboration with Jimi Hendrix was thwarted by the guitarist's death. In the 70s he was more readily on show, leading different editions of an orchestra which played his now substantial book of originals, which had begun to be dappled by his interest in synthesizers and electronics. He toured abroad, and there were occasional records, but it was perhaps not until the 80s that he became truly lionized again. In his 70s he took up a regular residency at Sweet Basil in New York, and with the greater interest in the jazz past becoming manifest, people realized the scope of Evans's formidable legacy. His later bands, though, were often ragged and too dominated by modest talents: it wasn't clear whether he really enjoyed the rock beats that they often fell into or was simply too passive to exert any influence. The breathtaking beauty of his music of the late 50s and early 60s was never reasserted. Gentle and amiable to the

last, he entertained a final project with Miles Davis based on *Tosca*, but it was too late for both men and nothing came of it. He slipped away to Mexico in March 1988 and died there of peritonitis.
**Out Of The Cool** (Impulse!)

# Herschel Evans
TENOR SAXOPHONE
*born* 9 March 1909; *died* 9 February 1939

Jo Jones called him 'the greatest jazz muscian I ever played with in my life', and when you consider that Lester Young was in the same band with Evans and Jones, it's some compliment. Evans and Young were together in the Count Basie band for less than three years. A Texan, Herschel played in numerous 'territory' bands before joining Basie. If he was the Coleman Hawkins to Lester Young's Lester Young, they made a formidable team, and while Young's solo spots on Basie's records are always delightful, one tends to regret that Evans had fewer chances, because he died so young. Perhaps the classic performance is 'Blue And Sentimental' (1938), a typical piece of bruising romanticism from what should have become a major voice on the tenor. As it was, Evans collapsed on the bandstand at a dance in Hartford, Connecticut and died a few weeks later from heart disease. For all their rivalry, as Basie himself remembered, 'nobody missed him more than Lester'.
**Count Basie, *The Complete Decca Recordings*** (MCA)

# Orrin Evans
PIANO

An outstanding talent among the ranks of younger American pianists. Evans grew up in New Jersey but made his mark on the Philadelphia scene, where he worked for several leaders and began making records of his own. He subsequently shifted to New York, but has since gone back to Philadelphia. His five albums for Criss Cross (1996–2001) work both as a demonstration case for some of the talents which the label has been fostering – besides Evans himself, John Swana, Tim Warfield, Ralph Bowen and others – and a show of his own work as

player and composer. His writing is full of twists and quirks and sets some tough challenges for the players, and occasionally his own playing has almost too rococo a bent, but at his best he is a communicative and rigorous player, genuinely full of ideas.
*Listen To The Band* (Criss Cross)

## Sandy Evans
TENOR AND SOPRANO SAXOPHONES
*born* 29 June 1960

Evans has been involved in several of the better Australian jazz initiatives in recent years. She began playing saxophone in the 70s and was soon involved in the all-star group Ten Part Invention, founded in 1985. She was a founder member of Clarion Fracture Zone (1989–98) and has also led groups of her own. Although she lived and worked in both Scotland and the USA for a spell, she is known mostly in her native country and recently won one of the first Australian Jazz Awards for excellence there.
*Clarion Fracture Zone, What This Love Can Do* (Rufus)

## Don Ewell
PIANO
*born* 14 November 1916; *died* 9 August 1983

Based in his home town of Baltimore, Ewell missed out on some of the attention accorded to Ralph Sutton, a similar stylist, since he aligned himself more closely with New Orleans originals and revivalists rather than the Condon Chicago clan. He worked under Bunk Johnson, Sidney Bechet and Kid Ory in the 40s and 50s, and enjoyed his highest-profile gig in the Jack Teagarden band of the late 50s. He remained in New Orleans after Tea's death and was often seen in Europe, but his life was clouded after his daughter's early death and he passed away himself not long afterwards. Stride, boogie and ragtime all fell easily under his fingers, and his best records deserve more recognition than they've received.
*Man Here Plays Fine Piano!* (Good Time Jazz)

## Jon Faddis
TRUMPET, FLUGELHORN
*born* 24 July 1953

Dizzy Gillespie kept a paternal eye on Faddis's early progress, from R&B bands in his native California to stays with Lionel Hampton and eventually Gillespie's own occasional touring big band. The young trumpeter certainly reminded the listener of Gillespie at his most daredevil, although at this point Faddis relied too much on showmanship and chops-busting high notes. His career on record has never really got going – there were a couple of often awful albums for Epic, and some better work for Concord – but after years of session-work he secured a prestigious position as MD of the Carnegie Hall Jazz Band in 1993, an ensemble that did much fine work as a friendly rival to the Lincoln Center Jazz Orchestra. Faddis was, however, devastated when Carnegie Hall withdrew their support of the Band at the end of 2001. It's not too late for an enterprising label to give the pugnacious Faddis the chance to show what he's learned over ten years of hard work.
*Legacy* (Concord)

## Al Fairweather
TRUMPET
*born* 12 June 1927; *died* 21 June 1993

Much of Fairweather's career was spent in tandem with Sandy Brown. They worked together in Edinburgh in the 40s, and not long after he moved to London in 1953, they were together again in a new band, which Fairweather more or less took over. Their records together are certainly directed by Fairweather's powerful lead and fuss-free arrangements. But after a spell with Acker Bilk in the mid-60s, Fairweather's career fell away and he turned to teaching full-time at the end of the decade, coming back for occasional reunions with (and subsequently tributes to) Brown, and eventually returning to Edinburgh. His canny partnership with Brown certainly produced British mainstream good enough to rival Humphrey Lyttelton's brand.
*Fairweather Friends* (Lake)

# Digby Fairweather
TRUMPET, VOCAL
*born* 25 April 1946

Richard John Charles Fairweather was the son of a choirmaster and tried out several instruments before settling on trumpet. He played as an enthusiastic amateur in the British mainstream before turning pro in 1977 and since then has been perpetually busy, as a musician, educator, writer and archivist – he founded a National Jazz Foundation Archive and usually has something to say on the issue of preserving the jazz heritage in the UK. Besides leading groups of his own, he has been in affable mainstream outfits such as the Pizza Express All Stars, the Kettners' Five, the Half Dozen, the Jazz Superkings and eventually the Great British Jazz Band, most of which run off his own unflappable good humour. Audiences seeing him for the first time are inevitably surprised at his embouchure, which is several inches to the right of where one might expect, but he squeezes out a very agreeable tone.
**Something To Remember Us By** (Jazzology)

# Fake Book

Fake books have been around since at least the 40s. They consist of a collection of simply presented musical scores, comprising standard tunes and, more often, jazz material, as an *aide-mémoire* or a crib sheet for musicians needing to grasp the essentials of a piece of music. The 'book' might be no more than a photocopied and loosely bound set of charts, which is mainly because most fake books are unauthorized and illegal, distributed almost on a word-of-mouth basis: they mostly violate music-publishing copyrights. Some fake books are more detailed than others, presenting not only a musical lead sheet but details on voicings, bass parts and accompaniments. Some are notoriously inaccurate, which has often led to widespread misconceptions around the tunes presented thus. The most famous is one called, ironically enough, *The Real Book*, which first appeared in Boston in the early 70s (and was seized on by students at Berklee College). It has been through some five subsequent editions.

# Charles Fambrough
BASS
*born* 25 August 1950

A Philadelphian, Fambrough first came to attention with Grover Washington in the early 70s, and went on to work through stints with Art Blakey and McCoy Tyner ('McCoy showed me how to play with endurance, Art gave me refinement'). Since then, he's been a busy freelance, but has tried to build a leadership career via some surprisingly star-studded sessions for the CTI label, which feature his interesting writing – although lately the sequence appears to have come to an end, and the bassist has been undertaking production duties for the independent label K-Jazz. A big man with a big sound.
**The Charmer** (CTI)

# Georgie Fame
VOCAL, ORGAN, PIANO
*born* 26 June 1943

'Georgie Fame' was bestowed by the pop hustler Larry Parnes, and Clive Powell (close associates still call him Clive) was in at the very start of the beat era, leading his Blue Flames on the London club scene, and getting into the charts with jazz-flavoured (though no one realized it at the time) hits such as Jon Hendricks's 'Yeh Yeh'. Fame was a regular in British pop all through the 60s and early 70s, although he also toured with Count Basie, and *Sound Venture* (1966), *The Two Faces Of Fame* (1967) and *The Third Face Of Fame* (1968) had the Harry South big band and charts by Tubby Hayes and others. His vocal style sounded like a more leathery Mose Allison, and he could scat and do vocalese as well as any American singer. Since his pop success died down, he's been a jazz-club regular, still recording frequently and sometimes working with his contemporary Van Morrison, and his band these days includes Guy Barker and Alan Skidmore as well as sons Tristan and James.
**Cool Cat Blues** (Go Jazz)

# Fantasy
RECORD COMPANY

First established in 1949 by two brothers, Max and Sol Weiss, Fantasy was begun as a way of getting Dave Brubeck on to record: he was even an investor in its early days. It latterly expanded to include such artists as Vince Guaraldi and Bill Evans, but it also serves as the overall name for what has since become the largest group of 'independent' labels in jazz. Saul Zaentz joined the company in 1955 and 12 years later led a buy-out from the Weiss brothers. He subsequently began buying up other catalogues: in the fullness of time, Fantasy had acquired Debut, Prestige, Riverside, Milestone, Stax, Contemporary, Good Time Jazz, Pablo and Specialty. All of these labels provided material for the group's series of Original Jazz Classics reissues, one of the most comprehensive programmes of its kind in the CD era, running to hundreds of releases. Not all of the group's commercial clout was based on jazz records: their biggest sellers by far were the hugely successful rock group Creedence Clearwater Revival. Zaentz, however, had in turn had the group informally up for sale for a number of years when it was finally acquired by another jazz independent, Concord Records, in 2004.

# Tal Farlow
GUITAR
*born* 7 June 1921; *died* 25 July 1998

Farlow's superfast technique was all the more remarkable in that he didn't even pick up a guitar until he was 21. He was with Buddy DeFranco in 1949, and from there joined the Red Norvo trio with Charles Mingus, later also working in Norvo's quintet. His playing in this period was fast and lucid, if not especially affecting: he had all the dexterity of the boppers, but there was a sort of glib ingenuity to a lot of it. Nine albums for Norman Granz parse his style as completely as it ever would be set down, and although the same easy facility can sometimes dull the listener's interest, much of his best work is in there. He more or less gave up working in music at the end of the 50s, pursuing a job as a sign-painter, and while he made *The Return Of Tal Farlow* (1969), it was a hesitant comeback, since he still played only part-time for much of the 70s. He was recorded more regularly by Concord in his later years, and returned to the touring circuit. A tall man with huge hands, he never lost his fluency on the guitar, and there's a more autumnal feel to his later music.
*Tal* (Verve)

# Art Farmer
TRUMPET, FLUGELHORN
*born* 21 August 1928; *died* 4 October 1999

Farmer's contribution to jazz was a model of taste, consistency and finesse. That makes it sound boring, but Art was so inventive a player that, like Zoot Sims or Jack Teagarden, he seemed almost incapable of performing below a certain level. Although he was born in Iowa (with his twin brother Addison, 1928–63, who played bass), he grew up in Phoenix, and eventually changed from sousaphone to cornet in a local marching band. From 1945 he began playing on the West Coast, where he performed with several big bands, occasionally going out on tour, and in 1953 he moved over to New York, where he worked with Teddy Charles, Horace Silver and Gerry Mulligan: on Mulligan's 1958 version of 'My Funny Valentine', Farmer's beautiful playing makes Chet Baker seem pallid. But he had already begun recording as a leader, with Prestige, from 1953. By 1958 his playing was at its peak: *Portrait Of Art* (Contemporary) and *Modern Art* (United Artists) are brimful of detailed, intricately poised trumpet playing, where Farmer's reluctance to bite off his notes makes his playing on each track seem all of a piece. In 1959, he and Benny Golson formed The Jazztet, one of the great New York bands of its day, where the contrast between Farmer's persuasive style and Golson's aggression paid many dividends. The group had run its course by 1962, and during this period Farmer switched more or less exclusively to the flugelhorn, although he still picked up the trumpet occasionally, mostly for section-work. He led a quartet with Jim Hall and then another small group with Jimmy Heath, but he also found work in Europe, and maintained a home in Vienna for many years from 1968. Where others of his generation were puzzled by the way jazz had gone, Farmer calmly carried on

working, in small groups and in orchestral settings, and the 80s in particular found him on golden form, leading some superb recordings with Clifford Jordan and staging various reunions with Benny Golson. He also began playing what he called the flumpet, which was a hybrid of trumpet and flugelhorn. If he occupies a middle ground somewhere between Miles Davis and Bobby Hackett, Art surrendered nothing to either man when it came to spinning out a lyrical solo, and his discography as a whole must be among the most satisfying in all of jazz.
**Blame It On My Youth** (Contemporary)

## Joe Farrell

TENOR AND SOPRANO SAXOPHONES, FLUTE
*born* 16 December 1937; *died* 10 January 1986

Farrell began playing in Chicago, and arrived in New York in 1959 with a penchant for a Getzian sound that in the end took him towards a hotter and often power-packed delivery. He freelanced and did much studio work in the 60s, with a few more starring roles – in the Jones–Lewis Orchestra, and with Chick Corea and Elvin Jones. Creed Taylor signed him to CTI and he made four records for him as a leader: some of the best and least compromised music on the label. He rejoined Corea as the saxophonist in the first edition of Return To Forever, and drifted through fusion for the rest of the decade. Always a wild man, he had his health destroyed by drink and narcotics, and by 1984 he was almost destitute.
**Moon Germs** (CTI)

## Claudio Fasoli

TENOR AND SOPRANO SAXOPHONES
*born* 29 November 1939

Fasoli didn't get a record out under his sole leadership until he was nearly 50. He was based in Milan in the early 60s and played in the modern circle of Franco Ambrosetti and Guido Manusardi, then in the fusion group Perigeo and in a quartet with Franco D'Andrea. In the 90s he recorded for Ram, Soul Note and Splasc(h), interesting sets which displayed the surprise switch between a light-bodied tenor and a more plangent soprano approach.
**Ten Tributes** (Ram)

## Nick Fatool

DRUMS
*born* 2 January 1915; *died* 26 September 2000

As able as any of the best Dixieland drummers, Fatool enjoyed a protracted and busy career. He was first in New York in 1937, and later worked with Benny Goodman and Artie Shaw, before going to Los Angeles in 1943. He subsequently spent much of his time as a studio man, with many leaders, mostly in a traditional-to-swing idiom. By the 60s he was pre-eminent in the field of small-group Dixieland drumming, and he put some spark into the bands of Pete Fountain and others. Fatool finally made an album under his own name for Jazzology at the age of 72, and was still working well into the 90s.
**Pete Fountain, Pete's Place** (Coral)

## Malachi Favors

BASS
*born* 22 August 1937; *died* 30 January 2004

Favors recorded with Andrew Hill as far back as 1955, and he was in the circle of musicians who worked with Richard Abrams in Chicago in the early 60s. But his great association was with the Art Ensemble Of Chicago, which grew out of working alongside Roscoe Mitchell, and it lasted the rest of his life with only a few diversions into other projects. He added an extra name (Maghoustous) and delighted in face-painting and costume, which, with his diminutive stature and customary beaming visage, gave him a pocket-mandarin look, and his playing, while it presented little in the way of extended techniques, was completely in tune with the Ensemble's journeyings. He sometimes picked up other instruments – harmonica, banjo – but the bass was his thing. Among a few other associations was one with Kahil El'Zabar's Ritual trio. While other members wrote more for the group, his tune 'Tutankhamun' was an AEOC classic. His death in 2004 was widely seen as the closing of the Ensemble's history, and while they have since made signs of carrying on, Malachi was in many ways their real heartbeat.
**Art Ensemble Of Chicago, People In Sorrow** (Nessa)

## Pierre Favre
PERCUSSION
*born* 2 June 1937

The Swiss drummer had orthodox jazz beginnings, playing with Dixieland and bebop
bands in his local environment in the 50s,
but he has since become a European eminence in the field of percussion. He played
in France, Germany and Italy in the 60s,
working for the cymbal manufacturers
Paiste for some of this period, and was in at
the start of European free music in the trio
and quartet led by Irène Schweizer. He
expanded his range all through the following decade, working with free players and
poets, studying orchestration, and eventually staging annual concerts with T V
Gopalakrishnann, the Indian percussionist.
Later collaborators have included Albert
Mangelsdorff and Don Cherry, and he has
occasionally renewed his associations with
Schweizer. Groups such as his four-man
Drum Orchestra have attempted to settle a
characteristic virtuosity into a formal setting which bridges the composition–
improvisation divide. The jazz content of
much of this work is often dispersed in
favour of a whistling-together of numerous
other musics, but when Favre is asked some
demanding questions, as in the duet record
with Schweizer, *Ulrichsberg* (2003), his conceptual baggage falls away and the powerful
improviser is restored.
*Window Steps* (ECM)

## Wally Fawkes
CLARINET
*born* 21 June 1924

Fawkes moved to England from his native
Canada when a boy, and took up clarinet in
his teens. He was good enough to be in the
pioneering George Webb's Dixielanders
from 1944, but his most famous association
came when he joined Humphrey Lyttelton's
first band in 1948, staying eight years and
forming a distinctive front line with the
leader. His juicily assertive playing then
turned up in a band of his own, The
Troglodytes: the name comes from his nickname 'Trog', which he uses as the byline in
his other working persona, as a cartoonist.
Latterly he has played at his own choosing,
sometimes showing up for a reunion with

Humph, although a few records for the
Stomp Off label in the 90s have shown him
still in strong voice.
*Flook Digs Jazz* (Lake)

## Irving Fazola
CLARINET
*born* 10 December 1912; *died* 20 March 1949

Louis Prima gave him the name 'Fazola',
allegedly out of 'fa, so, la', since otherwise
we would have had to settle for Irving
Prestopnik. A New Orleans man, Fazola
worked locally until he joined Ben Pollack in
1935. He went on to work with Glenn Miller
and Gus Arnheim, but his most renowned
gig was with Bob Crosby's Orchestra, even
though that lasted for less than two years.
Fazola played a superbly polished amalgam
of the bluesy New Orleans style and the
more elegant sound which Shaw and
Goodman brought to swing-era clarinet: he
was perfect for Crosby, whose Dixieland-
directed small group The Bob Cats featured
him on many of their best sides (he plays
the lead part on the unforgettable 'My
Inspiration', 1938). Faz may even have
indirectly helped create the Glenn Miller
sound: his doubling on saxophone for Miller
was so poor that the trombonist decided to
let a clarinet lead the reed section voicings.
He worked for several more leaders in the
40s but his health began to fail and anyway
he was always homesick for his native town.
A problem musician who liked both liquor
and a punch-up – many of his bosses
weren't sorry to see him leave.
**Bob Crosby, *The Bob Cats*** (Swaggie)

## Leonard Feather
PIANO, WRITER
*born* 13 September 1914; *died* 22 September 1994

Feather was the first jazz everyman. A
Londoner by birth, he studied piano and
clarinet at college and was soon in the thick
of the London music scene of the early 30s.
By 1934 he was a regular *Melody Maker* correspondent and he began visiting New York
the following year. He discovered George
Shearing (and produced his first London
sessions in 1938) and advised Benny Carter
to come to London. From 1940 he lived in
America, becoming a citizen in 1948, and he

became a familiar byline all over the American press, from *Down Beat* to *Esquire*, as well as broadcasting, organizing recording sessions, and occasionally composing and playing himself – mostly variations on the blues, such as 'Evil Gal Blues' for Dinah Washington and 'Jumping For Jane' for Coleman Hawkins. Leonard got embroiled in the bop vs tradition arguments in the 40s (he was on the side of the boppers), and he invented the famous Blindfold Test, where a musician is asked to comment on records without being told who the performers are – variations on this continue in the music press to this day. In 1960, Feather moved to Los Angeles and worked from there for the rest of his life. His *Encyclopedia Of Jazz*, first published in 1955, was one of the great jazz reference works of its day. Leonard never stopped hobnobbing with the players of the music he loved. Some unkind things were said about him over the years – such as a suggestion that he was auditioning for a place on the right hand of God – but he was a master professional in his field and a real gentleman.

**Leonard Feather 1937–1945** (Classics)

# Buddy Featherstonhaugh

CLARINET, TENOR AND BARITONE SAXO-PHONES
*born* 4 October 1909; *died* 12 July 1976

Featherstonhaugh worked with Spike Hughes and Bert Firman in the London scene of the 30s, and led a band of his own, the Cosmopolitans, which recorded four rare titles for Decca in 1933. He is best remembered for the spell he enjoyed as the bandleader for the BBC's Radio Rhythm Club during the latter part of the war, where his small group made numerous titles for HMV in a mainstream swing style. That was about it for Featherstonhaugh and jazz, though: he spent at least as much time racing cars as playing saxophone, and though he made one further rather boppish session in 1956, little more was heard from him. Hardly anything he did has made it to CD so far.

# John Fedchock

TROMBONE
*born* 18 September 1957

Born in Cleveland, Fedchock has been closely associated with the latter-day Woody Herman band: he joined in 1980 and became the MD in 1984, staying for a further three years; and he has been involved in the posthumous revivals of the Herman band. He also runs his own New York Big Band, first assembled in 1989 and brought together for occasional albums, featuring many of the premier names in the city. Their Reservoir albums are top-notch examples of what such a band of skilled pros can do with strong material. The trombonist was formerly married to Maria Schneider.

**New York Big Band** (Reservoir)

# Mark Feldman

VIOLIN
*born* 17 July 1955

A Chicagoan, Feldman went from private study to the studios of Nashville, where he made a decent living for a long time before making the move to New York in 1986. Since then he has been the violinist of choice for numerous left-field NYC projects, and has struck up notable associations with the likes of John Zorn, Dave Douglas, Uri Caine and Don Byron. At times he does seem like a token sound of the old world in an otherwise metropolitan-American ensemble, although his background is clearly rootsier than that. One of his projects was the string band Arcado, which he co-led with Mark Dresser and Hank Roberts. A solo record, *Music For Violin Alone* (1994), was beautifully played but not terribly interesting. Feldman has all the technique he can handle and in the right context he is a compelling voice.

**Arcado, Behind The Myth** (JMT)

# Victor Feldman

PIANO, VIBES, PERCUSSION
*born* 7 April 1934; *died* 12 May 1987

Feldman got off to a precocious start: he played drums in a family band from the age of seven, later switched to piano and was seeing what he could do on vibes by his teens. He was on the London stage and in films as a child actor, and sat in at jam sessions on the local bebop scene. He led several sessions for Tony Hall's Tempo label in the mid-50s, all sought after by collectors, then went to live and work in America. He toured with Woody Herman but then settled on the West Coast, and was soon in demand by leaders such as Howard Rumsey and Shelly Manne (he plays piano on Manne's superb *At The Black Hawk* sessions from 1959). A spell with the Cannonball Adderley group was really his final high-profile gig: though he played briefly with Miles Davis (he didn't record with him), thereafter he worked most frequently as a sessionman, in both rock and jazz situations (he plays vibes on Steely Dan's 'Razor Boy', to pick a single track). Feldman didn't so much fritter away his talent as settle it into situations where he played to orders, always impeccably. Records under his own name are mostly obscure and hard to run down, and many of them add up to little more than glossy easy-listening.

**Shelly Manne,** *At The Black Hawk Vols 1–4* (Contemporary/OJC)

## Lennie Felix

PIANO
*born* 16 August 1920; *died* 29 December 1981

Felix was training to work in his father's hairdressing salon when he began playing piano in London clubs, around 1938. After war service he continued in music, and played in London, Cape Town and the Far East, before joining Freddy Randall's band. During the trad boom Felix found himself in steady work as a trio leader, both in London and in Europe, where he once jammed with members of the Ellington band (on his telling Duke that he'd 'loved him all [his] life', Ellington told Felix, 'Well, don't stop now, baby!'). Felix's amalgam of Waller, Hines and Tatum kept him busy as a leader through the 60s and 70s, but he died after being knocked down by a car on a London street.

*In His Stride* (77)

## Simon H Fell

BASS, COMPOSER
*born* 13 January 1959

Working in the largely jazzless territory of Haverhill, Suffolk, Fell has assembled a formidable catalogue of recordings, bands and compositions. He is a talented large-scale composer whose works for both small and big ensembles include a tremendous amount of experimental activity – studio trickery and real-time complexities seamlessly integrated into forms where improvisational spontaneity and carefully structured form happily and productively coexist. He came to some prominence in the 80s in the brawling free-jazz trio Hession Wilkinson Fell (with saxophonist Alan Wilkinson and drummer Paul Hession) and is a virtuoso performer on the acoustic bass, but major recordings such as *Composition No. 12.5* (1990) and *Composition No.30: Compilation III* (1998) are ferociously ambitious and massive in scope (the latter requires a 136-page score, and even Fell describes it as 'unnecessarily complex, ornate and mathematical'). He releases much of the music on his own Bruce's Fingers label. An original force in the East Anglian countryside.

*Composition No. 30: Compilation III* (Bruce's Fingers)

## Maynard Ferguson

TRUMPET, FLUGELHORN, BANDLEADER
*born* 4 May 1928

A Canadian, Ferguson studied at Montreal's French Conservatory, and got his first starring role in the Stan Kenton band of the early 50s. His exceptional high-note facility made him the talk of the brass-playing world, and when he went freelance in 1953 he was much in demand for Californian session-work. He began leading his own big bands in 1957, an activity which he has basically stuck with until now, although in the harsher climate of the late 60s he scaled back to a sextet for a spell. The Ferguson big band was a hit festival attraction and he had a good ear for what audiences wanted: a round dozen albums made for Roulette between 1958 and 1964 offered a younger, just slightly hipper alternative to the Basie big-band sound, although in essence

Ferguson was no more forward-looking than the Count. His later albums for Columbia (1971–82) appear to be more compromised, since they include the likes of the theme from *Rocky*, but this was just Maynard's way of playing for the people. In the 80s and 90s he has bustled tirelessly on, leading a band he likes to call Big Bop Nouveau, and picking up various other horns – including valve-trombone and french horn, or his own invention, the firebird, a hybrid trumpet – during the course of a show. The dazzling range of old has inevitably been cooled off over the years, but in his 70s he is still partial to a bit of showstopping, and the best of the Roulette albums portray a musician pushing the merits of swinging playing in a period which tended to devalue such basic verities.
*Message From Newport* (Roulette)

# Festivals

Music festivals are a commonplace in every civilized country, and every kind of music is anthologized this way in the live medium. Whether presented over a single day, a weekend, a week or even longer, the jazz festival plays its part in the annual musical diary. While the celebratory aspect of festivals has a close kinship with early jazz performance, the music only slowly admitted the idea of itself as 'worthy' of the kind of stand-alone artistic appreciation which the festival is meant to encourage. It was, rather extraordinarily, the Australian Jazz Convention of 1946, organized by Graeme Bell and Harry Stein in Melbourne, which was most likely the first fully fledged jazz festival, although American entrepreneurs such as John Hammond and Norman Granz were already undertaking events which led in that direction. (Granz's Jazz At The Philharmonic concerts were akin to festivals in miniature: lots of big names presented as a package.) Nice and Paris hosted similar but more ambitious events at the end of the decade, inviting many American stars over to attend, and perhaps the most renowned of all jazz festivals, at Newport, Rhode Island, was first held in 1954. George Wein was responsible for much of what took place at Newport, and by the 70s he had established an organization to contract festival activity out to whoever wanted to stage it and could afford it.

In the meantime, almost every capital city in Europe and every state in the USA had at least had a go at presenting their own jazz festival. The rise of the festival mirrored the change in the way people listened to jazz: where once it was background music for drinking and partying, or an accompaniment for dancers, now it was sitting-and-listening music. By the end of the century, the format had become probably the most important medium of jazz presentation in the world. The European festival season, which runs broadly from late spring to early autumn, takes in so many events that at one time it became a tradition for many American musicians to summer in the old world and take advantage of the work situation. Massive events such as the North Sea Jazz Festival, held over a single weekend but taking in hundreds of performers on many stages, jostled for attention with smaller but beautifully proportioned festivals such as that in the little French town of Marciac, now internationally renowned. Big American events have moved on from the all-embracing Newport model: sponsored in some cases by a record label (Concord) or a magazine (*Playboy*), they frequently reflect the tastes of the organizers and the audience they expect; in those two cases, it would be mainstream-jazz lovers and well-heeled dilettantes respectively.

Sponsorship has, indeed, become a crucial issue for the jazz festival. Because the music is perceived as a marginal part of the culture, it has experienced many difficulties in attracting overall sponsorship, and festival organizers tend to seek a barrowful of sponsors, as well as bolstering their programmes with 'banker' acts to ensure ticket sales. This has led to festival programmes becoming compromised and bloated with musicians whose work often bears scant relation to the idiom of jazz: a defining example is the Montreux Jazz Festival, once a vital part of the live jazz calendar, but now more like an expensive showcase for acts who are being pushed by the big corporate players, and with at least as much rock as jazz involved. In other instances, the issue is sidestepped by simply having jazz as part of the remit of a festival which offers a broader contemporary overview. Either way, there is certainly a significant part of the jazz audience which only ever hears the music in a festival situation, and whose expectations and tastes are being defined by what they hear in that environment.

## Bobby Few
PIANO
*born* 21 October 1935

Few was playing on his native Cleveland scene from the early 50s, but he was scarcely noticed even when he arrived in New York in 1967 (at Albert Ayler's suggestion). He played with Ayler for a spell before emigrating to Paris in 1969, where he worked with other expatriates and local players such as Alan Silva and Frank Wright. But his period of most attention was when he worked as a sideman in Steve Lacy's group, starting in the early 80s and carrying on until the middle 90s. Few is a sterling contributor to some of Lacy's superior record dates of the period, even though the saxophonist often went pianoless even then: he had a knack of centring and solidifying a group which might have sounded wayward to many. Since leaving Lacy, though, he has not been very visible.
**Steve Lacy, *The Flame*** (Soul Note)

## Mongezi Feza
TRUMPET
*born* 1945; *died* 14 December 1975

Chris McGregor heard Feza playing in Cape Town when the trumpeter was still in his teens, and invited him to join the Blue Notes, who subsequently settled in London in 1965. He was a popular figure in the London jazz community and played in a crackly, carefree style which had a disarming streak of poignancy in it. In 1972 he settled in Scandinavia but was still playing in London occasionally; his sudden death curtailed a career which, it was posthumously recognized, had hardly been documented at all. His contributions to two Robert Wyatt records, modest as they were, offer some of the best surviving memories of him.
**Robert Wyatt, *Ruth Is Stranger Than Richard*** (Virgin)

## Firehouse Five Plus Two
GROUP

More a novelty group than anything, The Firehouse Five Plus Two (they seem never to have been without the two) came on like a more genteel version of Spike Jones, playing furiously fast Dixieland. Trombonist Ward Kimball first put the band together in 1949, mainly from amateur players who also worked in Walt Disney's animation unit. They were so successful that the group nearly foundered after conflicts with their day jobs in the early 50s, but they re-formed soon enough and lasted until 1971, their calling card being a dress code of firefighting uniforms, attire which didn't exactly confer much seriousness on the music. George Probert, who joined in 1954 and stayed 15 years, was probably their most notable performer. They built a loyal following among Californian audiences, and a measure of their popularity is that most of their records are, more than 30 years after their demise, still in print.
***Goes South*** (Good Time Jazz)

## Clare Fischer
PIANO, ARRANGER
*born* 22 October 1928

Fischer spent his teens in Grand Rapids, MI, where he mastered a wide range of instruments – keyboards, saxophones and cello among them. After university study, he got a job arranging material for The Hi-Lo's, and secured wider attention with a set of charts for a Dizzy Gillespie Verve album, *A Portrait Of Duke Ellington* (1960). He spent most of the 60s in a dual role as a commercial arranger and a jazz pianist: a string of albums in the latter capacity, for Pacific Jazz and Revelation, have never made it beyond a small cult following and urgently require CD revival. He has long had a great love for Latin rhythms, and much of his composing is in this vein, with 'Pensativa' perhaps his best-known piece in the idiom. In the 80s and 90s he was still doing charts for pop projects (Madonna was one artist who availed herself of his talents) while making occasional albums of his own, almost as an afterthought. Fischer's range in his own records has been unusually wide, and he hasn't been shy about doing kitsch and lightweight projects, which can seem curiously flimsy next to the often demanding listening of his solo piano sets. Perhaps it's all music to him.
***Surging Ahead*** (Pacific Jazz)

# Ella Fitzgerald
VOCAL
*born* 25 April 1917; *died* 15 June 1996

The queen of jazz singers – although whether she was the best of them is the sort of thing admirers can spend hours arguing over. She was born in Newport News, Virginia, but moved to Yonkers as an infant in a one-parent family. She lived with an aunt in Harlem after her mother died, but played truant from school and was almost homeless when she took part in a talent contest at Harlem's Apollo Theater and won first prize in the singing event. She looked too shabby to get a band singing job, but finally got one a year later when she joined Chick Webb's band. The young Ella had a light, girlish voice, but it was already smoothly authoritative: she learned tunes instantly and seemed able to master them straight away. She depped for both Billie Holiday and Helen Ward, but with Webb she became a swing-era star, with the perennial 'A-Tisket A-Tasket' becoming one of the most famous successes of the day. After Webb's death in 1939 she fronted the band herself, but she disbanded the orchestra three years later and embarked on a solo career.

The 40s were a mixed time for her: though seen as someone from the swing era, she handled bop vocals when she wanted to (helping make 'How High The Moon' a bopper's anthem), starred in duet recordings with Louis Jordan, Louis Armstrong and The Ink Spots, and recorded prolifically for Decca, although the label seemed unsure of how best to handle her as an artist. In 1949 she started working in Norman Granz's Jazz At The Philharmonic roadshow, usually backed by Oscar Peterson's trio with Ray Brown, who was then her husband; these events helped bring her to an international audience. But the LP era turned Fitzgerald's career into gold. She made some sublime duet sessions with Ellis Larkins, collected on *Pure Ella* (GRP, 1950–54), but when Norman Granz signed her to his new Verve label she began recording entire albums dedicated to the great American popular song composers. *The Cole Porter Songbook* (1956) was the first of them, spread over two LP records, and it was so successful that Granz had her follow the project up with sessions dedicated to Rodgers and Hart, Ellington, Berlin, the Gershwins, Arlen, Kern and Mercer. Perhaps nothing ever topped the Porter project – even in the 90s, in its umpteenth CD edition, it was still selling in the tens of thousands every year – but every album luxuriated in Fitzgerald's poise, perfect articulation (the surviving composers all loved the respect which this singer conferred on their work) and natural swing. Arranged mostly by Nelson Riddle, the music struck a balance between an orchestral suaveness and a jazzier syncopation, and Ella seemed to breeze through the charts.

Besides these records, though, she turned out dozens of other albums for Verve, each welcomed by what was now a large and worldwide audience. She continued to tour, mostly with the support of small groups and pianists such as Hank Jones and Tommy Flanagan, and though she endured an unhappy period with Capitol Records in the later 60s when Granz gave up Verve, recording some dreadful pop material, she was back with her longtime manager-producer when he started Pablo: several of her autumnal records for the label have some of her most considered work. Her scat singing is another aspect of her music which tends to divide the house: undeniably inventive and agile, in live performance it could become tediously repetitive. Most of her live concerts had their share of unfortunate spells, such as her annoying charge through her customary set-closer, 'Mack The Knife'. It is a commonplace to complain that she found no pathos in ballads and never drew tears from a lyric, but she wasn't that sort of singer: what you got from Ella, as with Sinatra, was a great performance, a fastidious and usually flawless interpretation. Long troubled by her weight and her failing eyesight, she had stopped performing by 1990, and her final years were reportedly sad and reclusive – a melancholy finale to a career which brought so much joy through her artistry.
**The Cole Porter Songbook** (Verve)

# Tommy Flanagan
PIANO
*born* 16 March 1930; *died* 16 November 2001

A godfather in Detroit's jazz community, Flanagan was working professionally from

his early teens, although the earliest part of his career was interrupted by army service. He worked with the likes of Billy Mitchell and Kenny Burrell on the city's club scene before eventually shifting his base to New York in 1956, where he became an indispensable part of the city's music, both in the studios and on dates: he plays piano on such major records as Sonny Rollins's *Saxophone Colossus*, Wes Montgomery's *The Incredible Jazz Guitar* and John Coltrane's *Giant Steps*. But he did some of his most high-profile work as an accompanist to singers, particularly Ella Fitzgerald, whom he played for during three different periods. By the late 70s, though, he preferred to work as his own boss in the trio idiom, and all through the 80s and 90s he made a steady stream of recordings – although mostly for European labels such as Enja and Timeless – which offer a profoundly individual take on the language of bebop piano, crafted with unfailing delicacy and refinement even as it was unfurled at fast tempos and in strong rhythmical characters. George Mraz partners him on many of these dates, and together they made a particularly sonorous combination. Although he was honoured by his musical community, it was rather shameful that American record labels latterly neglected this master musician: a single Blue Note album, *Sunset And The Mockingbird* (1998), became one of his final statements.
*Eclypso* (Enja)

## Brick Fleagle
GUITAR
*born* 22 August 1906

Jacob Fleagle started out on banjo and then played guitar in a variety of dance bands in the early 30s, before joining Joe Haymes in 1935. His great association, though, was with Rex Stewart: they played together on record on a number of occasions, under the leadership of either man, and Fleagle loved Rex's company. While he was a modest talent as a soloist, Fleagle had strong all-round musicianship: he wrote numerous arrangements, some taken up by Fletcher Henderson and even Duke Ellington, and the small-group sessions under his leadership were astutely marshalled as well. When bop came along, he retired more to the sidelines and got involved in publishing, even though

he remembered bop as 'considerable fun, much of it deliberate confusion'. His administrative career lasted for decades.
*Previously Unissued* (IAJRC)

## Herb Flemming
TROMBONE
*born* 5 April 1900; *died* 3 October 1976

A man of mystery, Herb Flemming may have been born in Montana, Honolulu, Egypt or none of the above (he once claimed that his father was Egyptian and his mother Tunisian, and his given name was Niccolaiih El Michelle). Whatever the truth of it, he was playing in James Reese Europe's army band in 1917 and thereafter worked on the New York scene, recording with such pioneers as Johnny Dunn and Perry Bradford. He toured Europe with Sam Wooding and eventually fetched up in Paris as MD for Josephine Baker. In 1935 he began a residency at the Sherbini Egyptian Club in Berlin, but returned to the US in 1937 and worked under many leaders before a long spell with Henry Allen, between 1953 and 1958. Europe eventually beckoned him again, and he visited France and Spain, settling in the south of the latter country at the end of the 60s. He was a familiar presence in Spanish seaside bands but declining health curtailed his playing and he eventually went back to America for the last time at the beginning of 1976. A lusty, uncomplicated player, he was a good match for Henry Allen and did most of his best recorded work with him.
**Henry Allen, *Red Allen Plays King Oliver*** (Verve)

## Bob Florence
PIANO, ARRANGER
*born* 20 May 1932

Florence was born in Los Angeles and has spent his working life there. He studied arranging at college and by the end of the 50s he was doing charts, for working big bands, singers and television. Much of his work has been buried away in commercial settings, but that has helped to pay for his most adventurous jazz work: he made a record for the small Carlton label as far back as 1959, but in the 80s and 90s he recorded more regularly with the kind of big band which such a stalwart of the LA session scene would have no difficulty in assembling. Florence likes an arrangement packed with detail and activity, and by now he's so skilful in the style that the music rarely sounds either overblown or overpowered by its mechanics. In the sometimes unfairly maligned tradition of West Coast big-band music, only Bill Holman has surpassed him for quality of writing over an extended period.

**Jewels** (Discovery)

## Med Flory
SAXOPHONES
*born* 27 August 1926

Meredith Flory came from Logansport, Indiana, but he is mainly associated with West Coast music. He was with Woody Herman in 1953, but went to California in 1956 and opened his account there with a group called Med Flory's Jazz Wave Orchestra, which lasted on and off until 1960, although he was also working as lead alto in the Ray Anthony band in the same period. In the 60s he was tied up with studio work, but in 1972 he co-founded (with Buddy Clark) a new group called Supersax which was dedicated to Charlie Parker and works as a homage to Bird, the book based around transcriptions of Parker solos. It has been a frequently impressive if often pointless ensemble. In the meantime, early Flory records such as *Jazz Wave* (1956) and *Med Flory Big Band* (1963) are rather more deserving of a revival.

**Supersax Plays Bird** (Capitol)

## Carl Fontana
TROMBONE
*born* 18 July 1928; *died* 9 October 2003

Fontana had remarkable chops and his skills never left him. Born in Monroe, Louisiana, he worked with Woody Herman and Stan Kenton in the early 50s, but his abilities led him towards studio work and through the 60s he was in both Las Vegas showbands and on numerous recording sessions. He joined in the mainstream revival of the 70s and toured with The World's Greatest Jazz Band, but he still only rarely secured limelight as any sort of leader, and his only

album in that regard was a single date for Uptown in 1985, *The Great Fontana*: he was still much in demand in Vegas. Retiring from that kind of work at last in the 90s, he was able to pick and choose gigs as he pleased. A series of live sessions made in 1993 at a venue in Phoenix, with Conte Candoli, was released after Fontana's death: they are a beautiful presentation of his huge sound, conversational licks and buttery good humour.

**The Complete Phoenix Sessions** (Woofy)

## Ricky Ford
TENOR AND SOPRANO SAXOPHONES
*born* 4 March 1954

A Bostonian, Ford first got attention with the posthumous Duke Ellington Orchestra in 1975, before joining the final Charles Mingus group and then subsequently playing in Dannie Richmond's band. He has often been feted as a talent deserving wider attention, but it's been a career whose promise has never been fulfilled, and since he started working in jazz education Ford's opportunities seem to have ebbed away. In a live situation he can be a tremendously exciting soloist, but his leadership career on record has never taken off: a series of studio albums for Muse sounded constricted and half-realized, and three albums for Candid have been occasionally momentous and not quite essential. Maybe the leader who used him best was Abdullah Ibrahim: Ford is very interested in the music's roots, and he responded handsomely to the tasks set by Ibrahim on *Water From An Ancient Well* (1985).

**Hot Brass** (Candid)

## Michael Formanek
BASS
*born* 7 May 1958

Formanek, from San Francisco, got off to an early start and was gigging with Joe Henderson and Tony Williams in the mid-70s, playing either acoustic or electric bass. After a move to New York in 1977 he focused on the stand-up bass and worked in an exceptionally broad range of projects. In the 80s it seemed he was moving towards the Downtown circle of players, numbering Tim

Berne, Marty Ehrlich and Greg Osby among his collaborators, and his own groups Loose Cannon, Wide Open Spaces and Beast Of Nature have been settled in that adventurous idiom. But he has continued to work in more mainstream situations, with Lee Konitz, the Mingus Big Band and many others. Besides his own instrumentalism, Formanek is a strong writer, importing devices from contemporary composition into a thoughtful jazz outlook. The wryly titled *Am I Bothering You?* (1997) has also found him tackling the bass solo album.
**Extended Animation** (Enja)

## Jimmy Forrest

TENOR SAXOPHONE
*born* 24 January 1920; *died* 26 August 1980

Forrest is thought of as a part of 'modern' jazz, and it's a surprise to discover that he was working with such a leader as the steamboat-bandleader Fate Marable, as far back as 1935. His first name association was with Jay McShann, in 1942, but he soon switched to the Andy Kirk band and stayed until 1948. A brief period with Duke Ellington was documented by only a single studio date, but Ellington (unwittingly) provided Forrest with his signature hit: a rolling shuffle called 'Night Train', which is based on Ellington's 'Happy Go Lucky Local'. Jimmy made five albums for Prestige at the beginning of the 60s, but a heart attack slowed him down, and it wasn't until he joined Count Basie in 1972 that he enjoyed his closing years. A typical St Louis tenorman – not quite as barrel-voiced as the Texas tenors, but still soaked in the blues, and happy to please an audience that liked R&B licks – 'Night Train' told all of the Jimmy Forrest story.
**Night Train** (Delmark)

## Sonny Fortune

TENOR AND SOPRANO SAXOPHONES
*born* 19 May 1939

Fortune grew up in Philadelphia and played on his local R&B scene early on. He moved from Elvin Jones to Mongo Santamaria to Buddy Rich to McCoy Tyner between 1968 and 1974, a progression which may say something about how difficult it was for a young

jazz musician to keep consistently congenial company during rock's heyday. But his highest profile was with the Miles Davis band which recorded the thunderous *Agharta* and *Pangaea* (both 1975), even though Fortune was with Davis for barely a year. After this he tried his luck with some leadership albums for A&M and Atlantic that sounded dangerously close to thin commercial fusion. The 80s were a wasteland for him, but in the 90s he made some uncompromising records for the European label Konnex and a pair of excellent sets for Blue Note, which unfortunately fared poorly in the marketplace. Once a relentless post-Coltrane type, in the Monk collection *Four In One* (1994) Fortune was shown to have calmed his style without taking the sinew and strength out of it. An able and underrecorded player who could use some thoughtful patronage.
**Four In One** (Blue Note)

## Al Foster

DRUMS
*born* 18 January 1944

Though born in Richmond, Virginia, Foster moved to New York as a child and started out on drums from the age of ten. He was busy in the city all through the 60s and his dedication to his family obliged him to turn down touring offers from such leaders as Miles Davis and Wes Montgomery. Eventually, though, he did join Davis in 1972, staying until the trumpeter went into his sabbatical in 1975. Thereafter he worked in all manner of groups until he once again joined Davis in 1980. The Davis association has probably helped cement the impression that Foster is one of the key drummers of his generation, and he has subsequently worked with other ex-sidemen such as Herbie Hancock. He remained very close to Davis on a personal level, staying in close touch with the trumpeter right up to his death: when he played on Joe Henderson's memorial record to Davis, *So Near So Far*, Foster played drums with a picture of Miles taped to his ride cymbal. While he is basically a post-bop stylist in the mould of Max Roach, Al became just as adept at playing groove and free rhythms of the kind that suited Davis's later music.
**Miles Davis, *We Want Miles*** (Columbia)

# Frank Foster

TENOR AND SOPRANO SAXOPHONES
*born* 23 September 1928

Although raised in Cincinnati, Foster first came to light on the Detroit scene, and after military service he joined the 1953 Count Basie Orchestra, staying for ten years and commanding the sound of the saxophone section, as well as contributing pieces to the band's book (his 'Shiny Stockings' is one of the most durable pieces in the Basie repertoire, as well as a jazz greatest hit, regularly covered by singers). After this he worked extensively as a writer, ran some small groups of his own and kept his big-band chops in order with two different groups, The Living Color and The Loud Minority, the latter still occasionally convened. He was tempted back into the Basie fold when asked to take over the Basie legacy band in 1986, and stayed with it for a decade. He has also done much work in jazz education. A master of most styles of saxophone playing, Foster has seemingly listened carefully to every post-war tenorman and made himself an invincible stylist in a swing-to-bop manner of absolute authority. Even in a casual blues jam such as Prestige's *All Day Long* (1957) his playing stands out for its decisiveness and elegance. Many of his own-name recordings are buried away on small labels and are out of print, but he has already left a legacy of playing, writing and bandleading which will leave a very deep mark on jazz history after bebop.

*Shiny Stockings* (Denon)

# Gary Foster

ALTO, TENOR AND SOPRANO SAXOPHONES
*born* 25 May 1936

Foster is a ubiquitous presence in the West Coast studios and has probably been on thousands of records in the past 40 years. Originally from Kansas, he went West in 1961 and struck up an enduring relationship with Clare Fischer, playing in both the big and small groups led by the pianist. He has been in many other big bands over the years and has seemingly had time to lead only a handful of records himself. His primary horn is the alto and he came up with an alternative to Lee Konitz's take on the Tristano-ite delivery: more rounded,

bluesless, but missing some of the penetrating ingenuity which Konitz displays. His collaborations with Fischer for the Revelation label enshrine some of his most creative playing and could certainly stand reissue.

*Grand Cru Classé* (Revelation)

# Pops Foster

BASS
*born* 18 May 1892; *died* 30 October 1969

Foster started on cello but soon went over to bass, and before 1914 he had already been playing with Freddie Keppard, Joe Oliver, Buddy Petit and many of the other principal lights in New Orleans. In the teens he worked in riverboat bands and (on dry land) in the Charlie Creath group, but in 1929, already pushing 40, he went to New York and joined Luis Russell. He was with him all through the 30s and is on most of the records where Russell backs Louis Armstrong. By the 40s, Foster's slap-bass style was anachronistic, but nicely in tune with the first stirrings of revivalism, and he is on many of the *This Is Jazz* broadcasts, as well as recording with Sidney Bechet and Jimmy Archey. He can be seen toting his bass with great enthusiasm in Roger Tilton's short film *Jazz Dance* (1954). Then came a regular stint with Earl Hines, and plenty of freelance work up until his death. The year before, Art Hodes recorded conversations and duets with the old man, a precious survival on the record cited.

*George 'Pops' Foster* (American Music)

# Pete Fountain

CLARINET
*born* 3 July 1930

Because Fountain pursued commercial success so effectively, it's hard to find his best work, which is hidden in among inoffensive but entirely forgettable easy-listening situations. Nobody playing a clarinet can build a catalogue like this any more. But Fountain, who'd played with various groups in his native New Orleans prior to 1957, was picked by bandleader Lawrence Welk to front a Dixieland unit on Welk's hugely popular TV show. The clarinettist was signed to Coral, who made more than 30 albums with him between 1960 and 1971. He ran his own club,

Pete's Place, picked up handsome pay cheques in Las Vegas and was a fixture in the days when 'light entertainment' still ruled American television. Although they actually only made a handful of dates together, he was very much a blood brother to Al Hirt. He was still playing his mild brand of Dixieland to hotel audiences in the 90s. Fountain wasn't a poor clarinet player, but he rarely did anything special on his records, mainly because he wasn't expected to. Acker Bilk's albums with strings might be a British counterpart to Pete, although Acker is a bluesier player.
*Pete's Place* (Coral)

## Fours

'Trading fours' means the swapping of alternating four-bar breaks between one soloist and another. While this is similar to a chase chorus, it is more akin to a dialogue between two members of the band, most often one of the horn players and the drummer – a device often used in the climactic chorus of a single performance, prior to a final statement of the theme.

## Panama Francis
DRUMS
*born* 21 December 1918

Francis led a long and busy jazz life. David Albert Francis (the 'Panama' came from Roy Eldridge, after the drummer's ever-present headgear) played in marching bands at school, and worked under Florida leaders such as George Kelly before going to New York in 1938, where he played with Eldridge and others. He was with Lucky Millinder from 1940, often working at the Savoy Ballroom opposite the Savoy Sultans, a band Francis loved: when he began leading on his own in 1946, it was the Sultans he modelled himself after. But it was an unsuccessful venture, and Panama joined Cab Calloway for five years from 1947. Then it was ten years of prolific studio work, although mostly on R&B sessions, and after that five years with Dinah Shore. In the 70s he toured Europe, and turned up on many of the mainstream sessions recorded by Black & Blue, before forming a new Savoy Sultans in 1979 and this time scoring a great success. The band

had New York appearances all through the 80s and became the now venerable drummer's starring vehicle.
*Everything Swings* (Stash)

## Cie Frazier
DRUMS
*born* 23 February 1904; *died* 10 January 1985

Frazier's style all but defines New Orleans drumming. He was masterful at slowly building tempos at a dance, brushing or tapping his way round the kit, making fast rhythms and crescendoes emerge with complete naturalness: 'A lot of drummers don't listen to the melody when they play, but I'm always following it, and sometimes I hum along. Those rock'n'roll drummers, they have a hard time with jazz.' He was in the thick of the city's music for his whole professional life, starting with Lawrence Marrero and Papa Celestin in the mid-20s, then with A J Piron, Wooden Joe Nicholas, Percy Humphrey and Kid Howard. From 1961 he was the most regularly encountered drummer at Preservation Hall, and he finally got to tour a little, visiting Europe and drumming with Kid Thomas Valentine, Jim Robinson, the Humphreys, Billie and De De Pierce and the Eureka Brass band, among many others.
**Percy Humphrey,** *Climax Rag* (Delmark)

## Free jazz

The new music of the 60s, at one time – rarely now – also referred to as the New Thing. Ornette Coleman's *Free Jazz* (1960) first put a name on what was going on, although Joe Harriott's *Free Form* (also 1960) came out at about the same time, and it was only Harriott's use of regular time (as well as his own obscurity) which made a crucial difference with Coleman's music. Like most jazz subdivisions, a hard-and-fast definition of free jazz is difficult, but it essentially covers musical improvisation without a preset harmonic structure, which lasts as long as the players deem it has a necessary life, without a repetitive chorus pattern. There are, though, different degrees of Free: it may be played in a particular key, it may not. There may be a theme; there may not. There may be no chorus structure, but the players may perform with an implied rhythmic framework or regularity; or they may not. Generally speaking, the more negatives there are or were, the more free the idiom, to the point where the 'jazz' element itself disappears and the music is simply free, or free improvisation, a language which, tellingly enough, was developed with a greater degree of intensity in Europe, which lacks the hard-to-escape jazz traditions of America.

Like most of the rest of jazz, free jazz rushed through its evolution in a matter of a few years: if Coleman's earliest recordings for Contemporary and Atlantic ushered the era in, Albert Ayler's extremism charged its remotest boundaries within five years. As usual, there were many forerunners and exceptions to the simple evolutionary path from hard bop to free jazz. Lennie Tristano had played an entirely improvised group piece called 'Intuition', with Warne Marsh and Lee Konitz, as far back as 1949, and Cecil Taylor's earliest recordings in 1955 approach free jazz from a different direction. John Coltrane took on those elements of free jazz which made sense in his journeyings, without ever quite feeling free. A figure such as Eric Dolphy seems to perch on the divide between free playing and bop orthodoxy. Paul Bley moved from bop to free and back again, yet was latterly able to accommodate the playing of a European free giant such as Evan Parker. Archie Shepp, perhaps the figure most in the vanguard of free playing as an expression of 60s black militancy, which is an important subtext in the music's position in that decade, has subsequently become more like a vaudevillian with a touch of Ben Webster about him. Given that free jazz seems by implication a play of expression without frontiers, it's curious to recall that most considered it 'over' by the end of the 60s: during the following decade, jazz-rock and a mainstream revival suggested a period of retrenchment, after ten years of saxophone screamers and a fundamentally aggressive face put on this new music. But free improvisation, as the Europeans had it, had actually commenced a slow and still unfolding evolution of its own, while American free jazz became another mode of expression for improvisers working within the capacious classroom of jazz vocabularies.

# Nnenna Freelon
VOCAL
*born* 27 July 1957

Freelon was an administrator in the field of health care, but had sung gospel music in her youth and sang locally in Durham, North Carolina, during the 80s. Ellis Marsalis heard her at a festival gig and from there she won a contract with Columbia, resulting in three strong records which were perhaps a shade unlucky in their timing: she was slightly too soon to benefit from the current wave of interest in jazz singers. Likened to Sarah Vaughan at the outset, her voice and delivery have matured into a powerful but sweet-toned instrument which she has used on a very broad range of material, moving to Concord after she left Columbia. She is also busy in jazz education, and considers getting an audience started at a pre-college age is the only way to build an audience of 'thinking, improvisational human beings'.
*Soul Call* (Concord)

# Bud Freeman
TENOR SAXOPHONE
*born* 13 April 1906; *died* 15 March 1991

Bud Freeman and Coleman Hawkins settled the tenor saxophone into jazz, and though Hawkins got most of the credit, Freeman did more than his part. He already sounds in control of matters on the 1927 'Nobody's Sweetheart', by the McKenzie–Condon Chicagoans, and by the end of the decade his style was basically secure. He didn't much care for the rhapsodic approach to ballads which Hawkins preferred, and rather than running out melodies he liked to chew a solo into rough-edged bits: he always fitted better into Dixieland situations than Hawkins did. His riff-crazy setpiece 'The Eel', first recorded in 1933, stuck with him to the end. He spent the 30s working with various swing bands: when he joined Tommy Dorsey in 1936, the singer Edythe Wright even announced it on one of Dorsey's records. Bud led some fine small-group records at the end of the decade, then ran society bands before going into the army. On his return, he took the somewhat amazing step of studying with Lennie Tristano for a spell, then freelanced: he went to live in Chile for a time, but missed the music, and returned to tour as a solo. Bud loved London, visiting several times before making his home there in the latter part of the 70s, and his many appearances at the Pizza Express are treasured memories for those who saw him. By this time he had settled into a more mainstream groove, cooling off the grittier side of his playing, but he still liked Dixieland and worked with The World's Greatest Jazz Band for three years. He was still playing in his 80s, but failing sight obliged him to end his career. Later recordings can make him sound a little halting in his delivery, but that was mainly how he chose to smooth out his style: Bud never liked to play long lines.

**Swingin' With The Eel** (ASV)

## Chico Freeman

TENOR AND SOPRANO SAXOPHONES, FLUTE
*born* 17 July 1949

Von Freeman's son has had a steady but finally disappointing career – at least in terms of fulfilling the promise of his early music. After various studies, he arrived in New York during the loft jazz boom and gigs with Elvin Jones and other leaders built up his reputation. With his own groups, Freeman suggested that he might become one of the great saxophone influences of the day, using a thorough knowledge of both in and out playing to drive a sound which was as grandly beautiful a tenor voice as has been heard in the aftermath of Coltrane. The classic *Spirit Sensitive* (1978), a programme of standards and ballads from a player who might have deemed such a move to be counter-revolutionary, is still a breathtaking listen, and in person Chico was a formidable presence. But the major-label contract only belatedly arrived (a brief and uninspiring period with Elektra Musician), Freeman threw in his lot with the 80s jazz supergroup The Leaders – an enjoyable but pointless ensemble – and eventually decided to mix straight-ahead playing with quasi-fusion in the electric line-up of Brainstorm. By 1999 he was involving himself in education and his playing career had tapered off altogether.

**Spirit Sensitive** (India Navigation)

## Russ Freeman

PIANO
*born* 28 May 1926; *died* 28 June 2002

Freeman disappeared from jazz after 1965 or so, beckoned by the lucrative field of film and TV work, but in the 50s he was one of the smartest pianists on the Californian scene. He had already been backing some of the leading boppers on their visits to the West Coast when he began playing and recording with Art Pepper and Chet Baker, from 1953 – although he refused to go to Europe with the trumpeter, that gig eventually going to the star-crossed Richard Twardzik. There was a long stint with Shelly Manne from 1955, although he was absent when Manne was making his immortal sessions at The Manne Hole and The Black Hawk for Contemporary. Only twice did Russ make his presence felt latterly: on Art Pepper's comeback date *Among Friends* (1975), and on a delightful set of duets with old friend Shelly Manne, *One On One* (1982). Although he basically worked from a bebop vocabulary, Freeman had such a strong left hand that he often sounds more like a particularly modernistic swing player.

**One On One** (Contemporary)

## Von Freeman

TENOR SAXOPHONE
*born* 2 October 1922

The godfather of modern Chicago jazz has never really left his local scene. Although he played with a navy band during the war and then for a brief spell with Sun Ra, he has mostly been his own boss ever since, although during the leaner period of the 60s he toured in blues revues. While he employed sidemen ranging from Ahmad Jamal and Andrew Hill to Malachi Favors and Richard Abrams, his own profile was rarely other than low away from his home town, and it wasn't until the later 80s that he toured internationally. After thousands of gigs – from vaudeville to barmitzvahs – his occasional association with son Chico in a two-tenor group finally brought him some attention, and the irony has been that, with the fad for rediscovering forgotten heroes, Von's profile and reputation have easily outdone Chico's in recent times. A gruff-toned, hard-swinging player with a notably idiosyn-

Buddy Bolden's band of the early 1890s, with the leader second from left at the back. What did they sound like?

King Oliver's Creole Jazz Band, with Louis Armstrong, Joe Oliver, Baby Dodds, Honore Dutrey, Bill Johnson, Johnny Dodds and Lil Hardin, at the time of their 1923 records.

Bix Beiderbecke, the original young man with a horn.

Duke Ellington's team of 1931 – half-way between Cotton Club jungle and 'His Famous Orchestra'.

Dizzy Gillespie in the bebop uniform of beret, horn-rims and goatee, directing rhythmical traffic in 1948.

Django Reinhardt,
the gypsy legend.

On clarinet, Sidney
Bechet.

Humphrey Lyttelton (with Keith Christie on trombone) rocks the Hammersmith Palais in the first wave of British trad in 1951.

Chet Baker, the second young man with a horn.

Benny Goodman as The King Of Swing.

Charlie Parker, Thelonious Monk, Charles Mingus and Roy Haynes perform at the Open Door in New York, 1953. Gallery admission: $1.00. Great days.

Backstage at Jazz At The Philharmonic:
Stan Getz warms up, Ella cools off.

cratic approach to the beat, and his music is perhaps the rougher, nastier side of the Chicago coin, as compared with Johnny Griffin's equally energetic but suaver and more refined delivery. In his 80s, he is, along with fellow local legend Fred Anderson, the acknowledged master of his home turf. Brother George (b 1927), who plays guitar, has also kept the faith with the local scene, although brother Bruz (b 1921), a drummer, worked on the West Coast and eventually settled in Hawaii.
*Have No Fear* (Nessa)

# Fresh Sound
RECORD COMPANY

Operating out of Barcelona, Fresh Sound made a name for itself in the 80s by issuing quality facsimile pressings of many important (mostly American) albums of the 50s and 60s, drawn from such hitherto neglected catalogues as HiFiJazz, Jazz West and Peacock, as well as RCA and Pacific Jazz. This was the first time this had been done on such a scale outside Japan. In the 90s, while continuing this work into the CD era, under the stewardship of Jordi Pujol the label began recording new sessions, again by many neglected figures – including Eddie Bert, Frank Strazzeri, J R Monterose and Charlie Mariano – as well as unexposed artists on their Fresh Sounds New Talent subsidiary, which in the new century had quickly established an important archive of work by the likes of Brad Mehldau, Mark Turner, Ethan Iverson, Bil McHenry and numerous others.

# Paolo Fresu
TRUMPET
*born* 10 February 1961

One of the key figures in new Italian jazz, Fresu is not so significant as, say, Gianluigi Trovesi or Giorgio Gaslini in terms of composing or group leading, but as a performing voice he is peerless. Like many brass players in the region, he started out playing in the local marching band in Sardinia, and showed no interest in jazz until he was nearly 20. His early albums for the Italian independent Splasc(h) show him working out a way of putting something of

himself into a blueprint of soft hard bop, and latterly – after writing for theatre especially – he has fashioned a small-group music which has a notably individual bent. It's a pat conclusion to suggest that Italian melody and sunshine offer the most distinctive colours in this music, but it would be hard to mistake Fresu's records for those of an American group. He has made numerous sets with his long-standing quintet, and others where he works in a duo with bassist Furio Di Castri, both men adding a discreet dappling of electronics. Signing to a European branch of RCA in 1996 has given him some valuable exposure, although as usual American business has resisted offering a European any significant exposure. His sound on the trumpet is quite gorgeous: brassy, full, but shaded to a whisper at times, and cast very much to a Miles Davis outline which he seems happy to acknowledge.
*Melos* (RCA)

# David Friedman
VIBES
*born* 10 March 1944

Juilliard study led to a career that might have been based around the New York Philharmonic, with which Friedman played in the early 60s. But from 1970 onwards he was with major leaders such as Wayne Shorter and Horace Silver, and he formed a partnership with fellow vibesman Dave Samuels that gave rise to recordings of various duo and quartet line-ups under the heading Double Image. Friedman is, perhaps, a percussionist whose main instrument happens to be vibes, and he is a significant technician and educator. But that may have prevented him making any particular impact on record, and it's difficult to come up with anything he's done which has real claims on the casual ear. The listed set, with Jane Ira Bloom, includes some of his most charming and attractive work.
*Of The Wind's Eye* (Enja)

## Don Friedman

PIANO
*born* 4 May 1935

Raised in San Francisco, Friedman began playing on the Los Angeles scene in the middle 50s: one notable early gig was with Ornette Coleman, in 1957. But a move to New York in 1958 brought him to wider attention, and he began recording under his own name in 1961. Since then, he has managed to play with equal facility in almost every kind of jazz setting, working with leaders as disparate as Jimmy Giuffre, Clark Terry, Attila Zoller and Lew Tabackin. If, at first, he sounded like little other than a gifted Bill Evans man, that notion was quickly dispelled by such records as *Dreams And Explorations* (1964), built around a sequence of intense originals which have a lick of Tristano about them but owe something to the climate of freedom which was abroad in the New York jazz of the period. In some ways, Friedman was unable to see through the implications of that set, since recording opportunities became scarcer and he moved more comprehensively into education from the 70s onwards. In the 90s, though, he came back to more regular recording. If some of the heat has gone out of his style, there's a compensating elegance, even majesty, in his delivery, and a fine sequence of discs for Steeplechase are well worth following.
*My Romance* (Steeplechase)

## David Friesen

BASS
*born* 6 May 1942

Friesen worked in the 60s and early 70s without winning much attention, and with his first record as a leader, *Star Dance* (1977), he found some small fame for playing in a way which bridged jazz sensibilities with something approaching the onset of New Age music. Much of his work since then has idled in that margin, although he can play demanding straight-ahead music when he wants to, in the company of such as Dave Liebman and Michael Brecker. He has appeared and recorded as a soloist, although that music tends to reside in the dreamier climes he seems fondest of.
*Two For The Show* (ITM)

## Johnny Frigo

BASS, VIOLIN
*born* 27 December 1916

Born into the poorest part of Chicago, Frigo took violin lessons from the son of a junk collector (until he moved away and John could no longer afford the fare). He began playing bass in the city's clubs in the early 30s (and won a tip from Al Capone). Then he joined Chico Marx's orchestra, which played the Ben Pollack book, and roomed with fellow sideman Barney Kessel. In the later 40s he led his own trio, The Soft Winds, with Herb Ellis and Lou Carter, and in the 50s was back in Chicago, playing bass as a sessionman and violin on country-music radio shows. Eventually he settled on violin as his sole instrument, and in his 80s he has become a festival favourite, touring and storytelling incessantly. Not a bad songwriter – 'Detour Ahead' is one of his – he finally got his own name at the top of a record with *Debut Of A Legend*, in 1994, aged 77.
**With Bucky Pizzarelli,** *Live from Studio A In New York City* (Chesky)

## Bill Frisell

GUITAR
*born* 18 March 1951

Frisell has become the premier purveyor of jazz as a rummage sale of Americana. His background is perhaps disappointingly unromantic for such a figure: rather than any backwoodsmanship, he was raised in Denver, studied in Colorado and at Berklee, and with Jim Hall, and only his father's abilities on tuba and bass suggest the rootsiness which commentators always ascribe to his music. His early progress was, surprisingly, made in Europe, where he made contact with the ECM axis in 1978–9 and began recording with the likes of Eberhard Weber and Jan Garbarek, leading his own sessions for the label from 1982. But his most important association came to be the one with John Zorn, who started hiring him in 1984 and engaged the guitarist for numerous Naked City albums as well as *Spillane* (1986) and *News For Lulu* (1987). His other principal sideman work has been with Paul Motian, with whom he recorded a string of albums in the 80s and 90s.

Frisell's own-name records have grown into a voluminous and rather complicated cycle. The ECM sessions such as *In Line* (1982) and *Lookout For Hope* (1987) balance impressionism and pastoralism in about equal measure, but since 1988 he has been recording for Elektra/Nonesuch and this has grown into a partnership between a jazz musician and a major label of unusual longevity. It helps that Frisell is an amenable collaborator who doesn't mind any rock associations – the Zorn affiliation has been a boon in that regard, and he has also served alongside Elvis Costello. But his own projects have been ingeniously marketed as simultaneously radical, accessible and experimental.

He toyed with the guitar-synthesizer in the 80s, but has since decided that he gets all the variety he needs out of an approach based around very thick sustain, digital delay and a trademark control of volume which lets him swell and decay his sound in a particularly idiosyncratic way. This sound is spread over his many Elektra/Nonesuch records, which otherwise take in putative soundtracks to Buster Keaton silents, cover choices from Madonna to Aaron Copland, acoustic quartet and sextet sessions, and particular projects such as *Nashville* (1996) and the all-solo *Ghost Town* (1999), where he seems to be annexing a specific stratum of American music from a recitalist's vantage point. By the time of *The Intercontinentals* (2003), a set of pieces which proposes missing links between several different old- and new-world musics, the listener can feel either beguiled or exasperated by Frisell's outreach. The music is often exquisite, in a way that can equally often suggest an embalming. Though he used to be characterized in his interviews as an overly modest, even bumbling introvert, Frisell is a shrewd and sometimes cold-eyed operative, and a key performer in the music at century's end and beginning.
*Ghost Town* (Elektra Nonesuch)

## Dave Frishberg
PIANO, VOCAL
*born* 23 March 1933

Frishberg isn't much of a singer, but he is an excellent pianist and a very fine songwriter, and one can forgive the quality of the vocals

on his own records, where he sometimes sounds like an older and jazzier Randy Newman. He studied journalism in college and after military service made his way to New York in 1957, where he worked as an intermission pianist in clubs before accompanying the likes of Ben Webster, Bud Freeman and Bobby Hackett. He arranged a beautiful album for Jimmy Rushing, *The You And Me That Used To Be* (RCA, 1972), by which time he had moved over to Los Angeles and begun making his own records, which subsequently emerged on Concord and Fantasy. His songs are a long drink of American wry, and beautifully pitched: they include 'My Attorney Bernie', 'Peel Me A Grape', 'Blizzard Of Lies', 'Quality Time', 'Do You Miss New York?' and his lyric for Bob Dorough's tune 'I'm Hip'. He has done his best to disprove the contention which a supply sergeant in the air force gave him: 'Jazz is okay, but it ain't got no words.'
*Live At Vine Street* (Fantasy)

## Tony Fruscella
TRUMPET
*born* 4 February 1927; *died* 14 August 1969

A pretty boy who played nice, lyrical, sometimes quite hot trumpet, Fruscella played around the New York scene of the early 50s and might have followed something like Chet Baker's career path if he'd been a little more talented and a little less easily led astray. Besides some very mixed live recordings, his only album, *Tony Fruscella* (Atlantic, 1955), is an interesting set which offers a snapshot of a melodious, thin-toned but thoughtful musician. He was already a narcotics addict, though, and by the 60s his playing career was virtually finished.
*Tony Fruscella* (Atlantic)

## Bob Fuller
CLARINET
*born* c1898; date of death unknown

Fuller's music is an entertaining relic of the first Jazz Age. His background is obscure, but he was touring with Mamie Smith in the early 20s, and thereafter he appears on scores of record dates, mostly in the accompaniments to blues singers, although there are numerous examples of his playing in what might be termed the New York barrelhouse style of such groups as the Three Monkey Chasers and the Kansas City Five. He plays with proud intensity on the straighter blues pieces, but there are so many vaudevillian touches in his work – somewhat in the manner of such clarinet comedians as Wilton Crawley – that a lot of it amounts to an acquired taste. By the end of the decade he seems to have known that his time in jazz was over: he later worked as a prison warder.

## Curtis Fuller

TROMBONE
*born* 14 December 1934

Perhaps the premier trombonist in the hard-bop movement, Fuller's neat facility and unemphatic methods typify the honest toil of the genre, as well as its occasional faceless-ness. He worked with Yusef Lateef in his native Detroit before arriving in New York in 1957, quickly establishing himself in a scene which wasn't long on trombonists. His glory years were with The Jazztet (1959–60) and Art Blakey's Jazz Messengers (1961–5), but his most famous entry remains what is basically a cameo role, on John Coltrane's *Blue Train* (1957). Fuller made three albums of his own for Blue Note and a few more for Impulse! in the 60s, but he became disenchanted with the business approach of jazz labels and since then has been seen more often in touring bands than before microphones. The best work of this reliable player draws, inevitably, on the J J Johnson style, allied with a sobriety which can tame any hints of wildness. In a time when trombonists have come to favour a more expressionist method, Fuller now seems a rather remote figure.
**Curtis Fuller Vol 3** (Blue Note)

## Gil Fuller

ARRANGER
*born* 14 April 1920; *died* 26 May 1994

Fuller had the odd distinction of being one of the first bebop arrangers, even though the orchestral manner of the early bop idiom was never too successful. He began writing for such leaders as Jimmy Dorsey and Les Hite in the early 40s, and made the acquaint-ance of Dizzy Gillespie while the latter was with Hite. In New York from 1945, he published some of the early bop compositions and wrote charts for Gillespie's sextet and big band: 'One Bass Hit', 'Oop-Bop-Sh'Bam', 'That's Earl Brother', and particularly 'Things To Come' and 'Manteca' are all notable Fuller efforts. By the end of the decade his charts were in many bands' books, and he tried leading his own orchestra in 1949 (it recorded only four titles), but thereafter he went into real estate and engineering, the latter his original subject of college study. In some ways Fuller's charts are prophetic of some brave new world of big-band writing, but it was one which never really came into being: if it presaged anything, it was the rise of Stan Kenton's more pretentious side (and Kenton was one of the few for whom Fuller did some later work, in the 60s). The pioneer arranger did one more album with Dizzy Gillespie in 1965 and then disappeared from the music.
**Gil Fuller And The Monterey Jazz Orchestra With Dizzy Gillespie** (Pacific Jazz)

## Walter Fuller

TRUMPET, VOCAL
*born* 15 February 1910

Fuller's only period of prominence was with the Earl Hines band. He'd come to Chicago in 1925 and joined Sammie Stewart's orchestra, but Hines hired him in 1931 and aside from one brief spell Fuller stayed until 1940. He was one of Hines's best soloists, hot in the Armstrong manner (and his singing was straight out of Pops, too) but with enough wrinkles of his own to make his solos more than worthwhile. After leaving Hines he led small bands of his own, but none of them were recorded and even though he was still playing in the 80s he made no further impact on jazz.
**Earl Hines, *1933–34*** (Classics)

## Funk

Developed out of the black-slang adjective 'funky', originally a bad smell, playing 'funky' denoted a grooving, boisterous take on the hard-bop idiom as it developed through the 50s, with Horace Silver as its avatar, pointing the way towards the soul-jazz of the 60s. Once Silver started coming up with titles such as 'Opus De Funk', the word entered the jazz vocabulary for all time. But funk as an idiom is really an outcropping of the soul music of the 60s, where repetitive structures are played through in patterns of syncopated rhythms, usually in duple time. These can attain their own fierce complexity and demand a playing where, instead of the jazz musician's looseness, the 'tightness' of the funk player is an absolute virtue. Contemporary players such as Christian McBride love the opportunity to play both jazz and funk, in part because the widely differing disciplines present different kinds of challenges to the virtuoso player. Ironically, while a singer such as James Brown is seen as a godfather of funk, it is the instrumentalists who have shaped much of the idiom: funk is a style set by the players, not the singers of soul. Consequently, the great funk bands are exactly that – *bands* of performers, such as The Ohio Players or War. While there may be space for improvisation within funk, it is more a music of *variation* around its basic principles. Funk's heyday was the early 70s, before the pop audience lost interest in instrumental music.

# Fusion

The idea of terming any jazz subset as 'fusion' is a little amusing, given that the music itself – despite notions of jazz 'purism' – is at root a unique fusion of numerous elements of other musics. By and large, though, 'fusion' came into use in the 70s as an alternative term for the more immediately descriptive 'jazz-rock'. It has latterly been used to characterize more or less any melding of jazz principles with characteristics drawn from some other contemporary idiom – hence jazz-rock, jazz-soul, jazz-funk, jazz-reggae (a rare one), jazz-rap, jazz-hip-hop or jazz-ambient may more easily be grouped by exhausted commentators as 'fusion'.

# Kenny G
SOPRANO SAXOPHONE
*born* 31 December 1959

Kenneth Gorelick is possibly, poor fellow, the most despised musician with any jazz

associations. A sessionman on Barry White records in the late 70s, he started to be featured as a soloist and eventually signed to Arista as a stand-alone artist in the early 80s. Cannily produced, the records put his distinctively limp and adenoidal sound on soprano sax in the middle of softly cushioned, light-fusion backgrounds. 'Songbird' was a huge instrumental hit which sent him hurtling to an unlikely but durable success as one of America's most bankable and failsafe sellers of records: he has reputedly sold more than 30 million albums since then. Mr G's music is inoffensive enough – if it were really objectionable it wouldn't have earned that kind of success – but what has irked jazz musicians and fans everywhere is that he is even *perceived* as a jazz artist. There is almost no improvisation in his records, and he is really an instrumental pop artist, in the way that Liberace and Mantovani once were. But the industry continues to categorize him as a jazz man, and place his records at the top of the industry's jazz charts.

# Milt Gabler
PRODUCER
*born* 20 May 1911; *died* 20 July 2001

Gabler was the first of the independent jazz record men. He worked in his father's radio store in Manhattan and founded the Commodore Music Shop there in 1935, the first specialist jazz retailer, and realizing the demand for deleted rarities began pressing up old masters on his United Hot Clubs of America (UHCA) label; this eventually led to the Commodore label itself (qv). He held jam-session concerts in 1941 and joined Decca later that year, initially to assist in reissue projects but eventually as a full-time A&R man. Perhaps his most ambitious project at the label was his three-record *Satchmo: A Musical Autobiography* (1957), but he was involved in all of their jazz work to some extent until leaving in 1973. In his final years he helped Mosaic with the reissue of all his old Commodore masters, a wonderful legacy from a fan to the music he loved.

# Steve Gadd
DRUMS
*born* 9 April 1945

The first of the studio superdrummers, Gadd built on the Buddy Rich tradition of virtuosity and applied those skills to at least as much rock and funk as jazz. He studied in New York, worked with Chuck Mangione while the latter was enjoying some of his fusion success, and by the end of the 70s was among the leading studio rats of the scene, working at a prodigious rate for whoever was paying. His eminence was such that he was probably the drummer producers most wanted to use on a high-profile project, and in Japan he had godlike status. In combining speed, power, dexterity and precision, Gadd has never had many rivals, advancing techniques in areas of pop and soul music which in the past had settled for feel and power as their absolutes. He worked with the Manhattan Jazz Quintet and his own Gadd Gang in the 80s and 90s, but slowed the pace of his involvement and now works as and when he chooses. The likes of Dave Weckl have built on his advances since.
*The Gadd Gang* (Columbia)

# Slim Gaillard
PIANO, GUITAR, VOCAL
*born* 4 January 1916; *died* 26 February 1991

Jazz's leading 'character' probably influenced nobody and left a suitably bizarre legacy on record, but he was unquestionably one of a kind. It is uncertain whether Gaillard was born in Cuba or Detroit. He stayed in Crete, following an ocean voyage, as a teenager, but he made show business his medium when he returned to Detroit and worked in a duo with Slam Stewart as 'Slim and Slam', which became a hit on radio as well as in clubs. The team enjoyed Hollywood success for a spell before Gaillard was drafted. Back in civilian life, Slim led a new trio with Bam Brown and Scatman Crothers, turned up on record dates with Charlie Parker and Dizzy Gillespie, and worked on his new language of Vout, which seemed to consist primarily of adding '-oroonie' to the ends of many words (this is why, when he was introduced to Mickey Rooney, Slim inquired of the actor what his surname was). He even had a Vout dictionary printed and distributed to

schools and colleges. 'Opera In Vout', which is really a ragbag assemblage of Slim's greatest hits to this point, was memorably set down at one of the Jazz At The Philharmonic recordings. He had a sonorous baritone voice, which sometimes sounded like a surreal Billy Eckstine, and he could play guitar and piano with a thunderous inattention to detail. He faded from sight in the later 50s but turned up again in the 80s, singing largely about food, and latterly making his home in London. For all his jubilant bonhomie, Slim was a secretive man, and hardly anybody knew where he lived or what he was doing most of the time. He set out to write an autobiography, but although he collected at least one advance for it, the manuscript never materialized. A hustler to the end.
*Slim Gaillard Rides Again* (Dot/Verve)

# Barry Galbraith
GUITAR
*born* 18 December 1918; *died* 13 January 1983

Galbraith made a name for himself on the New York scene of the early 40s and had two periods with Claude Thornhill before spending most of his time as a sessionman in the 50s and 60s. An unemphatic but sophisticated player, nothing was too tough a challenge and his playing on such a demanding date as George Russell's *Jazz Workshop* (1956) is as skilfully carried off as that on a rote hard-bop or vocalist session. In the 70s he settled into a teaching career. His only album as a leader, the rare *Guitar And The Wind* (1958), features him in front of many of his sessionman pals.
**George Russell,** *Jazz Workshop* (RCA)

# Eric Gale
GUITAR
*born* 20 September 1938; *died* 25 May 1994

Gale trained as a chemist but his penchant for the guitar led him into playing with R&B bands in the early 60s. He played that kind of music as well as organ-combo jazz when he moved to New York, and Creed Taylor hired him in 1969 as the in-house guitarist for CTI, although he never got to make an album of his own for the label. In the 70s his lean, hard-bitten style was softened a

little on some basically dreary sets for Columbia, and he joined the sessionman band Stuff for a time. He made a single date as a straight-ahead player, 1987's *In A Jazz Tradition*, but his career had petered out by the time of his death from lung cancer.
*A Touch Of Silk* (Columbia)

## Richard Galliano
ACCORDION, BANDONEON
*born* 12 December 1950

Galliano seems to have come into jazz almost by accident. Although he actually studied trombone, his father was an accordion teacher who taught him the instrument as an infant. He worked in a variety of musical settings in Paris from the early 70s, but an association with Chet Baker drew him closer to the jazz mainstream and in the 80s and 90s he steadily built a growing circle of playing-partners which has involved Louis Sclavis, Philip Catherine, Aldo Romano, Ron Carter and Enrico Rava. Along with Dino Saluzzi, he has investigated the music of Astor Piazzolla extensively and has made a plausible and rhapsodic fusion of Piazzolla's tango base with a freewheeling style of improvisation. Extensively recorded in recent years, he works a small corner of a large music, and though it feels like an acquired taste, record by record he's impressive.
*Laurita* (Dreyfus)

## Joe Gallivan
DRUMS
*born* 8 September 1937

Gallivan has had an extraordinary career. In his teens he played in Latin and jazz groups in and around Miami (where he also studied), and in 1960 he moved to New York, playing with Duke Pearson and co-leading a rehearsal band that had many of the leading hard boppers in it at one time or another. He went back to Miami and began a long and continuing association with the reeds player Charles Austin: they worked as a duo, and in a big band, and though the music was poorly documented it seems to have been a groundbreaking mix of jazz, rock and electronica. Gallivan took a tape of some of it to Igor Stravinsky, who listened with full concentration for an hour and told him he should be signed to Columbia. Back in New York, Joe hooked up with Larry Young: their trio Love Cry Want (with a guitarist named only 'Nicholas') opened more fresh territory, although their only recordings weren't finally issued until the 90s. Gallivan went to Europe in 1976 and worked with Elton Dean and Keith Tippett, as well as in Paris and the rest of Europe, and even in Hawaii. He pioneered further exploration of electronic and computer-based percussion and, back in London, led a trio with Paul Dunmall called Neon Lighthouse, as well as a big band, Soldiers Of The Road, which glittered with stars of the British scene. In the 90s he decamped for Hawaii again, where he worked a weekly gig in one of the bars and had everyone from George Benson onwards sitting in. Joe always resembles a member of one of Frank Zappa's early bands (or possibly Zappa himself), and he is a natural nomad who nevertheless enjoys a quiet night in talking. His huge body of work is scattered and almost impossible to assemble, but he is in his way a unique spirit in post-bop jazz.
*Innocence* (Cadence)

## Hal Galper
PIANO
*born* 18 April 1938

Galper studied at Berklee in the 50s and worked in the Boston area, often as house pianist at one of the clubs there. He toured with Chet Baker before settling in New York in 1967, and then freelanced under many leaders. By the middle 70s he was a very experienced hand, and was able to engage the Brecker brothers in a quintet which he led later in the decade. He then joined Phil Woods and was in his working band all through the 80s. Galper has little that's idiosyncratic in his style: he's more a safe all-round pair of hands, starting from a classic bebop system and covering blues tonalities and a certain harmonic adventurousness when he feels like it. In the 90s he became more involved with teaching and recorded rather less often.
*Reach Out* (Steeplechase)

# Vyacheslav Ganelin
PIANO
*born* 17 December 1944

The Ganelin Trio were a jazz sensation of the 80s. The Russian Ganelin had formed a band as far back as 1964, but then he joined forces with Vladimir Tarasov (drums, 1969) and Vladimir Chekasin (saxophones, 1971). They worked regularly in the USSR, and an East German concert dating from 1979 was recorded and the tapes smuggled out, eventually being released in the West by Leo Feigin's Leo label. In pre-glasnost days the group seemed to be breathing revolutionary fire and freedom, and when they went to perform in London in 1984 they caused enormous interest. Ganelin supplemented his keyboard work with electronics and other instruments, and the music was an often bizarre mix of free jazz, third-stream, vaudeville and bebop. But many were either bewildered and disenchanted, or saw the Trio as more clownish than musical. Leo continued to release Ganelin Trio music, as well as projects by the individual members, and eventually the group split up, Ganelin himself moving to Israel. There was a reunion of the original group in the new century. Ganelin solo has been an interesting if unpredictable proposition, producing ballet music and a rock opera in addition to piano records.
*Live In East Germany* (Leo)

# Allan Ganley
DRUMS
*born* 11 March 1931

Ganley worked at the tail end of the British dance-band era, with Bert Ambrose, before playing with modern leaders such as John Dankworth and Kenny Baker, as well as his own Jazz Today Unit and (with Ronnie Ross) The Jazzmakers. By the end of the 50s he was recognized as one of the premier British sticksmen, playing at Newport with The Jazzmakers and then going on to work in the Tubby Hayes group during the early 60s. For three years he was the in-house drummer at Ronnie Scott's Club, backing the visitors as well as the local men, and though he spent the late 60s and early 70s in Bermuda, he also studied at Berklee for a period. When he returned to Britain in 1976 he led an occasional big band, doing much of the writing himself, and it is still sometimes convened. In the meantime, this most accomplished and swinging of modern drummers still plays as many club gigs (and games of tennis) as ever.
**Tubby Hayes, *Down In The Village*** (Redial)

# Jan Garbarek
TENOR AND SOPRANO SAXOPHONES
*born* 4 March 1947

The young Garbarek was transfixed by the sound of John Coltrane, and amazed when he saw the Coltrane quartet perform in Oslo in 1963, although he also followed Dexter Gordon, who played regularly in Oslo. Still in his teens, he began working in the George Russell group, which was touring Europe, and started playing alongside Jon Christensen and Terje Rypdal. This group made its first record for ECM in 1970, *Afric Pepperbird*, and it was the start of an association with Manfred Eicher's label which continues to this day. Besides his own records, Garbarek also recorded extensively with the Bobo Stenson trio and with Keith Jarrett's 'European' trio, which was essentially the same group but with Jarrett in for Stenson. And he also turned up as a guest sideman on numerous sessions, with Bill Connors, Gary Peacock, Charlie Haden and others. He formed a new touring group with Eberhard Weber, David Torn and Michael Di Pasqua which toured in the 80s, and in the 90s a further quartet with Weber, Rainer Bruninghaus and Marilyn Mazur. Garbarek's music has emerged in a very patient unfolding across decades of thoughtful work. More than any other musician, his sound established a cliché about Nordic jazz being chilly, baleful and romantically gloomy, even though – particularly on such early records as *Tryptikon* (1972), with Edward Vesala and Arild Andersen – it is often much earthier than that. *Dis* (1976), where he played against the sound of a wind harp placed on the edge of a Norwegian fjord, is still a breathtaking listen, not only for the eerie sound of the North Sea winds moving through the harp's strings, but for the tonal strength and clarity of Garbarek's own playing, on both tenor and soprano. While he has investigated Norwegian folk sources at times, he mostly uses original material, and his long association with

Eicher has encouraged a refined use of the studio's possibilities, with records such as *All Those Born With Wings* (1987) crafted out of multiple overdubs. In 1993, his career took another step forward with the world-wide success of *Officium* (1993), a collaboration where he improvised saxophone lines against the singing of renaissance vocal music by The Hilliard Ensemble: it became a surprise hit around the world, and Garbarek and the Ensemble have gone on to re-create it in suitable live settings. Some have regretted that the jazz content in his music has seemed to ebb away, although with so many saxophonists content to plunder Coltrane's vocabulary in ordinary post-bop settings, Garbarek's preference for his current direction could almost be seen as a refreshing alternative. He does tend to attract some quasi-spiritual flannel in the writing about him by admirers, much as his sometime playing partner Keith Jarrett does: better to see this softly spoken, soccer-crazy Norwegian as a gently humane and idiosyncratic voice on an oversubscribed instrument. His daughter Anja is a successful pop singer in her home territory.
*Dis* (ECM)

## Laszlo Gardony

PIANO
born 3 July 1956

Hungary has had little influence on jazz, and Gardony is one of his country's few ambassadors for the music. Having spent some years studying at home, he exported himself: he was at Berklee in the early 80s, where he played and recorded with Tommy Smith's Forward Motion band, and latterly joined the faculty there. Most of his featured recording, though, has been done in his own country. A fluent and technically commanding player, he has the international language of the music under his fingers, although what there is of himself is either harder to divine or far below the surface.
*Reflection Of A Clear Moon* (Accurate)

## Lou Gare

TENOR SAXOPHONE
born 16 June 1939

Gare played with Mike Westbrook in the early 60s, but the partnership he formed with Eddie Prévost at much the same time turned out to be much more important, leading to the formation of AMM, which he played with until 1975 (latterly, the group consisted of only Gare and Prévost working as a duo). He relocated to Exeter in the late 70s and worked quietly down there, subsequently reuniting with AMM for long enough to make *The Nameless Uncarved Block* (1990). Gare is as low-profile as a leading member of his community – the British free-music pioneers – could be, which is saying something, and about as self-effacing as a saxophonist can aspire to be, which is saying something more. The record cited comes from his duo period with Prévost, and evidences his originality.
*To Hear And Back Again* (Matchless)

## Ed Garland

BASS
born 9 January 1885; died 22 January 1980

Ed Garland, known variously as 'Montudi', 'Tudi' or simply 'Nap', began playing in New Orleans in the first years of the 20th century, playing a washtub bass. He probably worked with both Buddy Bolden and Freddie Keppard, but Kid Ory was his main associate, although he went to Chicago around 1914 and eventually hooked up with Joe Oliver. In 1921, he travelled to the West Coast, and never really left: the New Orleans revival happened without his presence. He was on the Spikes' Seven Pods Of Pepper record date of 1921 (with Ory) and thereafter played at local dances, a modest career which lasted until the early 40s, when he once again hooked up with Ory. He stayed with the trombonist-leader for a further ten years, leaving his largest legacy of recordings: a slap-bass style which he probably helped to create, and the occasional arco feature. Thereafter, in a career which lasted well into the 70s, although encroaching blindness eventually obliged him to stop playing, Montudi kept working, a real pioneer whose work is now accounted only by historians.
*Kid Ory, Creole Jazz Band 1954* (Good Time Jazz)

# Red Garland
PIANO
*born* 13 May 1923; *died* 23 April 1984

Garland took some time to escape obscurity, even though he'd played with many leading jazz musicians: he was in the Billy Eckstine big band for a few weeks, worked at the Down Beat Club in Philadelphia for two years, and then backed Coleman Hawkins and Lester Young during the early 50s. But it was his time with Miles Davis, in the trumpeter's quintets of the later 50s, which sealed his eminence. By this time he had filtered together Count Basie, Bud Powell and Ahmad Jamal into a style which sounded light, bluesy, skittishly discordant, and – above all – tinkling in the right-hand register, an effect which Davis particularly enjoyed. Red ran up a large number of albums for Prestige and its various subsidiaries, mostly in the trio context, and though they inevitably tend to sound the same, his playing has its own kind of intensity: on a 1962 date which would be his last for nearly ten years, he played a notably poignant 'Nobody Knows The Trouble I've Seen'. The steam went out of his career, and he eventually returned home to Dallas, although there was a comeback of sorts from 1977. For the best of Red, though, the Davis records are hard to beat.
**Miles Davis,** *Cookin' With The Miles Davis Quintet* (OJC/Prestige)

# Tim Garland
TENOR AND SOPRANO SAXOPHONES
*born* 19 October 1966

Garland, born in Ilford, was one of the first 80s graduates from the Guildhall School to make an impact on the music: his 1988 debut *Points On The Curve* was cut only three years after he took up the saxophone. He co-formed the jazz-folk group Lammas in 1990 and also ran a strong post-bop quintet with Gerard Presencer, as well as turning up in several other London-based bands. In the last couple of years he has been in charge of a big band, the Dean Street Underground Orchestra, which performs regularly at Soho's Pizza Express, and an association with Chick Corea's group helped win him a contract with the American independent Stretch. Like Guy Barker, Garland has been leaving it relatively late to make a mark as a leader, but he is a talented post-bop player who surely has it in him to assert a more imposing presence on record than he managed with the somewhat whimsical Lammas.
*Made By Walking* (Stretch)

# Erroll Garner
PIANO
*born* 15 June 1921; *died* 2 January 1977

Garner may have been the greatest natural in jazz. He never learned to read music ('Hell, man, nobody can hear you *read*!') and he taught himself the piano, developing a style which belongs to no special era or school except his own. He grew up in Pittsburgh and played on the radio there as a child wonder. When he went to New York in 1944 he was soon at work on 52nd Street, subbing for Art Tatum before forming his own trio with bass and drums – a format that Garner played a large part in establishing as one of the basic jazz instrumentations. He liked the boppers, writing tunes for Charlie Parker (and letting the ever-insolvent Bird keep the royalties), but his own playing, unique as it was, had more to do with the swing era, thumping out patterns of block chords with the left hand while the right drew stentorian variations on the melody. It should have sounded preposterously overblown, but Erroll's style is all about a grand good humour, and his rocking beats and passages of counterpoint were designed to entertain without making the music seem merely crowd-pleasing. Crowds, however, were mightily pleased, and Garner became one of the most successful and best-loved musicians of any jazz period. He recorded prodigiously for Columbia in the 50s (*Concert By The Sea*, 1955, is one of the best-selling jazz albums of all time), toured constantly, and left a huge catalogue of both live and studio albums. Whether playing at a fast bounce or crawling through the slowest of ballads, Garner's monumental swing seems to have captivated audiences which otherwise cared little for any kind of jazz. Like Monk, he had a taste for unlikely ballads in particular ('When A Gypsy Makes His Violin Cry', for instance), and also like Monk, he left behind one immortal ballad of his own: 'Misty', an idea which came to him on a plane flight. His friend Jimmy Rowles

called him 'Ork', in tribute to the way he made the piano sound like a full orchestra.
**Concert By The Sea** (Columbia)

## Carlos Garnett
SAXOPHONES
*born* 1 December 1938

Garnett is a Panamanian who moved to New York in 1962 but made little impact until the 70s. He joined Art Blakey in 1969, but it was a brief association with Miles Davis (1972) which brought him to wider attention. Five modish albums for Muse in the early and middle 70s garnered him a modest cult reputation, with their stirrings of an exotic fusion that hinted at a global outreach, but Garnett didn't sustain any impact and his career was pulled up short by a drugs problem. He came back in the 90s with some competent new records that haven't provoked a great deal of interest.
**Under Nubian Skies** (High Note)

## Kenny Garrett
ALTO AND SOPRANO SAXOPHONES, FLUTE
*born* 9 October 1960

Garrett's career subdivides neatly into Miles and post-Miles. His early steps, going from his native Detroit to New York at the beginning of the 80s, were unremarkable, but when he joined Miles Davis in 1986 he toughened and matured into a soloist who could go toe-to-toe with any of the trumpeter's latter-day hornmen, and he stayed until the Davis band came to an end. Given his Detroit roots, it's appropriate that there's a good flavour of Junior Walker-style blues licks in his playing, which can otherwise be as loquacious and many-noted in its delivery as that of any other post-bop saxophonist. Garrett signed a solo deal with the WEA group of labels as far back as 1989, and a steady stream of records has kept him in the forefront of attention, even if none of the resulting discs quite lifts itself to a classic plateau so far. He's a communicative player, who likes listeners to be excited and persuaded by his music, and he's gradually worked away from existential solos and towards a more songful, even carefree manner. Funk sometimes invades his milieu, but never at the expense of his

jazz vocabulary. The record below is the author's favourite, but each of the sets has something to commend it.
**Simply Said** (Warner Bros)

## Michael Garrick
PIANO
*born* 30 May 1933

The Enfield-born Garrick took the mixing of poetry and jazz more seriously and substantially than anything done in the American beat era or after. An English graduate, he also led a quartet and from 1962 onwards began performing regularly at events where leading poets read their work, interspersed with performances from the Garrick group: a fine sampler can be heard on *Poetry And Jazz In Concert* (Argo). For the rest of the 60s he divided his time between sideman work in the Rendell–Carr Quintet and leading his own groups, which at different times included Tony Coe, Joe Harriott, Shake Keane, John Marshall, Henry Lowther and Art Themen: the records, made mostly for the Decca offshoot Argo (suggesting that the parent label saw them as pseudo-classical works) are now sought-after collectors' pieces. In the 70s and 80s he became more heavily involved in music education, at Wavendon and the Royal Academy Of Music, but continued to lead groups and make records: there was a greater emphasis on extended composition, with suites dedicated to Hardy, Tolkien and Peter Pan, and pieces which displayed a deep interest in English string writing and liturgical music. The jazz content has occasionally been somewhat set aside, but Garrick has gone his own way and seems unafraid of whimsicality or the burdensome English habit of writing at ponderous length.
**Down On Your Knees** (Jazz Academy)

## Jimmy Garrison
BASS
*born* 3 March 1934; *died* 7 April 1976

One wonders what must have been going through Jimmy Garrison's mind as, surrounded by the perpetual thunder of his bandmates in the John Coltrane quartet, without a bass amplifier and with the least gratifying role in the group, he carried on playing, in the one role which jazz had ascribed to him. He grew up in Philadelphia and played locally before moving to New York in 1959; a spell with Ornette Coleman, in 1961, prepared him for his long stint with Coltrane, which commenced in November of that year and ended only with the saxophonist's death. Despite the reservations suggested above, Garrison actually fitted into the group with great acuity, supplying a traditional walking role on the more straight-ahead material and adventurous counter-melodies and conversational responses as the music changed. After the Coltrane group ended, he carried on playing with spiritual heirs such as Archie Shepp and in the new Elvin Jones group, but lung cancer killed him in 1974. His son Matthew (b 1970) is also a bass player.

**John Coltrane,** *A Love Supreme* (Impulse!)

# George Garzone
TENOR AND SOPRANO SAXOPHONES
*born* 23 September 1950

Garzone has spent much of his career in jazz education, graduating from Berklee in 1972 and thereafter working in faculties in Massachusetts and New York, but he's kept his hand in as a player too. His most notable setting is with John Lockwood (bass) and Bob Gullotti (drums) in The Fringe, a trio that has kept a regular gig going in Boston almost continuously since 1972. There have been plenty of sideman roles for him on record, but his handful of dates for NYC, both as nominal leader and with The Fringe, are the best places to find him: *Fours And Twos* (1996), where he goes head to head with Joe Lovano, received little attention but is a beautiful context for the playing of both men. Like many educators, perhaps, Garzone has a chameleonic bent, but he can play with a massive authority which, when touched a little by frenzy, can be tremendously exhilarating to hear.

**Four's And Two's** (NYC)

# Giorgio Gaslini
PIANO
*born* 22 October 1929

Gaslini has divided a long career between jazz and symphonic music, sometimes bridging the two worlds. He was playing with his own jazz trio as early as 1947, spent much of the 50s composing and conducting, and formed a famous quartet with Gianni Bedori, Bruno Crovetto and Franco Tonani, which played in factories and hospitals as often as concert halls, a determined attempt by the leader to bring jazz close to the Italian people. In 1968, he recorded a piece called 'New Feelings' with free-playing luminaries such as Don Cherry and Steve Lacy, a characteristic mix of serialism and free form. He wrote his first jazz opera, a piece dedicated to Malcolm X, as far back as 1970 (and followed it with another on Othello in 1997). Through the 70s and 80s he was busy with live work, as well as recording albums with some extraordinary agendas: a set of Schumann in jazz, a brilliant Monk recital, a set of Albert Ayler pieces. In the 90s he wrote busily for the Italian Instabile Orchestra and created a programme based around Jelly Roll Morton's music. Gaslini's aim of 'total music', where jazz, pop, serialism, classical form and electro-acoustic approaches are synthesized into his own grand design, seems pompous and utopian, but more than perhaps any other contemporary figure he has come close to making such an alliance work. Even if some of the more ambitious undertakings may seem too much for the uncommitted, there is always the delicious pleasure in his own piano playing, which the Monk record capitalizes on to brilliant effect.

**Gaslini Plays Monk** (Soul Note)

# Jacques Gauthé
CLARINET, SOPRANO SAXOPHONE
*born* 12 June 1939

Born in Gaujac, Gauthé received clarinet lessons from Claude Luter in his teens and was soon leading Dixieland groups of his own; his Old Time Jazz Band was one of the best French groups in the idiom. In 1972, he moved to New Orleans and was made welcome by the local musical community: his Creole Rice Jazz Band became a familiar fixture in the city, and Lu Watters was impressed enough to allow him to use his old band name, which turned the group into the Creole Rice Yerba Buena Jazz Band. Gauthé's playing is a trenchant homage to the old masters of the style, with Sidney

Bechet a particular influence, and his records for GHB and Stomp Off are lively and authoritative examples of the vintage music made new for today.
**Creole Jazz** (Stomp Off)

## Charles Gayle
TENOR AND SOPRANO SAXOPHONES, PIANO
*born* 28 February 1939

Gayle's early jazz experience is somewhat mysterious: he was in New York in the 60s and was in the free-jazz scene 'off and on', in his own words, but didn't record in this period and was barely even known to audiences until the end of the 80s. He had started on piano, bass and trumpet, but it was his performances on tenor saxophone which secured his eminence: a huge, braying sound, phrases that writhe like tormented pythons and a cacophony of split tones and freak-register sounds, his music is as tumultuous as anything in the saxophone canon since Albert Ayler. In the 90s he recorded numerous albums – solo, and with various small groups – which offer exhaustive documentations of an exhausting music. Titles such as 'Holy Faith', 'Hymn Of Redemption', 'Daily Bread' and 'His Crowning Grace' suggest the religious fervour which attends Gayle's muse, and the results do seem to approximate some witness to Revelations. But the cited record also shows how, with William Parker and Rashied Ali, Gayle can provide striking evidence of how the jazz tradition represented by Coltrane can evolve into new forms. Allegedly homeless many times and earning a subsistence living as a street musician, Gayle might appear to have gone out of his way to avoid compromise. His music, though, speaks in a loud and fiercely provocative voice of its own.
**Touchin' On Trane** (FMP)

## Wilton 'Bogey' Gaynair
TENOR SAXOPHONE
*born* 11 January 1927; *died* 13 February 1995

Gaynair came out of Kingston, Jamaica, where he had led his own groups; he moved to Europe in 1955 and settled in Germany, where he did most of his professional work, in groups led by Kurt Edelhagen and Peter Herbolzheimer. But he is still best known for a single record he cut for Tony Hall's Tempo label in London, *Blue Bogey* (1955): it is so rare and sought-after that collectors around the world have been known to pay over $1,000 for a copy of it. Bogey Gaynair was a capable player in the swing-to-bop tradition represented by Lucky Thompson and Don Byas: while he lacked the individuality of such contemporaries as Joe Harriott and Dizzy Reece, he left a small and expensive legacy.
**Blue Bogey** (Tempo/Jasmine)

## Gianni Gebbia
SAXOPHONES, CLARINET
*born* 1 May 1961

A native of Palermo who taught himself to play alto sax, Gebbia has made his way through free jazz with seemingly careless abandon. In fact, he has schooled himself meticulously, has mastered circular breathing and extended techniques, and can hold his own in exalted free-music company (he even joined in the latter stages of New York loft jazz when he visited as a teenager). His all-solo album *Body Limits* (1996) is freedom tutored by an almost classical rigour. There can be something simultaneously dry and eerily off-centre about his playing which makes it an acquired taste, but the trio record with Peter Kowald and Günter Sommer, *Cappuccini Klang* (1992) remains an absorbing and vivid document of what this group could do.
**Cappuccini Klang** (Splasc(h))

## Jonathan Gee
PIANO
*born* 6 March 1959

The Israel-born Gee has been an ebullient presence on the British scene since the later 80s. A strong accompanist, clever writer and punchy small-group leader, he touches bases with several styles and has worked patiently towards wider recognition, making himself known on the international festival circuit: a recent record includes material from a live set in Azerbaijan. His regular trio with Steve Rose (bass) and Winston Clifford (drums) has a lot of road experience, and Gee has lately taken to singing, a little.
**Chez Auguste** (Jazz House)

# Matthew Gee
TROMBONE
*born* 25 November 1925; *died* 18 July 1979

Originally from Houston, Gee arrived East in time to catch the tailwind of the bebop era, performing with Dizzy Gillespie and Illinois Jacquet among other leaders. He mustered a modest sideman discography during the hard-bop years of the late 50s, with a single 1956 session for Riverside, *Jazz By Gee*, to his credit; but his most significant playing took place when he was with the Duke Ellington Orchestra, joining in 1959 and staying on and off until 1963. Thereafter he did very little of significance and it was rather poignant to find him at an Ellington reunion concert in 1975, years after his time with the band. Gee had an old-fashioned, brassy attack which didn't sit all that well with the smooth facilities of hard bop: Duke got the best out of him on their sessions together.
**Duke Ellington,** *Blues In Orbit* (Columbia)

# Herb Geller
ALTO AND SOPRANO SAXOPHONES, CLARINET
*born* 2 November 1928

Geller worked in New York with Claude Thornhill's band at the end of the 40s, married the pianist Lorraine Walsh, and then moved back to his native Los Angeles in 1951, soon getting regular studio work in the West Coast elite: 'When I wasn't in the studios, I was in burlesque houses, playing for stripteasers.' Following his wife's premature death in 1955, he worked with Benny Goodman for a time, toured Europe, and settled in Germany, first in Berlin, then taking over Rolf Kühn's job as one of the leading lights in the NDR in Hamburg, where he still lives. A strong, bluesy alto player with a stylistic debt to both Charlie Parker and Benny Carter, Geller's sound was less honeyed than the typical West Coast timbre, but his musicianship was always impeccable, and he was as likely to be found on a Bert Kaempfert session as a straight-ahead date during the 60s. He finally retired from the NDR in 1994, and now freelances on dates and record sessions, setting down some enjoyable music for Alastair Robertson's Hep operation, and playing with pals such as Jiggs Whigham when he gets the chance. His *Playing Jazz* (1995), a memoir of his career fashioned in the manner of a musical, is an entertaining departure from his main work.
**To Benny And Johnny – With Love From Herb Geller** (Hep)

# Gennett
RECORD COMPANY

Harry, Fred and Clarence Gennett were managers at the Starr Piano Company of Richmond, Indiana, and they gave their name to the record label which the company commenced in 1917. They began recording jazz as early as 1919, with discs by the New Orleans Jazz Band, but moved forward in earnest with music by Ladd's Black Aces (aka Original Memphis Five) in 1921, the New Orleans Rhythm Kings, and eventually King Oliver and Jelly Roll Morton in 1923. These discs inaugurated a series which was designated on the labels as a 'race record', and for the rest of the 20s Gennett had some of the best black and white hot music of the decade under their aegis. The onset of the Depression killed off the label, which was discontinued in 1930, although the company carried on in other forms; but its great legacy of jazz recording helped disseminate the music on a wide scale, and collectors today still prize King Oliver Gennetts in particular above most other kinds of jazz record.

# Fatty George
CLARINET, ALTO SAXOPHONE
*born* 24 April 1927; *died* 29 March 1982

Franz Georg Pressler was an important figure in post-war Austrian jazz. He ran a bop group, The Hot Club Seven, in the 40s, but also played clarinet in a swing style, and most of his music drifted between the trad-swing idiom and a cooler style of bebop. His 50s group The Two Sounds Band included Joe Zawinul and Oscar Klein, and George ran the Viennese club The Jazz Casino before it closed in 1958. After that, he opened Fatty's Saloon, which became one of the major Austrian jazz clubs. In the 70s, he was still playing with his Chicago Jazz Band, with Oscar Klein still on hand.
*Fatty '78* (MPS)

# Stan Getz
TENOR SAXOPHONE
*born* 2 February 1927; *died* 6 June 1991

An eavesdropper once heard the saxophon-ist practising a few lines, followed by his own voice sighing, 'The incredibly lovely sound of Stan Getz.' It was a case of vanity justified. All through a long and eventful career, Getz's pealing sound wooed and seduced audiences. He played alto sax and bassoon in his Philadelphia high-school orchestra but was already playing in New York at 16, having gone out to tour with Jack Teagarden. Next came jobs in the big bands of Stan Kenton, Jimmy Dorsey and Benny Goodman, and he worked briefly on the West Coast as a solo before joining Woody Herman at the end of 1947. As the key sound in Herman's 'Four Brothers' sax section he made a notable impact, which he built on further with an extended ballad solo on Herman's 1948 recording of 'Early Autumn', a lingering memory of the end of the swing era which is definitive in the minds of many listeners. From 1949, still only 22, Getz began leading small groups of his own, and this set the pattern for the rest of his career. Early bands with Al Haig, Jimmy Raney and Horace Silver made some scintillating records for Roost, and when Getz signed to Norman Granz's new Norgran label in 1952, it initiated a superb sequence of records, including *At The Shrine* (1954), *West Coast Jazz* (1955) and *The Steamer* (1956). Getz's phrasing had all the facility and agility associated with bebop, yet his golden timbre and a yearning edge on his melody lines set him aside from bop's jitters – even though the saxophonist had been, like many of his contemporaries, a heroin addict since his Kenton days. He toured both Europe and the US, joining Granz's JATP circus at one point, but his addiction brought health problems and in 1958 he decamped for Denmark, thereafter working in Europe for three years.

On his return in 1961 he found the new voices of Coltrane and Coleman in the ascendant, and he was suddenly last year's man: but 1962 saw his star rising again with an association with Charlie Byrd and a Brazilian sound that led to the hits 'Desafinado' and 'The Girl From Ipanema', creating the sudden boom in bossa nova music. Granz recorded a rapid-fire sequence of albums to capitalize on it, and though

Getz would later express dismay at what he saw as too much attention on this side of his work, it was music which settled his career into affluence (and it did point up the shapely beauty of his playing exceptionally well). He returned to a more straight-ahead sound as the 60s progressed and used new talents such as Gary Burton and Chick Corea among his sidemen. In the 70s, he looked down his nose at jazz-rock but was neverthe-less tempted in the direction of soft fusion on some poor records for Columbia. In the following decade, though, he reasserted his most convincing side with a new contract with Concord that produced some impec-cable records; and his audience had never really gone away. He eventually returned to a major label when he signed to Polygram, and despite one further album of prettified fusion made at Herb Alpert's behest, he cut some final dates with Kenny Barron and others which show the 'incredibly lovely sound' still rich and ravishing, bathed in an autumnal glow.

Cancer had begun to overtake him by the time of his final recordings, but he battled on to the very end, never anything less than an exceptionally cussed character. Getz dis-liked fools, and didn't seem to care too much for a lot of intelligent people, either. Ronnie Scott maintained that 'I got my bad back bending over backwards to accommo-date Stan Getz', and woe betide sidemen taking a wrong turning or promoters not ful-filling a whim. Getz is a hard musician to copy – there is a truculent side to his play-ing, as well as the beautiful one, and while he had favourite licks his finest playing has a sailing, inevitable feeling to it which is nearly impossible to simulate. Nevertheless, tenor players trying a smoothly rhapsodic approach to a tune will always be called Getzian. For a long time he was considered to be just the best of the many tenor players who appropriated much of Lester Young's style ('Nice eyes,' the man himself approv-ingly told the young Stan), but Lester was buried a long way back in the music of the mature Getz: a magnificent jazz musician.
*Focus* (Verve)

# Tiziana Ghiglioni
VOCAL
*born* 25 October 1956

Ghiglioni has become the leading Italian jazz vocalist, working a strikingly individual ground between standards singing, art-song and entirely free terrain. She didn't begin singing professionally until 1980, but quickly progressed from working with Italian players to using her big, arresting voice alongside such notable players as Steve Lacy, Mal Waldron and Lee Konitz. Her sextet Streams was succeeded by a quintet with Umberto Petrin, and projects dedicated to Duke Ellington and the Italian composers Luigi Tenco, Giorgio Gaslini (a frequent collaborator) and Lucio Battisti. She is still comparatively little known outside her own territory, partly through a lack of opportunity to perform elsewhere and also because her records have largely been for 'local' Italian labels. But her mixing of challenging material, melodic improvisation and timbral variation might be considered prescient: as some contemporary singers have turned away from jazz-vocal routine in search of fresh ground, they may end up working in the kind of areas Ghiglioni was working in the 80s and 90s.
*Spellbound* (YVP)

# Ghost Band

An ensemble – usually of orchestral size – which carries on performing the work of a deceased bandleader, using that musician's name on the marquee. The first notable example of a ghosted leader was Glenn Miller, who died at the height of his fame: there have been 'Glenn Miller Orchestras' ever since, often under distinguished leadership (Buddy DeFranco led one such group for a number of years). The most 'authentic' ghost bands use players who were original sidemen under the leader in question: better still, they may be led by an ex-sideman. The best example is the Count Basie band, which has enjoyed continuous existence since its leader's death in 1984, under (consecutively) Eric Dixon, Thad Jones, Frank Foster and Grover Mitchell. A tribute band, which is more a phenomenon of the rock age, spawning countless examples of anonymous groups apeing famous ones, is not quite the

same thing, although the Syd Lawrence Orchestra, which for many years xeroxed the Glenn Miller style, was almost a ghost band. Now that Lawrence himself is deceased, he has a ghost band of his own.

# Mike Gibbs
BANDLEADER, ARRANGER
*born* 25 September 1937

Born in Salisbury, Rhodesia (present-day Harare, Zimbabwe), Gibbs learned piano and then trombone before going to study at Berklee in 1959. He moved on to win a scholarship to the Lenox School in 1961, where he studied with Gunther Schuller and others, and after that studied on a scholarship at Tanglewood. In the meantime, he had been working extensively with Gary Burton, who went on to record a number of Gibbs compositions. In 1965 he moved to the UK, played in groups led by Graham Collier and John Dankworth, and then began leading bands of his own. The late 60s and early 70s were his golden years: his writing was a vivid synthesis of traits he had mined out of Gil Evans, Messiaen, Copland and others, and compared to some of the more sober composers working on the British scene his music sounded thrilling. He was quick to acclimatize to rock as a musical resource, and *Just Ahead* (1972) has some of his best work, albeit in an on-the-hoof live recording. 'Family Joy' and 'Sweet Rain', the latter a near-hit for Stan Getz, show how much he had to offer to the jazz repertory simply as a composer of attractive themes. But he wasn't recorded much as a leader during this period, and his decision to return to the US in 1974 as a composer in residence at Berklee dissipated his impact: he has never really lived up to his early promise since, interesting as much of the music has been, partly because little of what he has done has been documented. Gibbs has worked somewhat nomadically in the US (he quit the Berklee post in 1983), Europe and the UK (where he resettled in 1986), with work for film and dance mingling with occasional orchestral jazz pieces. *Europeana Jazzphony No 1* (1994) was a piece of almost bashful hubris which Gibbs just about carried off, and *Nonsequence* (2001) had some attractive new writing for both US and German musicians. Like many composers in a large-

scale jazz idiom, though, he is dependent on financial resources which are only seldom forthcoming.
***Big Music*** (ACT)

## Terry Gibbs
VIBES
*born* 13 October 1924

A native of Brooklyn, Gibbs worked as a drummer before being drafted and returned from the army with vibes as his next instrument. He played with several big bands (particularly Woody Herman) and, as the swing era passed away, with smaller groups before a spell with Benny Goodman. He led his own small bands before a move to Los Angeles in 1957, where studio work allowed him to play with a semi-regular big band in the evenings on the LA club circuit. Gibbs kept many tapes of these performances and they have been released in several volumes as 'The Dream Band'. He worked on television with Steve Allen, a foothold that brought him numerous MD positions on TV in the next decade, and made seven albums for Emarcy and five for Verve between 1956 and 1962 – although hardly any of this music has, surprisingly, made it to CD so far. An uncomplicated and swinging soloist who can suggest a bridge between Lionel Hampton and Milt Jackson, Gibbs is a loyal jazz lover who returned to extensive touring in the 80s and is still in fine form. His son Gerry is an accomplished drummer and Terry himself still assembles a Dream Band for live performances.
***Dream Band*** (Contemporary)

## Gene Gifford
ARRANGER, GUITAR
*born* 31 May 1908; *died* 12 November 1970

Gifford's jazz contribution is based around his work writing scores for the Casa Loma Orchestra. His up-tempo pieces called for skilful, driving playing, his ballads were lush and sentimental, and these two faces made up the approach of one of the most successful bands of its day, even though a central weakness – partly blandness, partly an inability to create a genuinely swinging feel – has left the music sounding much more dated today than many of its competitors.

'Casa Loma Stomp', 'White Jazz', 'Black Jazz' and the band's theme tune, 'Smoke Rings', were among the best of Gifford. Having joined the cooperative in 1930, he stayed until the end of the decade, then freelanced but gradually drifted more into engineering and consultancy work.
**Casa Loma Orchestra, *Maniac's Ball*** (Hep)

## Gig

A night's work for a musician. Or it could be a week, or a residency: 'going to the gig' means attending a particular engagement, but 'the gig' covers whatever the user wants it to. An ordinary nine-to-five job can just as easily be described as 'my regular gig'. As a verb, 'gigging' is also in use. 'I went to a great gig last week' is how the fan partakes of the dialect.

## Astrud Gilberto
VOCAL
*born* 30 March 1940

Forever typecast as the voice of 'The Girl From Ipanema' in 1963, Astrud – who was at the time married to the song's composer, João Gilberto – has ever since made a career out of the most modest singing talent. Bossa nova singing scarcely even exists as a 'style', and all Gilberto had to do on her sessions with her husband and Stan Getz was sing as demurely, quietly and evenly as possible. She made a few albums for Verve in the later 60s but since then has been busier as a touring artist. Thousands have been charmed by what she does, although if she'd had to make do without her original hit it's hard to imagine her securing any kind of success.
**Stan Getz and João Gilberto, *Getz/Gilberto*** (Verve)

## John Gill
TROMBONE, DRUMS, BANJO
*born* c1953

Gill was introduced to Dixieland by his father at an early age, when he wanted to play drums, and he foreswore The Beatles as a result. Driven on by hearing Lu Watters on record, he then encountered the Turk

Murphy group, and was eventually invited by Murphy to join as a banjoist. By the 80s, Gill had emerged as one of the leading young traditionalists on the West Coast, and he has since gone on to lead groups in tribute to Murphy, as well as such bands as the Novelty Orchestra Of New Orleans and The Dixieland Serenaders. Ransacking the often neglected repertoire of teens and 20s hot jazz and dance, the groups are among the most accomplished and enthusiastic keepers of a flame which has also been maintained by such American independent labels as GHB and Stomp Off. Almost anything with Gill's name on it is guaranteed to be worth hearing. Under his own leadership he tends to divide his time between trombone and banjo (as well as doing some singing), but his work on the Silver Leaf Jazz Band's *New Orleans Wiggle* (1999) shows that he remains a brilliant drummer in the classic style.
*Looking For A Little Bluebird* (Stomp Off)

# Dizzy Gillespie
TRUMPET, VOCAL
*born* 21 October 1917; *died* 6 January 1993

John Birks Gillespie grew up with his eight siblings in Cheraw, South Carolina, and mostly taught himself the trumpet. He went to Philadelphia in 1935 and began playing in a local band led by Frankie Fairfax, where he made friends with Charlie Shavers and picked up his lifelong nickname, on account of a penchant for clowning around. Two years later he was in New York, scuffling for a job and eventually taking one of the trumpet chairs in the Teddy Hill band, because he sounded a bit like the previous incumbent, Roy Eldridge. He stayed two years (and visited Europe) but moved to Cab Calloway's band in 1939, where he became one of the star players, his Eldridge influence beginning to be displaced by an even more daring approach: after hours at Minton's in Harlem, he sat in with schemers such as Kenny Clarke and Thelonious Monk and tinkered with musical ideas that pointed towards a whole new sound. He was sacked from the band in 1941 after an argument with the leader and took on bits and pieces of work, before playing in a Philadelphia club where Charlie Parker often sat in. Both men then joined the Earl Hines band, staying for a year (a period during which no

recordings were made), before Dizzy was hired by Billy Eckstine as MD for his new big band. Early in 1945, a Gillespie–Parker small group finally held an important engagement in New York, at The Three Deuces club, and it caused a sensation among musicians, effectively the unveiling of bebop. This was backed up by some of the first small-group bop recordings, for small labels such as Guild and Manor. Years of work and self-challenge had polished and driven Gillespie's playing to an electrifying level: as the message-bearer of bop's complexity and innate daring, his trumpet style brimmed with sensational ideas, enthrallingly executed. Although his tone sometimes betrays a thinness compared with some of those who followed him, it is also unflattered by the recording quality on many of the earlier bop sessions. With Parker, he was partnering the personification of bop's intensity: no wonder audiences were stunned, or in some cases repelled. At the end of 1945, Gillespie took a new sextet to the West Coast – the unreliable Parker was only occasionally in attendance – and played a residency at Billy Berg's club, although Californian audiences were sometimes indifferent to the new music. Back in New York, he had a second try at forming his own big band, the first attempt having quickly foundered a year earlier. Despite almost constant economic difficulties, the orchestra hung on until 1950, the only real bop big band which ever existed. Chano Pozo's addition to the rhythm section and originals such as 'Manteca' (1947) made explicit Dizzy's interest in the possibilities of Afro-Cuban music, and there were radical charts in the book from such hands as George Russell, Gil Fuller and Tadd Dameron, as well as such sidemen as John Lewis, Milt Jackson and Sonny Stitt. But Gillespie was forced to disband in 1950 – in common with every other big-band leader, he felt the cold wind of an economic downturn. Slimming down to a sextet – which included John Coltrane – Gillespie carried on, for a time trying his hand at record production with his own Dee Gee label, although this went under quickly enough. He visited Europe early in 1952, and the following year saw one of his final appearances with Parker, at the celebrated Massey Hall concert in Toronto, with Bud Powell, Max Roach and Charles Mingus (the hall was half-empty owing to the concert's clashing with a big sports event). Norman Granz signed him to a record contract, where he 'met' the likes of Stan Getz and Roy Eldridge in the studios. During this period, he began playing a trumpet with an upturned bell, reputedly the consequence of an accident to one of his horns: it let him hear his own playing better.

In 1956 he went on a tour of the Middle East sponsored by the State Department, with a new big band, which he kept together for a time until another disbandment in 1958. Thereafter he worked with small groups during the 60s: James Moody was his regular front-line partner, and the music was nice if relatively uneventful. Gillespie seemed to save his best for projects such as Lalo Schifrin's setting *Gillespiana* (1960): as outstanding as his small-group work was, something about playing in front of an orchestra always seemed to take him up a notch. He ran for presidential office in 1963 ( Jon Hendricks sang the campaign song, 'Vote Dizzy!') and was unsuccessful, but life on the road always kept him busy· he never kept away from bandstands for long. Granz signed him again when he started his new Pablo label, and there were a few goodish late records, although throughout the LP era record-making never seemed to bother Gillespie too much: one reason why his work is relatively undiscovered by the casual jazz audience is his lack of a signature album to come out of this period. By the 80s, he was jazz's most revered modernist, and bebop's great survivor: he always credited the steadying influence of his wife of many years, Lorraine, who kept him out of the trouble many of his contemporaries looked for. His lip was no longer as strong, but the sense of fun was undiminished, and he toured in honour of his 70th birthday with the old enthusiasm. Five years on, New York's Blue Note club put on a long celebration in honour of his impending 75th birthday, but his health had begun to fail and by the end of the year his powers had gone.

Among the compositions which he left behind were such bebop classics as 'A Night In Tunisia', 'Anthropology', 'Salt Peanuts' (which Jimmy Carter sang with him at the White House) and 'Groovin' High', and with 'Manteca' he ushered in the whole era of Latin jazz: his final big band he called The United Nation Orchestra, which shows how far his music had stretched. There was no greater entertainer in jazz, and no finer musician. One of Dizzy's visual trademarks was his enormously distended cheeks while blowing into the horn, a condition one doctor christened Gillespie's Pouches. Trumpet teachers always admonish their students not to puff out their cheeks while playing: but what aspiring trumpeter would not want to look and sound like Dizzy Gillespie? *Birks Works* (Verve)

# John Gilmore
TENOR SAXOPHONE
*born* 28 September 1931; *died* 20 August 1995

Gilmore's presence in modern jazz works almost by proxy. Although his name is really known only to dedicated followers of the music, his influence seems manifest in the work of John Coltrane, Pharoah Sanders and many other saxophone orators, who may have appropriated many of Gilmore's own methods: the truth of this is unclear, as are so many issues surrounding Gilmore and others who worked extensively for the bandleader Sun Ra. Gilmore played in air force bands in the early 50s and joined Sun Ra in 1954: although he spent various sabbaticals away from the guru, he basically stayed with Ra for the next 40 years. There are a handful of mostly obscure dates with other leaders, such as Andrew Hill, Art Blakey and McCoy Tyner, and the sagacious and dedicated Gilmore was often exasperated by Sun Ra's leadership; yet he basically never left the Arkestra. While he had a peerless technique and could break into false registers and otherwise push the horn to its most extreme measures, this was a product of the most dedicated practice and application, involving hours of work on the saxophone every day. Ra himself called him 'Honest John'. Gilmore was effectively his leader's deputy in the later years of the Arkestra, and helped the ensemble to carry on after Ra's death; but he died himself within two years.
**Sun Ra,** *The Magic City* (Evidence)

# Vince Giordano

BASS SAXOPHONE, TUBA, BASS
*born* 11 March 1952

Giordano might have been born 50 years late. A New Yorker, he was playing tuba and banjo in high school, and when his friends were probably listening to Ten Years After and Led Zeppelin, he was in a rehearsal band playing Paul Whiteman arrangements. That group eventually became the New Orleans Nighthawks (partly in tribute to the Coon–Sanders Nighthawk Orchestra of the 20s), and it played gigs on whatever was left of the 'society music' circuit in the 70s and 80s. By the end of that decade, Giordano was established as an authentic antiquarian, playing bass sax and tuba in re-creations of long-ago music, and getting work from the likes of Leon Redbone and Woody Allen. He also looked up Bill Challis, the original arranger for Whiteman and Jean Goldkette, and persuaded him to re-create some of his scores for a recording project. Having collected more than 30,000 original arrangements from his beloved Jazz Age, though, Giordano suddenly gave it all up: he sold his entire library, and seemed to go into a retirement, although he has recently been playing again.
*Quality Shout!* (Stomp Off)

# Greg Gisbert

TRUMPET
*born* 2 February 1966

A jazz-family offspring – his mother played cornet, and his father worked as both a saxophonist and pianist – Gisbert studied at Berklee and then worked for Buddy Rich and the ghost Woody Herman band, in the later 80s. Since then he has freelanced widely. He is a characteristic post-bopper with a big sound and a fluent command of the style, even though he doesn't see himself as a bebop player, and he has a pragmatic approach to his trade: 'It has been literally a means of survival, and that's the first and foremost reason why I play the trumpet right now.'
*The Court Jester* (Criss Cross)

# Ira Gitler

WRITER
*born* 18 December 1928

The Boswell of the bebop/hard-bop eras, Gitler worked for Prestige in the early 50s but has otherwise freelanced as a writer for more than 50 years, writing countless reviews, interviews, sleevenotes and books. Ira made it his business to be a part of the scene, and consequently befriended many of the major and minor figures of those times, and the best of his work is vivid and steeped in jazz lore: his oral history, *Swing To Bop*, gets under the skin of 52nd Street's greatest era like no other.

# Jimmy Giuffre

CLARINET, SAXOPHONES, FLUTE
*born* 26 April 1921

Giuffre grew up in Dallas and studied at North Texas State College. He was writing for big bands (Boyd Raeburn) before he even played with them. In 1947 he composed one of the most durable pieces in Woody Herman's book, 'Four Brothers', and after a spell with Buddy Rich eventually joined Herman as a saxophonist in 1949. From there he went to California and began playing and recording with Shelly Manne, Howard Rumsey and Shorty Rogers. In 1956, he recorded the rather extraordinary *The Jimmy Giuffre Clarinet* for Atlantic, which featured him on B♭ clarinet in settings which ranged from solo to curious woodwind ensembles: the version of 'My Funny Valentine', for clarinet, oboe, cor anglais, bassoon and bass, is among the most haunting of transformations. After this he performed and recorded with a trio of himself, Jim Hall and Ralph Pena on bass (later replaced by Bob Brookmeyer). Their Atlantic albums produced another enduring hit in 'The Train And The River', which the group perform in the concert film *Jazz On A Summer's Day*. Giuffre was still playing tenor and baritone as well as clarinet, but his 1961–2 trio with Paul Bley and Steve Swallow found him back with clarinet only. Their Verve and Columbia albums, which offered free playing as a subdued counter-face to Ornette Coleman, were again remarkable, while steadfastly refusing to find an audience: when the admiring Manfred Eicher reissued

them on ECM in 1992, they hardly sold at all. Giuffre carried on experimenting with styles and formats: in the 70s his group with Kiyoshi Tokunaga (bass) and Randy Kaye (drums) looked at folk and non-American idioms, and in the 80s he led a quartet with electric bass and keyboards which might be described as Weather Report pared back to the bone. By this time, Giuffre was playing soprano sax and bass flute as well as his familiar horns, and there was a memorable reunion with Steve Swallow and Paul Bley in 1992–3. Giuffre has sometimes been humourlessly derided as a mere experimenter, or a narrow aesthete, but such is the fate of most quiet pioneers. In his meticulous concern for timbre and texture, his music is a unique part of the jazz literature.
**The Jimmy Giuffre Clarinet** (Atlantic)

## Ralph Gleason
WRITER
*born* 1 March 1917; *died* 3 June 1975

Gleason helped create *Jazz Information*, one of the earliest American jazz magazines, and served as its first editor in 1939, before going on to long stints at *Down Beat* and as the weekly music columnist for the *San Francisco Chronicle*. He co-founded the Monterey Jazz Festival in 1958 and, unlike many of his generation, took an interest in rock music rather than cover his ears. His genial visage looks out from the back covers of many record albums for which he contributed sleevenotes.

## Tyree Glenn
TROMBONE, VIBES
*born* 23 November 1912; *died* 18 May 1972

Glenn is probably most renowned for his stint in Duke Ellington's orchestra, but that actually lasted only four years (1947–51). He had spent time in many 30s bands and was with Cab Calloway for six years prior to joining Ellington. With Duke, he played trombone and specialized in the kind of plunger-mute features which used to belong to Joe Nanton, but in the 50s he played as much vibes as trombone, leading his own small groups in New York and working on radio and televison (sometimes as an actor).

His bands featured some high-profile names, including Lester Young and Hank Jones at different times, but the six albums he made for Roulette were largely unremarkable. In the mid-60s he joined Louis Armstrong's All Stars and again played for Duke Ellington, who died only six days after Glenn himself.
**At The Roundtable** (Roulette)

## Globe Unity Orchestra
GROUP

Founded by Alex von Schlippenbach, initially for the purpose of performing his composition *Globe Unity* in 1966, this occasionally convened ensemble is perhaps the most renowned free-music group of its kind. While the line-up has fluctuated over the years, it is in the main made up of first-generation European free players such as Schlippenbach, Evan Parker, Peter Brötzmann, Paul Lovens, Gerd Dudek and many others. It has recorded mostly for FMP, although both recording and concert activity have been scarce in recent years, just as the notion of 'Globe Unity' seems ever more remote and unattainable.
**20th Anniversary** (FMP)

## Victor Goines
TENOR AND SOPRANO SAXOPHONES, CLARINET
*born* 6 August 1961

Goines is of the same generation as the Marsalis brothers, and he was also taught in New Orleans by Ellis Marsalis, although this wasn't until he was almost into his 30s: previously he had worked as a maths teacher. Although the records under his own name have been a little disappointing, Goines has a talented touch on both saxophone and clarinet, and he has often played the latter with the Lincoln Center Jazz Orchestra.
**Sunrise To Midnight** (Rosemary Joseph)

## Harry Gold
BASS SAXOPHONE
*born* 26 February 1907

A stocky man who seemed no bigger than the bass saxophone which was his favourite instrument, Harry Gold worked through most of the eras of British jazz. He began playing on the dance-band scene of the late 20s, and that career took him through the next decade, when he also began arranging for the BBC Dance Orchestra. His own small group The Pieces Of Eight recorded regularly during the 40s, a traditional-to-mainstream outfit which benefited from the high polish of Harry's arranging skills. As that style of jazz playing died away – Gold was too modern for trad, too old-fashioned for modern jazz – he worked more frequently as an arranger, but his career revived in the 80s and in his own eighth decade he was still to be found at club gigs with a newly formed Pieces Of Eight. Nobody in jazz played the bass sax for longer than Gold.

*Live In Leipzig* (Gold)

## Don Goldie
TRUMPET, VOCAL
*born* 5 February 1930; *died* 19 November 1995

His real name was Goldfield, inherited from his father Harry, who was one of Paul Whiteman's longest-serving trumpeters. Goldie played Dixieland in his teens with Art Hodes, but first made his name in Jack Teagarden's group, working as the lead trumpet between 1959 and 1963. His brash, Armstrong-influenced style (and corny singing) didn't go down well with many Teagarden admirers, but in all likelihood he held the group together, tired as the leader had become. After Teagarden's death, Goldie toured with small groups of his own and inherited Bobby Hackett's mantle as the lead trumpet on some of Jackie Gleason's later easy-listening albums. He ran his own booking agency and was still doing festival dates in the 80s, but there was tragedy ahead: a debilitating illness left him depressed, and he took his own life in 1995.

*Brilliant!* (Argo)

## Larry Goldings
ORGAN, PIANO
*born* 28 August 1968

Goldings has largely stuck by the Hammond organ as his main means of expression, although while briefly signed to Warners he did essay some acoustic-piano music, which he has seemingly set to one side again. Born in Boston, he studied in New York and formed his trio with Peter Bernstein and Bill Stewart as far back as 1986: it's still doing service, and they have recorded some excellent records for the independent Palmetto label. Some of his other associations include those with Maceo Parker, John Scofield and Dave Stryker. Goldings can play in a more traditional Hammond-jazz idiom, but he has asserted a more wide-ranging brief, tackling the organ as an impressionist instrument, playing softly as often as aggressively, and seeking to create a collective identity with the other members of his trio.

*Sweet Science* (Palmetto)

## Gil Goldstein
KEYBOARDS
*born* 6 November 1950

Sometimes it seems as if Goldstein is on a mission to single-handedly insinuate the profoundly uncool accordion into a position of jazz prominence. He did sideman work in the 80s with Gil Evans, Billy Cobham and Jim Hall, and soon began moving in elite sessionman circles, where he might be called on for a cameo with David Sanborn or Pat Metheny. Latterly he has become very prolific as an arranger-producer, himself playing keyboard instruments of both an acoustic and an electric disposition – but his trademark remains the accordion. So far it still seems like a lonely crusade.

**Mike Stern,** *Standards* (Atlantic)

## Vinny Golia
WOODWINDS
*born* 1 March 1946

Golia trained as an artist, and although born in New York and based there until 1972, he is renowned as one of the great organizational and documentary figures in the Californian avant-garde, where he has run his own Nine Winds label since the 70s. He is fascinated by the entire woodwind family, and his albums usually convene a shopful of saxophones, clarinets and flutes of varying size and timbre (it was quite a shock when he released an album of pieces for solo B♭ clarinet in 2001). Nine Winds has a very Californian outlook: a number of its releases come close to New Age music, albeit of a comparatively terse nature, but those records which feature Golia and his most frequent playing companions – Wayne Peet, Rob Blakeslee, Ken Filiano, Alex and Nels Cline, Bert Turetzky – are made of sterner stuff, sometimes fiercely free in their outlook. Besides working in small combinations, Golia also has a Large Ensemble, which has defied the impossible economics of running a free big band, although the title of one of his compositions for it – 'Pilgrimage To Obscurity' – may say something about its wider impact. A scholar of the world's knowledge in how to play his various horns, Golia is a great can-do personality and his now extensive catalogue is one of the music's relatively undiscovered riches.

**Nation Of Laws** (Nine Winds)

## Benny Golson
TENOR AND SOPRANO SAXOPHONES
*born* 25 January 1929

Philadelphia-born, Golson was working in R&B bands when he joined first Tadd Dameron, then Lionel Hampton and Earl Bostic, but his first major exposure came when he played with Dizzy Gillespie in 1956, also contributing to the band's book. He then went to Art Blakey's Jazz Messengers in 1958, and thereafter created The Jazztet with Art Farmer, which lasted until 1962. Golson's work as a saxophone soloist has often been undervalued over the years: he has an authoritative delivery which could often, at fast tempos, develop into a pell-mell frenzy, held in check only by his composerly bent. Yet it's his writing which Golson will surely be remembered for. He certainly picked up some ideas from Dameron, but few of his contemporaries have matched Benny's gift for writing sophisticated lines which retain an often unshakeable familiarity once heard. 'Whisper Not', 'Along Came Betty', 'Killer Joe' and 'Are You Real?' from his Messengers days are all fine examples of this, but his signature piece is surely 'I Remember Clifford', a memorial to Clifford Brown which stands alongside 'Round Midnight' as a definitive jazz ballad. In the 60s he disappeared into Hollywood and television writing, but in the 80s he began appearing as a performer again and he has enjoyed a surprising Indian summer in the recording studios, his powers as a soloist seemingly undiminished.

**Groovin' With Golson** (Prestige)

## Eddie Gomez
BASS
*born* 4 October 1944

Technique is something which Gomez possesses in superabundance. Although born in Puerto Rico, he grew up in New York and he was making waves on that scene from his early 20s, playing with stylists as remote from each other as Marian McPartland and Giuseppe Logan. His major association was with Bill Evans and he stayed in the pianist's trio for a little over ten years, from 1966. Since then he has largely been a hired gun and has shown little interest in working as a leader, at least on record. With Evans, Gomez took the Scott LaFaro legacy still further, pushing the bass forward as a solo voice and creating solos of sometimes jaw-dropping fluency, but following the Evans gig he hasn't really found a context to make his virtuosity create anything of lasting worth. Hearsay tells of a renowned musician remarking that he would rather work with Saddam Hussein than Gomez again. This may be unfair.

**Bill Evans,** *You're Gonna Hear From Me* (Milestone)

## Nat Gonella
TRUMPET, VOCAL
*born* 7 March 1908; *died* 7 August 1998

Gonella idolized Louis Armstrong, and when he sang a hit version of 'Georgia On My Mind' (1932) with Roy Fox's band, he sounded like a London version of the great man. The trumpeter worked his way round various dance bands before settling in with Lew Stone, where he formed a band-within-a-band called (inevitably) The Georgians. They were popular enough to go out on their own, and Nat's round of records, gigs and broadcasts made him the leading star of British jazz by the end of the decade, the vocal and trumpet combination still modelled on Armstrong (his brother Bruts, who also played trumpet, worked as a sideman in the band). Gonella played in military bands during the war, tried a brief and miserable flirtation with bebop, and then worked

through the dying era of the music halls before forming yet another version of The Georgians in 1959, which rode along with the trad boom before that too came to an end. Nat finally stopped playing trumpet in the 70s, but he never quit singing: in his ninetieth year, though basically retired and living in Gosport on the south coast (where a square was named after him), he recorded for the final time with Digby Fairweather, who loved having Gonella as a guest star on gigs. A great showman, who probably did at least as much as Louis Armstrong in raising a generation of jazz fans in pre-war Britain.
**The Nat Gonella Story** (Philips)

## Paul Gonsalves
TENOR SAXOPHONE
*born* 12 July 1920; *died* 14 May 1974

Gonsalves is always remembered as an Ellingtonian, but after various minor jobs he actually came to prominence as a member of the Count Basie orchestra, joining as a replacement for Illinois Jacquet in 1946. He made quite a name for himself with Basie (on such sides as 'Robbin's Nest', 1947), but Wardell Gray became the Count's new tenor star and, after a brief period with Dizzy Gillespie, Paul won the tenor chair in the Ellington band which had just been vacated by Ben Webster, in 1950. He remained with Ellington for the rest of his life. 'Mex' became, after Johnny Hodges, Duke's most featured and reliable soloist: it was an irony of this position that Gonsalves himself was constantly beset by drug and alcohol problems, and Ellington had to be at his most tolerant to hold on to his difficult star. His great moment came at the 1956 Newport Festival: Ellington's band had been in something of a slump, but an otherwise routine set was suddenly electrified by a marathon Gonsalves solo on 'Diminuendo And Crescendo In Blue', which provoked hysteria in the audience and put Ellington on the cover of *Time*. It was too bad for Mex that he was regularly obliged to repeat the trick in years to come, when his manner was actually a good deal more oblique and remote from rabble-rousing. Gonsalves developed a style which relied on very long, unbroken sequences of notes which teased the borders of tonality and often slipped back and forth between playing on the chords and outside

them altogether – a startlingly 'modern' approach which David Murray in particular has often expressed his regard for. Coupled with a tone which had a vulnerable, vocalized strain to it, it lent Gonsalves a strikingly individual platform, even on the ubiquitous tenor saxophone. He never fell back on clichés because, as Dan Morgenstern once put it, 'he couldn't remember them'. A session where Ellington featured his tenorman on every tune was set down in 1962 (*Featuring Paul Gonsalves*), but sadly it wasn't released until after both men had gone. Gonsalves died suddenly in London in 1974: his boss followed him, only ten days later.
**Duke Ellington, *Ellington At Newport*** (Columbia)

## Babs Gonzales
VOCAL
*born* 27 October 1916; *died* 23 January 1980

Like Slim Gaillard or Leo Watson, Gonzales loved spinning a yarn, and his life story is a little difficult to pin down. His real name was Lee Brown, he was born in Newark, NJ, and he studied piano there and learned to play the drums a little. He was with Charlie Barnet and Lionel Hampton in the early 40s, but being hidden in a big band wasn't really his style, and in 1946 he formed Three Bips And A Bop with Tadd Dameron and (guitarist) Pee Wee Tinney. Gonzales came up with the tune 'Oop-Pop-A-Da' (as well as such others as 'Lop-Pow', 'Dob Bla Bli' and 'Weird Lullaby'), and when Dizzy Gillespie had a hit with it Babs toured with the Gillespie orchestra. He cut a few more sessions with a sometimes starry personnel (including J J Johnson and Art Pepper) – another tune was called 'Prelude To A Nightmare' – before joining James Moody as a singer-manager, and then spending time in Sweden. Besides doing stints as a radio DJ and as Errol Flynn's driver, he clowned his way through the next three decades, writing two books of autobiography and making occasional albums, some of them consisting of comic routines told while he tinkled away at the piano (these were issued mostly on Expubidence, which might have been his own record label). Jazz didn't take Gonzales any more seriously than he took jazz, which was probably just as well for both parties.
**Babs Gonzales 1947–1949** (Classics)

## Dennis Gonzalez

TRUMPET
*born* 15 August 1954

A renaissance man of the south-west, Gonzalez is a second-generation Mexican-American who played a key role in asserting the identity of the avant-garde in an area of the US not normally associated with it. Moving to Dallas in 1977, he established the Dallas Association for Avant-Garde And Neo-Impressionistic Music, the resulting Daagnim label documenting his music and that of like-minded spirits. He visited London in the 80s and formed the New Dallas London Sextet while there. One of his very best records is *Stefan* (1986), made for Silkheart, by a quartet featuring himself and John Purcell. Dennis likes to play softly and lyrically as often as forcefully, and he likes to find the truth and point in even the most opaque performance. A schoolteacher and a painter as well as a musician, he was quiet for much of the 90s, but emerged again in the new century, playing and recording in new groups featuring his two sons.
**Stefan** (Silkheart)

## Jerry Gonzalez

TRUMPET, PERCUSSION
*born* 5 June 1949

A New Yorker, Gonzalez was playing both conga and trumpet from an early age and he played in a Latin-jazz group in high school with his bassist brother Andy (b 1951). In 1970 he took on a full-time musical career and played with Dizzy Gillespie and Eddie Palmieri before forming his own Grupo Folklórico Y Experimental Nuevayorquino, a jazz and Afro-Cuban fusion, which eventually turned into another group, The Fort Apache Band, which Gonzalez has run since with a varying personnel stretching to 12 musicians at some times and five at others. Their live work and records have displayed one of the most gripping mixes of jazz and Hispanic music thus far essayed, although outside their own turf the music has had comparatively little impact. Gonzalez has also done much specialist sideman work in the rare role of a trumpet-percussion double.
**Fire Dance** (Milestone)

## Benny Goodman

CLARINET
*born* 30 May 1909; *died* 13 June 1986

One of 12 children, Goodman grew up in Chicago and learned some music at his local synagogue but got his real grounding with the noted classical teacher Franz Schoepp. A fast learner, he was good enough to be playing gigs at 12, and was listening to all the best clarinet players in the city, from Leon Roppolo to Jimmie Noone. He got his union card at 14 and in 1925 joined Ben Pollack's band in Los Angeles, although they returned to Chicago soon after. He went to New York with Pollack in 1928, though by this time he was openly contemptuous of the leader and quit altogether after being ticked off for wearing dirty shoes. For five years he worked as a studio freelance, with Ted Lewis, Red Nichols, Ben Selvin and others, and in 1933 he started bandleading on records for Columbia, with John Hammond, a close ally, involved in the production work. A year later he was bandleading in public, with a respectable book and a few superior Benny Carter charts, and he won an important radio slot as the house band for NBC's *Let's Dance* series. Fletcher Henderson was drafted in as principal arranger, and his charts gave the band a solid jazz backing, reviving such earlier 20s pieces as 'King Porter Stomp'. By 1935 Goodman had important players such as Gene Krupa and Teddy Wilson in the band, and began recording with both of them in a spin-off small group; he also had a new contract with RCA under his belt. But Goodman's band failed to click in performance in New York, and an ensuing tour didn't seem to be going much better until the night of 21 August 1935, at the Palomar Ballroom in Los Angeles. Undecided between sweet and hot playing, Goodman tried a few swingers and the crowd went wild (it's portrayed in a somewhat more genteel way in *The Benny Goodman Story*, Hollywood's 1955 biopic). Some suggest that the swing era kicked off here.

From that point, Goodman grew stronger with every month. He brought in Lionel Hampton to join the already-established trio, which meant he had two significant black musicians in his team, a remarkable departure at the time; hired key men such as Ziggy Elman, Vido Musso and Harry James; and had Jimmy Mundy and Edgar

Sampson add to the band's book. A 1937 residency at New York's Paramount Theater had teenagers flocking to hear the 25-year-old's band, and in January 1938 Goodman hit a notable peak with a Carnegie Hall concert, fortunately recorded, which featured guest soloists from other bands and cannily cemented Goodman's eminence as 'The King Of Swing', evidenced by the furore created by such setpieces as 'Sing Sing Sing'. At the same time, Goodman had to see out some sudden losses from the band, including James and Krupa. In 1940, troubled by poor health, Goodman disbanded altogether, but by the end of the year he was back in action: Hampton and Elman had gone, but Cootie Williams arrived from the Duke Ellington band. There were other new faces: singers Helen Forrest and Peggy Lee, and guitarist Charlie Christian, as well as, briefly, Sid Catlett, who drove the band like no other. Goodman's own playing was still firmly placed front and centre on the band's records and broadcasts, and titles such as Eddie Sauter's 'Clarinet A La King' reinforced his number one position. But as the swing era wound down, the musician in Goodman became curious about the new music of bebop, and in 1947 he took out a fresh sextet as well as an orchestra, and recorded music for Capitol Records in something approaching the new style. The records sound like Goodman playing at bebop rather than with it, and he gave up on the idea. In the 50s he began touring for the US State Department, and there were some triumphant appearances ahead: the Far East (1956), the Brussels World's Fair (1958), the USSR (1962). He mostly worked in the US with small-sized groups, but much of his time was also taken up with the classical repertoire. As far back as 1938 he had been playing Mozart in public, and he went on to commission clarinet settings from Bartók, Copland and Hindemith, as well as playing most of the 20th-century classical clarinet repertoire, the lessons with Schoepp certainly paying their way.

Goodman spent most of his adult life in the forefront of popular entertainment, and he was a tough and recalcitrant customer who made life difficult for plenty of his musicians. Many Goodman sidemen spoke fearfully of 'The Ray', a stare from the leader which would be the silent prelude to either some devastating rebuke or a peremptory dismissal. His embattled progress from a very poor background may have instilled a perfectionism which unquestionably carried him through a long career with no loss of ability: his later records may sound a little more settled in their delivery, but the clarinet is a very difficult instrument to play at Goodman's level and he maintained his mastery through a lifetime of dedication. Next to Artie Shaw's almost brittle elegance, Goodman sounded warmer and less buttoned-up, but there was never a piece of music that he wasn't master of. Even on the seemingly desultory tours of the 60s and 70s there were challenging things in the band's book, and perhaps only bop defeated him. It may have been hyperbole to have called him 'The King Of Swing' in an era when Ellington, Basie and others were also at a peak, but Goodman himself could hold his own on anybody's stage and the tough Jewish kid from Chicago could have given any doubter a very fierce argument.
*The Birth Of Swing* (RCA Bluebird)

# Mick Goodrick
GUITAR
*born* 9 June 1945

Goodrick has been influential without gathering in much of a name career for himself, perhaps in part because he has preferred to stay mainly in the Boston area. He worked in a duo with Pat Metheny in the early 70s, and the pair of them also worked in the Gary Burton band of the same period (*Ring*, from 1975, shows both Goodrick and Metheny to fine advantage). In the 80s and 90s he was content to continue mainly in a sideman role, in such bands as Charlie Haden's Liberation Music Orchestra and Jack DeJohnette's Special Edition, although he also teaches at the New England Conservatory. Most of his recording has been done for European labels, particularly ECM, RAM and CMP: his limpid, fingerpicked style of phrasing contrasts with a thick electric tone, and the pastoral-sounding results do resemble the kind of music Metheny has gone on to make, though in a less widescreen ambience.
*In Passing* (ECM)

# Bobby Gordon

CLARINET

*born* 29 June 1941

In his youth, Gordon studied with Joe Marsala on Long Island, and in the 60s he worked in Chicago clubs, with Muggsy Spanier and others. He also made three albums of clarinet mood-music for Decca, but they didn't make him a star. In the 70s he was back in New York and playing at Condon's, and then toured regularly as a sideman with Leon Redbone. Latterly he has lived and worked in San Diego, where he now records for the Arbors label in the swing-revivalist idiom.

***Don't Let It End*** (Arbors)

# Dexter Gordon

TENOR SAXOPHONE

*born* 27 February 1923; *died* 25 April 1990

Born in Los Angeles, Gordon started on clarinet and alto and eventually moved over to the tenor by the time he was 17. He joined Lionel Hampton's band in 1940 and stayed three years, before freelancing on the West Coast and taking one of the saxophone chairs in Billy Eckstine's big band. In 1945 he arrived in New York and slipped into place among the new beboppers, though Gordon never really seemed like a bop musician: even in this company his playing had a slow-talking quality which set him apart from musicians such as Sonny Stitt, or even Lucky Thompson. He sparred with fellow tenorman Wardell Gray in a series of duels both on and off record, but his career stalled altogether when he served time for narcotics offences between 1952 and 1954. He was incarcerated for a second time in 1956 and didn't reappear until 1960, when he took a role in the play *The Connection* (as did Jackie McLean and Freddie Redd). Blue Note made some strong comeback records, including the fine *Go!* and *Dexter Calling* (1962), but he then went to Europe and found the welcome so agreeable that he basically remained there for the next 15 years, basing himself in Copenhagen. Dozens of sessions made at the Café Montmartre have survived, and his only other records during this period were made for Prestige on brief return visits to the US. But he was in turn given a prodigal's welcome when he did visit America again in

1976, and the following year he went back to stay. Bruce Lundvall signed him to Columbia, provoking a call from Ahmet Ertegun: 'You just did the greatest thing! You signed Dexter Gordon!' But the records were in the end nothing special. Dexter's huge sound and giant tread had given his music a deeper potency than ever, but he too often fell back on quotes and much of the music took on a merely ambling feel. In his prime, his music had a kind of jovial gravitas at its heart, building on Lester Young's example without succumbing to Lester's waywardness, and he was a great influence on the likes of Coltrane and Rollins. There was no better man to play the role of Dale Turner, supposedly an amalgam of Young and Bud Powell, in Bertrand Tavernier's 1986 film *Round Midnight*, and the sad thing about the music on the score is that Gordon's playing has begun to sound as slow and clouded as Young's was in decline. By the end of the decade his poor health, exacerbated by many years of heavy drinking, was finally failing: he died of cancer, cirrhosis and kidney failure.

***Go!*** (Blue Note)

# Joe Gordon

TRUMPET

*born* 15 May 1928; *died* 4 November 1963

Gordon's brief career – he was burned in a fire and subsequently died from his injuries – left some tantalizing examples of hard-bop trumpet playing. A Bostonian, he played locally in the 40s and worked with Charlie Parker and Art Blakey, and on one of Dizzy Gillespie's tours in the following decade. He moved to Los Angeles in 1959 and made a fine album for Contemporary there, *Lookin' Good* (1961), but the best examples of his fiery and lucid work are on the multiple volumes of Shelly Manne's group recorded live at San Francisco's Black Hawk club in 1959.

**Shelly Manne, *At The Black Hawk Vols 1–4*** (Contemporary)

# Jon Gordon

ALTO SAXOPHONE

*born* 23 December 1966

Gordon is a New Yorker who got his start in some classic bop combos – with Red Rodney and the Phil Woods orchestra – before going on to freelance and lead his own groups. He has a stacked knowledge of bop repertory and a sound and delivery which mix a joyful exuberance with darker and more thoughtful original writing, and although some excellent records for Criss Cross and Double Time haven't really reached a large audience, the best of them portray a mature and authoritative voice.

*Along The Way* (Criss Cross)

## Max Gordon
CLUB OWNER
*born* 1903; *died* 11 May 1989

Gordon was born in Lithuania and was part of the generation which went to America in the first years of the new century. He tried studying law, but preferred writing, and he took to running a coffee house in Greenwich Village. He opened his first club, The Village Vanguard, in February 1934, on Charles Street, although it moved to 7th Street a year later, where it remains to this day. The Vanguard was a mixed kind of place for the first 20 years of its life, blending music, folk singers and stand-up comedy, but by the mid-50s jazz had taken over (Max's other club, The Blue Angel, remained diverse, although it eventually closed in 1964). Gordon was present on most nights of its existence, and never retired. His autobiography, *Live At The Village Vanguard*, is a genuine memoir and a real page-turner, one of the most entertaining of jazz books. He loved the music and its characters and, small, feisty and astute, he managed to make a jazz business work for over 50 years.

## Wycliffe Gordon
TROMBONE
*born* 29 May 1967

Raised in Waynesboro, Georgia, Gordon begged his mother to get him a trombone after his older brother had one: 'I was listening to all the popular music my friends listened to, but I'd keep going back in the garage and put on a jazz record.' Wynton Marsalis heard him in 1988 and he spent seven years in the Marsalis touring band, also working with the Lincoln Center Jazz Orchestra, and recently he has been through

a burst of record-making for the Nagel Heyer and Criss Cross labels, ambitious and often surprising sets which have touched on gospel music as well as the expected post-bop and blues. 'We need to have more name recognition, and we, the trombonists, have to do something about that.'

*What You Dealin' With* (Criss Cross)

## Danny Gottlieb
DRUMS
*born* 18 April 1953

Primarily regarded as a fusion drummer, Gottlieb is an unusually sensitive example of the species, and much of his work has been coloured by a sense of restraint which could be regarded as rare for any drummer. A student of both Mel Lewis and Joe Morello, he met up with Pat Metheny when they were both members of the Gary Burton groups in the middle 70s, and he subsequently spent several years playing drums in Metheny's own band. In 1981 he formed a working partnership with bassist Mark Egan, eventually called Elements, a mix of American and Latin influences which typified Gottlieb's interest in a fusion which leaned towards world music rather than jazz-rock. In the meantime, he also freelanced and did a lot of session-work. In the 90s he formed the Contempo Trio with Mark Soskin and Chip Jackson. Gottlieb has also done some high-priced rock and soul gigs and seems quite unsnobbish about whom he plays with. The record cited, a rare solo outing for a major label, has an interesting range of both musicians and settings and is a fine sampler of the breadth of Gottlieb's interests.

*Whirlwind* (Atlantic)

## Jimmy Gourley
GUITAR
*born* 9 June 1926

Some think Gourley is a Frenchman, but he was born in St Louis and played in dance bands before serving in the navy; on his discharge he worked in Chicago. In 1951, though, he went to Europe and settled in Paris for some three years, playing with Henri Renaud in a regular band and working on the Parisian club scene. His style was

much like that of Billy Bauer and Jimmy Raney, a cool player with an almost reticent skill and a light, vibratoless tone – a rare sound in the post-Reinhardt continental scene of that time. He returned to Chicago in 1954 but three years later was back in Paris again, playing at the Mars and the Blue Note and accompanying Stan Getz and (on his final gigs) Lester Young. Kenny Clarke drummed with Gourley and in the 60s they toured together, the guitarist also working with organists Lou Bennett and Eddy Louiss. He ran a club in the Canary Islands at the start of the 70s, but then returned to Paris and has played in Europe since, making an occasional visit to the US and a handful of records under his own name.
*The Left Bank Of New York* (Uptown)

## Brad Gowans
VALVE-TROMBONE
*born* 3 December 1903; *died* 8 September 1954

Gowans actually played a surprising range of instruments – clarinet, saxophone, cornet – but settled on the valve-trombone in the 30s, having worked in New York on and off for a decade (he led a band called Gowan's Rhapsody Makers which recorded three sides for Gennett in 1926–7). He was one of the first jazz players to make a real go of that instrument, although the silkier role which it subsequently took on certainly wasn't his style, which was more upfront and suited his major playing jobs of the 40s, working with Eddie Condon's circle and taking a regular role at Jimmy Ryan's. He later played with Jimmy Dorsey, but cancer curtailed his career in the end.
**Eddie Condon, *1938–1940*** (Classics)

## Dusko Goykovich
TRUMPET, FLUGELHORN
*born* 14 October 1931

Born in the Yugoslav town of Jajce, Goykovich studied in Belgrade in the 40s and early 50s and then moved to Germany, where he played in radio orchestras and dance bands. He went to study at Berklee in 1961 and for a time was one of the horn players in one of the best of Woody Herman's trumpet sections, alongside Bill Chase and Don Rader. Later in the 60s he

returned to Germany, and was featured in the Clarke–Boland Big Band and in Peter Herbolzheimer's orchestras, as well as taking on the leadership of the Munich Big Band. Besides the orchestral side to his playing, he has also worked prolifically as a small-group leader, recording in that role for Enja. Goykovich plays in a style which is securely in the American bop idiom, although he is old enough to have swing-band music running through much of what he does. There is a cliché about his playing being imbued with Slavonic folk music, but it is actually hard to divine any such thing: the long-ago album *Swinging Macedonia* (made for Philips in 1966) is about the only specific nod to any such roots. Better to hear him as a European jazzman who long ago adopted American accents and made them his own.
*Soul Connection* (Enja)

## Conrad Gozzo
TRUMPET
*born* 6 February 1922; *died* 8 October 1964

Though he died young, Gozzo was a busy and accomplished lead man who is on a great many records. He started with Isham Jones's orchestra as early as 1938, and in the 40s served under Benny Goodman, Artie Shaw, Woody Herman and Boyd Raeburn. In the 50s he was in his element as a studio man, often playing with many of the name big bands even when he wasn't a full-time member. His sole album as a leader, *Goz The Great* (RCA, 1955), is very scarce and hasn't been reissued, but sooner or later some company will rectify that.
*Goz The Great* (RCA)

## John Graas
FRENCH HORN
*born* 14 October 1917; *died* 13 April 1962

Graas emerged from the Indianapolis Symphony to join Claude Thornhill's band in 1942. He was with Tex Beneke after the war and then joined Stan Kenton's Innovations In Modern Music Orchestra, but he did most of his work in Hollywood in the following decade, writing for television but also a regular on many West Coast jazz records. He is half of the exhilarating duo in Shorty Rogers's 'Coop De Graas' (the other one is Bob Cooper), and he embarked on a series of albums for Decca and Emarcy which feature his writing for medium-sized ensembles. The music can sound pernickety in the Californian manner of that time but often bounces with freshness and a curiously sober kind of exuberance. He throws in some unexpected humour in both his music and his titles: one piece is called 'Will Success Spoil Rock 'N' Roll?' But he died young of a heart attack.

*Jazzmantics* (Decca)

## Paul Grabowsky

PIANO
*born* 27 September 1958

Grabowsky is one of the strongest talents to emerge from the modern Australian scene. He studied in Melbourne and New York and then spent some time in Europe, staying in Munich for five years, before returning to Melbourne in 1985. Since then he has built an interesting discography, which includes small-group work and much grander pieces: he has had several commissions for film soundtracks and founded the Australian Art Orchestra, although that group seems to have only a peripheral relationship with jazz. The record cited represents the fruits of a trip to New York where he recorded with some local stars, but it features some very characterful writing and suggests that Grabowsky has much to say in even familiar jazz idioms.

*Tales Of Time And Space* (Warner Bros Australia)

## Robert Graettinger

COMPOSER
*born* 31 October 1923; *died* 12 March 1957

Graettinger played sax in some 40s big bands but composing was his *métier*, although he had precious little of his music performed and recorded. He began writing for Stan Kenton in 1947, and Kenton's band was probably the only jazz-orientated orchestra that would have thought of tackling Graettinger's difficult, sombre, sometimes fantastical music. Kentonians remember Graettinger travelling with the band for months at a time, simply to study the way each musician played so he could write more effectively for them. His output con-

sists of around a dozen pieces (all included on the disc cited), with the three-movement *City Of Glass* (1951) the eerie masterpiece. Gunther Schuller noted admiringly that Graettinger's music owed little or nothing to the reigning influences of the day (Stravinsky, Schoenberg and Bartók). He lived a pauper's lifestyle and died young.

**Stan Kenton,** *City Of Glass* (Capitol)

## Kenny Graham

SAXOPHONES
*born* 19 July 1924; *died* 17 February 1997

Kenny Graham's Afro-Cubists were a seminal part of the London scene of the 50s. They recorded dozens of sides for Esquire between 1951 and 1955, and Graham varied the line-up between seven and 12 players: his version of 'Flamingo' (1953) has four tenor saxophonists and three percussionists. Graham began on banjo and changed to saxophone in the mid-30s, working with Nat Gonella and Victor Feldman before he started his own band. Many of the best players in London passed through the ranks of the band and Graham's music was a strange fusion of bop, small-band swing and an exotic kind of impressionism, with the 'Afro-Cubism' expressed via multiple percussionists and titles such as 'Dance Of The Zombies' and 'Wha' Happ'n Sah?' But they were the first band to play at both Studio 51 and The Flamingo, two of London's premier modern clubs, and the first to broadcast on the BBC programme *Jazz For Moderns*. Graham became ill in 1958 and thereafter spent most of his time writing music (often for Humphrey Lyttelton, a long-time champion of his work) and only occasionally performing.

**Various Artists,** *Bebop In Britain* (Charly)

## Jerry Granelli

DRUMS
*born* 30 December 1940

Granelli grew up in San Francisco and played drums there with Vince Guaraldi and Denny Zeitlin in the 60s. He then based himself in turn in Boulder, Seattle, Berlin and Nova Scotia, teaching and performing in a wide range of settings and groups. He didn't really get himself on to record as a leader

until the 90s, but has since then come up with some striking and imaginative projects, including *I Thought I Heard Buddy Sing* (1992), a record based around Michael Ondaatje's book about Buddy Bolden, and *Broken Circle* (1996), which mixes an original suite inspired by native American history with covers of material by Peter Gabriel, Charles Mingus and Prince. His son Jerry is also a working musician.
***Broken Circle*** (Songlines)

# Norman Granz
IMPRESARIO, PRODUCER
*born* 6 August 1918; *died* 22 November 2002

One of the few men to make a million out of jazz, Granz could at least say he did it honourably and without having his musicians work on any kind of plantation. A Los Angeles jazz fan, he began organizing Sunday jam sessions in 1942 at a Beverly Hills club, which gradually grew into full-scale concert promoting. By 1944 he had held his first Jazz At The Philharmonic concert, at the Los Angeles Philharmonic Auditorium, which was essentially a simulation of the jam-session format he had started out with, and from there the concerts grew into something which was, by the middle 50s, a worldwide bandwagon. Then he got into record production: he established the Clef label in 1946, Norgran in 1953, and Verve in 1956, which absorbed the activity of the other two. He managed artists such as Ella Fitzgerald and Oscar Peterson, as well as overseeing the production of most of his record dates. By 1960 he had moved his base of operations to Switzerland, but carried on his JATP activity: although there was always something packaged and artificial about the kind of atmosphere the gigs were meant to engender, it certainly brought many major jazz names before audiences who would otherwise have never bothered to seek them out individually – and Granz always ensured that the musicians got top dollar and were looked after. He always knew when to get out of a situation: he sold Verve in 1967, and after that, as far as he was concerned, it was history (a little sadly, he refused to attend the label's 50th anniversary celebration in 1994). In 1973 he started again with a new label, Pablo, which used many of the artists he

had enjoyed long associations with: Ella, Oscar, Count Basie, Dizzy Gillespie. In 1987, he sold that too.

To his credit, Granz set by example a standard for treating musicians decently, and never tolerated any idea of a racial divide. His legacy is a complex one: he made something of a circus out of jazz presentation, and his records were professionally satisfying but rarely surprising. If he was a jazz entrepreneur first and foremost, he also seemed to set an unspoken agenda for how he felt his artists should perform. All that said, without Granz there would probably be an awful lot missing from jazz documentation from the 50s onwards.

# Stéphane Grappelli
VIOLIN
*born* 26 January 1908; *died* 1 December 1997

Grappelli spent most of his youth in orphanages and as a street urchin. But his otherwise impoverished father eventually got him a violin, and he learned that and the piano and began playing in Parisian bars and clubs in the early 20s, moving over to the piano as his main instrument for a time but reverting to the violin around 1930. He was soon cronies with Django Reinhardt, and the two co-founded the Quintette Du Hot Club De France in 1934 – violin, three guitars and bass, a more or less unprecedented combination and certainly so in a jazz environment. For five years it was the principal performing medium for both men, and through scores of records the music went round Europe and as far as the US. Grappelli moved to England in 1939 and stayed through the war years, often playing with George Shearing. After hostilities ended he returned to France and resumed his relationship with Reinhardt. After the guitarist's death, the violinist was content to drift along from gig to gig and country to country, and most of the 50s and 60s passed happily and uneventfully for him. But at the end of the 60s, his career unexpectedly started to warm up again. He visited the US for the first time in 1969, and charmed Newport Festival audiences, which pulled him back into the growing jazz festival circuit. He visited England again and toured with a 'Hot Club Of London' line-up, with Diz Disley and Denny Wright, the first time he had played in that format since his Reinhardt days. Albums with fellow violin maestro Yehudi Menuhin crossed him over into the classical–MOR audience, and by the 80s he was a delighted and revered international-musical leader with audiences of every stripe following his work. From there, he kept up a busy schedule right up until 1995: though frail and suffering from shingles and other conditions, he said he felt as if any aches and pains dropped away as soon as he began playing. Grappelli's playing hardly changed across 60 years. He remained in thrall to the swing idiom, and though his improvising perhaps grew more expansive – just as jazz itself did, with longer record playing-times and more varieties of instrumentation – it maintained the same sweetness and beguilingly romantic feel. Playing with performers such as Martin Taylor late in his life also kept him current, although there was something ageless about his delivery anyway.

*1992 Live* (Birdology)

# Milford Graves
DRUMS
*born* 20 August 1941

Even more so than Sunny Murray, Graves approached free-jazz drumming with a deconstructive and radical approach. A New Yorker, he started playing his drums with his hands rather than sticks, and was as interested in African, Cuban and even Indian drumming styles as jazz, studying with a tabla teacher in his teens. He was in charge of a Latin band from 1959 until the early 60s, and from 1964 was a leading presence among the New Thing players in the city, working with Paul Bley and the New York Art Quartet and recording a duo album for ESP with fellow drummer Sunny Morgan the same year. After intermittent work with Albert Ayler and others he moved into education, teaching at Bennington College from 1973 until the 90s. During this period he played only occasionally in public and hardly recorded at all, but later records with David Murray and others reasserted his qualities as a drummer. A 'colourist' who likes to get finely tuned and complex sounds from his instruments, Graves has worked a rather lone furrow, in some ways less influential than Murray because of a

thinner documentation on record. But he has been a prescient force in establishing a more worldly outlook on jazz rhythms.

**With David Murray, *Real Deal*** (DIW)

# Georg Gräwe
PIANO
*born* 28 June 1956

Gräwe has been busy on the German improvising scene since the late 70s. One remarkable initiative of his was the Grubenklangorchester, which set the coal mining songs of the Ruhr into an improvising context. Mostly, though, he does solo and trio work, one long-standing setting being a threesome with Gerry Hemingway and Ernst Reijseger. He has his own label (Random Acoustics) and has formed some alliances with the Chicago scene, where he spends part of each year. His music tends to teem with precise detail, and if it weren't improvised, a lot of it would sound like new chamber music. Those expecting Bobby Timmons licks are advised to stay clear, but Gräwe rewards a patient ear.

***Sonic Fiction*** (hat ART)

# Wardell Gray
TENOR SAXOPHONE
*born* 13 February 1921; *died* 25 May 1955

Like his regular sparring-partner of the 40s, Dexter Gordon, Gray was an unusual mix of swing and bop ingredients. He learned clarinet as a boy in Detroit, and joined Earl Hines's reed section before moving to Los Angeles in 1945. He began his friendly duels with Gordon there, recording a typical one on 'The Chase' (1947), and then joined the Benny Goodman small band, which was the leader's one hesitant foray into bebop. He went to New York with Goodman, and spent a period with Count Basie's big band and subsequent small group. Gray's career was, like his best playing, something of an improvisation, never settling anywhere long and with an unlucky streak: his records under his own name were for small labels, and none of them were well prepared, often featuring him in jam-session situations. He had a lighter style than Gordon and could get around the tenor with a fluency which was just this side of glibness: one wonders where

he might have gone next. But his was another life shadowed by narcotics, and he died in rather mysterious circumstances, possibly from a heroin overdose: his body was found in the desert outside Las Vegas.
*Memorial Volume One* (Prestige/OJC)


# Bennie Green
TROMBONE
*born* 16 April 1923; *died* 23 March 1977

Green joined the Earl Hines band in 1942 and stayed, aside from military service, until 1948, joining a second time in 1951. In the 50s and 60s he mostly led small groups of his own, and though he turned up in hard-bop situations for Blue Note (three albums as leader) and Prestige (a further three), he never sounds as if that was his favoured dialect, and his sound is more in the heartier swing tradition. He was with Duke Ellington for a brief spell at the end of the 60s but thereafter played mostly in Las Vegas bands. Bennie is affectionately remembered by collectors of the period, though none of his records has ever reached much of a wider audience.
*Soul Stirrin'* (Blue Note)


# Benny Green
PIANO
*born* 4 April 1963

Though he was born in New York, Green's family moved West when he was young and his father, a tenor saxophonist, helped introduce him to jazz. He worked in the Bay area when a teenager but returned to New York in 1983 and worked extensively with the three leaders who really shaped his approach to the music: Betty Carter (1983–7), Art Blakey (1987–9) and Freddie Hubbard (1989–92). He then joined Ray Brown for several years while working in his own trio (with Chris McBride and Carl Allen), which recorded a sequence for albums for Blue Note (he has since moved to Telarc). One of his idols is Oscar Peterson, and he has appeared and recorded with Peterson on a number of occasions. Critics have been somewhat harsh on Benny, possibly because he sees himself as an entertainer of audiences rather than a piano soliloquist: 'I want to play music that has the blues as its core and

shows my bebop influence, but the most important thing is that the music swings and is happy.' Green is a polite and cooperative fellow who refuses to talk down to his audience, and his virtues are increasingly rare in an introverted world of jazz piano; he is a natural and necessary successor to the Peterson manner. The playful ebullience of his playing can be captivating.
*Naturally* (Telarc)


# Bunky Green
ALTO SAXOPHONE
*born* 23 April 1935

Green came from Milwaukee and divided his time between there and New York, touring with Charles Mingus in 1956, and eventually settling in Chicago. He won a contest in a 1964 collegiate festival which allowed him to tour North Africa, where he was fascinated by the local music, and on his return he made three albums for Argo/Cadet. But these had little impact, and from 1972 he was involved principally in education, teaching in Chicago and Florida. Green's sound is hard bop with an oddly ambiguous edge, sometimes sour, sometimes abrasively mournful. He has rarely been seen or heard of outside his chosen turf, although Steve Coleman engaged him for a 1995 European tour. His handful of records are little known but personal and often strikingly effective.
*Heal The Pain* (Delos)


# Charlie Green
TROMBONE
*born* 1900; *died* February 1936

Green grew up in Omaha and played in tent and vaudeville shows, a training which shows up well in the accompaniments he recorded with many of the classic blues singers of the 20s, particularly Bessie Smith. But his principal gig was with the Fletcher Henderson band, which he joined in 1924 and finally left in 1930. He had a heavy, almost rasping sound, but could get around the slide-horn with a dextrous touch and while his soloing lacks the last ounce of finesse which Jimmy Harrison and Benny Morton brought to their work, he still counts among the better trombonists of that age. An exuberant trencherman, he found

more work with New York bands after his Henderson years, but died from the effects of tuberculosis in a Harlem hospital: the legend that he froze to death on his doorstep after an evening on the town is false.
**Fletcher Henderson, *1925–26*** (Classics)

# Dave Green
BASS
*born* 5 March 1942

The Mr Reliable of British bass players has worked apparently without stopping for the past 40 years. Among his principal gigs have been those with the Rendell–Carr Quintet (1963–9), Humphrey Lyttelton (1966–82), Stan Tracey (late 60s and much of the 70s), Ronnie Scott (70s and 80s) and Lillian Boutte (middle 90s). But it is likely that every major American visitor to the UK over the past four decades has had Green's smooth, unfussy time behind him or her at some point. The price for that unassuming excellence has been a certain anonymity, perhaps, although Green has occasionally led a group of his own, the band Fingers – which worked through the early 80s – being one example.
**Stan Tracey, *Portraits Plus*** (Blue Note)

# Freddie Green
GUITAR
*born* 31 March 1911; *died* 1 March 1987

Originally from Charleston, Green went to New York as a teenager, and after anonymous club work was offered the guitarist's chair in the Count Basie band when John Hammond persuaded the leader to hear him. He became part of the invincible All-American Rhythm Section, his imperturbable chording slotting in perfectly beside the pulse of the others, and while he sought no special attention as a player, his quiet mastery was eventually recognized as a piece of jazz immortality. Thereafter he was in the band more or less without interruption until the leader's death, although Green missed out for a brief period when Basie slimmed down to a small group at the end of the 40s. Finding a solo by him on a Basie record is tough to say the least, but his signature sound is a necessary part of one of the band's great 50s hits, 'Li'l Darlin''.
**Count Basie, *The Atomic Mr Basie*** (Roulette)

# Grant Green
GUITAR
*born* 6 June 1935; *died* 31 January 1979

Green's father was a blues guitarist and Grant played in St Louis R&B groups before Lou Donaldson, who heard him there, all but ordered him to try his luck in New York. He found a patron early on in Blue Note's Alfred Lion, who cut his first date with Green as a leader in 1960 and used him on no fewer than 15 different sessions in 1961. Green's style remained tied to his grounding in the blues, only rarely taking any kind of chordal approach and improvising in clear, simple lines which always had the soulful feel which Lion especially loved. His best records, including *Green Street*, *Grantstand* and *Feelin' The Spirit*, have a strong quota of blues and even gospel material, and they stand notably aside from Wes Montgomery, the major new influence on guitar in this period. He continued making records until later in the 60s, when he was inactive for a time, and two records made on his comeback for the label in 1969 are enfeebled by poor material and fail to recognize his strengths. His early-70s records are similarly wayward, although, with typical irony, were probably more successful in audience terms.
**Green Street** (Blue Note)

# Urbie Green
TROMBONE
*born* 8 August 1926

Green has fair claim on being one of the major jazz trombonists. But who can name one of his albums or cite one of his solos? His payback for being an absolute master on the most anonymous of jazz horns has been a kind of honoured obscurity. He was with Gene Krupa in the 40s, then with Woody Herman's Third Herd, but his proficiency inevitably directed him towards a studio career, and despite some featured appearances as a leader with RCA, ABC and Bethlehem most of his playing is hidden. He led one of the Tommy Dorsey ghost bands for a spell in the 60s, and thereafter ran small groups of his own, which now and then have had some featured recordings. In the microcosm of a track where he has a featured role, Green sounds huge and invincible.
**Let's Face The Music And Dance** (RCA)

## Burton Greene
PIANO
*born* 14 June 1937

Greene studied classical piano in Chicago in the 50s, and when he arrived in New York in 1963 he was soon involved in the burgeoning free-jazz scene, working in a group with Alan Silva, taking a prime role in the Jazz Composers' Guild and recording *You Never Heard Such Sounds In Your Life* for ESP. He went to Paris in 1969 and eventually settled in Amsterdam. Greene seems to have fished around in various genres – Indian music, klezmer, electronics and plain free improvisation – without finding a line to earth, or even many sympathetic listeners. In the 90s, he made something of a comeback by recording some records for Bob Rusch's labels – the disc cited is about the best of them – although the music continues to be an often impenetrable jumble. John Hammond once recommended him to George Wein, who responded: 'That cat plays the piano bench, he don't play the piano.'
***Throptics*** (CIMP)

## Sonny Greenwich
GUITAR
*born* 1 January 1936

Greenwich has, on account of indifferent health, played only occasionally and scarcely even considers himself a jazz musician, yet his documented work suggests a player looking for some surprising and uncovered territory. He played at first in R&B bands in Toronto but moved over to jazz in the 60s and, under a Coltrane influence, began playing in a swarming style which was very different to most directions in jazz guitar at the time: he managed to get a week at The Village Vanguard in 1968, and even turns up with Miles Davis the following year, but thereafter he performed only infrequently: live and broadcast material from the 80s and 90s finds him using guitar-synthesizer, and he made a duet recording with Paul Bley in 1994. Alternately hypersensitive and flooding with notes, his music is a curio which has further suffered from generally poor production values on record.
***Bird Of Paradise*** ( Justin Time)

## Sonny Greer
DRUMS
*born* 13 December 1895; *died* 23 March 1982

Ellington's drummers are a favourite talking point among his admirers, and they tend to be divided on the merits of the man who served longest in that capacity, William Alexander Greer. He worked with Elmer Snowden in New York before Ellington got there, and was soon in the small group which the pianist led at the start of his major career. A renowned hustler and all-round sharp point, Greer rousted and elevated the Ellington band for the next quarter-century. He built his drum set-up into an arsenal of percussion, adding chimes for 'Ring Dem Bells' (1930), and featuring in a famous photograph with his bandleader where the two men stand surrounded by what looks like a shopful of percussion instruments. While Greer survived the 40s, his drinking and a style which seemed old hat in the bebop era told against his longer endurance, and just as Ellington had cased out Wellman Braud a decade earlier, he brought in a second drummer (Butch Ballard) and Greer, outraged, took his leave. His stick-twirling flamboyance makes Greer exciting to see in the surviving footage of the 'old' Ellington bands, and he was surely the greatest showman Duke ever had, in the drum role or anywhere else. If he wasn't the most subtle or inventive drummer, it's hard to imagine hearing the 30s band with anyone else at the kit. He carried on working and playing into his old age, and in his 80s he could still be seen in the city, still very sharp.
**Duke Ellington,** *Never No Lament* (Bluebird)

## Larry Grenadier
BASS
*born* 6 February 1966

Grenadier took up electric bass at 11, so that he could join his brothers in a family rock band, but he switched to acoustic and began working in jazz clubs in and around San Francisco in the early 80s. As the decade wore on he began gaining high-profile gigs – with Stan Getz, Joe Henderson and Tom Harrell – and eventually went to New York, where he has been a prolific sideman ever since; perhaps his most attention-winning role has been in Pat Metheny's recent straight-ahead trio music. Grenadier has a thick, rather old-fashioned sound that sits with a fluency and adaptability which has earned him his current position as a sought-after bassman. His brother Phil is a trumpeter, and another brother plays guitar.

**Pat Metheny, *Trio 99–00*** (Warner Bros)

# Drew Gress

BASS
*born* 20 November 1959

Gress has mostly done sideman work, although he was a co-leader of the fine group with Phil Haynes, Joint Venture. Having studied in the Manhattan School Of Music, he became a regular presence on the city's new-jazz scene and worked with such leaders as Ellery Eskelin and Tim Berne. His own band Jagged Sky has been active since the middle 90s but has done little on record.

**Joint Venture, *Mirrors*** (Enja)

# Al Grey

TROMBONE
*born* 6 June 1925; *died* 24 March 2000

Grey came out of the navy and joined Benny Carter before moving through various big bands; finally he settled in with the Count Basie Orchestra in 1957, staying four years and becoming eminent as one of Basie's most colourful and reliably interesting soloists. After leaving the band in 1961, he spent the rest of his career freelancing and forging ready partnerships with old friends such as Jimmy Forrest and Buddy Tate. Fond of the plunger mute and a belly-laugh humour in his improvising, Grey was for a long time something of a throwback to a departed age of expressive trombone playing, which only proved his prescience when the likes of Ray Anderson came along. He recorded seven albums for Argo in the early 60s and was still performing right up to the end of his life, even if he was finally playing his slide-horn from a wheelchair.

**The Thinking Man's Trombone** (Argo)

# Johnny Griffin

TENOR SAXOPHONE
*born* 24 April 1928

The fastest tenorman of them all, Griffin could get around the horn with incredible velocity: on *Introducing Johnny Griffin* (1957), the bewildered Max Roach appears to be shouting at him to slow down. He came out of Chicago at 17 to join the Lionel Hampton band, and then went with his fellow sideman Joe Morris into an R&B group which enjoyed much success at the end of the 40s. Hard bop was really Griffin's thing, though. After he came out of the army in 1954 he led his own bands in Chicago and worked with Thelonious Monk, rarely if ever outfoxed by the pianist's unpredictable ways. Griffin recorded extensively for both Blue Note and Riverside, the albums not always well-shaped or organized, yet every one of them holds some exhilarating passages where the explosive tenor sound all but pounces on the listener. It helped that Griffin was accurate to the point of meticulousness: very few jazz improvisers have handled both ends of the executive spectrum with such finesse. In 1960, he formed a two-tenor partnership with Lockjaw Davis which produced plenty of the expected fireworks as well as musical insight, their Monk treatments working especially well. He found a warm welcome in Europe in 1963, and chose to stay on, eventually settling in France, where he has been ever since. A sinewy little man with a crafty smile, Griff has played much as he pleases since then, still making new appearances on record – a recent duo session with Martial Solal worked particularly well – and touring both in Europe and the US. He has slowed down a little, but he's still not exactly Ben Webster.

**The Congregation** (Blue Note)

# Henry Grimes

BASS
*born* 3 November 1935

Grimes played on the Philadelphia scene in the 50s, and he performed in several groups at Newport in 1958, where he can be spied in *Jazz On A Summer's Day*. At the beginning of the 60s he was still playing with leaders such as Sonny Rollins, but he became increasingly involved in free jazz, cutting his own trio date for ESP in 1965, and playing with Cecil Taylor, Albert Ayler, Don Cherry and other leading lights. But then he mysteriously abandoned music at the end of the 60s, and seemed to have disappeared from jazz altogether, denying further exposure of his meticulous technique in both arco and pizzicato playing. In 2003, he was rediscovered, living in a hotel room in Los Angeles: he told of having to 'get out of New York before I totally broke down'. He had sold his bass years earlier and worked at menial jobs. Yet despite having scarcely touched the instrument for 30 years, he began performing again and within a year was earning plaudits for the renewed power and authority of his playing in the free idiom.

**Cecil Taylor,** *Unit Structures* (Blue Note)

# Tiny Grimes

GUITAR, VOCAL

*born* 7 July 1916; *died* 4 March 1989

Along with Rufus Harley, Grimes is one of the two black American jazzmen to base a large part of his work around wearing a kilt. Lloyd Grimes began as a drummer, switched to a four-string guitar in 1937, and then teamed up with Slam Stewart before the pair of them formed a trio with Art Tatum. The pianist may have been the star of that particular show, which was a sensation on 52nd Street and everywhere else, but Grimes, who had been listening to Charlie Christian, was by no means a dunce on his instrument. He managed to get himself in on the beginning of recorded bop by making 'Tiny's Tempo' with Charlie Parker in 1944, then worked in his own groups until he moved in on the growing wave of rhythm and blues. His gimmick was to call the group The Rockin' Highlanders, which is where the kilts came in. By the 60s he was back doing more straight-ahead music, and by the end of the decade he had begun to visit Europe on a regular basis. Despite occasional spells of poor health he was still playing well into the 80s. The record cited shows up most sides of his talent.

**Tiny In Swingville** (Swingville/OJC)

# Don Grolnick

KEYBOARDS

*born* 23 September 1947; *died* 1 June 1996

Grolnick was rather a late bloomer in jazz: a philosophy scholar, he joined Billy Cobham's band Dreams as the keyboard player in 1971, and this led to a diary full of studio work, as often as not in rock situations. In 1985, he finally released an album under his own name, the infernally catchy *Hearts And Numbers* (Intuition), which was full of ingenious instrumentals where the likes of Michael Brecker were let loose. He went on to create two exceptional albums for Blue Note, *Weaver Of Dreams* and *Nighttown*, where an all-star line-up (the Breckers, Marty Ehrlich, Joe Lovano, Dave Holland) worked through a fascinating sequence of originals and standard revisions. This band even managed to tour Europe in 1994, which is some testament to the respect Grolnick mustered among such players. Tragically, there was only one further studio album, since Grolnick was taken by cancer in 1996.

**Nighttown** (Blue Note)

# Groove

Like much jazz argot, the likely origin of this lies in sexual slang, but a groove is a repeated, inherently rhythmical musical pattern. Andy Kirk's 'In The Groove' (1937) set the standard use for the term, and when Lionel Hampton asked his audiences, 'Is everybody in the groove?', he was inviting their participation in a mutual feeling of well-being which a swinging piece of music would serve to underscore. 'Grooving' is an adjective which can be applied to a performance which is of unmistakeable quality, although again it is the rhythmical element which determines the feeling: a top-quality rhythm section would probably be considered a 'grooving' one. Thus 'groove-based music' is likely to be aimed primarily at dancers, and 'hitting a groove' can be much the same as feeling at one with the rhythm. Beware, however, the word 'groovy', which is completely uncool and cannot be used in a jazz context without provoking mocking laughter.

# Richard Grossman
PIANO
*born* 14 November 1937; *died* 2 October 1992

Grossman began playing jazz in
Philadelphia in the 50s, with the city's hard-
bop groups, before turning towards free playing in the 60s. In the 70s he played in rock
ensembles and then shifted base to Los
Angeles, where he worked as a soloist and
a trio leader. Though he never achieved
much fame outside his immediate circles,
Grossman was a surprising and dramatic
voice in his idiom, mixing free playing with
stark structural concerns in a way which
makes both his solo and his group music
intensely absorbing. His Nine Winds records,
with members of the Vinny Golia circle of
players, are fine enough for us to feel
acutely disappointed at the lack of further
documentation and at his premature death.
***Trio In Real Time*** (Nine Winds)

# Steve Grossman
TENOR AND SOPRANO SAXOPHONES
*born* 18 June 1951

Grossman was the first of the saxophone
prodigies picked up by Miles Davis during
the trumpeter's fusion period. He was only
18 when Davis engaged him to play on the
first of several sessions, and he stayed for
around a year. Critics were largely unimpressed, but with the hysterical atmosphere
surrounding Davis and his numerous
players, this is still probably the most
famous association of Grossman's career.
For the rest of the 70s, Grossman moved
through various leaders without making
much impact, and he eventually chose to
settle in Europe and go out as a solo. While
he mostly played the soprano with Davis,
his subsequent work has been almost
entirely done on tenor, and he has settled
into a temperate climate of standards dates
with the best rhythm section he can find.
American labels have largely ignored him,
and most of his recording has been done in
Italy (Red) and France (Dreyfus).
***In New York*** (Dreyfus)

# Marty Grosz
GUITAR, VOCAL
*born* 28 February 1930

Marty's father George was an artist who left
their native Germany for America in 1933,
and the family remained a part of various
cultural circles: Grosz remembers meeting
Bertolt Brecht as a boy. He took up the
guitar in his teens and led a Dixieland small
group called The Cellar Boys – one of the
sidemen was a long-time collaborator, Dick
Wellstood. After army service he moved
to Chicago and began a long stint of club
work with small groups of various kinds,
although one gig was a long residency (on
banjo) at The Gaslight Club. In the 70s he
went back to New York and became a fixture
in the numerous swing-revivalist groups
which worked there and on the American
jazz festival circuit. Since then he has
recorded regularly as both leader and sideman and is in great demand for gigs both in
the US and in Europe: favourite partnerships include work with Keith Ingham, Ken
Peplowski and Peter Ecklund, and for a while
he was with Wellstood, Joe Muranyi and
Dick Sudhalter in The Classic Jazz Quartet,
which Grosz wanted to call The Bourgeois
Scum. A driving rhythm player who dislikes
solos and most enjoys playing for dancers,
Grosz has become the great raconteur of his
scene: 'I used to clown around in the band-
room backstage, and one of the guys said,
hey, do that on stage, because we need all
the help we can get.' He is a master at rediscovering forgotten material from the 20s
and 30s (samples: 'There's A Wa-Wa Gal In
Agua Caliente', 'Wedding Of The Painted
Doll') and while audiences hang on his every
word, the music is usually very good too, as
are the records.
***Music I Learned At My Mother's Knee And Other***
***Low Joints*** (Jazzology)

# Growl

The growl sound is an integral part of jazz
expressionism, though it is used mainly by
brass players. It describes the rasping edge
which is used to discolour the tone, producing a dirty, bluesy effect. The first master of
growl playing was Bubber Miley, whose
work in the early Ellington band was one of
the things which made Duke decide to

'forget all about the sweet music'. His replacement, Cootie Williams, carried on in the same manner. While growling fell out of favour with the boppers, its hint of vaudeville inappropriate to that kind of jazz, it re-emerged in the sound of the R&B sax-ophonists and is still an orthodox part of trad and swing playing.

## GRP
### RECORD COMPANY

GRP grew out of a production company founded by Dave Grusin and (drummer) Larry Rosen, which turned into a record label – distributed by Arista – in 1978. Its main focus was on a light style of fusion, exemplified by such artists as Lee Ritenour and Grusin himself, and eventually it became part of MCA in 1990 (which, in turn, led to its current situation as part of the huge jazz holdings of Universal Music Group). As a stand-alone label, GRP had numerous sales successes, with Ritenour, Diane Schuur, Billy Cobham, Chick Corea, Dave Valentin and others, but its musical policy was ruthlessly directed towards radio-friendly music and a house style which dis-couraged individuality and which led inexorably to the rise of smooth jazz as a potent force in American jazz radio. In other words, it had a profoundly damaging influ-ence on jazz in terms of audience expec-tation (anything difficult was immediately outlawed) and artistic impact (one sound-alike record after another). For a time, GRP was also used as an imprint for reissues of everything from early American Decca material to albums from the Impulse! cata-logue, but this seems to have faded in recent years, and since Grusin left himself in 1994 the label has largely died away as a pres-ence, though its unfortunate legacy remains.

## George Gruntz
### KEYBOARDS
*born* 24 June 1932

A tirelessly ambitious force in international jazz relations, Gruntz has led numerous star-studded ensembles over many decades now. Born in Basel, he studied there and in 1956 joined Flavio Ambrosetti's group as the pian-ist, a role he held down for some ten years.

In the meantime he led a trio of his own which backed many American visitors, and went on to gain a bigger profile as the pian-ist in the Phil Woods European Rhythm Machine (1968–9). He then took on organiz-ational roles: at the Zurich Schauspielhaus (1970–84) and the Berlin Jazztage (1972–94), positions which enabled him to enormously expand his circle of contacts. This assisted in developing the George Gruntz Concert Jazz Band, a large ensemble first founded in 1972 and which Gruntz took over completely by 1978. Since then it has toured and recorded regularly, making albums for ECM, Enja and TCB, and playing countless gigs under George's boisterous direction. Over some 25 years of work, the leader has been able to attract a formidable line-up of participants, from both the USA and Europe: a brilliant, entrepreneurial fundraiser, he has kept the project intact, even though the music is often ambitious and only indirectly crowd-pleasing. As a composer, Gruntz is a bit of a magpie: one of his early records was called *Jazz Goes Baroque* (1965), and he has also come up with ballets, oratorios, a cantata and a large-scale piece for percussion orches-tra. His jazz orchestra is in some ways a throwback to the days of the Clarke–Boland Big Band, and in some ways takes a view similar to that of the Mingus Big Band. Either way, the music is usually a lot of fun.
***Blues 'N Dues Et Cetera*** (Enja)

## Dave Grusin
### KEYBOARDS
*born* 26 June 1934

Grusin's career might have amounted to little more than comfortable hack-work: he was MD for Andy Williams in the early 60s, wrote TV and film music, and played key-boards behind Sarah Vaughan and Carmen McRae in the early 70s. But his own label GRP, co-founded with Larry Rosen, made him a wealthy man and a powerful force in American music, driving their artists on to primetime jazz-orientated radio and taking a major role in the creation of the smooth-jazz genre, which grew out of the polite fusion albums which GRP specialized in. Grusin himself recorded several examples of the style, including a notably discouraging tribute album to Duke Ellington. He eventu-ally left GRP in 1994 after its immersion in the MCA label system, and has since done projects for N2K. Scarcely a note of any of the 'jazz' music under his own name is worth bothering with.

**Homage To Duke** (GRP)

## Gigi Gryce
ALTO SAXOPHONE
born 28 November 1925; died 17 March 1983

As a player, Gryce was a capable if finally unremarkable Parker disciple, but his excellent skills as a composer have left a deeper mark. He studied at a very high level – Alan Hovhaness in Boston, Nadia Boulanger and Arthur Honegger in Paris – but turned up in the more prosaic surroundings of the Lionel Hampton big band in 1953. His own Jazz Lab quintet and Oscar Pettiford's group occupied him during the middle 50s, and quintet records for Prestige documented his music between 1959 and 1961. But jazz seems to have discouraged him, and soon after the last of these he disappeared into the public-school teaching system. His legacy is a fine book of tunes, which have mystifyingly never been given due homage, even in an age when rediscovering jazz composers is de rigueur: among them are 'Nica's Tempo', 'Minority', 'Casbah', 'Speculation', 'Stupendous Lee' and 'Up In Quincy's Room'. There are claims that he wrote symphonies, ballets and chamber music; if so, they seem lost to posterity.

**Jazz Lab** (Columbia)

## Vince Guaraldi
PIANO
born 17 July 1928; died 6 February 1976

It was no irony that Wynton Marsalis made an album in homage to Guaraldi's work: the trumpeter was part of a generation or two of American youngsters for whom the music on the Charlie Brown cartoons was some of the first jazz they ever heard. The San Francisco native got his start in the Cal Tjader groups of the early 50s, a piquant pairing as both would turn out to be great populists. Besides working with Tjader, he played in the Woody Herman band and others, but began making his own albums for Fantasy, mostly in a trio and small-group format, and by the end of the 60s there

were dozens of them. Guaraldi played pop-jazz of the most infectious and likeable kind: he was no great improvising force, and some of his work (such as a jazz mass) totters towards pretension, but compared to what would come out of the smooth-jazz era it was smart and satisfyingly lightweight material, which his durable hit 'Cast Your Fate To The Wind' (1962) exemplifies. His Charlie Brown music, though, full of funky electric piano, is what jazz remembers him for.

**A Boy Named Charlie Brown** (Fantasy)

## Frank Guarente
TRUMPET
born 5 October 1893; died 21 July 1942

Max Harrison garlands Guarente as 'the first important jazz musician born outside the USA', and on recorded evidence – mostly the numerous sides he made with the prolifically recorded group The Georgians – it is hard to disagree. He was born in Montemiletto, a village near Naples, and went to the US in 1910; he apparently made friends with Joe Oliver (while working in a bank by day) and began playing on the local New Orleans scene, although after army service he headed north, and eventually joined the Paul Specht orchestra in Atlantic City in 1921. The Georgians were a small group drawn from the Specht ranks, and they cut dozens of titles between 1922 and 1927, those up to the end of 1924 featuring Guarente, who leads and solos in a clean, lyrical, sweet-toned style which is easy to hear, fancifully or otherwise, as a precursor of Beiderbecke. He visited Europe with Specht and enjoyed much success there with a later version of The Georgians, but when he returned to the US in 1928 he found that jazz had moved swiftly on and he never made much more progress, working mostly as a studio musician and under leaders such as Victor Young. He was in Tommy Dorsey's 1942 band when he died at only 48 years of age.

**The Georgians** (Retrieval)

## Johnny Guarnieri
PIANO
born 23 March 1917; died 7 January 1985

Guarnieri was all music. His father taught, and the younger Guarnieri started on classical piano at ten. But hearing Art Tatum made him want to play jazz, and he joined Benny Goodman in 1939 and Artie Shaw in 1940 – he played harpsichord in Shaw's Gramercy Five – and managed to fit in CBS studio work along with jam sessions, sideman gigs with Billie Holiday, Slam Stewart and Lester Young, and almost nightly work on 52nd Street. By the end of the decade he was broadcasting every night with his own band, and in the 50s he became an NBC staffer. Guarnieri could play in any style, but his basic one was a light, at times frolicsome variation on stride: perhaps playing came too easily to him, for the surviving recordings under his own name at times seem almost flippant in their delivery. In the 60s he was going out as a solo again, holding down a sequence of hotel residencies, and he became a generous and much-liked teacher, recording some solo sessions for the independent TazJazz label late in life. He died while still out on tour.

*Johnny Guarnieri 1946–1947* (Classics)

# George Guesnon
BANJO, GUITAR
*born* 25 May 1907; *died* 6 May 1968

'Creole George' was a New Orleans altar boy who became, in his own words, a 'black sheep'. He worked as an apprentice plasterer, but began sitting in with cabaret bands and by 1928 he was playing for Papa Celestin and Willie Pajeaud. In the early 30s he toured with Sam Morgan's band; later he joined the Rabbit Foot Minstrels. In 1940 he tried his luck in New York but had little success, and went home to New Orleans a year later. From the 50s onwards he remained a regular in the city's music, often playing with Kid Thomas Valentine and appearing at Preservation Hall. In his later years this master of traditional banjo grew aggrieved at a life of struggle, and often 'put up my guitar and banjo never to play them again'; while Al Hirt earned thousands of dollars a week, 'in the end we wind up with the dry bones, that and nothing more'.

*The Creole Blues Of George Guesnon* (Icon)

# Friedrich Gulda
PIANO
*born* 16 May 1930; *died* 27 January 2000

One of the few performers in this book who can justify his place in both classical interpretation and jazz improvisation; perhaps Previn is his only rival in that regard, and Gulda was a much more ambitious improviser than the American. Gulda studied in Vienna and made his classical concert debut in 1944, going on to play at Carnegie Hall six years later. But while his career flourished in that direction, he also became fascinated by jazz, and another six years later he was playing at Birdland (with a band which cut a studio album for RCA), as well as playing in the Austrian All Stars alongside Joe Zawinul. From 1960 onwards, his output was prodigious and often extraordinary. He formed several jazz orchestras, culminating in the Euro-Jazz Orchestra (1965–6), which bulged with eminent players, and took up flute and baritone sax in addition to the piano. He founded a jazz competition in Vienna, worked in the trio form, and tried his hand at free jazz in a threesome called Anima. He sang, hiding under the name Albert Golowin (and behind a fake beard). He organized three mighty festivals in Austria in the 70s, at one of which he played a duet with Cecil Taylor, and in the 80s he played duos with Ursula Anders and often worked alongside Zawinul at major Viennese presentations. In the early 90s he formed his Paradise Band, and based a musical around it. This all ran alongside his classical ouput, which also included a good deal of formal writing. His records often had very little distribution outside Germany and Austria and are relatively unknown to the wider jazz audience, and there are scandalously few available on CD: , *From Vienna With Jazz* (1964), *Ineffable* (1965), *As You Like It* (1970) and *The Long Road To Freedom* (1971) are a mere handful of those which deserve a greater reputation. Also a clever and often mischievous writer on music – he wrote and had published his own obituary, a year before he died – Gulda now seems like a genuine pioneer, whose music has sometimes been sniffily dismissed on the tedious and fallacious grounds of being too European and unswinging. His music deserves a full reappraisal.

*The Long Road To Freedom* (MPS)

## Lars Gullin
BARITONE AND SOPRANO SAXOPHONES
*born* 4 May 1928; *died* 17 May 1976

Born in Visby, Gullin started on bugle and
clarinet (in a military band) and also played
folk music on the accordion in his teens. But
he turned to first alto and then baritone in
Swedish dance orchestras, and the baritone
took up his time from 1951 onwards. He was
with Arne Domnérus until 1953 and thereafter mostly led his own groups, as well as
working prolifically as a composer and
arranger. All through the 50s and early 60s
he fashioned music of a beautifully personal
kind, with Swedish tradition – specifically
the choral music and the romantic-classical
movement – running through it, in addition
to the received forms of American jazz.
Compositions such as 'Danny's Dream',
'Manchester Fog' and 'The Yellow Leaves'
Love To The Earth' are uniquely bittersweet
and melodious, the writing seemingly a
direct extension of his own style on baritone, which sounds different to any
accepted swing or bop convention – light,
heartfelt but never sentimental, he seemed
to make the baritone into a feminine instrument rather than a bluff low-register one.
Word of his accomplishment spread, visiting
Americans asked to play with him, and he
even had records issued in the US, a rare
honour indeed for a European jazzman.
Records such as *Portrait Of My Pals* (1964)
showed his skills expanding further, but one
unfortunate American trait Gullin did succumb to was a narcotics dependence, and
his career in the 60s and 70s lost impetus.
Latterly he spent more time composing, one
late work being *Jazz Amour Affair* (1970), for
a full symphony orchestra. He was still touring as late as the year of his death, although
the steam had long since gone out of his
career, and with hindsight much of it seems
tragically wasted. Gullin is still feted in his
own country, though, and moves have
recently been made to release a vast archive
of private and live recordings of his work.
His son Peter (1959–2004) was also a fine
baritone player, and he too died young.
**Lars Gullin Volume Two 1953** (Dragon)

## Ulrich Gumpert
PIANO
*born* 26 January 1945

Uli Gumpert was one of the leading personalities in free playing in East Germany.
While he has occasionally worked outside
Germany, it hasn't happened too often,
and in consequence he is rather less well
known than such contemporaries as Alexander von Schlippenbach. FMP recorded
him extensively in the 70s, with drummer
Günter Sommer as one regular partner, and
his playing in the Zentrall-Quartett has been
one place to catch him in more recent times.
Gumpert tackles free playing from what
sounds like a classical rather than a jazz
background.
**'N Tango Für Gitti** (FMP)

## Russell Gunn
TRUMPET
*born* 20 October 1971

Gunn was born in Chicago but grew up
mostly in St Louis, where he started on trumpet and was encouraged by Oliver Lake. He
moved to New York in 1994 and soon had a
bristling reputation as a contender, working
with both the Branford Marsalis Buckshot
LeFonque group and the Lincoln Center
Orchestra, and recording a fast string of
records for both Warner Bros and the independent High Note label. His 'Ethnomusicol-
ogy' concept was scattered through them
and both hip-hop and jazz material jostled
side by side. The problem was – in spite of
sometimes inflammatory material concerning critics and other nuisances – none of it
really created either a furore or significant
sales, and Gunn moved to Atlanta at the
start of the new century. Considered simply
as a trumpet player, he still has claims to be
up there with Roy Hargrove as one of the
sharpest of the younger men on the horn.
**Ethnomusicology Vol 1** (Warner Bros)

## Mats Gustafsson
BARITONE AND SOPRANO SAXOPHONES, FLUTE
*born* 29 October 1964

Born in Umeå, Gustafsson got into music via
his mother's Little Richard collection ('Of
course, he's still the king of everything'), but

when he heard Sonny Rollins in 1980 he took up the saxophone, moved to Stockholm and found himself especially interested in the European avant-garde. He began forming alliances with such contemporaries as Kjell Nordeson and Raymond Strid, out of which came bands such as Gush and the AALY Trio, and Gustafsson energetically made contacts around the world: he was around at the start of the explosion of Chicago's new improv scene in the early 90s, and has played regularly with Ken Vandermark and others from that scene. He is an energy player who still likes to find an almost rarefied detail in his own playing, and some of his solo projects – especially the Steve Lacy homage *Windows* (1999) – show him to be intrigued by how breath and air move through the circuitry of a saxophone. The AALY Trio show off his wilder side. A personality who believes strongly in free music's need to diversify and communicate, he is likely to have much more to say in his area yet.

**The Thing** (Crazy Wisdom)

# Rene Gustafsson

GUITAR

*born* 25 August 1933

Something of a connoisseur's guitarist, Gustafsson is also a godfather of Swedish modernism: playing in a Jimmy Raney style, he was in several crucial Swedish groups of the 50s and early 60s, and has been a close confrère of Arne Domnérus in particular. Perhaps too modest to really assert his presence, he has nevertheless helmed a few record dates over the years and played as a sideman on probably hundreds more.

**Rune At The Top** (Metronome)

# Gutbucket

'Gutbucket' playing is out of the traditional end of jazz, and consists of playing as lowdown and dirty as possible. It's a nice irony that several groups using the word either in their name or in one of their tunes have often been homely and polite. Gutbuckets were originally used to catch the drips from saloon beer kegs.

# Barry Guy

BASS

*born* 22 April 1947

Guy was in almost at the start of free music in London. He had been studying composition at Guildhall when he fell in with the expanding circle which included Evan Parker, John Stevens, Paul Rutherford and Derek Bailey, and played in the Spontaneous Music Ensemble, Amalgam and Howard Riley's trio, all in the late 60s, before forming Iskra 1903 with Bailey and Rutherford. Unlike the others, though, he also followed a career in contemporary- and period-music performance and secured an important reputation as a performer in that sphere. Ever since, Guy has juggled the two sides of his musical life, although latterly he has focused more on the improvisational side. At the same time, he has sought to impose a composer's discipline on the idiom, and out of that paradoxical situation came the London Jazz Composers' Orchestra, which has been one of his favourite vehicles since the early 70s. Barry's partner, Maya Homburger, is a period-performance violinist and their work together is documented on the Maya label. Guy countered the problem of the bass being almost inaudible in loud improvisation by using an amplifier early on. His solo works are some of his best statements on the improvisation–composition divide, but he is a master of the instrument in any jazz-related situation and it is interesting to conjecture on how he would sound playing something like time: his work with Riley is one of the few occasions he has approached this. If his music sometimes has a dour, rather British edge to it, he is still regarded with high esteem in European circles.

**London Jazz Composers' Orchestra, Ode** (Incus)

# Tommy Gwaltney

CLARINET, VIBES

*born* 28 February 1921

Gwaltney started on clarinet, but added the rare double of vibes when he suffered a damaged lung during war service and had to stop playing the horn for a time. He was only a part-timer when he appeared on Bobby Hackett's *Gotham Jazz Scene* (1957), but steadily took on more work and by the end of the decade he became interested in running festivals, which he organized in his home state of Virginia during the 60s, as well as opening his own club, Blues Alley in Washington DC. Among regular accomplices were guitarists Charlie Byrd and Steve Jordan, and he became a regular at the Manassas Festival, usually in Dixie-to-mainstream situations. Latterly he focused on the clarinet, tired of lugging the vibes around. While largely unsung outside his local terrain, Gwaltney qualifies as an eminent regional jazzman, and his relatively few records have many delightful moments. *Goin' To Kansas City* (Riverside)

# Bobby Hackett
CORNET, TRUMPET
*born* 31 January 1915; *died* 7 June 1976

Hackett started out on ukulele and guitar, but switched to the cornet and played in his home town of Providence before moving to first Boston and then, in 1937, New York, where he began working with Joe Marsala. Benny Goodman had him in the Bix Beiderbecke role at his 1938 Carnegie Hall concert, and then he began working at Nick's, which started a long association with Eddie Condon. Hackett tried out with his own big band but it quickly failed, and in 1941 he joined Glenn Miller's orchestra: his solo on 'A String Of Pearls' is one of the great moments in that band's discography. At this point, Hackett was a warm-to-hot stylist whose sound had Louis Armstrong and Bix Beiderbecke battling it out for supremacy, and after working as an NBC staffer he actually went on to work with Armstrong in the 1947 Town Hall concert. He then moved to ABC for more studio work, and in 1951 was pestered by the comedian Jackie Gleason to play as the solo brass voice on a sequence of mood-music albums. They became an unexpected (by Capitol, the releasing label) success, and in later years Hackett didn't disguise his feelings that Gleason had exploited him: 'All in all I made about 30 or 40 thousand. Gleason has probably cleared a couple of million.' The string arrangements were mild and unimpressive, but the beauty of Hackett's work is inviolable: by this time he had burnished his playing to a gorgeous lustre. He also made some fine Dixieland sets for

Capitol, some with Jack Teagarden, and cemented a partnership with the musician he liked to play with most of all, Vic Dickenson. In the 60s and 70s, besides owning his own hi-fi business for a time and briefly starting a record label, he played with Dickenson, Glenn Miller's memorial orchestra and Tony Bennett: he delivers the languorous obbligati on Bennett's great hit 'The Very Thought Of You' (1966). One of his most regular associations – and his last, in the final months of his life – was with Benny Goodman. In the end, the sweeter side of Hackett's playing was the one which brought him most success, but it had been made more resilient by his years of Dixieland routine, and the way he would decorate a standard tune became one of the most satisfying pleasures in the jazz of the LP era.
**Jackie Gleason, *Music To Change Her Mind*** (Capitol)

# Charlie Haden
BASS
*born* 6 August 1937

Haden's family was from Shenandoah, Indiana, and he played in their family hillbilly band until he was in his teens, mostly at the piano. Inspired by his brother, he switched to bass, and by 1957 he was working in Los Angeles clubs, the most notable association being with Paul Bley, in the group which Ornette Coleman and Don Cherry sat in with. He joined the new Coleman quartet in 1959, and performed with them in New York and on their Atlantic sessions, although a narcotics problem obliged him to stand down in 1960. Haden's elemental style was strikingly different to the sort of virtuosity of such contemporaries as Scott LaFaro, yet his concern for easygoing accompaniment and an earthy kind of swing helped rationalize and translate some of the leader's music into a more familiar jazz dialect. After a period of rehab, he worked his way back into the music and by 1966 was ensconced with Coleman again. In the 70s he divided his time between Coleman's music, Keith Jarrett's 'American' quartet with Dewey Redman and Paul Motian, and his own Liberation Music Orchestra project, where revolutionary songs of different origins received a dra-

matic jazz treatment. When Coleman largely abandoned his acoustic format, Haden, Redman and Ed Blackwell formed Old And New Dreams as a Coleman repertory band and recorded for Black Saint and ECM. The Liberation Music Orchestra remained Haden's major performing vehicle, but in 1986 he formed Quartet West, with Alan Broadbent, Ernie Watts and Larance Marable, effectively a homage to the repertory of old Los Angeles film and standards music, which Haden described as a 'dedication to beauty'. Their string of albums for Verve were some of the most successful mainstream jazz records of the 80s and 90s. He also became prolific as a sideman, with Pat Metheny, Kenny Barron, Hank Jones, Joe Lovano and many others. An unrepeatable mix of political artist, jazz revolutionary and country boy, Charlie is a crucial contributor to the last half-century of the music. Latterly a hearing problem has found him protecting his ears from feedback in live performance with a surrounding glass screen, although he is not beyond using it to get a chuckle from the audience. A terrible complainer who still has the ability to laugh at himself, his bass can sound sluggish and even weary in less sympathetic contexts, but in the right place he is nothing but magisterial, every note seemingly absolutely right. His two daughters achieved some notoriety for a time in a valley-girl kind of rock band.
**Haunted Heart** (Verve)

## Shafi Hadi

ALTO AND TENOR SAXOPHONES
born 21 September 1929

Born Curtis Porter in Philadelphia, Hadi played in R&B bands at the start of the 50s and was a distinctive contributor to several Charles Mingus groups later in the decade: he is especially fine on *The Clown* (1957) and *Tijuana Moods* (1957), and he contributed some haunting solos to the Mingus soundtrack for the John Cassavetes film *Shadows* (1959). After this, though, he slipped from view, reputedly working in New York as a painter in the 60s.
**Charles Mingus,** *Tijuana Moods* (RCA)

## Tim Hagans

TRUMPET
born 19 August 1954

Hagans is an accomplished trumpeter who has threatened but not quite realized great things. He played with Stan Kenton in the early 70s but left for Sweden in 1977, a territory where he has forged and retained several links, initially through Thad Jones's last big band. He returned to the US in 1982 and worked extensively as a sideman, besides teaching; but in the early 90s he was signed to Blue Note and made a sequence of judiciously crafted records which started out in intelligent hard bop and ended in Milesian fusion. But the records had no fortune in finding an audience. While Hagans remains in demand for his skills, the feeling is that his moment has basically passed.
**Audible Architecture** (Blue Note)

## Bob Haggart

BASS
born 13 March 1914; died 2 December 1998

Haggart's career was almost as long and distinguished as that of his fellow bassist Milt Hinton. He started out on guitar (George Van Eps was one of his teachers) but switched to bass in his teens and began working semi-professionally. He actually turned down offers from both Tommy Dorsey and Benny Goodman, instead joining up with the initial personnel of the Bob Crosby band in 1935. Haggart was with them until the break-up of the orchestra in 1942, and contributed much to the band's book, including the novelty hit 'Big Noise From Winnetka', 'South Rampart Street Parade' and 'Dogtown Blues'; but he was at least as gifted as a ballad writer, responsible for both 'What's New' and the instantly memorable 'My Inspiration'. He then went into studio work before renewing his partnership with Crosby colleague Yank Lawson: they worked throughout the 50s in the Lawson–Haggart Jazz Band, and made a string of albums for Decca (although the last one, *Boppin' At The Hop* from 1959, showed how even a Dixieland group had to try and turn rock'n'roll tricks). In the 60s, Haggart was a regular at businessman Dick Gibson's annual jazz parties, and eventually Gibson aided Haggart and Lawson in forming The

World's Greatest Jazz Band, which relaunched the careers of several old-time Dixielanders – though it was never quite as successful (or as Greatest) as Gibson had hoped. By the end of the 70s that enterprise had also died out, but in the 80s and 90s Bob still found plenty of time to play and record, his swinging, direct style unimpaired by the passage of time. He was also fond of golf and painting. An 80th-birthday celebration assembled many of Bob's surviving playing friends, and was extensively recorded by the Arbors label.

*Hag Jumps In* (Arbors)

## Joe Haider
PIANO
*born* 3 January 1936

Haider studied piano in Munich in the early 60s and became interested in the contemporary jazz being played there. He became the in-house pianist at the city's Domicile club, which he eventually took over as manager, and accompanied the usual contingent of visiting Americans there. But he also forged links with several of the leading Swiss players, founding a quartet called Four For Jazz and directing the Swiss Jazz School in Berne in 1970. Back in Munich, he co-led a big band with Slide Hampton, and later founded the EGO label, which documented his music and that of other German players. Haider's bop-rooted style took on some of the characteristics of free and modal playing as time went on. His music isn't well known outside his own circle, and he has in the end recorded comparatively little.

*Café Des Pyrénées* (Calig)

## Al Haig
PIANO
*born* 22 July 1922; *died* 16 November 1982

While bebop had many lost souls, Haig's case is a queer mixture of indifference and misfortune. His first influence on piano was Teddy Wilson, and after playing in a coastguards' band, he began working in New York at the end of 1944, gaining the attention of Charlie Parker and Dizzy Gillespie and appearing with them on some of the important early bop recording dates. While he also worked in big bands – with Charlie Barnet

and Jimmy Dorsey – Haig continued to turn up on small-group bop record sessions, and he played regularly with Parker again during 1948–50, as well as with Stan Getz, Coleman Hawkins and Jazz At The Philharmonic. Haig's style was suitably mercurial and virtuosic for his bebop surroundings, but he sounded like the emotional opposite of Bud Powell: calm, relaxed, intuitively responsive. He sounded as fine with Getz as he did with Parker. His fingerings were peerlessly smooth and even, and though he was seldom heard on well-recorded pianos, the poise of his playing cuts through with surprising effectiveness. But after 1952, Haig's jazz career instantly dissipated. He was briefly with Chet Baker, but they quickly fell out, and aside from a few brief episodes he remained professionally active as a pianist outside Manhattan, but only in cocktail situations. In 1968, his wife was found dead at their home, and Haig was subsequently tried for her murder but acquitted. Oddly, this commenced his re-emergence as a jazz performer: he began playing regularly in New York again, and a flurry of late recording activity – much of it of the highest quality, even though again he was often unlucky from a production point of view – showed that his talents were undiminished. The author heard him in London in 1981, and has never forgotten Haig's beautiful playing. He remained an exemplar of bebop piano, even though his expressiveness was nuanced, even diffident, and nearly at odds with the idiom he so thoroughly mastered.

*Invitation* (Spotlite)

## Sadik Hakim
*born* 15 July 1919; *died* 20 June 1983

A bit player in the bebop story, Hakim (then known as Argonne Thornton) was playing piano in Chicago when Ben Webster heard him and invited him to join his group in New York, in 1944. He roomed with Charlie Parker and played on the 'Thriving On A Riff' session for Savoy. He then toured with Lester Young. Hakim never found much attention after that, but he played in Canada for a time and eventually moved to Montreal in the 60s, before moving back to New York a few years before his death.

**Charlie Parker,** *The Complete Savoy Sessions* (Savoy)

## Pat Halcox
TRUMPET
*born* 17 March 1930

Halcox has been Chris Barber's most faithful sideman, joining in 1954 and staying ever since, although illness obliged him to take a temporary retirement in the early 90s. As befits such a loyalist, he began as a New Orleans purist of sorts but has broadened his style and manner of delivery as the Barber band itself branched out into many musical areas, and besides playing a calm and direct lead, he can solo in whatever idiom Barber himself has selected for the occasion. On the boss's annual summer leave, Halcox has occasionally availed himself of the opportunity to play with other bands, with sessions such as the Lake CD (drawn from three different sets during 1978–9) among the results. Not that he exactly goes avant-garde.
*Pat Halcox All Stars* (Lake)

## Edmond Hall
CLARINET
*born* 15 May 1901; *died* 11 February 1967

Hall came from a distinguished musical New Orleans family: his father was in the Onward Brass Band, one of the leading groups in the city at the end of the 19th century. The young Hall began working in various local groups and was with Buddy Petit for two years before trying his luck in Georgia and Florida. He moved to New York in 1928 and a year later was one of the star members of the Claude Hopkins orchestra, which kept him busy until 1935. Although he went briefly with Lucky Millinder, after this he worked exclusively in small groups, and he was a regular at Café Society and on Eddie Condon's Town Hall broadcasts. He turned down an offer from Duke Ellington to replace Barney Bigard and then went to Boston in 1946, before returning to the Condon circle. He was back in the limelight again in 1955 when he joined the Louis Armstrong All Stars, but the sameness of the shows bored him and he went freelance again in 1958. There were European tours ahead (including a memorable one with Chris Barber) and Ed Hall was an honoured guest in whatever situation he went to. Intensely dedicated to his instrumentalism,

he had a driving delivery with a pinched vibrato on the end of a line and a growling timbre when he really dug in. Although most of his work was in Dixieland situations, he felt just as comfortable in the small-group swing idiom, and his presence on the Vic Dickenson 'mainstream' sessions for Vanguard showed how warmly he could work in that style. Art Hodes remembered that 'When Ed came to a gig, he came to play. No attitude. No ego trip.' He died suddenly following a heart attack.

Hall's family turned out to be quite a dynasty. Five of his brothers played instruments: Edward Jr (1905–?) played tuba, although not professionally; Robert (1899–?) played clarinet and saxophones and played in New Orleans until retiring from music in 1941; Clarence (1903–69) was a saxophonist who played in traditional New Orleans groups and went on to be an R&B player with Dave Bartholomew in the 40s; and Herb (1907–96) was another fine clarinet player, who had a long career and played under many leaders, although his name was always rather in the shadow of his brother's eminence.
*Profoundly Blue* (Blue Note)

## Minor Hall
DRUMS
*born* 2 March 1897; *died* 16 October 1959

A spirited drummer in an old New Orleans style, Hall was at work in the city in the teens of the century but moved to Chicago in 1917 and never really went back. His most famous association was with Kid Ory: having played for him several times previously, he joined permanently in 1945 and stayed 11 years. A bit of a show-off, he nevertheless gave Ory's band a real kick in their Good Time Jazz sessions. His brother Tubby (1895–1946) was also a drummer.
*Kid Ory's Creole Jazz Band* (Good Time Jazz)

## Bengt Hallberg
PIANO
*born* 13 September 1932

The aristocrat of Swedish jazz. Hallberg's egalitarian approach admits almost every kind of music to his interpretation: he has recorded swing and bop, light and heavy

classical music, accordion albums, vocal works. He was involved in the Swedish dance-band scene from the late 40s and toured Scandinavia with Stan Getz and Lee Konitz when still in his teens. When he moved from his native Gothenburg to Stockholm in 1954, mainly to study composition, he was already the leading pianist in his country. As time passed, his cool, almost neutral early style became more assertively swinging, although he never surrendered the urbanity of his touch. But Swedish light and popular music took up much of his time from the later 50s, as composer and arranger, and though he made occasional records in a trio format there weren't too many. In the 70s and 80s he recorded much more regularly, principally for Phontastic, mixing solo and group work and often improvising on classical themes – or, indeed, on whatever he was asked. At a 'request' concert of solo piano in 1994, the first tune he picked out of a box of audience suggestions was the theme from *Dallas* (which he then imperturbably played). Now semi-retired, he can look back on a busy life in music, and one which in a certain way exemplifies one European attitude to jazz – not as an isolated art in itself, but as part of a broad sweep of popular musics, travelling through and among 20th-century audiences.
*Hallberg's Happiness* (Phontastic)

# Andy Hamilton
TENOR SAXOPHONE
*born* 26 March 1918

The Jamaica-born Hamilton worked in the US in the late 40s, mostly as a labourer, before moving to England in 1949 and settling in Birmingham. Although not really playing full-time until his old age, Hamilton has been a group leader ever since, with his West Indian Modernists (who never recorded) and Blue Notes being his principal bands. He has been a paterfamilias in Birmingham jazz circles for decades, holding workshops and advising younger players, and he finally made an album of his own in 1991, three years after being named Birmingham's jazz musician of the year (which took only 39 years to achieve). In his 80s, he is still playing regularly, and some of his sidemen should also be up for long-

service medals: pianist Sam Brown has been with him for more than 40 years.
*Silvershine* (World Circuit)

# Chico Hamilton
DRUMS
*born* 21 September 1921

The amazing Foreststorn Hamilton is probably the longest-serving drummer-bandleader of them all. He grew up in Los Angeles and was already playing with the likes of Dexter Gordon and Charles Mingus when in high school. After military service, he worked briefly with Jimmy Mundy and Count Basie before touring regularly with Lena Horne and doing studio work with Gerry Mulligan. By 1955, he was ready to lead groups of his own, but he chose to avoid the routine of a typical hard-bop formation and instead set up a five-piece of winds, cello, guitar, bass and drums. It found a ready audience in the later 50s, and Hamilton proved to have a sharp eye and ear for emerging talent: he brought in Jim Hall, Eric Dolphy, Paul Horn and Ron Carter among others. The group recorded one of the finest of all jazz film soundtracks, *The Sweet Smell Of Success* (1957), and the band's book was quietly progressive in its way. In the early 60s, Hamilton decided to change tack a little, and brought in brass to replace the cello, and elements of soul-jazz began to move in. He still toured regularly, and expanded to a septet in the later 60s, recording for Impulse!; but he also established an agency for composing jingles and advertising music. During the 70s he tried his hand at a more fusion-based approach, but latterly he has gone back to an acoustic setting, although guitars are these days a fixture in a Hamilton band. His own playing has sought no dramatic departures from the Jo Jones tradition he grew up with, but his solo record from 1993, *Dancing To A Different Drummer*, emphasizes the melodious tone he likes to try and get out of the kit, and the sheer good humour which lights up so many of his records and working groups is here too. Besides those names listed above, Charles Lloyd, Larry Coryell, Eric Person, Arthur Blythe, Arnie Lawrence, John Abercrombie and Gábor Szabó are all musicians who passed though the Hamilton academy at some point.
*The Dealer* (Impulse!)

# Jimmy Hamilton
CLARINET, TENOR SAXOPHONE
*born* 25 May 1917; *died* 20 September 1994

Hamilton started as a brass player, then switched to reeds and began working with Lucky Millinder and Teddy Wilson at the beginning of the 40s. But Duke Ellington hired him as Barney Bigard's replacement in 1943, which settled his career course, as he stayed until 1968. While he was featured primarily as a clarinettist, Hamilton sometimes turned to the tenor saxophone too, and it is his defining trait that the smooth, emollient style of his clarinet sound was partnered by a rough, blistered tone on the tenor. Ellington employed him with his usual deftness, disguising that Hamilton never had all that much to say on the clarinet beyond polite conversation. Away from Ellington he made five albums under his own leadership, and *It's About Time* (1961), for Prestige's Swingville imprint, is about the best of them. After leaving Duke he went to live in the Virgin Islands, and though he made occasional appearances in the US (featuring in John Carter's Clarinet Summit in 1983), he spent his final years there.
**Duke Ellington, *The Far East Suite*** (RCA)

# Scott Hamilton
TENOR SAXOPHONE
*born* 12 September 1954

Hamilton has one of the loveliest of tenor saxophone sounds – floating in between weightless and heavy, dark and light, he can drift through a line with such ardour that it can sweep the most sceptical listeners off their feet. There were numerous sceptics when he emerged on the American scene, working first in New England before going to New York in 1976, where he formed an alliance with Warren Vaché, played with some of the surviving swing masters (including Roy Eldridge and Benny Goodman) and established a rep as the coolest young fogey in the music. Scott sounded like a sleek composite of Zoot Sims and Ben Webster, talked like Jack Nicholson, and was generally lionized by an audience that felt modern jazz had somehow gone astray from timeless mainstream values. He signed a deal with Concord and he has recorded prolifically with them ever since, in practically every conceivable situation that could have suited him, as well as backing singers (Rosemary Clooney especially) and touring with various all-star Concord groups. Hamilton found himself especially welcome in England, which has become almost a second home for him, and his regular stints at the Pizza Express in London's Dean Street have surely qualified him for blue-plaque status there. Even if his style is derived from many illustrious forebears, he is easily identifiable as himself, and few saxophonists have conveyed the urgent art of improvisation with quite such easygoing charm. As he once told Francis Davis, 'I might incorporate the principles of another era, but we're improvisers. We're making it up as we go along, the way jazz musicians have always done.'
***Plays Ballads*** (Concord)

# Jan Hammer
ORGAN, KEYBOARDS
*born* 17 April 1948

Hammer's talents were largely wasted in jazz. He was born in Prague and played with Miroslav Vitous while still in his teens. Following the Russian invasion of Czechoslovakia in 1968 he settled in the US, and worked in and around Boston, eventually joining the Mahavishnu Orchestra in 1971 and playing a full battalion of electric keyboards. He then played with Billy Cobham's Spectrum, formed his own bands and drove much of the music during Jeff Beck's brief fusion period of the late 70s. But his hit music for the TV series *Miami Vice* in the 80s brought him so much attention and work for film and television that he more or less abandoned jazz. Hammer's music is often so heavily cloaked in electronic effect that the creativity in it is obscured, but he was an interesting keyboard thinker and his absenting himself from more demanding jazz territory is perhaps a pity. One of his best appearances on record is on John Abercrombie's *Timeless* (1974), where his playing is subtle and beguiling, although the jazz-rock thunder of the Mahavishnu music is probably more representative of what he wanted to do.
**Mahavishnu Orchestra, *Birds Of Fire*** (Columbia)

# John Hammond

PRODUCER AND IMPRESARIO
*born* 15 December 1910; *died* 10 July 1987

With his eternal crew-cut and Ivy League jackets, Hammond blew like a tornado through American music for decades. He was born rich with a private income and went to Yale, but was more fascinated by the culture of Harlem and spent much of his time campaigning in his own way for racial equality in the arts and elsewhere. He began producing record sessions in the early 30s, and among those whom he championed very early on were Billie Holiday, Count Basie and Benny Carter. He helped send Benny Goodman on his way (and introduced him to Charlie Christian). He set up the famous From Spirituals To Swing concerts at Carnegie Hall at the end of the 30s, and wrote with gusto about his many enthusiasms in the music press of the time. Although bebop didn't impress him, he helped establish the 50s mainstream idiom with the sessions he produced for Vanguard, and in the 60s he went on discovering new voices, having worked extensively at Columbia and other labels over the years: Bob Dylan, Aretha Franklin and Bruce Springsteen were among his later excitements. A generous man who loved his patrician role, Hammond sometimes seemed a difficult person to like, an easy one to admire.

# Johnny Hammond (Smith)

ORGAN
*born* 9 December 1931; *died* 4 June 1997

He started out as John Robert Smith, playing piano in Cleveland clubs, then became Johnny Hammond Smith after changing to the organ. By 1971 he was plain Johnny Hammond. In New York from 1958, he was soon signed up by Prestige as one of their rivals to Jimmy Smith, and he reeled off 22 albums for them through the 60s and early 70s (plus four for Riverside). Hammond had his own favourite devices, like every organist, and liked to build solos to a rollicking final chorus; across dozens of records, though, his style hardly evolved, and even with all those tries Prestige never got a bona

fide classic out of him. He made some sets for Kudu in the 70s which saw him trying out banks of synthesizers, but eventually the organ won him back and there were more records for Milestone to come. Like his surviving contemporaries, Hammond enjoyed some late limelight when the organ-jazz genre came back to prominence in the 90s.
*Black Coffee* (Prestige)

# Gunter Hampel

VIBES, BASS CLARINET, SAXOPHONES
*born* 31 August 1937

Hampel was born in Göttingen and studied architecture as well as music, before becoming intrigued by the first stirrings of free jazz in his country. He formed Birth Records at the end of the 60s to start documenting his own groups, which often included Perry Robinson and singer Jeanne Lee, whom he married. A 1969 session also included Anthony Braxton and Willem Breuker. He began his Galaxie Dream band in 1972, and the Birth catalogue filled up with studio and on-the-hoof live records; he has also made all-solo records where he plays vibes, flute and reed instruments. Hampel is something of a loner in his sphere: he has seldom appeared as a sideman (the 1989 Cecil Taylor concerts were an exception) and he has toured his music into rarely scouted territories such as Asia, South America and the Middle East. While he is an accomplished player on his various instruments, he tends to downplay virtuosity.
*Jubilation* (Birth)

# Lionel Hampton

VIBES, PIANO, DRUMS
*born* 20 April 1908; *died* 31 August 2002

Hampton's jazz was excitement, from first to last. He grew up in Birmingham and learned something about drumming from a nun at a Holiness church. He then moved to Chicago and studied drums and xylophone in a boys' band sponsored by the *Chicago Defender*. There were plenty of local groups who offered him a job, and eventually he went to Los Angeles with the Les Hite band, although he also worked and recorded there with Paul Howard. In 1929, he was with

Hite's band when it began backing Louis Armstrong, who encouraged him on vibes, as did the dancer Gladys Riddle, whom Hampton married. His career progressed only slowly, though he led groups of his own, but it wasn't until Benny Goodman sat in with him at the Paradise Café in Los Angeles that matters began to move quickly. Goodman featured him in his new trio and quartet, and RCA Victor began recording him in all-star small-group formats, where he engaged the cream of whichever band was in town to jam alongside him. These ebullient sessions are a snapshot of many of the great swing-era players in comparatively loose and amiable frameworks, although Hampton himself, whether playing vibes, singing, thundering away at the drums or snapping off two-fingered piano features, stands as tall as anyone.

In 1940, he finally formed a big band of his own, and it persisted in one form or another for the rest of his career. For most of its long history it was something of an academy, with such as Dexter Gordon, Charles Mingus, Illinois Jacquet, Dinah Washington, Betty Carter, Wes Montgomery, Quincy Jones, Art Farmer and Clifford Brown – to pick only names from the 40s and early 50s – all getting an early break in their careers. Hampton (and Gladys, who remained a notably fearsome example of the 'jazz wife' for the rest of their marriage) ran a tough, tight ship, which contrasted somewhat with the mayhem which the Hampton band could create on stage. The touring programme could last hours, with one hellraising feature after another, and riff tunes such as 'Hey Ba-Ba-Re-Bop' and the perennial 'Flying Home' dominated the band's book. In some ways it was a throwback almost to vaudeville, but the musicianship on hand took it to a higher level, and none tried harder than Hamp himself. Besides, it was also prescient of what lay ahead: 'Oh, Rock' was one prophetic title from the early 50s, and Hampton was never shy of adopting a dance craze such as 'The Hucklebuck'. His own playing set the standard for what the vibes could do, at least in the time prior to Milt Jackson's breakthrough, and his famous extended solo on 'Stardust' at a 1947 Gene Norman Just Jazz concert showed the extraordinary liberties he could take on a ballad feature – it became a favourite setpiece, though never a mere routine, as the surviving renditions are all different from each other.

Many have complained that Hampton's rabble-rousing approach had no musical rewards beyond the band's early life, but while he gave the people what they wanted, live recordings from the 60s and 70s show that both band and leader had plenty to say to more demanding jazz fans too. By this time, the band had become a dynasty, and reunions with old sidemen were also frequent. While he still worked with the big band, Hamp also established a 12-piece group, Jazz Inner Circle, and, in the 90s, a gang of old-timers named The Golden Men Of Jazz. He was close to Norman Granz for much of his recording career in the LP era, and made numerous albums with Oscar Peterson and others in the Granz elite, although he also enjoyed stints with Columbia and RCA. Away from the music, he was an activist on housing issues and used much of his own money in that direction; in addition, a staunch Republican, he campaigned for more than one presidential candidate. Honoured at the end of the century as one of the last great men of a vanished jazz era, but illness finally obliged him to leave playing behind.
*Stardust* (MCA)

## Slide Hampton
TROMBONE, ARRANGER
*born* 21 April 1932

Hampton grew up in a musical family in Indianapolis but first went to New York with Buddy Johnson's orchestra, in 1955, and he then worked with Dizzy Gillespie and Maynard Ferguson. His own octet became his main composing and performing vehicle in the 60s (four fine Atlantic albums are in need of reissue), and he also acted as MD for a big band which backed soul singers. He travelled to Europe with Woody Herman in 1968, and liked it enough to stay six years, leading a big band with Joe Haider. On his return to the US, he began leading a multi-trombone band, World Of Trombones, and was in the cooperative group called Continuum. By now among the most respected arranger-composers in his midstream field, he worked as MD for Gillespie's United Nation Orchestra from the late 80s, and carried on his alliance with the trumpeter until Dizzy's death; he is still a member of the Gillespie Reunion Orchestra, and the latest incarnation of his trombone band musters no fewer than 14 exponents of the horn. Slide is modest about his own abilities, always praising others' skills before his own, and complaining that 'my writing for saxophones is sad, man', but his thoughtfully assured work as composer, arranger and persuasive MD is about as accomplished as it gets. He always feels that trombonists are natural arrangers: 'They sit in the middle of the orchestra, and hear everything'.

**Somethin' Sanctified** (Atlantic)

# Herbie Hancock
KEYBOARDS
*born* 12 April 1940

Hancock studied piano from an early age, and was a classical prodigy in his home town of Chicago, playing Bach and Mozart on concert platforms when barely into his teens. At college he majored in electrical engineering (which would come in useful later) and composition, but when he went to New York in 1961 it was as a jazz player, with Donald Byrd's group: Blue Note's Alfred Lion was impressed enough by his playing on a Byrd album session to offer him his own date, and *Takin' Off* (1962) spawned an immediate jazz hit in the infernally catchy original 'Watermelon Man'. By 1963 Hancock was clearly hot property in New York, and Miles Davis enlisted him for his new quintet (at the 'audition' Davis asked Hancock to play a ballad: at its conclusion, he merely said, 'Nice touch'). His five years with Davis were Hancock's golden period of creativity. He fitted in handsomely with Davis's pre-electric music of this era, comping behind soloists with a glittering, literate ease (Hancock once suggested himself that he preferred to accompany rather than solo), interacting smartly with Ron Carter and Tony Williams, and lifting notes off the keyboard with a lustrous, rhapsodic tone which suggested his classical finesse imbued with a knowing sense of blues and bop grammar. While he contributed less to the Davis book than Wayne Shorter did, his own composing continued to blossom on his own-name recordings, for Blue Note and subsequently Warners: 'Maiden Voyage', 'Dolphin Dance'

and 'Speak Like A Child' sounded like instant standards, and Hancock has never again approached the casual mastery of this writing. *Empyrean Isles* (1964) and *Maiden Voyage* (1965) evoke a jazz-pastoral idiom which few others – Hancock included – have approached in quite the same way since. It is certainly the Hancock of this period which has been such a powerful influence on modern jazz piano. He wrote the score for *Blow Up* (1966), although his subsequent adventures in soundtrack music, including the awful *Death Wish*, were less distinguished.

Affected by the winds of change Davis was manipulating, Hancock also sought the fresh fields of electric music at the end of the decade. His sextet music of 1969–71 was lively, often juicily 'ethnic' long before that flavour became fashionable, and bolstered by the grand jazz chops of such sidemen as Johnny Coles and Joe Henderson; but Hancock's own piano was being steadily supplanted by synths and clavinets and the like, and by the time of *Headhunters* (1973) the leader had gone over to jazz-funk, which was at least a variation on the jazz-rock most of the competition were trying. That record and band became a benchmark in his career, and it was one he spent the rest of the decade trying to duplicate, with decreasing returns. By the early 80s he was going pop with a shameless enthusiasm, typified by the baby-soft *Lite Me Up* (1982), yet at the same time he was hedging his bets by playing acoustic, straight-ahead gigs and recording with Chick Corea, Wynton Marsalis and the VSOP supergroup. His hit single 'Rockit' (1983) was seen as revolutionary by some, although now it sounds more like an instrumental novelty: either way, it was his last appearance in the pop charts. Since then, Hancock has chased success on several fronts. He still plays in nostalgic line-ups such as the 1992 Tribute To Miles band, and in an occasional (acoustic) duo with Wayne Shorter. His *The New Standard* (1995) put up an all-star group to tackle a bunch of rock tunes by the likes of Peter Gabriel and Don Henley: his record company's idea, it lasted one album and one tour. A re-formed Headhunters project worked out much the same two years later. Hancock holds on to a huge following among a certain part of the jazz audience: the Us3 hit 'remix' 'Cantaloop' (based on 'Canteloupe Island' from *Empyrean Isles*) kept him current among listeners who still think Miles Davis and his various sidemen were the only people who mattered in modern jazz. But there is relatively little among the ponderous and jumbled discography of the past 25 years which really stands up to much scrutiny. A shrewd man with an enormous ego, in his middle 60s Hancock seems to be casting around for something useful to play, although his eminence is surely pretty safe.

*Maiden Voyage* (Blue Note)

## Captain John Handy

ALTO SAXOPHONE, CLARINET
*born* 24 June 1900; *died* 12 January 1971

He played guitar and mandolin with father John Senior and brothers Julius and Sylvester in a family band, before taking up clarinet and moving to New Orleans in 1918. Although busy in the city's music from then on, he didn't record until very late into the revivalist era and it wasn't until the Preservation Hall period of the 60s that he really asserted himself as a leader and personality (the 'Captain' came from his way of letting everone know what he wanted at a rehearsal). But he recorded and performed busily for the last decade of his life, with most of the leading players of the scene. By this time the alto saxophone had long since become his main instrument, and he played it with an iron tone and a broad vibrato, his style even pointing towards the manner of the major R&B saxophonists.

*Capt. John Handy & His New Orleans Stompers Vol 1* (GHB)

## Craig Handy

TENOR AND SOPRANO SAXOPHONES
*born* 25 September 1962

Handy is a can-do player whose full-bodied sound can fit into most American styles. He grew up in California and played in schoolmate Peter Apfelbaum's Hieroglyphics Ensemble, but in the 90s he did most of his work on the East Coast, with such leaders as Steve Coleman, Geri Allen, Betty Carter and Herbie Hancock. He has a more modest track record as a leader, with a few discs to his credit, but on the evidence of those band-

leading isn't really his forte: he's more a front-line ingredient who can peel off strong-hearted solos to order.

**New York Connexion, *Along Came Jones*** (Sirocco)

## John Handy

ALTO SAXOPHONE
*born* 3 February 1933

Although often confused with the older New Orleans musician, John Handy was very much his own man. He started on clarinet in his native Dallas, but moved to California and picked up the alto sax, working mostly on the blues circuit. He moved to New York in 1958, where he played on *Mingus Ah Um*. He was leading his own band in 1965, which made the celebrated set caught on *Live At The Monterey Jazz Festival* (Columbia, 1965): with a sound as tough and forthright as Charlie Parker's, with a blazing high register, these were his peak years. Although it would be unfair to say his career fell away, he didn't really create much out of changing times. A saxophone concerto, which he had long worked on, was performed but not recorded, a band with Indian musicians might have been a bit ahead of its time, but his later John Handy's Dreamland, similarly cast, seemed to have little to say. He had a great dance hit in 1976 with 'Hard Work', but it was a one-off, and much of his time since has been spent in education. Considering the best work under his own name and with Mingus, it's been an often disappointing career.

*Live At The Monterey Jazz Festival* (Columbia)

## W C Handy

COMPOSER, CORNET
*born* 16 November 1873; *died* 28 March 1958

'The Father Of The Blues' was born before anyone else in jazz. He began playing in minstrel shows at the end of the 19th century, and then toured with his own groups, into the teens of the new era. Handy was fortunate in receiving musical tuition when young, since he was able to formalize and copyright scraps of tune and fragments of what would become primal blues and jazz themes, many of which he may have simply heard somewhere rather than composing them himself. Either way, it meant that such bedrock material as 'St Louis Blues', 'Memphis Blues' and 'Beale Street Blues' are all credited to him. The sessions he made with his Memphis Orchestra in 1917 – ten issued titles for Columbia – are rather disappointing, with no jazz and not that much ragtime in them, cast as they are more in the novelty-military band style of the time. He founded a publishing company which made his fortune, and thereafter worked less as a performer, although he toured occasionally and cut an all-star recording date in 1939. By the 50s he had lost his sight, but he still attended functions and concerts in his honour.

## Jake Hanna
DRUMS
*born* 4 April 1931

Hanna worked mostly in the Boston area during the 50s and early 60s, having had his first gig at 14 (prior to military service). He spent two years with Marian McPartland and a further two with Woody Herman, but then won a stable gig on the Merv Griffin TV show, which lasted ten years and caused him to settle in Los Angeles. Since then he has worked in every kind of mainstream situation, and was for many years effectively the house drummer at Concord, appearing on dozens of their small-group dates and leading a handful of discs of his own. Born too late to be a swing-era man, he nevertheless styled himself more on the master drummers of that period than on the bop school.
**Al Cohn,** *Nonpareil* (Concord)

## Sir Roland Hanna
PIANO
*born* 10 February 1932; *died* 13 November 2002

Part of the unimpeachable group of Detroit bebop pianists, Roland Hanna worked quietly in heavy company: in the 50s he was with Thad Jones, Benny Goodman and Coleman Hawkins, and from there he passed into the even more demanding company of Charles Mingus and Sarah Vaughan. He was less often visible in the later 60s, but that was because he was touring in Africa, particularly Liberia, and as a result of that the

Liberian government made him Sir Roland Hanna. He never left behind his association with Thad Jones, and he was with the Jones–Lewis Orchestra between 1968 and 1974. He later created the New York Jazz Quartet, and was involved with Mingus Dynasty and the Mingus *Epitaph* Orchestra.
**Live At Maybeck Recital Hall** (Concord)

## Hard bop

Hard bop was the settling-down of bebop. By the early 50s, when the jangled nerves of original bebop had been calmed, the music slowed a little, became harmonically darker, bluesier and collectively more trenchant. Instead of soloists flying every which way, performances took on a chunkier feel, the pieces more specifically interlocking. It was timed with the emergence of the long-playing record format, and individual pieces ran for longer, and were less like a race to the end of the record. Rhythm sections became more like engine rooms. The raw material of hard bop was perhaps best exemplified in the compositions of Horace Silver, whose music sounded funky and bluesy, and was shot through with a sanctified feel that had the flavour of gospel music, although none of its piety. Major hard-bop groups such as Art Blakey's Jazz Messengers, the Cannonball Adderley Quintet and The Jazztet each worked their variations on the formula, and labels such as Blue Note and Prestige catalogued the movement. While hard bop lasted through the 50s and well into the 60s, it eventually turned into soul-jazz, and the more open-ended term 'post-bop' has more currency now.

## Wilbur Harden
FLUGELHORN
*born* 31 December 1924; *died* June 1969

Harden was from the South, and started out in R&B bands before going to Detroit in the mid-50s. His jazz career was telescoped into a period which lasted less than three years. He began playing with Yusef Lateef in 1957, and the following year made four sessions for Savoy, three of which had John Coltrane as a sideman: the saxophonist's presence advertised their existence, and they were subsequently reissued under his name, even

though Harden's playing has considerable flair and elegance of its own. He took the then-rare step of playing flugelhorn rather than trumpet, and the resulting music is an interesting variation on the timbres of Coltrane's work with Miles Davis. But illness interrupted his career only a year later, and he seems to have never recorded again.
**Tangyanika Strut** (Savoy)

## Bill Hardman
TRUMPET
*born* 6 April 1933; *died* 5 December 1990

Hardman is remembered as a resilient hard-bop footsoldier, but at his best he was considerably more. He was first inspired by Louis Armstrong, and was only later won over by bebop. He made his first appearances on record as *Jackie's Pal* (1956), as a protégé of Jackie McLean, but within a couple of years he had also played with Charles Mingus, Art Blakey and Horace Silver. His style was couched in familiar boppish language, but he had an expressive side which went back to Armstrong and Roy Eldridge, and though he was nearly always recorded as a sideman, he made his mark on a band without fuss or excessive pointing. He led a band called Brass Company in the early 70s, which attempted to re-create the Miles Davis–Gil Evans collaborations, without much success. In the 80s, his old friend Junior Cook became a partner in a good late hard-bop band, and Hardman made a few albums of his own for Muse; but nothing brought him much more than routine respect. He decided to move to Paris in 1988 and died there two years later.
**Art Blakey, Art Blakey's Jazz Messengers With Thelonious Monk** (Atlantic)

## Otto Hardwick
ALTO SAXOPHONE
*born* 31 May 1904; *died* 5 August 1970

Hardwick was an early confidant of Duke Ellington, with whom he played on and off until 1928, and if Johnny Hodges hadn't come along he might be better remembered than he is. He went to Europe in 1928 and played with Noble Sissle, but was bandleading back in New York two years later. Eventually, he went back to the Ellington

fold, and this time stayed until 1946, when he decided to get out of music altogether. He liked bestowing nicknames: 'Swee' Pea' (Billy Strayhorn) and 'Little Jazz' (Roy Eldridge) were two of them. He also doubled on clarinet, violin and bass sax, and despite his exotic first name he was mostly called 'Toby'.
**Duke Ellington, 1925–26** (Classics)

## Roy Hargrove
TRUMPET
*born* 16 October 1969

Hargrove was a precocious starter: Wynton Marsalis heard him when visiting Dallas in the 80s, and he went to Europe with Frank Morgan at 17. He began making records under his own name for RCA in 1989, and subsequently shifted to Verve, touring meanwhile with small groups. He has tried his hand at string and Latin projects, formed an 11-piece band named Crisol, and has lately tackled the hip-hop idiom with a new band, The RH Factor, although he stops short at electronic manipulation of the trumpet. As a player, Hargrove has a golden sound and is as mercurial on the horn as any of his peers. His difficulty seems to be in doing something which really stands out as exceptional: after a dozen albums, some of which dwell in the faddish domain of record-company concepts, there has been no sign of a masterpiece, and in his mid-30s Roy is starting to look like a journeyman.
**With The Tenors Of Our Time** (Verve)

## Harlem Hamfats
GROUP

The Harlem Hamfats were a unique mix of styles and personalities. Formed in 1936, they recorded dozens of titles for Decca, and were great jukebox favourites in the later 30s. Joe and Charlie McCoy played guitar and mandolin, an injection of Mississippi blues; Herb Morand, the trumpeter, came out of New Orleans; and Odell Rand was a lawless, exuberant clarinettist. Morand and Joe McCoy also sang, and the material included knockabout numbers such as 'Let's Get Drunk And Truck' and 'The Garbage Man'. Their blending of blues and barrelhouse jazz pointed the way towards

Louis Jordan and the R&B groups of the 40s, although the Hamfats broke up in 1939.
**The Harlem Hamfats** (Document)

# Rufus Harley
BAGPIPES
*born* 20 May 1936

Harley was a high-school saxophonist, but it was hearing the Scottish pipers at John F Kennedy's funeral which sent him towards the least likely of jazz instruments. He formed a group and impressed Atlantic Records sufficiently for them to have him make four albums in the late 60s. His best-known appearance, though, was on a Sonny Rollins tour of Europe in 1974, which vastly entertained his audiences. Though seen less often in recent years, he was still performing into the 90s. The sometimes wayward pitching of the pipes at least allowed him to entertain blues tonalities, and his album covers, with Rufus decked out in full Highland regalia, are collectors' pieces.
**Scotch And Soul** (Atlantic)

# Harmolodics

Ornette Coleman coined this term as a broad description of his music from the 70s onwards. As a musical principle, it seems to consist of the idea of instrumentalists convening to play a single melodic line, regardless of the varying pitches and tonalities each player is contributing. Coleman has the capacity to expand on this at great length, but his explanations have been so idiosyncratic that nobody – including the musicians who have worked alongside him – seems to really understand the theory. There is a suspicion that Ornette doesn't, either.

# Billy Harper
TENOR SAXOPHONE
*born* 17 January 1943

A power player in the tradition of Sonny Rollins and George Coleman, Harper is a steadfast improviser whose music has been little heard in recent years. He arrived in New York in 1966, and worked with Art Blakey, Max Roach, Lee Morgan and the Jones–Lewis Orchestra, as well as starting an association with Gil Evans: he was one of the star soloists in the Evans orchestras of the earlier 70s, but eventually decided that too much fusion was creeping in, and abandoned the gig. In the 80s he concentrated on leading his own quintet, which became a stable band including Francesca Tanksley and Eddie Henderson, playing Harper material which offered a convincing thesis on post-Coltrane improvising and small-group work. But it was never a fashionable group, and Harper found more work in Japan than in New York: the quintet has made only a handful of records in 20 years.
**If Our Hearts Could Only See** (DIW)

# Philip Harper
TRUMPET
*born* 10 May 1965

# Winard Harper
DRUMS
*born* 4 June 1962

The Harper Brothers, as their family band was styled, came out of Atlanta as teenagers, and won attention as part of the young lions wave of the 80s when they formed their group in 1985. It lasted seven years and made some inventive records for Verve in a post-bop style, although the attention on them didn't lead anywhere much. Since then, Winard has largely been the more successful of the two, in demand as a freelance and making records of his own as a leader. Philip is a capable if not especially individual trumpeter.
**Artistry** (Verve)

# Tom Harrell
TRUMPET
*born* 16 June 1946

Harrell grew up in San Francisco and did big-band work before joining Horace Silver in 1973, staying four years. He then freelanced and did session-work before joining Phil Woods's group in 1983, staying until 1989, during which time his playing became widely known and admired. Harrell's great skill is in synthesizing many of the major trumpet voices of the past few generations into a manner which balances fire and restraint to an alchemical nicety. His playing

can work to a timetable of almost impassive logic, one impeccable phrase following another, yet he has the kind of rapt lyricism which makes him close kin to a player such as Kenny Wheeler – and, like Wheeler, he is a composer of often inspirational effectiveness. The Woods group toughened and extended his range, and ever since he has freelanced with many captains. His own career as a leader has matured only slowly: major labels fought a little shy of him for a long time, since he suffers from a form of schizophrenia which has him on constant medication, and there was an unspoken worry among several companies that he would be a difficult figure to market and promote. But he did eventually sign with RCA in 1996, and has steadily created a strong body of own-name work.
*Labyrinth* (RCA)

## Joe Harriott
ALTO SAXOPHONE
*born* 15 July 1928; *died* 2 January 1973

In recent years, Harriott has been presented almost as a jazz martyr, which both obscures and complicates his surviving music. He was born in Kingston, Jamaica, and grew up in an orphanage, before playing in local dance bands. In 1951 he moved to Britain and played on the London scene: Tony Kinsey, Ronnie Scott and Tony Crombie were among the leaders he worked for, but his health was affected by tuberculosis. In 1959, though, after coming out of hospital, his music took an abrupt sideways shift: having all but perfected a Parkerian bebop vocabulary, he devised a kind of jazz where abstraction and free form overtook the rules of bop discipline, a striking parallel to Ornette Coleman's contemporaneous work in the US. Unlike Coleman, Harriott worked with a piano (Pat Smythe), and his music depended less on solo improvisation and more on the constant interaction of ensemble lines, incorporating silences and unusual shapes (hence his preference for 'abstract' over 'free' as a description). Shake Keane, Coleridge Goode and Harriott were all Jamaican immigrants, and they introduced a further Caribbean element to the group, which otherwise had a strangely European feel, very different to anything going on in American jazz. Their brief

sequence of records, though, attracted only modest public attention: one of them, *Abstract* (1962), was issued in America, but the rest quickly became collectors' pieces and remained unavailable for decades, only finally reissued (on the author's initiative) in the 90s. By the time of *Movement* (1963), Harriott was already scaling back, since the record mixed his more challenging music with simpler, blues-based pieces. The Harriott quintet eventually dispersed, and Harriott took what work he could (he had sometimes appeared as a guest soloist with Chris Barber's band). In 1966, he began working with the Indian violinist John Mayer on a project which eventually released the two records of *Indo-Jazz Fusions*, although this was much more Mayer's concept than Harriott's. By the turn of the decade, like fellow saxophonist Tubby Hayes, Harriott struggled to find an audience, and his last years were spent going out as a solo with local rhythm sections. One writer remembers seeing him in these years, and wondering that Joe seemed to spend more time playing on the pub fruit machine than attending to his music. His legacy on record sounds curiously landlocked, a fusion before its time, yet one which, for all its dramatic implications, sounds private and belonging only to its rather lonely creator. Harriott died of cancer.
*Abstract* (Redial)

## Barry Harris
PIANO
*born* 15 December 1929

The grandmaster of bebop piano and one of the great teachers in the music. Harris was a leading player in the strong Detroit circle of jazz musicians in the early 50s, and he was busy enough there to resist the temptation to move to New York – until the end of the decade, when he joined Cannonball Adderley's group for a brief spell and then settled in New York. He made five outstanding albums for Riverside early in the 60s, and three more for Prestige later in the decade, which showcased his huge authority on bebop material: the prevailing soul-jazz movement had no impact on his playing, and *Magnificent!* (1969) is a textbook exercise in the timeless qualities of bop as a creative idiom. Coleman Hawkins favoured

Harris as one of his last piano players (and told him, 'I don't play chords, I play movements'), and Harris helped care for Hawkins during his final illness. In the later 70s, the pianist went to live with Thelonious Monk in the Baroness de Koenigswarter's home, and remained there after both passed away. Though he dislikes travel, he has toured widely, and became known as one of the premier teachers in the music: he opened the Jazz Cultural Center in New York in the 80s, and students have always spoken of his teaching methods in the warmest terms. He came back after suffering a stroke in the early 90s, and is still playing handsomely: 'I'm a bebopper. I believe strictly in Diz and Bird, I don't think the music has gone any further.'

***Magnificent!*** (Prestige/OJC)

## Beaver Harris
DRUMS
*born* 20 April 1936; *died* 22 December 1991

Harris grew up in Pittsburgh and in his teens played baseball professionally, but after military service he played drums and went to New York in 1962. Although he wasn't really a free drummer in any sense, he fell in with the New Thing school of players, including Albert Ayler, Marion Brown, and especially Archie Shepp, whom he regularly played behind. In 1968 he formed 360 Degree Music Experience, initially with Dave Burrell and Grachan Moncur III, and that band became his major vehicle for most of the rest of his career, although he also freelanced with other players and often reunited with Shepp. Harris was really a swing drummer, disguised by his context, and at his best he could rationalize even the most out players. Latterly, though, his playing became more erratic and in the end 360 Degree Music Experience took on a shambolic edge.

**Archie Shepp,** *U-jaama* (Uniteledis)

## Bill Harris
TROMBONE
*born* 28 October 1916; *died* 21 August 1973

It is hard to think of a more ingenious, funny or capable trombonist than Bill Harris. Born in Philadelphia, he played

locally in a semi-professional capacity before eventually travelling to New York and joining Benny Goodman in 1943: although only briefly with Goodman, he was featured regularly enough to acquire a strong reputation. His most renowned association was with Woody Herman: in four separate stints with Herman's orchestra, the last in 1959, he set down numerous quick-witted solos, and although it's rare that a trombonist is the one who makes you sit up and listen, this was always the case when Harris went out front on a Herman record. Norman Granz put him into various Jazz At The Philharmonic situations (his long solo on 'Stompin' At The Savoy' from *Jam Session #6*, 1954, shows how many fresh paragraphs he could get out of such a hackneyed script) and he led some groups of his own, but there were unfortunately few opportunities for him to lead his own groups on record, and eventually he followed his friend Flip Phillips to Florida, where he largely remained. Harris is one of the few soloists who seems both spontaneous and entirely in control of where he's going: he liked to stroll through a sweet, lyrical passage and then upend it with a sudden blast, and he could undercut sentimental performances or play gently in the face of surrounding thunder. While admirers will point to a collected Herman edition as the best of Harris, the disc cited, one of his disgracefully few leadership dates, is terrific.

***Bill Harris And Friends*** (Fantasy/OJC)

## Craig Harris
TROMBONE
*born* 10 September 1953

Harris studied theory at college with Ken McIntyre, and played with Sun Ra in the late 70s. In the 80s he was in the thick of New York's new jazz, doing sideman work with David Murray, Lester Bowie and others, and leading his own groups: Tailgater's Tales was perhaps the principal one, with a multiple brass line-up, although it eventually slimmed down to a more conventional quartet. He also played in Slideride with Ray Anderson, Gary Valente and George Lewis. Some of his records have been muddled affairs, made for the JMT label, and his big-bodied and muscular playing is probably best heard with David Murray, who has a knack for getting the best out of Harris.

**David Murray,** *Picasso* (DIW)

# Eddie Harris

TENOR SAXOPHONE, KEYBOARDS, REED TRUMPET

*born* 20 October 1936; *died* 5 November 1996

An extraordinary musician. His roots were in Chicagoan gospel music and he played vibes and tenor sax at school before touring Europe in army bands. In 1960, back home in Chicago, he recorded a version of the theme from the film *Exodus* for Vee-Jay, and it became a million-seller. Vee-Jay then put him to work on other filmscore music (*Jazz For Breakfast At Tiffany's*, *Eddie Harris Goes To The Movies*), but none of these really clicked and in 1966 Harris signed to Atlantic. At around this time he began experimenting with electric saxophone, switched back and forth between rock and jazz rhythms for accompaniment, and between 1966 and 1973 managed to record some 20 albums for his label. His barnstorming set at Montreux in 1969 with the Les McCann group threw out another hit in 'Compared To What', and began a partnership with McCann which was occasionally reconvened almost up until the saxophonist's death. He was a favourite at the Newport Festivals, and liked to startle audiences with some new piece of bravado: one innovation was playing both trumpet and trombone with reed mouthpieces (and then playing the saxophone with a brass equivalent). The electric sax was his most successful idea, reaching full expression on such albums as *Excursions* (1973) and *Is It In* (1974), but it wasn't a development that found favour elsewhere (only Ian Underwood of The Mothers Of Invention adopted the idea at length) and in the end Harris reverted to an acoustic horn. In 1973 he made an album with Jeff Beck and Steve Winwood, *E.H. In The U.K.*, but that too was a one-off. Nay-sayers had been complaining about Harris ever since *Exodus* and he got some of his own back in the self-penned 'Eddie Who?', which actually became a great favourite with his audiences. Many musicians, though, revered him, and his compositions began to be more widely played – although 'Freedom Jazz Dance', the most successful, had been popular since the

60s. He was still working on the club circuit when he became ill in 1996. The final irony is that although Harris spent much of his time artificially altering his tone, his 'pure' tenor sound – hollowed out and oddly speech-like – was absolutely unmistakeable.

*Exodus To Jazz* (Vee-Jay)

# Gene Harris

PIANO

*born* 1 September 1933; *died* 16 January 2000

Harris taught himself piano and as a GI he played in army bands during the early 50s. In 1956 he formed The Three Sounds, with Andy Simpkins and Bill Dowdy: their simple, straight-ahead interpretations of standards and blues became very popular, and the group recorded a long sequence of albums for Blue Note which were among the label's most commercially successful. It was a formula which seemed foolproof, but after Dowdy and Simpkins left, Harris stumbled into a feeble backwater of fusion, which his final Blue Note albums document with unfortunate clarity. In the 80s he returned to acoustic trio music, and reasserted his eminence as one of the leading artists at Concord Records; he also toured with the Philip Morris Superband, as leader and fea-tured soloist, to considerable success. Harris's communicative music never lost its appeal and he was a great favourite with audiences up until his death: a natural show-man, one of his favourite remarks to an audi-ence was 'If you leave here with a smile on your face tonight, remember that Gene Harris put it there.'

**The Three Sounds,** *Introducing The Three Sounds* (Blue Note)

# Little Benny Harris

TRUMPET

*born* 23 April 1919; *died* 11 February 1975

Harris was a key witness in phase one of the bebop story. He was part of the jam-session circle which helped brew up the first stir-rings of the music in New York, and he came up with some of the early bebop themes, taking a hand in Parker's 'Ornithology' as well as 'Reets And I' and 'Little Benny Leaps' (aka 'Bud's Bubble'). He was a regular on 52nd Street and played in numerous groups during the 40s, but he drifted away from the music and by the middle 50s he had moved to the West Coast. Harris is usually dismissed as a minor figure, but that is a little unfair: his recorded solos suggest a perfectly capable player, although one inevitably in the giant shadow of Gillespie, Navarro and the other masters.

## Stefon Harris
VIBES
*born* 23 March 1973

The vibraphone hasn't attracted many recent converts, and of those Stefon Harris is, along with Matthias Stahl, the most exciting. He studied classical percussion at the Eastman School before being inspired – by a Charlie Parker record – to go towards jazz, and by the middle 90s he was working with such leaders as Max Roach and Bobby Watson. Blue Note took an interest in his work and he played with their New Directions group with young paterfamilias Greg Osby, before starting to make records of his own for the label. Although an unequivocally modern player, Harris's primary influence is Milt Jackson. His records thus far have been a mix of high-octane virtuosity and a sometimes rather ponderous approach to ensemble composition, but when he gets clear space to improvise he is a sparkling, sometimes ecstatic player.
**Black Action Figure** (Blue Note)

## Donald Harrison
ALTO AND SOPRANO SAXOPHONES
*born* 23 June 1960

A New Orleans man as well as a Berklee graduate, Harrison was in one of the last Jazz Messengers front lines with Terence Blanchard, and they went on to play together in a quintet which recorded for Columbia and Concord. Since then he has searched to find a niche for himself, with mixed success. He has played with Eddie Palmieri and Roy Haynes, and has divided his time between New York and New Orleans. His hometown roots often break through in his music: his father, 'Big Chief' Donald Harrison, performed regularly with the Guardians Of The Flame Indian tribe at the city's Mardi Gras, and in *Indian Blues* (1991) the saxophonist specifically explored his family connections. Two later albums for Impulse! had some excellent music, but Harrison's difficulty is that he is one of many admirable players entering middle age with no particular brief.
**Nouveau Swing** (Impulse!)

## Jimmy Harrison
TROMBONE
*born* 17 October 1900; *died* 23 July 1931

Harrison toured in minstrel shows and moved to New York in 1922. He worked briefly with Duke Ellington, but he found his niche when he joined Fletcher Henderson in 1927: for three years he was one of Henderson's brightest stars, a soloist of power, flexibility and maturity, who duplicated the kind of impact Jack Teagarden was having on the white bands he played in. He and Teagarden became fast friends, and the image of these two outgoing men as the easygoing kings of their instrument is irresistible. It is fascinating but pointless to conjecture where Harrison's skills might have taken him: he was operated on for stomach cancer in 1930, and never really recovered.
**Fletcher Henderson, *1927–1928*** (Classics)

## Max Harrison
WRITER

The most insightful and penetrating of all the English writers on jazz, Harrison's work is unfortunately rather scattered and not easily accessed, although his contributions to the two volumes of *Essential Jazz Records* crystallize much of his thinking. He has done long service as a critic of both classical and jazz music, and there is no other writer in the field who has had so much to say on both disciplines, starting in the middle 50s. After completing his contributions to *Essential Jazz Records*, though, he decided to step down from further jazz commentary and concentrate on his classical work.

## Antonio Hart

ALTO SAXOPHONE
*born* 30 September 1968

Hart came to prominence in the group of another young voice, Roy Hargrove, staying with him for some five years from 1988. That won him his own engagement with the RCA Novus label, and his records there reveal a confident if rather shallow stylist, easily in command of a post-bop vocabulary but not seeming to have much to say with it. After he began leading his own groups he seemed to grow into his role, and the later *Here I Stand* (Impulse!, 1997) has a good deal more power in it. Like so many others, though, Hart has found himself one of a crowd of talented players, at a moment when modern instrumentalists are not much in demand.
*Here I Stand* (Impulse!)

## Billy Hart

DRUMS
*born* 29 November 1940

Hart is a hugely prolific musician, playing on hundreds of albums and with every kind of contemporary jazz player. He was neighbours with Buck Hill in Washington DC and began playing with him; later he worked with Shirley Horn, then Jimmy Smith, before touring with Wes Montgomery. In 1968 he moved to New York, and expanded his associations to take in fusion (with Herbie Hancock, in the early 70s), the modal mainstream (McCoy Tyner) and the grand manner (Stan Getz). Hart seems like the most open-minded of drummers: he is content with playing straight time as efficiently as possible, but he likes the more impressionistic end of the spectrum just as much. Busy as he is as a sideman, he has led only a handful of records, although on reputation alone he counts as one of the senior figures in jazz drumming.
*Oceans Of Time* (Arabesque)

## Clyde Hart

PIANO
*born* January 1910; *died* 19 March 1945

Hart died young from tuberculosis, which halted an interesting progress. He started with big bands and played on numerous small-group sessions in the later 30s; then he found himself involved in some of the early bebop record dates, cutting 'Red Cross' with Tiny Grimes and Charlie Parker, and 'Groovin' High' with Dizzy Gillespie. His playing there suggested that he was ready to tackle the new idiom on its own terms. In addition, his earlier work shows a literate and unclichéd mind at work.
**Dizzy Gillespie, *1945*** (Classics)

## Johnny Hartman

VOCAL
*born* 13 July 1923; *died* 15 September 1983

Hartman came out of Chicago and turned up on a few ballad solos in the late bebop era, with Dizzy Gillespie in particular. He was a baritone much in the Eckstine mould, savouring the words and rolling them around in his mouth, although he had a less voluptuous tone than Mr B. Thereafter he worked as a club singer, and his great moment came in 1963 when Bob Thiele engaged him to sing on a ballad album with John Coltrane. Despite the unlikeliness of the alliance, it turned out very well, and figures as a pleasing interlude in Coltrane's otherwise tumultuous discography of the period. He continued working until his death.
**John Coltrane And Johnny Hartman** (Impulse!)

## Michael Hashim

ALTO AND SOPRANO SAXOPHONES
*born* 9 April 1956

Hashim came to attention when he joined the Widespread Depression Jazz Orchestra in 1976, an early example of the jazz-repertory band which he eventually took over. He went to New York with that band and subsequently led small groups of his own, although he also took every chance to learn from such seniors as Roy Eldridge and Jimmy Rowles. Hashim has a bumptious, intense approach to jazz repertory: his records for Stash and Hep have found him setting himself unusual challenges, putting Fats Waller into a determinedly contemporary idiom, and making Strayhorn and Kurt Weill material into powerful sources.
**Keep A Song In Your Soul** (Hep)

# George Haslam
BARITONE SAXOPHONE
*born* 22 February 1939

Born in Preston, Haslam started in part-time mainstream bands, maintaining a day gig as a mechanical engineer. But free music came to fascinate him, and in the 80s he turned wholeheartedly to that style. He founded his own SLAM label, which has grown to approaching 100 releases, documenting his own work and that of Mal Waldron, Steve Lacy, Howard Riley and many others. He is also an inveterate traveller, believing that every connection made leads to some useful next step along the road, and he has visited and played in Argentina, Cuba, Hong Kong and Eastern Europe. His baritone playing initially sounded more enthusiastic than accomplished, but he has grown into an improviser of considerable stature himself, and also likes the taragato.
**With Mal Waldron,** *Waldron–Haslam* (SLAM)

# Stan Hasselgård
CLARINET
*born* 4 October 1922; *died* 23 November 1948

Hasselgård's brief career had hardly started before it was over. As a young man he played in amateur groups in Uppsala in Sweden, and he then worked professionally with Arthur Österwall and Simon Brehm before going to New York early in 1947. He got himself involved in the music scene and then shifted over to Los Angeles, where he befriended Barney Kessel and Red Norvo: they all worked together on a four-title date for Capitol, which was one of his few legitimate studio sessions. Benny Goodman heard him at a club and, struggling with a bebop idiom which Hasselgård seemed comfortable in, the older man seemed to take the Swede on as a protégé. But Goodman suddenly disbanded the group which featured Hasselgård, and the latter then played in a new small group which had Max Roach on drums. He was killed in a car accident when en route to California once more. There is very little of Hasselgård's playing left: he was in America during the period of one of the 40s recording bans, and much of what he did there exists only as air-shots. But what survives suggests that he

was very close to establishing a style for bebop on the clarinet.
*At Click 1948* (Dragon)

# hat Hut
RECORD COMPANY

In 1974, Werner Uehlinger founded the curiously named hat Hut after a character in the paintings of Klaus Baumgärtner. Based in Switzerland (and for much of its life sponsored by Swiss banking interests), the label was at first dedicated to the work of saxophonist Joe McPhee, but soon other musicians came into the fold, notably Steve Lacy, the Vienna Art Orchestra, and numerous little-known figures from both the European and the American avant-garde. In the 80s the label began to mutate, and established different series under different names: hat Musics, hat ART and eventually hatOLOGY as its main title. While McPhee remains one of its stalwarts, it has expanded into several categories, including contemporary composition as well as more familiar strands of modern jazz (represented by the likes of Lee Konitz and Ran Blake). More than most labels, though, Uehlinger's catalogue is capital-A art music. These days he issues releases as limited editions of a few thousand, which the sleeves baldly admit. As a catalogue of adventurous new music, it must be accounted one of the premier entries.

# Dick Hawdon
TRUMPET
*born* 27 August 1927

Born in Leeds, where he still lives, Dick Hawdon started out in the Yorkshire Jazz Band, recording tracks for Tempo, before moving to London at the start of the 50s. He was skilled and open-eared enough to expand his traditional approach and play both in that style and with the modern outlook of Tubby Hayes and Don Rendell (and Jimmy Deuchar – 'Jimmy taught me everything I knew'). By the time he had spent five years as one of the leading players in the John Dankworth Orchestra, Hawdon seemed ready to take on a starring role as a British modernist, but 'it was getting silly, there were no gigs', and he chose instead to join

Terry Lightfoot in 1962, for the regular work. He also did studio and variety work in the 60s, and became a regular at the swish London nightspot The Talk Of The Town, which 'started off with good acts like Tony Bennett but eventually got around to Cliff Richard'. He took up bass as well as trumpet, and took on a lecturing job at Leeds College, which became his principal gig and lasted him into the 90s. In his retirement, he likes listening to Yo Yo Ma and King Oliver.

**Tubby Hayes, *The Swinging Giant Vol 2*** ( Jasmine)

# Hampton Hawes

PIANO
*born* 13 November 1928; *died* 22 May 1977

A master pianist whose work is, these days, unfairly slipping into neglect. Largely self-taught, he played on the Los Angeles scene with such leading musicians as Dexter Gordon and Sonny Criss, and Howard McGhee took him on as a pianist in 1950. Following military service, Hawes worked as a part of the West Coast scene and made eight fine albums for Contemporary, including *All Night Session!*, three records cut at a single stretch which, at the time, seemed like a real marathon. But Hawes was imprisoned for five years for narcotics offences, and it wasn't until he received a pardon from President Kennedy in 1963 that he returned to the scene. *The Green Leaves Of Summer* (1964) was fine enough to suggest that he had lost none of his skills, and reaffirmed the calibre of a style which was unique in its way: he had the executive flair of the bebop giants, but it was mixed in with a funky feel which suggested a close kinship with Horace Silver's kind of playing. The title piece of *The Green Leaves Of Summer*, though, hinted at a further rhythmic sophistication which was very particular to Hawes. But the 60s weren't especially kind to him. He found enough to keep him busy, but his kind of playing was out of fashion and by the 70s he was trying quasi-jazz-rock settings with electric keyboards, which led him nowhere. He died before he could take his ideas any further. His autobiography, *Raise Up Off Me* (1974), is a raw and direct look at a difficult jazz life.

**The Green Leaves Of Summer** (Contemporary)

# Coleman Hawkins

TENOR SAXOPHONE
*born* 21 November 1904; *died* 19 May 1969

The saxophone was made for jazz, and sooner or later it would have achieved eminence as a front-line instrument. But it was Hawkins who secured its importance, and set down the template for a first generation of jazz saxophonists. He took up the C-melody instrument at an early age and was performing for dancers when in his teens, and in 1921 he played in a Kansas City theatre orchestra, where Mamie Smith heard him and eventually (his parents at first disapproving) gave him a job in her touring band. 'Bean' (derived from 'Stringbean', a comment on his skinny young self) switched to the tenor saxophone and made his first records with Smith's Jazz Hounds, and in 1923 he began looking for work in New York. Fletcher Henderson hired him for some record dates and invited him to join his new band in January 1924: it was the start of a ten-year association. Considering the freakish sounds other saxophonists were making at the time, the impact of Hawkins's early featured spots is still astonishing: his passage on the Vocalion recording of 'Dicty Blues' is an amazing solo for 1923. In this period he was still relying heavily on the beat, and using much of the slap-tongue vocabulary which was the saxophone's accepted dialect, but already he was pushing an individual temperament and a more masculine, rugged approach. Sitting near Louis Armstrong in the Henderson band opened his ears further: next to the already brilliant Armstrong, Hawkins was still a comparative beginner, but he soaked up everything the trumpeter was doing, especially rhythmically. Following his progress on Henderson's records over ten years is like watching someone steadily open a door: he plays more independently of the beat, ornaments melody lines with increasing assurance, and enlarges an already full-voiced timbre. On a rare small-group, 'outside' date such as the 1929 session with The Mound City Blue Blowers, he plays a fuming solo on 'Hello Lola' and a lustrous one on 'One Hour'. By the early 30s, his was seen as the dominant saxophone voice, and despite the input of such contemporaries as Charlie Holmes, Johnny Hodges, Frankie Trumbauer and Jimmy Dorsey, everyone followed Hawkins.

The Henderson band was booked for a tour of England in 1934, but when it fell through Hawkins decided to go by himself. He had such a successful time in London that he remained for five years, touring the continent, recording with Django Reinhardt and The Ramblers Dance Orchestra, and living a star's life. On his return to the US in July 1939 he picked up where he had left off, despite the arrival of such new saxophonists as Lester Young. Hawkins formed a new band and in October he recorded, to close out a studio date, an almost impromptu version of 'Body And Soul': consisting of just two choruses of tenor saxophone with only a discreet accompaniment, its spontaneous perfection stunned other musicians, reaffirmed Hawkins's mastery and even won him a popular hit – 'Even the squares like it,' mused the bewildered Hawk.

He briefly led a big band, but aside from the leader's own playing it was a flavourless group, and he went back to small bands for the rest of the 40s. Bop piqued his interest, and he was one of the few older players to take an immediate hand in the music, recording with Gillespie, Parker, Navarro and J J Johnson soon enough. He played all over the US and still cut plenty of records, one highlight being 'Picasso', a completely acapella tenor solo which was loosely based on the 'Body And Soul' chords. At the start of the LP era he was recorded comparatively infrequently, but by 1957 he was making albums for Prestige and Riverside and there was a terrific burst of recording towards the end of the decade. He was happy to play in Jazz At The Philharmonic packages, and on dates with old friends such as Pee Wee Russell and Henry Allen: having lived through every jazz era and contributed to all of them, he had something to say in most situations. There were some gorgeous sessions with Ben Webster, and one of his favourite front-line partners was Roy Eldridge. But the youngest of the new men did pose some questions which even Hawk couldn't quite answer: a session with Sonny Rollins in 1963 was less successful. His tone hardened and the vibrato sometimes became more of a shake, but Hawkins was still playing powerfully in the middle 60s. He continued to visit his old European haunts, performing at venues such as Ronnie Scott's in London. Scott remembered when Ben Webster dropped by to tell Hawkins that 'My daddy took me to hear you play', whereupon Hawk would growl, 'Ben, you're older than shit'. His last two years saw a steady decline in his health, but he still toured Denmark in 1968 and played a final concert with Eldridge the following April: living on soup and brandy finally wore him out.

*Body And Soul* (RCA)

# Erskine Hawkins
TRUMPET
*born* 26 July 1914; *died* 12 November 1993

'The Twentieth Century Gabriel' began his career as one of many Louis Armstrong impersonators, leading the 'Bama State Collegians in his home town of Montgomery before going to New York with them in 1934. Hawkins's flamboyance as a front man was popular in Harlem clubs, and eventually they followed Chick Webb as the house band at the Savoy Ballroom. They signed to Bluebird (after a period with Vocalion) in 1938, and a year later had a major hit with 'Tuxedo Junction', which propelled Hawkins and his band to the forefront of the swing-era orchestras. They made scores of records all through the 40s, surviving the decline of the big bands better than most, and it wasn't until 1953 that Hawkins finally scaled back to a smaller group. For all the leader's showmanship and finesse, there was something workmanlike about the band: although in its time it could draw audiences as big as any for Basie or Lunceford, the records only rarely found an extra spark of originality, and soloists such as Dud Bascomb, Avery Parrish and Haywood Henry were more reliable than inspirational. As a result, Hawkins's huge output is today largely forgotten, and his own playing – capable enough in the Armstrong manner – all but unknown. Eventually he shifted to New Jersey and the Catskills and he was still playing in resort hotels into the 80s. *The Hawk Blows At Midnight* (1960), a solitary late album for Decca, found him still in fine shape.

*The Original Tuxedo Junction* (Bluebird)

# Clancy Hayes

BANJO, VOCALS

*born* 14 November 1908; *died* 13 March 1972

Hayes was really a vaudevillian, popular on radio during the 30s, who fell in with jazz when he joined the original line-up of the Lu Watters Yerba Buena Jazz Band in 1940. He stuck with Watters through the 40s, then joined up with the Bob Scobey band and stayed all through the next decade, light relief from the more 'serious' revivalist work of that band. He later guested with other revivalist groups and did solo work.
*Swingin' Minstrel* (Good Time Jazz)

# Edgar Hayes

PIANO

*born* 23 May 1904; *died* 28 June 1979

Hayes was a schooled musician and toured the South with his own groups during the 20s. But he was unnoticed until he joined the Mills Blue Rhythm Band in 1936, acting as one of their main arrangers. In 1937 he began leading his own band, and it was a good one, with Clyde Bernhardt, Henry Goodwin and the young Kenny Clarke in the line-up, and decent charts by Hayes and Joe Garland. Their records are rather let down, though, by too many indifferent vocals, and their hit version of 'Star Dust' is untypically sweet. Hayes departed for the West Coast in 1942, and made some V-Discs there; otherwise he mostly played in clubs, and away from wider attention.
*Edgar Hayes 1937–1938* (Classics)

# Harry Hayes

SAXOPHONES

*born* 23 March 1909

A doughty veteran of the London music scene, Hayes was playing as a teenager with Fred Elizalde at the Savoy, and from there moved through the dance-band scene of the 30s and early 40s: he spent some time with dreary orchestras such as those of Maurice Winnick and Sidney Lipton, but he also backed Louis Armstrong on tour and worked with Valaida Snow. In the middle 40s he broadcast regularly with his Radio Rhythm Club Sextet, basically a pick-up group of some of the better London sessionmen, and

they made dozens of 78s for HMV in a modest small-group swing style; they have been unfairly neglected in the reissue field. He was with Ambrose and Kenny Baker in the 50s and led more small groups of his own, eventually retiring from performance in the 60s to run musical instrument and record retailing businesses.

# Louis Hayes

DRUMS

*born* 31 May 1937

Hayes started playing drums for Yusef Lateef in Detroit, although he was at the time too young to work in clubs and had to leave in 1956. He spent three years in Horace Silver's quintet and then six years with Cannonball Adderley, forming one of the great rhythm partnerships of the time with bassist Sam Jones. After a spell of free-lancing he began leading groups of his own, and there were some very fine bands ahead: with Freddie Hubbard, Woody Shaw, Joe Henderson, Junior Cook and many others. He spent some time in McCoy Tyner's trio and big band in the 80s but has since largely returned to leading his own groups: 'I'm not a person that can follow another person's concept too long.' A swinging drummer in the manner of the vintage hard-bop players, and a great campaigner for the acoustic form.
*Louis At Large* (Sharp Nine)

# Tubby Hayes

TENOR SAXOPHONE, VIBES

*born* 30 January 1935; *died* 8 June 1973

British jazz's greatest prodigy picked up the saxophone at 12 and within three years was staggering his peers with his virtuosity. He worked under various London leaders in the early 50s, including Kenny Baker, led an octet for a spell in 1955, and then formed The Jazz Couriers with fellow tenorman Ronnie Scott. Hayes's style was fast, exuberant, almost indecently accomplished: other saxophonists were in despair at the ease of his delivery, which seemed to require no woodshedding and had no inner demons. The records he made for Tony Hall's Tempo label – particularly *Tubby's Groove* (1959) – brandished this facility with a nearly insolent bravado, recalling Sonny Rollins at his most imperious. With Scott, in The Jazz Couriers, Hayes put up a band which had the mettle of the American hard-bop groups (one of their originals was even called 'Message To The Messengers'), and which set a standard that no European band could match. In the early 60s Hayes began leading his own quintet, and their records for Fontana are classics of their kind, particularly the live (at Ronnie Scott's) sessions caught on *Down In the Village* and *Late Spot At Scott's* (1962), where Hayes also plays vibes in addition to his tenor work. But the kind of mainstream-modern jazz Hayes excelled in lost its impetus as pop dominated the 60s, and Tubby's career was interrupted by heart illness, not helped by a narcotics problem. He had earned the respect of his American peers, recording two albums in the US, and to this day he is remembered by many American jazz musicians who have otherwise little interest in British jazz; but his occasionally convened big band was too costly to maintain, and he had no record-company affiliation in the later 60s, a shameful neglect by the industry. He hardly played between 1969 and 1971, and then underwent a second heart operation, but died shortly afterwards. Brilliant and failsafe, his music can seem, with hindsight, too easy, even as it is flooded with notes and brimming with energy: sometimes Tubby seems to have little to say, beyond the facts of his own executive skills. He is nevertheless recalled with enormous affection by countless British jazz fans.

**Down In The Village** (Redial)

## Graham Haynes
CORNET
*born* 16 September 1960

Haynes seemed like a potentially major contributor in the middle 90s. He had studied with Jaki Byard and played in early editions of Steve Coleman's Five Elements band before spending three years in Paris, following the African music scene there. On his return to New York he signed to Verve and made some striking music with some unusual ensembles, a fusion of seemingly exotic elements which actually worked on *Transition* (1996) because he seemed to

believe in his ideas and distilled them in his acrid brass playing. But a follow-up record went nowhere and he currently seems adrift. Roy Haynes is his father.

**Transition** (Antilles)

## Roy Haynes
DRUMS
*born* 13 March 1925

Haynes was one of the youngest players to (just) be in on the first generation of bebop. Born in Roxbury, Massachusetts, of Barbadian parents, he first played drums in Boston groups and toured with both Luis Russell and Lester Young in the mid-40s, before finding himself in the company of Bud Powell and Charlie Parker in New York at the end of the decade. He worked in Parker's quintet for some three years, as well as with Sarah Vaughan for a long stretch of the 50s. But Haynes never settled for too long behind one leader, and he began bossing groups of his own from the early 50s too: quintets, quartets and trios have been his favourite situations, and he has shied away from doing any big-band work. Despite many high-profile associations, though, Haynes has never quite enjoyed the kudos and respect accorded to Max Roach. It is interesting to conjecture on the affinities and differences in their adjacent styles, and on how influential each has been. Haynes admits that after he first saw Roach playing in New York, 'I got rid of my tom-toms and used only one cymbal.' He has ever since used a kit of modest size – possibly in keeping with his own slight physical stature – and plays with a pushy insistence which is powerful without crowding his fellow players. *Cracklin'* (1963), a quartet date with the howling Booker Ervin, is a fitting example of Haynes's adroitness and cunning intensity. In all, though, he led only a dozen album sessions during the LP era, playing a kind of fusion with his Hip Ensemble (early 70s) before going back to acoustic situations in the 80s and 90s. Players of a generation or two later have always enjoyed having Roy in the band: Chick Corea, Pat Metheny and Gary Burton are three examples. In his 80th year, the trim drummer is still playing with great heart.

**Cracklin'** (New Jazz/OJC)

## Kevin Hays

PIANO
*born* 1 May 1968

Hays began gathering attention in New York circles from the late 80s: he worked in several of Bob Belden's groups (an association which in all likelihood assisted in his getting a contract with Blue Note), and was then in such fast company as the Harper brothers' band, Joshua Redman and Seamus Blake. Three albums for Steeplechase and three more for Blue Note charted a move from smart acoustic post-bop to a kind of retro-fusion with old-fashioned electric keyboards, as documented on some of the Blue Note sets: Hays has a notably personal touch on the Fender Rhodes, for instance. But Blue Note didn't pursue further recordings, and Hays is currently more visible as a sideman again.

*Ugly Beauty* (Steeplechase)

## J C Heard

DRUMS
*born* 8 October 1917; *died* 27 September 1988

Heard started as a tap-dancer in vaudeville and took up drums in his teens. He worked locally in Detroit before joining Teddy Wilson's big band in New York in 1939, and thereafter proved himself an asset to numerous bands, including those of Benny Carter and Cab Calloway. Norman Granz made him a regular on Jazz At The Philharmonic in the 50s, and that opened the door to his working in both Japan and Australia as a leader – still dancing and singing in addition to his drum work. Back in the US, he drummed for Coleman Hawkins and Roy Eldridge, and latterly worked with groups of his own in California and Detroit. Heard was among the last survivors of a generation of swing drummers that played with tact, grace and no little finesse. He apparently invented the names James Charles for himself, since nobody believed that his given names were nothing more than J C.

*Jazz At The Philharmonic In Tokyo* (Pablo)

## Albert 'Tootie' Heath

DRUMS
*born* 31 May 1935

The junior Heath brother, Albert has had a low-profile career with many high-profile names. His debut on record (1957) was with John Coltrane; he played in The Jazztet, and went to Scandinavia in 1965 to work as the house drummer at the Café Montmartre; and he was the first drummer in Herbie Hancock's sextet (1968). Although he gave up music for a time in the middle 70s, he was drawn back in again and became the last drummer to play in the Modern Jazz Quartet, after Connie Kay's death. He has also worked in The Heath Brothers' family band. A skilful and crafty exponent of bebop drumming, he might fairly wonder why he has received comparatively little acclaim for his playing over the years.

*The Jazztet At Birdhouse* (Argo)

## Jimmy Heath

TENOR AND SOPRANO SAXOPHONES
*born* 25 October 1926

'Little Bird' was the nickname which the young Jimmy Heath acquired on his local Philadelphia scene at the end of the 40s: he played alto then, got around the saxophone with suitably prodigious authority, and was already running big bands by the time he was 21. In the early 50s he switched to tenor and worked for a spell with Miles Davis (who didn't remember him very kindly in his autobiography). A narcotics problem kept him away from regular playing but he was very busy as a composer-arranger, and from the end of the 50s he was again very active as a performer. Art Farmer became a favourite front-line colleague, and they worked together in a quintet in the second half of the 60s. He began working with his brothers on a semi-regular basis in the 70s, and led small groups of his own, which have unfortunately been not too well documented: *You've Changed* (1991) is an instance of how good Heath's quartet of the time was. He has, in all, not been too lucky with recording: six albums for Riverside in the early 60s constitute his principal body of work, a spotty group which has some outstanding music along with some lesser records. His skills as an arranger and

composer have perhaps distracted attention from his tenor playing, which has genuine power and a quiet originality: imagine a Coltrane without the excess of notes and the self-conscious questing, and you are close to the unfussy power which Heath conveys at his best. His book of tunes is, though, plump with excellence: 'Gingerbread Boy', 'C.T.A.', 'Gemini', 'The Thumper', 'Sleeves' and 'Sassy Samba' are a few among many inventive and memorable themes.
**Really Big!** (Riverside)

# Percy Heath

BASS
*born* 30 April 1923; *died* 28 April 2005

The eldest of the Heath brothers is a gentle spirit whose great qualities have been modestly cloaked by the circumstances of his career. He didn't take up the bass until 1946, following his air force service, and played with brother Jimmy alongside Howard McGhee; then he worked with Dizzy Gillespie's small group before enlisting with the Modern Jazz Quartet in 1952. This kept him busy for the next 22 years – although he also played on numerous album dates as a sideman, with everyone from Ornette Coleman to Paul Desmond – and during the MJQ's brief retirement he worked with Jimmy once again in The Heath Brothers' Band, a group which has been occasionally revived ever since. Back with the MJQ, he stayed until the last hurrah and is now the sole survivor of the original band. Latterly he has also taken up the cello. Heath's lovely sound and uncomplicated, gregarious swing have raised the collective spirits on scores of record dates. Although he had several features with the MJQ, these mattered less than the beautifully apposite playing he contributed to their every date. In his 80th year, he finally led an album of his own, *A Long Song* (2002), and it is a charming record.
**Modern Jazz Quartet, The Last Concert** (Atlantic)

# Ted Heath

BANDLEADER
*born* 30 March 1900; *died* 18 November 1969

Heath probably belonged to an era before jazz. He played trombone in the dance-band scene of the 20s and 30s (and he is on Charles Penrose's record of 'The Laughing Trombone'), and didn't take to bandleading himself until 1944. From that point he created and built up the most powerful and impressive orchestra of its kind Britain has ever had, although how much of a jazz group it was is open to much debate. On one hand, Heath encouraged interesting and challenging music: he re-created some of the best swing-era hits, he had such creative spirits as Stan Tracey and Kenny Baker in his ranks, and at one point he even commissioned scores from Tadd Dameron. He also followed everything that was happening on the American big-band scene. On the other, he insisted on a serried perfectionism among his musicians, disliked any sense of improvisation, and welcomed middle-class gentility as warmly as any hint of jazz excitement. His big hits – 'Swingin' Shepherd Blues', 'The Faithful Hussar', 'Hot Toddy' – worked to a near-military timetable, not so different in their way to the music of Bert Kaempfert and James Last a decade later. At least he was well served by the Decca engineers, for whom he made numerous albums: the sound of the Heath band was always impressive. He retired from bandleading in 1964, but a kind of ghost band has functioned more or less ever since, often under the direction of one of his long-serving sidemen, Don Lusher.
**Listen To My Music** (Hep)

# Dick Heckstall-Smith

TENOR AND SOPRANO SAXOPHONES
*born* 26 September 1934; *died* 17 December 2004

Dick took up soprano saxophone in his teens and was a Bechet soundalike – 'But I was like Bechet with a nail stuck in his head'. He played trad with Sandy Brown in the late 50s, then, by now primarily on tenor, moved through a gaggle of sometimes unlikely situations: Ballets USA, Alexis Korner, Graham Bond, John Mayall, and finally Jon Hiseman's group Colosseum, where he played a steaming sort of rock-jazz. He briefly led a band of his own in the early 70s but then left music for academic study until forming a new group, the fondly remembered Big Chief, in 1976, as well as touring in an occasional partnership with Don Weller as The Tough Tenors. In the 80s he played with Bo Diddley, Jack Bruce and

others and formed another new band, DHSS, before going out with Big Chief again in the 90s. Heckstall-Smith was never any kind of purist, and much of his playing was done in groups that had little to do with any sort of mainstream jazz, but in situations such as Colosseum or Big Chief he blew tremendously gutsy and impassioned tenor. His legacy on record is rather disappointingly scattered and hard to pin down or even locate. He was also a very entertaining writer, and left some poignantly hilarious accounts of his days in the blues-rock field of the 60s.
*Live 1990* (L + R)

# Neal Hefti
ARRANGER
*born* 29 October 1922

Hefti played trumpet with Charlie Barnet and Woody Herman in the early 40s, but his talents lay elsewhere: he had tried arranging in his teens, and with Herman that interest was nurtured. By the end of the decade he was writing full time, for Harry James and then for Count Basie. It was his work with Basie which established his credentials: slick, smooth and smartly tailored to that band's best resources, Hefti's charts coupled precision and momentum quite irresistibly, and his scores for *The Atomic Basie* (1958) are definitive in their way. He occasionally led a big band of his own (his wife was the singer Frances Wayne) but by the 60s he had disappeared into television, with his music for *Batman* making his fortune, and his only records of the period are TV and pop arrangements.
**Count Basie, *The Atomic Basie*** (Roulette)

# Bob Helm
CLARINET
*born* 18 July 1914

Though primarily a clarinet man, Helm started on brass instruments, went through the saxophone family and also played guitar by the time he was in his teens. He began working with Lu Watters and Turk Murphy as early as 1936, and he was part of Watters's Yerba Buena Jazz Band, first in 1940 and then on and off until 1950. He then switched allegiances and spent much of the next 30

years in Murphy's band. The grand old man of Californian revivalism, he was still playing in the 80s and 90s and made an album under his own name for Stomp Off at the age of 80.
**Turk Murphy, *Turk Murphy's Jazz Band Favourites*** (Good Time Jazz)

# Gerry Hemingway
DRUMS
*born* 23 March 1955

An important and powerful presence in the American avant-garde of the past 30 years. He was already playing in the idiom in the 70s and gave a solo concert as early as 1974. He followed this with establishing his own label, Auricle, and releasing a solo drum album there. He was in BassDrumBone with Ray Anderson and Mark Dresser, one of his most frequent collaborators, and in the Anthony Braxton quartet with Marilyn Crispell and Dresser. In the 90s he ran a quintet, although this has subsequently dispersed, and he still plays solo regularly as well as collaborating with many of his major peers. Hemingway's interest in a world of rhythm has led him to investigate drumming styles of many different disciplines, MIDI sounds, electronics and whatnot, but his abiding love for Art Blakey's playing tends to centre him in jazz forms more readily than some free players, and he can play straight time beautifully when he wants to.
**Electro-Acoustic Works 1984–95** (Random Acoustics)

# Julius Hemphill
ALTO AND SOPRANO SAXOPHONES
*born* 24 January 1928; *died* 2 April 1995

Born in Fort Worth, Hemphill began playing clarinet there and eventually blew saxophone in R&B bands. In 1968 he moved to St Louis and took part in the activities of the Black Artists Group there, but his real work commenced when he went to New York, where he was one of the first musicians to run his own record label, Mbari, and create all-solo records such as *Blue Boyé* (1977). *Dogon A.D.* (1972) and *Coon Bid'ness* (1975) are also key works which premiere some of the early music of players who would be

important figures in the nascent loft scene of the time. He joined Oliver Lake, David Murray and Hamiet Bluiett in the World Saxophone Quartet in 1976, but continued to lead groups of his own, also duetting with cellist Abdul Wadud. Hemphill always had big agendas on his mind: compositionally, he was interested in works for multiple saxophones, of which *Long Tongues* (1987) was a seminal example, and he created and directed other grand works involving mixed-media of varying kinds. Elektra Musician recorded his big band in 1988, and while his bigger pieces took up much of his time, his own improvising on both alto and soprano was always powerful and affecting. But he was plagued with poor health in the last ten years of his life, and was eventually playing from a wheelchair. A lot of Hemphill's work either went undocumented or was scrappily set down: he should be remembered as a major figure of his time, but circumstances may militate against that. Two of his students, Tim Berne and Marty Ehrlich, have at least kept much of his inspiration alive.
*Roi Boyé And The Gotham Minstrels* (Sackville)

# Eddie Henderson

TRUMPET
*born* 26 October 1940

Henderson's jazz playing has been only a part of his working life: he has academic qualifications in both zoology and medicine, besides having served in the air force for three years. He studied trumpet and music theory, though, as far back as the early 50s, and began playing more regularly from the end of the 60s: with John Handy, Herbie Hancock (in the pianist's early-70s sextet), Joe Henderson and others, although latterly he has performed and recorded mostly as a leader. Miles Davis gave him encouragement early on, and much of Henderson's work sounds to have been crafted out of the acoustic music of Davis's middle-60s music. If he seems to have little to say in terms of originality, at his best he personalizes that idiom with care and dignity.
*Dark Shadows* (Milestone)

# Fletcher Henderson

PIANO, BANDLEADER, ARRANGER
*born* 18 December 1897; *died* 29 December 1952

The elegant, urbane Henderson was a crucial contributor to the music's progress. His mother taught piano, his background was middle class, and he qualified in degree studies in mathematics and chemistry at Atlanta University. But instead of any scientific career, the shy Fletcher ended up as a song-demonstrator for a music publisher in New York, from there becoming the talent scout for the new Black Swan record company. He played piano behind some of the singers and started to drift towards band-leading, and by 1924 he was experienced enough to gain an offer to run the house band at the Roseland Ballroom. His first 'band' records were made as early as 1921, but it took a couple of years for some of his familiar sidemen to fall into place, and by 1923 the seeds of Henderson's band had been sown: Don Redman was there in April, and Coleman Hawkins arrived in August. The early sides are mostly stiff and unexciting with very little jazz in them, although Hawkins was impressive from the start. Two things changed everything: the promotion of Redman to musical director, and the arrival of Louis Armstrong in 1924. Redman began to introduce hotter and more interesting material, including his own arrangements and originals, and Armstrong galvanized the band and altogether stunned New York's musical community: on some Henderson records, he takes a solo and the whole band suddenly seems to shift up a gear. The trumpeter left in 1925, but his legacy was a fast-maturing and powerful jazz orchestra. Redman continued contributing most of the band's book until he too left, in 1927, whereupon the diffident Henderson began arranging himself, and proved unexpectedly good at it, with charts such as 'King Porter Stomp' and 'Down South Camp Meeting' playing to the band's strengths. Like most of the bands of the time, he had a frequent turnover of personnel, but the orchestra was a magnet for fine players and Henderson hired a litany of major talents during the late 20s and early 30s: Joe Smith, Rex Stewart, Benny Carter, Henry Allen, Lester Young, Ben Webster, Dicky Wells, Buster Bailey and Joe Thomas were some of the musicians who worked for Henderson during 1926–34, and his only real rival as a leader in the city was Duke Ellington at The Cotton Club.

In spite of all this success, Henderson's temperament was a poor match for his vocation, and he was a feeble disciplinarian. He was involved in a serious car crash in 1928, and thereafter grew listless. After 1930 or so the quality of the band's records started to decline: for every good one there was a commercial spacefiller, and the leader didn't seem to care much either way. He began selling arrangements to Benny Goodman in 1934 to help defray bills, and though it's an exaggeration to say that these charts pushed Goodman's band towards the kingdom of swing, the likes of 'King Porter Stomp' took on a commercial life which the Henderson band had scarcely enjoyed. Henderson himself continued to lead groups less frequently after this, but he made his last records as a leader in 1941: this final band still had such strong players as Benny Morton, Eddie Barefield and Sandy Williams, but it sounded like a perfunctory swing orchestra. He worked for Goodman as a staff arranger and played piano in his sextet for a time, and then went back to bandleading, before a stroke ended his career in 1950.

*A Study In Frustration: The Fletcher Henderson Story* (Columbia)

# Horace Henderson

PIANO, ARRANGER
*born* 22 November 1904; *died* 29 August 1988

Fletcher's brother was no mean musician himself. He began leading bands from the early 20s and worked in and around New York (sometimes using his brother's name in order to attract more listeners). There was a confusing period of crossover between bands led by Fletcher and Horace during the early 30s: six titles made under Horace's name in October 1933 were really by Fletcher's band, and he claimed authorship of numerous significant charts in Fletcher's book anyway. He finally led five excellent sessions for OKeh in 1940, although the first of them was credited as 'Fletcher Henderson Conducts Horace Henderson And His Orchestra'! After army service he worked for Lena Horne, and thereafter in Las Vegas and Denver as the leader of small groups.

Horace's jazz contribution is a little enigmatic, given the lack of certainty surrounding exactly what he wrote, but his credited work suggests that he certainly rivalled Fletcher's own arranging and he was a more than capable pianist too.

*Horace Henderson 1940* (Classics)

# Joe Henderson

TENOR SAXOPHONE
*born* 24 April 1937; *died* 30 June 2001

Other musicians called Joe 'The Shadow', a homage to his elusiveness: quietly spoken and never one to make a scene. His muscular sound and intense delivery often seemed entirely at odds with his personal demeanour. Born in Lima, Ohio, he began playing in Detroit at the end of the 50s, toured the club circuit with Jack McDuff and for a time played behind The Four Tops in Las Vegas: one of the curiosities of his career is that his otherwise hardcore playing has sometimes serviced popular groups. He co-led a band with Kenny Dorham, which got him on to Blue Note as a solo artist, and he also played with Horace Silver for a spell. *Inner Urge* (1964), where he plays with McCoy Tyner and Elvin Jones, finds him spinning fresh ideas away from the John Coltrane axis which most tenor playing was then in debt to. In the 70s he was living in San Francisco, where he played for a time with the rock group Blood Sweat & Tears, and signed to Milestone, where he cut some fine records. His tone grew both stronger and more malleable, and his playing was full of unusual shapes and phrase-lengths, as well as squalling cries which could sound like a soul singer's wail. Joe's best tunes – 'Recorda-Me', 'A Shade Of Jade', 'Punjab', 'Isotope' – became important parts of the hard-bop book. By the 80s his career had subsided somewhat, but a beautiful two-volume set for Blue Note, *The State Of The Tenor* (1985), reminded many listeners of his excellence, and when he signed to Verve in 1990 he produced an album, *Lush Life*, which became a huge jazz best-seller and entirely revitalized his career. His sound had lost some of its power and grittiness, but his ideas had become more quizzical and were no less surprising. Three more records followed and Henderson enjoyed his late-blooming eminence, but by the end of the century The

Shadow had gone back into himself and he quietly withdrew from further work.

*The State Of The Tenor* (Blue Note)

# Jon Hendricks
VOCAL
*born* 16 September 1921

In the era of rap, Hendricks might seem like a prescient talent. He spent his adolescence in Toledo, singing on local radio stations, and after army service he studied law in college as well as playing drums. On Charlie Parker's advice he gave up the legal side and went to New York, where he began working with Dave Lambert and Annie Ross in what eventually became a hit act on record (*Sing A Song Of Basie*, 1957) and in live performance. Hendricks was the writing talent for the trio, setting lyrics to jazz material by Basie, Horace Silver and others, and the group lasted (with Yolande Noble eventually replacing Ross) until 1964. In 1968, Hendricks moved to Europe and stayed six years, before returning home and establishing a vocal group based around members of his family. Since then he has turned up in numerous situations as a vocal guest star and grandmaster of a black vocal tradition which, in many ways, he was one of the founders of: certainly the rap movement owes him a debt. Hendricks's ingenuity and dexterity in fitting words to jazz melodies and improvisations has never been matched, but in a sense it is a one-dimensional act: for all his musical chutzpah, there is something vaudevillian about his work, which the onset of rap does consign to the past. He has never been very fortunate as regards recording: like Betty Carter, he is an in-person one-off whose legacy will be best retained in people's memories of live events, and it is still the Lambert, Hendricks & Ross albums which do him most justice.

*Sing A Song Of Basie* (Columbia)

# Ernie Henry
ALTO SAXOPHONE
*born* 3 September 1926; *died* 29 December 1957

Henry is a notable example of a musician whose jazz contribution survives entirely because of records: if he'd never made some

featured recordings he wouldn't even have enjoyed footnote status. As it is, he began playing in New York bebop circles as a teenager, and he turns up as a sideman on some of Tadd Dameron's recordings and in Dizzy Gillespie's big band. He is one of the somewhat bewildered sidemen on Thelonious Monk's *Brilliant Corners* (1956), and Riverside gave him the chance to lead three albums of his own, the final one issued posthumously (he died of a heroin overdose). Often sloppily executed and poorly organized, his records suggest an intense Parker disciple with a hankering to make his mark somehow, the surviving music a surprisingly vivid testament.

*Seven Standards And A Blues* (Riverside/OJC)

# Nat Hentoff
WRITER
*born* 10 June 1925

Hentoff was the conscience of jazz journalism for many years. He worked on a Boston radio station and studied at Harvard in the 40s, and in the following decade he wrote for *Down Beat* and drew as close as he might to many of the major New York jazz figures of the day. His books *Hear Me Talkin' To Ya* (1955, with Nat Shapiro) and *The Jazz Life* (1961) were the first real efforts to explore the community of jazz musicians as an articulate group of working individuals, rather than stars or novelties or untouchable artists: Hentoff's straight demeanour put across the personalities of his subjects with uncommon candour. He co-edited one of the best of all jazz magazines, the short-lived *Jazz Review* (1958–61), but thereafter worked primarily as a journalist specializing in issues to do with civil liberties, a beat which he has patrolled into the new century in *The Village Voice* and elsewhere. Nevertheless, through occasional sleevenotes and columns, he maintains a jazz presence.

# Hep
RECORD COMPANY

Established in 1974 by the curmudgeonly and indomitable Alastair Robertson, Hep commenced as a reissue label – mostly of swing-era material – but has steadily grown into an important member of Europe's senior chapter of independent jazz companies. Robertson has put out a large number of remastered collections of both studio dates and transcription material, by bands such as those of Tommy Dorsey, Claude Thornhill, Boyd Raeburn, Earl Hines, Harry James and many others. But he has also sponsored new records by musicians who appeal to his more or less mainstream tastes. Spike Robinson, Don Lanphere, Joe Temperley, Michael Hashim, John Hart and Jimmy Deuchar are among those represented in what is now a large and valuable catalogue: Robertson refuses to compromise on quality in his reissue work, and he engaged the meticulous John R T Davies to do most of his remastering on those projects.

# Peter Herbolzheimer

TROMBONE, BANDLEADER
*born* 31 December 1935

Born in Bucharest, Herbolzheimer went to Germany as a teenager before spending time in Detroit, where he played guitar in clubs; only when he returned to Germany did he take up the trombone. He then sat through years of playing in radio and dance orchestras before forming his own Rhythm Combination And Brass in 1969, a band which has endured in one form or another ever since, and which has attracted high-calibre players from Europe and America (Art Farmer, Herb Geller) as well as local musicians. Herbolzheimer writes or arranges most of the material himself, and it is a skilful, watertight approach which mixes swing, bebop, blues and dance-orchestra music into a form which is unmistakeably middle-European, even as it can stand its ground with all but the best American big-band music. Despite the neutral feel of much of it, the Rhythm Combination And Brass discography bulges with classy playing.
*Friends And Silhouettes* (Koala)

# Woody Herman

BANDLEADER, CLARINET, ALTO SAXOPHONE, VOCAL
*born* 16 May 1913; *died* 29 October 1987

Herman spent most of his life as an entertainer. He danced and sang in vaudeville from the age of ten, and he worked in some of the touring bands of the early 30s (Tom Gerun, Gus Arnheim) before setting up on his own in 1936 with the nucleus of the Isham Jones orchestra. 'The Band That Plays The Blues' was pretty uncompetitive at first, with an indifferent book and only Herman's indomitable personality to buoy them up, but by 1939 things were improving fast and the great hit 'Woodchoppers' Ball' in that year – a tune which Herman continued to play for the rest of his career – gave them their real start. The band worked up until 1946, gaining important new personnel such as Neal Hefti, Ralph Burns, Conte Candoli, Bill Harris, Flip Phillips, Shorty Rogers, Sonny Berman and Billy Bauer along the way, and 'Herman's Herd' (retrospectively called the First Herd) were by the mid-40s one of the leading swing bands in America. But Herman temporarily disbanded in 1946 and came back with the Second Herd a year later, with the famous sax section of Stan Getz, Zoot Sims, Herbie Steward and Serge Chaloff: their feature on Jimmy Giuffre's 'Four Brothers' was a classic of its time, and so was Getz's rhapsodic solo on 'Early Autumn' (1948). Herman's 40s recordings are rightly cherished by big-band admirers as nonpareil examples of the genre – excellent charts by Burns and others, top-drawer soloists and playing of communal heart which spoke much about Herman's ability to get the best out of a band. He disbanded again in 1949 and slimmed down to a sextet for a time, but the Third Herd came into being in 1950 and Woody carried on touring. By the end of the decade he was back to a sextet, but the Fourth and effectively final Herd was assembled in 1961 (thereafter it became either the Swinging or the Thundering Herd).

Herman's music was kept fresh by his ability to spot and adapt trends without undermining the basic character of his swinging big band. He nodded to bebop in the 40s, and adapted to hard-bop, soul-jazz and funk trends in the 50s and 60s, bringing pieces such as 'Opus De Funk' and 'Watermelon Man' into the band's book, alongside Herman perennials such as 'Wildroot' and 'Apple Honey'. The band's personnel was subject to a regular turnover, but it remained in fine shape to the end: the edition which cut *Woody's Winners* (1965), one of the most exciting of all his records, was

stuffed with talent, and many of today's senior modern players got their start in a Herman band. Perhaps some of his late 60s and 70s material was too modish even for Herman, but Woody seemed to approach all of it in the same spirit of entertaining the people, and he never tried to 'improve' them the way his surviving contemporary Stan Kenton did. His own playing on alto and clarinet stayed strong, his singing – he had an agreeable light tenor – was often delightful, especially on an album of Al Jolson tunes (*The Jazz Swinger*, 1966), and in the 70s he even took up the soprano saxophone. Away from performance, though, his life took on a sad aspect. The IRS began pursuing him for unpaid taxes in 1967, and they hounded him for the rest of his days, eventually impounding his home and seizing all his assets. This didn't help his health, which declined rapidly in the last year of his life.
***Blowing Up A Storm!*** (Columbia)

## Vincent Herring
ALTO SAXOPHONE
*born* 19 November 1964

Herring couldn't wait to get involved in New York's jazz scene, arriving from California in 1982 and busking for dollars until he found his way into the Lionel Hampton Orchestra. From there, he has freelanced prodigiously: one of his favourite associations was with Nat Adderley's group, where he could sound as much like his idol Cannonball Adderley as he pleased, and this inevitably won him 'New Cannonball' plaudits. But he is happy to work either in his own groups or with post-bop bands which suit his intense, bluesy, acerbic style, which has gathered in a few more expressive quirks along with his basic influence. Though he has never had a major-label affiliation, Vincent has never been short of a recording session, and with Eddie Allen he actually founded a company to produce other artists.
***Simple Pleasures*** (High Note)

## Fred Hersch
PIANO
*born* 21 October 1955

Born in Cincinnati, Hersch studied at Boston before working in New York from 1977. Early associations with Art Farmer, Joe Henderson and Stan Getz helped put his name on the map, and he began recording as a leader and soloist from 1986. Most detect a strong Bill Evans influence in his work, but as he has said, 'if you're a white guy who plays tunes with a trio they're going to put you there'. In fact, Hersch has often encountered what might appear improbably avant-garde situations for him – such as a trio with Marty Ehrlich and Gerry Hemingway – which have either gone unnoticed or unrecorded. His career took a major step forward with his series of 'theme' albums for Elektra Nonesuch, with recitals dedicated to Monk, Strayhorn, Rodgers and Hammerstein, and Cole Porter, each of which has included some of the most sheerly beautiful piano playing of recent times. He still teaches at Boston and tours regularly as a soloist. Of his approach as a soloist, he has said, 'to me chords are not stacks of things: each note in a chord is a voice that wants to move somewhere'.
***Fred Hersch Plays Rodgers And Hammerstein*** (Nonesuch)

## Conrad Herwig
TROMBONE
*born* 1 November 1959

Herwig epitomizes the kind of prodigious advances which trombone players have made on their traditionally unruly instrument. He studied in Texas in the late 70s before big-band work with Buddy Rich and the Toshiko Akiyoshi orchestra, and has since then freelanced widely. Coltrane's music is very important to him – he did an entire album of Trane tunes reworked to a Latin pulse, and he has covered several of his pieces on his other own-name records – and his powerhouse technique and light-footed tread give his music a distinct lift, although the several discs he has made as a leader still don't quite evade some longueurs of post-bop orthodoxy.
***Unseen Universe*** (Criss Cross)

## Eddie Heywood
PIANO
*born* 4 December 1915; *died* 2 January 1989

Heywood was taught by his bandleader-father and freelanced in New York in the

late 30s before leading his own groups. He had a hit with a version of 'Begin The Beguine' in 1944 and his groups were a popular draw in the city's nightspots, but their records sound very tame, with even the likes of Vic Dickenson and Doc Cheatham obliged to play very politely. Heywood had some curious health problems, including temporary paralysis of the hands, which interrupted his career, but by the 50s he was playing in a style which sounded not too different from the piano schmaltz of Frankie Carle, and his later records – there were plenty of them, for Decca, Mercury, RCA, Coral, MGM and Liberty – court an easy-listening audience. He was still, though, playing in New York in the 80s.
*Eddie Heywood At The Piano* (Mercury)

# Al Hibbler

VOCAL

*born* 16 August 1915; *died* 24 April 2001

Hibbler was a singer who drifted in and out of jazz. Born blind, he sang with local bands in Memphis in the 30s, did some work with Jay McShann's band, but found his fame as a featured singer with Duke Ellington's orchestra during 1943–51. 'Flamingo' was probably his biggest hit with Ellington. A barrel-voiced baritone in the Billy Eckstine mould, the amazing thing about Hibbler was his bizarre pronunciation and diction: as Will Friedwald put it, 'Hibbler growls, rasps and grunts almost like he's belching', and sometimes he doesn't sound too different from the Dick Van Dyke school of American Cockney. He had a hit with 'Unchained Melody' in the 50s, made some typically odd albums for Decca and a single one for Reprise in 1961, and recorded a one-off meeting with Roland Kirk in 1971.
*Torchy And Blue* (Decca)

# John Hicks

PIANO

*born* 21 December 1941

A ubiquitous presence in New York jazz for the past 40 years, Hicks moved there in 1963, having studied in St Louis and at Berklee. He spent a period in Art Blakey's Jazz Messengers before moving on to the Betty Carter group and Woody Herman's big band, and though he was with Carter again

in the later 70s he has since worked mostly as a freelance and as a leader of his own small groups. Among an uncountable number of associations, he has enjoyed particular musical success with Cecil McBee and Elvin Jones in The Power Trio, and with George Mraz and Idris Muhammad as The Keystone Trio, as well as with Bobby Watson, Arthur Blythe, David Murray, Ricky Ford, Peter Leitch and Eric Alexander. Hicks does nothing dramatically innovative in terms of the modern piano tradition, and much of what he plays emanates from the McCoy Tyner brand of virtuosity, but he has a rare sense of authority which turns seemingly every engagement with the piano into something with a recitalist's dignity. As if acknowledging that, he has spent much of his recent discography (for High Note) fashioning a series of homages to older piano masters, from Earl Hines to Billy Strayhorn. His occasional brushes with avant-gardists such as Murray have only deepened the power of his playing, and he must be, along with Kenny Barron, the safest pair of hands in American jazz piano.
*Beyond Expectations* (Reservoir)

# J C Higginbotham

TROMBONE

*born* 11 May 1906; *died* 26 May 1973

Jack Higginbotham played in obscurity on the vaudeville circuit in and around Atlanta before he finally went to New York in 1928. He made up a great team with Henry Allen in the Luis Russell Orchestra and stayed there three years, before working with Fletcher Henderson and others, eventually rejoining Russell in 1937 when that band was backing Louis Armstrong, who loved Higgy's playing. His barking delivery and uproarious sound emerge with Falstaffian good humour on his featured moments, and a solitary 1930 session by J C Higginbotham And His Six Hicks produced the classic 'Give Me Your Telephone Number'. He rejoined Henry Allen's small group and worked with him through the 40s, and thereafter worked as a freelance, although he often played with Allen again. A solitary 1966 session, *Higgy Comes Home*, is rather disappointing: better to find him bursting through on many of the warmest 78s of the 30s and 40s.
*Henry Allen, 1944–1947* (Classics)

# Billy Higgins

DRUMS

*born* 11 October 1936; *died* 3 May 2001

The mere presence of the perpetually smil-ing Billy Higgins was enough to raise the capabilities and ambitions of whatever group he was playing in: few musicians have ever communicated such buoyancy and musical uplift, even when playing a familiar, procedural kind of jazz. He was born in Los Angeles and worked in R&B and rock groups there in the 50s, then hooked up with the likes of Don Cherry (Higgins co-founded The Jazz Messiahs with Cherry) and Ornette Coleman: he is on the first Coleman Contemporary album, and some of the Atlantic sessions, although he was denied a long stay in New York through permit prob-lems due to narcotics. He remained busy in California through the 60s and 70s, and by the 80s he had become formidably prolific on both record dates and sideman touring. Regular partners included Cedar Walton, Clifford Jordan and Sam Jones, but Higgins gave of his best to whoever engaged him, and his thrilling playing – propulsive, power-ful but idiosyncratically relaxed, never sug-gesting rush or anything even for a moment overdriven – was a comfortable bedrock for everyone at the front of the stand. He rarely led sessions of his own – a handful of dates for European labels, none of them that special, are about it – but few drummers were so widely recorded. He remained a stal-wart of the Los Angeles scene, co-owning a club called World Stage, but he was finally reduced by illness and twice underwent a liver transplant. In his final years he often played with Charles Lloyd, and their final sessions together, released as both a CD and a DVD, are a moving farewell.

**Ornette Coleman, *Change Of The Century*** (Atlantic)

# Eddie Higgins

PIANO

*born* 21 February 1932

Higgins was raised in Andover, Massachusetts, but for much of his career he was associated with Chicago's jazz scene, playing on the club scene there from 1950. In 1970 he moved over to Cape Cod, and also worked in Florida. A strong, two-handed player with experience in the Dixieland, swing and bop idioms, Higgins was only rarely recorded early on but has been more prolific in the CD era. He is married to the singer Meredith D'Ambrosio.

***Zoot's Hymns*** (Sunnyside)

# Andrew Hill

PIANO

*born* 30 June 1937

Hill's strange career has moved him in and out of visibility in a way which is as unpre-dictable and tantalizing as much of his enig-matic writing and playing. He was born in Chicago (although it has often been claimed that he came from Haiti, this is not the case), and in the early 50s was studying with Paul Hindemith before embarking on a career in local clubs and R&B bands (a single trio record, with Malachi Favors, dates from this period). He went to New York in 1961, where he caught the attention of Alfred Lion, and recorded a sequence of albums for Blue Note: although none of them have ever sold well, they have a huge critical repu-tation, particularly the masterful *Point Of Departure* (1964), a sextet record which bridges hard-bop convention and avant-garde leanings with unique authority. Hill's own style, in some debt to Thelonious Monk in particular, has a way of suggesting strange and undiscovered ideas – rhythmi-cally and harmonically – without quite loos-ing himself from the familiar cycles of bebop piano. Hill's arrival at Blue Note coincided, though, with the label's dissi-pation, and many of his sessions were shelved or are difficult to locate. He recorded little in the 70s, spending much of his time caring for his terminally ill wife, and isolated albums for Soul Note (and a single Blue Note date in 1989) arrived like bulletins from a semi-forgotten outpost. In the past 15 years he has recorded more regu-larly and was a JAZZPAR recipient in the new century. He remains a musician with few precedents, seemingly beholden only to himself. His pieces appear to be whole and unabashedly complete, like freshly tutored folk songs, yet are open to limitless interpretation, and the subtlest interpret-ative insights. While it is very much piano music, he engenders exceptional perform-

ances from horn players who have worked with him, from Eric Dolphy to Greg Osby.
*Point Of Departure* (Blue Note)

## Buck Hill
TENOR SAXOPHONE
*born* 13 February 1927

Hill has scarcely ever been sighted outside his native Washington DC. He was playing in local clubs as far back as 1943, but he didn't make a record under his own name until 1978 and from the 60s until the 90s he was never more than a semi-pro player, otherwise earning a living as a mailman. He is a terrifically gutsy swing-bopper, relying in the main on standards and blues but blowing past any sense of stale material by sheer force of conviction, even though he likes to acknowledge Lester Young as an important influence. Entirely ignored by major labels – who is going to sign up a part-timer from Washington? – he has nevertheless managed to set down some admirable sessions for Steeplechase and Muse, and in 1995 he managed to sneak on to a Verve date when long-time admirer Shirley Horn had him play – beautifully – on her *The Main Ingredient*.
*This Is Buck Hill* (Steeplechase)

## Teddy Hill
BANDLEADER, TENOR SAXOPHONE
*born* 7 December 1909; *died* 19 May 1978

Hill worked in various New York bands – he wasn't much of a saxophonist – and decided to have a try at leading his own in 1932. He proved to be a much better front-man than section-player, cutting a dashing figure and getting in some fine talent: Roy Eldridge, Chu Berry, Frankie Newton, Russell Procope and Dicky Wells worked for Hill at various points, and Dizzy Gillespie played his first recorded solo as a member of Hill's 1937 line-up. In 1940, he quit the limelight to manage Minton's Playhouse in New York, where he dispensed with the older style of music and brought in Kenny Clarke as the leader of the house band, helping, though he didn't know it, to get bebop under way. He was still at Minton's when it ended its live music policy at the end of the 60s.
*Uptown Rhapsody* (Hep)

## Earl Hines
PIANO
*born* 28 December 1903; *died* 22 April 1983

Hines grew up in Pittsburgh and played the organ in church and piano at parties. He was bandleading in the city as early as 1924, then moved over to Chicago and was soon among the city's leading musical lights, working mostly with Louis Armstrong at the Sunset Café and Jimmie Noone at the Apex Club. He recorded with both men, and is the co-star of several of the later Armstrong Hot Five titles, as well as the duo of 'Weather Bird' which is a battle royal between two virtuosos. The meat of Hines's methodology was already set in place: sometimes called a 'trumpet style', primarily because of the sharply delineated melody lines, and tremolo effects which were used much as a horn player uses vibrato. His most dramatic departure from what other pianists were then playing was his approach to the underlying pulse: he would charge against the metre of the piece being played, accent off-beats, introduce sudden stops and brief silences. In other hands this might sound clumsy or all over the place, but Hines could keep his bearings with uncanny resilience. He took a band into the Grand Terrace at the end of 1928, and stayed there ten years: though it was run by the Mob, it proved to be a congenial enough home, and Hines broadcast regularly from there and made many records (one announcer said, 'Here comes Fatha Hines through the deep forest with his children' – 'Deep Forest' was the band's signature tune – and 'Fatha' became Earl's nickname ever after). The band got better as the 30s went on: initially not much more than a backdrop for the leader's playing, by the end of the decade there were good Budd Johnson charts in the book and Billy Eckstine had arrived as a singer. In 1942, there were some distinguished new recruits in Sarah Vaughan, Dizzy Gillespie and Charlie Parker, but they left to join Eckstine's new group and Hines eventually disbanded his band in 1947.

He joined Louis Armstrong's All Stars in 1948 and stayed three years, although the old magic of 20 years before was largely missing and Hines resented Armstrong's style of leadership. He worked mainly in San Francisco in the 50s and recorded only occasionally; by 1964 his career was in the doldrums, but Stanley Dance had him give a series of New York concerts that year and the results wowed both audience and press. By the end of the decade he was an international touring attraction, playing solo and in small groups with old friends such as Budd Johnson. His 60s and 70s records include some of his best work: the scattershot ebullience of his earlier music has been reined in without losing too much of the original daring, and a programme of Duke Ellington pieces recorded not long after that leader's death is a formidable homage which finds the great pianist still in towering form. He was still playing in the weeks leading up to his death.

***Tour De Force*** (Black Lion)

## Terumasa Hino
TRUMPET, FLUGELHORN
*born* 25 October 1942

Born and raised in Tokyo, Hino started on trumpet at nine, and found himself loving both Louis Armstrong and Miles Davis. By the late 50s he was playing in swing-styled bands, but joined the important Hideo Shiraki group in 1964, and began leading his own bands from 1967. He scored some notable festival successes and eventually decided to move to New York in 1975. By this time, his style had taken on influences from all over the contemporary jazz spectrum, and a record such as the excellent *Into The Heaven* (1970) suggests a declamatory Miles Davis disciple with plenty of wrinkles of his own, notably an almost sentimental attraction to lyrical ballad playing and the capacity to play calmly and quietly even over a fierce backbeat. Since then, Hino has recorded frequently as both leader and sideman and remains a favourite at home (he divides his time between America and Japan), without quite recording a masterpiece or achieving a grander popularity. He made several albums for Blue Note's Japanese Somethin' Else imprint in the 90s. His brother Motohiko (1946–99), who often worked with him, was a fine drummer.

***Alone, Alone And Alone*** (Denon)

## Milt Hinton
BASS
*born* 23 June 1910; *died* 19 December 2000

One of the longest-serving of all jazz musicians, 'The Judge' could claim to have played tuba with Freddie Keppard, yet was around long enough to enjoy and participate in celebrations for his 75th, 80th and 90th birthdays, the latter in the new century itself. He grew up in Vicksburg, Missouri, and moved to Chicago in 1919, where he became involved in the city's music as a brass bassist, eventually switching to the string instrument around 1930. His major move was to join Cab Calloway in 1935, and he stayed until 1951, freelancing on record dates and keeping an eye on what the boppers were doing via his close friend Dizzy Gillespie. Thereafter he was never short of work for the next five decades. He played with jazz musicians of almost every style and inclination, from Coleman Hawkins and Joe Venuti to Branford Marsalis, and he took snapshots of most of them: a keen photographer from the start, he accrued an enormous archive of pictures. Hinton was also busy as an educator, and as a piece of living history with a keen and articulate memory he was treasured into his old age. Almost anything he played on would serve to show his impeccable time and harmonic knowledge, but the disc cited below also has him reminiscing about his teeming past, with a cast of old friends alongside.

***Old Man Time*** (Chiaroscuro)

## Hip

Every jazz listener aspires to be hip, which is the insiderish state of ease and familiarity with whatever is 'happening'. These days it is more likely to be deemed a sought-after state among fans than musicians: if you're a bona fide jazz musician, it's hard *not* to be hip. It mostly arose out of the bebop/beatnik dialect of the late 40s and early 50s, and was at one time designated as 'hep', although anyone using that term today is definitely not hip. One always describes *others* as hip, or otherwise: anyone saying 'I'm hip' is asking for trouble. Beware also the more elongated 'hipster', which is basically someone trying too hard to be hip (cf the *Seinfeld* character Kramer being considered a 'hipster doofus'). It is, of course, desirable to be both hip and cool, though these characteristics should ideally have a symbiotic relationship.

## Al Hirt
TRUMPET
*born* 7 November 1922; *died* 27 April 1999

Hirt was, like Pete Fountain, a very successful musician whose jazz status suffers from too much popularity. A New Orleans native, he was conservatory-trained and played with late-swing bands such as Tommy Dorsey's and Ray McKinley's. But he found his niche back in New Orleans, playing what many felt was mere tourist Dixieland but which won a huge audience via his contract with Audio Fidelity, a hi-fi label that gave him wide exposure. His RCA albums – there are at least 30 from the 60s and early 70s – built on that and turned him into a national celebrity. He was a skilful technician and a powerful executant of a kind which American audiences have always loved (hence his billing as Al 'He's The King' Hirt), and at his worst he drove the Harry James style to its spectacular limit, but once past the Christmas and strings albums there is a surprising amount to enjoy. Outside the US he was hardly known at all, which doubtless bothered him little.
*Horn-A-Plenty* (RCA)

## André Hodeir
COMPOSER
*born* 22 January 1921

Hodeir's work as a composer and a writer of jazz criticism is in a sense all of a piece: he edited the French magazine *Jazz Hot* in the late 40s, and books such as *Toward Jazz* (1962) have presented a sharp-eared and predictably acute insight into the musical processes behind jazz playing, as he hears them. He trained as a composer at the Paris Conservatoire, recorded as a violinist with Django Reinhardt and then formed the Jazz Groupe De Paris in 1954, entirely to play his own music: though not much recorded, what there is remains fascinating, and the music collected on *Jazz Et Jazz* (1959–60) is a glimpse of a rarely discussed area, the French modernism of the 50s. He sub-

sequently moved in the direction of larger-scale works and film music, and latterly focused primarily on writing.
*Jazz Et Jazz* (Fontana)

## Art Hodes
PIANO
*born* 14 November 1904; *died* 4 March 1993

Born in the Ukraine (and he was never exactly sure in which year), Hodes came with his family to New York in 1910 but later settled in Chicago, where he played piano in saloons and worked steadily, though without drawing much attention to himself. The keenest of observers and listeners, he prospered in Chicago's gangster era, with a good sense of when to keep his head down; then he moved to New York in 1938, where he had his own radio programme, started a record label (Jazz Record) and co-edited a magazine, also called *The Jazz Record*, which ran for four years in the middle 40s. He sometimes found trouble when soapboxing for the kind of jazz he loved – the tradition, blues and boogie woogie – and there were now-forgotten feuds with bop-inclined critics. He returned to Chicago in 1950 and never really stopped working: he still wrote (for *Down Beat* and *The Chicago Record*), in a conversational, wryly humorous style which was underpinned by a serious loyalty to the music. But his own playing, distilled out of the scores of pianists he had heard and followed, was the acme of Chicago's blues and traditional music: 'What was important was that you listened to the music when you got up, and went somewhere to play during the night. Always there was the turntable, the needle and the handful of records; your school books.' He recorded prolifically all through the 60s, 70s and 80s, with his few surviving contemporaries and with enthusiastic bands who might have been a couple of generations younger, and he toured both the US and Europe regularly until a stroke ended his career in 1991.
*South Side Memories* (Sackville)

# Johnny Hodges
ALTO SAXOPHONE
*born* 25 July 1907; *died* 11 May 1970

The favourite alto player of so many other musicians – John Coltrane was convinced that he had no peers on the saxophone – Cornelius Hodge (the 's' was added later) actually began on the improbable soprano instrument as a teenager, and received a lesson or two from Sidney Bechet, but soon enough switched to the alto. He worked alongside Bechet in some groups, dividing his time between Boston and New York in the early 20s, and he joined Chick Webb's band in 1926. But it was when he joined Duke Ellington, in May 1928, that Hodges found his destiny. By this time he had accrued a surprising maturity and command on what was still a jazz instrument finding its feet: barely 21 years old, he already mustered an effulgent tone and a way of ornamenting a melodic line which took the example of Bechet's prodigious virtuosity to a place which spoke of refinement, even luxuriance. His early solos with Ellington, as on 'Stevedore Stomp', still have the feeling of old-fashioned hot music about them, but by the time he became a regularly featured soloist in the early 30s the full expressive power of his delivery was becoming manifest. Ellington relied on his improvising on dozens of records, and in the late 30s Hodges was himself the nominal leader of several small-group sessions where the personnel was drawn from the Ellington band: the likes of 'Squatty Roo' (1938), a blistering concerto at a medium-up tempo which often brought out the best in him, were magnificent. He was a powerful blues player too, but Ellington realized that the Hodges which audiences liked best was the rhapsodist, and features such as 'Warm Valley' (1940) and 'Magenta Haze' (1946) were some of the most evocative works in the band's discography.

In 1951, Hodges felt like a change and led his own small group for a few years, recording for Norman Granz's Verve; but in 1955, tiring of the work of leading a band, he went back, and though he maintained an occasional regime of separation as a recording artist – cutting numerous sets with Wild Bill Davis and Earl Hines, and leading two classic sessions of small-group Ellingtonia, *Back To Back* and *Side By Side* (1959) – he basically stayed loyal to Ellington for the rest of his career. Although he had a sometimes sardonic outlook on his position in Ellington's music, he must have known that nobody else framed his playing so persuasively. He could seem almost icy in his detachment at times, allowing his eyes to roam an auditorium during a concert solo but only for the purpose of counting the exits to settle a wager, yet the molasses tone and perfectly judged licks kept his playing indecently fresh and oddly youthful. Nicknamed either 'Jeep' or 'Rabbit' (after a penchant for lettuce), Hodges was happy to let Ellington create new settings for him right to the end: 'Isfahan' from *Far East Suite* (1966) is a rapturous display of yearning, and the sessions for *New Orleans Suite* (1970) were to have featured him once again on the instrument which he had scarcely touched for years, the soprano sax. Instead, he died halfway through the recording, while visiting his dentist in New York.
**Back To Back** (Verve)

# Bendik Hofseth
TENOR AND SOPRANO SAXOPHONES
*born* 19 October 1962

At one point Hofseth seemed ready to become a surprise crossover star in 90s jazz. Having studied and played in comparative obscurity in Oslo, at 25 he took over Michael Brecker's chair in Steps Ahead and worked with that group for six years, in the meantime also establishing a solo career and playing with John McLaughlin. Hofseth's characteristically Nordic tone and brusque note-spinning made him seem like a plausibly rockier alternative to the prevailing Garbarek sound in Norwegian jazz, and he dabbled in fusion projects under his own name. But his impact seems to have petered out, at least internationally, over the past few years.
**Colours** (Verve)

# Jay Hoggard
VIBES
*born* 28 September 1954

Hoggard's interesting music has teetered on the brink of wider recognition, but in the end he is a rather marginalized figure. He began on vibes at 16 and visited Europe with Clifford Thornton, but it was a period studying in Tanzania which really determined some of his interests: he learned the West African balo, and subsequently the balafon, and his music since has been among the more distinctive attempts at threading African percussion techniques into a post-bop perspective. While he led groups of his own, played and recorded solo, and found himself linked in with the Young Lions movement of the early 80s, Hoggard's timing wasn't quite right: he was too early to capitalize on the mixing of jazz with world music, and too rootsy (or folksy) to really make an impact on the audience which followed the Marsalis generation. Since joining the faculty at Wesleyan University (where he originally studied philosophy) he has largely taken up his time with education, and Steve Nelson and Stefon Harris have stolen some of his thunder.

**The Little Tiger** (Muse)

# Allan Holdsworth

GUITAR
*born* 6 August 1946

The Bradford-born Holdsworth played in the British fusion bands Nucleus and Colosseum before joining Soft Machine in 1973, where he came to prominence: if McLaughlin was fast, Holdsworth was almost absurdly quick around the fretboard, and his improvisations with the group still amaze for their precision and the lucid geometry of his ideas. He then went to the US and played in Tony Williams's Lifetime. Based mainly in America, he has turned up in various fusion projects which seem to drift between jazz and rock moorings, never quite settling in at one point or the other. He sometimes uses a guitar-synthesizer. Like many musicians with a superabundance of technique, he can seem at a loss for the right context, and perhaps too few of the records under his own name really do justice to what is essentially a very musical and inventive mind.

**Wardenclyffe Tower** (Cream)

# Billie Holiday

VOCAL
*born* 7 April 1915; *died* 17 July 1959

Holiday contributed so much to her own legend through the misleading and grossly inaccurate memoir *Lady Sings The Blues* that it has taken a half-dozen biographers to get close to many of the facts of her life. On her birth certificate, her name is Elinore Harris, but as a girl she was known as Eleanora Fagan, given the nickname Billie, baptized as Elenore Gough and sometimes called Madge. In her teens she went back to Billie, and took her father's name of Holiday (though at first she used it as 'Halliday') when she started singing. Born in Philadelphia, abandoned by her father, she went to join her mother in New York in 1929, and reputedly worked as a prostitute. Around 1930 she started singing in Harlem clubs and was heard in one in 1933 by John Hammond, who set her up for record dates with Benny Goodman, and then began regular studio dates with pick-up groups under the direction of Teddy Wilson. These sessions continued until 1942, and on record after record the wonderful lightness of her voice, the easy fluency of her way with lyrics, the simplicity of her floating, beguiling approach to the beat captivate the listener. Perhaps she never made a better record than one of the titles at her first session with Wilson, 'Miss Brown To You': after the exhausting, frayed-nerves feel of what would be her latter-day records, one goes back to it and falls in love with Holiday all over again. Besides Holiday herself, the records feature stellar work from the likes of Lester Young, Roy Eldridge and Wilson himself, and the music can stand among the best small-group jazz records ever made.

Away from these records, though, Holiday's career only slowly picked up speed. She was with Count Basie in 1937 and Artie Shaw in 1938, but a residency at Café Society in Greenwich Village gave her something of a cult following, which was built on further by her signature record of 'Strange Fruit', an art-song about a lynching, made for the small Commodore label. In the 40s she signed to Decca and began making a speciality out of poignant and sometimes doom-laden ballads. Often her life seemed to be pursuing a tawdry imitation of some of her lyrics: 'Don't Explain', which almost amounts to an abused woman's confession, comes uncomfortably close to her own predi-lections, involving herself with a succession of unfortunate relationships and marriages, as well as a dependence on hard drugs and liquor. By the time she signed to Norman Granz's Clef label in 1953, her voice was tat-tered and worn, although when the spirit took her – and it often did – she could sum-mon her resources and give great perform-ances. But the girlish swing of her first records was a memory. Granz got some fine work from both singer and band on the best of these dates, but by the time she signed to make some new records for Columbia in 1958, her voice sounded close to a death rattle, and *Lady In Satin* (1958) is a dis-turbing listen. She collapsed in May 1959, and on her hospital bed she was arrested for narcotics possession, a final indignity of the sort her life had become wretchedly familiar with.

Since her death, Holiday's star has grown ever brighter. Many admirers are attracted more by her tragic mystique than her musicianship, and it is sad that her early music is nothing like as well known as the records she made in the LP era. She was a great natural: though she said that much of her inspiration came from Louis Armstrong's singing, her behind-the-beat delivery and the supple elegance of her phrasing have the individual grace and strength of a singular jazz musician, which is what sets her apart from so many merely interpretative singers. Whether one hears her as a tragic heroine or a great musician whose resources were systematically eroded, Billie's music, at its best and worst, has endured with a rare intensity.

*Lady Day Swings!* (Columbia)

# Dave Holland

BASS
*born* 1 October 1946

Holland was a quick learner. He studied at London's Guildhall School when in his teens, and by 1968 he was spotted as one of the most adept and musical bassists on the London scene. He might have remained there and worked a comparatively unevent-ful career, but his life changed in a few days when Miles Davis heard him in London in 1968 and within days Holland had gone to New York and joined the new, electric Davis

group, playing on *In A Silent Way* and *Bitches Brew*. It was an association which effectively set up the rest of his career, even though he left in 1970, along with fellow sideman Chick Corea, and began playing in the acoustic quartet Circle. When that group disbanded in 1972, the bassist found himself in demand from numerous quarters.

He carried on playing with fellow Circle member Anthony Braxton, and also recorded cello pieces with guitarist Derek Bailey, but instead of moving towards abstraction, which would have doomed him to the sidelines, he also worked effectively with more mainstream spirits such as Stan Getz and Lee Konitz. He did play at some length with Sam Rivers in the 70s, but there-after he has never really flirted with the jazz avant-garde again. Instead, his playing part-ners have included Pat Metheny, Herbie Hancock, Michael Brecker and other near-superstars.

Holland has been assiduous in creating a body of work as a leader. *Conference Of The Birds* (1972) was a beautifully modulated ses-sion where Braxton and Rivers performed almost as a pair of Blue Note saxophonists, on a sequence of charming compositions, and the later ECM *Emerald Tears* (1977) was a lyrical solo record; but Holland has been preoccupied mainly with records and tours by a quintet, a line-up which has at various times included Steve Coleman, Robin Eubanks, Steve Wilson, Steve Nelson and Chris Potter. In this environment, Holland's interest in unusual times has been explored from every direction, to the point where dif-ficult and contrary structures and settings have been distilled into smoothly effective pieces of post-bop repertory. It is one of the most specifically virtuosic groups in jazz, and it draws its fundamental strength from the leader's own impeccable playing: the precision and rapidity of his articulation, together with the sonorous, almost vocal tone which attracted Davis, make his every saying a pleasure. That said, both records and concerts – perhaps exemplified by the live *Extended Play* (2002) – can be intimidat-ingly 'musicianly', technique sometimes holding sway over content. Lately Holland has also recorded and toured with a big band, playing his music in that field.

*Conference Of The Birds* (ECM)

# Major Holley

BASS

*born* 10 July 1924; *died* 25 October 1990

'Mule' Holley took up the bass while doing navy service in the 40s. He played in California before returning to his home town of Detroit, performing regularly with Rose Murphy, and when he visited London with her in 1951 he stayed on and worked as a BBC studio man for five years. Back in the US, he worked the rest of his career mostly as a freelance: Roy Eldridge, Jimmy McPartland and Buddy Tate were among the leaders he played with frequently. Holley wasn't much of a soloist – he liked to play arco and sing along, somewhat in the manner of a more grouchy Slam Stewart – but as a timekeeper he was solid and steady and as adaptable as any who had enjoyed the kind of career he had.

**Coleman Hawkins,** *Today And Now* (Impulse!)

# Red Holloway

ALTO AND TENOR SAXOPHONES

*born* 31 May 1927

James Holloway is from Helena, Arkansas, but he might almost have been a Chicago bluesman: he worked the Southside clubs there in the late 40s, alongside all the local masters. In the 60s he joined in the soul-sax trend, cutting four typically spirited albums for Prestige, but it's really in his senior years that he's made a bigger mark on the music, touring as a guest solo and turning up in boisterous jam-session situations. He worked in a partnership with Sonny Stitt in the late 70s, and when he gets together with someone such as Clark Terry (*Locksmith Blues*, 1989) great fun is assured. He's a mighty player, but at this point, when he plays the blues, it's to have fun rather than torch the soul.

**Locksmith Blues** (Concord)

# Bill Holman

ARRANGER, TENOR SAXOPHONE

*born* 21 May 1927

Holman's association with Stan Kenton's orchestra, playing in the band as a sideman and contributing charts during 1952–6, was crucial in establishing his career. From there he wrote for other groups – Maynard Ferguson, Terry Gibbs, Gerry Mulligan's Concert Jazz Band – while continuing to contribute to Kenton's book, and in 1966 he gave up playing altogether after problems with his teeth and focused entirely on writing. Besides the inevitable work for television, and commissions from Europe as well as the US, Holman began leading an occasional big band in Los Angeles from 1975, which after many years of work made some records in the 90s (though regrettably none since): so finely crafted and inventive are the scores and playing that they should rank with the best big-band albums of the modern era.

**A View From The Side** (JVC)

# Charlie Holmes

ALTO SAXOPHONE

*born* 27 January 1910; *died* 12 September 1985

Holmes grew up in Boston with Johnny Hodges and, like Hodges, he eventually picked up the alto saxophone and went to New York in 1927. For most of the rest of the 20s and the 30s he worked for Luis Russell, including that bandleader's various backing gigs for Louis Armstrong and others. On the occasions where he steps out on Russell's records, he sounds soulful and exuberant. In the 40s he played with Cootie Williams and John Kirby, but there wasn't much other work and in the 50s and 60s he was more or less out of music, coming back one final time to play a few gigs in the 70s with Clyde Bernhardt.

**Luis Russell,** *The Luis Russell Story* (Retrieval)

# Richard 'Groove' Holmes

ORGAN

*born* 2 May 1931; *died* 29 June 1991

The big man of jazz organ played in New Jersey clubs before being signed by Pacific Jazz in 1961, and he went on to make further albums for Prestige in the second half of the 60s. His whomping bass lines gave him a rocking solidity which perhaps surpassed some of his organ-playing colleagues, although many of his records fall into the familiar trap of being too samey which the whole genre can fall prey to. He enjoyed a brief renaissance towards the end of his life, along with the rest of the Hammond organ-grinders, although he died while that revival was still under way.

*Misty* (Prestige/OJC)

## Tristan Honsinger
CELLO
*born* 23 October 1949

Honsinger studied classical cello at Peabody Conservatory but fled to Canada to escape the draft in 1969 and while there fell in with free-jazz players in Montreal. He shifted over to the Old World in 1974 and settled in Amsterdam, from there building a network of associations which led to work with many of Europe's leading free players, including Derek Bailey, Gunter Christmann and Irène Schweizer. He has subsequently been based in both Italy and Britain. The record cited is an exhilarating, entirely solo recital dating from 1998, which gives an idea of his expressive range, from Bach-like exercises to madcap circumlocutions which disguise a shrewd grasp of both structure and detail.

*A Camel's Kiss* (ICP)

## William Hooker
DRUMS
*born* 18 June 1946

Hooker played rock in Hartford and free jazz in California before arriving in New York in time for the loft-jazz experiments of the middle 70s. He has never really left that scene and its untempered ideals since, holding down a succession of day jobs in order to perform some of the most radical and uncompromised free playing: he plays with horns, guitars, poets and organists, in every kind of combination, and has managed to rattle off a chaotic discography of both live and studio work, stretched across a variety of tiny local labels. Stylistically indebted to pretty much any free drummer one could name, his playing drives and dictates the pace in all of his music.

*Great Sunset* (Warm-O'-Brisk)

## Elmo Hope
PIANO
*born* 27 June 1923; *died* 19 May 1967

Named after St Elmo, the patron saint of sailors, Hope began in R&B bands (where one of his fellow sidemen was Johnny Griffin). After playing on a Clifford Brown date for Blue Note, Alfred Lion recorded Hope in a trio situation, and then with a quintet. He was a strange mix of Monk, Powell and his own startling originality, which tends to surface in the middle of a tune like a flash of lightning. Certainly a track such as 'Mo Is On' (1953) has a whirling energy all its own. But there's a disjunctive feeling to much of Hope's playing, as if even he isn't sure what he's doing from moment to moment. As a composer, he came up with some fascinating pieces, and it's a little surprising that the fad for rediscovering forgotten jazz composers has so far left him out: the likes of 'Barfly' and 'Mirror-Mind Rose' certainly cry out for a comeback in the repertory. Hope didn't miss out on work – he recorded for Contemporary and Prestige, and with John Coltrane, Harold Land, Frank Foster and other high-profile hornmen, in both California and New York. But narcotics ruined him, and he did time for drug offences. His wife Bertha (who cut an album of duets with Elmo) remains a gifted pianist herself, and she is still recording.

*Trio And Quintet* (Blue Note)

## Claude Hopkins
PIANO, BANDLEADER
*born* 24 August 1903; *died* 19 February 1984

A tough and single-minded bandleader, Hopkins always had good orchestras, but they have left only a modest mark on the music's history. By the end of the 20s he had already toured Europe, worked for the Theater Owners' Booking Association and held down important New York club residencies; in 1931 he captured a prime spot at the Savoy Ballroom, which brought him a record contract with Columbia (and later Decca). The records are a rather disappointing lot, with exciting early arrangements such as Jimmy Mundy's 'Mush Mouth' (1932) misleading, since by the later 30s the band sounds almost faceless. Yet Hopkins stayed popular: he took over from

Cab Calloway at The Cotton Club and carried on with a large group until 1940, after which he toured in small groups and revues. He was still doing this kind of thing right up till the 80s. He found the company of swing mainstreamers very congenial for latter-day sessions such as *Let's Jam* (1961) and *Swing Time!* (1963) and his own piano playing – which he was never shy about featuring – was a pleasing if unexceptional distillation of such greater contemporaries as Hines, Wilson and Tatum.
**Claude Hopkins 1932–1934** (Classics)

## Fred Hopkins
BASS
*born* 11 October 1947; *died* 7 January 1999

A native Chicagoan, Hopkins was involved with the AACM early on and performed in a trio with Henry Threadgill and Steve McCall as early as 1971, although they had yet to start calling themselves Air. When they did, around 1975, this group became the main focus for Hopkins's activity, although he also did sideman work with David Murray, Oliver Lake, Don Pullen, Arthur Blythe and others. Following Air's dispersal in 1985, he went back to freelance work and formed Stringdom, a duo with cellist Dierdre Murray. He had been in New York since 1975 but returned to Chicago in 1997, although this versatile and much-admired bassman was not destined to live much longer.
**Air, *Air Time*** (Nessa)

## Horn

Pretty much any jazz instrument can be a 'horn'. While a 'horn section' refers to the brass and/or reeds, a jazz musician can say, 'I have to pack up my horn and get out of here', and could be referring to a trumpet, a piccolo or even a double bass.

## Paul Horn
FLUTES, CLARINET
*born* 17 March 1930

Arguably, Horn was way ahead of his time. He studied flute at university and joined Chico Hamilton's quintet on the West Coast in 1956. In the early 60s his house was a popular hangout for musicians (partly because Horn had a pool, and many liked to drop in for a swim) and the likes of Miles Davis would sit around and talk music for hours. Horn began making records in a somewhat vague chamberish idiom and was the principal soloist in a typically faddish piece by Lalo Schifrin, *Jazz Suite On The Mass Texts* (1965). Horn visited India in 1967 and joined The Beatles in becoming a follower of TM, subsequently decamping to Canada, where he had his own TV show for a time. Since then he has worked prolifically in a rather hard-to-identify style which might be called world music (Horn prefers the epithet 'universal'). Jazz forgot about him a long time ago.
**In India** (Blue Note)

## Shirley Horn
VOCAL, PIANO
*born* 1 May 1934

She grew up in Washington DC, and having studied piano and composition she brought together her first trio when she was 20. Although she acquired a strong reputation among musicians, it wasn't until the admiring Miles Davis got her a slot at The Village Vanguard in 1961 that her career went anywhere at all. Even then, after recording a couple of unremarkable albums for Mercury and one for ABC, she rarely left her Washington base. In 1978 she began making records for Steeplechase and in the 80s commenced a series of regular European festival visits. But it was her contract with Verve, beginning with 1987's *I Thought About You*, which gave her a belated breakthrough, and she has recorded a long series of albums for the label. She still preferred to work with her regular trio of Charles Ables (bass, who died in 2001) and Steve Williams (drums), which was together for many years. Shirley's sparse piano, breathily behind-the-beat phrasing and liking for tempos which are so slow that they barely seem to be moving at all go together to make a unique artist, who's been more influential than many listeners realize: would Diana Krall sound the way she does, without Shirley's example?
**Loving You** (Verve)

# Hot

Inevitably, this is the opposite of 'cool' playing, and its use goes back as far as ragtime, which used titles such as 'Too Much Mustard' to imply music emerging at a high temperature. 'Playing hot' was what set the first generation of jazz players aside from their more conservative colleagues: fast, swinging playing, with emphatic use of the beat, are what connoisseurs of so-called 'hot dance' music wait for on the thousands of generic dance-band discs made during the 20s and pre-swing-era 30s. So 'hot' basically equalled 'jazz' in its earliest days. As a variety of expression began to be accommodated within the music, though, the term 'hot' began to sound almost quaintly anachronistic, and it has little place in a modern jazz vocabulary. It is still in use, though, as part of the language of traditional jazz, since it is often part of the title of many of the tunes anyway.

## Avery 'Kid' Howard
TRUMPET
*born* 22 April 1908; *died* 28 March 1966

Although Howard began in New Orleans music by playing drums with Andrew Morgan, in the early 20s, he was inspired by Chris Kelly's example to take up the trumpet. In the 30s and 40s he worked with some of the leading brass bands, and he began a long association with George Lewis in 1943. But by the end of the 50s Howard was at a low ebb: he was one of the first musicians Barry Martyn saw when the drummer went to New Orleans in 1959, and Martyn was shocked at his wasted appearance. The advent of the regular music at Preservation Hall helped revitalize him, and he came back from a near-fatal decline to record regularly in the early 60s, leading his bands with a doughty vigour.
*Kid Howard's La Vida Band* (American Music)

## Darnell Howard
CLARINET, ALTO SAXOPHONE, VIOLIN
*born* 25 July 1901; *died* 2 September 1966

Howard enjoyed a remarkably long jazz life: he played with W C Handy in 1917, and was touring Europe with the New Orleans All Stars in the year of his death. He worked under several leaders in Chicago in the early 20s before becoming a regular with King Oliver, but when he joined Earl Hines in 1931 he had found his most successful job. Hines featured him regularly as a soloist and Howard stayed with him until 1937, leading his own groups during the pianist's summer breaks. Work was scarcer in the 40s and he repaired radios as well as playing music, but he had a successful stint with Muggsy Spanier in the early 50s and finally rejoined his old boss Hines in 1955, playing regularly at San Francisco's Hangover Club. While he did his best work on clarinet, Howard was also a violinist of some skill, and he can be heard in that capacity on some of Hines's earlier records.
**Earl Hines,** *1932–1934* (Classics)

## Noah Howard
ALTO SAXOPHONE
*born* 6 April 1943

Howard was a first-generation free player whose music had a contrary shyness about it – he never sounds comfortable with the kind of sonic aggression which Albert Ayler and Archie Shepp invested in. Nevertheless, when he moved to New York in 1965 – from his native New Orleans – he found himself in the front ranks of the New Thing, recording for ESP and playing in Paris and Belgium at the end of the decade. He helped found the New York Musicians' Organization in 1971 and started releasing records on his own Altsax label, but he became more elusive when he went back to Europe, where he has mostly lived since, although some recent records have emerged on the American Cadence label. Howard's trust in his own melodic imagination gives his music its balance and fertility, and he isn't afraid of mixing free thinking with more conventional post-bop playing. It is also informed by his wanderings, which at one time took him to Africa, and on the record listed he says, 'I'm Noah Howard – of the world.'
*In Concert* (Cadence)

# Paul Howard

SAXOPHONE, BANDLEADER

*born* 20 September 1895; *died* 18 February 1980

Howard led one of the very best bands in California in the 20s. He had already worked with King Oliver and Jelly Roll Morton when he formed a quartet in 1924, The Quality Four, which eventually expanded into a full orchestra, and in 1927 he worked at San Diego's Cotton Club for two years. Paul Howard's Quality Serenaders grew into a powerful, swinging outfit, and the 12 sides they cut for Victor in 1929–30 (with a line-up including Lawrence Brown, Lionel Hampton and the fine trumpeter George Orendorff) showcase a band that could hold its own with all but the hottest competition on the East Coast. When the band eventually split up, Howard worked for other leaders through the 30s until he once again led a band which had a long residency at Virginia's in Eagle Rock (1939–48). A staunch union man and a committed professional, Howard carried on playing for many years and then enjoyed a long retirement from the business.

# Freddie Hubbard

TRUMPET

*born* 7 April 1938

Hubbard's youthful music set him up to be an immortal force on his instrument, and his crashing decline is salutary and saddening. Born in Indianapolis, he learned trumpet (as well as french horn and tuba) in a high-school marching band, and he was part of a local group named The Jazz Contemporaries before moving to New York in 1958. His big sound, swaggering delivery and the melodic bloom he could put on otherwise bluesily charged improvisations soon had him set up as one of the coming men on his instrument, and after working with a few leaders he eventually replaced – a piquant move – Lee Morgan in the Jazz Messengers in 1961. Blue Note had already signed him as a solo, and his sequence of early records for the label – *Open Sesame* (1960), *Ready For Freddie* (1961) and *Hub-Tones* (1962) – establish his budding greatness with an almost insolent ease. He surpassed Morgan in terms of technique and smartness of tone, and while there

sometimes seemed to be a strange blandness at the very core of some of his solos, this hardly detracted from their capacity to excite. Meanwhile, he had also worked on such new-jazz documents as Eric Dolphy's *Outward Bound* and Ornette Coleman's *Free Jazz* (both 1960): while he can seem like the uncomprehending straight man in these situations, he certainly took much away from them, and he credited Dolphy in particular for opening his ears to different styles of playing. After leaving Blakey in 1964 and holding down a brief job with Max Roach, Hubbard worked primarily as his own leader, although he still took occasional sideman roles: nobody ever used him better than Herbie Hancock did for both *Maiden Voyage* (1965) and *Empyrean Isles* (1966), where his natural lyricism blossoms as on few other records.

From 1966 he began recording for Atlantic, and the albums began to capsize into confused seas of funk, experimentalism and – occasionally – plain jazz. Creed Taylor signed him to his new soft-focus label CTI in 1970, started with a great record (*Red Clay*), and then drove Hubbard's talent into a dead end of near-Muzak. Despite winning a Grammy for one of the albums in 1972, Hubbard's sales began to decline and by 1977 he was touring with VSOP, the reunion group with Wayne Shorter and Herbie Hancock. It prefigured the way his career would move in the 80s, since he steadily left the trappings of fusion behind and went back to an almost sentimental kind of hard bop. There were trumpet jousts with Woody Shaw (who outplayed him on *Double Take*, 1985) and moments where some of his old greatness would glimmer through, but Hubbard had already mixed himself up too many times: unsure of where his best setting lay, he ended up committing nothing to anything. In 1993 he damaged an already troubled lip, and has seemingly never fully recovered his playing skills, although this hasn't always prevented him from treating paying audiences with disrespect.

*Ready For Freddie* (Blue Note)

# Peanuts Hucko
CLARINET, TENOR SAXOPHONE
*born* 7 April 1918

Hucko worked with several of the prominent swing orchestras at the beginning of
the 40s, but his most featured role came in
Glenn Miller's Army Air Force band, where
he played mostly clarinet. He switched to
more of a Dixieland role when he hooked
up with the Eddie Condon clan later in the
decade, and he turns up on numerous
records from the 50s in this kind of jazz
idiom. Eventually he became one of Louis
Armstrong's All Stars in 1958, although he
stayed only a couple of years, and after that
he kept busy with such groups as The
World's Greatest Jazz Band and his own Pied
Piper Quintet, which often featured Ralph
Sutton. This work lasted him well into
the 90s. A fast, clean player, Hucko (the
'Peanuts' was a nickname he earned as a
boy, from his love of that food) wasn't an
eccentric in the Pee Wee Russell tradition,
and his fluency and reliability may have
got him further as a result.
*Swing That Music* (Starline)

# Spike Hughes
BASS
*born* 19 October 1908; *died* 2 February 1987

Hughes's long life was full of music, but his
jazz career lasted barely five years. Patrick
Cairns Hughes (his father was a cellist and
composer) studied music in Vienna and
began playing bass in London dance bands
in 1929. He recorded some 40 titles as a
leader for Decca (as the leader of his
Decca-Dents, Three Blind Mice – who accompanied Jimmy Dorsey on a London visit –
and Dance Orchestra), all of them approaching jazz from the direction of warmly played
dance music. He also wrote arrangements
for C B Cochrane, a *Harlem Symphony* and a
ballet, *High Yellow*, before going to New York
in 1933 and staying long enough to cut 14
titles with a group of black players that was
basically the Benny Carter band of the day
(and which included Henry Allen and
Coleman Hawkins). But he abruptly abandoned performance altogether, although he
still wrote criticism for *The Melody Maker*
for some years afterwards, and went back to
the classical world. There is still some mystery about this departure, but at least
Hughes donated a considerable body of
work to the early stirrings of English swing,
even if much of it is these days little known.
*Spike Hughes Vols 1–4* (Kings Cross Music)

# Daniel Humair
DRUMS
*born* 23 May 1938

Although considered a leading force in
French jazz for more than 40 years, Humair
is actually a Swiss, born in Geneva, who only
moved to Paris when he was 20. But he was
soon playing with the best musicians in the
city, as well as backing visitors, and spent
the next decade freelancing, working with
The Swingle Singers and Martial Solal – the
latter a favourite and long-standing association – then spending four years with Phil
Woods (from 1968) before leading bands of
his own. He has experimented with bands of
different shapes and sizes, but always seems
to prefer a return to the trio form, where he
can be both a group player and a powerful
individual presence: *Quatre Fois Trois* (1997)
celebrates that in four different line-ups. As
with many Europeans of his generation, the
circumstances of his career obliged him to
develop a broad stylistic versatility: a cultured man who also spends a lot of time
with a paintbrush and easel, he seems to
have had no trouble with that, and he has
performed with musicians of such widely
differing disciplines as Lee Konitz, Ellery
Eskelin, Joachim Kühn and Marc Ducret.
*9–11 P.M. Town Hall* (Label Bleu)

# Helen Humes
VOCAL
*born* 23 June 1909; *died* 13 September 1981

Humes started young: she cut four titles for
OKeh as a 'classic blues' singer when she
was barely 18 (a mix-up over her date of
birth led some to believe that she was even
younger). In the 30s she began working as a
big-band singer, and her break came when
Count Basie took her on (as a replacement
for Billie Holiday) in 1938. Although Helen
never won anything like the success and
notoriety which her predecessor enjoyed,
like her opposite number Jimmy Rushing
she could sing blues and perform as a jazz

singer with equal and beguiling assurance, and she stayed for three successful years. In the 40s she worked as a solo and with Teddy Wilson, eventually going out in package tours, and had regular work in Red Norvo's groups. She settled briefly in Australia in the early 60s but returned home to tend to her ailing mother, and thereafter enjoyed a new popularity as a club singer. Humes had a beautifully unselfconscious, fluent style, which lent dignity to bawdy material and a sweetness to hackneyed ballads, and even into her old age she retained a girlish quality in her delivery: while some of her albums have an off-the-cuff quality, there is something outstanding in all of them, and her series of Contemporary albums made around the turn of the 60s are unstintingly delightful. Compared to many of her peers, she remains undervalued and unfairly neglected.

**Songs I Like To Sing** (Contemporary/OJC)

# Percy Humphrey
TRUMPET
*born* 13 January 1905; *died* 22 July 1995

# Willie Humphrey
CLARINET
*born* 29 December 1900; *died* 7 June 1994

The Humphrey brothers came from a renowned New Orleans family: their father was Willie Sr (1879–1964), and their grandfather Jim (1859–1935) led the Eclipse Brass Band. Willie was already working at 14 and played with Freddie Keppard and King Oliver before moving to St Louis in 1925, staying for seven years. Thereafter he returned to New Orleans and remained a musical force there until his death. Percy, though, was more inclined to be a bandleader: he ran his own groups from 1925, and though he held down a variety of day jobs for many years, he found time to lead his own group, the Eureka Brass Band (from 1947) and the Preservation Hall Jazz Band, which he was still leading into the 90s. Both men lived for their music: Willie liked to sing and dance as well as play, and Percy was still playing until a few weeks before he died. Both men were recorded without any real dedication until they were past what might be thought of as their prime, but the sheer doggedness of New Orleans jazz fires

up the documents they left behind: Percy played with the short-breathed, punched-out phrasing which is the Crescent City signature, and Willie followed his own variation on the George Lewis style. A third brother, Earl (1902–71), was a trombonist.

**Preservation Hall Jazz Band, New Orleans** (Columbia)

# Pee Wee Hunt
TROMBONE
*born* 10 May 1907; *died* 22 June 1979

Hunt's jazz career fell into two distinct phases. He studied at Ohio State University and joined Jean Goldkette in 1927, but he became a mainstay of the Casa Loma Orchestra in 1929, staying until 1943 and acting as one of the principal soloists in that highly drilled ensemble. After that he worked as a disc jockey and in a navy band, but when he formed a Dixieland sextet in 1946 he struck gold again: signed to Capitol Records, he made a sequence of lively although faintly comic records, and had a major hit with a rickety-tick version of 'Twelfth Street Rag' in 1948, a record which all but sums up the clockwork feel of a certain strain of traditional jazz in this period. Capitol dropped him in 1955 and his career faded away.

**Dixieland Classics** (Capitol)

# Charlie Hunter
GUITAR
*born* 23 May 1967

Hunter's mother serviced and repaired guitars, and he bought his own first instrument at 12. His college years were spent in and around the Bay Area of San Francisco, and he became intensely involved in the club scene there, taking in a mixture of organ-combo jazz, hard bop, funk, rap and college rock. Besides signing to Blue Note and recording a series of albums for that label, Hunter also ran a parallel band called TJ Kirk which recorded for Warners. He has always been interested in going his own way on the guitar: he started with a seven-string instrument (using five guitar and two bass strings), following a style more in keeping with Larry Young's organ work than any guitar influences, and subsequently added a

third bass string to go up to eight. Hunter's fingerpicked delivery moves the virtuosity of Stanley Jordan up a notch, and while much of what he does – across an eclectic series of records, which have included a tribute to Bob Marley – appeals to rock ears, he is a jazz guy through and through.
**Natty Dread** (Blue Note)

## Chris Hunter
ALTO SAXOPHONE
*born* 21 February 1957

Hunter was a very bright light in the British jazz of the 80s. A close confrère of Guy Barker, he was, like the trumpeter, a graduate of NYJO and a busy and successful face on the London session scene of the early 80s, leading his own group and winning a star soloist role in the Gil Evans Orchestra during the same period: this led to his settling in New York, with a sound which resembled a close relative of the David Sanborn wail. But little he has done since the end of the 80s has had any far-reaching impact, and with no records under his own name in print his career seems to have tailed off very disappointingly.
**This Is Chris** (Paddle Wheel)

## Robert Hurst III
BASS
*born* 4 October 1964

Hurst grew up in Detroit and played bass in rock bands before working in local jazz clubs. In 1985, he won the bass role in the Wynton Marsalis band, playing on the trumpeter's important *J Mood* (1985), and ultimately made the transition to the Branford Marsalis group, working with that leader during his high-profile stint on *The Tonight Show*. After Marsalis's departure from that position, though, Hurst has been notably less prominent. He made a couple of albums of his own for DIW and is as accomplished and authoritative as expected from an individual who has held down the engagements he has. Making further progress as a leader will be a challenge for him, though.
**Robert Hurst Presents Robert Hurst** (DIW)

## Bobby Hutcherson
VIBES
*born* 27 January 1941

Hutcherson's career has had its share of stops and starts, and it has told against his real eminence being fully recognized. Raised in Pasadena, he was inspired by Milt Jackson to take up the vibes, and by 1960 was playing in the Los Angeles area. He first attracted some attention in a group led by Billy Mitchell and Al Grey, travelling with them to New York, and since he took on what would have been the pianist's role in that band, he also played chords with four mallets, although he preferred to use two and did so on most of his recordings. Once in New York he came to the attention of Blue Note's Alfred Lion, who recorded him extensively as both leader and sideman: he is on important albums such as Dolphy's *Out To Lunch!* (1963) and Andrew Hill's *Judgement!* (1964), but his own 1965–6 sessions are outstanding. Eschewing both the prettiness of the vibes and the conventionally bluesy delivery of Jackson, Hutcherson's music had an abstract side which only Walt Dickerson approached, yet he kept hold of the slow vibrato that Jackson espoused, and his group records are notable for their textured, almost palpable interleaving of sounds, a democracy of intention which makes album titles such as *Dialogue* (1965) and *Components* (1966) seem particularly apposite. Yet they fared comparatively poorly with even the jazz public, and have only been intermittently available since. Hutcherson remained with Blue Note until the early 70s but his later albums for the label descended into pseudo-fusion, and in the later 70s he was back on the West Coast. He formed a group with Harold Land, The Timeless All Stars, in 1981, and often worked with McCoy Tyner: the best of their duo performances, especially on the sublime *Manhattan Moods* (1993), touch on an almost delirious romanticism. Which suggests something of the way Hutcherson's career has gone: he has enjoyed very little label sponsorship since his Blue Note days (a brief dalliance with Verve in the 90s resulted in only a single album), and the toughness of his early work has been displaced by an accomplished though more conventionally persuasive delivery.
**Dialogue** (Blue Note)

# Gregory Hutchinson

DRUMS
*born* 16 June 1970

Hutchinson has been a ubiquitous drumming presence on the New York scene of the past 15 years or so. Betty Carter had him in one of her groups of the early 90s, and from there he has gone on to work with dozens of other players, mostly in a relatively conventional post-bop style: he shows little interest in (or has had little opportunity for) working in any kind of fusion or crossover situation. He works particularly well in the piano-trio format, seemingly uninterested in pushing himself to the front of the stand.

**Eric Reed, *Pure Imagination*** (Impulse!)

# Jason Hwang

VIOLIN
*born* 12 May 1957

Asian-Americans have thus far formed only a limited presence in American jazz. Hwang's dramatic music opens some fascinating possibilities for future development. He went to New York in 1979 to study film production and began making the customary wide circle of musical acquaintances: by the 90s he had played alongside such disparate figures as Billy Bang, Henry Threadgill, Vladimir Tarasov and Anthony Braxton, and had toured South Korea with the percussion ensemble Samul Nori. Although he has formed various bands of his own, it is the Far East Side Band which has so far been the best vehicle for Hwang's own playing: a fierce improviser on acoustic and electric violin, he draws on a variety of Eastern disciplines, and likes to think theatrically – 'Consider the composition a stage with specific lighting and props.' Ritual and stage convention are boldly interspersed with an improviser's imagination. Some of the music thus far has suffered from a missing visual element, but the set listed below has many riveting moments.

***Caverns*** (New World)

# Margie Hyams

VIBES
*born* 1923

Before she married Rolf Ericson and retired in 1950, Hyams seemed ready to establish herself as a considerable voice on the vibes. She joined Woody Herman's First Herd in 1944 and led a small group of her own later in the decade, but it was her in the end brief stay in George Shearing's quintet which really established her quick-witted and adroit playing as something to hear. Little was heard from her subsequently, although she did take up teaching.

**George Shearing, *Verve Jazz Masters*** (Verve)

# Ken Hyder

DRUMS
*born* 29 June 1946

Born in Dundee, Hyder started as an Elvin Jones fan, but he found himself caught up in traditional Scottish music too, and was among the first to try and create what has lately become a modish blend, Scottish folk and jazz. His band Talisker, formed at the start of the 70s, were a formidable proposition in person, with the saxophonists Davie Webster and John Rangecroft making up a powerful front line, but their records did little justice to the band. Hyder's subsequent progress has been a pilgrimage of sorts, which has found him travelling to Siberia and forming musical alliances with Tuvan singers, Inuit and Japanese musicians, and whoever else his open ears hear as a kindred spirit. If he has largely left jazz behind, his pioneer work and frontier spirit deserve recognition.

**Bardo State Orchestra, *Wheels Within Wheels*** (Impetus)

# Dick Hyman

PIANO, ORGAN
*born* 8 March 1927

Hyman's career can fairly be described as unique. He had classical lessons as a boy and tootled along with records on clarinet, but in 1947 he won a radio competition where the prize was a dozen lessons with Teddy Wilson, which set him on his way. By 1949 he was playing in New York clubs, and proved capable of backing both the boppers

and swing players. His versatility helped him get a job as a staffer at NBC, where he played every kind of popular music, and he was a regular in the recording studios, although often hiding behind pseudonyms and rattling off albums which cashed in on such crazes as an unlikely one for parlour tunes played on a honky tonk piano. In the 60s he began using electric keyboards, playing organ behind Bobby Hackett and becoming one of the first jazzmen to investigate synthesizers. In the 70s and 80s, he came into his own as a repertory specialist (his group the Perfect Jazz Repertory Quintet helped establish the idea of the jazz past as an area for rediscovery), and recorded all of Scott Joplin's music, as well as pieces by the stride masters and homages to Waller, Ellington and others. His concerts and lectures became masterclasses in the history of jazz piano, and he seemed as interested in Cecil Taylor as in James P Johnson. His ability to mimic Art Tatum's methods is dazzling. While it can be difficult to discern the 'real' Hyman in amongst all this scholarly ingenuity, nobody has made a more persuasive case for reinvigorating the dustier areas of the jazz past, and his record of duets with John Sheridan, *Forgotten Dreams* (2001), tackled perhaps the last unexposed field available to him, the remote legacy of 'novelty' piano. Debonair, twinkling and discreetly passionate, his playing is, for all its outreach, very personal at its best.
*Forgotten Dreams* (Arbors)

## Susie Ibarra

DRUMS
*born* 15 November 1970

Ibarra emerged in the middle 90s as a striking new voice in her field. A Sun Ra concert decided her on going into music, while studying art in New York, and she studied with Milford Graves, who encouraged the polystylistic approach she brings to drumming. A player of terrific energy who can suddenly fall into passages of quiet and restraint, she has done some powerful work on record already: duos with former husband Assif Tsahar and with Derek Bailey and Mark Dresser, and a brilliant trio record with violinist Charles Burnham and pianist Cooper-Moore.
*Radiance* (Hopscotch)

## Abdullah Ibrahim

PIANO, SOPRANO SAXOPHONE
*born* 9 October 1934

Born Adolph Johannes Brand in Cape Town – a name he shortened to Dollar Brand in his early years, by which name he is still sometimes known – Ibrahim soaked up whatever music he heard in the South African townships of his youth, a vivid mixture of gospel music, rhythm and blues and local dance music. He played piano in dance-orientated groups before forming his own group, The Jazz Epistles, in 1960: the line-up featured Hugh Masekela and Kippie Moeketsi besides Ibrahim, and they were the first black South African group to have their music recorded at album length. He left for Europe in 1962 and came to the attention of Duke Ellington, who encouraged him and helped him find work at some of the leading European festivals. Shifting to New York in 1965 he became caught up in the free-jazz scene there, although he recorded little: one exception was a duet record with Gato Barbieri. In 1968 he left the US and eventually returned to South Africa, where he adopted the Islamic name Abdullah Ibrahim and settled his music back into the more personal style he had started out with. From that point, his playing and groups established a strongly personal idiom which drew on African, European and American sources in a notably peaceful alliance, even when much of Ibrahim's music had political and passionate points to make. His love for the playing of both Ellington and Monk floods through his own pianism, and his ability to create seemingly simple yet inexhaustible melodies certainly owes much to Monk's example. He formed a series of groups of differing sizes – Universal Silence, African Space Program, Kalahari, The African Band – and in 1973 commenced a long-standing relationship with the German independent label Enja, which continues to this day, resulting in dozens of recordings. His septet Ekaya was formed in 1983 and has been one of his most durable vehicles, but he still performs regularly in trio and quartet settings and has lately produced several works for piano and orchestra. In 1990, having again lived variously in Swaziland, Europe and the US, he returned to South Africa and has since become closely involved with the indigenous music of Cape Town.

Ibrahim became something of a touch-stone for liberal audiences who wanted to hear an authentic voice of South African freedom during the apartheid era, and while some of his music is marked with greatness, he is perhaps not quite as remarkable as his admirers would contend: too many of his recordings display a thinness of resource and a falling back on familiar devices at the very moments where one might hope for catharsis. But he has certainly created a book of naggingly catchy melodies, and it is surprising that more of them have not been explored by other players. A charismatic individual with a ready laugh, never the sombre-wise-man some part of his legend might suggest, he doubtless enjoys his stature, and he still delights audiences around the world.

*Africa Tears And Laughter* (Enja)

## ICP
GROUP/RECORD COMPANY

Han Bennink, Willem Breuker and Misha Mengelberg founded the Instant Composers Pool in 1967, a cooperative which set some of the new jazz activity in the Netherlands on to a firm footing. While Breuker's input was concerned with his own composed music for the Breuker Kollektief, Bennink and Mengelberg would work primarily as an improvising duo. Breuker left ICP in 1974 and most of the activity since then has been based around the ICP Orchestra, which is led by Mengelberg although Bennink also performs in it. ICP also began as a record label at the time of the collective's initial activity, and it has continued thus into the CD era: many of the early records are now rare and highly collectable.

## Klaus Ignatzek
PIANO
*born* 4 November 1954

Ignatzek has worked prolifically on the German scene since the late 70s, playing first in a duo with alto saxophonist Jochen Voss, then leading trios and small groups and performing solo. He has a thorough understanding of hard-bop piano, as documented by its original American practitioners, and that has led many of his

records towards a rather anodyne and re-creative cul de sac. Some of his later records have more of a chamber-jazz feel.
*Reunion* (Acoustic Music)

## Improvisation

One participant in a marketing survey on the music complained that 'The trouble with jazz is that they stop playing the tune after a while', which at least tackles the central ingredient in jazz musicianship head on. Making up new material in the context of an otherwise structured performance had been part of music-making for hundreds of years before jazz, and it is interesting to ponder what such distinguished improvisers as Beethoven would have made of an idiom where that spontaneous creativity is inescapable. Improvisation remains the way jazz is most forcefully characterized: not so much inventing something completely new every time as turning the impossibility of playing something *exactly* as before to the music's advantage. An improvisation will most likely be based on some aspect of the material being performed – a new melody on a settled chord sequence, perhaps, or an old melody given a new embellishment – and the improviser will do his or her best to personalize it in such a way that what emerges is fresh, different music. Ragtime and early jazz appear to have had little in the way of distinct improvisation, and were characterized more by ornamentation, subtle displacement and tonal variation. It was the rise of the improvising jazz soloist, as personified by Louis Armstrong in the 20s, which settled a mantle of 'making it new' on the jazz musician, a demanding and often exhausting responsibility: for how many can truly 'make it new' every time? Most improvisers instead draw on their personal catalogue of phrases and ideas, and see what turns up along the way. Billie Holiday suggested that 'I never sing a song the same way twice', and it is that almost helpless spontaneity which the aspiring jazz musician seeks to emulate. 'Improvisation' (or simply 'improv') is also sometimes used as shorthand for the school of free improvisation, which tries to solve the problem of how to make something new out of existing material by having no premeditated material to begin with.

## Peter Ind
BASS
*born* 20 July 1928

Born in Uxbridge, Ind played bass while studying at Cambridge, and he departed for New York in 1951, one of the very few English players brave enough to make the trip permanently at that time. He studied with Lennie Tristano and played with many members of the Tristano circle, as well as musicians as diverse as Coleman Hawkins and Paul Bley. He moved over to the West Coast in the 60s and eventually returned to England later in the decade. He built up his Wave record label, originally created in 1961, which released rare material from his New York days, as well as new music; and established a London club, The Bass Clef, which was a proud mainstay of jazz performance until its closure in 1994. Peter has mustered a few firsts along the way – including the initial concerts by a solo bassist – and in recent years, his flowing head of hair undiminished by time, he has been bringing back much of the Wave catalogue in CD form.
*Looking Out* (Wave)

## Keith Ingham
PIANO
*born* 5 February 1942

A scholar born too late and a compulsive unearther of forgotten Tin Pan Alley tunes, Ingham is a versatile musician with a benign kind of tunnel vision. A Londoner who began playing in Hong Kong nightclubs while on government service, he backed British mainstreamers and American visitors on his return, and worked in a duo with his then wife, singer Susannah McCorkle. In 1977 he made a permanent move to New York and continued to back singers (including Maxine Sullivan and Peggy Lee) while constantly adding to his knowledge of the more arcane areas of the jazz repertory. He has been a frequent sidekick of Mary Grosz, and the titles of some of his records (such as *Out Of The Past* and *Music Of The Mauve Decades*) give some idea of his affections. At the same time, he is one of the few pianists who can convincingly line up John Lewis's 'Skating In Central Park' and Richard M Jones's 'Jazzin' Babies Blues' on the same

record. His playing is dapper and quick, if not resoundingly personal: perhaps he has sacrificed a notably individual touch to his interests. Any one of his records will offer much pleasure.
*The Back Room Romp* (Sackville)

## Institute Of Jazz Studies

Presided over by the avuncular Dan Morgenstern, the IJS is probably the most distinguished jazz archive in America. It was founded by Marshall Stearns in 1952 and was transferred to the Rutgers University campus in New Jersey in 1966. Morgenstern has been in charge since 1976. Besides a vast library of books, records, documents and memorabilia, it has built up a large body of oral histories.

## International Sweethearts Of Rhythm
GROUP

Formed in 1939 and led by vocalist Anna Mae Winburn, this was the first all-female big band in America and remains the best-known example of a rare species. It worked through the war years and eventually toured both America and Europe, but it made only a small number of recordings and the best of the band is to be heard mostly on AFRS transcriptions. While none of its members went on to careers of any real note, Winburn continued to lead other editions of the Sweethearts after the original group broke up later in the 40s.

## Irakere
GROUP

Founded in 1973 by some of the leading players on the Havana scene – including Chucho Valdés, Arturo Sandoval and Paquito D'Rivera – the group became missionaries for Cuban jazz at a time when that territory enjoyed no prominence at all among the wider jazz audience. Their American tours of the late 70s caused a good deal of excitement, although by the time the group had built an international reputation both Sandoval and D'Rivera had left to pursue their own careers. Valdés, however, continued leading the group into the middle 90s, and they became great favourites in London in particular, playing at Ronnie Scott's on a regular basis. After a few years, though, the group's music hardened into formula and routine, and their later records are dreary.

**The Legendary Irakere In London** ( Jazz House)

# Ike Isaacs
GUITAR
*born* 1 December 1919; *died* 11 January 1996

Born in Burma, Isaacs moved to London in 1946. Too old for rock'n'roll, he was one of the few British-based guitarists who owed most of their style to Django Reinhardt (though he preferred to play acoustic, much of his studio and other work was done on electric guitar), and he was a regular on the BBC, and in many studio situations. He toured with Stéphane Grappelli and had constructive partnerships with Diz Disley and Martin Taylor, although in 1981 he moved back east and settled in Sydney, where he worked at the Australian Guitar School. A lifelong student of guitars and the techniques they needed, Isaacs was an unassuming but delightful player with very few leadership credits to his name: *The Ike Isaacs Touch*, an album made for World Record Club in the 60s, is a collector's piece worth reviving on CD.

**The Ike Isaacs Touch** (WRC)

# Mark Isham
TRUMPET
*born* 7 September 1951

Isham is a superior kind of jazz dilettante. A player in both jazz and classical music, he turned up on a few obscure record dates in the 70s (such as Art Lande's beautiful *Rubisa Patrol*, 1976), but started doing filmscore writing soon after and that has taken up much of his time since. But a handful of 'legitimate' studio projects have thrown out a particularly delicate-tough sort of music, a kind of essay on post-bop and how it might sound as an intellectual pop music. He is less interested in the ambient groove form preferred by Jon Hassell, but the studio craft exhibited by both men builds a bridge

between their styles. A project dedicated to rekindling the music of Davis's *In A Silent Way* was interesting but a tad too specific: Isham works better from his own blank canvas.

**Blue Sun** (Columbia)

# Italian Instabile Orchestra
GROUP

This is a characteristic and beneficial conceit by the modern Italian jazz movement. It was co-founded by Pino Minafra and promoter Riccardo Bergerone in 1990, and consists of a gathering of some of the leading Italian jazz musicians, including Minafra, Mario Schiano, Giorgio Gaslini and others. Although only occasionally convened, and often only in 'festival' situations, the group has already established a strong book of original compositions (contributed by its members on a democratic basis) and recorded a number of CDs, including a recent collaboration with Cecil Taylor. Eclectic, energetic and bursting with creative good humour, it is the kind of genial body which any 'local' jazz environment could benefit from.

**Skies Of Europe** (ECM)

# Vijay Iyer
PIANO
*born* 1971

Iyer is an Indian-American whose recent progress has resulted in some startling music. He grew up in upstate New York and is self-taught on piano, subsequently studying at Berkeley and working in Bay Area groups with such as Steve Coleman, George Lewis and Liberty Ellmann. His quartet with saxophonist Rudresh Mahanthappa is one of his groups; another is the trio Fieldwork, now with saxophonist Steve Lehmann. His lack of any formal training has granted a notably fresh feel to his playing: 'What I wanted, as a pianist rooted in the percussive aspects of pianists like Ellington and Randy Weston, was to use rhythm as the central structural element.' He and Mahanthappa are part of a generation of Indian-Americans whose music will be intriguing to follow.

**Fieldwork, Your Life Flashes** (PI)

# David Izenzon

BASS
*born* 17 May 1932; *died* 8 October 1979

Izenzon's brief and curtailed jazz career has a poignant resonance. Born in Pittsburgh, he played locally (with Dodo Marmarosa and others) before moving to New York in 1961. There he hooked up with Ornette Coleman, and worked in the trio which recorded *Town Hall 1962* (1962) and *At The Golden Circle* (1965). The latter recordings especially demonstrate the creative power of Izenzon's playing, particularly brilliant with the bow: there are moments where he seems to be in such a closely argued dialogue with Coleman that one wishes that there had been many more documents of their work together. While he also recorded with Archie Shepp and Bill Dixon, though, Izenzon's career never really gained any further momentum, and his personal life was subsequently taken up with caring for his handicapped son and working towards a professional qualification in psychotherapy. At the time of his early death, jazz had largely forgotten him.
**Ornette Coleman,** *At The Golden Circle* (Blue Note)

# Jackie & Roy

VOCAL DUO

Roy Kral (1921–2002) worked on the Chicago club scene and met Jackie Cain (b 1928), whereupon the duo of Jackie & Roy began a career which lasted into the 90s. They joined Charlie Ventura's band in 1948, Kral also playing piano in that group and contributing arrangements, and for a time were the hippest vocal act in the music, setting ingenious vocalese pieces alongside straighter ballad singing. They married in 1949 and continued to work in Chicago and Las Vegas in the 50s and early 60s, though Jackie took some time off to raise a family (Anita O'Day deputized for her on occasion). They shifted base to New York in 1963 but carried on performing, doing commercials, and generally maintaining a loyal following. Their records should be better known to the mainstream jazz audience but are best known to followers of cabaret and theatre music: three albums for ABC (1957–9) and three more for Columbia (1960–63) are all due a revival.
*In The Spotlight* (ABC-Paramount)

# Chubby Jackson

BASS
*born* 25 October 1918; *died* 1 October 2003

Jackson grew up in New York and took up the bass in his teens. His first major engagement was with the Charlie Barnet orchestra, but his stint in Woody Herman's First Herd (1943–6) is still the association for which he is best remembered: he gave the Herman band a powerful rhythmic kick, and he was a natural showman and gregarious enough to pester the leader into taking on both Ralph Burns and Neal Hefti as contributors to the band's book. After the Herd split up, he ran a club (The Esquire), worked with Charlie Ventura and eventually led his own big band for a brief spell: their 1951 session for Prestige is a tremendously sought-after rarity for jazz LP collectors. After that he turned up on television and freelanced in Las Vegas and Los Angeles. Arthritis eventually curtailed his career, but Chubby kept an eye on the jazz scene until the end, and his son, Duffy Jackson, is a drummer whose showbiz inclinations are very much a chip off the old block.
*Chubby's Back!* (Argo)

# Cliff Jackson

PIANO
*born* 19 July 1902; *died* 24 May 1970

Born in Culpeper, Virginia, Jackson moved to New York in 1923 and played as an accompanist to many of the classic blues singers before forming his own band, The Krazy Kats, which cut twelve sides in 1930 ('The Terror' has long been a collector's favourite). In the 30s and 40s he recorded occasionally, with Sidney Bechet and others, but worked mainly as the house pianist at sundry New York clubs, work which lasted up until his death, as well as sometimes accompanying his wife, Maxine Sullivan. In the 60s he finally made some solo recordings which gave his playing a rare spotlight: he was an old-school stride player who hadn't forgotten ragtime, and they show a dignified and elegant professional at work.
*The Stride Piano Of Cliff Jackson* (Fat Cat's Jazz)

# D D Jackson
PIANO
*born 25 January 1967*

Born in Ottawa of African-American and
Chinese parents, Jackson studied in New
York with both Jaki Byard and Don Pullen,
and he has been active in the city's musical
community since the start of the 90s. He
has put together a brisk and often exciting
discography, mostly for the Canadian Justin
Time label, although he was signed to RCA
for a couple of albums. Jackson has appropriated something of Pullen's voluminous
style, expanded to accommodate a more
effusively romantic feel, and he has a sense
of outreach which is perhaps typical of
jazz's move towards a polycultural position.
David Murray and Hamiet Bluiett have been
among his favourite collaborators thus far.
*Anthem* (RCA)

# Javon Jackson
TENOR SAXOPHONE
*born 16 June 1965*

The last tenorman in the final Jazz
Messengers line-up, Jackson has sought to
find and hang on to a popular audience without a great deal of success. He cut a couple
of sets for Criss Cross at the beginning of the
90s and then went to Blue Note for four
albums (oddly enough, the first was one of
the very few records produced by Betty
Carter). All of these have some intermittently powerful music in them, but none
counted as any kind of jazz hit, and Javon
seems to have found himself in a mild quan-
dary over direction. Though stylistically he
is firmly in the post-bop saxophone mould,
he's tried on material by Al Green and Stevie
Wonder, and his latest effort *Easy Does It*
(2003) sets him up with an organ/guitar
band and plenty of backbeats. It sounds
good, but if Jackson – as he has asserted –
likes to take risks, they never seem to be
taken on his records.
*Pleasant Valley* (Blue Note)

# Milt Jackson
VIBES
*born 1 January 1923; died 9 October 1999*

Jackson took up the vibraphone when at
high school in Detroit, and he wasn't a bad
singer, spending some time working in a gospel quartet. But Dizzy Gillespie heard him in
Detroit and in 1945 offered him a job, first
with his sextet and then with the big band.
Jackson's debut on the session which produced 'Anthropology' (1946) showed that he
was already fully conversant with bebop and
unfazed by playing an instrument which
hardly seemed like the most appropriate for
the style. He went on to work in small
groups with other leaders and with Woody
Herman's big band before rejoining
Gillespie's sextet in 1950. But it was the first
sessions by the Milt Jackson Quartet, for
Prestige in 1952, which decided his direction
for the next 20 years, since the group
evolved into the Modern Jazz Quartet and
became a busy and prolific recording and
touring ensemble. Jackson fitted into the
group as well as he fitted into any band he
played with: he was the principal improviser
in the band, although improvising was not
really the MJQ's forte. Away from it, he continued to make records of his own, and
occasionally play with other groups: there
was a fine series of albums for both
Riverside and Atlantic, and meetings with
John Coltrane and Wes Montgomery. When
the MJQ went into abeyance in 1974, it was
generally thought that this had been due to
Jackson's restlessness with his own career,
although he was happy to join the re-
formed ensemble in the 80s, and stayed
until its final 1997 appearances. In the
meantime, Norman Granz began recording
him for Pablo, and he recorded a whole
string of sessions for that label; his final
association was with Quincy Jones's Qwest
operation. 'Bags' was one of the rare jazz
performers whose work was all of a piece,
and always interesting. He took the vibes
into the hi-fi era by slowing the oscillator on
the instrument, giving him a more luxuriant tone. He could swing at any tempo, and
his slow playing was rich and eventful without being crowded. Perhaps the key to his
consistency and longevity, though, was his
mastery of playing blues: his own tunes
always seemed to be irreducibly simple
blues pieces such as 'Bags' Groove', and he

was quite content to play entire sets of blues, always finding something fresh to say. A neat pencil of a man with lugubrious eyes and a compensating huge smile, he was an indispensable part of jazz for five decades.
*Wizard Of The Vibes* (Blue Note)

## Oliver Jackson
DRUMS
*born* 28 April 1933; *died* 29 May 1994

Jackson played drums in his native Detroit in the 40s, but decided to try variety and formed a duo with fellow drummer Eddie Locke. They went out as a drumming and dancing team, Bop And Locke, in 1952, which enjoyed some success, but changing tastes and a lack of work made them give it up in 1957. Thereafter Jackson freelanced and toured both Europe and the US, sometimes with the Lionel Hampton band and, for much of the 60s, with Earl Hines. In the 70s, the French label Black & Blue used Jackson as their regular drummer, and he turns up on most of their sessions with everyone from John Lewis to Lockjaw Davis. He was still touring up to the end and the record cited was made only a few months before he died.
*The Last Great Concert* (Nagel Heyer)

## Quentin Jackson
TROMBONE
*born* 13 January 1909; *died* 2 October 1976

Claude Jones was Jackson's brother-in-law, and encouraged him to take up the trombone, subsequently helping him get a gig with McKinney's Cotton Pickers in 1930. Thereafter Jackson was a regular sideman with Don Redman, and then spent eight years with Cab Calloway. But his major association was as one of Duke Ellington's trombonists: he joined after the death of Tricky Sam Nanton, and established his plunger-mute solos as the glorious successor to Nanton's pioneering work. After 11 successful years, 'Butter' Jackson left Ellington in 1959 and worked for a variety of leaders during the 60s, from Count Basie to Charles Mingus. Latterly he played less often, but his final association was with the Jones–Lewis Orchestra. The record cited features some of his ripest playing, in a congenial gathering of Ellingtonians.
**Billy Strayhorn,** *Cue For Saxophone* (Felsted)

## Ronald Shannon Jackson
DRUMS
*born* 12 January 1940

Jackson's career scarcely started until he'd already been in jazz for many years. He was part of the Fort Worth musical community in the late 50s and early 60s and moved to New York in 1966, where he played with both Charles Mingus and Albert Ayler. It was the free end of things which he preferred: although largely away from professional music for much of the 70s, he came back as a recruit to Ornette Coleman's Prime Time, Cecil Taylor and James Blood Ulmer (1979). That experience set him up for The Decoding Society, a band which he led through various incarnations for the rest of the 80s and much of the 90s. With a line-up that mixed horns, guitars and sometimes vibes (Khan Jamal) and violin (Billy Bang), it was a polyglot ensemble driven by Jackson's propulsive rhythms – an enigmatic feel which could suggest swing, funk and march rhythms pulped together – and nurtured on his own, often very hummable writing. Vernon Reid was a key member of the band for much of the 80s, and they recorded a sequence of albums for the Island subsidiary Antilles, a rare example of major-label patronage for demanding music. Jackson also played in Power Tools, a short-lived trio with Bill Frisell and Melvin Gibbs, and the improv supergroup Last Exit. In the later 90s he seemed less visible, although the Knitting Factory label released a tranche of live and reissued recordings, and a heart problem slowed him down a little in the new century. Jackson was a busy achiever with a twinkling smile, and his music can fairly be described as a genuine fusion – brainier and more emotive than chops-driven jazz-rock, but still sometimes prey to technique and showmanship at moments where it should be connecting on a more direct level. His assembled recordings remain fascinating, though.
*Decode Yourself* (Island)

# Tony Jackson

PIANO
*born* 5 June 1876; *died* 20 April 1921

'Real dark and not a bit good-looking, but he had a beautiful disposition,' remembered Jelly Roll Morton, who considered Jackson the finest of all the early New Orleans pianists. He was the regular performer at Gypsy Schaeffer's in the Storyville district, and all who heard him recalled his excellent voice, singing both blues and popular tunes, and a memory for material which was peerless, playing every tune anyone could remember. He was also, as Morton alluded to, 'one of those gentlemen that a lot of people call lady or sissy', and he spent his later years in Chicago, where attitudes were more free-thinking. Although he wrote 'Pretty Baby' and other tunes, there is nothing else left to remember Jackson by: he never recorded.

# Willis Jackson

TENOR SAXOPHONE
*born* 25 April 1928; *died* 25 October 1987

'Gator Tail' Jackson grew up in Miami and played in local bands before a long stint as a sideman with Cootie Williams, beginning in 1948. He began leading small groups of his own in the early 50s, sometimes backing his then-wife Ruth Brown, and he became a strong draw on the chitlin circuit. His records for Prestige were popular on black jukeboxes, and some two dozen LPs kept him busy before microphones all through the 60s. As that market declined, so did Gator's career, although he carried on where he left off when Muse signed him later in the 70s. There is little in his discography which really endures and the music all sounds alike after a while, but the live records do bring back much of the atmosphere of his heyday.
*Live! Jackson's Action* (Prestige)

# Pim Jacobs

PIANO
*born* 29 October 1934; *died* 3 July 1996

Born in Hilversum, Jacobs formed his first trio in 1954, and the singer Rita Reys joined the group in 1957 (she and Jacobs later married). Pim and Rita were a familiar double-act on the Dutch scene through the 60s and 70s, and the pianist made numerous sets for Philips and CBS in a good-natured Garner–Peterson style (he was also a TV producer and occasional impresario). Very little of the music made it beyond the Dutch borders, and although the set listed below has been available as a Japanese CD, it is hard to find.
*Come Fly With Me* (Philips)

# Illinois Jacquet

TENOR SAXOPHONE
*born* 31 October 1922; *died* 22 July 2004

Jacquet's tempestuous style brought a new wildness to saxophone playing in the 40s, and perhaps to jazz altogether. Though born in Louisiana, he grew up in Houston, where his father ran a big band. He tried both soprano and alto before settling on the tenor: this was after Nat Cole had recommended him to Lionel Hampton, who didn't need a new alto man at that point. He burst into prominence by playing a characteristic solo on Hamp's biggest hit, the 1942 version of 'Flying Home', but didn't stay with that leader for long: instead he shifted to Cab Calloway's and Count Basie's orchestras, although more significant was an appearance at the first Jazz At The Philharmonic concert in 1944. This institutionalized his rabble-rousing side into a failsafe way of stirring up excitement at a typical JATP jam, to which he was often asked back. In the meantime, he performed with his own small groups, and started touring Europe as a regular guest star in jazz packages and at festivals. This kind of touring regimen lasted him well into the 70s, and he also cut entertaining if unambitious records for Argo, Cadet and Prestige, some of which also featured his bassoon playing. By this time the 'Texas tenor' style which he had all but patented had cooled off: originally marked by nearly screaming high notes, which helped to work audiences into a frenzy, his original Coleman Hawkins influence had been returned to a more languid though still full-blooded delivery. His ballad playing owed much to Hawkins, too, and when he began leading a big band in the 80s – originally peopled by players drawn from his students at Harvard, where he taught – his playing took on even more gravitas, with ballads being subjected to a rhapsodic steaming. He missed the 1994 Verve 50th anniversary concert because he couldn't agree terms with the organizers, which denied both sides a piquant historical moment. Otherwise, he carried on with the big band and with occasional small groups, until shortly before his death. Jacquet's influence wasn't all that profound in jazz terms – saxophone hysteria was largely confined to the R&B idiom, at least until the free players of the 60s – but he helped to please many a crowd during a period when audiences had grown uneasy with the aspirations of bebop. His older brother Russell (1917–90) toured with him early on (and with two other brothers, drummer Linton and saxophonist Julius), before leading a big band of his own, which was not at all a bad outfit on the basis of their 1946 recordings. Russell played trumpet and sang blues capably, and in 1983 he again worked with Illinois in New York, although he enjoyed little attention later in his career.

*Swing's The Thing* (Verve)

## Bent Jaedig
TENOR SAXOPHONE
*born* 18 October 1935; *died* 2004

Jaedig's big sound in the swing-tenor idiom was a fixture on the Danish jazz scene for many years. Though he grew up in Copenhagen, he did some of his early professional work in German groups, with Albert Mangelsdorff and others, in the mid-50s. He divided his time between that setting and the Danish environment, and latterly worked mainly in Denmark, as a small-group leader, in radio big bands, and with Horace Parlan and Niels Jorgen Steen.

*The Red Lightning* (Music Mecca)

## Jam (session)

To 'jam' is to improvise on one's instrument, and a jam session is a basically informal gathering of musicians, playing for the fun of it. Jam sessions originated as after-hours encounters where players gathered away from their regular gigs and explored new ideas or simply jousted with each other (although the competitive streak associated with the 'cutting contest' is not really a part of the cooperative jam session). Inevitably,

smart entrepreneurs began staging jam sessions for audience interest – Jazz At The Philharmonic is a prime example – and by the middle 50s genuine jam sessions had become rare. They made something of a comeback in later decades as a counter to the prevailing orthodoxy which was being established via jazz courses at music colleges. Some New York clubs still treat certain nights of final sets as 'the jam session', where all comers can sit in, while a night-owl audience bears witness.

## Ahmad Jamal
PIANO
*born* 2 July 1930

Jamal worked in his native Pittsburgh without attracting much attention before he formed his first trio in 1951. From there, playing in Chicago and New York, he quickly established an influential sound: the piano, guitar (Ray Crawford) and bass (various players, including Israel Crosby) established a lightly swinging music which could sound either flimsy or lean and incisive, sometimes both during the course of a performance. His hit version of 'Billy Boy', a folk song given a bouncily rhythmical treatment, sums up Jamal's earlier music: the two hands working in specific roles, the right a tinkling counterpoint to the elastic left. When Vernell Fournier (drums) replaced Crawford, Jamal came up with his most successful album, *At The Pershing* (1958): live albums have always brought out the best in him, and by this time the advocacy of Miles Davis – who appeared to love Jamal's trilling, spacey improvisations and trim feel – had given the pianist a bountiful credibility, with Davis's own pianist Red Garland seemingly obliged to follow in that style. Jamal opened his own Chicago club for a spell, then began touring again with various new trios. By the end of the 60s he had built up a huge discography on Cadet and Argo, although many of the records were thin on quality, and in the 70s and 80s he moved further towards a noodling sort of easy listening, buffed up with horns and strings. In his 60s, though, Jamal seemed to repent to some extent, and went back to an acoustic trio, which has toured widely and enjoyed more success in Europe than he has known before. The later records for Telarc

and Birdology have certainly been among his best and most powerful statements, a lingering look through the jazz composing tradition with his own interpretations assuming a mature grace.
*At The Pershing* (Chess)

# Khan Jamal
VIBES
*born* 23 July 1946

Born Warren Cheeseboro, Jamal is an interesting and adaptable musician whose music only occasionally surfaces on record and in performance. He took up vibes in the early 60s and was one of the few players on the instrument to try and find a place for it in free jazz, working in The Cosmic Forces at the end of the 60s and with Byard Lancaster in Sounds Of Liberation. He has often been attracted to fierce saxophonists, and besides Lancaster has worked with Frank Wright, Charles Tyler and Jemeel Moondoc. He worked in the unlikely situation of Ronald Shannon Jackson's Decoding Society for a spell in the 80s and turned up in Europe to record with the likes of Tyler and Johnny Dyani. In the new century he has been a little more visible on record, for CIMP and Jambrio. African beats seem to flow through his playing, and while he can infiltrate his way into most free situations, his rhythmical qualities determine his sound, melodious without submitting to standard vibes prettiness.
*Balafon Dance* (CIMP)

# Bob James
KEYBOARDS
*born* 25 December 1939

James made an uneventful trio record in 1962 which premiered his style of bop piano, and then recorded a curious set for ESP in 1965, with Barre Phillips, which mixed acoustic playing with *musique concrète*. But these were red herrings for a career which soon turned commercial. He worked as MD for Sarah Vaughan until 1968, then did session-work and arranging for Creed Taylor's CTI operation. He has since made a lucrative career as an executive, and cut a sequence of deadening soft-fusion records, some of them with the tedious group Fourplay, as well as

going the way of the misguided and arranging classical music for synthesizers.
*Hands Down* (Tappan Zee)

# Harry James
TRUMPET
*born* 15 March 1916; *died* 5 July 1983

James got his early schooling in his father's circus orchestra, and some might suggest that he never really left the circus behind. He was in New York by 1935, and his early records with Ben Pollack's band are almost painfully exciting: the likes of 'Spreading Knowledge Around' feature trumpet daredevilry of the highest order. Between 1937 and 1939 he was in Benny Goodman's orchestra, where he quickly became the star soloist after Goodman himself, and he then formed his own band: still only 23, he was soon in charge of one of the most commercially successful white bands. He had two of the best vocalists of the day, Frank Sinatra (1939–41) and Dick Haymes (1941–4), and began recording sides that were more like supercharged light music than big-band jazz – 'Ciribiribin', 'Carnival Of Venice', 'Trumpet Rhapsody' and the hugely successful 'You Made Me Love You' settled down his earlier hot style into a brash mellifluousness. He married Betty Grable and ruled as one of the kings of American entertainment, but like many others suffered when the big bands went into decline – for a while he scaled back, but if anything the records took a turn back towards jazz, and by the end of the 50s James could boast fine Neal Hefti and Ernie Wilkins charts in his book and a strong personnel. He spent many years based in Las Vegas, but never gave up touring, and even when his era had long since gone he was still bandleading right up until the 80s. James could stand a revival of interest: when he wasn't pleasing circus crowds he could be a thoughtful improviser, and though the slurping vibrato and almost whinnying phrasing of his hits is a distraction, that may have been the price of being, allegedly, the best-selling jazz musician of all time. He was certainly an important influence on many British trumpeters, notably Humphrey Lyttelton and Kenny Baker.
*Trumpet Blues* (Capitol)

## Stafford James

BASS
*born* 24 April 1946

Another in the legion of dependable bassists who have swarmed through the music in the past 50 years, James took up the instrument while he was stationed in the military in New Orleans in the 60s. He then worked steadily with an eclectic list of leaders, among them Woody Shaw, Sun Ra, Roy Ayers, Gary Bartz, Slide Hampton and Jimmy Heath. From time to time he led small groups of his own, which became more prominent when he settled in Paris in 1989; latterly, though, he has been less visible on the international scene than he once was.
**Woody Shaw, *Lotus Flower*** (Enja)

## Jon Jang

PIANO
*born* 11 March 1954

Jang (his original name is Jang Jian Liang) can fairly claim pioneer status in the development of Asian-American jazz. He grew up in California and graduated at Oberlin before returning to the San Francisco area, where he became a prominent activist in the promotion of various aspects of the Asian-American arts scene. After gaining some attention as a member of Fred Ho's Afro-Asian Music Ensemble in the mid-80s and founding the Asian Improv record label, he has been a leader or prime mover in a number of significant groups: the Pan-Asian Arkestra and the African-Chinese Sextet (which included David Murray and Billy Hart) were two of them. As a pianist, Jang is a thoughtful, even modest executant: his solo record *Self-Portrait* (1999) is reflective and unambitious, which contrasts with the fiercer music on such discs as *Tiananmen!* (1993) and *Immigrant Suite No 1* (1997), where the sometimes uneasy alliance of Chinese and Western instruments makes an intermittently powerful mark. Jang has made little apparent impact outside the US and it would be fascinating to hear him in some of the multicultural situations which have become fashionable programming devices on the European festival circuit.
***Tiananmen!*** (Soul Note)

## Guus Janssen

PIANO
*born* 13 May 1951

Born in Heiloo, in the Netherlands, Janssen followed Dutch free music in the 60s with great interest – 'We used to confront friends with Willem Breuker's first duo record with Han Bennink' – then studied in Amsterdam and played in a group with his drummer-brother Wim. Since then he has recorded small-group music for such labels as Claxon and Geestgronden, and though he claims to have never really worked in any mainstream jazz idiom, 'I have the idea that the conceptions of strict forms confronted with the anarchy of free forms enriched my music a lot.' He is certainly a strikingly individual player, and his trio with Wim and bassist Ernst Glerum overflows with fresh ideas, very different to what is normally encountered in this instrumentation.
***Zwik*** (Geestgronden)

## Lars Jansson

PIANO
*born* 25 February 1951

Raised in Uddevalla, Jansson studied classical piano and trained as a dentist, but the lure of Miles Davis's and Mose Allison's music drew him into playing jazz. His major break came when Arild Andersen hired him (1975) as the keyboard player in the group which recorded several fine albums for ECM. At the end of the 70s Jansson began leading his own groups. He is an impressionist with a sliver of steel in his make-up: the ubiquitous Bill Evans influence which has infected so many European pianists is there in what he does, but his style leans towards a darker and more opaque harmonic substance, with his fastidious improvising keeping moody meandering at arm's length. His writing for big band – with the Tolvan Big Band and, most recently, the Bohuslan Big Band – has a livelier, more obviously muscular bent to it.
***Ballads*** (Imogena)

# Joseph Jarman

SAXOPHONES
*born* 14 September 1937

Jarman put much of the fire and bite into the Art Ensemble Of Chicago's music. He took up the saxophone while playing in army bands in the middle 50s, and on returning to Chicago he took a fast interest in the new music which the city was spawning at the beginning of the 60s, working with both Muhal Richard Abrams and Roscoe Mitchell and taking a founding role in the AACM. His own band of the middle 60s featured pianist Christopher Gaddy, who died young, but it was perhaps inevitable that he would join forces with the other members of the nascent Art Ensemble at the end of the decade. Jarman's onstage demeanour with the AEOC was unfailingly extravagant: he would be decked out in costumes and face paint, singing, stepping and suddenly abandoning theatre for an incendiary solo – like Roscoe Mitchell, he took a full armoury of reed and woodwind instruments on to the stage. Away from that, he is a serious and stately figure, with a profound involvement in Buddhism and philosophy. His musical activity became more sporadic in the 90s and he formally left the Ensemble in 1993, although he has reunited with the surviving members on occasion.
**Art Ensemble Of Chicago,** *People In Sorrow* (Nessa)

# Keith Jarrett

PIANO
*born* 8 May 1945

It is entertaining to learn that jazz piano's most capital-A artist had some of his first professional experience touring in his teens as a piano soloist with Fred Waring's Pennsylvanians. But from there he went to Boston, studying on a one-year scholarship to Berklee before moving to New York in 1964. Art Blakey heard him at a jam session and offered him the piano chair in the Jazz Messengers, in December 1965, but Jarrett only stayed three months. From there, he burst through to prominence as the pianist in Charles Lloyd's group, which began enjoying success on the rock-festival circuit and brought Jarrett's in-performance showmanship at the keyboard into full public glare. After Lloyd disbanded the group in 1969, Jarrett began playing with trios of his own, and was then hired (June 1970) by Miles Davis, playing only organ at first but then – after Chick Corea's departure – electric piano as well. This on-and-off spell with Davis lasted until December 1971, and from that point onwards Jarrett decided not to use electric keyboards again. He had made a solo record for the new ECM label, *Facing You*, just before leaving Davis, and this dramatic set – full of sweeping romantic piano music – all but ushered in a new age of acoustic jazz which seemed almost to set its face against the prevailing winds of jazz-rock.

Through the next decade, Jarrett recorded with an 'American' group (Dewey Redman, Charlie Haden, Paul Motian) and a 'European' one (Jan Garbarek, Palle Danielsson, Jon Christensen), as well as chronicling a great trove of solo music – multidisc piano recitals and church organ records, plus settings for his piano with string arrangements. Almost from the start, listeners were sharply divided on Jarrett's merits: an admiring and worldwide audience flocked to hear him perform what appeared to be extended improvisations, stretching the blueprint of *Facing You* into epic meditations which sometimes featured Jarrett's groans and cries and extravagant body language almost as much as his keyboard work. Detractors took a view which John Litweiler's description summed up: 'the ostinato sections yield to hymns, sweetly pathetic melodies, up-down keyboard chases, strife resolving in bombast, and a wide variety of other stuff'. Following the prodigious success of *The Köln Concert* (1975), Jarrett's most renowned solo record, ECM seemed to encourage an almost obsessive documentation, as in the ten-LP set *The Sun Bear Concerts* (1976), although this was no more an indulgence than a classical pianist recording a Beethoven cycle. In the 80s, Jarrett did indeed begin to tackle the classical repertory, recording Barber and Shostakovich, but he also seemed to retrench into the jazz tradition by forming a still ongoing trio with Gary Peacock and Jack DeJohnette, which took the American standards songbook as its primary source of material, although there have subsequently been episodes of free playing by the band.

Enormously influential in the way that

Bill Evans once was, Jarrett's kingly stature hardly declined as the 90s progressed, and he also took to decrying what he saw as the state of conservatism in jazz via open letters and speeches to concert audiences. But he was suddenly halted by the onset of chronic-fatigue syndrome in 1996, and while he has subsequently restarted his performing and recording regimen, some of the voltage may have gone out of his activity. Jarrett's position hasn't always been helped by supporters who have built his undoubted talent into godlike eminence, and there have been foolish claims made both for and against him. There are some simple virtues in his playing which any listener can surely respond to: gorgeous melodies, patiently evocative development which can lead to genuinely transcendent climaxes, beatific ballad playing. But it can be hard to tune out musical (and non-musical) matter which is likely to have dismayed as many as it has enraptured.

**The Köln Concert** (ECM)

## Clifford Jarvis
DRUMS
*born* 26 August 1941; *died* 26 November 1999

Jarvis was a strong hard-bop drummer who never quite made it to the top in a crowded field. A Bostonian, he studied at Berklee (with Alan Dawson) and moved to New York at the end of the 50s, recording with several of the hard-bop leaders, and also making occasional entries into Sun Ra's Arkestra, an engagement which lasted into the 70s. Since he also worked with Pharoah Sanders and Sonny Simmons, he seemed at ease in both bop and free situations. He visited Europe with both Ra and Archie Shepp, and found it congenial enough to eventually settle in England in the 80s – an authentic American veteran in a scene full of aspiring young players. In the later 90s, though, he was less visible and recorded little, and he died in London at the end of the century.

**Freddie Hubbard, *Hub-Tones*** (Blue Note)

## Bobby Jaspar
TENOR SAXOPHONE, FLUTE
*born* 20 February 1926; *died* 4 March 1963

Born in Liège, Jaspar started on the saxophone in his teens, and though he studied as a chemist, music beckoned him and he went to Paris in 1950 to get involved with the French bop movement. He led groups of his own and worked with the likes of Henri Renaud, and took every chance to play with visiting Americans: one of them, Blossom Dearie, married him in 1956. This led to an American stay, and his playing won a surprise approval from a New York scene which was traditionally sceptical of European players. Jaspar's light tone recalled a Lester Young influence, but his phrasing was more modern than that, and in addition he was particularly adept and incisive on the flute, an instrument which had gained little support from his contemporaries. There were stints with J J Johnson, Jimmy Raney, Donald Byrd and even Miles Davis, and he returned briefly to Europe in 1961; but problems with both narcotics and his heart led to his demise. A handful of records under his own name are a rather mixed lot, but his best performances – as in the disc listed, recorded live in London in 1962 – make one regret his early death even more.

**The Bobby Jaspar Quartet** (Mole Jazz)

## André Jaume
SAXOPHONES, CLARINET
*born* 7 October 1940

Jaume heard Sidney Bechet in his native Marseilles, and picked up the clarinet as a result. He found his way to modern jazz 'without any logical progression' and went to Guy Longnon's jazz school in 1964. Since he rarely left Marseilles and has never been involved in the Paris scene, Jaume has seemed a tangential figure in his country's jazz, but he built up several intriguing associations in the 70s and 80s, with the likes of Joe McPhee, Jimmy Giuffre and Raymond Boni. Werner Uehlinger's hat Hut operation documented him in this period, and subsequently the CELP label has set down many records. Jaume has tried associations with gamelan and other musics which haven't always worked, but his penchant for the clarinet has helped keep that member of the

reed family relevant, and there are a handful of his CDs which should be in every jazz library, even if his reputation is still confined largely to an audience of connoisseurs.
**Clarinet Sessions** (CELP)

## Jazz

1. The word itself is impossible to trace to any specific origin. While it may have emerged out of African-American slang for sex, there are also other possible derivations, such as the French *jaser* ('to chatter or prattle'), or the Bantu verb *jaja* ('to play music'). It began to be used in print around 1914, although the first group to employ the word in their name – and in the description of their performances – remains the Original Dixieland Jazz (or Jass) Band, which first recorded in 1917. By 1919, when the English music hall comedian Jack Pleasants recorded a song called 'I Went A-Jazzing', the term was widely used, but not necessarily in any musical context: it could just as easily be used to describe a display of odd behaviour, an eccentric dance, an unspecific musical cacophony, or even an attempt at deceiving someone. The broader phrase 'all that jazz' subsequently carried a cargo of sarcasm: in everyday speech, someone might say that 'he told me everything was fine, and all that jazz'. Musicians such as Duke Ellington became dismayed and disenchanted with the negative connotations of the word, and shied away from its use; Miles Davis regarded it as almost a racist term. Yet in the contemporary era, Wynton Marsalis has insisted on its primacy, and refuses to turn away from it, instead suggesting that 'jazz' covers a coherent and living tradition. For every listener who sees 'jazz' as the most fitting heading over a powerful genre, though, there is another who half-humorously refers to jazz as 'the j-word', reluctant to articulate a noun which can still suggest something difficult, dangerous or even depraved to an unwitting outsider.
2. Defining the music is no less difficult than seeking the genesis of the word. It came into being in the early 20th century as a music drawn from a number of different sources – African and European-American in origin – and personified by two principal characteristics: a syncopated rhythmical element which has come to be called 'swing', and

some improvisational input, which could come from a soloist inventing a new melodic line or an ensemble simply playing the material in a spirit of free-flowing spontaneity, necessarily departing, however slightly, from a written score or a premeditated direction. If both of those features are missing, it is difficult to see how the music can be described as jazz. While African-Americans take the principal responsibility for its creation and early development, from the beginning jazz displayed numerous borrowings from other folk and art musics, and it in turn fed into subsequent musical forms such as rhythm and blues, soul and rock 'n' roll. In the new century, it is as much a global dialect of expression as an established tradition, and in theory it can be played by any number of musicians – from a soloist to multiple orchestras – and on any instruments.

## Jazz At The Philharmonic

The entrepreneur Norman Granz staged a concert at the Los Angeles Philharmonic Auditorium on 2 July 1944, a benefit in support of legal aid for the defendants in a murder trial. Granz assembled a dozen jazzmen – including J J Johnson, Nat Cole, Meade Lux Lewis and Les Paul – and the music consisted of a series of loose-knit performances with the ambience of a jam session. It was successful enough to make Granz want to carry on with the idea (though not, subsequently, for charitable purposes), and by the end of 1946 he was promoting similar events in other cities on a monthly basis, although the name Jazz At The Philharmonic was retained. By the 50s these had become institutionalized tours of several weeks' duration, and eventually Granz brought them to Europe and Japan as well as the American circuit. When he heard a set of transcriptions of the first concert, 'I realized you could never get that in a studio, where you get a controlled performance', and thereafter he set about recording as many of the performances as possible, and issuing them on his own labels. JATP, as it became known, was the backbone of Granz's jazz business interests and made him a wealthy man, the concerts growing to involve such stars as Ella Fitzgerald, Charlie Parker, Dizzy Gillespie, Oscar Peterson and Coleman

Hawkins, and regular bands such as the Modern Jazz Quartet and Duke Ellington's orchestra: yet his fierce interest in the well-being of the performers ensured that they were handsomely paid and comfortably looked after during a JATP stint. Right until the end – the final JATP concerts took place in the early 80s – the jam-session feel persisted at the concerts, if only in the concluding melee which usually featured various instrumentalists jousting with each other in informal battles. The issued recordings of JATP run to scores of albums, although they have never satisfactorily been issued on CD: a set of the 40s sessions (running to ten CDs) was issued by Verve in 1998, but they have still not tackled the rest of this bulky oeuvre, to the exasperation of collectors.

## Jazz Centre Society/Jazz Services

First established in 1968, the Jazz Centre Society was a London-based body, organized by musicians and friends of the music who felt that one way or the other British jazz was getting a raw deal in terms of work opportunities, funding and recognition by the cultural establishment. While some might argue that nothing has changed much in 35 years, the JCS took some major steps towards ameliorating that situation, organizing concerts, providing touring and management support, and proceeding towards a point where the funding for a National Jazz Centre could begin to become a reality, in 1978. Warehouse premises were eventually acquired for that purpose, but the company established to oversee the project eventually foundered, in circumstances which have never been properly explained. The JCS, nevertheless, turned itself into Jazz Services in 1983, and continues to this day to provide touring support and educational and other services, primarily for the community of jazz musicians. Funded largely by the Arts Council and directed by the tireless and indefatigable Chris Hodgkins, it has been a priceless resource which countless British musicians have benefited from both directly and indirectly.

## Jazz Composers' Guild/ Jazz Composers' Orchestra

Bill Dixon founded the Guild in 1964, to promote the playing of free jazz in New York without becoming beholden to the established system of nightclubs and booking agents, which had been widely discredited during the hard-bop era and was in any case unsympathetic to the then-new music. The likes of Cecil Taylor, Carla Bley, Michael Mantler, Archie Shepp and Sun Ra were involved, but like so many musician-run cooperatives, it didn't last long and was dissolved a year later. Bley and Mantler nevertheless established a Jazz Composers' Guild Orchestra, later the Jazz Composers' Orchestra, which in turn led to the Jazz Composers' Orchestra Association. The JCO commissioned and performed new works by leading players of the free movement, and the JCOA recorded and released them via a New Music Distribution Service, which also handled other jazz labels. However, the JCO, which was only an occasional enterprise at best, disbanded in 1975, and the NMDS collapsed in the 80s, with a lot of jazz labels eventually owed a lot of money. Freedom and sound organization don't always mix well.

## Jazz Crusaders

See the CRUSADERS.

## Jazz Jamaica

See GARY CROSBY.

## Jazzmobile

Billy Taylor, one of the most proactive American jazz musicians in terms of organizational know-how, got this initiative off the ground in 1965. It promotes the performance of the music within a local-community environment, by sponsoring concerts on a mobile stage which is set up in Harlem, Brooklyn and other New York locations, and the events have involved the participation of many major players over the years.

Taylor has remained President of the organ-ization and Dave Bailey has been the direc-tor since the late 60s. Jazzmobile activities have been expanded to include numerous educational programmes, a symptom of the gathering momentum of jazz education, although this was first undertaken as far back as the early 70s.

## Jazzology
RECORD LABEL

This is the principal and original label of a group which has expanded to become a prime source for classic American tra-ditional jazz. Under the ownership of George H Buck, it began almost as a one-off enter-prise in 1949 to issue sessions by clarinettist Tony Parenti, and little more was under-taken until 1954, when the subsidiary label GHB was launched. Working out of Columbia, South Carolina, Buck started recording new albums in the traditional style – mostly it was New Orleans jazz on GHB and a more Chicago-styled music which came out on Jazzology, including numerous sessions by Wild Bill Davison and others – but he also began acquiring the cata-logues of other independent labels. By the 80s, the group had taken over a whole string of independents: Circle, Icon, MONO, Jazz Crusade, American Music, Solo Art, Jazz Record, Monmouth-Evergreen, Audiophile and Progressive were among those absorbed, and the group had fair claims to rival even the Fantasy Group as a voluminous archive of American jazz. American Music in particu-lar was used to issue scores of rare and hitherto unheard or unrevived New Orleans sessions. Audiophile and Progressive fea-tured issues of a more MOR or mainstream-modern persuasion. Rarely advertising product or otherwise servicing the industry, Buck's group of labels seem to survive entirely on word of mouth and the loyalty of a large group of diehard fans.

## Jazz Passengers
GROUP

Originally just the duo of Roy Nathanson (alto sax) and Curtis Fowlkes (trombone), the group grew into a septet in the late 80s and began working in New York at that time.

From instrumental beginnings the group evolved into a kind of ongoing jazz cabaret, recalling the work of Carla Bley and Frank Zappa and relying a good deal on its theatri-cal leanings. To this end, guest vocalists were seconded into the group, and an often surprising list they were: the record cited includes Jimmy Scott, Bob Dorough, Mavis Staples, Jeff Buckley and Deborah Harry. The ex-Blondie singer did, indeed, become a regu-lar Jazz Passenger and toured with the band until her former group was reconvened. In the new century, the Passengers seem to have curtailed their activities somewhat.
*In Love* (High Street)

## Jazz-rock

It was perhaps inevitable that jazz's har-monic sophistication and scope for improvis-ation would be combined with the more visceral excitements of rock music, specifi-cally its aggressively simple rhythms and the power drawn from its amplified instru-mentations. It didn't really happen, though, until the end of the 60s, when such musicians and/or groups as Miles Davis, Ian Carr's Nucleus, Soft Machine, Don Ellis, Herbie Hancock and The Jazz Crusaders set down music which began to make the characteristic rapprochement. It was two-way traffic: rockers such as the members of Soft Machine liked the finesse and gravitas which the jazz ingredients bestowed on their idiom, while Davis probably observed the kind of young, attractive audience which Jimi Hendrix was playing to and wondered why his old acoustic jazz didn't fit in with that scene. It was a period when rock still had plenty of leeway for an audience inter-ested in individual instrumental prowess – guitar heroes such as Alvin Lee of Ten Years After and Jimmy Page of Led Zeppelin were cheered for their marathon solos, a situation now unthinkable in the midst of pop music's present conservatism – while the adventurous technological climate, of new sounds emerging all the time from synthesi-zers, guitars and a rapidly advancing record-ing-studio culture, presented an interesting new field for jazz players who felt they wanted a change from the irreducible acous-tic line-ups of the hard-bop group. As a result, the early and middle 70s were jazz-rock's golden age. Several of the sidemen

Davis had gathered around him for such pioneering records as *In A Silent Way* and *Bitches Brew* went on to be jazz-rock giants, including John McLaughlin (Mahavishnu Orchestra), Chick Corea (Return To Forever), Joe Zawinul (Weather Report) and Tony Williams (Lifetime). Zawinul especially set a scintillating creative pace with Weather Report's records of the period. In a related area, The Crusaders (formerly The Jazz Crusaders) and The Brecker Brothers played jazz solos over funk-orientated rhythms, and were lumped in with the rest of the jazz-rockers.

Even by the middle of the decade, though, jazz-rock was losing its impetus: the brainy virtuosity of Corea's music, for instance, was soon enough wasted on the rock end of his audience, and the more interesting edges on the music of Weather Report and John McLaughlin began to be smoothed away. By the end of the decade, people were calling the genre 'fusion' instead of 'jazz-rock', suggesting that the various ingredients in the style had become so comprehensively pulped that a more distinct nomenclature was no longer appropriate. In the later 80s, jazz-rock seemed to settle into two camps which were practically in opposition: the tough-minded, almost interiorized music exemplified by the M-Base group of musicians, including Steve Coleman and Greg Osby, and the comforting, almost soporific style of smooth jazz, which became an accepted radio format in America and brought lucrative careers into the hands of such players as Kenny G, Dave Koz, Najee and Boney James, whose music is so denuded of jazz content that it is little more than instrumental pop. As the 90s progressed, several of the jazz-rock heavyweights of 20 years earlier began making comebacks, including Herbie Hancock's Headhunters, John McLaughlin reverting to all-out fusion after a period of pastoral playing, and Chick Corea's unfortunate Elektric Band. But more typical, perhaps, of the music best feeding the jazz-rock audience (whoever that may now be) is the work of Bill Frisell: soaking up influences and stylistic traits from a planet's worth of music, Frisell nevertheless satisfies listeners who still like to (albeit surreptitiously) shake their heads in time to a guitar solo.

# Jazz Warriors
GROUP

Jazz Warriors was for a time the most palpable example of the new wave of black British jazz in the 80s. It was the first all-black British big band of the post-war jazz era, drawn from the numerous musicians who were working on the London scene at the time of its formation (1985). There is some controversy over whose was the guiding hand in the Warriors' formation – both Gail Thompson and Courtney Pine have claimed that credit. The band also involved Steve Williamson, Philip Bent, Gary Crosby, Claude Deppa, Mark Mondesir and Cleveland Watkiss among others. Crosby and the veteran trumpeter Harry Beckett proved to be the key forces in the band: Crosby, a born organizer, helped create working opportunities, and Beckett rehearsed the group and arranged much of its music. The group always had something of an 'outsider' status, partly because many of its members came from backgrounds other than jazz (soul and reggae), and partly because they sought to work outside the small and not especially welcoming jazz-venue circuit of that time. Although they recorded a single album for Antilles (*Out Of Many, One People*, 1987), the Jazz Warriors seemed to drift apart, perhaps because too many of its individual members were seeking to concentrate on their own careers. Crosby has, however, overseen the group's interrupted progress, over many changes of personnel: the latest incarnation is as Tomorrow's Warriors, and is once again made up of young, aspiring musicians with an eye on the future.

# François Jeanneau
SAXOPHONES
*born* 15 June 1935

Jeanneau is a premier French modernist. He was playing in the traditional idiom as far back as 1955, with Raymond Fonseque's group, but was playing hard bop with George Arvanitas in the early 60s and began soaking up the influence of John Coltrane. He was, however, out of jazz for a decade, and on reappearing in the middle 70s he unveiled a tough modern style which was burnished by a particularly rich and attractive tenor sound. Jeanneau didn't make too many records, though, and the few which appeared didn't gather much attention. He became the initial leader of the government-sponsored Orchestre National de Jazz in 1986–7. He has latterly followed a French trend in investigating a mix of jazz with African music.

*Techniques Douces* (Owl)

## Eddie Jefferson
VOCAL
*born* 3 August 1918; *died* 9 May 1979

Jefferson had a mostly luckless career. He worked as both a dancer and a singer in his teens and by 1940 was trying his hand at scat singing, only to decide to take the different route of setting words to the melodies of improvised solos: 'Taxi War Dance' (Lester Young/Count Basie) and 'Body And Soul' (Coleman Hawkins) were two examples. But he had little in the way of recording opportunities and he must have felt chagrined when King Pleasure, who basically copied his style, had a hit with Jefferson's own variation on 'Moody's Mood For Love', in 1952. But it did at least open the door for Jefferson himself to start recording. He went on to manage (and sing with) James Moody's group for long spells in the 50s, 60s and 70s, while also making occasional featured dates of his own for Prestige and Riverside. While his voice was less smoothly appealing than Pleasure's, he was really the originator of the vocalese style, and was just starting to gain wider recognition as such – when he was murdered by a gunman outside a Detroit nightclub in 1979.

*Body And Soul* (Prestige)

## Hilton Jefferson
ALTO SAXOPHONE
*born* 30 July 1903; *died* 14 November 1968

'Jeff' was a valuable stalwart in several of the best black bands of the swing era. He started with Claude Hopkins in 1926 (which was long before that band began making records), then went with Chick Webb, McKinney's Cotton Pickers, Hopkins again (this time he is on a few of their sessions), Fletcher Henderson and Benny Carter, spending much of the later 30s with either Hopkins or Webb. He was with Cab Calloway for most of the 40s and was regularly featured, but in the 50s work fell away somewhat, and though he was still playing almost up until his death he filled in his time with other jobs. Unremembered in comparison with many other swing-era soloists, Jefferson had an immaculate sound and he unobtrusively bettered every saxophone section he played in.

*Cab Calloway, 1941–1942* (Classics)

## Herb Jeffries
VOCAL
*born* 29 September 1916

Jeffries led something of an extraordinary artistic double-life. He was a band singer in the early 30s with Earl Hines and others, but then began acting in low-grade Westerns as 'The Bronze Buckaroo', a singing cowboy. In 1940 he became Duke Ellington's male singer, scoring a major hit with 'Flamingo' (1942). Thereafter he mostly sang as a solo on the club circuit, but he made only a handful of long-playing records in the 50s and his eccentric sound – oilier even than Billy Eckstine's timbre – was difficult to locate. He was still singing in the 90s, and decided to go back to being The Bronze Buckaroo and sing country music.

*Duke Ellington, The Blanton–Webster Years* (Bluebird)

## Billy Jenkins
GUITAR
*born* 5 July 1956

The amiable Jenkins is a master of English absurdity, as well as a thoughtful and ingenious musician. He played in 70s rock groups such as Burlesque and the duo Trimmer & Jenkins, settings that stirred art-rock with punk attitude, and in the 80s he was a sideman with Ginger Baker. But it's been his own groups and orchestras which have fashioned a uniquely personal music, drawing on jazz, rock and blues, but using English anti-pastoral themes as the concept: Jenkins sees dedications to his hometown, Bromley, and the Greenwich one-way traffic system as the logical subject matter for a suburban British musician, and his music could in some ways be seen as a jazz-orientated equivalent of such post-modern

English rock music as Blur and The Fall. His principal performing vehicle has been the Voice Of God Collective, which has been made up of a large pool of players, although his Blues Collective (Jenkins now claims to be a blues player rather than any kind of jazz musician) has lately secured more prominence. The near-legendary *Scratches Of Spain* (1987), which comes with cover art with the word 'Billy' emblazoned on it in much the same way as 'Miles' appears on its role model's sleeve, is an essential early document, but the more recent *Suburbia* (1999) and *Life* (2001) are primal Jenkins.
**Suburbia** (Babel)

# Freddie Jenkins
TRUMPET
*born* 10 October 1906; *died* 12 July 1978

Another of Duke Ellington's legion of characterful trumpeters, Jenkins joined Duke in 1928 and spent six busy years with the leader. Early films of the Ellington band catch glimpses of his onstage abandon, fanning his trumpet and generally showing off, but his playing backed up the showmanship and he has many fine moments on records of the period. A lung infection obliged him to quit in 1934, although he commenced playing again shortly afterwards and was with Duke for another brief spell before further illness made him leave the music business altogether at the end of the 30s.
**Duke Ellington, *1929*** (Classics)

# Leroy Jenkins
VIOLIN
*born* 11 March 1932

Born in Chicago, Jenkins started on violin, switched to alto in high school, but amazingly enough decided to stick with what was a very unfashionable jazz instrument. He taught in the school system in Mobile and Chicago in the early 60s but was soon caught up in the early days of the AACM. As part of the Creative Construction Company, he recorded in Paris with Anthony Braxton in 1969, before ending up at Ornette Coleman's house in New York. Eventually, he formed the Revolutionary Ensemble in 1971 with Sirone (bass) and Jerome Cooper (drums), a group which practised relent-

lessly for six hours a day and recorded four albums which offer some of Jenkins's most vivid work. His rough sound and fierce attack recall the fiddlers of old black string bands, yet this is countered by a carefully nurtured elegance which can sound like a European romantic survival. The Ensemble broke up after seven years, and Jenkins has pursued a sometimes erratic course since, forming an almost jokey R&B kind of band named Sting ('I felt pinched being an avant-garde type') and otherwise working in small-group contexts which occasionally get the best out of him. Barring the Revolutionary Ensemble records, which have never been easy to find, nothing in his recorded work compares to the solo record cited, a powerful and combustible recital which has a bad-tempered beauty all its own.
**Solo** (India Navigation)

# Jack Jenney
TROMBONE
*born* 12 May 1910; *died* 16 December 1945

Jenney is still remembered mainly for one tune that he played on: Hoagy Carmichael's 'Stardust'. He was in the 1940 Artie Shaw band which recorded it, and his eight-bar solo is a few seconds of perfection, but the 1939 version he recorded with his own band, where he takes a musing journey through the tune and comes up with a beautifully pointed dialogue with the original melody, is a benchmark of swing-era trombone, as fine as anything Teagarden or Dorsey played in the same era. He had come up through the ranks of New York big bands in the early 30s, but his own band was a financial disaster and he moved on to Shaw and then Benny Goodman. Alcohol had all but ruined his health by 1945, and he died that year following an appendectomy.
**Stardust** (Hep)

# Jean-François Jenny-Clark
BASS
*born* 12 July 1944; *died* 6 October 1998

A superbly accomplished musician. Jenny-Clark's early death from cancer robbed listeners of what should have been much more from an intensely versatile and inquisitive mind. In his teens he was already

playing in Paris with Aldo Romano, and while he took the customary route of backing visiting Americans, he also found his interest piqued by the free music of the day, and he played with figures as diverse as Steve Lacy, Barney Wilen, Gato Barbieri and Don Cherry. At the same time, he could be found playing composed music by Stockhausen and Berio. All through the 70s, 80s and early 90s he was busy in numerous groups: he had a technique which took him from in to out without any hint of unease, and his beautiful sound lent improvisations a formidable elegance to go with their spontaneity. Jenny-Clark made a single album of solos and duos, *Unison*, in 1987, but otherwise rarely featured on the front of the marquee.
**Paul Motian, *Le Voyage*** (ECM)

# Ingrid Jensen
TRUMPET
*born* 12 January 1969

Although Jensen has accrued a reputation as a New York player, she is actually a Canadian who studied at Berklee in the 80s and then went to Europe to work with the Vienna Art Orchestra. She remained there for a time before shifting to New York in 1993, where she has since worked with a range of players and in both small and large groups: Maria Schneider has deployed her to good effect, and in 2003 she recorded some of the Miles Davis–Gil Evans charts as a soloist with the Scottish National Jazz Orchestra. Jensen has made only a handful of discs under her own name, none of which have made an indelible mark: she is a powerful and accomplished soloist, but does tend to sound best as an executant of other musicians' ideas.
**Higher Grounds** (Enja)

# Papa Bue Jensen
TROMBONE, BANDLEADER
*born* 8 May 1930

Papa Bue is Denmark's answer to Chris Barber: he actually played alongside Barber in the 50s, and has run his Viking Jazz Band in one form or another since 1956. They have been fixtures at trad-orientated festivals and on the venerable supporting circuit ever since, and have recorded prolifically:

there are at least 20 CDs in print, and a full discography might have given Tolstoy some problems. Although this kind of music has often been unkindly recorded and packaged down the years, the Vikings at their best strike a good balance between archaeological work, improvisation and good-time fun.
**Everybody Loves Saturday Night** (Timeless)

# Jørgen Grunnet Jepsen
DISCOGRAPHER
*born* August 1927; *died* 24 August 1981

Although a Dane, Jepsen wrote for the Swedish *Orkester Journalen*, primarily through contributing discographies of some of the major jazz musicians. He expanded this work into book form, and eventually prepared *Jazz Records 1942–1969*, a multi-volume work which picks up where Brian Rust's discographies leave off. It was the first attempt at codifying an exceedingly complex area and remained the standard work for many years, until competing versions by Walter Bruyninckx and Tom Lord took centre stage.

# Jerry Jerome
TENOR SAXOPHONE, CLARINET
*born* 19 June 1912; *died* 17 November 2002

Jerome played fine swing-styled saxophone for more than 60 years. He spent five years studying to be a doctor, but eventually gave it up for music, and he joined Glenn Miller in 1936. Benny Goodman hired him to replace Bud Freeman in 1938, and when that orchestra disbanded, he went over to Artie Shaw. For much of the 40s, though, he worked in radio, and latterly television: he set up his own business as a writer of commercials, and also did A&R for Apollo records – 'I did a Winston commercial that was on the air for ten years, and every 13 weeks I received another check. How else can you send four kids to college?' Eventually, in 1972, he decided to take the old folks' route and retire to Florida, but he still played local gigs and was effectively rediscovered in the mid-90s by Arbors Records, who recorded him at length in two two-disc sets of archive and new pieces and Jerry's entertaining reminiscences. The 1996 date – 'Everything in four, with a good solid

feel' – found the old fellow still in strong fettle.
**Something Old, Something New** (Arbors)

## Egil 'Bop' Johansen
DRUMS
*born* 11 January 1934; *died* 4 December 1998

A Norwegian who taught himself drums and threw himself into the local Oslo scene, 'Bop' Johansen actually decided to decamp for Sweden in 1954, and there he remained. He played with just about every modern jazz musician who set foot in the country and is on countless sessions as a sideman; occasionally he led a few dates of his own, particularly with the gang of veterans in Jazz Inc. His final association was with the Brazz Brothers quintet, with whom he played regularly in the last ten years of his life – they were, ironically enough, a Norwegian band.
**Jazz Inc, Walkin' On** (Dragon)

## Jan Johansson
PIANO
*born* 16 September 1931; *died* 9 November 1968

Johansson studied engineering in Gothenburg, but gave it up for music and he was working as a professional from the middle 50s. He played with Gunnar Johnson and toured with Stan Getz, before beginning work as a leader at the start of the 60s. Johansson had a meteoric few years: most of what he did on record is compressed into the period 1960–68, which still accounts for some 20 albums' worth of music. He struck up a few close musical dialogues – with Georg Riedel, Arne Domnérus, Rune Gustafsson and a few others – and he was busy writing scores for the Radiojazz-gruppen from its inception in 1967. His most individual trait was a fascination with original folk material, not only from Sweden, but also from Russian, Hungarian and other sources. He seemed able to integrate these themes into a piano style which covered much of the instrument's jazz history, as well as covering such pieces as Ornette Coleman's 'Una Muy Bonita'. His own writing extended across an equally broad range, some of it almost jokey, some amazingly original. His revision of 'A Night In Tunisia' for the Radiojazzgruppen (on *Den*

*Korta Fristen*, 1967) shows what he could do with a big ensemble. Although he is still hardly known outside Sweden, many musicians from his own country acknowledge a considerable debt to his composing and playing and much of his best work has been reissued on CD by the Heptagon label. What else he might have gone on to create is, sadly, an unanswerable question: he was killed in a car accident on the way to a concert.
**8 Bitar Johansson/Innertrio** (Heptagon)

## Sven-Åke Johansson
DRUMS, VOCAL
*born* 1943

The Swede found himself involved in the very first wave of Euopean free jazz: he was in the trio with Peter Brötzmann which cut such epochal records as *For Adolphe Sax* (1967), and he then worked with Rüdiger Carl, Manfred Schoof, Ernst-Ludwig Petrowsky and especially Alex von Schlippenbach, with whom he formed a long-standing duo partnership: originally it was simply a piano/drums dialogue, but Johansson became increasingly interested in his vocal capabilities, and it has latterly been a kind of avant-garde *Lieder* setting. Johansson has also written operettas. This has taken some of the interest away from his drumming, but he has renewed his attention to that side of his music-making in recent years, especially in the very fine *Six Little Pieces For Quintet* (1999), which he describes as 'early free jazz on period instruments'.
**Six Little Pieces For Quintet** (hatOLOGY)

## Bill Johnson
BASS
*born* c1872; *died* 2 December 1972

Johnson was the oldest player in King Oliver's Jazz Band, yet he outlived every other member of that group. He was born somewhere in Alabama around 1872 and he was playing guitar and bass in New Orleans at the turn of the century. He toured with the Original Creole Band a few years later (on bass and mandolin) and must be accounted among the first to spread the new dialect of jazz further afield than New

Orleans; the group got as far west as California. He was working with Joe Oliver when the leader made his first two sessions for Gennett in 1923, this time playing banjo (he's the one who makes the enthusiastic shout of 'Oh play that thing!' on 'Dipper Mouth Blues'), and he later recorded with Johnny Dodds and others; there is a single coupling made for Brunswick in 1929 where he leads a group with Georgia Tom Dorsey and Frankie Jaxon. He carried on working in Chicago in the 30s and 40s but subsequently retired to Texas, where he lived to a biblical age.

**King Oliver, *The Complete*** (Retrieval)

# Budd Johnson

SAXOPHONES, CLARINET, ARRANGER
*born* 14 December 1910; *died* 20 October 1984

Johnson was an important back-room figure in jazz who never quite got his due as an instrumental voice. Born in Dallas (his brother Keg was a trombonist who sometimes worked with him), Albert Johnson worked in his home state before settling in Kansas City at the end of the 20s. His first important work, though, was with Earl Hines in Chicago, where he was a stout member of the reed section and began writing charts for the band's book ('Grand Terrace Shuffle' is a classic from this period). In the 40s he worked for various leaders but surprisingly found himself involved in the first wave of bebop, sharing a front line with Dizzy Gillespie and replacing Dexter Gordon in the Billy Eckstine band. Thereafter he freelanced or worked for numerous leaders as a hired gun, eventually returning to the Earl Hines small group of the mid-60s and then running his own JPJ Quartet in the first half of the 70s. Johnson managed to put together a huge discography without, like so many of his contemporaries, ever quite setting down the immortal LP which would have secured his library reputation. Though he liked the rhythmic felicities associated with the Lester Young school, tonally he was at the lean end of the Hawkins model, and he could play a blues with unshakeable assurance. Perhaps the best of him can be found on *Budd Johnson And The Four Brass Giants* (1959) and *Let's Swing* (1961). A gracious, much-liked man, who always appeared to be wearing a smile for the camera, Budd seemed to

have been around jazz for ever, and it felt surprising that he was in the end only 74 when he died.

***Let's Swing*** (Prestige)

# Bunk Johnson

TRUMPET
*born* 27 December 1889(?); *died* 7 July 1949

It's impossible to say for certain when Johnson was born. He always claimed 1879 as the year, which went without being questioned until many years after his death, when researchers began arguing that he may actually have been born ten years later, based on census records and other evidence. Still, at the time of Johnson's celebrated second career in the 40s, nobody disbelieved that the man they were hearing and dealing with was in his 60s. The early part of his career, though, still has much uncertainty about it. He claimed to have played with Buddy Bolden in the 1890s (had he been born in 1879 he would have been older than Bolden), and in the early 1900s he worked with the bands of Frankie Dusen and Henry Allen. Around 1914 he left New Orleans and joined various travelling shows and circus bands on the Southern circuit, settling in Houston for a time, and this way of life seems to have kept him busy up until the 30s. He moved to New Iberia in 1931 and played there for a time, but was obliged to stop in 1935 when he lost his teeth. Rediscovered in 1938, and given a new set of dentures and a new horn, he began practising again and in 1942 made his first recordings for Bill Russell's Jazz Man label, with Jim Robinson and George Lewis in attendance. Johnson's first comeback music had a liveliness to it which he rarely captured again, although at this point he still sounds a little out of practice. Nevertheless, he was quickly acclaimed as living history, and he began working in San Francisco, Boston, New York and New Orleans, although it wasn't enough to keep him in full employment and he had already become contrary and difficult. Sidney Bechet, who worked with him in Boston, became exasperated at Johnson's drinking, and when the band with Robinson and Lewis was reassembled for a 1946 engagement in New York, the unpredictable Bunk cursed out his men on the stand. The records, though, suggested Johnson was in

better heart: his clear open tone bypassed the showy tricks of many hot players, and his almost courtly kind of swing certainly recalls the virtues of brass playing of the pre-jazz era. He had recorded a brass band session for American Music in 1945, which also re-established a link with the past. In 1947 he moved to New York and played with both old and young hands, including Jimmy Archey and Omer Simeon, and on his very last session – again with a more Dixieland-orientated crew, including Ed Cuffee and Garvin Bushell – he played pop tunes and ragtime numbers rather than the New Orleans standards he had worked on before. He went back to New Iberia and died in 1949 after suffering two strokes. Johnson is – along with the sideman whose playing he never seemed to like much, George Lewis – the recurring icon of New Orleans jazz, and the rallying point for everyone who decided that there was a 'purism' to follow in appreciating that music. It would have been fascinating to hear what the young Bunk might have sounded like, but even in his autumnal recordings one can surely hear echoes of a music which, by the time they were made, had already all but vanished.
**Bunk's Brass Band And Dance Band 1945** (American Music)

## Charlie Johnson
PIANO
*born* 21 November 1891; *died* 13 December 1959

Johnson may have been a very important pianist (Sam Wooding, who heard him early on, suggested that he was already playing jazz when his contemporaries were still doing ragtime) and the boss of an outstanding band: he was leading the regular outfit at New York's Smalls' Paradise for ten years from 1925, and with a line-up that included – at various points – Benny Carter, Sidney De Paris, Jabbo Smith, Pike Davis, Jimmy Harrison and Edgar Sampson, it was replete with talent. Victor sides such as 'The Boy In The Boat', 'Walk That Thing' and 'Hot Bones And Rice' (1928–9) offer some of the hottest New York jazz of its period, equalling Ellington and Henderson. But Johnson had no luck with management, made only a few records, and when the swing era began to stir was already an also-ran. In the end he left behind only 14 titles and plenty of

stories about his style of laissez-faire organization. Although he played occasional gigs in Harlem in later years, he was basically out of music by 1940.
**The Complete Charlie Johnson Sessions** (FDM)

## Gus Johnson
DRUMS
*born* 15 November 1913; *died* 6 February 2000

Johnson came from Texas and played in Kansas City, joining Jay McShann's band there in 1938. He freelanced after the war and was with Count Basie, joining the pianist's octet in 1950 and staying on for the re-formed big band and proving particularly adept in both roles: it was only when appendicitis put him in the hospital that Basie took on a replacement in 1954. After this, Johnson worked behind singers (particularly Ella Fitzgerald and Lena Horne) besides doing more big-band work with Woody Herman and Gerry Mulligan. He joined The World's Greatest Jazz Band in 1969, staying until 1975, and thereafter freelanced on the festival and swing-revival circuit until illness obliged him to retire in 1990.
**Count Basie, Dance Session** (Clef)

## Howard Johnson
TUBA, BARITONE SAXOPHONE
*born* 7 August 1941

Not too many have followed his example, but Johnson has pioneered the use of the tuba in post-bop jazz. He started on baritone and took up the tuba not long afterwards, settling in New York in 1963 and working several sides of the spectrum: free jazz with Bill Dixon and Archie Shepp, soul-jazz with Hank Crawford, and particularly the small-group music of Charles Mingus. Session-work proved to be his most viable occupation and he is on many blues and rock records, but versatility is something that comes easily to him: he has played trumpet, cornet, flugelhorn, penny whistle, clarinet and bass clarinet on records in addition to his regular horns, and his long stints with various Gil Evans orchestras, Carla Bley, McCoy Tyner and George Gruntz's Concert Jazz Band have broadened his horizons further. But what Johnson surely likes best are his own bands featuring multiple tubas: he had a tuba quartet called Substructure in 1966, and his later band Gravity, first formed in 1968 and still convened whenever he has the opportunity, has featured up to nine tubists and a rhythm section. If this music doesn't exactly sound fleet, the fluency which Howard has brought to the tuba has at least given an improbable horn solid jazz status.

*Gravity!!!* (Verve)

## J J Johnson

TROMBONE

*born* 22 January 1924; *died* 4 February 2001

Although he was born James Louis Johnson, he answered to 'JJ', a nickname picked up from his habit of initialling his arrangements, and he subsequently made JJ his legal name. He had begun writing charts while with Benny Carter's band in the early 40s, his first important engagement, although he had previously played with Fats Navarro in a touring group led by Snookum Russell. After leaving Carter in 1945, he spent a period with Count Basie and then settled in New York, working at the heart of the new bebop scene. By this time his trombone playing had matured from a fast, full-toned and declamatory manner into a *very* fast, light-bodied, supremely targeted delivery: nobody got around the horn with the same agility and on-the-nose accuracy as JJ. He mixed with the best of the boppers, turning up on some of Parker's Dial titles and leading his own dates for Savoy, while also touring with Illinois Jacquet's group (where Johnson was surprised to find the leader very interested in the new music and encouraging of the trombonist's adventures). He joined Dizzy Gillespie's big band in 1949 and was a part of the Miles Davis nonet, but music wasn't paying his bills and he stopped playing for a time to work as a blueprint inspector. On his return, in 1954, he cut some outstanding sessions for Blue Note, as well as playing masterful solos on Davis's *Walkin'* session for Prestige. But what turned his career around was forming a trombone duo with Kai Winding, the band coming to be called Jay and Kai. It lasted for only a couple of years (besides occasional reunions in the 60s), yet records for Prestige, Savoy and Columbia were all warmly received and the music – though

rather blandly conceived around the simpatico tones of the two leaders – struck a chord with audiences. After this, Johnson led his own band and recorded for Columbia, wrote some large-scale works (*Perceptions* was one such, recorded with Dizzy Gillespie as principal soloist in 1961) and taught. After 1970, when he moved to Los Angeles, he became much more involved in film and TV scoring, and largely left jazz performance behind, though he sometimes played for fun. The price Johnson paid for his peerless virtuosity on the trombone was a soupçon of blandness: in his bebop heyday he often sounds as if he is improvising as some sort of academic exercise, and with the rise of a new expressionism on the trombone in recent years, his methods have to some extent gone out of style. Yet his choice of notes and the warmth of his delivery in his late-50s and early-60s music overcomes any worry that he is coasting through it, and there is much to be rediscovered in the records he made in this period. It was a pleasure to find him returning to more active duty as a leader-performer in the late 80s, and though there was a cloud cast over this time with the illness and subsequent death of his wife Vivian in 1992, his final records, including the lovely *The Brass Orchestra* (1996), find him in suitably magisterial voice. Sadly, depressed by a worsening illness of his own, he took his own life in 2001.

*The Eminent JJ Johnson Vol 1* (Blue Note)

## James P Johnson

PIANO

*born* 1 February 1894; *died* 17 November 1955

Johnson was old enough to bridge the worlds of ragtime and jazz piano. His family, originally from New Jersey, moved to New York in 1908, and while the young Johnson also took classical lessons, by 1913 he was busy as a piano soloist in some of the dance clubs in the city's black neighbourhoods. He made piano rolls before he cut records, but his first three solo sides – 'Harlem Strut', 'Keep Off The Grass' and one of his signature pieces, 'Carolina Shout' – were made in 1921 and are among the first real jazz-piano recordings. Even more so than Jelly Roll Morton's earliest solos, Johnson's music shows ragtime being left behind and jazz taking over: he plays with a jauntiness and a free-flowing accuracy which is, in its way, a definitive 'stride piano' style, yet is at the same time more personal and less repetitive than much in that idiom. His compositions share ragtime's trait of a series of inter-linked melodic strains, but thereafter they are subtly dispersed and improvised upon, and there seem to be echoes in his music of very distant influences: church music, country dances and rural blues, all of which is hinted at by such titles as 'Mule Walk' and 'Blueberry Rhyme'. Johnson continued working in Harlem and was an inspiration to the young Fats Waller, Duke Ellington and many others, a champ at cutting contests and a prolific man in recording studios: he backed many blues singers (including Bessie Smith) and led band dates of his own too. He began writing for the Broadway stage with *Runnin' Wild* (1923), and though he had no block-buster hits he was a solid professional writer whose work was respected. But his larger-scale works – *Yamekraw* (1927), an orchestral piece with a piano part played by Waller at the Carnegie Hall premiere, *Harlem Symphony* (1932) and *Symphony In Brown* (1935) – received scant attention in an age when black Americans weren't meant to do that kind of thing. After a relatively quiet period, Johnson re-emerged as a performer at the 1938 From Spirituals To Swing concerts and began recording for Blue Note. But his health was declining and he suffered a series of strokes; even so, Eddie Condon and others in that circle were delighted to have him on piano whenever possible. In 1951, a final stroke left him paralysed and he never played again.

*Snowy Morning Blues* (GRP)

## Ken 'Snake Hips' Johnson
BANDLEADER
*born* 10 September 1914; *died* 8 March 1941

Johnson moved to England in 1929 from his native British Guiana: a fine dancer, he began working as a choreographer, and got as far as America before returning to England in 1936. He began dancing with a black band named The Jazz Emperors and eventually took over leadership of the group, which then expanded to a larger orchestra and incorporated more West Indian musicians. It has achieved a some-

what legendary status in British jazz for its excellence, involving such key players as Leslie 'Jiver' Hutchinson, but the 16 titles they made for Decca and HMV are often not much more than capable dance music and at this distance it's hard to tell how good the band may have been. Not much survives of Johnson's legacy, besides some fleeting film appearances: he was killed when a bomb landed on London's Café de Paris in 1941.

## Marc Johnson
BASS
*born* 21 October 1953

Johnson first came to prominence as the bassist in Bill Evans's final trio, and after that he worked regularly with Stan Getz and John Abercrombie, although a burgeoning career as a freelance may have discouraged him from staying in one group for too long. His 80s quartet Bass Desires – with John Scofield, Bill Frisell and Peter Erskine – was something of a supergroup of its day, and fine as their two ECM albums are, the group was even more exciting to hear live, and it's a pity that they made no further records. Since then, Johnson has built up a broad list of playing partners in both Europe and the US, although his work as a leader has stalled somewhat: a single and fine album for Verve, *The Sound Of Summer Running* (1997), was never built on further. A technically adroit player with a grand sound, Johnson's thoughtful writing needs further documentation.

**Bass Desires** (ECM)

## Osie Johnson
DRUMS
*born* 11 January 1923; *died* 10 February 1966

Johnson grew up in Washington DC and was playing professionally by the time he was 18. After navy service he worked in Chicago, with Earl Hines and others, and in the next decade he was busy mostly as a studio sessionman in New York, doing many television gigs (he plays in the famous *Sound Of Jazz* telecast, 1957) and turning up on a vast number of records. He made a couple of ten-inch albums as a small-group leader for Period (1955), now extremely rare, and also took a starring role on *A Bit Of The Blues*

(RCA, 1956), where he was featured as a singer rather than playing the drums.
**Paul Gonsalves, *Tell It The Way It Is*** (Impulse!)

## Pete Johnson
PIANO
*born* 25 March 1904; *died* 23 March 1967

Johnson was the third man in the famous boogie-woogie triumvirate which dominated the style at the end of the 30s (Meade Lux Lewis and Albert Ammons were numbers one and two). Born Kermit Holden in Kansas City, Johnson worked locally and became one of John Hammond's discoveries, causing a sensation at the 1938 From Spirituals To Swing concert at Carnegie Hall. Besides working with Ammons and Lewis, he struck up a great partnership with singer Joe Turner, and the pair made many records together up until 1955. Johnson was as much a master of his style as his two contemporaries: his 1939 solo session for Solo Art is an object lesson in how much variation can be called out of the blues and boogie idioms. Some of his later dates are subject to routine, but the tracks with Turner (such as 'Roll 'Em Pete') are always exuberant. He stopped playing in 1958 after suffering a stroke and his appearance at the Newport Festival that year turned out to be a farewell.
***Pete Johnson 1938–1939*** (Classics)

## Plas Johnson
TENOR SAXOPHONE
*born* 21 July 1931

Although he started on soprano, Johnson soon switched to tenor and played with his brother in a band in New Orleans. In 1954 he arrived in Los Angeles, and though he did some work with the Johnny Otis revue, he spent most of his time as a studio session-player, contributing rollicking (and sometimes tender) solos to hundreds of rock'n'roll, R&B and middle-of-the-road records of every conceivable stripe. He was in the band for the television show fronted by Merv Griffin all through the 70s and early 80s, and since then has turned up in various all-star situations, and even fronted a record or two of his own. As dependable as nightfall, Plas is in everybody's collection even if they don't realize it. While he could

play in any style to order, his 'natural' is a bluesy, swing-styled delivery with a touch of Johnny Hodges.
***The Blues*** (Concord)

## Philip Johnston
ALTO AND SOPRANO SAXOPHONES
*born* 22 January 1955

Johnston divided his time between New York and San Francisco in the 70s but eventually settled on the East Coast. With Joel Forrester, he co-led the four-sax-and-rhythm Microscopic Septet (1979–92), as well as such other groups as Public Servants (80s) and Big Trouble (90s), the latter band recording for Black Saint, Avant and Eighth Day Music and setting down some of Johnston's most vivid work: offbeat arrangements, with a careful use of structure, covering Herbie Nichols and Steve Lacy tunes as well as Johnston's own.
***Philip Johnston's Big Trouble*** (Black Saint)

## Pete Jolly
PIANO
*born* 5 June 1932; *died* 6 November 2004

Jolly (real name Peter Ceragioli) moved from New Haven to Los Angeles in the early 50s and was soon established as a regular in the West Coast jazz of that fertile period, recording with many of the familiar figures in the scene all through that decade and the 60s. Latterly he played more in film and TV, but still did club gigs and in the 80s and 90s he went back to playing more frequently in a live setting. Some of his own-name records offer playing in a rather trivial style, sometimes resembling a slightly frantic cocktail-piano mood, but his better music swings in an agreeably powerful manner.
***Little Bird*** (Ava)

## Carmell Jones
TRUMPET
*born* 19 July 1936; *died* 7 November 1996

Although he remains a favourite among LP collectors, Jones never found much in the way of wide acclaim and in the end his career tailed off dramatically. He grew up in Kansas City and began leading groups there around 1959 after military service, but in 1960 he moved to California and enjoyed his most productive period there in the early 60s. Gerald Wilson used him to fine effect as one of his orchestra's best soloists, and Jones's own records of the period – *The Remarkable Carmell Jones* (1961) and *Business Meetin'* (1962), both for Pacific Jazz – show how he was taking the Clifford Brown manner to a place where it sat comfortably with the straight-ahead style of that time. There was one Prestige album to come, and a year with Horace Silver's group (he plays on the splendid *Song For My Father*, 1965), but Jones then spent the rest of the 60s in Europe and American jazz more or less forgot about him. Eventually he returned to Kansas City around 1980, and though he was occasionally sighted thereafter, his career faded away.

**Business Meetin'** (Pacific Jazz)

## Claude Jones

TROMBONE
*born* 11 February 1901; *died* 17 January 1962

Jones deserves to be ranked among the best of the early jazz trombonists. He played with McKinney's Cotton Pickers through most of the 20s, performing at first in a flexible Miff Mole style, but some of his best work was with Fletcher Henderson, whom he joined for a two-year stay in 1929. It was something of a late coming-out, since Jack Teagarden and Jimmy Harrison had already set up new agendas for the trombone, but by the time of one of his best records, Henderson's 1931 'Sugar Foot Stomp', Jones had his fat sound and quick, agile phrasing in full harmony with each other, and his strongest solos have a remarkable impact. In the 30s he enjoyed further prominence with Don Redman and especially Cab Calloway, and in 1944 he spent five years in the Ellington orchestra, playing valve-trombone. But music wasn't always on Jones's mind: he owned a sausage-manufacturing firm for a spell, and eventually he left playing behind altogether in the 50s when he became a mess steward working on ocean liners. He died on board ship during a voyage in the winter of 1962.

**Fletcher Henderson, *1931–1932*** (Classics)

## Darryl Jones

BASS
*born* 11 December 1961

Darryl 'The Munch' Jones was one of the later fusion musicians to be made a star by Miles Davis. The trumpeter plucked him from obscurity to play in his 1983 band, and Jones worked with Davis on and off for the rest of the 80s. His distinctive, almost twanging sound is a constant in Davis's records of the period, and Jones seemed to be a favourite onstage foil for the old man. Since then, despite various guest-star roles, he hasn't really found a significant niche, and he certainly hasn't put his own name on a distinctive record.

**Miles Davis, *We Want Miles*** (Columbia)

## Dill Jones

PIANO
*born* 19 August 1923; *died* 22 June 1984

One of the few Welshmen to enjoy a significant jazz career, Jones studied music in London at the end of the 40s and before the decade was out he had enjoyed spells with Humphrey Lyttelton and Harry Parry. The latter association helped get him into broadcasting, and he introduced the BBC's *Jazz Club* show for some years in the 50s. He was busy with several different leaders in London during that decade, shifting easily between the various shades of mainstream-to-modern, but in 1961 he took the famous plunge and settled in New York, and for the rest of his life (cut short by cancer in 1984) he was busy there, as a sideman with the Chicagoan style of bands that worked at Ryan's and Condon's, as a member of the JPJ Quartet with Budd Johnson, and as a soloist himself. In the latter role he especially liked to play stride piano, of which he was one of the superior exponents in an age when it had largely fallen into disrepair. These days he is half-forgotten by British audiences – his discography is rather scattered, and the fine record cited has yet to appear on CD – perhaps because he left a long time ago and seldom came back. But he deserves to be remembered as one of British jazz's most worthy exports.

**Up Jumped You With Love** (77)

# Elvin Jones

DRUMS

*born* 9 September 1927; *died* 18 May 2004

The youngest of the three Jones brothers came out of the army in 1949 and began working with Thad in the Billy Mitchell group in Detroit. Having next toured with Charles Mingus, he arrived in New York in 1956 and was an in-demand freelance in that scene before joining the John Coltrane quartet in late 1960, a move that effectively fulfilled his destiny by conjoining him with one of the great jazz innovators of the day. Jones's own style had moved in a steady progression towards the kind of development he would express fully in Coltrane's company: he didn't depart from the bop-drumming tradition of Clarke and Roach, but he moved it dramatically onwards. His great advance was to introduce a polyrhythmic feel as standard: it wasn't unusual for him to be playing metrical subdivisions of the underlying beat which suggested two or three drummers working to complementary ends. The cross-rhythms which Art Blakey introduced as a variety into his basic style became the meat and matter of Jones's delivery. Yet instead of introducing incoherence, the very rightness of his drumming made it sound beautifully logical: for all its complexity of accent and tone, it sounded natural and, in the context of Coltrane's quartet, essential to the momentum of the music. The central dialogue in the quartet is often held as that between Coltrane and Jones, who had gone beyond Blakey by pushing the drummer's role into a foreground where he took on an equal role in the conversation. This new freedom pointed towards both the free players of the next half-generation and the fusion drummers of the one after that: it was of further significance that Jones played louder than any drummer who came before him. For five years, Coltrane's music was driven relentlessly by Jones, but when Rashied Ali was engaged as a second drummer, Elvin chose to take his leave: extraordinarily, his first gig after leaving was on a Duke Ellington tour of Europe. Thereafter he began leading bands of his own, often of two saxophonists, bass and drums, and the music – as set down on a group of late-period Blue Note albums – was dense and challenging, using young players such as Dave Liebman and Steve Grossman. Leading small groups sustained the rest of Jones's career. He resisted the temptations of fusion and, although he sometimes used guitarists, kept an acoustic band. From 1985 he spent much of his time based in Nagasaki, where his wife came from, but in the 90s he was still touring and often working in America again: among his later sidemen were Sonny Fortune, Javon Jackson, Delfeayo Marsalis, Joey Calderazzo and Ravi Coltrane. Despite his wild-man reputation in his younger years, Jones was an outgoing and good-natured man who was always kind to younger musicians: Dave Liebman regarded him as a second father during the time they worked together.

**John Coltrane,** *A Love Supreme* (Impulse!)

# Etta Jones

VOCAL

*born* 25 November 1928; *died* 16 October 2001

Jones began singing in her teens, and by the time she was 16 she was touring with Buddy Johnson and making her first records (at Leonard Feather's behest). She then spent time as the singer with Earl Hines's group and did club work in the 50s, but a contract with Prestige led to a surprise hit in 1960, 'Don't Go To Strangers', which was successful enough to ensure regular appearances on black jukeboxes and a string of fine albums for the label. Jones's heavy, pleading style was delivered in a big voice that she handled with a deceptive lightness: like Shirley Horn, she relished slow tempos and could personalize a song without taking excessive liberties with melody or phrasing. In the later 60s and 70s her career slipped back a gear, but she came into her own once again with her albums for Muse and High Note in the 80s and 90s: usually backed by a band with the supremely accomplished Houston Person (who was her partner for many years), Etta's voice became even more sumptuous, the delivery more majestic, and an album created as a Billie Holiday homage, *Sings Lady Day* (2001), was resplendent – poignantly so, given that she died only months after it was completed.

***Don't Go To Strangers*** (Prestige)

# Hank Jones

PIANO
*born* 31 August 1918

Jazz has never wanted for pianists with long careers, and Hank Jones is up there with the most remarkable of them. Although associated with the Detroit school of pianists, he was born in Vicksburg and grew up in Pontiac, Michigan (where his brothers Thad and Elvin were born). He was already performing locally in his early teens, and eventually went to New York in 1944: there he worked at first with swing-era players such as Hot Lips Page, Andy Kirk and Buster Bailey, but he was also listening to the new bebop players, and was soon adept in playing in both idioms. His natural style, though, was that of a deferential ensemble player with acute harmonic understanding and unerring instincts, and that led him in the direction of an accompanying role: he duly worked as Ella Fitzgerald's pianist between 1947 and 1953, which also introduced him to Norman Granz's Jazz At The Philharmonic roadshow. After this he freelanced in New York, and then worked as the regular pianist at Savoy Records for many of their sessions: *Have You Met Hank Jones?* (1956) is a little masterpiece from this period. In 1959 he began an association with CBS as a staff musician, playing on the *Ed Sullivan Show* and numerous other engagements, while also doing many record dates. This lasted until the late 70s, when he joined the Broadway musical *Ain't Misbehavin'*, which brought him to a further, largely non-specialist audience. Since the early 80s, as an acknowledged elder statesman, he has worked with The Great Jazz Trio (originally Jones, Ron Carter, Tony Williams), and otherwise as he has pleased: he enjoyed a contract with Verve in the 90s which brought about such projects as the surprising *Sarala* (1995), which paired him with African musicians. Hank Jones all but defines urbanity in the jazz idiom. Hardly any of his records are individually well known as such, and he has played through a career which has been carried off in a kind of continuous shadow: even when he has been in a high-profile gig, the spotlight has never seemed to be on him. Restraint and fine taste have marked all of his music, but that suggests a rather dry, uninvolving musician: fairer to say that Hank's immaculate touch and quiet ingenuities always deserve the listener's finest attention.
*Have You Met Hank Jones?* (Savoy)

# Jimmy Jones

PIANO
*born* 30 December 1918; *died* 29 April 1982

Jones practised his craft with quiet perfectionism. Though born in Memphis, he grew up in Chicago, where he played with Stuff Smith before moving to New York in 1944. He found his forte when he began playing for Sarah Vaughan in 1947: although he was ill for a time, he basically remained her accompanist for the next ten years, demonstrating a tact and generosity in this role which might be a model for a pianist working behind a singer. Besides this regular gig, he worked prolifically as a sideman in the studios and struck up a particularly loyal association with various Ellington sidemen. This led him to an arranging and conducting role, which brought him the job of MD for Ellington's stage show *My People* (1963) and secured a role as an occasional dep for Duke himself in the 60s. He also worked as an accompanist for Ella Fitzgerald in this period. Reticent as his style might seem, Jones was a lucid and inventive thinker, sequencing passages of detail and sophistication even while doing nothing to upset or distract whomever he might have been playing for. His work on Kenny Burrell's Ducal homage *Ellington Is Forever* (1975) serves as a wonderful summary of his virtues.
**Kenny Burrell,** *Ellington Is Forever* (Fantasy)

# Jo Jones

DRUMS
*born* 7 October 1911; *died* 4 September 1985

Papa Jo Jones came out of Chicago to work with carnival bands and territory groups: he was on piano and vibes, but switched back to the drums when he joined the Count Basie band in 1934, staying until 1948. With Basie, Freddie Green and Walter Page, Jones made up the 'All-American Rhythm Section' which powered the orchestra: obliged to play lightly and gracefully, in order not to overpower the subtle dynamics established by the other three, Jones came up with a new emphasis where the pulse of the beat was switched from the bass drum to the hi-hat cymbal. The paradigmatic shift from the two-beat music of the 20s to the swing era's four-four time was crystallized in Jones's playing. He also found new things to do with the basic kit: playing with brushes, and placing the rimshot in places which accented unexpected beats. He didn't much care for effects such as the wood-block or chimes: Jones was the quintessen-tial kit drummer. On definitive Basie per-formances such as 'One O'Clock Jump' (1937) or 'Swinging The Blues' (1938), Jones is masterful without becoming intrusive. After he left, he toured with Jazz At The Philharmonic, helped establish the 'main-stream' lineage with his playing on the celebrated Vanguard sessions of 1953–4, and spent the rest of the 50s and 60s work-ing in small groups, choosing performers (Coleman Hawkins and especially Roy Eldridge among them) whom he could recognize as kindred spirits in a harsh world for a dedicated musician. He gradually slowed down, and worked less often: illness brought his career to a close at the begin-ning of the 80s. A fierce, proud man, Jones felt he had paid more dues than most, and he was probably right.

**Count Basie, *The Original American Decca Recordings*** (MCA)

## Jonah Jones

TRUMPET, VOCAL
*born* 31 December 1908; *died* 30 April 2000

Born in Louisville, Kentucky, Jones worked locally until joining New York-based big bands in the early 30s, eventually teaming with violinist Stuff Smith, with whom he struck up a vaudevillian duo partnership. Then he joined the Cab Calloway band in 1941, staying for 11 years. After this it was back to New York lounges, and that might have been the end of Jones's story if it hadn't been for *Jonah Jones At The Embers*, an LP which sparked an improbable hit with a quartet version of 'On The Street Where You Live'. Capitol had him cut a further 16 albums in a similar vein, the Armstrong-derived trumpet swaggering through a set of standards, with Jonah's occasional singing adding to the fun. Album collectors prize some of these records more for the covers

than the music – many feature expensive-looking trollops rather than the smiling Jones himself – but lightweight as it was, it was a good act, and kept the trumpeter into a comfortable old age. He worked the festi-val circuit in the 80s and though he eventu-ally retired, he still liked to pick up the horn from time to time. Very little of his work has so far emerged on CD.

*I Dig Chicks* (Capitol)

## Max Jones

WRITER
*born* 28 February 1917; *died* 1 August 1993

Although he learned saxophone and founded the High Wycombe Rhythm Club in 1935, Jones was basically a writer and com-mentator on jazz, one of the leading figures in the British critical scene of the post-war period, a prolific and always entertaining wordsmith. Although he also worked for the specialist press, Jones's great association was with the *Melody Maker*, commencing in the 40s and lasting until the 80s, when he retired. On the occasion of one of the maga-zine's milestones, he reluctantly took the daring step of allowing his otherwise ever-present beret to be photographed by itself: he had lost his hair owing to a medical con-dition in the 40s, and only allowed the pic-ture to be taken after he (temporarily) passed the headgear out from under the door of a bathroom cubicle. Jones was amus-edly tolerant of everything that happened in the bop era and after, but he basically remained a Louis Armstrong man for the duration of his critical life.

## Norah Jones

VOCAL, PIANO
*born* 30 March 1979

Jones was a singer and pianist with some experience of working as a club act when, early in the new century, she auditioned for Bruce Lundvall in his office. After a few minutes he had heard enough, and immedi-ately offered her a deal to sign with Blue Note. A daughter of Ravi Shankar, she was all but unknown when her first record, *Come Away With Me*, came out, but it has gone on to become Blue Note's biggest-selling record ever and a follow-up album has been almost as successful. Jones isn't a jazz musician, but her sexily languorous vocals and a backing which has the feel of a drowsy coffee-house band have proved surprisingly irresistible to a worldwide audience, and now other labels are looking for their own Norah. It is the kind of failsafe record which a jazz label prays for, since the success can bankroll many less successful projects.

*Come Away With Me* (Blue Note)

## Oliver Jones
PIANO
*born* 11 September 1934

Canada's other most famous jazz-piano export (he actually studied with Oscar Peterson's sister Daisy) is a stylish and grand-hearted player, very much a kindred spirit to the great Oscar. For the larger part of his career, though, he worked in relative anonymity. Between 1963 and 1980 or so he backed the Canadian MOR singer Kenny Hamilton, and after that worked in Montreal clubs, particularly Biddle's. Later in the decade he began visiting both America and Europe to work, but he throttled back on his appearances in the mid-90s and retired altogether in 1999, a rare example of a jazz musician deciding he had said enough even though still in excellent fettle. He was recorded prolifically by the Justin Time label during his peak years, and every record demonstrates his class: swing-to-modern showpieces, full of notes, and if never quite as sparkling as Peterson at his peak – an inevitable point of comparison which Jones probably felt he could never evade – there was always plenty to listen to.

*From Lush To Lively* (Justin Time)

## Philly Joe Jones
DRUMS
*born* 15 July 1923; *died* 30 August 1985

Joe Jones from Philadelphia had plenty of local experience before he moved to New York in 1947. Although he didn't really get on to record in this period, he played behind many of the leading boppers, then worked with Joe Morris and Ben Webster before building up a wider book of associations which eventually led to work with Miles Davis, who liked having Jones behind him

on otherwise indifferent local jobs. This led to the trumpeter engaging him full-time when he put together his famous 1955 quintet. He stayed, aside from one spell away, until 1958, when his unreliability due to drug problems caused the hitherto tolerant Davis to finally cry enough. But Jones was by now enough of a major player to find work easily enough, and he was a prolific studio artist all through the early 60s; in 1958, he had made *Blues For Dracula* for Riverside, the title piece a steal from a Lennie Bruce routine (Jones and Herb Geller had often worked with Bruce on the West Coast). He went to Europe during a brief spell with the Bill Evans trio and stayed in London for two years from 1967, then spent three years in Paris before finally returning to Philadelphia. Jones's career was regularly interrupted by personal difficulties, but as a musician there were few players who could have bettered his work in any of the many groups he played with. Though he could drum with tremendous force and aggression, he was also one of the great brush-players in jazz, and the toughest of horn players out front could find themselves in a direct dialogue with what was coming out from the kit: leaders as different from each other as Davis, Evans and Dexter Gordon each found him an inspiration. In his last years, he worked with the Tadd Dameron tribute group Dameronia, and in the percussion quartet Pieces Of Time. His own records as a leader were mostly only so-so affairs, but there are scores of albums where he can be found playing outstanding jazz drums.

**Miles Davis,** *Milestones* (Columbia)

## Quincy Jones
ARRANGER, COMPOSER, PRODUCER, TRUMPET
*born* 14 March 1933

Jones's jazz career was eventually far outstripped by his work in popular music, and as a consequence his best work in the idiom has become comparatively neglected. He grew up in Chicago and Seattle and learned trumpet from the age of 15, then did a stint in the Ray Charles band. He studied in Boston but got his next break when he joined Lionel Hampton in 1951, touring in one of the superior editions of Hampton's working band, and recording in Paris on one of their European jaunts. He was an unexceptional trumpet soloist, but that soon fell into the shadow of his composing and arranging, which he began to develop as a freelance around this time, writing for everyone from Tommy Dorsey to Count Basie. He did another tour as MD with Dizzy Gillespie in 1956 but afterwards signed a contract with Mercury and worked as a producer for Barclay Records in Paris, where he did in-house work with the likes of Eddie Barclay and Harry Arnold. He toured Europe with the show *Free And Easy* and worked with the same band on a jazz tour (although it ended up almost broke). But in 1961 he was back in New York and doing pop A&R for Mercury, where he launched such careers as that of Leslie Gore: it was quite a breakthrough for a black in what was very much a white business. Jones was devilishly handsome and laden with charm, and while he carried on with pop work (as well as engagements for Count Basie and Frank Sinatra), he found the wherewithal to make records such as *The Great Wide World* (1960), *Big Band Bossa Nova* (1962) and *The Quintessence* (1962). Hollywood beckoned too, with the scores for *Mirage* (1965) and *The Pawnbroker* (1966). But eventually his own-name records began to swap jazz for pop content, and by the 70s, rich, influential and seemingly with an infallible commercial touch, he mingled making likeable dance music of his own with top-of-the-line pop projects such as the production of Michael Jackson's *Off The Wall* (1977).

Jones sustained that effortless mix of cool and gravitas through the 80s: nobody refused one of his calls, and it is hard to imagine any other musician being able to assemble the all-star cast which appeared on his *Back On The Block* (1989), almost an essay on the many musics which had informed his career, and which emerged on the imprint which he started under the auspices of Qwest/Warner Bros. The skill and suaveness of his arranging and composing in the 50s had long since been supplanted by a slick hummability, but at least the best of Jones's early work can be easily accessed in other people's discographies. By the end of the century, though, his influence had waned, and he does now seem to belong to the past: in his 70s he could hardly be expected to still be in the forefront of pop production, but Jones does come from an era where a deployment of instrumental

prowess still meant much in record production, and the technocrats who rule pop record-making now are a different breed. He remains one of the formidable figures of American music of the past half-century, and a redoubtable icon to more than one generation of black performers in particular. *Back On The Block* (Qwest)

# Richard M Jones
PIANO
*born* 13 June 1892; *died* 8 December 1945

Jones is mainly associated with Chicago jazz of the 20s, but he had a lot of musical work behind him at that point already. He was playing in the Eureka Brass Band of New Orleans (as an alto-horn player) as early as 1902, and in the teens of the century he was among the more significant small-group leaders in the city, having switched to piano. In 1918 he decamped for Chicago, and worked as a record A&R man and for Clarence Williams's publishing house, as well as cutting records of his own: there were eight sessions by Jones's Jazz Wizards – basically a pick-up band – made during the 20s, and he made two more in 1935 using the same name. An unexceptional player himself, he had a good ear for a capable musician, and the surviving music is an enjoyable memory of some of the Chicagoan music of its time. He never left music behind, organizing record dates and jam sessions even in the year of his death. *Richard M Jones 1923–1927* (Classics)

# Sam Jones
BASS, CELLO
*born* 12 November 1924; *died* 15 December 1981

He was old enough to be a first-generation bebopper, but Jones didn't really come to any prominence until he left his native Florida – where he worked in local bands – and arrived in New York in 1955. He was good enough to find himself in demand by several of the hard-bop leaders, but eventually he settled in with the quintet led by his fellow Floridan Cannonball Adderley. There, along with drummer Louis Hayes, Jones became part of one of the grooviest and most swinging rhythm sections in the music, staying until 1966, when he joined

Oscar Peterson's trio: in the meantime, he also led three record dates of his own for Riverside, and turned in sterling sideman work on many other sessions for both that label and Blue Note. In the 70s, he formed another long-standing alliance with Cedar Walton and Billy Higgins, where Sam again proved that in a congenial setting there were few bassists to touch him in setting out the fundamental verities. As a soloist he never did anything very remarkable, beyond playing rock-steady pattern-work that carried its own head-nodding appeal. In his final years he led an occasional biggish band, but in the end lung cancer took him off the scene. His cello playing was featured from time to time, although not much he set down really suggested that the instrument had a lot to say in a hard-bop context.

**Cannonball Adderley, *At The Lighthouse*** (Riverside)

## Thad Jones
CORNET, TRUMPET, FLUGELHORN
*born* 28 March 1923; *died* 20 August 1986

Jones began performing alongside his older brother Hank when in his teens, and after army service he played in dance bands before spending three years working with Billy Mitchell in Detroit (brother Elvin was also in the band). In 1954, he joined Count Basie's trumpet section and stayed almost ten years. He also cut the first records under his own name in this period, and record producers weren't shy about building him up: the first was *The Fabulous Thad Jones* (Debut), and the third was *The Magnificent Thad Jones* (Blue Note, 1957, with its unforgettable cover photo of Jones in Times Square). Basie didn't give him all that much prominence as a soloist, but he did begin to feature Jones's writing, and after leaving Basie and a period of freelancing Thad joined forces with drummer Mel Lewis to form a rehearsal band in 1965: in the end the Jones–Lewis Jazz Orchestra ran until 1978 and made 15 albums. Jones's playing has sometimes been overlooked in favour of his composing for big bands, which found full expression in his partnership with Lewis: as a soloist, though, he was rarely less than outstanding, bringing a challenging modern slant to high-end bebop playing. The Jones–Lewis band often had many of

the best New York musicians in its ranks, and they needed to be good: Jones's arrangements were tough and intricate, yet were creative and contemporary enough to have subsequently become a staple part of the curricula of many college bands. But the partnership ended suddenly: Jones had formed professional links with Danish jazz, and abruptly left New York to work there in 1978, leaving the slightly bewildered Lewis to carry the Orchestra on. Thad worked with a new big band, Eclipse, in Scandinavia, but finally came home in 1985 when offered the leadership of the posthumous Count Basie band, although he died himself the following year. He left a book of outstanding big-band music and many great performances on record, and ballad players often turn to his one immortal entry in that idiom, 'A Child Is Born'.

**Jones–Lewis Jazz Orchestra, *Central Park North*** (Solid State)

## Wallace Jones
TRUMPET
*born* 16 November 1906; *died* 23 March 1983

Having arrived in New York from his native Baltimore in the mid-30s, Jones found a gig with his cousin, Chick Webb, before moving on to first Willie Bryant and then Duke Ellington (1938–44). Duke only occasionally featured Jones, but his muted playing in particular can be heard to advantage on concert versions of 'Creole Love Call' and 'Black And Tan Fantasy', and he appears to have been a reliable section-man. After leaving Ellington, the trumpeter played with a few other bands but by the end of the 40s he was out of music altogether.

**Duke Ellington, *Carnegie Hall January 1943*** (Prestige)

## Herbert Joos
TRUMPET
*born* 21 March 1940

Born in Karlsruhe, Joos started on bass before taking up the trumpet around 1960. His starting point in jazz was hard bop, but he graduated to the free end of things and during the 70s he was a regular in that sector of the German scene, recording a pioneering all-solo album, *The Philosophy Of The*

*Flugelhorn* (1973), where he actually played eight different instruments, and group records for JAPO and FMP. Joos favoured quiet settings and open space, occasionally inflected by electronic manipulation, and his work from the perioid has some resemblance to Leo Smith's. He resurfaced rather surprisingly in the 90s with an impeccable album of Billie Holiday ballads for Emarcy, but the record disappeared very quickly. Joos is an accomplished graphic artist and he has contributed artwork to many jazz books and records.
***Blow!*** (FMP)

## Clifford Jordan

TENOR SAXOPHONE
*born* 2 September 1931; *died* 27 March 1993

Jordan grew up in Chicago (where his classmates included Johnny Griffin and John Gilmore), and played locally until he went to New York in 1957, working with Max Roach and Horace Silver. He co-led a quintet with Kenny Dorham and spent the early part of the 60s working for either Roach again or Charles Mingus. Later in the decade he toured Europe as a solo, began his own label (Frontier records, although the album eventually came out on Strata East) and formed a long-standing quartet with Cedar Walton, Sam Jones and Billy Higgins, which set down some of his best work: Jordan had a big, toasted tone in a magisterial hard-bop style, and had already done some fine work for Blue Note (*Cliff Craft* and the duet record with John Gilmore, *Blowing In From Chicago*, both 1957), but the Strata East set *Glass Bead Games* (1973) shows that he had, perhaps inevitably, taken on the more oblique influence of Coltrane. In the 80s he made something of a comeback after a quiet period, cutting some superb records with Art Farmer and Slide Hampton and eventually forming a big band which played regularly at Condon's in New York: on the evidence of its one record, *Down Through The Years* (Milestone, 1991), the band was as good as live reports suggested. But Jordan had to give up playing after he contracted lung cancer.
***Glass Bead Games*** (Strata East)

## Duke Jordan

PIANO
*born* 1 April 1922

Born Irving Stanley Jordan in New York, he took a cameo role in bebop: he was with the Savoy Sultans at the beginning of the 40s, and played piano for Charlie Parker in 1947–8. Stan Getz hired him in 1952–3 but the pianist felt he didn't get enough space and went on to work in numerous other groups, touring Europe with Rolf Ericson and playing in the stage production of *The Connection*. Duke was rather unlucky with American labels – his sole Blue Note, *Flight To Jordan* (1959), was a rare example of him getting his own date – and he disappeared from the scene altogether in the 60s, emerging again in 1972. In 1978 he left America for good and settled in Copenhagen, where one of his great admirers, Nils Winther, recorded him at great length for Steeplechase. Although based in bop, his style owed much to the more delicate inspirations of Teddy Wilson, and it was a manner which didn't transfer very easily to recordings: too many of his albums sound too much alike. As a composer, he came up with one bona fide classic: 'Jordu', which has been recorded many times.
***Flight To Jordan*** (Blue Note)

## Kidd Jordan

*born* c1932

TENOR SAXOPHONE

Jordan played in New Orleans R&B bands in the 50s, but most of his life has been spent in the public education system, teaching music in high schools and then joining the Southern University before founding the Heritage School in 1990. He co-founded the International Arts Quintet with Alvin Fielder in the 70s, which has worked on and off since, although it has hardly made any records, and he has instead found more exposure with such leaders as Dennis Gonzalez, Joel Futterman, Sunny Murray and Fred Anderson. Jordan could have ended up like Ornette Coleman, moving from R&B to free playing, but rather than following Ornette's boppish leanings he hung on to the R&B shouting and wailing style, seeking a way to bring that into free and abstract situations. His son Kent (b 1958) plays flute, recorded a single album for Columbia in 1988, and has sometimes turned up as a sideman alongside Ellis Marsalis and Elvin Jones. A daughter, Rachel, also plays flute.

**With Fred Anderson,** *Two Days In April* (Eremite)

soon – and at a surprisingly young age – to appreciate the kind of revival of interest in his music which such projects as *Joe Jackson's Jumping Jive* and the London musical *Five Guys Named Moe* would later inspire.

*Louis Jordan & His Tympany Five* (JSP)

## Louis Jordan
ALTO SAXOPHONE, VOCAL
*born* 8 July 1908; *died* 4 February 1975

There was probably no more comprehensive an entertainer in jazz than Louis Jordan: Chris Barber, who featured him as a guest star with his own band in the 60s, likened the experience to being dragged along by a wild horse, and that was at a point long after Louis's golden years. His father taught him the saxophone and enlisted him to play with his own Rabbit Foot Minstrels, on the Arkansas vaudeville circuit, when the young man was still in his teens. He moved on to other local groups before shifting over to Philadelphia. He spent two years with Chick Webb from 1936 and eventually, in New York, formed his own band, The Tympany Five, which began recording in 1938 and proceeded to make scores of sides for Decca. The remarkable thing about them is no matter how formulaic and familiar Jordan's style became, he managed to imbue almost every disc with a zesty enthusiasm which kept the act improbably fresh. It's a testament to his durability that, six decades later, such pre-rock songs as 'Is You Is Or Is You Ain't My Baby?', 'Caldonia' and 'Choo Choo Ch' Boogie' are still relatively familiar. The language of his lyrics was steeped in neighbourhood black wisdom, which helped keep him a jukebox favourite, but the fizz and vitality of The Tympany Five's playing was just as important: Jordan himself was an able soloist on alto, and the rest of the group played in a swinging jump-band style which paved the way for the more hard-bitten R&B idiom of the 50s (Jordan was, perhaps, too good-humoured to let the bluesier side of his music predominate, preferring to make his points through a good-natured irony). By the 50s he had begun to sound a little dated, but trouper that he was, he kept going, and remade many of his old hits for Mercury. In the 60s and early 70s he was still performing, although he died too

## Ronny Jordan
GUITAR
*born* 29 November 1962

A Londoner, Jordan picked up on the George Benson style (at least, the part of it that came straight from Wes Montgomery) and turned it into a surprise chart hit on a 1991 treatment of Miles Davis's 'So What', which strung the familiar melody over a snapping hip-hop beat and created an instrumental pop ready-made which has regularly turned up in trailers and commercials. Nothing else he has done since has been remotely as catchy or successful, but it has brought him the opportunity to record for three different major labels, and with 2003's *At Last* he reaffirmed how formulaic smooth jazz was where he was heading all along. Jordan isn't a bad guitarist, but he has nothing to say beyond his basic Bensonese, despite a recent press quote that insists: 'I've got a lot to say and a lot of different ways to communicate.'

*The Antidote* (Island)

## Sheila Jordan
VOCAL
*born* 18 November 1928

Sheila Dawson from Detroit was in love with bebop as soon as she heard it, and began singing vocalese lines in a group which used Charlie Parker material. She moved to New York in 1951, married Duke Jordan a year later (they were divorced in 1956) and sang in clubs before she made a single album for Blue Note on George Russell's recommendation: one of only a handful of vocal discs issued by Alfred Lion on that label, *Portrait Of Sheila* (1962) remains a masterpiece in its idiom. It is so good that it makes one angry that Jordan had so few opportunities to record when her voice was in its first bloom. She scarcely recorded at all again until the middle 70s, despite a few touring trips to Europe, where she recorded a duo record

with Arild Andersen in 1977. There was teaching in New York and a duo formed with Harvie Swartz before she and Swartz joined a quartet led by Steve Kuhn (1978–81). All this time she had done secretarial work at a job she started in 1966, where her colleagues had no idea of her jazz vocation, and when laid off in 1987 she finally turned to a full-time singing career. Since then she has worked and recorded steadily in both the US and Europe, recognized as a giant in her field: her singing is, outside of Betty Carter's, the most improvisational and immediately creative of any jazz vocalist, freely interpreting songs and melodic lines and using material from contemporary poetry and jazz standards as well as originals and the standard songbook. She continues to explore the duo form with the acoustic bass, and Cameron Brown has been a favourite partner in that regard for some years. It continues to be a source of regret that she was not recorded more often in her prime, but her singing and artistry have remained amazingly fresh and alive.
*Portrait Of Sheila* (Blue Note)

## Stanley Jordan
GUITAR
*born* 31 July 1959

Jordan was something of a one-season wonder. Though born in Chicago he grew up mostly in California and was soon playing in high-school rock bands before studying music at Princeton. Although he did some sideman work, he was still mostly busking when he made a self-produced solo album in 1982 which eventually came to the attention of Bruce Lundvall at Blue Note, who signed him to the label. *Magic Touch* (1985), his debut for the label, was a surprise hit. It showcased Jordan's ingenious virtuosity, using his fingers to tap on the guitar's strings at both ends of the neck, enabling him to play multiple melody lines and counterpoint. It wasn't a new technique, but Jordan was probably the first to base an entire improvisational style around the notion, and on pop covers such as 'Eleanor Rigby' it made a melodious, coolly entertaining sound. While he made other albums for Blue Note, though, Jordan's career lost all momentum and he all but disappeared in the 90s, although in the new century

Lundvall again had him recording for Blue Note. Not quite smooth jazz yet rarely tough enough to sit strongly in more assertive company, Stanley's music does seem like an amiable cul de sac.
*Magic Touch* (Blue Note)

## Taft Jordan
TRUMPET
*born* 15 February 1915; *died* 1 December 1981

Jordan is fondly remembered as a second-string Ellingtonian, even though he was actually with Chick Webb's band for much longer. Webb heard him in 1933 playing in an after-hours club, and hired him as his Armstrong clone – 'Taffy' was a Louis man through and through. He stayed until 1941, tried out as a bandleader himself, then joined Ellington in 1943 and stayed four years. He is marvellous on an almost impromptu 'Tea For Two', done as a spacefiller at one of Duke's Carnegie Hall concerts. Jordan got through a lot of studio work in the 50s, and managed to record a pair of albums under his own name, for Mercury and Moodsville. In the 60s and 70s he did more theatre and studio work, occasionally sighted by jazz audiences. Never a star, but when a Jordan solo comes up on a record, it's usually worth stopping to listen.
*Mood Indigo – Taft Jordan Plays Duke Ellington* (Moodsville/OJC)

## Theo Jörgensmann
CLARINET
*born* 29 September 1948

The German clarinettist is one of the few to make a solid go of his instrument in an unequivocally modern setting. He first emerged in the Contact Trio in the early 70s and was even playing a kind of jazz-rock in the group Out, but thereafter he worked mainly with his own small groups. Other ventures included the Grubenklangorchester, with Georg Gräwe, which used for its repertoire songs emanating from the Ruhr, and a four-man clarinet band, CL-4. He has recorded quite frequently, but mostly for small German labels, and most of his work from the vinyl era is unfortunately out of print. The record cited, a duo with bass

clarinettist Eckard Koltermann, is a handsome instance of Jörgensmann's mature work: only rarely does he depart from conventional clarinet techniques and sounds, yet he creates music of uncompromising modernism and striking individuality.
*Pagine Gialle* (hatOLOGY)

## Anders Jormin
BASS
*born* 7 September 1957

Jormin grew up in the Swedish town of Jönköping and studied piano in Gothenburg before electing to switch to the double bass. In the 80s he worked with both local (Rena Rama) and international figures and groups, but latterly he has concentrated on his own groups and projects, and his style has expanded from a typical hard-bop grammar into a much more wide-ranging remit which includes Scandinavian repertory of different kinds, and choral and South American music. Some of these directions have tended towards the kind of northern brooding exemplified by *Nordic Light* (1987), but his solo record *Alone* (1990) shows in particular his interest in vocal music as a source for instrumental inspiration.
*Alone* (Dragon)

## Julian Joseph
PIANO
*born* 11 May 1966

Joseph was in the thick of the new London jazz scene of the mid-80s when he won a scholarship to Berklee in 1985. He spent a brief period in the Branford Marsalis quartet – an astonishing breakthrough for a British musician – and returned permanently to London in 1990, although his reputation has garnered him a good deal of significant work abroad. He recorded three albums for the major label East West, and fronted a concert series at Wigmore Hall with such illustrious guests as Johnny Griffin and Eddie Daniels. In 1995, he led a big band at his own concert in the Albert Hall's annual Promenade series, although those who saw it tend to remember his excruciating announcements more than the music. Joseph is also a regular on BBC radio. Astutely managed by his brother James, Julian continues to be one

of the most high-profile British jazz performers, and it's to be hoped that this charming and powerful musician is better documented and produced on record than he has been so far. A third brother, John, is a trumpeter.
*The Language Of Truth* (East West)

## Ekkehard Jost
WRITER, BARITONE SAXOPHONE
*born* 22 January 1938

Jost was studying music in Hamburg when he became interested in the burgeoning free-jazz scene which was boiling up in Germany at that point, and he sought out the likes of Peter Brötzmann and played with them. He has performed in an on-and-off way ever since, occasionally making records and sometimes doubling on accordion and other instruments. But it is as a writer and theoretician that he has made his mark, and much of his working life has been spent in academia in any case. His 1974 treatise *Free Jazz* tackles one of the most difficult parts of the jazz oeuvre and analyses and extrapolates clear musical principles from a scene which was, to outsiders, beset by musical chaos. Although much of his subsequent writing has failed to make it into translation, Jost remains a clear-headed writer whose work should be ranked with that of the best jazz commentators.

## Jump

Jump music bridges the swing-era setpieces with the somewhat less polished, more mobile music of the small groups of the 40s who were still playing music based in the swing idiom but were looking towards rhythm and blues. Although most of the big bands had a title such as 'One O'Clock Jump' (Count Basie) somewhere in their book, this was more of a generic term used to cover some of the liveliest pieces tailored for dancers. The master of jump music, as it came to be seen, was Louis Jordan, whose recordings of the middle 40s are textbook examples of the style – a small group of horns and a rhythm section playing riff themes, simple blues pieces and pop tunes enlivened and particularized, in Jordan's case, by bumptious vocals and wryly humorous lyrics. The later interest in small-group swing as a revivalist idiom has had its share of jump music, but there jump has become absorbed into a more wide-reaching overview.

## Vic Juris
GUITAR
*born* 29 September 1953

Juris is a jazz guitarist who is clearly aware of the blandishments of fusion but has hardened his stance rather than taking the soft option. He did, in fact, spend a large part of his early career in the Barry Miles group playing jazz-rock, from the late 70s and into the 80s, but he also played hard bop with Richie Cole and soul-jazz with Don Patterson and Wild Bill Davis. In the 90s he spent a long stint in Dave Liebman's quintet, but came into his own more as a leader himself: one project was a quintet called 5 Guitars Play Mingus. His qualities come out best in an outstanding series of records for Steeplechase, where he approaches a catholic choice of material and produces playing which is calm, technically proficient, but endowed with a generous inventiveness – on acoustic and electric guitars and even the guitar-synthesizer.
*Songbook* (Steeplechase)

## Tiny Kahn
DRUMS
*born* c1923; *died* 19 August 1953

Norman Kahn was a very big man, which is how he got his nickname. He was one of the many New York drummers who powered the music through its nightclub years of the 40s and early 50s. He played with such late-swing bands as those of Georgie Auld and Charlie Barnet in the 40s, and he fitted in especially well with Chubby Jackson's swing-to-bop orchestra, composing 'Tiny's Blues' and turning in a fine arrangement of George Wallington's 'Godchild' for that group. His arranging was subsequently also in demand by other leaders, but he had no real chance to make an impact in the changing scene of the 50s, since he was felled by a heart attack in 1953.
**Stan Getz, *Jazz At Storyville*** (Roost/EMI)

## Max Kaminsky
TRUMPET
*born* 7 September 1908; *died* 6 September 1994

Although in the main associated with the Condon clan, Kaminsky actually began in Boston and in the early 30s was working there as well as in Chicago and New York. He soon acquired a rep as an excellent lead man, and was sought after by various leaders – Goodman, Shaw, Dorsey, Miller – although it was Artie Shaw's band which the trumpeter worked with most. Following the war, he made the best of a club situation which was becoming tougher for the more traditional musicians, though when Birdland opened 'I blew the first note in there', and he even got to jam with Charlie Parker on a CBS television show. Max remained on view in the kind of places where the Condon gang would gather through the 50s and 60s, and managed to find time to write an excellent memoir, which suggested he never took the game for granted: 'No matter how great is the job you're playing one week, next week you may just be a guy out of work.'
**Eddie Condon, *The Town Hall Concerts*** ( Jazzology)

## Richie Kamuca
TENOR SAXOPHONE
*born* 23 July 1930; *died* 23 July 1977

Kamuca sounded like a star soloist in the Stan Kenton (1953) and Woody Herman (1954–6) bands, but though he then settled on the West Coast as a solo, he never quite progressed to a point where he won a bigger reputation. His work in the Shelly Manne group which cut the formidable *At The Black Hawk* (1959) for Contemporary, now spread across five separate CDs, shows how good he was: a Lester Young disciple with enough rhythmical vim to bolster his affectingly pale tone, he was a blowing musician of unusual thoughtfulness. He went back East in 1962 and spent a longish spell with (of all people) Roy Eldridge, but when he returned to LA in the 70s he spent his last years in studio work. Three Concord albums, set down not long before his death from cancer, have never been reissued.
**Shelly Manne, *At The Black Hawk Vols 1–4*** (Contemporary)

# Kansas City

New Orleans and Chicago had clearly defined jazz flavours early on, while New York was a bit too cosmopolitan to have a single stye of 'New York jazz'. Kansas City was perhaps in between those two points. Crystallized in the work of Bennie Moten's band of the early 30s (and, subsequently, the Count Basie orchestra which emerged from Moten's legacy), it was orchestral music, swinging to a more fluid pulse than that of other areas, involving a prevalence of 12-bar blues material and so-called 'head' arrangements based around an instrumental riff or a gathering of riffs. The style wasn't confined to Kansas City, though: it is a little more accurate to call it a Southwestern jazz, since it also took in bands and musicians working as far afield as Dallas and Oklahoma City.

## Egil Kapstad
PIANO
*born* 6 August 1940

Kapstad is an exemplar of the first wave of Norwegian post-bop jazz. His style is couched in terms which are close to those of his admitted major influence, Bill Evans, but he brings to his playing a coolly incisive kind of romanticism, and the unpretentious elegance of his improvising clears away a lot of the clutter which often attends pianism in the Evans style. While he has often worked with quartets including a saxophonist, some of his best music is in the piano-trio idiom, and the record cited – which takes in material by eight separate Norwegian composers – is a wonderful homage to his surroundings.
***Remembrance*** (Gemini)

## Jan Kaspersen
PIANO
*born* 22 April 1948

A clever and boisterous improviser and group leader, the Copenhagen-born Kaspersen is a bright light in his native jazz. He worked with various 'local' bands in the late 60s and 70s before leading groups of his own and recording extensively (mostly for the Olufsen label) as a solo in the 80s

and 90s. He has a lifelong passion for the music of Thelonious Monk and has played many of the master's compositions on record, and his own writing often sounds as if it has a strong Monkian bent. But his bands frequently work to a humorous agenda which doesn't, for once, undercut the musical content too much.
***Live In Sofie's Cellar*** (Olufsen)

## Dick Katz
PIANO
*born* 13 March 1924

Katz numbers such figures as Teddy Wilson (with whom he studied in the 40s), Benny Carter and Al Haig among his principal influences. In the 50s he freelanced in New York under a large number of leaders, in small groups and big bands (Oscar Pettiford's, for one), and backing singers, including Carmen McRae, Nancy Harrow and Helen Merrill, with whom he toured in the early 60s. He struck up a close alliance with Roy Eldridge from that time, who told him, 'Don't play all that crap, man, tell a story. Don't go runnin' off at the mouth.' That advice was well learned: Katz's mature work, although he has recorded only very rarely as a leader, is full of space, tiny felicities and lightly abstruse musings, which suggest not only the classical elegance of Wilson but the more modern traits of Monk and others. He co-founded the Milestone record company in 1966 with Orrin Keepnews, and did some production work there, but latterly returned to full-time playing and teaching.
***3 Way Play*** (Reservoir)

## Connie Kay
DRUMS
*born* 27 April 1927; *died* 30 November 1994

Kay's career suggests a capable, slightly indifferent man who was content to have a steady gig and didn't feel he had to worry too much about the sort of music he was playing. He was doing paying gigs already by 1939 and in the 40s and early 50s he played with everybody from Miles Davis and Cat Anderson to The Clovers, Stan Getz and LaVern Baker. In 1955 he took over from Kenny Clarke in the Modern Jazz Quartet, and with that he had found his steady gig:

he was with them until the 1974 annulment, and then rejoined when they restarted in 1981. In the interim he was as catholic as ever in his choice of work, even taking on the job of house drummer in the last years of Eddie Condon's club. John Lewis rarely gave him a feature in the MJQ, but only because Kay didn't seem to like them much: 'Sacha's March' was his only regular solo in their later years. Despite suffering a stroke, he played his final gig with the band in the month before he died.

**Modern Jazz Quartet, *Echoes*** (Pablo)

# Shake Keane

TRUMPET

*born* 30 May 1927; *died* 10 November 1997

Ellsworth Keane: poet, schoolteacher, college principal (Georgetown), Minister of Culture (St Vincent), and sometime jazzman. He moved to the UK from St Vincent when he was 25 to study English literature, but also played with Joe Harriott on the London scene and their work together, up until 1965, led to a strain of free jazz entering into the British vocabulary. Shake (the nickname derives from 'Shakespeare', through the poetry link) had the chops for bebop but often preferred to play in a particularly spare and oblique manner, and after he went to play as a soloist with the big Kurt Edelhagen band in Cologne, he gradually slipped away from jazz, and back to poetry and academe. In the 90s, he unexpectedly resurfaced, having been offered an amnesty by the US government after living there illegally, and played a reunion tour of England with Michael Garrick: but his time had gone, and after playing at a concert in support of a cancer research charity, it was cruelly discovered that he had the disease himself. Keane was never as well-recognized as Harriott, and the only album under his own name, *That's The Noise* (1961), is unremarkable.

**Joe Harriott, *Abstract*** (Redial)

# Orrin Keepnews

PRODUCER

*born* 2 March 1923

Keepnews became arguably the most significant of jazz record producers. He began writing jazz journalism when he came out of the army at the end of the 40s, then (with old friend Bill Grauer) began organizing a reissue programme of some of RCA Victor's jazz material for the new LP era. In 1953, he and Grauer founded Riverside, quickly among the up-and-coming jazz independent labels, and Keepnews himself produced many of Riverside's most important records, particularly those involving Thelonious Monk and Bill Evans. Evans named his tune 'Re: Person I Knew' in anagrammatical honour of his producer. In the 60s he co-founded Milestone and latterly ran production work at Fantasy, a company which subsequently acquired Prestige, Riverside and Milestone. In the 80s he established the Landmark label at a time when jazz independents were thought to be struggling, but he subsequently sold this off to Muse. Since then, he has mostly worked on reissue projects (such as RCA's vast edition of all their Duke Ellington holdings) and written copious sleevenotes and commentaries. Keepnews is not shy of claiming his credit in the jazz of the LP era, but considering what he had a hand in creating, he has a right.

# Geoff Keezer

PIANO

*born* 21 November 1970

Since both of his parents taught the piano, it's unsurprising that Keezer was something of a keyboard prodigy, and he joined one of the last editions of the Jazz Messengers in 1988. Since then he has put up his flag alongside numerous leaders – Art Farmer, Jim Hall, Ray Brown and fellow young master Christian McBride – while trying to make his solo career go places. He's had some success in that regard, but a brief association with both Blue Note and Columbia seems to have left him out in the cold as far as a major-label deal is concerned. Keezer is quite an ambitious writer as well as a revisionist: *World Music* (1992) included a startling new look at 'It's Only A Paper Moon' as well as a bagful of rather complicated originals, and at this stage Geoff may have been trying a little too hard. Recently (with McBride) he has been playing electric keyboards as well, somewhat in the style of old-fashioned fusion. In person, though, he is rarely less than the most exciting player on the stand, and a good producer may yet get a masterpiece out of him.

*Turn Up The Quiet* (Columbia)

# Roger Kellaway
PIANO
*born* 1 November 1939

Although he studied classical piano, Kellaway's first gigs were as a bassist, but by the early 60s he was on piano and playing with both the Al Cohn–Zoot Sims group and the Clark Terry–Bob Brookmeyer quintet. This was in New York, but in 1966 he moved to California to join Don Ellis, and became busy in film and TV work, as well as acting as MD for pop and MOR record dates, working with Bobby Darin and Singers Unlimited as well as jazz players. He returned East in the 80s and took on more straight-ahead work, but in the 90s he moved back West and resumed much of his scoring duties. Kellaway has thus far set down comparatively few discs under his own name, but over four decades of recording he has been involved in hundreds of albums. Without making much fuss about it, he has crossed and recrossed boundaries and been comfortable with seemingly any genre. He ran the Cello Quartet (cello, piano, bass and drums) for much of the 70s, scored *A Star Is Born* (1976), wrote orchestral works including a ballet, and tinkered with electronic and *musique concrète*. Yet his duo set with Ruby Braff, *Inside And Out* (1995), was entirely congenial to both men, and musicians such as Michael Moore and Guy Barker delight in his musical company. His trio and solo work is notable for sheer musical high spirits, even when he is playing technically taxing material, and the set cited has the quality of eavesdropping on a clever fellow who can play anything he chooses.

*Live At Maybeck Recital Hall Vol 11* (Concord)

# Peck Kelley
PIANO
*born* 1898; *died* 26 December 1980

John Dickson Kelley was a Houston man who ran bands in his native city in the early 20s. The most famous edition was known as Peck's Bad Boys, which at one time or another included Jack Teagarden, Pee Wee Russell and Johnny Wiggs. While he had occasional sojourns away from the city – his reputation as a real piano virtuoso had spread far and wide as the decade wore on – Kelly never liked being away from home for long, and he turned down all offers to either play for others or make records. Eventually, he was persuaded to cut a couple of record dates, in 1957, after he had retired: he still had a lot of facility, and could play some very difficult stuff, although the context was rather flat. And that was all.

*Peck Kelley Jam* (Commodore)

# Brian Kellock
PIANO
*born* 28 December 1962

Kellock has taken a leading role in the new Scottish jazz of recent years. Born in Edinburgh, he worked locally with such contemporaries as John Rae and as an accompanist to Carol Kidd in the late 80s and early 90s, and has latterly begun to build a powerful reputation as a trio leader and soloist. He has a firm and wide-ranging grasp of piano styles, able to conceive and execute an evening of Fats Waller's piano pieces one day and deliver a set of hard-edged modern piano the next, which might set Lennie Tristano pieces alongside his own originals. He is also a fearless collaborator, and has recorded two albums with saxophonist Tommy Smith where he comfortably holds his own against Smith's mercurial playing.

*Live At Henry's* (Caber)

# Jon-Erik Kellso
TRUMPET
*born* 8 May 1964

Kellso is from Dearborn, Michigan. In his teens he soaked up his parents' Ellington and Goodman records, and began playing in Dixie-styled groups, eventually working with James Dapogny's Chicago Jazz Band. By the 90s he was a prominent player in the new swing mainstream, touring widely and doing festivals and extensive sideman work. His records display a confident though easygoing stylist in the vein of late-swing models such as Billy Butterfield and Ruby Braff.

*Chapter 1* (Arbors)

## Chris Kelly

TRUMPET

*born* c1885; *died* 19 August 1929

Kelly is, at this distance, among the most mysterious of the earliest New Orleans pioneers. He arrived in the city around 1915 and after some years of work took over a band led by Johnny Brown, which rapidly became among the most popular groups of its kind. Kelly himself dressed in whatever clothes he could find to stand up in, yet listeners loved his curious showmanship, and on his famous setpiece 'Careless Love Blues' – where he reputedly used a plunger mute to great advantage – the audience would all but swoon to the sound of his trumpet. George Lewis was one of his regular playing partners in the 20s, but Kelly's own behaviour grew strange and difficult owing to his heavy drinking, and like Keppard and Bolden before him he became fallible: he died of a heart attack in 1929, and at his funeral the city turned out en masse to commemorate the passing of a favourite son. Yet he made no records and was never photographed.

## George Kelly

TENOR SAXOPHONE, PIANO

*born* 31 July 1915; *died* 24 May 1998

Kelly was a busy second-feature player, and his career stretched from playing piano for Ma Rainey when he was 12 through to playing European festivals only months before his death. He worked as a saxophonist for various 'territory' leaders during the 20s and 30s but moved to New York in 1941 and played with Al Cooper's Savoy Sultans. He freelanced through the 50s and early 60s, then left music for a spell before returning in the next decade to play piano for The Ink Spots. Back on tenor, he joined Panama Francis's Savoy Sultans but eventually left to form his own Jazz Sultans, which lasted into the 90s.

*George Kelly Plays Don Redman* (Stash)

## Wynton Kelly

PIANO

*born* 2 December 1931; *died* 12 April 1971

Dead at 39 from a heart attack, following an epileptic fit, Kelly now seems like a master

of his idiom whose music has been consistently underappreciated. His only real period of prominence was when he was with the Miles Davis group of 1959–62. Before that, he had played in both R&B and jazz groups as a teenager, backed Dinah Washington and run his own trio. Davis hired him in February 1959, replacing Bill Evans (although both of them play on *Kind Of Blue*), and Kelly's bright, catchy yet almost fiercely tightened delivery – the right hand articulating notes and clusters with an icy decision – is deepened by a blues feel which makes both solos and accompaniments oddly compelling. It was a template which others soon picked up on, but Kelly's career never really went anywhere after he, Paul Chambers and Jimmy Cobb left Davis to set up on their own. They also backed others, including Wes Montgomery (making the superb *Smokin' At The Half Note*, 1965, with the guitarist), but by the end Kelly was playing solo and doing more sideman work in and around New York. His own-name sets for Riverside, Vee Jay and especially Verve have never enjoyed much notice and repay the best attention.

*It's All Right!* (Verve)

## Stacey Kent

VOCAL

*born* 27 March 1968

Kent is an expatriate American who lives in London. She studied at Guildhall and began singing on the London circuit in the early 90s, eventually gaining a contract with Alan Bates's Candid label. A small-voiced singer with a coolly persuasive delivery, Kent is more an interpreter of standards than any kind of jazz artist, but her sequence of albums have struck a surprisingly powerful note with a growing international audience, possibly of listeners who were previously, in Kenny Davern's phrase, 'melody-starved people'. She has been an able self-publicist by appearing regularly as a radio presenter, as well as touring regularly in both Europe and the US.

*The Tender Trap* (Candid)

# Stan Kenton

PIANO, BANDLEADER
*born* 15 December 1911; *died* 25 August 1979

Stan Kenton always excited extremes of opinion. He led big bands of sometimes elephantine proportions, played Wagner transcriptions, and fashioned orchestral concepts which strike the unsympathetic as impossibly pompous. Yet he was a generous leader, a man who liked to play for dancers, a good pianist and an underrated composer. His orchestras – starting in 1940 with his first 14-piece group – included perhaps the greatest group of soloists and arrangers of any big band dynasty, and his legacy to American music still resonates loudly today, through the time and resources he put into the college circuit and music education. He played piano in various 30s dance bands before setting out on his own, and during the war years the Kenton Orchestra gathered together a devoted audience for its fine, precise playing and a book of charts that at least suggested the stirrings of high art: Kenton's theme tune itself was called 'Artistry In Rhythm'. Pete Rugolo joined as staff arranger in 1945 and brought many extraordinary scores to the band's book. The leader twice disbanded and re-formed his ensemble, first as the Progressive Jazz Orchestra (1947) and then as the Innovations In Modern Music Orchestra (1950), which stretched to 43 players at its peak. Kenton inevitably had to disperse these forces for economic reasons, but they still left some dazzling results, and big-band admirers the world over remember every Kenton line-up up until 1960 or so with fierce admiration. Soloists included many stellar names of the period – from Art Pepper and Zoot Sims to Shelly Manne and Maynard Ferguson – and besides Rugolo, the composer-arrangers included Bill Holman, Robert Graettinger, Bill Russo, Shorty Rogers and Gerry Mulligan.

Kenton recorded for Capitol for many years and left a huge string of albums – his enjoyably epic portrayal of *West Side Story* was a Grammy winner – and when they eventually let him go, he formed Creative World, a label of his own, which poured out further records until his death. The so-called 'Mellophonium' orchestra came along in 1961 and Kenton's Los Angeles Neophonic Orchestra followed in 1965, although, as

before, the leader couldn't financially sustain either venture. He began holding clinics at universities, and thereafter it was the college audience which kept the Kenton band on the road. Besides Wagner, Stan kept a weather eye on what was clicking in popular music, and he also did cover versions of Blood Sweat & Tears songs. There were fewer stars in his latter-day bands (Peter Erskine is a notable exception) but the Kenton Orchestra is perhaps the ongoing model for the numberless college big bands which are still at work all over America. Years after his death, Kenton's music is still debated and celebrated at regular fan conventions on both sides of the Atlantic. Disliked by critics, but his place in the music is secure though curiously lonely.
***West Side Story*** (Capitol)

# Robin Kenyatta

ALTO AND TENOR SAXOPHONES, FLUTE
*born* 6 March 1942; *died* 26 October 2004

The former Prince Roland Haynes – he took his adopted name in homage to Jomo Kenyatta – found himself, following military service, involved in New York's October Revolution of free jazz in 1964. He worked and recorded with stalwarts of that scene such as Bill Dixon and Roswell Rudd, and after a spell of touring in Europe he eventually settled there in 1970, where he recorded *Girl From Martinique* (1970), perhaps his signature session, for ECM. He ran his Free State Band in Paris, with Joachim Kühn and others, but returned to New York in 1972. In the 80s he moved to Switzerland, where he died (in Lausanne) in 2004. Kenyatta's career had many interesting quirks in its earliest period, combining a genuine interest in African musical timbres with his own bluesy alto delivery, and it was a pity he wasn't recorded in more favourable circumstances early on. As it was, too many of his later adventures were spoiled by inappropriate fusions and borrowings from reggae, disco and seemingly whatever else came into his mind.
***Girl From Martinique*** (ECM)

# Freddie Keppard

TRUMPET

*born* 27 February 1890; *died* 15 July 1933

Keppard was the second 'King' of New Orleans brassmen, although he didn't start on the cornet until he was 16, after which he 'became to be the greatest hot trumpeter in existence', according to Jelly Roll Morton. His Olympia Orchestra soon had many of the best men in New Orleans in its ranks at different times (Picou, Bechet, Noone, even Joe Oliver as a deputy for the leader). Eventually, looking for new pastures, Keppard went to Los Angeles and gave his band over to A J Piron, around 1914. On the West Coast he played with his Original Creole Band, but never took up the opportunity (reputedly offered) to make records: had he done so, he might have beaten the Original Dixieland Jazz Band to the starting line. He toured and then settled in Chicago in 1918, where he set up a new band, although he also played with the bands of Doc Cook and Erskine Tate (finally making his first records). He also recorded a handful of small-group sides with Johnny Dodds and others. His meagre legacy on record makes it hard to discern how great Keppard really was, but certainly the best sides, such as 'Here Comes The Hot Tamale Man' and 'Stockyards Strut' (both 1926), feature an aggressive, power-packed player with what sounds like a delivery that could quickly reach boiling point in the right setting. Next to contemporary work by Armstrong and others it sounds comparatively primitive, and may argue for Keppard as the last great ragtime player rather than the first jazz trumpeter. Either way, Freddie 'always was after women and spent every dime he ever made on whiskey' (Morton again). He was penniless and all but forgotten when he died in Chicago at the age of 43.

*The Complete Recordings* (Retrieval)

# Kenny Kersey

PIANO

*born* 3 April 1916; *died* 1 April 1983

Born in Ontario, Kersey began working in the Detroit area in his teens and by 1936 he was in New York. He became the house pianist at Café Society in 1938, recording with Billie Holiday and others, and followed Mary Lou Williams into the Andy Kirk band before being drafted. In the 40s and 50s he played all over New York, favourite partners including Buck Clayton (he is on some of the trumpeter's jam session records for Columbia) and Henry Allen. The only records under his own name were a handful of sides made for Savoy in 1946, but he turns up on many other sessions made before a stroke obliged him to retire in 1958.

**Buck Clayton, *All The Cats Join In*** (Columbia)

# Barney Kessel

GUITAR

*born* 17 October 1923; *died* 6 May 2004

The 20-year-old Kessel can be spotted among the musicians in the celebrated short film *Jammin' The Blues*. He grew up in Muskogee, Oklahoma, and there was always both a bluesy feel and a countryish lilt to his playing. He worked in several big bands, particularly Artie Shaw's, in the twilight of the swing era, a clear disciple of the Charlie Christian style, and he plays on Charlie Parker's 'Relaxin' At Camarillo' date for Dial (1947). But his proficiency led him towards Californian studio work, and for much of the 50s and 60s he was doing dates involving every kind of music: to pick one otherwise anonymous example, he plays the delicious figures on The Coasters' hit 'Smokey Joe's Café' (1958). He did do some touring with Oscar Peterson in 1952–3 and with Jazz At The Philharmonic, and he made a dozen albums of his own for Contemporary between 1953 and 1965, several of them featuring some of his best work, as well as four albums by The Poll Winners, a trio with Ray Brown and Shelly Manne. Kessel's very facility sometimes tells against his playing being more interesting than it is, but his ability to play apposite fills and solos in a confined space can often be a pleasure in itself, and when he began making records for Concord he also featured in the Great Guitars group with Charlie Byrd and Herb Ellis. Fittingly, though, his final albums were made for Contemporary again. In 1992, he suffered a severe stroke which ended his playing career, and sadly led to a long and debilitating illness.

*To Swing Or Not To Swing* (Contemporary)

# Keynote
RECORD COMPANY

Another of the leading independent jazz labels of the 40s, Keynote was started by Eric Bernay in New York in 1940. Initially it had little to do with jazz, releasing records of folk, classical and theatre music, but under the stewardship of Harry Lim the company began producing jazz sessions in 1943. For three busy years, Lim produced some of the best small-group swing sessions of the period, involving Coleman Hawkins, Lester Young, Earl Hines and other major names, as well as bringing in new talents such as Dave Lambert, Lennie Tristano and George Barnes. John Hammond replaced Lim in 1947 and the label, rather curiously, then went back towards classical music, although it was eventually sold to Mercury a year later after getting into financial difficulties. Most of the material has been reissued in the CD era.

# Steve Khan
GUITAR
*born* 28 April 1947

The son of songwriter Sammy Cahn, Khan had previously played piano and didn't take up the guitar until he was 20. From the early 70s, though, he was busy as a New York session musician on rock and jazz dates, playing with The Brecker Brothers for a spell before leading his own group Eyewitness in the 80s. For most of this period Khan settled into a role as a fusion stylist, playing hard in the jazz-rock vernacular of the time, and *Tightrope* (1977) is a notably effective showcase for top chops with a band of fusion Young Turks. In the 90s, though, he followed the example of many others and throttled back into a more classic kind of boppish jazz guitar, which he also proved to be very good at, and the disc cited seems to work a very plausible ground between the two points.
*Got My Mental* (Evidence)

# David Kikoski
PIANO
*born* 29 September 1961

Kikoski grew up in New Jersey, studied at Berklee, remained in Boston for a time playing local gigs, but fetched up in New York in 1985 and has spent the past 20 years as a busy sideman and occasional leader. He had one shot at major-label status with a set for Epic's offshoot Epicure in 1994, but otherwise most of his work has been done for independent operations, and his Criss Cross albums hold his best work. Quite a prolific writer, he isn't shy about featuring his own tunes, and for once the interpreter makes the composer's pieces seem clear and fresh and unmuddled by extravagant improvisations.
*Almost Twilight* (Criss Cross)

# Masabumi Kikuchi
PIANO
*born* 19 October 1939

Kikuchi hasn't quite gained the international recognition afforded to either Toshiko Akiyoshi or Yosuke Yamashita, but he is as interesting a player as they and his rather scattered recordings are worth seeking out. He studied in his native Tokyo in the 50s and briefly went to Berklee in 1968, working with the likes of Sonny Rollins and Joe Henderson along the way, and during the 70s he worked with leaders as illustrious as Elvin Jones and Miles Davis. Less was heard from him during the 80s, but in the following decade he made several records with a trio named Tethered Moon (himself, Gary Peacock and Paul Motian), which tackled such unusual repertoire as material associated with Edith Piaf. A solo record, *After Hours* (1995), is one of the most patiently worked and slowly unfolded piano albums of recent times. Tethered Moon can sometimes sound like a sterner version of the Jarrett Standards Trio (and Kikuchi does the Jarrett singalong too), but the records so far have been very gracefully distilled.
*Chansons De Piaf* (Winter & Winter)

# Rebecca Kilgore

VOCAL, GUITAR
*born* 24 September 1949

Becky Kilgore started out as a guitarist in western swing and swing-revivalist bands in the 80s, but soon made a more significant mark as a singer. While she still works with such bands as the country group Cactus Setup, the Portland-based vocalist has won more attention handling jazz and show tunes in the company of such congenial personalities as Dave Frishberg (who reads her moves perfectly) and Dave McKenna. She has a medium-sized voice which manages to personalize and inhabit lyrics without showing any trace of mannerism or pretentiousness – an act of invisible craft which is very rare indeed among the glut of contemporary jazz-orientated singers.
**Not A Care In The World** (Arbors)

# Al Killian

TRUMPET
*born* 15 October 1916; *died* 5 September 1950

Killian moved to New York, from his native Birmingham, Alabama, when in his teens, and he worked his way through the ranks of a number of big bands in the late 30s, eventually moving between the orchestras of Count Basie and Charlie Barnet in the following decade. Bop caught his approving ear and he played at Billy Berg's in California in 1947 as the leader of a bebop group, although the verdict was that he didn't really have the chops for the music. Then he joined Duke Ellington and stayed for some three years. He met his end at his Los Angeles home, shot by his reputedly psychopathic landlord.
**Count Basie, The Jubilee Alternatives** (Hep)

# Jonny King

PIANO
*born* 2 February 1965

King leads a double life as a New York copyright lawyer and an accomplished jazz pianist. He plays in an expansive post-bop idiom and has one or two illustrious sideman gigs to his credit (Joshua Redman, Eddie Harris), while leading groups of his own, and he is a characterful composer. Besides all this, he

wrote *What Jazz Is* (1997), which is one of the best introductory books a new fan can acquire as a jazz primer, full of musicianly insight which still takes the listener's side without talking down to him or her.
**Notes From The Underground** (Enja)

# Pete King

CLUB OWNER, TENOR SAXOPHONE
*born* 23 August 1929

Although the 'other' Peter King in British jazz played tenor in London circles in the early 50s, he is rightly best known as the longtime business partner of Ronnie Scott, and co-proprietor of the club in London's Soho district which still bears Scott's name. While Scott effectively fronted the operation, King ran most of the business side and still does, some years after Scott's death. As much a Soho institution as a jazz one – 'The thing about Soho, it was always a bit naughty – not really bad, just naughty' – King has been through all the ups and downs of running a jazz club and come out usually smiling, although the smile is always a bit warmer when he sees every table in the club full of punters. He has also dabbled a little in motor racing. Indifferent health has slowed him a little in recent years, but he has a loyal team of lieutenants to support him.

# Peter King

ALTO SAXOPHONE
*born* 11 August 1940

King's consummate grasp of the bebop idiom is so complete that he seems to breathe the language, and it's appropriate that it was hearing Charlie Parker which made him move from the clarinet to the alto when in his teens. Ronnie Scott engaged him to play the opening stint at the new Scott club in 1959, and ever since he has been a favoured son there. In the 60s (then often playing tenor more than alto) and 70s he worked steadily enough with both big bands and small groups, although he was less lucky in his recording engagements than some and didn't actually cut an album under his own name until 1982's somewhat ironically titled *New Beginning*, for Spotlite. In the 90s he made a sequence of dates for the Miles Music label, which gave him a more substantial discography, although he turns up under many other flags: with John Dankworth, Colin Towns, Charlie Watts, Stan Tracey and the BeBop Preservation Society, and as an occasional sideman with visiting Americans. King has been such a fixture in British jazz for so long that he is somewhat taken for granted, but loyal audiences hold him in fierce esteem. While his rhythmical language and scouring tone remain bop signatures, he has taken on bits and pieces from Coltrane and others and has deepened his style as the years have gone by. There are still too many one-day dates in his discography and a sympathetic label and producer can surely get a masterpiece out of him yet.

*Tamburello* (Miles Music)

## Tony Kinsey
DRUMS
*born* 11 October 1927

Kinsey grabbed his early opportunities with both hands. He worked on the *Queen Mary* and visited New York regularly enough to have lessons with Cozy Cole and, on orchestration, with Bill Russo. John Dankworth used him as the drummer in the earliest editions of the Johnny Dankworth Seven, and from 1953 or so Kinsey mostly led his own small groups. He was a dynamic and swinging straight-ahead drummer and his quartets and quintets of the 50s and 60s had some of the best London horn players in them: Joe Harriott, Ronnie Ross, Don Rendell, Les Condon, Jimmy Deuchar and Peter King at one time or another, and sessions for Esquire and Decca caught all concerned in crisp fettle. In the 70s and 80s he often wrote for TV, documentaries and commercials, but he has never stopped playing jazz and runs occasional big bands and, renewing his old alliance with John Dankworth, small groups.

**Various Artists,** *Bebop In Britain* (Esquire)

## John Kirby
BASS
*born* 31 December 1908; *died* 14 June 1952

Kirby grew up in an orphanage, went to New York as a trombonist, but then changed to tuba and was still playing that when he joined Fletcher Henderson in 1930 – although, like most other bass players, he had also started on the switch to the stand-up bass violin. He stayed four years with Henderson and then worked elsewhere until he was hired as the regular leader at New York's Onyx Club on West 52nd Street. Frankie Newton and Leo Watson were involved at first, but eventually the personnel stabilized around Kirby, Charlie Shavers, Russell Procope, Buster Bailey, Billy Kyle and O'Neil Spencer. Maxine Sullivan (whom Kirby married in 1938) also sang vocals. The leader contributed some originals but Shavers did a lot of the arranging, and their chamber-jazz style – which often involved a gentle jazzing of such classics as the Sextet from *Lucia di Lammermoor* and something which was turned into 'Bounce Of The Sugar Plum Fairy' – became a major hit on radio and on record, as well as in the club. The numerous records work to a careful timetable, and often trade in pianissimo qualities which were entirely different to those of other small-group swing bands (and oddly antithetical to the playing of Shavers and Bailey elsewhere). After four successful years, the band began to come apart, and eventually Kirby had to disband altogether in 1946, Sullivan having divorced him too. Drink and diabetes hampered his further progress and he was nearly forgotten when he died in 1952, in California. The Kirby sextet hinted at things to come – Tristano, West Coast neatness, perhaps the whole wave of cool jazz itself – without really influencing any player or school too much. Heard one at a time, the records remain, for all their novelty elements, smoothly enjoyable setpieces which grant John Kirby his modest niche in the history.

*John Kirby 1938–1939* (Classics)

## Andy Kirk
BANDLEADER
*born* 28 May 1898; *died* 11 December 1992

Kirk came from a dysfunctional family and, though born in Kentucky, was raised by relatives in Denver. He amused himself on various instruments and eventually settled on tuba and bass sax (like Jimmie Lunceford, he studied for a time with Wilberforce Whiteman), playing around Denver, New

York, Dallas and Tulsa. He took over a band called The Dark Clouds Of Joy and began making records with it in 1929: they became regulars in Kansas City and were soon one of the top outfits in the Southwest. For most of the 30s they remained based in Kansas while undertaking regular tours and making numerous records. Mary Lou Williams, who joined Kirk when she was 19 in 1929, stayed until 1942 and was arguably the pivotal musician in the band during the 30s, as soloist, arranger and composer: her 'Walkin' And Swingin'' (1936) is one of the great Kirk records. But Kirk could also, at different times, boast such soloists as Irving Randolph, Ben Webster, Lester Young and Dick Wilson. Vocalist Pha Terrell garnered a big hit for Kirk with the 1936 'Until The Real Thing Comes Along', which inevitably was at the sweeter end of things, although all along the leader liked playing the more romantic dance music as much as the swinging material. A new generation of players kept the band and music fresh during the 40s, and there was no let-up in their recording: among the new players were Don Byas, Kenny Kersey, Al Sears, Jimmy Forrest, Howard McGhee (who was featured on the classic 'McGhee Special' in 1942), Fats Navarro and even, very briefly, Charlie Parker. Eventually, though, Kirk decided to disband in 1949, and though he led the occasional pick-up group thereafter, he went into other areas of endeavour such as real estate. His discography approaches 200 individual recordings, and though the band had relatively few of the sort of signature recordings which elevated Ellington and Basie, it is a surprisingly consistent and credible body of work, the later records often offering as much interest as the early ones. In his final years, Kirk was again active in the business, though this time as an official of the Musicians' Union, and he died in New York in his 95th year, having outlived most of his swing-era rivals.

*Andy Kirk 1936–1937* (Classics)

# Rahsaan Roland Kirk

SAXOPHONES, FLUTES, ETC
*born* 7 August 1936; *died* 5 December 1977

Kirk is forever regarded as a one-off genius whose eclecticism and entertainer's panache endeared him to the jazz community. Blind

from an early age, he was a precocious saxophonist in his school band and was playing at dances in his native Ohio by his mid-teens. After a dream where he saw himself playing several horns simultaneously, he found a manzello and a stritch, two forgotten instruments, at a music shop, and taught himself to blow these and the tenor at the same time. This kind of showmanship brought him to wider attention and he began recording in the late 50s, before joining Charles Mingus in 1961 and starring on the chaotic passages of *Oh Yeah*. From there he became an international touring performer, and a much-loved regular at Ronnie Scott's: he was performing there during a police raid, and the irate Pete King had to point out to an officer trying to make Roland stop playing that he was blind. Kirk recorded prolifically for Mercury, Limelight and Atlantic, his albums for the latter label becoming ever more extravagant in terms of instruments, settings and studio effects. His Limelight albums are among his best, particularly *Rip, Rig & Panic* (1965), although the live experience of *Here Comes The Whistle Man* (1967) is indispensable, and a quite tumultuous version of 'If I Loved You' and the handsomely arranged date with a Benny Golson orchestra suggests that for all his 'audio dreams', Roland was often at his best in essentially romantic music. Too many of his later records feature too much nonsense, and listeners coming to them cold may wonder what all the fuss was about with Kirk: when confined to a straight-ahead, swinging role on the tenor alone, he usually created his most lasting music. Far from being timeless, he was very much a product of his heyday, the 60s and early 70s: he suffered a terrible stroke in 1975 which left him partially paralysed, and forced back into action too soon by the debilitating costs of medical care, he probably wore himself out. At 41 he died as a result of a second stroke.

*Rip, Rig & Panic* (Limelight/Verve)

# Kenny Kirkland

PIANO
*born* 28 September 1955; *died* c13 November 1998

Kirkland grew up in New York and studied at Manhattan School Of Music. His first key alliance was with Wynton Marsalis, and he worked in the trumpeter's band until 1985.

He remained a close associate of Branford Marsalis, playing with him on *The Tonight Show* and on several of his albums; he also did high-profile sideman work with Sting, Courtney Pine and Kenny Garrett. Yet his own career suddenly seemed to fall away as the 90s progressed: he made only a single album under his own name, a disappointingly muddled set for GRP, *Kenny Kirkland* (1991), and he never found a way to make his breadth of interests cohere into an audience-winning style. Even so, he was greatly admired by other musicians as both player and composer, and the New York community was shocked at the news of his death: when his body was discovered in his apartment, he had already been dead for several days. Branford Marsalis named *Requiem* (1998), the pianist's last appearance on record, for him.

**Wynton Marsalis, *Black Codes From The Underground*** (Columbia)

## Ryan Kisor
TRUMPET
*born* 12 April 1973

The precocious Kisor won the Thelonious Monk/Louis Armstrong trumpet competition in 1990 and was soon studying and playing in New York. His career seemed to be going at a meteoric rate when Columbia signed him for a couple of records around this time, but like many others he was quickly dropped by the major label and has since worked his way back mostly via sideman work: with the Lincoln Center Jazz Orchestra (Wynton Marsalis regards him very highly), Carnegie Hall Jazz Band and the Mingus Big Band, and with George Gruntz's ensemble. He rarely sounds like an original but Kisor is still delightful to listen to (and the Columbia records were unfairly overlooked): at his best his playing fizzes with a kind of sly abandon.

***Power Source*** (Criss Cross)

## Harry Klein
BARITONE SAXOPHONE
*born* 25 December 1928

It seems like damning him with faint praise to hear Klein described as 'one of the most popular baritone saxophonists in England'

in the middle 50s, as *Grove* does: how many others were there? Klein started on alto, in the dance-band era of the 40s, but went over to the baritone in the following decade and held down roles with Kenny Baker, Ronnie Scott, Victor Feldman, Tommy Whittle and the Jazz Today group; some of his best playing was set down with Tony Kinsey. His group The Jazz Five, with Vic Ash, turned out a modest classic in *The Hooter* (1960), one of the very few British jazz albums of the period to be given a full American release (on Riverside). Latterly he mostly did studio work, again back on alto more often than not, but his great-hearted baritone sound is one of the most enlivening things on the 50s dates he took part in.

**The Jazz Five, *The Hooter*** (Tempo/Riverside)

## Manny Klein
TRUMPET
*born* 4 February 1904; *died* 31 May 1994

Manny Klein probably made more records than most other American trumpeters. His three brothers were also musicians (Dave Klein, also a trumpeter, was one of Ted Lewis's first hot soloists), and after subbing for Bix Beiderbecke in the Paul Whiteman band, Mannie played on hundreds of New York studio dates up until 1937. He can be heard taking fine solos on records by The Boswell Sisters ('It's The Girl', 1931) and Adrian Rollini ('Sugar', 1934), to pick two out of many, and when he moved over to the West Coast in 1937, he did the same thing, playing on numerous soundtracks and studio sessions of every kind all through the 40s and 50s. It was a cruel blow to this peerless pro when a stroke in 1973 left him unable to read music, but his lip was intact, and he still turned up at festivals and special occasions until shortly before his death.

## Oscar Klein
TRUMPET
*born* 5 January 1930

Although born in Graz, Austria, Klein formed his first group (the Florence Dixieland band) in Florence, then played with The Tremble Kids in Switzerland in the 50s before subsequently playing with the

Dutch Swing College Band for four years from 1959. Having started as a guitarist (he took up trumpet because nobody else in his band played one) he set up a guitar school in Innsbruck and eventually settled in Basel. A frequent partner of Fatty George, he has become a familiar figure to middle-European audiences, turning up on television on a regular basis and taking on what amounts to a variety artist role.
*Moonglow* (Nagel Heyer)

# John Klemmer
TENOR SAXOPHONE
*born* 3 July 1946

Klemmer lucked out with his records for ABC in the 70s, which set his saxophone against puling backings of fusion-lite and electronics in what might, with a little imagination, be seen as prototype Kenny G music. Klemmer is a better saxophonist, but the records had minimal jazz content. He had previously worked in his native Chicago and made some uneventful sets for Cadet. He disappeared from sight in 1981 following a breakdown and aside from a couple of odd glimpses in the late 90s has hardly been heard from since. His 1998 set *Simpatico* turned out to be made up of old tapes with overdubbed ocean noise: retro New Age, perhaps.
*Arabesque* (ABC)

# Eric Kloss
ALTO, TENOR AND SOPRANO SAXOPHONES
*born* 3 April 1949

Kloss attended a school for blind children, where he learned saxophone, and he was already gigging (with Richard 'Groove' Holmes among others) in Pittsburgh when in his middle teens. Between 1966 and 1970 he made ten albums for Prestige, in varied company, and while some of them are little more than prentice hard bop, Kloss took an ambitious course, stirring in prototype jazz-rock, funk and free elements, and enlisting many heavy-duty sidemen, including Booker Ervin, Cedar Walton, Chick Corea and Dave Holland. His own style was marked by a kind of rough-and-ready virtuosity, as if he had the chops for something special but couldn't quite decide what to do with his

abilities. He was a familiar touring presence in the 70s and 80s and made some more records for Muse, but since the early 90s he has been mostly involved in education, still based in Pittsburgh.
*In The Land Of The Giants* (Prestige)

# Earl Klugh
GUITAR
*born* 16 September 1954

The Detroit-born Klugh is a capable guitarist and it's a pity that his career has been dedicated to creating a succession of boring, soft-focus albums which set the stage for the smooth-jazz onslaught of the 90s. He sticks to acoustic guitar and plays in a melodious style that slots into place with the carefully sculpted backings. Early on, he was involved in rather more energetic music: he was with Chick Corea's Return To Forever for one season, and has sometimes traded licks (in a very gentlemanly way) with George Benson. The later records, though, have no imperatives other than to soothe.
*The Best Of Earl Klugh* (Warner Bros)

# Jimmy Knepper
TROMBONE
*born* 22 November 1927; *died* 14 June 2003

Knepper left a ghostly impression on the music: ubiquitous but hidden, a very particular individual who nevertheless melts into the background, whose playing and presence seem fleeting and hard to remember. He grew up in Los Angeles and studied there, in the meantime playing in big bands (Charlie Spivak, Charlie Barnet, Woody Herman) in the late 40s and early 50s. Charles Mingus hired him as a replacement for Willie Dennis, and it was a bittersweet relationship. While Knepper came to prominence via Mingus's groups and records (particularly *East Coasting*, 1957, and *Blues And Roots*, 1959), and stayed on and off until 1962, the leader lost his temper with the trombonist at a rehearsal in 1962 and smacked him in the mouth, causing an injury which thenceforth obliged Knepper to limit the range of his playing. Thereafter he took a more circumspect role for a time, playing in Broadway pit bands and re-emerging to take the trombone chair in such

groups as the Jones–Lewis Orchestra, the Jazz Composers' Orchestra and some of Gil Evans's various groups. Somewhat surprisingly he played with Mingus again in the late 70s and later toured with Mingus Dynasty. In the 80s and 90s he seemed to take whichever jobs appealed to him: having invested money in property many years earlier, music became more of a matter of pleasing himself. Over a career of 50 years he led only four or five albums, none of them particularly special. His consistency and clean attack – fast, but not quite as neat and tidy as the J J Johnson style – also glove his personality, although he could play with a gruff timbre that nodded to some of the more expressive players of his instrument.
**Charles Mingus, *Blues And Roots*** (Atlantic)

# Knitting Factory
VENUE, RECORD LABEL

At one time in the late 80s, The Knitting Factory seemed like the coolest jazz club on Earth. It was founded as a performance space by Michael Dorf and Louis Spitzer (who didn't last long – Dorf took over most of its activities by the end of the first year) in an old building on New York's Houston Street which had once, indeed, been a knitting factory. Jazz began to creep into what was originally a multicultural performance space and after a year or so it was the main impetus of the club. The so-called Downtown group of players – spearheaded by the likes of John Zorn, Wayne Horvitz, Marty Ehrlich, the 29th Street Saxophone Quartet and others – became regulars, and so did Andrew Hill, Charles Gayle, James Blood Ulmer and many more. Its surroundings were archetypally pokey but felt right. The KF eventually shifted to larger premises on Leonard Street in 1994 and started its own record label; and Dorf expanded his now formidable brand into festival surroundings, taking a stake in George Wein's JVC Festival and sending packages of bands overseas. But after many years of what appeared to be notable success, the financial side began unravelling, and disgruntled musicians, distributors and magazines who had sold them advertising began to count the cost. The Knitting Factory continues, but a lot of people are still reputedly owed a lot of money and Dorf appears to have stepped down.

# Hans Koch
SAXOPHONES, CLARINETS
*born* 12 March 1948

From the seemingly (to outsiders, at least) hopeless position of Switzerland, Koch has built a strong body of work as a free improviser. While that territory has little in the way of tradition in this area to act as a support, Koch has worked steadily through the 80s and 90s with such kindred spirits as Werner Ludi and Franz Koglmann. His own records take a surprisingly tough and combative line in the idiom.
**Hardcore Chamber Music** (Intakt)

# Franz Koglmann
TRUMPET
*born* 22 May 1947

Koglmann's music is a fierce critique of cultural attitudes and hegemonies and jazz is only a part of it. Born in Mödling, Austria, he studied in Vienna, played in a group called The Masters Of Unorthodox Jazz and founded his own Pipe record label. Having already visited the US, he began forming alliances with sympathetic minds – Steve Lacy, Bill Dixon, Albert Mangelsdorff, Lol Coxhill – and in the 80s established some new groups of his own, incuding the Pipetet and Pipe Trio, KoKoKo (with Klaus Koch and Eckhard Koltermann) and the Monoblue Quartet, which also featured Tony Coe. Werner Uehlinger of hat ART began recording him extensively and there were some outstanding records: the provocative and mildly notorious *A White Line* (1989) paid homage to a continuum of Bix Beiderbecke, Stan Kenton and Shorty Rogers; *Cantos I–IV* (1992) is a sumptuous setting for the 17-strong Pipetet; *L'Heure Bleue* (1991) mixes originals and recompositions for the Monoblue Quartet and a duo of Koglmann and Misha Mengelberg. His own precise but often radiantly lyrical playing articulates every patient step in the music. Latterly he has established an imprint of his own, Between The Lines, and among more recent records *Fear Death By Water* (2003) is one of his most coolly scathing projects to date, almost a musical equivalent to *The Way We Live Now*. Koglmann's suggestion that he has 'a greater affinity for the expressions of a melancholy decadence than the spon-

taneous joy of improvising; I cannot see swing as the one and only saving criterion' is tantamount to anti-jazz in some contemporary quarters. But his music is a compelling argument for a new jazz aesthetic altogether.
*Cantos I–IV* (hat ART)

## Eero Koivistoinen
TENOR AND SOPRANO SAXOPHONES
*born* 13 January 1941

One of the first Finnish modernists to make an impact outside his country, Koivistoinen studied in his native Helsinki and at Berklee in Boston in the early 70s, having already made an impact at the 1969 Montreux Festival. Some of his albums from the 70s have recently been reissued, and though dated in some ways they show how he was trying to make something happen out of various fusion borrowings. In the 80s and 90s he went back to a more secure, post-bop situation and cut a couple of all-star American records, *Picture In Three Colours* (1983) and *Altered Things* (1991). A busy composer in film and TV work, and his later music works an agreeable line between a free-thinking approach and carefully scored and detailed base material.
*Sometime Ago* (A Records)

## Hans Koller
TENOR SAXOPHONE
*born* 12 February 1921

Koller studied in Vienna before war service, and after his discharge he worked in the Hot Club Of Vienna before moving to Germany, where he was quickly in the thick of the new music, playing in the New Jazz Stars with Albert Mangelsdorff and going on to form a quartet, also leading workshops in Hamburg. While he played most of the saxophone family, it was on tenor that he made his strongest mark, and while he recorded steadily in the 60s and 70s little enough of this work has been reissued on CD, and much of Koller's best music – often shifting from bop situations towards a much freer way of thinking – is hidden. He became increasingly interested in saxophone groups and formed all-sax ensembles which stretched to seven members at one point.

He eventually retired from playing in 1995, and there is a Hans Koller prize for achievement by Austrian musicians presented annually in his honour. He has also worked extensively as an abstract painter.
*Relax With My Horns* (Saba)

## Krzysztof Komeda
PIANO
*born* 27 April 1931; *died* 23 April 1969

Komeda's career was conducted partially in secret: a qualified doctor (real name Krzysztof Trzcinski), he used the name Komeda to disguise his activities from the Polish authorities. Yet he became a hit at Polish jazz festivals in the later 50s and over the next dozen years turned out a prodigious body of work – jazz small-group music, film- and theatre scores, folk-influenced songwriting, jazz with poetry. He wrote the music for dozens of films, most famously the Roman Polanski features *Knife In The Water*, *Cul de sac* and *Rosemary's Baby*, spending his last two years in Hollywood at the suggestion of the director himself. While comparatively unexceptional as a soloist or improviser himself, Komeda's work is a fascinating conflation of many strands of Polish and European musics, jazz and contemporary composition. Much of it was recorded and he could number such important collaborators as Bernt Rosengren, Zbigniew Namysłowski and Tomasz Stańko among his sidemen, with the latter two particularly outstanding on the magnificent *Astigmatic* (1965), a key document of jazz in Europe in the 60s. But the records, though they have made it to CD for the most part, are always difficult to find, and this tends to enhance the somewhat enigmatic history of this musician: in rather mysterious circumstances he suffered injuries which put him into a coma while in America, and though flown home he never regained consciousness.
*Astigmatic* (Power Bros)

## Toshinori Kondo
TRUMPET
*born* 15 December 1948

Kondo studied in Kyoto and arrived in Tokyo in 1972, where he played with Yosuke

Yamashita before forming trios of his own. He played with Derek Bailey on one of the guitarist's Japanese visits (Bailey advises to always go shopping with Kondo, since he is matchless at getting a discount on shop prices) and from there he moved to New York, although British audiences saw him in a Company Week in 1979. Kondo's style had by now gone from a liberated freebop approach to full-on free playing, getting a strange series of accents out of the open horn and using mutes to find effects which Miles Davis might have winced at. He returned to Japan in 1982 but continued to keep in touch with the global free scene before forming the Tibetan Blue Air Liquid Band, later the IMA (International Music Activities): greeted with dismay by some as a noisy fusion band, it was a lot more interesting than that and one of their records, *Konton* (1987), was given an international release by Sony. IMA lasted through the 90s, although it recorded less often and appeared mostly in Japan. Kondo has more recently returned to free playing, appearing with Peter Brötzmann's Die Like A Dog group, while investigating the possibilities of hip-hop fusion and working with turntable and laptop operators. Much of his energetic career has been conducted away from Western eyes – besides music, Kondo has been a male model for cosmetics, an author, a TV actor and a well-known face-about-Tokyo – but he remains a compelling improviser and a startlingly inventive musical thinker.

**Konton** (Sony)

# Klaus König
TROMBONE, COMPOSER
*born* 31 December 1959

König is a German trombonist whose main contribution has been brought about by his interest in large-scale works. He studied music theatre in Cologne, and there's more than a touch of the theatrical about the big works he has been fortunate enough to have recorded by the Enja label in the 80s and 90s: they are typical pieces of European composition–improvisation which have some striking moments amidst a lot of what might be deemed to be procedural music.

**The H.E.A.R.T. Project** (Enja)

# Lee Konitz
ALTO SAXOPHONE
*born* 13 October 1927

Konitz studied clarinet as a boy in Chicago (the model which his parents bought him came with an offer which included free lessons with Lou Honig, who also taught Johnny Griffin). He later took up tenor sax and began working professionally in 1942, eventually doubling on alto, which became his premier instrument. Not long afterwards he first met Lennie Tristano, who became an early mentor and teacher, and after a spell with Claude Thornhill's band, he hooked up with Miles Davis and came to perform in the nonet which was responsible for the *Birth Of The Cool* sessions. He also made some striking records with Tristano at this time, including the Capitol sessions which produced 'Crosscurrent' and 'Intuition' (1949), arguably the first free-jazz vehicles. But he broke away from Tristano not long afterwards and had a steady job with Stan Kenton's band in 1952–3. It was really his final big-band work: thereafter he played mostly in small groups, often under his own leadership. In the 50s there were memorable encounters with Gerry Mulligan and Warne Marsh, and oustanding records for both Atlantic and Verve: the latter contract culminated in *Motion* (1961), a thrilling trio record with Elvin Jones on drums, which in the CD era was expanded to a three-disc archive with all the unreleased material. In his earlier days, Konitz's alto sound was based around a smooth legato line, and he is often credited with establishing the most convincing counter to Charlie Parker's domination of bebop alto: it was, though, neither uninflected nor free of vibrato – 'I was listening to some of my early records with Stan Kenton and oy vey! It was very schmaltzy!' Instead of Parker's brimming variety, Konitz preferred a long line which swung in a different way, precisely tailored but touching deftly on harmonic ambiguities as it unreeled. After *Motion*, though, Konitz suddenly found work scarce and he recorded and performed very little for a time, taking in students instead. By the end of the decade his stock was back up and he found himself much in demand in Europe, recording for such labels as Storyville and Steeplechase in the 70s and touring with Warne Marsh. He formed an occasional nonet, and worked in duet with several pianists, including Martial Solal, Michel Petrucciani and Harold Danko.

His music is informed by a compulsion to remain an improviser, and not a licks specialist or a mere pattern-player, strategies which he has often been critical of in others: 'Because I've had so much experience playing, I realized that it's possible to really improvise, and that means going into it with a so-called clean slate.' This has led him to investigate the medium of solo records, playing in Derek Bailey's Company, and generally taking on performing situations where he has much less of a safety net than most veterans of his experience would be prepared to encounter. When coupled with a tone which has now taken on a bruised, sometimes furry quality, it lends his playing a unique mix of adventure and vulnerability. In the 80s and 90s he became amazingly prolific as a recording artist, cutting dozens of records for numerous independents and still turning up on a major from time to time: two records with Brad Mehldau and Charlie Haden emerged on Blue Note, and Columbia sponsored a quartet date. He divides his time between New York and Cologne, where he lives with his third wife, and he survived a severe bout of illness and has come back playing more strongly than ever.
*Motion* (Verve)

## Peter Kowald
BASS
*born* 21 April 1944; *died* 21 September 2002

Kowald started on tuba and then switched to acoustic bass. He was a founder member in Peter Brötzmann's trio from 1965, and is on such early documents as *For Adolphe Sax* (1967): already a formidable player, he took to the new free-playing idiom immediately and with characteristic gusto. Besides his association with Brötzmann, he took a leading role in the Globe Unity Orchestra, and worked with such up-and-coming names as Pierre Favre, Evan Parker, Gunter Christmann and Alex von Schlippenbach, and in bands of his own. All through the 70s, 80s and 90s, Kowald worked to expand his areas of performance and his own understanding of improvised music. While some of his first-generation contemporaries preferred to maintain a small circle of playing

associates, he constantly welcomed new collaborators and fresh fields of discovery. He recorded for the FMP label throughout this time: two especially notable projects were three volumes of duets, one each devoted to players from Europe, Asia and the USA, and a quite remarkable record, *Was Da Ist?* (1995), which might be the finest of all bass solo collections, showcasing his wonderful sound and bringing all the detail in his playing into a rich close-up. He always enjoyed the chance to work with fellow bassists, among them Barry Guy, Joëlle Léandre and William Parker, and the opportunities of mixed media intrigued him too. His sudden death, in New York in 2002 from a heart attack, shocked the free-music community and he was greatly mourned by the huge number of musicians and listeners he had played for and inspired.
*Was Da Ist?* (FMP)

## Roy Kral
See JACKIE & ROY.

## Diana Krall
VOCAL, PIANO
*born* 16 November 1964

Krall is the most successful Canadian export since Oscar Peterson (or, perhaps more pertinently, Joni Mitchell). She went to Berklee in the 80s and played in Toronto clubs, at first working as a pianist alone. But it was her voice which would make her fortune, a direction initially encouraged by Jimmy Rowles. She moved to New York in 1990 and made her first album in 1992, followed by *Only Trust Your Heart* (1994). But it was her switch to Impulse! and her work with producer Tommy LiPuma which turned her career around. What had been a fairly staid nightclub-trio act, with Krall crooning somewhat dispassionately over a conventional backing, became the sexiest and hottest new formula in jazz. The husky contralto she uses – 'I sound like my grandmother, she apparently had the same catch in her voice that I do' – began to be paired up with seductive material such as 'Peel Me A Grape', and suddenly everyone was listening to the singer rather than the pianist. Under LiPuma's shrewd direction, the records *Love*

*Scenes* (1997) and the almost cloyingly lush *When I Look In Your Eyes* (1998) achieved platinum sales and global success, and Krall was the number one singer in jazz, even though the largest part of her audience in all likelihood knew little and cared less about that kind of music. Krall has continued to tour with a trio, but it is now performing in major concert halls and on black-tie occasions. Her marriage to the rock singer-songwriter Elvis Costello meant that *The Girl In The Other Room* (2004) was stacked with originals and pieces co-written with her husband: how this will square with an audience that would rather hear her singing 'The Look Of Love' is hard to divine as yet, but the record hasn't been as commercially successful as some of her previous ones.

*Love Scenes* (Impulse!)

## Wayne Krantz

GUITAR
*born* 26 July 1956

Krantz was a welcome addition to the 90s jazz scene since he appeared to have figured out some new routes in the tiring genre of jazz guitar. He had been working in New York since the mid-80s, with Billy Cobham, Leni Stern and others, but a trio he formed with Lincoln Goines and Zach Danziger displayed a surprising and notably individual identity, mixing post-bop improvisation, rock, country and electronic styles into something which emerged as a clear-headed fusion rather than an eclectic mishmash. A couple of albums for Enja set down some of it in fine style, and when Krantz formed a new trio (with Tim Lefebvre and Keith Carlock) later in the decade, they played a weekly gig at the city's 55 Bar for several years and the prolific Krantz began steadily releasing material via his own website.

*Greenwich Mean* (Wayne Krantz)

## Carl Kress

GUITAR
*born* 20 October 1907; *died* 10 June 1965

Kress played banjo and guitar on the New York scene of the 20s and he is involved in many of the best sessions to come out of the studio of that time: with Miff Mole, Frankie Trumbauer, the Dorseys and others. In the 30s he played more session-work and his jazz credentials waned a bit, but in 1961 he formed a duo with George Barnes, which lasted until his death. Some duets he made with Eddie Lang and Dick McDonough, early in the 30s, are little classics of their kind, Kress's strummed swing a perfect feed for the others.

## Volker Kriegel

GUITAR
*born* 24 December 1943; *died* 15 June 2003

Kriegel's great period was the 70s, when he ran the group Spectrum (with Eberhard Weber) and the slightly later Mild Maniac Orchestra; he also helped to found the United Jazz And Rock Ensemble with Wolfgang Dauner, and the record label Mood. He had previously come to prominence as a member of the Dave Pike Set. Kriegel's music favoured a cooler kind of jazz-rock than the overheated model of Return To Forever and their ilk, and his writing for his groups was light, harmonically imaginative and careful to put the chops of the band in a useful context. It sometimes approximates TV-theme music, but it was at least a refreshing change from the American model. Kriegel attracted a major fan base on his home German scene but the music never travelled quite as well, and very little of it is internationally available now. As a guitarist he was himself an interesting blend of jazz and rock influences. He more or less gave up public playing in his last decade, preferring to write and work at his second vocation, which was as a cartoonist.

*Spectrum* (MPS)

## Ernie Krivda

TENOR SAXOPHONE
*born* 6 February 1945

Like a number of other reed players, Krivda got his start by playing in a polka band. He switched to alto and then tenor, doing big-band work during the 60s, and then held down a regular gig in Cleveland at a bar called the Smiling Dog Saloon. In 1975 he moved over to Los Angeles, tried his luck in New York but eventually went back to Cleveland in 1979. Since then he has played

locally without really getting much national prominence, although his records – he has been especially favoured by the Cadence and CIMP labels, which have recorded him extensively – have been more widely distributed. Krivda is an extravagant saxophonist with a fat sound and a boisterous, sometimes renegade style of improvising. He still loves to do big-band work and his groups Fat Tuesday Big Band and Swing City were surprisingly effective recent vehicles.
*The Band That Swings* (Koch)

# Karin Krog

VOCAL

*born* 15 May 1937

Krog to some extent broke the mould of Scandinavian female singers performing jazz. Where most had followed the girlish style of Monica Zetterlund, using a generic accent to confer a kind of naive charm on English lyrics, Krog from the start took a more mature and thoughtful style, even though her voice was not an especially powerful or wide-ranging instrument. Her early work (collected on the now hard-to-find Verve compilation *Jubilee*) mixed boppish material with more conventional swing-standards interpretation, and she was soon a regular on the European festival circuit, eventually visiting America in 1967, where she worked with Don Ellis's big band. She continued a busy regimen of playing live and recording all through the 70s and 80s, also working as a television producer in her native Oslo. Her own label, Meantime, was established in 1987, and besides issuing new work she has also bought back the masters of some of her earlier dates. She has often worked in collaboration with her partner, John Surman, which has assisted in her exploration of such fields as electronic music and the fringes of avant-garde composition. There are few vocalists who have tackled the kind of range exemplified by such projects as *Bluesand* (1999), a dark and finely etched series of duets with Surman, and the musing recital (with Steve Kuhn) of standards and originals in *Where You At?* (2002).
*One On One* (Meantime)

# Gene Krupa

DRUMS

*born* 15 January 1909; *died* 16 October 1973

The Chicagoan was still in his teens when he made his first impact on record, as part of the seminal band which made the four titles by McKenzie And Condon's Chicagoans in 1927. But it was not a star-making debut: for the next seven years he often played in ordinary dance bands and pit orchestras and took whatever work there was going in New York and Chicago. Joining Benny Goodman in 1934, however, eventually proved a turning point for the dashing Krupa, by this time on his way to becoming the showman who would enthral the young audiences of the swing era. By the time he left in 1938 (following a quarrel with the leader), Krupa was a star, as much a visual dynamo on stage as a driving force behind the drums. He played in both Goodman's small-group and orchestral recordings, and brought the house down with 'Sing Sing Sing' at the Carnegie Hall concert which was a benchmark in the leader's success story. Yet he went on to great success of his own as a leader: by the early 40s the Krupa orchestra was one of the very top swing bands, and with soloists such as Roy Eldridge and Anita O'Day doing the vocals, there was real musical quality to go with the crowd-pleasing of which Krupa was an almost helpless exponent. There was a brief and potentially catastrophic interruption in 1943: Krupa was arrested and briefly jailed for 'contributing to the delinquency of a minor', a more or less trumped-up charge which amounted to his hiring an underage assistant, although he had the charge revoked on appeal. He went back to Goodman and then Tommy Dorsey for a spell, but re-formed his big band and enjoyed much further success: later 40s titles such as 'Up An' Atom' and 'Disc Jockey Jump' revitalized his idiom, and there were some strong swing-to-bop players in the new ranks, such as Urbie Green and Frank Rehak. In 1951, though, he disbanded again, and went back to small groups. Jazz had moved on and he no longer enjoyed the same eminence, but Jazz At The Philharmonic gave him an appropriate outlet for his kind of musical fireworks, and there were drum battles with Buddy Rich which Norman Granz organized: Rich liked outplaying the older man, who acknowledged his superiority, but there was a mutual affection between the two men, the greatest pair of showmen the drums have seen. Krupa took life a little easier (he had a heart attack in 1960), had his life story filmed by Hollywood (with Sal Mineo in the title role), and occasionally went to Goodman small-group reunions, the last of them taking place only months before the drummer's death. Flashy and brilliant, the man who 'made the drummer a high-priced guy' was often described as vulgar, whatever that means in jazz. Like Rich, he had his own ideas about how to swing a band, and they didn't always chime with everyone else's. But it is difficult to think badly of a man who brought so much exuberant joy to the music.

*Drummer Man* (Verve)

# Joachim Kühn

PIANO
*born* 15 March 1944

Kühn's music is a tough and sometimes daunting realm where his early years as a concert pianist coexist with a broad range of jazz interests. He grew up in Leipzig and studied music there, but in 1961 he went over almost entirely to jazz: 'Free jazz was the new music. When I heard Ornette Coleman play, I knew that this was the music I wanted to make.' He moved to the West in 1966 and worked in Hamburg with his brother Rolf: they played in America together and recorded an album there for Impulse!, *Impressions Of New York* (1967). There were many associations which lasted through the 70s, and for a time Kühn was under contract to Atlantic and lived in America, but in 1984 he returned to Paris and formed a long-standing trio there with J-F Jenny-Clark and Daniel Humair. Kühn might fairly claim pioneer status as an improviser who drew on his classical knowledge (like Friedrich Gulda before him, though in a different way), and brought in techniques such as playing the piano's interior. His records sometimes end up desiccated, as if he is working out ideas and procedures for his own benefit and is careless of the listener's response, but his great virtuosity makes piano aficionados sit up. In 1996 he finally got to work with his original influence when he recorded a duet album

with Ornette Coleman, *Colors* (1996), and that experience may have led to the ambitious solo set *The Diminished Augmented System* (1999), where he plays music by himself, Coleman and J S Bach. What sets him apart from many third-stream dabblers is the feeling that he has a thorough knowledge of every kind of music he tackles.

*Colors* (Verve)

# Rolf Kühn

CLARINET
*born* 29 September 1929

Kühn played clarinet in wartime dance bands in Leipzig. That experience stood him in good stead when he went to live in the US, since he played in Benny Goodman's orchestras (sometimes subbing for the leader) and in the Tommy Dorsey ghost band. Back in Germany, he directed the NDR Studioband (a television orchestra) and worked in small groups with his younger brother Joachim: the record cited is a fine sampler of their work together, and the title piece, 'Music For Two Brothers', is a remarkable duet performance, as much for Rolf's uncompromisingly 'modern' clarinet as for Joachim's keyboard virtuosity. In the 70s he tried his hand at fusion, a pretty dramatic departure for a clarinet player, though it is a testament to his skills that the instrument doesn't sound all at sea. Thereafter he worked more often in theatre and TV music, although every so often he has emerged to make a jazz record.

**With Joachim Kühn, *Music For Two Brothers*** (MPS)

# Steve Kuhn

PIANO
*born* 24 March 1938

Kuhn studied as a child with Margaret Chaloff (Serge's mother – 'She was like a surrogate mother to me') and after graduating from Harvard he got his start on record in Kenny Dorham's group (*Jazz Contemporary*, 1960). He then spent six weeks in the John Coltrane quartet before moving over to Stan Getz's group. Later in the 60s he moved to Stockholm, making several European alliances, and though he went back to the US in

1971 his most significant recordings in that decade were made for ECM, four records based around his own, somewhat impressionistic, writing. He led a fine quartet which had Sheila Jordan as vocalist, but then drifted away from jazz for a time, and latterly he has recorded and performed mostly in the standards idiom. Kuhn's music is sometimes deceptive: he seems to almost take pains not to club the listeners with virtuosity, but he likes musicianly quotes and ingenious bits of piano business. His decision to mostly play standards, though, has left him without a notably individual position in what is now a very crowded field.
*Trance* (ECM)

## Sergey Kuryokhin

PIANO
*born* 16 June 1954; *died* 9 July 1996

Kuryokhin was certainly a one-off. Born in Murmansk, he studied to some extent in Leningrad but was basically a self-taught musician. What he heard of American jazz fired his enthusiasm, and he hooked up with Vladimir Chekasin and Anatoly Vapirov. But any kind of anti-establishment music was fine by Kuryokhin, and besides working in jazz ensembles he played in underground rock groups of every kind. His first record was a solo set, *The Ways Of Freedom* (1981), and it was the West's introduction to his work since the master tapes were smuggled out of the USSR and released by Leo Feigin of Leo Records (who inevitably became Kuryokhin's patron in the outside world). He barnstormed his way through the 80s, visiting London, playing orchestral works with jazz and rock soloists, and leading groups which he always called Pop Mechanics, even though their personnels varied wildly. Perestroika seemed to blunt the edge of his work: what was there to rail against in an unrepressed Russia? It is hard to get a handle on this probably brilliant man's work, since it is so all over the place, full of bawdy comedy and classical repose, often sitting next to each other. He never swings and he frequently sounds as much a classical guy as a jazz man, but he left a jumbled and sometimes delicious legacy. His death from cancer martyred a madcap spirit.
*Sergey Kuryokhin* (Leo)

## Billy Kyle

PIANO
*born* 14 July 1914; *died* 23 February 1966

Kyle came to prominence as the pianist and one of the arrangers for the John Kirby Sextet, which he joined in 1938, and after war service he led his own bands and often worked with Sy Oliver. But he will always be remembered for his association with Louis Armstrong's All Stars, a band he joined in 1953 and stayed with until he died. His style was much akin to that of his illustrious predecessor in the group, Earl Hines, but he took a more unassuming role and played as though the spotlight should always be on the boss. He was still on tour with the band at the time of his unexpected death.
*Billy Kyle 1937–1938* (Classics)

## Joe LaBarbera

DRUMS
*born* 22 February 1948

The youngest of the three jazz-playing LaBarbera brothers has had the most prominent career. He worked with Woody Herman in 1972 but it was a high-profile stint with Chuck Mangione at the time of the trumpeter's greatest success (1973–7) that brought him attention. Thereafter he freelanced until joining what turned out to be the final edition of the Bill Evans trio, in 1979. In the 80s he went back to a hired-gun role, sometimes working with brother Pat in the JMOG (Jazz Men On The Go) quartet. John (b 1945) is a trumpeter who did big-band work before working primarily as a commercial arranger and educator. Pat (b 1944) is a fine tenorman in the Coltrane lineage, who settled in Canada in 1974 and has been a part of that country's jazz midstream ever since.
*JMOG, JMOG* (Sackville)

## Steve Lacy

SOPRANO SAXOPHONE
*born* 23 July 1934; *died* 4 June 2004

As Dave Liebman put it: 'He's the epitome of art for art's sake. He goes his own way, he plays everybody's stuff – koto guys, Russian poets, guys standing on their heads – and it's always Steve Lacy.' The inspiration of

Sidney Bechet got Lacy started on the soprano: at that time he was still Steven Lackritz, but Rex Stewart – one of the older Dixielanders whom the young saxophonist ended up playing with in this period – christened him 'Lacy' as an easier alternative. He recorded a few sessions in that idiom in the early 50s, but after a brief period of study his curiosity took him towards a much more modern jazz outlook, and in 1955 he joined Cecil Taylor's group, an extraordinary leap by any standard, and on the basis of their few recordings one which suited him unexpectedly well. He spent four months in one of Thelonious Monk's groups, beginning an association with that music which Lacy mused on for the rest of his playing life: John Coltrane came to check the group out at The Village Vanguard, and not long afterwards he took up the soprano himself. Lacy then formed a quartet with Roswell Rudd which was devoted entirely to playing Monk's compositions. Thereafter, though, he turned to his own kind of free playing, which usually started out from one of his steady, contemplative compositions and made a step-by-step journey to some remote place. In 1965 he went to Europe and worked there with various musicians, among them Don Cherry and Michael Mantler, and formed a quartet with Enrico Rava, Johnny Dyani and Louis Moholo, which went to Argentina and was stranded there for a time. He went back to New York, but found the working climate there unresponsive, and went back to Europe, first to Italy, then to Paris, where he lived from 1970. All through the next decade he performed and recorded prolifically, putting together a quintet which had Steve Potts as a fellow saxophone voice on alto and soprano, Irene Aebi (Lacy's wife) on cello and vocal, Kent Carter's bass and Oliver Johnson's drums. Besides this group, which performed such epic pieces as 'The Woe', Lacy's response to the Vietnam war, the leader worked with improvisers of every conceivable background and began performing solo concerts. The Lacy group added Bobby Few (piano) and replaced Carter with Jean-Jacques Avenel in the 80s and carried on adding to a prodigious body of work. Lacy's sound had settled into its maturity: each note and phrase carefully laid out, the sound classical and rounded and just occasionally gargled or mutilated, one movement leading inexorably to the next even

though the spontaneity of development seems palpable. He never played fast and he never sounded ruffled. He occasionally visited America to play again, and had a brief spell on RCA's Novus imprint, but otherwise he still recorded for European labels such as hat ART and Soul Note, and took on occasional projects such as that devoted to the music of Herbie Nichols. Grander works such as The Cry (1999) mingled with more solo records (including one for John Zorn's Tzadik imprint, whose Jewish agenda Lacy seemed to regard with amusement). At the start of the new century he decided to leave Paris and return to America, but it proved to be a brief final period, since he was diagnosed with cancer and died the following year. Lacy's style and manner were so inimitable that, although many musicians claim his influence, none have ever really tried to sound like him: no other performer pursued such a particular course for so long, went into it so deeply, and yet remained absolutely themselves throughout. His body of compositions – most of them given succinct titles such as 'Stamps', 'Trickles', 'No Baby' or 'Wickets', and many with a dedication to an artist of a different discipline altogether – is a bottomless archive of ideas, and perhaps more than any other musician he quietly insisted on the links between his own work and the inspirations and motivations derived from other areas of the arts. His humorous, serious approach to the making of jazz music is already much missed by his many admirers.
*The Way* (hatOLOGY)

# Tommy Ladnier
TRUMPET
*born* 28 May 1900; *died* 4 June 1939

Ladnier's style was a somewhat rickety mix of old and new. He had arrived in Chicago around 1917 and worked with a variety of leaders, including Ollie Powers, Lovie Austin and King Oliver, and in between stints in Europe with Sam Wooding's band he worked with Fletcher Henderson in New York during 1926–7. Ladnier's sound wasn't especially lovely and he liked to emulate the wah-wah delivery of King Oliver to some extent, but his occasionally brittle phrasing nevertheless swung the line in its own way, and hearing Louis Armstrong had clearly – on the evidence of his solos with Henderson – cleaned up and streamlined his attack. The Depression left him in poor shape and he had a drink problem, but after working as a tailor in partnership with Sidney Bechet he worked with the saxophonist in the New Orleans Feetwarmers: their 1932 session for Victor is chaotic but exciting. Although he worked on and off during the 30s there wasn't much left of Ladnier's story: Hugues Panassié got him to record a final session in 1938, where he is clearly ailing, even though the playing has a bluesy poignancy about it. He died the next year of a heart attack.

*Goose Pimples* (Topaz)

## Scott LaFaro
BASS
*born* 3 April 1936; *died* 6 July 1961

LaFaro changed everything for the modern bassist. Since the swing era the bassist's role had steadily though very slowly expanded, but LaFaro put it on a fast track. He had earlier tried clarinet and saxophone but settled on the bass in his late teens, and by 1955 he was on the road, arriving in Los Angeles and playing with Chet Baker and recording with Hampton Hawes and Victor Feldman. He worked in and around California for 18 months before going to New York, where he joined the Bill Evans trio with Paul Motian. His studio and live recordings with Evans unveiled his ideas in full to a startled jazz world: instead of mere timekeeping and simple counterpoint, he drove the bass into an ensemble prominence which no other player had dared execute. The sound he got off his instrument was still substantial, but by setting the strings differently through lowering the bridge on the instrument, he allowed faster fingering, and in his playing with Evans he often sounded like a guitarist, so fleet and sensitive in timbre were his lines. Instead of simple timekeeping, he suggested a freely moving pulse, open to appropriate though not disruptive variation, and it was significant that he also fitted in well with Ornette Coleman's music: he plays on both *Free Jazz* and *Ornette* (both 1960). Much of this might have failed if LaFaro hadn't also displayed a genuine melodic gift, improvising lines with a sparkling freshness and a beautifully limber feel. If there was a downside to his inno-

vations, it came in creating the need for bassists to take on amplification (although it is surprising to observe just how clear the dazzling live music from the Evans Village Vanguard sessions is, even though they were recorded on a simple reel-to-reel with a single microphone). But LaFaro can hardly be held responsible for a development which would surely have happened anyway. It was a terrible blow to Evans and the rest of the jazz community when LaFaro was abruptly taken by a fatal car accident in July 1961. What else might he have gone on to play?

**Bill Evans,** *The Complete Live At The Village Vanguard 1971* (Fantasy)

## Guy Lafitte
TENOR SAXOPHONE
*born* 12 January 1927; *died* 10 July 1998

Lafitte was playing with gypsy bands in the late 40s but established himself in Paris around 1950, playing in various traditional to swing contexts. He had a long residency at Les Trois Mailletz in the 50s, and was with Georges Arvanitas and Christian Garros in the Paris Jazz Trio. Often sought out as a playing partner by visiting Americans, Lafitte flourished on the French festival circuit, and he developed a particular closeness with the Marciac Festival: he was in attendance there every year from 1978 until his death. A grand tenorman in the Hawkins tradition, Guy never lost his great-hearted tone: even *Crossings* (1997), a duo session with bassist Pierre Boussaguet made when the saxophonist was already ill, bursts with that wonderful sound.

*Lotus Blossom* (Black & Blue)

## Biréli Lagrène
GUITAR
*born* 4 September 1966

Lagrène was a child prodigy in the so-called gypsy tradition of guitarists, and *Routes To Django*, made when he was 14, showed him already blissfully sailing through the Reinhardt style. He quickly became a regular on the festival circuit in both Europe and the US – as much a novelty act in terms of appeal as anything else – and began working with other guitarists in the expected multi-instrument duels. His music hasn't really developed very far, but he was pretty impressive to start with and on all of his many records there are passages to either amaze or bewilder in terms of the technical bravado. Searching for a context has rather inevitably led him towards flirting with full-on jazz-rock, although on the evidence of *Front Page* (2000) he would do better to leave well alone.

**Routes To Django** (Antilles)

## Cleo Laine
VOCAL
*born* 28 October 1927

Clementina Campbell joined the Johnny Dankworth Seven in 1952 as their regular singer, Cleo Laine, and her 50s work is in some ways among her most appealing from a jazz point of view. She married Dankworth in 1958 and since then they have been seen as an inseparable musical partnership, still performing in both Britain and the US. Her broad range helped her with a stage career in the 60s, doing such musicals as *Show Boat* and *Colette*, and she has also done classical repertoire besides making a hugely successful career as an MOR singer. Her chocolatey tone and majestically mannered phrasing and diction are as individual as they come, even though the jazz-vocal historian Will Friedwald placed her in his 'Must To Avoid' category.

**Shakespeare And All That Jazz** (Fontana)

## Papa Jack Laine
DRUMS, ALTO HORN
*born* 21 September 1873; *died* 1 June 1966

Laine never recorded, but he took a noted patrician role in the earliest years of the music in New Orleans. His Reliance Brass Band, formed in the early 1890s, was basically a marching band which acted as a training ground for players who later turned out to be among the leading white (and Creole) New Orleans musicians, including Nick LaRocca, Tom Brown and Sharkey Bonano. The sound of the band was most likely akin to a military ragtime orchestra, and it was popular enough for Laine to have had up to five different Reliance bands running at any one time. He was retired from music by the time King Oliver was making records, but lived on into a very old age.

## Oliver Lake
ALTO AND SOPRANO SAXOPHONE
*born* 14 September 1942

Lake didn't come to any prominence until he had already turned 30, having worked as a teacher in St Louis and played in R&B groups. He was a founding figure in the city's Black Artists Group, but then moved to Paris in 1972 and stayed two years before moving base to New York. His 70s music, as a leader on the loft-jazz scene and in collaboration with the members of the World Saxophone Quartet, set him up as one of the major leaders of the day: records such as *Life Dance Of Is* (Antilles) suggested a populous vision where jazz, funk and poetry intermingled vividly if sometimes awkwardly. His own playing, especially on alto, had some of the jumpy exuberance of Eric Dolphy (and both *Prophet*, 1980, and *Dedicated To Dolphy*, 1994, have made Lake's debt to that musician clear), but with an earthier and more specifically bluesy bent. His Jump Up band of the 80s seemed to be stretching for crossover success, setting his solos against reggae and R&B rhythms, but the records never quite succeeded and already seem dated. Lake appears to enjoy any context where he can take an active role, but for all his more populist leanings, he is often at his most convincing when he works from a blank canvas: the solo excursion *Matador Of 1st And 1st* (1995) is a memorable summary of work done and issues considered, and his early set of duos with Julius Hemphill, *Buster Bee* (1978), still has great power and beauty. His own label Jump Up has documented his work in recent times, after previous affiliations with Black Saint and Gramavision.

**Matador Of 1st And 1st** (Jump Up)

## Ralph Lalama
TENOR SAXOPHONE
*born* 30 January 1951

Lalama is an old-school big-sounding tenorman. He came up via the last-gasp big-band grounding of Woody Herman, Buddy Rich and the Jones–Lewis Orchestra in the

70s and 80s, and has freelanced since then, although he is also an experienced teacher in New York's musical colleges. He's the kind of player who would never have enjoyed much solo documentation had it not been for a label such as Criss Cross, which has offered him a sequence of enjoyable leadership records. A large and somewhat flatly inflected sound carries the notes, which are often pawkily chosen: if Lalama can run the changes with anyone, he prefers taking his time. His brother Dave (b 1954) plays piano.
*Music For Grown-Ups* (Criss Cross)

## Nappy Lamare
GUITAR
*born* 14 June 1905; *died* 8 May 1988

The 'Nappy' came from a middle name of Napoleon, but this may have been an invention of Hilton Joseph Lamare, who came out of the New Orleans scene of the 20s to join Ben Pollack's band in 1930, and subsequently the Bob Crosby band, which he stayed with until it was disbanded in 1942. After the war he freelanced and led a Dixieland band of his own on a weekly television show, before joining forces with fellow ex-Crosbyan Ray Bauduc in a band called The Riverboat Dandies. He was still playing this kind of good-natured jazz into the 80s.
**With Ray Bauduc, *On A Swinging Date*** (Mercury)

## Donald Lambert
PIANO
*born* 12 February 1904; *died* 8 May 1962

Lambert grew up in New Jersey, and in the end spent most of his professional life there. Having taken piano lessons from his mother, he began playing in Harlem venues towards the end of the 20s and quickly gathered an impressive reputation as a leading player of the stride style. But he made no records and in 1936 he went back to New Jersey, working two long residencies there which kept him occupied right up until his death. Though he occasionally went back to his old stamping grounds, and set down four titles for Victor in 1941, his reluctance to leave his own neighbourhood has resulted in his name drifting into obscurity.

The record cited is made up of informal tapes made at Wallace's Bar, where he held his last residency.
*Meet The Lamb* (IAJRC)

## Lambert, Hendricks And Ross
VOCAL GROUP

The three cool cats were Dave Lambert, Jon Hendricks and Annie Ross, each an accomplished singer in their own right: when they were hired to record an album of Basie tunes with a group of other singers, the unsatisfactory results led the trio to re-record the whole session using just their own, overdubbed voices. *Sing A Song Of Basie* (1957) turned out to be an unexpected hit, and from there the group became a working unit, mixing scatting and vocalese to jazz melodies. For four years the group was a hot property, touring the US to great acclaim and recording four further albums (one was not inaccurately called *The Hottest New Group In Jazz*). But after Ross had to leave the band through illness, she was replaced by Yolande Bevan and the steam went out of the act, which disbanded two years later. Backed by a small group led by pianist Gildo Mahones, the music still sounds fresh, a genuine one-off which later vocal bands such as New York Voices have tried to emulate without quite catching the original zip of the trio.
*Sing A Song Of Basie* (Impulse!)

## Byard Lancaster
ALTO SAXOPHONE
*born* 6 August 1942

Lancaster energed from the Philadelphia scene (where he had worked with Sonny Sharrock and Stanley Clarke in the early 60s) and arrived in New York in 1965, recording in a Sunny Murray group for ESP and then in a broad range of playing situations. By the mid-70s he had worked with Sun Ra, McCoy Tyner and Larry Young, and had gone as far afield as working with Memphis Slim and some avant-garde rock groups, having spent time in several European countries as well as the US. These days he is based in Philadelphia again and one regular

playing partner is the cellist David Eyges. Lancaster's rough, bruising alto style has never found overwhelming favour with audiences and he is generally held in higher esteem by musicians.
**Sunny Murray,** *Quintet* (ESP)

# Harold Land
TENOR SAXOPHONE
*born* 18 February 1928; *died* 27 July 2001

Land worked locally in California before going to Los Angeles in 1954, where almost immediately he joined the Clifford Brown–Max Roach quintet. He disliked their touring schedules, though, and two years later opted for home turf by joining the LA-based Curtis Counce band. He then began making records of his own, for Contemporary and Hi-Fi. Land's astringent tone and the individuality of his ideas allowed him to stand tall in heavy company all the way through his 50s period, and his playing on such records as Counce's *Exploring The Future* (1958), *Harold In The Land Of Jazz* (1958) and above all the outstanding *The Fox* (1959) seems as fresh and absorbing as it was five decades ago. He recorded much less in the 60s, but Gerald Wilson featured him as a soloist on several of his orchestral records, and in the 70s he began leading a cooperative venture with Blue Mitchell. By this time he had let John Coltrane's music get under his skin, and he sounds like a more calculating, less spontaneous musician, but by the time of his valedictory *A Lazy Afternoon* (1994) he seems at peace with everything he's heard in jazz. Known only to diligent admirers of the music, he is one of many musicians whose reputation deserves to be greater.
**The Fox** (Hi Fi/OJC)

# Art Lande
PIANO
*born* 1 January 1947

A somewhat mysterious figure, Lande is originally from New York but was playing keyboards on the West Coast in the early 70s, with Steve Swallow and others. His great moment came when he formed a quartet (with Mark Isham, Bill Douglass and Glenn Cronkhite), Rubisa Patrol: their eponymous 1976 album for ECM is enduringly beautiful. Since then he has surfaced occasionally, often in illustrious company – recording with Gary Peacock, Isham and Nguyên Lê – but often delivering playing which sounds more like New Age noodling than anything with a jazz backbone. He is still based on the West Coast.
**Rubisa Patrol** (ECM)

# Nils Landgren
TROMBONE, VOCAL
*born* 15 February 1956

Landgren grew up in rural Sweden and played drums in his town marching band before taking up the trombone (his mother was a Jack Teagarden fan). He studied in Stockholm before joining the rock group Blue Swede, and ever since he has divided his time between rock, funk and jazz. He founded the first edition of the Landgren Unit in the early 80s before establishing a large-scale soul band, which didn't last long ('We were too jazzy for the rock clubs, and not jazzy enough for the jazz clubs'). This eventually led to the Landgren Funk Unit, which mixes James Brown with straight-ahead hard bop, and includes sidemen such as Esbjörn Svensson. But Landgren has also investigated his Swedish folk roots in projects such as *Swedish Folk* (ACT, 1997), a series of acoustic duets with Svensson which are disarmingly lovely. It's perhaps to be hoped that he doesn't entirely neglect that side of his music, since recent work has found him heading up what may be a dead end of imitation funk.
**Fonk Da World** (ACT)

# Steve Lane
CORNET
*born* 7 November 1921

Lane is one of the longest-serving bandleaders in British jazz. He began playing with his own trad groups in the early 50s and was still attempting to perfect an idiom which he sees as representative of a golden age some 50 years later. Ragtime became an obsession early on, and while Colyer and Barber largely left that music behind, Lane continued to mix authentic rags into sets that were otherwise devoted to blues and more familiar trad staples. He co-founded the VJM label, which documented his own work over many years as well as putting out many important reissues. Lane's groups (usually going under the name The Southern Stompers) sometimes sounded excessively proper and tight, but since he wasn't seeking anything loose or wild, he got the result he wanted. Hardly any of his work has made it to CD so far. He had a profound distaste for the way the music business went: as long ago as 1973, he said that 'if Louis Armstrong came along today he probably wouldn't make it'.

*Just Gone* (Major Minor)

## Eddie Lang
GUITAR
*born* 25 October 1902; *died* 26 March 1933

Born Salvatore Massaro, he studied violin in his home town of Philadelphia but changed to guitar and began playing duets with his school friend Joe Venuti. In 1924 he joined Red McKenzie's group The Mound City Blue Blowers, which toured the US and even spent a season in London (influencing such groups as The Gilt-Edged Four), and when he returned to New York he was quickly in huge demand as a sessionman, for singers, dance-band dates and small-group hot music. Among the bands he performed with live were those of Roger Wolfe Kahn, Jean Goldkette and Adrian Rollini, and in the studios he continued his partnership with Venuti, cutting duets, sessions by the Venuti Blue Four and a few dates by the 'Ed Lang Orchestra'. He played duets with the blues guitarist Lonnie Johnson and cut a memorable date with Johnson and King Oliver under the band title The Gin Bottle Four: in both cases he was labelled as 'Blind Willie Dunn'. Lang's facility, single-string solos and lovely, singing tone set him apart from every other white guitarist of the time. Solo records such as 'April Kisses' hint at a Neapolitan sweetness in his make-up, but the sides with Venuti and a title such as Tommy Dorsey's version of 'Tiger Rag', where Lang plays whiplash accompaniment, show a more pugnacious talent. He tends to play the rhythm role in his duos with Johnson, but brings great invention to it, and his all-round skill helped push the guitar into an ascendancy over banjo as the

rhythm-section instrument of choice. In 1929, he and Venuti joined the Paul Whiteman orchestra, and Lang was subsequently put on a retainer as Bing Crosby's accompanist. But he died, possibly through being over-anaesthetized, following an operation on his tonsils, after having suffered throat problems for a number of months. He left a huge legacy of recordings – Raymond Mitchell's Lang discography runs to more than 350 pages and details hundreds of sessions – and a standard for all later guitarists to aspire to.

*Joe Venuti & Eddie Lang* (JSP)

## Don Lanphere
TENOR AND SOPRANO SAXOPHONES
*born* 26 June 1928; *died* 12 October 2003

For many years Lanphere remained something of a mystery to bebop fans. He recorded a handful of small-group sides at the end of the 40s with Fats Navarro and Max Roach, and his solos on 'Go' and 'Stop' (issued by New Jazz in 1949) are exciting enough to make one shout for more. After some big-band work, though, he was arrested for narcotics possession and he subsequently worked primarily at his parents' music shop in Wenatchee, Washington. He reappeared towards the end of the 50s and rejoined the Woody Herman band for a spell, but he was in trouble with the law again in 1961 and left music altogether for a long time. In the 80s, after a religious conversion and a long period of rehabilitation, he got his career going again, and enjoyed something of an Indian summer for the independent Hep label, working with Larry Coryell and Bud Shank among others. He resettled in Seattle and taught, playing occasional gigs until shortly before his death. The quicksilver delivery of old throttled back a little, but Lanphere remained a skilful exponent of his bop-derived improvising.

*Don Lanphere/Larry Coryell* (Hep)

## John LaPorta
ALTO SAXOPHONE, CLARINET
*born* 1 April 1920

LaPorta may be a minor figure, but he deserves better than the snooty dismissals he has elicited in some quarters. Having played in the big bands of Bob Chester and Woody Herman he began studying with Lennie Tristano in 1946, and seven years later he joined Charles Mingus and Teo Macero in forming the Jazz Composers' Workshop, recording with both of those leaders as a sideman. LaPorta's best work was as a clarinettist, particularly on the record cited, although the little-known *The Most Minor* (Everest), though virtually impossible to find, is worth hearing. Both show a Tristano-derived style given a dryly passionate airing. But LaPorta mostly worked in education from then on, serving on the Berklee faculty for many years and writing for the bands there.

**The Clarinet Artistry Of John LaPorta** (Fantasy)

# Ellis Larkins

PIANO

*born* 15 May 1923; *died* 29 September 2002

A gracious gentleman of the piano for decades, Larkins was a prodigy, playing Mozart in Baltimore when only 11, but steady work in jazz clubs brought him to New York, where he worked regularly at such Manhattan haunts as The Blue Angel and Café Society in the 40s and 50s. Besides solo and trio work, his other great forte was as an accompanist to singers. Some of Ella Fitzgerald's best work of the early LP era (such as *Ella Sings Gershwin*, 1950) has Larkins at the piano, and he later worked with Joe Williams and particularly Anita Ellis. His distillation of what he liked in Tatum, Wilson and others came out as singularly his own: the melody carefully out front, and what he called a 'kind of imaginary big band, which directs the voicings' when he played an improvisation. Deferring to singers over many years helped him acquire a sly elegance which made one realize that he was often directing the music even as he appeared to be merely comping. He carried on playing in clubs and taverns and listening rooms into the 90s. Larkins led only a handful of albums over the years, but the duets with Ruby Braff on Irving Berlin tunes have a special appeal.

**With Ruby Braff, *Calling Berlin Vol 1*** (Arbors)

# Pete La Roca

DRUMS

*born* 7 April 1938

He remains best known by this name, which he adopted when doing regular work as a timbale player in New York Latin bands, but Peter Sims is the one he prefers these days. He came to prominence in the later 50s in New York's hard-bop circles, and was a regular in the Blue Note studios, getting one featured album (*Basra*, 1965, long a collectors' favourite) as well as a host of sideman appearances. As the 60s wore on, though, he found musical styles turning in a direction which displeased him, and he more or less stopped playing and qualified as a lawyer. He began leading occasional groups again at the start of the 80s and it was a nice touch when Blue Note again gave him a record date in 1997, where he led a strong band of veterans including Dave Liebman and Jimmy Owens. A thoughtful and smartly accomplished musician.

**Basra** (Blue Note)

# Nick LaRocca & The Original Dixieland Jazz Band

CORNET

*born* 11 April 1889; *died* 22 February 1961

LaRocca was committed to the idea that jazz came into being under his direction, and as a white New Orleans brass player he was at least in the right city. In the teens of the new century he fell in with other young musicians eager to try and play the new hot music, and while on a trip to Chicago with Johnny Stein's Dixie Jass Band he and trombonist Eddie Edwards formed a breakaway unit, which came to be called the Original Dixieland Jass Band. When they took the group to New York they were a sensation: they rattled the fixtures when they played at Resenweber's restaurant, and rocked post-war smart society. By beating Freddie Keppard (who was suspicious of recording) to the punch, they became the first group to make jazz records, in 1917. LaRocca's drive kept the ODJB going until 1925, and took them around the world, including a long stay in London and an audience with King George (they made him laugh). While the

group was, artistically speaking, almost at a standstill as early as 1919, its imprint was indelible: staple tunes such as 'Livery Stable Blues', 'Clarinet Marmalade' and 'Tiger Rag' still follow the ODJB's model to this day when played by revivalist bands. LaRocca himself was a big influence on Bix Beiderbecke, and relished his limelight: 'I confess we're musical anarchists!' he told one reporter. But once New York's dance bands had assimilated the ODJB's energies, the Originals began to sound stuck in a single groove, and LaRocca, exhausted, disbanded the group in 1925. There was a brief reunion in the middle 30s, but it was too early for real revivalism at that point and LaRocca went back to his home city, earning his living in the building trade. Unrepentant, he insisted to his last breath that he and his gang were the real originators of jazz, as their publicity machine had once asserted. Their records today sound like ancient history; yet nothing quite dims the fuming, clangorous sound which the ODJB sent around the world.
*The Original Dixieland Jazz Band 1917–1921* (Timeless)

## Prince Lasha
ALTO SAXOPHONE, FLUTE
*born* 10 September 1929

One of the Fort Worth community of players who worked locally with Ornette Coleman in the 50s, Lasha then moved to California in the middle 50s and while there made two albums for Contemporary which might, in their way, have made up something towards a West Coast manifesto for the new music (Sonny Simmons was also on them both). But they didn't really lead him anywhere: he went to New York and recorded with Eric Dolphy (*Iron Man*), but then moved to Europe before going back to California. In the 70s and 80s he surfaced only rarely. His slightly reedy alto sound and woodsy flute are individual enough, but the documentation doesn't amount to much.
*The Cry* (Contemporary)

## Last Exit
GROUP

An improvising supergroup which lasted for a few explosive records and years. Bill Laswell (bass) was quite likely the prime mover in assembling the band, which also included Peter Brötzmann (saxophones), Sonny Sharrock (guitar) and Ronald Shannon Jackson (drums). Their live appearances were very loud and hugely exhilarating, and it helped that the four men were players who worked at a high creative level rather than semi-competents armed with too much power. It is hard to choose between their few records, mostly derived from live shows, and the one cited must have given Herbie Hancock (who sits in on one track) a fright. The death of Sharrock in 1994 brought the group to an end, although it rarely performed in the 90s in any case.
*The Noise Of Trouble* (Enemy)

## Bill Laswell
BASS
*born* 12 February 1955

Laswell probably wouldn't see himself as any kind of jazz musician, but he has had an important influence on a generation of players who see jazz as, at least, a central part of their musical make-up. Born in Salem, Illinois, he arrived in New York in 1978 and quickly became a central figure in the city's No-Wave movement, where punk, funk and the avant-garde were stirred into a multicultural mix that mirrored some of the then-current upheavals in rock music, from a more self-consciously 'artistic' perspective. Art music is, perhaps, Laswell's idiom: as much as he has drawn on popular musics, rhythms and textures, he is no more a 'street' musician than was Charlie Parker. For a time in the 80s he was a hot producer in the popular field, following a major hit with Herbie Hancock's 'Rockit' (1983), and he helmed projects for Mick Jagger and Motorhead as well as running the Celluloid and Axiom labels, where anyone from Billy Bang to Buddy Miles could be making records. His most renowned setting as a performing musician, after the initial impact of his group Material, was the supergroup Last Exit, with Ronald Shannon Jackson, Peter Brötzmann and Sonny Sharrock. His Miles

Davis remix project *Panthalassa* (1998) was perhaps not quite as controversial as some might have expected. Laswell is a taciturn, deadpan figure of completely unshockable disposition, whose time may have passed: the all-inclusive nature of his projects and philosophy are no longer so novel in a world obsessed with eclecticism, and maybe even he has run low on new stones to overturn.
**Baselines** (Elektra)

# Yusef Lateef
SAXOPHONES, OTHER WIND INSTRUMENTS
*born* 9 October 1920

The remarkable Lateef has been playing jazz for more than 60 years. He started on alto, then switched to tenor, and in the 40s worked with Lucky Millinder and Ernie Fields before settling in Chicago in 1949. He was briefly with Dizzy Gillespie's big band but had to leave owing to his wife's illness. At this time he was still plain Bill Evans, but he changed to Yusef Lateef when he became a Muslim. Now in Detroit, he began working again in the mid-50s and made small-group records for Savoy and Prestige, mostly on tenor, though he also took up flute at Kenny Burrell's suggestion. At this point he sounds like a bluff, hard-swinging tenorman in the grand manner, and these records offer much straightforwardly enjoyable blowing. But as the Detroit scene declined, Lateef relocated to New York around 1960, and besides leading his own groups he joined Cannonball Adderley's band for two years from 1962, an attractively dark foil to the leader's customary cheeriness. He also began making records for Impulse!, an association which produced some of his best work: the first, *Jazz 'Round The World* (1963), showcased his new interest in bassoon, oboe, shenai and argol, and the subsequent *Live At Pep's* (1964) showed them in a live context. In the later 60s and 70s he moved labels to Atlantic, and made some of his most extravagant work, several records mixing up jazz, funk, gospel, poetry, assorted grunting and weird electronics, and latterly these moved in the direction of near Muzak. In 1981, he spent four years teaching in Nigeria, and since his return he has continued on a course which might be described as Yusef's world music: his own label, YAL, has documented sprawling works which seem to be couched in a discouraging dialect of New Age mysticism, sometimes in collaboration with the Californian drummer Adam Rudolph, and the music has been wispy and insubstantial to match. Yet there have also been some remarkable two-tenor fisticuffs with the likes of Archie Shepp, Von Freeman, Ricky Ford and René McLean, which suggest that Lateef's prowess on tenor remains considerable. An enigmatic man.
**Live At Pep's** (Impulse!)

# Latin jazz

Given the rich diversity of popular and folk musics which exist in South America, grouping their collective fusion with American jazz as 'Latin jazz' does seem a patronizing simplification. But the term has come to signify any blending of jazz with a prominent streak of Latin American music. This usually works out as a jazz instrumentation of horns set against one of the dance rhythms which typify Latin music. Historically, there has been an element of Latin music in jazz from the beginning. Habanera and tango rhythms can be heard in some ragtime music, and the tango in particular suggests the 'Spanish tinge' which Jelly Roll Morton loved, and which featured in such Morton tunes as 'The Crave'. But it wasn't until the 40s, with the arrival of Machito on the New York bandleading scene, and the pioneering fusions sponsored by Dizzy Gillespie in his big-band music, which resulted in the arrival of such signature themes as 'Manteca', that a specific strain of Latin jazz came into being. Over the next ten years, the 'Latin number' became a regular element on records and in live sets, with new steps such as the mambo and the cha cha cha becoming familiar to dancers (even Perry Como declared that 'Papa Loves Mambo'), and hard-bop composers such as Horace Silver tinkering with Latin rhythms in their writing. These were duly followed in turn by the bossa nova and the samba in the next decade, both imports from Brazil, while Cuba provided the style that came to be called salsa, although this has for the most part remained a dance music which otherwise has little to do with jazz. As these various flavours have become more universal, the idea of Latin jazz has become more blurred, and by the end of the century it had become, like such terms as 'fusion' and 'world jazz', all but impossible to define with any specificity.

# Christof Lauer
TENOR AND SOPRANO SAXOPHONES
*born* 25 May 1953

Lauer's playing mixes the brawny, impassive power which is Michael Brecker's bequest to a generation of saxophonists, with a more classical emotional backwash sometimes intruding into his improvising: on ballads, when he's simply playing the tune and steering clear of note-spinning, he's at his best. His early playing in the 70s was done in bands in both Germany and Austria (where he studied for a time) and since then he has figured in many situations: with Jasper van't Hof, Joachim Kühn, Volker Kriegel, Carla Bley and the United Jazz And Rock Ensemble. His own records give the impression of a huge, sometimes loutish sound which he has difficulty in directing towards a real result, but in cooler moments he can be very impressive.
*Evidence* (CMP)

# Cy Laurie
CLARINET
*born* 20 April 1926; *died* 18 April 2002

A Londoner who – like many other clarinettists in the British trad movement – modelled his playing on that of Johnny Dodds, Laurie led his own bands through the 50s and ran a popular club in London's West End. He had some illustrious sidemen and associates, but by the end of the decade other musicians had overtaken him and he gave up on music altogether, going to India to meditate and proving himself ahead of The Beatles at least. He returned to Britain and by the early 70s was based in Essex: everything had, of course, changed, but Laurie's capable playing still won audiences and he continued working in revivalist programmes into the 80s.
*Blows Blue Hot* (Lake)

# Elliot Lawrence
BANDLEADER, PIANO
*born* 14 February 1925

Lawrence's big bands were really superior dance orchestras, but he was himself a useful arranger and pianist and he commissioned scores by some of the better composers of the period. He worked in this capacity on and around the East Coast during the 50s and among his seven albums for Fantasy were *Plays Gerry Mulligan Arrangements* and *Swinging At The Steel Pier* (both 1956), the latter featuring charts by Al Cohn. He continued bandleading into the 60s but became increasingly involved in TV work, which he was still doing in the 90s.
*Elliot Lawrence Plays Gerry Mulligan Arrangements* (Fantasy)

# Hubert Laws
FLUTE, SAXOPHONES
*born* 10 November 1939

The elder of the two horn-playing Laws brothers, Hubert studied classical music in his native Houston and was a founder member of The Jazz Crusaders (before they took that name). In the 60s he did studio and sideman work and made some sets of his own for Atlantic: by this time he had begun to specialize on flute, and in the 70s he mixed jazz situations with classical work, occasionally trying to bridge the two genres, notably with a series of sets for CTI. An impeccable technician, Hubert has settled for mediocre recordings: he may have helped legitimize the flute as a jazz horn, but the results have been profoundly unmemorable, although his various sponsors have clearly had no ambition to challenge him. Brother Ronnie (b 1950) has gone the soul-jazz route on tenor, and has really fared no better.
*The Laws Of Jazz* (Atlantic)

# Hugh Lawson
PIANO
*born* 12 March 1935; *died* 11 March 1997

Lawson began working in his native Detroit in the mid-50s, with Yusef Lateef and others, and moved to New York to freelance later in the decade. He worked as a sideman in many post-bop groups all through the 60s, 70s and 80s, and while he was a generous technician and a fine accompanist, little he did as a soloist or leader really caught the imagination. Perhaps his most notable hour came when he helped organize a group of seven pianists called The Piano Choir: two albums for Strata East documented their work in the early 70s.

**The Piano Choir,** *Handscapes I* (Strata East)

## Yank Lawson

TRUMPET
*born* 3 May 1911; *died* 18 February 1995

Lawson joined Ben Pollack's band in 1933 and from there became one of the major soloists in the new Bob Crosby band. He quit in a quarrel over money and then joined Tommy Dorsey. In the 40s he worked mainly as a freelance: his big sound and full-of-beans approach to playing blues enlivened most of the bands he was in, and he was rarely short of a gig. But in 1951 he joined up with his old Crosby associate Bob Haggart in the Lawson–Haggart Jazz Band, recording a string of albums for Decca which saw them through the decade, even though some of them were frankly commercial. In the 60s he was playing more at reunions of old comrades than anything, but the Lawson–Haggart combination came together again in The World's Greatest Jazz Band, which started in 1968 and lasted ten years. In his 70s and 80s, Lawson still played with much of his old fire and he was a father figure among the remaining originals of American Dixieland. He was still on tour when he suffered a fatal heart attack at 83.

***Ole Dixie*** (ABC-Paramount)

## Daunik Lazro

ALTO AND BARITONE SAXOPHONES
*born* 2 April 1945

Like many European saxophonists of a particular age, Lazro started under the spell of Sidney Bechet: but free jazz was what he ended up playing, at the beginning of the 70s. Some of his early work was recorded by hat Hut, and Lazro also worked alongside that label's great subject, Joe McPhee. But the 80s weren't especially kind to him as far

as recording opportunities were concerned, and only recently has he been more visible again. He comes from Chantilly, and try as he might to sound biting and angry, there's a sweetness and even some Gallic charm at the heart of his music, which comes out particularly well in the disc cited below, a series of duets with violinist Carlos Zingaro.

***Hauts Plateaux*** (Potlatch)

## Nguyên Lê

GUITAR
*born* 14 January 1959

Born in Paris but of Vietnamese parentage, Lê has brought an unusual background into jazz. He has made specific reference to his roots on the *Tales From Viêt-Nam* record (1995), but this is rather less successful than some of his other projects, which lend a more personal touch to jazz, rock and fusion material. While his own style seems to derive mostly from such American models as Jimi Hendrix and Bill Frisell, his best music suggests that he can put his own spin on what is now a very crowded and overbearingly eclectic idiom. He mostly works with his own groups and in the company of such as Marc Johnson, Peter Erskine and Danny Gottlieb, but he has also toured with Tommy Smith.

***Three Trios*** (ACT)

## Joëlle Léandre

BASS
*born* 12 September 1951

Although Léandre is a prominent name in free improvisation, her background is in contemporary composition rather than jazz. She studied in Paris in the late 60s and subsequently did the same in Buffalo, NY, where she worked with both Morton Feldman and John Cage. On her return to Europe later in the 70s she moved towards free playing and for the past 20 years she has been among the major voices on her instrument, working with many of the premier free players in Europe, Japan and the US. Records have only rarely captured the impact of her in-person performances, which are always intensely dramatic and often feature her wordless vocalizing. She has made something of a speciality out of

the duo format, often with other bassists, including William Parker and Kazue Sawai.
*C'Est Ça* (Red Toucan)

## Mike LeDonne
PIANO, ORGAN
*born* 26 October 1956

LeDonne studied at the New England Conservatory and settled himself into the New York scene in the early 80s. Since then he has held down some strong sideman gigs with such groups as the Art Farmer–Clifford Jordan Quintet and as one of Milt Jackson's regular accompanists. In the 90s he came to more prominence as a leader, recording extensively for Criss Cross and Double-Time. While he mostly plays his own forceful take on bop piano, he sometimes moves over to the Hammond organ, and is a notably deft executant on that instrument.
*Waltz For An Urbanite* (Criss Cross)

## Jeanne Lee
VOCAL
*born* 29 January 1939; *died* 24 October 2000

A challenging, powerful and strikingly individual singer, Lee died without ever really reaching the public or the attention which her talents merited: even in the most popular category of jazz performers, there are some who never get a break. While she started on the Ella Fitzgerald route by winning a talent contest at the Harlem Apollo, Lee then studied modern dance at college and began working in a duo with pianist Ran Blake, which won some critical raves early on (for *The Newest Sound Around*, RCA, 1961) but never came to much public attention. In 1964 she moved to California, and on a 1967 visit to Europe she began working with Gunter Hampel, whom she later married. She often performed with Hampel's groups, into the 80s, and also worked with such spirits of the avant-garde as Anthony Braxton and Cecil Taylor. In the 90s her voice remained a grand and moving instrument, as what was probably her final featured record, *After Hours* (Owl, 1994), demonstrated: a duo with Mal Waldron, it fields a remarkable intensity. But Lee seemed caught between art-music, improvisation and a more accessible kind of jazz sing-

ing, and while she is in some ways a comparable figure to Betty Carter, she remains even less well known to the wider audience for jazz singing.
*The Newest Sound Around* (RCA)

## Julia Lee
PIANO, VOCAL
*born* 13 October 1902; *died* 8 December 1958

Julia Lee And Her Boy Friends were a popular act for Capitol Records in the 40s: it was actually a studio band of varying personnel, which the lissom-voiced Lee fronted in a light-toned variation on the up-and-coming R&B idiom, mixing winsome ballads with saucier material such as 'King Size Papa'. Actually, Lee was already a veteran performer. She had been performing in Kansas City theatres as far back as 1916, subsequently in the context of the group fronted by her brother George (1896–1958), a minor local bandleader. She remained a local favourite in the city for most of her life, and was still making records into the 50s.

## Tony Lee
PIANO
*born* 23 July 1934; *died* 2 March 2004

Lee was one of the great stalwarts of the London post-war scene, and his trio worked for some 40 years (from 1961) as the informal in-house rhythm section at West London's venerable venue The Bull's Head, in addition to which he played countless small gigs all over the city. A lightly swinging player in the Hank Jones manner, whose occasional records were a pendant to a career which all but defined the journeyman role of the local jazz musician in England.
*Close To You* (Mainstem)

## Cliff Leeman
DRUMS
*born* 10 September 1913; *died* 26 April 1986

A veteran of scores of Dixieland and big-band playing situations, Leeman put in close to half a century of work in jazz. He grew up in Portland and worked in both classical music and variety before joining Artie Shaw in 1937. Thereafter he worked under many of the major swing bandleaders in the 30s and in several small groups in the 40s. In the 50s he gravitated to the Eddie Condon circle of players and struck up an alliance with Yank Lawson and Bob Haggart, which led to his appearing on most of their records. In the 60s and 70s he played with Peanuts Hucko, Bobby Hackett, Joe Venuti and others, and was in the final edition of The World's Greatest Jazz Band.

**Eddie Condon,** *Jam Session Coast To Coast* (Columbia)

## Gene Lees
WRITER
*born* 8 February 1928

A piercingly shrewd commentator who is nevertheless prone to tremendous bouts of narcissism and tunnel vision, Lees is one of the more vivid American writers on the music. He was editor of *Down Beat* for a time, and has published jazz biographies and collections of critical writing; he is also a capable lyricist and has worked with several distinguished composers in that category. But he is probably most famous (or notorious) for his Newsletter, a private monthly publication which mixes his often one-sided rhetoric with more considered essay work.

## Michel Legrand
PIANO, COMPOSER
*born* 24 February 1932

A pretty good piano player in a lightly boppish style, Legrand's real talents are as composer and arranger. After studying in Paris, he was turning out commercial arrangements before he was 20 and soon flew to prominence as a composer of film scores. Songs such as 'What Are You Doing The Rest Of Your Life' have made his fortune, but Legrand has never left behind his jazz interests: he made a one-off classic in *Legrand Jazz* (1958), a striking set of arrangements which brought together Miles Davis, Ben Webster and John Coltrane on the same sessions; he has cut occasional discs where he leads small groups from the piano; he completed two gorgeous collaborations with Stéphane Grappelli, *Legrand Grappelli* (1992)

and *Douce France* (1995), which were among the violinist's favourite sessions; and he formed a big band in the 90s which reinterpreted some of his great hits. A martinet in the studio and not one to suffer fools with good grace, Legrand's jazz adventures may only have been executed when they suited him, but they have surely been worth documenting.

*Legrand Jazz* (Philips)

## Peter Leitch
GUITAR
*born* 19 August 1944

Leitch grew up in Montreal and played locally there and in Toronto before moving to New York in 1983. There he has mostly led his own small groups and played in duos with, in particular, Gary Bartz, John Hicks and Ray Drummond. He has been extensively recorded by the New York independent Reservoir. On most of the several records, Leitch sounds like a very wise and experienced head: his playing has much of the quiet, cooled elegance of Jim Hall, allied to a more straightforwardly boppish approach and an ability to play easily next to such different players as Bartz and Hicks.

*Colours And Dimensions* (Reservoir)

## Brian Lemon
PIANO
*born* 11 February 1937

A pro's pro, Brian Lemon has been an anchorman in British jazz for 40 years. He grew up in Nottingham and was working at the local Palais at 16 while visiting the two local jazz clubs, and he still likes the trad and Dixieland that got him into jazz. On arriving in London in the 60s, he found there were many opportunities for a pianist: cocktail bar gigs, BBC work at Maida Vale, or depping for Dudley Moore at The Establishment Club. Visting Americans, from Milt Jackson onwards, liked Lemon's unflappable and perfectly apt style, and he has worked with players of most temperaments ('I never play with anybody far out because I don't feel that kind of thing, but I bend slightly without realizing it'). Only occasionally working as any kind of bandleader, in the 90s Lemon found a patron in

John Bune, whose independent label Zephyr has put together a catalogue of more than 30 CDs, most of them featuring the pianist in some capacity. As Bune says, 'there isn't anybody who doesn't want to play with him'. In the last couple of years, though, arthritis has slowed down the otherwise unconquerable Lemon.

*But Beautiful* (Zephyr)

## Leo
RECORD LABEL

Founded by and named after (his daughter's idea) Russian émigré Leo Feigin, this British label was established in London in 1980 primarily to document what was underground jazz coming out – smuggled out, usually – from the then USSR. Its first releases included important material by The Ganelin Trio, Vladimir Chekasin and others, and Feigin's almost single-handed devotion to this music and the cause of its artists helped bring them to the West. Since perestroika, some of the revolutionary chic has left the label, but Feigin had long since diversified in any case. He now operates out of a rural location in Devon, where he has built a catalogue stretching into hundreds of releases, mostly of new jazz and free music: among those who have contributed major records to the list are Anthony Braxton, Sun Ra, Cecil Taylor, Evan Parker, The Remote Viewers, Mat Maneri and many others. The ebullient Leo continues making new discoveries among his artists and there is no more enthusiastic spokesman for his missionary work.

## Harlan Leonard
SAXOPHONES, BANDLEADER
*born* 2 July 1905; *died* 10 November 1983

Leonard joined Bennie Moten's band in Kansas City as early as 1923, and he was still there in 1931, when he went with the breakaway unit under Thamon Hayes, the Kansas City Sky Rockets. This group he took over in due course, and as Harlan Leonard's Rockets they became the most popular band in the city in the later 30s. Concentrating on local turf, the band never aspired to the nationwide success which Count Basie went on to enjoy, and good though they clearly were

there are only 23 recorded tracks to remember them by, all recorded in 1940. Henry Bridges (tenor) and Fred Beckett (trombone) were among the soloists, and there are six arrangements by the young Tadd Dameron, but in the end Leonard became a footnote in the history. He disbanded in 1945, and eventually spent his remaining working years as an IRS official.

*Harlan Leonard 1940* (Classics)

## Bill Le Sage
PIANO, VIBES
*born* 20 January 1927; *died* 31 October 2002

Formerly starring on ukulele and drums, Le Sage came out of the army in 1948 and worked in John Dankworth's groups. He took a few lessons from Lennie Tristano while in New York in 1950, and began to try his hand at vibes in 1953, which he went on to play in Kenny Baker's Dozen. He co-led a group with Ronnie Ross for much of the 60s and also led a ten-strong band called Directions In Jazz, before forming the Bebop Preservation Society in 1969, which turned out to be an occasional but long-lasting repertory band. Unpretentiously skilful on both piano and vibes, Le Sage's book of compositions could do with a second look.

*Pied Piper Of Hamelin* (Spotlite)

## Jack Lesberg
BASS
*born* 14 February 1920

A Bostonian, Lesberg played violin before having to fill in on bass in the group he was working in. This led to his working in New York, where he played with such diverse figures as Willie 'The Lion' Smith and Leonard Bernstein (classical stuff). He became a regular in the Condon circle, and from there went on to work with, to resort to the cliché, too many leaders to mention, although what he mostly played was Dixieland of some kind. He was still playing all through the 80s.

**Bobby Hackett,** *Live At The Roosevelt Grill* (Chiaroscuro)

# Stan Levey
DRUMS
*born* 5 April 1926; *died* 19 April 2005

Raised in Philadelphia, Levey started out as a boxer, and at first the fight game sustained him even after he'd moved to New York and begun moving through some distinguished company (Coleman Hawkins, Thelonious Monk, Art Tatum); but too many minor injuries obliged him to concentrate on the kit. Although not usually considered as a leader among bop drummers, Levey nevertheless played for most of the major boppers yet was less lucky with being in on the right recording sessions. He played with all sorts of leaders and in big bands too, eventually settling into the regular spot as Stan Kenton's drummer between 1952 and 1954. That took him to California, where he liked the air, and he stayed there throughout the 50s, busy with session-work and with numerous leaders, and happy to back up either Stan Getz or Ben Webster or Dexter Gordon. In the 60s he took to playing for singers, joining the Paul Smith Trio while they were supporting Ella Fitzgerald, but some of the enjoyment had gone out of it for him and he eventually chose to move from music to his second love, photography, which has preoccupied him since. Levey's unobtrusiveness has perhaps told against his receiving wider recognition: a crisp, exacting kind of attack (very different to, say, Shelly Manne's) allowed him to propel the group with superb effectiveness without dominating the sound. As busy as he was in the studios, he only ever led four albums himself.
***Stanley The Steamer*** (Bethlehem)

# Milcho Leviev
PIANO
*born* 19 December 1937

In the UK at least, Leviev is still known mainly for a stint as the leader of a quartet which had Art Pepper as its saxophonist (1980), but he has had a considerable career either side of that. He studied in Sofia and directed both the Bulgarian radio big band and the Sofia Philharmonic during the 60s. He departed for West Germany in 1970 and a year later went to the US, where he eventually became a citizen. In the 70s he had a long association with Don Ellis, and in the

80s he tried his hand at jazz-rock in the group Free Flight before steady work in California, and eventually a senior post in jazz education. Leviev's straightforward post-bop style hasn't received much attention on record and he has made only a small number of discs for minor labels.
***Blues For The Fisherman*** (Mole)

# Rod Levitt
TROMBONE
*born* 16 September 1929

Levitt will remain forgotten until some enterprising soul reissues in full his marvellous sequence of Octet records from the mid-60s (one for Riverside, which has now reappeared, and three for RCA). A capable trombonist with the likes of Dizzy Gillespie and Sy Oliver in the late 50s, Levitt might have stayed as merely a name in the brass section if he hadn't formed the eight-piece group which recorded the albums in question – a fascinating sequence of sessions where Levitt's originals cover a broad stylistic range involving satire, impressionism and much closely patterned musical argument. Besides Levitt himself, the star player in a band of comparative nobodies is trumpeter Rolf Ericson, but the whole group shines, and the music compares very handsomely with similar sessions by George Russell and Gil Evans (Levitt did, indeed, play on Evans's *Pacific Standard Time* sessions in 1959). The difference may lie in the trombonist's wry and sometimes mordant humour. Unfortunately, the records took him nowhere, and after 1966 he spent much of his time running a company which made commercials.
***Solid Ground*** (RCA)

# Jed Levy
TENOR SAXOPHONE
*born* 12 August 1958

Levy studied in Boston in the 70s and was closely influenced by the teaching of Jaki Byard, 'of all the great musicians I have worked with, one of the only ones I would call a genius'. Since then he has worked as a freelance in New York and Boston. Levy's only rarely been featured as a leader on record, but on the basis of his two

Steeplechase albums he is a tenor player of sometimes overwhelming strength and authority, an almost classical player taking a very different course to the Michael Brecker model.

*Sleight Of Hand* (Steeplechase)

# Lou Levy

PIANO

*born* 5 March 1928; *died* 23 January 2001

Although a Chicagoan who worked in both that city and New York in the early part of his career, Levy is known primarily as a West Coast player. He was with Woody Herman's Second Herd in 1948, but after this took time away from music and in 1955 he established himself on the Los Angeles scene. Stan Getz liked him as an accompanist: Levy is on *West Coast Jazz* (1956) and *The Steamer* (1957), and the pianist worked him with Getz again on and off into the 90s. While also doing sideman work with many of the West Coast's usual suspects, he was further prized as an accompanist by singers, and played frequently with Peggy Lee, Ella Fitzgerald, Anita O'Day and June Christy. A gracious adjunct to a voice or a soloist, Levy's playing when soloing had a tougher, more virtuosic streak, with his Powell and Tatum influences melting into a powerful matrix of his own. Some late albums for Verve, made at Jean-Philippe Allard's instigation, include some of his best work. Lou was much liked by the LA musical establishment: an enduring problem with narcotics led to a final period of rehabilitation which Herb Alpert provided.

*Lunarcy* (Verve)

# George Lewis

CLARINET

*born* 13 July 1900; *died* 31 December 1968

Bunk Johnson may have been the fountainhead of the New Orleans revival, but Lewis was its real father figure and its enduring icon. Born George Joseph François Louis Zeno, he didn't start on the clarinet until he was around 18, and he began working in New Orleans in the early 20s, with Buddy Petit and his own New Orleans Stompers. He was busy throughout the 20s but never worked outside the city and as a result never made any records. Work was scarcer in the 30s, and though he was still playing in dance halls he also had a regular job as a stevedore. When Bunk Johnson made his first records in 1942, one of the session organizers, David Stuart, went to see Lewis at Johnson's suggestion: 'I never saw such a clarinet in all my life, held together by elastic bands and bits of wire. Then he stood there and played like an angel.' Lewis then recorded regularly with Johnson (though the two men eventually had a somewhat stormy relationship) and Kid Shots Madison, as well as with his own groups. His sound in the 40s, as preserved by the records, seems as beautiful as Stuart remembered: Lewis's home-made technique introduced careless regard for pitch at times, but the serenely vocalized tone and courtly elegance were unique, and he played with wonderful spirit. There was a triumphant visit to New York in 1945 but Lewis disliked being away from home for too long and he re-established himself back in New Orleans in the following years. By 1950, with the revival in full swing, he had become the venerable godfather of his kind of jazz. As the decade wore on he was persuaded to tour more frequently, and often played in California. Eventually, he also visited Europe and Japan, playing with Ken Colyer in England, and wherever he went he was accorded a hero's welcome. Lewis was recorded prolifically: he made studio records for Verve and Riverside, but there are countless surviving live sessions, such as a vast trove of material recorded by the American Folklore Group of Miami University in 1952, as well as concert recordings from his overseas travels. There must be dozens of versions of his most famous setpiece, 'Burgundy Street Blues', a poignant solo turn which, for all its familiarity, never sounds as if it's been played one time too many. Among his later music, he often recorded with Kid Howard and his many appearances at Preservation Hall, from 1961 up until the year of his death, were frequently documented. Rough without being sloppy, folk-like but with its own kind of urbanity, the music of this slight, frail-looking man is for many the very heart of New Orleans jazz.

*Jazz At Vespers* (Riverside)

# George Lewis

TROMBONE
*born* 14 July 1952

Lewis was born in Chicago, started on trombone at nine, and was studying theory with Muhal Richard Abrams before he was 20. Although he mastered every style of playing on the horn, he has suggested saxophone players as his prime influences, and his musical interests have progressed in a steady direction away from his own instrumentalism. He began playing in Anthony Braxton's groups in 1976, while making several challenging records under his own name: *Solo Trombone Record* (1975), *Shadowgraph 5* (1977) and *Homage To Charles Parker* (1979) involve several leading figures of the Chicago avant-garde and they retain a surprising freshness many years on. He began playing in real-time with computers programmed to respond 'improvisationally', and eventually recorded and performed less and less frequently, preferring academic study and teaching (it hasn't assisted that he has very rarely been interviewed). *Endless Shout* (1997), which ranges from a four-part piano work to a full-scale orchestral 'conduction' (see BUTCH MORRIS), samples his more recent music to fine effect. Although documentation of his music is comparatively thin, the best of it suggests that Lewis has built on the experimental Chicagoan new music of the 60s more intricately and successfully than most.
***Endless Shout*** (Tzadik)

# John Lewis

PIANO
*born* 3 May 1920; *died* 29 March 2001

Lewis grew up in New Mexico and studied music there before going into the army: while stationed in Europe he formed a close friendship with Kenny Clarke, and on his return to the US he went to New York in 1945 and began working on the bebop scene. In 1946 he joined Clarke in Dizzy Gillespie's big band, besides studying at the Manhattan School Of Music. He is on a few key sideman sessions in this period – such as the Charlie Parker date which produced 'Parker's Mood' (1948) – and he also backs Lester Young on some of the saxophonist's sessions for Verve. But it was his work with Clarke and

Milt Jackson in what eventually came to be called (in 1952) the Modern Jazz Quartet which settled the rest of his career, and it is discussed under the entry for that group. Away from the MJQ, though, Lewis pursued a number of related musical interests. He directed the annual School Of Jazz at Music Inn in Lenox, Massachusetts in the later 50s, was MD of the Monterey Jazz Festival during 1958–62 and developed Orchestra U.S.A. as a performing vehicle for his third-stream compositions during 1962–5. He wrote filmscores, a ballet and other works, which were recorded on both Atlantic and RCA, and in the 80s and 90s he did occasional solo work and recording, including Bach duets with his wife Mirjana. Most of this music has fallen into a state of obscurity, which hasn't been assisted by a generally uncomprehending and mystifyingly hostile critical regard for Lewis's work. Stylistically, he was almost a diametric opposite to bop pianists such as Bud Powell: a gentle, filigree player, favouring delicate counterpoint over any kind of aggressive comping (which also set him aside from a fellow 'classicist' such as Dave Brubeck), whose piano playing was regularly accused of a kind of spineless conservatism, a charge which was also levelled at his composing. While he doubtless borrowed from the European antecedents who clearly fascinated him, his music is better heard as a notably individual response to an idiom otherwise crowded with shouting, jittery music. Such records as *Original Sin* (1961) and *European Windows* (1958) have been all but forgotten, but remain intriguingly set aside from the jazz mainstream, and the occasional records where his piano took centre stage (such as *The John Lewis Piano*, 1958) are all worth rediscovering. Even so, his finest writing was reserved for the MJQ, and the best of it is as accomplished and inspiring as anything in jazz after Parker. While the classical tradition absorbed him, he also – as he once told the author – loved blues, and regarded the earliest records by Muddy Waters as some of the finest music of the 20th century. In his last years he recorded a pair of albums for Atlantic, *Evolution* and *Evolution II* (1999–2000), which were a beautiful summary of his career.
***The John Lewis Piano*** (Atlantic)

## Meade 'Lux' Lewis

PIANO

born 4 September 1905; died 7 June 1964

Lewis's tune 'Honky Tonk Train Blues' (1927) was first recorded while he was playing in bars and brothels in Chicago and Detroit, and wasn't even issued until 18 months later, by which time he was working (with his friend Albert Ammons) as a taxi driver. Although it didn't win much attention at first, it has become acknowledged as the first masterpiece of boogie-woogie piano, and it was belatedly hearing it which set John Hammond on a mission to find Lewis and have him record again. That didn't happen until 1935: in between, Lewis continued driving and playing piano. He made more records for Hammond, but there was no breakthrough until the 1938 From Spirituals To Swing concert at Carnegie Hall, which catapulted Lewis, Pete Johnson and Albert Ammons to fame. Alfred Lion recorded Lewis for Blue Note, and several of the pieces are superb: the five-part 'The Blues' (1939) is Lewis at his finest. His inventiveness within the boogie form and his unalloyed feeling for blues playing set him apart from many of his contemporaries in what was for a time the most popular piano music in America. By the middle 40s, though, the craze had died away. Lewis carried on playing through the 40s and 50s, but he seemed to grow bored with his own style, and some later recordings sound decidedly tired. He was killed in a car accident.
Meade Lux Lewis 1927–1939 (Classics)

## Mel Lewis

DRUMS

born 10 May 1929; died 2 February 1990

Lewis was already working full-time when in his mid-teens, and by the time he came to join Stan Kenton in 1954 he had a lot of experience behind him, including a stint with Ray Anthony, who didn't like the drummer's real name of Sokoloff and insisted he change it. After two years with Kenton he settled on the West Coast and busied himself with small-group studio work, but in 1960 he was back in New York with Gerry Mulligan's Concert Jazz Band and he went back into studio work there. In 1965 he co-formed a big band with Thad Jones, primar-

ily for recording work, but as it garnered a weekly gig and toured Europe it became a more fixed outfit, which lasted in this form (using a pool of the best New York players) until 1979, when Jones abruptly left for Sweden. After that, Lewis got in Bob Brookmeyer to help as MD and chief arranger, and the Monday night residency at The Village Vanguard continued unabated. Lewis was enormously liked and admired by his men, and while he continued to do other studio jobs it was the Orchestra which kept him going, even through the cancer which eventually brought his life to an end, some years after he had been diagnosed with the disease. For all the small-group music he played, it was as a big-band drummer – where he could steer a large ensemble through difficult music without losing any sense of the overriding power of the ensemble – that he excelled.
Live At The Village Vanguard (Solid State)

## Ramsey Lewis

PIANO

born 27 May 1935

Lewis played piano in Chicago in the quartet led by saxophonist Wallace Burton in the early 50s, and when Burton was drafted, the pianist took over the remaining trio. It was a popular local act and they started making records for Argo in 1958, but all of seven years later the Lewis Trio found overnight fame when their instrumental take on the pop tune 'The In Crowd' sold a million. Thereafter Lewis made more soundalike records in the same vein and continued to make a lot more money than he had a year or two earlier, although the original group quarrelled and split up. In some ways, Lewis has lived off that unexpected success ever since. In the 70s and 80s he made mostly tiresome potions of jazz, funk and disco, which all sound a lot more dated than 'The In Crowd'. In the 90s, seemingly aware that he might do better to fall back on his talent, he has done more straight-ahead playing, but in what is now a very full marketplace his music doesn't display a pressing need to exist.
The In Crowd (Argo)

## Ted Lewis
CLARINET, VOCAL
*born* 6 June 1890; *died* 25 August 1971

A master of jazz as vaudeville, Lewis worked in tent shows and the like before moving to New York and playing clarinet in Earl Fuller's band. He was leading groups of his own from 1919 and a decade later was among the highest earners in his field, fronting his band in a top hat and tails, singing (or rather, in the Rex Harrison style, talking) his way through often egregiously sentimental material, and sometimes giving his sidemen some space: since they often included Dave Klein, George Brunies, Muggsy Spanier, Jack Teagarden, Jimmy Dorsey and Benny Goodman, that was no bad thing. Detractors tend to remember Lewis's sometimes unspeakable clarinet playing, which could sound like an extended gargle and reflected his pre-jazz background, but there are lovely moments on many of the records and a genuine best-of from his scores of Columbia sides made between 1922 and 1932 would do the band justice. The indefatigable Ted carried on hoofing well into the 60s.
*Classic Sessions 1928–1929* (JSP)

## Vic Lewis
BANDLEADER, GUITAR
*born* 29 July 1919

A great hustler, the London-born Lewis learned guitar in the 30s and went to New York in 1938, recording there with Bobby Hackett. He served in the RAF during the war and then formed a Dixieland band with Jack Parnell, which eventually turned into a big band somewhat in the style of Stan Kenton's orchestra. He carried on in much the same fashion in the 50s but in the 60s turned his hand to artist management, securing many famous showbiz names on his books. This kept him busy into the 80s, but he also made new big-band records with Shorty Rogers and formed a West Coast All Stars, which made the set of Bill Holman charts on the record cited.
*West Coast All Stars Play The Music Of Bill Holman* (Mole)

## Victor Lewis
DRUMS
*born* 20 May 1950

A distinguished drummer of the modern era. Besides learning drums, Lewis studied classical piano, and after graduating from Nebraska University he moved to New York and began working there in 1975: one of his first gigs was with Woody Shaw, and he became a regular in the trumpeter's music. Since then, he has worked continuously and built up a formidable discography, displaying a conservative style which relies more on deftness and subtle power than showmanship. Among his most notable gigs have been those with Stan Getz (for much of the 80s), John Hicks, Bobby Watson and Kenny Barron. He has also led groups of his own, although they have been only sporadically recorded, with not especially remarkable results.
**Bobby Watson, *Post-Motown Bop*** (Blue Note)

## Lick

When the imagination fails, fall back on licks. The lick is a phrase or a sequence of notes which might be a favourite device of the player executing them, used to cover a sudden shortage of inspiration or an otherwise blank spot in a solo. Every improviser has favourite licks, whether they admit to them or not, and on a bad night a musician might feel they are doing little other than playing licks. A lick can also be used as a starting point in making something new, though, particularly if it is then passed into the musical conversation and someone else makes something fresh out of it. Some licks can be so particular to a player that other players might copy them, as in, 'I heard him using some Stan Getz licks in there.'

## Dave Liebman
TENOR AND SOPRANO SAXOPHONE, FLUTE
*born* 4 September 1946

Liebman studied at New York University but had already been playing gigs since he was 14, fascinated by Coltrane's music and jamming in free-jazz situations for hours. After some experience playing in rock music he worked with Elvin Jones for two years from

1971 and then spent a year with Miles Davis. He formed his own band, Lookout Farm, which made one record for ECM: this marked the start of his long association with pianist Richie Beirach. He then led two further bands, a quintet with Terumasa Hino and John Scofield (whom he recommended to Miles Davis) and another band with Beirach, Quest, which lasted through most of the 80s. He continues to lead small groups of his own while also recording prolifically in a variety of contexts, from all-solo records to groups which seem like Liebman's idea of world jazz (of which the multicultural Lookout Farm was a kind of prototype). Besides this busy regime, he has become an important figure in jazz education: 'It's better to have good music than no music. You can't plead for ignorance – that doesn't help anybody.' His own education appears to have been much based around the lessons of John Coltrane: Liebman is one of the great scholars of Coltrane's music, and his educational role has given him an insight into and an overview of the way jazz has gone and is going which is almost unrivalled among working musicians. For a long spell he gave up on the tenor and played soprano almost exclusively, but these days he works on both horns again. A prolific output on record has resulted in a rich discography which is similarly hard to match in terms of its variety and achievement.
*Homage To John Coltrane* (Owl)

## Terry Lightfoot

CLARINET
*born* 21 May 1935

Lightfoot's first band was the Wood Green Stompers, but they became Terry Lightfoot's Jazzmen (and supported Kid Ory on tour in 1959), and he has led traditional bands ever since, aside from a spell in the early 80s when he ran a pub. The various Lightfoot line-ups have included some fine players – Dickie Hawdon, Roy Williams, Colin Bates and Ian Hunter-Randall among them – and the leader's own clarinet is a reliable sound, but their records have often tended to be a motley collection of genuinely played trad material and the showbiz end of the style, which can be as bad as trad-haters often insist. Their albums for Denis Preston's

Lansdowne operation are probably the best things recorded under Lightfoot's leadership. Of late, his daughter has been singing with the current incarnation of the band.
*Alley Cat* (Columbia)

## Kirk Lightsey

PIANO
*born* 15 February 1937

Lightsey's career took an awful long time to get going. He trained as a classical pianist in his home town of Detroit, but in the 60s backed Motown artists as well as the great Lovelace Watkins, dividing his time between the Motor City and Los Angeles (one of his few jazz dates in the period was on the group of Prestige albums Chet Baker made with George Coleman). He finally won some attention when he gigged with Dexter Gordon at the end of the 70s, and he went on to play piano with the cooperative group The Leaders, which led to records of his own for Criss Cross, Sunnyside and other independent labels: one, a Nat Cole homage, features his own vocals (*From Kirk To Nat*, 1990). He later went to live in Paris. Lightsey is hard to pick out as an individual player, but his broad experience lends his music much gravitas.
*Isotope* (Criss Cross)

## Abbey Lincoln

VOCAL
*born* 6 August 1930

Lincoln's career has followed a strange course. She grew up as part of a large family on a Michigan farm, and in the early 50s moved to California, where she began singing in clubs, using various professional names, although she was Abbey Lincoln when she made her first recordings with a Benny Carter orchestra in 1956. At this point she sounded like a genteel example of the 'girl singer' of the period, but by the time of *Abbey Is Blue* (1959) and *Straight Ahead* (1961) she was a more personal and dramatic vocalist, her material beginning to take a more political slant, a direction which her marriage to Max Roach (1962; they parted in 1970) encouraged. She began recording polemical material and worked more extensively as an actress: if anything, though, this

direction almost capsized her recording career, and she didn't make another American record until 1979's *What It Is* for Columbia. In the 70s and 80s she made some European records but they were poorly produced, and it wasn't until she signed a new deal with Verve in 1991 and made the acclaimed *You Gotta Pay The Band* that she reclaimed her audience and repu- tation. By now her voice had started to fray, but she compensated with a sharper musical intelligence and a gentler and more express- ive purpose. While some of her influence can be heard in Cassandra Wilson's work, Lincoln is very much *sui generis*: a magnetic performer, a distracted and offbeat stylist, she is a better folk singer than the narciss- istic Nina Simone, even though jazz is abso- lutely her idiom.
**You Gotta Pay The Band** (Verve)

# Lincoln Center Jazz Orchestra
GROUP

First formed as part of the Lincoln Center's 1988 concert series Classical Jazz, the Orchestra – under the long-term artistic direction of Wynton Marsalis – has become New York's most eminent big band and one of the premier large jazz ensembles. They have toured the world extensively in the past ten years besides conducting a busy pro- gramme of concerts on their home turf; there have been occasional stand-alone records, although they have also worked as the large ensemble on some of Marsalis's own-name projects. Specifically honed by their leader as an all-purpose repertory ensemble, able to perform scores by Fletcher Henderson and Thelonious Monk alike, the LCJO has received adverse comment – for treating their subject matter as museum pieces – but audiences have been mostly delighted.

# Ove Lind
CLARINET
*born* 29 June 1926; *died* 16 April 1991

Lind was besotted with the Benny Goodman small-group style, and from his early days with The Swinging Swedes (1952–4) he worked variations on that manner in most of what he did. He and bassist Gunnar Almstedt formed a quartet in 1954 which lasted some eight years, after which Lind worked in MOR music before helping to spark the considerable interest in revivalist swing which ran through Swedish jazz in the 70s and 80s. Lind's many records for Phontastic, Columbia and other labels may be derivative of his role model's style, but in their coolly effective way they are a thoroughly enjoyable reminder of the vir- tues of that kind of jazz.
**Swinging Down The Lane** (Phontastic)

# John Lindberg
BASS
*born* 16 March 1959

Originally from Detroit, the gangling Lindberg moved to New York in 1977 and didn't waste any time: he formed the String Trio Of New York, with Billy Bang and James Emery, played in the Human Arts Ensemble with Joseph Bowie, began a regular associ- ation with Anthony Braxton and toured in a trio with Jimmy Lyons and Sunny Murray. This youthful period still has some of Lindberg's best work: virtuosic, fresh playing with both fingers and bow, and a rare sense of how to balance playing in structured and free situations. In 1981 he went to live in Paris but returned two years later and lived in Newburgh, upstate New York. From there he has built up a strong catalogue of record- ings through into the new century, for Black Saint and latterly Franz Koglmann's Between The Lines, often involving unusual instru- mentations and unexpected groupings of personalities and still seeking the finest bal- ance between freedom, form and compo- sitional detail.
**Bounce** (Black Saint)

# Nils Lindberg
PIANO
*born* 11 June 1933

Lindberg's music is an archetypal Swedish marriage of jazz and the country's classical traditions. While studying in Stockholm in the 50s he played sideman gigs with such residents as Benny Bailey and Putte Wickman, and by the early 60s his

composing and arranging had become well known and admired. A *Symphony No 1* was performed by an orchestra featuring many star soloists from the city (and was subsequently issued on CD by Dragon, 35 years after it was recorded in 1963), and Lindberg's other major works from the period – *Sax Appeal*, *Trisection* – are haunting and full of fine writing. Thereafter he has carried on composing, often in a romantic orchestral vein but seldom leaving jazz too far behind: *Saxes Galore* (1979), *Melody In Blue* (1993) and *Lindberg Mitchell Paulsson* (1992) are among the results, though little of this music has carried very far outside Sweden.
**Sax Appeal & Trisection** (Dragon)

## Rudy Linka
GUITAR
*born* 29 May 1960

One of the handful of Czech jazz players to make an impact outside their own country, and sometimes it seems that Linka is used mainly as the source of puns for album-title and headline writers ('Czechs And Balances', 'Always Double Czech' etc). He is an able and good-natured player who now lives in New York and has made some European albums, mostly for Enja, which display an American approach crafted to his own ends.
**Always Double Czech** (Enja)

## Alfred Lion
PRODUCER AND LABEL OWNER
*born* 21 April 1908; *died* 2 February 1987

Lion was spellbound by the sound of the Sam Wooding orchestra when they played at his local skating rink in Berlin in 1924. He became fascinated by American jazz, and emigrated to the US in 1938, where he attended the From Spirituals To Swing concert at Carnegie Hall, and subsequently recorded the boogie-woogie pianists who played there for a new label, Blue Note Records. One of the first independent jazz companies, Blue Note endured under Lion's direction (with his partner Frank Wolff) into the 60s. He personally supervised almost every recording session, and built up an outstanding archive of contemporary black jazz of the 50s and 60s. Tiring of a business which had always been run on a shoestring,

he eventually sold out to Liberty in 1966, and after an unhappy year where he had to deal with a new corporate image, he left altogether. When EMI relaunched Blue Note in 1985, Alfred was guest of honour at their gala concerts in New York and Japan the following year, but his weak heart was failing and he died in 1987. His sensitive patronage and sense of fair play gave many black musicians respect and reward in an era when they were often routinely exploited by the record business.

## Melba Liston
TROMBONE, ARRANGER
*born* 13 January 1926; *died* 23 April 1999

Liston played trombone in high school in Los Angeles and she joined Gerald Wilson's band in 1943. After five years the orchestra disbanded, but she had a job offer from Dizzy Gillespie; by this time she had been writing arrangements for some years. She toured briefly with Billie Holiday in 1949 and found the experience miserable, causing her to leave music altogether for a spell, but she was tempted back by Gillespie in 1956 and played in and wrote for some of his State Department tours. In 1958 she commenced her longest association, with Randy Weston, writing for his *Little Niles* album and contributing to his other projects over the next few years. While she continued to work as a performer, with Clark Terry and others, writing and arranging was by now her long suit and she also composed for commercials and television. She led her own band, Melba Liston and Company, in the early 80s but was forced to stop playing after a stroke in 1985. The faithful Weston, however, encouraged her to write again, and she contributed to some of his albums of the early 90s. More a musicians' favourite than someone who found much fame with the jazz public, Liston's skilful and often demanding scores have been comparatively little recognized.
**Randy Weston, *Little Niles*** (United Artists)

# Booker Little

TRUMPET
*born* 2 April 1938; *died* 5 October 1961

The star-crossed Little hardly had time to get his career started. He came from Memphis, part of a small but eventually significant group of players which included George Coleman and Charles Lloyd, and studied in Chicago, where he was playing with Max Roach at the age of 20. He already sounds a considerable talent on the drummer's *Deeds Not Words* (1958), and by the time of his recordings with Eric Dolphy (*Far Cry*, 1961), and the three albums he made under his own leadership, it was clear that here was a thrilling young talent. He had an unusually gentle sound for a trumpeter, at times almost Chet Baker-like, with a clean open tone and a bright but not sharp intonation, but his choice of notes and fluent exposition of subtle and often difficult ideas pointed towards a genuinely innovative talent. Like his sometime playing partner Dolphy, he hinted at the way free jazz would go while remaining loyal to an essentially orthodox post-bop vocabulary (it was piquant that, like Dolphy, he also took part in Coltrane's sessions for *Africa/Brass*, 1961). It's often been suggested that Little was the next step on from Clifford Brown; and all the more tragic that, like Brown, he was halted in his earliest prime. Illness which suggested a condition akin to arthritis struck him down and he died of uraemia.
***Booker Little*** (Time)

# Fud Livingston

CLARINET, TENOR SAXOPHONE
*born* 10 April 1906; *died* 25 March 1957

Livingston's music is a tiny window on a seldom-explored area of New York jazz. He worked as both a player and an arranger for such key white bands as The California Ramblers and Ben Pollack's orchestra in the mid-20s, and his sideman work with Miff Mole, Red Nichols and Frankie Trumbauer is even more adventurous. His masterpieces, 'Feelin' No Pain' and 'Imagination', have the same distant feel of French impressionism which haunted Beiderbecke, and when played by such skilful musicians as the Nichols–Mole axis the results are still fascinating. His clarinet playing is often mistaken for that of Pee Wee Russell (they sometimes shared reed duties on a date) and is similarly, quirkily, intriguing. But Livingston became a chronic alcoholic. As late as 1939 he was writing charts at the request of Bob Zurke, but thereafter he slipped from sight and died forgotten in 1957.
**Miff Mole, *Slippin' Around*** (Frog)

# Charles Lloyd

TENOR AND SOPRANO SAXOPHONES
*born* 15 March 1938

Lloyd's unpredictable career has had some rollercoaster qualities to it. He grew up in Memphis and was involved in the early R&B scene there, before he moved to California in the mid-50s. Listeners first heard him on record with the Chico Hamilton group in 1961, at this point on alto and flute, but under the influence of John Coltrane he switched to tenor, spent a brief period with Cannonball Adderley, and then began leading groups of his own. His key moment was when he organized a band with Keith Jarrett, Cecil McBee and Jack DeJohnette, which in 1966 caused a small sensation at the Monterey Festival – lining up mostly alongside West Coast rock groups – and recorded *Dream Weaver* (1965), *Forest Flower* (1966), *Love-In* (1967) and *Journey Within* (1968). Lloyd latched on to a tailwind which was then blowing through that part of America, where listeners were as likely to applaud his band as The Grateful Dead, and for much the same reason – instrumental jamming, be it jazz- or rock-derived. Besides his own catchy tunes and songful tenor – which sent the Coltrane influence in a more beatific direction than its originator chose – the group could boast a bona fide new star in Jarrett, whose showmanship also won over audiences. By the end of the decade it was almost all over: Jarrett and DeJohnette had moved on, and Lloyd himself became involved in teaching and meditation and drifted off the live circuit. There was a brief comeback when Michel Petrucciani persuaded him out of what was effectively a retirement, in 1982, but it wasn't until the end of the decade, when he formed a new quartet and began making records for ECM, that Lloyd made a full return to duty. The extremes of opinion which his early work had once excited were now forgotten, and by now Lloyd was enjoying an elder states-man's breadth of experience. His ECM work has set him among many stalwarts of the label, although recent collaborators such as Brad Mehldau and the late Billy Higgins – who cut some of his most poignant final music with the saxophonist – have been just as significant.

*Forest Flower* (Atlantic)

## Jon Lloyd
SAXOPHONES
*born* 20 October 1958

Lloyd became a stalwart of the London free-improv scene in the 80s, and played with most of the leading figures as well as lead-ing groups of his own. Most of the work done under his own name grapples with the structure–freedom divide, and seeks to make the most convincing case for looking after both sides of the spectrum. Records for Leo and hat ART make a strong case for his arguments.

*By Confusion* (hat ART)

## Joe Locke
VIBES
*born* 18 March 1959

Locke was on the New York scene by 1980, leading bands of his own and playing with such leaders as Eddie Henderson, Ronnie Cuber and (as an arranger) Grover Washington Jr. His own projects have offered a very broad range of sympathies: straight-ahead vibes and rhythm, quasi-fusion projects, albums of pop covers and impressionist, chamberish music. But he stands very tall in a line of virtuoso vibes players, and there's little in any of them which sounds like compromise or music made just to sell records. He considers him-self 'a two-mallet player who holds four mal-lets' because he uses the 'second' mallets to play chords rather than single lines. As with so many American players, much of his work has been done for European labels, in this case Steeplechase and Sirocco.

*Wirewalker* (Steeplechase)

## Mark Lockheart
TENOR AND SOPRANO SAXOPHONES
*born* 31 March 1961

Lockheart is one of the London-centred musicians who found prominence in the middle 80s: with Loose Tubes, Django Bates and Billy Jenkins. His band Perfect Houseplants, a quartet, worked through the 90s, although Lockheart's ambitions as a writer led him to augment it with extra musicians and the one record under his own name, *Through Rose-Coloured Glasses* (1998), features carefully scored if some-times fussy pieces for 12 musicians. As a saxophonist his considerable tech-nique lets him command most playing situations.

*Through Rose-Coloured Glasses* (Subtone)

## Didier Lockwood
VIOLIN
*born* 11 February 1956

Lockwood has done more than most to push the violin forward as a convincing 'modern jazz' instrument, although even his virtu-osity hasn't really persuaded a large audi-ence of the instrument's appeal. First influenced by Jean-Luc Ponty, he worked with the avant-rock group Magma and by the end of the 70s was playing both acoustic straight-ahead music and fusion of varying stripes, although he prefers to use an acous-tic instrument himself rather than any kind of electric violin. He recorded regularly in the 80s and 90s, on all-star dates and hom-age records, and generally gave the impres-sion that he is a very talented musician who is a bit stuck for a genuinely meaningful situation.

*New York Rendezvous* (JMS)

## Giuseppi Logan
ALTO SAXOPHONE
*born* 22 May 1935

Logan achieved a mild notoriety when he moved to New York in 1964 and started play-ing free jazz in the New York vanguard of that movement. His two albums for ESP (both 1965) both featured plenty of appropri-ate noise, but once the moment had passed there seemed to be very little to commend in his work and there was nothing much to report after that.

**Giuseppi Logan Quartet** (ESP)

# Jean-Loup Longnon
TRUMPET
*born* 2 February 1953

Scarcely known outside his native France, Longnon is a Parisian with a prodigious command of the trumpet vocabulary, from Dixieland to bebop settings. He started out with such groups as The Dixie Cats and the Milt Buckner band, but by the latter part of the 70s he was leading his own occasional big band and dividing his time between swing playing and a more boppish outlook. Longnon has a firm sound which he doesn't try to Gallicize in any way: he plays as he hears 'those bebop princes, whose humour had nothing equal to their generosity'.

**Bop Dreamer** (Pygmalion)

# Loose Tubes
GROUP

Formed in 1984, Loose Tubes gathered together many of the leading young lights on the London jazz scene of that day. Twenty-one musicians made it among the biggest of big bands, and the group could draw on a considerable pool of writing as well as playing talent: particularly from Django Bates, Iain Ballamy and Steve Berry. The music was a lightly exotic blend of jazz, rock and sundry 'world' musics and the whole stew was leavened by a streak of British humour, which may have militated against the music travelling very well outside its own country. Managed by Colin Lazzerini, the group managed to release three albums and was a great concert draw in its day, but it ran out of steam as the decade closed and its various leading lights were concerned to do more of their own thing. It was sometimes asked why there were no black or female musicians in the group.

**Open Letter** (Editions EG)

# Jeff Lorber
KEYBOARDS
*born* 4 November 1952

Lorber is a brilliant technocrat whose peripheral relationship with jazz is intriguing in its way. Classically trained, he studied at Berklee in the early 70s, and while there began transcribing and studying the music of many modern jazz pianists. His first significant band was named The Jeff Lorber Fusion, and included Kenny G(orelick) among its sidemen, and Lorber began turning out albums in a light but ingeniously constructed idiom which tailored jazz principles to a cold but ruthlessly logical result: everything in them made smart musical sense, but any sense of spontaneity was entirely calculated. In the 80s and 90s he worked out of Los Angeles as a producer – of both instrumental and pop artists – and became a major figure in American radio's smooth-jazz format, although most of his work was actually a lot tougher and more musically stringent than most of the other music in that style. Lorber's keyboard-dominated music is layered and luxuriant: he sets out for a result in the studio, and he seems to stop at nothing to get it.

**The Best Of Jeff Lorber** (Verve)

# Eddy Louiss
PIANO, ORGAN
*born* 22 May 1941

His father Pierre played trumpet and ran his own group, and Eddy worked with him and also sang in The Double Six of Paris in the early 60s. He played both organ and piano behind many visitors to the Paris scene later in the decade, and though he occasionally worked abroad, it wasn't until he recorded with Stan Getz on *Dynasty* (1971) that he really made an impact outside his local circuit. His jazz career since has been a matter of intermittent sightings: he has also worked in variety (the fate of many organ players), but over the years has managed to build an impressively diverse discography, with a big band, Multicolor Feeling, duets with Michel Petrucciani, Franco-African fusion projects and a record by an even bigger band called Fanfare (41 players strong). Louiss often comes across as a good foil rather than a great individualist, but the

1968 record cited features playing of tremendous guts in the company of René Thomas and Kenny Clarke.

*Trio* (Dreyfus)

## Jacques Loussier

PIANO
*born* 26 October 1934

Loussier's trivial music has been ubiquitous for decades. He studied the classics at the Paris Conservatoire and did hack-work accompanying cabaret singers in the 50s, before hitting on the idea of jazzing J S Bach: the result was a trio, Play Bach, with Pierre Michelot (bass) and Christian Garos (drums), which set familiar Bach pieces in the context of a jazz rhythm section. Four albums made in the style for Decca in the early 60s went on to become international bestsellers, and through the use of one of the pieces in a celebrated series of British TV commercials for a brand of cigar, Loussier's sound remained naggingly familiar. He formed a new trio in the 90s and starting pillaging the works of Ravel, Vivaldi and Satie, having run out of Bach. Some respected writers have made themselves look foolish trying to legitimize Loussier's music in sleevenotes to his records: it's a useless novelty.

*Play Bach* (Decca)

## Joe Lovano

TENOR AND SOPRANO SAXOPHONE
*born* 29 December 1952

Lovano grew up in Cleveland and played with his father's band before studying at Berklee (where classmates included Bill Frisell and John Scofield). Until the mid-80s he mostly did big-band work, with Woody Herman and the Mel Lewis Orchestra, but his role in the Paul Motian small group brought him much wider attention, and subsequent gigs with Tom Harrell and Scofield increased his profile. In 1990 he signed to Blue Note as a solo artist, and since then has become a hugely prolific performer both on record and in person, a guest star on a large number of records in addition to more than a dozen sets under his own name for his parent label. Lovano's dark, big sound on both tenor and soprano has become ubiquitous. His earlier playing

is more in the grand tenor tradition of Webster and Rollins, but the influence of free playing has latterly introduced multiphonics and investigations of extremes of timbre, particularly on tenor. The price on this direction is the presence of a cold abstraction in much of his improvising: for all their many-noted configurations, his solos can sound starved of real melody, and there's an almost brutal edge to a lot of it which stands in for warmth. He is so widely admired, though, that he has become tiresomely familiar as a star sideman: he might be the very rare case of a jazz musician who's been making too many records.

*Universal Language* (Blue Note)

## Paul Lovens

DRUMS
*born* 6 June 1949

Watching Lovens play is almost as exhilarating as hearing him: a diminutive man who seems to ride his drum kit like a jockey, flashing around it and creating the most exorbitant yet intensely controlled and refined racket. Though he played some rock music early on, he has been a free improviser for most of his music-making career, with the Globe Unity Orchestra and the Alex von Schlippenbach group with Evan Parker, in duo with fellow percussionist Paul Lytton (who co-founded the Po Torch label with him) and with musicians from Gunter Christmann to Mats Gustafsson. He sometimes plays the musical saw, but otherwise everything he does has to do with percussion.

**With Alex von Schlippenbach and Evan Parker,** *Swinging The Bim* (FMP)

## Frank Lowe

TENOR SAXOPHONE
*born* 24 June 1943; *died* 19 September 2003

Lowe was from Memphis and his first inspiration was King Curtis. By the time he'd joined Sun Ra in 1966, though, he was well versed in where the tenor saxophone had gone in jazz, and he was leading his own groups from the early 70s. Billy Bang was one favourite partner: for a while they worked together in a group named The Jazz Doctors, which had both men dressed for

the operating theatre. For the most part, Lowe favoured small groups which can roam freely but still work from compositional germs. There is no bebop in his playing, but the example of the R&B tenor school left its mark, and he liked to play concisely and to the point. He may never have topped the brilliant quintet date *The Flam* (Black Saint, 1976), but other latter-day records such as *Bodies And Souls* (CIMP, 1995) found him in great heart.
**The Flam** (Black Saint)

# Mundell Lowe
GUITAR
*born* 21 April 1922

Lowe has probaby been busier for longer than any other jazz guitarist. He was playing country music as well as swing at the end of the 30s, and in the 40s carried on in the same eclectic style: with Ray McKinley, Benny Goodman, Fats Navarro, Billie Holiday and Charlie Parker, among others. He was basically a studio man in the 50s, working for NBC and making albums of TV-theme jazz for RCA. He was still playing gigs in the 60s, mainly on the West Coast, but also wrote for television himself and headed up such curious sessions as *Tacet For Neurotics* (1960) and *Blues For A Stripper* (1962). He joined in the fun of the small-group swing revival of the 80s and 90s and recently made some fresh records for Nagel Heyer.
**Porgy And Bess** (RCA)

# Henry Lowther
TRUMPET
*born* 11 July 1941

An impeccably reliable sideman and soloist, whose unassuming position has denied him the grander reputation he deserves. He grew up in Leicester, where his father taught him to play the cornet (for sideman work with the Salvation Army), but he was involved in the contemporary London scene from the early 60s and has most likely worked with every major British jazz leader, including Mike Westbrook, Mike Gibbs, Kenny Wheeler, Stan Tracey, Graham Collier, Barbara Thompson and John Surman. But his first album as sole leader, *Child Song*

(1970), was not transferred to CD until 2005, and Henry's great skills have often been buried away. As a lyric improviser he is probably the equal of the far more widely known Kenny Wheeler.
**Stan Sulzmann, *Birthdays Birthdays*** (Village Life)

# Werner Lüdi
ALTO AND BARITONE SAXOPHONES
*born* 22 April 1936; *died* 20 June 2000

Born in Poschiavo, Switzerland, Lüdi was excited by the arrival of free playing and he was playing with Gunter Hampel as early as 1962. Yet he quit playing altogether in 1967 to enter the more lucrative world of advertising, and it wasn't until the 80s that he showed up again. Soon enough he was working with the likes of Hans Koch and Paul Lovens, and formed an occasional partnership with Peter Brötzmann. Lüdi was a heart-on-sleeve player who didn't care whether he sounded plushly romantic at one moment or turned to anarchic violence the next: if that's how he felt, that's how he played. Brötzmann in particular enjoyed playing with him and he dedicated a project to Werner after the latter's sudden and unexpected death.
**Brain Drain** (Unit)

# Jimmie Lunceford
BANDLEADER
*born* 6 June 1902; *died* 12 July 1947

Nobody led a smarter, more on-the-button big band than Lunceford. He started out as a saxophonist, having studied music in Nashville, and he played in Harlem clubs before going to teach music in Memphis. Out of this came a student band which at first played in summer resorts and then gradually found some momentum, eventually basing itself in Buffalo, with Lunceford taking over as full-time leader in 1933. They were soon in The Cotton Club, and after two sessions for Victor they began a long series of recording dates for Decca. Within a couple of years, Lunceford's was among the most admired and popular bands in the country. After initial arrangements by Will Hudson and Willie Smith (and a single contribution by Lunceford himself, the remarkable

'Stratosphere', 1936), Sy Oliver, who was playing in the trumpet section, became the principal writer for the band. Although the band could always boast a few good soloists – Smith, Joe Thomas, Oliver himself, Snooky Young – they mattered less than the martial precision and supremely professional swing which the band created as a unit, which the band's stagecraft matched: collective vocals, choreographed displays. Oliver's departure in 1939 proved to be a turning point of sorts: although Billy Moore brought in some strong new charts, the strength of the band's output faltered, although the leader kept his men going on a punishing schedule. The best Lunceford records – 'White Heat', 'Rhythm Is Our Business', 'Organ Grinder's Swing', 'For Dancers Only', 'Lunceford Special' and 'What's Your Story, Morning Glory?' – take their place among the leading swing-era memories. But the musicians in the band were less happy about their leader's approach to business: they were notoriously among the poorest-paid performers in the major orchestras, and following a walk-out by many of the leading players in 1942, the band declined further (Lunceford blamed the problems on his manager). Yet the band still made records, right up until their leader's sudden death in 1947, and the later sessions actually suggest a stronger renewal. Under long-time sideman Ed Wilcox, the band continued until 1950, but its time was gone.

*Jimmie Lunceford 1939–1940* (Classics)

## Jesper Lundgaard

BASS
*born* 12 June 1954

Lundgaard's career has been a model of quietly effective work. Born in the Danish town of Hillerød, he began as a guitarist before starting on bass around 1970, studying at Århus University and playing locally in the middle 70s. By 1979 he was settled in Copenhagen, where he has been the bassist of choice for any number of visiting Americans, as well as working with expatriate Bob Rockwell in The Repertory Quartet (several fine albums for Music Mecca). The record cited, a series of duets with fellow bassist Mads Vinding, may not be entirely typical of Lundgaard's usual work, but its lyricism and understated virtuosity seem to sum up the measure of the musician.

**With Mads Vinding, *Two Basses*** (Touché Music)

## Carmen Lundy

VOCAL
*born* 1 November 1954

Carmen has followed a rather characteristic path for a singer of her time and vocal range. She was in operatic training before choosing to go the jazz route, moving to New York in 1978, and working the club circuit as singer-with-trio. She toured with a Broadway production, *Sophisticated Ladies*, and eventually moved over to the other coast in 1991. She has recorded regularly as a leader, though always for smallish labels, and while she is adept enough in jazz, gospel and soul stylings, no one strand in her work stands out enough to catapult her into the top commercial range: if she's too pop for some jazz ears, she's too musicianly (and, at this point, too old) to really annex any pop success.

***This Is Carmen Lundy*** ( Justin Time)

## Curtis Lundy

BASS
*born* 1 October 1955

Carmen's younger brother was an R&B guy until his sister pointed him in the direction of jazz. He was closely associated with Bobby Watson in the 70s and 80s, and also spent five years in the boot camp of Betty Carter's band, from 1982. Curtis seems to have been either selective or a little unlucky in his sideman gigs, which were relatively infrequent during the 90s, although he often turned up in the company of John Hicks, and his own albums as a leader have been creditable showcases for some excellent bands.

***Against All Odds*** ( Justin Time)

## Don Lusher

TROMBONE
*born* 6 November 1923

The first gentleman of English trombone. Like several other British jazzmen, he got his start in a Salvation Army band, but after war service he played in The Squadronaires and

in Geraldo's dance band before joining Ted Heath in 1953, a gig that lasted until 1962 but which Lusher has been perennially associated with, since he has regularly been prominent in Heath orchestra revivals. Don has done countless record dates and was a familiar instrumental voice behind Frank Sinatra and other big-ticket singers. He is modest about his own impeccable work: 'I'm a musical shop assistant, really, with being in sessions so much. You have to play the way they want it, and it doesn't hurt me to do that because I'm not a tremendous jazzer.'
**The Don Lusher Big Band Pays Tribute To The Great Bands** (Horatio Nelson)

## Claude Luter
CLARINET, SOPRANO SAXOPHONE
*born* 23 July 1923

Luter's regular partnering of Sidney Bechet during the American's French years (roughly 1949–55) remain his international claim to fame, but he had already become a considerable force on the French traditional scene, having led groups in the style since the early 40s. He also appeared alongside other visiting Americans, including Rex Stewart, Mezz Mezzrow and Albert Nicholas. In the 80s and 90s, by now an honoured veteran of the music, he appeared in New Orleans itself, a respected son from a very different background.
**Red Hot Reeds** (GHB)

## Brian Lynch
TRUMPET
*born* 12 September 1956

Lynch incarnates all the virtues and highlights of hard-bop trumpet: fast and fierce playing, a glittering tone, high-wire pyrotechnics but utterly safe assurance. He studied in Wisconsin before arriving in New York in 1981, where he worked with such totemic outfits as Horace Silver's band, Art Blakey's Jazz Messengers (the final edition), the Toshiko Akiyoshi Orchestra and the Mel Lewis Orchestra. He also followed a parallel career in salsa music (where trumpeters are always in demand), and became a sideman for Eddie Palmieri. More recent steady gigs have been with Phil Woods and a Blakey tribute band. Lynch has a deep knowledge of his

specialist subject and made a very good fist of the record cited, which nods to nine different trumpeters. He may purvey a stereotypical kind of excitement, but he plays exciting jazz all the same.
**Tribute To The Trumpet Masters** (Sharp Nine)

## Jimmy Lyons
ALTO SAXOPHONE
*born* 1 December 1931; *died* 19 May 1986

Lyons learned the saxophone and played bebop in his teens, but he didn't gain any attention until he began playing with Cecil Taylor in 1961, an association which lasted on and off until his death. His tone on alto had a wounded, almost a crying quality, and when situated in the eye of the storm which Taylor's groups would customarily create, it had the effect of humanizing music which might otherwise have seemed forbiddingly abstract. But he was obliged to find non-musical work during the 60s in addition to his gig with the pianist, and it was not until the 70s, when he also taught, that he worked at music full time. Besides Taylor's music, he was also involved with groups of his own, often with his partner Karen Borca on bassoon, and though few of his own pieces suggested much more than a prop for his improvising, his sound remained a singular element in the free music of the 70s and 80s. He died from the effects of lung cancer.
**Push Pull** (hat Hut)

## Jimmy Lytell
CLARINET
*born* 1 December 1904; *died* 28 November 1972

Born James Sarrapede – he took his adopted surname from a silent film star – Lytell replaced Larry Shields in the Original Dixieland Jazz Band in 1922, then enjoyed a prolific stint with the Original Memphis Five and its many pseudonymous offshoots. Stylistically, he was a transitional figure between the harsh and jangling accents of Shields and the smoother facility of Jimmy Dorsey. He never really left his old associations behind, even though he went into studio work in the 30s and 40s: he was back with his old front-line colleague Phil Napoleon in the trumpeter's re-formed Memphis Five in the late 40s, and played with Miff Mole on the trombonist's final studio date.

**Original Memphis Five, *The Columbias 1923–1931*** (Retrieval)

# Johnny Lytle
VIBES
*born* 13 October 1932; *died* 15 December 1995

Lytle started out as a drummer, with Ray Charles and Gene Ammons, but he changed over to vibes in the mid-50s and after that usually led his own groups. Unlike most of his contemporaries on the instrument, though, Lytle chose to work in a setting which had more in common with instrumental R&B than hard bop, using organ and guitar as part of his backing band and working from simple blues-based and funky material. While none of this music troubled the jazz mainstream too much, Lytle was very popular in black neighbourhoods and his albums – and there were many of them, for Jazzland, Riverside and Solid State in the 60s, and Muse and Milestone in the 70s – sold steadily. He was rediscovered during Britain's jazz-dance revival in the 80s and even appeared in London in 1989.

**The Village Caller** (Riverside)

# Humphrey Lyttelton
TRUMPET, CLARINET
*born* 23 May 1921

Lyttelton had a toff's background, going to Eton and serving in the Grenadier Guards, but he was already more interested in playing jazz and joined George Webb's Dixielanders in 1947, branching out on his own a year later. The early Lyttelton bands were in thrall to hardcore ideas of revivalism (though not as severe as Ken Colyer's brand), and were closely modelled on the lessons of the Armstrong Hot Fives and Sevens. But it wasn't long before the leader both softened and built on that approach, shifting perceptibly towards the small-group swing idiom which, by the middle and late 50s, had become the centre of his bands' sound. In 1954 Lyttelton hired Bruce Turner to play both clarinet and alto saxophone (a move which outraged trad purists at the time), and by the end of the decade he had Tony Coe, Jimmy Skidmore and Joe Temperley

making up a full saxophone section. The Lyttelton bands recorded prolifically for Parlophone, and the material mixed everything from Bessie Smith's 'Young Woman's Blues' and Sidney Bechet's 'The Onions' to catchy originals, Humph's composing pen coming under the influence of Buck Clayton (with whom he also made some jovial two-trumpet sessions). He even had a chart hit in 'Bad Penny Blues', although the leader later admitted that the key element in that success may have been Joe Meek's curious engineering of Johnny Parker's piano part. In the 60s, besides writing for *Punch* and commencing his long-standing jazz programme for BBC Radio, Lyttelton carried on bandleading, making a sequence of fine albums for Black Lion before starting a label of his own, Calligraph, which has documented his output since the 80s and has lately reissued some of his earlier material (the label name also refers to Lyttelton's other specialist skill, calligraphy). Humph has become familiar to the British public as a radio personality as well as a jazz musician, chairing the long-running quiz *I'm Sorry I Haven't A Clue*, but British jazz musicians and audiences alike owe him a huge debt for literally decades of proselytizing on behalf of the music. Still leading the Humphrey Lyttelton band – which these days includes young talents such as saxophonist Karen Sharp alongside veterans like Jimmy Hastings – the remarkable Humph has now been bandleading for longer than Duke Ellington. It's still a pretty good band, too.

**The Parlophone Sessions** (Calligraph)

# Paul Lytton
DRUMS, PERCUSSION, ETC
*born* 8 March 1947

Lytton took up drumming in his teens, and it is a surprise to learn that this most unconventional of percussionists actually spent some time (1967) in the National Youth Jazz Orchestra. But by the end of the decade, having financed his way in music via a parallel career in dentistry, he was playing the freest kind of improvisation, with such fellow devotees as Evan Parker and Barry Guy. He has been working in a duo with Parker ever since, a grouping which was expanded in 1983 to make up a trio with Guy. In 1975 he moved to Belgium and formed an alliance with fellow percussionist Paul Lovens, founding a cooperative and the label Po Torch. Lytton's approach to his various drumkits has little or nothing to do with any sense of jazz rhythm: he likes to exploit them for sound, and while this could be described as based around textures and tone colours, Lytton's music-making tends to evade such simple rationales. At different times he has worked with set-ups of enormous size and complexity, sometimes with such ancillaries as an amplified egg slicer, often with live electronics. It is an eerie, unfathomable counterpart to Parker's own extreme sound-world. Compared to many of his contemporaries, Lytton has recorded relatively infrequently, but of late he can also be found on record with the King Ubu Orchestra and Phil Wachsmann.

**Parker/Lytton,** *Two Octobers (1972–1975)* (Emanem)

# Harold Mabern Jr

PIANO
*born* 20 March 1936

Mabern was in the thick of the fertile Memphis music scene from an early age, playing with such contemporaries as George Coleman, Booker Little and Hank Crawford in his teens. He went to Chicago in 1954 and joined the group MJT + 3 before going to New York in 1959. He took on some illustrious gigs while in New York during the 60s, including time with Miles Davis, Sonny Rollins, Freddie Hubbard and Wes Montgomery, but none of these in the end brought him much individual fame, and in the 70s his profile was less prominent. In the 80s he worked extensively with George Coleman, re-establishing the Memphis axis as an important part of post-bop jazz. Recently he has performed regularly with the Chicagoan saxophonist Eric Alexander, and has asserted a position as one of the godfather figures of post-bop piano.

*A Few Miles From Memphis* (Prestige)

# Teo Macero

PRODUCER, TENOR SAXOPHONE
*born* 30 October 1925

Macero's association as Miles Davis's record producer is so high-profile that many aren't even aware of his work as a musician himself. He learned to play tenor sax in his parents' club, Macero's Tavern, and studied at Juilliard from 1948. In 1953 he joined Charles Mingus's Jazz Workshop and played on some of the bassist's early albums, but he was rather more interested in working as a composer and theoretician, and along with Gunther Schuller he exemplified a trend among a few composers that led to the so-called 'third stream' music of the time: the titles of two of his few own-name records, *Explorations By Teo Macero* (Debut, 1954) and *What's New?* (Columbia, 1956), are typical. But he joined Columbia Records in 1957 and began producing jazz records there: after the triumph of *Kind Of Blue* in 1959, he and Davis worked closely for the next 24 years, despite a stormy relationship in the studio which is evidenced by surviving tapes that show each man cussing the other out. In Davis's electric period, Macero's role became even more crucial: the recent release of the unedited versions of the *In A Silent Way* and *Bitches Brew* material demonstrates palpably how skilful Macero was in making sense out of what was often near chaos. Besides this work, he never stopped composing, producing hundreds of works for orchestra, small groups, film and television, although little of it is easily accessible to any interested listener. In the 80s, he also produced one of the albums by the English collective Loose Tubes.

*Explorations By Teo Macero* (Prestige)

# Machito

BANDLEADER
*born* 16 February 1908; *died* 15 April 1984

Frank Raúl Grillo, aka Machito, squeaks into this book, even though his relationship with jazz, no matter what evidence is thrown up in his favour, is basically peripheral. His eminence is really based around Cuban music and salsa. Although born in Florida, he grew up in Havana, and during the 20s he sang with numerous bands who worked in the musical clubs in the city (his nickname is a

derivation of *macho*, bestowed by his family since he was the first son after three daughters). In 1937 he returned to the US and continued working in Cuban groups there before forming the Afro-Cubans in 1940, with Mario Bauza as its musical director. They subsequently shared concert stages with the Stan Kenton orchestra, and played with some of the leading boppers of the period, who often guested on Machito's own records. In the end, though, the group played primarily for the audience for Cuban music, and while there were many points of crossover with jazz, the broader range of Machito's music remains unknown to the jazz audience at large. Machito himself finally became the grand old man of his genre, and was still touring and playing regularly in the 80s: he died while visiting London on yet another engagement.
***Machito & His Salsa Big Band*** (Timeless)

## Mahavishnu Orchestra

See JOHN MCLAUGHLIN.

## Kevin Mahogany

VOCAL
*born* 20 July 1958

Mahogany got his start as a saxophonist and didn't begin singing until he was 18. He sang in R&B bands in his native Kansas City before focusing on jazz as his preferred medium. In the 90s he seemed set to go places as a major figure in jazz singing: three albums for the Enja label were followed by two more for Warner Bros, and his dark but flexible baritone was handsomely applied to a broad range of material which he seemed at ease with and in control of (he even managed to make something poignant out of Barry Manilow's 'When October Goes'). But the records didn't find much of an audience and he seems for the moment to have slipped back into the margins.
***Another Time, Another Place*** (Warners)

## Joe Maini

ALTO SAX
*born* 8 February 1930; *died* 8 May 1964

A nasty piece of work, Maini came from Providence, Rhode Island, but spent most of his playing career in Los Angeles. He had already done time for narcotics offences before he went to Hollywood in 1951, and he became fast friends with Lenny Bruce, at that time trying to establish a career himself. Maini was a strong and effective altoist in the Parker manner, and he held down jobs in many of the better West Coast groups without really making a name for himself as the kind of player a label would back: he never recorded as a leader. By 1964 his career wasn't in good shape, and he met a bad end, dying in a game of Russian roulette.
**Terry Gibbs,** ***The Big Cat*** (Contemporary)

## Mike Mainieri

VIBES
*born* 4 July 1938

Having studied classical percussion, Mainieri began playing vibes and at 18 joined the Buddy Rich band, staying until 1962. He already had a prodigious four-mallet technique, and he subsequently worked through the 60s and 70s as a session musician, becoming a prime mover on the New York studio scene. He formed Steps (Ahead) in 1979, an acoustic fusion supergroup which enjoyed several years of high-profile success until its disbandment in 1986. Thereafter Mainieri often worked away from jazz, producing music for commercials and the like, although a reconstituted Steps Ahead has been intermittently active and has recorded for his own label NYC.
**Steps Ahead,** ***Modern Times*** (Elektra)

## Mainstream

Originally, 'mainstream' was coined to describe the kind of small-group swing which was making something of a comeback at the start of the 50s, an assertion of the primal values of 'good swinging jazz' at a time when bebop had driven a lot of the old jazz audience away. Early mainstreamers (though they never saw themselves as such) were men such as Ruby Braff, Buck Clayton and Vic Dickenson, and the diverse backgrounds of those three men let one know that the term was always going to be exceedingly flexible in its use. As time went on, 'mainstream' took on more of a revivalist use as the swing era drifted further into the past. Latterly, 'mainstream' has come to mean almost any jazz style which hews close to the middle of the road at any one time: these days there can be mainstream trad, mainstream swing or mainstream bebop.

## Duke Makasi
TENOR SAXOPHONE
*born* 21 November 1941; *died* 25 November 1993

Although one of the major saxophonists in his country, Makasi's career was all but stifled by the overriding situation in his native South Africa. Born in Port Elizabeth, he settled in Johannesburg in 1971 and played with such groups as Roots and his own Spirits Rejoice, but he never travelled outside his native region (aside from a visit to Lesotho in 1976, where he played with Joe Henderson). Little of his work on record has been made generally available, although his fine playing can be heard with Abdullah Ibrahim, as a sideman.
**Abdullah Ibrahim,** *African Herbs* (The Sun)

## Adam Makowicz
PIANO
*born* 18 August 1940

Born in Czechoslovakia and raised mainly in Poland, Makowicz studied classical piano but jazz took his ear early on. He based himself in Warsaw and worked with the bands of Michal Urbaniak and Zbigniew Namysłowski, following Urbaniak's lead into fusion in the early 70s. He was a 'discovery' of John Hammond later in the 70s and made a New York debut in 1977, moving there permanently the following year. For a few seasons, Makowicz was considered a major new voice on the American piano scene: he liked to mix Chopin into his jazz playing, already laden with a Tatumesque technique, and in the 80s and early 90s he recorded for both RCA and Concord. But more fashionable younger talents have superseded him and he has had little attention lately.
**Live At Maybeck Recital Hall** (Concord)

## Tony Malaby
TENOR SAXOPHONE
*born* 12 January 1964

Malaby has been busy since the early 90s yet has only recently gained much attention. He grew up in Tucson and studied in Arizona, before taking on further studies in New Jersey and then moving to the West Coast. In 1995 he settled in New York and has steadily increased his profile, recording with such prime movers as Tim Berne and Marty Ehrlich. Malaby has a dark tenor sound and improvises lines of often startling detail and complexity.
**Dave Scott–Tony Malaby** (Nine Winds)

## Radu Malfatti
TROMBONE
*born* 16 December 1943

Born in Innsbruck, Malfatti went the route common to many of his middle-European generation, starting in Dixieland and moving quickly into free jazz. By 1970 he was in Amsterdam with the likes of Paul Lovens and Peter Kowald, and in the early 70s he was in London, playing there with Elton Dean and fellow trombonist Nick Evans (their band was called Nicra). Since then he has based himself in Zurich, East Berlin and Cologne, getting in the thick of things each time. Like such fellow slide-horn players as Gunter Christmann and the Bauer brothers, Malfatti relishes the essential dourness of the trombone and peps it up with deadpan drolleries of the kind which make the free trombonists a school in and of themselves. Although he has played to great effect on big canvases, such as the London Jazz Composers' Orchestra, he is probably at his best in small groups where he can make every gesture count.
**With John Butcher, Paul Lovens, John Russell, Phil Durrant,** *News From The Shed* (Acta)

## Raphé Malik
TRUMPET
*born* 1 November 1948

Malik studied in Massachusetts but quit before completing his courses and stayed in Paris for a spell, where he played with Frank Wright. He first made a mark as a member of the Cecil Taylor Unit, from 1975 to 1981. This remains his most notable sideman work on record, but he has also led a long-standing quintet with a stable personnel (Brian King Nelson, Larry Roland, Dennis Warren and, until his death, Glenn Spearman). He remains based in Massachusetts. Malik is basically an old-fashioned practitioner of energy music, although his time with Taylor introduced sophistications and skills into his thinking which have enabled him to cut away mere rhetoric; he also prefers decisive, brassy tones over sputtering, expressionist effects. The Berlin performance on *21st Century Texts* (1991) is a vintage set by the quintet.

**21st Century Texts** (FMP)

# Russell Malone

GUITAR
*born* 8 November 1963

Malone has achieved more by association than anything under his own marquee: the Georgian guitarist was with Harry Connick between 1990 and 1994 and then joined Diana Krall's group in 1995, catching a ride with what became the hottest commercial property in the music at that point. He is a very able technician, able to pick out lines at a speed to rival John McLaughlin (hear the *tour de force* of 'Jingles' on *Black Butterfly*, 1985). His best ability, though, is to play complementarily in a group situation, which is why he fitted so well with Connick and Krall. As a solo/leader – on an instrument which is already overpopulated with performers – he may lack the necessary charisma to make a significant mark, and so far neither Columbia nor Impulse! has managed to get a really successful record out of him.

**Black Butterfly** (Columbia)

# Stefano Maltese

ALTO SAXOPHONE
*born* 14 January 1955

Maltese is from Palermo and his music seems soaked in the heat and tranquillity of southern Italy. He has worked with small groups and the bigger Open Music Orchestra, which recorded his big project *Sombra Del Sur* (1992), and he is interested in unusual combinations of instruments and the sound of multiple reeds. Charles Mingus sounds like an obvious influence and Maltese put together a Mingus project in 1998. His own playing flirts with entirely free abstraction but a 1995 meeting with Evan Parker on *Double Mirror* wasn't very successful.

**Sombra Del Sur** (Splasc(h))

# Junior Mance

PIANO
*born* 10 October 1928

The most cheerful of blues-playing pianists, Mance grew up in Chicago and was working there with Gene Ammons by the time he was 20. He played with Lester Young in New York but returned to Chicago to become the regular pianist at the Bee Hive club, where he backed the many visitors who blew through the city. Later in the decade he was with both Cannonball Adderley and Dizzy Gillespie, as well as backing Dinah Washington, and from the early 60s he has worked steadily as a piano-trio man, occasionally backing singers such as Joe Williams but mostly headlining the gigs himself. He has played all over Europe and America and is still a regular and welcome visitor to the UK, with plenty of records for Jazzland, Riverside, Capitol and Atlantic behind him. Mance's familiar groove is probably a bit too familiar by now, but in person he is always worth hearing.

**The Soulful Piano Of Junior Mance** (Jazzland)

# Joe Maneri

CLARINET, ALTO AND TENOR SAXOPHONES
*born* 9 February 1927

Maneri worked in almost complete obscurity for decades. In the late 40s he performed in New York groups which played traditional music of the Balkans, while at the same time working in a jazz ensemble which improvised on 12-tone themes that followed Schoenberg's doctrine. In the 50s he was recording free music and adding *musique concrète* touches, and he wrote a piano concerto which was played by the Boston Symphony in 1960. He also fell in with the Gunther Schuller circle of third-streamers, although nothing came of it in terms of recordings. In the 90s, he finally began to get on to record, in groups with his son Mat, making records for both hatOLOGY and ECM: they unveiled a testing, sparse, melody-starved but exacting kind of free music, a paradoxical blend of aggression and restraint. Maneri might not quite qualify as a lost genius, but his long-undocumented music has its own peculiar virtues.

***Three Men Walking*** (ECM)

# Mat Maneri
VIOLIN
*born* 1969

Maneri worked informally in his father's groups before leading his own trio, Persona (which his father then subsequently joined). The younger Maneri's style does seem to be a chip off the old block: dry, almost parched playing which hasn't any sweetness or noticeable warmth to it. He doesn't go in for much in the way of 'extended techniques' on the violin but it's not pretty music and it takes its strength from intellectual and conceptual rigour, despite his experience playing such warm-blooded repertoire as klezmer and European folk music. Most of his playing is done on an ordinary violin but he sometimes picks up the viola or an electric violin.

***Fifty-One Sorrows*** (Leo)

# Albert Mangelsdorff
TROMBONE
*born* 5 September 1928

Mangelsdorff brought a new virtuosity to the trombone. Previous players had settled for either the expressive approach of a Vic Dickenson or the trim fluency of Miff Mole, but the German sought to take the instrument up a level in terms of possibility, and sought to duplicate some of Coltrane's ideas about multiphonics, a disarming undertaking for the instrument. His brother Emil (b 1925), who played clarinet and alto sax, introduced him to jazz, and though Albert started on guitar he switched to trombone in 1948 and played with small groups and big bands based in Frankfurt in the early 50s. He co-led a hard-bop band with Joki Freund before establishing a new quintet in 1961 which was later considered one of the

key German groups of its time, despite recording only two LPs (one, *Now Jazz Ramwong*, was even released in the US, although in a badly edited version). By the late 60s Mangelsdorff's personal evolution had passed from cool to hard bop to free playing, and he fitted into the ranks of the Globe Unity Orchestra without any stylistic discomfort. His exceptional technique helped him introduce a chordal vocabulary into trombone playing, which he exploited extensively, particularly in his 70s records for MPS, the one label which documented him with any real commitment at that time: *The Wide Point* (1975) matched him up with Elvin Jones and Palle Danielsson, *Trilogue* (1976) was by a trio with Jaco Pastorius and Alphonse Mouzon, and *Live In Montreux* (1980) settled him in with J-F Jenny-Clark and Ronald Shannon Jackson. He also recorded three tempestuous LPs with the Peter Brötzmann group. While Mangelsdorff chose to retain many elements of his hard-bop vocabulary in his playing, his innovations in timbre pointed the way for such players as Gunter Christmann and Radu Malfatti, and he managed to bring an unfashionable instrument into many unexpected areas: he also played with the John Surman–Barre Phillips–Stu Martin trio, and has been a regular in the United Jazz And Rock Ensemble. Although regularly showered with acclaim as one of the few Europeans of his time whose music has extensively travelled, Mangelsdorff has actually not been recorded as frequently as some think, and even now far too much of his best work languishes on out-of-print records.

***The Wide Point*** (MPS)

# Chuck Mangione
TRUMPET, FLUGELHORN
*born* 29 November 1940

A minor hard bopper, Mangione co-led a group with his pianist brother Gap, The Jazz Brothers, which made a few sets for Riverside before the trumpeter joined the Jazz Messengers in 1965. He stayed two years, although this period of the band isn't well documented (the Limelight album *Buttercorn Lady* shows what Mangione could do on the elegant solo on his own 'Recuerdo'). Thereafter his career seemed to stall until he suddenly found himself a fusion star of the middle 70s: it was a track called 'Land Of Make Believe' which initially did the trick, and in 1977 *Feels So Good* sold an astonishing two million copies, although its unchallenging mix of sweetly memorable melodic hooks and Latin-lite rhythms was really competing in the Herb Alpert arena. Mangione's success lasted a few years and helped pave the way for smooth jazz's ascendancy, but by the end of the 80s his run had come to an end and he actually quit playing in 1989. A 1998 comeback, *The Feeling's Back*, was utterly feeble. Mangione did most of his hits playing on the flugelhorn: its mellow tootling suited his environment perfectly.

**Feels So Good** (A&M)

# Winston Mankunku
TENOR SAXOPHONE
*born* 21 June 1943

Mankunku is another of the South African jazz players whose best work has either been lost or is undocumented, in large part owing to the country's former system of apartheid. Born in Cape Town, he played with the leading local players in the 60s but chose not to follow the example of several of his colleagues and remained in the country. Although he was discouraged enough by his situation to almost give up music during the 70s, he later returned to active playing and fared better in the 80s and 90s. Even so, his records are scarcely known outside his own country.

**Jika** (Nkomo)

# Herbie Mann
FLUTE, BASS CLARINET
*born* 16 April 1930; *died* 1 July 2004

Although much of his work was sniffily dismissed as mere populism for many years – a not entirely unjustified charge – Mann became a great enduring spirit, and while his huge discography has its share of flim-flam, there is much good music there too. Though he was born in Brooklyn, his first important work was done on the West Coast in the middle 50s, where he began writing music for television, and made records for Bethlehem, Prestige and Riverside. One surprising first was *Great Ideas Of Western Mann* (1957), an album done entirely on bass clarinet. The flute, though, was Mann's speciality, and its essential perkiness has driven every group and style he put up. He formed an Afro-Jazz Sextet in 1959, imported the bossa nova from Brazil in 1961 (an idiom which suited him perfectly), toyed with jazz-rock in the later 60s, and even had a go at reggae and disco in the 70s (he ended up calling one of his latter-day groups Jasil Brazz). *Memphis Underground* (1968) predates the early fusion albums of Miles Davis, but the multiple guitars, basses and keyboards followed a similar pattern, even though Mann's cheerful brew was in the end nothing like Davis's preening darkness. A long association with Atlantic spawned a mountain of albums all through the 60s and 70s and into the 80s, although more recently Herbie went with independents and in particular has his own label, Lightyear. A lot of his beats go clip-clop and you need a photographic memory to even vaguely recall a lot of his solos, but at their best Mann's various syntheses had a liveliness all their own, and he might fairly have claimed credit for a great deal of pioneering in the various fields of fusion. Besides, nobody got more mileage out of puns on their name (*Family Of Mann, Evolution Of Mann, Our Mann On Flute* etc, etc).

**Memphis Underground** (Atlantic)

# Shelly Manne
DRUMS
*born* 11 June 1920; *died* 26 September 1984

Although Manne is always associated with West Coast jazz, he was a New Yorker who got his start with the Joe Marsala group in 1940. After serving in the US Coast Guard (where he was stationed not far from the city, and was thus able to keep his hand in on the New York scene), he worked primarily in Stan Kenton's orchestra from 1946, until he moved to Los Angeles in 1951. From then on he was a major force in Californian jazz as sessionman, leader and club owner. He was a regular in the studios for such leaders as Shorty Rogers, helmed the Poll Winners trio with Barney Kessel and Ray Brown, and ran his own quintet from 1955, as well as leading numerous sessions for

Contemporary. *Modern Jazz Performance Of Songs From 'My Fair Lady'* (1957) became a hit album, and the label had Manne record other 'Broadway' albums as follow-ups. Four live records made at The Black Hawk by the 1960 edition of Manne's quintet were all classics, but there were also dates recorded at his club, Shelly's Manne-Hole, which he ran until 1974. Manne was a consummate professional and master of his craft: he handled near-avant-garde dates such as *The Three* (1954) with the same aplomb as booting along Shorty Rogers & His Giants. He played on Ornette Coleman's first album for Contemporary, as well as on Tom Waits's *Small Change* (1977), and he handled every gig with the same unfussy skill. Richard Bock's Contemporary albums caught his beautiful sound at the kit particularly well, but Shelly always sounded good. On the day of his sudden death from a heart attack, he was, as usual, booked into a studio.

*At The Black Hawk Vols 1–4* (Contemporary/ OJC)

# Wingy Manone
TRUMPET, VOCAL
*born* 13 February 1900; *died* 9 July 1982

Joseph Manone (the 'Wingy' came from his missing right arm, lost in a childhood accident) was an outstanding New Orleans trumpeter, although that was often hidden by his other entertaining skills. He spent most of the 20s touring, working in Chicago, St Louis and New York, although he did manage to record a session in New Orleans (as Joe Manone's Harmony Kings) in 1927. In 1930 (as Barbecue Joe & His Hot Dogs) he recorded a session for Champion in Richmond, Indiana, which included 'Tar Paper Stomp', possibly the original of the famous 'In The Mood' riff. But he didn't really find much of an audience until 1934, back in New York, when he began making records on a regular basis. One of them, 'Isle Of Capri', became a hit, though more for Manone's goofy vocal than for the jazz content, and thereafter the leader mugged his way through dozens of sides for Vocalion and Bluebird, all the way into the 40s. He became pals with Bing Crosby and went to work with him in Hollywood, subsequently turning up on Bing's radio show, but by the 50s he had decided to settle into his routine

in Las Vegas nightclubs. One has to search through Manone's records to find the best of his trumpet work – he was a particularly strong lead player – but the ebullient personality is in front of the listener from the first bar. He was still touring in the 60s and 70s, though clearly tiring of a business which had moved a long way on from his kind of entertainment.

*Wingy Manone 1936* (Classics)

# Michael Mantler
TRUMPET
*born* 10 August 1943

Along with his one-time wife Carla Bley, Mantler helped organize the Jazz Composers' Guild in New York in 1964, and subsequently the Jazz Composers' Orchestra. It was a rather fearsome agenda Mantler set for his players: he once ticked off a drummer for daring to play eight bars in straight time. From the 70s onwards he has specialized in unremittingly bleak and mordant large-scale compositions which sound more like a mix of contemporary composition and art-rock than anything much to do with jazz, reinforced by his use of vocalists such as Robert Wyatt and Jack Bruce. His trumpet playing, once featured rather effectively on 1985's *Alien* (even though, as Brian Morton once put it, it sounds 'like the work of a man who hasn't seen daylight for 20 years'), seems to have been put out to grass.

*Folly Seeing All This* (Watt)

# Frank Mantooth
PIANO, ARRANGER
*born* 11 April 1947; *died* 30 January 2004

Mantooth set a formidable standard among *fin-de-siècle* big-band arrangers. He had worked in US air force bands before studying piano in Vienna in the 70s, but he returned to the US in 1981 and created a large and accomplished body of work as writer-arranger. Scores of his charts have entered the repertory of modern college and youth big bands, in both the US and Europe, and he was busy in education; but his best legacy is probably the series of records he made for the West Coast Sea Breeze label in the 80s and 90s. Mantooth said little that was new, but he could marshal a band's resources and give them nourishing musical substance with complete aplomb, and his music captures the American sound of a big orchestra swinging through a timeless style of playing better than most such ventures. His early death in 2004 shocked the big-band community.

*A Miracle* (Sea Breeze)

## Guido Manusardi
PIANO
*born* 3 December 1935

Although he qualifies as one of the god-fathers of modern Italian jazz, Manusardi has actually spent a lot of time away from his own country. He played dance music in his teens before travelling through Europe, and he lived in Sweden during 1959–67, where he began making a reputation and his first records. He then divided his time between Romania, where the folk music cap-tivated him, and Sweden, and only settled back in Italy in 1974. Since then he has recorded prolifically and led numerous small groups. His own writing is coloured by his various travels – *The Village Fair* (1996) is a brilliant evocation of folkish melodies in a jazz setting, and *Doina* (2000) is a setting of ten Romanian themes – but his playing is rooted in a more conventional jazz tradition, with Erroll Garner and Oscar Peterson not-able influences.

*The Village Fair* (Soul Note)

## Fate Marable
PIANO
*born* 2 December 1890; *died* 16 January 1947

Marable seems to have only rarely played on dry land. He began working on Mississippi riverboats in 1907, and within ten years he was leading bands and recruiting new young players for what came to be a kind of float-ing university of music. Marable was a tough taskmaster and among the many musicians whom he brought along in his bands were Louis Armstrong, Henry Allen, Gene Sedric and both Dodds brothers. Long after jazz had moved on from its riverboat phase, he was still leading groups: later stu-dents included Earl Bostic and Jimmy Blanton. Marable was eventually laid off in 1941 and thereafter played piano in clubs.

On the evidence of the one disc that he made, two titles for OKeh in 1924, he wasn't an outstanding player himself: it is an awful record. When jazz was young, though, Marable helped it drift downstream and into the ears of many who would later spread the gospel.

## Rita Marcotulli
PIANO
*born* 10 March 1953

From a musical family (her sister sings opera), Marcotulli studied classical piano in her native Rome and has worked there in the jazz community since the early 80s. She hasn't travelled much and many of her records are on rather hard-to-find small Italian labels, but she is a powerful player and has invested faith in her own com-posing, creating a book of tunes with a rhythmically strong core. Two records for Label Bleu have had wider distribution and include some of her best work.

*The Woman Next Door* (Label Bleu)

## Michael Marcus
SAXOPHONES
*born* 25 August 1952

Marcus is perhaps the only saxophonist working who has specifically built on the leg-acy of Roland Kirk: he has played in hom-ages to Kirk, recorded with former sideman Jaki Byard, and does the Kirk thing of play-ing more than one horn at once, as well as tackling the stritch and the manzello, Roland's eccentric horns. Aside from this, his main thing is the baritone saxophone, although he also has a go at other members of the family. Originally from San Francisco, he played in blues bands before moving to New York in 1982. Though his playing has a sometimes shaky relationship with pitch, Marcus is a garrulous and entertaining improviser and often makes the kind of joy-ful racket which audiences loved about his spiritual forebear. It makes a change from yet another Michael Brecker clone.

*In The Center Of It All* (Justin Time)

# Steve Marcus

TENOR AND SOPRANO SAXOPHONES
*born* 18 September 1939

Marcus went a journeyman's route through the various options for a jazz saxophonist in the 60s and 70s. He started in Stan Kenton's band (1963), then played with Herbie Mann and Woody Herman, although he also led groups of his own: one, The Count's Rock Band, featuring Larry Coryell and Herbie Hancock, made two albums for Vortex, and another, a quartet with Daniel Humair, Miroslav Vitous and Sonny Sharrock, cut an album for STV. He continued in a fusion vein for the early 70s, still working with Coryell, but then went back to hard bop and joined Buddy Rich's band in 1976 and stayed until the leader's death. Since then he has divided his time between fusion and straight-ahead playing: he worked as MD for a Rich memorial band and recorded two albums in that capacity.
**Buddy Rich Big Band,** *Burning For Buddy* (Atlantic)

# Rick Margitza

TENOR AND SOPRANO SAXOPHONES
*born* 24 October 1961

The self-effacing Margitza is another Miles Davis graduate: having studied in Detroit, he moved to New York in 1989 and was hired by Davis for a season. Since then he has led his own groups and freelanced as a sideman. Blue Note signed him in the early 90s and made three albums, all of them with some excellent music, but as with so many signings of that period Margitza didn't stay the course and he has since worked for smaller labels. A thoughtful saxophonist with an intelligent lining on his brawny post-Brecker sound, Margitza surely has a lot more interesting music in him yet.
*Hope* (Blue Note)

# Tania Maria

PIANO, VOCAL
*born* 9 May 1948

The energetic Maria is a popular live performer, although her many records suggest a talent that doesn't translate easily to disc. A teenage star in her native Brazil, she settled in Paris in 1974, began working on the festival circuit, and relocated to the US in 1981. She began making records for Concord, and her style – basically a mix of Brazilian pop, Latin fusion and a lick or two of post-bop piano – makes for an entertaining night out and not something to return to very often.
***The Real Tania Maria: Wild!*** (Concord)

# Charlie Mariano

ALTO AND SOPRANO SAXOPHONES
*born* 12 November 1923

Mariano grew up in Boston and decided on a jazz career when he heard the playing of Lester Young. He began playing on the local scene in the late 40s (and made his first records as a leader there), then joined Stan Kenton in 1953, which led to his settling in Los Angeles for a time, although he felt he was more of an East Coast man. He returned to Boston in 1958 and married the pianist Toshiko Akiyoshi, with whom he ran a quartet for some years: *Toshiko–Mariano Quartet* (Candid, 1960) is their classic statement. He also played with Charles Mingus and is on some of that leader's best work for Impulse!. But eventually he moved on to Europe, after a period of travel which piqued his interest in Indian music, which he has often followed since, learning to play the wayward Indian reed instrument the nagaswaram in addition to his customary alto and soprano. He did some brilliant work with Eberhard Weber's Colours group in the later 70s, and was also in the United Jazz And Rock Ensemble. Latterly based in Cologne, he continues to perform and record across a wide spectrum of groups. Somewhat of a free conservative – 'I like form, and I wince if I hear a melody played too "out"' – Mariano has worked in bop, fusion and several strains of what might be called world-jazz, and has brought a gently probing intelligence to all of them.
***Toshiko–Mariano Quartet*** (Candid)

# Dodo Marmarosa

PIANO
*born* 12 December 1925; *died* 9 September 2002

Marmarosa's extraordinary piano intro to Charlie Parker's 'Relaxin' At Camarillo' alone marked him as an out-of-the-ordinary

talent. But his career never really got much
further. He grew up in Pittsburgh, and
joined Gene Krupa in 1942 and Artie Shaw in
1944, coming to real prominence with some
of his features there. Two years later he was
in Los Angeles and began working with the
boppers: he is on a number of important
sessions of the period, the Parker date being
only one of several where his dexterity, melodic imagination and rhythmical ingenuity
set him aside from many note-spinning boppers. But he became ill and went home to
Pittsburgh, thereafter scarcely surfacing at
all until making a single album, *Dodo's
Back!*, for Argo in 1961, as well as some
sessions with Gene Ammons. After that he
disappeared again, but was unexpectedly
'rediscovered' when researcher Robert
Sunenblick uncovered some rare 50s and
60s tapes of the pianist at work, and
recorded a poignant interview with the
gentleman who preferred to call himself by
his real name, Mike Marmarosa (all documented on *Dodo Marmarosa, Pittsburgh
1958*, Uptown).
**Dodo Lives** (Topaz)

## Lawrence Marrero
BANJO
*born* 24 October 1900

Marrero's father Billy led the Superior
Orchestra of New Orleans, and Lawrence got
his start with him, although by 1920 he was
himself leading the Young Tuxedo Orchestra
(which his brother Eddie played bass in). He
worked in and around the city during the
20s and 30s but became best known for a
long association with George Lewis, which
began in the late 30s. Marrero sometimes
doubled on electric guitar, but Lewis liked
the steady sounds of his banjo, and he also
turned up on many of the first sessions of
the New Orleans revival, with Bunk Johnson,
Wooden Joe Nicholas and others. Illness
obliged him to stop touring with Lewis from
1954, although he still played gigs in New
Orleans until his death.
**George Lewis, *Trios And Bands*** (American Music)

## Joe Marsala
CLARINET, TENOR SAXOPHONE
*born* 4 January 1907; *died* 3 March 1978

An unassuming barrier-breaker, Marsala was
one of the few small-group bandleaders to
front a mixed-race combo in the 30s and
40s. He had grown up in Chicago and led a
largely uneventful career there at first, often
playing with Wingy Manone's groups, and in
1935 he went to New York with Manone's
band and eventually took over the trumpeter's steady gig at The Hickory House in
Manhattan. From 1937, Joe led the group
there for over a decade: he married the harpist in the band, Adele Girard, and headed a
line-up which mixed musicians of different
generations as well as colours: besides Hot
Lips Page, Chuck Wayne, Dave Bowman and
Zutty Singleton, there were youngsters such
as Earl Bostic, Shelly Manne, George
Wallington, Neal Hefti and Buddy Rich. The
Marsala band broadcast regularly from the
venue and Marsala's only 'outside' gig in the
period was occasional work with Eddie
Condon. But in 1948 he disbanded the
group, slowed down his performing schedule and eventually went into music publishing full time. His clarinet solos are
always worth waiting for on the records:
dark, musing and woodsy in timbre.
**Joe Marsala 1936–1942** (Classics)

## Branford Marsalis
TENOR AND SOPRANO SAXOPHONES
*born* 26 August 1960

The eldest of the Marsalis brothers actually
started on alto sax, which he played in his
early stint in Art Blakey's Jazz Messengers,
but he is primarily a tenor and soprano
man. He joined Blakey in 1980 after studying at Berklee, although he was only in the
band for five months, and then joined
brother Wynton's quintet. Like his brother,
he signed a contract with Columbia and
released the first of numerous albums for
them in 1983. Miles Davis used him as a sideman in 1984, and then came the great turn-
around, when he joined the new group
formed by rock star Sting in 1985, a move
which incurred Wynton's very public dis-
approval. Although he played with Sting a
few more times in the 80s, he largely
recorded and toured with his own quartet,

although in 1992 he took over as the house bandleader on NBC's *The Tonight Show*, where he acted as a foil to the show's new front-man, Jay Leno. After three years he was tired of it, and he abandoned the post, leaving behind the band he had put together for the job with guitarist Kevin Eubanks in charge. After a brief dalliance with a jazz hip-hop group called Buckshot LeFonque (the name borrowed from a Cannonball Adderley pseudonym), which resulted in one tour and one album, he has worked with straight-ahead small groups ever since.

Branford is the funny one in the Marsalis clan. Blessed with a somewhat un-American dry wit, he is a devastatingly shrewd critic of jazz culture, bolstered by the familiar Marsalis trademark of supreme self-confidence. While he has shown little interest in the kind of evangelical role Wynton has adopted, he goes about setting a standard in his own way. His saxophone playing brims with the steely bravado and lorryload of technique that marks out the generation of players which he helped to bring to prominence, but he is a warmer stylist than many of his contemporaries and though he can drift off into prolixity there is seldom the sort of technique-for-its-own-sake feeling which permeates Michael Brecker's music. His numerous records for Columbia (including one record of classical saxophone music) are satisfying yet often give off an air of detachment, as if – and perhaps he is in this way most like Wynton – he isn't that bothered about individual records and prefers the big picture of live playing and overall presence. In 2002, however, on leaving Columbia, he embarked on a record label of his own, Marsalis Music: although it has so far released one piece of extraordinary hubris, a record which covers such untouchable material as 'A Love Supreme' and Sonny Rollins's 'The Freedom Suite', the other results have been among Branford's most engaging moments, including a Marsalis 'family' record where he plays alongside Wynton again. They sound so fine in this context that one regrets how their paths have so often diverged since the early 80s.

***The Steep Anthology*** (Columbia)

# Delfeayo Marsalis
TROMBONE
*born* 28 July 1965

The third Marsalis brother has mostly been more active – or, at least, more high-profile – as a record producer, a subject he studied at Berklee, than as a trombonist (or 'trambonist', as he seems to prefer it). He began producing albums by his brothers, particularly Branford's Columbia sessions, in the 80s, as well as records for Courtney Pine and others. In the 90s he sought a higher profile as a performer himself, and led his own groups and cut a couple of albums of his own. As a stylist he seems to adopt a stance somewhere between the deadpan fluency of J J Johnson and the more expressive sounds which are the favoured contemporary timbre. Jason (b 1977), the youngest of the four musician-brothers, is a drummer who has worked primarily in the New Orleans circle of players, leading groups which have recorded for the Basin Street label and playing with Irvin Mayfield in the New Orleans 'fusion' group Los Hombres Calientes.

***Musashi*** (Evidence)

# Ellis Marsalis
PIANO
*born* 14 November 1934

The patriarch of what has become America's First Family of Jazz, Ellis played locally in New Orleans in the 50s and formed the American Jazz Quintet with his contemporaries Ed Blackwell and Alvin Batiste. But his career didn't get him too far, and he began teaching music in schools and taking sideman gigs with Al Hirt. He was still doing club work in the 70s while also teaching at university, but after the fame of his sons began to spread, Ellis found himself something of a celebrity too, and he signed as a solo to Columbia, although the records turned out to be more workmanlike than remarkable. His basic bebop style has its idiosyncrasies, but he is clearly more significant as a teacher – having instructed many up-and-coming players – and as a role model to his respectful sons. Scott Hamilton remembers playing with him at the Hiatt in New Orleans in the era before Wynton's emergence, 'and he was telling us how his

son was gonna be a big star. We thought, oh yeah, sure.'
**A Night At Snug Harbor, New Orleans** (Evidence)

# Wynton Marsalis

TRUMPET
*born* 18 October 1961

A tremendous, noisy debate has surrounded this remarkable man for more than 20 years. He got off to a very early start in New Orleans, encouraged by his father to study both jazz and classical music, and he was a strong and fast enough learner to be playing a Haydn concerto with the New Orleans Philharmonic at the age of 14. He then studied at Tanglewood and Juilliard before joining Art Blakey in 1980. Marsalis immediately imparted a new seriousness to the then rather fading Jazz Messengers, he and his brother playing in sharp suits on the stand and even revitalizing their leader. In 1981 he toured in a quartet with Herbie Hancock and signed to Columbia as a leader, recording and releasing *Wynton Marsalis* (1981) before leaving Blakey and forming his own quintet, with Branford also involved. Although it was in formal terms a straight-ahead hard-bop band, there was something implicitly exciting about the group, as if, by their freshness and dedication to giving their all to the music, the Marsalises were reinventing that particular wheel and making an audience listen with new ears.

Already an articulate and outspoken figure, the trumpeter appeared to relish his rapidly growing eminence and set out a position where he seemed to be reclaiming the music after years of crossover misuse: 'Miles in the 70s, that's not jazz,' he would opine, and some felt a cold, reactionary draught. But Marsalis was ready to answer anything with his own music. He recorded steadily and prolifically for Columbia, although there were changes in his band personnel soon enough: Branford left in 1985, and when the trumpeter learned that he was to join a band led by Sting, he was openly disapproving. Meanwhile, Marsalis gathered in players who epitomized his own playing stance, including Jeff 'Tain' Watts, Wessell Anderson, Herlin Riley, Marcus Roberts, Kenny Kirkland, Reginald Veal, and Robert Hurst, and besides making jazz albums he also recorded pieces from the classical trumpet repertoire, winning a Grammy award in both categories in 1984. In 1987, there came a major turning point: he helped establish a jazz programme at New York's Lincoln Center, previously a bastion of classical culture, and went on to be artistic director of successive programmes there, leading to the creation of a stand-alone jazz division in 1995. This powerful position in the city's cultural politics has brought him probably as much criticism as praise, and much of it has been openly vitriolic. His programmes have been seen as exclusive and misleading: as an overview of jazz history, the avant-garde has been ignored, the contributions of white musicians have been seemingly downplayed, and an orthodoxy has been established around the twin historical poles of Louis Armstrong and Duke Ellington, Marsalis's greatest inspirations. Yet he can easily counter his detractors: it has brought steady work to 1,200 musicians, sponsored numerous new-music commissions every year, and given jazz education a huge boost in the US. As a public platform for jazz in a previously unwelcoming cultural establishment, Lincoln Center's contribution via Marsalis and his work has been incalculable.

Education has been an extraordinary priority for him: no musician since Dizzy Gillespie has been more involved in outreach to other musicians, and he has gone into probably hundreds of schools and colleges to speak to young people about jazz, as well as identifying and encouraging scores of budding players, from Roy Hargrove and Wycliffe Gordon to Ali Jackson and Eric Lewis. His Southern charm and informality have gone hand in hand with a shrewd understanding of how the jazz business works: one of the major changes which Marsalis has effected has been to make the music into something more like a business where the performers can ask for serious remuneration. As far back as the early 80s, when he first went to Europe, he began asking for top dollar. But the abiding complaint which many have is that, on a musical level, his own work has nothing of the innovator about it, although this does pander to a cliché about jazz being judged on the number of barriers it breaks down. While he has a notably individual sound – an experienced listener can surely spot him within 16 bars or so of a trumpet solo – it is put in the service of a playing style which does not pretend to be that of a visionary. His early playing was mostly made up of gestures from the hard-bop masters, from Freddie Hubbard to Woody Shaw, and as he has expanded his powers, latterly he has chosen to explore a more specifically expressive sound, deliberately harking back to such old spirits as Bubber Miley, Roy Eldridge and, inevitably, Armstrong. The change can be easily followed in his records: the crisp, almost dazzling essays on bop in *J Mood* (1985), the rambunctious flirting with the edges of free playing in *Live At Blues Alley* (1986), the dissertation on New Orleans in *The Majesty Of The Blues* (1988), the jazz-goes-to-church *In This House, On This Morning* (1992), and a record each in homage to Thelonious Monk (1994) and Jelly Roll Morton (1999). For a demonstration of how much trumpet he can play on a record, it is hard to beat the ebullience of *Live At The Village Vanguard* (1990–94), no fewer than eight CDs of music covering his various stints at New York's most famous club over a five-year period.

As a composer, his ambitions have sometimes outstripped his abilities: the huge *Blood On The Fields* (1994), which won a Pulitzer Prize, has a tremendous impact in person, but on record feels at times like a very long haul, and the even more gargantuan *All Rise* (2001), with the involvement of two orchestras in a 12-movement piece, does seem like a grand folly. Yet Marsalis is a restless man, and he never seems to dwell on one work for very long: 'It might disappear, but if it's of sufficient quality, it will come back. If not, it shouldn't.' Though he made dozens of albums for Columbia, relatively few earned anything approaching best-seller status, and perhaps they were content to let him go when he eventually signed a new deal with Blue Note in 2002 – the deal done by the man who had originally signed him to Columbia 20 years earlier, Bruce Lundvall. At the end of 2004, the Lincoln Center's new jazz performing spaces were opened amid much ballyhoo in the city: an incredible feat of fund-raising if nothing else, and further palpable evidence that Marsalis is moving mountains in the name of jazz.

***Live At The Village Vanguard*** (Columbia)

# Warne Marsh

TENOR SAXOPHONE
*born* 26 October 1927; *died* 18 December 1987

Marsh tried his hand at all sorts of instruments before settling on the tenor, and by the time he was 17 he was playing gigs. Following his military service he began studying with Lennnie Tristano in New York, and of all the pianist's pupils it was Marsh who followed through his musical and philosophical doctrines to their logical limit, setting all his musical agendas thereafter by the motives Tristano had instilled. But he had little opportunity to make records: beside a few sideman gigs with Tristano and a duo session with Lee Konitz for Atlantic, Marsh made only three other official albums in the 50s and 60s, although he also played informally with musicians such as Peter Ind and Clare Fischer. He played long, intensely relaxed lines in a buffed grey tenor tone which deliberately eschewed any kind of extravagance of timbre or rhythmical idiosyncrasy: it was a paradigm of 'linear' improvisation, nothing on show for its own sake and every potential emotional outburst suppressed in favour of a coolly effective whole. In the age of Rollins and Coltrane (let alone Ayler), it was scarcely a popular position to take, and Marsh knew it, but like so many jazz musicians he relied on the attentions of a small but dedicated audience. The attentive were always rewarded with playing of freshness and spontaneity, which only revealed itself to genuine listeners. From the early 60s he mostly divided his time between the East and West coasts, but earned his living principally by teaching, although he also cleaned swimming pools and repaired televisions in leaner times. In the later 70s and 80s he toured more widely, visiting Europe several times and again working in tandem with Lee Konitz, and the advocacy of fans such as Anthony Braxton assisted. His biography *An Unsung Cat* reveals a complex man of contrasting temperaments. He died during a performance at a club in Hollywood.

***Star Highs*** (Criss Cross)

# Eddie Marshall

DRUMS
*born* 13 April 1938

Marshall has unobtrusively added value to several significant modern groups. His first important gig was with the Toshiko–Mariano quartet in 1960, and he moved on (after army service) to playing with Stan Getz before working in pop situations. He then settled in San Francisco and became the in-house drummer at the city's important Keystone Korner club, working there through the 70s and backing many visitors. Although a heart condition slowed him down, he continues to work and teach in San Francisco, and his sons also work in music.

**Art Pepper,** *San Francisco Samba* (Contemporary)

# John Marshall

DRUMS
*born* 28 August 1941

Marshall has participated in many of the leading British groups of the past 40 years. In his 20s he worked for such leaders as Michael Garrick, Graham Collier, Mike Westbrook and Keith Tippett, but his major associations were with the early stirrings of British jazz-rock: he played with Ian Carr's Nucleus between 1969 and 1971, and then spent a long nine years with Soft Machine. Seeing Marshall in this period was always exciting and often fairly exhausting: a master of virtuoso, polyrhythmic playing that seemed to blitz together jazz and rock approaches, with Soft Machine he played as fast and hard as most of his American contemporaries in the idiom, and even if he didn't quite have Billy Cobham's super-human dexterity and power, he wasn't far behind, and his lengthy solo features could be awe-inspiring. His subsequent ventures have been a little more quiescent, working with Eberhard Weber, various John Surman groups, Theo Travis and Kenny Wheeler, but he remains a formidable presence, although he seems to perform in Britain comparatively rarely.

**Soft Machine,** *Softs*

# Kaiser Marshall

DRUMS
*born* 11 June 1899; *died* 3 January 1948

As Joseph Marshall remembered it, they looked for a title to bestow on this impressive new drummer from Georgia, and since the familiar titles such as 'King' were all already taken, they settled on 'Kaiser'. Marshall worked with Fletcher Henderson during his early years as a bandleader, staying until 1929, and during the 30s he depped in many of the major New York bands, including those of Duke Ellington, Cab Calloway and Chick Webb. In the 40s he carried on working as a freelance: some of his last work on record was with the Mezzrow–Bechet Quintet, and he cut his last record with them only weeks before he died from food poisoning.

**Fletcher Henderson,** *1927* (Classics)

# Wendell Marshall

BASS
*born* 24 October 1920

Born in St Louis, Marshall was Jimmy Blanton's cousin and it was Blanton's example which inspired him to take up the bass. Which made it all the more appropriate that he joined Duke Ellington's orchestra in 1948, having already worked in son Mercer's band. Marshall stayed with Duke until 1955 and then won the role of in-house bassist at Prestige Records, which gave him a sideman role on dozens of albums from the period. Dependable and able to move easily between hotter and cooler styles of playing – and unfazed if having to turn in a few solo bars, at a time when bassists did comparatively little spotlit work – Marshall is a somewhat undersung and forgotten figure on his instrument. That is in part due to his deliberately low profile, for after leaving Prestige in 1963 he worked mostly in Broadway pit orchestras and retired altogether in 1968.

# Claire Martin

VOCAL
*born* 6 September 1967

Martin is a superior jazz-pop singer, whose career on record has thus far been a sometimes awkward, occasionally triumphant

crossing between the two sides.
London-born, she worked on cruise liners
and in America before basing herself back in
London from 1991 and recording a sequence
of albums while basically doing time on the
club circuit. She has a likeably punchy way
with a quick tempo and delivers ballads
with a cool and faintly detached air, as if she
doesn't want to put her faith in the Krall
style of crooning. She tried to go more the
way of a rock synthesis with *Perfect Alibi*
(2000), but that market has few places for a
30-something singer at present and she continues to drift, a little undecided, between
styles.
**Make This City Ours** (Linn)

## Pat Martino
GUITAR
*born* 25 August 1944

A disastrous interruption to his career may
have cost Martino a more prominent awareness among the huge audience for jazz
guitar. Born in Philadelphia, he started out
in the organ-combo jazz which was hot in
the city in the early 60s, playing with the
likes of Jack McDuff and Groove Holmes
before leading his own groups late in the
decade. He made records for Prestige, Muse
and Warner Bros (the latter more in a lite-
fusion mode) and established a reputation
as a fast, hard-hitting but stringent improviser, with a penchant for playing in octaves
in the Wes Montgomery style. But he suffered an aneurysm in 1980, which brought
on memory loss and an almost complete
breakdown in his ability to play. He
struggled his way back, and after a number
of false starts began performing again in the
90s. Since then, he has signed with Blue
Note and re-established his career, although
some of the old facility has been replaced by
an aggressive and rather dour approach
which is less appealing than his previous
manner.
**Consciousness** (Muse)

## Barry Martyn
DRUMS
*born* 23 February 1941

They called him 'Kid' Martyn at first, which
wasn't unjustified or patronizing: this
Londoner was only 15 when he formed his
first band, and he was as purist in his
approach as Ken Colyer, modelling his
groups on the sound of the George Lewis
bands of the 50s. Martyn embarked on his
first pilgrimage to New Orleans in 1961, still
only barely out of his teens, and he began
recording and studying with the old-timers
of the city's music, starting his own label
(Mono) and himself playing with such local
old masters as Percy Humphrey and Kid
Sheik Cola. Thereafter he divided his time
between England and the US, but eventually
became an American citizen and settled first
in Los Angeles and later in New Orleans
itself. While he still visits Britain and
Europe regularly to play, he has become an
honoured and honorary member of the New
Orleans musical community, doing as much
as anyone to document – via recordings and
oral histories – and preserve the music of
the city, and researching old recordings for
labels such as American Music. Along the
way, he has made himself into a master of
his adopted city's music, and his cigar-
chomping presence has enlivened the spirit
of a music which might otherwise have
fallen into disrepair long ago.
**Vintage Barry Martyn** (GHB)

## Hugh Masekela
TRUMPET, VOCAL
*born* 4 April 1939

Along with Abdullah Ibrahim, Masekela was
for a long spell jazz's most famous exile, and
one of the few African players to create any
lasting impact on a world stage. Born in
Witbank, South Africa, his first gig – with the
African Jazz Revue – set the tone of all his
future playing, since it mixed a received
bebop form with the looser and more dance-
able sound of mbaqanga, which originated
in the townships. After a spell with the
important local group The Jazz Epistles he
left his homeland in 1960 and went to study
at London's Guildhall, before another move
to California. There he made records for his
own Chisa label and made occasional visits
to Africa, before moving to Botswana in
1982, although he returned to the US in
1985. There were associations with Fela Kuti
and Miriam Makeba, Masekela's ex-wife,
which produced intermittently interesting
music. Masekela finally settled back in South

Africa following the end of the apartheid era, and he continues to tour as an ambassador for his country's great black music. As a player himself, Masekela has an appealing, forthright sound, and he brings some gravitas to his musical settings by dint of who he is: but far too much of his work on record has been based around insubstantial and simplistic fusions of jazz, Afropop and light music which sometimes come very close to making Hugh sound like Herb Alpert. One sometimes wonders how many more interesting players from the region must have been lost.

*African Connection* (Impulse!)

## Phil Mason
CORNET
*born* 10 April 1940; *died* 2002

Mason's fiercely enthusiastic cornet playing was a tonic for many years in the often parochial British traditional scene. He began playing in London with Eric Silk's band in the middle 60s, joined Max Collie in the 70s, and thereafter led groups of his own – not in an especially purist style of any kind, but with a generous approach to a standard repertoire which he held in a loyal high esteem.

*Hush Hush* (Lake)

## Rod Mason
TRUMPET
*born* 28 September 1940

Mason arrived on the London trad scene in 1960, and besides leading some groups of his own he spent periods with Monty Sunshine (1962–5) and Acker Bilk (1971–3). Since then he has mostly worked as his own leader, although he spent a period with the Dutch Swing College Band in the 80s and that led to his working mainly in Europe, usually with his Hot Five – a suitable band name, since much of his playing is on a direct line from vintage Louis Armstrong.

*Rod Mason's Hot Five* (Timeless)

## Cal Massey
COMPOSER, TRUMPET
*born* 11 January 1927; *died* 25 October 1972

Massey played trumpet with Jay McShann in the 40s, but he subsequently made his mark as a composer. He led a group in Philadelphia in the later 50s which performed his music, but nothing was recorded until 1961, and he meanwhile contributed pieces to other albums: John Coltrane recorded 'Bakai' and 'The Damned Don't Cry' (originally for *Africa/Brass*, although it was left off the original album), and Freddie Hubbard, Jackie McLean and Lee Morgan also set down some of Massey's tunes. The one record under his own name, *Blues To Coltrane* (Candid, 1961), has some intriguing music but sounds under-rehearsed and too diffident. Massey later played with Archie Shepp but had no further opportunities to record his own music. His son Zane (b 1957) is an accomplished tenorman in a freebop style.

*Blues To Coltrane* (Candid)

## George Masso
TROMBONE
*born* 17 November 1926

Masso played with Jimmy Dorsey's band after serving in the army, but for most of the 50s and 60s he preferred teaching to playing professionally. In 1973 he began performing again, playing with Benny Goodman and Bobby Hackett, and since then he has become a regular participant in many of the small-band swing groups which have kept that idiom available to modern audiences. A gentlemanly stylist with an occasional salty twist which recalls the Bill Harris approach, Masso has been a bonus in many of the records made in this vein in the past decade or so.

*That Old Gang Of Mine* (Arbors)

## Carmen Mastren
GUITAR
*born* 6 October 1913; *died* 31 March 1981

Mastren played in a family band as a boy and moved to New York in 1935, joining Tommy Dorsey a year later and becoming a a key member of that band: besides his strong rhythm work, he was a gifted soloist and smart arranger. He left in 1941 and basically worked as a studio musician thereafter, playing for NBC until 1970 and then freelancing as he pleased. His oddest recording project was probably a studio date called *Banjorama* (1957), which featured Mastren, Bucky Pizzarelli and Robert Dominick on banjos and had Dick Hyman masquerading as 'The Renowned Ricardo'!

**Tommy Dorsey, *1936*** (Classics)

# Mat Mathews

ACCORDION
born 18 June 1924

The accordion no longer carries quite the opprobrium it once did among jazz audiences, thanks to the efforts of Astor Piazzolla and Gil Goldstein among others, but Mathews must have felt like he was walking into the lion's den when he first fronted a group at the Newport Jazz Festival. A Dutchman, he went to the US after escaping from a Nazi death camp and working in European clubs. In 1952, he formed a band in New York and during the 50s played something like bebop on the instrument, recording for Brunswick and Dawn and sharing an album of live music from Newport with Toshiko Akiyoshi. He was behind the New York Jazz Quartet/Ensemble, which also numbered Herbie Mann and Joe Puma among its members, but eventually returned to Holland, where he often worked in film and TV scoring. Ahead of his time.

**The Modern Art Of Jazz By Mat Mathews** (Dawn)

# Ronnie Mathews

PIANO
born 2 December 1935

Mathews got his start backing the standards vocalist Gloria Lynne in 1960, and from there he did sideman work with Sonny Stitt, Max Roach and Roy Haynes, also taking on a stint with Art Blakey at the end of the 60s. Narcotics problems kept him off the scene for a while, but by the middle 70s he was playing full time again, and he features on Dexter Gordon's *Homecoming* comeback album for Columbia (1977). Thereafter he worked sometimes as a leader, besides playing sideman roles and teaching in New York.

Mathews has never been much in the limelight, and some of his appearances have suggested a note-spinning modal player in the McCoy Tyner cast, but a few trio records – particularly the one below – have been enjoyable for playing of lived-in dignity.

**Dark Before The Dawn** (DIW)

# Matty Matlock

CLARINET
born 27 April 1907; *died* 14 June 1978

Julian 'Matty' Matlock was something of an aristocrat among Dixielanders. He grew up in Nashville, played in Southern orchestras as his start, and went to New York to join Ben Pollack in 1929. Along with many of his fellow sidemen he stayed on when the Pollack band turned into the Bob Crosby orchestra in 1935, although latterly he spent more time writing arrangements for the band than performing in it. In 1942 he headed for Hollywood, where he wrote and led some groups of his own, often backing Bing Crosby on his Decca record dates and appearing in the film *Pete Kelly's Blues* as the combo leader. In the 60s and 70s he was busy playing again, at Dick Gibson's Jazz Parties and on tour, visiting Europe in 1972. With his usually sparkling clarinet and his all-round writing skills, he offered a rounded musicianship which was rare in his part of the jazz lexicon.

**Pete Kelly's Blues** (Columbia)

# Bennie Maupin

SAXOPHONES, BASS CLARINET
born 29 August 1940

Detroit-born, Maupin played saxophone in high school, then moved to New York in 1963 and worked in relative obscurity until joining Roy Haynes in 1966. He was one of the players involved in the studio sessions for Miles Davis's *Bitches Brew* (1969), and a year later he began an association with Herbie Hancock, working with him through most of the 70s. Maupin took a significant part in records such as *Headhunters* (1973), and many years later he was – seemingly as a guy looking for work – involved in the Headhunters reunion. But in those situations he sounds like Hancock's stooge: on his own, in the ECM one-off *Jewel In The*

*Lotus* (1974), and in his strange, retro-styled record with Patrick Gleeson, *Driving While Black . . .* (2000), he sounds like his own man.
**Jewel In The Lotus** (ECM)

# Billy May
ARRANGER, TRUMPET
*born* 10 November 1916; *died* 22 January 2004

Like Glenn Miller or Gordon Jenkins, May is a big-band figure whose relationship with jazz is tangential. He actually played with both Miller and Charlie Barnet in the early 40s, and then worked as a studio player, although by the 50s most of his work was as an arranger. He made a sequence of albums of his own for Capitol in the 50s, a mix of sweet big-band swing and easy listening, as well as doing arrangements for such singers as Frank Sinatra, whose albums with May were the 'swinging' end of his 50s repertoire. May carried on working through the 60s, 70s and 80s, eventually an honoured figure in big-band arranging.
**Frank Sinatra, *Swinging Session*** (Capitol)

# Tina May
VOCAL
*born* 30 March 1961

Born in Gloucester, May mixed working as an actress with jazz singing from the early 80s. In the past 15 years she has steadily built up a body of work which portrays a mature and thoughtful interpreter of the standards-songbook, as well as one whose tastes extend into more rarefied areas of repertoire. She has a strong and wide-ranging voice which has its idiosyncrasies of intonation and enunciation, although these only add to a delivery which is notably free of cliché and of following other jazz-singing role models.
**One Fine Day** (33 Jazz)

# Bill Mays
PIANO
*born* 5 February 1944

A Californian, Mays got his start accompanying singers such as Sarah Vaughan and Al Jarreau in the early and middle 70s. He switched coasts and settled in New York in 1984, and since then has worked in small groups, in Bob Minzter's big band, and frequently in a duo format with different bass players. A graceful player, but little he has set down on record really lingers in the mind, although a couple of recent records for Palmetto suggest a sudden focusing of his talents.
**Summer Sketches** (Palmetto)

# Lyle Mays
KEYBOARDS
*born* 27 November 1953

Mays sometimes seems more like a technician than a musician. He got his start in Woody Herman's band in 1975 but then joined fellow Midwesterner Pat Metheny in the guitarist's quartet, and that association has endured ever since. Mays is Metheny's main co-writer and handles all the keyboard orchestration on his many records: he was an early starter in getting state-of-the-art synthesizers into jazz-orientated music, and he clearly has great knowledge of their use. Much of what he does on Metheny's records is deft and suitably beguiling, although as an improviser he doesn't seem up to much: but that is not the point of his role. Away from Metheny he has made a few records of his own, all notably dreary.
**Pat Metheny, *Still Life (Talking)*** (Geffen)

# Louis Mazetier
PIANO
*born* 17 February 1960

Mazetier divdes his time between playing jazz piano and working as a radiologist. He played in French traditional circles before becoming a founder member of Paris Washboard (1987), and he has also recorded some collections of ragtime piano. A demonstrably ebullient and witty player, he brings both a natural zip and the proper feel of authenticity to material which it is very easy to get wrong.
**With Neville Dickie, *If Dreams Come True*** (Stomp Off)

# Marilyn Mazur

PERCUSSION
*born* 8 January 1955

Though born in New York, Mazur moved
with her family to Denmark as a child and
has been based there since. She worked as
either drummer or percussionist with various Danish groups, and secured some attention in Pierre Dørge's New Jungle Orchestra,
but a four-year stint with Miles Davis, from
1985, inevitably put her into the spotlight.
Since then, besides working on her own projects, she has also had a starring role in Jan
Garbarek's touring band, and she brings a
little electricity with her acoustic set-up into
what can sometimes be a rather studious
ensemble. Mazur suggests no single tradition in her work: she may be that rarity,
a genuinely worldly rhythm player. It was a
nice acknowledgement of her work by her
own country when she won the Danish
JAZZPAR Prize in 2001.
**All The Birds** (Stunt)

# Robert Mazurek

CORNET, ETC
*born* 1966

Mazurek's career has taken some unlikely
turns. Although born in New Jersey, he has
spent most of his time in Chicago, playing
on the local hard-bop scene in the 80s and
working with such local heroes as Eric
Alexander. In 1992, he spent some time in
Scotland, after deciding to take a group over
to the Edinburgh Festival, and recorded for
the very traditionally minded Hep label; but
in 1995, he embarked on a complete change
of direction back in Chicago after playing
with guitarist Jeff Parker, and started to move
into the region of Don Cherry's free playing.
This in turn led to an association with the
circle of young Chicagoans who were trying
to mix up jazz procedures with rock and
electronic composition, and Mazurek subsequently became a key member of the
Chicago Underground Trio, often contributing as much in the way of electronics as brass
playing. While the group's music is often
more heavy on texture than event, it's an
agreeable and creative change from turning
out hard-bop licks.
**Chicago Underground Trio, *Possible Cube***
(Delmark)

# M-Base

A cooperative gathering, informally organized by a group of musicians based at that
time (around 1984) in Brooklyn, NY: the principal individuals involved were Steve
Coleman, Greg Osby, Graham Haynes,
Cassandra Wilson, Geri Allen and Gary
Thomas. The name is derived from Macro
Basic Array of Structured Extemporizations,
not quite as snappy a title as the one
chosen. The M-Base sound, as evidenced by
the recordings of Coleman's Five Elements,
and the bands of Osby, Thomas and Wilson
– all of whom were at that time recording
for the Austrian company JMT, effectively
the house label for the music – resided in a
sort of brainy, inscrutable kind of fusion:
driven by angular, almost spidery funk
rhythms, dry harmonic content, and melody
lines planned with an algebraic logic, the
music was a fascinating alternative to what
was at the time seen as the prevailing orthodoxy of the neo-bop music of Wynton
Marsalis and his contemporaries. As cool as
Konitz, as austerely cerebral as Tristano, this
was a modern black music denuded of the
sweat and upfront emoting of funk and
R&B, even as it staked a claim on a young,
self-aware audience. Even a sceptic such as
Branford Marsalis acknowledged the value
of putting a label on what they did.

M-Base did not last very long. The main
participants either faded from the scene
(Haynes, Thomas), or went eclectic (Allen) or
popular (Wilson). Yet all bar Thomas went
on to major-label deals. Osby has become a
young grandmaster of a polystylistic
modern idiom, which has left Coleman to
remain as M-Base's premier keeper of the
spirit: his music continues to expand
further on his original manifesto of
Structured Extemporizations.

# Cecil McBee

BASS
*born* 19 May 1935

McBee has quietly and without any undue
fuss built a large discography and a huge list
of associations, in both 'in' and 'out' situations. He arrived in New York in 1964, having previously played in military bands, and
through the 60s and 70s worked with
dozens of leading players: Wayne Shorter,

Charles Lloyd, Sam Rivers, Alice Coltrane, Abdullah Ibrahim, Chico Freeman, Joanne Brackeen and Norman Connors are some of them. He was a member of The Leaders and every so often he has stepped out as a leader himself, although that initiative never seems to last for too long. Some of his superior later work has been with the Japanese pianist Yosuke Yamashita. The best thing to say about his playing is that it always seems to fit just right, whoever is out front and in charge.

*Unspoken* (Palmetto)

## Christian McBride

BASS
*born* 21 May 1972

McBride's affections are divided equally between James Brown and Ray Brown: he loves both on-the-one funk and the feel of 4/4 jazz time, and he sees no contradiction in declaring a similar loyalty to both. He studied bass and classical music in his home town of Philadelphia and arrived in New York in 1989, quickly securing work with such leaders as Roy Hargrove and Freddie Hubbard, and he began an association with Benny Green in 1991. Thereafter he was in constant demand as the hottest young bassist on the scene. The beauty of McBride's style is the way classicism mixes with funk and neither side has the upper hand: he brings the same dedication to both. While his jazz work has a much stronger presence – by the end of the century he had already performed with many of the major active figures in the music – he has made a point of pursuing his interests in the more popular idiom, and his recent solo work (*Vertical Vision*, 2002) investigates fusion as a possible area of activity too. A cheerful and outgoing man, he will surely be a valuable part of jazz for many years to come.

*Number Two Express* (Verve)

## Steve McCall

DRUMS
*born* 30 September 1933; *died* 24 May 1989

McCall was primarily a serving soldier in the American avant-garde of the 70s and 80s. He played in R&B bands in his native Chicago before becoming involved in the

AACM in 1965, and thereafter he was on hand to drum for many of the leaders of the movement. He was in Paris during 1967–70, and thereafter his major association was with the trio Air, with Henry Threadgill and Fred Hopkins, although he also played with such leaders as Arthur Blythe and David Murray. He led some groups of his own, but never on record.

**Air,** *Air Lore* (Novus)

## Les McCann

PIANO, VOCAL
*born* 23 September 1935

McCann's busy career has been full of incident, although in the end there has been little enough which really stands out as important. Born in Lexington, Kentucky, he trained as both a singer (in which capacity he once appeared on Ed Sullivan's TV show!) and as a pianist, and he worked in California nightclubs at the end of the 50s before signing to Pacific Jazz and recording a sequence of quite successful albums. For much of the 60s he pursued a style which was his own rather bodacious variation on soul-jazz, and his partnership with saxophonist Eddie Harris led to a hit track with 'Compared To What', from their 1969 *Swiss Movement* record. His 70s discography is a chaotic muddle of jazz, blues, gospel and pop music and the original albums are barely worth keeping. In the 80s and 90s he was touring with Harris again, and enjoying a modest renaissance. Lately, poor health has curtailed his keyboard playing, but he's still singing. John Scofield remembers playing a show around the time he did one of his Blue Note albums in dedication to McCann's kind of music, and hearing a voice in the audience shouting out, 'Yeah! Les McCann! All right!' When John peered out to see who it was, he recognized the cheerleader. It was Les.

*Swiss Movement* (Atlantic)

## Ron McClure

BASS
*born* 22 November 1941

McClure's major early association was with the Charles Lloyd group, starting in 1967 and lasting a couple of years. After this he worked mainly as a freelance, with a few

significant associations: with Dave Liebman, Lee Konitz, Richie Beirach. While he has played in some fusion situations and has used the electric bass in that context, his principal work has been in a reflective post-bop mode, and he has led a number of sessions of his own for Steeplechase in particular in that context.

**Sunburst** (Steeplechase)

# Rob McConnell
TROMBONE, BANDLEADER
*born* 14 February 1935

The Canadian trombonist played in Toronto dance bands before joining Maynard Ferguson in 1964, though he soon returned to Canada, where he worked mainly as a studio pro. He originally formed his Boss Brass outfit to work as a studio ensemble for light-music material, but eventually he added a reed section, and by 1976 it was a full-scale big band which worked as a concert orchestra too. Signed to Concord, McConnell delivered a long series of what were basically soundalike albums: though the music packed the expected punch, the band always sounded like what it originally was, a middle-of-the-road studio team. They only rarely ventured far from their Canadian base, and lately McConnell has scaled back to a smaller ensemble, which on recent evidence is rather more characterful.

**Brassy And Sassy** (Concord)

# Susannah McCorkle
VOCAL
*born* 1 January 1946; *died* 19 May 2001

McCorkle was born in California but was living in Paris in the early 70s when she discovered jazz singing and started performing herself. She moved to London in 1972 and began working with Keith Ingham (to whom she was married for a time), singing the standards book, and in 1979 she settled in New York. She recorded and performed live steadily enough over the next two decades, although she never seemed to have much luck with her career: two affiliations with minor labels left her earlier records in limbo, and while she went on to make a fine sequence of CDs for Concord, many of them are blemished by errors of judgement in

picking material – she wanted to mix contemporary and older songs, and often the newer pieces didn't sound right. But her best performances feature a husky, finely nuanced delivery that honours good material and is coolly affecting in a notably modern way. Had she been 15 years younger, she might have capitalized on the new fad for jazz singers which emerged in Diana Krall's wake. But she had long suffered from depression, and one day in 2001 she abruptly took her own life.

**Hearts And Minds** (Concord)

# Dick McDonough
GUITAR, BANJO
*born* 1904; *died* 25 May 1938

McDonough was a southpaw who started leading his own groups while still in his teens before getting involved in New York's dance-band scene. Though he started out on banjo and mandolin, he realized that the guitar was going to be the coming instrument, and along with Eddie Lang he dominated the New York studios in the later 20s, recording with all the elite white jazz players as well as on commercial dates. He carried on in much the same manner during the 30s, recording some fleet duets with his friend Carl Kress, but a fondness for drink began to ruin his health and he collapsed and died while doing another studio job for NBC.

**Various Artists**, *Pioneers Of The Jazz Guitar* (Yazoo)

# Brother Jack McDuff
ORGAN
*born* 17 September 1926; *died* 23 January 2001

Eugene McDuffy started his jazz career on bass, working in Chicago with Johnny Griffin and others, but decided to move over to the piano in the middle 50s. This in turn gave way to the Hammond organ, and by 1960 he was leading his own groups in the newly popular organ-combo format. Prestige signed him in that year and he recorded a long sequence of albums for the label, usually with a horn player or two along for the ride, mostly in the studio but sometimes live as well. Besides these sets he also made three for Atlantic, and in the 70s he made

yet more records for Blue Note and Cadet. McDuff assimilated the popular fads for funk and near-disco rhythms along the way but basically kept faith with his bebop style: less of an expressionist than Jimmy Smith and some of his contemporaries, and his albums have stood the test of time better than many in the same idiom. His career was somewhat in the doldrums in the 80s but was boosted by the revival of interest in the organ-jazz style, and Concord signed him in the 90s, where he resumed his easy-going delivery, now deep enough to lend every performance a massive authority. Joey DeFrancesco sparred with him on a few late sessions, to delightful effect.

*Tough 'Duff* (Prestige/OJC)

# Gary McFarland

VIBES, ARRANGER

*born* 23 October 1933; *died* 3 November 1971

McFarland blazed a brief and mercurial trail. Though he was born in Los Angeles, he went to Oregon in his teens and studied at the State University; during his military service he learned to play vibes, and in the second half of the 50s he studied composition and eventually went to Berklee. In 1961, he began moving in exalted company, arranging for Anita O'Day and Stan Getz, and having his own tunes picked up by such as John Lewis (who gave him significant early encouragement) and Gerry Mulligan ('Weep' and 'Chuggin'' for the Concert Jazz Band). He made seven albums for Verve and four for Impulse!, including projects with star soloists such as Bill Evans and Clark Terry, and from 1965 led a vibes-fronted quintet of his own, which had a kind of soft-fusion feel. There were four further albums for a label he helped to found, Skye, but McFarland seemed to have lost his way after an exciting start, and his attempts at becoming a mood-music baron left him adrift from the high ground of jazz composition which would have sustained his reputation. He died of a heart attack at 38, a condition apparently worsened by a drink problem. Very little of his work has been widely reissued, and a homage project involving his best music wouldn't come out of turn.

*The Gary McFarland Orchestra, Guest Soloist Bill Evans* (Verve)

# Bobby McFerrin

VOCAL

*born* 11 March 1950

McFerrin was the son of two opera singers, but originally studied as a pianist before he concentrated on his voice. Having already played in jazz small groups, he performed in a duo with Jon Hendricks in 1979 and thereafter started working as a solo with accompaniment, making some headline performances in 1981–2 which led to his being signed to Elektra Musician. From 1983, though, he worked mostly by himself, for at least a large part of his concerts, occasionally enlisting a guest star to perform a dialogue with him, and his 1984 album *The Voice*, with its virtuoso one-man displays, catches some of his most vivid work. McFerrin's very broad vocal range, his fine control, improvisational skills and use of expressive devices from a porcine grunt to a skylark falsetto, made him a unique figure in American music: yet his performances soon left jazz behind and stretched towards a kind of vocal circus act, climaxing with his irritating habit of enlisting members of the audience to 'accompany' him vocally, a shameless if well-meant display of democracy in action. On record, McFerrin has had trouble finding a sound context for his prowess. His biggest success was the exasperating 1989 hit 'Don't Worry, Be Happy', but aside from that his albums have registered little in the way of lasting impact, and misguided crossover projects such as *The Mozart Sessions* (1996) have only underlined how difficult it is for him to find a sensible milieu. His Voicestra, a dozen singers from various disciplines and backgrounds, makes a remarkable sound in their seemingly improvised mantras, but again one wonders what the musical point really is. And compared to Phil Minton, McFerrin often seems more like a counterfeit improviser than a genuine one.

*The Voice* (Elektra Musician)

# Bernie McGann

ALTO SAXOPHONE

*born* 22 June 1937

A veteran Australian modernist, McGann was born in Sydney and started playing there in the late 50s: one of his early playing companions was drummer John Pochée,

whom he is still performing with. He then lived and played in New Zealand and Melbourne before returning to the Sydney scene. His style and sound have toughened over the years, building on an early Paul Desmond influence to create a broad palette which encompasses the Ornette Coleman end of the scale as well, although he prefers to suggest that he has listened to everybody and taken on this and that. A couple of his sessions were released in England on the Emanem label in the 80s, but otherwise his work has only been documented on Australian labels, and not too well: after a solitary 1967 session he didn't record again for 20 years, and has so far completed a mere five CDs under his own leadership. Besides his own small-group work, he has played with the large group Ten Part Invention, where his skills add much to the band's sound.
***Bundeena*** (Rufus)

## Lou McGarity
TROMBONE
*born* 22 July 1917; *died* 28 August 1971

McGarity's first significant gig was with Benny Goodman's band (1940–42), and thereafter he worked with Raymond Scott before enlisting in the Eddie Condon circle of musicians. McGarity's easygoing style and attractively full sound was an appealing change from the more barking manner of many of the Dixieland trombonists, and besides sticking with the Condon clan he also did much studio work in the 40s and 50s. Latterly he suffered from heart problems, which often interrupted his career thereafter, but he managed to cut a pair of albums under his own name in 1959–60.
***Some Like It Hot!*** (Jubilee)

## Howard McGhee
TRUMPET
*born* 6 March 1918; *died* 17 July 1987

'Maggie' was a fine trumpeter, but his misfortune was to emerge at a moment when the competition was at first Dizzy Gillespie, Fats Navarro and Miles Davis, and then Clifford Brown: good though he was, he ended up as an also-ran in bebop. He was born in Tulsa, and worked in Midwestern bands before joining Lionel Hampton and Andy Kirk. He joined Coleman Hawkins's small group in 1944, and plays some terrific solos on their sides for Capitol. He went to California with Hawkins and remained there for a time, long enough to take part in some of Charlie Parker's Dial records: he plays on the tormented 'Lover Man' session of 1947. He then joined Jazz At The Philharmonic and toured with that operation, gaining wider attention as a result, and by 1949 he was winning best-trumpet polls. But in the 50s his career fell away: heroin addiction took its toll on him, and he made only a handful of records in the period when he should have been asserting his qualities and making a name as a leader. *Maggie's Back In Town* (1961) marked something of a revival, and he began working regularly with Teddy Edwards. But McGhee's playing had declined: his phrasing, previously a confident blending of bop and swing devices, became less certain, even though some later records with Edwards suggest a man coming to terms with his limitations in a sometimes moving way. He was still playing into the 80s, although the business had long since left him behind. Every photograph shows him wearing dark glasses: he was self-conscious about a childhood accident which resulted in his losing an eye.
***On Dial: The Complete Sessions*** (Spotlite)

## Chris McGregor
PIANO
*born* 24 December 1936; *died* 26 May 1990

McGregor was, with Abdullah Ibrahim, the focal point of South African jazz in exile. He studied piano in Cape Town and led jazz groups there in the early 60s before forming The Blue Notes with Mongezi Feza, Dudu Pukwana, Nick Moyake, Johnny Dyani and Louis Moholo, a mixed-race group which clearly stood little chance in its own country of working at all. They left South Africa in 1964 and played in France and Switzerland before McGregor and his companions settled in England. The pianist and his players started to take on free-jazz influences, and the music on *Very Urgent* (Polydor, 1967) is an often clumsy mix of the new developments with the more conventional, boppish feel of their previous music, along with the group's store of African melody. McGregor's impulses, though, led him more towards larger ensembles, and after trying to get a big band off the ground, he put together the Brotherhood Of Breath at the end of the decade, mixing his Blue Note sidemen with leading British free players. The group worked occasionally but left little in the way of a recorded legacy, and in 1974 McGregor decamped for France. He still returned to the UK for gigs, with his surviving comrades from the old days, and there was more big-band work completed, but in the 80s it felt as if the pianist had absented himself from what was then a thriving new jazz scene in the UK, and despite a couple of late records his latter-day contributions were modest. On a straightforward musical level, McGregor never approached Abdullah Ibrahim's creative output: he was a heavy man to be around, and there was something almost shamanic about him, but once his presence was gone, it was clear how thin his legacy would seem to listeners who had never heard his groups in person. If it wasn't for the Ogun label, which sponsored most of his recorded work, there would be even less to remember him by.

*Blue Notes For Mongezi* (Ogun)

# Jimmy McGriff

ORGAN
*born* 3 April 1936

McGriff learned from the masters, studying with Jimmy Smith and Richard 'Groove' Holmes, and put what he learned to constructive use: he signed to the Sue label in 1962, and almost at once scored a big hit on the soul charts with 'I've Got A Woman'. His funky organ-combo sound was a typical soul-jazz mix, but it leaned much closer to the soul end, and his Sue albums have a stronger jukebox orientation than those of his contemporaries. He went on to record another string of albums for Solid State, and in the 70s he did the same for Groove Merchant. As time went on, though, McGriff's sound moved back towards jazz, and in the 80s he signed to Milestone and formed a regular partnership with Hank Crawford, with the records still emerging at steady intervals. The sound has settled into a middle-aged spread, but McGriff's bluesy, generous music has the warm appeal of a bowl of hot stew.

*I've Got A Woman* (Sue)

# Kalaparush Maurice McIntyre

TENOR SAXOPHONE
*born* 24 March 1936

McIntyre is something of a lost soul among those musicians who created Chicago's jazz avant-garde in the 60s. He was a founder member of the AACM and he plays on the seminal record *Sound* by Roscoe Mitchell (1966). He went to New York in 1969 but was soon back in Chicago, and then tried New York again in 1974, playing on the loft scene there, but he never won great interest for his music and despite a few promising gigs with the Ethnic Heritage Ensemble and a few other groups, he was reputedly reduced to busking in the city in the 90s. A comparatively recent record for CIMP, *Dream Of* (1998), is the only recent evidence of his playing.

*Forces And Feelings* (Delmark)

# Makanda Ken McIntyre

ALTO SAXOPHONE
*born* 7 September 1931; *died* 13 June 2001

Ken McIntyre (he added 'Makanda' around 1990, when he learned that the Zulu word meant 'big head') was a second-string figure in the early 60s avant-garde. Born in Boston, he studied there and made a couple of strong early records in 1960–61, which had Eric Dolphy among the personnel. But he gave up the struggle of earning a living from his playing early on, and spent most of his life in education, teaching first in public schools and then in colleges: he was still teaching in the late 90s. In the 70s he made a series of albums for Steeplechase and he worked off and on in Europe and the US whenever the opportunity arose, but his quirky compositions and often convoluted playing suggested directions which were carried through more convincingly by other players.

*Looking Ahead* (Prestige)

# Dave McKenna
PIANO
*born* 30 May 1930

McKenna worked quietly and was well known only to other musicians for many years, in part because of his often working away from familiar jazz climes. He started playing in Boston groups at the end of the 40s, and did time with Woody Herman and Charlie Ventura before mostly playing in small groups through the 50s and 60s: horn players such as Bobby Hackett and Zoot Sims liked his sympathetic but hard-swinging manner, and he built up an encyclopedic knowledge of American songs that let him handle anything that came up on the stand. He moved to Cape Cod towards the end of the 60s and worked mainly in piano bars for much of the time, where he was left to his own devices; but a contract with Concord brought him to an international audience for the first time, and all through the 80s and 90s he made many records for the label, toured with some of their 'label' bands, and worked regularly with fellow mainstreamers Scott Hamilton and Warren Vaché. A large man who seems to put his full weight behind his playing, his prodigious output can sometimes feel undifferentiated, although that is more the consequence of a consistency of approach and taste: he knows what he likes to do, and he does it his way, unfurling songs by looking after their melodies ahead of driving a fast tempo. As the century wound down, he went into semi-retirement.
*My Friend The Piano* (Concord)

# Red McKenzie
VOCAL, ETC
*born* 14 October 1899; *died* 7 February 1948

William 'Red' McKenzie was a Runyonesque hustler: Eddie Condon thought he looked like 'a mad bartender', but they became fast friends and McKenzie got Condon his first record date in 1927. By then, he was already going places, having led The Mound City Blue Blowers for three years, and the group moved from a novelty band to a genuine hot ensemble. Red himself buzzed out vocal lines through a comb and paper, but that didn't get in the way of guest soloists such as Coleman Hawkins on the great 'Hello

Lola', from 1929. The MCBB worked on through the 30s, although latterly it was just a name for a straight dance band which McKenzie led as a singer. But his life went sour on him: his wife died, he moved back to his home town of St Louis, and though he later rejoined the Condon circle he had spoiled his health, mostly through drinking, and he died of cirrhosis.
*Mound City Blue Blowers* (Timeless)

# Ray McKinley
DRUMS
*born* 18 June 1910; *died* 7 May 1995

McKinley lived a long and busy life in big-band music. Born in Fort Worth, he played in bands which toured the south and west before joining the Dorsey Brothers in 1934, subsequently sticking with Jimmy after the siblings parted company. In 1939 he formed a new band with Will Bradley, which cashed in on the swing-era fad for boogie-woogie setpieces arranged for orchestra, and during war service he joined the Glenn Miller AAF band. He ran the band with Jerry Gray after Miller's death and he was still leading 'ghost' versions of the Miller orchestra until the late 60s, after which he led small groups for a few years – before taking over yet another Miller band from Tex Beneke, which took him into the 80s. While not much remembered as any kind of stylist, McKinley was an absolute pro at the kit, knowing exactly how to get the orchestra to sound right, and he most likely did more than anyone to keep Miller's legacy musically intact and relevant for audiences of more than one generation.

# McKinney's Cotton Pickers
GROUP

Bill McKinney (1895–1969) formed this band in Springfield, Ohio, around 1919, and they enjoyed local success playing as much novelty music as dance tunes: trumpeter John Nesbitt looked after the band's book of arrangements, and McKinney fronted the group. Jean Goldkette heard them in Detroit and suggested a name-change to McKinney's Cotton Pickers. He also hired Don Redman to build the band's material, and in 1928 they finally made their first records for Victor. Although they were contractually obliged to stay in Detroit, it was soon obvious that this was one of the best orchestras of the day, boosted by some of Redman's best writing and enlivened by soloists such as Nesbitt, Prince Robinson, Joe Smith and Claude Jones. The group was eventually allowed to tour more widely, but Redman quit in 1931 to run his own band and they went into a decline from that point, despite input from Benny Carter, and Joe Smith and Rex Stewart joining for a time. They made no more records after 1931, but left a fine legacy in their 53 issued titles. McKinney led various editions of the band until the early 40s, by which time they had been comprehensively sidelined by the music's progress. **Put It There** (Frog)

## Hal McKusick

ALTO SAXOPHONE
*born* 1 June 1924

McKusick was a section-player in many big bands in the 40s and early 50s, but he's best remembered as a studio man who led some interesting dates of his own for a number of different labels in the latter part of the 50s. His RCA set *The Jazz Workshop* (1956) was recorded contemporaneously with George Russell's of the same title, and features material by Russell, Jimmy Giuffre, Gil Evans and others: a quietly compelling record with some starkly challenging music, although *Triple Exposure* (Prestige, 1957) and *Cross Section: Saxes* (Decca, 1958) also have some fine and rewarding music. McKusick's own playing was soft-toned and wryly inventive. After this burst of activity, though, he doesn't seem to have recorded again as a leader, although he still did studio work into the 70s and carried on playing into the 90s with small groups. He is also a pilot.
**The Jazz Workshop** (RCA)

## John McLaughlin

GUITAR
*born* 4 January 1942

The Yorkshire-born guitarist mainly taught himself to play, starting with the blues, and when he moved to London in the early 60s

he played on the R&B circuit, particularly in Graham Bond's group. Bond's vaguely mystical leanings probably turned his head eastwards, although most of his early appearances on record were in prosaic surroundings such as Sandy Brown's *Hair At Its Hairiest*. McLaughlin spent nine months playing with Gunter Hampel in Germany before recording a set with John Surman, *Extrapolation* (1969), which suggested a talent suddenly bursting into maturity: smartly inventive tunes which were vehicles for some outstanding improvising by both men. It was the start of a couple of whirlwind years for McLaughlin: he joined Tony Williams's Lifetime in America, and played on the sessions for the Miles Davis albums *In A Silent Way*, *Bitches Brew* and *Jack Johnson* (for which Davis gave him the helpful advice, 'Play it like you don't know how to play the guitar'). Lifetime, with Williams, Jack Bruce and Larry Young, made ferocious music, but McLaughlin was dissatisfied with the way the group worked and he very likely had ambitions to be a star himself. In 1971, he formed the Mahavishnu Orchestra – the name came from Sri Chinmoy, a guru the guitarist had become beholden to on a spiritual level – and the band was an almost immediate hit on the college-rock circuit as well as with more tolerant jazz fans. For sheer musclebound power and the exhilarating sense of straining after ecstasy, the original Mahavishnu music was unrivalled and monumental. Billy Cobham's drums drove the band more furiously even than Tony Williams did in Lifetime, in part because he was less of a jazz drummer than Williams, and McLaughlin, violinist Rick Laird and keyboard whiz Jan Hammer piled on the improvisations with just the right amount of bravado and abandon. More than any other group, the Mahavishnu Orchestra gloried in the moment when rock, jazz and, crucially, technology – the new world of effects which were coming out of guitars and keyboards at that point – all collided and fused.

Inevitably, it wasn't too long before it began to atrophy: after *The Inner Mounting Flame* (1971) and *Birds Of Fire* (1973), and the stopgap live set *Between Nothingness And Eternity* (1973 – although that did include one of their finest moments, the almost crazed 'Sister Andrea'), all McLaughlin could think of was to bring in a full orchestra for the drearily pretentious *Apocalypse* (1974).

Despite an idea that McLaughlin was introducing a new style of clean living into jazz and rock (some hope), the band fell apart, and in 1976 he tried the acoustic Indian-jazz-rock fusion of Shakti, which toured occasionally. Having settled in Paris, he drifted between styles for much of the 80s and early 90s, playing in a trio with Al Di Meola and Paco de Lucía, trying other small-group formats and vacillating between acoustic and electric guitars. He signed to Verve at the beginning of the 90s and peeled off a variety of records and projects: a glum all-acoustic homage to Bill Evans, a rowdy fusion band called Free Spirits, a retrospective collection called *The Promise.* Shakti also came back together, under the rubric 'Remember Shakti'.

By now McLaughlin was a veteran with a large body of work behind him, and if he had little left to prove, it started to look as if he had little left to say as well, especially on the instrument which was now swarming with performers. It can often seem as if there is very little jazz in his music: his sweeping virtuosity has a hard, metallic edge to it, he never swings in the way that jazz guitarists 'usually' do, and his improvising is more akin to running impetuously through a labyrinth of modes, where the object is to build dazzling edifices of many, many notes. McLaughlin's arrival, though, was perfect timing: a jazz-orientated guy who loved the opportunities in a visceral, excessive rock situation, he came along just at the right moment.

*The Inner Mounting Flame* (Columbia)

# Jackie McLean
ALTO SAXOPHONE
*born* 17 May 1931

McLean lived in a New York neighbourhood full of musicians, and when he took up the alto there were plenty of people to play and practise with, including Sonny Rollins and Bud Powell. He started playing with Miles Davis – who was, like McLean, a narcotics addict at the time – and made his first records with him in 1951, before setting out as a leader himself and also working with Art Blakey's Jazz Messengers. He signed to Prestige in 1956 and made a sequence of exciting but often raggedy hard-bop albums for them: at this point his sound was a

direct evolution of Charlie Parker's blues playing, with a sour edge that he never quite got rid of, suggesting a microtonal flatness in most of his solos. He lost his cabaret card because of his drugs problems and couldn't work in New York for a time, but he was engaged to perform in the jazz play *The Connection*, with Freddie Redd's group, and toured with it to London, a gig which lasted on and off until 1963. In the meantime, he started making albums for Blue Note, eventually recording some 20 sessions for them all through the 60s: he reputedly used to take his pet monkey (featured on the cover of *Capuchin Swing*, 1960) into Alfred Lion's office, in order to get the Blue Note boss, who despised the animal, to give him a fresh advance. His Blue Notes demonstrate a player facing up to the new music and wondering what to do about it: records such as *Let Freedom Ring* (1962) and *Destination . . . Out!* (1964) suggested an awkward truce between his natural inclinations and the burdensome freedoms of the new jazz. In 1968 he began teaching at the University of Hartford, Connecticut, and started working with deprived children, and almost since then his musical career has taken something of a back seat. He made records for Steeplechase in the 70s, sometimes with his son René (b 1946) as a second saxophonist, and in the 90s he made moves towards becoming more active again as a performer; but later records for Verve and the revived Blue Note suggest a player whose best work is in the past. McLean's tart, often unlovely sound and astringent improvising have tended to divide listeners: for some he is an impassioned master of bop in its final stages. Others find him prolix and too often unconvincing.

*Bluesnik* (Blue Note)

# Dave McMurdo
TROMBONE
*born* 4 March 1944

Although he was born in the London suburb of Isleworth, McMurdo is a Canadian trombonist, who worked in Vancouver in the 60s and Toronto in the 70s. He was a sideman in some of the best of the country's large ensembles before forming his own Jazz Orchestra in 1988, a fine vehicle for the work of a number of writers besides McMurdo

himself, whose few records suggest a powerful midstream ensemble somewhat in the manner of the Clarke–Boland Big Band.
*Fire And Song* (Sackville)

# Harold McNair
SAXOPHONES, FLUTE
*born* 5 November 1931; *died* 7 March 1971

McNair was born in Kingston, Jamaica, but did all his important work in London. Before moving to England he played in the Bahamas, Cuba and Florida, and then took one of the alto chairs in Quincy Jones's 1960 big band, but from 1961 onwards he was based primarily in London. Besides leading groups of his own, he played with bands led by Mike Carr and Phil Seaman, and formed an unlikely association with the pop singer Donovan, recording his 'Lord Of The Reedy River'. McNair made a point of featuring flute playing as well as alto and tenor saxophone and was a capable soloist, but these days he is remembered mainly by record collectors as a cult figure: his *Affectionate Fink* album (Island, 1965), which also features Ornette Coleman's sidemen David Izenzon and Charles Moffett, is among the most highly prized of British jazz LPs. McNair died of lung cancer.
*Affectionate Fink* (Island)

# Big Jay McNeely
TENOR SAXOPHONE
*born* 29 April 1927

McNeely was the greatest sax honker of them all. Almost from the start of his career, he decided to keep 'serious' jazz at arm's length. Although he started playing in his native city of Los Angeles with contemporaries such as Hampton Hawes, he preferred to be involved with the new R&B groups of the day, and was soon playing with Johnny Otis in 1947. In this environment, he built up a style which depended entirely on almost bawling through the tenor saxophone: while some have likened this to the holy-roller stye of gospel preaching, it is in reality more akin to a cat with its tail on fire. But it went down a storm on the club circuit which Big Jay 'And His Mad-Cap Deacons' began playing for, with his brother Bob also an accessory, since he played baritone sax in the band. 'Playing Of Mad-Cap Sax Star Excites Crowds To Hysteria' howled a headline in *Ebony* magazine (1953), and the wild fervour of early rock'n'roll shows was tailor-made for McNeely. As soon as that scene began to decline, though, so did Big Jay's popularity, although he carried on working in Los Angeles clubs through most of the 60s. In the 90s he found a ready-made niche in rock'n'roll revival shows.
*Swingin'* (Collectables)

# Jim McNeely
PIANO
*born* 18 May 1949

A Chicagoan, McNeely went through much musical training: his father played piano, his brother was a working bassist, and Jim studied clarinet and composition at university. After choosing to focus on piano, he began getting gigs in the middle 70s and enjoyed some high-profile relationships: Stan Getz, Joe Henderson and Art Farmer were some of the leaders he worked for in the 80s. His writing brought him work in the Thad Jones–Mel Lewis Orchestra, and subsequently for several European big ensembles as well, particularly in Scandinavia: in 1998 he began directing the celebrated Danish Radio Big Band. McNeely plays composer's piano: abrim with ideas, but often rather modestly presented, so an inattentive listener can miss some of the detail of his thinking (on his Maybeck recital disc, he almost casually recasts one standard in all 12 keys). His arranging and composing has a following among musicians, less so among listeners: Jim's probably destined never to be much of a front-man.
*Live At Maybeck Recital Hall Vol 20* (Concord)

# Jimmy McPartland
CORNET
*born* 15 March 1907; *died* 13 March 1991

Jimmy McPartland always treasured Bix Beiderbecke's words of encouragement: 'I like you, kid. You sound like me, but you don't copy me.' A Chicagoan who was part of the so-called Austin High School Gang of players, he was only 17 when hired as Bix's replacement in the Wolverine Orchestra. He went on to join Ben Pollack's band in 1927 and started recording with the Red McKenzie–Eddie Condon circle, already a strong and outgoing player (much more so than Beiderbecke ever was). In the 30s he freelanced in New York, sometimes playing in the band led by his guitarist brother Dick (1905–57), and he was in residence at Nick's in New York before army service during the war. While in Europe he met pianist Marian Turner, and they were married in Germany in 1945. Thereafter, although their marrriage eventually broke up, they worked regularly together, and by the 50s McPartland was among the most eminent Chicago-style players in the music. He was busy with club work in New York and Boston, took on a few acting roles, and made some of his best records early in the LP era, including *Shades Of Bix* (1953), *Jimmy McPartland's Dixieland* (1957) and *The Music Man Goes Dixieland* (1958). Although work for him dried up in New York, he toured widely in the 60s and 70s and up until the end of his long life he was still a great-hearted player. He and Marian remained close friends, living in the same apartment building, and during the week before he died, they remarried.

**Shades Of Bix** (Brunswick)

# Marian McPartland
PIANO
*born* 20 March 1918

The first lady of jazz piano was born in Windsor, in the heart of England's home counties. Marian Turner was obliged to follow her mother's wishes and learn the violin until she was 14, but she went on to the English music-hall circuit as part of a four-piano act led by Billy Mayerl. She played for the troops during the hostilities and met Jimmy McPartland while he was on war service; they married in 1946, and went to live in America the following year. While New York was unlikely to be a welcoming environment for a white Englishwoman presuming to play jazz piano, McPartland nevertheless made her own way, establishing a trio besides playing in some of Jimmy's groups. In 1952 she began a long residency at The Hickory House, a club at 144 West 52nd Street, which lasted until 1960, and for much of the time her playing partners were Bill Crow and Joe Morello: although she made only a few records during this period,

they show how her style developed from a basic swing-piano idiom into a thoughtful and beautifully cadenced delivery which took on traces of bebop. From 1960 she toured extensively, usually with a trio, and over the years has employed a large number of sidemen, from Steve Swallow and Dave Bailey to Eddie Gomez and Billy Hart. She started her own record label, Halcyon, in 1969, which ran for some ten years before she finally secured a long-lasting affiliation with a sympathetic label when Concord signed her: since then she has created a large body of work for the label, of solo and trio sessions and music with occasional guest stars, including a fine date with Benny Carter. It is one of the best sequences of piano records from the past two decades.

Away from simply playing, Marian has led a very busy life. She began working with children in music education in the 50s and has continued since. She is a funny and perceptive writer, and her collection of essays *All In Good Time* is a delightful read. She worked as a disc jockey for a time and in 1978 began hosting a series called *Piano Jazz* for National Public Radio in the US, where she chats and reminisces with another musician – usually but not always a pianist – and the two play solos and duets. It was so successful that it continued into the new century, and a considerable number of programmes have been issued on CD. Despite her many years in the US, she has retained her British citizenship and she still visits home from time to time, still with the gracious manners of an English gentlewoman.

**In My Life** (Concord)

# Joe McPhee
SAXOPHONES, CORNET, TRUMPET
*born* 3 November 1939

McPhee has mastered the very rare double of saxophone and brass. He started out on trumpet and played that instrument in army bands in the early 60s, but in 1968 he taught himself the saxophone, and the tenor has since become his major horn. He began moving in free-jazz circles at the beginning of the 70s and in 1975 went to Europe for two years, where he started a long and enduring association with Werner Uehlinger's hat Hut operation (all the early hat Hut records feature McPhee). Returning to America, he later based himelf in Poughkeepsie, NY, although he has recently settled in France. Though somewhat better known in Europe than at home for many years (largely through the hat Hut association), McPhee became a ubiquitous figure on record in the 90s and has set down a tremendous amount of music in recent times. He is an unusual repository of classic saxophone sound – a solo performance is as likely to conjure up the timbre of the swing masters as readily as any extremism – and an openness to the most abstract setting and situation. Collaborators have included Raymond Boni, Evan Parker and André Jaume, and his every recording has something unpredictable about it, even when the music doesn't always succeed.

*Tenor* (hatOLOGY)

## Charles McPherson
ALTO AND TENOR SAXOPHONES
*born* 24 July 1939

McPherson spent his teenage years in Detroit, in the middle of its most fertile period as a jazz city, and he began lessons with Barry Harris. He moved to New York aged 20, and was hired by Charles Mingus, with whom he stayed on and off until 1972. He had mastered the bop vocabulary so faithfully that he was often regarded as little more than a Parker copyist, but as time went on the altoist inhabited the style so securely that he sounded more fully and engagingly his own man. There was a sequence of albums for Prestige which sometimes sounded like potboilers, but by the 90s, even though the saxophonist was sighted less frequently, he sounded close to magisterial, and a couple of dates for Arabesque featured some terrific music. In a romantic irony of sorts, he overdubbed the saxophone parts for sections of the soundtrack to Clint Eastwood's *Bird* in 1988.

*McPherson's Mood* (Prestige/OJC)

## Tommy McQuater
TRUMPET
*born* 4 September 1914

The Scottish-born trumpeter moved south at the start of the 30s and worked on cruise liners before joining the London dance-band scene and playing in the bands of Jack Payne and Lew Stone. After hours he would play in The Bag O'Nails or The Nest, jamming into the small hours. He worked in Benny Carter's group and then joined Ambrose's band, where he worked alongside Danny Polo, playing on some of the clarinettist's small-group dates. During the war he joined The Squadronaires, with his great pal George Chisholm, and then 'it felt different after the war, in a way. You didn't see so many dinner suits walking around.' In the 50s and 60s he was busy with studio freelance work, under such leaders as Cyril Stapleton, playing behind many showbiz legends. He went on to teach a number of British trumpet players and has enjoyed a long retirement, still going out to hear music whenever he can. One of the earliest hot players in London, and for many years one of the very best.

**George Chisholm,** *Early Days 1935–1944* (Timeless)

## Carmen McRae
VOCAL
*born* 8 April 1920; *died* 10 November 1994

McRae studied as a pianist but she was in love with Billie Holiday's singing and modelled her early style on her. She married Kenny Clarke in 1944 and was billed as 'Carmen Clarke' for her first recorded vocals, as a singer with Mercer Ellington's orchestra in 1946. By the middle 50s she had separated from Clarke and was Carmen McRae again, working as an intermission act at Minton's in New York, and making a single ten-inch album for Bethlehem. In 1955 she signed to Decca and made a sequence of seven outstanding records, although they have been mystifyingly neglected in the CD era: her voice had moved away from Holiday's style, taken on something of the high-art mannerism of Sarah Vaughan, but was basically an individual instrument which moved enigmatically between sweetness and a uniquely bitter aftertaste – no jazz singer has ever used sarcasm and a dark wit in the way that McRae did. From this point she worked regularly as a solo, usually with a trio accompaniment, and she made records for such labels as Columbia (two superb 1962 albums), Atlantic, Mainstream, Concord and, her final association, RCA Novus, for which she recorded homages to

Thelonious Monk and Holiday. A jazz singer through and through – no other vocalist has dared essay a Monk tribute record, and she managed that at the age of 68 – Carmen had a combative career. Her temper caused fall-outs with sidemen and record companies, and she had a sometimes tempestuous relationship with her material: Atlantic tried to get her to cover contemporary pop tunes, but those songs she deigned to sing she often turned on their heads, as in her stark, extraordinary treatment of Paul Simon's 'The Sound Of Silence'. Her voice deepened and darkened over the years and her large, blazing eyes seemed to stare down audiences. But she left a very fine discography on record and its comparative lack of recognition is unfortunate. She latterly suffered from asthma, had a bad attack of it following an engagement in 1991 and never sang again.

*Sings Lover Man* (Columbia)

## Jay McShann
PIANO, VOCAL
*born* 12 January 1916

The last great spirit of Kansas City jazz was actually born in Muskogee, Oklahoma, and he began playing in Tulsa and Arkansas in the early 30s. In 1936 he started playing in a trio in Kansas City, which grew to become a sextet and finally, in 1939, a big band. They began recording for Decca in 1941, although after an early hit with 'Confessin' The Blues', which featured Walter Brown's vocal, 'we never got a chance to record what we really wanted – we had a fantastic book, but we recorded very little of that stuff.' The surviving records do include much fine swinging music, though, with McShann's men running the classic KC gamut of blues, riffs and head arrangements. There is also the bonus of hearing Charlie Parker on his first sessions, since he joined McShann in 1941: 'Hootie Blues' and 'The Jumpin' Blues' are startling glimpses of the young Parker. McShann took the band to New York but had to do army service in 1943. He re-formed the orchestra in 1945, although he eventually scaled back to a small group, and though using both Parker and Gillespie at different times, he wasn't tempted by bebop: 'You couldn't dance, tap your foot or snap your fingers to bop. I didn't want to play music I could get no feeling from.' He went back to Kansas in 1950 and has been based there since, although he has also toured Europe extensively, as a soloist, a small-group pianist and a big-band leader, taking a group to Europe in 1989 with charts by Ernie Wilkins. A pianist of tremendous authority, 'Hootie' is a master of blues playing in particular, and although he recorded little in the 50s and early 60s, a now extensive discography has caught him all the way through the later part of the LP and CD eras.

*My Baby With The Black Dress On* (Chiaroscuro)

## Medeski, Martin And Wood
GROUP

John Medeski (b 1965) grew up in Florida and studied piano there, before moving to Boston in 1983 and becoming involved in the city's jazz scene. He toured with a group which included bassist Chris Wood (b 1969), and together with drummer Billy Martin (b 1963) they formed the trio Medeski, Martin And Wood in 1991. The group began recording for Gramavision, with Medeski using a battery of often lo-fi electric keyboards to go with the piano, and started touring on the college-rock circuit, where they became an unlikely success – unlikely, at least, in that jazz-orientated groups weren't supposed to do well in that context. They have since been credited with starting a trend for 'jam bands', other small groups of a similar nature, which rather than working to an orthodoxy of jazz improvisation prefer the simpler and more visceral appeal of rock jamming. Signing to Blue Note in 1998, the trio turned in probably their best work with *Combustication*, and here the shallow and often rickety eclecticism of their earlier records was more polished and finessed. Since then, though, the group's seemed stuck for ideas on how to progress, and *Uninvisible* (2001) sounded suspiciously like both comedy and self-parody, hopping from genre to genre with neurotic abandon. If anything personifies the cloudy waters which jazz has fished through in search of popular appeal – and the likely pitfalls along the way – it's probably this group.

*Combustication* (Blue Note)

# John Mehegan

PIANO
*born* 6 June 1916; *died* 2 April 1984

Mehegan left behind a scant discography and what there is isn't exactly epochal, but he is an interesting figure by dint of his writings. Working in New York from 1941, he had an entirely unremarkable playing career but taught at the Metropolitan Music School (1946–58) and Juilliard (1947–64), as well as working as a newspaper critic. An interesting sidebar is his trip to South Africa in 1959: he was obliged to leave since he was encouraging the work of black players, but he may have had a briefly important role in influencing the direction of a number of players, notably Abdullah Ibrahim. He also wrote four detailed books on the art of jazz improvisation. Mehegan's two Savoy albums suggest an original though often inscrutable approach: standards are coldly reharmonized, and a set of duets with Eddie Costa is set up to work as a fusion of 'modern jazz' with classical counterpoint. The sleevenotes to one of them are written by someone named Uncus, who speculates on how it would have sounded if Handel had 'blown on a set of changes'.
*Reflections* (Savoy)

# Brad Mehldau

PIANO
*born* 23 August 1970

Mehldau studied in New York from the late 80s, worked as a sideman in several post-bop groups and then began leading a trio: with Larry Grenadier and Jorge Rossy, this has become his preferred working group. He made a couple of sets for the Spanish Fresh Sound label but his Warners debut, *Introducing Brad Mehldau* (1995), was his introduction to American audiences, although New York musicians had already spread the word about his talents. Mehldau's progress since has been absolutely compelling to follow. He has recorded a sequence of albums for Warners (although he has recently moved over to Nonesuch), mostly by his trio, although there have been two solo records and one, *Largo* (2002), where the group was augmented with other players along with some studio experimentation. Aside from the disappointing first solo set, each record

has seemed like a beautifully finished essay on contemporary piano jazz as well as an advance on the previous one. He personally resists being compared with Bill Evans, considering that that is the standard reference point for all white pianists, and he certainly has much more variety in his style than Evans: many improvisations are fuelled on complex cross-rhythmical content, and lushly as he sometimes plays, there is a compensating astringency which sounds more like Paul Bley's sinewy lyricism. He is a brilliant interpreter of Thelonious Monk – the Mehldau–Monk interpretative dialogue might be the most remarkable going on in jazz at present – but he also searches for other material in surprising places, and his covers of Radiohead and Nick Drake tunes have set a trend in jazz players looking at rock themes. He has also done some exceptional sideman work, with Lee Konitz, Charles Lloyd and Joshua Redman. Perhaps the best comparison is with Keith Jarrett, not in terms of sounding like him, but in his focus on the acoustic piano recital: if anyone can succeed Jarrett as an audience draw for this kind of music, it is surely Mehldau.
*The Art Of The Trio, Vol 1* (Warner Bros)

# Myra Melford

PIANO
*born* 5 January 1957

Melford studied classical piano but grew bored with the idiom and left the piano alone until later studying in Washington. She moved to New York in 1984 and formed a powerhouse trio with Lindsey Horner (bass) and Reggie Nicholson (drums), smartly documented on *Jump* (1990). She became a fixture on the city's alternative jazz scene and worked with larger groups, edging towards free music but relying on a book of originals which suggest a lively mix of influences, tied together by her trademark rhythmical momentum.
*The Same River, Twice* (Gramavision)

# Gil Melle

SAXOPHONES
*born* 31 December 1931; *died* 28 October 2004

Melle was an archetypal Greenwich Village bohemian. He grew up in New Jersey and was a talented painter as a boy (calling his style 'primitive modern'), and by the time he was in his teens he had also amassed a huge collection of Duke Ellington records. He began playing in New York clubs from the age of 16, and Alfred Lion heard him there and recorded him for four ten-inch Blue Note LPs. Melle designed his covers and did some other artwork for Blue Note, and he also introduced Lion to the man who would become his regular engineer, Rudy Van Gelder. But Melle's best work was the three albums he later made for Prestige: he was a more interesting composer and group leader than improviser, performing mainly on baritone saxophone. In 1964 he moved to Los Angeles and began writing film music; later in the decade he formed a group called The Jazz Electronauts. Subsequently he worked more in the visual arts and with computers.

*Primitive Modern* (Prestige/OJC)

## George Melly

VOCAL
*born* 17 August 1926

Melly somehow barged his way into becoming the premier singer of British trad in the early 50s, even though he was often either absolutely awful or drunk (or both). His regular gig was with Mick Mulligan's Jazz Band, an outfit which could be equally shambolic, but by sheer persistence both vocalist and band made their way to some degree of excellence. This entire era is captured by *Owning Up*, a disgracefully funny read and one of three brilliant books of autobiography by the singer. In the 60s Melly wrote the comic strip *Flook*, turned up regularly on TV and radio, offered a critique of every art movement which came his way, and carried on singing. In the 70s he joined forces with trumpeter John Chilton, and their long association (including a regular and riotous New Year residency at Ronnie Scott's) continued until Chilton's retirement at the end of 2002. Melly has since struck up a new partnership with Digby Fairweather's group. George's maximum-volume suits, hats, Bessie Smith lecture and ability to beg cigarettes off strangers in bars continue to delight his faithful followers. Although he has to do most of a gig sitting down and is now saddled with an eyepatch, he is clearly

determined to work the boards until he drops.

*Puttin' On The Ritz* (Legacy)

## Misha Mengelberg

PIANO
*born* 5 June 1935

The patrician spirit of the Dutch avant-garde was actually born in the Ukraine: his father Karel was a composer and conductor who worked in Kiev until moving with his family to the Netherlands in 1938. Misha studied piano at The Hague's Royal Conservatory, but by 1959 was already performing jazz. He formed a quartet with Piet Noordijk, played with Eric Dolphy on one of the saxophonist's final European visits, and began playing with his long-time musical partner Han Bennink. They formed the Instant Composers Pool (ICP), with Willem Breuker, in 1967. Since then, aside from teaching and composition, he has been a busy and in-demand performer around the world: besides his duo with Bennink, he has worked with Company, in various ICP groupings (usually eight or ten in number), in the Herbie Nichols Project, and with sundry groups of his own devising. Like Bennink, he has a formidable ability in mixing high art and fairly low comedy, a rotund presence at the piano who might drift away into chamber music, a Monk tune or a heartbreaking lament. His larger-scale ICP music is emotionally complex and structurally ingenious.

*The Root Of The Problem* (hatOLOGY)

## Don Menza

TENOR SAXOPHONE
*born* 22 April 1936

Although he has created some strong small-group music, Menza's real home is the modern big band. In the 50s he played in army bands, gave it all up on leaving the service, then started again and joined Maynard Ferguson's big band in 1960. He went to Europe for four years, but on his return in 1968 joined Buddy Rich, a pressure-cooker environment which suited his crisp, no-nonsense delivery just fine. Besides this gig, he worked with Stan Kenton, Louie Bellson, Woody Herman and Bill Berry, and finally led a big band of his own on the West Coast from 1975. In the 80s and 90s he played in theatre orchestras and taught more, but he later began leading big bands in Las Vegas again.

**Buddy Rich,** *Mercy, Mercy* (Pacific Jazz)

# Helen Merrill
VOCAL
*born* 21 July 1929

Born Jelena Ana Milcetič, a name she used on her final album for Verve, Merrill is unique among jazz singers. She began singing in the late 40s, performing with bebop players, although after her marriage she worked less until signing to Mercury records in 1954. Her first album, which Clifford Brown worked on as a principal soloist, set down her style: a coolly effective voice which specialized in ballad tempos, a stark delineation of lyrics and no scatting or anything of the kind. She made five albums for the company (issued on the Emarcy imprint) and held her own in the tough, torch-singer environment of the 50s: the only criticism she remembers receiving was from Dinah Washington, who told her she should get better shoes to wear on stage. In 1959, following her divorce, she moved to Italy for four years, then returned to the US in 1963. But the business had largely forgotten about her, and she worked little and recorded less, finally establishing her own production company in 1980. She occasionally worked in a duo with the English pianist Gordon Beck, and made a couple of sets for the French Owl label which also involved Steve Lacy and Gil Evans, both longtime admirers of her singing. In 1989 she finally signed to a major label again (ironically enough, it was the Emarcy imprint at Polygram). Her albums of the 90s were remarkable: although her voice had inevitably lost some of its bloom, her power to distil the contents of a lyric and starkly sing was even more concentrated than before. *Brownie* (1994), a homage to Clifford Brown, was especially remarkable.

**Brownie** (Verve)

# Merseysippi Jazz Band
GROUP

Formed in Liverpool in 1949 and lasting through the rest of the century and into the new one, this is a great British/Northern institution. Several members, particularly founding fathers Frank Robinson (piano) and Nob Baldwin (banjo and guitar), who were still playing after 50 years, were with the band for decades. The band played fierce, uncomplicated trad from the start – unusually, mostly with a two-trumpet front line – and though they may have mellowed, the spirit of the playing has only deepened. The discography isn't all that large, and much of what has been set down was done in their 50s salad days. In 2003, they won a British Jazz Heritage award, which was scarcely undeserved.

**The Merseysippi Jazz Band** (Lake)

# Louis Metcalf
TRUMPET
*born* 28 February 1905; *died* 27 October 1981

The teenage Metcalf played with Charlie Creath's band in St Louis, but moved to New York in 1923 and played behind blues singers on record dates. By the time he joined Duke Ellington in 1927 he was a smart player, with a clear and sweet tone that was a piquant counterpart to Bubber Miley's rasping solos. He is also on some of King Oliver's Victors. In the 30s he toured Canada and the Midwest before going back to New York, and he continued working in the city well into the 60s: but he led no record dates during the 78 era, and the only later evidence of his playing is on a couple of rare small-label albums.

# Pat Metheny
GUITAR
*born* 12 August 1954

In terms of record and concert-ticket sales, Metheny is surely the most popular jazz musician of the modern era, although some might argue that the whole thing is a case of mistaken identity. A Midwestern boy from Lee's Summit, Missouri, he didn't take up the guitar until he was 13 and was soon hooked on Wes Montgomery's style: yet by the time he had enrolled at Miami University he was good enough to be appointed as a teacher in his second year, and by 1973 was teaching at Berklee. A year later he began playing in Gary Burton's group, and then formed a quartet with three pals from student days, Lyle Mays, Mark Egan and Danny Gottlieb. This group cut several best-selling albums for ECM, and in the meantime Metheny also played with Joni Mitchell and in a quartet with Charlie Haden, Dewey Redman and Paul Motian. A visit to Brazil also inculcated an affection for Latin rhythms. By the early 80s, buoyed up further by constant touring, Metheny had built a huge American following, and when he signed to Geffen in 1985 he was backed by significant major-label promotion. The result was The Pat Metheny Group becoming an attraction which was almost on a par with the stadium-rock bands in the US. Metheny had also perfected a signature sound which involved his otherwise clean, full tone being subjected to a digital delay device which thickened and expanded his sound without resorting to the kind of distortion effects which were standard business among rock guitarists. Coupled with Mays's shrewd keyboard orchestrations, the group had a sound which appealed to progressive-rock listeners, fusion fans and plain old lovers of guitar heroes: in total, a lot of people. Yet Metheny did it without sacrificing jazz credibility, and he hung on to this further by using his success to swing projects which smaller fish could never have countenanced: jazz-superstar gigs with Herbie Hancock and Dave Holland, the *Song X* (1985) album with Ornette Coleman, a solo thrash called *Zero Tolerance For Silence* (1994), the gorgeous album of duets with Haden, *Beyond The Missouri Sky* (1996), and the oddball encounter with Derek Bailey at The Knitting Factory which led to the three-disc *The Sign Of 4* (1996).

Alongside all this, Metheny has calmly continued touring with the PMG, playing marathon sets that unfailingly appease the hardcore audience which might blanch at the likes of the Bailey project. All this makes him sound like a very calculating man, but the affable Metheny seems to find little in the way of paradox in his career. What can dismay some sympathetic but not fanatical listeners is the way his embrace of electronics regularly leads him towards clichés which he himself may have created: too many of his live improvisations seem to end up in a monotonous wailing which is, in its way, only a few beats away from heavy-metal excess. For all its loyalty to the ideals of jazz improvisation, the PMG does, uncomfortably often, sound like a brainy prog-rock group with particularly nostalgic leanings: a piece such as 'Last Train Home' sums up the thick strain of sentimentality in Metheny's music. And he couldn't care less.

*Letter From Home* (Geffen)

## Metronome

*Metronome* was one of the leading American jazz magazines, founded in the 30s and published regularly until 1961: their annual poll resulted in the winners being organized into bands for recording dates, a practice which started in 1939 and lasted until the middle 50s. Some of the 'Metronome All Stars' dates of the 40s are particularly good. 'Metronome' was also used as the name for one of the leading Swedish jazz record labels, established in 1949, which recorded many of the leading Swedish modernists, although after 1960 its jazz activity all but ceased.

## Hendrik Meurkens
HARMONICA
*born* 6 August 1957

Still a rarity in jazz and likely to remain so, the harmonica has lately relied on only elder statesman Toots Thielemans and comparative youngster Meurkens to keep it alive in the music. Unsurprisingly, it was hearing Thielemans which made the vibes-playing Meurkens entertain the idea of moving over to the unloved wind instrument. A Hamburger, he worked in German film and television for much of the 80s but in the following decade he began making records for Concord in a Latin-inflected style, having spent some time in Brazil too. He is a skilful player and he makes a plausible case for modern harmonica jazz, but lacking the gravitas and sly ebullience of Thielemans he does sound as if he's in the wrong game.

*October Colors* (Concord)

## Mezz Mezzrow

CLARINET
*born* 9 November 1899; *died* 5 August 1972

Milton Mezzrow played the role of 'colourful character' to the hilt. He hung around with the young Chicagoan jazz crowd of the 20s, turned up on a handful of record dates, then went to New York in 1929, working as a freelance during the 30s. He played with Sidney Bechet and Tommy Ladnier on some of their 'comeback' dates, led a mixed-race band which was a surprise for its time (1937), and eventually got the King Jazz label off the ground in 1945, leading to a long string of sessions by the Mezzrow–Bechet Quintet, settings in which he manages to just about hold his own with the overpowering Bechet. This seems the more surprising because Mezzrow was usually a dreadful musician. John Chilton opines that 'Mezzrow was essentially a folk and blues musician for whom conventional technique was irrelevant', although that hardly excuses playing of often diabolical ineptitude on most of his records: rarely has such a prominent jazzman left such a dispiriting legacy of playing. He shifted over to France in the 50s and guested with various bands there. His other main claim to jazz notoriety was his book, *Really The Blues*, a glaringly sensational memoir which ends with his suggesting that his ashes be made into one of his records and given to a kid who should then play it until he's sick of it and tosses it away. It didn't happen.
**King Jazz Vol 1** (GHB)

## Pierre Michelot

BASS
*born* 3 March 1928

Michelot has been a notable witness and participant in French jazz, from bebop onwards. He played and recorded with Kenny Clarke and Coleman Hawkins as far back as 1949, and he also did sideman work with Sidney Bechet and Django Reinhardt. All through the 50s he was on call as the bass man for visitors for club dates in Paris, and in 1959 he joined Jacques Loussier's trio, playing Bach for the next 15 years. On a more modern note, he also played in the trio HUM with René Urtreger and Daniel Humair. In the 70s and 80s he did studio work but was still regularly sighted on jazz gigs, and it was a nice touch for Bertrand Tavernier to cast him in *Round Midnight* (1987), since he had played with Powell and Young during the 50s.
**Dexter Gordon, Our Man In Paris** (Blue Note)

## Palle Mikkelborg

TRUMPET
*born* 6 March 1941

Although Mikkelborg has been active in Danish music since 1960, it wasn't until many years later that an international audience knew much about him. He worked in the big bands which played on Danish radio in the 60s. In the 70s he led a quintet called Entrance, which worked in the kind of impressionistic fusion which he came to specialize in, and turns up as sideman on several ECM albums of the period. Given that his own sound has the feel of a Nordic Miles Davis, it was appropriate that he compose *Aura* (1985), an extended concerto for Davis which the trumpeter rightly regarded as a particularly fine vehicle: it sounds more interesting as a context than anything any of Davis's other latter-day collaborators came up with, an update on Gil Evans's veils of sound. Since then, Mikkelborg has continued to create a variety of extended, medium- to large-scale works, sometimes using himself as a soloist.
**Miles Davis, Aura** (Columbia)

## Joakim Milder

TENOR AND SOPRANO SAXOPHONES
*born* 24 September 1965

Milder is a quiet, major voice among Swedish modernists. He began making records at the end of the 80s, mainly for Dragon and Mirros, which present a particularly individual stance. He often plays softly, eschews an open-voiced timbre, avoids licks and improvises lines that are fragmented by changes of time and delivery, pocked with silences. He has mostly worked in conventional instrumentations – usually just sax and rhythm, trio or quartet – but some new records for a label of his own, Apart, suggest he is looking to interact more with other horns. It is in some ways typically Scandinavian jazz, but idiosyncratic for all

that. He has also worked as a sideman with Tomasz Stańko and Fredrik Norén, and is an expert on cameras: sometimes he will visit a country just to attend a camera auction.
*Monolithic* (Apart)

## Butch Miles
DRUMS
*born* 4 July 1944

Miles acquired an unfortunate reputation as a crashingly insensitive drummer while with the Count Basie band: he was with them during 1975–9, and some of his solo features rank with the most tedious instances of big-band drumming in history. Yet away from this context he has done much fine work. He often sounds better in small-group situations, where he seems to scale back his prodigious energy and play for the band. He led his own group, Jazz Express, in the 80s and 90s, and rejoined the Basie ghost orchestra in 1997, not quite a reformed character, but not so bad.
*Cookin'* (Nagel Heyer)

## Ron Miles
TRUMPET
*born* 9 May 1963

Miles has done some interesting work, although his output on record so far has been sometimes inscrutable. He has mostly worked away from the obvious jazz centres of America, living in Denver from his early teens, studying there and working in the Boulder area with saxophonist Fred Hess. He came to more attention via an association with Bill Frisell, playing on the guitarist's *Quartet* (1995) album, and with Ginger Baker. His Gramavision albums suggested an ambitious group composer, even if the music had a sometimes obscure and cryptic side, and two more recent efforts for Sterling Circle, including a duet album with Frisell, offer a mix of back-porch musing and music with a tough contemporary edge.
*Laughing Barrel* (Sterling Circle)

## Milestone

A record company co-founded by Orrin Keepnews and Dick Katz in 1966: quite a courageous undertaking at a time when the jazz record business was struggling against the rise of rock. They had six years of independence before selling the label to Audio Fidelity, and from there it was acquired by Fantasy, which kept it afloat and signed such major names as Sonny Rollins and McCoy Tyner to the roster (Rollins has remained there to this day). For a time it was used as a reissue label for old Riverside material, but latterly it has become a 'new' jazz label again.

## Bubber Miley
TRUMPET
*born* 3 April 1903; *died* 20 May 1932

Although Miley was, in a sense, a man with one trick up his sleeve, it was so good that he helped the music turn a corner. He started on trombone but switched to cornet, and he toured with Mamie Smith's Jazz Hounds – his presence is probably but not wholly confirmed on some of her 1921–2 records – and then settled down in New York when he joined Elmer Snowden's Washingtonians, which subsequently turned into the Duke Ellington orchestra. Miley's expressionist style harked back in some ways to vaudeville, but – perhaps with Ellington's contextual guidance – he had a forward-looking edge on his solos which took his King Oliver influence a step ahead. Oliver's wa-wa playing was adapted by Miley's use of a plunger mute to secure an even more dramatic voicing on the trumpet, and he and fellow sideman Joe Nanton shared a vocabulary which suited Ellington's 'jungle' period at The Cotton Club to a tee. Miley's growling delivery soon enough became the talk of New York brass players. But by 1929, drinking and fast living had taken a toll on him, and his playing became unreliable. Ellington hired Cootie Williams with the brief to follow in Bubber's stylistic footsteps. Meanwhile, Miley made some desultory late sides for Victor and had a show built round his talents, but he died of tuberculosis. In 1941, the ever-reflective Rex Stewart recorded a tune called 'Poor Bubber'.
**Duke Ellington, *1927–1928*** (Classics)

# Eddie Miller

TENOR SAXOPHONE, CLARINET
*born* 23 June 1911; *died* 1 April 1991

Miller grew up in New Orleans (where Leon Roppolo heard him play clarinet and said, 'It's not how many notes you play, kid, it's how you play 'em') but moved to New York in 1928 and eventually joined the Ben Pollack band. He was one of its stars when it evolved into the Bob Crosby orchestra – the most songful of clarinettists and a tenor player of unruffled smoothness who still had heat and light in his delivery. Like Bud Freeman with Tommy Dorsey, Miller brought a suaveness to the reed section which streamlined a Dixieland approach without excessively gentrifying it. His clarinet solos on 'Wolverine Blues' and 'South Rampart Street Parade', two of the band's best records, were classic moments of the swing era. After the Crosby band broke up, Miller led a few groups and did much studio work, rejoining his old colleague Matty Matlock in the *Pete Kelly's Blues* combo in the 50s, and then working as a freelance into the 80s, with Crosby reunions and guest-star tours ahead of him. 'The Little Prince' was a sweet-natured man who was loved by seemingly everyone who played with him.
**Bob Crosby, *The Big Noise*** (Halcyon)

# Glenn Miller

TROMBONE
*born* 1 March 1904; *died* c15 December 1944

Miller was never very close to the warm end of jazz. A country boy from Iowa, he began on trombone at 12 and eventually joined Ben Pollack's band in New York in 1926, already trying his hand at arranging. He then freelanced as part of the New York studio circle, although as a hot player he was always second-best to Jack Teagarden and Tommy Dorsey. By the mid-30s he was ready to try out with his own band, but after one disbandment and a second poor start things looked bleak until 1939, when Miller won a pair of residencies which enabled him to broadcast from New York and New Jersey. By 1940 the band was a great hit, and even began appearing in films (*Sun Valley Serenade* became a big success around the world). The Miller 'sound' – a reed section where the clarinet doubles one octave

higher on the melody – became a signature effect in the American dance music of the war years, and Miller (a diehard patriot) himself enlisted, forming a new band to perform for the troops at the end of 1942. In 1944 it was based in England, where it completely outclassed all the native dance bands, broadcasting regularly for the BBC. One December night Miller set off for France to arrange the details of a forthcoming visit, but his plane disappeared and he was presumed dead.

As a leader, Miller was, like Dorsey, a martinet who demanded loyalty and every detail in its place. Jerry Gray's seamless arrangements suited his book perfectly, and his vocal group, The Modernaires, added a further distinctive sound to such hits as 'Chattanooga Choo Choo'. Going through Miller's huge discography can be dispiriting since so much of it is made up of sentimental dance tunes (Marion Hutton and Ray Eberle also did a lot of singing); yet while it was a supremely sleek dance orchestra, it is Miller's jump tunes which are best remembered, from 'In The Mood' to 'American Patrol'. The actual jazz content was minimal: Bobby Hackett's celebrated solo on 'A String Of Pearls' was perhaps the only real hot moment in the band's history. But Miller continues to have a huge following, as untouchable in his way as Vera Lynn and FDR, and he is an irreplaceable part of 20th-century nostalgia. Rumours have sometimes circulated that, rather than being killed in a plane crash, he was found dead in a French brothel and the whole matter was hushed up; but this may belong in the 'Elvis Sighted On Moon' file.
***The Popular Recordings*** (RCA)

# Harry Miller

BASS
*born* 25 April 1941; *died* 16 December 1983

Born in Cape Town, Miller went to London in 1961 and played in Geraldo's dance orchestra and in Don Brown's band, but found his niche as a member of London's movement of young modernists, playing with the likes of Mike Westbrook, John Surman and Brotherhood Of Breath. Perhaps his most effective gig was in the Mike Osborne Trio, with Louis Moholo, a fiery and electrifying group, but he also led his own band, Isipingo, in the 70s. He helped found Ogun

Records in 1973, but four years later he moved to the Netherlands to work on the free scene there. 'Aitchy' was a serenely adaptable player, fitting in with Chris McGregor's township feel as easily as he did in the more acerbic and grainy music of Osborne. He died following a car accident in his adopted base of the Netherlands.
*Children At Play* (Ogun)

# Mulgrew Miller

PIANO
*born* 13 August 1955

Born in Greenwood, Mississippi, Miller played piano in an R&B band at high school, then studied jazz at Memphis State (where he often heard Phineas Newborn, a considerable influence). He played with the Ellington band of the late 70s before joining two great on-the-road academies: Betty Carter ('She won't let you go to sleep') and Art Blakey ('Even when he was sick he could outplay everybody on the bandstand'), in between playing with Woody Shaw for two years. After leaving Blakey in 1986, aside from a period with Tony Williams, Miller has mostly been his own leader, or has cherry-picked choice sideman jobs with singers. Although perhaps difficult to pick out in a blindfold test, Miller has synthesized all the major strains in modern piano and come up with a powerful, all-encompassing style which has not quite had the best fortune in album success: a period with RCA at the beginning of the 90s created some magnificent records which failed to create any real impact, and he is at the awkward stage of in between young lion and old master. His particular ability to mix power with sensitivity in a directly communicative way, though, makes him the natural heir to both Herbie Hancock and McCoy Tyner.
*Hand In Hand* (RCA Novus)

# Punch Miller

TRUMPET, VOCAL
*born* 24 December 1897; *died* 2 December 1971

Ernest Miller (the 'Punch' nickname derived from his twin sister, who was Ernestine Judy) began playing in New Orleans in the teens of the century, and after army service he played there and in touring bands before settling in Chicago in 1926. Miller was a flashy, showy player who won a strong local reputation but never quite found himself on the right record dates or in the most up-and-coming bands: he never actually led a record session until the 40s. By that time, he had been a regular in Chicago for 20 years, and he finally went to New York (in a carnival group) in 1947, where he had some brief impact before returning to show bands and R&B revues. In 1956 he went home to New Orleans and worked there for the remainder of his life, surviving a serious illness in 1959 and becoming involved in the music at Preservation Hall from its opening in 1961. His later records show a bullish if technically reduced player. The film *'Til The Butcher Cuts Him Down*, completed in the last year of his life, shows Punch fighting against his terminal illness and enjoying some final limelight.
*Punch Miller's New Orleans Band 1957* (504)

# Lucky Millinder

BANDLEADER
*born* 8 August 1900; *died* 28 September 1966

Lucius Venable Millinder was a showman-entertainer with a fine ear: he never learned to read music but remembered every note of an arrangement. He worked as a dancer and MC in Chicago clubs before starting to lead bands, and moving to New York he took over the Mills Blue Rhythm Band, which eventually went out under his own name. After a period in the doldrums, he took a new group into the Savoy Ballroom in 1940 and enjoyed great success there. Young players such as Lockjaw Davis, Thelonious Monk and Cat Anderson passed through the ranks, and by the middle of the decade Millinder was catching a ride on the upsurge in rhythm and blues, with Wynonie Harris handling vocals and Bullmoose Jackson and Lucky Thompson in the reed section. It lasted until 1952, when he tried his hand at other jobs, working for a spell as a DJ.
*Lucky Millinder 1943–1947* (Classics)

# Irving Mills
AGENT, PUBLISHER
*born* 16 January 1894; *died* 21 April 1985

Mills was a key business face in American music between the wars. He sang for dance bands in his teens but in 1919 – with his brother Jack – established a music-publishing firm, and as this business grew he also worked as a manager and talent scout. His biggest catch was Duke Ellington, who signed to Mills's operation in 1926, but he also handled the work of several other major black bandleaders, including Fletcher Henderson, Benny Carter and Cab Calloway. Mills took label credits on some of the studio pick-up bands he recorded in the 20s and 30s, and he also got composer credits with Ellington for working on the lyrics of such tunes as 'Mood Indigo' and 'Sophisticated Lady'. Mills made a lot of money out of jazz but compared to some of those working at that end of the business in his time he was much more angel than devil. He lived to a ripe old age and was still busy in his business as late as the 60s.

# Mills Blue Rhythm Band
GROUP

The 'Mills' was Irving Mills: the band had been started by drummer Willie Lynch, in New York in 1930, but when Mills took over as manager he planted his name at the front. They went through a few leaders before Lucky Millinder took over in 1934, and he eventually bestowed his name on the group. By the time of Millinder's steward-ship, though, the original glory days of the MBRB were probably over. Their hottest records were made early on – 'Blue Rhythm', 'White Lightning', 'Rhythm Spasm', 'Wild Waves' (all 1931–2) – and they never quite found an arranger who could give them a solidly individual identity. Ed Anderson, their first trumpet, was the outstanding soloist in the band's early days. Eventually, the orchestra split up altogether in 1938.
*Rhythm Spasm* (Hep)

# Pino Minafra
TRUMPET
*born* 21 July 1951

Minafra's exuberant music has been a joy-ous part of recent Italian jazz. In the 80s, after graduating from the conservatory at Bari, he worked in bands with Roberto Ottaviano and (a notably kindred spirit) Carlo Actis Dato, before going on to curate the Europa Jazz Festival di Noci and helping to set up the Italian Instabile Orchestra. In the 90s he founded the Sud Ensemble, a sex-tet which sums up many currents in Italian music, from brass bands to folk to jazz. Their one major record, *Sudori* (1995), is so good that it is a shame that Pino seems to have been too busy to make more. His own trumpet playing, puckish and pugnacious, is in the spirit.
*Sudori* (Victo)

# Johnny Mince
CLARINET
*born* 8 July 1912; *died* 23 December 1994

Mince moved through the ranks of several American orchestras, starting with Ray Noble (1935), then Bob Crosby (1936) and finally Tommy Dorsey (1937–41), where he did his best work, taking warm solos with Dorsey's Clambake Seven and often cutting through the sound of the full band when he got his chance on Dorsey's more circum-spect records. If he wasn't always the most interesting of soloists, his agile technique helped Dorsey compete with the clarinet sounds coming off Goodman and Shaw records. In the 40s he embarked on studio work, and from the 70s he appeared in many nostalgia and revivalist shows.
*Tommy Dorsey, 1938* (Classics)

# Kosuke Mine
TENOR SAXOPHONE
*born* 6 February 1944

Born in Tokyo, Mine started on alto in a group led by Masabumi Kikuchi, from 1969, but subsequently switched to tenor. He spent some time in New York, tried his hand at fusion, but largely went back to an acous-tic and straight-ahead format in the 90s. Mine made some albums for the Japanese

arm of Verve at this point, a handsome showcase for his reflective compositions and sinewy delivery, which owed something to Joe Henderson's influence but had his own spin. Still prolific at home, his music, like that of most Japanese post-boppers, hasn't really succeeded in travelling elsewhere.
*In A Maze* (Verve)

# Charles Mingus
BASS, COMPOSER
*born* 22 April 1922; *died* 5 January 1979

Mingus evaded stylistic boundaries and straddled genres with a lusty, furious intensity that lasted 40 tempestuous years. He grew up in Los Angeles, where he had a frustrating time with both the trombone and the cello and eventually settled on the double bass, receiving lessons from Red Callender. He took some composition tuition, and began writing his first pieces as early as 1939: one of them, 'what Love', wasn't recorded until the 60s. He played with Louis Armstrong's big band in 1942, and from there took further lessons on the bass, from a classical musician named Herman Rheinschagen: his early dedication to accruing a complete technical mastery set Mingus aside from most other bassists of his generation. Still based in Los Angeles, he continued to work in clubs during the middle 40s and sometimes sponsored his own record dates, often billed as 'Baron' Mingus. In 1947 he found a place in Lionel Hampton's touring band, with whom he recorded the feature 'Mingus Fingers', but he only stayed a year; after that, he became part of the Red Norvo Trio, with Tal Farlow, recording for Discovery. In 1951 he settled in New York, where he worked with a variety of leaders and established his own record label, Debut, in 1952. This began documenting Mingus's work during the period, which was increasingly marked by an acknowledgement from other musicians that he was one of the masters of his instrument: despite a dreadful temper and resorting to violence at seemingly every opportunity, he had the highest musical respect from his peers. He co-founded a Jazz Composers' Workshop with such kindred spirits as Teddy Charles and John Laporta, and in 1955 finally began leading significant groups of his own, with such sidemen as J R Monterose, Mal

Waldron, Bud Powell, Elvin Jones, Jackie McLean, Bill Hardman and Eddie Bert. The groups gigged around New York and at the Newport Jazz Festival, and achieved some stability when Dannie Richmond, who became Mingus's closest musical confrère, arrived on drums at the end of 1956.

The period 1957–65 was Mingus's golden age. He worked continuously with a core group that usually numbered around seven or eight musicians: among his sidemen were some of the most individual players of the time, including, besides some of those already mentioned, Booker Ervin, Eric Dolphy, Jimmy Knepper, John Handy, Pepper Adams, Roland Kirk, Ted Curson, Jaki Byard, Roland Hanna, Charles McPherson, Richard Williams and Charlie Mariano, all of whom blossomed and did a lot of their best work under the leader's direction. They were the performers in Mingus's 'workshop', not so much a band but a giddy, revolving ensemble where players came and went at the leader's whim, where musical projects of the grandest kind started and stopped just as abruptly, and where the conflicting ambitions of nightclub jazz and the concert platform constantly collided. There were European tours, hungrily documented by semi-official recordings, and festival appearances, but all of these were simply addenda to a formidable group of studio recordings: *Blues And Roots* (Atlantic, 1959), *Mingus Ah Um* (Columbia, 1959), *Charles Mingus Presents Charles Mingus* (Candid, 1960), *Oh Yeah* (Atlantic, 1961), *The Black Saint And The Sinner Lady* (Impulse!, 1963) and – most outrageously titled of all – *Mingus Mingus Mingus Mingus Mingus* (Impulse!, 1963) are only the most important in an astonishing body of work. In its mixing of grand compositional ambition – particularly the mighty *Black Saint And The Sinner Lady*, the one Mingus artefact which seems to specifically nod to his great influence, Duke Ellington – and spontaneous, jam-session feel – the sort of atmosphere which pervades most of the records at one time or another, even though it is jamming on an exalted scale – Mingus's music on record is surely unique. A concert at New York's Town Hall in 1962, planned as a celebration of his progress, turned out to be a shambles, with the hot-tempered Mingus smacking Jimmy Knepper in the mouth (and ruining his embouchure), and the recorded results a piecemeal travesty which took many years to be properly presented on record.

After the European tour of 1964, though, Mingus lost some of his notoriety. Compared to some of the new figures on the free-jazz scene, he was no longer such an outlaw. His personal life drifted into turmoil: in debt, and depressed, he withdrew from performing for a time, only to be forced back into it by his financial position. He assembled new bands and enjoyed a fresh prominence when the long-awaited (by its author, at least) publication of his autobiography, *Beneath The Underdog*, took place in 1971. He assembled a new repertory of Mingusian characters for his bands, including George Adams, Jack Walrath, Don Pullen, Hamiet Bluiett, Hugh Lawson and others, with the faithful Dannie Richmond back in the fold. Compared to the earlier records, the 70s albums seem tame and conventional, but on their own terms they are full of fine music. In 1976, though, Mingus's health began to fail, and although he collaborated with the singer-songwriter Joni Mitchell on a final project, his spirit was spent.

His legacy is complex, and yet universal. So much of the music of the past 30 years has its pre-echoes in the work of the various Mingus bands: one can hear him in the music of such diverse figures as David Murray, Misha Mengelberg and John Zorn. His passion for the jazz past of Ellington and Jelly Roll Morton prefigured the revivalism of today, even though he might have sneered at it; his insistence on instrumental excellence is followed in the high standards of execution which have become a norm among young players. His berating of inattentive audiences looks forward to a state where jazz is respected as art-music, yet the noisy, turbulent feel of all his own bands asks listeners to participate in a communal, unstuffy exhilaration. He didn't like free jazz and he scorned players who did no more than copy Charlie Parker's licks, but he couldn't evade the principles which he knew underscored jazz's real achievements. The many obsessions of this extraordinarily difficult man continue to haunt the music, some 30 years after his death.

**Mingus Ah Um** (Columbia)

# Mingus Dynasty/Mingus Big Band/Mingus Orchestra

Charles Mingus's widow Sue has informally overseen a number of group projects in connection with the posthumous performance of her husband's music. The first, Mingus Dynasty, was a small group of six or seven players, initially formed in 1979 with Dannie Richmond as the authentic guiding spirit. This was succceeded in the early 90s by the more rambunctious and big-scale Mingus Big Band, which continues to tour and has held weekly residencies in New York. The Mingus Orchestra has occasionally been convened as a rather more respectful vehicle. Of the three, the Mingus Big Band, which routinely uses musicians from a pool drawn from some of the superior New York jazz players, has the greatest cachet, and it has made a number of suitably celebratory albums.

**Mingus Big Band, *Blues And Politics*** (Dreyfus)

# Phil Minton
TRUMPET, VOICE
*born* 2 November 1940

A genuine radical among British improvisers, Philip Watcyn Minton was born in Torquay and began playing jazz there at the end of the 50s. He moved to London in the early 60s, playing trumpet and singing with Mike Westbrook's group, although he subsequently moved abroad, first to the Canary Islands and then Sweden. In 1972 he was back in London and rejoined Westbrook, appearing as one of his principal voices through much of the composer's work of the 70s and 80s. Besides this, he developed further his interest in vocal free improvisation, and was soon enough considered a major player in that movement, working with percussionist Roger Turner (a long-standing duo), Veryan Weston, Gunter Christmann and in many ad hoc groupings. Minton's huge range and operatic intensity bring him to the furthest edges of what the human voice can do in sung performance: in person he can be a transfixing artist, but even on record his musicianship is often shockingly confrontational, even as it can evoke poignancy and a queer sense of joy.

***A Doughnut In One Hand*** (FMP)

# Bob Mintzer
TENOR SAXOPHONE
*born* 27 January 1953

Mintzer is a multi-reedsman specializing in tenor and with a prodigious facility at writing and arranging for the kind of supercharged big bands that were the bequest of such leaders as Buddy Rich and Stan Kenton to post-bop jazz. He was a sideman with Rich and with the Jones–Lewis Jazz Orchestra in the 70s, then fronted big bands of his own, did sideman work with fusion groups such as The Yellowjackets and worked on tutorials and music for student ensembles. He has recorded many of his own big-band charts for albums on the audiophile label DMP. In person, Mintzer's orchestras probably have much more impact than they do on record, but most don't get the opportunity to hear them that way. On disc, they tend to sound strong but prepackaged.
*Latin From Manhattan* (DMP)

# Billy Mitchell
TENOR SAXOPHOPNE
*born* 3 November 1926; *died* 18 April 2001

Mitchell spent some time in New York at the end of the 40s with Lucky Millinder's orchestra and then took over Gene Ammons's chair in the Woody Herman Second Herd, but he returned to Detroit in 1953, where he led a small group featuring Thad and Elvin Jones. His own style was cast in a hearty swing-to-bop manner which was steeped in the sort of blues feeling which made his next move, joining the Count Basie orchestra, an entirely logical one. He was with Basie between 1958 and 1961 and then formed a sextet with Al Grey. Mitchell rejoined Basie later in the 60s for a brief spell and during the 70s and 80s he freelanced in New York. All through the 60s, 70s and 80s and into the 90s he also ran a house-band gig at clubs owned by Sonny Meyerowitz: the final one ended when Sonny's Place eventually closed in 1997. Mitchell's playing appeared in many sideman situations on record but in a career stretching nearly a half-century he fronted fewer than a dozen records of his own. Don Schlitten, who loved spotlighting undervalued players on his Xanadu label, got

some great music out of him on *De Lawd's Blues* (1980).
*De Lawd's Blues* (Xanadu)

# Blue Mitchell
TRUMPET
*born* 13 March 1930; *died* 21 May 1979

Richard Mitchell (the 'Blue' was a high-school nickname) played in R&B bands in the Miami area in the middle 50s, before impressing Cannonball Adderley and going to New York to make his first dates for Riverside. He joined Horace Silver in 1958 and stayed for six years, playing on many of Silver's best Blue Notes, and when Silver split up that edition of the band, Blue and fellow hornman Junior Cook carried on working together. Mitchell had seven dates of his own for Blue Note, and his burnished hard-bop manner was gradually turned towards soul-jazz – which in a sense brought him full circle. He worked with Ray Charles and John Mayall before eventually settling in Los Angeles, and his final jazz work (before succumbing to cancer) was in a band with Harold Land which recorded for Concord. Honest, unflashy and more songful than bluesy, Blue's playing was refreshingly free of showboating, even though he may have lacked the edge of ambition which could have taken his records on to the very highest level.
**Horace Silver, *Finger Poppin'*** (Blue Note)

# George Mitchell
TRUMPET
*born* 8 March 1899; *died* 27 May 1972

'Little Mitch' played on only two major groups of recordings – the early sessions by Jelly Roll Morton's Red Hot Peppers, and the discs by the New Orleans Bootblacks/Wanderers, which were akin to the Armstrong Hot Five minus Armstrong – but his playing was authoritative enough to make him a major figure among the trumpeters of his time. Raised in Louisville, he began playing in Chicago around 1920 and worked with numerous leaders, but it was his playing on the sessions mentioned, all crammed into 1926–7, which really set out his stall: with the Bootblacks/Wanderers (a total of eight titles) he plays a strong but democratic lead

which at times seems to liberate Kid Ory and Johnny Dodds from Armstrong's overwhelming delivery, and with Morton he is beautifully versatile and adroit, swinging the principal line, taking firecracker breaks and using the mute to particular effect on titles such as 'Grandpa's Spells'. But after 1927 his career abruptly wound down, and he more or less left music in 1931 for a steady job elsewhere.
**Jelly Roll Morton, Vols 1–5** (JSP)

## Red Mitchell

BASS, PIANO
*born* 20 September 1927; *died* 8 November 1992

Red Mitchell unobtrusively made himself into a profoundly important part of postbop jazz. He played bass (having started on piano) with Woody Herman during 1949–51, but eventually settled in Los Angeles and was an important part of both the live and studio scene there between 1955 and 1961. He regularly partnered Shelly Manne at recording dates and was as effective with Hampton Hawes and André Previn as he was with Ornette Coleman on the latter's *Tomorrow Is The Question* (1959). His band with Harold Land made a single album for Atlantic and *Get Those Elephants Out'a Here* (1958) was made with his brother Whitey, also a bassist, and trumpeter Blue Mitchell, as 'The Mitchells'. Red tired of prevailing American attitudes in the 60s and departed for the more welcoming climes of Stockholm in 1968: he only finally went home for good in 1992, just months away from his death. Even hidden away in Sweden, though, he managed to make many records and was always in demand. As a bassist, he was an unassuming kind of virtuoso, developing techniques which helped him deliver horn-like solos, such as sounding notes with his left hand on the neck of the bass, and latterly using a tuning in fifths (rather than the normal fourths) that deepened his sound, and enabled him to deliver slurred solos which could be almost speech-like (and he would sometimes grumble along in accompaniment). A wonderful example is his delicious duet with Helen Merrill on 'Some Of These Days' (*Clear Out Of This World*, 1991). While less often cited in bass family-trees than Scott LaFaro, Red could claim his own significant role. His all-

solo record *A Question Of Interdependence* (1988) is *sui generis*.
**With Lee Konitz, *I Concentrate On You*** (Steeplechase)

## Roscoe Mitchell

SAXOPHONES, PERCUSSION
*born* 3 August 1940

Along with Muhal Richard Abrams, Mitchell was the key musician in Chicago's rising avant-garde in the 60s. His sextet of the early 60s (which never recorded) featured himself alongside Joseph Jarman and Henry Threadgill, and later groups which worked following the formation of the AACM in 1965 included musicians such as Lester Bowie and Malachi Favors, who would go on to join Mitchell in the Art Ensemble Of Chicago. *Sound* (1966) was the first important statement of the new music from Chicago, and it remains a compelling experience, Mitchell and his group creating a new jazz aesthetic out of small sounds and interrelating music and silence, a very different approach to the Coltrane–Ayler axis. While the AEOC took up much of Mitchell's activity over the next three decades, he also maintained a busy schedule of separate solo and group work. Many of his major works were set down on such 70s albums as *Nonaah* (1975) and *L–R–G/The Maze/S II Examples* (1977), which mixed solo saxophone pieces with complex group works, but in the 80s and 90s he also recorded with such groups as his Sound Ensemble, New Chamber Ensemble and The Note Factory. All this music-making displays a profoundly thoughtful approach to textures and dynamics, the possibilities of chamber-musical form as a useful context for improvisation, and always his own and varied vocabularies on the saxophone family (bass to sopranino): only Anthony Braxton has pursued such a thorough investigation into saxophone sound. While some of the later records suggest, perhaps, a thickening of the creative arteries, Mitchell's patient journey has been a genuine odyssey.
***Sound*** (Delmark)

# Hank Mobley
TENOR SAXOPHONE
*born* 7 July 1930; *died* 30 May 1986

Mobley grew up in New Jersey and took up the alto sax around 1948, but discouraged by Charlie Parker's omnipresence he soon switched to tenor. He played mostly with Paul Gayten's R&B band until 1954, when he spent time with Dizzy Gillespie's sextet and then joined what would become the first edition of Art Blakey's Jazz Messengers. He stayed two years, and then worked with Horace Silver, Thelonious Monk and Miles Davis, besides embarking on a long and fruitful recording career with Blue Note: besides numerous sideman appearances, he cut more than 20 albums as a leader for the label. Mobley has always been a favourite among jazz LP collectors, and although never deemed to be much of an influence, he was actually more highly regarded than some think: many British musicians of the 50s and 60s sought out what were then his very hard to find records. In the age of Rollins and Coltrane, his 'round sound' seemed comparatively tepid, but it was allied to a brilliant understanding of how to make the beat work for a soloist. On his greatest records, *Soul Station*, *Roll Call* and *Workout* (1960–61), he seems to time every inflexion of his melodic line with some aspect of the underlying pulse, and some of his solos have a cliffhanger aspect which he unfailingly rights by the end. While some of his later records fell prey to Blue Note's search for popular hits, he remained a consistently absorbing player. But in other respects his career was luckless. Narcotics kept interfering – he spent time in prison either side of his Miles Davis stint in 1961 – and after the Blue Note era had ended, his health declined. A booking at the North Sea Jazz Festival in 1985 caused great excitement among the faithful, but it never transpired, and Hank died the following year.
*Workout* (Blue Note)

## Modal jazz

It all started, supposedly, with Miles Davis and *Kind Of Blue*. Chafing against compositions which were stifling with chord changes, Davis looked to organize his music around modes – either the diatonic scales of the European classical heritage (Phrygian, Dorian, Lydian or Mixolydian), or nondiatonic scales of the sort found in flamenco music (which particularly attracted Davis). The vagueness of the term, though (as with many jazz 'definitions') also allows modal jazz to be based on a simple major or minor mode. Its main characteristic lies, perhaps, in what it is not: a performance locked into an unyielding grid of a chord progression. Davis had, in fact, already set down a classic 'modal' performance in the 1958 'Milestones', from the album of that name, although it was the music of *Kind Of Blue* which sounded like a manifesto, and introduced the idea of a more breathing, flexible, open-ended modern jazz. Not necessarily an easier one to play, though: charging through the flying chordal sequences of bop may have presented one kind of technical challenge to an improviser, but working against a static backdrop of a mode was demanding in a different way. Ironically, Davis if anything went back to chords in much of his 60s music, while sidemen such as John Coltrane pursued modes to their limit. All this happened concurrently with Ornette Coleman's arrival, with music which went further by abandoning a tonal centre, an idea which Davis himself eventually embraced in his fusion phase. As he told the author in 1985, 'I tell them [my musicians], don't fuck around trying to find a tone centre.'

## Modern jazz

Nothing can be modern for very long, but 'modern jazz' has enjoyed a surprisingly long life as an expression. It first meant bebop and hard bop, or the latest phase of the music as it stood in the 50s. This is very likely what Chuck Berry meant when he said, in 'Rock 'N' Roll Music', 'I've got no kick against modern jazz/Except they try to play it too darn fast.' Since then, though, succeeding waves of jazz activity have also been referred to as 'modern', so almost anything which isn't 'traditional' can fit the bill. Han Bennink has been known to shout out, 'This is very modern!', as he attacks his drumkit. Perhaps the safest definition of modern jazz is that it is the music listened to by moderns.

# Modern Jazz Quartet
GROUP

Milt Jackson, John Lewis and Kenny Clarke
had played together in Dizzy Gillespie's big
band in the 40s, and with Ray Brown they
cut some quartet titles for Prestige in 1951,
under the name Milt Jackson Quartet. The
following year, Percy Heath arrived to
replace Brown: Lewis advised him to brush
up on his technique, he took some lessons
from Charles Mingus, and they played their
first gigs as the Modern Jazz Quartet, at a
club in Greenwich Village. Ten people came
to the first date, but it was enough for Bob
Weinstock to sign them to Prestige as an
ongoing project. Their early progress wasn't
too rapid: they recorded only 22 titles
between then and July 1955, although these
already included such staples of the MJQ
repertoire as 'Django', 'Delaunay's Dilemma'
and 'Ralph's New Blues'. But they became
known as a festival attraction, and their
career on record went up a gear when they
signed to Atlantic in 1957. The format for the
group's performances varied little: a book
of elegant, finely turned compositions by
Lewis, some blues from Jackson, and the
unobtrusive lift given by the rhythm section
(Connie Kay came in for Clarke in 1955,
when the latter found the direction of the
group not to his taste). They began touring
the world, and though the group effectively
had an extended vacation every summer to
allow Lewis to engage in other projects, they
remained in demand right up until their
first retirement in 1974, at the behest of
Jackson, who wanted to try other things.

Refined, restrained, introverted and tasteful: the adjectives were as often used in a
pejorative way as in a positive one, and
Lewis in particular came in for criticism, supposedly for putting a dusty 'classical' coat
on bebop principles and keeping Jackson's
talents under wraps. Yet the vibesman's
music was never framed in a better light
than in the MJQ, and there were other
quietly revolutionary things they did: putting jazz into concert halls at a time when it
was still seen as an unworthy music by
many hierarchies, creating album-length
works which embraced long-form at a point
when much jazz was still tied to the jukebox. And for every classical indulgence in
Lewis's compositions, there was the underlying and rarely distant feel of the blues in
every set the MJQ played, a bracing rootsiness which the quartet never gave up on.
Their large discography includes many outstanding records, including *Odds Against
Tomorrow* (1957), *European Concert* (1960),
*The Comedy* (1962), *Lonely Woman* (1962)
and *Blues At Carnegie Hall* (1966), and when
they reconvened the group in 1982 their
stately demeanour had grown and lent majesty to much of what they did. Kay's health
declined and when he died in 1994 Tootie
Heath took over the drum chair. The group
played its final concert in 1997.
*European Concert* (Atlantic)

# Kippie Moeketsi
ALTO SAXOPHONE
*born* 27 July 1925; *died* 1983

Born in Johannesburg, Moeketsi began playing in the 40s and in the following decade
he started working with Dollar Brand and
Hugh Masekela, which eventually led to the
formation of the seminal group The Jazz
Epistles. After that group dissolved, he
joined Davshe's Jazz Dazzlers, who went to
London in 1961 to play in the stage musical
*King Kong*, but on his return he found that
things were growing tougher for a black jazz
musician: his work pass and saxophone
were confiscated and he drifted out of music
until the 70s. He joined the African Jazz
Pioneers in 1982 but died a year later. There
is little enough on record to remember him
by, and much of that is scattered and hard
to find.
*Jazz Epistles Verse 1* (Gallo)

# Charles Moffett
DRUMS
*born* 11 September 1929; *died* 14 February 1997

Moffett was part of the Fort Worth circle of
musicians in the 50s and he soon befriended
Ornette Coleman. He played trumpet before
taking up drums in college, and then played
with Little Richard in 1953, although for
most of the 50s his main activity was as
a high-school teacher. He went to join
Coleman in New York in 1961, but this
coincided with the saxophonist's virtual
retirement from playing, and in the meantime Moffett led groups of his own: unfortunately, a quintet with Carla Bley, Pharoah

Sanders and Alan Shorter went unrecorded. He then toured with the Coleman trio which made *At The Golden Circle* in Stockholm (1965), as well as playing on a handful of other records. The Stockholm recordings show up all his virtues, which display a buoyantly swinging style over a free pulse, an uncluttered and generous delivery. In 1970 he moved to California and directed a music school there, and thereafter he worked in jazz only occasionally, although a few late recordings were made with Frank Lowe and Sonny Simmons. After some years of indifferent health he died in 1997. His sons Charnett and Cody carry on the family tradition.

**Ornette Coleman,** *At The Golden Circle* (Blue Note)

# Charnett Moffett

BASS
*born* 10 June 1967

Charles Moffett's youngest son has become the most prominent of the Moffett siblings (his name is a contraction of Charles and Ornette). A precocious youngster, he played bass in his father's family band at the age of seven and was working with Wynton Marsalis by the time he was 16. All through the 80s and 90s he was busy as a high-profile sideman, with both Wynton and Branford Marsalis, Wallace Roney, Kenny Garrett, Ornette Coleman and many others. Fast, accurate and powerfully assertive, Moffett is an exemplar among a generation of young bassists, but if he has leadership ambitions they have so far not been well realized: a 1987 set for Blue Note and a subsequent one for another label were disappointingly slight in content. His brother Cody (b 1961) is another skilful and prolific sideman who has similarly made no real mark as a leader.

**Ornette Coleman,** *Sound Museum: Hidden Man* (Verve)

# Louis Moholo

DRUMS
*born* 10 March 1940

Moholo is the last survivor of the great group of South Africans who played such a large role in the British jazz of the 60s and 70s, following their exile from their own country. Born in Cape Town, he was leading his own groups from the age of 16 and he joined Chris McGregor's Blue Notes in 1963, not long before they secured a passage to Europe. There, Moholo played with Roswell Rudd and in Steve Lacy's quartet with Johnny Dyani and Enrico Rava. Eventually he rejoined McGregor and his band Brotherhood Of Breath, and based himself in London. He worked with important 70s bands such as Mike Osborne's Trio, Dudu Pukwana's groups and Harry Miller's Isipingo, and subsequently led bands of his own, such as Viva La Black and Spirits Rejoice. Any who expect Moholo's drumming to sound 'African', rather than belonging to the greater jazz tradition, might be disappointed, since he is a master of bop, rock and free playing as much as he is an exponent of the kind of music which he and his compatriots brought to Europe 40 years ago. His encounter with Cecil Taylor at the 1988 Berlin event celebrating the pianist's music was a triumphant display of his finest chops.

*Viva La Black* (Ogun)

# Miff Mole

TROMBONE
*born* 11 March 1898; *died* 29 April 1961

Mole was the first jazz trombonist of any consequence, and by the mid-20s he was an acknowledged master; but his subsequent eclipse was both sad and a salutary lesson in how quickly tastes in jazz can change. A few years older than several in his circle, he was already a skilled technician on his horn when he began making records with the Sam Lanin-sponsored group which became known as either the Original Memphis Five or Ladd's Black Aces, from 1921. Mole's agility, quickfire tonguing and neatly unemphatic articulation released the slide-trombone from its often clownish role in early jazz, and for the first time proposed it as a valid solo instrument. From 1925 onwards he was closely linked with cornetist Red Nichols: they worked together as king-pins on hundreds of sessions on the New York recording scene, whether in studio dance bands or in the coolly hot settings of such bands as The Five Pennies and Miff's Molers, the one group which Mole himself nominally led. In 1929, Miff (his real Christian names were Irving Milfred) disappeared into the NBC orchestra, where he sat out the Depression, and by the time he made records again under his own name, in 1937, his era was already over, his bluesless style long since trumped comprehensively by Jack Teagarden and Jimmy Harrison. He joined the Condon circle in the 40s, and linked up with Muggsy Spanier for a time, but alcoholism began to take its toll; and although he managed to make occasional dates (Lee Wiley had to urge him through a single solo on one of her 50s sessions), Miff was all but finished. Booked to play at the 1960 Newport Festival, he arrived only to find that it had been cancelled because of unruly audiences. Debilitated by hip operations, he died in 1961, so poor that his trombone was impounded to help pay for his funeral.

**Doggin' Around** (Frog)

## Lars Møller

TENOR SAXOPHONE
*born* 17 September 1966

Møller is from Copenhagen but has opened his receptors wide: he studied in New York, spent three years in New Delhi working in Indian classical music, and was taught composition by Bob Brookmeyer. This experience informs a post-bop style which is big and powerful in the modern manner. His records are a satisfying document of a career in progress, moving from conventional, Coltrane-ish quartets to grander settings for larger groups.

**The Pyramid** (Stunt)

## Nils Petter Molvaer

TRUMPET, ELECTRONICS
*born* 18 September 1960

Molvaer has become something of a figurehead of a Norwegian 'underground', which mixes elements of jazz with hip-hop, ambient and other shadings of electronic music. He played in a more or less conventional post-bop style while a member of the Masqualero group in the 80s, and then went on to create a broad portfolio of work with such leaders as Marilyn Mazur and Jan Eberson, but his own records, starting with

1997's *Khmer*, have taken a much more singular route. What set Molvaer aside from American models trying this tack – or, indeed, the ambient music of the sometimes Eurocentric trumpeter Jon Hassell – was his rooting these forms in the recognizably Nordic aesthetic which many other players had helped establish, setting the improvisational elements in a framework which had a bloodless, chilled quality. Determinedly unsexy music, which he has gone on to evolve further across other records, although the jazz content does seem to be fading away.

**Khmer** (ECM)

## Grachan Moncur III

TROMBONE
*born* 3 June 1937

Son of veteran bass player Grachan Moncur (1915–96), Moncur toured with Ray Charles before moving to New York and joining The Jazztet in 1962. Thereafter he played an interesting role on the New York scene of the period: while he showed a predilection for the free end of the jazz spectrum, his sober and clear cut style of playing owed more to the classic style of bop trombone, and he ended up mixing the free and hard-bop vocabularies to often intriguing effect. As a sideman he recorded with Jackie McLean, Marion Brown, Archie Shepp and Joe Henderson, as well as recording two fine albums for Blue Note as a leader. In 1974 he completed a large-scale work, *Echoes Of Prayer*, for the Jazz Composers' Orchestra, and thereafter divided his time between teaching and playing alongside friends such as Shepp, Frank Lowe and Nathan Davis. Only rarely recorded as any kind of leader, he has had to settle for a minor role in the modern progress of the music, but even as a bit player he has brought some absorbing material to the table.

**Evolution** (Blue Note)

## Thelonious Monk

PIANO
*born* 10 October 1917; *died* 17 February 1982

For better or otherwise, the music of this strange, contradictory man has become perhaps the central text in jazz composition after Ellington. He was born Thelonious Monk in Rocky Mount, North Carolina, and added 'Sphere' as his middle name while in his teens. His family moved to New York when he was four, and he began playing piano in church when a boy, sometimes touring with an evangelist. By the early 40s he was working as the house pianist at the Harlem club Minton's Playhouse, where he, Kenny Clarke (who played drums in the group) and Dizzy Gillespie began working out – on the bandstand and elsewhere – the theoretical and practical formulae which would lead to the birth of bebop. After a brief period as pianist in Lucky Millinder's band, he joined the Cootie Williams orchestra in 1944, a band which made the first recording of Monk's latterly celebrated ballad 'Round About Midnight'. Still virtually unknown to the jazz public, he then played in Coleman Hawkins's small group during 1944–6, and by now word about his unpredictable prowess had got out: Ike Quebec suggested to Alfred Lion of Blue Note that he record this unusual pianist, and when Lion began recording Monk he was so excited by the initial results that he quickly took down more sessions, all of which eventually emerged in the LP era as *Genius Of Modern Music Vols 1 & 2* (Blue Note). Monk's style was a unique assemblage of old and new: he could sound like the stride piano masters, and there was a powerful Duke Ellington influence at work, but what he played was angular, analytical, pared away: he seemed to want to get to the bones of material which was already fat-free. While he appeared to embody some aspects of bebop, in other ways he seemed set against its jittery spillage of notes. Themes such as 'Off Minor', 'Epistrophy', 'Misterioso' and 'Well You Needn't' were as clipped and inscrutable as their titles. Yet his sideman work with Charlie Parker – on airshots and on the 1950 session which produced the likes of 'Bloomdido' – showed how skilfully he could work with bop's premier improviser.

In 1951 he was briefly imprisoned on a probably trumped-up narcotics charge, and lost his New York cabaret card as a result, so for a few years he had to settle for working on record rather than on a bandstand, and in 1952 he signed a new deal with Prestige Records. His appearance on a 1954 date with Miles Davis prickled with tension, but the music was magnificent. Then Orrin Keepnews signed him to Riverside, where he produced some of his most finished and rich recordings: the group date *Brilliant Corners*, the solo *Thelonious Himself* and the quartet session with the saxophonist who at this period started working with him on live dates, *Thelonious Monk With John Coltrane* (1956–7). His composing touched on a broader range, from the excruciatingly difficult 'Brilliant Corners' and 'Gallop's Gallop' to almost catchy pieces such as 'Rhythm-A-Ning' and 'We See'. It had taken some time, but Monk had somehow become a popular figure: he toured with his quartet (Charlie Rouse became his long-time horn player in 1958), had a celebrated concert of his works in an orchestral setting at New York's Town Hall (1959), and eventually moved on from Riverside to sign to the major label Columbia in 1962. Yet this marked the beginning of a creative impasse. His composing slowed to barely a trickle of new pieces, and his live performances began to take on a rote nature with the quartet, although it was still the kind of music which many aspiring bands would have loved to have got near.

The Columbia albums drifted towards studio chores, although Monk's penchant for throwing in an oddball standard (such as his cruel portrayal of 'Lulu's Back In Town', 1964) freshened up some of the programmes. By the end of the decade, his strange demeanour was becoming increasingly bizarre. On the 1971 Giants Of Jazz tour, Dave Liebman remembered him as being 'like Lon Chaney', lying flat out on tables most of the time and groaning if spoken to. Admirers such as Steve Lacy – who once had a band which played nothing but Monk tunes – helped disseminate his work further, but Monk himself seemed to have lost interest in his own music. He made a final appearance at Newport in 1976, but Whitney Balliett found it 'mechanical and uncertain', and thereafter he retreated to the home of a long-time patron and friend, Baroness Nica de Koenigswarter, in New Jersey: Monk's wife Nellie (for whom he wrote 'Crepuscule With Nellie') visited to cook for him, a strange arrangement, and Monk died there in 1982, having not touched a piano for years and seemingly entirely withdrawn from the world.

Since his death, there has been much conjecture as to whether he may have suffered from a mental illness for a long time, the old 'eccentricities' a symptom of a genuine malaise. His legacy is a book of some 70 compositions, of which one at least, 'Round Midnight', has become the most celebrated and frequently covered jazz ballad of the modern era. If he was still comparatively neglected as a composer at the time of his death, that has now entirely changed: his music is seen almost as a testing ground for modern musicians, and everyone has a go at one of the tunes sooner or later. It is a collective resource which, for its infinite variety within a small, carefully codified point of view, is unrivalled in the jazz idiom. And even as that resource continues to nourish improvisers to this day, it is probably best heard through the composer's own irreducible interpretations.

***Thelonious Himself*** (Riverside/OJC)

## T S Monk, Jr

DRUMS
*born* 27 December 1949

Monk's son started out in rock groups but played in his father's quartet in the early 70s. He also played fusion and funk music, and in the 80s switched to drum machines, although he went back to the kit at the end of the decade. In the 90s he finally seemed set on addressing his father's legacy, and he formed small groups which played more in a hard-bop style, leading eventually to the band Monk On Monk, a ten-piece group that reinterpreted his father's original music. His albums for Blue Note from this period were an exceedingly mixed lot, but the *Monk On Monk* album turned out much better than it might have done. Since then, Monk has gone back to a funkier style, and his label N2K has enjoyed some crossover success with other artists.

***Monk On Monk*** (N2K)

## Ade Monsbourgh

SAXOPHONES, CLARINET
*born* 17 February 1917

'Lazy Ade' Monsbourgh is a senior spirit in the doughty field of Australian trad. He was playing as a sideman with Graeme Bell as far back as the early 30s, and went to Europe with him in the 40s, although he also visited England as a solo in 1951–2 and recorded there with Humphrey Lyttelton. He had a long and busy career on and off record until the 70s, when he basically retired, although he has occasionally turned up as a guest star since.

***Lazy Ade & His Late Hour Boys*** (Swaggie)

## Monterey Jazz Festival

One of the major American festivals, founded in 1958 by Ralph Gleason and Jimmy Lyons and held annually (September) on the Monterey County Fairgrounds, California. Originally a challenging mix of familiar jazz forms and stars and specially commissioned new material, the programming atrophied to some extent towards the end of the 20th century, although that may have been no more than symptomatic of the ageing of the jazz festival as any kind of innovative event.

## J R Monterose

TENOR SAXOPHONE
*born* 19 January 1927; *died* 26 September 1993

Monterose had a single great year: it was 1956, when he cut his solitary album as a leader for Blue Note and played as a sideman on Charles Mingus's *Pithecanthropus Erectus* and Kenny Dorham's Café Bohemia sessions. On the evidence of that material, he was an idiosyncratic hard bopper with plenty of ideas, although they were delivered in an unfashionably tight and tensed-up tone. He had some sideman work after that and was occasionally caught by microphones on local gigs in upstate New York: he was still playing in the 90s, but at that point the music had long since passed him by.

**Charles Mingus,** ***Pithecanthropus Erectus*** (Atlantic)

## Wes Montgomery

GUITAR
*born* 6 March 1925; *died* 15 June 1968

Montgomery learned the guitar in his teens, and developed a technique based around his thumb rather than a pick, supposedly because it made a quieter sound and didn't disturb his family when he was practising. Although he was with Lionel Hampton for a spell at the end of the 40s, he returned to his native Indianapolis around 1951 and worked at a day job while playing on the local circuit at night. His brothers Monk (drums, 1921–82) and Buddy (vibes, b. 1930) often worked alongside him, and their group was at first known as The Mastersounds, although they eventually became better known simply as The Montgomery Brothers. During this period, Wes established himself as one of the masters of his instrument. He had trademarks, particularly playing in unison octaves, which eventually became almost the whole direction of his style, but he took the swing dialects of Charlie Christian into the modern world of hard bop more capably than any other guitarist, lightening the bluesier style of Kessel and Burrell with melodic ingenuities that have kept his work for Riverside (for whom he recorded all through the early 60s) wonderfully fresh. He began touring more widely in the early 60s and suddenly found himself a hit-maker when he started recording for Verve in 1964, and melodious if relatively tame pop covers such as 'Goin' Out Of My Head' went into the charts. By 1968 he was being moulded as a full-scale middle-of-the-road star, and was having to say things like 'There's a jazz conception to what I'm doing, but I'm playing popular music and it should be regarded as such.' His sudden death from a heart attack left questions about his future work unanswered. It's been almost obligatory to look down on Montgomery's later, orchestrated music, but compared to most of today's smooth jazz it is bursting with character and life. Either way, he left an indecently rich legacy of fine records, many of which remain benchmarks for jazz guitar.

*Incredible Jazz Guitar* (OJC/Riverside)

# Tete Montoliu

PIANO
*born* 28 March 1933; *died* 24 August 1997

Blind and half-deaf, Montoliu still managed to create a prodigious body of work. He grew up in Barcelona and began playing jazz in the middle 50s, soon leaving the jazz-starved Spanish scene and working in France, Italy, Germany and Denmark, where he became the house pianist at Copenhagen's Café Montmartre for a period in the middle 60s. Eventually he returned to Spain and began working as a soloist and a trio leader: in his heyday of the 70s and early 80s, he recorded prolifically for Nils Winther's Steeplechase label, and set down many albums which highlighted his garrulous swing-to-bop style. He also recorded with Anthony Braxton (something of a mismatch) and George Coleman. Montoliu's music has a sometimes tiresomely virtuosic flavour and his albums tend to pall at length, but he was a perhaps surprisingly sympathetic accompanist (to Ben Webster, among others) and on ballads he could find an agreeably rhapsodic flavour.

*The Music I Like To Play* (Soul Note)

# Montreux Jazz Festival

Founded by Claude Nobs, this annual Swiss festival has become perhaps the most famous European jazz event, and was first held in 1967. The shrewd Nobs realized early the long-term value of the festival's musical content and ensured that every event was recorded, retaining most of the rights. In its early days it was held at the Montreux Casino but has since expanded into a number of venues. From the 70s onwards pop and rock concerts and artists began to creep into the programming, and major record companies started using the event to showcase priority artists: over the last dozen years or so the jazz content has, indeed, become almost secondary, and its title is these days something of a sham.

# James Moody

TENOR AND ALTO SAXOPHONES, FLUTE
*born* 26 March 1925

Although Moody was in at the start of bebop, he presented an acceptable face of the music to doubters: he sounded a little like Dexter Gordon, another bopper whose style really derives from an earlier matrix, and his jukebox hit 'Moody's Mood For Love' (1949, and actually his first record on alto rather than his customary tenor) suggested a kinship with the swing masters in the way they'd treat a ballad. Before that, he'd worked in Dizzy Gillespie's big band in the mid-40s, then with Miles Davis in Europe, where he stayed until 1951. He ran a small band of his own in America throughout the 50s, but recorded comparatively little, and it wasn't until he signed with the small Argo label that he was busy in the studios. Although not very highly regarded (and seldom reissued), this sequence of albums has much to enjoy – such as the bluesy big-band charts of *Last Train From Overbrook* (1959) – and also demonstrates what a fine flute player Moody was as well. Some of his best-known work was with the Dizzy Gillespie small group that toured during the 60s, but after that he was somewhat hidden in low-profile gigs until – like so many others – he was rediscovered as an elder statesman in the 90s, and made a sequence of patchy but enjoyable records for Warner Bros. A droll stage demeanour has made him popular with audiences, and he always insists on being called 'Moody', never 'James'.

*Young At Heart* (Warner Bros)

# Jemeel Moondoc

ALTO SAXOPHONE
*born* 5 August 1951

Although Moondoc grew up in Chicago and started playing there, he seems to have had little to do with the city's jazz scene: instead, he studied in Boston and played in R&B bands there. After hearing a Cecil Taylor record he made his way to Wisconsin, where Taylor was teaching at the time, and sat at that master's feet. Then, in 1972, he moved to New York. He played and led groups on the loft jazz scene there, and has since then worked steadily and prolifically in various American free-jazz circles, making a number of records for the Midwestern label Eremite. His music oscillates between free playing and a more structured post-bop approach, and groups such as his Jus' Grew Orchestra have some of the tenacious intensity of Taylor's group music, though not quite the clarity of focus.

*Fire In The Valley* (Eremite)

# Brew Moore

TENOR SAXOPHONE
*born* 26 March 1924; *died* 19 August 1973

If there was ever a clone of Lester Young, it was Brew Moore, who unashamedly worshipped and emulated his mentor's playing. He grew up in Mississippi and worked in various Southern cities before getting his chance in New York, in 1948, where he worked with Claude Thornhill and Machito and played in small groups when he had the chance. There were only a handful of record sessions under his own name by the time he decided to settle in Europe in the early 60s, and though he shuttled back and forth between Copenhagen and New York, he never really got his career going again. He died after falling down some stairs in his Danish home.

*The Brew Moore Quintet* (Fantasy)

# Dudley Moore

PIANO
*born* 19 April 1935; *died* 27 March 2002

Moore was better at comedy than he was at jazz, but he played very decent piano in a light Erroll Garner style and probably beckoned quite a few otherwise reluctant listeners in the direction of the music. He got a gig with John Dankworth's band early on (1960), but reading and rehearsing charts appealed less than leading his own trio, and he played in London clubs before finding a grander showbiz success in *Beyond The Fringe* and his subsequent partnership with Peter Cook. Moore never left his affection for jazz behind, though, and even in his movie-star years was pleased to play the occasional gala or talk about the music.

*Genuine Dud* (Decca)

# Glen Moore

BASS
*born* 28 October 1941

Moore worked in New York with Zoot Sims and others in the early 60s, but his career took a different turn when he joined the Paul Winter Consort in 1970 and subsequently became a founding member of the band Oregon (suitably enough, since he was from Portland himself). Besides his work there, he has gone on to do occasional solo work, duos with Ralph Towner and Larry Karush, and projects which build on the world-jazz direction which Oregon have largely pursued.

**With Ralph Towner,** *Trios/Solos* (ECM)

# Michael Moore
BASS
*born* 16 May 1945

Moore's avuncular demeanour and choice of basically conservative playing situations have tended to disguise a very keen, sharp-eared player who does a lot more than most bassists on his kind of gig. He grew up near Cincinnati and toured with Woody Herman in the middle 60s before going to New York. There he vacillated between mainstream playing with the likes of Ruby Braff and Jake Hanna, and more 'modern' settings with Freddie Hubbard. The mainstream end took precedence, and he commenced a long-standing duo with guitarist Gene Bertoncini. For a time he lived in India and London, but he returned to New York soon enough and has continued to play in small-group formats which give him space and time to give of his best. He is as fast and proficient as any bassist since Charles Mingus, but his speed and skill are mostly put at the service of melodic improvising and counterpoint in a genial swing-styled idiom.

# Michael Moore
ALTO SAXOPHONE, CLARINET
*born* 4 December 1954

Moore grew up in California and studied in Boston before moving to New York, but following a visit to the Netherlands in 1978 he settled there permanently two years later and has become a fixture in Amsterdam's music scene.

# Oscar Moore
GUITAR
*born* 25 December 1912; *died* 8 October 1981

Nat Cole's guitarist never escaped the association of working with that illustrious leader: he was with Cole between 1937 and 1947 and his quietly snappy lines and fills gave the King Cole Trio much of their hipness and character. After this he worked in a trio with his brother John and made a handful of albums as a leader, including one session from 1965 which nodded to his old boss after the latter's death.

*Oscar Moore Quartet* (Tampa)

# Ralph Moore
TENOR SAXOPHONE
*born* 24 December 1956

Moore must have been tired of being referred to as a young and up-and-coming talent, a description which persisted into his mid-30s. He was born in London, of an American father and English mother, and he went to live with his father in California in 1972, where he studied saxophone. He played in Horace Silver's groups in the early 80s and thereafter steadily added to a burgeoning CV, playing under a number of distinguished leaders, but his career as a solo artist has sputtered out after a few strong records which failed to catch much attention. Latterly he played in the house band on *The Tonight Show* on American television.

*Rejuvenate!* (Criss Cross)

# Jason Moran
PIANO
*born* 21 January 1975

Born in Houston, Moran studied there before moving to New York in 1994, where his sideman work eventually took him into the Greg Osby group (Osby actually hired him on his drummer's recommendation, and at that point hadn't even heard him play): a brilliant teaming, where the musical dialogue between Moran and Osby reached astonishing levels of creativity. Moran has since begun working as a group leader himself, and records as a solo for Blue Note. The teeming resources of his music might exemplify the breadth and outreach of jazz as it currently stands in the hands of its most creative new minds: interpretations of Schumann, Ravel, James P Johnson and Afrika Bambaata, and compositions of his own which reflect two intriguing influences, Jaki Byard and Andrew Hill, both of whom he studied with privately. His series of

'Gangsterism' compositions use as their root a piece by Hill, 'Erato'. Already embraced by a wider musical establishment – he has received a commission from the organization Chamber Music America – Moran's future progress is likely to be compelling, and he is adamant about working within his chosen idiom: 'I don't understand people who say there's nothing new in jazz.'
**Black Stars** (Blue Note)

# Airto Moreira
PERCUSSION
*born* 5 August 1941

Moreira lived in Brazil until he was 27: playing Brazilian music, folk, a little Latin jazz, probably whatever came his way. He also began collecting percussion instruments, and by the time he and his wife Flora (Purim) moved to Los Angeles in 1967, he had scores of them. In 1969 he began touring with Miles Davis, and this set him up for a career where he became the percussionist of choice with numerous star groups and leaders – Weather Report, Stan Getz, Return To Forever. It is a position he has largely maintained ever since, although he and Flora also work extensively as the leaders of a lite-fusion group, which still tours constantly. Moreira is a bystander in the jazz of the past 30-something years, just occasionally doing something more than making up the numbers.
**Chick Corea, *Return To Forever*** (ECM)

# Joe Morello
DRUMS
*born* 17 July 1928

Morello's principal gig was drummer with the Dave Brubeck Quartet, through most of its greatest years: he joined in 1956, after working with Marian McPartland for some years, and stayed until 1967. With Brubeck, Morello was deft, smart and a canny improviser: his famous feature on 'Take Five', the group's great hit, became his most familiar setpiece, but he negotiated Brubeck's often difficult music with a calm and spruce ingenuity that regularly lifted the band through what might have been rocky waters. It was appropriate that, after this, he worked mostly as a drum instructor and an ambassa-dor for manufacturers such as Ludwig: there were no better exponents of how musical a kit could sound. Latterly he has played and led occasional groups of his own, although increasing blindness has curtailed his activity.
**Dave Brubeck, *Time Out*** (Columbia)

# Frank Morgan
ALTO AND SOPRANO SAXOPHONES
*born* 23 December 1933

Young Frank heard Charlie Parker when the master was still with Jay McShann, and that was enough to make him want to start out on alto. His family went to Los Angeles in 1947 and he worked on the bebop scene there in the early 50s. But drugs had already caught hold of him, and he went to prison on narcotics offences in 1955 (where he befriended Art Pepper). *Introducing Frank Morgan*, which came out the same year, turned out to be a premature showing. In the 80s, many years after his first jazz steps, Morgan was suddenly rediscovered and began working as something of a born-again survivor. He made albums for Contemporary, Antilles and Telarc in the late 80s and early 90s which showed his bebop chops still in fine order, and has recently made a new record for High Note. As with the latter-day Pepper, he plays with a chastened and sometimes bitter dignity.
**Bop!** (Telarc)

# Lanny Morgan
ALTO SAXOPHONE
*born* 30 March 1934

Morgan is perhaps typical of a generation of West Coast players who did impeccable work on probably hundreds of records without their names or faces ever getting specific recognition. He worked in big bands before doing military service in the later 50s and then played for Si Zentner and Bob Florence, although in 1960 he went East and spent six years in the Maynard Ferguson orchestra. He returned West in 1969 and resumed activity as a studio player and as a small-group sideman and leader. He has fronted only a handful of not especially remarkable albums in a 50-year career.
**Pacific Standard** (Contemporary)

# Lee Morgan

TRUMPET

*born* 10 July 1938; *died* 19 February 1972

The most extravagantly talented trumpeter of his generation – even though his talents were often dispersed or misplaced or simply, as in the later part of his brief career, taken for granted. He grew up in Philadelphia and was in love with jazz from an early age: Reggie Workman remembered how 'he knew about everybody from Pops right on up to today, yet he amalgamated it into his own sound'. By the time he was 18 he was good enough to secure a gig with Art Blakey's Jazz Messengers (and make his first LPs), but this lasted only a few weeks, and he then joined Dizzy Gillespie's orchestra until it disbanded in 1958. Blakey took him on again and he stayed until 1961. In this period, Morgan was all flash and fire and high spirits, and perhaps not much more than the sum of his influences (primarily Fats Navarro and Clifford Brown), but with Blakey his sound became thicker and some of the shrillness hardened and settled down. Aside from another period with Blakey in 1964–5, he thereafter freelanced, mostly as a member of his own groups. Alfred Lion recorded him almost obsessively for Blue Note: he cut more than 20 sessions for the label as a leader and appeared as a sideman on dozens of others. His playing took on a technically more challenging cast, using half-valved trumpet sounds and shying away from bebop pyrotechnics and into a more thoughtful though still demanding procedure. It was something of an irony that his track and album *The Sidewinder* (1964), a catchy groove tune, became Blue Note's biggest hit and the piece of music which pushed the label towards its first real sales success: its simple boogaloo setting wasn't really where Morgan was heading. Nevertheless, thereafter Lion constantly tried to get him to repeat the trick on his albums.

Much of his work from the later 60s has been undervalued, although it's true that in place of the old exuberance there is a sometimes troubling and clouded feel to his playing, as if there was something heavy on his mind; and many of his best solos are hidden on obscure Blue Note dates, far away from *The Sidewinder*. The hit sustained him through a period when his kind of jazz went into a steep commercial decline: he refused to go towards fusion or the kind of sellout which Donald Byrd embraced, and he even took part in the Jazz And People's Movement, protesting at the disrespect jazz received from the American cultural establishment. He was playing at a club called Slug's, in New York, on a cold night in 1972, when a long-standing female friend found him with another woman in the club, and shot him dead with his own pistol.

*The Sidewinder* (Blue Note)

# Sam Morgan

CORNET, BANDLEADER

*born* 18 December 1887; *died* 25 February 1936

The eldest of the four Morgan brothers, Sam was born in Bertrandville and played in brass bands before moving to New Orleans itself in 1915. He began leading groups there and was soon a considerable figure, despite suffering a stroke in 1924. His brother Isaiah also had a good band, which Sam joined in 1925, and he eventually took over its leadership. In 1927, Columbia recorded eight titles by the group, a precious part of the very small amount of 'authentic' New Orleans music recorded in the 20s. The best titles, including 'Mobile Stomp', 'Bogalousa Strut' and 'Steppin' On The Gas', have a drive and exuberance which is as invigorating as anything recorded in the original Jazz Age, as well as demonstrating the classic New Orleans ensemble feel in full cry. The band remained popular but didn't record again, and Morgan had another stroke in 1932 and effectively retired from music not long after. Isaiah (1897–1966), a trumpeter, subsequently worked in and around Biloxi before he retired in the 50s; Andrew (1901–72), who played clarinet and alto sax, remained busy in the city's music right up until his death; and Albert (1908–74), who played bass, moved on from New Orleans to play in New York in the 30s, where he spent some years with Cab Calloway. In the 40s and early 50s he played in Boston, and eventually he settled in Los Angeles, where he worked with revivalists such as Joe Darensbourg. Between them, the Morgans brought much to jazz, but nothing really surpassed the electrifying early records under Sam's name, which three of them played on – only Albert was missing.

*Papa Celestin & Sam Morgan* (Azure)

# Dan Morgenstern
WRITER, CUSTODIAN
*born* 24 October 1929

Morgenstern grew up in Vienna but left before war broke out and spent the next nine years as a refugee in Scandinavia. He moved to New York in 1947 and was soon caught up in jazz. He began working as a writer on the music in the 50s and served as editor on several magazines while also writing sleevenotes, producing concerts and lecturing. In 1976 he became director of the Rutgers Institute of Jazz Studies, which he has overseen since and has helped grow into one of the world's major jazz archives. An outstanding writer with a rare ability to bring readers close to musicians he has himself been close with for many years, Dan is perhaps the single most knowledgeable and sympathetic communicator on jazz his (adopted) country has ever produced.

# Butch Morris
CORNET, CONDUCTOR
*born* 10 February 1947

Morris is a Californian who worked in such enclaves as the Horace Tapscott circle in the 70s before touring Europe with Frank Lowe and – crucially – working the New York scene with his famous contemporary, David Murray. While Murray's subsequent work took a less *outré* course, though, Morris looked for more ambitiously remote fields to work in. Besides writing chamber works, he began to develop a system which he christened 'conduction' – which boils down to conducting a band of improvisers through a performance. The object appears to be to find another way of balancing the ingredients of form, freedom, composition and improvisation under the conditions of a spontaneous live performance. This has led to some stormy situations: he once rebuked guitarist Derek Bailey for not following his directions, whereupon Bailey calmly packed up and left the stage; and a tour where Morris conducted a British band reputedly ended in acrimony, yet led to the formation of the London Improvisers' Orchestra. The ten-disc *Testament* collection is a suitably exhausting trip through Morris's efforts in this direction, which at least has resulted in a lot of festival work for him. It seems a pity

that the various conductions have obliged him to put down his cornet of late, since *Burning Cloud* (1993), by a trio with J A Deane and Lê Quan Ninh, suggests he has much of interest to say on the horn.
*Testament* (New World)

# Joe Morris
GUITAR
*born* 13 September 1955

Morris is a formidable player, even in an age when the guitar hardly wants for virtuoso performers. Inspired by John McLaughlin, he began working around the Boston scene in the late 70s, where he met up with Matthew Shipp. Since then he has recorded regularly (originally on his own label Riti, although this is now in abeyance since Morris is in such demand elsewhere), and played with the inevitable gaggle of bands of his own, in varying sizes and working through disciplines from funk to entirely free playing. Morris can play at head-spinning velocity, even while executing lines of almost pernickety precision: the acoustic solos on *No Vertigo* (1995) are a particularly vivid illustration of his facility. Rather than going the Frisell route, he prefers a direct and uncomplicated sound on electric, and he also likes to pick up the mandolin or the banjulele. Although he went through a lean spell at the beginning of the 90s, Morris has since been prolifically recorded by a variety of labels.
*No Vertigo* (Leo)

# Thomas Morris
CORNET
*born* c1899; *died* after 1940, exact date unknown

Little is known about Morris, but he was a busy man in the New York studios of the 20s, cutting more than 150 sides between 1922 and 1927. He was a strong blues accompanist behind many singers during the early part of this period, including Sara Martin and Rosa Henderson, and he went on to lead several dates of his own, notably the 1926 sides by his Hot Babies, which variously included Rex Stewart, Jabbo Smith and Joe Nanton besides Morris himself. The toughness of his sound was somewhat undercut by a fondness for crabbing his tone, but he left some rootsy and enjoyable music behind him. In the 30s he joined a religious group and gave up music altogether; nobody knows what became of him.

**When A 'Gator Hollers** (Frog)

# James Morrison
TRUMPET, TROMBONE, SAXOPHONE, PIANO
*born* 11 November 1962

Morrison's instrumental facility is so wide – he plays many instruments, all of them with high executive skill – that he's often seemed too clever by half. He was born in Boorowa, Australia, and studied in New South Wales before coming to some attention alongside Red Rodney in 1986 and then with the Philip Morris Superband. Like many Australian celebrities, Morrison has failed to make a lasting international impact: he toured with a notably strong band in the mid-90s (which included Mark Nightingale, Brian Kellock and Rickey Woodard in the line-up) but his records have largely failed to last the course. *Snappy Doo* (1990) was one of the more extraordinary feats in modern jazz record-ing, a big-band set where Morrison played every brass and reed instrument, but it did call to mind Dr Johnson's retort about a dog on its hind legs. His best record is *Two The Max* (1991), with Ray Brown, Benny Green and Jeff Hamilton.

**Two The Max** (East West)

# Dick Morrissey
TENOR AND SOPRANO SAXOPHONES
*born* 9 May 1940; *died* 8 November 2000

Morrissey toyed with various instruments before settling on the saxophone at 18: by the time he was 21 he had completely mas-tered the horn and developed a powerhouse sound and delivery which his first album, *It's Morrissey, Man!* (1961) showcased to impressive effect. He ran his own quartet in the middle 60s, which set down some of the best British jazz of its time, but Dick looked towards fresh fields with the jazz-rock group If and by the 70s was touring America with the band. He met guitarist Jim Mullen while playing in the horn section for The Average White Band, and their Morrissey–Mullen group was a very successful band of its time (1976–85, with occasional reunions). Dick

was still playing beautifully up till 1990 or so, but illness took him off the scene and by the mid-90s it was clear that he wasn't going to play again. Along with Tubby Hayes, Morrissey was the top young tenorman of his scene in the 60s, and the thunderous excitement of his playing is rekindled by the records. Even in the com-paratively placid music of Morrissey–Mullen he could still offer playing of great heart.

**It's Morrissey, Man!** (Redial)

# Benny Morton
TROMBONE
*born* 31 January 1907; *died* 28 December 1985

Morton joined Fletcher Henderson's band at 19, and from there worked for Chick Webb (1928–31), Don Redman (1931–7) and Count Basie (1937–40), bringing to each band a thoughtful, accomplished manner: while some of his early solos with Henderson are in more of a shouting style, he softened and matured that approach as time went on. In the 40s he worked in swing-styled small groups, and later found steady employment in Broadway orchestras, before working in swing-revivalist groups in the 60s and 70s such as The Saints And Sinners and The World's Greatest Jazz Band. Never a flam-boyant or characterful player in the manner of some of his trombone contemporaries, Morton was a reliable musician whose best playing is handsome and literate.

**Edmond Hall, Profoundly Blue** (Blue Note)

# Jelly Roll Morton
PIANO, VOCAL
*born* 20 October 1890; *died* 10 July 1941

Born Ferdinand Joseph Lamothe, Morton's first music was playing guitar in New Orleans string bands, but he started on piano when he was ten, and was good enough to play in the parlours of the city's Storyville district by the time he was 15. Exactly what he played is uncertain, but in all likelihood he followed the pattern of the other piano players in the city, learning rags and marches and popular classical and dance tunes. For the next dozen years he led a picaresque existence of hustling in pool halls, pimping, working in blackface minstrel shows and playing a lot of piano, all through Florida, Mississippi and Alabama: the account he left Alan Lomax in *Mr Jelly Roll* is a priceless memory of the times. He finally went West and arrived in Los Angeles in 1917, where he settled for six years and established a princely reputation among musicians. By the time he went to Chicago in 1923, recording an extensive series of piano solo treatments of his own music for Gennett, his music had matured into a marvellously vivid idiom of his own: while the core of the pieces goes back to ragtime and the blues, they are elaborated on and embellished with such skill and ingenuity that they still seem alive and fresh, even through the dim recording quality. But the solos were a prelude to the brilliant small-group recordings of 1926–7, by Jelly Roll Morton's Red Hot Peppers: the pianist orchestrated his music in such a way that it was tightly drilled and rehearsed, yet free-flowing, zinging with the electricity of the breaks by the individual players, and sonorous in the use of countermelodies and ensemble harmony. The best of these records, including 'Grandpa's Spells', 'Black Bottom Stomp', 'Jelly Roll Blues' and 'Dr Jazz', are as fine as jazz would get in the 20s, and Morton reigned as one of the masters of Chicago's music scene. But his move to New York in 1928 coincided with the start of a fall in his fortunes. The later Peppers sessions show his inventiveness already starting to decline, although there were still some superb records, and his later piano solos are full of interest; yet Morton never shook off his vaudeville past, something which began to date him in a rapidly changing jazz world, and the hokum element in records such as 'Sidewalk Blues' sounded old-fashioned in the city where Ellington and Henderson held sway.

The 30s were a disaster for him. He was dropped by Victor, and the consequences of an unfortunate publishing agreement with the Melrose brothers, which he fought against for years, denied him many of the royalties due when the swing era turned a piece such as 'King Porter Stomp' into a hit. He was reduced to playing in pit bands until he was more or less rediscovered in 1938 by Alan Lomax, a folklorist working for the Library Of Congress, who recorded hours of his reminiscences and a number of piano solos which showed that his mastery was intact if just a little rusty. Outraged by a broadcast where W C Handy was feted as jazz's father figure, he wrote to the press that 'it is evidently known, beyond contradiction, that New Orleans is the cradle of jazz, and I, myself, happened to be the creator in the year 1902'. There was a final date for Victor, and some sessions made for the small label General, but despite composing and thinking about new projects to the end, Morton's health was gone: he drove to California in 1940, and died there the following July. Disliked by many of his contemporaries for his loud mouth, jazz's first great composer went to a lonely grave. The modern advocacy of his work by Wynton Marsalis and others is some overdue justice for his wonderful music.

*Jelly Roll Morton Vols 1–5* (JSP)

## Mosaic

RECORD COMPANY

In 1981, Michael Cuscuna was researching Thelonious Monk's Blue Note recordings for its parent label when he realized that there was enough in the way of out-takes and unissued material to make a deluxe edition of all the music worthwhile – the kind of thing a major label might not want to do, but a limited-edition, 'boutique' label for jazz-connoisseur collectors would be well equipped to provide. Thus was Mosaic Records born, masterminded by Cuscuna and his business partner Charlie Lourie. Since then, Cuscuna has researched and prepared some 250 boxed editions of complete chapters from the works of various jazz artists or labels: benchmark issues have included a complete edition of Commodore sessions, Nat Cole's Capitol trio dates (which ran to dozens of LPs), and numerous sets dedicated to major Blue Note artists. Sets are licensed from their respective owners for a limited period, and are available until they have sold out or the licence has expired. Prepared with the most fastidious attention to detail and the highest standards of remastering, the sets are considered to set the standard for all jazz reissues. Lourie died in 2000 but Cuscuna carries on the company's work.

## Sal Mosca
PIANO
*born* 27 April 1927

Mosca learned piano with various teachers but it was the influence of Lennie Tristano, whom he studied with between 1947 and 1955, that really directed his playing: unlike some of Tristano's students, Mosca remained great friends with his mentor. He often worked with Lee Konitz in the 50s and 60s, and again in the 70s with Konitz and Warne Marsh, but for the most part he has performed as a soloist or trio leader. While Tristano's methods inform most of what he does, he is an intense and complex improviser whose investigations of standard material are labyrinthine yet clear-headed and in some ways very easy to follow – possibly because, as he has said, 'under all that complex improvising, there is always the simple melody as your guide'. He has actually been recorded very infrequently over decades of musical activity.
*A Concert* (Jazz Records)

## Bob Moses
DRUMS
*born* 28 January 1948

Moses has been an interested party in a number of significant post-bop ventures. He started as a percussionist in Latin bands, and in 1966 co-founded Free Spirits with Larry Coryell, a group which was among the first stirrings of what might be called jazz-rock. He then worked with Roland Kirk and Gary Burton before another modestly ground-breaking group, Open Sky, featured him with Dave Liebman and Frank Tusa. For the rest of the 70s and 80s he mostly freelanced, although he did have the opportunity to record some of his large-scale music when Gramavision sponsored the release of *When Elephants Dream Of Music* (1982) and *Visit With The Great Spirit* (1983), colourful jumbles of influences from jazz, Afro-Cuban and African music with a sometimes dark and brooding edge to them. But none of his albums really reached a significant audience, even though he is an avowed populist when it comes to music-making.
*Visit With The Great Spirit* (Gramavision)

## Danny Moss
TENOR SAXOPHONE
*born* 16 August 1927

Moss was rather hidden in the rank and file of British jazz for a long time. He began playing in RAF bands in the 40s, then worked with British big bands, including those of Ted Heath, Oscar Rabin and John Dankworth, eventually leading his own small group in the 60s. Thereafter he did much studio work in the sessionman's golden age of the 70s and was a regular with London's Pizza Express All Stars in the 80s. In 1989 he and his wife, the singer Jeannie Lambe, went to live in Australia. Ironically enough, his career has taken something of an upturn since then: he has been extensively recorded as a soloist and leader by the Nagel Heyer label (the proprietor unabashedly considers Moss the finest saxophonist currently playing) on his regular return visits to Europe, and his big, meat-and-potatoes sound and delivery have been handsomely documented as a result.
*Weaver Of Dreams* (Nagel Heyer)

## Sam Most
FLUTE
*born* 16 December 1930

Most began as a reed player in big bands at the twilight of the swing era, but he increasingly turned to flute as his specialist instrument and pioneered its use in a bop environment. His Bethlehem albums of the middle 50s include some of his best work and he often turned up as a sideman on the label's other sessions; but the instrument remained a marginal one in jazz of the period. Most joined Buddy Rich in 1959, thereafter playing on the West Coast and in Las Vegas, mostly in sessionman roles. Sam was a typical Don Schlitten 'rediscovery' in the 70s and he made four albums for Xanadu, before going on to teach and occasionally co-lead a group with his brother Abe (b 1920), a clarinettist whose career was primarily taken up with studio work.
*Sam Most Plays, Bird, Bud, Monk And Miles* (Bethlehem)

# Bennie Moten

PIANO, BANDLEADER

*born* 13 November 1894; *died* 2 April 1935

Moten's band was, over a dozen years, the cradle of Kansas City jazz. He began playing piano in the city's bars in 1918, with a trio, which steadily expanded its personnel until, in 1923, they made their first records, as a sextet. Moten's OKeh sides are primitive and unsubtle, with the eccentric clarinet of Woody Walder (who sometimes just blew through his mouthpiece) taking up a lot of space. By the time of his first sessions for Victor in 1926, the band had begun to move towards its mature self. Moten started to lure away players from his great KC rival Walter Page and his Blue Devils, and by 1929 the bandleader had added Hot Lips Page, Bill Basie and Jimmy Rushing to his line-up: eventually Page himself joined too. The group's sound had grown huge, virtuosic, and indomitably swinging, via one of the best rhythm sections in the music (Basie, Page, Willie McWashington). There was a fine range of soloists and a strong hook to go with them. The band toured widely and sometimes endured a 'Battle Of The Bands' with rival outfits. But the Depression started to take its toll on touring ensembles, and a near-disastrous outing in 1932 almost finished the band (although the extraordinary records they made at this time, ten astonishing titles cut at a single date in December, make one wonder why the orchestra didn't find more success). The leader had an up-and-down struggle over the next two years, but the band seemed to be back to its best at the beginning of 1935, booked into a Chicago engagement, when Moten abruptly died after a mishap during a minor hospital operation. His legacy lived on – under Count Basie's stewardship.

*Band Box Shuffle* (Hep)

# Paul Motian

DRUMS

*born* 25 March 1931

Following his military service, Motian settled in New York in 1954 and for the rest of the decade worked prolifically with a broad variety of leaders, from Thelonious Monk to Coleman Hawkins. But his most important association was with Bill Evans, in the trio (1959–62) which also featured Scott LaFaro. While LaFaro's dramatic innovations and Evans's playing attracted the most attention, Motian played his part in the group's progressive tendencies, playing in a more interactive and less accompanying manner and adding to the freeing-up of the drummer's role which was being explored elsewhere by Elvin Jones and others. Motian always picked the best pianists to work with: in the 60s he played for Paul Bley, Keith Jarrett and Mose Allison, the latter a partnership which he renewed in the 90s on some of Mose's late Blue Note records. He moved closer to free jazz via Bley and an association with the Jazz Composers' Orchestra, although in the end he only took it so far, preferring to work within fluid structures rather than empty space. After the Jarrett quartet disbanded in 1977, his principal activity was as a leader himself: with trios, at first with players such as David Izenzon and Charles Brackeen, and then in a long-standing group with Joe Lovano and Bill Frisell, first convened in 1981. This band recorded extensively for JMT, as did a later vehicle, The Electric Bebop Band, which doubled up electric guitars and saxophones. The drummer has also done other high-calibre work with Masabumi Kikuchi, Enrico Pieranunzi and Tom Harrell. Listeners tend to be divided on the merits of Motian's playing: the more insinuating style of his earlier period has been supplanted by an often noisy, even brash delivery which some of his more extrovert playing companions may have encouraged – when playing with a musician such as Pieranunzi, he reverts to his older style. His composing also has a sometimes obfuscatory feel to it, and his albums covering other material, such as the *Motian On Broadway* series, tend to be stronger. A long-promised autobiography has, disappointingly, so far not appeared: he is a great storyteller and has a huge fund of anecdotes.

*Le Voyage* (ECM)

# Mound City Blue Blowers

GROUP

Red McKenzie started this trio in 1924, almost as a city slicker's version of a backporch country trio: McKenzie played comb-and-paper, Jack Bland did banjo and guitar, and Dick Slevin played kazoo. They were a novelty hit on record and made numerous sides under this name, with Eddie Lang subsequently joining in too. McKenzie later revived the name for much larger groups of more conventional instrumentation, which recorded up until 1936.

## Alphonse Mouzon
DRUMS
*born* 21 November 1948

Mouzon's work has never been too much admired by the jazz audience, mainly because he's spent so much time in more popular idioms. This heresy started in the 60s, when he moved to New York and played behind the likes of Roberta Flack and Roy Ayers. He was the first drummer in Weather Report and lasted a year in a group which admittedly went on to have a high turnover of drummers, then played for McCoy Tyner and Larry Coryell. But he was at least as interested in leading his own groups, which usually pushed more in the direction of funk than jazz, and in the 70s and 80s he set down an enjoyably cluttered string of records for various labels which cheerfully mixed up genres: a 1982 set for Polydor was called *Step Into Funk*, but a few years later he followed that with one called *Back To Jazz*! For the most part, funk has suited him better because Mouzon is one of the loudest and hardest-hitting drummers outside of John Bonham. In 1992 he founded his own record label, Tenacious.
**Funky Snakefoot** (Blue Note)

## Famoudou Don Moye
DRUMS
*born* 23 May 1946

Moye was the last man to join the Art Ensemble Of Chicago, enlisting in 1970 having already toured in Europe over the previous two years. Although he has also played in numerous other situations – with Don Pullen, Julius Hemphill, The Leaders, Arthur Blythe and others – he has never really established himself as a singular force away from the AEOC, and aside from a desultory 1975 solo album there is very little to tabulate in his work away from that environment.
**Art Ensemble Of Chicago,** *Urban Bushmen* (ECM)

## MPS
RECORD COMPANY

Established in 1968 by Hans Georg Brunner-Schwer, MPS (Musik Produktion Schwarzwald) worked out of its boss's base in the Black Forest and quickly established itself as one of the leading European jazz labels. Brunner-Schwer had a particular interest in jazz piano, and set down albums by pianists ranging from Oscar Peterson to Cecil Taylor: Peterson's *Exclusively For My Friends* sequence of albums were among the label's most renowned releases, but there were many others, and by the end of the 70s the company had more than 500 albums in its catalogue. It was significant in mixing European artists (Albert Mangelsdorff, Volker Kriegel, Martial Solal) with Americans (Peterson, George Shearing, Sun Ra). The label was eventually acquired by Polygram/ Universal, although it has been disgracefully neglected in reissue terms of late.

## George Mraz
BASS
*born* 9 September 1944

Mraz grew up in Czechoslovakia and studied in Prague, but his first jazz experience was in playing in a Munich club in 1967, where he followed the customary European procedure of backing American visitors. He moved to the US a year later and studied at Berklee before touring with Oscar Peterson and settling in New York. Mraz found American jazz welcoming, and he was busy all through the 70s and 80s as a sideman, in situations ranging from the conservative bop language of Hank Jones to the close-to-far-out feel of the Quest group. He carried on this activity in the 90s and beyond, but also made a particular rapprochement with his roots: during the course of a solo contract with Milestone which resulted in a number of fine small-group records, he completed a set based around Moravian folk melodies, a unique homage from an expatriate to his deepest roots.
**Morava** (Milestone)

# Bheki Mseleku

PIANO, TENOR SAXOPHONE
*born* 3 March 1955

Born in Durban, South Africa, Mseleku had a strange career: it may be over, it may not. He taught himself to play the piano and visited the US in 1977 with a band called Malombo, then settled in Sweden. He played there with John Dyani and other kindred spirits but didn't make any records. In 1985 he began living in London, where, despite mixing with some of the major names on the new jazz scene there, he still didn't make much progress. Eventually, he made a record of his own material for the small World Circuit label, in 1991, and he then came to the attention of Verve, who signed him to a multi-album deal. Mseleku's music sounds to be in the characteristic South African tradition of Abdullah Ibrahim, with rolling, Ellingtonian melodies and interesting structural touches, and he built on it by also playing saxophone and piano simultaneously to create multiple melodic voicings. Yet after three albums with Verve, which never really made much international impact, and an American tour where he played piano for Joe Henderson, he more or less disappeared, with rumours about health problems. A reserved and shy man, Mseleku seems to have been a little overwhelmed at the prospect of a major label's requirements; perhaps he simply preferred a quieter life.
*Timelessness* (Verve)

# Idris Muhammad

DRUMS
*born* 13 November 1939

Muhammad was born Leo Morris in New Orleans, where he tried to get lessons from Paul Barbarin (the veteran drummer thought the young man was too good to teach). He played behind soul singers in the 60s and backed Lou Donaldson before doubling as the drummer in the stage musical *Hair* and as an in-house sessionman for Prestige, both during 1969–73. He is a regular on dozens of records in the soul-jazz and organ-combo field from this period. Since then he has turned his hand to a huge number of jazz groups and playing situations, from the old-time feel of Doc Cheatham's jazz to such up-to-the-minute leaders as John Scofield and David Murray. He is one of the few musicians of his generation to have moved from prominence as a rock and soul player – he backed such major figures as Sam Cooke and The Impressions early on – to the high end of modern jazz performance. He made eight albums in the 70s as a leader, highly collectable among rare-groove fiends, although none of them are actually all that good: his finest playing is elsewhere.
**Ahmad Jamal, *The Essence*** (Birdology)

# Jim Mullen

GUITAR
*born* 2 November 1945

A redoubtable musician whose place at the high end of British jazz is part hard graft, part sweet inspiration. A Glaswegian, he started as a bassist but by the early 60s was doing gigs on guitar, eventually moving to London at the end of the decade to do rock and session-work. He toured the US with The Average White Band in 1976, where he met up with Dick Morrissey, and their Morrissey–Mullen outfit became the leading British pop-fusion outfit: it may have been commercially pitched by their record company, but both men ensured there was full-on jazz playing to go with the catchy tunes. In the 80s and 90s Mullen worked on the London scene as a group leader, as well as playing with such American visitors as Gene Harris and Jimmy Smith and often accompanying singers such as Claire Martin. Jim's own albums have latterly been full of gorgeous playing, tough and tender by turns, and his set of music based around Robert Burns pieces is definitive. He is also an implacable enemy of smooth jazz and corporate interference in musicians' work: 'It's the world we live in, unfortunately, but I'm fighting it all the way.'
**Burns** (Black Box)

# Gerry Mulligan

BARITONE SAXOPHONE
*born* 6 April 1927; *died* 19 January 1996

Mulligan was a man of paradoxes. He wrote many of the most precise and considered scores in modern jazz, yet he loved the freedom and spontaneity of jam sessions. He was one of the prime architects of cool, yet his own playing could be as fiercely hot as that of any hard bopper. He ran one of the most famous small groups in jazz, but his heart was surely with the big-band form. Born in New York, he started on piano (which he sometimes returned to on recordings), then tried out virtually the whole saxophone family. Moving to Philadelphia in 1944, he began writing arrangements, and then joined Gene Krupa as staff arranger in Los Angeles. Back in New York, he wrote for Claude Thornhill and was a key contributor to the Miles Davis 'Birth Of The Cool' sessions: it rankled with him in later years that he never got that much credit for his involvement. He made some sides with a tentet in New York, then went back to Los Angeles and formed a new quartet with trumpeter Chet Baker and no pianist. Their residency at a little club called The Haig caused a sensation, with queues around the block, and the subsequent recordings for Dick Bock's Pacific Jazz label showed why: irresistible Mulligan originals such as 'Walkin' Shoes' mixed with standards in clean, sonorous lines, and the results sounded like evergreen classics from the first auditioning. But Mulligan was using heroin, and only a three-month incarceration enabled him to get off the habit. He carried on with various four-man line-ups after Baker's departure, with Bob Brookmeyer, Jon Eardley and Art Farmer among his partners, and 'met' various saxophonists in the Verve recording studios, including Johnny Hodges, Ben Webster and Stan Getz. On the celebrated *Sound Of Jazz* telecast, he plays in the band that accompanies Billie Holiday and stands tallest of all.

In 1960, he assembled his Concert Jazz Band, which also recorded for Verve: a very different animal to the typical shouting big band, its light feel and sometimes silky sound was a beautiful vehicle for Mulligan scores such as 'Blueport', but it flew in the face of jazz trends and economies and didn't last long. After this, Mulligan became a star sideman with Dave Brubeck and eventually mustered a new big band, The Age Of Steam (referring to the saxophonist's long-standing love of locomotives). The Concert Jazz Band was also occasionally brought together again, as was a 'Rebirth Of The Cool' band which took a fresh look at Mulligan's old scores (and settled them to his satisfaction). 'Jeru' went from the cool uniform of shades and crew-cut in the 50s to bearded longhair in his old age, but while he never again quite found the popular audience he had enjoyed with the quartet, his later music and recordings still have the mark of greatness on them, and his achievements as arranger and composer now seem among the most formidable in any jazz era. As a saxophonist, he made the baritone seem both light and limber while never shying away from its deep-sea timbre: another paradox.
*The Original Quartet* (Blue Note)

## Mick Mulligan
TRUMPET
*born* 24 January 1928

The leader of Mick Mulligan's Magnolia Jazz Band, whose ribald adventures in post-war English trad are given a rib-tickling recounting in George Melly's memoir *Owning Up*. Mulligan himself came from Harrow and played honest trumpet: the records stand up reasonably well, though they never really aspired to the kind of dedication shown by Chris Barber and Ken Colyer. The leader packed it all in in 1962, when the boom for their kind of music was dying fast, and he has sensibly never sought to make any kind of comeback.
*Ravers* (Lake)

## Multiphonics

It is a simple thing for a keyboard player or a guitarist to produce several notes at once, but for brass and wind players it is another matter entirely. Anyone who has had a go on a saxophone or a trumpet for the first time knows they can unexpectedly produce multiphonics via their own lack of expertise, but to do it deliberately and with fine control requires exceptional skill and dexterity. Having said that, very few musicians have found the effect worthwhile at any length. Albert Mangelsdorff, renowned for playing chords on the trombone, and extending his range further by 'humming' an extra note into the mouthpiece, is one of the very few to make it a consistent part of his playing aesthetic.

# Jimmy Mundy

ARRANGER, TENOR SAXOPHONE
*born* 28 June 1907; *died* 24 April 1983

Mundy played in various bands in Chicago
and the Midwest before joining Earl Hines in
1933, where his variation on the Hawkins
archetype won him some solo space in the
reed section, although he was soon contributing to the band's book with charts such as
'Cavernism' and 'Fat Babes'. From there he
moved to Benny Goodman's 1936 band, as
a staff arranger, and soon became one of
the principal writers for that band. While
many of Mundy's themes were more like
sequences of riff variations than any
through-conceived charts, he knew the
strengths of whomever he was writing for
and he helped Goodman garner numerous
successes. He did much the same for Count
Basie in the 40s, and thereafter freelanced in
California and New York, latterly often doing
rote commercial work away from jazz
altogether. He did, though, do enough work
under his own name during 1937–47 to be
gathered in on a single CD, which is the disc
cited.
*Jimmy Mundy 1937–1947* (Classics)

# Joe Muranyi

CLARINET, SOPRANO SAXOPHONE
*born* 14 January 1928

A Pops man through and through, Muranyi
played in the last edition of the Louis
Armstrong All Stars (1967–71), and has ever
since been fiercely dedicated to Armstrong's
legacy. Before that he produced albums and
played in New York Dixieland groups, and
afterwards he formed another close alliance
with Roy Eldridge. He was in The Classic Jazz
Quartet with Marty Grosz, Dick Wellstood
and Dick Sudhalter, and since then has freelanced and played with Dixieland and
swing-revivalist groups of various temperaments, often coming out as the most individual and amusing voice in the band.
*The Classic Jazz Quartet* (Jazzology)

# Mark Murphy

VOCAL
*born* 14 March 1932

Murphy started out as a pianist, took up acting and singing and made his first records in
the latter capacity in 1956. The singer of
*Meet Mark Murphy* was all clean-cut lines
and lounge-lizard style, and both Decca, who
released his first records, and Capitol, who
did the next three, tried to make a college
idol out of him. But rock'n'roll singers were
doing better with a young audience, and at
Riverside, in 1961–2, he cut his best early
work, *Rah!* and *That's How I Love The Blues*.
Hanging out with Jack Kerouac and Allen
Ginsberg brought out the beat-poet side of
the singer, although the records stuck to a
middle ground, and his limber, handsome
voice was given mostly familiar material. In
1963 he moved to London and worked in
Europe for ten years, both acting and singing, although what little popular audience
he had drifted away, and on his return to
the US he rebuilt a career as a 'strict' jazz
singer. His Muse albums of the 70s and 80s
were widely studied by aspiring singers and
with the likes of *Bop For Kerouac* (1981) he
finally had the chance to use beat and bebop
material in an authentic homage to those
schools. London's dance-jazz revival of the
80s honoured Murphy's work, and he
returned to Europe as something of a
legend. In the 90s and the new century his
art has, if anything, deepened further:
recent albums for High Note have found the
vocal timbre starting to fray but the artistry
unimpaired and perhaps even more daring
in terms of rhythm and improvisation. A
huge influence on Kurt Elling and other
singers with genuine jazz aspirations rather
than mere songbook-singing, Murphy is,
along with Sheila Jordan, the surviving great
voice from the original post-bop era.
*Bop For Kerouac* (Muse)

# Turk Murphy

TROMBONE
*born* 16 December 1915; *died* 30 May 1987

Murphy, Lu Watters and Bob Scobey ruled
the revivalism based around San Francisco.
While California was never previously
thought of as any kind of centre for traditional jazz, the unbridled vigour which the

musicians brought to their small scene brought about a remarkable school of players. Murphy was a sideman for Watters from 1937, and they began attracting real attention with the timely Yerba Buena Jazz Band, formed in 1940 to play at San Francisco's Dawn Club, just in time to catch the first sparks of vintage revivalism. After navy service, Murphy carried on with Watters for a spell before forming his own band in 1949, which lasted into the 80s and became an institution in its scene, playing at such important venues as Hambone Kelly's, Easy Street and Earthquake McGoon's. Murphy himself played rumbustious tail-gate trombone and he led numerous record dates: few leaders have managed to record for Atlantic, Columbia, Verve, Roulette and RCA, but Murphy succeeded. Like Watters, Turk is still revered among the community of players he fostered, and his unpretentious but surprisingly durable music – mystifyingly despised by many American critics, over many years – still has a great following.
**New Orleans Shuffle** (Columbia)

# David Murray
TENOR SAXOPHONE, BASS CLARINET
*born* 19 February 1955

Murray's music, a restless, teeming river of activity, has unfailingly enlivened jazz for the past 30 years. He grew up in California and played in R&B bands before going to New York in 1975 and immediately making an impact on the loft scene there. In collaboration with college pal Stanley Crouch, Murray seemed to charge full-tilt to the head of the scene, and for a few years he appeared to be everywhere: recording solo albums, quartets and his favourite octet combination; forming an occasional big band; joining James Blood Ulmer in the Music Revelation Ensemble; taking a role in the World Saxophone Quartet; and recording albums at a pace which at the time seemed incredible, although he subsequently suggested that he felt he had so much going on then that he should have recorded even more. Early on he was regularly compared with Albert Ayler (and his tune 'Flowers For Albert' is one of his best-known), but the ruthless extremism of that saxophonist was not really Murray's style: when asked about influences, the name he

always brought up was Paul Gonsalves, and although the wildest aspects of his early work (particularly his live solo records) touch on the likes of Ayler, much of what he was already doing referred back to classic elements of the jazz tradition. On tenor, he displayed a big, brawling sound which regularly flew into false registers, and he took the slightly unusual step of choosing to double on bass clarinet rather than soprano (claiming that the latter instrument was 'too feminine'). Yet his ballad performances suggest a line going back to Ben Webster, even as they unfold with a kind of bruising rapture.

While his earliest records came out on a plethora of labels, he subsequently recorded prolifically for the Italian Black Saint operation, for the Japanese DIW label and most recently for the Canadian Justin Time imprint: aside from a brief period on Columbia, he has never enjoyed a significant tenure at a major label and most of his albums have been sponsored by non-American companies. Some of his finest work has been caught in the albums by his octet, particularly *Ming* (1980) and *Murray's Steps* (1982), but as ubiquitous as his records have become there are very few which are undeserving. In the 90s he expanded his range further, recording a homage to the Grateful Dead and (since relocating to Paris in 1997) forming an Afropop–jazz mix called Fo Deuk Revue, as well as playing with the Gwa-Ko Masters: Murray remains one of the few contemporary American jazz players to perform regularly with African musicians. He remains active in the World Saxophone Quartet and, at 50, still seems ready to look for new musical areas to explore, even if the sheer bravado of his earliest work has inevitably cooled off.
**Ming** (Black Saint)

# Dierdre Murray
CELLO
*born* 1951

Murray played in classical, jazz and folk situations in New York from an early age. On record, she has tended to be a sidewoman rather than a leader: she contributed significantly to records by Hannibal Marvin Peterson, David Murray and particularly Henry Threadgill's Sextet, and also worked in a regular duo with Fred Hopkins, a partnership that was only closed with the latter's death in 1999. Latterly she has been rather more involved in composition.

**Henry Threadgill, *You Know The Number*** (RCA Novus)

## Don Murray
CLARINET
*born* 7 June 1904; *died* 2 June 1929

As tragic jazz deaths go, Don Murray's is up there with Frank Teschemacher's. He played with the New Orleans Rhythm Kings early on before working for Jean Goldkette, where he got to know Bix Beiderbecke and Frankie Trumbauer: he takes the clarinet role on the Bix & His Gang sessions, and at least one respected judge thinks that he plays at least as well as Beiderbecke on those records, beautifully inventive throughout. His few other featured dates were with Joe Venuti and Trumbauer, but he died after fracturing his skull in a fall.

**Bix Beiderbecke, *Bix & Tram*** (JSP)

## Sunny Murray
DRUMS
*born* 21 September 1937

The words most often used in connection with Murray's style are 'waves' and 'colours', which sound an unlikely mixture for a drummer who started playing drums for Henry 'Red' Allen. Everything changed for Murray when he met and began playing with Cecil Taylor in 1959. Over the course of three years, and very occasional gigs, they set about formulating a trio music (with altoist Jimmy Lyons) which pushed free jazz into a new area, where the pulse existed but was uncountable and rhythmically open-ended. On the celebrated Café Montmartre recordings of 1962, Murray's time seems to ebb and flow around Taylor's piano. He sometimes played with knitting needles rather than sticks, used the cymbals to create a constantly rising and falling hiss that resembled breakers on a shore, and began looking for ways to make the kit resonate and speak, in direct conversation with the other players. It was the next step after Elvin Jones, and by the time Murray had begun playing with Albert Ayler *(Bells*, 1965)

he had all but abandoned any idea of time-keeping. It was a style which, influentially speaking, probably found more favour with European drummers than Americans, and Murray was one of many free players who based themselves in France between 1968 and 1971. Since then, he has worked steadily if often in rather low-profile situations, mostly as a group leader, and frequently in duo situations, with such players as Charles Gayle and Sabir Mateen. Sometimes he softens his style to move back to a more boppish feel, but that is a grandmaster's privilege: this gentle giant of a man moved jazz drumming on a few notches.

**Cecil Taylor, *Nefertiti, The Beautiful One Has Come*** (Revenant)

## Muse
RECORD COMPANY

Joe Fields founded this label in 1972 and set out to record what was then the least fashionable area of jazz: hard bop. Artists such as Woody Shaw, Sonny Stitt and Houston Person, all of whom struggled to find any interest elsewhere despite their eminence, were recorded at varying length, and Fields and various producers – Don Schlitten, Michael Cuscuna and others – built up what in time became a formidable catalogue. In the 80s, Fields shopped around further: he bought the Savoy catalogue in 1985, sold it on six years later, and then acquired Landmark. Muse's archive could boast some 600 titles by 1997, but it was then sold to 32 Jazz, which itself has now gone bust and the current status of the catalogue is uncertain. In the meantime, Fields held on to many of his artist contracts, and he and son Barney have since started two new labels, High Note and Savant, which carry on the dedication to straight-ahead acoustic music.

## Vido Musso
TENOR SAXOPHONE
*born* 16 January 1913; *died* 9 January 1982

On record, Musso is one of the most solidly reliable saxophonists of the swing era: he turns up with Kenton, Goodman, James, Herman, Krupa and Tommy Dorsey, and his solos and section-work seem completely dependable. But he was a difficult character, an extrovert who tried his damnedest to be a successful bandleader himself yet never quite managed it. He co-founded Kenton's orchestra in 1935 then went elsewhere; he took over Bunny Berigan's band after the trumpeter's death but couldn't make it work. In the meantime, he took his gruff sound and boisterous delivery through all the bands mentioned, and eventually fetched up with Kenton again in 1945. There, his solos had some of the qualities which Illinois Jacquet brought to the Lionel Hampton band, but Musso never got on with bebop, and as the music became more modern, he drifted. His final record found him playing rock'n'roll saxophone on *Teenage Dance Party* (Crown, 1957).

**Stan Kenton, *1947*** (Classics)

# Wolfgang Muthspiel

GUITAR
*born* 2 March 1965

The Austrian guitarist first came to attention working in a pairing with his trombonist brother Christian (b1962), Duo Due. He studied at Berklee in the late 80s and secured a contract with Polygram in 1989, which resulted in a sequence of likeable records which mixed a sober fusion style with tougher jazz material. Since then he has been less conspicuous in the crowded environment of jazz guitar.

***Loaded, Like New*** (Amadeo)

# Muzak

Originally the corporate name for an organization formed in the 60s to provide recorded music for supermarkets, hotel lobbies and other workplaces in need of soothing sounds, it subsequently became a generic term for any kind of music which melts into the background and has no discernible emotional content or reason to exist other than to fill what would otherwise be quiet space. The term 'elevator music' fulfils the same function. Smooth jazz is often considered by its detractors to be little more than Muzak. Come to that, a lot of people unsympathetic to any kind of jazz regard the music of, say, Bill Evans to be little other than Muzak, too.

# Amina Claudine Myers

PIANO, ORGAN, VOCAL
*born* 21 March 1942

Myers became a minor player in Chicago's AACM scene in the middle 60s before going to New York in the 70s and Europe in the 80s. One close association was with Lester Bowie, and she is on some of the trumpeter's quintet records. She has a powerful voice in a gospel-blues tradition and recorded an album of Bessie Smith pieces for Leo (she was, in fact, the first artist on Leo Records) in 1980, but her subsequent foray into a fusion setting for RCA Novus was little short of disastrous. A team-player rather than any kind of individualist, she has never topped her cameo role on Arthur Blythe's glorious version of 'Just A Closer Walk With Thee' (*Blythe Spirit*, 1984).

***Salutes Bessie Smith*** (Leo)

# Simon Nabatov

PIANO
*born* 11 January 1959

Nabatov is a Muscovite with an exciting, comprehensive grasp of jazz piano styles. He studied at the Moscow Conservatory, where 'the stuff we heard came from all different kinds of records, without any sense of connections or chronology. There is definitely something unique in the way Russians view style.' He emigrated to the USA in 1979, studied at Juilliard and jammed with Wynton Marsalis, before playing in various New York groups. Nabatov came to more prominence, though, when he moved to Cologne in 1989, since when he has worked in a surprisingly broad range of bands, from swing-styled music with Wolfgang Schluter to ambitious, extended small-group composition on projects such as *The Master And Margarita* and *Nature Morte* (both issued on Leo). Nabatov's solid knowledge of 20th-century piano music sometimes crowds a technique which could stand with Tatum and Taylor, but he is working his way through some absorbing ideas.

***Nature Morte*** (Leo)

# Nagel Heyer
RECORD COMPANY

Hans Nagel Heyer set this label up in 1992, at first to release copious numbers of both live and studio sessions by players in the contemporary swing and Dixieland mould. In the new century, though, they seem to have made a fairly dramatic change of tack, with recent records featuring post-bop players such as Donald Harrison, Wycliffe Gordon and a number of contemporary European players.

# Zbigniew Namysłowski
ALTO SAXOPHONE, TROMBONE
*born* 9 September 1939

For a long time, Namysłowski was the only Polish jazz musician known beyond his own borders. He worked on both cello and trombone before turning to the alto: he toured Europe with the Polish All Stars and was the trombonist in the New Orleans Stompers, but he switched direction completely on taking up the alto and then formed his own band, presciently (though inaccurately) called The Jazz Rockers. This gave way to a quartet, which toured Europe frequently in the 60s and recorded an album for Decca in 1964, *Lola*. Since then, he has continued an uninterrupted career of playing and recording, although not too much of his work has subsequently been widely distributed. He played on Krzysztof Komeda's famous *Astigmatic* album and recorded a further important set of his own, *Winobranie* ('Wine Feast') in 1973, which became something of a Polish bestseller and portrays much of his interest in combining jazz themes with native folk material. Without the sponsorship which his contemporary Tomasz Stańko has enjoyed at ECM, Namysłowski tends to remain a marginal figure, and since many of his influences are obscure to Western audiences, he has been largely bracketed as an exotic. His own playing is a vinegary take on the sound of the American hard-bop masters.
*Winobranie* (Muza)

# Ray Nance
TRUMPET, CORNET, VIOLIN, VOCAL
*born* 10 December 1913; *died* 28 January 1976

Ray Nance was a fine asset to Duke Ellington, and a versatile one: he played excellent hot trumpet, picked up the violin for occasional features, sang in an attractive and full-chested baritone, and was somewhat of a showman. He did little of note before Ellington took him on in 1940, and his talents blossomed in Duke's trumpet section: he plays the fine (and much-copied) solo on the original version of 'Take The "A" Train' (1941), and the delicate violin part on Mercer Ellington's 'Moon Mist' (1942), which was often a favourite live piece in Ellington's 40s concerts. He stayed until 1963 – he had originally taken over Cootie Williams's trumpet chair, and Cootie came back after Nance moved on. Some thought that – certainly in comparison with Williams – Nance was a lesser figure among Duke's trumpets, but the recorded evidence hardly supports that view. He carried on working with swing-styled small groups until his death.
**Duke Ellington,** *Never No Lament* (Bluebird)

# Joe 'Tricky Sam' Nanton
TROMBONE
*born* 1 February 1904; *died* 20 July 1946

Nanton played in a handful of New York bands before Duke Ellington hired him in 1926. Although a few of his early solos on record are played on the open horn – and sound comparatively tame – Nanton came into his own with the plunger mute, following Bubber Miley's example and creating a gallery of effects which ranged from a tigerish growl to what sounded like an elephant yawning. Sometimes he made audiences laugh – as in his awesome solo on the 1943 Carnegie Hall concert version of 'Black And Tan Fantasy' – and his style was deliberately limited, gestural rather than seeking any musical imperative. Yet every time he steps forward on an Ellington record, he unfailingly grabs the listener's attention, and Ellington always looked for new ways to feature him, such as in *Black, Brown And Beige*. He suffered a stroke in 1945 and had to stop playing for a spell, but he was soon back with the band, although his time was fast running out: he died in a San Francisco hotel room, three days after making his last recordings with the orchestra.

**Duke Ellington,** *Early Ellington* (GRP)

## Phil Napoleon

TRUMPET

*born* 2 September 1901; *died* 30 September 1990

Born in Boston, Filippo Napoli went on to become one of the most recorded trumpeters in jazz, mainly through the enormous amount of work he set down with a huge number of studio bands in New York in the 20s. He often pops up as the soloist in eight or 16 bars of a hot dance record, although his powers in this respect were a notch below those of some of his peers, and he was valued most as an impeccable sectionman, a role which sustained him through the leaner times of the 30s. He did, however, lead the Original Memphis Five from its inception, and the hundreds of sides by this ground-breaking group (none of whose members came from Memphis) are still much loved by collectors of the period. Napoleon's solid lead helps to set the records ahead of those by such similar bands as the Original Indiana Five. He left full-time playing to sell instruments in the 40s, but took up the horn again in 1949 and led a strong Dixieland group at Nick's in New York (their several Capitol albums have been ignored so far by CD reissues). At the age of 65, he opened his own club in Miami, led the band, and carried on playing into the 80s. Though largely unknown to the casual audience, Napoleon should be remembered as a pioneer among white trumpeters. Four of his brothers were also musicians, and nephews Teddy and Marty (the latter a capable pianist) also went into the business.

*Live At Nick's* (Jazzology)

## Lewis Nash

DRUMS

*born* 30 December 1958

Nash grew up in Phoenix, Arizona, and after various studies arrived in New York in the mid-80s. One of his first 'name' gigs was in the Betty Carter group which also included Benny Green, but Nash was quickly established as the kind of drummer who could play supportively and responsibly for musicians of any generation, and he became a favourite of such senior figures as Art Farmer and Tommy Flanagan as well as playing with his contemporaries. He has a crisply direct style which relies more on integrating the band than showmanship and solo work. Outings as a leader have been very rare, probably because he is in such constant demand as a sideman, but a single set with his name out front for Evidence (1989) is as good an example as any of his powers.

*Rhythm Is My Businss* (Evidence)

## Ted Nash

ALTO SAXOPHONE

*born* 28 December 1959

The son of Dick Nash (b 1928), a trombonist who freelanced widely on the West Coast from the 60s to the 90s, and the nephew of Ted Nash (b 1922), a fine saxophonist and big-band veteran who also did much studio work in California. The younger Nash has been busy on the New York scene since the late 80s. He has worked in the Lincoln Center Jazz Orchestra and has featured Wynton Marsalis as a sideman on two of his own records, which have thus far been an absorbing and accomplished take on some of the multifarious directions small-band music is moving in in Manhattan of late. The record cited, which features a line-up of sax, trombone, violin, accordion and two drummers, is particularly inventive.

*Sidewalk Meeting* (Arabesque)

## National Youth Jazz Orchestra

See BILL ASHTON.

## Fats Navarro

TRUMPET

*born* 24 September 1923; *died* 7 July 1950

Navarro was one of bebop's most complex personalities. Dead at 26 from tuberculosis, an illness made worse by his heroin addiction, his career on record is telescoped into less than five years and is a fascinating legacy. He was born in Florida and was touring with territory bands as a teenager before enlisting with the Billy Eckstine band and making his base in New York. Navarro arrived just as bop was taking off and his facility on trumpet allowed him to master the intricacies of the idiom quickly; yet much in his playing suggests it distils rather than exemplifies bop principles. He was recording with the likes of Kenny Clarke and Coleman Hawkins before hooking up with Tadd Dameron, whose compositions and band suited the trumpeter almost perfectly. Although he toured with Jazz At The Philharmonic and Lionel Hampton, it was the Dameron groups which gave Navarro his best opportunities on record, and his playing on such records as 'The Squirrel' and 'Our Delight' (1947) is extraordinary: 'I'd just like to play a perfect melody of my own, all the chord progressions right, the melody original and fresh – my own.' A thinker and a sensitive man (his cruel nickname, Fat Girl, which referred to his size and high speaking voice, must have hurt him), Navarro made an oddly suitable front-line partner for Charlie Parker, and their airshot recordings – the last made only weeks before Navarro's death – are scintillating. With his superbly full tone, the trumpeter pointed out a way to elaborate at bebop speed without sounding frenzied, and his example was a prescient one which would be echoed in the brief, succeeding careers of Clifford Brown and Booker Little.

*The Complete Fats Navarro On Blue Note And Capitol* (Blue Note)

## Naxos Jazz
RECORD COMPANY

Klaus Heyman's budget-priced classical label changed everything in that sector of the music industry, bringing low-cost but high-quality performances into an area which had previously been dominated by major labels and big-ticket orchestras and conductors. Their move towards jazz in 1995 presented an intriguing direction. For a long time, the high cost of full-price CDs had deterred many listeners from investigating work by unfamiliar musicians: perhaps Naxos could pull off the same trick in jazz as they had in the classical repertoire. Thus far, though, the results have been unimpressive on all sides. Initially curated by the pianist Mike Nock, the first 50 or so releases included only a sprinkling of genuinely outstanding records among many merely average ones, and sales were largely disappointing: as a result, Naxos have now moved more towards reissuing out-of-copyright jazz from the pre-LP era, an area where they compete directly with other labels doing much the same sort of thing.

## Buell Neidlinger
BASS
*born* 2 March 1936

Neidlinger studied cello in New York and played classical music before joining a Dixieland ensemble, Eli's Chosen Six, in 1954. In 1955, though, he switched direction completely and joined Cecil Taylor's group, staying until the early 60s. He then went back mostly to classical music, working in Houston and Boston, before shifting to Los Angeles in 1970 and teaching there, as well as working as a studio professional. In the 80s his label K2B2, run with saxophonist Marty Krystall, documented work which stretched in the direction of country music – they had a band called Buellgrass for a time – and in 1995 it released perhaps the most finished of Neidlinger's various solo projects, a set of Herbie Nichols tunes arranged for horns and a string trio, reportedly fulfilling a wish Nichols himself had once expressed to the bassist. Since then the label appears to have largely gone dormant, but Neidlinger's various adventures in American music make up a beguiling journey altogether.

**Cecil Taylor,** *Jazz Advance* (Blue Note)

## Louis Nelson
TROMBONE
*born* 17 September 1902; *died* 5 April 1990

The most honest and unpretentious of trombonists, Nelson was a familiar presence in New Orleans's city's music for decades. He played on riverboats and in the city's music joints from around 1925, and though he was also working as a postman when the New Orleans revival started in the early 40s, he kept his hand in with such leaders as Kid Thomas Valentine and Kid Howard. From the early 50s he was a regular sidekick to

Valentine, an association which lasted until the 80s, as well as being a regular at Preservation Hall with Percy Humphrey and others. Much of his early work was in the big-band environment of Sidney Desvigne's orchestra, which made him sound a mite too sophisticated to some of his colleagues, but if he wasn't quite as completely down-home as Jim Robinson, he wasn't exactly Miff Mole, either. He was still playing at Preservation Hall until a few weeks before his death: hurt in a bad car accident at the end of March 1990, he died shortly afterwards.

*Live In Japan* (GHB)

## Louis 'Big Eye' Nelson
CLARINET
*born* 28 January 1885; *died* 20 August 1949

Nelson (born Louis Delisle) was old enough to have played with most of the early New Orleans masters, and aside from a brief spell in Chicago with Freddie Keppard he spent virtually all his working life in the city. This kept him away from recording microphones, but in his last ten years he ran a regular quartet at Luthjens', and he made a few records with Kid Rena in 1940 and a handful under his own name right at the end of his life. Perhaps inevitably, these souvenirs offer only glimmers of what Louis might have sounded like in his prime – he was certainly held to be one of the best clarinet men on the scene – but even past his prime there is still evidence of his strong tone and no-nonsense technique.

*Big Eye Louis Nelson* (American Music)

## Oliver Nelson
ALTO AND TENOR SAXOPHONES, ARRANGER
*born* 4 June 1932; *died* 27 October 1975

If Nelson had only been responsible for *The Blues And The Abstract Truth* (1961), one of the most perfectly played, arranged and pro-grammed of all jazz albums, he would have been an immortal; but he contributed much else to the jazz book of his time, and it's sad that the business preferred to send him in the direction of commercial scoring. He was playing second alto for Louis Jordan in the early 50s before military service, and then studied theory in Washington before work-ing back in New York with Louie Bellson and Quincy Jones. He began getting steady work as an arranger-composer – *Afro/American Sketches*, an inventive pastiche of various black-music forms, was recorded in 1961 – as well as recording small-group albums as a leader. Besides the above-mentioned master-piece – which has an extraordinary band including Eric Dolphy, Freddie Hubbard and Bill Evans – he made seven albums for the Prestige group of labels and more for Impulse!, most of which showcased his tenor and alto work, lugubrious but prone to burst-ing into a sudden tear-up. By the middle of the decade he was in demand for both festival commissions and film and TV work, and he played less: much of his big-scale work has a tiresome edge, involving effortful European borrowings, but such fine setpieces as 'Walk On The Wild Side' for Jimmy Smith created a personal space for Nelson within the arrang-ing continuum. Most of his later time was spent writing cop-show music for television and film, and his sudden death in 1975 – from a heart attack, although a drink problem didn't do his health any favours – curtailed a career that might have had much interesting music in it yet.

*The Blues And The Abstract Truth* (Impulse!)

## Steve Nelson
VIBES
*born* 11 August 1954

Nelson is still thought of by some as a youngish lion, and it may surprise them to find out how long he's been on the scene: he began gigging with Grant Green as long ago as 1974. He has been in New York since 1976 and has built up an enormous list of credits as sideman and session-player: it may assist him that although the vibes aren't exactly the most in-demand of jazz instruments, the ranks of vibes players aren't overpopulated, either. Nelson is either content with his side-man status or he's been unlucky with his own projects, since he hasn't released a record under his own name since 1989. But he keeps close company with Bobby Watson and Mulgrew Miller in particular, and Dave Holland has used him rather ingeniously as an open-ended source of harmony in his small groups.

**Dave Holland, *Not For Nothin'*** (ECM)

# (New) Black Eagle Jazz Band

GROUP

A grand old name among American traditionalists – although the band was actually put together by an expatriate Englishman, cornetist Tony Pringle (b 1936), in 1971. Since then it has followed Pringle's brand of diehard trad, not quite as purist as his original influence, Ken Colyer, but never as loose as the typical American Dixieland gang. They have made many records, with such long-serving sidemen as Eli Newberger and Pam Pameijer, and have appeared on such labels as GHB, Stomp Off and Lake, as well as their own BE set-up.

*Jersey Lightning* (Stomp Off)

# Phineas Newborn Jr

PIANO

born 14 December 1931; *died* 26 May 1989

On his appearance, Newborn was considered in some quarters the most sensational new pianist since Art Tatum, but his career went spectacularly wrong. He played in R&B bands in Memphis in the late 40s: his father was a drummer, and the younger Phineas played in his band until he was 'discovered' by John Hammond, which led to his playing in New York and being signed by Atlantic. In the latter part of the 50s he was seen as a player of huge promise, with a formidable two-handed technique and a garrulous way of interpreting standard material. He recorded for both Atlantic and RCA and played with Charles Mingus and others, but the records he made didn't quite click – RCA in particular seemed to have no real idea how to manage his talent – and by 1960 he was already adrift. He shifted to Los Angeles and began recording for Contemporary, but he then went through two broken marriages and a series of mental breakdowns. By the end of the decade he had managed to make four albums for Contemporary, but his career was in the doldrums and he returned to Memphis, still undergoing mental trauma. Preparing for a comeback, he was then mugged and had his fingers broken, but in the latter part of the 70s he somehow managed to start performing again. *Look Out! Phineas Is Back* said a 1976 album for

Pablo, but it was too late, and despite intermittent work in the 80s his time had gone. A case history of a fine talent largely ruined by circumstance.

*Here Is Phineas* (Atlantic)

# David 'Fathead' Newman

TENOR AND ALTO SAXOPHONES

born 24 February 1933

Newman has handled the double of R&B and jazz saxophonist better than almost anyone else. He grew up in Dallas and worked in local bands before moving to the bigger league of Lowell Fulson and T-Bone Walker, eventually joining the new star Ray Charles in 1954 and staying ten years. He played baritone and tenor with Charles, but ironically his most famous setpiece, Paul Mitchell's irresistible 'Hard Times', was recorded on alto (his old friend and fellow Charles sideman Hank Crawford played baritone on the 1958 date). He made further records for Atlantic in the 60s and worked for Herbie Mann and Red Garland, before leading his own bands and acting as guest star with everyone from Aretha Franklin and Dr John to Roy Hargrove and Don Braden. Fathead's hard, dark sound personifies one side of the Texas-tenor lineage, and whatever the surroundings, he seems ready to give his best. His nickname was bestowed by a high-school teacher, who caught him learning parts by ear rather than reading them: unflattering, but it doesn't seem to bother him. Recent sets for High Note have found the old warrior still in great form.

*House Of David* (Atlantic/Rhino)

# Joe Newman

TRUMPET

born 7 September 1921; *died* 4 July 1992

A stalwart swing-styled trumpeter, the dapper Newman personified a particular yet rather anonymous jazz stylist: a big-band pro who could step out front with ease, yet was never quite a star by himself. Born in New Orleans, he joined Lionel Hampton in 1942 before three separate stints with Count Basie's band in the later 40s. He eventually went back to Basie's ranks yet again in 1952, and this time stayed nine years: his sharp, lit-up style suited the section, and he could also play with the easeful lyricism of his predecessor Harry Edison when he wanted to. He made quite a number of small-group records under his own name during the 50s, for RCA, Roulette, Coral and Jazztone, but after leaving Basie his career settled into a genteel jog: he was a regular sideman with Benny Goodman, worked for an educational trust called Jazz Interactions, and guested with touring groups and played in pit bands. Most of his own-name records are rather hard to find and, as with many of his contemporaries, his best work is scattered, but Newman's best playing is fine enough to stand tall with any other swing-orientated trumpeter.

*Good 'N' Groovy* (Swingville/OJC)

## New Orchestra Workshop
GROUP

A cooperative group made up of many of Canada's circle of free-jazz and post-bop players. Among the prime movers are Paul Plimley, Lisle Ellis and Paul Cram, and while the collective has been only occasionally convened since its inception in 1977, it has run several successful concert series and worked with invited guest stars of the order of Marilyn Crispell and George Lewis, some of these events being documented on record.

*The Future Is N.O.W.* (Nine Winds)

## New Orleans Jazz

It is not merely romantic to say that jazz was born in New Orleans, and all of the music's original sons certainly worked in the city in the first two decades of the 20th century. Numerous theories have been put forward as to why jazz should have chosen this bustling seaport to be born in, and its comparative tolerance and cosmopolitanism – as well as a kind climate, which put a lot of music in the streets as well as under roofs – played their part. As a cradle of jazz civilization, though, New Orleans always had a sort of purism about it which the first generation of jazz musicians went back to at the time of the revival of 'New Orleans jazz' in the 40s. The polyphonic feel of the 'classic' New Orleans ensemble tended to set it apart from – and, some might argue, behind – the music as it developed in Chicago and New

York. Louis Armstrong may have been a New Orleans homeboy, but he did his important work outside the city, and the solo style which he pioneered was almost antithetical to the city's roots: New Orleans music is primarily an ensemble sound, going back to the first marching bands. Thus the groups of such different individuals as Bunk Johnson, Kid Thomas Valentine, George Lewis, Paul Barbarin and Kid Sheik Cola all worked to a cooperative principle, no matter how strong the leader may have been.

## New Orleans Rhythm Kings
GROUP

The principals in the group were all from New Orleans, and they were proud of a style which derived directly from their hometown music: but the NORK never actually played in New Orleans, and their influence was in the end directed on Chicago jazz rather than anything from their native city. The three prime movers were cornetist Paul Mares, trombonist Georg Brunis and clarinettist Leon Roppolo, and while they knew each other from their adolescent days, they actually formed a group for a residency at Chicago's Friars Inn nightclub around 1921. As an eight-piece band, they cut their first eight titles for Gennett in 1922 (as Friar's Society Orchestra), but by the following year they were the New Orleans Rhythm Kings, under which name they made a further 22 titles. Although the music was dustily recorded by Gennett's acoustic process, the crackle of the band still comes through, more than 80 years on. As a white New Orleans band, they were following in the footsteps of the Original Dixieland Jazz Band, but they had also absorbed the kind of music that King Oliver's groups had been playing in Chicago ahead of them – Mares in particular resembles an Oliver disciple. They could also boast, in Roppolo, the best white clarinet player of his day, a skilful and continuously inventive player whose solos on their records still impress. Their material, too, was jazz-based, rather than pop tunes given a hot treatment. The group split up in 1923, but re-formed back in New Orleans and made a few final records before dispersing again.

*New Orleans Rhythm Kings 1922–1925* (Retrieval)

# Newport Jazz Festival

The most durable American jazz event has changed entirely since its inception in 1954, when it was organized by founders Louis and Elaine Lorillard and directed by the owner of Boston's Storyville Club, George Wein. He eventually took over the event altogether and it has been held annually ever since, although in 1972 it shifted to New York City, subsequently took the name of chief sponsor Kool in 1981, and when they were in turn supplanted by JVC it became, from 1986, JVC Jazz Festival New York. Wein has shrewdly packaged the event over the years. He realized early on that an occasional rock'n'roll figure wouldn't hurt ticket sales, and Chuck Berry played there in 1958; even Jethro Tull were on the bill in 1969. The most famous Newport event was the 1958 Festival, on account of the movie filmed there, *Jazz On A Summer's Day*, probably the most renowned of all jazz films. There were some stormy events: Newport City Council cancelled the 1961 Festival altogether following two years of crowd disturbance, and there was a riot in 1971, which most likely obliged Wein to move location the following year. Initially an outdoor, three-day occasion, it now runs for ten days and uses many of the most upscale music venues in Manhattan. Wein has also sent the 'Newport' brand around the world, using the name for concert tours of Europe and Japan.

# David Newton
PIANO
*born* 2 February 1958

The Glaswegian has become a familiar figure in London's jazz environment since moving there in the 80s. He has often worked with Martin Taylor, has frequently accompanied singers – Carol Kidd and Stacey Kent in particular – and has put together a thoughtful series of albums of his own, which showcase a delicate lyricism on ballads backed by a tougher approach to jazz material.
*In Good Company* (Candid)

# Frankie Newton
TRUMPET
*born* 4 January 1906; *died* 11 March 1954

Newton has been rather regularly cited as an unjustly forgotten trumpet star of his day: the trouble is, as with so many other talented players, he isn't associated with a series of recordings famous enough to dispel the obscurity which passing time deals out as a matter of course. This, despite recording with Bessie Smith (on her last date), Maxine Sullivan and Billie Holiday. He was in New York by the end of the 20s, working with Cecil Scott and Chick Webb, before going with Charlie Johnson and Teddy Hill. He backed Maxine Sullivan on her classic 'Loch Lomond' but left that group before it became the successful John Kirby outfit. He led his own groups on record dates for Variety, Bluebird, Blue Note (one of their first sessions) and Vocalion, and the surviving 24 titles are bursting with his playing – his solos simmer rather than light flames, with a restful tone and an unusual avoidance of familiar licks. He worked at several major venues in the 40s but nobody wanted to record him, and his career slipped away. Newton found solace in painting and social work. He was prone to illness, and he eventually died of gastritis in 1954.
*Frankie Newton 1937–1939* (Classics)

# James Newton
FLUTE
*born* 1 May 1953

Newton is a great rarity, a flute-only specialist. In high school in Los Angeles he played bass guitar and most of the saxophones, but it was the flute which took his ear most kindly, and he fell in with other young blades on the scene such as David Murray and Arthur Blythe in the early 70s. By 1977 he had decided to play the flute exclusively, and perfected a technique which is among the most advanced heard in a jazz context, playing multiple tones and creating a dense weave of sound on projects such as the all-solo ECM record *Axum* (1981). He played on the New York loft scene while it was still active, and he continued to work with Murray – regularly into the 90s, in both small groups and Murray's big band – and with Anthony Davis. For the most part,

though, he has tended to shift his activity away from a jazz context. He played regularly with Jon Jang, with Indian musicians and in contemporary-composition ensembles, work which has settled him more comfortably in an art-music idiom: some of his rather occasional own-name records have drifted towards New Age music, very different to the authoritative Duke Ellington repertory set *The African Flower* (1975), which was Newton's one album for Blue Note.
***Axum*** (ECM)

# New York jazz

Unofficially the jazz capital of the world, since the 20s at least, New York is more the place where jazz musicians go to be a part of the number one, all-embracing scene, rather than somewhere that acts as a cradle of any identifiable style. In the 20s, New York jazz meant either the mingling of black idioms which was being played in Harlem clubs, from stride piano to the new orchestral jazz of Fletcher Henderson and Duke Ellington, or the politer, society-band hot music which most of the white orchestras were playing, with their spin-off in the small-group music of Red Nichols and Miff Mole. In the 30s, as clubs and music rooms proliferated and the swing era grew in momentum, New York musicians directed the future traffic: they took the music into the new style of bebop, and though other jazz developments such as New Orleans revivalism emerged from elsewhere, they were still somehow legitimized when the musicians went to New York to play. In the 50s and 60s, while such New York-based musicians as Miles Davis, John Coltrane and Sonny Rollins were active, the city easily maintained its eminence; and in the 70s, loft jazz sprouted out of a single Manhattan neighbourhood, much as the so-called Downtown school of the next decade also did. Perhaps jazz is too universally spoken these days for New York to claim the same authority, but while such powerful figures as Wynton Marsalis continue to hold court there, it will still be the music's capital city.

# New York Voices
VOCAL GROUP

Originally a quintet established in 1987, New York Voices are now founder members Darmon Meader, Peter Eldridge and Kim Nazarian, plus Lauren Kinhan, who replaced Caprice Fox and Sara Krieger. They specialize in a somewhat showbizzy take on the Lambert Hendricks & Ross style of presentation, though it's done with a supercharged musicality which comes through delightfully in performance; the records are perhaps rather more manufactured in feel (although since most records are like that, it's not a very fair criticism). Their first albums were made for GRP and they have since moved to Concord.
***Hearts Of Fire*** (GRP)

# Albert Nicholas
CLARINET
*born* 27 May 1900; *died* 3 September 1973

Although he was just a few weeks older than George Lewis, Nicholas was never the same kind of revivalist: more than any other New Orleans clarinettist of his generation, he kept an outgoing and open-eared approach to jazz developments, while staying basically his own man. He studied with Lorenzo Tio (both father and son) and worked in Buddy Petit's band at the start of the 20s, going on to lead his own groups and eventually leaving for Chicago in 1924, where he joined Joe Oliver's band. From there, he travelled widely, playing in Shanghai, Cairo and Paris, and in the 30s he was with Luis Russell's band, sometimes taking a solo on records with Louis Armstrong. Though he left the music business for a time at the start of the 40s, he was playing again by 1945, taking part in sessions with Bunk Johnson and Kid Ory but also forming a trio with Ralph Sutton and Art Trappier. Still a wanderer, he went to Europe in 1953 and never really went back, aside from a few return visits, and he spent the rest of his days working in festival bands and with local traditional groups of various stripes and levels of ability. Nicholas – his uncle was Wooden Joe – remained a New Orleans man, but he was adaptable to most playing situations and he was still a strongly individual player in his final years.
***Baden 1969*** (Sackville)

# Big Nick Nicholas

TENOR SAXOPHONE, VOCAL
*born* 2 August 1922; *died* 29 October 1997

Nicholas played in the bands of Earl Hines and Lucky Millinder in the 40s, became a great pal of Hot Lips Page, and then joined Dizzy Gillespie's big band. He was a familiar face in the Harlem clubs of the early 50s, singing as well as playing tenor, but work dried up and he left New York to live in Virginia. He had hardly been heard from in years when he suddenly reappeared in New York at the end of the 70s, and over the next few years he made his only records as a leader there. Soulful swing-to-bop was his principal style, and John Coltrane remembered him well enough to compose 'Big Nick', recorded for Impulse! in 1962.
*Big Nick* (India Navigation)

# Wooden Joe Nicholas

CORNET
*born* 23 September 1883; *died* 17 November 1957

Joe Nicholas worked with King Oliver in New Orleans in the teens of the century, and formed his own Camelia Band in 1918. But he went unrecorded until the years of the New Orleans revival. Bill Russell heard him for the first time in 1943, playing 'Tiger Rag' at Graffanini's Beer Parlor: 'I will never forget the terrific impact – Wooden Joe's attack almost blew me out of the room.' Russell recorded him in 1945 and 1949, and the records are a faded but lively testimony to his mighty sound. Joe used a six-piece band because 'they can do all and more than a big band. In an eight- or nine-piece band there are always some dummies.'
*Wooden Joe Nicholas* (American Music)

# Herbie Nichols

PIANO
*born* 3 December 1919; *died* 12 April 1963

A mysterious and elusive figure, Nichols has been haunting the jazz of the past 20 years much more readily than he did in his own lifetime. He studied piano in New York and began playing in bands in 1937; following his military service he drifted around the New York club scene of the 40s, taking what work he could find, and paying close atten-

tion to some of his peers: he was the first to write an article on Thelonious Monk's music, in a black magazine called *Music Dial*. Mary Lou Williams recorded four of his tunes, and he co-led one date for Savoy in 1952, but it wasn't until Alfred Lion of Blue Note finally offered him a date in 1955 that Nichols got himself on to record in a serious way. Lion was excited enough by the music to cut 30 titles across five different sessions, and they were a fine showcase for Nichols's strange music. Titles such as 'Orse At Safari', 'Love, Gloom, Cash, Love', 'Cro-Magnon Nights' and 'Shuffle Montgomery' alone suggest that Nichols was no ordinary thinker, and his playing is quite a tough listen: he is more abstruse and difficult than Monk, ideas darting past before they settle in the mind, and in otherwise steady, mid-tempo settings he used rhythmical ideas which derail expectations. Lion never used him as a sideman on any other dates and left eight titles unissued: the records sold poorly in Nichols's lifetime, and he went back to club work, dying of leukaemia in 1963. As a final cruelty, many of his original, unpublished compositions were reputedly destroyed in a flood at his father's apartment, years after his death. Yet projects led by long-time Nichols admirers such as Misha Mengelberg, Roswell Rudd and Frank Kimbrough have brought many of the pianist's tunes into something approaching the standard post-bop repertoire, and today he is lionized by musicians, if not listeners.
*The Complete Blue Note Recordings* (Blue Note)

# Keith Nichols

PIANO, VOCAL, TROMBONE
*born* 13 February 1945

Nichols started on both piano and trombone as a youth in Essex, and studied at Guildhall while also playing in traditional groups. His main interest, from early on, was in re-creation, and doing it as well as possible – on hearing his first King Oliver record: 'to my young ears it was bloody dreadful' – and he began wondering what those bands would really have sounded like in person. He visited the US in the early 70s and wrote arrangements and played with such groups as the New Paul Whiteman Orchestra, before leading a long-standing group with Alan Cohen, the Midnite Follies Orchestra. Since then he has guested with many European and American revivalist groups and worked on some major record projects involving re-creations of ragtime as well as the music of Oliver, Fletcher Henderson, Bix Beiderbecke and others, sometimes researching previously unplayed and unrecorded originals. Through utterly meticulous study and networking to locate the best and most sympathetic players, Nichols's projects have achieved a superb empathy with the original music, and have managed it without taking all the fun and sparkle from the originals, which is usually the problem with this kind of work. His own playing – mostly piano – is skilled and exuberant, like his singing.

*Henderson Stomp* (Stomp Off)

# Red Nichols
CORNET, TRUMPET
*born* 8 May 1905; *died* 28 June 1965

Loring Nichols (the nickname came from his flame-coloured hair as a youth) was the top trumpet man in New York jazz of the 20s – that is, if you liked the kind of stylized and, some would say, effete music which Nichols and his circle practised, both on their own record dates and in the hundreds of sessions they made as sessionmen for the leading white dance orchestras of the time. Since that kind of music has been out of fashion almost since the original Jazz Age came to an end, Nichols's reputation has unfairly suffered ever after. He was born in Ogden, Utah, where his father, a music teacher, encouraged him to study the cornet, and he was playing at dances before he was even in his teens. By 1922 he was playing in bands in the New Jersey area, and soon enough started leading groups of his own. He began making records before he was 20, and by the time he was 21 he was the most in-demand and busy sessionman in New York: he and trombonist Miff Mole were the two kings of the scene. As a leader, recording for Brunswick, the group name he regularly used was Red Nichols And His Five Pennies, even though the band could sometimes number a dozen players, and for other labels he used a string of pseudonyms: The Wabash Dance Orchestra (Duophone) and The Red Heads (Pathé) are just two among many. The Five Pennies records were widely admired by other musicians working in the

same milieu, particularly in Britain, and while they seem tame and even puny next to Armstrong's Hot Fives or Morton's Red Hot Peppers, it was different music, often metronomically arranged and delivered. Nichols himself played in a dancing, angular way, picking his way through the harmonies and using a clean and penetrating tone: he had none of Beiderbecke's poignancy and little of his luminous sound, and that has always hurt his reputation, too. In 1930, he was 25 and seemingly with nowhere else much to go: the Depression cut back on everybody's recording duties, and he played in pit bands and with a modest big band of his own; but there was plenty of work on the radio and Red had nothing of the jazz purist about him, was always happy to play commercial charts. In the 40s, a new version of the Pennies came together, and he spent most of the rest of his life busy doing club work. The biopic *The Five Pennies* (1959) sparked a fresh interest in his career, and he made new records for Capitol, his stye intact. He was playing in Las Vegas when he died suddenly from a heart attack.

*Red Nichols & Miff Mole 1925–1927* (Retrieval)

# Maggie Nicols
VOCAL
*born* 24 February 1948

Nicols, who moved to London from her native Edinburgh in 1964, is a doughty performer who has battled her way through decades of largely undernourished and unrecognized work in free improvisation, occasionally heading in a more straight-ahead jazz direction. Her primary influence was Annie Ross, and she got her grounding with the London club pianist Dennis Rose – 'Dennis would immediately find my key and it was like singing on a cushion.' She worked with dance bands and in strip clubs in the 60s before meeting some of the new London improvisers, and she credits John Stevens for taking her from bebop to free singing. In the 70s, deeply involved in the women's movement, she helped to create FIG (Feminist Improvising Group) with Lindsay Cooper, an unforgettable group in performance, and the later Contradictions. Listing all her subsequent associations would take up a great deal of space, but they include the groups Very Varied, Loverly, No Rules OK, Cats

The man from Hamlet, North Carolina: John William Coltrane.

Art Blakey's Jazz Messengers perform at the New School, New York, in January 1956. Spot Hank Mobley, Doug Watkins, Horace Silver and Donald Byrd in the line-up.

(*left to right*) Art Farmer, Gerry Mulligan, Frank Rosolino and Bud Shank from the 1958 film *I Want To Live*

Miles Davis with Ralph Burns and Terry Gibbs,
some time before his Prince Of Darkness days.

The saxophone colossus, Sonny Rollins in
1965.

Melting the harmonies: Bill Evans performing
in Copenhagen in 1964.

Downtown emeritus: John Zorn in London in 1989.

Greg Osby in 1992.

Joe Zawinul at the Marciac Jazz Festival, 2002.

Harmolodics made easy in 2003: Ornette
Coleman keeps score.

Cradle, a French-based group called Méchantes, Keith Tippett's Tapestry, Pulse, Les Diaboliques and long-standing duos with Pete Nu and Julie Tippetts. In the new century she has formed a trio with saxophonist Caroline Kraabel and viola player Charlotte Hug. Her singing still often touches on the song form when she chooses, but is more to do with a free-flowing use of sound, speech and vocal effects, sometimes approaching confessional theatre, which can be joyous or starkly poignant. She still runs workshops and open evenings in London on a regular basis. Too little of her work has been recorded over the years, and even less is easily available by this unique artist.
**Nicols And Nu** (Leo)

## Lennie Niehaus

ALTO SAXOPHONE
born 1 June 1929

Niehaus grew up in Los Angeles and spent most of the 50s in Stan Kenton's band. He did, though, moonlight on his own recording dates, mainly for Contemporary, and made some appealing if fundamentally lightweight music on most of them: arranged with needlepoint precision, with his own airy alto playing at the heart, they now sound like characteristic music of the sort which frankly gave West Coast jazz a rather anaemic reputation. Much better is *I Swing For You*, a solitary 1957 date for Emarcy. In the 60s he worked mainly as a TV and film-music arranger, a job which kept him busy right into the 90s, since he began an association with Clint Eastwood which resulted in his organizing much of the original music for Eastwood's Charlie Parker movie *Bird* (1986). In the new century, he visited London and conducted a big band through some of his own arrangements.
*I Swing For You* (Emarcy)

## Phil Nimmons

CLARINET
born 3 June 1923

Nimmons was the other Canadian on Norman Granz's Verve label. He worked as a dance-band musician in Vancouver in the 40s before a spell studying at Juilliard, then went on to lead groups for the CBC, where he wrote much music for radio and television. He recorded two albums for Verve with his group Nimmons 'N' Nine, but their scarcity today hints at the reluctance of American jazz fans to open their doors to a Canadian arranger. Actually, *Nimmons 'N' Nine* (1960) is a very agreeable set of charts in a personalized take on the West Coast style, and the leader went on to make several more Canada-only albums. Phil was subsequently involved in jazz education, but he still makes occasional records, and the 2000 date *Sands Of Time* on Sackville showed that his chops were still in good order.
**Nimmons 'N' Nine** (Verve)

## Sal Nistico

TENOR SAXOPHONE
born 2 April 1940; *died* 3 March 1991

Nistico was one of the best soloists Woody Herman ever had: a tough nut in the tenor section who could stand up and take the most blistering solos while still finding a lick of astringency when he had to. He worked in the Mangione brothers' band before joining Herman in 1962, and though he also had spells with Count Basie and Don Ellis, he stayed on and off until 1971. At the end of the 70s he was living in Europe, and he sometimes visited the UK on tour, once with Chet Baker and once as a guest of the Stan Tracey quartet.
**Woody Herman, *Verve Jazz Masters*** (Verve)

## Mike Nock

PIANO
born 27 September 1940

Nock might be one of the only two New Zealanders ever to make any international impact on jazz. He studied at Berklee and settled in Boston, where he backed many touring visitors; and his Fourth Way was formed in 1968, a pioneer fusion group, although their three albums attracted little attention (Michael White, who went on to play with Pharoah Sanders, was the violinist in the band). Nock went on to tinker around with electronic music and eventually relocated to Australia, but he became more visible again when hired by the budget label Naxos to be their chief A&R man: unfortu-

nately, after some adventurous records this initiative seems to have come to an end.
***Not We But One*** (Naxos Jazz)

# Jimmie Noone

CLARINET
*born* 23 April 1985; *died* 19 April 1944

Noone is generally acknowledged as one of the masters of New Orleans clarinet playing, yet his records have latterly enjoyed very little awareness and his influence on a broad span of jazz players has been all but forgotten. He arrived in New Orleans around 1910 and practised with Sidney Bechet before joining forces with Buddy Petit and forming the Young Olympia Band in 1914. Noone then went to Chicago in 1917 and toured with Freddie Keppard, before joining King Oliver in Chicago: he plays on a handful of Oliver's 1923 sessions, but by this time he had moved on to work for other leaders. After a spell with Doc Cook's orchestra, he led his own band at Chicago's Apex Cub, which recorded some renowned sessions during 1928: they were Noone's finest hour, and a benchmark for jazz clarinet in the later 20s. His sound had a classical security, full and rich in every register, and the Apex Club band was a strikingly new instrumentation: alto sax taking the lead, clarinet as counterpoint, and three layers in the rhythm section, including Earl Hines. They recorded prolifically between 1928 and 1931, and Noone held court in Chicago as one of the kings of the scene, but in a sense he remained a provincial musician: he hardly ever played in New York, and by 1938 he was touring in the South. At the end of his life, the New Orleans revival was under way, and it is likely that he would have capitalized on it: he was playing club dates with Kid Ory in the year of his death. But he had been a trencherman all his life, and his fondness for food led him, in the opinion of his son, to eat himself to death. Clarinettists remained in awe of Noone's abilities, even though the records have fallen out of favour: problematically, many of them are tarnished by poor vocals and indifferent material, as handsomely as Noone himself always plays. His son, Jimmy Jr (1938–91), also played clarinet and soprano sax.
***Jimmie Noone 1928–1929*** (Classics)

# Charlie Norman

PIANO
*born* 4 October 1910

'Papa Piano' is a smiling eminence among Sweden's senior jazz establishment. A dance-band musician from the 30s, he picked up on the fad for boogie woogie early on, and caused something of an upset when he recorded a boogie version of 'Anitra's Dance' from *Peer Gynt*: the Grieg Foundation were decidedly not amused. In the 50s and onwards he led small groups in a swing style, and he often played as an accompanist to Alice Babs. His few CD-era recordings remain a delightful souvenir of a musican who always loved jazz.
***Papa Piano*** (Phontastic)

# North Sea Jazz Festival

A festival which just grew and grew and grew. The first event, held in The Hague, took place in 1976, under the auspices of organizer Paul Acket, and the aim seems to have been to corral as many performers and events as possible into what remains a strictly three-day span of activity. Simultaneous performances take place on some 15 different stages in the festival's venue complex, and a spectator trying to negotiate everything going on is subject to battle fatigue within a few hours. Nevertheless, by the end of the century the event was attracting audiences in excess of 60,000 in number, and it has fair claim on being the most densely populated event of its kind in the jazz calendar.

# Red Norvo

XYLOPHONE, VIBES
*born* 31 March 1908; *died* 5 April 1999

The first and last xylophone player in jazz, although he switched over to vibes soon enough. Joseph Norville was born in Beardstown, Illinois, and actually started out on the marimba, before changing to the xylophone, the sort of skill which could more easily get him work in vaudeville (he developed an act where he played the instrument while simultaneously tap-dancing). He then started leading bands, and shifted to Chicago, where he joined Paul Whiteman's band and met his first wife, Mildred Bailey. After leaving Whiteman he freelanced, often in an informal partnership with Charlie Barnet, the two men sharing record dates. But Bailey's burgeoning popularity assisted Norvo's own career, and for a time they were billed as 'Mr And Mrs Swing'. Their marriage eventually broke up (they divorced in 1945), but Norvo remained close to her, and in the meantime he led big bands and small groups. By 1945 he had switched permanently to the vibraphone, and in a famous record date he was in charge of a group featuring Charlie Parker and Dizzy Gillespie. In 1947 he moved to California, and eventually established a trio with Charles Mingus and Tal Farlow: almost by accident, the deferential Norvo briefly became an avatar of cool jazz with this group. Other players came and went in the place of these sidemen, and by 1956 Norvo had moved on again, leading small groups of varying sizes and renewing an old relationship with Benny Goodman. In the 60s and 70s he suffered from heart and hearing problems, but carried on working and was still touring Europe and elsewhere when he suffered a stroke in 1986 and thereafter stopped performing. Having lived through several jazz eras, Red deserved his eminence; little he did as a soloist had any lasting impact, and even when he went over to the vibes he still favoured the hard, vibratoless sound he got from the xylophone. His main contribution was as an organizer and bandleader, fronting bands which featured everyone from Frankie Trumbauer to Charles Mingus.

*Dance Of The Octopus* (Hep)

## Adam Nussbaum
DRUMS
*born* 29 November 1955

Like all of the drummers in his style – which stretches from a basic post-bop to the most chops-directed end of fusion – Nussbaum has racked up a huge list of sideman credits over 20-something years of work. He was a New Yorker, and his first significant gig was with John Scofield: Nussbaum was in the guitarist's group from 1978, and also did several sideman gigs alongside him. Thereafter his credits are far too numerous to mention, in both Europe and America. He walks a line

somewhere between the musclebound approach of Dennis Chambers and Dave Weckl and a much more deliberate manner in the jazz tradition: his work with John Abercrombie, for instance, shows up his 'sensitive' side, even though these distinctions are sometimes pretty pointless. He seems to have no leadership ambitions whatsoever.

**John Abercrombie, *Tactics*** (ECM).

## Dick Oatts
ALTO AND SOPRANO SAXOPHONES
*born* 2 April 1953

Originally from Des Moines, Oatts moved to New York in 1977 and took the first alto chair in the Jones–Lewis Orchestra. He also played in other small groups, particularly Red Rodney's quintet, where he worked with pianist Garry Dial, and they went on to co-lead a band for a time. Since the early 90s he has mostly fronted his own trios and quartets, often with the bassist Dave Santoro. Nils Winther of Steeplechase likes Oatts's muscular bebop style and has recorded several albums with him.

*All Of Three* (Steeplechase)

## Hod O'Brien
PIANO
*born* 19 January 1936

O'Brien ('Hod' is derived from his middle name, Howard) made records as long ago as 1957 but has only intermittently had much visibility. He played with Oscar Pettiford's quintet and as a sideman with J R Monterose, and then spent two years as house pianist in a Staten Island club, but he gave up music to study maths and psychology in the 60s. By 1974 he was playing again and he briefly opened a club with Roswell Rudd, the St James Infirmary. Latterly he has done sideman work and in the CD era he recorded as a leader for the first time, making solidly enjoyable music in a boppish vein for the independent labels Criss Cross and Reservoir.

*Opalessence* (Criss Cross)

# Jimmy O'Bryant
CLARINET
*born* 31 December 1896; *died* 24 June 1928

O'Bryant seems to have come from Arkansas, but he was a leading figure in the Chicago gang of players which recorded for Paramount in the middle 20s, starting with the Lovie Austin group, and then with King Oliver, Jimmy Blythe, and in support of several of the blues singers who cut discs for the label. Little enough is known about him, but his best records reveal a bluesy but dedicated and quite sophisticated player: although he started out in vaudeville, there is very little hokum in his playing, and he could stand his ground with his most gifted contemporaries. There are enough records under his own name to suggest that he was a reliable studio man, and the likes of 'Drunk Man's Strut' and 'Down To The Bricks' suggest that he could hold his own with another regular in the Paramount studios, Johnny Dodds.
**Lovie Austin,** *1924–1925* (Classics)

# Anita O'Day
VOCAL
*born* 18 October 1919

O'Day's extraordinary career has lasted more than 60 years. The former Anita Belle Colton sang in Chicago clubs in the late 30s and joined Gene Krupa in 1941: a hip, upfront member of the band, rather than one of the sequinned canaries which were the stereotypical band singers of the day. 'Let Me Off Uptown', where she chaffed with Roy Eldridge, was a major hit for both her and the band. She then moved to Stan Kenton's orchestra, as the first of his three great female singers, and spent another period with Krupa before working as a solo. Norman Granz signed her in 1954 and she enjoyed a long and fruitful association with Verve, which showed all the virtues of her style. At fast tempos she was incomparable, lighter and more fluent than Ella, less regal but more daring than Sarah Vaughan: she could scat with a dancing ease, and bent lyrics and melodies with more imagination than anyone prior to Betty Carter. On ballads she was less individual and there is sometimes a flip quality to her treatment of more poignant lyrics, but it stems from a musicianship which was tough-minded and unsentimental. Her LP records were never as popular as they might have been and compared to some of her contemporaries her best work is often hidden: it took a Mosaic reissue to finally put all of her Verve records out on CD. But her career was in any case often troubled and interrupted by narcotics problems. She was twice jailed for drugs offences and almost died from an overdose in 1966. Matters were back on better tracks in the 80s, when she started her own record label, Emily, and she continued to sing in clubs and occasionally tour in the 80s and 90s. But a bad fall which left her with a broken arm resulted in a long period of hospitalization at the end of the century, even though she managed to give a concert on her 80th birthday. She visited London and performed there early in 2004: it was a very strange event, and a sad sight for those who remembered her electrifying performance in the film *Jazz On A Summer's Day* (1958).
**Anita O'Day Sings The Winners** (Verve)

# Chico O'Farrill
TRUMPET, ARRANGER
*born* 28 October 1921; *died* 27 June 2001

O'Farrill moved to New York in 1948 from his native Havana, and divided his time there between writing charts for jazz orchestras – Dizzy Gillespie, Benny Goodman, Stan Kenton – and Latin bands of the sort led by Machito. In the 60s he wrote more frequently for television and drifted away from jazz, but in the 90s he came back to more frequent big-band work, led a regular orchestra at New York's Birdland and made a few final recordings, of which the overwhelmingly exuberant *Heart Of A Legend* (1999) was a rousing homage to a life spent in Latin and Afro-Cuban music. His son Arturo has carried on some of his father's work and has also worked as a pianist with Carla Bley and others.
**Heart Of A Legend** (Milestone)

# Ogun
RECORD COMPANY

Founded by Harry and Hazel Miller and Keith Beal, in London in 1973, Ogun documented some of the strongest left-field

British jazz of the 70s at a time when that music was entirely out of favour with the major record labels: the music of Miller, Mike Osborne, Alan Skidmore, Elton Dean, The Blue Notes, Trevor Watts, Keith Tippett and others. The output slowed in the 80s and 90s and much of the earlier catalogue still awaits CD release, but it remains an important resource.

# Dave O'Higgins
TENOR AND SOPRANO SAXOPHONES
*born* 1 September 1964

O'Higgins grew up in Birmingham and moved to London to study in 1983. After spells with the NYJO and Sax Appeal, he was soon in the forefront of the new London jazz of the 80s and took a major role in Roadside Picnic, one of the few bands of the era to win a major-label contract. Since then he has steadily built on this progress without quite threatening any household-name status, perhaps because British jazz is still sorely under-supported by its homegrown music industry. O'Higgins has a positively ironclad tone in the grand Rollins manner and he can play with superb fluency; if he could translate his instrumental gifts to a recording of genuine stature he could break out of the inhibiting cycle of low-profile work which holds back so much British jazz. He has also proved to be a capable force in jazz education.
*All Good Things* (EFZ)

# OKeh
RECORD COMPANY

Along with Gennett and Paramount, the most important of the jazz labels of the 20s. It came out of a company established to look after the American operations of the German Odeon label, and the first OKeh release came out in 1918. The A&R man Fred Hagar took a chance on recording some songs by Mamie Smith in 1920, and 'Crazy Blues' and other titles were such a success that they led to the formation of a so-called 'race' series of releases. Clarence Williams became the A&R man for New York and Richard M Jones did the same in Chicago. OKeh's roll-call includes many of the most significant series of 20s jazz recordings: King

Oliver's Jazz Band, Louis Armstrong's Hot Five, Bix & His Gang, Bennie Moten's earliest orchestral sides, Joe Venuti's Blue Four, and much music by Frankie Trumbauer, Duke Ellington, Earl Hines and others. Columbia took over the operation in 1926 but it continued unabated, and the race series was only terminated in 1934 during the Depression. The label was revived by CBS in 1938 and continued to be used into the 50s, mainly for R&B records. But its glory days were undoubtedly those of the original Jazz Age, and collectors' pulses still quicken at the sight of the famous 'large orange' OKeh label.

# Itaru Oki
TRUMPET
*born* 10 September 1941

Oki learned koto as a child in Kobe – his mother was a koto teacher – and moved on to trumpet in his teens: he even had a lesson with Kenny Dorham when the trumpeter visited Osaka in 1956. He played in bebop groups in Tokyo in the 60s but drifted in the direction of free playing and eventually settled in Paris. Not much of his subsequent work has been well documented on record, but there are some Japanese records for Trio and dates with Noah Howard and Michel Pilz. Oki plays in a fanciful style which still has some of his old bebop leanings in it, and he has a taste for the unusual, also playing various kinds of flute and a variation on Art Farmer's flumpet.
**With Michel Pilz,** *One Year: Afternoon And Evening* (FMP)

# Tiger Okoshi
TRUMPET
*born* 21 March 1950

Okoshi briefly promised to be an interesting force, but his career seems to have entirely petered out. He moved to the US in the early 70s from his native Japan and studied at Berklee, leaving to join Buddy Rich in 1975. He did some strong sideman work with Gary Burton but his own band, usually called Baku, took more of a fusion-orientated line and made some interesting records for JVC which already sound rather dated, although the surprising Armstrong

homage of *Echoes Of A Note* (1993) was a then unfashionable departure which holds up much better.
**Echoes Of A Note** (JVC)

## Joe 'King' Oliver
CORNET
*born* 11 May 1885; *died* 8 April 1938

The second 'King' of New Orleans brassmen was a proud and imposing man whose ignominious final years were a terrible humiliation. He made only slow progress in his native New Orleans, working as Bunk Johnson's deputy on some gigs, and he was still working for other leaders, including Kid Ory and Richard M Jones, into the teens of the century. Joe worked hard on his own playing and by 1918 he was ready to move to Chicago, where he eventually joined Bill Johnson's group at the Royal Gardens. In 1920 he finally formed a group of his own, including Honoré Dutrey, Johnny Dodds and Lil Hardin, and worked busily in the city before playing in San Francisco and Los Angeles; but it was when he moved back to Lincoln Gardens in Chicago and hired Louis Armstrong as the second cornet that Oliver really moved up a gear. His great year was 1923: the sensational two-cornet breaks which he and Armstrong devised captivated audiences and had musicians spellbound, and the records by Oliver's Creole Jazz Band, as he had named it, catch at least a part of what must have been an enthralling live group, although almost everyone who heard both the records and the in-person music claimed that the discs were only a shadow of what they were really like. Nevertheless, Oliver managed to set down, in 'Dipper Mouth Blues', perhaps the first great jazz solo on record, a three-chorus blast based around a simple figure that he colours with a wa-wa effect that was the King's particular trademark. Never an ambitious or extravagant soloist in the way Armstrong would become, much of his playing was based around his collection of trumpet mutes, novelty effects which rooted his style in a pre-jazz age, even if he recognized which way the music was going: he kept Armstrong in his shadow and was tough on his men on the stand, and it helped make the Creole Jazz Band the major group which it was. But by the end of the year, it had

broken up: Armstrong was on his way to New York with Lil, and Oliver went on tour with a new outfit. As King Oliver's Dixie Syncopators, they eventually made further records – a larger group with saxophones in the line-up, but the results seem disappointing after the records of 1923; yet there are many rousing moments and individual pieces such as 'Wa Wa Wa' (1926) suggest that Oliver could still marshal a stomping, powerful group. He was playing in New York in 1927 and did well at the Savoy Ballroom, but he supposedly turned down the job that went to Duke Ellington at The Cotton Club and his band dispersed. He signed to Victor and led what amounted to dates with studio pick-up groups, often not playing himself: terrible problems with his teeth, which had long been exacerbated by his habit of drinking on the stand from a bucket of sugared water, had left his own chops shaky and unreliable, and the records are a very mixed lot. From 1930 he toured with undistinguished groups and made no more records after 1931. Five years later, Louis Armstrong was on tour in Savannah when he ran into the humbled Oliver, running a little fruit stand and working as a janitor, his old authority cruelly destroyed.

Of all the leading names in early jazz, Oliver is one of the hardest to assess. He left a decent number of recordings, but few of them really do more than hint at the stature he enjoyed in his heyday. Armstrong all but worshipped him as a sideman in his band, yet Oliver's influence is something he seems to be trying to escape rather than follow in his own playing. Oliver's use of mutes must have impressed players such as Bubber Miley, but the simplicity of his playing was itself old-fashioned by the middle 20s – rather like that of his contemporary, Johnny Dunn. Blues playing, though, brought out his best side: the rare duo record he made with Jelly Roll Morton, 'Tom Cat Blues' (1924), and some of his sideman work with Clarence Williams, show how affecting he could be. As a set of irreplaceable documents, though, the sessions by the Creole Jazz Band are without peer in their time.
**King Oliver's Creole Jazz Band – The Complete Set** (Retrieval)

# Sy Oliver

TRUMPET, ARRANGER, COMPOSER
*born* 17 December 1910; *died* 27 May 1988

Melvin Oliver was a very smart young man: his ambition as a teenager was to read law, and his nickname was a derivation from 'psychology'. But music played an important part in his home life, too, and before he was 20 Oliver had learned trumpet and begun arranging for bandleaders such as Zack Whyte and Alphonso Trent. He joined the up-and-coming orchestra of Jimmie Lunceford in 1933, playing in the trumpet section and writing charts, and he soon proved indispensable to Lunceford's progress, coming up with original compositions and a surprising number of variations of old popular songs such as 'Annie Laurie'. The best of Oliver with Lunceford is stunning in its mix of sophistication and straightforward, swinging appeal: 'Swinging Uptown', 'Stomp It Off' and 'Organ Grinder's Swing' epitomize the precise, all-parts-working style which Oliver excelled at. He was also a very capable trumpet soloist (often with the mute) and an agreeable band singer. At the same time, Oliver was contributing charts to the Benny Goodman book, and he was eventually poached by Tommy Dorsey in 1939, for whom he wrote 'On The Sunny Side Of The Street' (and earned the lifelong admiration of Frank Sinatra). After military service, Oliver tried out with his own band – the surviving records are rather good, and comparatively little known – and thereafter went into more of a backroom capacity, doing studio arrangements for singers on record dates and leading orchestras, although there were no big-band albums under his nominal leadership in the LP era. At the end of the 60s he went back to performing again, leading a nine-piece group which recycled his charts (and tried out a lot of new ones) and carried on working through the 70s. Fastidious and urbane, he lent a metropolitan refinement to all his work which has helped it endure.
**Jimmie Lunceford, *1934–1937*** (Classics)

# Olympia Brass Band

GROUP

Although it sounded like one of the several long-established brass bands of New Orleans, the Olympia was actually only founded in 1962, by Harold Dejan. Usually a ten-piece group, it became a frequently recorded ensemble and played regularly at Preservation Hall, with the participation of such musicians as Kid Sheik Cola, Emanuel Sayles, Cie Frazier, Emanuel Paul and Milton Batiste.
**Dejan's Olympia Brass Band In Europe** (77)

# Junko Onishi

PIANO
*born* 16 April 1967

Onishi made her debut as a youthful virtuoso following her Berklee studies, arriving in New York in 1989. She won a contract with Somethin' Else, the Japanese arm of Blue Note, and made a sequence of beguilingly enthusiastic records: two sets recorded at The Village Vanguard, with the heavy-duty support of Reginald Veal and Herlin Riley, are especially effective, showing her tackling material as diverse as 'Blue Skies' and 'Brilliant Corners'. But a subsequent and rather jokey neo-fusion record seemed to leave her at a stylistic dead end. She is based in Japan again and one wonders if she will make further international progress.
**Live At The Village Vanguard II** (Blue Note)

# Orchestre National De Jazz

GROUP

Governments have sometimes offered a surprising amount of support – given the traditional lack of interest by cultural establishments in sponsoring jazz – in funding jazz orchestras of different kinds. The French ministry of culture paid for the start-up of this ensemble in 1986, and it seems to be continuing. A music director is chosen and is asked to serve a two-year term, and the orchestra – made up of a picked group of contemporary players – plays concerts and makes the odd record; over a dozen have emerged so far. There have been some excellent albums and the Orchestra has surely done some fine evangelical work at home, though thus far the music hasn't crossed too many national frontiers.
**Monk Mingus Ellington** (Label Bleu)

## Oregon
GROUP

Oregon are almost the fall guys for a raft of prissy, inconsequential and pseudo-exotic music-making which has been created in their wake: their own music has been, for the most part, much tougher and more substantial. The original members – Ralph Towner, Paul McCandless, Glen Moore and Collin Walcott – were all members of the Paul Winter Consort and went on to form their own group in 1970. At a time when most of the attention was on the new electric music of jazz-rock, Oregon went in the opposite direction while ending up at a similar kind of destination: using woodsy acoustic instruments, from cor anglais and violin to tabla and sitar and 12-string guitar, they came up with a blend of carefully scored pieces which amounted to back-porch chamber music and settings which had a substantial degree of improvisation and an underlying jazz pulse. Moore's bass work was the primary line back to a jazz feel, given that there was no drummer involved (Walcott played tablas and a limited amount of percussion), but with the virtuosity of Towner often suggesting the participation of a horn soloist, the group was in a state of carefully orchestrated tension which such pieces as 'Icarus', 'Witchi-Tai-To' and 'Silence Of A Candle' celebrated. Their early records for Vanguard and Elektra in the 70s remain their best work, while the concept was still fresh. They suffered a bad setback when Walcott was killed in 1984: his replacement, Trilok Gurtu, was another polystylistic spirit, but the group was never the same, and some of their later records can sound almost like pastiches of themselves. In the meantime, overpopulated categories such as New Age and world music often featured groups which took their cue from Oregon's pioneering work, and came up with much drearier results.
*Distant Hills* (Vanguard)

## Original Dixieland Jazz Band
GROUP

See NICK LAROCCA.

## Original Memphis Five
GROUP

The Five first came together around 1917, although they disbanded and re-formed before they began making records in 1921, first as Ladd's Black Aces (basically a pseudonym used by the Gennett label), and then under the rubric which was used for scores of sessions and individual titles until 1931. Other group names such as The Savannah Six and Jazzbo's Carolina Serenaders were used by much the same personnel. The prime instrumental voice in the band was trumpeter Phil Napoleon, but Frank Signorelli (piano), Miff Mole (trombone), Jimmy Lytell (clarinet) and Charlie Panelli (trombone) were all early regulars, and some of the later discs featured the Dorsey brothers and others. Although many of the records are more like hot dance music than jazz, there was a high content of genuine Dixieland and jazz-based material, and Napoleon, Mole and Lytell always give of their best.
*The Columbias 1923–1931* (Retrieval)

## Niels-Henning Ørsted Pedersen
BASS
*born* 27 May 1946; *died* 19 April 2005

It seems surprising that NHOP, as he is always known, was only in his late 50s when he died, such was the length and breadth of his career. He was playing in Copenhagen's jazz clubs when he was only 14, and three years later the skills of this young man had become so renowned that he was asked to join the Count Basie Orchestra (he had to turn them down, since he was still at school). He became the regular bassman at the Café Montmartre, and is on dozens of in-person recordings made there as a result. In 1972 he began a long association with the Oscar Peterson trio, which took him to every part of the jazz touring world and brought him his widest fame. After 1987 he was his own leader for the most part. Like many great sidemen, he had some difficulty coming up with groups and albums of special distinction under his own leadership, but NHOP's natural reserve made him a somewhat unlikely front man in any case. Very few bassists have approached his dexterity on the instrument, and although he was most at home in relatively conventional bop and swing situations, the way he managed to make complex and quicksilver patterns seem graceful and unshowy provided a tremendous lift to any group.

*This Is All I Ask* (Verve)

## Anthony Ortega
SAXOPHONES, CLARINET, FLUTE
*born* 7 June 1928

Tony Ortega came out of the army and into Lionel Hampton's band, going with them to Europe and staying long enough to make records in, of all places, Oslo. In 1954 he was back in Los Angeles, went to New York for a couple of years but returned West in 1958. Work was scarce and he played in anonymous situations before playing as one of the soloists on Quincy Jones's soundtrack for *The Pawnbroker* (1965), and then making a couple of albums for the West Coast independent Revelation. These have always enjoyed something of a cult status, and Werner Uehlinger decided to reissue them on his hat ART label in the 90s. Ortega grafted some aspects of free playing on to his basic bebop grammar, but it didn't get him much beyond cult status, and he remained a player on the Los Angeles session scene, though he was also a regular visitor to France in the 90s and made some late records for Evidence.

*New Dance* (hat ART)

## Kid Ory
TROMBONE
*born* 25 December 1886; *died* 23 January 1973

Ory came from a poor background and was supporting his family as a labourer in his teens, but he always liked music and started on banjo before moving to the trombone. He played in New Orleans bands in the early years of the century and by 1910 or so he

was leading his own group, which grew into one of the most prominent in the city: he eventually numbered King Oliver, Sidney Bechet, Johnny Dodds, Jimmie Noone and Louis Armstrong among his sidemen, although since the band never made any records it's impossible to make any judgement on how good they were. But Ory did lead the first record date by a band of black New Orleans players, under the incongruous name Spikes' Seven Pods Of Pepper: 'Ory's Creole Trombone' was one of the titles, and it was made for the tiny Nordskog label in 1921 in California, where Ory had been playing successfully for the previous two years. By 1925 he was in Chicago, taking part in the imperishable sessions by Louis Armstrong and Jelly Roll Morton, but later in the decade he was working in minor bands and he went back West in 1930. By 1933 work was so scarce that he gave up music altogether, and spent the rest of the decade as a cook, a postman and a chicken farmer. But the New Orleans revival brought him back: in 1942 he was playing again, with Bunk Johnson and others, and from 1945 he was up to full strength as a bandleader, holding down residencies in Los Angeles and San Francisco (where he had his own club in the 50s), making records for Good Time Jazz and Verve, and even playing at Disneyland in the 60s. His own playing never changed much, if at all: with a raucous tone, short-breathed phrasing, a fondness for using a mute but a reluctance to take much in the way of solos, he was an ensemble player who was always happy when there was a strong trumpet man nearby (and he used picked players such as Teddy Buckner and Marty Marsala in the 50s). He never wrote much – 'Ory's Creole Trombone' was about it, although he was happy to collect royalties off 'Muskrat Ramble', which was actually written by Louis Armstrong – and managed his money with a chicken farmer's shrewdness, enabling him to retire to Hawaii in 1966.

*This Kid's The Greatest* (Good Time Jazz)

## Mary Osborne
GUITAR
*born* 18 July 1921; *died* 4 March 1992

Osborne played banjo in her family string band as a child, and she was broadcasting every week on local radio when she was

only 12. She joined a trio as a bassist when she was 15, but gave that up when she heard Charlie Christian and immediately switched to electric guitar. She went to New York around 1940 as a member of the Buddy Rogers band, and then freelanced there and in Chicago: she is on record with Coleman Hawkins (on his terrific date with Fats Navarro and J J Johnson), Mary Lou Williams and Mercer Ellington in this period, and also cut some trio sessions of her own for various labels, displaying a very capable swing-to-bop style. But the 50s marginalized her: she played on radio shows and cut a single album for the small Warwick label, *A Girl And Her Guitar*, but she eventually settled in California, where she ran a company making guitars with her husband, the trumpeter Ralph Scaffidi. In 1990 she played a date at The Village Vanguard: it was close to half a century after her first gigs on 52nd Street.
***Now And Then*** (Stash)

# Mike Osborne
ALTO SAXOPHONE
*born* 28 September 1941

Osborne is a sadly lost resource: illness has kept him off the scene since 1982, and what should have been his prime years have been denied to him. He grew up in Hereford but moved to London to attend the Guildhall School and was soon in the thick of the capital's contemporary scene, playing with Mike Westbrook, Mike Gibbs, the Brotherhood Of Breath and others. In the 70s he often worked as a duo partner of Stan Tracey's, as well as leading his own trio. Ossie was a tempestuous player in the manner of Jackie McLean, moving from in to out strenuously but with terrific passion: rather than settling for bebop fluency, he made improvising sound tough and resolutely hard-won. Although he made several albums for Ogun in the 70s, none of them have so far been reissued and there is very little at present to remember him by. The set listed was made in 1970 and is not one of his best, but it's the only easily available Osborne.
***Outback*** (FMR)

# Greg Osby
ALTO AND SOPRANO SAXOPHONES
*born* 3 August 1960

Perhaps the master musician of his generation and an outstanding thinker, group leader and organizing force in jazz's continuing progress. Born in St Louis, where he worked in R&B bands in his teens – Osby has paid specific homage to this period in his record *St Louis Shoes* (2003) – he studied in Washington and at Berklee in the early 80s, although he departed before graduating to tour with Jon Faddis. In 1983 he was doing sideman work in New York, where he began making some of the associations which would lead to the M-Base collective: with Steve Coleman, Gary Thomas, Cassandra Wilson, Marvin 'Smitty' Smith and others. Dismayed at the apparent conservatism in the jazz essayed by the neo-bop movement of the early 80s, M-Base set out a different agenda. In its way, it was almost akin to the original boppers' rejection of swing orthodoxy: in search of progressive development, they used funk and electronics, and rhythmic and harmonic structures of such complexity that they felt hotly abstract and emotionally inscrutable, a direct counter to the sentiment and nostalgia perceived in their contemporaries' direction. Osby's records for the independent label JMT were steeped in this approach, but the results – often poorly produced – tended to sound like fusion taken down a rather blind alley, where the music feels tense with possibility yet sounds unfulfilled. His own playing, though, already had a pointed intensity which was gloved by a seemingly ice-cool demeanour, and when he signed to Blue Note in 1990 the stage was set for his major advances. The early records seemed like a discouragingly messy continuation of the JMT music, bringing in a harp and a muddle of other ideas, but by the time of *Black Book* (1994) and *Art Forum* (1996), Osby had begun to shed some of the excess baggage and his music suddenly vaulted ahead. He assembled new groups of amazingly creative and exciting players, including Jason Moran, Mark Shim, Rodney Green, Nasheet Waits and Stefon Harris, and while the music seemed to settle back into a more boppish idiom, it was bop taken to a very advanced state, calling for razor-sharp thinking and reflexes. Using such concepts as rhythmical

cells and the supposed orthodoxy of jamming situations (such as on the extraordinary *Banned In New York*, an on-the-hoof live date from 1998), Osby has seemed to rethink a classic tradition and make it release new energies and directions almost at will. His series of Blue Note records in the past ten years have been an absolutely compelling sequence and, as he rather ruefully admits, he has been approached for advice and support by scores of aspiring musicians, already a senior figure in his 40s.
**Banned In New York** (Blue Note)

## Roberto Ottaviano
SOPRANO SAXOPHONE
*born* 21 December 1957

Ottaviano has played a thoughtful part in the new Italian jazz of the past two decades. He got his start in one of Pino Minafra's groups in the early 80s and he began making records of his own in 1983, leading a sextet and a quartet which both included Paolo Fresu in their ranks. His Six Mobiles group, a band consisting entirely of brass and woodwinds, is one of his more venturesome projects, but Ottaviano is fond of a challenge and his other settings have included an overdubbed solo set (*Otto*, 1991) and a trio with Pierre Favre and Irène Schweizer. He is one of the few to specialize in soprano sax and is, unsurprisingly perhaps, a Steve Lacy disciple: he even followed in that master's steps by recording in a duo with Mal Waldron (*Black Spirits Are Here Again*, 1996).
**Hybrid And Hot** (Splasc(h))

## Harold Ousley
TENOR SAXOPHONE
*born* 23 January 1929

Ousley learned tenor sax while at high school in Chicago, and he played in circus and R&B bands for much of the 50s, as well as honking on a few rock'n'roll records. In the 60s he turned up in soul-jazz groups and in the 70s he was more of a big-band guy. Never one for the existential long solo, his cheerful and off-the-top sound has enlivened quite a few otherwise plain records. The Chicago label Delmark sponsored a record date by him in 2000: nothing special,

but a nice acknowledgement of a long career.
**Grit-Gittin' Feeling** (Delmark)

## Out

Playing 'out' means improvising which is outside the harmonic structure of the piece being performed – a flirtation with free jazz, perhaps, in an otherwise straightforward bop theme. Out playing came along in the early 60s, but latterly 'out' tends to be used as a description for any sort of unconventional though not wholly free playing. 'In' playing is its opposite, playing exactly to the rules.

## Jimmy Owens
TRUMPET
*born* 9 December 1943

A doughty foot-soldier in the broad terrain of post-bop and fusion, Owens has played on scores of records and in numerous bands, only rarely gaining any significant attention along the way. He played under numerous leaders in the 60s – Slide Hampton, Charles Mingus, Hank Crawford, Max Roach – took a chair in the first Jones–Lewis Jazz Orchestra and moved through the big bands of Clark Terry, Count Basie and Duke Ellington. He was versatile enough to then play in Billy Cobham's Spectrum in the early 70s, and has latterly mostly led small groups of his own while taking a significant role in jazz education, playing a major part in several of New York's jazz teaching initiatives. He has had a miserly exposure as a leader on record himself: instead, find his agile, elegant playing on such sessions as the Billy Taylor record cited below.
**Billy Taylor & The Jazzmobile Allstars** (Taylor Made)

## Tony Oxley
DRUMS
*born* 15 June 1928

Oxley got his start as a drummer in military bands, but he led a bop-to-free group in his native Sheffield in the early 60s and hooked up with like-minded souls Derek Bailey and Gavin Bryars, in a trio named after an obscure British composer, Joseph Holbrooke. This started out as a free-jazz group but ended up as a band playing nothing but free improvisation – possibly the first to do so in the UK. When he eventually came south to London, Oxley managed to get the gig as the house drummer at Ronnie Scott's Club, a post he held for several years and which brought him into contact with numerous visiting American players. It was a some-what different style to the one he was pursu-ing in his own groups, though, recorded almost by chance in two records made for the British arm of CBS while they were hav-ing a momentary aberration and sponsoring free music: *The Baptised Traveller* (1969) and *Four Compositions For Sextet* (1970) were the surprising results. It was basically his idea to start the improv independent label Incus, although Evan Parker and Derek Bailey sub-sequently took on most of the work. Oxley worked through the 70s and 80s in sundry free groupings and eventually decamped for Germany, where he is still based. His kit-playing evolved from a basic free-jazz style into a clattery, combustible approach where electronics mixed with queer assemblages of percussion devices which sometimes looked like a portable scrapyard, although Oxley has mastered a wide range of techniques and he can play with subtlety as well as bull-dozing strength. In the 80s, never short of a surprise, he began working closely with Cecil Taylor, and they continue as a duo or trio (often with bassist William Parker) to this day.

*The Tony Oxley Quartet* (Incus)

# Makoto Ozone
PIANO
*born* 25 March 1961

Another Japanese pianist of formidable skill and virtuosity, Ozone studied at Berklee, where he began working with Gary Burton (and subsequently joined the vibist's group). More recently he has gone out as a solo, and has recorded a group of albums for Verve. He ran into difficulties when his work permit ran out in 1989, but carried on with festival work, and in 1999 he managed to return to the US. Ozone has been writing and playing in a more classically directed idiom of late, performing the Mozart Double Concerto with Chick Corea: whether he makes much progress in his jazz career may be down to whether or not he comes up with a signature record.

*Three Wishes* (Verve)

# Pablo
RECORD COMPANY

Norman Granz's final venture in the jazz record business was established in 1973, some six years after Granz had sold his Verve operation. Essentially, Pablo carried on where Verve had left off: Granz re-signed his favourite musicians, including Ella Fitzgerald, Oscar Peterson, Count Basie and Milt Jackson, brought in such simpatico mainstreamers as Zoot Sims, and effectively made a star out of Joe Pass, who moved from being a merely admirable second-division player into a superstar of jazz guitar. There was nobody remotely avant-garde or even particularly fashionable on Pablo: although a subsidiary called Pablo Today was commenced in 1979, it presented exactly the same face as the rest of the oper-ation. Besides studio dates, Pablo issued many live recordings from the Montreux Jazz Festival and elsewhere. After 15 years, Granz called time once again, and sold Pablo to the Fantasy group of labels, where it still resides.

# Pacific Jazz
RECORD COMPANY

Although it has never quite enjoyed the reputation of its illustrious contemporaries Blue Note and Prestige, Pacific Jazz was of equal importance – particularly as it was the most significant jazz independent operating on the West Coast of the US. Richard Bock started the label in 1952, snapping up the Gerry Mulligan quartet with Chet Baker as his first star signing, but also going on to record the earliest work of such luminaries as Jim Hall, Art Pepper, Wes Montgomery, Chico Hamilton, Les McCann and Joe Pass, as well as a large body of work by The Jazz Crusaders and the big-band recordings of Gerald Wilson's orchestra. After recording Ravi Shankar in 1958 Bock began a World Pacific subsidiary to release that sort of music, although it didn't secure the same prominence as his base label. Coincidentally,

Dick Bock became tired of the independent jazz business around the same time as Alfred Lion did: like Lion, he sold out to Liberty, in 1965, and though he continued to advise on new projects, he eventually left to go into film editing around 1970. Today, EMI, the present owners, have folded the Pacific Jazz library into Blue Note's holdings, although a healthy proportion of the material is still available on CD.

## Oran 'Hot Lips' Page

TRUMPET, VOCAL
*born* 27 January 1908; *died* 5 November 1954

Things never quite fell right for Page. Born in Dallas, he played behind blues singers early on and he got as far as New York in Ma Rainey's backing band. Then he fetched up in Kansas City, working first for Walter Page and then for Bennie Moten. He joined what eventually became the new Count Basie orchestra in 1936, after first working in a small group, but he was tempted away from Basie's ranks by Joe Glaser, Louis Armstrong's manager: the charming Hot Lips, an Armstrong follower through and through, was seen by the wily Glaser as insurance should anything go wrong with his primary charge, and Page's problem was that nothing ever really did. There was plenty of work for him in New York: he led small groups of his own and played featured solos behind Joe Turner and in Joe Marsala's band, eventually taking one of the chairs in Artie Shaw's orchestra in 1941, although it didn't do him much good. He tried a big band of his own and then switched back to small groups, but by the end of the 40s bop was the new thing and he began to sound *passé*. Page continued to make records, playing and singing in a meaty style of blues, and there are enough recordings from the period to fill up four CDs, but precious few of them have had much currency since. The thing that he probably loved above all was to play at jam sessions, not something which was likely to do much more than keep his reputation safe among his fellow musicians, and his death at 46 was a melancholy conclusion.
*After Hours In Harlem* (High Note)

## Walter Page

BASS
*born* 9 February 1900; *died* 20 December 1957

Page worked around the Midwest in Kansas City and Oklahoma City in the early 20s, and eventually founded his own band, Walter Page's Blue Devils, in 1925. He collared some of the best of the local players – Lester Young, Buster Smith, Count Basie – at various points, and was the great rival of Bennie Moten, but the band made only a single record in 1929 and Page never quite had Moten's acumen. In the end he joined Moten's group himself in 1931, and from there moved on to the new Basie band in 1935. As part of the pianist's outstanding rhythm section, Page's rock-solid time and unflustered swing was a key part of the four-way conversation. J Bradford Robinson has pointed out that, recording for Decca, the Basie outfit never benefited from the clarity which Duke Ellington enjoyed at RCA, and Page's presence is thus never as clearly heard as Jimmy Blanton's is with Ellington: often he is more felt than actually distinguished in the ensemble. He stayed until 1943, when he was drafted, and though he spent a further spell with Basie later in the 40s, thereafter he worked mostly in small groups, taking a notable hand in the Vanguard sessions led by Vic Dickenson and Buck Clayton's 'Jam Session' dates of the early 50s. Much admired as a bandleader and father-figure to many of the graduates of Kansas City, Page's early death has left him sometimes neglected in the histories of the pre-war music.
**Buck Clayton**, *A Buck Clayton Jam Session* (Columbia)

## Marty Paich

PIANO, ARRANGER
*born* 23 January 1925; *died* 12 August 1995

Paich was arranging for army bands during his military service and by the early 50s was a regular on West Coast record dates, writing for bands such as Stan Kenton's, playing piano for Shelly Manne and Shorty Rogers, and – with the Marty Paich Dek-Tette – acting as a studio backing for Mel Tormé (probably his best work on record) and others. One other jazz date which shows off his strongest style is Art

Pepper's *Plus Eleven* (1959). He later went into film and television and left jazz behind. Paich was an adept but doodling pianist; his crisp, neat arrangements were a smart match for Tormé, and he also did sound work for Ella Fitzgerald and Anita O'Day.
**Mel Tormé,** *Swings Shubert Alley* (Verve)

## Eddie Palmieri
PIANO
*born* 15 December 1936

Palmieri was born into a New York Puerto Rican community, and his music has been a family affair: he began playing in his uncle's band at 13 and his brother Charlie led some successful bands of his own. His career has been based around Afro-Cuban music which jazz has filtered into regularly though inconsistently. He began bandleading himself around 1960, with the formation of Conjunto La Perfecta, which lasted until 1968: a brass-heavy outfit, it backed Cal Tjader on the important *El Sonido Nuevo* (Verve, 1966), a landmark in the development of salsa music. Palmieri re-formed it in the 70s and also worked with other players in the salsa genre, and by the 90s he was using jazz players such as Brian Lynch and Donald Harrison, part of a trend for hard-bop types to moonlight in Latin bands of different sorts. Palmieri's own lusty, extravagant piano playing is usually at the heart of the groups, and while none of his records really sit squarely in a jazz pocket, there's no real reason why they should.
**El Sonido Nuevo** (Verve)

## Hugues Panassié
WRITER
*born* 27 February 1912; *died* 8 December 1974

France had no more passionate and pro-active jazz fan than Hugues Panassié. He toyed with the saxophone himself, but his talents lay elsewhere: he co-founded the Hot Club De France in 1932, the leading organization of French jazz followers, wrote a quantity of books and journalism, edited *Jazz Hot* during two periods, established the Swing label, and, while in New York, got Tommy Ladnier and Sidney Bechet back on record after their careers had been in the doldrums. All through the 30s and early 40s he was the kingpin of his scene, but things went awry after bebop made its appearance: Panassié didn't disguise his dislike of the new music, and he became as anti-progressive in his way as Ken Colyer. He lost credibility among more liberal French fans as a result.

## Andy Panayi
FLUTE, SAXOPHONES
*born* 18 January 1964

Panayi has become a stalwart member of the modern London scene, working widely as a session- and section-man and sometimes leading his own groups. He started on flute and has paid a lot of attention to that instrument, but he is a capable and fluently hot player on most of the saxophones. His parents are Greek Cypriots and his dad is pretty useful on the bouzouki.
**Blown Away** (Jazz House)

## Tony Parenti
CLARINET
*born* 6 August 1900; *died* 17 April 1972

Though he grew up in New Orleans and was playing in bands there from the age of 14, Parenti didn't really become a name musician until the 40s. He was, though, one of the few bandleaders to actually be recorded in New Orleans during the 20s: there are two sides for OKeh, six for Victor and ten for Columbia, although they had little impact at the time. Parenti went to New York around 1928 and played in studio bands for much of the next dozen years, touring with Ted Lewis from 1939. In the 40s he became eminent as a Dixieland leader, and he was the first musician to make records for the Jazzology label: thereafter he played in that style right up until his death, at clubs and festivals, and on record for George Buck's group of labels. Parenti was also one of the few Dixielanders to keep playing the ragtime repertoire, even after it had gone out of fashion.
**Ragtime Jubilee** (Jazzology)

# Tiny Parham
PIANO, ORGAN, BANDLEADER
*born* 25 February 1900; *died* 4 April 1943

His nickname was misleading: Hartzell Parham was a huge man. He was raised in Kansas City and began making a name for himself on the Chicago scene of the mid-20s. He led a series of recording sessions for Victor, which are these days remembered only by specialists of the period, yet which include a lot of fine and unexpectedly idiosyncratic music: instead of simple blues and barrelhouse music, Parham's brand of Chicago jazz mixed an almost schmaltzy feel on some pieces with some strikingly individual turns of phrase, and pieces such as 'The Head Hunter's Dream', 'Pig's Feet And Slaw' and 'Cathedral Blues' are as intriguing as their titles, with notable contributions from such sidemen as Punch Miller, Darnell Howard and Junie Cobb. After this burst of activity, though, Parham slipped back into obscurity in the 30s, and he spent his final years playing the organ in ice rinks and theatre lobbies.
*Tiny Parham 1928–1930* (Timeless)

# Paris Reunion Band
GROUP

Mike Hennessey helped create this group, which was originally organized as a vehicle in homage to Kenny Clarke, and was supposed to feature the drummer's own playing: but he died before it could play any music, and thereafter it went out as a touring group during 1985–8. Many European fans remember it fondly, as it offered a glimpse of a number of players who hadn't been easily visible on jazz stages for some time: Joe Henderson, Woody Shaw, Dizzy Reece, Kenny Drew, Grachan Moncur II and Curtis Fuller among them, making it something of an all-star hard-bop ensemble. Their one featured album on Sonet was, though, nothing out of the ordinary.
*French Cooking* (Sonet)

# Paris Washboard
GROUP

A gem among the many European revivalist bands. It originally fell into place as long ago as 1970, when the Gilbert Leroux Washboard Group came into being, a title which was retained until 1987, when they became Paris Washboard, with Leroux (washboard), Daniel Barda (trombone), Alain Marquet (clarinet), Louis Mazetier (piano), although Leroux was eventually replaced by Gérard Bagot (washboard) in 1990. A front line of trombone and clarinet goes back as far as The Louisiana Five in 1919, but it has hardly ever been convened since. While based in the city of their title, the Washboarders have travelled the trad touring world and delighted audiences everywhere: the music is full of characteristic high jinks, but it keeps a faithful hold on material which mixes authentic James P Johnson and Fats Waller tunes with in-the-spirit originals. Their long sequence of records for Stomp Off are consistently delightful.
*One More Time!* (Stomp Off)

# Charlie Parker
ALTO SAXOPHONE
*born* 29 August 1920; *died* 12 March 1955

If any one individual personifies a romantic idea of jazz – in his instrumental prowess, creativity and brutal destiny – it is Charles Parker, often called 'Bird' or 'Yardbird', saxophonist, narcotics addict and wayward genius of a music which seemed to almost burn out with him. Parker was born in Kansas City and left school at 15, already determined to become a full-time musician. He played at jam sessions and in unremarkable local groups until visiting New York in 1939 and staying for something like a year before returning to Kansas City, armed at least with jam-session experience. He then joined Jay McShann's band, with whom he made his first recordings ('Listen to the Bird blow!' recalled McShann, more than 60 years later) and from there he moved on, in late 1942, to Earl Hines's orchestra, and thence to the Billy Eckstine big band. During this period he was one of the participants in the Minton's Playhouse jam sessions which were effectively the crucible of bebop. By the time 1945 was under way, Parker had all the constituent parts of his style in place.

Although Parker did in some ways advance his art as time went on, he shares with many of the other jazz innovators – including Louis Armstrong, Bix Beiderbecke,

Ornette Coleman and Albert Ayler – a sense that he quickly understood what he had to say and wasted no time in saying it. He introduced such formal breakthroughs as improvising off the top of the chord sequence of a standard melody (something he reputedly realized while jamming on Ray Noble's tune 'Cherokee'), but the matter of his musicianship was at once more subtle and more upfront than that. He made everything seem inevitable, even simple, although what he was doing was immensely sophisticated in comparison with most of his contemporaries. While Dizzy Gillespie and Thelonious Monk had toiled towards the formal innovations of bebop during those countless hours of jamming and thinking and talking at Minton's, Parker came along and grasped the verities and played through them at the drop of a proverbial hat. His many hours of practice disguised his facility to a degree, but by the time of his coming out, his saxophone tone had matured and hardened into a fearsomely confrontational sound: even though he was often recorded in less than ideal conditions during his career, it is remarkable how his saxophone sound cuts through even the worst of low fidelity. It is this aspect of his playing, more than any other, which has kept his music alive to a modern audience: a single phrase from Parker's saxophone can erase the passage of decades by virtue of its vivid, seemingly immortal immediacy.

For all his individuality of timbre, though, it is Parker's rhythmic language which is most startling and enduring. Harmonically, he works from a relatively limited basis: as with many of the leading boppers, he was content to work mostly from a handful of familiar chord sequences as the model of his 'original' compositions. But his rhythmic imagination seemed limitless. In moving so comprehensively away from the simple four- and eight-bar divisions which tended to be the swing improviser's grammar, he introduced a fabulous complexity which required exceptional resources to master. Melody lines might be compressed, stretched, ornamented or otherwise made new, bursts of notes could be followed by unexpected rests, accents would fall in unlikely places. In some ways, Bird was the ultimate licks-player: the Parker scholar Thomas Owens has identified how he kept something like 100 formulae under his fingertips, phrase-shapes and patterns which he would refer to across the course of an improvisation, each one subject to the continuous variation which is the improviser's prerogative, and defence against predictability.

All this emerges in his body of recorded work, which can almost be divided down the middle, between his studio sessions – in the main, three corpuses of work for the Savoy, Dial and Clef (subsequently Verve) labels – and a huge number of live recordings, which more than doubles the size of his studio legacy. The Savoy and Dial material exists mostly in multiple takes of each tune, revealing further Parker's abilities to vary his approach. The band sessions featured such playing partners as Miles Davis, Max Roach, Dizzy Gillespie, Howard McGhee and Duke Jordan, but Parker's genius dominates every record. The Dial contract arose out of the trip Parker and Gillespie made to the West Coast at the end of 1945: although Gillespie eventually returned East, Parker stayed in Los Angeles. By this time, he had been addicted to heroin for some time, and had developed a gargantuan appetite for excess: drugs and alcohol dominated every day, yet miraculously seemed to have little effect – at this stage – on his capacity to play, which led some to believe that Parker's example was to be followed to achieve the right state to play the music in, a disastrous idea which ruined many lives. Matters came to a head at the notorious record date which produced the tortured 'Lover Man', after which Parker collapsed. He was confined at Camarillo State Hospital and emerged in 1947, eventually returning to New York, where he formed the quintet with Davis (who in later years had very little good to say about Parker).

Between then and 1951 Parker enjoyed his greatest years of success. He was feted as the master of his idiom, a club was opened in his name (Birdland), he signed to Norman Granz's operation and made records with strings and Latin groups, and he visited Europe in 1949 and 1950. His playing survives in numerous broadcast and unauthorized recordings, including many taken down by an obsessive fan, Dean Benedetti, who haunted backstage areas and recorded Bird on a portable machine (the surviving discs were eventually recovered from the Benedetti family and issued in the 80s in a

Mosaic edition). There were new studio encounters with Gillespie and Monk (a memorable date from 1950), and though some felt that Granz tried to prettify Parker's music in the wrong way, few would quibble with much of his playing on the best of the Clef sessions. But his problems with narcotics began to drag him down: his cabaret licence was revoked in 1951, banning him from playing in New York, and he was kept from the city's club scene until late in 1953. There was still wonderful music to come – a celebrated concert at Toronto's Massey Hall in 1953, to cite one occasion – and there are hints in his later work of how he might have addressed the further evolution of his own playing. But debts and an alcohol problem which was probably even worse than his narcotics addiction wore him down. He was committed to Bellevue Hospital in 1954 at his own request following a suicide attempt, and played his final gig in March 1955, dying a few days later at the home of Nica de Koenigswarter. The eventual cause of death was lobar pneumonia, but his bloated body was wrecked in any case: his coffin was so heavy that the pallbearers at his funeral almost dropped it.

The wonder of Parker's music is that it still sounds modern, 50 years after his death. He died before the LP era had got fully under way, and one can only guess at what he might have done with the long form of the album: 'I can definitely say that music won't stop. It will continue to go forward,' he told an interviewer late in his life. For many, the playing in 'Scrapple From The Apple', 'Parker's Mood', 'Now's The Time', 'Ah-Leu-Cha', 'Bluebird', 'Bird Gets The Worm', 'A Night In Tunisia' and so many others is as far forward as jazz music will ever get.

*The Complete Savoy And Dial Studio Recordings* (Savoy)

# Errol Parker

PIANO, DRUMS
*born* 30 October 1930; *died* 2 July 1998

Parker was an enthusiastic witness in the music who never really broke through on his own account. Born in Algeria, he went to Paris in the 40s as an art student and fell in with the local jazz scene, before going back to his studies and leaving music alone in the early 50s. He then played piano behind Don Byas and recorded as a solo for a few labels, scoring a minor hit with a tune called 'Lorré' in 1963. He moved to New York in 1968 and moved over to drums, leading various bands which culminated in a regular tentet, although their records on his own Sahara label suggest an ambition which had a long way to go before it came into focus. Parker's most interesting idea was a kit drum set which dropped the snare and used a more African line-up of individual drums. His autobiography *A Flat Tire On My Ass* is a sometimes unreadable ramble, which was finally published a few years before his death.

*A Night In Tunisia* (Sahara)

# Evan Parker

TENOR AND SOPRANO SAXOPHONES
*born* 5 April 1944

Britain has produced only a handful of genuinely significant jazz figures, and Parker may be the most important of all of them. He began playing the alto saxophone but soon enough, having heard John Coltrane, moved over to the tenor, and he played with the pianist Howard Riley in an early-60s quartet largely inspired by Coltrane's music. He moved to London from Birmingham in 1966 and began playing in the free-music circle which was developing in the city at this point, making connections with John Stevens and the Spontaneous Music Ensemble, and Derek Bailey and the Music Improvisation Company, which lasted for a period from 1968 until the early 70s. At this point, Parker's sound was a raw and fact-finding matter, his manner already starting to test the extremes of his technique and looking for alternatives to prevailing free-jazz role models. In addition to his work on the British scene, he was building associations in Europe: with the Peter Brötzmann group which cut the epochal *Machine Gun* (1968), with a quartet including Pierre Favre, Irène Schweizer and Peter Kowald, and in the trio with Alex von Schlippenbach and Paul Lovens which has become his most enduring association. By 1974, when he made his initial solo soprano saxophone recordings – *Saxophone Solos* (Incus) was actually recorded at his first solo performance of any kind – Parker's mature style was already firmly in place, and though he inevitably amplified it further over the next three decades, the improvisations on this record are still startling: using circular breathing, advanced tonguing and multiphonic techniques, he was able to fashion what sound like, on first impact, dialogues between more than one horn. In a typical solo performance, individual motifs may be subjected to a fusillade of repetitions where their constituent parts are altered and microscopically varied, the individual notes moving as in a dance of molecules, the dynamics under constant review. If it sounds like a dry, abstract or dispassionate music, the intensity of Parker's delivery can be mesmerizing, the complexity of his structures close to overwhelming.

While he has created a large body of solo work, Parker's principal activity does, though, continue to be found in group contexts. The trio with Schlippenbach and Lovens still tours annually and has a similarly large number of records under its collective belt. Parker ran the independent label Incus with Derek Bailey for many years, but following a falling-out in the late 80s they have gone their separate ways and what was also a fruitful musical partnership has not been reconvened. As time has gone on, Parker's natural gregariousness in his musical life has brought him a huge number of associations: besides working with probably every leading player in the free-music community at some time or other, he has also played in such bands as the various editions of the Charlie Watts orchestra, with Jah Wobble and Scott Walker, and with such American jazz performers as Paul Bley and Cecil Taylor. In the past decade he has recorded more prolifically than ever before, for a multiplicity of labels, and has set aside some of his own taboos – playing solo on tenor, which he had previously avoided, and experimenting with electronic manipulation of sound. His Electro-Acoustic Ensemble has been one major recent initiative in his work, but he considers that there is now a limitless terrain for the free improviser to pursue – 'everything is open sky'. As far as he has moved on from his original inspiration, John Coltrane, one can easily imagine the departed saxophonist being fascinated by and impressed with Parker's progress.
*The Snake Decides* (Incus)

# Johnny Parker
PIANO
*born* 6 November 1929

Parker's most famous hour remains his boogie playing on Humphrey Lyttelton's 'Bad Penny Blues' (1956), which for many is what made the record a hit. He had already been with Humph for some years but left to go solo a year later, although he only worked on and off for much of the 60s. He joined Kenny Ball in 1967, and after a period away went back in 1969 and stayed ten years. He has freelanced since, although indifferent health has curtailed his appearances. Parker looks like a right young tearaway on the cover of a solo EP he made in the 50s, but he was a fine and strong-handed player in both the traditional and boogie idioms.
**Humphrey Lyttelton,** *The Parlophones* (Calligraph)

# Knocky Parker
PIANO
*born* 8 August 1918; *died* 3 September 1986

John William Parker started out playing in Western swing bands in Texas in the 30s, and did little in a jazz context before working with Zutty Singleton at the end of the 40s. Much of his professional life was subsequently spent in education, in Kentucky and Florida, but he also focused his playing activity on music of the ragtime era, recording many of the works of Scott Joplin and other rag composers at a point where they had yet to get the full rediscovery treatment. He also did the same service for Jelly Roll Morton's piano music.
*Knocky Parker* (GHB)

# Leo Parker
BARITONE SAXOPHONE
*born* 18 April 1925; *died* 11 February 1962

Parker didn't have a great deal of competition, but the wisdom is that he was one of the best of the bebop baritones. He originally played alto, but while with Billy Eckstine's big band in 1944–5 he changed over to baritone, and he made some small-group records of his own for Savoy as well as turning up on a few other bebop dates. Parker's style was halfway into the feel of bop, but he also had the booting delivery which was more like the style of an R&B player. Narcotics problems more or less brought his career to a halt, until he was effectively rediscovered by Blue Note, who managed to get two album sessions out of him only months before his death from a heart attack.

*Rollin' With Leo* (Blue Note)

## Leon Parker

DRUMS
*born* 21 August 1965

The New Yorker was busy on the Manhattan scene from the middle 80s, leading groups of his own, taking high-profile sideman gigs with Jacky Terrasson and others, and playing in a style which relied on a pared-back kit: he learned drums without a hi-hat cymbal and a floor tom, and he subsequently went back to that kind of instrumentation. Some albums for Columbia hinted that he might become a star of sorts, but the records didn't sell and Parker's choices of material suggested another talent that was being spread too thinly in the service of eclecticism. He has since relocated to France.

*Belief* (Columbia)

## Maceo Parker

ALTO SAXOPHONE
*born* 14 February 1943

Parker's robustly cheerful brand of jazz-funk has made him a widespread hit on the live circuit, although his records tend to be nine-day wonders. He has impeccable R&B credentials, working as a sideman with James Brown in the 60s and for two subsequent periods in the 70s and 80s, as well as with Bootsy Collins. His later work is all in the same chunky, funky bag, nothing brand-new but spirited and professionally rousing, and when he has such old sparring partners as Fred Wesley and Pee Wee Ellis along for the ride, as on the live record cited, it's all taken in good part.

*Live On Planet Groove* (Minor Music)

## William Parker

BASS
*born* 10 January 1952

'The Mayor' has become something of a god-father to America's contemporary avant-garde, a prolific musician who has grown into his seniority steadily and patiently. He took up the bass in high school in the Bronx and listened to the music of the time, particularly Coltrane and Coleman, and he was soon involved in New York's radical circles, taking a role in the loft jazz of the middle 70s and working with one of his long-time associates, Cecil Taylor, as early as 1974. From the 80s onwards he became a significant force in his community as an organizer and activist, starting up festivals, running collectives and leading community arts initiatives where jazz was sometimes only a part of the activity: his wife Patricia is a choreographer, and he has often worked alongside dance artists. Since the CD era began he has been recorded almost continuously as both sideman and leader: besides Taylor, whom he has worked with in trio and larger settings, some of the other artists he was worked with frequently are Peter Brötzmann, Bill Dixon, Jemeel Moondoc, Charles Gayle, David S Ware and Matthew Shipp. His own bands In Order To Survive and the big-scale Little Huey Orchestra have been rich areas of activity. Parker's playing defies the subterranean and back-of-the-stage feel which the bass often falls into in jazz, instead taking a powerful solo role, and integrating both pizzicato and arco work into a single, authoritative voice.

*O'Neal's Porch* (AUM Fidelity)

## Horace Parlan

PIANO
*born* 19 January 1931

Parlan suffered from polio as a child; as a result his right hand was weakened, and his piano manner features a compensating strength in his left hand which has given him an unusual individuality within a basically conventional post-bop approach. He grew up in Pittsburgh but moved to New York in 1957 and immediately joined Charles Mingus's group. Thereafter he worked with some distinctive leaders, including Booker Ervin, Lou Donaldson and Johnny Griffin,

and he recorded six albums for Blue Note as his own boss. But he was one of the many who found the jazz life tough as rock took hold of the entertainment business, and in 1973 he moved to the more welcoming climes of Copenhagen, where he has been based since. His later work, mostly for the Steeplechase label, finds him in congenial settings where his bluesy yet unmannered style is often engaging. Perhaps, though, he has never quite found a way to make his playing truly coveted by an audience.
**Speakin' My Piece** (Blue Note)

## Parlophone
RECORD COMPANY

Some will be surprised to learn that The Beatles' home label is actually German in origin. The first Parlophone 78s came out in Germany prior to the First World War, and in Britain it was established in the early 20s as an affiliate for the Lindström company's activities. But the label was soon used for a broad range of popular music, from comic songs to hot dance and jazz, and its early red labels feature many fine American records – including such black artists as Sara Martin and Clarence Williams – making their British debuts. British record collectors remember this as perhaps the most important of all the 78 labels for jazz, as it was filtered into the UK: in the later 20s and 30s, with its purple and then pale blue and magenta labels, in various 'New Rhythm Style' series, it released many masterpieces – by Armstrong's Hot Five, Beiderbecke, Ellington and others from the OKeh catalogue – in master pressings, and the tradition carried on into the 40s when swing and bop records superseded the older material. There were also homegrown jazz records by Harry Hayes, Johnny Dankworth, Humphrey Lyttelton and others. And then The Beatles eventually came along.

## Jack Parnell
DRUMS, BANDLEADER
*born* 6 August 1923

Parnell was at the heart of British live entertainment for decades. His uncle, Val Parnell, was a leading impresario whose weekly staple *Saturday Night At The London*

*Palladium* was one of the principal British television variety showcases, and Jack's leadership of the orchestra lent him a powerful stature. Before that he had played in RAF bands, spent seven years with Ted Heath, and led his own big band in the early 50s, which included such modernists as Ronnie Scott and Jimmy Deuchar. Twenty years at ATV, including the *London Palladium* shows, found him working with many of the showbiz world's leading entertainers. But Parnell was a capable big-band drummer in any case, and he latterly worked with and directed smaller groups, sometimes conducting the London Jazz Orchestra on some of Laurie Johnson's shows in the 90s. Records under his own name, though, are relatively few in number: Jack was too busy with other gigs.

## Harry Parry
CLARINET
*born* 22 January 1912; *died* 18 October 1956

Mainly because they've never been reissued properly, Parry's fine records of the 40s have been particularly neglected. Born in Bangor, he played in brass bands as a boy and took up the clarinet in his teens. He moved to London in 1932 and worked on the dance-band scene there, eventually leading a sextet of his own which was engaged by the BBC in 1940 as the house band for their *Radio Rhythm Club* programme. Parry's Goodman-influenced style and smart arrangements fitted in neatly with the BBC's requirements, which were to provide lightly swinging music without frightening too many horses, but in their way the surviving records have genuine pep and inventive writing. George Shearing and Tommy Pollard were among Parry's sidemen.
**Jazz in Britain 1919–1950** (Proper)

## Hermeto Pascoal
VARIOUS INSTRUMENTS
*born* 22 June 1936

As capacious as jazz has become, it seems like a narrow category for the extravagant Pascoal, who began working in family bands in his native Brazil when he was 11. He played on radio shows there in the 50s and led his own band during the 60s. Airto

Moreira got him into jazz circles later in the decade, and Pascoal worked alongside Miles Davis, Donald Byrd and others, although he eventually settled over on the West Coast. He has toured and performed almost constantly since, working with a small group of Brazilian musicians but often expanding to fit the situation: he became a great favourite in the UK in the 80s, appearing like a lightning bolt to organize and rehearse large groups of British players in his music and tour the results. None of this has translated very well to record, and none of his compositions has really broken through to any great familiarity, but Hermeto's genial music is very beguiling. Among the instruments he plays are saxophones, flute, keyboards, guitar and percussion, but he is surely the only person in this book who has actually played a live pig on stage (he uses it as a percussion instrument – whether it joins in vocally or not is up to the pig).
*Fest Dos Deuses* (Philips)

## Joe Pass
GUITAR
*born* 13 January 1929; *died* 23 May 1994

Pass was a late-blooming jazz star. He was working with Charlie Barnet as a teenager, and after service with Uncle Sam's navy he spent his 20s and early 30s in Las Vegas – although he also had problems with narcotics, and served time in prison as a consequence. His first record as a soloist was made with fellow inmates at the Synanon Foundation for drug rehabilitation. There were some lightweight sets for Pacific Jazz, but it wasn't until Joe was in his 40s that he came to Norman Granz's attention. Granz built Pass into one of the new jazz stars of the 70s, recording him with Oscar Peterson and Ella Fitzgerald and anyone else available on the Pablo roster, and more importantly establishing him as a solo artist: the *Virtuoso* series of one-man albums placed a new imprimatur on solo, straight-ahead guitar at a point where the instrument had otherwise been completely annexed by rock. Pass became an international touring attraction as both soloist and small-group performer, and he recorded prolifically from that point right up until his death. More a synthesizer of historical trends than any kind of innovator, Joe's steely, unflappable poise in his

delivery masked a considerable power: as sweetly toned and luxuriant as his playing was, he disliked situations that might put him or his listeners to sleep, and he encouraged a degree of connoisseurship among his audience that defied the tag of easy listening. Granz might have been guilty of creating a production line of too many similar Pass records, but with hindsight it's agreeable that he set down as much as he did. He remains one of the few guitarists to essay an important style entirely out of fingerpicking.
*Virtuoso* (Pablo)

## Jaco Pastorius
BASS
*born* 1 December 1951; *died* 22 September 1987

Pastorius grew up in Florida, where he was a multi-instrumentalist before settling on bass guitar (an arm operation curtailed his desire to play drums). Although he wrote charts for jazz orchestras, most of his teens were spent playing funk, rock and reggae. He was heard by a member of Blood Sweat & Tears and was offered an album deal with CBS in 1975; then he joined Weather Report, and was suddenly a star, taking on distinguished sideman jobs with the likes of Joni Mitchell and alerting a generation of bass players to the singing, almost lubricious sound of the fretless bass guitar. He stayed with Weather Report for some six years before setting out on a doomed solo career: there were strange projects involving big bands, steel pan orchestras and jazz-funk ensembles where chaos would sometimes reign, although Pastorius's composing instincts usually saw him through. But his behaviour became erratic and mysterious, and by 1987 he was living what amounted to a vagrant's life. He died following a beating outside a club, where the unrecognized bassist was trying to get in past an unrelenting bouncer. As far as the music under his own name is concerned, he never surpassed that initial CBS album. But electric-bass players everywhere still bow to his influence, and still try to replicate the virtuosity of his style.
*Jaco Pastorius* (Columbia)

## John Patitucci
BASS
*born* 22 December 1959

A Brooklynite, Patitucci studied on jazz bass but played rock in his teens. When he went to university in California he moved on to the acoustic model and was working as a sessionman until he met Chick Corea in 1985, when he took on the bass role in both the electric and acoustic groups led by the pianist. He also began cutting sets under his own name, from 1987. Patitucci has become a small-scale superstar on his instrument and can probably book a ticket with any all-star rhythm section that goes out to tour. He can handle seemingly any situation he's put into, but as with so many such talents his own music can leave the uncommitted listener unmoved. *Another World* (1993) is a modish blend of world music, fusion and jazz, but it has its likeable moments.
**Another World** (GRP)

## Pat Patrick
SAXOPHONES
*born* 23 November 1929; *died* 31 December 1991

Patrick was one of Sun Ra's most loyal side-men. He first played with the Saturnian bandleader in Chicago around 1950, when the great man was mostly working with small groups in burlesque houses, but he was a charter member of the Arkestra and worked with it almost continuously until the middle 70s, when he became involved in education; even then he periodically returned to the ranks. For the most part he played baritone saxophone, although – like most of Ra's troops – he doubled on what-ever wind instrument seemed necessary at the time. While his Arkestra persona was mostly in a squalling free-jazz idiom, he also worked with other leaders in the 60s and 70s: these included such disparate figures as Willie Bobo, Thelonious Monk and even Duke Ellington.
**Sun Ra, *The Magic City*** (Saturn/Evidence)

## Don Patterson
ORGAN
*born* 22 July 1936; *died* 10 February 1988

Patterson has a modest following among admirers of the organ-combo jazz which was at its height in the 60s. He played primarily in the Philadelphia area, and Prestige released no fewer than 18 albums of his music during the 60s and early 70s, but there was nothing Patterson did which wasn't done at least as well by other per-formers in the style. He made a few more records for Muse but at the time of his death was largely forgotten: the organ-jazz revival of the 80s and 90s didn't quite arrive in time for him to benefit.
**The Exciting New Organ Of Don Patterson** (Prestige)

## 'Big' John Patton
ORGAN
*born* 12 July 1935; *died* 19 March 2002

Pretty much all you need to know about Kansas City's John Patton is set down in the six minutes of 'The Silver Meter', the irresist-ible groove tune which leads off his Blue Note debut, *Along Came John* (1963). He toured with Lloyd Price in the 50s, then joined the gang of club combo leaders who came in the wake of Jimmy Smith's success. Patton never made it to Smith's level, but his several Blue Note dates are enjoyable enough and after years of obscurity he popped up again at the behest of (of all people) John Zorn, who had him appear on *Spillane* (1985). He enjoyed some further limelight on visits to Europe, when hailed as a leader in his genre (like every other Hammond player who came back in the 80s and 90s).
**Along Came John** (Blue Note)

## Alcide 'Slow Drag' Pavageau
BASS
*born* 7 March 1888; *died* 19 January 1969

A grand old man of New Orleans bass play-ing, Pavageau didn't even take up the instru-ment until he was 40, having previously strummed guitar on the streets of the city.

His principal association was with George Lewis, joining the clarinettist in 1944 and continuing for a quarter-century, although he also appeared with Kid Howard and Percy Humphrey among other New Orleans leaders. His slap-bass style was perhaps the real bedrock of Lewis's ensemble sound, simple but entirely effective. Pavageau's nickname came from his youthful adeptness at the slow-drag dance popular at the beginning of the 20th century. He died following a street mugging.

**George Lewis,** *The Beverley Caverns Sessions* (Good Time Jazz)

## Cecil Payne
BARITONE SAXOPHONE
*born* 14 December 1922

Payne is an accomplished if lesser light in the pantheon of baritone boppers. He worked with numerous leaders from the late 40s onwards – Dizzy Gillespie, Illinois Jacquet and James Moody among them – then, in the 60s, in big bands run by Machito, Woody Herman and Count Basie. In the 90s he has surprisingly done more work as a leader than ever before, basing himself in Philadelphia, recording new albums and bossing a team of original old-timers calling themselves The Bebop Generation. The later recordings suggest an unquenched enthusiasm to play, although his executive powers have diminished.

**The Connection** (CP Records)

## Nicholas Payton
TRUMPET
*born* 26 September 1973

Payton's huge sound and suitably booming delivery turned many heads when he first emerged out of New Orleans at the end of the 80s: here was a trumpet man who sounded like the natural Louis Armstrong successor that Wynton Marsalis wanted to be, at least some of the time. Appropriately enough, Payton began working with members of the Marsalis circle at the start of the 90s, but he also worked as MD in the more modern surroundings of Elvin Jones's Jazz Machine band. Since then, he has strolled down a line which is a convenient divide between past and present. He signed

to Verve and made records which either reinvented his New Orleans roots (*Gumbo Nouveau*, 1996) or made his Armstrong leanings explicit (*Dear Louis*, 2000). And then he headed over to Warners and made *Sonic Trance* (2003), a set which mixed straight-ahead playing with almost avant-garde electronic settings; and Payton has also recently played with Greg Osby. Through all of this, he still sounds like a very good trumpet player.

**Dear Louis** (Universal)

## Annette Peacock
VOCAL, PIANO
*born* 8 January 1942

Often more of a silent contributor than a participant, Peacock's participation in jazz has been a matter of a small but very telling oeuvre. She married bassist Gary Peacock in 1960 and found herself part of New York's new jazz of the early 60s: she actually went to Europe with Albert Ayler, but her own writing assumed precedence and she subsequently composed a small but remarkable body of original music, which her new partner, Paul Bley, began using regularly. Aphoristic but coolly lyrical, tunes such as 'Blood', 'Closer', 'Mr Joy', 'Touching' and 'Albert's Love Theme' remained in Bley's book for years and he played them almost obsessively. In 1968, Peacock and Bley began working together in an electronic group called The Synthesizer Show, using some of the early Moog synthesizers, but this approach was later abandoned and Peacock moved to live in England in 1974. In the 70s and 80s she worked almost as a sort of singer-songwriter, her skinny but alternately sexy and detached voice musing through her own material, and she collaborated with a diverse group of players and bands, although for a lot of the time she seemed to entirely disappear. She subsequently went back to the US, but Manfred Eicher started recording her music again in the 90s, and Marilyn Crispell's album of her music, *Nothing Ever Was, Anyway* (1996), was a timely reminder of her powers as a composer.

**An Acrobat's Heart** (ECM)

# Gary Peacock

BASS

*born* 12 May 1935

Peacock has moved through more jazz idioms, more comfortably, than almost any other bassist. He started on piano, which he played in army bands, and he worked with Attila Zoller and Hans Koller in Germany before moving to California in 1958, where he did gigs with leaders as diverse as Shorty Rogers and Paul Horn. He went to New York in 1962, and although initially disappointed at what was going on managed to play with a formidable group of leaders, including Paul Bley, Albert Ayler, Jimmy Giuffre and Bill Evans. He also worked briefly with Miles Davis later in the 60s, but left music for a time to study macrobiotics and philosophy. In the middle 70s he resumed playing with Paul Bley, which began an association with ECM: he has since made solo albums for Manfred Eicher, and been the bassist in the Keith Jarrett Standards Trio, which has brought him his biggest audience. Peacock's inquisitiveness and interest in open-ended situations has seen him through a diversity of gigs which may be unrivalled. He has a big strong sound but is at least as interested in playing quietly and melodiously. Of his own playing, he has said: 'I don't play bass lines. The people around me tell me what to play. Because I'm listening. That tells me what comes up.'

***Tales Of Another*** (ECM)

# Duke Pearson

PIANO

*born* 17 August 1932

Born in Atlanta, Columbus Calvin Pearson (the 'Duke' was bestowed by an uncle, who was an Ellington fan) studied piano and trumpet, but dental problems obliged him to give up the latter, and he arrived in New York around 1959, where he played with Donald Byrd and briefly with The Jazztet. Byrd introduced Pearson to Alfred Lion of Blue Note, and there the pianist began to take on an A&R and production role. He made 11 albums for the label, none of which counted as best-sellers, but they quietly carried on the label's straight-ahead tradition at a time when it was moving more towards funk and crossover music. He was able to form a fine big band during the same period which managed two albums: there is a wonderful arrangement of 'A Taste Of Honey' on *Introducing Duke Pearson's Big Band* (1968). As the label began to wind down, though, Pearson became homesick for Atlanta and returned there in 1971. Multiple sclerosis overtook him in the middle 70s and he was forced to give up playing.

***Sweet Honey Bee*** (Blue Note)

# Santo Pecora

TROMBONE

*born* 31 March 1902; *died* 29 May 1984

Pecora was a New Orleans trombonist who, in the end, had a longer and more successful career than many more highly regarded names. He is on some of the early sessions by the New Orleans Rhythm Kings, and from there went to work in big bands during the 30s. In the 40s he found steady work as a studio musician in Hollywood, but he went back to New Orleans and Chicago in the 50s and was busy as a Dixieland leader, in which capacity he recorded for Clef and Vik.

***Dixieland Mardi Gras*** (Vik)

# Bernard Peiffer

PIANO

*born* 23 October 1922; *died* 7 September 1976

Peiffer began playing in France in the 40s, and while he did sideman work with Django Reinhardt and others it was his work as a soloist and small-group leader which got him attention – strong enough to catch the ears of some influential judges, and encouraging enough for him to try his luck in the US in 1954. Peiffer's rather elaborate technique sat him squarely on the Art Tatum bench, and it wasn't surprising that American critics were impressed – or that, for all his skills, he never made much headway in an environment where even Tatum himself was scarcely a household name. He settled in Philadelphia, where he eventually died in 1974, and worked primarily on the club circuit there, but aside from a few records at the end of the 50s – including the absurdly titled *Modern Jazz For People Who Like Original Music* (1960), which seems to invite obscurity with open arms – he never found much interest from record companies.

***The Astounding Bernard Peiffer*** (Decca)

# Dave Pell
TENOR SAXOPHONE
*born* 26 February 1925

Some see West Coast jazz of the 50s as a trivialization of the 'real thing', but Pell went one further and trivialized the idea of West Coast jazz. He was a regular sideman in Les Brown's band until 1955, and then led groups of his own – mostly an octet – which sounded rather like a parody of the dinkiest aspects of the West Coast style. Even though he had players of the calibre of Benny Carter, Art Pepper and Mel Lewis on the albums, they sounded not much different to a cooler version of Pee Wee Hunt's Dixieland (Pell encouraged the lack of seriousness by dressing up as Napoleon for his sleeves and making concept albums such as *Swingin' In The Old Corral*). He subsequently went into record production but reformed his octet in the 80s.

***I Had The Craziest Dream*** (Capitol)

# Ken Peplowski
CLARINET, TENOR SAXOPHONE
*born* 23 May 1959

Peplowski grew up in Cleveland, where he got his start in the Tommy Dorsey ghost band, touring Europe when he was in his late teens. He went to New York in 1981 and played clarinet in Dixieland bands. Since then he has worked steadily in the small-group swing idiom, dividing his time between clarinet and tenor, and playing with such cronies as Warren Vaché, Howard Alden and Marty Grosz (the Grosz–Peplowski duo is one of the most entertaining acts on the live circuit, since they share a similar sense of humour). Peps recorded a long sequence of fine albums for Concord in the 80s and 90s, and he has cultivated an attractive approach to both instruments which is reliable without growing too predictable.

***A Good Reed*** (Concord)

# Art Pepper
ALTO SAXOPHONE
*born* 1 September 1925; *died* 15 June 1982

Pepper's sensational career – he called his autobiography *Straight Life*, which given the facts of it seems like a savage irony – is a totemic example of jazz's inhumanity to man. Frederick Spencer's dry remark – 'the index entries in Art's autobiography read like a book about crime, not music' – hardly seems an exaggeration. He grew up in California and took up the saxophone and clarinet before he was in his teens, working in Benny Carter's and Stan Kenton's big bands before going into the army. When he came out he went back with Kenton, where he became one of the orchestra's star soloists: bop had taken over his style, but he played it with a pointed, almost fastidious refinement, which was at the same time never as cerebral-sounding as Lee Konitz's otherwise similar approach. After 1951 he went out as a solo, but heroin addiction had already taken over his life and most of the next two decades were a wasteland of drug abuse and its consequences, illuminated – almost like flashes of lightning – by spells of brilliant music-making. His albums for Aladdin and Savoy were impressive enough, but those for Contemporary are among the finest of their time: Pepper's sinewy elegance and almost intuitive musicality are best understood through the circumstances of *Meets The Rhythm Section* (1957), a remarkable date played with what was then Miles Davis's rhythm section, which he recorded at no notice, after two weeks without practice and during one of his most difficult narcotics periods. In between jail sentences and incidents such as committing armed robbery, he eventually switched to the tenor, listened to what Coltrane was doing, and rejoined the jazz fray in 1968 with a stint in Buddy Rich's band. After a period of inconclusive rehabilitation in the early 70s he finally re-emerged as a solo force: he formed a long-standing quartet with George Cables, made records for Galaxy, and toured intensively. And he talked constantly, on and off the bandstand, amazed that he was still alive and playing. Pepper admirers are somewhat divided on the merits of his latter-day work: there are new and often off-colour traits in his playing which Coltrane's example seems to have instilled, and listening back to the almost pure stream of melody in his 50s improvising, something seems to have been irrevocably altered somewhere. Yet the best of his later music is intense and profoundly felt, his ballad playing a sometimes pitiless portrait of the artist. Art never got away from his demons, though. Hospitalized the week before his death, he still managed to have cocaine smuggled in to his room: 'I want to be high when I die.'

**Art Pepper Meets The Rhythm Section** (Contemporary)

## Jim Pepper
TENOR SAXOPHONE
*born* 17 June 1941; *died* 10 February 1992

A Native American who was a product of the Creek and Kaw tribes, Pepper brought something of his proud heritage into the jazz domain, although in the end he wasn't able to suggest a great individuality in his own playing, which added tinges of free jazz to what was basically a boppish style. He worked in crossover groups of different kinds in the 60s, but spent most of the 70s away from music, working as a fisherman in Alaska. He came back as a sideman with Charlie Haden and made a sequence of records for Enja and Nabel: it seems sad that no American label was interested in recording his music. The tune 'Witchi-Tai-To', which he first recorded with the rock band Everything Is Everything in the 60s, was effectively his signature piece, based on a Peyote chant.

**The Path** (Enja)

## Ivo Perelman
TENOR SAXOPHONE
*born* 12 January 1961

Perelman moved from his native São Paulo to Boston in 1981, and he stayed at Berklee for a year. Thereafter he worked in Los Angeles, Rome and New York, and by the 90s he was starting to make records under his own name. Although he categorically denies the influence of both Gato Barbieri and Albert Ayler (he sees Coltrane as his primary model), Perelman's style is very much in their lineage at least: a screaming player whose outbursts are nailed to an underlying control and sense of form which sets him on a significantly more purposeful course than many energy players. An all-solo record, *Blue Monk Variations* (1996*)*, shows how much he can make out of one piece of material, endlessly running the tune inside and out. He has (until *The Ventriloquist*, 2001) avoided making records with other horn players but with so much sound coming out of his own instrument – many of his sessions have a marathon-endurance quality about them – this hardly seems like an insufficiency, and he has been prolifically recorded already. He also plays cello, although an entire set dedicated to that instrument (*Strings*, 1998) was undistinguished. Lately he has turned to painting, and has apparently been 'discovered' in that capacity, which may have curtailed his musical activities for a while.

**Sad Life** (Leo Lab)

## Danilo Perez
PIANO
*born* 29 December 1965

A Panamanian, Perez studied classical piano and then went to Berklee, graduating in 1988. He had already begun playing with Jon Faddis and others, and was in Dizzy Gillespie's United Nation Orchestra; he then worked as a freelance in New York, although he has since returned to Boston as a member of the faculty at the New England Conservatory. Perez has been groomed as a possible star by Impulse!, recording a handful of records for the label, but while he keeps the sometimes fatuous excess of Afro-Cuban musicians such as Arturo Sandoval at arm's length, he also falls into the trap of note-spinning at times, and the record cited, an attempt at setting Thelonious Monk's music to Afro-Latin pulses, feels phoney and contrived.

**PanaMonk** (Impulse!)

## Bill Perkins
TENOR SAXOPHONE
*born* 22 July 1924; *died* 9 August 2003

Perkins was among the most likeable of the West Coast players. He played with Woody Herman and Stan Kenton in the 50s, and while he also did his share of studio work he had but a single album to his name during the period, *On Stage*. During the following decade he went more wholeheartedly into studio work, sometimes doubling as an engineer, and in the 70s he enjoyed stints with the *Tonight Show* band, as well as taking part in sundry West Coast reunions by Shorty Rogers, the Lighthouse All Stars and others. He survived a bout of cancer in the early 90s and made a number of fine latter-day sessions under his own name: Lester Young haunted his playing, and Perkins built over that influence with a lovely, streaming melodic vocabulary which makes his appearances on record a consistent pleasure.

**The Right Chemistry** (Jazz Mark)

## Carl Perkins

PIANO
*born* 16 August 1928; *died* 17 March 1958

Originally from Indianapolis, Perkins arrived in California in 1949. His left hand was handicapped by a bout of polio as a child, and he developed a crabwise method of playing which had his left arm set almost in parallel with the keyboard. Another player wrecked by drug addiction, Perkins was dead by 1958 and left only a single album under his own name and a group of sideman sessions, including dates with Art Pepper, Dexter Gordon and, in particular, the Curtis Counce group, which made a sequence of Contemporary albums that have long been collectors' favourites. Perkins liked to pick off phrases with a horn-like delivery and he conspicuously avoided many of the conventions of bebop piano. On his very last date, with Harold Land, he contributed 'Grooveyard', the one Perkins tune to enter the jazz repertory.

**Curtis Counce, *You Get More Bounce With Curtis Counce*** (Contemporary)

## Rich Perry

TENOR SAXOPHONE
*born* 22 July 1955

Perry spent most of his early career as a big-band section-player. He joined the Jones–Lewis Jazz Orchestra in 1977 and took a memorable role in Maria Schneider's regular New York big band, where his calmly authoritative work was one of the principal voices in their regular gigs in the city. In small-group situations he has worked regularly with Harold Danko, and Nils Winther of Steeplechase has recorded him prolifically as both leader and sideman in the past decade or so. He has a softly articulated sound, reserved rather than bland, which carries his ideas in a steadily flowing measure that can take an entire album to insinuate their way in: he does nothing to surprise or startle, and stays loyal to his own idea about the architecture of a solo.

**Beautiful Love** (Steeplechase)

## Charli Persip

DRUMS
*born* 26 July 1929

Persip has been a busy and ubiquitous presence in jazz since the early 50s, without really making a significant mark as a leader or individual influence. He started out in R&B bands in New Jersey, and after a brief spell with Tadd Dameron worked with Dizzy Gillespie for five years from 1953. Besides other freelancing, he then formed his own band, The Jazz Statesmen, which made a solitary album for Bethlehem in 1960, before a busy spell of studio work in hard-bop small groups. He went back to the soul circuit in the later 60s and toured as Billy Eckstine's drummer, before going into educational work and eventually forming his own Superband, a bop-orientated big band which has recorded only seldom but which showcases his style as well as anything he has recorded.

**Roland Kirk, *We Free Kings*** (Mercury)

## Houston Person

TENOR SAXOPHONE
*born* 10 November 1934

As full-bodied and comforting as home-baked pie, Houston Person's tenor sound has been an attractive refuge in post-bop jazz. He didn't start on the saxophone until he was 17, then went into the army and emerged to play in organ combos on the chitlin circuit of the 60s. In a sense, he's never gone away from that format: he likes bluesy settings on a low simmer, and his empathy with recording situations has lat-terly led him into a production career in addition to his own playing. He backed his partner Etta Jones on numerous recording projects up until her death, and he has a large discography of his own on Muse and High Note.

*My Romance* (High Note)

## Åke Persson

TROMBONE
*born* 25 February 1932; *died* 5 February 1975

'The Comet' was so accomplished that he was a star in his native Sweden at the age of 18, playing with Simon Brehm and Arne Domnérus, as a sideman with Art Farmer and Stan Getz, in Harry Arnold's Radio-bandet, and eventually as one of the solo lights in the Clarke–Boland Big Band, although his steadiest gig through the 60s and 70s was with the RIAS orchestra of Berlin. Mellifluous and vibrant, too much of his later playing was hidden away in the larger orchestras he chose to work in, although that was a sign of the times for a jazz trombone player. He took his own life in 1975, much mourned by his fellow members of the Clarke–Boland band.

*The Great Åke Persson* (Four Leaf Clover)

## Bent Persson

CORNET, TRUMPET
*born* 6 September 1947

Persson is a brilliant mimic of the original styles of hot trumpet as they stood in the 20s: leaders such as Keith Nichols have used him to handsome effect on some of their revivalist projects, although he is a more than capable and imaginative soloist in his own right. He emerged on the Swedish tra-ditional scene in the 70s, a long-standing member of the Kustbandet group, and besides leading occasional bands and record-ing projects of his own he played the solo parts on the audacious *Louis Armstrong's 50 Hot Choruses For Cornet*, a direct re-creation of the solos and breaks which Armstrong once recorded on to wax cylinders for the Melrose publishing company, never since found but existing in manuscript form.

*Jazz, Blues And Stomps* (Kenneth)

## Hannibal Marvin Peterson

TRUMPET
*born* 11 November 1948

Born in Smithville, Texas, Peterson moved to New York in 1970 after playing locally and studying at North Texas State, where he was one of the stars of its big band. He began a long association with Gil Evans, appearing in most of the arranger's sub-sequent bands, as well as other sideman work and projects such as his Sunrise Orchestra (actually a quintet) and groups with George Adams and John Hicks. After a serious illness he changed his name to Hannibal Lokumbe and embarked on a mis-sion to play jazz to school and church audi-ences, moving on to create large-scale works such as *African Portraits* (premiered in 1990 and eventually recorded five years later) and a play, *Diary Of An African American*. From 1999 he spent three years doing com-missioned work in New Orleans. Often operating away from the sight of the jazz media and only rarely recorded in recent years, Peterson has to some extent slipped into the margins, but he is an ambitious and perhaps even a visionary figure: *African Portraits* had little of the ballyhoo which attended Wynton Marsalis's *Blood On The Fields*, but some commentators felt it a far more successful embracing of aspects of African-American history. His own trumpet playing mirrors his outreach: there are glimmers of every part of jazz history in it.

*African Portraits* (Teldec)

## Oscar Peterson

PIANO
*born* 15 August 1925

Peterson's contribution to jazz is of incalcu-lable value, since he is one of the few figures to attract and commune with a large, popu-lar audience across literally decades of work, even as the music has been subject to count-less attacks on its health and viability in the business world of the arts. Much credit for that might go to his long-time manager, Norman Granz: Peterson was a favourite on Canadian radio in the 40s and he did club work in his native Montreal when Granz heard him and brought him to Carnegie Hall in 1949 for one of his Jazz At The Philharmonic concerts. The pianist's style offered nothing new to American audiences, but the ebullience and skill of his mixture of Art Tatum, Nat Cole and Teddy Wilson spoke so clearly to listeners that they responded with an enthusiasm which has been as enduring as Peterson's own career. The pianist formed his first trio in 1952, with Ray Brown and Irving Ashby, and though the guitarists sometimes changed, this lasted until 1959, when Ed Thigpen came in as a drummer and the guitarist's role was dropped. Meanwhile, in addition to his JATP work, Granz recorded Peterson at great, almost consuming length, as both a leader and an accompanist: he is on Verve albums by Ben Webster, Lester Young, Louis Armstrong, Benny Carter, Coleman Hawkins and Ben Webster, Sonny Stitt and Dizzy Gillespie, and as diverse as these talents were, Peterson brought a sympathetic and enlightened approach to each session while remaining, surprisingly, himself. His own records of the 50s were sometimes cast in a rather perfunctory role by producer Granz, but there were outstanding episodes: live sessions from 1957 were particularly fine, and the new trio with Brown and Thigpen resulted in the best of Oscar's Verve recordings. *Porgy And Bess* (1959), the five discs of *The London House Sessions* (1961) and especially *Night Train* (1962), the last being perhaps the most durable of all his records, will sum up the style of a certain jazz era for many listeners, even if Peterson himself was in some ways remote from what else was going on in the music at that time.

In the later part of the 60s, after Verve's closure, he shifted to the German label MPS and made another renowned set of records, *Exclusively For My Friends* (1963–8), but Granz eventually brought him back to an American home when the new label Pablo commenced operations, and Peterson recorded albums at a faster rate than ever, as the producer lined him up alongside everyone else on the label's roster in addition to his own featured records. It was a period where there seemed to be a movement to try and take Oscar more 'seriously': it was true that jazz critics had tended to take him for granted for a long time, and were sometimes openly hostile about his perceived levels of success, which brought him television series as well as residencies

on most of the world's leading concert platforms. Peterson's later work often took on more rococo elements – the Tatum influence pushing further forward, perhaps, as the Nat Cole one declined – but the qualities which his audience most enjoyed, such as the jubilant improvising and the unfailing commitment to swinging, never failed to stay front and centre. His composing – never a great priority for him – had sometimes had a functional quality, but it began to assume a more reflective and autumnal feel, often going back to his Canadian roots for inspiration.

In the 90s, he was by now an honoured veteran of the music, but his health began to decline: always a huge man, heart problems and a stroke impaired the use of his left hand, but with typical resilience he continued performing and gradually increased his facility to something like its old level. Through much of the 70s and 80s he had played mostly with Niels-Henning Ørsted Pedersen and Martin Drew, but as he cut down on touring commitments he no longer kept a regular group. His final association on record has been with the Telarc company, and he has still managed to deliver more than a dozen new albums to them. The sheer size of his output means that Oscar's work will always be in some senses undervalued: nobody can be so prolific and make every utterance indispensable. But what a wonderful lifetime of music he has gifted to his listeners.
*Night Train* (Verve)

# Ralph Peterson Jr
DRUMS
*born* 20 May 1962

Peterson played in funk bands in and around Atlantic City but he moved over to jazz in his late teens and studied both drums and trumpet at university. By 1983 he could be spotted as one of the emerging 'young lions' of the New York neo-bop scene, and he was in the group Out Of The Blue as well as with David Murray, Jon Faddis and Wynton Marsalis. Peterson plays in a hyperactive, almost furious style, the kind of post-Elvin Jones playing which became the familiar virtuosic groove of New York drummers in the period, although few played it with Peterson's kind of flair. He began leading groups of his own, assisted by a contract with Blue Note, and although slightly set back by some personal problems (which he chronicled, after a fashion, on his 1994 set *The Reclamation Project*), he has carried on leading his own bands, often under the rubric The Fo'tet, with such regular sidemen as Bryan Carrott (vibes) and Steve Wilson (saxes), most recently documented on the independent Criss Cross. He still makes the most tremendous racket behind his soloists: perhaps he is the real inheritor of Art Blakey's mantle.

*The Art Of War* (Criss Cross)

## Buddy Petit
CORNET
*born* c1897; *died* 4 July 1931

After Buddy Bolden, Petit was the most famous of the early New Orleans masters who never managed to make a record: ever since, scholars of the period have pondered on how good he really was. Born Joseph Crawford (Petit was his stepfather's name), he began playing in the early teens of the century and soon worked alongside some of the best musicians in the city. He worked for a brief spell with Jelly Roll Morton in California, but soon returned home and from then until his death he was a regular and popular figure in New Orleans and neighbouring cities, working in dance halls and on the riverboats. Had he gone to Chicago, he might have made a bigger name for himself; but it never happened.

## Umberto Petrin
PIANO
*born* 15 May 1960

Petrin's brainy style has a touch of the dilettante about it – he worked as an art critic, a poet and a book reviewer before he made much headway in jazz – but his work on record suggests a notably individual point of view. He worked mainly in Milan from the middle 80s and started making records for the independent Splasc(h) label, mixing together an interest in Monk and Tristano and coming up with a post-modern jazz perspective which can be irritatingly knowing yet full of unpredictable turnings. The record cited is a recital of Monk tunes which

is, in its way, as striking as Giorgio Gaslini's look at similar material.

*Monk's World* (Splasc(h))

## Michel Petrucciani
PIANO
*born* 28 December 1962; *died* 5 January 1999

Surely nobody who ever saw and heard this formidable man will ever forget him and his music. He was born into a French musical family: his father played guitar, his brothers guitar and bass, and Michel worked in the family band from an early age. He went to Paris in 1980 and began recording there: despite suffering from osteogenesis imperfecta, which restricted his growth and gave him health problems for all of his adult life, he developed a piano style which was swooningly romantic and seemed, to some listeners, to represent the incarnate successor to Bill Evans's music. His early records especially are laden with effusive playing which sometimes suggest Keith Jarrett in more decisive mode, but as he went forward he became more considered and diverse. He always kept heavy company, recording with such giants as Jim Hall, Wayne Shorter, Roy Haynes and Eddie Gomez, and he secured a contract with Blue Note in 1985, which brought him to a wider audience, enabling him to move to New York in 1999. There was a brief period where he dabbled in a kind of fusion, but he went back to straight-ahead playing in his final years. There was always a sense that Petrucciani was living on borrowed time, even as his music exuded a palpable *joie de vivre*, and in the end he died from pneumonia, worsened by complications arising from his physical condition.

*Pianism* (Blue Note)

## Oscar Pettiford
BASS
*born* 30 September 1922; *died* 8 September 1960

Pettiford came from a large musical family, and he learned to play various instruments in what amounted to a touring vaudeville family band based around Minnesota. He went to New York as one of the two bassists in Charlie Barnet's orchestra in 1943, and from there he played on the nascent bebop scene before going to California with Coleman Hawkins, but was soon back in New York and leading bands on 52nd Street. He joined Woody Herman in 1949, practised cello while recovering from an accident in which he broke his arm, and then led more groups in New York. Eventually he led his own big band for a spell in the middle 50s, but inevitably it didn't last long, and he then went to Europe in 1958, playing in France, Germany and Scandinavia before his sudden demise from a stroke. Everyone who heard Pettiford in person seems to agree that he always sounded better than his records: on both bass and cello, he played with a lively, almost pneumatic style, supportive of the soloists but always ready to assert his instrument's singularity. His tunes 'Tricotism' and 'Bohemia After Dark' became staples of the hard-bop repertoire.

**The Oscar Pettiford Orchestra In Hi-Fi** (ABC-Paramount)

# Barre Phillips

BASS

*born* 27 October 1934

Phillips moved to New York from his native San Francisco in 1962, and began playing with free-jazz leaders such as Archie Shepp and Paul Bley. He worked in Jimmy Giuffre's trio and went to Europe with George Russell before working in a trio with Attila Zoller. Like many of his generation and inclination, Phillips found the climate more welcoming in Europe, and he went to live in London in 1967, although France eventually proved more congenial and he moved there permanently in 1969. His *Journal Violone* album marked the first-ever record of solo bass playing (1968), and he went on to work in The Trio with John Surman and Stu Martin. Thereafter, Phillips was somewhat buried away in Europe: he made some interesting records for ECM, including a renewal of his old association with Bley (*Time Will Tell*, 1994), and has forged playing partnerships with various free players. His own style is a sometimes humorous and good-natured kind of free playing, devoid of much of the angst which sometimes accompanies the genre and full of melodious lines and conversational interplay.

**Mountainscapes** (ECM)

# Flip Phillips

TENOR SAXOPHONE

*born* 26 March 1915; *died* 17 August 2001

Flip started on clarinet, but hearing Frank Trumbauer on 'Singin' The Blues' made him settle on saxophone. He worked at local (Brooklyn and New York) gigs, making little impact until he joined Woody Herman's First Herd in 1944: he made a name here as an extrovert soloist, which caught the attention of Norman Granz, who made him a regular at his Jazz At The Philharmonic tours for ten years from 1946. For decades this conferred a reputation of mere rabble-rousing on Flip – which he was certainly capable of – while hiding away many more considered performances and a particularly noble manner on ballads (it is intriguing to hear him alongside Hodges, Carter, Parker and his main man Ben Webster on the 'Ballad Medley' from Granz's *Jam Session #1*). At the end of the 50s, Phillips decamped to Florida, where he kept a day job managing an apartment building while playing in the evenings. He guested with Woody Herman at the 1972 Newport Festival and developed a taste for more regular gigging again, although he mostly remained in the Florida area, when he wasn't tempted out for tours or occasional New York gigs with like-minded souls such as Scott Hamilton and Kenny Davern. He was still making records in the 90s and said a remarkable farewell with *Swing Is The Thing!* (1999), the big sound still intact at 86. Flip's later records contain much to enjoy, but the compilation of some of his best tracks for Granz shows his various sides to advantage.

**Flip Wails** (Verve)

# Sid Phillips

CLARINET

*born* 14 June 1907; *died* 24 May 1973

Philips worked on the London dance-band scene with Ambrose and others from the early 30s, but he is best known for the many records he made with his own Dixieland-orientated groups from the late 40s onwards, recording many singles and early LP sessions with groups which featured such future stars as Kenny Ball. The music was a trim and rather polite kind of English Dixieland, but it kept that music alive at a time when British jazz was caught between trad purism and the new strains of bebop. He was still playing into the 70s.

*Hors D'Oeuvres* (ASV)

## Pick-up groups

A band of players organized casually for the purposes of a particular record date or, though this is less likely, a live session: not quite an ad hoc grouping, but one which has been put together as a matter of con-venience, and may never play in exactly that combination again. Although this might sound like a recipe for, at the least, a less than coherent performance, since the organizer wants a good result they are likely to have engaged the most appropriate players they can find for the situation. Some pick-up groups have created results bordering on the sublime: examples might be Teddy Wilson's bands supporting Billie Holiday, or the pre-war Victor sessions by Lionel Hampton.

## Alphonse Picou
CLARINET
*born* 19 October 1878; *died* 4 February 1961

Picou was playing in New Orleans bands, par-ticularly the Excelsior Brass Band, in the 1890s. He went on to stand next to King Oliver in Louis Keppard's orchestra and was one of the first players in Papa Celestin's Tuxedo Orchestra, where he is credited with having come up with the clarinet part on 'High Society'. He spent occasional periods in Chicago in the teens and 20s, but other-wise remained in New Orleans, busy enough until he decided to let music take a back seat at the start of the 30s. The revivalist era of the 40s saw him playing again, but he could do much as he pleased: his work as a tinsmith had made him wealthy enough to invest in property. In his 80s he was still playing locally, although he never did get on to record very much.

**Oscar Celestin, *The 1950s Radio Broadcasts*** (Arhoolie)

## Enrico Pieranunzi
PIANO
*born* 5 December 1949

Born in Rome, Pieranunzi was attracted to jazz piano by an Erroll Garner record, although he studied classical piano before beginning to play in small groups in the city. He was the house pianist at Music Inn during the early 70s, and toured with Art Farmer, before beginning to get on record with small groups of his own. He credits work with Chet Baker during 1980 as help-ing him develop a more 'singing' style, and a later encounter with Bill Evans's music (about whom he has written a book) leading him towards a more relaxed and lyrical approach. In the 80s he worked with the Space Jazz Trio, with Enzo Pietropaoli and Roberto Gatto, as well as in trios with Marc Johnson, Paul Motian and Joey Baron. Pieranunzi has built up a sizeable discogra-phy, at first with Soul Note and Enja, then YVP, and most recently EGEA and CamJazz. His distillation of influences has led him to a beautifully cultured and, for all its thought-fulness, outgoing music: his frequent work with Johnson and Baron, who aren't given to noodling, has strengthened his trio work, although the Mediterranean feel of his solo music is at least as engaging. He writes mostly in minor keys: 'Major keys seem to have the answers. I like questions.'

**Con Infinite Voci** (EGEA)

## Billie Pierce
PIANO, VOCAL
*born* 8 June 1907; *died* 29 September 1974

## De De Pierce
CORNET, VOCAL
*born* 18 February 1904; *died* 23 November 1973

A husband-and-wife team which was central to the New Orleans revivalism of the 50s and 60s. Billie was from Florida and worked on the black theatre circuit in the 20s before settling in New Orleans, where she married De De in 1935. The cornetist was born in the city and met Billie when both worked in the George Lewis band. They played in some of the roughest places in the city in the 40s and early 50s, and when De De lost his sight and Billie also became ill, they gave up music, only to return to the scene later in the decade. They were familiar figures at Preservation Hall in the 60s and a fair number of studio and live recordings have survived. De De's lead could sometimes be shambolic and he clearly relied heavily on the tough-voiced Billie, who played stomping piano in the proper style. While she took most of the vocal duties, De De also sang in Creole patois, a style which has all but vanished since. Although their music was sometimes further let down by the quality of bandsmen they had, at their best they played some of the deepest, rootsiest jazz that the New Orleans style could boast – sober, joyful and almost sanctified in its intensity.

*Jazz At Preservation Hall II* (Atlantic)

# Billy Pierce
TENOR SAXOPHONE
*born* 25 September 1948

Pierce studied in Nashville and at Berklee, playing in funk and soul groups more than in any jazz situation, and he didn't really take a hand in jazz until the end of the 70s, when he began a long-standing association with pianist James Williams. He then spent two years with Art Blakey's Jazz Messengers, and in 1986 joined the Tony Williams band, staying until its dispersal in 1993. Pierce made a handful of intermittently impressive records as a leader himself, plying a boisterous variation on the hard-bop sax repertory, but little has been heard from him in the new century.

*William The Conqueror* (Sunnyside)

# Nat Pierce
PIANO, ARRANGER
*born* 16 July 1925; *died* 10 June 1992

Pierce began playing with bands in the Boston area in the early 40s. When he joined Woody Herman in 1951 he found a more settled niche: he played piano for Woody, wrote charts, and in the 60s even acted as the orchestra's road manager. By the mid-50s he was well-known enough to be getting work from numerous sources: he masterminded the arrangements for the famous *Sound Of Jazz* telecast, played with Lester Young and Ruby Braff, and led his own occasional big band ('A bunch of guys

wanted to get together to play'). Pierce became used to depping for leaders: he played the Basie role on the Lambert, Hendricks & Ross album *Sing A Song Of Basie*, covered for the Count himself when the latter was ill during the 70s, and filled in for Stan Kenton when that leader was ill in 1972. He moved West while working for Carmen McRae in the 70s, and struck up a partnership with drummer Frank Capp: their Capp–Pierce Juggernaut was the big-band vehicle for most of Nat's later scores, although he also took the piano role on many small-group dates for Concord. More a functionary than any kind of personal stylist, Pierce was the kind of musician who kept wheels dependably turning. It would be agreeable to see his 1957 big-band album for RCA – the last ever recorded at the old Savoy Ballroom in Harlem – restored to print.

*Juggernaut Strikes Again* (Concord)

# Dave Pike
VIBES
*born* 23 March 1938

Originally from Detroit, Pike went to Los Angeles in 1953 and he began playing on the city's hard-bop scene a year or so later, a regular at the Hillcrest Club and eventually playing alongside Paul Bley there. He went to New York in 1960, and a year later made *It's Time For Dave Pike* for Riverside, although he then toured with Herbie Mann for some years rather than leading on his own. What changed course for him was a move to Europe: in 1967 he was in Berlin, where he formed a band with Volker Kriegel which enjoyed much success and recorded for MPS, with tunes such as 'Walkin' Down The Highway In A Raw Red Egg' and the use of sitar and other exotica suggesting that Pike was keying in to the spirit of what were then psychedelic times. Pike returned to the US in the mid-70s and worked in and around California, before going back to New York, but he broke his arm and had to spend a long time recuperating. He has only been intermittently visible since then, although he has shuttled between Europe and the US and made occasional records. Pike's 60s music has long enjoyed a somewhat ironic following, but he is a solid player in a straight-ahead bop style when he wants to be.

*Masterpieces* (MPS)

# Jean-Michel Pilc
PIANO
*born* 19 October 1960

The Parisian pianist worked as an engineer until the late 80s, and from then played with a broad range of French performers before shifting operations to New York in 1995. Since then he has gone on to make a series of trio records for the Dreyfus label which suggest a player of great ambition and often startling ideas about approaching other people's material: the music on the disc cited, for instance, includes some hair-raising revisions of 'So What', 'Rhythm-A-Ning' and 'Scarborough Fair'. He also has a sense of humour, as in an earlier original called 'My Köln Concert', which lasts for two minutes. Pilc has tended to divide listeners thus far, sometimes suggesting an almost arrogant and incommunicado talent, but that's sometimes the way with modern artists.
***Welcome Home*** (Dreyfus)

# Michel Pilz
BASS CLARINET
*born* 28 October 1945

What's happened to this gifted and unusual musician? He began working in Manfred Schoof's group as far back as 1968, and in the 70s he took an engaging role in the free-music scene of middle Europe, leading groups of his own as well as working with Schoof, Alex von Schlippenbach and Itaru Oki. In choosing to stick entirely to the bass clarinet, and playing it in an often melodic and shamelessly songful way, he was very much a school of one. But little has been heard from him in a long time.
***Carpathes*** (FMP)

# Courtney Pine
TENOR AND SOPRANO SAXOPHONES
*born* 18 March 1964

Pine dominated the so-called British jazz revival of the 80s, and he has continued to enjoy much limelight since as probably the most famous British jazz player under 50 (the under-40s he has just left behind). He took up the saxophone at 15, and although it's not clear whether he started in jazz or reggae bands, both played a strong part in his early musical undertakings. Eventually jazz took up more of his time, and he got some valuable experience working in some of John Stevens's informal groups, before himself forming the Abibi Jazz Arts collective, designed to increase interest in jazz among British black musicians. In 1985, rumblings around the London scene pushed him forward as the leading voice in the emerging new movement, and when he was signed to Antilles, an offshoot of the major label Island, and released his first record in 1986, the British media ate up the story about Pine as the charismatic new face of British jazz, a brilliant piece of marketing. Fortunately, Pine himself was able to back up the hype with his own playing, which had blossomed into a powerful and virtuosic saxophone voice; and it helped that he retained his interest in reggae and other popular forms, rather than following a Wynton Marsalis line towards any sort of jazz purism. He toured the US (*The Empire Strikes Back* was the headline in *The Village Voice*), played alongside young American masters including Kenny Kirkland and Jeff 'Tain' Watts, but decided against any permanent move to the US and remained based in London. For the rest of the 80s, he continued to build his reputation: he played cameos on pop records and was the British jazz representative at the huge Nelson Mandela birthday concert in 1987.

Since then, he has settled into a productive if sometimes nondescript round of touring and making occasional records. A series of albums for Antilles, and then various other branches of the Polygram empire, came to an end when he took the surprising line of releasing a disc under his own imprint, *Devotion* (Destin-E), in 2003; but his records had, for all their worldly outreach, taken on board a mass of black-music influences from reggae to hip-hop and back again, often hiding his saxophone-playing skills in convoluted and overstacked surroundings. In a curious way, Pine seems to have ended up as something of a loner: he rarely takes any kind of sideman role any more, has long since given up on his association with the Jazz Warriors enclave (Gary Crosby has assumed a much more patrician role than Pine), and his studio work, where he often ends up playing most of the tracks himself, effectively removes him from any

jazz dialogue. His concerts, though, remain exuberant affairs, even though it can seem a pity that such a powerful musician spends a lot of time with crowd-pleasing nonsense. The encouraging thing about *Devotion* was a renewed commitment to making his music about the black British experience: as his American audience has drifted away, his focus remains on his own kind of roots.
*Journey To The Urge Within* (Antilles)

## Armond Piron

VIOLIN
*born* 16 August 1888; *died* 17 February 1943

Piron represents a different sort of New Orleans music to that of many of his contemporaries. He was playing in the city from the beginning of the century, but his groups were more in the 'society' strain of music played for dinner dances and the like, and the records he made in New York during 1923–5, as Piron's New Orleans Orchestra and featuring Lorenzo Tio and others, suggest an outlook that had rather more to do with ragtime than jazz. He did, though, write a tune which has become an enduring part of the traditional repertoire, 'I Wish I Could Shimmy Like My Sister Kate', which was one of the several pieces published by the Piron & Williams Company, which he established with his sometime sideman, Clarence Williams. Piron latterly worked on riverboats.

## Bucky Pizzarelli

GUITAR
*born* 9 January 1926

Pizzarelli spent years in settings where jazz played only a modest role: he was an NBC staffer from 1954, and didn't have any high-profile gigs until he began working with Benny Goodman in 1966, which became a regular association. Since then he has been in demand for festival gigs and in touring small groups; he also sometimes plays in a family band with his sons John and Martin. Although he once wrote a tutorial called *Power Guitar*, Bucky's elegant style runs down from Charlie Christian and George Van Eps. He plays a seven-string guitar, which allows him to add his own bass line when he solos, and he turns up in many

mainstream groups of the kind much recorded by Concord and Arbors.
**Kenny Davern**, *Breezin' Along* (Arbors)

## John Pizzarelli

GUITAR, VOCAL
*born* 6 April 1960

Of all the cool new male vocalists who emerged in the 90s – in the wake of Harry Connick, though in this case that may be coincidental – John Pizzarelli may be the most talented. He originally preferred rock, and tried out on the trumpet, but eventually he went over to guitar and began playing in a duo with his father Bucky in the 80s. RCA signed him as a singing and playing solo act and he made a string of successful albums for them, although he has since relocated to the Telarc label. His trio (with brother Martin on bass and Ray Kennedy on piano) regularly turned up on TV and in a Broadway show, and the elegant Pizzarelli had the air of man-most-likely-to for much of the decade. While this brought him steady work, he hasn't quite hit stardom, but fortunately he has his talent to fall back on: a swinging guitarist in the manner of his father, but his singing tends to divide the house, although he taps into the Nat Cole vein more effectively than perhaps any other contemporary singer. Some of his originals are rather good, and Leiber and Stoller's 'Style Is Coming Back In Style' belongs absolutely to him.
*Dear Mr Cole* (RCA Novus)

## Lonnie Plaxico

BASS
*born* 4 September 1960

Plaxico played in hard-bop bands before joining Wynton Marsalis for a spell in 1982. The following year he joined Art Blakey's Jazz Messengers, but the activities of the M-Base group later in the decade were more to his liking, and he took up the electric bass to go with the acoustic instrument. Jack DeJohnette used him as bassist in Special Edition for some five years, but since 1993 Plaxico has freelanced or led bands of his own. He made some albums for Muse which were in a disappointingly lightweight pop-fusion vein, and a single set for Blue Note in

2001 didn't fare a great deal better. But the record cited, a recent set for the independent Sirocco, is better, getting closer to a personal idiom where funk and modal jazz make a convincing truce.
*Rhythm And Soul* (Sirocco)

# King Pleasure
VOCAL
*born* 24 March 1922; *died* 21 March 1981

Eddie Jefferson started vocalese, the trend for setting lyrics to instrumental solos, but King Pleasure made a hit out of the form when his 'Moody's Mood For Love' struck the charts in 1952. This came after he won a talent contest at the Apollo Theater in Harlem. Like many hitmakers, Pleasure didn't last long: he only mustered enough material for one ten-inch album on Prestige, although he later turned up again on a couple of obscure dates for HiFi and United Artists before drifting altogether from sight. But the Prestige tracks are terrific in their way: the problem with vocalese is that, once heard, it can be irritating to have the words lodged in the memory when listening back to the originals. Pleasure's real name was the slightly less impressive Clarence Beeks.
*King Pleasure Sings* (OJC/Prestige)

# Paul Plimley
PIANO
*born* 16 March 1953

Plimley's important contribution to Canada's free-jazz scene has received little wider appreciation, although that can be put down to that entire community having scant international recognition. He started playing free music in the 70s and co-founded NOW, the New Orchestra Workshop, in Vancouver in 1977, still a focal point for many Canadian improvisers. Plimley has twice spent periods of study with Cecil Taylor, and there is certainly something of Taylor in his playing, although he brings touches of oddball humour and even a circumspect sentimentality into a sweepingly inclusive piano style. The record cited is a solo recital, but he has often performed with Lisle Ellis, and once in a meeting with tabla player Trichy Sankaran, which is great fun.
*Everything In Stages* (Songlines)

# Pony Poindexter
ALTO SAXOPHONE, VOCAL
*born* 8 February 1926; *died* 14 April 1988

Norwood Eugene Poindexter played clarinet, alto and soprano in high school in New Orleans, and when his family moved to California he began playing in nightclubs. After army service he joined Billy Eckstine's big band, and then mostly led his own groups in the San Francisco area. Eventually, from 1964, he went to live in Europe, staying until the end of the 70s. While there he played in a lively if hardly profound bebop style, although his few European records are highly sought-after by collectors for their scarcity. He went back to the US in 1979, but illness curtailed his playing and he latterly appeared mostly as a singer.
*Pony's Express* (Epic)

# Ed Polcer
CORNET
*born* 10 February 1937

Polcer began playing Dixieland cornet in Condonite circles in New York in the 60s, although he was only a part-time musician. He eventually became co-owner of Condon's in 1979 and finally became a full-time musician during the following decade, working in Dixie-mainstream bands and leading groups of his own, sometimes touring with the likes of Kenny Davern. Bobby Hackett recommended him to Benny Goodman as a sideman in the 70s, and that says something about Polcer's amiable and melodious style.
*A Salute To Eddie Condon* (Nagel Heyer)

# Ben Pollack
DRUMS, BANDLEADER
*born* 22 June 1903; *died* 7 June 1971

'May it please you – Ben Pollack,' he says as a sign-off line at the end of many of his records from the 20s, and Pollack was always eager to please. Born in Chicago, he played with the New Orleans Rhythm Kings before leading his own dance band, which had many fine players – Benny Goodman, Jimmy McPartland, Jack Teagarden were just some of them – most of whom were disrespectful of Pollack's musical conservatism and effeminate singing. Pollack carried on as front man until 1934, but most of his band quit in 1934 over the leader's engagement of his girlfriend Doris as the band's singer, and Pollack had to regroup with a new and less effective line-up. Decca dropped him after 1938 and he then led small groups in California for a time, but worked more frequently as a restaurateur and an agent. He was still bandleading in the 60s, though, and being successful at it: but declining health, debts and, possibly, a bitterness at failing to get his due led him to take his own life in 1971.

*The Dean Of Swing* (ASV)


## Danny Polo
CLARINET
*born* 22 December 1901; *died* 11 July 1949

Polo had several years in Chicago jazz behind him when he went to Europe in 1927 with a band led by George Carhart. The group toured through the continent and Polo lived in Berlin and Paris before eventually settling in London in 1929. For the next ten years he was a pivotal figure in the London dance-band scene, playing with Ambrose and recording with Spike Hughes, Philip Lewis, Ray Noble and others, as well as making records under his own name with some of the best of the British hot players: Tommy McQuater was a great pal, and still remembers Polo as one of the best musicians he played with. Polo's elegant and almost cool playing breaks through on many British records of the period, but eventually he sailed home to New York, where he worked with Coleman Hawkins, Joe Sullivan and Jack Teagarden before joining Claude Thornhill in 1942, an environment where his playing must have seemed right at home. He was still with Thornhill when he suffered a heart attack in 1949.

**George Chisholm,** *Early Days* (Timeless)


## Herb Pomeroy
TRUMPET
*born* 15 April 1930

Pomeroy spent most of his working life in music education, and most of it has been in and around Boston. He played there with Charlie Parker in 1953 before a spell with Lionel Hampton's band, and in 1955 he

started teaching at Berklee. He led a big band which had a long residency at The Stables club, and he often led other orchestras at festival events, frequently with ex-students of his in the line-up; but Berklee was the mainstay of his working life, and he retired in 1995 after 40 years of dedicated service which helped make the college's jazz programme the educational powerhouse it is today. In consequence, his appearances on record are comparatively rare.

*Band In Boston* (United Artists)


## Valery Ponomarev
TRUMPET
*born* 20 January 1943

Russian jazz won an avant-garde profile in the 80s via Ganelin, Kuryokhin and others, but Ponomarev was a Muscovite hard bopper long before their appearance. He performed on what there was of the Soviet jazz circuit of the 60s and then defected in 1973, eventually joining Art Blakey's Jazz Messengers in 1977, though that was not a vintage period for the band. He then put together a band of his own, Universal Language, which has endured on and off since, with different line-ups. Ponomarev was probably perceived as something of a novelty item in pre-glasnost days, but all through his career on record he has played with a polished and inventive approach which might be undersung since there are so many other trumpeters doing the same.

*A Star For You* (Reservoir)


## Jean-Luc Ponty
VIOLIN
*born* 29 September 1942

Ponty remains a one-off in the music, and while he has set a fine example for anyone attempting to play the violin in a modern jazz setting, he has almost closed off the chapter too: it remains an instrument with little if any allegiance among mainstream modernists, and only avant-garde players have really sought fresh fields with it. Born in Avranches, his father a violin teacher, the young Ponty studied ferociously to become a concert player and went to the Paris Conservatoire, but jazz took his ear (although he first played the music on clarinet and tenor

sax), and by 1962 he was playing in a group with Jef Gilson. He made sensational appearances at the Antibes (1964) and Monterey (1967) festivals, building an audience on both sides of the Atlantic, and two years later he was recording with Frank Zappa (*King Kong*, an album which first came out on Pacific Jazz), and Ponty was experimenting with electric violin. He led a band of his own in Paris which leaned towards free playing, but then settled in the USA and, following in Jerry Goodman's steps, he played with Frank Zappa and in a new version of the Mahavishnu Orchestra. From 1975 he was a jazz-rock leader in his own right, recording a long sequence of albums for Atlantic, playing mostly an amplified and effects-treated violin, eventually switching to a five-string instrument which gave him a wider range. Ponty's fusion sometimes fell foul of the usual excesses of jazz-rock – absurdly fast solos, and material calculated to stun listeners rather than seduce them – but there was always a compensating sweetness at the core of much of his music, and his own playing married consummate technique with an inescapably romantic streak, no matter how disguised it might have been by electronic bombast. By the 90s he had begun to look towards the world-music aesthetic which he espoused on records such as *Tchokola* (1991): although the music occasionally sounds merely dinky, Ponty manages to communicate something deeper. Sometimes one regrets that the dashing virtuoso of his first records, where he played with the likes of Daniel Humair and Michel Portal, was long since lost to acoustic jazz, but Ponty has travelled his own way and made much enduring music as he has gone.
*Aurora* (Atlantic)

## Odean Pope
TENOR SAXOPHONE
*born* 24 October 1938

Pope went to Philadelphia as a child, and began learning saxophone there: Max Roach took him on briefly as a sideman in 1967, and it was an association which was renewed on and off down the years. In the 70s he was involved in various freebop situations, including the cooperative group Catalyst, and Saxophone Choir, which set

eight horn players alongside a rhythm section. Latterly he worked mostly with a trio, sometimes in a fusion flavour: *Almost Like Me* (Moers, 1990), though impossible to find on CD, is worth trying to locate. Pope's grand and rather slow-moving sound has felt somewhat out of step with the pace of jazz developments in recent times, and the records by his Saxophone Choir and other projects do feel as if they belong to a past chapter of the avant-garde.
*The Ponderer* (Soul Note)

## Lenny Popkin
ALTO SAXOPHONE
*born* 30 May 1941

Popkin is, along with Richard Tabnik, the last of the Tristano-ite saxophonists. He began studying with Lennie Tristano around 1967, and worked on gigs both with Tristano himself and with Sal Mosca. Since the 70s he has been closely associated with Connie Crothers, and most of his playing on record has been in her company. It is lonely work: they are keepers of a flame which has all but died out in the rest of the jazz business, and their label, New Artists, is scarcely known to any but hardcore followers of this strain of the post-bop vocabulary. Inevitably, Popkin has affinities with such previous Tristano-men as Lee Konitz and Warne Marsh, but his dedication to the principles espoused by his teacher seems unswerving, and some stringently powerful music has resulted.
*Jazz Spring* (New Artists)

## Al Porcino
TRUMPET
*born* 14 May 1925

Porcino's huge list of sideman credits typifies a can-do generation of mobile and unpretentious jazz players. He started performing in big bands around 1943, and worked with everyone from Tommy Dorsey and Stan Kenton to Charlie Parker and Chubby Jackson during 1945–55. He went over to Los Angeles after that, and did big-band work with Terry Gibbs as well as countless studio pop and orchestral dates. In the later 60s and 70s he was back East, and playing with the Jones–Lewis Orchestra and others, even leading his own big band for a spell. In the 80s he was in Europe, still running big bands and celebrating his 70th birthday in Munich with a gathering of old musical friends.

**Terry Gibbs,** *The Exciting Big Band Of Terry Gibbs* (Verve)

## Michel Portal
CLARINET, SAXOPHONES
*born* 27 November 1935

Much of Portal's early experience in performing was entirely outside jazz. He studied at the Paris Conservatoire in the 50s and became a proficient exponent of the works of contemporary composers, specializing in clarinet, as well as playing with light-music orchestras. He seems to have somehow found his way into jazz, in part via performing some of André Hodeir's music, and that led him in the somewhat unlikely direction of free jazz: by the end of the 60s he was playing with Sunny Murray, Anthony Braxton and John Surman. Since then he has appeared and worked with a very broad spectrum of players, including Martial Solal, Jack DeJohnette and a musician whom he once taught, Louis Sclavis. On record, Portal's music has touched a bewildering variety of bases: his work for the Label Bleu label has been detailed and absorbing, but some recent CDs for Universal, where he plays with such unlikely bedfellows as Vernon Reid and Tony Hymas, have been close to disastrous.

***Arrivederci Le Chouartse*** (hatOLOGY)

## Art Porter
ALTO AND SOPRANO SAXOPHONES
*born* 3 August 1961; *died* 23 November 1996

Porter came from Little Rock, Arkansas – his dad was a local jazz pianist – and he toured under various leaders in the 80s, spending some time working in Chicago with Jodie Christian and others. He came to prominence, though, in the early 90s, when Verve signed him as a prototype smooth-jazz saxophonist of a more incisive and creative bent than most in the genre: while his records were produced by Jeff Lorber to appeal to the appropriate radio format, Porter's own playing was often hot, abrasive and power-packed, much closer to David

Sanborn than Gerald Albright. He was drowned in a boating accident while visiting a festival in Bangkok.

***Pocket City*** (Verve Forecast)

## Chris Potter
SAXOPHONES, BASS CLARINET
*born* 1 January 1971

Potter was a prodigy: he moved to New York (from school in South Carolina) at 18, and was working with Red Rodney's group while studying in Manhattan. By the time of his first record, *Introducing Chris Potter* (1993), he was already a seasoned pro and an in-demand sideman. The sheer verve and clean-limbed spirit of his early records is a tonic, and it was in a sense surprising that Potter served a long apprenticeship at independent labels – two records for Criss Cross and six for Concord – before eventually signing to Verve in 2000. When the Paul Motian Electric Bebop Band played a London residency in 1992, Potter and Joshua Redman were together in the group for a single night, and it was Chris who clearly got the better of the exchanges. He has already recorded so prolifically as a sideman that he's in danger of becoming too familiar: no great original, but a superbly confident and resourceful executant. While he is primarily a tenorman, he likes to bring at least a couple of other horns on to a date. His Verve sessions to date have had their doleful side as well as the expected quota of top playing: hopefully he won't be overcome by a case of existential saxophone angst.

***Vertigo*** (Concord)

## Tommy Potter
BASS
*born* 21 September 1918; *died* 15 March 1988

Bassists were mostly on the witness stand during the bebop era, given an unglamorous role compared with the drummer, asked to provide strong and steady though unobtrusive pulses, and scarcely ever called upon to take a solo of any sort. As far as records were concerned, they suffered further: the poor conditions which many of the bebop masterpieces were set down in usually gave the bassist the worst sound of all. Tommy Potter worked imperturbably through all of this.

He was in the Billy Eckstine big band of 1944–5, where he met Parker and Gillespie, and was in Parker's quintet between 1947 and 1950, as well as taking part in numerous other record dates of the period. He continued to be busy all through the 50s and early 60s, also playing with such diverse figures as Harry Edison and Artie Shaw, and by the end of the 60s he was out of music full time and worked mainly in hospitals. Listen closely to many of the great Parker records: there he is, on time, doing the right thing.

**Charlie Parker,** *The Complete Savoy And Dial Studio Recordings* (Savoy)

# Bud Powell
PIANO
*born* 27 September 1924; *died* 1 August 1966

A mental case who suffered numerous nervous collapses, who behaved irrationally on an almost continuous basis, and who abused himself further with heroin use and heavy drinking, Powell was also one of the masters of the bebop idiom, even if his music seems to balance precariously between executive brilliance and a capitulation to a kind of narcotic delirium – almost a manifestation of bop's state of jangled nerves. He was part of the inner circle at Minton's Playhouse in the early 40s, where Thelonious Monk kept an eye on his progress, and he began playing in Cootie Williams's orchestra in 1943. But things started to go awry for him as early as 1945, when he was hospitalized supposedly following a racial beating, and though he quickly returned to the 52nd Street scene, recurrent problems led to him having ECT later in the decade. While he didn't take part in any of the early major bebop record dates, his own first records as a leader in 1947 unveiled his early style brilliantly, showing the influence of such earlier masters as Nat Cole and Teddy Wilson, but with a careering right hand which, as many commentators have suggested, was the pianistic equivalent of Charlie Parker's explosive lines. His almost brittle delivery underscored the piano's existence as a percussion instrument, and the role of his left hand – sparsely marking out chords which blipped into unexpected spaces, dissonant and startling even if one follows that hand rather than the right – quickly became standard

practice for bebop piano, even though none really approached Powell's momentous personification of the style. Alfred Lion recorded him for Blue Note later in the decade with a band including Fats Navarro and Sonny Rollins, and 'Ornithology' is a beautiful instance of Powell in his prime. But there was a two-year gap before his next session for Blue Note. His behaviour became increasingly strange, and even Parker, hardly the epitome of good sense when it came to personal conduct, didn't want him in his band. Lion set up another date for Blue Note in 1951, and it didn't start auspiciously: Powell tried to kill Lion's cat, disappeared for 90 minutes just as they were about to start playing, and then rushed headlong through the date. His 50s work for Blue Note included some astonishing work, such as 'Un Poco Loco' and 'The Glass Enclosure', yet even by 1953 his playing had begun to decline, marked by misfingerings and dead ends. Even a below-par Powell was worth hearing and he made some further records for RCA and Roulette later in the decade, but by 1959 he was in a very fragile state and went to live in Paris for five years, a celebrity away from home, and while his life was settled to some extent, his musical powers continued to diminish rather than recover. As with Lester Young, who, like Powell, was in part used as the basis for the Dale Turner character in Bertrand Tavernier's *Round Midnight*, Powell's playing became careful and self-conscious, and although many public and private recordings have survived from his Paris years, the best moments are often hidden or spoiled. He went back to America in 1964 on the promise of work, but was already suffering from tuberculosis and cirrhosis, and though he was supposed to return to Paris he never did: after a hopeless final Carnegie Hall concert in 1965, he died from his TB condition in 1966.

*The Amazing Bud Powell* (Blue Note)

# Mel Powell
PIANO
*born* 12 February 1923; *died* 24 April 1998

Powell worked under his original name of Melvin Epstein on the New York circuit of the late 30s, and became Mel Powell when he joined Benny Goodman's sextet in 1941. On being drafted, he went to Europe and played with Glenn Miller and others, but he was back with Goodman in 1945. His great technique and scintillating touch had something of Art Tatum about them, and Powell's playing seemed to delight the hard to please Goodman. But he went into a period of classical study, with Paul Hindemith and others, which eventually took him away from jazz altogether. There were some 1953–4 sessions for Vanguard, part of the new mainstream which came into focus at that point, where Powell led some impeccable groups in this 'new' style, but then he went into composition and was only rarely sighted in jazz thereafter, making a brief appearance on a jazz cruise in 1986 and a final date for Chiaroscuro a year later.

*Borderline/Thigamagig* (Vanguard)

## Seldon Powell

TENOR SAXOPHONE AND FLUTE
*born* 15 November 1928; *died* 25 January 1997

A doughty sessionman, Powell had a terrific sound on tenor and it's too bad that he didn't have more opportunities as a featured player. He studied classical music early on and went to Juilliard after his military service in 1953, but he had already established himself as a pro player and he began turning up on many record dates from the mid-50s onwards. Much of the 60s was spent doing TV work, and thereafter he played on soul records and in very occasional feature roles: Gerry Mulligan hired him to take the tenor solos for his JVC Festival band in 1987. He made only two albums under his own name, for Roost in 1956, which are hardly known even to collectors, but they would make a splendid reissue.

*Seldon Powell Plays* (Roost)

## Specs Powell

DRUMS
*born* 5 June 1922

Gordon Powell was one of the great group of New York drummers who swung the music during the 30s and 40s. Although he started out on piano, he played drums with Edgar Hayes, and besides work with other bandleaders he had a steady job as a studio man with CBS from 1943. Erroll Garner used him on some of his 50s dates, although thereafter he was sighted less frequently on record. Specs made one delightful session as a leader for Roulette, *Movin' In* (1957), where the cover showed the bespectacled drummer perched with his feet up in a removal van. So far, it's never been reissued.

*Movin' In* (Roulette)

## Chano Pozo

PERCUSSION
*born* 7 January 1915; *died* 2 December 1948

Pozo was in jazz for a few weeks. He was a Cuban who had somehow found his way to New York in 1947, where he played a Carnegie Hall concert in September which featured him alongside Dizzy Gillespie's orchestra, unveiling the new idea of Afro-Cuban jazz. There were record dates with Gillespie ahead, which saw him featured on the likes of George Russell's 'Cubano Be – Cubano Bop'. But Pozo was a desperate character, who had already had run-ins with hoodlums in Havana and New York, and he was murdered in a Harlem bar one night in 1948. Nobody is sure whether it was over drugs, money, a simple argument, or whatever.

*Dizzy Gillespie, **The Complete RCA Victor Recordings** (Bluebird)*

## Gerard Presencer

TRUMPET
*born* 12 September 1972

Presencer came through the ranks of the NYJO – at 11, he was one of their youngest-ever performers – and at weekends played in a pub residency run by his jazz-mad father. His very first recording, a Barcelona club date with Tete Montoliu and Peter King released by Fresh Sounds, shows how amazingly confident and accomplished he was at 15. Like many prodigies, he has sometimes struggled since to find his best context. Charlie Watts has hired him for several of his touring groups, he played the soundalike trumpet solo on Us3's worldwide 'Cantaloop' hit in 1992, and he has since dabbled in various projects on record which mix fusion with more straight-ahead playing. However, education looks to be his principal activity for the foreseeable future, since he holds

significant teaching posts at both the Royal Academy in London and the Berlin Hochschule. The sheer dazzle of his playing can be thrilling, and a well-resourced record label will surely get something exceptional out of him eventually.
*Platypus* (Linn)

## Preservation Hall

'Preserving' the jazz past has been a trend in the music for at least 60 years. It became almost an obsession for some of those who drifted around the edges of the New Orleans musical community. One of them was Larry Borenstein (1919–81), an art and curio dealer who also dabbled in real estate, and who regarded New Orleans jazz as a folk art akin to the paintings he bought and sold. He began turning his art store on St Peter Street into a performance space around 1955, and it eventually grew into such a regular business that Borenstein opened an adjacent building entirely for these performances, which was christened Preservation Hall in 1961. Under the management of Allan and Sandra Jaffe, it became perhaps the most important venue for the music in the city, and a Preservation Hall Jazz Band was established as a sort of house band, a group which eventually (from 1963) undertook tours of the US and elsewhere – Kid Thomas Valentine even led a State Department tour to the Soviet Union in 1979. Leaders of the groups at different times included Valentine, Percy Humphrey and Kid Sheik Cola, and many of the great surviving main-stays of the local music performed either in the PHJB or at the Hall itself. By the end of the century most of the old-timers had gone, and the PHJB now included Europeans (Lars Edegran, Orange Kellin) and 'modern' New Orleans men (Michael White, Wendell Brunious) among their number. But the institution endures, still carefully preserved.

## Prestige
RECORD COMPANY

Bob Weinstock founded the label in 1949, and was quick to begin recording many of the most progressive musicians of the day: early signings included Gene Ammons, Sonny Stitt, Sonny Rollins, Stan Getz and Wardell Gray, and as the 50s progressed, he added Miles Davis, Thelonious Monk, John Coltrane and many others to the roster. Rudy Van Gelder did many of the recording dates as engineer, just as he did for Blue Note. Like most of the independent labels, Weinstock was strapped for cash much of the time, and when a major made someone an offer he was never able to hang on to his artists, as happened with Davis and Coltrane. But the Prestige catalogue of the 50s bulged with masterpieces, with some of the best of Rollins, Davis and the Modern Jazz Quartet. A celebrated remark – 'the difference between Prestige and Blue Note is two days of rehearsal time' – sums up the perceived departure point between the two principal jazz independents, but Weinstock was as shrewd as Lion and Wolff and he was able to expand further in the 60s: three new imprints, Swingsville (mainstream), Bluesville (blues) and Moodsville (broadly, jazz for around midnight), expanded the catalogue further, and Weinstock jumped on the trend for soul-jazz, building what was easily the leading representation of the genre – only Jimmy Smith escaped him. Other musicians such as Gene Ammons recorded throughout the label's lifetime. Eventually, though, Weinstock sold up, and the label was passed on to Fantasy in 1971, which was at least another independent. And, unlike Lion and Richard Bock, Weinstock got decent money.

## André Previn
PIANO
*born* 6 April 1929

Previn's jazz work may only be a small part of his CV these days, but for a long time he could have been numbered among the most popular jazz pianists in America. When he went to the US in 1943 he soon found him-self in demand as both pianist and arranger, and in 1947 some sessions for RCA brought him considerable success. His Contemporary albums of the late 50s found him addressing either individual show-scores (a fad begun by the hugely successful *Modern Jazz Performance Of Songs From My Fair Lady*, 1957) or Broadway composers, and with the likes of Shelly Manne and Red Mitchell in support they're a beguiling sequence of records, Previn's early Tatum influence slightly displaced by his interest in bebop piano. He moved over to Columbia in 1960 and recorded a further 13 albums, but these were more in an easy-listening vein and Previn's classical vocation was by this time taking precedence. In the 90s he began making the occasional trio record again. More than a dilettante, less than indispensable, Previn the jazzman is perhaps best heard as an interesting diversion.

*Pal Joey* (Contemporary/OJC)

# Bobby Previte
DRUMS
*born* 16 July 1957

Previte arrived in New York in 1980, where his skills soon got him into the swing of the city's jazz–new music fringe. It was a fertile time for brainy crossovers, and Previte was closely involved with the likes of John Zorn, Wayne Horvitz, the New York Composers' Orchestra and Tim Berne. Since then, he has led various bands of his own: Empty Suits (acoustic–electric fusion), Weather Clear, Track Fast (straight-ahead), Latin For Travelers (improvising rock bar-band), The Horse (post-Miles fusion). He does most of the writing for these groups himself, and he also gets plenty of commissions: from the Moscow State Circus and the International Puppet Festival, to name two improbable associations. The diminutive Previte likes to have fun when he plays, and though there are occasional hints of the fatalism which afflicts a lot of New York's Downtown music, the energy and high spirits of the leader's playing usually carry things over such troughs. Perhaps the only pity is that these groups don't stay together and get documented for long enough to create a substantial impression.

*Weather Clear, Track Fast* (Enja)

# Eddie Prévost
DRUMS
*born* 22 June 1942

'The Art Blakey of Brixton', as he was known for a time, has concentrated most of his playing career on the AMM ensemble, but away from that he has played free jazz and improvisation with a number of other groups, including Supersession and Resoundings,

and he has also worked in duos with Evan Parker and Marilyn Crispell. An acute commentator on musical culture as well as a drummer with an idiosyncratic and impeccably responsive outlook; much of his work has been documented on his own CD label, Matchless.

**With Evan Parker,** *Most Materiall* (Matchless)

# Sammy Price
PIANO, VOCAL
*born* 6 October 1908; *died* 14 April 1992

Price started out as a dancer, working on the Texas vaudeville circuit of the 20s, and he then began leading his own bands, making his first record in 1929 (a single title for Brunswick). He moved through various cities before taking a job for Decca in New York in 1937, where his task was to accompany their blues performers; and his own Price's Texas Blusicians began recording three years later, making lively jump and boogie music, the sidemen including Lester Young, Shad Collins and Emmett Berry. During the 40s he mostly worked as a solo in New York clubs, making records for Mezz Mezzrow's King Jazz label for a time, and he went to France to appear in the celebrated Nice Jazz Festival of 1948. He spent the early 50s in Dallas, where he ran nightclubs, but went back to New York and thenceforth based himself there. From the 60s onwards he was a frequent visitor to Europe, and later on he made some lovely duet records with Doc Cheatham. Little of Price's playing was truly individual or outstanding, but he became a great survivor whose mix of blues and swing playing set out its own modest place in the music's history, which in the end he was involved in for most of the way.

**With Doc Cheatham,** *Black Beauty* (Sackville)

# Julian Priester
TROMBONE
*born* 29 June 1935

Priester has found himself in a very broad range of playing situations, but at heart he is a bop slideman with an unpretentious outlook. He grew up in Chicago and played blues with Muddy Waters before joining Sun Ra's band for three years. In 1956 he joined Lionel Hampton and toured with him, and

then worked in Dinah Washington's accompanying band (he left after she started making advances). For much of the 60s he freelanced on hard-bop record dates and in theatre orchestras, making a single date of his own for Jazzland (*Spiritsville*, 1958), and another for Riverside (*Keep Swingin'*, 1960); after six months with Duke Ellington he joined Herbie Hancock's sextet in 1970, staying three years. Hancock eventually cut down the group ('he decided to play a more commercial variety of jazz'), and Priester moved to San Francisco. He made two records for ECM, *Polarization* and *Love, Love*, which used electronics, and later settled in Seattle, where he works on the faculty at Cornish College and plays with some of his graduates in a small group.
**Keep Swingin'** (Riverside/OJC)

## Brian Priestley

PIANO
*born* 10 July 1946

Priestley's a Mancunian by birth, and his cultured tones were familiar to London listeners for many years in the 70s and 80s as the presenter of one of the best jazz radio series, *All That Jazz*, and he has also been a regular and perspicacious commentator on the music in print. Away from all that, Priestley plays his own learned kind of swing-to-bop piano and is a great scholar of Duke Ellington's music, having transcribed many of the composer's pieces for performance.
**Who Knows** (33 Records)

## Louis Prima

VOCAL, TRUMPET
*born* 7 December 1911; *died* 24 August 1978

Prima is one of the great jazz funsters. He grew up in New Orleans (his brother Leon was a good trumpeter) and worked in Chicago and Cleveland before moving to New York in 1935, where he held down a residency at the Famous Door club and began making a long sequence of records for Decca, which started out with genuine New Orleans sidemen such as George Brunies and Sidney Arodin and hot jazz performances but eventually became little more than a framework for Prima's goofy vocals

and blustery trumpet. Prima became a big hit on radio but decamped for Hollywood, where he turned up in movies and mugged his way through 15 more years of regular work and record-making. In the 50s he began a new kind of act, which featured his wife, Keely Smith, and traded on the new taste for rock'n'roll, and it helped get him into Las Vegas. His trumpet style was akin to an over-the-top Louis Armstrong, but he never entirely put the horn in its case and even in his Vegas years he still played. Modern audiences will know him best, though, as the voice of King Louie in Disney's cartoon version of *The Jungle Book*.
**The Wildest!** (Capitol)

## Russell Procope

CLARINET, ALTO SAXOPHONE
*born* 11 August 1908; *died* 21 January 1981

Procope had an entirely unremarkable career before he joined Duke Ellington. He was a schoolmate of Benny Carter's and he played on some of Jelly Roll Morton's Victor sides before he duly joined Carter's band in 1929, thereafter moving over to Chick Webb's orchestra. In the 30s he was with Fletcher Henderson, Willie Bryant and others, and in 1938 he joined John Kirby's small group, where he became well-enough known, although here his playing was more notable for its neutral qualities than anything and didn't upset Kirby's careful designs. In 1946, he filled in for the absent Otto Hardwick in Ellington's band, and remained there until Duke's death. As with so many others, Ellington brought out the very best in his capable if reserved sectionman, and Procope's easeful alto and ripplingly bluesy clarinet were home at last. He always spoke highly of his boss, and after Ellington's passing he led a tribute group called Ellingtonia.
**Duke Ellington, *Masterpieces*** (Columbia)

## Progressive jazz

It might sound modern, but progressive jazz really belongs to a distant past these days. Stan Kenton liked the term, and he applied it to his big band of the late 40s, as he tried to take listeners and musicians alike on an 'adventure in modern music'. A few other leaders of the time seemed to be going in the same direction, particularly Boyd Raeburn, who came up with one of the great tune titles in 'Boyd Meets Stravinsky' (1946). The third-stream movement of the late 50s might also have been called progressive, since that harboured similar inclinations to confer the legitimacy of 'straight' music on disreputable jazz; instead, it was called third stream. Nothing much since has been referred to as progressive jazz, as if the innate snobbery of the term is too obvious to need stating. Progressive rock, though, suggested the wisdom of the old homily about those not knowing their history being doomed to repeat it.

## Pseudonyms

Jazz musicians have often hidden their real identities on record dates behind a pseudonym, usually for the purposes of evading a contractual obligation of some sort. This kind of thing has been going on since the beginning of jazz on record. The English ragtime banjo player Olly Oakley, for instance, was listed on labels as Fred Turner, Signor Cetra, Jack Sherwood, Mr F Curtis, Frank Forrester and Tim Holes (and even then Oakley's real name was Joseph Sharpe!). In the 20s, prolific studio musicians such as Red Nichols and Harry Reser disguised their bands under a multitude of alternative titles. Sometimes it was more a matter of sheer carelessness: Jelly Roll Morton was labelled as Jelly Roll Marton on his very first record. For their single coupling on Brunswick (as opposed to the rest of the series on OKeh), Louis Armstrong's Hot Five were listed as Lil's Hot Shots; and guitarist Eddie Lang, who was white, was disguised as Blind Willie Dunn for his duets with Lonnie Johnson, who was black.

By the 40s, pseudonyms had become more knowing. Charlie Chan turned out to be Charlie Parker, and nobody was fooled. Sometimes a bit of tomfoolery was deliberately disguised: a kitsch Woody Herman recording of 'Oh Gee, Say Gee, You Oughta See My Gee-Gee From The Fiji Isle' was credited to Chuck Thomas & His Dixieland Band. The hard boppers also joined in the fun. Cannonball Adderley disguised himself as Buckshot La Funke on a Louis Smith date for Blue Note, a name which Branford

Marsalis revived many years later for a band name of his own. Tony Scott didn't want his presence advertised on a Milt Hinton session, so he called himself A J Sciacca – which happened to be his real name. The Art Salt who played on Shorty Rogers's *Cool And Crazy* turned out to be Art Pepper, and there is an example of an entire album named after a pseudonym: Billy Strayhorn's *Cue For Saxophone*, which was named after the principal soloist Cue Porter, aka Johnny Hodges.

These days a simple escape clause along the lines of 'Mr X appears by kind permission of Label Y' takes care of contractual difficulties, so pseudonyms are no longer what they were. But occasionally something crops up: it's strange how the mysterious trumpeter E Dankworth, who appeared on the debut album by Marcus Roberts, sounds just like Wynton Marsalis.

## Tito Puente

PERCUSSION, BANDLEADER
*born* 20 April 1923; *died* 31 May 2000

Puente is another musician whose standing in Latin music has sometimes crossed him over into the jazz sector. He was born in New York and was raised in Spanish Harlem, playing in bands led by Machito and others, and after naval service and a period of study at Juilliard he went on to form his own group and became one of the principal leaders of Afro-Cuban music for dancing in the city. This lasted until the end of the 60s: Puente made scores of records, but there were really only a handful that had much in the way of jazz input, including one with Woody Herman, *Herman's Heat And Puente's Beat* (1958). He came back to full strength after a period of decline when the salsa boom of the 80s took hold, and from there he was again very popular until his death, latterly leading a group which came to be called the Latin Jazz Ensemble, with guest soloists such as Phil Woods. Even then, the jazz content was slight enough.
*Un Poco Loco* (Concord)

# Dudu Pukwana
ALTO SAXOPHONE
*born* 18 July 1938; *died* 30 June 1990

Born in Port Elizabeth, Pukwana played piano before he took up the alto, and he led a band of his own, the Jazz Giants, before joining Chris McGregor's Blue Notes in 1963. He joined their exodus from South Africa and worked in Europe before settling in London in 1965. Besides continuing his association with McGregor, he led his own bands Spear, Assagai and Zila, and anyone who was part of the audience on the London jazz scene of the 70s in particular will remember these groups with affection: Pukwana brought an authentic touch of South African passion and sunshine to what was then an often drab and insular community, and he could enliven and enrapture the most routine pub gig and its audience. Dudu also recorded with such fellow expatriates as Johnny Dyani, as well as with free players, including Han Bennink and Misha Mengelberg, and was always an explosive and exciting freebop stylist; but the records under his own name are rather disappointing, and with hindsight it seems tragic that so little of his music was really documented in its best and most vibrant colours. His sudden death in 1990 left his adopted community grieving at his abrupt departure.

**Johnny Dyani,** *Witchdoctor's Son* (Steeplechase)

# Don Pullen
PIANO
*born* 25 December 1941; *died* 22 April 1995

Pullen was a strange pianist. Listeners can be left gasping at his virtuosity: only Cecil Taylor, who is always cited as either influence or direct musical kin when Pullen is discussed, played more notes and got more unquenchable velocity out of the keyboard. Yet Pullen's background was in gospel and R&B settings, he liked to play organ in soul-jazz bands, and he preferred boppish rhythm sections rather than the kind of polyrhythmic onrush which Taylor has long favoured as his accompaniment. Many of his records come on like a stylistic collision. He studied medicine in Charlotte, NC, but preferred music, and was soon (1964) playing in the free vanguard with the likes of

Giuseppi Logan. Most of his work, though, was with soul bands, and he even accompanied Nina Simone for a spell, before joining Charles Mingus's group in 1973. Two years later he went out on his own as a leader, and in 1979 formed a long-standing partnership with another ex-Mingusian, George Adams, in a quartet which lasted until 1988. After this he recorded as soloist and trio leader for Blue Note, but eventually he was overcome by cancer. Pullen's huge, swarming style at the piano asked for particularly sympathetic sidemen, and *Random Thoughts* (1990), for instance, seems to find him held back by the able yet curiously inappropriate playing of James Genus and Lewis Nash. His right hand, endlessly ripping out glisses and clusters from the keyboard, is what ties him to Taylor, but unlike Cecil, Pullen was content with exploring what he could do with relatively simple cells of harmony and rhythm. His solo performances, where he could play unfettered, catch the essence of a generous and thoughtful spirit.

**Evidence Of Things Unseen** (Black Saint)

# Bernard Purdie
DRUMS
*born* 11 June 1939

'Pretty' Purdie (the nickname comes from his surname) played with both Louis Armstrong and Dizzy Gillespie in his time, but jazz is not really what he does. He moved to New York in 1960 and immediately began working in R&B and soul groups, backing James Brown and King Curtis and eventually acting as MD for Aretha Franklin during the early 70s. His volume of activity in the studio almost inevitably meant that he played with jazz musicians at various points, but a record such as *Soul Is . . . Pretty Purdie* (Flying Dutchman, 1972) points up that a kind of soul-jazz-rock was about as close as he was going to get to leading a genuine jazz album. In the 80s he was often in company with Hank Crawford and in the 90s he sometimes played drums for Jack McDuff.

**Hank Crawford,** *Roadhouse Symphony* (Milestone)

# Flora Purim
VOCAL
*born* 6 March 1942

The Brazilian singer began working with Airto Moreira in the middle 60s; they later married, but by then she had moved to first Los Angeles and then New York, where she sang in one of Stan Getz's Latin groups. Her breakthrough came as a member of Chick Corea's Return To Forever in 1971, where her wispily light and airy singing – a lot more musical, at least, than Astrud Gilberto's – helped cross the group over towards a more popular audience. In the later part of the 70s she worked as a solo, with records such as *Open Your Eyes You Can Fly* (1976) making a soft truce between a confected studio pop and Latin music, but when this direction dried up she began working with Airto again and they have, for the past 20 years, worked as a sort of Latin family act, touring and performing for club audiences around the world.

**Return To Forever, *Light As A Feather*** (Polydor)

# Jack Purvis
TRUMPET
*born* 11 December 1906; *died* 30 March 1962

Jazz seems to have been something of a lark for Purvis. He played in dance bands in Kentucky and managed to perform in Europe during 1928, then joined Hal Kemp's band in New York a year later. Somehow he managed to get OKeh to sponsor three record dates of his own in the same period: at the first he played what were labelled as 'trumpet solos', one of them called 'Copyin' Louis', although it is actually the other side, 'Mental Strain At Dawn', which sounds like an Armstrong pastiche, and perhaps the tracks were labelled the wrong way round. The second dates found him in the incredible company of Coleman Hawkins, J C Higginbotham and Adrian Rollini, although Purvis's own playing suggests he was no slouch. He did studio work in California and worked in other bands in New York, but his life was always a mystery and music had to take its place beside other, possibly nefarious, activities: gun-running, smuggling and fighting as a mercenary were some of his alleged interests, and he was later reported as playing in a prison band, which would

add up. Not much is known of his later activity, but it seems he may have taken his own life in 1962.

**With Louis Armstrong, *Satchmo Style*** (Parlophone)

# Ike Quebec
TENOR SAXOPHONE
*born* 17 August 1918; *died* 16 January 1963

Quebec had a beautiful timbre – a heavy-rolling sound that could beseech or confront, and it was timeless enough for him to be able to play in a 40s swing combo or a 60s samba setting and make both sound right for him. He started out as a pianist, switched to the tenor sax in 1940 and played in a band called The Barons Of Rhythm in New Jersey before freelancing on the New York scene. Cab Calloway gave him a job in 1944 and he stayed seven years, but at the same time he was recording for Blue Note as a small-band leader (the 'swingtet'). He became close with Alfred Lion, Blue Note's boss, and gave him some tips on people to record: it is likely that he pointed Lion in the direction of Thelonious Monk, for one. After leaving Calloway he had a relatively quiet time of it, but in 1959 he went back to Blue Note as an A&R man, recommending Dexter Gordon and others, and he made some more records for the label. The masterpiece is the ballad collection *Blue And Sentimental* (1961): despite a preponderance of slow tempos, Quebec plays with magisterial intensity and makes the record into a monument. Not too long afterwards he had to stop playing, and he died of lung cancer in 1963.

***Blue And Sentimental*** (Blue Note)

# Alvin Queen
DRUMS
*born* 16 August 1950

Queen worked busily in American jazz from around 1970: he toured with Charles Tolliver's group, and played gospel music and as a freelance with Pharoah Sanders and others. In 1979, he moved to Europe and settled in Geneva, where he established his own label, Nilva, and plays with other expatriates and locals, as well as such visitors as John Patton and Bennie Wallace.

Although Nilva seems to have gone quiet of late, he continued to be a presence in middle Europe during the 90s, playing in a forceful swing-to-bop style which has tied in neatly with his working opportunities.
*Glidin' And Stridin'* (Nilva)

## Gene Quill
ALTO SAXOPHONE
*born* 15 December 1927; *died* 8 December 1988

Quill was really a section-man: he grew up in New Jersey and he played in many of the bands that worked in and around Atlantic City, including those of Claude Thornhill and Gene Krupa, and he is on many studio dates playing either dance or swing music in the 50s. But he remains best-known for an occasional partnership on record with Phil Woods: both played a fierce kind of bebop which came in on a direct route from Charlie Parker, and records such as *Phil Talks With Quill* (Epic, 1959) and *Phil And Quill* (Prestige, 1957) featured the kind of sparring which was commonplace on many of the studio dates of the time. After 1960 Quill never got any further featured roles, and illness eventually cut short his career as a sessionman.
*Phil And Quill* (Prestige)

## Paul Quinichette
TENOR SAXOPHONE
*born* 17 May 1916; *died* 25 May 1983

Quinichette was saddled with the nickname Vice-Pres because of the similarity of his sound to Lester Young's, and it didn't really do him any favours (even though he had informally studied with Young in the early 30s). He grew up in Denver and played with local bands before going to New York around 1946. A spell with Count Basie (1951–3) brought him to wider notice and he recorded some sessions for Emarcy which were successful enough to encourage him to go solo. But he never really broke through to the front ranks after that; stylistically a little adrift from his times, he was really a swing man rather than any kind of hard bopper, and his Basie association never went away (three of his 50s dates were titled *For Basie, Basie Reunion* and *Like Basie*). One unexpected encounter was a blowing date with John

Coltrane in 1957, which surprisingly turned out very well. Quinichette left music altogether in the 60s, and though he began playing again in the 70s, poor health eventually sidelined his career.
*Cattin' With Coltrane And Quinichette* (OJC/ Prestige)

## John Rae
DRUMS
*born* 8 June 1966

Rae is the son of bassist Ronnie, himself a significant force in British jazz for many years in the trad-to-mainstream field. The drummer has been recording since his debut (at 16) with Tommy Smith, and his groups the John Rae Collective and the folk-jazz fusion Celtic Feet are powerful contributors to the new Scottish scene of today. A natural leader with a busy but powerfully inventive style, Rae is something of a binding force among many of the leading Scottish players. His brother and four sisters are also musicians.
*Celtic Feet* (Caber)

## Boyd Raeburn
BANDLEADER, SAXOPHONES
*born* 27 October 1913; *died* 2 August 1966

Raeburn's music has been entirely neglected by modern audiences, even though he might stand in the same wings as Stan Kenton and Claude Thornhill, as a baron of mood-music leaning towards jazz – sometimes spectacularly so. He led nondescript dance bands in the 30s, but changed direction in the early 40s, when he took on a succession of arrangers – George Finckel, George Handy and Johnny Richards – who revolutionized the band's book and introduced some very challenging scores. Sidemen such as Sonny Berman, Hal McKusick and Dodo Marmarosa came in, and singer Ginnie Powell was one of the best band vocalists of the day. There are some daft but intriguing titles in the band's sessions for Savoy and elsewhere, including 'Dalvatore Sally' and the immortal 'Boyd Meets Stravinsky', and Raeburn can claim the distinction of cutting the first version of 'A Night In Tunisia'. But the public didn't go for this stuff, and by the end of the decade

Raeburn's best men had moved on; and since he had no talent for arranging or composing himself (bizarrely, he took up the bass saxophone as his main instrument around 1946), he went back to dance-band work, and was out of music altogether by the end of the 50s.

**Boyd Meets Stravinsky** (Savoy)

# Ragtime

'Ragged time' was the original description of the way 19th-century instrumentalists would syncopate the rhythms in a popular tune: on a piano, the melody line would receive this kind of treatment with the right hand, while the left usually conducted a simple and regular bass pattern. This became known as 'ragging' a tune, and the pieces themselves became 'rags'. Ragtime was developed mostly as a piano music, and the practice of constructing rags out of a sequence of 16-bar strains became standard among the early masters of the idiom, including Scott Joplin, James Scott and Tom Turpin. But as it became popular, it was also played and recorded as a band music, and for other instruments. Much early ragtime on record is played on the banjo, by Vess Ossman, Olly Oakley and other pioneers, since that instrument recorded far better than did the piano in the primeval era of the gramophone – no records exist of Joplin, for instance, although many ragtime pioneers made piano rolls for use on pianolas and similar instruments. By the time Irving Berlin wrote 'Alexander's Ragtime Band' (not actually a rag) in 1911, the idiom was a world-wide craze, even though its successor, jazz, was already on the way. But the multi-thematic strictness of ragtime continued to inform the playing of many first-generation jazz musicians, including Jelly Roll Morton and Eubie Blake, and the entire stride-piano school owes much to ragtime principles. The first records by the Original Dixieland Jazz Band more or less called time on ragtime, although 'jazz' and 'ragtime' were inter-changeable for a long time as descriptions of this upheaval in popular music: Muggsy Spanier's Ragtime Band of the late 30s played no rags and performed entirely in the Chicago idiom of the 20s, but nobody complained about their name. In the late 40s, though, scholars began taking an inter-est in ragtime again, and a group such as Tony Parenti's Ragtimers addressed some of the old tunes again. The British trad move-ment of the 50s saw the likes of Ken Colyer and Chris Barber dedicating whole records to their idea of strict ragtime, and the huge success of the music in the 70s movie *The Sting* sparked an unlikely fad for a ragtime revival. These days it stands as part of the repertory of popular music, as it stretches back over a century or two: a few modern piano virtuosos still specialize in recitals of the form.

# Ram Ramirez
ORGAN, PIANO
*born* 15 September 1913; *died* 11 January 1994

Born in Puerto Rico, Ramirez was raised in New York and was playing piano from a very early age. He worked as a sideman for numerous outfits, going to Europe with Bobby Martin's band in 1937, and then work-ing with Frankie Newton, John Kirby and Sid Catlett back in New York, sometimes leading small groups of his own. Ramirez was a swinging player with a good mastery of stride rhythms, but he never had much of an impact as a leader, and it wasn't until he took up the organ in 1953 – inspired, like many others, by the example of Wild Bill Davis – that Ramirez really found an idiom he could make a mark in. He could impro-vise extravagant fantasies out of simple materials at the organ: his 25-minute romp through 'Robbin's Nest', egged on by an enthusiastic crowd, is the astonishing high-light of *Live In Harlem* (1960), a real collec-tor's piece which never stops swinging, even when Ramirez holds down the same chord for minutes on end. He subsequently toured Europe with T-Bone Walker, and went back more regularly to the piano, touring with the Harlem Blues And Jazz Band in the 80s. The royalties for 'Lover Man', which he co-wrote, hopefully warmed his later years.

**Live In Harlem** (Black & Blue)

# Freddy Randall
TRUMPET
*born* 6 May 1921; *died* 18 May 1999

Randall should be remembered as one of the most individual figures in British jazz. A

Londoner by birth, he began making waves on the local jazz scene in the late 40s, and by the 50s was leading a group which had many of the best players in the Chicago-orientated British style: yet none of them had the assurance and intensity of Randall himself, who played so fiercely that he might have been a blood brother to Muggsy Spanier and Bill Davison (Max Harrison once suggested that an entrance and departure by Randall on a record was akin to having an electric current switched on and off). His health gave him some trouble, but Randall had a fine band with Dave Shepherd in the early 60s and another with Shepherd and Danny Moss in the 70s, which kept his music alive at a time when there was otherwise little local encouragement for the style: by then, though, some of the power in his music had been calmed by a more mainstream focus. Subsequently, he played on more of a part-time basis, becoming involved with care for the elderly, and by the 90s he had more or less given up playing. Randall's great records might be counted among the finest of all British traditional jazz records: he had a rare gift for inspiring a band, and at his best he could have cut any comparable British trumpeter.
*His Great Sixteen* (Dormouse)

# Doug Raney
GUITAR
*born* 29 August 1956

Jimmy's son is, like his father, a fine and accomplished player, although stylistically he is rather more disposed to a thoughtful, modal style than his father. He started out as a rock player but soon enough went over to jazz, of a straight-ahead kind, and after touring with his father in Europe he remained in the old world, where he has made a long series of records for Steeplechase and has toured as a solo or a guest.
*Something's Up* (Steeplechase)

# Jimmy Raney
GUITAR
*born* 20 August 1927; *died* 10 May 1995

Originally from Louisville, Kentucky, Raney began making a mark on the New York and Chicago scenes of the late 40s, and when he hooked up with Stan Getz in the early 50s (both had been sidemen with Woody Herman) he set down some of the benchmark guitar playing of his day on Getz's various sessions for Storyville. Raney has routinely been cited as a major influence on his instrument, and listening to the freshness of his playing on these dates – cool, boppish, but with an almost surgical precision in the solos – one can hear why other players might have been impressed. Yet over quite a long career he actually recorded comparatively little, and even then in situations which were largely away from the spotlight. After working with Getz he played with Red Norvo, then in Europe, and then back in New York; after a brief reunion with Getz in 1962, he went into studio work and finally went back to Louisville in 1968. He was 'rediscovered' in the 70s, and thereafter enjoyed something of an Indian summer, sometimes touring and recording with son Doug. He died in a Louisville nursing home following a stroke. Right up until his final sessions, Raney was an impeccable player: every line in a solo is as clean as a whistle, every harmonic point deftly made. He was less in thrall to the pell-mell atmosphere of bop than Tal Farlow, and though he is sometimes cited as an innovator, it's hard to see exactly what he introduced into the music.
*The Master* (Criss Cross)

# Ernest Ranglin
GUITAR
*born* 19 June 1932

Born in Manchester, Jamaica, Ranglin taught himself the ukulele and then the guitar, and played in hotel bands in the Bahamas and on the Jamaican studio scene of the late 50s and early 60s, taking a hand in the early days of ska and bluebeat music. He moved to London in 1963, appointed as an A&R man for the small label Island by founder Chris Blackwell, and he worked at Ronnie Scott's (and in Scott's own band) while there. He subsequently divided his time between London, Jamaica and the US, and formed a partnership with Monty Alexander which resulted in some of his most jazz-orientated recordings. Ranglin has really cast his net too wide to be considered a jazz man: an honoured elder of Jamaican music and very likely a key figure in the history of

crossover, he is a great veteran of numerous popular styles.
*Below The Bassline* (Island)

## Enrico Rava

TRUMPET
*born* 20 August 1939

Rava studied piano and played trombone in Turin, but Miles Davis's playing made him switch to trumpet, and he found himself involved in the new-jazz scene in Rome in the middle 60s: he toured with Steve Lacy's quartet, and from there built up some associations in the US and in South America, while also playing in the European free scene, with the Globe Unity Orchestra and other groups. His 70s albums for ECM contain some of his best work: a distillation of some free-jazz tenets mixed with a fundamentally lyrical sound, with plenty of Miles Davis in it though coloured also by a Mediterranean love of sweeping melody. In the 80s and 90s he worked in an eclectic range of settings: electric music with his Electric Five, duos with Lee Konitz and Enrico Pieranunzi, orchestral pieces and dedications to the operatic repertoire. Some of these have, inevitably, been considerably more effective than others, but Rava's best music has a lived-in elegance which speaks of a compassionate imagination, and his return to ECM with *Easy Living* (2004) reasserted some of his best virtues.
*The Pilgrim And The Stars* (ECM)

## RCA Victor

RECORD LABEL

The origins of one of the world's great record labels go back to 1901, when the gramophone pioneer Eldridge Johnson established Victor in New Jersey in 1901. It had close links with the Gramophone Company in the UK, sharing record masters for release in both territories, and the American arm had plenty of ragtime in its catalogue even before they recorded James Reese Europe (in 1913) and the first records by the Original Dixieland Jazz Band (1917). When Nat Shilkret became their chief A&R man in 1926, the label stepped up its jazz input, recording Jelly Roll Morton, King Oliver, Duke Ellington, Bennie Moten and many more, as well as setting down some of the best of the New York dance orchestras. Victor was sold in 1929 and became R(adio)-Victor Company of America, or RCA Victor, which continued its jazz commitments, and it dominated much of the swing era with artists such as Ellington, Tommy Dorsey, Benny Goodman, Lionel Hampton and Artie Shaw. In the LP era, the jazz content waned somewhat, although they still had fine records by Sonny Rollins, Paul Desmond and others, and they tended to lag behind Columbia and Warner Bros in their modern jazz catalogue. In the 80s, RCA was eventually taken over by the German BMG (Bertelsmann Music Group), which coincided with a fresh initiative in recording new jazz via the Novus imprint. Like so many major-label jazz activities, though, this died out soon enough. In the new century, BMG and Sony have merged, creating another humungous entertainment company; but thus far no indication of new jazz activity has been sighted.

## Jason Rebello

PIANO
*born* 29 March 1969

Rebello got off to a remarkable start – perhaps too much so. He was still studying piano at London's Guildhall when he began playing on what was then a vibrant scene full of young talent, and he was quickly signed by the British arm of BMG–RCA, which engaged Wayne Shorter to produce Rebello's debut. His records for the label tended to obscure a considerable straight-ahead talent under self-conscious originals and nods in the direction of fusion and crossover: when Rebello got clear space to play, he was clearly a thoughtful and creative improviser. In 1996 he left music altogether for a spell but came quietly back a year or so later and eventually made another record for an independent label, before going on tour with Sting as band pianist. Whether he will find himself quite so much in the limelight again remains to be seen.
*A Clearer View* (Novus)

## Sonny Red (Kyser)
ALTO SAXOPHONE
*born* 17 December 1932; *died* 20 March 1981

His full name was Sylvester Kyser, but he was always listed on records as 'Sonny Red'. He played a minor role during the height of the hard-bop era, working with Barry Harris in his native Detroit, and then with Art Blakey, Curtis Fuller and various leaders during the 60s. A single Blue Note album, *Out Of The Blue* (1960), and three others for Jazzland, are all prized in their original form by collectors, but Red played little that was distinctive in his field and he was heard from only rarely in his later years.
***Out Of The Blue*** (Blue Note)

## Freddie Redd
PIANO
*born* 29 May 1928

Redd played on the New York scene in the early 50s in a variety of situations, including bebop and R&B groups, and he toured Sweden with a band assembled by Rolf Ericson in 1956. On his return he worked in San Francisco for a spell before undertaking the project by which he is still best remembered, writing the music for Jack Gelber's jazz play *The Connection*, and taking a part in the performance: it played in New York, Paris and London during 1959–61, and the music was recorded by Blue Note. Redd made one other album for Blue Note, but thereafter he led a somewhat picaresque existence, playing all over the US, Europe and Canada, turning up in London to play on James Taylor's debut album, and only finally returning to the US in 1974. Thereafter he lived mostly on the West Coast, where he has occasionally performed. Had it not been for *The Connection*, jazz might have lost sight of Freddie a long time ago, but his enjoyably funky take on the hard-bop idiom has endured through those Blue Note sessions.
***Music From 'The Connection'*** (Blue Note)

## Vi Redd
ALTO AND SOPRANO SAXOPHONES, VOCAL
*born* 20 September 1928

Redd's father was a drummer and, with her high-school classmate Melba Liston, she began playing jazz in her teens; but she went into social work as her vocation and only began performing regularly in the 60s. In 1962 she made records for both Jazzland and Atco – the latter was called *Lady Soul*, some years in advance of the title being bestowed on Aretha Franklin – where she mixed playing alto with singing. She toured in Europe and the US later in the 60s and subsequently divided her time between performing, teaching and working with handicapped children. She has received little critical attention, but in her way she is a unique performer, crossing between blues, soul and jazz and never thinking that there could be any kind of barrier between the three.
***Lady Soul*** (Atco)

## Dewey Redman
TENOR SAXOPHONE
*born* 17 May 1931

Redman is a saxophonist greatly admired by many fellow musicians, whose work has never much broken through to wider acclaim. He grew up in Forth Worth, Texas, and divided his time between schoolteaching and working as a musician until he moved to San Francisco in the middle 60s. Eventually he joined Ornette Coleman's band in New York from 1967, besides forging associations with Charie Haden and playing in Keith Jarrett's 'American' quartet in the early 70s. Thereafter he has worked mainly as a freelance on his own account, although he has also enjoyed associations with the Coleman 'repertory' group Old And New Dreams and played in his own small groups. Redman's mournful, vocalized sound is something set apart from the mainstream of post-Coltrane saxophone players, and though he has only rarely worked as a leader on record, showing little ambition in this direction, his music is an individual and perhaps unique part of the post-bop jazz landscape: an introverted player who likes to play the extrovert, he wanders an intriguing line between in and out.
***In London*** (Palmetto)

## Don Redman

ALTO SAXOPHONE, ARRANGER
*born* 29 July 1900; *died* 20 November 1964

Redman emerged out of West Virginia as a prodigy who had music running all the way through him. He moved to Pittsburgh and joined a band led by Billy Paige, and arrived in New York with that outfit, only to form an alliance with Fletcher Henderson, who was then forming his first group. Redman stayed with Henderson for four years: he established the band's book, watched what happened when Louis Armstrong came into the orchestra, and revised his ambitions accordingly. The best of his early, pre-Armstrong arrangements suggest that he would have been a significant force anyway, but the trumpeter's example led him away from the more staid style of Henderson's early dance music and in the direction of a wholehearted jazz approach. But the band-leader Jean Goldkette poached him in 1927 to write for McKinney's Cotton Pickers, and within a year or so he had turned that band into one of the best of its kind. He played in the group himself – though never an out-standing soloist, he could handle clarinet and alto sax duties respectably enough – and also revealed a talent as a vocalist, in a confidential, half-sung, half-spoken way. In 1931 he finally went out on his own, and led an orchestra until 1940: it was never a hit band, but it worked steadily enough, and it recorded some of Redman's most inspired arrangements, including 'Chant Of The Weed', 'Shakin' The African' and other striking originals. But after 1940, Redman was largely sidelined in jazz. He wrote for other leaders and took a band to Europe in 1946, and in the 50s most of his professional life was spent working as MD for Pearl Bailey; but the eminence he had enjoyed in the 20s and 30s was behind him. He was one of the first to hear jazz as an ensemble music, which could incorporate the individuality of breaks, solos and the dialogue between sections into an orchestrated whole, but Redman's contribution still awaits its full due.
*Shakin' The African* (Hep)

## Joshua Redman

TENOR SAXOPHONE
*born* 1 February 1969

Joshua is the son of Dewey Redman, although he had little contact with his father during his childhood and grew up in Berkeley, California. He turned away from studying law at Yale in order to pursue a career in music, and after winning the 1991 Thelonious Monk Saxophone Competition he toured with Jack DeJohnette and then secured a contract with Warners. Redman's early records, starting with *Joshua Redman* (1992), were thrilling documents: here was a superbly accomplished saxophonist, aware of the tradition but not in thrall to it, a show-man but not someone who showed off for its own sake, and an instrumentalist who pushed almost teasingly at stylistic barriers without blowing into inaccessible areas of the avant-garde. Young and smart and immediately attractive, he seemed like a god-send to the jazz scene of the early 90s, and with major-label backing, too. But almost from the start, things seem to have slid away from him: the records grew self-conscious, a backlash began, and his funda-mentally conservative take on acoustic jazz sounded reserved in a time when crossover began to seem important again. Redman has mixed acoustic, straight-ahead records with sets by a trio of himself, Sam Yahel (organ) and Brian Blade (drums), but the appeal he had ten years ago seems to have signifi-cantly drizzled away. He remains a very fine saxophone player, and perhaps it is time that this was acknowledged regardless of the winds of fashion.
*Wish* (Warner Bros)

## Dizzy Reece

TRUMPET
*born* 5 January 1931

Alphonso Reece grew up in Kingston, Jamaica, with such contemporaries as Joe Harriott, and he began playing trumpet in his teens. After working with Jamaican bebop groups he arrived in London in 1948, and divided his time between Britain and playing on the continent in the early 50s. In London, he played with Kenny Graham and Tony Crombie and led small groups of his own, making records for Tony Hall's Tempo label. A fiery but knowing stylist, Reece borrowed from many of his American contemporaries without sounding too much like any of them, and his records have always enjoyed a following. He moved to New York in 1959 and Hall, always an admirer, recommended him to Alfred Lion of Blue Note: Hall managed to record him with Art Taylor and Donald Byrd, who were brought in from Paris, in London – *Blues In Trinity* was listed as a French session, but this was a subterfuge to get round the British union ban. Reece made two more albums for Blue Note but never found much in the way of jazz stardom. He has made a few records since and occasionally surfaces, as in a tour with the Paris Reunion Band in the 80s.

*Blues In Trinity* (Blue Note)

## Eric Reed
PIANO
*born* 21 June 1970

A Philadelphian, Reed played piano in church and after his family moved to Los Angeles in 1981, he worked in Gerald Wilson's big band. He became a Wynton Marsalis protégé and played with the trumpeter at different times during the 90s, as well as making records of his own. Along with Cyrus Chestnut, Reed is one of the few contemporary musicians to address gospel music as a significant part of his stylistic make-up, and that is integral to an otherwise typically outgoing and virtuosic approach. He has been bounced between various record labels but at the moment seems to have a home at Nagel Heyer.

*Mercy And Grace* (Nagel Heyer)

## Tony Reedus
DRUMS
*born* 22 September 1959

A nephew of pianist James Williams, Reedus studied at Memphis State University but was on his way to New York soon enough and played in Woody Shaw's band during the early 80s. Since then he has worked primarily as a freelance. Two excellent records as a leader were made late in the 80s but since then Reedus seems to have been given no further opportunities to be out front. A big and intense performer who does, nevertheless, play for the band.

*The Far Side* (Jazz City)

## Dianne Reeves
VOCAL
*born* 23 October 1956

Reeves's solo career took a long time to get going. She grew up in Denver and was heard with her high-school band by Clark Terry in 1973, who gave her some featured spots in his own groups. She moved to Los Angeles later in the 70s and worked as a session singer, and then with the fusion bands Caldera and Night Flight, before going back east to New York and working with Harry Belafonte. Her break finally came when she was signed to Blue Note, then rebuilding its new artist roster, in 1986, and she has recorded for them steadily ever since – one of the few artists to remain on the label since that time. Reeves has had an awkward time of it in some ways. She emerged as a solo performer at a point when jazz singers weren't especially good business, prior to the boom initiated by Cassandra Wilson and Diana Krall, and most of her records have offered a self-conscious mix of jazz, soul and even folkish material, with a variety of backings. But persistence, and the label's loyalty, have paid off, and she has lasted the course better than many of her contemporaries. She has a grand voice somewhat in the Dinah Washington mould, and her own songwriting does more than merely fill up space.

*The Grand Encounter* (Blue Note)

## Reuben Reeves
TRUMPET
*born* 25 October 1905; *died* 25 September 1975

Reeves worked mainly in Chicago in the 20s, and his fame rests primarily on the 20 issued titles made for Vocalion by Reuben 'River' Reeves And His Tributaries, all but four of them dating from 1929. He was no genius as a player, but the music is agreeably hot in the Chicago manner of the day, and there is also some fine work from Omer Simeon and Darnell Howard. Reeves subsequently spent a period in Cab Calloway's trumpet section in New York, but eventually

he returned to Chicago and drifted into obscurity.
*The Complete Vocalions* (Timeless)

# Hans Reichel
GUITAR
*born* 10 May 1949

A pioneer in guitar strangeness. Reichel started as a self-taught violinist (in which capacity he has recorded duets with Rüdiger Carl), but became interested in rock and took to the guitar. Apparently dissatisfied with conventional instruments, he has made a speciality out of 'prepared' guitars, double-necked instruments with the two necks facing in opposite directions, the daxophone (an invented percussion instrument) and other oddball innovations of his own. The results are sometimes fantastical solo records and performances, although Reichel often plays melodically and he doesn't seem to be much interested in effects pedals and the like.
*Wichlinghauser Blues* (FMP)

# Rufus Reid
BASS
*born* 10 February 1944

An accomplished bass-for-hire, Reid has been a regular in the music since the early 70s, when he became the in-house bassist at Segal's Jazz Showcase for some five years. In 1976 he went to New York, where he has been based since, playing for many different leaders. In the 90s he co-led a post-bop group with the drummer Akira Tana, Tana-Reid, and he has led the odd session of his own. A duo record with Michael Moore, *Doublebass Delights* (1997), is entertaining, but best heard only once. Reid has a suitably fine and rich sound, and is sensible enough to realize that bass solos aren't what everyone in the room is waiting for.
*TanaReid, Looking Forward* (Evidence)

# Ernst Reijseger
CELLO
*born* 13 November 1954

The bespectacled Reijseger was a fine addition to the Dutch improvisation scene

of the 70s. He started working with Han Bennink and other familiars towards the end of the decade and since then has enjoyed a plentiful supply of playing partners, including Gerry Hemingway (in his quintet), with Bennink and Michael Moore in The Clusone 3, in the ICP Orchestra, in a duo with Louis Sclavis and with a trio led by Ettore Fioravanti, Belcanto. Where his cello counterpart Tristan Honsinger is determined to shed his playing of anything melodious and sweet, Reijseger is quite happy to use conventional techniques and forms as part of his playing, and a record of duets with Franco D'Andrea, *I Love You So Much It Hurts* (Winter & Winter, 2000), is a charmer. The solo record cited leaves him to his own devices, and they are bountiful.
*Colla Parte* (Winter & Winter)

# Jack Reilly
PIANO
*born* 1 January 1932

Reilly has led a mildly exotic career in jazz backwaters. He studied classical piano until he was 16 and then studied with Lennie Tristano and George Russell. He didn't have much exposure, aside from some appearances with John LaPorta, and played quietly on the New York scene of the late 60s before a stay in Norway. He established a jazz curriculum at Mannes School in New York and then took a position at the New England Conservatory. In the meantime he had been active as a composer, creating a jazz requiem and sundry extended piano works, and some records for Revelation presented a style which sounded steeped in classical technique without drying out a palpable feel for improvisation. Reilly has since recorded some extravagantly conceptual solo CDs and is an inveterate letter-writer.
*The Brinksman* (Revelation)

# Django Reinhardt
GUITAR
*born* 23 January 1910; *died* 16 May 1953

Reinhardt's music spoke to an audience which went far beyond the jazz specialists. He was raised in a gypsy community not far from Paris, starting on violin and then guitar, and the most critical event of his early years was a serious injury sustained to his hand in a caravan fire when he was 18: as a result he was unable to use two fingers of that hand, and was obliged to come up with an alternative method of fingering strings. He subsequently began working in a duo with the salon singer Jean Sablon before working in a new group which involved his brother Joseph, also a guitarist, and the violinist Stéphane Grappelli, which was eventually called the Quintette Du Hot Club De France. The combination of Grappelli and Reinhardt was the most sensational thing in jazz since Venuti and Lang, and the copious records they made for Decca, HMV and Swing in the pre-war years attested to their fast popularity. Word travelled quickly about Reinhardt's virtuosity, and he made records with American jazz royalty in pre-war Paris, including Coleman Hawkins, Benny Carter, Rex Stewart and Bill Coleman. The cliché regarding Reinhardt's eminence is that he was the first jazz musician outside the United States of any consequence, a typical piece of American hubris. What attracted other musicians was the flash of Reinhardt, his indomitable way of swinging, and his easy versatility: he could take the typical guitarist's role of accompanist but was able to slip quickly into a solo setting and perform with all the forcefulness of a Hawkins or Carter. The sound he got out of the guitar – wonderfully resonant, accentuated by his use of silences and unexpected phrases which might allow a single cadence to sound like the chime of a bell – always attracts the ear, and as forcefully as he usually plays (a necessary procedure for someone using an unamplified guitar) there is often a lovely tenderness in his pre-war playing, which is set down in his most famous original theme, 'Nuages'. Pair him with the helplessly romantic Grappelli, and it was not surprising that the Quintette's music won over so many listeners.

After the outbreak of war in 1939, Grappelli remained in London and the Quintette broke up. Reinhardt travelled through Europe, tinkered with a big band and a new quintet with Hubert Rostaing, and toyed with large-scale composing, but never really settled into anything: his capricious temperament, which had so often exasperated Grappelli, often let his ambitions down. Duke Ellington sent for him in 1946 and he visited the US to guest with the Ellington band, already intrigued by what he had heard about bebop, but he did not take America by storm and by 1947 he was back in France and in his native community once more. He eventually changed over to electric guitar, which hardened his playing a little, although even in his later recordings his virtuosity and powers of invention seem largely intact. Yet Reinhardt always seems to belong to that golden age of the 30s and the QHCF, even if he did keep his ears open for the new developments which had emerged from Charlie Christian's fingers. He died from a stroke at the age of 43. Tellingly enough, any attempts to pay homage to him, such as Martin Taylor's *Spirit Of Django* project, always focus on his earlier work. His son Babik (b 1944) is also a guitarist, and though he has tried to set out his own space in the music, he has often wound up playing in settings which pay tribute to his father's work.
*Django Reinhardt Vols 1–5* (JSP)

# Emily Remler
GUITAR
*born* 18 September 1957; *died* 4 May 1990

'I may *look* like a nice Jewish girl from New Jersey, but inside I'm a 50-year-old, heavyset black man with a big thumb, like Wes Montgomery.' Emily Remler was first inspired by Paul Desmond to play jazz, but it was hearing Montgomery that made her choose to be a guitarist. She studied at Berklee and in 1978 was playing in New Orleans, where she met Herb Ellis, who introduced her to Carl Jefferson of Concord. Her six albums for the label display a style which sounds like a bridge between the more traditional playing of Montgomery and the pastoral rock formations of Pat Metheny. She worked in a duo with Larry Coryell and went on to play with the more commercial set-up of David Benoit. The jazz world was shocked by the news of her sudden death, while on tour in Sydney, Australia. She died of a heart attack, allegedly induced in part by narcotics misuse.
*East To Wes* (Concord)

## Kid Rena
TRUMPET
*born* 30 August 1898; *died* 25 April 1949

Another almost-lost figure of early New
Orleans jazz, Rena (real name Henry René)
learned trumpet in the Colored Waifs' Home
at the same time as fellow inmate Louis
Armstrong, and he later worked with Kid
Ory before forming his own Dixieland Jazz
Band around 1921. He remained in the city
and stayed busy in that and other groups,
but he eventually stopped playing in 1947
after becoming ill. His only record date,
from 1940, shows his powers in decline, and
he plays no more than a straightforward
lead: at his peak in the 20s he was reckoned
to be among the most powerful trumpeters
in the city, able to hit resplendent high
notes and lead a group with rare authority.
His brother Joseph (1897–1973) played
drums, and quit music to become a preacher
in the 40s.
**Prelude To The Revival Vol 2** (American Music)

## Henri Renaud
PIANO
*born* 20 April 1925

Renaud was an important organizing force
for jazz in post-war France. He arrived in
Paris in 1946 and backed several American
visitors before leading his own groups,
including a big band in the early 50s.
Besides his work as a musician, Renaud
became involved in record production and
as a general fixer on the scene: he began
recording groups for the Swing label in both
Paris and New York. This side of his professional life eventually took precedence:
although he made two LPs released in the
US, he became a jazz A&R man for CBS in
France in 1964, and went on to produce
music programmes for radio and television.
His own music – a light, fat-free style somewhat akin to Hank Jones's playing – never
had much attention, but he got the job
done.
**The Birdlanders** (Period)

## Don Rendell
TENOR AND SOPRANO SAXOPHONES, CLARINET
*born* 4 March 1926

Rendell came up through the London dance-
band scene, with such bands as those of
Oscar Rabin in the 40s, and he then worked
in John Dankworth's septet in the early 50s
before forming groups of his own. He
worked under two American leaders, Stan
Kenton and Woody Herman, later in the
decade, while also making a few records of
his own: though primarily indebted to the
swing style of Lester Young, he inevitably
took on board much of the bebop language,
and the result was a personal synthesis
which is best heard in such records as *Play-
time* (Decca, 1958). He continued to expand
his style in the 60s, when he formed a quintet with Ian Carr which lasted between 1963
and 1969, making a series of latterly prized
though at the time largely ignored albums
for Columbia. In the 70s he did some of his
best work in a group he co-led with saxophonist Barbara Thompson, and he has
continued to play as a leader on the British
circuit while also involving himself heavily
in teaching.
**Space Walk** (Redial)

## Harry Reser
BANJO, GUITAR
*born* 17 January 1896; *died* 27 September 1965

Reser was one of the great fixers on the 20s
New York studio scene. He led countless
bands through numberless sessions, and
hundeds of records came out of it: a discography by Bill Triggs lists him playing as
the mastermind behind such groups as the
Tennessee Happy Boys, The Clicquot Club
Eskimos, The Kentucky Hot Hoppers, The
Six Jumping Jacks and The Rambling
Ragadors. Reser had his own repertory cast
of players such as Tommy Gott and Larry
Abbott, and his kind of jazz was often closer
to a Spike Jones novelty than real hot dance
music, but he played his part in the original
Jazz Age. Reser never retired from music: he
was still playing in theatre orchestras until
the end, and on the day of his death he went
down early to tune his guitar in the orchestra pit, where his colleagues subsequently
found him slumped in his chair.

# Allan Reuss
GUITAR
*born* 15 June 1915; *died* 4 June 1988

A measure of the esteem Reuss was held in can be gained by noting the number of solos he was allotted in his various sideman jobs: he played with several of the leading swing-era big bands, and in an age when guitarists were mostly seen and not heard, Reuss usually made his mark. He took over from George Van Eps (his old teacher) in the 1935 Benny Goodman orchestra, and from there went on to work with Jack Teagarden, Jimmy Dorsey and Harry James, as well as playing studio gigs on small-group dates. In the 50s he began to focus on teaching, and his public playing subsided.
**Jack Teagarden,** *1939–1940* (Classics)

# Revivalism

It can seem that as soon as one style of jazz was deemed to be 'over', somebody else started 'reviving' it. The original revivalism, though, was perceived to be the reawakening of interest in the kind of jazz played in New Orleans from around 1900 to the early 20s, before the rise of such soloists as Louis Armstrong changed the direction of the music. This coincided with the rediscovery of Bunk Johnson around 1940, and Bill Russell's founding of his American Music label, set up to document Johnson and many of his contemporaries while they were still around and playing. This in turn inspired young musicians to undertake their own kind of revivalism, which led to such groups as Lu Watters's Yerba Buena Jazz Band. In Europe, a similar thing occurred, with many youthful players taking their cues from the jazz of the 20s, as learned from records. In due course, swing and bebop have had their own revivals, as has hard bop and even free jazz. Thus far, post-modernism has escaped.

# Rita Reys
VOCAL
*born* 21 December 1924

Born in Rotterdam, she began singing with Dutch dance bands in the 40s and subsequently began working with small groups in more of a cool-jazz vein. She toured America in 1956 and made *The Cool Voice Of Rita Reys* for Columbia, with Art Blakey's Jazz Messengers as the backup band, although thereafter she worked mostly in Europe, recording prolifically in the 60s and 70s, often with her husband Pim Jacobs in support. Reys was, like the Swedish singer Monica Zetterlund, capable of charming audiences with her non-idiomatic pronunciation of English lyrics, but she was a swinging vocalist who thoroughly mastered her idiom.
**The Cool Voice Of Rita Reys** (Columbia)

# Mel Rhyne
ORGAN
*born* 12 May 1936

Rhyne made a single album, *Organizing*, for Jazzland in 1960, and although he also secured some eminence as a sideman with Wes Montgomery between 1959 and 1963 (the group broke up partly because lugging around the Hammond was proving too difficult!), little more was heard from him until the 90s, as he had buried himself away in Milwaukee. But he came back as a sideman with Herb Ellis, and then Gerry Teekens recorded a string of sessions with him for Criss Cross. The first was called *The Legend* (1991), which may have been protesting too much, although Rhyne was at least playing in an unhackneyed style (a little like Shirley Scott's), which stood aside from swarming blues lines and preferred perkily fingered melodies.
**Kojo** (Criss Cross)

# Rhythm and blues

While rock'n'roll is at least two steps removed from jazz and can't rate an entry here, rhythm and blues is another matter. The term itself actually came into being as recently as 1949, coined by the American record-industry newspaper *Billboard* as a replacement for what had previously been termed 'race' records – in other words, black music which aspired to popular status. This could have as easily encompassed all kinds of jazz, but R&B was a little more specific than that: it was mostly music with a vocal content, had an upbeat feel aimed at dancers, mixed a blues element with the more extrovert style of the jump bands of the 40s – a big band such as Buddy Johnson's and a small group such as Louis Jordan's were excellent examples – and, in terms of lyrical subject matter, was as often about dance crazes as words of love or hate. Instrumental R&B was often a matter of a featured saxophonist such as Earl Bostic or Big Jay McNeely blowing in front of a simmering rhythm section, in various degrees of extroversion. But it was singers such as Joe Turner and Wynonie Harris who became the real stars of rhythm and blues, and they were joined soon enough by women such as Ruth Brown and LaVern Baker: between them, these stylists ushered in the rock'n'roll era from the black, blues side of the fence, while Elvis Presley came in from the white, country side. There were offshoots of R&B such as the sweeter vocal music of doo-wop, and gospel music also took on some of the secular manners of R&B, if not the morals. The term might seem outmoded now if the industry hadn't clung on to it: today, *Billboard* still uses the term to describe what is ostensibly their black popular music chart, printed every week.

## Rhythm section

The engine room of any jazz ensemble is what drives the band, and the 'rhythm section' is usually the bassist and the drummer, plus any auxiliary percussionist(s). The pianist, if there is one, is regularly deemed to be a part of the rhythm section too, although their harmonic and solo roles are more upfront. Count Basie's 'All-American Rhythm Section' comprised four individuals, since guitarist Freddie Green was also a part of it, and was integral to the orchestra's propulsive yet light-footed feel.

## Buddy Rich
DRUMS
*born* 30 September 1917; *died* 2 April 1987

Rich was on stage for nearly 70 years. His parents were a vaudeville act, Wilson and Rich, and he appeared as the baby in the act before he had celebrated his second birthday. He was playing drums on Broadway stages at four, and was leading his own band on the circuit at 11. His first real jazz gig was

with Joe Marsala's band in 1937, and between then and 1945 he held down the drummer's role in a host of leading bands, including those of Harry James, Artie Shaw, Tommy Dorsey, Benny Carter and – his favourite gig – Count Basie, even though it was only as a fill-in for the drafted Jo Jones. Rich could be a handful for a leader – Tommy Dorsey famously remembered that 'there are three evil people in the world – Adolf Hitler, Buddy Rich and Alvin Stoller – and I've had two of them in my band!' – but he was a brilliant technician with incredibly fast hands and an almost punitive way of swinging the band. He then led an orchestra of his own for some two years, although it wasn't a great success, and was convened only intermittently later in the decade. He was perhaps inevitably featured at Jazz At The Philharmonic shows, and played on some important bebop record dates, though these tended to suggest that bop wasn't really what he did best.

In the early and middle 50s he worked with Harry James and eventually went over to leading a small group, as well as making a vocal record for Verve which showed off his surprisingly agreeable tenor. Rich was with James again in the 60s until he flew in the face of every conceivable fashion by reforming his own straight-ahead big band in 1966: it was a surprise success, as if making a lone stand against jazz's commercial decline appealed to big-band diehards everywhere, though Rich's unswerving showmanship ensured quality entertainment for paying audiences. The leader used the best arrangers and built up a quality book, and he mustered some excellent soloists of the order of Art Pepper, Don Menza and Pat LaBarbera, although it was Rich the public came to see and his nickname 'Superdrummer' wasn't worn lightly. The band did eventually disperse in 1974, but after working at his own club, Buddy's Place, in New York for a period, the indefatigable Rich came back with a big band again. What eventually wore him down was his heart: he had his first attack as early as 1959, and though he went through bypass surgery in the 80s – and was playing again within months – it finally gave out on him. In the end, Rich was a rather lonely survivor of what was, by then, a vanished era of touring big bands. His furious personality was famously explosive: a legendary tape exists

of him cursing out most of his band on their bus, which resulted in a mass firing (and re-hiring), not an uncommon occurrence. For many he was the greatest drummer in all of jazz, and probably the most significant fore-bear of the supreme technicians of the fusion era; others would call him a crashing bore. Yet he could also play deftly and help-fully, as he did with Art Tatum, Bud Powell and others. In the 50s, he recorded several drum 'battles' with the likes of his first influence, Gene Krupa (who unstintingly admired Rich) and Max Roach, but the best of him is in the shouting, roaring records he made with his 60s big band for Pacific Jazz.
*Big Swing Face* (Pacific Jazz)

## Johnny Richards
ARRANGER
*born* 2 November 1911; *died* 7 October 1968

Born Juan Ricardo de Cascales in Mexico, Richards was a child prodigy who was in vau-deville at eight and holding down an orches-trator's job by the time he was 15. He worked in London and Hollywood in the 30s as a filmscore writer, studied with Schoenberg, and led his own big band between 1940 and 1945. Back in Hollywood he began doing charts for Boyd Raeburn and Charlie Barnet, but it was his tenure as arranger for Stan Kenton from 1952 which won him real atten-tion from the jazz audience, and he led his own orchestras again in the late 50s and middle 60s, although in the end he made only a handful of full-length albums of his own music, notably *Walk Softly/Run Wild!* (Coral, 1958), *The Rites Of Diabolo* (Roulette, 1958), and *Wide Range* (1957) and *Experi-ments In Sound* (1958, both Capitol). Richards integrated modern classical and other influ-ences into a complex overview which resulted in intriguing if finally unpopular results: none of his albums have so far been reissued on CD. The studio pro Danny Bank remembered him as 'a kind of sadist. He used to write music that was so difficult and he would laugh. It would tickle him if it would throw a good player a curve.'
*Wide Range* (Capitol)

## Tim Richards
PIANO
*born* 23 June 1952

Though born a Londoner, Richards worked in the west of England in the late 70s, forming Spirit Level with saxophonist Paul Dunmall around 1979. He returned to London in 1985, although the music wasn't really flashy or attention-seeking enough for him to capitalize much on the jazz boom then emerging in the capital. Richards has since then done at least as much work in Europe as in the UK, and Spirit Level has lasted more than 20 years with various personnel changes, although Richards has latterly beefed it up into the nine-strong Great Spirit. Compared to, say, Django Bates, Richards is all but unknown as a jazz composer, but in his unpretentious way his music does have plenty of spirit.
*Great Spirit/Best Of Spirit Level* (33 Jazz)

## Jerome Richardson
SAXOPHONES AND WOODWINDS
*born* 15 November 1920; *died* 23 June 2000

Richardson led only a handful of records in his long career, but he is probably among the most-recorded saxophonists of his generation, playing in countless small groups and big bands from the 50s onwards. He was briefly in Jimmie Lunceford's band in 1941 and after the war worked with Lionel Hampton and Earl Hines before becoming a regular on the New York club scene. Master of most of the woodwind family, studio work was easy to come by for him and he played on studio dates of every kind all through the 50s and 60s. He was lead alto with the Jones–Lewis Jazz Orchestra for five years from its founding in 1965, but then moved to Hollywood and carried on as a ses-sionman, which kept him busy for the rest of the 70s and all through the 80s, although he increasingly did pop sessions rather than jazz dates. A couple of late 50s dates for New Jazz got him started as a leader on record, and there was little else until a valedictory session for the Swiss label TCB, *Jazz Station Runaway*, in 1997. Richardson's skills in play-ing to orders were one thing, but he was an ear-catching soloist too, especially on tenor.
*Roamin' With Richardson* (New Jazz/OJC)

## Dannie Richmond

DRUMS

*born* 15 December 1931; *died* 16 March 1988

Richmond started out as a saxophonist, and he was still working in that role when he played drums at a jam session in 1956, and did so well that he made the change straight away. He joined Charles Mingus later the same year, and remained Mingus's drummer of choice for most of the next 20 years. They were great carousing buddies as well as bandmates, and as a rhythm-section team they made up one of the most creative duos of their time. Richmond had a rare ability to turn his style on a dime, switching between the crisp propulsion of a signature hard-bop groove to quietness, and from there to freely moving pulses which showed he was paying attention to what the free players were doing. He did some 'outside' work in the 60s too, including working in a soul band called LTD, and in the 70s he even had gigs behind Joe Cocker and Elton John. After Mingus's death in 1977, Richmond worked with Mingus Dynasty, and then in a quartet with his former Mingus sidemen Don Pullen and George Adams, a setting which was about as close as he got to leading from the front. It was his death which eventually broke that group up.

*Mingus Ah Um* (Columbia)

## Mike Richmond

BASS

*born* 26 February 1948

Richmond is a very reliable pro whose recent low profile in recording and featured gig work is to be regretted. A Philadelphian, he studied with Jimmy Garrison in the early 70s before going out as a touring bassist-for-hire, recording with the likes of Stan Getz and Buddy DeFranco, although one of his best-remembered associations was with Jack DeJohnette's New Directions band. He acted as MD for Mingus Dynasty in the 80s and led a few sessions of his own, including a few very good dates for Steeplechase. His natural feel is for walking bass in the classic manner (and he has written a tutorial on the subject), and after exposure to some fancier and less effective modern techniques, the precisely swinging style of Richmond sounds all the more valuable. Education has probably taken up a lot of his time of late, since he has been a regular on the NYU faculty.

*Dance For Andy* (Steeplechase)

## Georg Riedel

BASS, COMPOSER

*born* 8 November 1934

Riedel was born in Czechoslovakia but moved to Sweden with his family when he was four. He was an early member of Lars Gullin's small groups in the 50s and has enjoyed a long association with Arne Domnérus, which has lasted into the new century. Besides doughty work as a mainstream-to-modern bassman, though, Riedel's great vocation is composing: his *Jazz Ballet* (1964) actually got an American album release in 1964, and besides this he has composed a large body of orchestral, chamber and jazz works, as well as many songs.

*Jazz Ballet* (Philips)

## Alex Riel

DRUMS

*born* 13 September 1940

Copenhagen's master sticksman began playing in traditional bands at the end of the 50s, and then took on the role of the house drummer at the Café Montmartre, the city's leading jazz venue, in 1963. Since then he has worked in various of the leading Danish jazz small groups, with Palle Mikkelborg, Jesper Lungaard and others, as well as in a rock band called Savage Rose. On record he has played with dozens of visitors and home-grown talents. Riel's straightforwardly swinging style always lifts the music, and it's been a pleasure in recent years to find him heading up some sessions of his own for the local Stunt label. Besides this, he is one of jazz's great jokers, able to spin puns into and out of a conversation and in more than one language.

*Rielatin'* (Stunt)

## Riff

A brief melodic phrase, mostly two or four bars in length, which is subject to repetition to form a central ingredient in the performance. Some 'tunes' can be made up of riffs ('One O'Clock Jump', from the greatest of all riff bands, the Count Basie Orchestra, is an exemplar), and riffs can be used as a counterpoint: Basie's band is again a good example, skilled as they were at devising riffs more or less on the spot as a backdrop to a soloist's venturings. Riffs were used in the early marching bands from New Orleans, and have always been a part of the blues: once riffs had become tiresomely familiar in the swing era, they were often appropriated by the R&B bands which came next. The boppers used riffs as themes, but they wouldn't have had them in a solo, which was far too obvious. Bassists have used riffs as the root of much modern jazz, and Paul Chambers's riff on Miles Davis's 'So What' ushered in a whole era.

## Knut Riisnaes
TENOR SAXOPHONE
*born* 13 November 1945

Riisnaes began working in a modern idiom on the Oslo scene of the later 60s, and since then has slowly built up a fine body of work on record. While he can work in a straightforward blowing context, and once made such a record with the visiting Red Holloway, he is in more of an introverted post-bop vein, delivering improvisations in a full and weighty tone which has a severe side to it. The recent *Touching* (2001) delivers a fine essay on the tenor-and-rhythm form, calmly personal rather than ambitious. His brother Odd (b 1953) also plays tenor saxophone and is similarly accomplished.
*Touching* (Resonant)

## Ben Riley
DRUMS
*born* 17 July 1933

Originally from Savannah, Georgia, Riley became a ubiquitous figure on New York's small-group scene of the 50s and 60s, and he is on dozens of records from the period. His most famous gig was as the drummer in Thelonious Monk's group of the early 60s, and that association sustained him into the 80s, when he decided to form a Monk repertory band with his former Monk colleague

Charlie Rouse, and the group Sphere (with Kenny Barron and Buster Williams as well) worked regularly until Rouse's death, latterly coming together again with Gary Bartz as a substitute saxophonist. In the meantime, Riley has continued to work regularly as a drummer for hire. Dick Katz has described him as 'one of the handful of master jazz accompanists. He also has a dance-like feeling, a subtle West Indian thing.'
**Thelonious Monk, *It's Monk's Time*** (Columbia)

## Herlin Riley
DRUMS
*born* 15 February 1957

Along with John Vidacovich, Riley is preeminent among modern New Orleans drummers. He actually divided his time between drums and trumpet during the 70s, and didn't go over to the kit full time until the early 80s, when he began playing with Al Hirt and then with Ahmad Jamal. Wynton Marsalis engaged him as his ensemble drummer in 1988 and he has worked with the trumpeter ever since, in both that group and the Lincoln Center Jazz Orchestra. Lately he has also been touring with his own quartet. Adaptable and a genial presence in the Marsalis group, he brings a stylish bonhomie which has considerably warmed up Marsalis's music in recent times.
**Wynton Marsalis, *Citi Movement*** (Columbia)

## Howard Riley
PIANO
*born* 16 February 1943

Riley's father played in dance bands in the 30s, and Howard learned himself in Huddersfield in the 50s. By 1960 he was playing three nights a week at the Dyers And Finishers Club, before studying at Bangor, and during his university years he met Evan Parker. After a year's fellowship study in America, he settled in London in 1967, formed a trio with Barry Guy and Jon Hiseman and began associating with the free scene centred on the Little Theatre Club – 'a fantastically productive time in London' – and he made two trio records for CBS at the end of the decade (he also remembers playing at a pub in Beckenham with John

McLaughlin, for which they got '30 bob each'). Since then he has worked steadily enough, particular associations including a duo with Keith Tippett and group work with Elton Dean, Eddie Prévost and other first-generation British free players, as well as teaching at the major London colleges. But his major activity in the past 30 years might be his solo work, which has now been extensively documented on record: flinty, bonily resilient music with a northerner's distrust of swank and an extensive range of approaches codified by a trenchant imagination that always wants to get to the heart of the matter. Although he has never enjoyed the faintly glamorous aura which has been conferred on Keith Tippett, there is no other British pianist whose music is so free of cliché and capable of turning up fresh material, even after decades of intensive work in the improvisation field.

*The Heat Of Moments* (Wondrous)

## Sammy Rimington
CLARINET AND ALTO SAXOPHONE
*born* 29 April 1942

Rimington was still in his teens when he first went to America with a British trad group (Ken Colyer's). He may be the most naturally gifted of British players in his idiom, which is spirited and authentic (if that loaded word has any meaning) New Orleans jazz. While his clarinet playing owes the usual debts to the music's masters, from Johnny Dodds to George Lewis, his saxophone playing has a broad-brimmed vibrato that sounds as if it were forged in the Crescent City, and he likes to play as freely as possible within that style: one can imagine him enjoying a gig in an Albert Ayler ensemble. He actually moved to the US in 1965, working with many New Orleans legends, before returning to Europe two years later. He has ever since been in regular touring mode, staying with various leaders for a spell – including Barry Martyn, George Webb and Chris Barber – but most often as a guest soloist. There was a surprising dalliance with an early kind of jazz-rock in the group Armada (1971), but Rimington soon enough went back to his roots. His legacy on record to date has been somewhat dependent on the company he keeps, but if Rimington is in the line-up, the listener can be sure of his ability to lift even a ramshackle semi-pro outfit's game.

*The Exciting Sax Of Sammy Rimington* (Progressive)

## Lee Ritenour
GUITAR
*born* 11 January 1952

Ritenour's nickname, 'Captain Fingers', signals the chopsmanship which his career has been based around. He studied in California and began working as a session guitarist in Los Angeles in the early 70s. He subsequently began touring with a late-70s jazz-funk group, and along with such powerful friends as Dave Grusin began to move in on the nascent smooth-jazz market of the 80s. He also tried playing to Brazilian rhythms, a further softening of what was hardly profound music to start with, and latterly formed his own imprint, i.e. (sic), at Verve, although corporate politics being what they are it seems as if this has already been abandoned. There is little which is sensational about Ritenour's style – it's too dull for that – but he has a strong following among guitar obsessives. His Montgomery tribute *Wes Bound* (1992) affects all the surface matter of that guitarist's approach and none of the spirit.

*Rit* (Elektra)

## Sam Rivers
SAXOPHONES, FLUTE, PIANO
*born* 25 September 1923

Rivers's parents were both professional musicians and he took up the saxophone while at college in Texas. He went on to study in Boston from 1947, where he struck up an association with Jaki Byard, and although word of him was getting out, he did little to try and build any kind of career, preferring to work almost in isolation. He had been on tour with, of all people, T-Bone Walker when he was hired by Miles Davis as his quintet's saxophonist in 1964, but found the music ultimately conservative and he instead went on to make a handful of records as a leader for Blue Note, along with some sideman work with Tony Williams and Andrew Hill. The Blue Notes have never enjoyed much popularity and compared to

some of his later work they're a sometimes raw mix of ideas, Rivers's out playing colliding with conventional forms, although the final *A New Conception* seemed like a retreat into standards playing. In 1968, Rivers began playing with Cecil Taylor's group, although that was among the most inchoate settings for either man, and in the early 70s he set up Studio Rivbea (named in part for his wife Beatrice), the first of the new-music venues set up in Manhattan's then cheap SoHo district, which presaged the start of loft jazz. Later in the 70s he toured extensively in a trio with Barry Altschul and Dave Holland, perhaps the first outlet to show off the extent of his multi-instrumentalism. Following the closure of Studio Rivbea at the end of the decade, Rivers worked in Europe and eventually resettled in Orlando, Florida, where he again became the focal point for a community of new-music players. By the end of the century he had accrued a reputation as a grand old man of the avant-garde: there were albums by an all-star Rivbea Orchestra, an all-solo record for FMP, and a guest appearance on a set by one of jazz's most dynamic new talents, Jason Moran. In his 80s, Rivers was still teaching, touring and performing. He is in some senses an old-fashioned spirit of the avant-garde, still looking to make new matter out of venerable free-jazz texts: an enigmatic campaigner.
*Inspiration* (RCA)

# Riverside
RECORD COMPANY

Established by Bill Grauer and Orrin Keepnews in New York in 1953, the label began as a reissue operation, drawing material from the 20s catalogues of Paramount, Gennett and others, but Keepnews was producing new sessions soon enough and by the end of the decade it had built an important listing of sessions and artists. Arguably the most significant albums were those by pianists: Keepnews made the earliest recordings by Bill Evans and continued working with him until 1962, and he developed a close relationship with Thelonious Monk, setting down many of his most accomplished records. Other important names included Cannonball Adderley and Wes Montgomery, and there was a series devoted to redis-

covering older musicians from Chicago and New Orleans, Riverside Living Legends. Grauer's death in 1963 halted the company's progress, though, and it was, like every jazz label at that point, not in good financial shape: it went bankrupt within 12 months. Fantasy eventually acquired the catalogue and it has been part of their holdings since the 70s.

# Max Roach
DRUMS
*born* 10 January 1924

Roach always had strong associations with black church music, his mother singing gospel and himself playing in church from an early age in North Carolina. He moved to New York in his teens and became the house drummer at Monroe's in 1942, inevitably falling in with the musicians working towards bebop. He joined Benny Carter's big band in 1944, but a year later was working with Parker and Gillespie on 52nd Street and in Dizzy's big band. He plays drums on most of Parker's important small-group sessions during 1947–9: he and Kenny Clarke had set down the primer for bop drumming, the pulse driven out from the ride cymbal, the 'bomb-dropping' bass-drum interpolations, the variations of rhythm and sound coming from the other parts of the kit. Roach was a more daring stylist than Clarke, less 'proper' in a way, and he was probably the figure who most inspired the likes of Roy Haynes to really think about their own approaches.

Roach continued working with Parker and Miles Davis while also studying composition in Manhattan School, and in 1952 he began an alliance with Charles Mingus which resulted in the formation of a record label, Debut. A year later he was over on the West Coast, where he formed a new band with Clifford Brown and Sonny Stitt, who was replaced first by Teddy Edwards and then by Harold Land. The Brown–Roach quintet began touring in 1954 and its reputation was enhanced by four brilliant records for Emarcy: Brown's creativity was surging towards a peak, Roach matched him, and Land and pianist Richie Powell played above themselves in such a sparkling context. Where Blakey's Jazz Messengers were setting down one kind of hard-bop blueprint, the Roach–Brown group suggested a less bluesy, more aristocratic kind of style. Land was replaced by Sonny Rollins in 1955, but the deaths of Brown and Richie Powell in a car accident the following June devastated Roach, although he re-formed a new band soon enough.

He did, in fact, continue to lead small bands of one sort or another from then until the early 90s. His first horn players after the dissolution of the Brown group were Kenny Dorham and Booker Little, Hank Mobley and George Coleman, and Julian Priester; Roach suffered badly from depression during this period and Priester remembers the leader punching him during a fraught club gig. The records became, if anything, even stronger and more challenging: *Deeds Not Words* (1958) and *We Insist! Freedom Now Suite* (1960) saw Roach opening up his music to the wider possibilities of studio work in the LP era, touching on freely paced structures and using barrier-nudging soloists like Little to bring a new immediacy to what he was doing. His then wife, Abbey Lincoln, performs on some of this music, and the politically aware Roach began using his work as a platform for cultural protest. Though the Debut venture had long since foundered, Roach and Mingus collaborated on an 'alternative' Newport festival in 1960, and a year later he stopped a Miles Davis concert at Carnegie Hall with a protest against the sponsoring African Research Foundation. As the decade wore on, though, Roach contented himself with letting his music do the talking. He recorded a largely solo album, *Drums Unlimited*, in 1966, which bridged his take on jazz tradition with an undogmatic approach to the way it could be opened into other areas of improvising. This led eventually to his all-percussion ensemble M'Boom, first established around 1970 and which continued into the 90s. He recorded comparatively infrequently in the 70s, for the most part leading a relatively conventional post-bop quintet, but in the 80s he was busier in the studios with both M'Boom and his own groups, and he also took to performing duos with some surprising collaborators – Archie Shepp, Max Roach and Cecil Taylor – where he lent regal authority and counterpoint to the free playing of his partners. The duo with Taylor has been convened on a number of occasions since, and there was also a concert duo recording with Dizzy Gillespie in 1989, a farewell to bebop from two of its

originators. Roach's body of work has an invincible look to it: there is little or nothing which looks like a studio chore or a producer's folly. His playing, particularly as a soloist, has a composer's refinement and particularity, as well as a master drummer's accomplishment; and he should be remembered as a principal among the many small-group leaders of the past 50 years.

*We Insist! Freedom Now Suite* (Candid)

## George Robert
ALTO SAXOPHONE
*born* 15 September 1960

Born in Geneva, Robert studied at Berklee in the early 80s and privately with Phil Woods. Since then he has worked steadily in his native country as a small-group leader, displaying a fecund imagination in what are mostly familiar post-bop situations, documented mostly on a series of enjoyable records for the Swiss TCB and Mons labels. He might feel a little held back by his country's utter lack of prominence in the style of jazz he works in.

*Featuring Mr Clark Terry* (TCB)

## Yves Robert
TROMBONE
*born* 17 January 1958

Robert worked in and around Marseilles from the late 70s, playing Dixieland to start with but working his way towards free playing via an association with André Jaume. He has subsequently worked as a sideman with Louis Sclavis, Steve Lacy and the Orchestre National De Jazz, although he has also led a few bands of his own. Trombonists often have to work hard at not sounding lugubrious, but Robert seems to positively embrace that aspect of his playing, and his sonorously mournful sound is especially well captured on a recent ECM project, cited below.

*In Touch* (ECM)

# Hank Roberts

CELLO
*born* 24 March 1954

The cello is a pretty intractable instrument in jazz terms, but Roberts did his best to make it work, although some of his projects sidetracked him into pointless crossover areas. He mixed together cello and trombone playing as a student, but subsequently focused on the string instrument and in the late 80s he began working with Tim Berne in New York, before finding himself in projects with Bill Frisell, the string trio Arcado and eventually something called the Esslinger Cello Projeckt. His own Birds Of Prey band was a fairly awful attempt at mixing avant-garde improvisation with funk. Not much has been heard of him lately, as he has gone more into teaching than performing. This seems like a negative notice, but Roberts was a compelling figure in performance: with his scarecrow-like frame and penchant for singing wordlessly along with his solos, he cut a uniquely eerie figure in the New York music of his day.
*Little Motor People* (JMT)

# Howard Roberts

GUITAR
*born* 2 October 1929; *died* 28 June 1992

Roberts was a creative thinker who, though, was content to bury himself away for most of his career as a sessionman. He grew up in Phoenix but moved to Los Angeles in 1950 and almost from the first was heavily involved in the studio scene there, playing on probably thousands of records up until the 80s. He is involved in plenty of the West Coast jazz sessions of the 50s but was just as likely to be performing on a mood-music record, and his most notable work from any jazz viewpoint is in the records under his own name. The four he made for Verve are particularly fine, and although those he cut for Capitol in the 60s tend to be presented as lightweight pop-instrumental records, Roberts can't help putting some interesting touches into even the thinnest of them, his knowledge of harmony and 20th-century compositional form often breaking through. He latterly became a respected teacher, and was writing regularly for *Guitar Player* magazine until shortly before his death.
*Good Pickin's* (Verve)

# Luckey Roberts

PIANO
*born* 7 August 1893; *died* 5 February 1968

Roberts was a grand figure in black music, yet only from time to time did he come into the jazz mainstream. After working as a child acrobat in Philadelphia, he started on piano around 1900 and moved to New York ten years later. In 1911 he had a musical comedy, *My People*, in production, and over the next 20 years this was followed by 13 others. 'Junk Man Rag', a much-covered tune in the ragtime era, was his first published hit, and its demanding virtuosity was reflected in most of Roberts's other tunes: he was a formidable executant, and he played his pieces in a fast style designed to dazzle. Roberts led his own bands in vaudeville and at society engagements but they weren't recorded and there is precious little of him on record until a set of piano solos made for Rudi Blesh's Circle label in 1946, which show his ebullient delivery of some of his hit pieces was unimpaired. From 1940 until 1954 he ran his own place, The Rendezvous Club, in New York, and he turns up on some of the Blesh *This Is Jazz* broadcasts of 1947. He was still writing and performing until the late 50s. Had he recorded more, Roberts might be mentioned more often in the company of Willie Smith, James P Johnson and Eubie Blake, but in the end he left us very little.
*The Circle Recordings* (Solo Art)

# Marcus Roberts

PIANO
*born* 7 August 1963

Nicknamed 'J Master' by Wynton Marsalis, whose band Roberts came to prominence in, the pianist has been busy and prominent in American jazz for almost 20 years. He lost his sight as a child through cataracts, and went on to study in his native Florida, where Marsalis heard him and subsequently hired him (in 1985) for his touring group. He was the first winner of the Thelonious Monk Competition in 1987, and made a series of surprisingly successful (in jazz-commercial terms) albums for RCA Novus, before subsequently making a further sequence for Columbia. He left Marsalis's group in 1991, although he did direct the Lincoln Center Orchestra on a 1994 tour, and has since often turned up in the Marsalis circle of ongoing projects. Roberts is a bit of a conundrum: obviously versed in all of the historical styles of the instrument, his own original thinking is generally a lot more interesting than his re-creative work in the repertory, which tends to come over as a particularly dogmatic history lesson on stride, blues or whatever he happens to be playing. The Ellington homage listed below is actually a set of originals, and is a lot more absorbing than most Ducal tributes. He has lately been experimenting with variations on the traditional rhythm section, and with his Columbia contract currently in abeyance, it's to be hoped that some of these are documented elsewhere.

*In Honor Of Duke* (Columbia)

# Herb Robertson

TRUMPET, CORNET
*born* 21 February 1951

Robertson's crackling, unpredictable sound has made him a regular contributor to the American avant-garde of the past quarter-century. He worked in his native New Jersey after studying at Berklee, and then became a regular in Tim Berne's groups all through the 80s, as well as making his first records as a leader for JMT. In the 90s and the new century he has divided his time between America and Europe, leading often somewhat ragtag ensembles which have gravitated more towards the open-ended and European style of free playing. Robertson's earlier music was more structurally orientated and it may be that he has yet to really nail his most effective balance between inside and out playing. The journey there, though, has often been pretty exciting along the way. His real name is Clarence: 'Herb' was bestowed by teenage friends, after Herb Alpert, when he first became interested in jazz trumpet.

*Certified* (Winter & Winter)

# Joseph Robichaux

PIANO
*born* 8 March 1900; *died* 17 January 1965

The nephew of John Robichaux, a great old-time New Orleans bandleader who led groups in the city for more than 40 years,

Robichaux played piano in many of the better bands in the precinct in the 20s, featuring on some of the sessions by the Jones And Collins Astoria Hot Eight in 1928. He formed his New Orleans Rhythm Boys in 1931, who cut 22 titles for Vocalion in New York in 1933, a rare example of a New Orleans band getting exposure at that time (one title was even issued in England on Rex). The group lasted until the end of the decade but did not record again, and Robichaux eventually disbanded it and worked in New Orleans as a solo. He later worked extensively as a sideman with George Lewis, and at Preservation Hall in the years leading up to his death.

# Ikey Robinson

BANJO, GUITAR
*born* 25 July 1904; *died* 25 October 1990

Robinson grew up in Radford, Virginia, and was quick to pick up several instruments, though he settled on the violin and played in his family band, before changing to banjo and working elsewhere in Virginia. He went to Chicago in 1926 and recorded as both a sideman (with Jelly Roll Morton) and a leader, before moving to New York around 1930 and playing on record sessions with Clarence Williams. He went back to Chicago later in the decade and continued leading small groups all the way into the 50s, although he made no records with any of them. In the 60s he was still working, with Junie Cobb and with Franz Jackson's group the Original Jass All Stars, and he toured Europe with them. On his 80th birthday he played at a concert in his honour. Robinson wasn't much of a soloist, but as a sturdy rhythm man he enjoyed a very long career.

**Junie Cobb,** *New Hometown Band* (Riverside)

# Jim Robinson

TROMBONE
*born* 25 December 1890; *died* 4 May 1976

Perhaps the most significant of all New Orleans trombonists, Robinson didn't start on the horn until he was 25 (while serving in France with the US army). Back home he stayed with the fine Sam Morgan band for ten years. Eventually, he became bored with

band residencies and played only occasionally until the New Orleans revival got under
way. Thereafter, he was busy with Bunk
Johnson and especially George Lewis, whom
he toured with until the clarinettist's death.
Robinson set the style for ensemble playing
on his instrument: a tough, no-nonsense
counterpoint to the trumpet and clarinet,
plenty of space in the line, and a way of barking out a note to denote a change of paragraph. He didn't solo very often and when
he did he could sound tense and almost viol-
ent – so his solos are actually worth waiting
for. In his 80s, he was still playing the same
way. He only rarely had his name out front
on a record date, but there is so much of
him with Johnson and Lewis that it hardly
matters.

**George Lewis, *The Beverley Caverns Sessions*** (Good
Time Jazz)

## Orphy Robinson
VIBES
*born* 13 October 1960

Robinson's often interrupted progress has
been a curious part of recent British jazz. He
played various instruments before settling
on the vibes, and from his teens worked in
London funk bands before coming to prominence with the Jazz Warriors and as a
Courtney Pine and Andy Sheppard sideman.
He seemed set for some sort of stardom
when signing to Blue Note and releasing two
albums in the early 90s, but that led
nowhere, the albums quickly vanished, and
despite sometimes convening bands of his
own he has only occasionally made his presence felt. Which hasn't stopped this likeable
musician challenging himself: he has
worked much more closely with the free-
improvisation camp than straight-ahead
jazz of late, and in 2005 was heard playing
steel pan in a duo with bass saxophonist
Tony Bevan.

**The Vibes Describes** (Blue Note)

## Perry Robinson
CLARINET
*born* 17 September 1938

Robinson is one of the very few to make a
go of creating a place for the clarinet in the
jazz avant-garde. His father was a folk-music
historian and performer, and Robinson
studied in New York and at Lenox School,
where he met Ornette Coleman. He then
spent two years in Europe before returning
to New York and eventually taking a role in
the Jazz Composers' Guild, turning up with
Henry Grimes on ESP and in Carla Bley's
*Escalator Over The Hill*. Thereafter, though,
he has never seemed to enjoy much luck
with his associations from a documentary
point of view. He spent a long period in
Gunter Hampel's group, led the bands Pipe
Dreams, Nightmare Island and Licorice
Factory (which used several clarinettists),
and has occasionally featured as a sideman,
although most of this work has been
scrappily recorded and only on minor labels.
As if acknowledging that his chosen horn
can't compete with free-jazz screaming,
Robinson has tended to work in semi-
pastoral and sometimes unusual crossover
settings, and the folk music of his father
sometimes surfaces in a bucolic turn of
phrase or two.

**Gunter Hampel, *Jubilation*** (Birth)

## Prince Robinson
TENOR SAXOPHONE, CLARINET
*born* 7 June 1902; *died* 23 July 1960

Robinson was respected as a fine player by
Coleman Hawkins and numerous others, but
he has barely left a mark on the music. He
learned clarinet in his teens and played in
local bands in his native Virginia before
moving to New York in 1923 and working
with a variety of groups, including Duke
Ellington's orchestra, as well as subbing for
Hawkins with Fletcher Henderson. He then
worked with McKinney's Cotton Pickers for
a number of years, where he took some of
his most striking features on record, and
also in studio groups during the 30s: he can
be heard taking solos with Clarence Williams
and Teddy Williams. He spent seven years
with Claude Hopkins from 1945, and was
still playing in the years leading up to his
death, including in a Henderson reunion
band. But he never led a band of his own on
record, and while his best playing, where it
can be found, is impressive, something
about his rhythmical language never quite
left the 20s behind.

**McKinney's Cotton Pickers, *Put it There*** (Frog)

## Scott Robinson
SAXOPHONES, CLARINET
*born* 27 April 1959

Robinson is doing more than anyone to bring back some of the more arcane members of the saxophone family into regular use. He has done one album (*Thinking Big*, 1996) which involves almost every member of the reed family, including the contrabass sarrusophone, and another (*Melody From The Sky*, 1998) where he's featured entirely on C-melody saxophone. The problem with both is that they tend to end up as novelty music, rather than plausible jazz. Robinson was a very young member of the Berklee faculty and is a natural scholar of his subject, which broadly speaking is the American pre-war popular repertoire, although he is a very sound man to have in any mainstream situation, and he's done a lot of session work. Perhaps it's no surprise that he's even performed with that other great fan of oddball saxophones, Anthony Braxton.
*Thinking Big* (Arbors)

## Spike Robinson
TENOR SAXOPHONE
*born* 16 January 1930; *died* 29 October 2001

Robinson started out on alto, in navy bands, and around 1950 he went to London as part of a band attached to the American Embassy. He then found himself in the thick of the London modern scene, and recorded for Esquire with some of the leading British players of that time. When he returned to America he became an engineer, and played in only a part-time capacity for some 30 years: when he finally retired from his job in 1985, he returned to the saxophone, by this time a tenor. Spike never forgot his time in Britain and he became a regular visitor in the 80s, before settling in the UK in 1989. Alastair Robertson, a great admirer, made many records with him for the Hep label. His languorous style and beautiful tone made him sound much like late-period Lester Young, minus the fluffs and the agonies. English audiences will always remember his immortal introduction to every piece: 'Here's another nice ol' toon . . .'
*It's A Wonderful World* (Hep)

## Phil Robson
GUITAR
*born* 28 February 1970

Robson moved to London from his native Derby to study at Guildhall School, and in the 90s he became a frequently encountered name on the scene as a sideman, as well as with his band Partisans, which he co-leads with Julian Siegel. Like most members of a generation who grew up with at least as much rock, funk, dance, folk and blues music in their ears as jazz, Robson has an eclectic range which lets him fit into most situations, but his own projects have shown a constructive and thoughtful progress which his alliance with the Babel label has capably documented.
*Partisans* (Babel)

## Sebastian Rochford
DRUMS
*born* 20 November 1973

The Aberdonian drummer has become something of a focal point for London's jazz in the new century. He arrived down south in 1997 and found sideman work in a number of situations, but his main interest has been in the groups Polar Bear, which he leads, and Pete Wareham's Acoustic Ladyland, which reworks some of Jimi Hendrix's material in a genuine jazz language. The shy and rather tongue-tied Rochford's own style mixes jazz and rock influences but ends up fairly squarely in the jazz corner. These groups take a central role in the F-IRE Collective, an informally organized gang of young players who are networking and seeking to establish playing and recording opportunities within an often indifferent London environment. Work in progress.
**Polar Bear**, *Dimly Lit* (Babel)

## Bob Rockwell
TENOR AND SOPRANO SAXOPHONES
*born* 2 May 1945

Rockwell is a talented and engaging saxophonist: but there are hundreds of them in America, and perhaps he made a smart move by basing himself (from 1983) in Copenhagen, where he has enjoyed a fruitful career. He was living in Minneapolis as a teenager, when he started on clarinet and tenor, then worked in Las Vegas shows before moving to New York and numerous sideman gigs in 1978. Since his move to Denmark he has been involved in many of the best local groups – including those of Jan Kaspersen and Jens Winther – and made a number of albums for Steeplechase, each showcasing his big sound and assured grasp of the post-bop idiom.

*Light Blue* (Steeplechase)

## Claudio Roditi
TRUMPET, FLUGELHORN
*born* 28 May 1946

Born in Rio de Janeiro, Roditi played locally before going to a jazz competition in Vienna in 1966. He then toured Europe before going back to Brazil, and next studied at Berklee before settling in New York in 1976. Ever since he has been a ubiquitous presence on that scene, leading his own small groups, sharing front lines with Paquito D'Rivera, taking a role in Dizzy Gilespie's United Nation Orchestra, and generally working out his idea of a fusion between his native Brazilian music and New York's contemporary jazz. Roditi is a very proficient player, though one does feel that he doesn't truly have a great deal to say: the record cited catches him at a very good moment, but most of his appearances on record tend to be forgotten as soon as they're over.

*Free Wheelin'* (Reservoir)

## Red Rodney
TRUMPET
*born* 27 September 1927; *died* 27 May 1994

Robert Chudnick was for a long time famous more by proxy – as Charlie Parker's trumpeter in 1949 – but in the 80s he made a slightly amazing comeback, and it didn't seem all that surprising at the time to find him in the bar at a south London pub where he was playing that evening. Rodney (the 'Red' inevitably came from his hair colour) toured with all sorts of big bands in the 40s and gained his greatest exposure in the Woody Herman trumpet section in 1948. He worked with Parker during 1949–50 and was sometimes billed as 'Albino Red' in order to

pass at gigs in the South (this brought about the funniest scene in Clint Eastwood's otherwise gloomy biopic *Bird*), but he became hooked on heroin and his career fell away in the 50s. At the end of the decade he was running society bands and making good money, but it only fed his drugs habit, and he moved to Las Vegas to work in 1960. In 1972 he suffered a stroke, but gradually worked his way back, and by the end of the decade he was playing serious gigs again. He was a great pleasure to hear in the last ten years of his life, the old bebop speed pared back but a new emphasis on flugelhorn bringing extra lustre into his work. Red's quintet also acted as an important seedbed of talent, introducing Dick Oatts, Garry Dial, Joey Baron and Chris Potter among others.

*Red Giant* (Steeplechase)

## Paul Rogers
BASS
*born* 20 April 1956

Rogers came to some prominence in the 80s, working with such veteran British modernists as Harry Beckett and Alan Skidmore; but his real forte was in the field of free improvisation, and he soon moved more or less exclusively into that field, making some memorable alliances with the likes of Evan Parker and Paul Dunmall. Rogers seeks nothing especially outlandish or misanthropic in his approach to the instrument, using the full arsenal of conventional techniques for fingers and bow, but his ideas are ambitious enough to extend the vocabulary of the instrument significantly. He is especially good in small, close-knit combinations, where he can be both a soloist and a combative ensemble voice. The recently released *Listen*, made up of solo concerts recorded ten years apart in 1989 and 1999, is a magnificent reminder of his talents, which have been much less available to British audiences since his decision to settle in France in 1992.

*Listen* (Emanem)

## Shorty Rogers

TRUMPET, FLUGELHORN, ARRANGER
*born* 14 April 1924; *died* 7 November 1994

Born Milton Rajonsky, Shorty was the biggest name in West Coast jazz. He studied in New York before going into the army, and on his discharge worked first with Woody Herman's First and Second Herds, and from there in the Stan Kenton band of 1950–51. Besides his own trumpet playing, which was delivered in a bright, almost humorously optimistic yet contrarily low-key style, Rogers's writing and arranging were also given early prominence in both bands' books. After leaving Kenton he worked on his own account as one of the busiest pro-fessionals on the Los Angeles studio scene, his music helping to create the idea of 'West Coast jazz' – bustling with incident, full of musicianly and quietly challenging ideas, his scores didn't suit grandstand players (with the exception of high-note specialist Maynard Ferguson) and called for a co-operative and very precise kind of executive skill. Partly for that reason, the idiom was subsequently criticized for being passionless and procedural, yet that argument seems absurd if one listens to the brilliant 1953 sessions released as *Cool And Crazy* (RCA), where Rogers and his Giants (to use the name they often worked under) work through some of the liveliest and most excit-ing big-band music of its era, even given the complexity of the scoring: setpieces such as 'Sweetheart Of Sigmund Freud' haven't lost their capacity to put the listener on the edge of their seat, even 50 years later. Rogers used the cream of the Californian studio men for these and other dates, and he made a sequence of orchestral records in this vein for RCA all through the 50s, as well as scor-ing for film and doing some surprising small-group work: his album *The Three* (Con-temporary, 1954), with Shelly Manne, and the remarkable *Collaboration: West* (Prestige, 1953), with Teddy Charles, show him experi-menting with free forms.

In the 60s he was in too much demand from Hollywood to pursue much of a jazz playing career, and the West Coast scene was in any case at a low ebb. But in the 80s he returned to more active duty, and toured with various reunion editions of The Giants: every gig he played found him wreathed in smiles, a musician who loved playing jazz and never lost his taste for the music which got him his start.
*Sweetheart Of Sigmund Freud* (Giant Steps)

## Mickey Roker

DRUMS
*born* 3 September 1932

Roker was born in Miami but began playing in jazz groups in Philadelphia, at the end of the 50s. He then shifted to New York and worked steadily under dozens of leaders, from Junior Mance and Ben Webster to Bobby Hutcherson and Clifford Jordan. He was an in-house drummer for Blue Note in the late 60s, and worked steadily with Dizzy Gillespie through the 70s. Norman Granz used him on many of his studio dates for Pablo in the 70s and early 80s, and while he then toured with Ray Brown's trio, he became tired of life on the road and has since preferred to spend his time at home in Philadelphia, working as and when he chooses.
**Lee Morgan**, *Live At The Lighthouse* (Blue Note)

## Adrian Rollini

BASS SAXOPHONE, VIBES
*born* 28 June 1903; *died* 15 May 1956

The nonpareil master of the bass saxophone defined the style of the instrument for all time – even though it led his career into a dead end. Rollini was a piano prodigy, giving concerts as an infant, and entered jazz when he joined Ed Kirkeby's studio band The California Ramblers in 1922. He is on hun-dreds of dance records made in the 20s, and though he didn't record as a leader himself until 1934, he is on many of the major sessions by Bix Beiderbecke, Frankie Trumbauer, Red Nichols, Miff Mole, Joe Venuti and Eddie Lang. Besides the bass sax, he also had a go at such peculiarities as the goofus and the hot fountain pen (a kind of clarinet). He also spent two years in London working in Fred Elizalde's band: Elizalde's dazzling record of 'Nobody's Sweetheart' shows Rollini at his best. The saxophonist made his monstrous instrument seem nimble and light-footed: he seemed able to switch between a bass and a front-line role without any effort at all, and fellow saxmen such as Coleman Hawkins and Harry Carney

were jealous. In the 30s he played vibes more and more and bass sax less and less: the big horn wasn't in such favour in swing-era settings, even though Rollini's later records where he plays it show no lessening of interest. He worked at New York's President Hotel until the mid-40s but eventually decamped to Florida and worked away from jazz. Film exists of Rollini playing vibes, yet there isn't a single frame known to exist of him playing the instrument with which he is for ever associated. His brother Arthur (1912–93) was a fine tenorman who spent several years with Benny Goodman.
*Swing Low* (Affinity)

## Dennis Rollins
TROMBONE
*born* 11 November 1964

Courtney Pine nicknamed him 'Badbone', and Rollins has used that name for his own bands, although he still works with Pine as a sideman. He was born in Birmingham and was playing in the National Youth Jazz Orchestra in 1985, before moving on to the Jazz Warriors a year later. A cheerful rather than a challenging soloist, he is as much in debt to funk players (Fred Wesley is the obvious role model) as he is to jazz trombonists, and the Badbone records offer up a likeable mix of funk, jazz and pop.
*Make Your Move* (Sound)

## Sonny Rollins
TENOR AND SOPRANO SAXOPHONES
*born* 7 September 1930

Theodore Walter Rollins started out on alto but changed to the tenor saxophone when he was 16. He was already playing in high-school bands, with Jackie McLean and Kenny Drew, and he made his first records in 1949 as a sideman. For the next five years he built up a portfolio of work on the New York scene, in the company of Charlie Parker, Max Roach, Bud Powell, J J Johnson and Thelonious Monk, and particularly with Miles Davis, both on record and on live dates. His progress was hampered somewhat by a dependence on drugs, but the youthful Rollins already had his huge, almost gleaming sound in place: where saxophonists often sought to mellow their timbre, Rollins,

perhaps following Parker's example, tried to harden and intensify his tone, giving it an almost metallic bite. During this period he composed a handful of tunes – 'Oleo', 'Airegin' and 'Doxy' – which would enter the jazz repertory, although since then he has shown a seeming reluctance to write many more. He joined the Clifford Brown–Max Roach quintet in 1955, and while there embarked on his own recordings, for Prestige, Blue Note and Contemporary. In the space of an amazing two-year period, from December 1955 to November 1957, he set down 12 albums under his own name which contain perhaps the single most sustained, creative saxophone playing anywhere in jazz on record: taking in such milestones as *Work Time*, *Saxophone Colossus*, *Tenor Madness* and *Tour de Force* for Prestige, *Newk's Time* and *A Night At The Village Vanguard* for Blue Note, and *Way Out West* for Contemporary, it showed his appetite for playing to be immense, his improvisational powers unquenchable. Gunther Schuller undertook a celebrated analysis of his solo on 'Blue Seven' from *Saxophone Colossus*, which proclaimed Rollins to be the creator of a new kind of thematic improvising, where the soloist builds an improvisation out of motifs drawn from the melodic theme, rather than merely taking off from the chord sequence. This was in part true, although much of what the saxophonist was playing didn't depart dramatically from the boppers' use of improvising formulae: he simply did it with a greater degree of sophistication and ever-more rhythmic ingenuity. Coupled with his iron-clad sound, it makes his playing from this period almost overwhelming in its exultant intensity: as Coltrane would with Elvin Jones, Rollins loved to spar with his drummers, and his work with Roach and with Philly Joe Jones on *Newk's Time* is tumultuous in its exhilaration. The music on the date at The Village Vanguard is fine enough to make one miserable at the thought of how many more live sessions with Rollins could have been taken down, and weren't. There was also his choice of material: bored with many of the overplayed standards, and gifted with a sometimes impish sense of humour, Sonny picked out tunes which nobody else thought of playing, including 'How Are Things In Glocca Morra', 'There's No Business Like Show Business' and

'Rock-A-Bye Your Baby With A Dixie Melody'. And he came out with a political statement of sorts, though an unspecific one, in *Freedom Suite* (1958), the title piece of which was perhaps his last major piece of composing. Saxophonists everywhere were in awe and despair of his talent.

In some ways, so was Rollins. Dissatisfied with many of his sidemen and with much in his own playing, he went into a period of seclusion in 1959 and didn't play again in public for two years, although he did spend time practising in the open air, on the Williamsburg Bridge. At the end of 1961 he returned, set up a new group with Jim Hall, and began making records for RCA (including a meeting with Coleman Hawkins). He listened to the avant-garde and briefly worked with Don Cherry, but it wasn't really for him, and he spent much of the 60s in what seemed like a state of indecision, although his work on the soundtrack to *Alfie* (1965) was still little short of marvellous. He finally went on another period of retreat, during 1969–71, before signing a new contract with Milestone which has lasted to this day. He has recorded prolifically enough for them, mostly on his own account: aside from a brief tour with the Milestone Jazzstars in 1978 (with McCoy Tyner, Ron Carter and Al Foster) he has worked as his own master, touring in bands which function effectively as backdrops for his own playing, and which have included such sidemen as Clifton Anderson, Mark Soskin, Victor Bailey and Stephen Scott. It has been a commonplace to encounter criticism of the post-1971 Rollins as a diminished player, and while the Olympian achievements of the middle 50s haven't been repeated, it would be unfair to expect that they would be. In fact, particularly in live performance, much of the old Rollins remained intact all through the 70s, 80s and 90s: on a good night, a grand improvisation would break away from the moorings of his accompanists and restore all his musical eminence. Many of the Milestone studio recordings have been comparatively prosaic and well-mannered, although his first record of the new century, *This Is What I Do* (2000), was a triumphant reminder of his mastery of the saxophone, even in his 70s. But there may be little more to come from him now: he has declared an intention to retire at 75 (and possibly write a long-awaited autobiogra-

phy), and, on a sadder note, the death of his wife Lucille at the end of 2004 may have made his mind up for him.
*A Night At The Village Vanguard* (Blue Note)

## Aldo Romano
DRUMS
*born* 16 January 1941

Although born in Italy, Romano has lived and worked most of his life in France. He played with the Paris circle of modernists in the early 60s and he moved close to the free end of playing when he played with the visiting Don Cherry in 1965–6. He was a regular sideman with Joachim Kühn, and accompanied Keith Jarrett on the pianist's first tour of Europe. After a period where he tinkered with jazz-rock in the early 70s, he went back to a more conventional post-bop style. In the late 80s he began working in a quartet with some of his Italian countrymen, including Paolo Fresu, Franco D'Andrea and Furio Di Castri, and their record of popular Neapolitan tunes, *Prosodie* (1995), was quite intoxicatingly lovely.
*Prosodie* (Verve)

## Wallace Roney
TRUMPET, FLUGELHORN
*born* 25 May 1960

Roney's exemplary technique and hard-hitting approach have been widely admired, but he has been saddled with a reputation as a Miles Davis copyist which he finds especially exasperating. Born in Philadelphia, he joined the Art Blakey group when he was 21, though he only stayed for six months or so. Freelancing in numerous New York bands, he eventually joined the Tony Williams quintet which formed in 1986 and recorded several sets for Blue Note. In 1991, he worked alongside the ailing Miles Davis at the latter's Montreux appearance with Quincy Jones, and earned the master's approval; this presumably led to his reprising the Davis role in Gerry Mulligan's Re-Birth Of The Cool group, and a subsequent tour with an all-star Davis Tribute band. While he has since then performed in numerous and diverse situations and led some strong groups and records of his own, the Davis ghost (early 60s model, perhaps) is very hard to lay in his playing. As if to step away from this, Roney has pitched much of his recent work in a more aggressive and unsparing idiom, sometimes with electronic support. However one wants to appreciate him, he is a proficient and likeable trumpeter, and he can get a lovely sound on ballads, Davisian or not. He is married to the pianist Geri Allen and they frequently work together.

**No Room For Argument** (Stretch)

## Ronnie Scott's Jazz Club
VENUE

England's most renowned jazz venue was established in London's Soho district in 1959 by saxophonist Scott with his business partner, Pete King. The original premises were at 39 Gerrard Street (known to habitués as 'The Old Place'), but the Club moved in 1965 to 47 Frith Street, where it has flourished ever since. Scott and King made a point of featuring American visitors for stays of a week or more at the Club, following an American model which was new to Britain at the time, and the venue became a regular stopover for such musicians as Ben Webster, Coleman Hawkins, Dizzy Gillespie, Zoot Sims, Dexter Gordon and numerous others, as well as the entire orchestras of Count Basie, Buddy Rich and Gil Evans, who somehow fitted on to the modest-sized stage. For many years it employed an in-house trio as support for the visitor, which for a number of years was led by Stan Tracey, and the 'support' act for the headliner has usually been British, which has sometimes led to amusing mixtures of styles: the singer Joan Armatrading, early in her career, once supported Cecil Taylor. As a focal point for London's jazz scene, it has been as indispensable as is The Village Vanguard in New York. In 2004, its future – never entirely stable or guaranteed, given the eternally parlous state of the jazz business – seemed assured when a new management structure and financing for the future was announced.

## Leon Roppolo
CLARINET
born 16 March 1902; died 5 October 1943

Roppolo's brief career was mercurial, and ended in a bizarre fashion. He learned guitar and clarinet as a youth, and played briefly in New Orleans around 1917 before touring in vaudeville, playing on riverboats and eventually ending up in Chicago. He joined a band led by Paul Mares in 1921, which eventually became the New Orleans Rhythm Kings, and Roppolo was the star player of the group: a natural master of the clarinet who sounded confident and inventive in every register, he stands out on their records, and contemporary accounts present him as the thinking, inquisitive player in a band of young maestros. He spent a brief period in New York, returned to New Orleans, played for a spell with the Halfway House Orchestra and then rejoined the new New Orleans Rhythm Kings. But something strange had happened to him, possibly a consequence of his fondness for reefers and alcohol: he suffered a mental collapse, and was confined to an asylum for the rest of his days, even though he managed to lead a band in his place of confinement and was let out to perform on a couple of occasions not long before his death. It was a queer and melancholy fate for a young man who might have gone on to much greater things.

**New Orleans Rhythm Kings,** *The Complete Set* (Retrieval)

## Denis Rose
PIANO
born 31 May 1922; died 22 November 1984

There is very little to remember Denis Rose by. He was an unassuming but regular figure on the London scene from the 40s to the 80s. He was quick to pick up on the possibilities of bebop, and was an almost professorial presence at the early sessions at London's initial bebop premises, Club Eleven: at the age of 26, he was somewhat older than some of the participants, and he is remembered by other musicians as a 'teacher' to many of the other players involved. But Rose hardly recorded at all: at one of his handful of dates, with a Ronnie Scott group, he played trumpet. For much of his career he played background music in clubs. Maggie Nicols remembers him with particular affection, crediting him as a guiding force in her development as a singer.

## Bernt Rosengren
TENOR SAXOPHONE
born 24 December 1937

Rosengren was the leading Swedish modernist of the 60s and 70s. A native Stockholmer, he made his first record as far back as 1959 (a Sonet LP entitled *The Beat Generation*!), and having worked in Poland (where he played on the soundtrack to Roman Polanski's *Knife In The Water*) and on tour with George Russell, he soon asserted himself as a premier voice in a community which would have to wait a long time for international recognition. Rosengren's basic hard-bop style was expanded soon enough by exposure to John Coltrane's music, but he has always asserted a careful grip on his own playing and there is very little wasted in his delivery of an improvisation. He later worked with Don Cherry and Lars Gullin, and recorded a classic of his country's music, *Notes From The Underground* (Harvest) in 1973. Since then he has played in a rather more conservative bop idiom, working in the groups Summit Meeting and his own bands convened to celebrate the music of Gershwin and Swedish poet Evert Taube. Rosengren hasn't always been as well documented as he should have been on record, but he is unquestionably one of the major players in his country's jazz.
*Notes From The Underground* (EMI/Harvest)

## Kurt Rosenwinkel
GUITAR
born 28 October 1970

Guitarists have become almost as important as saxophonists in contemporary jazz, and almost as ubiquitous, which makes it that much more difficult to assert an individual voice. Rosenwinkel has made a fair stab at it. He grew up in Philadelphia and took up the guitar at 12, becoming one of the few who tuned to jazz rather than rock, and he went to Berklee in 1988. His first important gig was as one of the guitarists in Paul Motian's Electric Be-Bop Band, and he has since worked in numerous New York groups and led bands of his own, winning a contract with Verve, although with that label's downsizing of its roster that may have been terminated. Rosenwinkel has a heads-down, unfussy and plain attack on guitar which has an almost classical feel at times, but on record he has mixed that in with tracks which sound like memories of progressive rock, a rather strange truce.
*The Next Step* (Verve)

## Michele Rosewoman
PIANO
born 29 March 1953

Rosewoman came to some prominence in the 80s as a composer and performer. She moved to New York from California in 1978, having studied South American and African percussion styles, and has mixed work in an Afro-Cuban idiom with an impressive quintet which at various times included Steve Coleman, Greg Osby and Gary Thomas, as well as a 14-strong band named New Yor-Uba, which was intended to create a celebratory performance of Cuban music in a New York context. Most of her recordings have been made for the European Enja label, and the earliest are the best: a 1999 record found her returning to some of her previous work, and some of the steam does seem to have gone out of her career.
*The Source* (Soul Note)

## Renee Rosnes
PIANO
born 24 March 1962

A Canadian by birth, Rosnes studied in Vancouver and Toronto before moving to New York in 1987. There she worked with three senior spirits: in Joe Henderson's all-female rhythm section, in Wayne Shorter's touring band (where she played electric keyboards), and with J J Johnson, who worked with her up until his death. She made her first record for Blue Note in 1990, and has enjoyed the loyalty of the label since, which has paid for some interesting and surprisingly left-field projects at times: given that she is at heart a straightforward and lyrical post-bop player who has done most of her work in small-group contexts, a record such

as the big-band world-music fusion of *Life On Earth* (2001) came out of an unexpected place. One gift she has is for making a surprise choice of material work for her, as in the title track of the compilation listed, which creams off some of the best of her Blue Note recordings.
**With A Little Help From My Friends** (Blue Note)

## Frank Rosolino
TROMBONE, VOCAL
*born* 20 August 1926; *died* 26 November 1978

Rosolino was exceptionally adept on the trombone, and he claimed he got his facility from attempting to copy the phrasing and technique of his brother, who was a gifted violinist. He worked in various trombone sections at the end of the 40s, notably Gene Krupa's, and eventually joined Stan Kenton in 1952. From 1955 he was based on the West Coast, and he turned up in numerous sessions before going the Hollywood studio route. In between times, he co-led a group with Conte Candoli. Like Milt Bernhart and Bob Enevoldsen, Rosolino could get around the slide-horn with a smooth facility, but he had a slightly more aggressive attack than theirs and he could punch through a chart with real finesse, and an occasional wry humour. He sometimes sang novelty vocals (as on Gene Krupa's 'Lemon Drop', which for a time gave him the nickname 'The Lemon Drop Kid'). But the end of his life was awful: in deep depression, he shot his two children and then took his own life. None of his original albums are currently in circulation, and the best of him is to be found with the likes of Howard Rumsey.
**Howard Rumsey, *Lighthouse At Laguna*** (OJC/Contemporary)

## Annie Ross
VOCAL
*born* 25 July 1930

Born Annabelle Short in Mitcham, Surrey, she went to Los Angeles at the age of three with her aunt, the singer Ella Logan, and worked as a child actress before returning to Europe as a cabaret singer. She worked with Kenny Clarke in Paris and they had a child together before Ross returned to the US, where she had hits with a tongue-twisting vocalese version of 'Twisted' (1952), a set-piece which has been much copied since, by Joni Mitchell and several others. She returned to London to star in the revue *Cranks*, which featured her alongside Anthony Newley, and then was back in New York to continue her singing career, this time as part of a trio with Dave Lambert and Jon Hendricks, which enjoyed some five years of resounding if debilitating success: exhausted by the constant touring, Ross left to come back to England in 1962. She ran her own club in London for a time (Annie's Room, which eventually closed in 1965), recorded some more albums – which are unjustly obscure, and deserve reissue – and in the 70s and 80s mixed this side of her work with more acting, turning up frequently on television and in films. In the 90s she was touring again as a solo, and although her voice had inevitably faded somewhat, Ross's rare imagination persisted. She can claim to be a unique figure in her idiom: she was at least the equal of her partners in Lambert, Hendricks and Ross, performed the tricky calling of vocalese with a simple fluency, and worked the divide between cool and emotive and 'theatrical' singing at least as well as any of her contemporaries. Her various solo records, in a scattered discography full of out-of-print and otherwise hard to locate items, can fairly rank with the best jazz vocal albums of the LP era.
**Sing A Song With Mulligan** (World Pacific/Capitol)

## Ronnie Ross
BARITONE SAXOPHONE
*born* 2 October 1933; *died* 12 December 1991

Although born in Calcutta, Ross moved to London from Scotland at the start of the 50s and worked in a band with Don Rendell, who was the one who got him to switch from tenor to baritone sax since Rendell played tenor himself. He went to the Newport Jazz Festival in 1958 to appear as a British representative in Marshall Brown's International Youth Band, although at 25 he was possibly a bit old for it. He returned there a year later with a band he co-led with Allan Ganley, and thereafter divided his time between small-group and big-band section work. Ross was only rarely featured out front, and his two great records, *Double Image* (1958) and *Cleopatra's Needle* (1968), are long out of print and impossible to find. Rock fans are unwittingly familiar with his beautiful playing, via the handsome baritone solo he plays on Lou Reed's 'Walk On The Wild Side'.

***Cleopatra's Needle*** (Fontana)

## Roulette

RECORD COMPANY

The company was established in 1957 by a group led by Morris Levy, a crook who had already exploited the New York jazz business for many years. Its mainstay was Count Basie's orchestra, who recorded numerous albums between 1957 and 1962, although the catalogue also contains significant holdings of Sarah Vaughan and Maynard Ferguson material. Levy wasn't much interested in jazz and was quite happy to turn Roulette into a pop label in the 60s. EMI eventually acquired the catalogue in 1989, and much of the best of it has been reissued.

## Charlie Rouse

TENOR SAXOPHONE
*born* 6 April 1924; *died* 30 November 1988

Although Rouse did front eight albums of his own during a long career of playing, he is always remembered as the saxophonist in Thelonious Monk's quartet. This position came up after many years of work in the music: he joined Dizzy Gillespie's big band in 1945, worked in R&B bands, had brief spells with Duke Ellington and Count Basie, was on Clifford Brown's first record dates, and then led a hard-bop quintet called Les (Jazz) Modes. As that band was petering out in 1959, he sat in with Monk at a New York gig and went on to stay for the next 11 years. Where Johnny Griffin didn't change his style at all with Monk, and played in the same headlong fashion, Rouse, previously a typically fluent bop player, meticulously adapted himself to Monk's music: his tone became heavier, his phrasing more careful, and he seemed to act as an interlocutor between his leader and the listener. In the 70s he studied acting for a time, and then found a new niche as a guardian of Monk's

music in the group Sphere, which acted as a repertory band for the pianist's music. He played a final tribute to his old boss a few weeks before his own death from lung cancer.

**Thelonious Monk,** *It's Monk's Time* (Columbia)

## Rova

GROUP

The most durable of all the saxophone quartets has been together since 1977, when the San Francisco musicians Jon Raskin, Larry Ochs, Andrew Voigt and Bruce Ackley combined and used their surname initials for their group name. The key difference between them and their near contemporaries the World Saxophone Quartet is the substantial body of original work they have created: while WSQ are only occasionally convened and rely on a relatively limited book, ROVA have a mass of material and have been given numerous commissions. Steve Adams replaced Voigt in 1988, but they did not become ROAA. While they retain a fundamental allegiance to jazz improvisation, much of their work revolves around complex scores. They have undertaken many visits to Europe (including two tours of the then-Soviet Union) and have a significant discography stretching over nearly 30 years. While the individual members do undertake 'solo' work away from the group, their greatest commitment is to ROVA itself.

***Bingo*** (Victo)

## Jimmy Rowles

PIANO
*born* 19 August 1918; *died* 28 May 1996

Nobody in jazz played a slow tempo as well as Jimmy Rowles. He had classical lessons as a child, but developed a taste for Teddy Wilson's playing, and went to college in Seattle, where he spent most of his time playing jazz. He settled in Los Angeles around 1942 and then worked in Lester Young's group, and in the big bands of Woody Herman and Benny Goodman. But during the 50s he worked mainly as a solo, and as an accompanist to singers. He worked in Hollywood clubs and played many studio sessions, while backing Peggy Lee, Billie

Holiday and Anita O'Day among others. A rehearsal tape exists of Rowles and Holiday working through some material, and it gives a rare and funny insight into the way both worked. He is on many jazz sessions of the period – with Stan Getz, Lee Konitz, Bud Shank, Benny Carter and more – and was an especial favourite of Ben Webster's, with whom he also played golf. This kind of thing kept him occupied during the 60s too, but eventually he moved over to New York in 1973 and he carried on in much the same vein. He is a superb part of many of Zoot Sims's later albums for Pablo, and he also accompanied Ella Fitzgerald for a spell at the beginning of the 80s, a decade when he also visited Europe to play in festivals. As time went on he took to singing himself, in a gruff, grandfatherly voice which was in its way as inimitable as his piano playing, which was always at its best in a slow but constantly swinging groove. Rowles loved the music of Ellington and Wayne Shorter, and had an encyclopedic knowledge of American songwriting: he would always bring a few unusual standards to a date, and many of the records he played on, whether it was his date or not, benefited from an idea for a surprising ballad or a forgotten swinger. For many years he had relatively few albums to his own credit, but there are later sessions for Xanadu, Musica, Contemporary, Black & Blue and Choice, all of which are worth hearing, and the date he did for Columbia with Stan Getz, named after his gorgeous original 'The Peacocks', is sheer bliss. His daughter Stacy is an accomplished trumpeter. Emphysema restricted his playing in his later years.
**The Peacocks** (Columbia)

# Ernie Royal
TRUMPET
*born* 2 June 1921; *died* 16 March 1983

Marshal Royal's brother was an excellent trumpeter. He worked alongside Marshal in the Lionel Hampton band of the early 40s, before going into Woody Herman's Second Herd (the first black to do so) and spells with Barnet, Ellington and Kenton. Thereafter he was most likely to be found doing studio work, holding down a staff role at ABC between 1957 and 1972, and regularly starring on Oliver Nelson and Quincy Jones

dates. A great high-note man, Ernie was remembered by fellow studio regular Danny Bank as a 'tune detective', hearing wrong notes in scores and calling for the band to stop – at his own calculated discretion. 'He would find something wrong in the last hour that would drive us over the time. Every time I saw Ernie on the job, I knew I was going to get overtime.'
**Quincy Jones, *The Birth Of A Band*** (Mercury)

# Marshal Royal
ALTO SAXOPHONE
*born* 5 December 1912; *died* 8 May 1995

The elder of the Royal brothers worked in his family's band until 1929, when he went to play in Los Angeles, from there moving into the Les Hite band and then Lionel Hampton's orchestra. He then played mostly as a studio musician until joining Count Basie's small group in 1951, leading to his assistance in forming a new Basie big band. Royal bossed the saxophone section for the next 20 years, his lush tone dominating the alto sound, and his stickler's approach to musical detail helping to assert the image of utter precision which the latter-day Basie band perfected. He finally moved on in 1970, settled back on the West Coast and played with other big bands, at jazz parties, and at Basie reunions, still entirely meticulous and methodical in his approach to playing lead alto.
**Count Basie, *The Count On The Coast*** (Phontastic)

# Gonzalo Rubalcaba
PIANO
*born* 27 May 1963

Rubalcaba's extravagant talent excited plenty of interest on his advent in the US, from his native Havana. He studied classical piano in his native city, and played in fusion groups before working with Dizzy Gillespie when the latter visited Havana in 1987. Two years later he played with Paul Motian and Charlie Haden in Montreal, and a subsequent appearance by the same group at the 1990 Montreux Festival was recorded for his Blue Note debut. He subsequently had travel problems owing to his visa being refused, but that was sorted out after he

resettled in the Dominican Republic, and he has since recorded several more records for Blue Note. Rubalcaba's swarming, note-spinning style seemed full of pianistic hubris at first, exciting as it could often be, and much of his playing seemed like a mishmash of classical virtuosity and a some-times hamfisted attempt at pegging this style to a jazz banner. But the more recent records, in a typically eclectic bunch of instrumentations and styles, have seemed to settle him down somewhat, and a lot of the nonsense has been filtered away.
**Supernova** (Blue Note)

# Roswell Rudd
TROMBONE
*born* 17 November 1935

Rudd pioneered the use of the trombone in American free jazz. He studied classical music at Yale and played in a Dixieland band before moving to New York around 1960, where he continued playing in the same idiom, working in the Condon circle for a time. But while taking lessons from Herbie Nichols, his allegiances changed, and he joined the group led by another ex-Dixielander, Steve Lacy, which played Thelonious Monk's music exclusively. He then recorded with Cecil Taylor and Archie Shepp, and joined John Tchicai and Milford Graves in the New York Art Quartet. Impulse! recorded a single album by him, *Everywhere*, in 1966, and he later figured in Charlie Haden's Liberation Music Orchestra. The 70s were a rather thin decade for his music-making: he wrote some pieces for the Jazz Composers' Orchestra, and returned to academia, where he taught ethnomusicol-ogy, although he also made ends meet by driving a taxi. Enrico Rava invited him to join a quartet, which made one fine album for ECM, but in the 80s he drifted into play-ing show music for hotel audiences, although he also initiated projects which would lead to the reconsideration of Herbie Nichols's music. In the 90s, he returned to more active jazz duty, recording with Elton Dean in London, and making some new records of Nichols's 'unheard' music for the CIMP label. Rudd's furry tone, mumbling phrasing and mixture of barks and growls and disjunctive ideas make him an often sur-prising member of any avant-garde frater-nity, but his interrupted and frequently compelling progress is an idiosyncratic jazz story of the past 40 years or so.
**Enrico Rava, *Quartet*** (ECM)

# Pete Rugolo
ARRANGER
*born* 25 December 1915

Rugolo went to the US from Sicily as a child and studied in San Francisco, one of his tutors being the composer Darius Milhaud. He got his break as a composer and arranger when he sold his first score to Stan Kenton, and between 1945 and 1949 he was one of Kenton's principal contributors. Rugolo's charts fitted exactly with Kenton's gen-eralized idea of playing 'modern music': ingeniously strewn with incident, yet com-pacted into the demandingly tight and wasteless format of the three-minute 78rpm side, Rugolo's music is often wholly remark-able in the way it avoids swing-era cliché, big-band bombast or anything else which was going on at the time. Curtly functional titles such as 'Monotony' (about which Charlie Parker said, 'Very weird, marvellous ideal'), 'Conflict', 'Impressionism', 'Lament' or 'Fugue For Rhythm Section' are superbly played by Kenton's men and still sound little less than extraordinary. Rugolo sub-sequently went into record production and writing for television, but he continued making records under his own name in the 50s: unfortunately, many of them were con-ceived almost as novelty records or exer-cises in showing off hi-fi systems or the new stereo process, as in the seven albums he made for Mercury during 1957–9. He did, however, before he left jazz behind altogether, write some hauntingly effective charts for some of June Christy's later Capitol albums.
**Stan Kenton, *1947 Vol 2*** (Classics)

# Hilton Ruiz
PIANO
*born* 29 May 1952

Ruiz grew up in New York in a Puerto Rican family and played with Latin bands and with Frank Foster's group when still in his teens. He studied for a time with Mary Lou Williams and then under various leaders

through the 70s, including Roland Kirk and Arthur Blythe. He began to come into his own as a leader in the 80s, and after some interesting but largely unremarkable records for independent labels he worked through several years at RCA's Novus imprint, leading small groups which mixed New York hard bop with Latin colours. Ruiz's great strength was his experience at the sharp end of New York jazz: unlike many of the musicians who imported Latin music into American jazz in this period, he didn't attempt the flashy note-spinning of many of the Cuban stylists, and his composing had a leaner, more effective substance to it. But the Novus period came to an end, and Ruiz has sometimes struggled for attention since: he made a couple of decent records for Telarc and some disastrously thin ones in what amounted to a smooth-fusion genre. Lately he has been sighted back in more demanding company, which is good news.
*Strut* (Novus)

## Howard Rumsey
BASS, LEADER
*born* 7 November 1917

Rumsey's career as a bassist wasn't crucial, but as a leader and entrepreneur he helped put the school generally known as 'West Coast jazz' on the map. He briefly worked with Stan Kenton in 1941 before going out as a freelance in southern California, and in 1949 he formed a band that took up a residency at the Lighthouse Café on Hermosa Beach. The original band was a straight-ahead bebop band, with Sonny Criss and Hampton Hawes, but in 1951 Rumsey re-formed the group around such names as Shorty Rogers and Shelly Manne. It lasted until the early 60s, even though there was a regular turnover of personnel, and Rumsey eventually managed and co-owned the club. There was a long sequence of albums for Contemporary, and most of the major West Coasters played in the group at one time or another. The club became a major place to hang out and listen. Shorty Rogers remembered: 'We'd start playing at two in the afternoon and someone would wander in, sit down in a bathing suit, have a beer. At two in the morning they're still at the same table, and it's been twelve hours!' By 1968, busy with management, Rumsey had

stopped playing himself, and he later opened another club on Redondo Beach.
*Music For Lighthousekeeping* (OJC/Contemporary)

## Jimmy Rushing
VOCAL
*born* 26 August 1902; *died* 8 June 1972

He grew up in Oklahoma City, where he learned piano with some assistance from his blues-playing uncle, from there playing at school dances until he began singing too, which quickly took over his musical life. In his student years he roamed around besides studying, and eventually fetched up in Kansas City, where he became a regular with Walter Page's Blue Devils (with whom he made his first record, in 1929) and then with Bennie Moten's band. From there it was inevitable that he end up in the new Count Basie band, and Rushing was the perfect singer for them: steeped in the blues but flexible and inventive enough with his voice to master all the new possibilities of jazz singing, he seemed to personify the combination of grace and earthiness which was Basie's speciality. He was with Basie almost continuously until 1950, setting down dozens of classic performances on record, but if anything his best years were still ahead: he led a band of ex-Basie-ites at New York's Savoy Ballroom, toured Europe as a solo and charmed audiences there and at festivals. His 50s albums, including *Little Jimmy Rushing & The Big Brass* (1958) and *Rushing Lullabies* (1959), update his style while clinging to its classic virtues. He was still busy with club residencies and tours all through the 60s. Although some of his later records were less sympathetically produced, his final album, *The You And Me That Used To Be*, completed in the year of his death from leukaemia, was handled with loving sympathy by the MD, Dave Frishberg. Jimmy was a huge man – his long-standing nickname, Mr Five By Five, was an affectionate remark on his stature – yet he handled himself with as much lightness as he did his singing.
*Rushing Lullabies* (Columbia)

# Bill Russell

PRODUCER, HISTORIAN, VIOLIN
*born* 26 February 1905; *died* 9 August 1992

Russell spent decades collecting, chronicling, recording and otherwise preserving the sound and spirit of authentic New Orleans jazz. As a young man, he studied composition in Chicago and New York, but in the 30s he began collecting early jazz records, and researching the artists. He helped in the rediscovery of Bunk Johnson ('I wasn't trying to re-create any old-time bands – I just wanted to record Bunk and get an idea how he played, how he sounded'), and founded a record label, American Music, which began intensively documenting the music of as many of the surviving New Orleans pioneers as he could find and persuade to make records, an initiative which played a strong role in the revival of the city's music. He subsequently became a jazz curator at Tulane University, even though he always considered himself a musician rather than a historian or a critic – and to that end, he then played himself in the New Orleans Ragtime Orchestra, which toured in the 60s and 70s. His vast archive eventually passed into a major library, the Historic New Orleans Collection.

# Curley Russell

BASS
*born* 19 March 1917; *died* 3 July 1986

Dillon 'Curley' Russell was a New Yorker who began playing in big bands in the early 40s before moving to the 52nd Street club scene and becoming involved in the early impetus out of bebop. He is on some of the important bebop sessions for Savoy Records, and was a regular sideman in Tadd Dameron's groups. From there until the middle 50s his name can be spotted with Thelonious Monk, Lester Young, Horace Silver, Art Blakey and others, but in the middle of the decade he sems to have drifted off the jazz scene altogether and he latterly found work with R&B bands.

# George Russell

COMPOSER, BANDLEADER
*born* 23 June 1923

Russell is one of the most difficult of all jazz figures to assess: genius or otherwise, he has contributed the elephantine Lydian Chromatic Concept Of Tonal Organization to the music, as well as a body of recorded work which mixes masterpieces with inconsequential ramblings. He played drums in local bands while at high school, but contracted tuberculosis while at college and it troubled his health for a number of years. It was during convalescence that he came up with his famous concept, which touches on a variety of aspects of both composition and improvisation, suggesting scales as a helpmate for the improviser and offering the composer a system where intervals are graded according to how far their pitches are from a single, central note. By the time he had recovered, Russell had begun writing for Dizzy Gillespie and others, coming up with such crucial 40s scores as 'Cubana Be – Cubana Bop', 'Ezz-Thetic' and 'A Bird In Igor's Yard', and working in the same circle as Gil Evans in New York. His book on the Lydian theory first emerged in 1953, and has been revised and expanded since, although musicologists and others have often scoffed at its plausibility and usefulness: Darius Brubeck called it an 'unbelievably turgid discourse burdened with jargon'.

Russell finally made some records of his own in 1956, starting with a group called The Jazz Workshop, and the brilliant *Jazz Workshop* set for RCA is a startling vindication of Russell the composer and group organizer, the music stacked with incident and ingenuity, yet unfolding with a jazzman's spontaneity and inevitability. This was the start of six years of remarkable work, which included the formation of his own performing sextet in which he played piano, and a sequence of records which are dazzling in their level of inventiveness, including *Live At The Five Spot* (1958), *Jazz In The Space Age* (1960), *Stratusphunk* (1960), *Ezz-Thetics* (1961), *The Stratus Seekers* (1961), and *The Outer View* (1962). Most of the records were dominated by Russell's original writing – unaccountably neglected by other jazz players since, although the music might be too closely associated with Russell himself to fully enter the wider repertory, and

the records are relatively little known – although there is at least one startling cover, the version of 'You Are My Sunshine' which Sheila Jordan sings on *The Outer View*. In 1963, though, Russell abandoned America for Europe, and went to teach in Sweden and Denmark. Almost from that point, his music began to lose its clarity and compactness. He wrote more for orchestras, and tinkered with *musique concrète* in pieces such as *Electronic Sonata For Souls Loved By Nature*; among his 'students' in these bands were Jan Garbarek and Terje Rypdal. Then he returned to the US in 1979, where he more or less stopped composing and went back to revising the Lydian theory, as well as working on the faculty of the New England Conservatory. In the 80s he began performing again with big bands in New York and London, conducting some of his greatest hits – which involved the diminutive Russell strutting around the orchestra as part of his conducting style – and it was all great fun, if hardly on the profound level of his early music: the later records do not stand up well away from the concert stage. As with Gil Evans, Russell let rock creep into his music without having that influence do him too many favours. In his old age he has been showered with awards and honours, but it seems strange that so much of his best work is hardly discussed or any longer performed.
*Jazz Workshop* (RCA)

## Hal Russell

SAXOPHONES, TRUMPET, VIBES, DRUMS
*born* 28 August 1926; *died* 5 September 1992

Russell was, in his way, a considerable presence in his local Chicago scene, but despite the espousal of numerous commentators concerning his overall importance, he is a minor figure whose work hasn't worn especially well. He played drums in high school in Detroit and from there worked with Woody Herman and Claude Thornhill, before moving to Chicago around 1950 and playing with a wide variety of players for the rest of the decade. He joined the much-discussed trio of Joe Daley's in 1959, a prototype free-jazz oufit who made a single record for RCA in 1963, but he otherwise did little of significance until the 70s, when he formed his first band in Chicago and added C-melody and tenor saxophones to his playing repertoire, as well as taking up the trumpet for a second time. In due course, this all led to his NRG Ensemble, a band which paved the way for some of the post-AACM music which has filled the city's jazz scene since, but on which – on the evidence of his records for ECM and Nessa – Russell has left few traces.
*The Hal Russell Story* (ECM)

## Luis Russell

BANDLEADER
*born* 6 August 1902; *died* 11 December 1963

Russell grew up in Gran Colombia (now Panama), played the piano in movie houses there, and went to New Orleans after a win in the local lottery. He took over the band previously led by Albert Nicholas, and from there moved to Chicago, where he worked under King Oliver, with whom he stayed until 1927. In New York, he took over another band, bolstered with some of the best sidemen available in the city, and worked through a series of residencies at some of the major venues in the city. His 1929–30 records for OKeh showcased some of New York's best big-band music of the time, and with soloists such as Henry Allen, J C Higginbotham, Albert Nicholas and Bill Coleman, there were few bands in the city that could touch Russell's. But he couldn't sustain his success, and other swing bands surpassed him. In 1935, he was hired by Louis Armstrong's manager, Joe Glaser, to be the permanent backing vehicle for the trumpet star (although Glaser fired the rest of the band in 1940, Russell was kept on for another three years). He made no more records under his own name, and eventually left music behind, working as a shopkeeper and a driver and, at the time of his death, teaching piano.
*The Luis Russell Story* (Retrieval)

## Pee Wee Russell

CLARINET
*born* 27 March 1906; *died* 15 February 1969

Born Charles Ellsworth Russell into a St Louis family, he took up the clarinet at 13 and was playing professionally within a few years, working in Texas bands with such contemporaries as Wingy Manone and Jack

Teagarden, and then in Frankie Trumbauer's orchestra back in St Louis. In 1927 he went to New York and remained there, fitting into the Red Nichols session-scene and working in Broadway pit bands and other dance orchestras: glimpses of him on record, such as the terrific Mound City Blue Blowers date with Coleman Hawkins in 1929, show a player of already fierce individuality. He began working with Louis Prima in 1935 and toured with him before returning to New York and a residency at Nick's in 1937. That settled him in with the Eddie Condon set, where he largely remained for the next dozen years or so, taking part in Condon's numerous broadcasts (where he is often the butt of the leader's jokes) and planting his quirky style in amongst hardcore Chicago Dixieland. Russell had by this time gone entirely his own way on the clarinet. It was a style made up of unorthodoxies: growling tones, queer alternations of softly melodious phrases and guttural, almost squawking attacks, the use of a slow and hefty vibrato which seemed to fall behind the beat yet was often miraculously righted to resolve a line or a whole solo. It was an ongoing brinkmanship which only Russell seemed the master of. But drink was all but destroying him, and after stints with Art Hodes in Chicago, Russell went to California and almost died from his condition. By 1951 he was back in action and playing and touring with his own and other groups, and he was on the bill of the first Newport Jazz Festival, since George Wein was a longstanding admirer of his. Although he often proclaimed himself to be sick of Dixieland, that was still what he mostly played, and what he usually played best; he latterly performed in what might be called quasi-modern contexts, duetting with Jimmy Giuffre, working in a band with Marshall Brown which covered tunes by Coltrane and others, and performing in a nutty mismatch with Thelonious Monk at the 1963 Newport Festival. There was even a record where he played against Oliver Nelson arrangements, *The Spirit Of '67* (Impulse!), the cover adorned with one of his paintings, a hobby which he took up in the 60s. His wife Mary had managed to get him back in something like good shape, but when she died of cancer he resumed drinking and rapidly went downhill. Russell was an undeniable one of a kind: his admirers regard him as something of a misunderstood genius, others drastically demur. Benny Goodman considered his playing comical. His best work remained in the older repertoire which he spent most of his career playing – on a good night, when the phrases fell just where he wanted them, he was supreme.

*Swingin' With Pee Wee* (Prestige)

## Babe Russin

TENOR SAXOPHONE
born 18 June 1911; *died* 4 August 1984

Russin played in the Red Nichols circle in New York from the late 20s, and after time spent as a staffer at CBS, he joined Benny Goodman in 1937, with whom he was basically associated, although he also worked for both Tommy and Jimmy Dorsey and led bands of his own. In the 50s he worked as a studio man in California, although he would occasionally join Goodman reunions. His solo moments with Goodman and others show a surging player in the Hawkins mould.

*Benny Goodman, 1937–1938* (Classics)

## Bill Russo

COMPOSER, ARRANGER
born 25 June 1928

Russo had lessons with Lennie Tristano in his teens and was studying law before moving over to orchestration: he contributed numerous charts to Stan Kenton's book in the early 50s, and later in the decade formed the Russo Orchestra, for the purposes of performing his own music, broadly in the third-stream genre which was modish at the time. Russo's work for Kenton is full of striking ideas, in such scores as 'Solitaire', 'Hall Of Brass', 'Portrait Of A Count' and 'Twenty-Three Degrees North, Eighty-Two Degrees West', and he set some even tougher challenges for the players in his own orchestral recordings, culminating in *The Seven Deadly Sins* (1961), a record scarcely known yet full of fascinating music. He lived in London at the start of the 60s and led the London Jazz Orchestra there, before returning to the US to work in Chicago and, for a period in the 70s, San Francisco. In the 90s he formed a new Chicago Jazz Ensemble to play a jazz

repertory by himself and many other composers, although it does not seem to have been recorded.
***The Seven Deadly Sins*** (Roulette)

## Brian Rust
DISCOGRAPHER
*born* 19 March 1922

The dean of early jazz discography was born in London and began collecting records from an early age: his memory is such that he can give you the exact date when he got his first jazz 78. He worked in the BBC record library for many years, and while there began working on the book which would eventually appear as *Jazz Records, 1897–1942*, the standard work on its subject and a remarkable feat of scholarship: it attempts to list every jazz record made in the period, anywhere in the world, and provide dates, personnel and release details. Now in its fifth edition, which emerged in 2002, the book is usually known to collectors simply as 'Rust'. In addition, its author has also produced discographies of labels, American and British dance bands, and music hall and musical comedy artists.

## Paul Rutherford
TROMBONE, EUPHONIUM
*born* 29 February 1940

A senior spirit in the British avant-garde, Rutherford made his early associations in, of all places, an RAF regional band, starting in 1958: there he met the likes of Trevor Watts and John Stevens. While studying at Guildhall, he helped found the Spontaneous Music Ensemble in 1965, and later the group Iskra 1903 with Barry Guy and Derek Bailey. While he has also worked in all the expected environments – with Globe Unity, the London Jazz Composers' Orchestra, Company and so forth – Rutherford's greatest skill may lie in solo improvisation. He is the most disjunctive of players: he never thinks in anything as long as a paragraph, and every phrase in an improvisation can appear to stand alone, even if the whole has its own peculiar momentum and direction. He likes such traditionalists as Jim Robinson, which actually squares with his delivery: unlike an expressionist such as Gunther Christmann,

he rarely practises excessive distortion or uses extra-musical paraphernalia. A period of illness kept him off the scene for a while, but in the new century he has returned to full strength.
***Trombolenium*** (Emanem)

## Terje Rypdal
GUITAR
*born* 23 August 1947

Born in Oslo, Rypdal took up the guitar in his teens, a big fan of The Shadows, and he was soon in a popular band named The Vanguards before going on to form a more successful one, Dream, in 1967, which also included Jan Garbarek in its line-up. He then studied electrical engineering at Trondheim before going back to the guitar, playing in one of George Russell's groups and renewing his association with Garbarek, with whom he started making records for ECM. While also playing in the pit band for *Hair*, he began to make albums of his own for ECM: unencumbered by much in the way of jazz influences, he has been able to create almost his own vocabulary for the electric guitar in an improvising context, using a sound which has tremendous density and sustain, skirling against often sparse rhythmic backdrops and static harmony, texture determining much of the musical shape and content. His 70s bands included dour sounds such as the trombone and a thick-sounding electric piano, and on the all-solo *After The Rain* (1976) each piece seemed like a brief, polished tone poem. In the 80s he led a rather clumping threesome called The Chasers, which seemed like his idea of a power trio, but more important to his progress has been what amounts to a parallel career as a contemporary composer: much of his work in this area has not been documented by ECM, but it includes a great deal of large-scale orchestral and chamber music. The recent *Lux Aeterna* (2000), with Palle Mikkelborg, might be seen a crossing point between his work as a performer and a composer. Rypdal is not much cited as an influence on other guitarists, but as Pat Metheny has recently pointed out, he was playing using many of the same stylistic elements as Bill Frisell, many years before the American. An important European musician, the scope of whose work asks for careful listening and investigation.

*Odyssey* (ECM)

## Sackville
RECORD COMPANY

Canada's leading jazz independent was established in 1968, in Toronto, by John Norris and Bill Smith, the team responsible for the magazine *Coda*. While its core artists have tended to be swing-mainstream players such as Buddy Tate, Ralph Sutton, Jay McShann and Doc Cheatham, it has also ventured into the avant-garde (Smith's principal interest) and recorded some particularly important sessions in the 70s by George Lewis, Julius Hemphill, Oliver Lake and Barry Altschul. In the 90s it also became a significant Canadian distributor for several other independents.

## Fats Sadi
VIBES
*born* 23 October 1927

Born in Andenne, Belgium, Sadi 'Fats' Lallemand started out in circus bands as a xylophonist, but was turned on to jazz and the vibes by hearing Lionel Hampton. He played in clubs in and around Brussels until 1950, when he moved to Paris and stayed ten years. He led a big band during this time and made records for Vogue and Swing before eventually returning to Belgium; many became familiar with him via his work in the Clarke–Boland Big Band, and he later toured the US with Caterina Valente. Milt Jackson liked and respected his work, and he played in both the swing and bop idioms, a fleet and imaginative player, who was still playing in his 70s on his home scene.

*The Sadi Quartet* (Ispahan)

## Johnny St Cyr
BANJO, GUITAR
*born* 17 April 1890; *died* 17 June 1966

'Play that thing, Mr St Cyr, lord!' exhorts Louis Armstrong, on the first record made by the Hot Five, 'Gut Bucket Blues', in 1925.

St Cyr had been doing just that since the early years of the century, at New Orleans picnics and in the bands of A J Piron and Kid Ory. He had started on a guitar which he made himself, but by the time he joined King Oliver in 1923 he used a six-string instrument which was a hybrid guitar-banjo, again of his own making. When he was making the records with Armstrong he was working with Doc Cook's Dreamland Orchestra in the city, and besides the Hot Five sessions he also plays on the best of Jelly Roll Morton's Red Hot Peppers dates. The Depression left St Cyr without much work, and he returned home to New Orleans and worked mainly as a plasterer. But he began playing again regularly in the 50s, with Paul Barbarin and George Lewis, and he led some sessions of his own, mainly collected on the record cited. He played at Disneyland with a band called the Young Men From New Orleans, in his final years. A versatile rhythm man and an inventive soloist, St Cyr participated in some of the most famous of all jazz records, and he stoutly played his part in all of them.

*Johnny St Cyr* (American Music)

## Sal Salvador
GUITAR
*born* 21 November 1925; *died* 22 September 1999

Salvador was always ahead of his time: he once released an album called *Music To Stop Smoking By* (Roulette, 1964), and he formed a big band in New York in 1958 which was effectively a rehearsal band (it sometimes subbed for Count Basie) and was the first such in the city. He was inspired to play jazz guitar when he heard Charlie Christian, and he then worked in Boston before joining Stan Kenton around 1952. He made an early LP for Blue Note in 1953, and otherwise freelanced during the rest of the 50s, before working with the big band, which lasted on an occasional basis until the middle 60s. He then taught and sometimes played in public, forming a fusion group as late as 1988.

*Music To Stop Smoking By* (Roulette)

# Perico Sambeat
ALTO SAXOPHONE
*born* 13 July 1962

A Valencian, Sambeat has been somewhat hidden in one of the least exposed jazz countries in Europe, but he started to get some wider recognition when he joined the Guy Barker group in 1996. He had previously been working in Barcelona's club scene from the mid-80s, and gave himself a brief taste of the New York jazz life too. Although he made one blowing record, *Dual Force* (1993), a live set made on a visit to Ronnie Scott's in London, his subsequent albums for Fresh Sound have been rather more thoughtful: *Ademuz* (1995), while attempting to integrate various Latin and jazz elements into a thickly textured whole, comes alive when Sambeat himself is soloing, in a style which has all the juice and exhilarating abandon of Cannoball Adderley in his pomp.
*Ademuz* (Fresh Sound)

# Joe Sample
KEYBOARDS
*born* 1 February 1939

Sample spent much of his professional life in the group The (Jazz) Crusaders, which he co-founded in his native Houston in the 50s and remained with until he decided to leave in 1987. In the 70s and 80s he also worked as a sessionman, and made solo records in a style which sounded like a smoother and less funky Crusaders. Recently he has done more solo work for Verve, although nothing he has done under his own name has surpassed what he did in the group he spent the most time with.
*Rainbow Seeker* (ABC)

# Dave Samuels
VIBES
*born* 9 October 1948

Samuels has been busy in jazz-related music for decades, although he has left no real mark on the contexts he's played in. He studied in Boston, and with Gary Burton and David Friedman, and himself taught at Berklee before moving to New York in 1974. He then formed an occasional duo with Friedman, and they sometimes recorded as a quartet (with Harvie Swartz and Michael di Pasqua) as Double Image. Samuels's major career break came when he joined the very popular light-fusion band Spyro Gyra in 1979, an association which lasted the best part of 20 years. He later formed a Caribbean Jazz Project. For all his undoubted proficiency, Samuels has been little other than a decorative agent in whichever context he's been involved with.
*Double Image* (Enja)

# David Sanborn
ALTO SAXOPHONE
*born* 30 July 1945

A passionate, intense, powerful musician who is in love with his vocation, Sanborn has nevertheless had an awkward relationship with jazz. He originally took up the saxophone as a kind of therapy: a polio sufferer who had to spend some of his youth in an iron lung, he began playing the horn to help strengthen his lungs, and the unusual posture he adopts when playing is as a result of that early training. In his teens he was already playing in R&B bands, inspired by the example of Hank Crawford, and after university studies he worked with Paul Butterfield's Blues Band (1967–71), and then as a kingpin among sessionmen. For a period in the 70s, Sanborn was equalled only by the Brecker brothers as the horn player that the rock elite wanted on their records: his appearance on David Bowie's *Station To Station* (1975) was archetypal of his stature, and he parlayed that eminence into a considerable solo career, starting with *Taking Off* (1975), which was the forerunner of a long and prolific sequence of records under his own name. In the later 80s, he slowed down on his work as a sessionman, and he has latterly been very choosy about the 'outside' projects he has played on. Sanborn's own records started out in a style which mixed jazz-rock with a light-funk dappling, and he has often been blamed for helping to get the smooth-jazz genre under way, a charge which he regards with something approaching contempt. Since he has never been much of a bebop player and controls his improvising within tightly mediated contexts, one can argue that there is very little of the legitimate jazz player about him, yet the harsh and sometimes

wrenchingly intense sound he gets out of
the alto can be as affecting as that of any
saxophonist since Parker. What he does is
play in sentences, telling, individual lines,
perfectly appropriate for the modern procedures of recording studios, less effective in
the accruing of memorable solos in the
grand jazz manner. He remains an inquisitive musician, playing live with John Zorn at
The Knitting Factory on one occasion, but
some of his recent work has been less
appealing. His records with Marcus Miller
producing, in the late 80s and early 90s, feature some of his most powerful work, but
lately he has taken to a more or less acoustic
jazz context, playing standards and straight
bebop tunes, and somehow they don't seem
to suit him at all.
*Close-Up* (Reprise)

## David Sanchez
TENOR AND SOPRANO SAXOPHONES
*born* 3 September 1968

Sanchez is regularly feted as a 'new star', but
he moved to New York from his native
Puerto Rico as long ago as 1988, and in some
ways his progress has been careful. He
played in various Latin and hard-bop bands
for the first couple of years, joined the Dizzy
Gillespie United Nation Orchestra in 1991,
and thereafter worked primarly as a leader,
although he has also played alongside Roy
Hargrove, Danilo Perez and Tom Harrell.
Sanchez began making records for Sony/
Columbia in the mid-90s and six interesting
discs have appeared, drawing on Puerto
Rican, Brazilian and Cuban sources, mixing
up instrumentations, and featuring his
extravagantly virtuosic tenor and soprano at
the eye of each group. Instead of the lavish
and sentimental approach which many
South American musicians have brought
into jazz, Sanchez looks for both clarity and
a purposeful complexity, playing in odd
times, and pushing his Rollins-like sound
into unusual shapes. It's perhaps surprisingly demanding music, and possibly for
that reason Sanchez hasn't quite caught
hold of the audience which Joshua Redman
and a few other younger stars have enjoyed.
*Travesia* (Sony)

## Pharoah Sanders
TENOR SAXOPHONE
*born* 13 October 1940

Sanders came from Little Rock, Arkansas
(Little Rock was also his nickname for a
time) and he played in R&B bands in San
Francisco before moving to New York in
1962, immediately slotting into the city's
free-jazz scene. He cut his debut, *Pharoah's
First*, for ESP in 1965, and by this time he
was already involved in what would prove
to be John Coltrane's final group, pairing
Trane in the front line and taking a more
hysterical trajectory than even the leader
would have countenanced: shrieking, howling lines that cared little for the niceties of
pitch and clarity. After Coltrane's death,
Sanders moved on to a band with Leon
Thomas, where he produced his greatest hit,
'The Creator Has A Master Plan' (also sung
by a bewildered Louis Armstrong on one of
his final sessions!). From there he led a
variety of groups and recorded for Impulse!,
a series of albums which have interesting
moments scattered among aimless and
sometimes nonsensical spacefilling. A
measure of Sanders's disarray can be taken
from his decision to try and make disco-
flavoured records towards the end of the
decade: was this really the banshee who had
stood next to Coltrane? In the following
decade, though, he retrenched and largely
reinvented himself – somewhat like Archie
Shepp – as a midstream-modern tenorman
with a sentimental attachment to old-time
ballads. In the 90s he became a regular touring artist, made some largely inconsequential new records for Verve, but still found a
ready audience for his playing, which now
included a notable piece of prestidigitation
where he appears to stop playing the saxophone and yet still produces sounds from
the horn. As with Alice Coltrane, one
wonders if Pharoah would have got very far
without his former boss's patronage.
*Karma* (Impulse!)

## Randy Sandke
TRUMPET
*born* 23 May 1949

Sandke has been involved in the music for a
long time. He played rock in a band with
Michael Brecker at the end of the 60s, but

he suffered a serious injury to his larynx in 1969 and didn't play trumpet again for a decade, performing instead on guitar. But in 1980 he returned to the horn, and then became a prominent member of the new mainstream circle which had emerged in American jazz, working with Bob Wilber, Ken Peplowski, Dan Barrett and others, as both a sideman and leader. While swing is his primary bag, Sandke is a smartly eclectic type when he wants to be and his brilliant record *Inside Out* (Nagel Heyer, 2000) pairs himself, Peplowski, Wycliffe Gordon and Scott Robinson with the 'modernists' Uri Caine, Marty Ehrlich and Ray Anderson, in an audacious fusion which turned out handsomely. More significant, though, was his remarkable *The Re-Discovered Bix And Louis* (1999), which puts the very trim New York All Stars to work on a set of virtually forgotten themes once associated with Armstrong and Beiderbecke. Sandke's own playing – with a beautifully light touch, but completely energized and assertive – embodies the skill and authority of his conceptual approach.

**The Re-Discovered Bix And Louis** (Nagel Heyer)

## Arturo Sandoval
TRUMPET, PIANO
*born* 6 November 1949

Sandoval can play pretty much anything he pleases on the trumpet, but the one thing which seems to elude him is jazz. A Cuban who got his start playing in street bands in his teens, he was one of the founding members of Irakere in 1973, staying eight years and thereafter touring with his own groups, visiting Europe frequently, although it wasn't until 1990 that he decided to defect to the US. Sandoval's superabundance of technique takes the approach of Dizzy Gillespie, Clifford Brown and Freddie Hubbard and impacts it all into an exasperatingly showy delivery which renders much of his playing meaningless. His records, full of one showstopping feat after another, aren't quite as exhausting as his concerts, but they have been produced with a similar lack of restraint and no sense of what to do with his talent. When he feels like a breather from the trumpet, he sits at the piano and does much the same there. Glimmers of what Sandoval can do at a lower level only

make one even more annoyed at what he does the rest of the time.
**Swingin'** (GRP)

## Nisse Sandström
TENOR SAXOPHONE
*born* 13 March 1942

Sandström got his start in the Swedish free-jazz scene of the early 60s, but he had shifted back towards a more boppish demeanour by the time he started making records under his own leadership, which wasn't until *The Painter* (Odeon, 1972). He subsequently worked with Red Mitchell and Rolf Ericson, making some further records for Phontastic, and in the gang of local heroes that made up the Jazz Inc and Summit Meeting groups. A Lestorian player with a lean and insidious way of playing, Sandström makes a quietly effective mark on his relatively few records.
**Jazz Inc, Walkin' On** (Dragon)

## Mongo Santamaria
PERCUSSION, BANDLEADER
*born* 7 April 1922; *died* 2 February 2003

Ramon Santamaria grew up in a poor part of Havana, and though he studied the violin as a child, it was as a percussionist that he made his mark when he moved to the US in 1950. While he had a steady gig with Tito Puente's orchestra, he also played with Dizzy Gillespie, and then in small groups with Cal Tjader. Like Ray Barretto, he did plenty of studio-session work as, sometimes, the token Latin-jazz man, but he also led numerous groups of his own, bolting brass and horn sections on to the *charanga* idiom, and moving easily between hardcore Cuban music, Latin jazz and the crossover-soul idioms which ran through the late 60s and pre-disco 70s. He also contributed one immortal tune to the modern repertoire: 'Afro Blue', recorded by everyone from John Coltrane to The Albion Band. Santamaria left a vast discography as both leader and sideman, and the best way to discover his work is probably through one of the several compilations which exist in the CD format. Not so much an innovator, more a standard-bearer for the beats and pulses which came out of his background, Santamaria immersed himself and his bands so deeply

in that rhythmical lexicon that he personified it. As with many such figures, though, his influence on jazz is difficult to quantify in any specific way: he brought the news from Cuba, and it spread far and wide.
**Skin On Skin** (Rhino)

## Heikki Sarmanto

PIANO
*born* 22 June 1939

Sarmanto was the first Finn ever to enrol at Berklee (in 1968), although he had already studied at the Sibelius Academy. A prolific composer in both the jazz and the contemporary classical idioms, he has been denied a wider reputation by working through a period when Finnish jazz was almost unheard by and invisible to an international audience. He was recording with quintets and sextets as far back as 1969, led a puckishly named Serious Music Ensemble in 1971 and also made a big band album in 1972. He has tried to accommodate jazz within symphonic, operatic and sacred music forms, although these settings have again gone largely unnoticed outside his own country. But in his own terrain he is regarded as one of the masters. Heikki's brother Pekka (b 1945) is a bassist who has worked more frequently with musicians outside the Finnish circle.
**Everything Is It** (Odeon)

## Bernardo Sassetti

PIANO
*born* 24 June 1970

Sassetti is from Lisbon, one of the least visible of European jazz territories. He backed numerous visitors to his home scene in the late 80s and early 90s, and came to the attention of British trumpeter Guy Barker, who engaged him for his international group, which recorded three albums. Sassetti has made several records under his own leadership for local labels but so far has yet to win much attention from the wider jazz audience. He is, though, a beautifully lyrical player and composer, whose melodious touch and fine articulation let him stand out as a cool alternative in even the most heated band.
**Nocturno** (Clean Feed)

## Heinz Sauer

TENOR SAXOPHONE
*born* 25 December 1932

Sauer began playing in Frankfurt in the 50s, and from 1963 he was a close associate of Albert Mangelsdorff, playing with him well into the 70s, before forming small groups of his own. Sauer's fundamentally bop-directed style has taken on other influences – late Coltrane, early free jazz, electronics – as he has gone forward, and it's a pity that his own groups have seemingly been offered few opportunities to record.
**Metal Blossoms** (L + R)

## Eddie Sauter

ARRANGER, COMPOSER
*born* 2 December 1914; *died* 21 April 1981

Sauter played drums and trumpet in New York bands before Red Norvo asked him to look after his band's book, in 1936. He later went solo as a freelance, turning in quality work for Benny Goodman and Artie Shaw, but a bad bout of tuberculosis left him unable to work for much of the 40s and he was almost forgotten when, with fellow arranger Bill Finnegan, he organized a band primarily for recording purposes in 1952. The Sauter–Finnegan Orchestra scored a few unlikely hits, in particular the infuriatingly perky 'Doodletown Fifers', which has become a light-music classic of a kind. Subsequently he did more scoring both in and out of jazz, and had something of a comeback in the idiom with three outstanding projects for Stan Getz in the 60s: the gorgeous charts for *Focus* (1961), the soundtrack to Arthur Penn's film *Mickey One* (1965) and the seriously inclined *Tanglewood Concerto* (1966). The early work with Norvo still has much charm, and Sauter's chart for Ellington's 'I Let A Song Go Out Of My Heart' (1938) is a handsome nod to the master; but his Goodman arrangements find him in full flight, with 'Clarinet A La King' (1941) a brilliant concerto for liquorice stick. Had it been done for a less popular soloist, the work with Getz might have gone into musicianly obscurity, but the saxophonist's stature has kept *Focus* in the racks over the years, and even though *Mickey One* is much less familiar it is a comparable achievement.
**Stan Getz, *Focus*** (Verve)

# Savoy
RECORD COMPANY

Savoy became the pre-eminent bebop label. Established by Herman Lubinsky in Newark, New Jersey, in 1942, it really began to take off as a jazz enterprise when Teddy Reig, a dedicated fan of the new music, began recording the leading boppers, starting in 1945. By the end of the decade Savoy had set down many of the defining statements of bop's first wave, including important sessions by Charlie Parker, Dexter Gordon, Miles Davis and Fats Navarro. At the same time, the label pursued the emerging popular idiom of rhythm and blues, and with Johnny Otis they had one of the major new stars of the style. When a West Coast office was opened in 1948, Erroll Garner was also brought on board, and Lubinsky became entrepreneurial enough to start buying up some of the smaller bebop labels, such as Regent, Discover and National. Reig left in 1952, but his successors, Lee Magid and Ozzie Cadena, carried on Savoy's work in both the jazz and R&B fields. In comparison with Blue Note and Prestige their jazz output was much smaller, but there were still significant new signings such as Cannonball Adderley and Yusef Lateef. After 1960, though, the jazz side of Savoy's business petered out as the label focused on a new initiative building their roster of gospel artists. After Lubinsky's death, the catalogue was sold to Arista in 1974, which commenced 30 years of reissue confusion. The material has since passed through various hands and reissue programmes have regularly stopped and started. Some new records were also made in the 90s.

# Scat singing

Jelly Roll Morton demonstrated the art of scat singing to Alan Lomax in some of his Library Of Congress recordings of 1938: 'Skip, scat, skoodle-dee-doo . . .'. The idea is to replace intelligible words with nonsense syllables which swing through the line, and approximate an instrumentalist's improvisation rather than the vocalist's recourse to a preset lyric, thus avoiding all the meaning that words imply. Louis Armstrong was often said to have invented scat singing on his 1925 record of 'Heebie Jeebies', where he reputedly dropped his lyric sheet on the studio floor and had to make up something on the spot, but the reality is that scatting of different sorts had been around much earlier: Will Friedwald has suggested the popular singer Ukelele Ike as a possible scat pioneer, and Morton himself claimed that he heard the form many years earlier. Armstrong, though, popularized it best, and in the 30s his example was followed by Cab Calloway, Leo Watson and ultimately Ella Fitzgerald (as well as Bing Crosby). Bebop itself may have taken its name from a scat rendition of a bop melody line, and bop singers such as Babs Gonzalez and Jon Hendricks used scat as part of their vocabulary. In the 60s, The Swingle Singers took scatting to the classical concert stage, their politesse about a light year away from Armstrong and Calloway, and in the other direction the free improvisers began inventing their own kind of scat, which reaches perhaps an ultimate state of departure from coherent language in the work of Phil Minton and Diamanda Galas. At the same time, bebop scat underwent a revival, just as bop itself did in the 80s, and Betty Carter and Kurt Elling brought a new degree of sophistication to scat singing from that direction.

# Phil Schaap
PRODUCER, BROADCASTER
*born* 8 April 1951

Anyone who has heard Schaap on the radio is in no doubt about his knowledge and enthusiasm. On his celebrated programme *Bird Flight* on the New York station WKCR, where he plays the music of Charlie Parker, he might speak for ten minutes about a three-minute track before eventually playing it. His father was a jazz scholar, and Phil has gone into the same line of business, working on the radio since his student days in 1970, as well as teaching and producing reissues of important jazz sessions of every sort. The music needs more devoted guardians like Schaap, although his obsession with minutiae can deter all but the most committed.

# Giancarlo Schiaffini

TROMBONE
*born* 23 October 1942

Born in Rome, Schiaffini worked with the Gruppo Romano Free Jazz in the 60s, and subsequently led bands of his own as well as working with most of the major European free improvisers and playing solo, making records for such Italian independents as Horo, Splasc(h) and Pentaflowers. At the same time, he has conducted a parallel career in the performance of contemporary classical music, earning dedications from the likes of Berio and Stockhausen, and his work with the Italian Instabile Orchestra bridges some of his different interests.
**As A Bird** (Pentaflowers)

# Mario Schiano

ALTO SAXOPHONE
*born* 22 July 1933

Schiano is one of the godfathers of free jazz in Italy. He began playing in Rome at the end of the 50s, but it wasn't until the founding of the Gruppo Romano Free Jazz in 1966 – initially as a trio, with Schiano, Marcello Melis and Franco Pecori, who were subsequently joined by Giancarlo Schiaffini – that he found any direction. After this Schiano moved into working with a number of different small groups in the 70s, investigating folk song as much as jazz form, and after a period of relative abstinence he returned to regular playing in the 80s, with a broad range of groups and players from across Europe (occasions well documented by the Splasc(h) label). Stefano Zanni's verdict seems perfect: 'a master of collective improvisation, able to combine Mediterranean lyricism, Neapolitan cabaret and irony, and southern Italian popular songs'. Unsurprisingly, for an artist so steeped in Italian manners, his music has made only a modest impact outside his local territory.
**Sud** (Splasc(h))

# Lalo Schifrin

COMPOSER, ARRANGER
*born* 21 June 1932

Schifrin was a piano prodigy in his native Buenos Aires, and studied in Paris with Olivier Messiaen, while also playing in some jazz groups there. Back in Argentina he played in small and large groups and formed a big band somewhat in Dizzy Gillespie's idiom before moving to New York in 1958. Gillespie hired him as his small-group pianist in 1960, and Schifrin went on to score *Gillespiana* for the trumpeter, one of Dizzy's most wholesome orchestral show-cases. Subsequently, though, Schifrin largely left jazz behind in favour of filmscore work (*Mission Impossible* is one of his famous ones), and only came back to active duty in the 90s with a series of albums and concerts based around a 'Jazz Meets The Symphony' concept, which could sound as portentous as its title suggests.
**Dizzy Gillespie, *Gillespiana*** (Verve)

# Alexander von Schlippenbach

PIANO
*born* 7 April 1938

Born in Berlin, Schlippenbach studied composition and piano in Cologne and played boogie woogie and in an Oscar Peterson style before moving on to Monk. He was in Manfred Schoof's quintet in the middle 60s, but a turning point came when one of the German radio stations, RIAS, commissioned him to create a large-scale score, *Globe Unity*, in 1966, which was performed by a specially assembled orchestra that used many of the leading players in what was becoming a pan-European movement of free-jazz musicians. It was successful enough to enable Schlippenbach to convene what became called the Globe Unity Orchestra on numerous other occasions, although only infrequently in the 90s and beyond. In the meantime, he formed small-group associations: a long-standing trio with Evan Parker and Paul Lovens, a similarly durable parnership with drummer and vocalist Sven-Åke Johansson, and a duo with his wife, pianist Aki Takase, which also led to the formation of the Berlin Contemporary

Jazz Orchestra. Schlippenbach was one of the first European pianists to approach the new forms of free jazz head on, and he still insists that what he plays is in that sphere, rather than the more amorphous category of free improvisation. While one can detect trace elements of such obvious forebears as Cecil Taylor in what he does, it's probable that Schlippenbach has arrived at his own free style independent of most such American influences (as his close contemporary, Peter Brötzmann, arrived at his own methodology). Thelonious Monk remains in the background of much of his playing, but Schlippenbach's melting pot of bop and classical ingredients has long since settled into an idiosyncratic manner of his own. The propulsive intelligence and complexity of his ideas as a pianist are perhaps best sought out in the many records he has made with Lovens and Parker.

*Swinging The Bim* (FMP)


# Don Schlitten
PRODUCER
*born* 4 March 1932

Schlitten was a New York art student in the 40s and played tenor saxophone, but it was as a fan and producer-entrepreneur that he would make his mark on the music. He started his own small label, Signal, in the early 50s, and from there worked as a producer at Prestige before pursuing more label activities of his own in the 60s and 70s, notably with Cobblestone and Xanadu, the latter in particular becoming something of a refuge for neglected artists of the bebop era at a time when that sort of music was distinctly out of fashion: Xanadu's valuable archive includes some of the best records by such artists as Al Cohn, Barry Harris and Jimmy Raney, although little of it has so far emerged on CD. Schlitten is also a noted photographer.


# Maria Schneider
COMPOSER, BANDLEADER
*born* 27 November 1960

Schneider studied jazz and composition before moving to New York in 1985, where she secured the two affiliations which set her on her way as a composer: working as a sort of apprentice to Gil Evans and following his methods, and studying with Bob Brookmeyer until 1991. In 1992 she formed her own big band, mostly of New York's jazz-session elite, and it held down a five-year residency at the Greenwich Village club Visiones. Schneider's star has risen steadily, winning her orchestral commissions from all over the jazz world, including the UK and Europe as well as America, but most of her music has been disappointingly sparsely recorded: there are just two CDs on the European Enja label, and in 2004 she finally released some more music, *Concert In The Garden*, which is only available via her own website: it was a genuine surprise when a record which was not even available in retail outlets won the Grammy award for Best Jazz Album in 2005. Her music is an elegant refraction of several strands in post-bop orchestration, suggesting the influence of her teachers as well as Thad Jones and Ellington, and while it can be difficult to point to things which are distinctively hers, her craft and lucid thinking seem to bring out the best in her players.

*Concert In The Garden*
(www.mariaschneider.com)


# Loren Schoenberg
TENOR SAXOPHONE
*born* 23 July 1958

Too young to go steady with modern jazz, it seems, Schoenberg instead opted to be an advocate primarily of the swing era. He studied in New York in the 70s and since then has worked prolifically as a sideman, with everyone from Howard McGhee and Panama Francis to Benny Goodman and Gunther Schuller. He has led a big band of his own and has conducted numerous other orchestras, as well as generally beating the drum for pre-bop jazz in particular, broadcasting and writing journalism and sleevenotes. Schoenberg is an able and fluent saxophonist, but he lacks the degree of individuality which some of the other swing revivalists have managed to inculcate into their own playing.

*Out Of This World* (TCB)

# Manfred Schoof

TRUMPET
*born* 6 April 1936

Schoof started out on piano and didn't
touch the trumpet until he was 17, and he
then studied compositon in Cologne. He was
with Alex von Schlippenbach in Gunter
Hampel's early 60s band before he led a
quintet (Schlippenbach, Gerd Dudek, Buschi
Niebergall and Jaki Liebezeit) which during
1965–8 set down some of the first free playing in middle Europe: unfortunately, a
single FMP album, released several years
later, is their only legacy. In 1969 he formed
the New Jazz Trio with Cees See and Peter
Trunk, which came to an end following
Trunk's death in a car accident at the end of
1973, and thereafter he formed a new band
which worked in a more impressionist,
modal style, with a lick of fusion via Rainer
Bruninghaus's keyboards. Latterly he played
in larger ensembles as a soloist, and with the
European Jazz Ensemble. Schoof's early free
playing mellowed into a more conservative
style, but he was never a noise-maker on the
trumpet, more a lyrical player whose thinking was broad enough to accommodate outside playing within an expansive, generous
style.
*Horizons* (Japo)

# Gene Schroeder

PIANO
*born* 5 February 1915; *died* 16 February 1975

Schroeder was one of Eddie Condon's most
faithful lieutenants. He had been in New
York for a few years before he joined the
Condon gang at Nick's in 1943, and he
moved from there to Condon's own club in
1945 and stayed for the next 15 years.
Schroeder's easygoing style wasn't too flash
or ambitious, but he was a swinging player,
and Condon liked the way he fitted in. After
he left Condon, the pianist went on to work
in other harmless Dixieland outfits,
although poor health curtailed his playing
in his final years.
*Jammin' At Condon's* (Columbia)

# Gunther Schuller

COMPOSER, AUTHOR
*born* 22 November 1925

Schuller played classical music all through
the 40s and 50s; his father was a violinist
with the New York Philharmonic, and
Schuller himself worked regularly at the
Metropolitan Opera. But he was at least as
interested in jazz: he played French horn on
some of the early Miles Davis nonet
sessions, and he befriended some of the pro-
gressives who were in Davis's New York
circle, including George Russell, Gil Evans
and John Lewis. He and Lewis founded the
Modern Jazz Society in 1955, and it started
ten years of activity which came to be called
– after one of Schuller's own phrases –
'third-stream' music, where elements of the
European classical tradition were combined
with jazz procedures. This brought about
such recorded projects as *Jazz Abstractions*
(1960) and the Modern Jazz Quartet's *Third
Stream Music* (1957), which featured several
of Schuller's works performed by the MJQ. It
generated a modest excitement, rather like a
more scholarly version of the Pre-Raphaelite
movement, perhaps, and it helped awaken
at least a part of the classical establishment
to the idea that jazz was a music which
deserved some kind of respectability (and
funding). The big band Orchestra USA was
another by-product of the time, again conducted by either Lewis or Schuller. Annual
concerts at Brandeis University were a feature of the movement, and Lewis and
Schuller also established a Lenox School of
Jazz, in Massachusetts, where Ornette
Coleman first made an impact. Schuller's
continuing influence brought jazz into the
hitherto for-classics-only environment of
Tanglewood in 1963, and four years later he
was appointed president of the New England
Conservatory, where he opened a jazz department and gave a resident composer job to
George Russell. His work as an author has
possibly had an even more widespread
influence: *Early Jazz* and *The Swing Era* are
huge and all but exhaustive accounts of
their respective periods, although they were
intended to be stages one and two of a trip-
tych: whether the third part, which was
meant to bring the jazz story up to the present, will ever appear is not known. Latterly,
Schuller directed a repertory orchestra at the
Conservatory, and his sons George (b 1958), a

drummer, and Ed (b 1955), a bassist, carry on in the family's jazz traditions. Whatever one thinks of third stream and its sometimes questionable merits, Schuller played a major part in the American cultural establishment's softening what was once a very unwelcoming attitude towards jazz.

*Jazz Abstraction* (Atlantic)

# Diane Schuur
VOCAL
*born* 10 December 1953

Diane 'Deedles' Schuur overcame the handicap of being blind from birth and has blustered through a successful enough career, although jazz-singing specialists often regard her with little in the way of respect. In the 70s she mainly sang in a pop setting, but Stan Getz heard her at the 1979 Monterey Jazz Festival and latterly played with her and encouraged her to pursue a jazz direction. She made a sequence of records for GRP which mixed shrill and entirely overheated performances with more effective work, and she went on to perform with both the Count Basie and Mel Lewis orchestras. Latterly she switched labels to Concord, where the results have thus far been comparatively temperate.

*Diane Schuur And The Count Basie Orchestra* (GRP)

# Irène Schweizer
PIANO
*born* 2 June 1941

Along with Alex von Schlippenbach and Howard Riley, Schweizer pioneered European free piano. Born in Schaffhausen, Switzerland, she played piano and drums in her teens, and moved to London as a language student in 1961, there soaking up the jazz scene and taking occasional lessons from Eddie Thompson. She returned and made her first recordings in Zurich in 1962, and from there formed a trio which worked in a freebop style that eventually worked towards entirely free playing. By 1968, Schweizer was in a new group with Pierre Favre and Evan Parker, and in the 70s she worked as co-leader of a group with Rüdiger Carl. A number of FMP records from the period document her powerful music: com-

plex, unbeholden to other free-playing models, full of sometimes cliffhanging drama – especially in her solo albums *Wilde Señoritas* (1976) and *Hexensabbat* (1977) – it asks for and rewards rigorous attention. Later in the decade she co-founded the Feminist Improvising Group with Maggie Nicols and Lindsay Cooper, which subsequently turned itself into the European Women's Improvising group in the early 80s. The label Intakt was founded in part to document her work, and for the past 20 years there has been a steady stream of records, including five different duo performances with drummers – Schweizer's own skills as a percussionist have always been a part of her concept at the piano. All of it suggests a musician still expanding her field of vision, and especially fine was the 2003 *Ulrichsburg*, another meeting with a drummer – Pierre Favre, whose association with the pianist now goes back almost 40 years.

*Chicago Piano Solo* (Intakt)

# Louis Sclavis
CLARINET, BASS CLARINET
*born* 2 February 1953

The marvellous Sclavis has been a mercurial creative force on the European scene since the early 80s. Born in Lyons, he moved from conservatory study to free improvisation in the middle 70s, and has whirled his way through a broad range of projects ever since. He has formed a Clarinet Trio, which mixed improvisation with recitals of scored modern compositions, and various editions of his own ensemble, which have included such sidemen as Yves Robert, Dominique Pifarély, François Raulin, Bruno Chevillon and Marc Ducret, and have tackled jazz-based originals, folk and dance music, compositions by Rameau and Ellington, theatre music, and, most recently, a project inspired by the streets of Naples, *Napoli's Walls* (2002). Not all of these have been equally or entirely successful, and Sclavis can sometimes move almost alarmingly between high comedy and stark, severe political art, as in some of the music on the record cited, which includes a threnody for the murdered Algerian singer Lounes Matoub. He is generous with space for his fellow musicians, which can sometimes also be a pity since it is rare that he is not the outstanding player on display. The duo record with Ernst Reijseger, *Et On Ne Parle Du Temps* (FMP, 1994), is one place to hear his own skills at length. While he does pick up the saxophone at times, it is the clarinet family which brings out the real Sclavis.

*L'Affrontement Des Prétendants* (ECM)

# Bob Scobey

TRUMPET

*born* 9 December 1916; *died* 12 June 1963

Scobey was one of the leaders of the Californian movement which sparked a revival in older jazz styles in the 40s. He played in San Francisco at the end of the 30s, partly as a sideman with Lu Watters's big band, and when Watters formed his Yerba Buena Jazz Band at the start of the new decade Scobey was first choice as lead trumpet. Following his army service he led bands of his own, and from then until his death he was a prime mover in the ensemble-based revivalism which enjoyed a great popularity in the area all through the 50s and early 60s. His 50s albums for Good Time Jazz, RCA and Verve are all classics in their way, with his regular gang of sidemen – including Clancy Hayes, Matty Matlock and Manny Klein – setting down unpretentious but mightily swinging documents of a music which has never enjoyed any kind of fashion since. Scobey spent his final years in Chicago, eventually taken by cancer, and his memory is still revered by followers of his style.

*Direct From San Francisco* (Good Time Jazz)

# John Scofield

GUITAR

*born* 26 December 1951

Scofield was too young to be a jazz man from the start, and inevitably he began playing in rock groups as a teenager, though he liked Wes Montgomery too. He went to Berklee in 1970 and by 1974 was working with jazz musicians, eventually joining Billy Cobham a year later. He went through a strange collection of bandleaders – from Charles Mingus to Chet Baker – in the later 70s and began leading groups of his own, which were recorded by the German label

Enja, since there seemed to be no interest in America. But Scofield's breakthrough came when the rejuvenated Miles Davis hired him in 1982 for one of the trumpeter's most successful latter-day bands, Scofield staying until mid-1985. Thereafter he was able to work as he pleased as a leader, as well as being in constant demand in a star-sideman role. A sequence of records for the American independent Gramavision led to a contract with Blue Note (1989–95) and then a stint with Verve (1996 to date).

Scofield's timing has rarely been less than perfect. He came along at a moment when the guitar was preparing to become a dominant jazz voice, yet needed a singular stylist to articulate it. His interest in blues and rock kept a communicative twist in playing which was otherwise heavily soaked in the polytonality espoused by improvisers such as Joe Henderson and McCoy Tyner, and as a composer he has a bookful of tunes which marry a lovely, serene lyricism with tough, bluesy essentials. He knows the seductive power of fusion as crowd-pleasing bombast, and tries to offset that by being self-aware enough to never go over the top – as he has said, the problem with guitar players is that, unlike saxophonists, they don't need to take a breath. He likes old-fashioned R&B-combo jazz, and made *Hand Jive* with Eddie Harris, partly in tribute to the old McCann–Harris group. His Blue Note albums include meetings with Bill Frisell and Pat Metheny, and for Verve he has gone down the route of the so-called Jam Band, which recently has taken a somewhat worrying turn: the awful *Überjam* (2000) found him almost destroying his signature sound via electronic trickery, although the subsequent *Up All Night* (2003) has redressed the balance. Many Scofield admirers, though, look back wistfully to his Enja and Gramavision albums as their man's creative high point: without the need to create album concepts or please major-label accountants, his music was then at its freshest and most unaffectedly creative. It's arguable, too, that Scofield has simply made too many records as both leader and sideman. But he is, along with Frisell and Metheny, the most significant and influential guitarist since Wes Montgomery.

*Still Warm* (Gramavision)

# Jimmy Scott

VOCAL
*born* 17 July 1925

Scott's peculiar career eventually achieved a state of grace. Born in Cleveland, he sang in church in a family quartet, and from those beginnings he toured in vaudeville, where his modest stature and oddly high-pitched voice earned him the nickname Little Jimmy Scott, these traits the consequence of a medical condition. He joined Lionel Hampton's group in 1948 and had a major hit with a ballad, 'Everybody's Somebody's Fool', but it was the last real success he had for many years. Decca recorded an album's worth of material where his pleading, contrite sensibility on standard material set him completely apart from the new wave of jazz baritones. But his solo career never really got started, and it wasn't until 1955 that he signed with another label, Savoy, which proved to be a poor choice: the few records were shabbily produced and sloppily packaged. He had one more bite at the cherry when Ray Charles sponsored an album, *Falling In Love Is Wonderful* (Tangerine, 1963), but it soon vanished and Scott was hardly heard from at all until he began performing again in the late 80s. Rediscovered for a final time at the start of the 90s, he has since become an object of fascination: a sequence of carefully produced albums for Warner Bros and Milestone make the most of his now frail but still affecting voice, his wayward approach to phrasing and bar lines and almost exclusive use of slow tempos rendering the albums often heartrending portraits of a withered but defiant artist.
*All The Way* (Sire/Warner Bros)

# Ronnie Scott

TENOR SAXOPHONE
*born* 28 January 1927; *died* 23 December 1996

While Scott holds a place at the head of the table in British jazz, his career as a player has a frustration about it which is, with hindsight, saddening. A Londoner, born Ronald Schatt, he began club work in his teens and played in dance bands (Ted Heath, Ambrose) after the war, taking his chance to hear New York jazz when he played on some of the transatlantic liners. He was one of the movers who helped get the London bop

venue Club Eleven going in 1948, and in the early 50s he established a band which, besides his own playing, featured some of the best of the young moderns then playing on the London scene, including Victor Feldman and Jimmy Deuchar. This lasted in various forms until 1957, when he formed The Jazz Couriers with Tubby Hayes, a two-tenor band which could brew up music of extraordinary excitement. Their few records show how good Scott really was: while the flash and exuberance of Hayes takes the ear immediately, it's the more authoritative, profound work of Scott which draws the listener in. In 1959, Scott and business partner Pete King established Ronnie Scott's Jazz Club, originally in Soho's Gerrard Street, and this venture took up much of the rest of his life, since it became one of the most eminent and durable venues of its kind in the world. Scott played there regularly with his own groups, which ranged from a quartet to an eight-piece band, and away from the club he toured occasionally, held down one of the saxophone chairs in the Clarke–Boland Big Band (some of his best solos on record), and briefly fronted an orchestra at the end of the 60s which accompanied visiting singers. Scott's playing deepened and became more individual as the years passed, absorbing matter from many of the American soloists who had played at his club, but keeping its tough, resilient and humorous core personal to Scott himself. His personal life, rather intrusively documented in a number of places, was lonely and marked by serious spells of depression, and the standard set of jokes which he told every night at the club, to fill in between sets, had something of Pagliacci about them. The most disappointing thing about his career was his reluctance to make records: aside from a few live sessions, there is only a handful of studio dates under his own name to remember him by. His suicide at the end of 1996 was a bitter finale.
*Live At Ronnie Scott's* (Columbia)

# Shirley Scott

ORGAN, PIANO
*born* 14 March 1934; *died* 10 March 2002

Scottie perhaps never quite got her due as a pioneer of jazz organ: like her fellow Philadelphian Jimmy Smith, she switched to the instrument from piano around 1955 (and Jimmy gave her a few informal lessons). She backed Eddie 'Lockjaw' Davis up until 1960 or so and then worked regularly with Stanley Turrentine, whom she married in 1961. But Shirley was already making records under her own name from 1958: she made two dozen for Prestige and a further eight for Impulse! in the 60s, trying out trio, quartet and even big-band settings. Never quite the manic performer which Smith was, Scott nevertheless put together an exciting and effective style out of bop lines, gospel and blues licks, and a canny understanding of the organ's expressive potential via vibrato and tone settings. It's a pity that many of her records were clearly dashed off by her labels with relatively little production work, but they each have their beguiling or explosive moments. She split up with Turrentine in 1971 and later went back to the piano as often as the organ; TV viewers could spot her as the bandleader on Bill Cosby's brief revival of *You Bet Your Life* in the 90s.

*Soul Shoutin'* (Prestige)

## Stephen Scott

PIANO
born 13 March 1969

Scott rushed through his early, New York years: he was a Young Talent Award winner in 1986 and was playing for Betty Carter at 18. Verve signed him as a solo artist four years later and he made four excellent records for the company, although he was subsequently dropped when that label began paring back on its jazz commitments. Since then he has dropped back into a sideman role for the most part: one high-profile gig which he has enjoyed has been with the touring Sonny Rollins group. Scott is a fleet fingered improviser, but he has also written some excellent tunes, and he's an accomplished all-rounder who needs sensible label patronage as he moves through his 30s.

*Vision Quest* (Enja)

## Tony Scott

CLARINET
born 17 June 1921

Scott was studying in New York when he began playing at the jam sessions at Minton's in the early 40s, and he quickly took on some of the early ideas of the nascent bebop idiom: the trouble was, he played clarinet, which would never find much of a foothold in bop. After playing in army bands he performed in small groups and big bands (Tommy Dorsey, Claude Thornhill, Duke Ellington) as well as working as an arranger and leading his own groups. None of them made a particular mark, but as the 50s went on he managed to make albums for RCA, Brunswick, Coral and Seeco, and his final quartet featured Bill Evans on piano: *A Day In New York* (Fresh Sound) documents its exceptional work. In some ways, Scott made a better fist of modernizing the clarinet than Buddy DeFranco, a very different kind of player – he mixed cool and hot approaches without any fuss or awkwardness, and the best of his records, although only rarely reissued and largely unknown except to scholars of the period, are very fine. However, everything changed for him when he took off to travel Europe and the Far East at the start of the 60s. He absorbed numerous influences from his travels and on his return recorded *Music For Zen Meditation* (Verve, 1965), a trio set for clarinet, Shakuhachi and koto, which was subsequently lionized by rock hippies: as a result, it has never been out of the catalogue since and is one of the all-time best-sellers in Verve's history. A follow-up later covered yoga meditation, and from there Scott eventually left to live and play in Italy. He has infrequently drifted into view since, recording occasional albums for twilight labels such as Philology, and devoting one entire project to a study of Billy Strayhorn's tune 'Lush Life'. Scott's career effectively divides into his New York bop days and his Euro-Asian, world-music aftermath: some of those 60s records certainly act as mild-mannered blueprints for aspects of the world music of the 80s and 90s.

*Music For Zen Meditation* (Verve)

# Phil Seamen

DRUMS
*born* 28 August 1926; *died* 13 October 1972

A funny, talented man – anecdotes abound
concerning his humour and idiosyncrasies –
Seamen was eventually destroyed by his
heroin addiction, and it was a notable waste
in British jazz. Born in Burton Upon Trent,
he started playing drums in the 40s, behind
the likes of Nat Gonella and in the Joe Loss
orchestra, but in the 50s he mixed big-band
work with Jack Parnell with small-band playing in some of the best modern combos,
including those of Ronnie Scott and Don
Rendell. He went on to do more fine work
with Tubby Hayes and Joe Harriott – he
plays on most of Harriott's important
records – and then divided his time between
R&B with Alexis Korner and a long stint as
the house drummer at Ronnie Scott's Club.
It was piquant enough when Seamen toured
with Ginger Baker's dreadful group Air Force
at the end of the 60s, since Baker had been a
pupil of his, but his last years were mostly
spent doing routine pub gigs on the London
circuit: if he had leadership aspirations, they
never got much beyond bossing a few small
groups. Seamen still played well at the end
of his life – the record cited finds him with a
1971 Tony Coe quartet, and preserves one of
his stage announcements – and though he
had something of a wild-man reputation,
that was mostly in comparison to the often
staid surroundings his career had regularly
settled him in. He was a strong and individual bebop drummer at heart, who was
adaptable enough to move across most jazz
boundaries.
**Tony Coe, *Some Other Spring*** (Hep)

# Al Sears

TENOR SAXOPHONE
*born* 21 February 1910; *died* 23 March 1990

Sears had already enjoyed a busy jazz career
before he joined Duke Ellington in 1944, but
as with so many other Ellingtonians, it was
that band which brought out his most
characteristic work. He was in New York by
1928, working for Chick Webb and Elmer
Snowden, before leading small groups of his
own until 1940 or so. He then played with
Lionel Hampton and Andy Kirk before joining Ellington, succeeding Ben Webster and
staying some five years: his sound was akin
to a more mobile, less decisive Webster. But
it was the 50s that made him his best living:
he joined the Johnny Hodges small band of
1951, gifted the leader a major hit with his
own tune 'Castle Rock', and then moved
over to R&B and publishing, playing tenor
solos on rock'n'roll records and generally
enjoying a more financially fruitful time
than he had with jazz. He later turned up
in Ellington reunions, but after 1960 his
playing days were largely behind him.
***Swing's The Thing*** (Swingville/OJC)

# Don Sebesky

ARRANGER
*born* 10 December 1937

Sebesky got his start as a trombone player
in big bands of the middle 50s, but he began
writing arrangements for the likes of Stan
Kenton, and by the middle of the 60s that
was his full-time musical occupation. In this
field, Sebesky enjoyed a considerable
amount of success, as well as plenty of
diverse opinion about his work. On one
level, his arrangements are pretentious and
overblown, and pander to the crowd; on
another, he has sometimes almost accidentally found a way to focus a talent in an
otherwise unpromising situation. The
exemplars of the latter are the charts he
created for some of Wes Montgomery's later
records: they may have sent Wes in the direction of easy listening, but they did it in
some style. Perhaps fortunately, Sebesky
largely left jazz after 1970, and on the evidence of the grotesque Bill Evans memorial
of *I Remember Bill* (BMG, 1997), it is just as
well.
**Wes Montgomery, *Bumpin'*** (Verve)

# Section/section-player

A section within a large ensemble is a group
of like instruments: a brass section, a saxophone section, and so on. Some instrumentalists have made a professional speciality
out of section-work, which calls for the discipline of precise dovetailing of executive
skills, rather than the individuality of the
soloist – although a section-player may be
obliged to take a solo at the leader's whim.
Veterans of section-work, who have played

alongside each other many times, some-times call each other 'section', in deference to their shared skills.

## Gene Sedric
CLARINET, TENOR SAXOPHONE
*born* 17 June 1907; *died* 3 April 1963

Gene 'Honey Bear' Sedric would have remained a largely unremarked-on player of the 20s and early swing era if he hadn't won the lucky break of joining Fats Waller in 1934. Before that, he came up in his native St Louis, playing in local and touring bands before joining Sam Wooding in 1925 and remaining a mainstay of the orchestra, on their European travels and elsewhere, until 1931. Given that Wooding's band worked largely outside the jazz mainstream, Sedric might have subsequently disappeared if Waller hadn't hired him to join Herman Autrey as the front line for Waller's 'Rhythm' group. He stayed until the pian-ist's death, touring and recording constantly, although, as with Autrey, on the records Sedric's clarinet and tenor are often obscured by the leader's shouting and gen-eral mayhem. Thereafter he worked as a leader himself, and with others such as Mezz Mezzrow, but his later recordings made no mark, and after a final appearance on the session with Dick Wellstood which appeared as *Uptown And Downtown* (Swing-ville, 1961), ill-health obliged him to retire from playing.
**Fats Waller,** *1937 Vol 2* (Classics)

## Zbigniew Seifert
VIOLIN, ALTO SAXOPHONE
*born* 6 June 1946; *died* 15 February 1979

Zbiggy Seifert was born in Kraków and studied both violin and alto saxophone there, although it was John Coltrane's tenor which was his abiding passion. He led a quar-tet, playing alto, which he performed with in the later 60s, but violin eventually took over his playing completely, while he was in a group led by Tomasz Stańko. In the 70s he came to wider attention, in bands led by Hans Koller, Joachim Kühn and Volker Kriegl, and he made some impact in America when he appeared at the Monterey Jazz Festival of 1976. He had a go at fusion,

but the results were rather less impressive than his Coltrane-inspired acoustic work, best caught on the often thrilling record cited, though it has yet to find CD reissue. There was, in the end, little enough of Sei-fert caught on record: he was killed by cancer when only 32.
**Man Of The Light** (MPS)

## Boyd Senter
CLARINET, ALTO SAXOPHONE
*born* 30 November 1899; *died* June 1982

Senter had at least one distinction: his first record was issued as by Jelly Roll Morton's Jazz Kings in 1924, even though Morton had nothing to do with it. The rest of his career is often more dismaying. He is one of the leaders of that group of clarinettists – includ-ing Ted Lewis, Woody Walder and Wilton Crawley – who used the instrument primar-ily as a vaudeville horn, getting some risible if energetically noisy music out of it on a surprisingly large number of records made in the late 20s. He also doubled on alto sax, on which he sounded much the same. He made a further ten rare sides for the Autograph label and two for Paramount before cutting 23 titles for Pathé, 26 for OKeh and 14 for Victor, his final session taking place in 1930, which suggests that Senter may have been a clown but he was a very popular one. The 'Jazzologist Supreme' was still playing after the war, although he eventually spent more time in the hardware business.
**Jazzologist Supreme** (Timeless)

## Session/sessionman
The session is usually a recording date (live 'sessions' are more usually called 'gigs'). A sessionman (women are allowed these days, but there are far fewer of them) is one who makes most of his professional living play-ing at sessions, which may or may not have jazz content. It's more likely that the jazz element is under strict control: most session-men are engaged to work on advertising jingles, backing work for singers, film soundtracks, or a horn chart for a pop record. There used to be more outlets for 'creative' session-work than there are now, in part because jazz was a more familiar

part of the popular music of the 50s and 60s. It's possible, with the rise of synthesizers and other electronic instruments, able to replicate more or less any other instrument, that the sessionman's days are numbered in any case.

## Doc Severinsen
TRUMPET
*born* 7 July 1927

Although Severinsen got his grounding in big-band work in the late 40s, he spent most of his career in television. He joined the band on Steve Allen's show in 1955, began helping Skitch Henderson on *The Tonight Show*, and took over the band altogether in 1967, staying until the orchestra was dispersed on Johnny Carson's retirement. As a result, Severinsen probably brought more jazz into American homes in the 60s, 70s and 80s than any other musician, even though much of what the band did was little more than produce fills and cues for guests. Severinsen brought a ready supply of wit to the job and he made sure that the band was stacked with jazz pros: two albums made for Amherst, while dominated by Severinsen's own rather glaring solos, prove what a good if conventional big band it was. Since the demise of the Carson era, Doc has continued to tour the Orchestra, although many of its alumni have now also retired or are gone.
**The Tonight Show Orchestra With Doc Severinsen Vol II** (Amherst)

## Bud Shank
ALTO SAXOPHONE, FLUTE
*born* 27 May 1926

A leading spirit and sound in the story of West Coast jazz, Shank was actually born in Dayton, Ohio, and studied at North Carolina University in the middle 40s. He played with Charlie Barnet and Stan Kenton, and after a brief period of military service shifted to Los Angeles in 1952. There he became one of the most prominent fixtures in the burgeoning studio scene of the time, playing on countless sessions based around the Shorty Rogers axis of musicians, as well as leading his own quartet, playing regularly in the Lighthouse All Stars, and making what amounted almost to novelty records

with Bob Cooper (Shank played flute, Cooper the oboe). At this point, Shank's alto was a fleet, supple bebop arrow, with less of a sharp point than Art Pepper's but similarly incisive. His flute, a double which helped get him much of his work, was in its way just as effective, and a partnership with guitarist Laurindo Almeida prefigured some of the Brazilian jazz of a few years later (he also made one exceptional date, *New Groove*, for Pacific Jazz in 1961, where he was featured on baritone sax). Shank was still a studio favourite all through the 60s, and some of his later World Pacific albums amounted to easy-listening renditions of pop tunes; he was just as likely to be heard on pop studio dates, and it wasn't until the formation of the L.A. Four in 1974, a quartet with Almeida, Ray Brown, and one out of Chuck Flores, Shelly Manne and Jeff Hamilton, that he reasserted his jazz credentials. They made a sequence of coolly agreeable albums for Concord, but after ten years Shank was tired of both that band and the studio scene, and he abandoned the flute altogether in order to concentrate on the alto. There were some reunions with the surviving members of the Shorty Rogers gang, but Bud was more interested in leading new small groups of his own, and he made a series of albums that found his old bebop style refashioned for modern times. Although sometimes his playing took on an arbitrarily fierce tone, there have been some handsome sessions along the way.
**I Told You So** (Candid)

## Sonny Sharrock
GUITAR
*born* 27 August 1940; *died* 26 May 1994

Sharrock sang doo-wop as a teenager, and began playing the guitar in 1959, going to New York six years later and becoming involved in the free-jazz scene rather than rock'n'roll. Since there weren't any real role models for him on his instrument in the idiom, he took to trying to emulate some of the saxophone players of the day, which engendered a style based on fast picking to approximate trills, a slide on the strings, and turning his amplifier up to way past 11, all of which created a caterwauling sound which could compete with such playing companions as Byard Lancaster and Pharoah

Sanders. He is on a very few records of the period, but none of them give much idea of what he could do, and one of the more representative, *Monkey-Pockie-Boo* (1970), with his wife, the untalented singer Linda Sharrock, is poor. Sharrock paid bills by working in Herbie Mann's touring groups for several years, and it wasn't until he was more or less rediscovered by Bill Laswell in the 80s that the guitarist began to get some recognition. In the improvising supergroup Last Exit he finally found a congenial setting, and his solo record *Guitar* (Enemy, 1986) is a torrid masterpiece of electric drones and tumult which is a prescient document of where the instrument would go later in the 80s and 90s. Sonny was always a little ahead of his time. He was finally set to receive something like his due in 1994, when he was engaged by RCA on a major-label deal: but he died of a heart attack a few days after signing the contract.

*Guitar* (Enemy)

# Charlie Shavers

TRUMPET

*born* 3 August 1917; *died* 8 July 1971

A trumpet master whose beautiful playing has become another casualty of the times: the record-makers of the LP era largely wasted Shavers's talents, and modern audiences must seek the best of him out on anthologies and compilations. A New Yorker, he started on piano and banjo and eventually settled on the trumpet, playing in minor groups before working alongside Dizzy Gillespie in the group led by Franke Fairfax. He then moved to Lucky Millinder's orchestra, but John Kirby signed the teenaged Shavers to join his sextet at the end of 1937. He stayed for some six years, although he also played on some other record dates: the one which produced '29th And Dearborn' with Johnny Dodds (1938) shows his impeccable blues playing. 'Undecided', his most memorable tune and a certified jazz imperishable, was introduced with Kirby, and though the often strict surroundings of the Kirby band hardly let Shavers fly, he found ways of adding brilliant bits of decoration to almost every record. In the end, he departed for big bands: principally Tommy Dorsey's, which he joined in 1945 and where he stayed on and off for almost 11

years. He was a regular at Jazz At The Philharmonic, quite capable of delivering the obligatory high-note finales, and toured with Benny Goodman and his own small groups, a regime which lasted well into the 60s. Shavers was exceptionally strong in the altissimo range, which occasionally led him into showboating, a trait which sometimes got him branded as a vulgarian (it didn't help that Shavers loved entertaining a crowd): somehow, though, this big man was able to dance and float through such passages, where Cat Anderson and Maynard Ferguson might have merely squealed. The sad thing was, as mentioned, the lack of support from record labels. He made some good records for Bethlehem, but most of the others were on cheap labels such as Everest and MGM, and it seems strange that Norman Granz never gave him a shot at studio leadership. In the end, he was felled by throat cancer, even though he was still just strong enough to play a final New York gig only weeks before his death, which occurred two days after Louis Armstrong's passing.

*Charlie Shavers 1944–1945* (Classics)

# Artie Shaw

CLARINET

*born* 23 May 1910; *died* 30 December 2004

A high-profile success which he would have preferred to have had buried in obscurity, aspirations to great art thwarted by commercial popularity, a theme tune called 'Nightmare', eight marriages and a retirement which lasted three times as long as his bandleading career: Artie Shaw's world was as unconventional as jazz could provide. He was born Arthur Jacob Arshawsky in New York but grew up in Connecticut, where he played sax from the age of 12 and began working in dance bands three years later. His career was nothing special until he returned to New York around 1930, where he began working mainly as a studio-session musician, finally forming his own group in 1936. This set out his stall from the start: rather than playing conventional dance material, he hired an eight-piece group and they played an original work of chamber music. Shaw then tried a more conventional band, but it didn't last long and Shaw disbanded, only to regroup later in 1937 with a new book. Within a year he had his break-through hit, an irresistible Jerry Gray arrangement of 'Begin The Beguine', and within weeks the Shaw band was a sensational rival to Benny Goodman's supremacy, with the leader's clarinet similarly prominent to Goodman's. But success didn't so much spoil Shaw as leave him aghast: he wanted listening audiences rather than jitterbugging kids, and he went as far as leaving his own band to the leadership of sideman Georgie Auld at the end of 1939. A year later, he recorded a hit version of 'Frenesi' with a studio band, which sparked off a new touring outfit, this time augmented by the string section Shaw had always hankered after, and there was a small group, Artie Shaw's Gramercy Five, which – as with Goodman – spotlit the leader's clarinet in a smaller setting, though Shaw went the unusual route of having Johnny Guarnieri play harpsichord rather than piano. It was another successful venture, but again the dissatisfied Shaw disbanded it, only for a third band to emerge at the end of 1941. This time America's entry to the war intervened, and in the Navy Shaw toured a forces band which was greeted with wild acclaim in the Pacific. After the war the same cycle of dispersal and regroupment continued, until Shaw led his final Gramercy Five for record dates in 1954. By now he was turning more to writing, having completed his autobiography, *The Trouble With Cinderella*, the previous year, and at this point he abandoned the music business altogether.

Shaw's fine technique and piping sound let him effectively go toe to toe with Goodman all through the great years of the swing era, and his capricious temperament and impatience with what he had to do to succeed made him just as awkward a figure: where Goodman was a martinet, Shaw was more like his own worst enemy. Landmark records such as 'Concerto For Clarinet' (1940) underscore his impeccable credentials as a clarinet player, but they also hint at suffer-ing-artist syndrome: Shaw never achieved anything immortal as a writer of prose, and his attempts at 'serious' music were trumped by his great hit records. Yet he was smart enough to realize that studio con-ditions only rarely brought out the best in the big bands, and when he helped in com-piling the definitive *Self Portrait* collection

of his best work for RCA Victor, he often picked broadcast versions of tunes over their studio counterparts. Like Goodman, he pioneered having black musicians in his otherwise white bands, giving work to Billie Holiday, Roy Eldridge and Hot Lips Page, and while he found time to woo Ava Gardner and Lana Turner, among several other spouses, he has left a substantial discogra-phy for a man who was always breaking up his own bands. In his old age, he was tempted out of retirement in 1983 to con-duct (though not play in) an orchestra that brought some of his old scores back to life, and the band continued – though usually under the stewardship of Dick Johnson rather than Shaw – into the 90s. He remained a tough talker with a vivid and candid memory, right up until a few weeks before his death.

*Self Portrait* (Bluebird)

# Clarence (Gene) Shaw
TRUMPET
*born* 16 June 1926; *died* 17 August 1973

An interesting trumpeter with a clean, mel-odious sound, Shaw had a walk-on role in hard-bop history. He took up the horn in the 40s and studied and played locally in his home town of Detroit, before going to New York in 1956. He spent a few stormy months with Charles Mingus and plays superbly on two Mingus classics, *Tijuana Moods* (RCA) and *East Coasting* (Bethlehem), but after a punch-up with the leader Shaw threw his trumpet away and didn't play again until 1962. Thereafter he made three albums for Argo under the name Gene Shaw: rarities, they are pleasing if unexceptional. After that his career went nowhere.

**Charles Mingus**, *Tijuana Moods* (RCA)

# Ian Shaw
VOCAL
*born* 2 June 1962

Shaw has been a fixture on the British jazz scene since the late 80s, but with hindsight it's clear that his timing has never been lucky. He sang standards and soul-pop tunes at a time when that kind of material was less fashionable, and has never much broken out beyond a club following: in recent years, he might have been hurt to see lesser singers such as Jamie Cullum win huge amounts of attention. He worked steadily through the 90s and is one of the handful of British artists of his ilk to make some impact in America: two albums for Milestone in the US have included some of his most mature and thoughtful singing. But part of his difficulty is that he mixes the worlds of jazz and cabaret singing, rather than jazz and chart-pop, and in his 40s, though it seems unfortunate to say it, he is probably too old to find the breakthrough which his career needs if it's to go up another level.

**Soho Stories** (Milestone)

# Woody Shaw
TRUMPET
*born* 24 December 1944; *died* 9 May 1989

Shaw became a tragic figure of his time: he was a brilliant and much-admired trumpeter, but his career never quite secured the stable position which would have allowed him to flourish, and he was dogged by some terrible misfortunes. He was raised in New Jersey (his father ran a group of gospel singers) and started on trumpet at 11. He had been working uneventful local gigs before a sideman job with Eric Dolphy in 1963, who then invited Shaw to join him on a European tour. Dolphy's death intervened, but Shaw made the trip anyway and found plenty of interesting gigs before returning home in 1965. Some high-profile sideman work followed – with Horace Silver, McCoy Tyner and Max Roach – but Shaw became a heroin addict, and ever after he couldn't quite shake off narcotics. Even though the kind of music he played – a particularly lyrical sort of hard bop – was entirely out of fashion in the 70s, he still held down creative gigs with Joe Henderson, Art Blakey, Bobby Hutcherson and Louis Hayes, and in 1977 Woody decided that his own time had come as a leader. There was a sequence of fine albums for Muse, Red and Enja, but a potentially important contract with Columbia in the end failed to lead him to any lasting success. He carried on band-leading in the 80s, but the impression that he had missed his time crept through the scene, and although he still played very well, a shadow had been cast over him: he became HIV-positive after using an infected needle, his sight began to fail through a hereditary illness, and in the end his teeth gave way and his playing petered out. Woody was, at his best, a major figure in the jazz of his time. Much has been made of his ability to be a hard-bop insider who could handle more outward-looking music, but it was his concern to play lyrically which really set him apart from the heat-seeking changes players of his generation. His best compositions – including 'The Moontrane' and 'Katrina Ballerina' – have a wistful quality married to a carefully logical outlook. Early in 1989 he lost an arm when he fell in front of a subway train at a Brooklyn station, and he died some weeks later. His recorded legacy is still only very haphazardly available on CD.

**The Moontrane** (Muse)

# George Shearing
PIANO
*born* 13 August 1919

Shearing might be one of the few jazz artists whose work has genuinely grown in stature in his old age: filled with deft pleasantries, everything he did up to the age of 65 or so was as blithely inconsequential as fairy cake. He grew up in a very poor family, one of nine children, and was born blind, learning the piano at a special school. He then played accordion and piano in various dance bands before leading small groups of his own, and by the mid-40s he was considered one of the most able and skilful of British jazz pianists, although at this point his style was a mixture of Wilson, Tatum, Hines and others. He went to New York in 1947 and settled there, eventually forming a quintet which debuted 'The Shearing Sound' in 1949, after two intensive years of club work by the leader as a solo and intermission pianist. Using an instrumentation of piano, vibes, guitar, bass and drums, Shearing hit on a nimble formula: the piano plays block chords (the melody harmonized with a chord of three notes in the right hand, the left playing the melody but an octave lower), while the upper melody note is doubled on the vibes and the lower by the guitar. On what was effectively the quintet's signature tune, 'Lullaby Of Birdland', the music sounds like the coolest of bebop distillations – bop without pain, or perhaps bop relaxing in the

lounge with an aperitif. It was tremendously successful, and after Shearing's initial sessions for MGM in the LP era he signed to Capitol, and made a long series of records in the same style. Eventually the quintet (by now really a sextet, since Shearing added a percussionist early on) was upholstered with strings, brass and whatnot, and the album covers featured glamorous sirens and titles such as *Latin Escapade* and *Blue Chiffon*. Some of his tunes entered the jazz repertory, though, such as 'Conception', covered by Miles Davis ('Miles didn't get the bridge right – he should have called it "Deception" or something'). Meanwhile, the quintet endured, although Shearing also worked in a trio, and he took to mixing classical and jazz repertoire. Eventually he disbanded the quintet altogether, in 1978, after many changes in personnel, and he worked frequently with Mel Tormé until the singer's death, an unusually simpatico partnership which made many albums for Concord. Shearing also worked for Concord as a solo, but his most interesting work has come since signing to Telarc at the start of the 90s: it has brought forth some of his wittiest and most engaging records, the old magpie approach to jazz piano thinned to an elegant and slightly misty, romantic sheen.
*That Shearing Sound* (Telarc)

## Jack Sheldon

TRUMPET, VOCAL
*born* 30 November 1931

Sheldon did the rare double of cool West Coast stylist and stand-up comedian. He was in Los Angeles by 1947, playing in air force bands before working with many of the best Californian groups of the 50s, including those of Curtis Counce, Jimmy Giuffre and Herb Geller. In the 60s he worked up a parallel act as a comic, which can be heard on *Oooh – But It's Good!* (Capitol), and he turned up frequently on American television during the period. Latterly he has gone back to a conventional jazz format, his playing a more outgoing variation on the Miles Davis brand of cool trumpet.
*Hollywood Heroes* (Concord)

## Dave Shepherd

CLARINET
*born* 7 February 1929

Britain's Benny Goodman – not quite fair or accurate, but Shepherd does that style as well as anybody – has been busy in jazz for more than a half-century. He played Dixieland with Freddy Randall and others in the early 50s, and was part of the slightly more modern Jazz Today Unit thereafter. He played with Randall again in the 60s and 70s and has shared stages with quite a few American giants in his time: Teddy Wilson, Gerry Mulligan, even Billie Holiday on her British visit. Some albums in dedication to the Goodman repertoire have brought out his imitative side, and Shepherd is a fine executant rather than a sterling individual, but he has been a bonus presence in recent times in the repertory groups the Pizza Express All Stars and The Great British Jazz Band.
*Tribute To Benny Goodman* (Avid)

## Archie Shepp

TENOR AND SOPRANO SAXOPHONES
*born* 24 May 1937

For a long time, Shepp seemed one of the most frightening members of the avant-garde, but in his middle age he became more like a grouchy-sounding teddy bear. He was raised in Philadelphia, studying drama rather than music at college, and while an out-of-work actor in New York (1959) he took up the alto saxophone to play in dance bands, an instrument he traded for the tenor when he became aware of John Coltrane's work. He was one of the earliest free-jazz players to be recorded, and he was documented with surprising frequency in the 60s, with Cecil Taylor, Bill Dixon, and then in the New York Contemporary Five with Don Cherry and John Tchicai. By the time of his leadership debut, *Four For Trane* (Impulse!, 1964), which was produced by Coltrane, Shepp's style was already mature and focused. While he was equipped to match saxophone screamers such as Albert Ayler and Charles Tyler, Shepp seemed to sense that this was a way forward which would soon be exhausted, and almost from the start his music was more wide-ranging and adaptable, adding compositional com-

plexity, familiar aspects of jazz expressionism (growls, slurs, note-bending), sudden
boppish flurries and contrastingly romantic
declamations which had a sardonic cruelty
to them. In his great records of the 60s –
*Four For Trane, Fire Music* (1965), *On This
Night* (1965), *Live In San Francisco* (1966) and
*The Way Ahead* (1968), all recorded for
Impulse! – he offers a primer for the diversity of the avant-garde within a unified and
carefully maximized use of resources. It
further helped that Shepp was that most terrifying thing to respectable society, a wither-
ingly articulate and intelligent black artist:
his numerous interviews and open letters
set out a devastating critique of his environment, his business, and the hoops an
African-American musician was still obliged
to jump through. He continued to work in
the theatre, but this time as a playwright,
and he later joined more than one
university faculty.

Yet much of the steam went out of
Shepp's music at the end of the decade, even
if his attitudes outwardly remained
unchanged. A trip to North Africa, where he
was recorded at the 1969 Pan-African
Festival, suggested only that he had little
musical common ground with those he tried
to perform with. *Attica Blues* (Impulse!, 1972)
was a broken-backed big-band project, and
thereafter Shepp's records seemed to slide
into disappointing mixtures of rambling
free-form and stilted repertory. He switched
from a dramatically inclusive playing vocabulary to a foreshortened one: his tone
weakened, he turned to an almost R&B style
of phrasing for a time, and he went into misconceived repertory excursions where he
played ballads and gospel pieces. Still touring with small groups in the 80s and 90s, in
performance he could veer between a suddenly rekindled intensity and a shambolic
and seemingly dishonest presentation.
Taking up blues singing was also not much
of a good idea. A few recent performances
on record have been close to embarrassing,
although, as so often, Shepp can suddenly
appear to wake up and rouse himself, and
some feel that one such occasion is caught
on *Live In New York* (Verve, 2001). It is hard
to argue, all the same, that Shepp has
carried forward the same kind of dignity
and creativity which still infuses the work of
such fellow veterans as Cecil Taylor.
*Fire Music* (Impulse!)

# Andy Sheppard
TENOR AND SOPRANO SAXOPHONES
*born* 20 January 1957

Sheppard got off to a rather slow start. He
grew up in Warminster, in the English West
Country, and didn't even take up the saxophone until he was 19. But he was already
playing in groups within weeks, and went to
Paris to play in Urban Sax and Big Band
Lumière. In 1985 he returned to England and
settled in Bristol, at a propitious moment:
the upsurge of interest in a young British
jazz scene was getting under way, and
Sheppard's outgoing command of most
modern styles quickly put him in the forefront. He signed to the Island Records offshoot Antilles, sharing the label with
Courtney Pine, and made three albums for
the label, starting with small groups and
leading to a big band named Soft On The
Inside. Other associations include an enduring one with Carla Bley and Steve Swallow,
in both Bley's big band and in the touring
small group which Bley and Swallow
muster. Sheppard changed labels to Blue
Note in the 90s, but some of the impetus
behind the British music had declined, and
he only managed a single record for them
before being dropped. Since then, he has
often worked with keyboardist Steve Lodder,
and has spent much of his time writing
music for film and television. Sheppard was
one of the brightest talents to emerge in his
time. Perhaps he should have persisted
longer with some of his projects: his small-
group records for Antilles suggest a matur-
ing band that had a lot of fine music in
them yet, and Soft On The Inside seemed an
almost premature leap into big-band work,
which was ultimately abandoned to go back
to more economically feasible small groups.
In the indulgent Bley–Swallow band,
Sheppard is mostly a colourful bystander.
His dark but polished tone and strength as a
melodic improviser make him unfailingly
enjoyable to hear; as ever, context is his
difficulty.
*Introductions In the Dark* (Antilles)

## Shorty Sherock

TRUMPET
*born* 17 November 1915; *died* 19 February 1980

Sherock worked steadily through a journey-man career. In the 30s he worked with Jimmy Dorsey and Bob Crosby, and then played for numerous other leaders, trying his hand at bandleading himself for a spell. He is on some of the early Jazz At The Philharmonic shows and is, frankly, the most excitable and least convincing of the soloists. He was a studio player for most of the rest of his career, and never really retired.

**Various Artists, *The Complete Jazz At The Philharmonic On Verve 1944–49*** (Verve)

## Bobby Shew

TRUMPET
*born* 4 March 1941

The inventor of the Shew-horn, a trumpet with one set of tubes but two bells, obviously has a sense of punning humour, and his sunnily disposed playing has featured in many American settings since his 60s spells with Woody Herman and Buddy Rich. He worked in Las Vegas for a long period and from there went on to be a star turn in the Toshiko Akiyoshi big band of the late 70s. But after that he decided to focus primarily on small-group playing, working primarily on the West Coast, although he has been a regular traveller to the Far East and Australasia. Shew is a tireless pro in the post-bop tradition, although much of his work as a leader has been rather hidden on small labels. The record cited takes him back to his roots, since he grew up in New Mexico and was surrounded by Latin music.

***Salsa Caliente*** (MAMA)

## Larry Shields

CLARINET
*born* 13 September 1893; *died* 21 November 1953

Shields was the oustanding player in the Original Dixieland Jazz Band. He was pals with Nick LaRocca in his teens, and the jangling attack of his clarinet is always the most striking thing on the ODJB's records, much more fluent and imaginative than anything LaRocca was doing. But he never went

on to make much of a mark anywhere else. After leaving the group in 1921, he worked in California and Chicago without creating any significant music, and then turned out for ODJB reunions until he drifted out of music altogether.

***The Original Dixieland Jazz Band 1917–1921*** (Timeless)

## Sahib Shihab

SAXOPHONES, FLUTE
*born* 23 June 1925; *died* 24 October 1989

Born Edmund Gregory in Savannah, Georgia, Shihab did big-band work in the early 40s but was involved in some of the pioneer bop sessions for Blue Note later in the decade, recording with Art Blakey, Thelonious Monk and Tadd Dameron. This, however, didn't do his career any special good, and he was doing day work and only occasionally playing at night until joining Dizzy Gillespie in 1953. There were some subsequent high-profile gigs (he cut a date with John Coltrane in 1957), but when he went to Europe with a Quincy Jones orchestra in 1959 he liked it enough to settle there, eventually basing himself in Copenhagen. Though he spent a period in Los Angeles in the 70s, Shihab was thereafter an honoured American in Europe, turning up in the Clarke–Boland group and radio orchestras. Though he could double on anything, Shihab's main horn was the baritone, and he got a beautiful, limber sound out of it, which he could effortlessly transfer to his delicate flute playing (there was a *Flute Summit* date with James Moody and Jeremy Steig in 1973). He made only a handful of discs under his own leadership, and his best surviving playing has to be searched out in other settings.

**Kenny Clarke–Francy Boland Big Band, *All Blues/ Sax No End*** (MPS)

## Matthew Shipp

PIANO
*born* 7 December 1960

A prolific and imposing presence in the jazz of the new century, Shipp has steadily grown into a tremendously powerful musician. Born in Wilmington, Delaware, he studied with Ran Blake at the New England Conservatory in the early 80s before moving

to New York, where he was soon involved in a circle of musicians including Ron Brown, William Parker, Whit Dickey and David S Ware. This has gradually expanded from duo and trio work with Brown and Parker to a quartet with Parker, Ware and several drummers to an ensemble which mixes free-jazz playing with electronics, turntables and sampling. Shipp's music is stuffed with references – to Monk, Taylor, a wealth of piano composers from other disciplines, and particularly Andrew Hill, who has belatedly become an important influence on new jazz pianists – but he is a free-thinking virtuoso who stands his ground and finds virgin territory in whichever combination of players or musical setting he is dropped into. It is often playing of inscrutable intensity – Shipp's interest in contrasting structures and tremendously dense voicings can sometimes starve the listener of melody – but a suddenly voluminous discography has many fascinating things in it, and he is almost unique among American pianists in moving towards a convincing case for both acoustic and electric improvisation and the bridge between what are still two distinct idioms.
*Equilibrium* (Thirsty Ear)

## Bob Shoffner
TRUMPET
*born* 30 April 1900; *died* 5 March 1983

Shoffner was raised in St Louis and played trumpet and piano in dance bands before serving in the US Army at the end of the First World War. He arrived in Chicago in 1921 and played in King Oliver's band as a successor to Louis Armstrong, and he is on most of the records made by Oliver's Dixie Syncopators for Vocalion. Besides these dates he is also on record with Lovie Austin, Jimmy O'Bryant and Luis Russell, and though he worked through the 30s he was only rarely sighted in the studios. He put music to one side in the 40s, but he picked up the horn again later in the 50s, when he became a regular trumpeter in Franz Jackson's revivalist band.
**Franz Jackson, *A Night At The Red Arrow*** (Pinnacle)

## Alan Shorter
FLUGELHORN
*born* 29 May 1932; *died* 5 April 1988

Many regard Wayne Shorter as something of an enigma, but his brother Alan was at least as mysterious. He started as a tenor player, working in a group with his brother, but switched to the flugelhorn after someone walked off with his saxophone. He eventually moved to New York some time in the early 60s, where he flitted through the free-jazz scene, turning up on records with Marion Brown and Archie Shepp, and on Wayne's *The All Seeing Eye* (1965), and he managed to record a single date for Verve as a leader, the curious *Orgasm* (1968). At the end of the decade he joined the small exodus to Paris by American avant-gardists and made one further record there as well as playing further with Shepp; but little more is known of his activities after 1971 or so. The announcement of his death in 1988 closed a frustratingly elliptical chapter: Shorter's brief contribution, particularly his playing on Archie Shepp's *Four For Trane* (1964), hints at a talent which merited much wider exposure.
**Archie Shepp, *Four For Trane*** (Impulse!)

## Wayne Shorter
TENOR AND SOPRANO SAXOPHONES
*born* 25 August 1933

The man who painted 'Mr Weird' on the side of his saxophone case in high school started on clarinet and then switched to tenor. He studied at New York University and following army service he played with a Maynard Ferguson group before joining Art Blakey's Jazz Messengers in 1959. Four years with Blakey sharpened and focused his playing to a formidable degree, his big, almost unruly sound given sinew by some strangely cryptic ideas about phrase shapes and construction. In Brian Case's brilliant phrase, hearing him was 'a little like being knocked down by a chess player'. Miles Davis enlisted him in 1964, and he was with the trumpeter for the next six years, in the meantime also recording a remarkable series of albums under his own name for Blue Note. As a composer, Shorter soon established himself as a rare individual in a genre otherwise full of functional writers. He often used familar devices, such as the standard AABA chorus form, simple bass patterns and conventionally swinging hard-bop rhythms, but his harmonic thinking and chord progressions introduced daring new sounds to what was by now very familiar terrain for the small jazz ensemble, and as a melodist, he was as creative as any composer then working. Some of his themes for Blakey, including 'Lester Left Town' and 'One By One', presage what he would go on to do, but his solo work and writing for Davis see him in full creative flow: 'Night Dreamer', 'House Of Jade', 'Speak No Evil', 'Tom Thumb', 'Chief Crazy Horse', 'Adam's Apple', 'Witch Hunt' and above all 'Footprints', one of the most frequently covered tunes in the modern jazz repertoire, are just some of the entries from a body of work which was all but unprecedented. By the time of 'Nefertiti' (1967), which seemed to suggest a whole new approach to group improvising, with the horns endlessly cycling through the doleful melody while the rhythm section goes into free-fall, Shorter was working at an extraordinary level. His own playing matched his writing for ingenuity: expressive effects would emerge with startling impact out of otherwise subdued, almost behind-the-hand playing, bluesy outbursts alternated with quizzical shape-shifting. It was a dramatic alternative to Coltrane's model, even though Trane had clearly had an impact on Shorter's own thinking.

After his work with Davis on *In A Silent Way* (1969), though, Shorter seemed to falter: his final Blue Notes were less impressive, as he sought to find a way of working within the emerging jazz-rock genre, and his co-founding of Weather Report with Joe Zawinul solved the problem for him by leaving most of the compositional input to the keyboardist, Shorter himself spending as much time now on the soprano as the tenor saxophone. Shorter fans often despaired of his stature within Weather Report, but since this was really Zawinul's band, Wayne's comparatively meagre compositional input was no real surprise. After the group disbanded, he seemed unsure of which way to go for a time, settling for occasional Miles Davis sideman-reunions with Herbie Hancock and others, and leading fusion bands of his own with often mixed results. In the 90s he seemed to finally settle back into a more creative position. An acoustic duet album with Hancock was disappointingly inconsequential, although concerts they did together were far superior. Eventually, back with a mostly acoustic set-up, he returned to steady live work and cut the recent records *Footprints Live!* (Verve, 2001) and *Alegria* (2002), which were widely acclaimed although, in comparison with his old achievements, pleasing but tame. Wayne is an enigmatic man, still perhaps the 'Mr Weird' of old: a conversation with him about music might quickly end up on the subject of astronomy or hieroglyphics. He has had some personal sadnesses, losing his wife in an air crash some years ago, and for all the riches his writing offers to musicians looking for interesting music to play on, there is something private and very particular about his music which he perhaps keeps to himself.
**Speak No Evil** (Blue Note)

# Don Sickler
TRUMPET
*born* 6 January 1944

Sickler is an ordinary post-bop trumpeter, but he has found his way to an influential position in New York jazz. He was closely associated with Philly Joe Jones from the late 70s and took over Jones's Dameronia project on the drummer's death in 1985. Since then he has performed in a variety of small and large bands, although his most regular work has been as a fixer of record dates, a producer and an MD for various one-off events at Carnegie Hall and elsewhere. He has also been very shrewd at building up a publishing business, which has now gathered in the publishing rights to the music of a large number of jazz players.
**Dameronia, *To Tadd With Love*** (Uptown)

# Side

Jazz fans show their age if they talk about 'sides'. It basically dates them to at least a familiarity with the era of 78rpm discs, when a jazz record had two sides, with one performance on each. Elsewhere in this book, one can find references to musicians making 'sides' for a certain 'label': that would be a group of performances for a single record company. Younger generations brought up on CDs, MP3s and the like must forgive this collector's indulgence.

## Sideman

A sideman is someone who's playing in the band but who isn't the leader. Their choice of instrument has no relevance. Thus far, the term 'sidewoman' has made no inroads into jazz vernacular: sexist it may be, but the original term abides.

## Ben Sidran

PIANO, VOCAL, PRODUCER, AUTHOR
born 14 August 1943

Sidran's career as a jazz polymath has created an entertaining body of music and a considerable stack of related work in several media. At university in Wisconsin he played in a rock band with Boz Scaggs and Steve Miller, and in 1967 he moved to England to study for a PhD at Sussex University, playing in sundry rock groups in the UK. In 1970, Capitol Records hired him as a producer working on the American West Coast, and he went on to make jazz programmes for television and for National Public Radio. Besides this activity, which lasted into the late 80s, he began performing as a group leader in his own right, playing and singing in a style borrowed mainly from Mose Allison, although Sidran laces his manner with a good slug of knowing, beat-inspired lyric-writing. His books *Black Talk* (1971) and *Talking Jazz* (1981), which mainly present him in conversation with jazz musicians, are an entertaining read, authenticated by his working knowledge of the professional's lot: 'What I've learned from jazz musicians isn't anything to do with the notes, it's an approach, how you go through the day.' His own records, many of them issued on a label he has run since 1990, Go Jazz, are sometimes depressurized by backings which tend to drift towards fusion-lite, but in person he is a hard-swinging entertainer with a lot of presence.
*Live At The Celebrity Lounge* (Go Jazz)

## Frank Signorelli

PIANO
born 24 May 1901; *died* 9 December 1975

Largely unremembered but actually something of a pioneer, Signorelli was, like his contemporary Jimmy Durante, in almost at the start of jazz on record: he played with both the Original Dixieland Jazz Band and the Original Memphis Five, and in the 20s he piled up a large number of sideman credits as part of the New York session scene. Unlike some of his contemporaries, though, Signorelli endured: he played with Bobby Hackett and Phil Napoleon in the 40s, and presided over a re-formation of the Original Memphis Five in the 50s, as well as recording in a duo with George Wettling. He also wrote some good tunes, among them 'I'll Never Be The Same' and 'Stairway To The Stars'.
*The Original Memphis Five* (Folkways)

## Alan Silva

BASS, OTHER INSTRUMENTS
born 22 January 1939

Silva seems deliberately elusive. His principal instrument seems to be the bass, but when he made his first record (for the New York avant-garde label ESP in 1965) he played only violin, cello and piano. He was right in the heart of the free-jazz upheaval which rocked the New York scene of the 60s, yet his own contribution was musically largely peripheral, and his playing on Cecil Taylor's *Unit Structures* and *Conquistador!* (both 1966) suggests that he was the weakest link in that chain. He retreated to France at the end of the 60s and organized unwieldy ventures such as his Celestial Communications Orchestra, which made a chaotic triple LP for BYG. After a long and enigmatic absence he returned in the 90s, playing synthesizers and MIDI keyboards as well as plain old bass, and re-forming a version of the CCO. Whatever the point and purpose of his music, it looks as if it's going to continue to take up a lot of time and space.
*Transmissions* (Eremite)

# Horace Silver

PIANO

*born* 2 September 1928

Horace Ward Martin Tavares Silver began playing locally in Connecticut clubs at the end of the 40s, and he was heard in this capacity by a visiting Stan Getz, who subsequently hired the pianist and used him on some of the saxophonist's early sessions for the Roost label. Silver joined forces with Art Blakey in 1952 in the prototype Jazz Messengers in New York: though initial recordings were under Blakey's name, by the time the personnel settled down in 1954 they were called the Jazz Messengers. Silver stayed two further years and contributed extensively to the band's book, but after he left he went on to form his own quintets, which played in much the same style, although leavened by his own good humour. He had already begun recording for Blue Note while with Blakey, and that association grew warmer and more dependable as time went on: Silver stayed with the 'old' Blue Note longer than any other artist, still recording with the company until well into the 70s, and he became the musician who was Alfred Lion's closest confidant.

Meanwhile, his working group – always two horns and a rhythm section – began to personify what would become the standard hard-bop small-band setting. Throughout a long career, he has almost exclusively used his own originals rather than relying on any standards, and his writing in the 50s soon established the blueprint for his idiom. It was a logical progression from the cooling of bop's original helter-skelter first phase: the rhythm section still played in a taut, bebop style, but the convoluted melodies of bop were traded for much simpler, almost motif-like tunes (one of his early successes, 'The Preacher', was actually hated by Alfred Lion at first, and it took a bit of subterfuge by Horace – saying that if they abandoned it, it would mean more studio time spent – to get it past his producer). They added a melodious bounce to a sound that was still unimpeachably modern, and hip. Silver employed a procession of outstanding horn players for the next 20 years, including Carmell Jones, Hank Mobley, Kenny Dorham, Art Farmer, Blue Mitchell, Junior Cook, Joe Henderson, Woody Shaw, Clifford Jordan and Randy Brecker, and his Blue Note albums were a remarkably consistent lot: the sequence he cut at the end of the 50s, in what was a glorious spell for jazz on record, included *The Stylings Of Silver*, *Further Explorations*, *Finger Poppin'* and the quite flawless *Blowin' The Blues Away*, and is still an enthrallingly fresh listen, even after some five decades of similar music-making by others following the formula.

Silver's own playing helped keep his groups on their toes, pushing and thrusting whether in solo or accompaniment and constantly varying the pace with a stock of ingenious licks. Aside from a break in the early 70s, he kept touring the group and, although some of his latter-day Blue Note sets have some modish and misconceived trappings, he was one of the few old-stagers who left the label with his honour intact, not tempted by fusion. He subsequently founded his own label in the 80s and toured with new groups, although there were spells when he was off the scene due to illness or family matters. He later signed again to both Columbia and Impulse!, now a godfather of his idiom, and perhaps the only sour note of the period was his decision not to appear at the celebratory concerts which relaunched Blue Note in the middle 80s: if one musician's work sums up the ideals and rewards of that label, it is Silver's.

**Blowin' The Blues Away** (Blue Note)

# Omer Simeon

CLARINET

*born* 21 July 1902; *died* 17 September 1959

Although born in New Orleans, Simeon played no part in the city's clarinet tradition: he didn't take up the instrument until his family had moved to Chicago in 1914. He was busy on the city's music scene in the early 20s, and in 1926 he was enlisted by Jelly Roll Morton for the pianist's first Red Hot Peppers sessions: Simeon's versatile sound – fruitily rich in the low register and pinchingly acerbic in the high one – makes a tremendous impact on those classic records. He then toured with King Oliver and Charlie Elgar before going back to Chicago, where he played first with Erskine Tate and then in Earl Hines's orchestra: although he didn't quite have the starring role he enjoyed in the 20s, he makes a mark on a number of Hines's records, and he stayed until 1937. In the 40s he secured a regular gig with Jimmie Lunceford, which carried on after the leader's death, and in the 50s he held down a regular role in the Wilbur De Paris band, featuring on that leader's notable series of Atlantic albums. Simeon's work never declined: he was as good in the De Paris band as he was with Morton, and his journeyman career often disguised a forthright talent.

**Jelly Roll Morton,** *Vols 1–5* (JSP)

# Norman Simmons

PIANO
*born* 6 October 1929

Simmons is one of the great accompanists. He played piano in his native Chicago in clubs such as The Studio Lounge and backed visiting horn players (when he asked Coleman Hawkins about tempos, Hawk simply replied, 'as fast as you can'). But singers especially liked him, and he supported Ernestine Anderson, Carmen McRae (for most of the 60s), Betty Carter, Anita O'Day and latterly Joe Williams. He is a gifted arranger, too, with several charts hidden away on records such as Johnny Griffin's *Big Soul Band*, but his patient and gentlemanly accompaniments are his real contribution to the music.

**Joe Williams,** *Ballad And Blues Master* (Verve)

# Sonny Simmons

ALTO SAXOPHONE
*born* 4 August 1933

Simmons has conducted much of his career in California, which – considering its isolation from the free-jazz activity centred on the East Coast – has all but marginalized his fierce and often genuinely angry music. He played in R&B bands in the 50s and subsequently worked with the few like-minded free players in his locale, including Prince Lasha, but a move east to New York at least resulted in one ESP album (*Staying On The Watch*, 1966) and the tremendous *Manhattan Egos* (Arhoolie, 1969), which he recorded with a band that included his wife, trumpeter Barbara Donald. He then moved back West, and eventually took a sabbatical from playing. His music in this period carries an impact exceptional even among the

players in this idiom: toughened by his R&B background, perhaps, he could deliver solos in the free idiom of coruscating power and strength. The 70s and 80s were a poor time for him: his marriage with Donald broke up, alcoholism interrupted his career, and he was reduced to playing as a street musician. In the 90s he enjoyed a surprise comeback, even managing to record two albums for the Warner Bros offshoot Qwest, and two further records for Bob Rusch's CIMP label reveal the outpourings of a furious musician, scathingly eloquent even as his music speaks to a tiny audience.

*Manhattan Egos* (Arhooli)

# Zoot Sims

TENOR SAXOPHONE
*born* 29 October 1925; *died* 23 March 1985

Did Zoot (John Haley) Sims ever make a poor record, or deliver a less than enjoyable performance? Mere consistency is the enemy of the creative jazz player, but Sims belied the maxim: a modest titan who made a virtue out of his impeccable reliability. His family were vaudeville performers and he started on clarinet before taking up the saxophone in his teens. His first important work was with Benny Goodman, starting in 1943, and after army service he was one of the 'Four Brothers' in Woody Herman's 1947 band. From there he worked with Buddy Rich, Goodman again, Elliot Lawrence and Stan Kenton, but from around 1953 his career was spent working as a freelance. He struck up an invincible partnership with his former Herman sideman Al Cohn: they toured and recorded as the leaders of an occasional but frequently convened quintet, which endured into the 80s. Besides this he gigged and recorded as a solo himself, as well as doing high-profile sideman work with Goodman, Gerry Mulligan, Clark Terry and others. He turns up on many record dates as an almost unannounced soloist, and always gives his best: one isolated example might be his solos on the debut record by songwriter Phoebe Snow (*Phoebe Snow*, 1974). For a long time his recording career as a leader had something of a laissez-faire quality to it, but in the 70s Norman Granz signed him to his Pablo label and finally took the cheerfully wayward Sims in hand: his Pablo albums, especially those with such simpatico spirits as Jimmy Rowles, place his wonderful, burnished-but-homely sound and compulsively swinging phrasing in a rounded context at last. Sims was routinely characterized as a Lester Young follower, but even at the time of Young's death Lester's shade had been comprehensively sidelined in Zoot's own playing: it surely belongs only to the man blowing the horn. There should have been much more of it for listeners to hear, but cancer brought about his passing just short of his 60th birthday.

*If I'm Lucky* (Pablo/OJC)

## Singers

What is a jazz singer? The question is at least as vexing as such other favourite teasers as 'What is swing?' Essentially, a jazz singer takes a preset text, usually a so-called 'popular song', and delivers a performance of it which is imbued with the characteristics of the jazz artist – adding improvisational ingredients to what would otherwise be a strict rendition of the tune, which could take in such techniques as ornamenting or altering the melody, falling behind or anticipating the beat, varying the tone of attack, or otherwise reshaping the performance as it might otherwise have been envisaged by the composer. The lyrics are only rarely, if ever, changed: that is one sanctity which the jazz singer preserves. Just as an instrumentalist seeks to be always swinging, so does the jazz singer: even an otherwise fairly literal aproach to a song can be jazzed by the subtlest introduction of swing. Most jazz singing began with, inevitably, Louis Armstrong, whose 20s vocals set the pace for the new idiom, but even so there are numerous pre-echoes of Armstrong's approach in the vaudeville and music hall traditions of both Europe and the US, just as there are seeds of jazz in ragtime and other popular strains of instrumental music. As decades passed, it was very hard to differentiate between pop and jazz singers until the advent of the rock'n'roll era: because rock didn't swing, pop singers thenceforth stopped being jazz singers, whereas previously it was entirely logical for Ella Fitzgerald to be a giant in both the jazz and popular fields. Jazz singers subdivide further into improvisers, scat-singers and exponents of vocalese.

## Zutty Singleton

DRUMS
*born* 14 May 1898; *died* 14 July 1975

Arthur Singleton makes a bizarre impact on his first important recordings, with Louis Armstrong's Hot Five: on 'Sugar Foot Strut' (1928) he sounds as if he's juggling cups with his teeth, although at these sessions he was actually among the first drummers to employ brushes and the 'sock' cymbal. He is even more inventive on the trio sides made with Jelly Roll Morton a year later, hearing the kit as a source of percussive sound as well as propulsion. By this time he had already done much work in New Orleans groups and was a figure who called for (and received) plenty of respect from his fellow musicians. He played all over the New York scene during the 30s, with players as diverse as Roy Eldridge, Sidney Bechet and the Condonites, and he led his own groups on and off as he chose. In 1943, he went over to the other coast and formed a surprise partnership with Slim Gaillard, which even put him behind Charlie Parker on one date. By the 50s he was back in New York, working even through lean times in the music, and he went to Europe to play with Bill Coleman too. For much of the 60s he was still to be found at Jimmy Ryan's on West 54th Street, but a stroke finally put an end to his playing in 1970. Zutty probably isn't remembered as much as he would have liked to have been, but he influenced many drummers who came after him and was, in his way, an innovator on his chosen instrument.

**Jelly Roll Morton, *Vols 1–5*** (JSP)

## Lars Sjösten

PIANO
*born* 7 May 1941

Born in Okarshamn, Sweden, Sjösten was part of the Swedish post-bop movement of the 60s, working in Eje Thelin's small group and backing numerous American visitors in Stockholm before spending a long period (middle 60s until 1976) as Lars Gullin's pianist. His own composing and bandleading have been only sparsely documented, but what there is of him on record shows a thoughtful and adroit stylist whose slightly quirky writing sets him at a useful distance from many of his contemporaries in a crowded idiom.

*In Confidence* (Dragon)

## Alan Skidmore
TENOR AND SOPRANO SAXOPHONES
*born* 21 April 1942

Skidmore followed in his father's business by taking up the saxophone in his teens, and after some desultory work on the British scene he did much work in Hamburg for the German radio station NDR in the later 60s. His 1970 quintet, which made the fine *TCB* (Philips, never reissued to date), gave him some attention as a leader, and in the 70s he began working with Georgie Fame – he still plays in Fame's band – as well as with the short-lived saxophone trio SOS, with John Surman and Mike Osborne. Skidmore was for many years something of a prophet without honour in his home territory: he continued to work frequently in German radio orchestras on the continent, and his bands Tenor Tonic (with Paul Dunmall) and a group dedicated to the legacy of his abiding influence, John Coltrane, were popular live draws which were documented on only a handful of albums. Latterly, he has enjoyed the sponsorship of Colin Towns's Provocateur label, and has recorded sessions with an African percussion group, Amampondo (subsequently Ubizo), which show his exultant style in full cry.

*The Call* (Provocateur)

## Jimmy Skidmore
TENOR SAXOPHONE
*born* 8 February 1916; *died* 23 April 1998

The elder Skidmore played guitar at first, and didn't touch the saxophone until he was 20. He played in the small swing groups of Harry Parry, Carlo Krahmer and Vic Lewis in the 40s, and in the following decade worked in the Jazz Today Unit and other small groups before joining Humphrey Lyttelton in 1956 and staying for four years. He was a comfortable match for Humph's easeful mainstream style, and fitted into the group beautifully, but after his departure his career never really went anywhere

much. His style of playing resisted the encroaching modernism of younger players, and perhaps he was never personally ambitious enough to push himself to the forefront. As a result he played mainly local gigs in later years, though he never retired: he played a gig with son Alan to celebrate his 80th birthday. His sole album as a leader, *Skid Marks* (DJM, 1972), is yet another British record still awaiting reissue.

**Humphrey Lyttelton, *Triple Exposure***
(Calligraph)

## Skiffle

In the main this was a peculiarly British phenomenon. While the word is probably part of the black argot of the 30s, relating to the dance music played at rent parties, it was taken up by members of the British trad movement of the 50s, seeking a variation on their normal style which introduced more of a folk-blues element. Ken Colyer had a 'Skiffle band' within his own group, which would sometimes do a skiffle set where Colyer played guitar and sang. But skiffle's great hit was 'Rock Island Line', made by a contingent from the Chris Barber band, with Lonnie Donegan singing: it made Donegan's career a success, and paved the way for bands such as those of Bob Cort and Chas McDevitt, made up of guitars, acoustic bass, washboard and sometimes harmonica or jug. Brian Bird, in his *Skiffle* (1958), opined that 'the future of skiffle would seem assured, and its scope unrestricted'. By the time Bird's book had made it into print, skiffle was already dead, and rock'n'roll had taken hold.

## Steve Slagle
ALTO SAXOPHONE
*born* 18 September 1951

Slagle studied at Berklee, before settling in New York in 1977. While his career as a leader perhaps hasn't developed very far, most of his records having been made for the Danish Steeplechase label, he is a distinctive voice in a large ensemble – Carla Bley and the Mingus Big Band have both featured him to advantage – and his bop-rooted style, slightly sour attack and unsentimental work

at slow tempos make him the sort of soloist one always looks forward to hearing.
***Alto Blue*** (Steeplechase)

# Cee Slinger
PIANO
*born* 19 May 1929

Slinger worked on the Dutch dance-band scene until becoming a regular feature at Amsterdam's Sheherazade Club, first as an accompanist to Rita Reys, then as the leader of The Diamond Five, a smart hard-bop out-fit with Cees Small (trumpet) and Harry Verbeke (tenor sax). The pianist opted for a day job in the steel industry from 1962, but still played occasionally, and went back into music full-time in 1974. Like many European players of his generation, he is well-known at home and has backed numberless visitors yet remains all but unknown outside his home turf. The Diamond Five made only a single album and a few EPs during its life-time, though there were a couple of later reunion albums, and a version of Theo Loevendie's 'Ruined Girl' is strangely haunting.
***Brilliant!*** (Fontana)

# Carol Sloane
VOCAL
*born* 5 March 1937

Born Carol Morvan, she originally appeared under the name Carol Vann, but at Larry Elgart's insistence changed her stage name to Sloane. As a singer, she's enjoyed a stop-start sort of career. A couple of decent records were made for Columbia in the early 60s, but it wasn't a good time for a new stan-dards singer to make a breakthrough, and though she worked steadily enough she made no more records and eventually moved to North Carolina in 1969. She returned to New York eight years later and picked up her career again, eventually moving to Boston in the 80s, where she began making repertory records for Contemporary and Concord. Her style often amounts to a kind of conspiratorial whisper, delicate, carefully nuanced, and making the most of every beat in a slow tempo.
***Sweet And Slow*** (Concord)

# Small Group

A misleading term in that a small group may have plenty of people in it: if it's not quite big enough to be a big band, a dozen players or so, then it's a small group. 'Medium' groups don't exist. A duo or a trio, however, is usually a duo or a trio, rather than a small group, which tends to need four or more players to qualify for the term.

# Bill Smith
CLARINET
*born* 22 September 1926

Although he is probably better known in contemporary music circles as the composer William Overton Smith, Bill Smith is a decent clarinettist, whose main association has been with Dave Brubeck, with whom he founded the octet which was Brubeck's main performing vehicle in the late 40s. He depped for Paul Desmond on occasion in the Brubeck quartet around 1960, and for a time led a bop-orientated American Jazz Ensemble. He again worked with Brubeck in the 80s and 90s, their sensibilities still in very close accord.
**Dave Brubeck,** ***Moscow Night*** (Concord)

# Bill Smith
WRITER, SAXOPHONES, DRUMS
*born* 12 May 1938

Though born in Bristol in the west of England, Smith has been a force in Canadian jazz for many years. He moved to Toronto in 1963 and joined *Coda*, the country's jazz magazine, initially as art director and later as co-publisher and editor. Besides his work on the magazine, Smith has led his own groups, broadly working in a freebop style, playing both saxophone and drums. He sub-sequently shifted base to Horny Island and plays locally there. He also co-founded the Sackville label with his fellow publisher, John Norris.
**With Joe McPhee,** ***Visitation*** (Sackville)

# Buster Smith
ALTO SAXOPHONE
*born* 24 August 1904; *died* 10 August 1991

Smith would scarcely hold on to even a footnote in jazz history if it wasn't for his influence on Charlie Parker. He had previously
spent some ten years in Walter Page's Blue
Devils in Kansas City, from the 20s through
to the early 30s, and he was in at the start of
Count Basie's new band; but he went out on
his own as a leader, and Parker was one of
his sidemen early on, although these bands
were never recorded. He went to New York
in 1938 and freelanced as both an arranger
and a section-player, with Pete Johnson and
others, but eventually left to resettle in
Dallas in the early 40s and spent the rest of
his career playing locally in R&B bands.
Atlantic Records made one session with him
in 1959, *The Legendary Buster Smith*, but it
was an indifferent and generic R&B kind of
record, and the question of exactly how
much influence he had over Parker's
developing style – significantly acknowledged by Bird himself – remains something
of an enigma.
**Pete Johnson, *1938–1939*** (Classics)

# Derek Smith
PIANO
*born* 17 August 1931

A Londoner, Smith worked on the British
mainstream scene of the 50s, with Kenny
Baker and other leaders, before leaving for
America in 1957. Based primarily in New
York, he has been busy there ever since,
although his appearances on record have
been comparatively rare. He undertook sideman duties with Benny Goodman, Benny
Carter and others, and spent five years with
Doc Severinsen's *Tonight Show* band. He
sometimes works in a duo with fellow pianist Dick Hyman. Smith's unfussily virtuosic
style is a buoyant and smiling distillation of
the Tatum–Peterson approach, full of dash
without losing his audience in mere note-
spinning, and his occasional albums are
usually delightful.
**High Energy** (Arbors)

# Jabbo Smith
TRUMPET, VOCAL
*born* 24 December 1908; *died* 16 January 1991

Born Cladys Smith in Pembroke, Georgia, he
grew up in an orphange in Charleston and
learned trombone and trumpet there, and in
1925 he joined Charlie Johnson's outfit in
New York, which was three years of steady
work that he built on with occasional record
dates as a freelance. He then toured with the
pit band for James P Johnson's revue *Keep
Shufflin'*, ending up in Chicago and staying
there as a new star of the trumpet. Smith's
daredevil approach was soon compared to
that of Louis Armstrong, but if he had any
pretensions to challenging Armstrong's eminence they didn't last (the impartial Red
Nichols remembered hearing them together,
and finding Louis easily the superior).
Brunswick signed him as a leader, and the
19 issued sides he made (as by Jabbo Smith's
Rhythm Aces) are full of trumpet bravado,
although – Omer Simeon aside, though even
he sounds below par – the rest of the Aces
weren't up to much and the records tend to
be a one-man show. Smith loved the high
life and became notorious for missing gigs,
and for much of the 30s he drifted around
the scene: a fine but solitary 1938 date produced four titles which hinted at what
Smith might have achieved if he'd paid
more attention to his career. He left music
altogether in the 40s but started a tentative
comeback in the 60s, which eventually
picked up momentum with festival appearances in the following decade and a stint
touring with the show *One Mo' Time* at the
start of the 80s. While he was hailed as a living legend, it was obvious that his technique
had fallen into disrepair, and his singing
was often more impressive than his latter-
day trumpet work. Smith's early playing set
the stage for a brilliant adventure which
never happened. He is often cited as an
influence on such trumpeters as Roy
Eldridge and Dizzy Gillespie, but it is actually hard to hear much of Smith in their
work, beyond a simple taste for excitement.
**Jabbo Smith 1929–1938** (Classics)

# Jimmy Smith

ORGAN

*born* 8 December 1925; *died* 8 February 2005

Wild Bill Davis and Milt Buckner had already done much of the pioneer work, but it was Smith who brought the Hammond organ into modern jazz. In Philadelphia, in his 20s, he had a very good ear – despite two periods studying harmony and theory he claimed never to be able to read music – and he worked as a pianist in routine R&B bands until he took up the Hammond at the age of 27. After a period of intensive practice before he made even a single public appearance using the instrument, he soon acquired a hot reputation in the Philadelphia area, and when he made his New York debut in 1956 – at the Café Bohemia – he was an almost immediate sensation. Within a year he had signed to Blue Note and made the first of dozens of albums for them, and created another sensation at the 1957 Newport Festival. Frank Wolff's first impressions of Smith – 'a man in convulsions, face contorted, crouched over in apparent agony, his fingers flying . . . the noise was shattering' – make clear what an impact Smith had. At a time when there was still very little electricity on jazz bandstands, the effect of Smith in full flow must have been enthralling. His simple style – a walking bass on the pedals, thick chords with the left hand, spidery decoration with the right and a smart use of the organ's stops to alter the attack and tone in the playing, getting rid of the old ice-rink vibrato and replacing it with a hot, almost chewy texture that was both ominous and mellowed – was bolstered by a rhythm guitarist and a punchy groove from the drums, and the formula was finished and available for endless recycling. To some extent, every jazz organist who has come after him has followed directly in Smith's footsteps, no matter how much they may have varied the details.

Smith worked continuously for the next 20 years. He moved from Blue Note to Verve in 1962, and recorded more ambitious projects, including the memorable Oliver Nelson orchestrations for *The Cat* (1964) and a fruitful alliance with Wes Montgomery. At the end of the 70s he opened his own supper club in Los Angeles, but he returned to touring in the following decade and was still playing in Japan, Europe and the US until

only weeks before his death. He made more records for Milestone in the 80s and had a brief reunion with the 'new' Blue Note, but made his last albums for another one of his old labels, Verve, in the 90s. By this time the real fire had largely left his playing and he had long since settled into a routine, but he remained an ornery character to the end, a great kidder and, when the mood took him, not a bad blues singer too.

*A New Star – A New Sound: Jimmy Smith At The Organ* (Blue Note)

# Joe Smith

TRUMPET

*born* 28 June 1902; *died* 2 December 1937

Bessie Smith's favourite accompanist, even ahead of Louis Armstrong, Smith was one of seven brothers, all of whom played the trumpet (one of them, Russell, went on to work with Joe in the Fletcher Henderson band). He moved to New York around 1920 and from there toured and recorded in bands accompanying Ethel Waters and Mamie Smith, as well as backing several other women in the classic-blues idiom on record. He joined Fletcher Henderson in 1925 and stayed three years, as one of Henderson's leading soloists: a thoughtful, almost cool player, staying mostly in the middle register and using the mute for gentle tonal colourings rather than anything glaringly expressive, and his sketchpad style was a genuine rarity among trumpeters of his era. His best work with Smith and Henderson has an almost luminous quality, which gleams through often poor recordings. He moved over to McKinney's Cotton Pickers in 1929, but drink had started to wreck his health, and despite a move to Kansas City early in the 30s he hardly played again.

**Bessie Smith,** *Complete Recordings* (Frog)

# Johnny Smith

GUITAR

*born* 25 June 1922

Originally from Birmingham, Alabama, Smith moved to New York in the 40s and soon found a job as a studio regular for NBC. In 1952 he scored a surprise hit with a single version of 'Moonlight In Vermont', which also featured a dreamy Stan Getz contribution, and this was enough to set up a sequence of 23 albums for his label, Roost. In 1958 he moved to Colorado and opened a music shop there, although he continued to play and made a handful of albums for Verve in the late 60s. He eventually retired from active playing in the 80s. Smith was that rarity, a player who could do smooth and sweet and manage it without losing musical interest: his many records are these days only much remembered by guitar connoisseurs, though.

**Moonlight In Vermont** (Roost/Capitol)

# Keith Smith

TRUMPET
born 19 March 1940

Smith played on the London trad scene of the late 50s and early 60s before going to America in 1964, where he managed to record alongside George Lewis in New Orleans. Eventually he managed to settle in the US, living and playing in various locations. Smith has been a canny self-publicist since, establishing a group (and brand name) called Hefty Jazz, and putting together showbiz-jazz packages including dedications to Hoagy Carmichael, Louis Armstrong and Dixieland jazz. His own trumpet playing is no more than a game variation on a fundamental Dixieland approach.

**Swing Is Here Again** (Lake)

# Dr Lonnie Smith

ORGAN, PIANO
born 3 July 1942

Sometimes confused with his close contemporary Lonnie Liston Smith. Dr Lonnie Smith sang in R&B groups before taking up the organ, subsequently touring with George Benson and numerous other leaders in the late 60s and 70s. He has also played behind numerous soul singers, from Esther Phillips to Dionne Warwick. Smith's organ playing takes few liberties with the standard organ practice established by Jimmy Smith and his contemporaries, and he has largely resisted the blandishments of fusion and its associations.

**George Benson, The George Benson Cookbook** (Columbia)

# Lonnie Liston Smith

ORGAN, KEYBOARDS
born 28 December 1940

Sometimes confused with his close contemporary (Dr) Lonnie Smith. Lonnie Liston Smith began working on the New York scene of the early 60s, and mustered a string of distinguished credits with Roland Kirk, Art Blakey, Pharoah Sanders and even Miles Davis. In 1974, he formed a fusion band, the Cosmic Echoes, which recorded a sequence of successful soul-jazz-rock albums that, with hindsight, represent something close to the nadir of their genre, sunk by tedious solos, soulless vocals and dismal disco rhythms. Nevertheless, the band continued into the 90s, although its jazz credibility is close to zero.

**Expansions** (Flying Dutchman)

# Louis Smith

TRUMPET
born 20 May 1931

Smith grew up in Memphis and after working as a high-school teacher moved to New York in 1957. His two Blue Note albums, *Here Comes Louis Smith* (1957) and *Smithville* (1958), were strong enough to suggest that he was set fair for a considerable career in the hard-bop scene of the day, but he was discouraged by the poor prospects for a musician such as himself, gave up on a playing career, and returned to teaching. He played occasionally in the 60s and 70s, and was finally recorded at length on a sequence of albums for the Danish Steeplechase label in the 80s and 90s; but these records have a semi-pro feel to them which suggests that Smith's best work is a long way behind him now.

**Here Comes Louis Smith** (Blue Note)

# Marvin 'Smitty' Smith

DRUMS
born 24 June 1961

For a time, Smith seemed likely to become one of the leading drummers in the music, but television has seduced him away from regular jazz work. He was busy as a freelance on the New York scene from the early 80s, ready to play for everyone from Steve

Coleman to Hank Jones, and his mastery of difficult time signatures and the most fearsomely complex music (Coleman's would be a good example) marked him out as a player of great potential. He was hired by Sting to play in his touring band in 1987, and he made the first of two albums for Concord as a leader himself. By the mid-90s he had racked up a very broad range of sideman credits, but in 1995 he became the drummer for *The Tonight Show*, first with Branford Marsalis and then with Kevin Eubanks. This has all but taken him away from outside work: a pity, although one can't begrudge any musician the opportunity of regular work.

*The Road Less Traveled* (Concord)

## Pine Top Smith

PIANO

*born* 11 June 1904; *died* 15 March 1929

Smith more properly belongs in a book on the blues, but his great setpiece, 'Pine Top's Boogie Woogie' (1928), set the style on record for the idiom of piano boogie woogie. As Smith played it, it was an instruction to dancers, together with his own exhortations to those on the floor. It was one of eight recordings he made in Chicago at the time, having previously worked in Birmingham and Pittsburgh. Having established a style at a single stroke, Pine Top left the scene, though not of his own volition: he was shot during a brawl in the Chicago club he was playing in.

**Various,** *The Boogie Woogie Masters* (Charly)

## Stuff Smith

VIOLIN

*born* 13 August 1909; *died* 25 September 1967

Leroy 'Stuff' Smith played in various Southern territories during the late 20s, joining up with the band of Alphonse Trent, which he eventually took over. Aside from a brief interlude in New York, where he played a few gigs with Jelly Roll Morton, he remained with those musicians and toured with them into the 30s. In 1936 he tried his luck again in New York, and secured a regular gig at The Onyx Club, where he led a sextet (including Jonah Jones) and began making records for Vocalion. He took the

group to Hollywood a year later, but subsequently went bankrupt, although he returned to action back in New York soon enough. Smith's unpredictable temper and jealous nature always seemed to stand in the way of his greater success: his career kept stopping and starting in New York and Chicago for the next 15 years. Influenced in probably equal terms by Joe Venuti and Louis Armstrong, his violin style mixed salty and sweet playing in roughly similar measure, with his strange, almost scraping tone and eerie intonation uplifted by a power-packed sense of swing, a momentum which would often take him racing past whoever his accompanists were. It often doesn't work on his 78-era records, but in 1956 he cut some LP sessions for Norman Granz's Verve, where he played with Dizzy Gillespie among others, which finally laid out the extent of his skills, although it often sounds as if microphones would never really catch Stuff the way he should have been heard. Though he was sometimes laid low by illness, his career continued to revive in the 60s: he became a festival hit, settled in Denmark in 1965, and more than held his own in the formidable company of Stéphane Grappelli, Jean-Luc Ponty and Svend Asmussen at the sessions which produced *Violin Summit* (Saba, 1966). He died the following year, the effects of alcohol and a wild-man lifestyle finally taking their toll.

*Stuff Smith/Dizzy Gillespie/Oscar Peterson* (Verve)

## Tab Smith

ALTO AND TENOR SAXOPHONES

*born* 11 January 1909; *died* 17 August 1971

Smith began playing in his home state of North Carolina in the 20s, and he went to New York at the start of the following decade. He appears on record dates with Henry Allen and Billie Holiday, and in 1940 he joined Count Basie's orchestra, moving from there to the Lucky Millinder band, and eventually to leading groups of his own. He was a big hit at the Savoy Ballroom, where his adaptable style on alto and tenor mixed sentimental balladry with effusive, jump-style music which would ultimately point the way towards R&B. In 1951 he moved over to St Louis and recorded regularly, enjoying jukebox popularity along with such contemporaries as Earl Bostic. Many of these records have been reissued by Delmark, and they stand up surprisingly well: Smith's good judgement led him away from the more fatuous repetitions of rock'n'roll saxophone, which in any case had yet to really get under way. By 1960 his career was largely over.

*Ace High* (Delmark)

# Tommy Smith
TENOR AND SOPRANO SAXOPHONES
*born* 27 April 1967

Smith was a genuine prodigy on the saxophone, whose rise to prominence coincided with the British jazz 'revival' of the 80s yet was carried through away from the London-centred limelight of that brief moment. He grew up in Edinburgh, started on saxophone at 12, and by the time he was 15 he was a local sensation, winning a scholarship to Berklee in 1984 and making his first records with his own band within a year. He then played with another Berklee-derived band, Forward Motion, and alongside one of his tutors, Gary Burton. In 1988 he made the first of a sequence of albums for Blue Note, the first British musician to be signed to the label in its new incarnation, and though the affiliation didn't last it helped build a platform for his international recognition. Since then, though, Smith has largely focused on his Scottish base. After a period with the independent label Linn, he established his own imprint, Spartacus, which releases his own material as well as that of his ex-wife Laura Macdonald, also a saxophonist. In 1995, he established the Scottish National Jazz Orchestra, which under his stewardship has become the leading jazz repertory ensemble in the country. His own discography has grown to considerable proportions and includes original writing for medium-sized ensembles, ballad records, settings of indigenous Scottish poetry (a particular interest of his), meetings with American musicians and two recent records of duos with pianist Brian Kellock. Deprived of the oxygen provided as a matter of course to London-based musicians by the local media, Smith remains a curiously undervalued talent even in the UK. Of the generation which emerged in the mid-80s, he might be the most outstandingly talented: a virtuoso player with a peerless command of the saxophone, an ambitious composer and bandleader, mindful of American and European influences but increasingly his own man on an instrument which is never short of practitioners, he is a genuinely remarkable musician, and as a focal point around which Scottish jazz has progressed in recent times, his importance is absolutely vital.

*Beasts Of Scotland* (Linn)

# Wadada Leo Smith
TRUMPET
*born* 18 December 1941

Smith's father was a blues musician, and the young man grew up in Mississippi surrounded by that music. He worked in army bands before joining the AACM in Chicago in 1967, and soon joined Anthony Braxton and Leroy Jenkins in the Creative Construction Company, which worked in Paris for a spell at the end of the 60s. On his return he formed New Dalta Ahkri, an ensemble with a floating personnel of between two and five players, and his own record label, Kabell. Smith's 70s music has a surpassing grace and meditative eloquence to it. He stepped entirely aside from the energy playing of a decade before, and though he employed a certain number of extended trumpet techniques, his main point of departure was playing as exquisitely and with as finely nuanced a delivery as possible. On the ECM album *Divine Love* (1978), the textures and interplay between the musicians are as rapt as anything in the jazz of the period. Smith also made a point of working with European players – he played in Derek Bailey's first Company gathering, and worked in a trio with Günter Sommer and Peter Kowald – and published some theses on the practice of improvisation. In the 80s, he converted to Rastafarianism, adopted the forename Wadada, and expanded his outreach further, working with dance and poetry groups, writing for the theatre, and working in Japan, New York and California. His discography, hitherto rather rarefied, has expanded much further, with the fusion band Yo Miles! addressing some of Miles Davis's electric music, and records such as the all-solo *Red Sulphur Sky* (Tzadik, 2001) and *Luminous Axis* (Tzadik, 2002) underlining that Smith, for all his conceptual complexities, is one of the most simply affecting trumpet players in the music.

***Divine Love*** (ECM)

# Willie Smith
ALTO SAXOPHONE
*born* 25 November 1910; *died* 7 March 1967

For many years, Willie Smith was considered as part of the great triumvirate of swing altos, along with Johnny Hodges and Benny Carter; yet today he is practically a forgotten figure. Born in Charleston, and later a chemistry graduate, Smith joined Jimmie Lunceford in 1929 and stayed throughout the band's glory years, finally leaving only in 1942. He led the saxophone section with exactly the masterly authority which Lunceford – the most disciplined of leaders – wanted, and his own musicianship (he wrote several fine charts for the band's book) was sumptuously refined. If Smith didn't quite have the creamy bluesiness of Hodges, he was probably Carter's equal as a soloist, and it's only the comparative obscurity of so much of the Lunceford catalogue which has submerged his reputation. For much of the rest of his career, he was again with a leader – Harry James – whose latter-day records are not much followed, and though he starred with Jazz At The Philharmonic for a time and even had a spell subbing for Hodges in the Ellington band, Smith must have felt like a nearly man, and he took refuge in alcohol, and eventually succumbed to cancer. During the entire LP era, he led only a single session, for GNP in 1965. The best of him is scattered through many sessions with Lunceford and James, and his alto solo on the former's 'Uptown Blues' is one for the ages.

**Jimmie Lunceford,** *1939–1940* (Classics)

# Willie 'The Lion' Smith
PIANO, VOCAL
*born* 25 November 1897; *died* 18 April 1973

With his cane, derby and cigar, William Henry Joseph Bonaparte Smith was one of the great characters in New York's jazz scene as it grew up in the beginning of the 20s. Like such fellow pianists as Jelly Roll Morton, James P Johnson and Fats Waller, he helped establish a school of New York piano playing, based around stride rhythms, but incorporating a good deal more ragtime than most of those mentioned above: originals such as 'Echoes Of Spring' have the delicacy and refinement of a quadrille, and Smith's delivery has more gaiety than bluesiness in it. To that extent, perhaps he is a lesser figure than his several great contemporaries, but the man himself was in no doubt about his prowess, and he loved the challenge of a cutting contest, mastering tunes in every conceivable key to beat the competition. He hardly made any records during the 20s, but he did play on the million-selling 'Crazy Blues' (1920) by Mamie Smith, and was forever aggrieved that he made no royalties from it. He had more luck in the 30s with some fine small-group swing dates, but later audiences were treated to one history lesson after another as The Lion swept through continents, singing, playing and discoursing on the history of jazz as he remembered it. Duke Ellington, who wrote 'Portrait Of The Lion' for him, said that 'I can't think of anything good enough to say about The Lion.'

***Pork And Beans*** (Black Lion)

# Paul Smoker
TRUMPET, FLUGELHORN
*born* 8 May 1941

Smoker was cautious about committing himself to a playing career. Although he performed with Dodo Marmarosa in 1961 and worked on and off with Bill Chase, Art Pepper and others, for the next 20 years he was primarily involved in education, teaching at college level in Iowa. In the 80s he moved away from his previous bop-orientated style towards the avant-garde, playing in several Anthony Braxton groups, joining Ellery Eskelin, Drew Gress and Phil Haynes in the cooperative Joint Venture, and shifting his base to upstate New York. He has since recorded extensively for CIMP and Nine Winds. Smoker's background in bop still informs his approach and even though he's mostly playing free, he finds space for bluesy touches, sparely crafted melodies and (on the record cited, which is aptly titled) a willingness to work from familiar material if it gets him somewhere interesting. A player who likes a kind of careful abstraction.

***Standard Deviation*** (CIMP)

## Smooth Jazz

Smooth jazz is essentially an industry term – that is, one that has not grown out of any musician-derived vernacular, which in itself makes it a rarity in the jazz vocabulary. It refers to the style of music created specifically for the American radio format which bears this name. 'Smooth jazz' was developed in the early 90s as a progression from the so-called 'quiet storm' format, which referred to the kind of lulling soul music which had grown up in the 80s as a soothing alternative to the more aggressive kind of black music then being peddled by the industry. 'Smooth jazz' was perceived as an instrumental (and therefore even more anodyne) variation on that style, where an instrumental 'voice' substitutes for a human one. Its origins can be traced as far back as the later music of Wes Montgomery and Grover Washington Jr, but its real pioneers are such instrumentalists as Kenny G, Bob James, Dave Grusin and David Benoit, and their immediate successors Boney James, Nelson Rangell, Norman Brown and Dave Koz. Most 'smooth jazz' players have very little to do with jazz: their music doesn't swing, and it has almost zero improvisational content. They are essentially instrumental pop musicians.

## Gary Smulyan

BARITONE SAXOPHONE
born 4 April 1956

Smulyan grew up on Long Island and started on alto, changing over to baritone when he joined Woody Herman in 1978. From there he enlisted in Mel Lewis's orchestra in New York, sticking with it when it became the Vanguard Jazz Orchestra, and he has followed the baritone man's usual lot by playing section-work in several other big bands. However, his cheerful and often nicely lyrical style is something he's been concerned to set out front too. He formed the Three Baritone Saxophone Band with Ronnie Cuber and Nick Brignola in the early 90s, has recorded regularly as a leader for Criss Cross and Reservoir, and has taken every opportunity to visit Europe and play with local rhythm sections.
*Homage* (Criss Cross)

## Pat Smythe

PIANO
born 2 May 1923; *died* 6 May 1983

Smythe gave up a career in the law to play jazz piano. His first notable association was in the Joe Harriott group which recorded Harriott's important albums at the start of the 60s, and he was also with Harriott on his later sets, including *Indo-Jazz Fusions* (1967). His own trios at various points featured John McLaughlin and Dave Holland, he backed singers and American visitors, and in the 70s he worked extensively with Kenny Wheeler. Smythe never got on to record much under his own name: three tracks for Columbia in 1962 were about it. The best of him is probably to be found on Harriott's records.
**Joe Harriott,** *Abstract* (Columbia/Redial)

## Jim Snidero

ALTO SAXOPHONE
born 29 May 1958

Originally a Californian, Snidero has been in New York since the early 80s and has held down numerous section- and sideman roles, occasionally stepping out as a leader and making records under his own name. He is a fierce player in a grand bebop alto tradition – 'Swing and soul – in that respect, Charlie Parker, Cannonball Adderley and Sonny Stitt are, for me, perfection on the alto' – but, like those players, he likes to underscore a significant romantic streak in his make-up, and a recent date with strings has made that even more manifest. Snidero is otherwise busy in jazz education, teaching at the New School University.
*Vertigo* (Criss Cross)

## Valaida Snow

TRUMPET, VOCAL
born 2 June 1904; *died* 20 May 1956

An extraordinary personality of the 30s, Snow was quickly forgotten when her era came to an end. One of three sisters who all became entertainers, she began working in Harlem cabarets as early as 1922, and she toured the US (and China) through the rest of the decade, singing, dancing, sometimes playing the violin but also blowing hot trumpet solos. In 1929 she visited Paris and spent two years touring Europe before returning and joining the band of the smitten Earl Hines for a spell. In 1934 she was in London, appearing in *Blackbirds Of 1934*, and over the course of two years she recorded 30 titles for Parlophone, a unique portrait of a jazzwoman in an era where scarcely any existed, and the records (usually labelled as by 'Valaida') seem to catch much of the exuberance of what was a sensational act: surely there's no better version of, for instance, 'I Wish I Were Twins' (her first issued side, from 1935) on record. She moved on through Europe and ended up in Denmark, where she had her work permit revoked after the Nazi occupation and was eventually interned, but she managed to secure a return to the US later in 1942. Although scarred by her experiences, she resumed her career and from the late 40s was still touring regularly, although mostly as a singer. She died following a series of shows in New York. Both her singing and her trumpet playing came on a line straight from Louis Armstrong, but she brought a thrilling gaiety of her own to her pre-war music, which her best records suggest in some style.

*Valaida Snow 1935–1937* (Classics)

# Elmer Snowden
BANJO, GUITAR
*born* 9 October 1900; *died* 14 May 1973

As an instrumentalist Snowden might seem to have a very marginal presence in the music's history, but he was an important man in New York jazz for many years. He worked in his native Baltimore in his teens, with Eubie Blake and others, primarily playing the banjo, and he took a group to New York in 1923 which included Arthur Whetsol and Otto Hardwick; when they were later joined by Duke Ellington, Bubber Miley and Charlie Irvis, the group, then known as The Washingtonians, became the nucleus of the Duke Ellington orchestra, which Snowden soon felt he was being pushed out of, and he duly left on his own account. But he was a very shrewd fixer who was soon enough running bands all over Harlem: at the Bamville Club, the Hot Feet Club, Smalls' Paradise, The Nest and the Furnace Club. Eventually, having already made a lot of money out of

the jazz business, Snowden took himself to Philadelphia in 1933, where he taught, led small groups and played in occasional society orchestras for the next 30 years. In 1963 he relocated again to California, and appeared at the Monterey Jazz Festival that year. A couple of records he made in 1960, *Harlem Banjo* (Riverside) and a duet session with Lonnie Johnson, *Blues And Ballads* (Bluesville), finally brought some attention to his banjo and guitar work, and it was impressive. He died just a year before his old sideman, Duke Ellington.

*Harlem Banjo* (Riverside/OJC)

# Martial Solal
PIANO
*born* 23 August 1927

Solal's stature as one of the few European musicians of his time to gain US recognition has endured for decades. He was born in Algiers and worked there until 1950, when he settled in Paris, formed a trio and played alongside such notables as Django Reinhardt, Lucky Thompson and Sidney Bechet. Word of his talents got out soon enough: Contemporary released a ten-inch LP called *French Modern Sounds* in 1954, and by 1961 Capitol could issue an album called *Vive La France! Vive Le Jazz! Vive Solal!*. The minutiae of Solal's career since take in scores for more than 20 films, an occasionally convened big band, solo recitals, meetings with such individuals as Johnny Griffin and Lee Konitz, and a considerable amount of activity in 'straight' composition in both the orchestral and piano idioms: but there are few whose dedication to the piano/bass/drums trinity have yielded such riches over such an extended period. Among his trio partners have been Guy Pedersen and Daniel Humair, and Gilbert Rovère and Charles Bellonzi (in the 60s), and he has latterly often worked with American players, such as Marc Johnson, Gary Peacock and Paul Motian. His style is a personal refraction of Tatum, Hines, Powell and other virtuosos of the swing and bop eras, but his brilliant executive touch, often fantastical imagination and capacity to reach the furthest extremes in an improvisation without quite losing sight of the shoreline make him all but unique. He is also one of the few pianists with an extensive 'classical' knowledge

who can use that resource without making it seem like a self-conscious graft. His large discography is rather scattered across labels which have not always done their best to keep it in print, but any record by Solal will have treasure on it somewhere, and his best records offer the best of modern jazz piano.
*Sans Tambour Ni Trompette* (RCA)

## Solo

Solo performances by a single individual have been a part of jazz since ragtime: pianists took the first solo honours, but virtually every instrument has subsequently been emancipated enough to allow them to be used for a solo performance in some part of the jazz idiom. Free improvisers have taken that to its extreme. But the 'solo' in an otherwise ensemble-driven performance is the moment when one member of the group steps forward and delivers an improvisation, which may be accompanied by other members of the group or not. The jazz content of many dance records of the 20s and 30s is often determined by their solos, or lack of them. Collectors of early records may ask, 'Does this one have any solos?', which determines whether there's any interest or otherwise.

## Lew Soloff

TRUMPET
*born* 20 February 1944

Soloff's father managed a nightclub and the young man listened to live music from an early age. He studied at Juilliard and Eastman and began playing in New York clubs from the middle 60s, working in both the jazz and Latin idioms. He joined Blood Sweat & Tears in 1968 and toured with them for five years; since then he has been among the leading studio and big-band trumpeters in New York. Soloff's ubiquity has meant that he has formed few distinctive associations, although he has been one of the regular soloists with Carla Bley's various bands and for some years he was the trumpeter with the Manhattan Jazz Quintet, a small group of New York pros which made a series of albums under the leadership of pianist David Matthews. Soloff is widely admired by other trumpeters as a formidable technician

and a master of the horn, but his relatvely few records under his own name have made little impact with listeners and many would most likely struggle to spot him in a blindfold test. He is a wine connoisseur and reputedly has a very fine cellar, lucky fellow.
**Manhattan Jazz Quintet, *Manhattan Blues*** (Sweet Basil)

## Günter Sommer

DRUMS
*born* 25 August 1943

For a long time 'Baby' Sommer was regarded as the Han Bennink of East Germany. Bennink was certainly an early influence on his free playing, which developed out of more boppish beginnings with groups in his native Dresden. From the late 60s onwards his main associations were with Friedhelm Schönfeld, Manfred Ludwig and particularly the pianist Ulrich Gumpert, who worked with him in a duo and as part of Gumpert's Workshop Band. He also developed a solo aesthetic, documented on such records as *Hörmusik* (FMP, 1979), and *Sächsische Schatulle* (Intakt, 1992). Sommer's playing has matured into a style which mixes orchestral timbres with the zany swing inherited from Bennink. The record cited shows how sympathetic a listener and collaborator he can be, in duo with pianist Irène Schweizer.
***Irène Schweizer/Günter Sommer*** (Intakt)

## Soul

The idea of 'soul' as a musical term came into use in the jazz of the 50s. Milt Jackson's *Plenty, Plenty Soul* (Atlantic, 1957) was an early instance of its use in an album title, and from there it was a short step to the creation of the soul-jazz movement, where the contours of straight-ahead hard bop were given a more 'spiritual' twist, taking on an influence which was primarily drawn from gospel music. Horace Silver's style, which comprehensively mixed the sacred (gospel) and the profane (funk), set the tone for soul-jazz, and the notion of soulful playing became a cliché soon enough, particularly in the numerous organ combos which flourished during the peak period of soul-jazz in the middle 60s. In the meantime, 'soul' itself became a musical category:

centred on black vocalists of the 60s whose style and delivery was closely linked to gospel music, yet who addressed themselves to secular material, it became the central idiom of black pop in that decade and beyond. But the notion of soul in music is inevitably hard to quantify, and latterly some black musicians have resented the idea of an innate 'soulfulness' as a racist stereotype.

## Eddie South
VIOLIN
*born* 27 November 1904; *died* 25 April 1962

It would be romantically convenient to portray South as a misunderstood virtuoso or a frustrated concert violinist, but he actually had a successful career and in the end his talent was never unrewarded. He studied the classical repertoire both privately and at Chicago College, then worked with Freddie Keppard and in Jimmy Wade's band before playing with Erskine Tate. In 1928 he went to Europe and studied further in Paris and Budapest. He fronted big bands of his own back in the US, recorded with Django Reinhardt (some classic sides) on a return trip to Paris in 1937, and returned to America a year later. South's full dark tone and impeccable swing suggested that if he had classical aspirations, he could still play jazz violin as well as anybody of that era. Records for Columbia in 1940, though, suggested that he felt comfortable with an inclusive approach which was likely to admit European salon and gypsy music as much as jazz: 'Hejre Kati', a relic of his stay in Hungary, became his theme, and at the same date he recorded 'Zigeuner' and 'La Cumparsita'. South was a regular on radio and was frequently seen on television in the 50s, but he made only a single record in the LP era, *The Distinguished Violin Of Eddie South* (Mercury, 1958), the title of which suggests something of how he was seen.
*Eddie South 1937–1941* (Classics)

## South Frisco Jazz Band
GROUP

Formed around 1960 in the Los Angeles area, this was a gang of experienced players in the revivalist idiom, formed in the spirit of the Turk Murphy and Lu Watters groups.

They included such familiar names of that scene as Bob Helm, Leon Oakley, Jim Snyder and Mike Baird, and they made numerous records for Stomp Off and other labels over a period of some 40 years. In the end the group called it a day because the various band members eventually came to live too far apart from each other to play together regularly, but the surviving discs showcase an ensemble of huge spirit and drive.
*Sage Hen Strut* (Stomp Off)

## Muggsy Spanier
CORNET
*born* 9 November 1901; *died* 12 February 1967

The long-faced Francis Spanier (nicknamed for the New York Giants manager Muggsy McGraw, since he was an aspiring ball player himself) came to exemplify an unpretentious and eventually old-fashioned strain of Chicago jazz: once his style was in place, around 1924, he never changed it in any way. He grew up in an orphanage after his parents split up, and learned the cornet there, going on to play with Chicago bandleaders such as Elmer Schoebel and listening to what King Oliver was doing. He made his first records with The Bucktown Five in 1924, then joined Floyt Town, a leader who never recorded, and cut some fine studio dates with the Chicago Rhythm Kings. Ted Lewis hired him in 1929 and he stayed until he switched to Ben Pollack's band in 1935, but a drink problem laid him low and he subsequently almost died from a perforated ulcer in 1938, saved by an operation at a sanatorium in Touro, his convalescence honoured by his famous blues tune 'Relaxin' At The Touro'. In 1939 he formed an eight-piece ensemble he named the Ragtime Band, which used as its repertoire material which in many cases dated back to that of the Original Dixieland Jazz Band. With fine players such as Georg Brunis, Rod Cless and Joe Bushkin in the line-up, the group made 16 classic recordings in what would turn out to be a harbinger of the revivalist idiom of the decade ahead. Yet while the discs are collectively known as 'The Great Sixteen', the band itself was a commercial failure, and Spanier had to break it up at the end of the year. His own playing on these sides was maginificent, a trim, wasteless kind of Dixieland lead horn, with a superbly effective use of the mute and a refusal to break too much out of the low and middle registers ('Get a piccolo,' he grumbled to someone who asked for more high notes). He then went on to record sessions with Sidney Bechet in the Bechet–Spanier Big Four, where he more than held his own with the usually tyrannical Bechet, although a venture with a big band was short-lived and unsuccessful. Thereafter he spent the rest of his career in small groups, sometimes working in the Eddie Condon circle, but mostly leading his own bands, in New York, Chicago and San Francisco (the Club Hangover, where he worked with Earl Hines). Spanier recorded off and on during the LP era, but he was content to play Dixieland warhorses, and while it's always a pleasure to hear him, his finest work is on those sessions from the late 30s. A lifelong smoker with a taste for booze, he was eventually stricken by what was probably emphysema, and his heart gave out.

*Muggsy Spanier 1939–1942* (Classics)

# Spasm Band

Rough-and-ready ensembles which proliferated in New Orleans during the early part of the century, these bands were usually made up of three or four players: one would probably be a banjo or guitar player, another would play a simple melody instrument such as a kazoo, and there would be at least one percussionist of some kind. The homemade feel of these groups would often extend to the instruments themselves, and the repertoire would be simple blues and pop tunes of the day. The skiffle boom of the 50s updated the style.

# James Spaulding
ALTO SAXOPHONE, FLUTE
*born* 30 July 1937

Spaulding didn't mean it to turn out that way, but he became a premier second banana on straight-ahead dates in the 60s and 70s. While doing army service he played in a local Indianapolis group, The Jazz Contemporaries, around 1956 – the line-up also including Freddie Hubbard and Larry Ridley. He studied in Chicago, joined Sun Ra for a spell, and played around the Midwest

before Hubbard asked him to go to New York in 1962. Thereafter he became the second horn in the front line on many dates for Blue Note in particular. Alfred Lion never quite got around to giving James his own date ('He wanted "Alligator Boogaloo" and stuff, and I had written some serious, straight-ahead bebop'), and suddenly the hard-bop era was over. Spaulding worked with the posthumous Ellington orchestra in 1974, then returned to his degree studies. He was only rarely sighted on record again until 1988, when Muse finally gave him the chance to lead his own sessions, which contain some of his best work. Entirely dependable as a sideman, his fast, unfussy work on both alto and flute has brightened dozens of records.

*Blues Nexus* (Muse)

# Martin Speake
SAXOPHONES
*born* 3 April 1958

Speake studied in London in the early 80s before co-founding the all-saxophone group Itchy Fingers, which made two albums and garnered some attention during the 80s British jazz boom. He has since then concentrated on solo projects, usually with just himself and a rhythm section, although he has also made a point of seeking out international figures to tour with, including Paul Motian and Ethan Iverson. While he has played most of the saxophone family, his principal horn is the alto, and he plays and phrases in a cool, almost mentholated style which has an attractively opaque feel to it.

*Secret* (Basho)

# Glenn Spearman
TENOR SAXOPHONE
*born* 14 February 1947; *died* 8 October 1998

Though Spearman was born in New York, his family moved West when he was young and at the end of the 60s he was working in California with such free players as Charles Tyler and Sonny Simmons. He lived in Europe for much of the 70s before going back to New York and from there to Oakland, and it wasn't until the late 80s that he began making a mark on record. His groups Trio Hurricane (with William Parker and Paul Murphy) and the Double Trio (two saxes, piano, bass and two drummers) were fine settings for his own playing, which tended towards herculean overblowing and an unstemmable full throttle, although he managed to introduce touches of subtlety even when going at full tilt. In some ways he was an old-fashioned free player, still in thrall to the power-playing of the late 60s, although since he'd lived through it he was entitled to be. His later records saw him slowing down as his illness (he died of liver cancer in 1998) took hold.

*Smokehouse* (Black Saint)

## Chris Speed

TENOR SAXOPHONE, CLARINET
*born* 12 February 1967

Speed studied classical clarinet before he took up the saxophone in his teens. His Seattle classmates included Jim Black, and he worked with Black and Andrew D'Angelo in a group called Human Feel, all of them shifting to New York in the early 90s. Since then he has done the customary thing and worked in a plethora of bands of varying sizes. Speed's concern to give seemingly equal time to both clarinet and tenor has brought about some interesting surprises: on *Iffy* (Knitting Factory, 1999) he uses the clarinet to front what amounts to a power trio, and a quartet with Black, Cuong Vu and bassist Skuli Sverrisson has created some crackling, often funny music – Speed may be a passionate player, but he likes a slice of the sardonic too.

*Emit* (Songlines)

## Spirits Of Rhythm

GROUP

Originally a trio of the brothers Wilbur and Douglas Daniels (tiples) and Leo Watson (tiple and vocals), the Spirits came into being when they were joined by guitarist Teddy Bunn, and subsequently percussionist Virgil Scoggins. They had a long and successful residency in New York at The Onyx Club, as well as in Hollywood and on tour, and their records brim with a mix of countrified strumming, Bunn's beguiling virtuosity and the almost surreal scatting of the madcap

Watson: it was a great and enduring act, which lasted well into the 40s.

*The Spirits Of Rhythm 1933–1934* (JSP)

## Splasc(h)

RECORD COMPANY

Peppo Spagnoli has presided over this leading Italian independent since it was founded (financially, as a cooperative) in 1982. The earlier releases were adorned by Spagnoli's abstract paintings, but the covers are a little more prosaic now. It has grown into a voluminous (several hundred releases) and peerless documentation of contemporary Italian jazz, with virtually every major figure in the country's music represented as either leader or sideman, and many lesser-known musicians given the chance to set down some of their music.

## Spontaneous Music Ensemble

GROUP

Established in 1965 by the London-based Trevor Watts and John Stevens, the SME quickly became the leading British free-jazz group, enlisting such players as Evan Parker, Derek Bailey, Kenny Wheeler, Barry Guy and Paul Rutherford. Its size and shape fluctuated over the next 18 years, Stevens remaining as the only continuous member. Stevens and Parker became the nucleus of the group in 1967, with Watts's departure, but Watts returned the following year and Parker himself departed. Other musicians came in and out on a more or less ad hoc basis, and at one point, when the group recorded *Face To Face* (Emanem, 1973), it was again down to a duo of just Watts and Stevens. Nigel Coombes (violin) and Roger Smith (guitar) came in to form a trio with Stevens between 1976 and 1992, and John Butcher (saxes) replaced Coombes for the last two years of the group's existence. Throughout its history, SME was always about group playing, the individual silenced in favour of the ensemble, 'the idea of a musician being part of a larger whole rather than a separate attraction' (Stevens). Austere, nonlinear and often remarkably quiet, the group's music was perhaps insufficiently documented con-

sidering its capacious history and importance, but Martin Davidson of Emanem has
trawled various sources to rebuild the
group's discography and make as much as
possible available. Ironically, in the light of
the above, it stands mostly as a personification of Stevens's musicianship and ideals:
driven by his unswerving conviction that
every gig was an important, unrepeatable
event, SME's music continues to be a
homage to his principles.
***Karyobin*** (Chronoscope)

## Spotlite
RECORD COMPANY

The Londoner Tony Williams established
this label in 1968. It began issuing broadcast
material from the 40s by Charlie Parker and
others, and was the first to reissue a complete edition of Parker's Dial sessions.
Williams began making new records in 1974,
and has built a substantial catalogue of
material by such players as Peter King, Guy
Barker, Brian Dee, John Horler and Harry
Beckett. In the 70s Williams also recorded
such veteran boppers as Al Haig, Joe Albany
and Red Rodney.

## Spyro Gyra
GROUP

Founded by saxophonist Jay Beckenstein
and pianist Jeremy Wall in 1974, this
American soft-fusion band is one of the
most durable groups of the past three
decades. Personnel have been subject to
numerous changes down the years, and Wall
stepped back from live playing duties to act
as the group's producer and chief composer,
although Beckenstein has remained as the
group's chief instrumental voice. Other
contributors have included Dave Samuels,
Julio Fernandez, Richie Morales and Scott
Ambush. The group got off to a slow start,
but following a worldwide hit with 'Morning
Dance' (1979) it steadily built on that success
to become enormously popular, although
sales have never quite broken through to
the Kenny G level. Beckenstein and Wall
have taken a musicianly approach to their
work, but in the end the music is at best
inoffensive and at worst drearily
routine.

## Square

At one time this was a withering put-down
in jazz argot: a 'square' was someone who
had no appreciation or understanding of
jazz, and it subsequently entered the general
language as a description of just about any
person who was unaware, lacking or simply
not-one-of-us. The irony is that, inevitably,
the term itself has become so antiquated
that anyone using it now is likely to be
pretty square themselves.

## Larry Stabbins
TENOR AND SOPRANO SAXOPHONES
*born* 9 September 1949

Stabbins began working with Keith Tippett
when he was still in his teens, an association
which continued into the 90s. Much of his
career has been spent in playing free music,
but he took a lucrative holiday from that
when he began playing with a post-punk-
pop trio called Weekend in 1980, which
eventually evolved into the more successful
Working Week in 1985. That group recorded
some mildly successful (in pop terms; in
jazz-sales terms, hugely successful) records
which piggybacked on the British jazz
'revival' of the middle 80s. Stabbins came
across as more like the token horn player in
the group, and the music was as soft and
substantial as marshmallow. He recently re-
emerged and made the solo record cited,
which shows his chops in decent order.
***Monadic*** (Emanem)

## Jess Stacy
PIANO
*born* 11 August 1904; *died* 1 July 1995

Stacy's playing lit up the swing era at some
unexpected moments. He played on riverboats before going to Chicago in the 20s, but
his career didn't take him very far until he
joined Benny Goodman in 1935, and though
the testy Goodman didn't give him a great
deal to do in the four years Stacy was there,
the pianist did take his chance at the celebrated 1938 Carnegie Hall concert, where a
surprise call to take a solo on 'Sing Sing
Sing' resulted in a brief improvisation
which all but stopped the show, seeming to
go against the grain of the customary

crowd-pleasing of what was otherwise Gene Krupa's vehicle. After leaving Goodman he played with the big bands of Bob Crosby and Tommy Dorsey, as well as leading his own group for a time (his then wife Lee Wiley sang vocals). But it wasn't a success, and from 1948 he worked over in California, mainly as a saloon pianist. Stacy was a clever and perhaps a naturally spontaneous improviser: 'I can hear what I'm going to do a couple of bars ahead, and when I get near the end of those bars a couple more open up.' But his playing was largely wasted as far as the LP era was concerned, with only *A Tribute To Benny Goodman* (Atlantic, 1956) making much of an impact. He was effectively retired by the mid-60s but made a final record of piano solos in 1977.

*Jess Stacy 1935–1939* (Classics)

## Standard

A 'standard' composition is one which has become a familiar vehicle in the jazz or popular repertoire. Singers of standards are likely to base their material around those tunes composed by the leading American songwriters of the middle of the 20th century, such as the Gershwins, Porter, Rodgers and Hart, Kern, Arlen and so on. For the most part, a standard has to have achieved a certain age before it can be deemed such (a Paul Simon song, for instance, is too young to be a standard). Jazz standards are themes by jazz composers which have become common currency in jazz repertory: examples might be Thelonious Monk's ''Round Midnight' or Benny Golson's 'Whisper Not'.

## Tomasz Stańko

TRUMPET
*born* 11 July 1942

Stańko studied at a music school in Kraków and went on to co-found, with Adam Makowicz, a group called Jazz Darings in 1962. A year later he was working with Krzysztof Komeda and he proceeded to lead his own quintet, as well as make alliances with some of the European free players, working in the Globe Unity Orchestra and elsewhere. He recorded with Edward Vesala and won his own ECM album date, *Balladyna*, in 1975, and in the 80s he con-

tinued with some of these associations as well as playing with Cecil Taylor, Ted Curson and Jack DeJohnette. He has really come into his own as a leader with the outstanding group of records he has made for ECM over the past decade: beginning with *Matka Joanna* (1994), and proceeding through four further albums, Stańko has asserted a persona which is rare in European jazz. Isolated from many of the media currents which impose themselves on jazz appreciation, he has been able to enact a remarkably unselfconscious journey which touches on an expressive idiom that seems somehow different to the standard post-bop approach, even though its defining characteristics are familiar enough. His trumpet works in a tersely lyrical, modal groove which is both outgoing and quietly meditative.

*Leosia* (ECM)

## Steeplechase

RECORD COMPANY

Established by Nils Winther in Copenhagen in 1972, Steeplechase has steadily grown and become one of the leading independent European jazz labels. Winther appears to produce every record and his principal interest is in bebop and its immediate derivations: he started with a Jackie McLean record, and has since built a catalogue running into hundreds of sessions, mostly studio dates but with a number of archive live recordings, such as location sets made by Dexter Gordon in Copenhagen in the 60s. There is absolutely nothing from either the traditional and Dixieland end of the music, or from what could be construed as the avantgarde: a solo Lee Konitz record is about as far out as Winther has ever got. He now has significant holdings by such artists as Konitz, Gordon, Duke Jordan, Kenny Drew, Harold Danko, Andy LaVerne, Dave Stryker, Ron McClure, Doug Raney and Rich Perry.

## Bobo Stenson

PIANO
*born* 4 August 1944

Born in Västerås in Sweden, Stenson played in mainstream circles before forming a quartet with Jan Garbarek at the start of the 70s which made a brief sequence of outstanding

records for ECM. He also worked in a trio with Palle Danielsson and Lennart Aberg, Rena Rama, which tinkered with the idea of fusing various European folk musics with jazz playing, and for a time he tried electric keyboards – 'I woke up one day with a ring in my ear and thought it was time to stop.' Latterly he has worked primarily in the trio format, and recent records with Jon Christensen and Anders Jormin have offered a wonderful distillation of his listening and playing: the record cited mixes original pieces with reworkings of Ives, Eisler and Berg, and is measured and thoughtful without losing the spontaneity of a jazz-based approach.
*Serenity* (ECM)


# Mike Stern

GUITAR
*born* 10 January 1953

Stern grew up in Boston and studied at Berklee, where his tutor, one Pat Metheny, put him up for a job with Blood Sweat & Tears, a band which he joined in 1976 for two years. He then moved on to Billy Cobham's new band and from there joined the 'comeback' Miles Davis group of 1981–2: although many audiences were dismayed by what they heard as Davis importing a heavy-metal guitarist into his band, the records reveal Stern to have been a more sensitive player than that. He then embarked on a long series of solo projects for Atlantic, some of them particularly astutely produced by Jim Beard, although he now appears to have been dropped by the label: mixing fusion approaches of varying degrees of light and shade, they have been intermittently successful, and Stern has toured with groups of different kinds in support of his records. He's clearly a talented man, but his output suggests that he produces his best music under careful guidance. His wife Leni (b 1952) is also a guitarist and singer, and has released a series of albums which are broadly in a fusion vein but which, in their more quirky way, are at least as interesting as Mike's projects.
*Play* (Atlantic)

# John Stevens

DRUMS, CORNET
*born* 10 June 1940; *died* 13 September 1994

Born in Brentford in west London, Stevens did his national service in the RAF and while playing in service bands made connections with Paul Rutherford and Trevor Watts. He became a significant figure on the London scene from 1963, working with Tubby Hayes, Ronnie Scott and others, while beginning to cultivate alliances which led him inexorably towards free music. For a time he ran a seven-piece group with Alan Skidmore and others which was couched in a hard-bop dialect, but his important group was the Spontaneous Music Ensemble, which he founded with Watts in 1965. Aside from his work with the SME, which runs through the rest of his career, Stevens was always a busy musician and catholic in his choice of musical fields. Among his bands of the 70s were Splinters (with fellow drummer Phil Seamen), Away (an unusually creative jazz-rock group which recorded two albums for Mercury), the John Stevens Dance Orchestra (a large ensemble, not really for dancing), a quartet with Watts, Barry Guy and Howard Riley, and John Martyn's trio with Danny Thompson. In the 80s he formed Detail, usually a trio or quartet; Folkus, a ten-strong ensemble; and Freebop, another large group, which found Courtney Pine and Evan Parker sitting in the same section. In the meantime, he continued playing with the SME, and was heavily involved in community education, becoming fascinated by the possibilities of teaching improvisation: 'If somebody says to me, "I can't improvise", I would find that very inspiring. Because I know that within a short time they will be doing it and saying, "Oh, is that it?"' John's own style was, in the end, irreducible. He began as a drummer who followed the hard-bop masters, but he gradually pared his kit down to its smallest essentials, often played very quietly, and found a way of drumming which sounded utterly free and spontaneous without losing its line to the jazz he had grown up with. His regular Friday-night sessions at the Plough, a pub in south London, became essential gatherings for free-music followers in the city in the 70s, and Stevens loved talking to his audience and trying to engage them in what he saw as a profoundly important matter, the act of making music. A tempestuous man with many private demons to go with his generous nature, his sudden death from a heart attack shocked the listening and playing communities to whom he had given so much.

**With Derek Bailey,** *Playing* (Incus)

# Herbie Steward
TENOR SAXOPHONE
*born* 7 May 1926

Steward might be unfairly characterized as the one of the Four Brothers whom everyone forgets. He played in Artie Shaw's big band before joining Woody Herman's Second Herd on its formation in 1947, where he played on the original recording of 'Four Brothers', but he left the band a few weeks later and his replacement, Al Cohn, often gets a 'Four Brothers' tag in his place. Steward then freelanced for a time, spent a period with Harry James, and ended up working in Las Vegas and as a Hollywood studio musician. Thereafter he spent very little time in jazz, although where he has popped up, his coolly insidious style suggests that he could have made some very agreeable jazz records if he'd had leadership opportunities in that direction.

**Woody Herman,** *Blowin' Up A Storm!* (Columbia)

# Bill Stewart
DRUMS
*born* 18 October 1966

Born in Des Moines, Stewart studied at Northern Iowa University and in New Jersey, and he settled in New York in 1989. A high-profile stint with John Scofield's group pushed him to prominence in the early 90s, and since then he has steadily grown in stature, working with many of the major American jazz leaders, although he is happy to do session gigs on small labels and he maintains a long association with the organist Larry Goldings. Stewart's style has much in common with Jack DeJohnette's playing, although he is a more easy-going and less obviously combative player than DeJohnette. He is also a very interesting composer, and two records which he made for Blue Note as a leader, *Snide Remarks* (1995) and *Telepathy* (1996), have something of a cult following among musicians,

although they cut little ice with the public and regrettably he hasn't had the chance to build on them.

*Telepathy* (Blue Note)

# Bob Stewart
TUBA
*born* 3 February 1945

Stewart started out as a trumpet player but took up the tuba in his teens, and eventually began gigging in the group Gravity, run by that other great low-brass specialist Howard Johnson. Since then he has largely performed as a freelance, for leaders who have demonstrated a penchant for a bass instrument which is something other than the string version: these would include Arthur Blythe (some of Stewart's most memorable work), McCoy Tyner, David Murrray and Charlie Haden. Stewart has led some groups of his own, including the First Line Band, but he always seems to give of his best in his sideman duties.

**Arthur Blythe,** *Blythe Spirit* (Columbia)

# Louis Stewart
GUITAR
*born* 5 January 1944

Born in the Irish town of Waterford, Stewart worked in showbands (an Irish manifestation of a dance orchestra with a slightly more Gaelic bent to it) before a visit to New York fired his interest in playing jazz. He then began backing visiting players, including Lee Konitz, and at the end of the 60s he joined Tubby Hayes's group before undertaking touring work with Benny Goodman. He was a sideman with Ronnie Scott and George Shearing later in the 70s, and since then has worked as a freelance in a variety of settings, recording as a leader mostly for the independent Jardis label. A perennially unruffled bebop stylist somewhat in the Tal Farlow mould, Stewart has rather more of a reputation among musicians than listeners, partly because he comes from a territory with very little jazz clout, and further because he has never had much interest from record labels: a sympathetic company could yet get a classic out of him.

*Overdrive* (Hep)

# Rex Stewart

CORNET

*born* 22 February 1907; *died* 7 September 1967

Stewart grew up in Washington DC and moved to New York around 1920, playing at first only in minor groups, but eventually winning a seat in the Fletcher Henderson band of 1926. He already worshipped Louis Armstrong, and felt discomforted at first trying to fill his shoes in the Henderson band, so much so that he quit for a time but returned in 1928, this time staying five years. Stewart also admired Bix Beiderbecke, and his own style, which he arrived at after struggling with an imperfect technique, mixed the influence of the two giants: he also developed a method of half-valving notes which gave them a particular, 'squeezed' quality that became unique to him. He also played with McKinney's Cotton Pickers and in 1933 led what must have been an exciting big band (with Ward Pinkett, Sidney Catlett and others), which never made any records. But his moment came when he joined Duke Ellington in 1934. Ellington soon had his talents perfectly set, with inimitable features such as 'Boy Meets Horn', which became his great setpiece with the band, and Rex enjoyed 11 years of limelight with the orchestra. His effusive style and 'chattering' sound (later capitalized on for an LP he made with Dicky Wells, *Chatter Jazz*, in 1959) then took him to Europe, where he enjoyed much popularity in the late 40s. The 50s found him semi-retired, but he turned out for Fletcher Henderson reunions in 1957, and then spent a brief period playing in Eddie Condon groups. In the 60s he emerged as a witty and entertaining writer on jazz, with a fine store of reminiscences, but he died suddenly of a brain haemorrhage.

**Duke Ellington, *1937 Vol 2*** (Classics)

# Slam Stewart

BASS

*born* 21 September 1914; *died* 10 December 1987

Stewart told how while studying at Boston Conservatory, he heard a violinist, Ray Perry, humming along with his playing, and Stewart decided to try the same trick with the bass, humming the melody an octave higher. He never stopped doing it, no matter how tiresome it became to his listeners. Slim Gaillard liked his style and they worked as a duo, Slim 'n' Slam, in the late 30s, with a perennial hit in 'Flat Foot Floogie'. Stewart went to Hollywood in 1943, where he became pals with guitarist Tiny Grimes, and from there they began working in a somewhat unlikely trio with Art Tatum, although – for all his seemingly clownish aproach – Stewart actually was steeped in music, and he could handle whatever Tatum was throwing around on the keyboard. He also played with Benny Goodman and Erroll Garner and even turns up on some early bop dates with Dizzy Gillespie. He was busy all through the 60s and 70s, a regular with Goodman, Rose Murphy and others, and he latterly formed a duo with Bucky Pizzarelli. While his solos aren't something to look forward to, Stewart was an exceptional ensemble bassist, and the high regard he enjoyed with Tatum and Goodman tells its own story.

**Art Tatum, *The Complete Capitol Recordings*** (Capitol)

# Sonny Stitt

ALTO AND TENOR SAXOPHONES

*born* 2 February 1924; *died* 22 July 1982

A favourite source of debate is the extent to which Stitt came up with his own style: how much he took from Charlie Parker, and how much came from inside. Originally from Boston, he joined the Billy Eckstine orchestra in 1944, then went to the Dizzy Gillespie sextet and big band. But he lost his New York cabaret card when getting into trouble over narcotics, and then spent time in Detroit and Chicago, concentrating for the moment on tenor sax (and very occasionally baritone). By 1950 he was back in New York and formed a frequently convened partnership with Gene Ammons. Thereafter he spent the rest of his life as a nomadic solo: there were occasional stints with Miles Davis (1960–61), Jazz At The Philharmonic, and the Giants Of Jazz (1971–2), but Stitt never stayed in one place for long. He began playing the alto again after Parker's death, and for a while he played it through the Varitone attachment, an electronic fad which he toyed with in the late 60s. As he grew older, Stitt settled into his alto style, and the Parker comparison began to seem redundant: both men were working off the

same sheet, but Stitt forced his own agenda on to the notes, and could sometimes call up the shades of Lester Young and Wardell Gray (who had once given him some informal lessons). He recorded a bewildering number of albums for at least 30 different labels: many of the sessions are entirely routine, since Stitt had seemingly little interest in posterity, but when at his best and with sympathetic accompanists he always proved the durability of hardcore bebop improvisation. He loved the challenge of a jam session: Art Pepper's recounting of one battle with Stitt (in his autobiographical *Straight Life*) is unforgettable. Sonny never came off the road, and died only a few days after flying home from his final concert in Japan.
**Keepers Of The Flame** (Camden)

## Kathy Stobart
TENOR SAXOPHONE
*born* 1 April 1925

Born in South Shields, Stobart moved to London in 1942 and played locally with a variety of leaders, eventually forming her own group, which performed briefly before breaking up in the early 50s. She then divided her time between raising her family (with her second husband, trumpeter Bert Courtley) and playing, including stints with Humphrey Lyttelton (celebrated in the ten-inch LP *Kath Meets Humph*, Parlophone 1957, included in the record cited) and in Courtley's own band. In the 70s she taught and led her own groups, playing in London and on cruise ships. A pioneer among postwar British jazzwomen, Stobart's tenor playing was, at its best, a smoothly effective and swinging sound which she handled with wonderful authority. Her final association was with Humphrey Lyttelton, returning to his line-up a final time before she retired early in the new century.
**Humphrey Lyttelton, *Triple Exposure*** (Calligraph)

## Stomp Off
RECORD COMPANY

Since 1980, Bob Erdos has been producing scores of outstanding examples of modern revivalist jazz from his base in York, Pennsylvania. Bob's affections lie with ragtime, hot dance music, and the Chicago and New Orleans styles of roughly 1924–35, and he has built an unrivalled catalogue of contemporary interpretations of this kind of material. American musicians such as John Gill, Marty Grosz, Jim Cullum, Ernie Carson, Hal Smith, the South Frisco Jazz Band, the New Black Eagle Jazz Band and the Grand Dominion Jazz Band line up alongside such Europeans as Bent Persson, Keith Nichols and Paris Washboard.

## Stop-time

The stop-time solo is an important part of traditional jazz, although with the increasing flexibility of the pulse it has largely disappeared from more contemporary forms. It is essentially a series of breaks rather than a solo: the rhythm section will play only on the first beat of every bar, as a kind of punctuating marker, for the duration of a chorus (or more), while the soloist has to carry the improvisation through. This heightens the drama of the solo by making it, in efect, an unaccompanied outburst with only a skeletal backing. The greatest example on record is surely Louis Armstrong's unimprovable solo on 'Potato Head Blues' (1927).

## Storyville
RECORD COMPANIES

The first Storyville label was founded by impresario George Wein in 1951, and grew out of recordings made at the club of that name in Boston (Storyville has older jazz links, since it was also the notorious brothel district of New Orleans, where many ragtime and early jazz pianists worked in the first years of the century). It recorded a variety of modern and mainstream musicians for a time, but Wein's other activities made him lose interest in the label and it folded later in the 50s. At the same time, another Storyville label, concerned primarily with recording traditional jazz, was founded in Denmark by Karl Emil Knudsen, and was also named after a club, although this one was in Copenhagen. This grew into a formidable catalogue of European trad, bolstered by broadcast material from American sources and other jazz. In the new century, it was still going strong.

## Billy Strayhorn
PIANO
*born* 29 November 1915; *died* 31 May 1967

Strayhorn studied music in Pittsburgh and when he sent one of his compositions to Duke Ellington in 1938 it was the start of an association which would last the rest of his life. Ellington began recording Strayhorn tunes such as 'Something To Live For' straight away, and before long the young man was subbing as pianist for Duke and became an associate arranger, which in practice meant that the two men worked very closely on much of the composing for the orchestra. Nicknamed 'Swee' Pea', after Popeye's offspring (Strayhorn had an eternally babyfaced look), Strayhorn composed several of the signature pieces in Ellington's book, including 'Take The "A" Train', 'Day Dream' and 'Chelsea Bridge', and he had a hand in many of those works principally credited to Ellington himself: scholars have been devoting much time of late to figuring out who did what. Away from writing, he was an effective, rather guileful pianist, playing a sideman role on small-group dates by Ellingtonians, although he led only a handful of sessions of his own, including the memorable *Cue For Saxophone* (Felstead, 1958). Stricken by cancer, he still wrote from his hospital bed: two late pieces wryly titled 'Blood Count' and 'U.M.M.G.' (Upper Manhattan Medical Group) showed his gifts undimmed. After Strayhorn's death, the Ellington orchestra recorded . . . *And His Mother Called Him Bill* (RCA, 1967), which ends with the bandleader playing the Strayhorn ballad he most admired, 'Lotus Blossom', alone at the piano.
*Cue For Saxophone* (Felstead)

## Frank Strazzeri
PIANO
*born* 24 April 1930

Though born in Rochester, New York, where he first began playing in clubs, Strazzeri is really a West Coast man. He went from Rochester to New Orleans, and then worked in Las Vegas before finally settling in Los Angeles in 1960. Since then he has worked steadily in the characteristically wide range of settings which a studio and session-player expects – everything from the Lighthouse All Stars and a regular late 60s gig at Donte's to touring with Elvis Presley and playing as the musical coordinator for the Chet Baker film *Let's Get Lost*. Strazzeri came to a late flowering as a leader on record when he made some recordings for Fresh Sound and Jazz Mark: *Little Giant* (1989), *Somebody Loves Me* (1994) and a duo record with Bill Perkins, *Warm Moods* (1991), offer pleasing results via his delicate touch and a concern to pick unusual tunes rather than standard warhorses.
*Little Giant* (Fresh Sound)

## String Trio Of New York
GROUP

Founder members Billy Bang (violin), James Emery (guitar) and John Lindberg (bass) established the group as an early example of polystylistic fusion from a jazz base: they have drawn from bluegrass and other string-band traditions, and there's an inescapable feel of chamber music about their more serene work. Yet it's a jazz group at heart, and a slightly complicated discography spread across four different independent labels is colourful and perhaps insufficiently recognized. Bang left the group in the 80s and his place has subsequently been taken by (successively) Charles Burnham, Regina Carter and Diane Monroe; recently the Trio appeared to have been relatively inactive, but they released a new album in 2003.
*Rebirth Of A Feeling* (Black Saint)

## Frank Strozier
ALTO SAXOPHONE
*born* 13 June 1937

Something of a lost figure (his one Steeplechase album was wistfully entitled *Remember Me*), Strozier was a powerful hard-bop saxophonist who never had much luck on record. He worked in his home town of Memphis in the late 50s, and was the alto player with MJT + 3, a group led by Walter Perkins. In New York, he worked for Roy Haynes and, tantalizingly, Miles Davis (a stay which went unrecorded); moving to California, he was with Shelly Manne and Don Ellis. But little he did garnered wider attention, and he abandoned jazz altogether in 1983, before returning in the 90s as a pianist. Strozier's mettlesome playing takes the ear whenever he gets a feature on a record, and it's too bad that such cases are comparatively rare.

**Roy Haynes, *Cymbalism*** (New Jazz/OJC)

## Dave Stryker
GUITAR
*born* 30 March 1957

Born in Omaha, Stryker worked on both coasts before significant spells with Jack McDuff and Stanley Turrentine. Working environments like those have steeped him in blues licks and hard-bitten entertainment, but he also has a full bebop vocabulary and usually finds space on his records for an attractively limpid ballad or two. Steeplechase have recorded him extensively as a leader, including three instalments of *Blue To The Bone*, which set him off against organ combo and fat horn section. Maybe he's best in an open-ended small-group setting, though.

***Passage*** (Steeplechase)

## John Stubblefield
TENOR SAXOPHONE
*born* 4 February 1945

Stubblefield blew lusty R&B tenor on his local Arkansas circuit in the early 60s, but moved to Chicago in 1967 and became deeply involved in the activities of the AACM. A band he led called The Hot Five – with Leo Smith, Amina Myers and Malachi Favors – unfortunately never recorded. The saxophonist moved to New York in 1971, and from that point became much in demand as sideman and section-player; he also led a quartet of varying personnel throughout the 80s and early 90s, but he has either been unlucky or not been much interested in recording as a leader, for a couple of unremarkable albums (for European labels) have been the only results. Latterly he has been heavily involved in jazz education, although he has sometimes depped for the busy David Murray when the latter has been absent from the World Saxophone Quartet. Like Murray, in fact, he has a partiality for the tenor's pinched highest register, which he loves to squeeze his way through. One

leader he has done some excellent work with is pianist Kenny Barron.

**Kenny Barron, *What If?*** (Enja)

## Richard Sudhalter
TRUMPET, AUTHOR
*born* 28 December 1938

Sudhalter started as a musician but has been at least as significant as a writer and commentator. He played cornet in high school and lived in Austria and Germany before settling in London in 1964, where he worked as a reporter for United Press. He also played in the Anglo-American Alliance and in Sandy Brown's group, while writing jazz journalism and co-authoring a book on Bix Beiderbecke. His interest in repertory led him to assist with the New Paul Whiteman Orchestra, and on his return to the US in 1975 he led various groups and played in The Classic Jazz Quartet with Marty Grosz, subsequently a regular associate. Sudhalter's playing is an agreeable amalgam of his many favourites on the horn, but his writing is more distinctive, and his masterpiece is the outstanding *Lost Chords: The Contribution Of White Musicians To Jazz, 1915–1945*, which in America's race-obsessed jazz establishment caused a lot of unwarranted heat but remains a fine study of its subject.

***The Classic Jazz Quartet*** (Jazzology)

## Idrees Sulieman
TRUMPET, ALTO SAXOPHONE
*born* 7 August 1923

Sulieman was almost accidentally in near the start of bebop on record: in between gigs with the big bands of Benny Carter and Cab Calloway, he worked with Thelonious Monk in 1947 and is on some of the pianist's first Blue Note dates. In the 50s he turns up with Max Roach, Dizzy Gillespie, Mal Waldron and others, playing effectively enough although without any great distinction. In the 60s he settled in Europe, and some of his best work was with the Clarke–Boland Big Band, which he played with for ten years. In the 90s he returned home to Florida, having taken up the alto sax for a time.

**Mal Waldron, *Mal 1*** (Prestige/OJC)

# Ira Sullivan

TRUMPET, SAXOPHONES

*born* 1 May 1931

Sullivan's proficiency on both brass and reed instruments marks him out as a rarity, and musically he has led a notably inquisitive career. In the 50s he worked mainly in Chicago, but thereafter he settled in Florida and disliked travelling far from home: as a result he made very few records, and most of his work was done away from taste-making audiences. His quintet with Red Rodney in the 80s, which involved a lot of original material rather than standard bebop, should have received more attention, but as it is three rather scrappy albums for Muse missed the spark of what was reputedly an outstanding group. He has continued to play in a variety of settings where his talents are on display, but again records have been few, and Sullivan is almost a textbook example of a musician whose lack of support from record companies – not entirely their fault – has marginalized a fine player, versed in bop but perfectly aware of what's happened since and prepared to take some of it on board.

*Sprint* (Elektra Musician)

# Joe Sullivan

PIANO

*born* 4 November 1906; *died* 13 October 1971

The youngest of nine in a Chicagoan family, O'Sullivan learned piano at school and subsequently studied at the city's Conservatory. He was already leading bands by the early 20s and joined up with the Red Nichols axis in New York later in the decade. He played solo at The Onyx Club before going over to the West Coast, where he was a favourite accompanist of Bing Crosby (one can hear Bing encouraging the pianist on their fine record of 'Moonburn'). Despite a serious illness, he also worked in the Bob Crosby band and led his own orchestra before returning to a trio format in California. By the 50s, despite spells with various members of the Condon clan, Sullivan was stuck with solo gigs in noisy nightclubs, and he felt – rightly enough – that jazz had largely passed him by. There was a modest comeback in the 60s, engineered by his friend, writer Richard Hadlock, but the pianist's health went down-

hill. Much of his best work on record is right at the beginning of his 'name' career: two solo sessions from 1933 and 1935 include rococo delights such as 'Little Rock Getaway' and 'My Little Pride And Joy', where his dexterity is matched with melodic ingenuity.

*Joe Sullivan 1933–1941* (Classics)

# Maxine Sullivan

VOCAL, VALVE-TROMBONE

*born* 13 May 1911; *died* 7 April 1987

Born Marietta Williams, the small-voiced Sullivan sustained a long and mostly delightful career on record and in person. She sang a version of 'Loch Lomond' with Claude Thornhill's band in 1937, which saddled her with an obligation to jazz up folk and neo-classical material for many years. She then worked with John Kirby's group, a perfect fit, and married the leader, although they divorced in 1942. She maintained a busy solo career, sometimes playing valve-trombone as well as singing, until 1957, when she decided to devote more time to her family, having married Cliff Jackson after her divorce, and that she'd had enough of doing the material she was stuck with; but she returned to singing in the late 60s. In the 70s and 80s she enjoyed an Indian summer of performing and recording, often with the new swing mainstreamers such as Scott Hamilton in tow, and she addressed her material with a freer approach than she did in her youth. 'Killing Time', from one of her final sessions, is among the most unaffectedly poignant interpretations of its kind.

*Close As Pages In A Book* (Audiophile)

# Stan Sulzmann

TENOR SAXOPHONE

*born* 30 November 1948

Sulzmann is a veteran of the modern London scene. He began playing at the Wimbledon Palais in 1963, and then joined the London Youth Jazz Orchestra (later the NYJO – Sulzmann plays on their first record, although he had actually left at that point). He played on the *Queen Mary* liner for a year and then worked on the London R&B scene before studying at the Royal Academy. Since the early 70s he has been busy as a sideman and with leading small groups of

his own, as well as working in European big bands and finally completing an orchestral project, *Birthdays, Birthdays* (1998). Some of his best playing, in his tough but malleable post-Coltrane style, is with Kenny Wheeler's small groups on *Flutter By, Butterfly* (Soul Note, 1987) and *Music For Large And Small Ensembles* (ECM, 1990).
*Treasure Trove* (ASC)

# Sun Ra
KEYBOARDS, BANDLEADER
*born* 22 May 1914; *died* 30 May 1993

He was born Herman Blount in Birmingham, Alabama, although as every schoolboy knows, he was really from the planet Saturn. He learned to play piano by watching his sister, and subsequently toured with a Chicago band, around 1933, although he subsequently returned to college in Alabama. For the next ten years he played in undistinguished groups in the Midwest, interrupted only by a brief and miserable spell in the armed forces. He then played in Fletcher Henderson's band in 1946, worked as a pianist in Chicago clubs, and bossed an occasional big band in the area, before forming a small group with saxophonist Pat Patrick in 1950 which eventually grew into a large ensemble. Blount had become fascinated by Egyptian studies, and he changed his name to Le Sony'r Ra, his legal name, although it would be shortened to Sun Ra for stage purposes. He called his group the Arkestra and insisted that he was a communicator from another race, sent here to help a people in darkness. From this point, the Arkestra began enlisting musicians who would, in some cases, stay for decades: besides Patrick, these would include John Gilmore, Marshall Allen and Ronnie Boykins. Dressed in suitably elaborate robes, Sun Ra and his men began formulating stage shows which might have seemed vaudevillian but which would sustain their reputation as genuine mystics. A record label, Saturn, was established in 1956: its chaotic discography was, by the time of the leader's death, so large and convoluted that it ran to hundreds of pages and possibly thousands of recordings. The 50s music was largely in thrall to hard-bop conventions, but as time went on it took on more percussive devices, brought in Latin influences, started to take on free-form elements, and eventually involved electric keyboards. Sun Ra shifted the operation to New York in 1961, and this initiated his most radical period, with such records as *The Magic City* (1965) as confrontational and powerful in their way as anything made by Shepp or Ayler. The Arkestra had relatively little regular work, but they rehearsed almost all the time, and Sun Ra's men were extraordinarily loyal – 'They're in the Ra jail, the best in the world.'

In 1968 Sun Ra moved base again, this time to Philadelphia. In the 70s, the Arkestra shows became bigger and grander: there were singers, dancers and acrobats involved, and Sun Ra himself added synthesizers and such instruments as the rocksichord to his own stage paraphernalia. Later, he went further by reaching back, playing old Fletcher Henderson arrangements alongside such greatest hits of his own as 'We Travel The Spaceways'. The group travelled the world and was honoured at last, through persistence as much as anything else, although Sun Ra had always attracted an audience outside jazz by dint of his sheer strangeness. He welcomed believers and would expound at length on his other-worldly philosophies. By the late 80s, age was slowing him down and the Arkestra began to lose its zest, but it carried on all the same, and even after his death it still exists, currently under the leadership of Marshall Allen. Although, as a whole, Sun Ra's work was too sprawling and individual to really be any kind of a general influence, much of what he did was routinely ahead of its time and prescient of things which have happened in music since, whether in jazz, rock or wherever. And he is surely still out there, somewhere.
*Space Is The Place* (Evidence)

# Monty Sunshine
CLARINET
*born* 8 April 1928

Sunshine was in at the start of London trad: he was in the first edition of the Crane River Jazz Band, and then joined Ken Colyer in 1953, staying on with the 'breakaway' band which was in turn led by Chris Barber. He plays the clarinet part on 'Petite Fleur' (1955), one of the biggest of the trad hits. In 1960 he began leading for himself, a situation which carries on to this day, though there

have been occasional reunions with Barber too. He retains a big following in Germany, where his style of playing has always ruled a certain kind of jazz roost, and his sweeping phrasing and wide vibrato remain intact.
*New Orleans Hula* (Stomp Off)

# John Surman
BARITONE AND SOPRANO SAXOPHONES, SYN-THESIZERS
*born* 30 August 1944

Born in Tavistock, Devon, Surman took up the baritone sax from an early age and studied in London in the 60s. He had been in one of Mike Westbrook's jazz workshops when still in his mid-teens, and he was a regular Westbrook sideman in the 60s, continuing to record with him into the 70s: he is the principal soloist on Westbrook's *Citadel/Room 315*. Besides plenty of other sideman work, Surman began recording with his own groups in 1968. He played with the fierce, free-jazz orientated The Trio (himself, Barre Phillips and Stu Martin) between 1969 and 1971, and then in the SOS trio with Mike Osborne and Alan Skidmore, one of the first groups where he began to use synthesizers as a backdrop to his own improvising. His own-name albums – including *Extrapolation* (1969) with John McLaughlin, *How Many Clouds Can You See?* (1968), the all-solo *Westering Home* (1970) and *Morning Glory* (1973) – showcased what might have been the most individual instrumental talent in European jazz at that time. He had mastered the baritone sax to such an extent that he brought some of the ferocious intensity of post-Coltrane improvising to the unwieldy instrument, and he explored its upper range to its furthest extremes, an unprecedented step. His doubling on soprano brought that instrument into equal focus with his baritone work, and his playing on *Westering Home* and with SOS explored his interest in multiple woodwind textures, another pioneering effort.

In 1979 he made his first solo album for ECM, combining saxophone improvisations with synthesizer patterns, and that approach has sustained much of his solo work since; but he has also convened an ongoing Brass Project for 11 musicians, performed with Paul Bley and some other ECM artists, and worked frequently with his wife,

the singer Karin Krog. Some who have followed Surman from his early days have sometimes regretted that some of the power and impact of his early work has often been displaced by the occasionally motionless pastoralism of his ECM music, although he continues to play in a quartet, even if it does not work in Britain very often. Before Surman, British jazz musicians seemed almost reluctant to take themselves out into the world. His adventures – with The Trio, and with Manfred Eicher's ECM – changed all that.
*Upon Reflection* (ECM)

# Ralph Sutton
PIANO
*born* 4 November 1922; *died* 30 December 2002

Sutton was perhaps the last of the great stride pianists – at least, among those who were first around when the idiom was young. He spent much of his youth listening to Fats Waller on the radio, and worked with Jack Teagarden before being drafted in 1943. After the war he rejoined Teagarden before working with small groups and ending up in the Eddie Condon circle of players. He moved on in 1956, and worked as a club player on the West Coast. In the 60s he was a regular at Dick Gibson's Jazz Parties, and he joined The World's Greatest Jazz Band at its inception in 1968. By the 80s he was an honoured veteran, and beginning to be perceived as a throwback to a vanished jazz era. He continued to tour both Europe and the US, his playing always in demand for its hugely swinging virtuosity in the stride idiom: his affection for Waller's music endured, and there would be something by Fats in every set he played. A stroke in 1992 slowed him down for a time, but he was soon back to full strength, and was recorded at length by several labels. Retirement never arrived: he passed away in his car, parked outside the venue where he was due to play another gig.
*At Café Des Copains* (Sackville)

## Esbjörn Svensson

PIANO, KEYBOARDS
*born* 16 April 1964

The Swede played in Fredrik Norén's hard-bop group in the 80s before forming his trio (latterly known as EST) with his long-time friends Dan Berglund (bass) and Magnus Öström (drums). Although some think that they leapt to a kind of overnight stardom, the trio had already made four records before their breakthrough set, *Winter In Venice* (Superstudio, 1997). A year earlier, the pianist had followed three interesting if not especially remarkable records with *Trio Plays Monk* (ACT, 1996), a dazzling homage to its dedicatee, where the group seemed to rethink the rhythmic bases for such well-worn pieces as 'I Mean You' and 'Rhythm-A-Ning' and made every track seem like something fresh, new and unhackneyed. *Winter In Venice* and its successor, *From Gagarin's Point Of View* (ACT, 1998), built on this achievement with great finesse: without resorting to any kind of electronics, the group suggested a *rapprochement* with rock in pieces such as 'Dodge The Dodo', and Svensson extrapolates what he wants from influences such as Keith Jarrett and the Chick Corea of *Now He Sings, Now He Sobs* ('I listened to that record thousands of times') and then uses them to his own ends, refreshingly free of rhetoric. Yet at this point, just as they were becoming a major international success, EST's records and performances began to slip towards what might even end up as self-parody. They began to introduce electronic textures very sparingly, but by the time of *Seven Days Of Falling* (2003) and *Viaticum* (2005), the music was starting to have more in common with Radiohead than Keith Jarrett, and much of the improvisational interest was being traded for mere textural tinkering. Svensson clearly has more to say yet, but at the time of writing his progress has become disappointing.
*From Gagarin's Point Of View* (ACT)

## Steve Swallow

BASS
*born* 4 October 1940

Swallow's talents as player and composer have sometimes been lost to indifferent contexts. He was only 20 when he began playing with Paul Bley's group, which went on to form the nucleus of the Jimmy Giuffre trio that recorded *Fusion* and *Thesis* (Verve, 1961–2). He then played regularly in Art Farmer's group with Jim Hall, joined Gary Burton in the Stan Getz group, and eventually moved on to Burton's own band in 1967. It was during this period that he switched over from the acoustic instrument to electric bass guitar, which he continued to play with Burton into the 70s. In the end he abandoned the acoustic bass altogether. He uses a pick on the bass guitar, fingers it more like a guitar than a bass, and secures a clean, almost rubbery sound from it that is as distinctive as anything the next generation of bassists (including Jaco Pastorius) would come up with. If anything, Swallow's style has been notably uninfluential: jazz bass is still more acoustic than electric, and those who do use the bass guitar tend to take their cues more from funk and rock players than Swallow's precise, clear vocabulary. In 1978 he began playing in Carla Bley's groups, and he ultimately became her partner: they have worked together in both her big-band and small-group music, although one often feels that these are little more than noodling contexts for his own playing. He continues to work with some high-profile players, including John Scofield, and his own small groups have been wholesome if not always very exciting vehicles for writing which deserves a tribute album of its own.
**With Gary Burton,** *Hotel Hello* (ECM)

## John Swana

TRUMPET
*born* 26 April 1962

A stalwart of the modern Philadelphia scene, Swana started playing trumpet at 11, and by the middle 80s was gigging regularly in the city as both a sideman and a leader. He started making records for Gerry Teekens's Criss Cross label in 1990 and has since then built up a sequence of sessions for the label which make a very pleasing case for his music, full of finely judged playing which can still get hot and a little bothered when the spirit catches hold of him. Given that this is currently unfashionable music he has not made much of a reputation outside his base, but Swana's playing will reward any sympathetic listener.

**John Swana And Friends** (Criss Cross)

# Harvie Swartz

BASS

*born* 6 December 1948

Swartz played in Boston and Denmark at the beginning of the 70s, and then moved to New York in 1972, where he accompanied singers and did a lot of studio work. In the early 80s he formed a String Ensemble with Erik Friedlander (cello) and others, and then mixed his time between sideman gigs in fusion bands with his own work as a leader: he led a fusion group of his own, Urban Earth, for a spell, and in the 90s he moved on to a Latin crossover group, Eye Contact, which led to his giving up the electric bass. Recently he seems to have reinvented himself as 'Harvic S'. Some of his best work was done in a duo with Sheila Jordan, as on the record cited.

**With Sheila Jordan, *Songs From Within*** (MA)

# Swing

Swing remains indefinable, which long ago led to the retort, 'If you have to ask what it means, you ain't got it', although nobody knows for sure who said that first, either. In a piece of music, it is a rhythmical property which conveys some sense of forward momentum: a mixture of an underlying regular pulse with minute variations of that pulse. As one feels a certain strain between those two points, so one feels swing – perhaps. Thus, there are countless ways of swinging, each variation contributing to what should be, in a true state of swing, a natural ongoing flow. According to Jon Hendricks, anything you do can swing, if you approach it in the right, jazz-directed attitude – so you can in theory swing while boiling a kettle.

'Swing' was also the music which evolved out of the big-band idiom fashioned by such leader-composers as Fletcher Henderson, Duke Ellington and others at the end of the 20s, which grew into the big-band era – often called 'The Swing Era' – of the 30s and early 40s.

# Swingle Singers

Assembled by Ward Swingle and Christiane Legrand in Paris in 1962, this was an ensemble of eight academically trained vocalists who recorded a series of very popular records which featured scat arrangements of familiar classical and baroque themes. The singers were given a lightly cushioned undertow from bass and drums, and the result was an agreeable confection which charmed audiences for much of the 60s with their dah-bah-dah kind of music. A succeeding group, Swingle II, focused more on newer music and was less successful.

**Jazz Sebastian Bach** (Verve)

# Gábor Szabó

GUITAR

*born* 8 March 1936; *died* 26 February 1982

Born in Budapest, Szabó played on his local jazz scene during the 50s before going to the US to study at Berklee in 1958. In 1962 he moved over to the West Coast, where he joined Chico Hamilton's small group, and in the late 60s he fronted groups of his own, although a series of records under his own name consisted largely of mixtures of pop covers and doodling stabs at a light kind of fusion. These leanings became more pronounced in a generally thin and depressing discography during the 70s. He latterly divided his time between Hungary and the US. Little of his surviving music has much mettle to it: a talented player who left a poor legacy of work on record.

**Jazz Raga** (Impulse!)

# Lew Tabackin

TENOR SAXOPHONE, FLUTE

*born* 26 May 1940

Tabackin was born in Philadelphia and studied music there, before doing military service and eventually settling in New York in 1965. He began playing in big bands such as the Jones–Lewis Orchestra, as well as in television groups such as Doc Severinsen's *Tonight Show* band, quickly acquiring a reputation as a pros' pro when it came to reading and leading a section. He married Toshiko Akiyoshi in 1969 and they moved to California in 1972, working together in a

group which eventually became the big band which was one of the finest of its era. Tabackin's solo work is well featured on their various records with the Orchestra, which eventually took root back in New York in the 80s, but he has also led small-group record dates of his own which feature his huge and expressive sound, a direct descendant of the Sonny Rollins approach that Tabackin has personalized to sumptuous effect. His Concord records as a leader find him at his best, and meetings with Phil Woods and Warne Marsh also put Lew on his mettle. Tom Waits wanted to use Zoot Sims for his *Small Change* record (1977), but Tabackin got the gig instead, and he turned in a brilliant performance on a record which most jazz fans are probably unaware of. Akiyoshi often made a point of featuring his flute playing, which has the same kind of authority as his tenor work.
*Tenority* (Concord)

## Jamaaladeen Tacuma
BASS
*born* 11 June 1956

Tacuma's strange style cut an interesting furrow through the jazz-funk of the 80s. Born Rudy McDaniel, he sang doo-wop in his teens and later played in funk bands before joining Ornette Coleman's Prime Time in 1975. This led to a close alliance with James 'Blood' Ulmer, both on and off record, and ultimately to his own series of albums for the independent Gramavision label: starting with *Show Stopper* (1984), they showcase him in an improvidently eclectic range of settings. Later he became a regular confrère of the Austrian saxophonist Wolfgang Puschnig, in groups which tended to lose his playing in a lot of rambling nonsense. Tacuma's very bright, nibbling style of articulation hews closely to the kind of performing which his fellow Prime Time members followed, that of playing a continuous 'solo' line while still following something like the bassist's traditional function in the ensemble. While he is surely a master of this approach, he's never really found a way of framing it to advantage in his own records and band projects. A four-bass and drums band, Basso Nouveau, went unrecorded.
*Show Stopper* (Gramavision)

## Tailgate

'Tailgate' is the traditional jazz method of playing trombone, as it developed in New Orleans. It involved using the slide to play portamento or slurring notes, which became an essential ingredient in the sound of the jazz-band front line: a musician such as Kid Ory was one of the early tailgate masters. The word seems to derive from the trombonist standing on the 'tailgate' of the vehicle which the band were travelling on, if they were playing in a parade or on the back of an advertising wagon: that gave the trombonist room enough to use the slide to full advantage.

## Aki Takase
PIANO
*born* 26 January 1948

Takase studied in Tokyo and has been in jazz for a long time already, although she didn't have too much impact outside Japan until the 80s, when she began working in both Europe and America. Like so many Japanese musicians, she has an enviable technique and a formidably wide stylistic grasp, which can sew together passages of abstraction and familiar jazz standards into a single performance. Her diminutive figure slamming out line after line of invention is certainly unforgettable once seen in performance. She has recorded with musicians as diverse as David Murray and Alex von Schlippenbach, but her solo recordings, where she relishes every leap into the void, are what must be heard.
*Le Cahier Du Bal* (Leo)

## Akira Tana
DRUMS
*born* 14 March 1952

Tana grew up in San Jose, California, and played both trumpet and drums as a boy, before playing in rock bands in his teens. He studied in Boston and worked locally with a variety of musicians before a move to New York in 1979. Aside from his work as a sideman, he is best known for the group TanaReid, which he formed as a co-leader with the bassist Rufus Reid in 1990, a hard-bop unit which was something like a little

Jazz Messengers in terms of its nurturing young front-line talent.
**TanaReid, *Looking Forward*** (Evidence)

# Horace Tapscott

PIANO
*born* 6 April 1934; *died* 27 February 1999

Tapscott's eminence as a guru to the Californian jazz community persisted for many years. He was actually born in Houston, but his family moved West in 1943, where he played trombone in a high-school band and later worked briefly in Gerald Wilson's orchestra. After some time spent playing in minor local groups, he toured with Lionel Hampton for two years from 1959, and eventually moved from the trombone to the piano because of problems with his teeth. In 1961, he embarked on the formation of a group which came to be called the Pan Afrikan Peoples' Arkestra, and this in turn led to a community body named the Underground Musicians' Association (UGMA), later renamed the Union Of God's Musicians And Artists' Ascension (UGMAA). At various times, dozens of musicians were involved, although comparatively little of the work was actually documented: Butch Morris, David Murray, Arthur Blythe and Roberto Miranda were among those who were associated with it at one time or another. Tapscott took it upon himself to establish his own label, Nimbus, to finally set down the work of his various groups, and by the time of his death it included ten volumes of solo piano music as well as group records by various editions of the Arkestra. Although he also set down some significant recordings elswewhere – particularly the acclaimed *The Dark Tree* (hatOL-OGY, 1989) – Tapscott's music remains all but undiscovered by the wider jazz audience, except the few who have actively sought it out. He died from cancer in 1999. Perhaps his real legacy is in the ongoing work done by such 'students' as Murray and Blythe.
***The Dark Tree*** (hatOLOGY)

# Joe Tarto

TUBA, SOUSAPHONE, BASS
*born* 22 February 1902; *died* 24 August 1986

Tarto was the brass-bass man of choice on the New York session scene of the 20s. He is on an enormous number of records made between around 1925 and 1930, in the company of such specialists as Red Nichols, Miff Mole, Bix Beiderbecke, the Dorseys and the rest of their circle, and he was not a bad arranger himself. Although, like the rest of his generation, he eventually went over to the acoustic bass, tuba and sousaphone were really Joe's thing, and though he spent the next few decades playing in pit bands and as a sideman in the Paul Whiteman orchestra, he was still playing in a group of his own, the New Jersey Brass Quintet, into the 80s.
**Red Nichols, *Red Nichols & Miff Mole 1925–1927*** (Retrieval)

# Buddy Tate

TENOR SAXOPHONE
*born* 22 February 1912; *died* 10 February 2001

Tate's sound exemplified a popular notion of the 'Texas tenors', big, embracing and to some extent one-dimensional. He actually started on alto and played briefly with Count Basie in 1934 before a spell with Andy Kirk; but he rejoined Basie to replace the lately deceased Herschel Evans in 1939, and stayed for ten years. Thereafter he went into small groups and ran a long-standing residency at a Harlem lounge, The Celebrity Club: it lasted until 1971, when the owners decided that something a little more modern was required, but in the meantime Tate had recorded and played regularly elsewhere. He toured as a solo and with Jay McShann and Milt Buckner, and by the 80s was still standing tall as one of the last of a tribe of pre-war saxophone giants, recording with younger men such as Scott Hamilton, and eventually fetching up in such gatherings of veterans as Lionel Hampton's Golden Men Of Jazz. Tate's records are somehow never quite as good as some remember them, and often fall into mere swing-based routine, but he could always provide a very good simulation of the great style of swing saxophone and the record cited basks in the opulence of his sound.
***The Ballad Artistry Of Buddy Tate*** (Sackville)

## Grady Tate

DRUMS, VOCAL
*born* 14 January 1932

Tate began to come to prominence when he arrived in New York in 1963, eventually getting a great deal of work as a drummer in both small-group and big-band situations. Norman Granz used him for many of his dates for Verve during the later 60s, and he also did a lot of work accompanying singers: a vocalist himself, although he rarely demonstrated it at this point, perhaps he could declare an affinity. He continued to play in all manner of mostly mainstream bands through the 80s and 90s, and began to be featured as a singer on a handful of projects, eventually getting a featured role on a Milestone album, *Body And Soul* (1992), which was perhaps not really worth the wait.

**Ray Brown, *Don't Forget The Blues*** (Concord)

## Art Tatum

PIANO
*born* 13 October 1909; *died* 5 November 1956

Although not born blind, Tatum had poor eyesight from an early age, which corrective surgery only slightly improved. His sight was further damaged by a beating in his teens. He learned music in a school in Toledo, and before he was 20 he was a regular in the city's nightlife, playing piano for tips at first but soon enough turning professional, and performing on the radio before the 20s were over. He went to New York in 1932 and made his first solo recordings a year later: his tumultuous version of 'Tiger Rag' must have caused a sensation straight away, but it was only the beginning of Tatum's achievements. He worked in Cleveland, Chicago and Hollywood during the rest of the decade, visited England in 1938, and then founded a trio with Tiny Grimes and Slam Stewart in 1943, embarking on a series of recordings for Capitol (who also had Nat Cole's trio, probably the model for Tatum's own set-up). Thereafter he worked primarily in club engagements, principally in New York and Los Angeles. While his recording regimen slowed around 1950 for a time, in 1953 he was signed by Norman Granz, who recorded him at great length as a soloist – in a series of LPs called *The*

*Genius Of Art Tatum* – and in group contexts, where he performed alongside such musicians as Lionel Hampton, Buddy DeFranco, Ben Webster, Benny Carter and Roy Eldridge. By then, Tatum's almost offhand genius was nearly taken for granted, and Granz's albums restored the idea of the pianist as the master player on his instrument. His command of the piano was so comprehensive and intense that the reaction of many listeners was simply to gape at his abilities. He suggested Fats Waller as his primary influence (Waller returned the favour by exclaiming 'God is in the house!' whenever Tatum walked in), and his early work does suggest a superhuman elaboration on the principles of stride piano; but Tatum integrated every kind of jazz piano technique into a delivery which simply blew past the sum of his influences. While he rarely composed pieces and worked from a lexicon of standard material which he returned to constantly over many years, he managed to introduce the subtlest variations into performances which became, in some ways, a kind of elevated routine: he would regularly offer audiences interpretations which sounded much as he had previously recorded them, and it was down to connoisseurship among his followers to discern how his art continued to develop. Although he seldom chose hectic tempos, every piece would teem with so much decoration that it appeared as if he was always playing fast, and into the scheme of each performance he would cram harmonic subtleties – substitute chords, unusual intervals – so deftly that an inattentive audience would hardly know what they had been hearing. It was a style which impressed and compelled every other virtuoso in the music, which brought Coleman Hawkins, Charlie Parker and practically every jazz piano player into the fold of Tatum's close admirers.

Granz's recordings effectively summarized and celebrated Tatum's art. While he never took the chance to stretch out, even in the new long-playing era – most of the individual tracks are still only three or four minutes in length – many of the solos are definitive statements on a large number of his favourite pieces. The group sessions also include almost numberless wonderful moments, the sessions with Carter, Webster and DeFranco in particular rising to almost

unbelievable peaks of creativity. In the end, the sessions turned out to be Tatum's swan-song. He continued an innocuous round of touring in modest venues, but his health, including a probable diabetic condition, was suffering, not helped by his enormous daily intake of alcohol. He died as a result of kidney disease a few weeks before his 47th birthday. One tragic aspect of his art is that, even in his later recordings, he was never particularly well recorded as a pianist. What would Tatum sound like, on a fine piano, in today's impeccable studio conditions?
**The Complete Pablo Solo Masterpieces** (Pablo)

## Art Taylor

DRUMS
*born* 6 April 1929; *died* 6 February 1995

'A' was another in the seemingly endless line of great New York drummers. He debuted on record behind Coleman Hawkins in 1951, and from that point onwards he was constantly busy. Some of his 50s gigs included spells with Buddy DeFranco, Bud Powell, George Wallington, Miles Davis, Donald Byrd and Thelonious Monk. He ran his own Taylor's Wailers for a time in 1956 and went to Europe with Byrd in 1958; finding the Old World much to his taste, he settled in France and Belgium and only went back to the US to tour. While in Europe he also began interviewing fellow musicians, the results being published in 1977 as *Notes And Tones*, a candid and revealing series of conversations. He finally returned home in 1984 and began bandleading again. The new Taylor's Wailers began to look like replacing Blakey's Jazz Messengers as a hard-bop academy, but AT himself became ill with cancer and he was forced to call time on his playing. If Blakey was the more powerful drummer, Taylor was nevertheless a master of the kit, and a creatively swinging force in every group he played for: he is on hundreds of hard-bop dates, and they all benefit from his presence.
**Taylor's Tenors** (Prestige/OJC)

## Billy Taylor

PIANO
*born* 24 July 1921

Although Taylor has had a busy enough career as a pianist, his real work in jazz has been as an educator and propagandist. He grew up in Washington DC and studied piano from an early age. He was in New York by 1944, where he subbed for Bud Powell in Dizzy Gillespie's band for a time, and he played for numerous leaders in various styles before eventually becoming the house pianist at the Birdland club in 1951. On record he worked mainly as his own leader, helming trios and larger groups for a number of labels, including Prestige, Roost, ABC-Paramount and Savoy. While little of his playing really makes an individual mark – his facility in the right hand mixes the bop stylists with the even more florid approach of Art Tatum – Taylor has always been good at reaching an audience, and in some ways it's surprising that his records aren't more widely known than they are. His real forte, though, has been away from mere playing. He began writing, lecturing and holding jazz workshops in the middle 50s, became a disc jockey on New York radio, and also became a regular on television, never missing the opportunity to beat the drum for jazz. He helped establish the Jazzmobile initiative in the city in 1965 and has remained devoted to it since. While he founded his own label, Taylor Made, in the 80s, his work on radio and as a speaker has continued to take up more of his time than actual playing. Honoured in his senior years as a great and loyal friend to the music and its performers, Billy also contributed one of the most significant political songs of the so-called civil rights era, 'I Wish I Knew How It Would Feel To Be Free', which for many years was the theme tune to a popular film review programme on British television, but which is better known in the US as an anthem of its time.
**It's A Matter Of Pride** (GRP)

## Cecil Taylor

PIANO
*born* 15 March 1929

Taylor grew up on Long Island and took piano lessons at his mother's behest. He briefly studied at the New England Conservatory and then played in R&B bands (one leader said to him, 'Boy, where is your left hand?', an incentive for greater ambi-dexterity), and with Hot Lips Page, before embarking on leading groups of his own. With sidemen including Steve Lacy, Dennis Charles and Buell Neidlinger, he cut an album, *Jazz Advance* (1956), one of the great debuts in jazz history, and played a resi-dency at The Five Spot club in New York. This attracted critical attention, but no real audience: Taylor continued to work only occasionally over the next five years, with Archie Shepp in place of Lacy, and made a handful of other records, but compared to Ornette Coleman's explosive arrival his music had only a modest impact at that point, despite an approach which was at least as free-thinking as Coleman's and per-haps even more 'revolutionary'. The music on the early records depicts a world where bebop is dissolving into open spaces, yet where tonality still endures; where the piano is an orchestra (or, as he would later suggest, 'eighty-eight tuned drums'); where chrorus lengths and bar-lines are vanishing, yet their outline remains. There are still numerous influences audible in Taylor's music at this point, including Ellington, Brubeck and Powell, but its restless activity and emotional complexity speak of another time rapidly rushing into view.

It wasn't quite that fast: Taylor had to work as a dishwasher to make ends meet, and a *Down Beat* 'new star' award in 1962 came at a point where he was hardly work-ing at all. Gil Evans sponsored an album where some of the pianist's compositions were premiered (*Into The Hot*, 1961), and then a re-formed Taylor group toured Scandinavia in the winter of 1962–3, where a trio performance at the Café Montmartre with Jimmy Lyons and Sunny Murray set down one of the essential early Taylor docu-ments. By the middle 60s, when he made such records as *Unit Structures* and *Con-quistador!* for Blue Note, there was little left of his older jazz influences, and live record-ings from the later 60s, with Sam Rivers and others, suggest a music that was becoming torrrential in its relentless urgency. The pian-ist would lead his groups through improvisa-tions which seemed to last for hours, driven as much by kinetic force as any musical imperative, and listening through them

could seem as demanding on the audience as it was for the musicians to play the music. By the 70s, this had throttled back again: his great solo records of the decade, including *Silent Tongues* (1974) and *Air Above Mountains* (1976), laid out many of his concerns with fascinating clarity, with his interest in contrasting structures and musical 'cells', from which great vistas were drawn, made powerfully manifest. The years of neglect and poverty were largely behind him: by the 80s he was a feted member of a worldwide avant-garde, and at the end of the decade, when a great festival was held in his honour in Berlin in 1988, the avant-garde world paid their respects back to him.

Taylor's generosity with his music has been one of the most pleasurable aspects of jazz of the past two or three decades. Unlike Ornette Coleman, who has been almost secretive about his work, Taylor has been prolifically recorded, outgoing with students and interviewers, and prodigious in the per-formance of his music, even into his old age. A trio with Tony Oxley and William Parker has been regularly convened, and Taylor's energy and creativity, in this context and with such other, disparate figures as Max Roach, Bill Dixon and Evan Parker, are enough to marvel at.

*Cecil Taylor In Berlin 1988* (FMP)

# Creed Taylor
RECORD PRODUCER
*born* 13 May 1929

Taylor's mission was to make jazz commer-cial without losing its artistic weight, but it proved to be an almost disastrous miscon-ception. He began producing records for Bethlehem in 1954, and from there moved to ABC-Paramount as head of A&R, where he founded the Impulse! imprint in 1960. A year later, he had moved on to Verve, where he began to put his ideas into operation: he dropped some of the more swing-styled musicians and JATP leftovers, and instead brought in Jimmy Smith, Bill Evans and Wes Montgomery, artists who could fit in with an enlightened new style. Taylor's idea was to create a kind of credible easy-listening, and Montgomery, in particular, was almost like his test case for success, a brilliant improviser whose none the less mellow and easy-on-the-ear timbre could surely be directed towards playing pretty for the people. Taylor moved on yet again, to Herb Alpert's A&M label, in 1967, and took Montgomery with him: the guitarist's final records dismayed many who loved his more straight-ahead work, yet somehow he managed to fulfil Taylor's ambition of mixing soothing music and high-calibre playing. Thereafter, though, Taylor began to overreach himself. He formed a company of his own, CTI, which signed George Benson, Freddie Hubbard and others, and though some of the albums were commercial hits, others were dramatic failures, and it went bust within a decade. Little of the music which was made for CTI today sounds much more than dismal. But Taylor set some wheels in motion: his work surely laid the foundations for the smooth-jazz boom of the 90s and beyond.

# John Taylor

PIANO
*born* 25 September 1942

Taylor is one of the few British musicians to sustain a significant international reputation. He came out of Manchester in the early 60s, largely self-taught, and he fitted right into the burgeoning new London scene, soon part of a circle which included Alan Skidmore, John Surman, Harry Beckett, Mike Gibbs, Kenny Wheeler and Norma Winstone, whom he married in 1972. He established the trio Azimuth, with Winstone and Wheeler, around 1977, making three albums with it for ECM, and since then he has freelanced as a leader himself, as a duo partner with Wheeler, Tony Coe, Stan Sulzmann and others, and with a group which has recorded under Peter Erskine's name for ECM. Musicians love playing with Taylor because he combines an accompanist's sensitivity with a soloist's largesse far better than most pianists. He likes the long seamless line, and although often alluded to as a Bill Evans disciple, his playing seems both like and unlike the American's: his melodies have a folkish bent that Evans would never have considered, and that has tended to disguise what is actually a powerful and often rhythmically aggressive delivery.
*Rosslyn* (ECM)

# Martin Taylor

GUITAR
*born* 20 October 1956

The most successful British jazz musician of his generation. Taylor began playing guitar as a child, in his native Harlow, Essex, and soon attained local stardom: 'He's a guitar wizard – at eight', said a headline in the *Harlow Citizen*. Most of his technique he picked up himself, but Ike Isaacs became a mentor to him, and he worked all through the 70s with British mainstreamers such as Dave Shepherd and Alan Elsdon, as well as playing on cruise ships. He began working with Stéphane Grappelli in 1979, an association which lasted into the 90s, and in his own music he moved steadily towards solo playing as his main activity. By the 90s, he was travelling the world as a solo guitarist and in great demand. His immaculate style has the knack of speaking directly to both the Joe Pass kind of jazz audience and the vast following which the guitar enjoys as a generic instrument: 'the way I play solo is more akin to classical guitar playing. The whole touch, finger-style playing . . . I've been really inspired by piano players, and I think of it in that way as being a complete instrument.' After a rather scrappy series of records, he eventually signed to the Scottish independent label Linn and recorded a fine series of albums for them, including two by his Reinhardt tribute group, Spirit Of Django. Sony signed him for what turned out to be two rather dreary sets aimed at the American radio market, but let him go after that (at least, he says, it opened up the Japanese market to him). He now records for an independent of his own, P3. Awarded an MBE for services to jazz music, Taylor's shrewdness and careful management of his career have nevertheless rather set him aside from the rest of British jazz: impeccably professional, he has instead mastered the broader idiom of guitar music.
*Solo* (P3)

# Sam 'The Man' Taylor

TENOR SAXOPHONE
*born* 12 July 1916; *died* 5 October 1990

Taylor had a busy if undistinguished sideman career from the late 30s in big bands, with Cootie Williams, Lucky Millinder and

Cab Calloway, but he came into his own in the 50s as a session musician, when he began fronting records which were either in the spirit of *Rockin' Sax And Rollin' Organ* (MGM, 1957) or the more romantically inclined *Blue Mist* (1955), a title which led to a number of sequels with either 'blue' or 'mist' in the titles. Another memorable concept was his 1958 date for Metrojazz, *Jazz For Commuters*. This season in the sun lasted him into the early 60s, but he disappeared after that.

**Blue Mist** (MGM)

## John Tchicai
ALTO AND TENOR SAXOPHONES
*born* 28 April 1936

Born in Copenhagen of a Danish mother and Congolese father, Tchicai took up clarinet and alto sax in his teens. After working in European festivals, he went to New York in 1962, where he joined Archie Shepp and Don Cherry in the New York Contemporary Five, after that playing with Roswell Rudd in the New York Art Quartet. Never a saxophone screamer, Tchicai favoured a melodic approach somewhat akin to Ornette Coleman's, although his sound had a slightly peeled quality which made his solos a dramatic contrast to those of many of his fellow musicians: he is certainly one of the odd men out on John Coltrane's *Ascension* (1965). He went back to Denmark in 1966 and led a band of his own, Cadentia Nova Danica, for some years, but later spent more time teaching than performing. In the 80s he switched from alto to tenor, getting a bigger sound in the process, and he enjoyed a long association with Pierre Dørge's New Jungle Orchestra, although he was otherwise on record comparatively rarely. A duo session with Misha Mengelberg, *Grandpa's Spells* (Storyville, 1992), was a timely reminder of his powers. In 1991, he settled in California to be near the rest of his family. Tchicai's career has often been conducted out of the jazz public eye, and his music is perhaps little more than an interesting diversion in the avant-garde developments of the 60s and beyond.

**New York Art Quartet** (ESP)

## Jack Teagarden
TROMBONE, VOCAL
*born* 29 August 1905; *died* 15 January 1964

The eldest of the four Texas Teagarden siblings – Charlie (1913–84) was a fine trumpeter, Norma (1911–96) an accomplished pianist and Cub (1915–69) a drummer who eventually quit the music business – Jack seems to have taken to trombone playing with an ease and skill that was all but unprecedented, at a time when the horn was the clumsiest and least accommodating of jazz instruments. He joined the local band of Peck Kelley in 1921, already impressing other musicians, but came to wider prominence in the New York scene of the middle 20s, with bandleaders Roger Wolfe Kahn and Ben Pollack. Although he could play with lovely sonority, it didn't stand in the way of his solos coming out pepper-hot, and flecked with blue intonations. He was already singing, too: 'That's A Serious Thing', made with an Eddie Condon group in 1929, showed how a lazy Texas drawl could establish a whole style of jazz vocals. Teagarden joined the big Paul Whiteman ensemble in 1933, hungry for some security, and was featured on many speciality pieces; but he decided to lead his own band from 1939. A poor businessman and slack disciplinarian, Tea wasn't really suited to bandleading, and he struggled through several years of at best modest success. He joined the Louis Armstrong All Stars in 1947 and the pairing of Teagarden and Pops seemed irresistible at first; yet the trombonist disliked his sideman status and the band's routine of one-nighters discouraged him. In 1951 he went back to leading small groups of his own: usually his was far and away the principal talent in the group, although he didn't seem to pay much mind to any shortcomings around him. He campaigned for years against an antiquated cabaret tax law which did not allow him to sing in clubs. His own playing remained close to impeccable, although his singing voice started to sound more exhausted than lazy, and his records in the LP era are a very mixed lot – many have yet to see CD reissue. Worn down by years of drinking, he died in New Orleans in 1964, still on the road. Although his best work is scattered across many years and under many flags – with Armstrong, Pollack, Bobby Hackett, Condon and others – the wonderful balance between inventive hot playing and the sweetly fluent, singing tone marks out almost any record he plays on as something special.

*The Indispensable Jack Teagarden* (French RCA)

## Temperance Seven
GROUP

Although first formed as far back as 1955, The Temperance Seven enjoyed a brief hey-day in the early 60s, when some of their singles managed to crack the top of the pop charts. Although the group were never entirely serious – how could any British band dedicated to playing dance and rag-time pieces from the teens and 20s be entirely serious? – there was always a dedi-cation to getting the spirit right which has lent their activity some credence. The band has seen numerous personnel changes (hardly surprising considering that it has lasted through five decades) although origi-nal drummer Brian Innes has been a con-stant. Paul McDowell played trombone and sang on the band's most successful records, and John R T Davies, better known for his studio remastering work, joined in 1959. Some of their early records are shocking – *The Temperance Seven + 1* (1961) is a slap-stick wreck of a session – but they did get better. It's hard to believe that this group once made it into the top ten.

*The Temperance Seven, 1961* (Parlophone)

## Joe Temperley
BARITONE SAXOPHONE
*born* 29 September 1929

Temperley came south from his native Fife to play in London dance bands at the end of the 40s, and after various associations he worked in Humphrey Lyttelton's band between 1958 and 1965. For the past 40 years he has been based in New York, taking the baritone player's necessary role in big-band saxophone sections – with Woody Herman, Clark Terry, Thad Jones–Mel Lewis and others – as well as studio work. But he has found a role as a paterfamilias since 1990, as the resident baritone man in the Lincoln Center Jazz Orchestra. He returns to the UK every so often and has made some small-group records for Hep, which display a con-

ventional, graceful approach to the swing-to-bop style.

*Nightingale* (Hep)

## Tempo
RECORD COMPANY

First established by the Tempo Record Society of London in 1946, it recorded new British groups playing in the traditional idiom and reissued out-of-print American material from the 20s. In 1953 it was taken over by Vogue, which halted the reissue series and slowed down the new material. In 1955, though, the label was unexpectedly reborn as a modern outlet. Tony Hall, a dash-ing and tireless supporter of the modern London scene, who did some freelance work for Decca, the company which had in the interim taken over Vogue, persuaded them to let him mastermind a series of new records using Tempo as the imprint. As a result, Hall managed to produce and release sessions by Tubby Hayes, Victor Feldman, Dizzy Reece, Jimmy Deuchar, Ronnie Scott and others, in what is, with hindsight, the most significant series of modern British jazz records of its time. While it only lasted a very few years, the label's reputation has continued to grow since its demise, and orig-inal Tempo pressings of these records are now worth a king's ransom to collectors.

## Jacky Terrasson
PIANO
*born* 27 November 1966

Terrasson grew up in Paris and went to Berklee before returning to Paris, where he worked for a time on the club scene. He moved to New York in 1990, and after winning the Thelonious Monk Piano Competition three years later he seemed set for a meteoric rise, signing to Blue Note a year later and embarking on a series of piano-trio records. These have had some impact, but Terrasson's musical expertise is let down by a shameless addiction to sen-sationalism. He takes a revisionist approach to standards which can leave them as un-recognizable cadavers, and the record cited wavers between sensitively created pieces and tunes where the group sprint from one end of the expressive spectrum to the other

with no sense of any musical logic. A meeting with Cassandra Wilson (*Rendezvous*, 1997) was hopelessly confused.
**Alive** (Blue Note)

# Clark Terry
TRUMPET, FLUGELHORN, VOCAL
*born* 14 December 1920

Nobody ever says a bad word about Clark Terry. As a brass player, bandleader, mentor and spokesman for jazz music, he is incomparable. He grew up in St Louis and played there in touring shows in the late 30s, before joining a navy band in 1942. He then worked with Lionel Hampton, in a group nominally led by George Hudson which Terry actually directed, and with Charlie Barnet's orchestra, before enlisting with Count Basie in 1948, subsequently also working in Basie's small group. In 1951, he moved on to Duke Ellington's orchestra, where he became an indispensable part of Duke's brass section, on both trumpet and flugelhorn – the latter an instrument which had thus far enjoyed very little jazz attention, and which Terry helped make into a significant part of the brass player's arsenal. Ellington featured him regularly, and in such setpieces as the *Such Sweet Thunder* suite (1957), his mischievous humour and improvisational exuberance often light the touchpaper for the whole band. After leaving Ellington, Clark found himself in constant demand. He was a studio regular all through the 60s and much of the 70s, held down a chair in the *Tonight Show* band (the first black staff musician at NBC), starred in Gerry Mulligan's Concert Jazz Band, co-led a quintet with Bob Brookmeyer, toured with Jazz At The Philharmonic, founded an orchestra (sometimes known as Clark Terry's Big B-A-D Band) which lasted on and off into the 80s, got himself in the thick of jazz education, and acted as an inspiration to numerous trumpet players as a result. Later groups, such as the nonet Clark Terry's Spacemen and the Statesmen Of Jazz, surrounded him with fellow veterans, but even when he was the eldest of the gang, nobody outdid Terry for musical energy. His instantly identifiable style is perhaps a mix of such forebears as Rex Stewart and, reputedly, a school of mellow-toned St Louis trumpeters who didn't otherwise gain much attention. On flugelhorn, which he increasingly adopted as time went on, he established a burring, beautifully melodious sound which more or less set the style for the instrument. While remaining a musician who belonged to the swing idiom, he had little trouble addressing the issues of bop, and has found himself amenable to pretty much any jazz situation. His vocal speciality is a tune called 'Mumbles', which he loves to throw out to audiences as an encore, a mush-mouthed assemblage of nonsense scat. He was seriously ill at the start of the new century but amazed everyone by playing again soon afterwards, still the irrepressible Clark Terry.
**Memories Of Duke** (Pablo/OJC)

# Frank Teschemacher
CLARINET
*born* 13 March 1906; *died* 1 March 1932

Teschemacher enjoyed a formidable reputation among musicians. He started on clarinet in 1925, was soon involved with the young Chicago school then coming together, and went to New York in 1928, where his hot, fluent playing made him a favourite in many bands. It is all the more disappointing that his relatively few appearances on record are, for the most part, nothing special, and fluffs and indifferent intonation spoil what are often interesting ideas. Max Kaminsky suggested that he 'froze up' in the recording studio and never gave of his best, but a serious drink problem probably didn't help either. He was killed when thrown from a car being driven by Wild Bill Davison.
**Eddie Condon, *1927–1938*** (Classics)

# Henri Texier
BASS
*born* 27 January 1945

Texier is a Parisian who's been involved in his city's jazz since his teens. He worked in the city's clubs in the early 60s, backing American visitors, and from there led small groups (including such players as Enrico Rava and Michel Portal) as well as doing sideman work. He was part of Phil Woods's band European Rhythm Machine for four years from 1968, and in the 70s he worked in a steadily widening vista: playing solo, trying free improvisation, using traditional French folk instruments and themes, playing with bagpipers and bell-ringers, writing film-scores, and touring all through southern Europe and north Africa, absorbing the local sounds and images – he has a significant interest in the visual arts too – as he went. Texier's discography accommodates most of these adventures, with a long list of records for the independent Label Bleu. Texier has the seniority to be able to assemble a band like the one for *Respect* (1995), which includes Lee Konitz, Bob Brookmeyer, Steve Swallow and Paul Motian, as well as taking on more personal projects such as the worldly *Mad Nomads* (1995).

**Mad Nomads** (Label Bleu)

## Eje Thelin

TROMBONE

*born* 9 September 1928; *died* 18 May 1990

Thelin's music, sometimes dour, sometimes nuttily sweet, never quite settled down, and was perhaps the better for it. He played Dixieland in his native Sweden when a teen-ager, and then played bebop with Putte Wickman before forming a quintet which secured success beyond his national borders in the early 60s. From 1967 he spent five years teaching in Austria, but he returned home in 1972 and worked as a composer, arranger and performer, taking on the bits of free jazz which appealed to him, dabbling in electronics, and experimenting with long-form and large-scale music. His final work, *Raggruppamento*, was made when he was already ill with cancer and he doesn't play on the recording, but its various textures and ideas make an agreeable summary of his work. The record cited shows off his quintet in full flow.

**At The German Jazz Festival 1964** (Dragon)

## Art Themen

TENOR AND SOPRANO SAXOPHONES

*born* 26 November 1939

Themen does the rather rare jazz double of saxophonist and orthopaedic surgeon. Given that he has never made music a full-time matter, his career has been busy, without his playing getting the kind of documen-tation it has deserved. He played in the London blues boom of the early 60s, and toured with the likes of Joe Cocker, before concentrating more specifically on jazz from the 70s. He was a long-standing sideman of Stan Tracey's, while also playing with Graham Collier, Dave Gelly, Michael Garrick, Al Haig and Henry Lowther, just occasion-ally leading a group of his own. As the Charlie Rouse to Tracey's Monk, Themen has played a delightful cameo role for many years, and it's a shame that no label has really taken the trouble to create a starring role for this individual stylist, whose tenor playing never sounds too much like anyone else's.

**Stan Tracey,** *Portraits Plus* (Blue Note)

## Bob Thiele

PRODUCER

*born* 27 July 1922; *died* 30 January 1996

Thiele had been in record production work for many years – he formed the Signature label in the 40s, and from there worked for Coral, Dot and Roulette – before he arrived at Impulse! in 1962, where he did his most important work. He directed much of John Coltrane's work for the label, cleverly pack-aging one of the most difficult propositions of the time and making much of Coltrane's music seem almost friendly in its outreach, as well as helming records by Pharoah Sanders and others on the label. In 1969 he formed his own label, Flying Dutchman, which has something of a cult following among vinyl collectors, given the often bizarrely eclectic range of artists it pro-duced, and he later set up the Doctor Jazz and Red Baron imprints through Columbia.

## Toots Thielemans

HARMONICA, GUITAR

*born* 29 April 1922

Others have tried it, but Thielemans is really the only musician to create a long-lasting career out of the jazz harmonica. Born in Brussels, he started on accordion and didn't actually try the harmonica until he was 17. Besides that, he also taught himself the guitar, and ever since has played guitar and harmonica and also added whistling to his list of accomplishments. He befriended the boppers at jazz festivals in Europe in the late 40s, played with Benny Goodman in 1950, and the following year emigrated to the US and eventually became a citizen. He was in George Shearing's groups for six years and then had a surprise solo hit with his tune 'Bluesette' (1961), which he originally recorded as a guitarist and whistler. While he is fair enough at both of these skills, though, it's his harmonica playing which is exceptional. On top of his bebop stylings he added the influence of John Coltrane's playing, and allied with his natural flair for improvising, the result has been a career full of whirling, delightful music, often in very demanding company: at the age of 78 he recorded a series of duets with Kenny Werner which showed his powers undimmed. Perhaps his best record, though, is the one cited, where he tackles composers such as Monk, Thad Jones and Wayne Shorter, and plays all of them with elegance and ingenuity.

*Only Trust Your Heart* (Concord)

# Ed Thigpen
DRUMS
*born* 28 December 1930

Ed's father Ben drummed for Andy Kirk for many years, and the younger Thigpen followed in the family business. Although born in Chicago, he was raised in California and started out behind Cootie Williams, before going into the army. In 1954, he backed Dinah Washington, then worked with Bud Powell before two long stints in piano trios: Billy Taylor (1956–9) and Oscar Peterson (1959–65), the latter an association which he is still best remembered for. After this, he freelanced as he pleased and played in Ella Fitzgerald's backing group before moving over to Copenhagen in 1972, where he still lives. Because he has mostly worked in situations where the spotlight is far from the drummer, Ed's work has perhaps been a shade undervalued, but he is a top-notch accompanist and can swing whatever band is in front of him with deceptive ease. He has become a great patrician influence in his adopted home and has made a fine series of albums under his own leadership for the Danish Stunt label.

*Out Of The Storm* (Verve)

# Jesper Thilo
TENOR SAXOPHONE
*born* 28 November 1941

A native of Copenhagen, Thilo studied clarinet at the Conservatory and worked in the band of modern Danish godfather Arnvid Meyer in the early 60s. From the mid-70s onwards he was leading bands of his own, as well as doing radio and big-band work. Thilo has set down a long sequence of albums for the Music Mecca label, and all of them showcase his beautiful, hearty sound and huge swing. He is in the mighty lineage of Zoot Sims, Dexter Gordon and Lockjaw Davis, but American voices have long since been subsumed into his own style, and there are few more accomplished saxophonists at work in continental Europe. It's only a shame that he works outside his home terrain so infrequently.

*Movin' Out* (Music Mecca)

# Third stream

Rarely has such a fashionable and potentially convenient term dropped out of common usage so quickly. Probably coined by Gunther Schuller around 1957, it was designed to describe an amalgamation of Western classical music and jazz – essentially, the supposed structural sophistications of the former combining with the vitality and spontaneity of the latter. This was somewhat different to the perceived respectability of a piece such as Gershwin's *Rhapsody In Blue*: there was a more premeditated and calculating motive behind a third-stream project. Yet the whole notion of an ongoing third-stream movement quickly fell apart, despite the vigorous canvassing by figures such as Schuller, primarily because, by the time the 'movement' had come into being, the process of diversification in postwar musical culture had already gone beyond the stage of uniting behind such a deliberately orchestrated initiative. This didn't prevent a great deal of interesting and often vital music being created under the 'third stream' banner: works by figures as diverse as John Lewis, Bill Russo, Don Ellis, Jimmy Giuffre and J J Johnson could all qualify as third stream. But most of these were simply conceived as stand-alone works which should be appreciated on their own merits rather than as representatives of a figurative school.

## Gary Thomas
TENOR SAXOPHONE, FLUTE
*born* 10 June 1961

Thomas has been in some high-profile jazz situations and his saxophone playing is widely admired, but his career seems to have completely stalled. Born in Baltimore, he first came to prominence in Jack DeJohnette's Special Edition, joining in 1985 and working with the drummer on and off for the next seven years (Greg Osby was also in the group, a formidably ferocious front line). While associated with many of the members of the M-Base enclave, Thomas was only a satellite member of that group. He also worked with Miles Davis's band before commencing his own leadership career on record. After three records for Enja, he was signed to JMT (and subsequently its successor, Winter & Winter), where he created a series of records which mixed fusion and funk settings with almost unconscionably dark and troubling playing, a very different feel to the usual music in this mould. He added rap ingredients for a time, but had abandoned these for the record cited, perhaps his most intense and focused work: the use of flute adds a strange lyricism, while the tenor is bruising and brutally eloquent. Yet Thomas has seemingly had no opportunity to add to this work, and after a gap of several years he has much ground to make up.
*Pariah's Pariah* (Winter & Winter)

## Joe Thomas
TENOR SAXOPHONE, VOCAL
*born* 19 June 1909; *died* 3 August 1986

Thomas started on alto in Horace Henderson's band, but switched to tenor and joined Jimmie Lunceford's orchestra in 1933. A showman and an extrovert with a shouting tenor sound, Thomas was nevertheless a loyal sideman, and even after many of his colleagues had fallen out with their leader, Thomas remained a Lunceford man: after Jimmie's death he took over the leadership, although he eventually decided to form his own band, which worked in a style

that shifted from swing to R&B: 'Big Foot' (1950) is a characteristic track. After 1951 he went into the family business of funeral parlours, but still played occasionally, and there was a comeback of sorts when he appeared at the 1970 Montreux Festival, which led to occasional work in Kansas City, where he had settled in his later years.
**Jimmie Lunceford, *1937–1939*** (Classics)

## Leon Thomas
VOCAL
*born* 4 October 1937; *died* 8 May 1999

Thomas's maverick career suggests a line back to such figures as Leo Watson and Babs Gonzalez. He moved to New York in 1958 and found what work he could as a singer, playing occasionally with Count Basie and later with a variety of small-group leaders, though he didn't get on record until his appearance with Pharoah Sanders on *Karma* (Impulse!, 1969). Thereafter he worked primarily as a leader, making a series of records for Flying Dutchman which have something of a cult following, and later turning up on small labels, although his career had slowed dramatically by the 80s, and it was only the interest in his early records which brought him some late attention in the 90s. Thomas's style was a wacky mix of blues, hippie mysticism, yodelling, scat, soul shouting and gospel preaching. He tends to come across best in minuscule doses.
***Spirits Known And Unknown*** (Flying Dutchman)

## René Thomas
GUITAR
*born* 25 February 1927; *died* 3 January 1975

Born in Liège, Thomas began working on the Paris scene in the early 50s, before moving to Montreal in 1956. From there, he made occasional visits to New York, where he worked with Sonny Rollins (he is on Rollins's *Brass/Trio*, 1958), and made his sole American record as a leader, the disc cited. He returned to Europe in 1961 and spent the rest of his career working steadily, touring with Stan Getz at the end of the 60s. Jimmy Raney was Thomas's idol, and he played his own remarkably fresh and clear-headed variation on Raney's approach: there is too little of him in featured roles on record. He died sud denly of a heart attack while working in Spain.

***Guitar Groove*** (Jazzland/OJC)

# Barbara Thompson
SAXOPHONES, FLUTE
*born* 27 July 1944

Though she studied clarinet in her teens, Thompson had no special interest in jazz until she heard Johnny Hodges playing with Duke Ellington, and she began to study the saxophone while at the Royal College Of Music. From the mid-60s she began playing on the London scene, eventually leading her own groups. Her primary performing vehicle has been the small band Paraphernalia, which has had a shifting personnel, although regular members have been keyboardist Peter Lemer and drummer Jon Hiseman, who is Thompson's husband. Away from this, she has played mainly in the United Jazz And Rock Ensemble, but for the most part Thompson's is the unusual case of a British musician who has taken care to focus very specifically on her own writing and performing context. Paraphernalia has often settled for a sometimes mundane rock feel to a lot of its music, which tends to disguise the leader's meticulous compositional detail, and her often complex harmonic thinking: as a soloist she also takes an unhackneyed line, sometimes playing two instruments simultaneously and keeping bebop licks at arm's length. Her performing has been interrupted by illness in recent years, but she insists that she is still working and has a full diary ahead.

***A Cry From The Heart*** (VeraBra)

# Sir Charles Thompson
PIANO
*born* 21 March 1918

Sir Charles (the knighthood came from that inveterate bestower of honours Lester Young) has made several telling contributions to jazz history. He wrote 'Robbins' Nest', a hit for Illinois Jacquet in the 40s; he played a key role in the sessions for Vanguard which originally coined the sobriquet 'mainstream jazz'; and he was versatile enough to be favoured by such disparate talents as Young, Charlie Parker and Buck

Clayton as an accompanist. Born in Ohio, he played mostly on the West Coast until moving to New York in the 40s. From the 50s onwards he has been sighted mostly in small-group situations, and has lived and worked in the US, Canada and Europe. In his 80s, he was still playing 'Robbins' Nest', and cutting music for the Chicago label Delmark, which often likes to support fondly remembered veterans. His piano style is, inevitably, in a classic mainstream bag: deft, economical, bluesily swinging.

***His Personal Vanguard Recordings*** (Vanguard)

# Eddie Thompson
PIANO
*born* 31 May 1925; *died* 6 November 1986

Thompson was a familiar figure on the London bebop scene of the 50s, and he was house pianist at Ronnie Scott's around 1959–60. In 1962 he left for New York and stayed ten years; in 1972 he came home and, despite sometimes working in a duo with Roger Kellaway, remained based in the UK until his death. Thompson was an eclectic improviser, who started with Art Tatum as his guiding star, and his style moved through queer phases that sounded as if he was trying on different suits as he went forward. Born blind, and an immaculate wit, he was a great one for getting an audience on his side: 'This one's called "When Your Liver Has Gone".' In the end, he went rather under-recorded, and only Hep's Alastair Robertson, who thought him a master, latterly made records with the pianist.

***Memories Of You*** (HEP)

# Gail Thompson
SAXOPHONES, BASS
*born* 15 June 1958

Thompson was a powerful activist and musician on the London scene for a long time, until illness obliged her to cut back. She played baritone sax with NYJO and went on to form bands of her own, Gail Force the most notable, as well as co-founding the Jazz Warriors in the mid-80s (there is some confusion as to who did what in the beginnings of that group, but with her can-do approach Thompson was surely a prime mover). She played with Art Blakey's

Jazz Messengers for a brief spell, but found she could not play the saxophone any longer because of what seemed to be a muscle problem: in response she took up the electric bass, but was eventually diagnosed with multiple sclerosis. Since then, she has worked primarily as a composer, and, ambitious as ever, has assembled big bands to play her latest work.

*Jazz Africa* (Enja)

## Lucky Thompson
TENOR SAXOPHONE
*born* 16 June 1924

Eli Thompson's career had its share of misfortune. In the early 40s, he played in the bands of Lionel Hampton, Billy Eckstine and Count Basie before moving from New York to Los Angeles, where he worked as a studio player and recorded prolifically: he is on some of Charlie Parker's Dial sessions, and he cut a pair of classic titles for Victor in 'Boppin' The Blues' and 'Just One More Chance' (1947), records which sum up his allegiance to Coleman Hawkins and Don Byas and his grasp of how that style could be used for bebop. He was back in New York in 1948 and for the next eight years played on record dates while also establishing his own publishing company. He toured Europe with Stan Kenton, and after an incident where he reputedly had an altercation with Joe Glaser and was made unwelcome in his old New York haunts, he settled in France, staying until 1962, picking up the soprano sax, and recording with local players. Back in the US his career was going nowhere, and eventually he returned to Europe, again living in France between 1968 and 1971. When he returned home for the last time, he taught for a period but eventually, embittered by the way his business had gone, Thompson virtually retired in 1974. His life since hasn't been much documented, but he has apparently lived in various parts of the US, gave away his horns in exchange for dental work, suffered a street mugging and was eventually taken into care in the early 90s. He is a proud and sometimes difficult man, whose beautiful sound on the tenor and a notably individual way with the soprano are now dispersed across a substantial but often obscure discography: there is wonderful playing on his 50s dates

with Miles Davis and Milt Jackson, and some of his later own-name albums are undeservedly neglected.

*Lucky Strikes* (Prestige/OJC)

## Malachi Thompson
TRUMPET
*born* 21 August 1949

Thompson was raised in Chicago and played R&B music before joining the AACM in 1969. He led small groups and played in large ensembles in the city before moving to New York in 1974. While he worked there busily enough, with Kalaparush Maurice McIntyre, Sam Rivers, Archie Shepp and others, Thompson had few opportunities to record, and eventually he formed his own Freebop band, which played in a style suggested by its name. Many saxophonists came and went in the line-up, but his most faithful partner was Carter Jefferson, who remained close to Thompson until his death in 1993. In the middle 80s Thompson left the US and settled in Vienna: he returned in 1989, having been diagnosed with lymphoma, but he recovered and has since led the Freebop band back in Chicago, recording with it regularly for Delmark, as well as taking a very prominent role in community arts programmes and disseminating the word about Chicago's musical tradition. This full-circle career has made him into a leading 'local guy' in American jazz and a great spirit in his own scene. The Freebop records have perhaps never quite found the final spark of excellence, but as a body of work they're a pleasing and often impassioned portrait of one aspect of Chicagoan jazz.

*Freebop Now!* (Delmark)

## Claude Thornhill
PIANO, LEADER
*born* 10 August 1909; *died* 1 July 1965

Like Raymond Scott and a handful of other American composers, Thornhill had a sideways relationship with jazz. Originally from Indiana, he worked with territory bands before moving to New York, where he wrote for several dance orchestras as well as MD'ing studio sessions. He ran his own big band from 1940, and after war service reconvened it in 1946. The Thornhill orchestra of

the late 40s is among the most admired of its kind – though more often by critics than the public, and even big-band fans might struggle to remember more than one or two titles by the orchestra. Gil Evans worked with Thornhill early on, and contributed several charts to the band's later book, as did Gerry Mulligan. But Thornhill's own writing was just as effective for his band, notably his charming original 'Snowfall', and the pianist was at least as interested in a faintly exotic kind of mood music as in jazz: his own charts for Schumann's 'Träumerei' and for 'O Sole Mio' are typical. It's a moot point to what extent the Thornhill–Evans axis brought about the Birth Of The Cool band, though hindsight certainly suggests that Evans's work in particular can be seen as a dry run for those celebrated sessions. The leader's heart, though, may have been more in the kind of sweetly turned society music represented by 'La Paloma', and if he influenced cool jazz, he surely also marked out the way for such light-music mandarins as Frankie Carle. Thornhill suffered a nervous breakdown and had some alcohol problems, but he still led bands in the 50s, largely playing for dancers.
*The 1948 Transcription Performances* (Hep)

# Henry Threadgill
SAXOPHONES
*born* 15 February 1944

A native Chicagoan, Threadgill started in gospel and R&B groups before taking a role in the development of the city's AACM. But it took the formation of the trio Air in the early 70s to bring him to wider attention. Along with Fred Hopkins (bass) and Steve McCall (drums), Threadgill fashioned a complex balance of written forms and free improvising, which owed something to the inevitable influence of Muhal Richard Abrams but took its own direction from the variety of sounds which the saxophonist could draw from his various instruments – lyrical, poignant, bitter. An album of ragtime tunes (*Air Lore*, 1980) offered a then-unfashionable link with jazz's remote past. Air lasted into the middle 80s but Threadgill eventually moved on to larger groups, often with queer instrumentations and even stranger names and tune titles. The Sextet had seven members, Very Very Circus

included trombone, two tubas and two guitars, and the more recent Make A Move and Zoo-Id persist with unusual horn and string combinations. Threadgill has had a surprising number of major-label associations over the years, recording for Arista, Island, RCA and Columbia, although that has worked against his music remaining widely available, since very little has been kept in catalogue by those companies. He is a genuine maverick, pursuing a sometimes baffling path. Here are some of his titles: 'Spotted Dick Is Pudding', 'Refined Poverty', 'Around My Goose'.
*Easily Slip Into Another World* (RCA)

# Three Sounds
GROUP

See GENE HARRIS.

# Steve Tibbetts
GUITAR
*born* 3 October 1954

A minor original whose occasional records seem like reports from a lonely American outpost, Tibbetts is a guitarist and soundscaper of an unassuming sort. Typically, he has been mostly documented by the German independent label ECM, who began recording him in 1981. Based in St Paul, Minnesota, he has studied percussion and various sorts of world music, but his records suggest a dense musical thinker with a penchant for big-screen sound. Records such as *Big Map Idea* (1981) and *The Fall Of Us All* (1993) posit a darker alternative to Pat Metheny's American pastorale, and one which similarly evades the sentimental nostalgia of Bill Frisell. Tibbetts may turn out to be more significant than either of them, even though he is by comparison almost unknown. Layered, heavily sustained electric guitars, deft use of studio loops, and the involvement of regular drum-partner Marc Edwards give his work its main ingredients. In 1999, he made *Å*, described as 'visionary fiddle music', with the Hardanger fiddle player Knut Hamre.
*The Fall Of Us All* (ECM)

## Timeless

RECORD COMPANY

Wim Wigt has quietly built this Dutch label into an institution among European independents, in the years since he started operating in 1975. Wigt's principal interest was in hard bop, and the mainstays of the label included, at various times, Cedar Walton, Art Blakey and Pharoah Sanders, as well as European performers and a series dedicated to traditional jazz, which has also sponsored a major series of 78-era reissues.

## Bobby Timmons

PIANO
*born* 19 December 1935; *died* 1 March 1974

One of the cadre of pianists who emerged from the local Philadelphia scene in the middle 50s, Timmons made his first real impact with Art Blakey's Jazz Messengers, whom he joined in 1958. Though he only stayed for a year (there was a brief reunion in 1961), he contributed at least one staple to the band's book in 'Moanin'', which defined the strain of gospel melody in hard bop at least as well as anything in Horace Silver's repertoire. He then joined the Cannonball Adderley group, where he came up with the natural successors to 'Moanin'' in 'This Here' and 'Dat Dere'. Yet these associations with two of the most popular hard-bop bands did little for his own subsequent career: a quiet, sensitive man, Timmons was not a natural leader, and although he drank from the same well as Red Garland and Ray Bryant, his music didn't quite gather in the elegance of the former or the ebullience of the latter. And he wasn't always lucky with recording: the excellent 1964 date *From The Bottom*, for instance, didn't manage a release until the 70s, when he was already suffering from the cirrhosis which would kill him in 1974. A string of dates for Prestige in the latter part of the 60s, when he was earning a living in clubs leading trios, had very little impact, and his career declined along with jazz's own struggles with rock.
***This Here Is Bobby Timmons*** (Riverside/OJC)

## Lorenzo Tio Jr

CLARINET
*born* 21 April 1883; *died* 24 December 1933

Tio was long a near legend to early jazz collectors, and he left very little of his work to remember him by. The Tio family was one of the major New Orleans dynasties, and Lorenzo Jr was a fourth-generation scion of clarinet players and teachers, who numbered Johnny Dodds and Barney Bigard among his pupils. He worked extensively with other leaders, including Papa Celestin and Armand Piron, but the happenstance of early jazz recording meant it largely passed him by, and only a few sides under Clarence Williams's leadership say much about his playing. From the middle 20s onwards he worked largely in New York, but he was too old to make a wider impact and he died suddenly in 1933.

## Keith Tippett

PIANO
*born* 25 August 1947

Born in Bristol, pianist Tippett has been a larger-than-life force in British jazz for decades. His early experiences were with church music, and the contrary traits of gospel exuberance and sacred solemnity continue to haunt his music to this day. He found his way into connections with like-minded spirits such as Elton Dean at the end of the 60s, and came to the attention of fellow West Countryman Robert Fripp, who engaged Tippett for King Crimson's *In The Wake Of Poseidon*, and its near-hit single 'Catfood'. Though this was a brief association, it is one which has served the pianist well to this day. Since then, Tippett has dispersed his energies between unwieldy big bands (the 50-strong Centipede, which made an unsatisfactory record for RCA, *Septober Energy*, and a 22-piece group, The Ark) and solo and small-group performances. His ensemble Mujician, which includes saxophonist Paul Dunmall, has been one of his most successful, and he has also performed with his wife, singer Julie Tippetts, and in duo with fellow pianist Howard Riley. Tippett's work calls for a certain suspension of disbelief: he can sound intolerably pretentious at one moment, profoundly moving the next, and his records have often teetered

between these two points. His use of
prepared-piano effects and a performance
aesthetic which aspires to a kind of pure
intuition may strike some listeners as sin-
cere and others as calculating. More than
many in his British idiom, he has the aura
of stardom about him. But some of his best
work is with the no-nonsense Riley, who
seems able to shut off Tippett's sometimes
overbearing ego and bring out the truly
sensitive musician within.
**Mujician I/II** (FMP)

## Juan Tizol
VALVE-TROMBONE
*born* 22 January 1900; *died* 23 April 1984

Born in Puerto Rico, Tizol moved to the US
in 1920, playing in minor groups until he
joined Duke Ellington's band in 1929. A fluent and mobile practitioner on his chosen
horn, Tizol proved an adaptable and useful
man for Duke to have around: he often
played with the saxophones rather than the
brass, and he brought some long-lasting
compositions into Ellington's book, two of
which – 'Caravan' and 'Perdido' – have
become among the most durable of jazz
standards. In 1944, he accepted an offer to
join Harry James, but for the next 15 years
he spent his time going back and forth
between James and Ellington, eventually
retiring to a quieter life in 1960. Tizol rarely
took solos and was a conscientious section-
man who was among the first on the stand:
his royalties on 'Caravan' alone should have
ensured him some dollars for his pension.
**Duke Ellington, *1937*** (Classics)

## Cal Tjader
VIBES, PERCUSSION
*born* 16 July 1925; *died* 5 May 1982

Tjader is an important, catalytic figure, but
exactly how important is difficult to quantify. A dancer and a drummer in his teens,
he worked with two major crossover figures
– Dave Brubeck and George Shearing –
before forming his own group in 1955. Latin
beats have always been a tributary rather
than a main current in jazz rhythm, but
Tjader made them the source of his playing,
although from the beginning there was no
clear obeisance to a particular style: Cuban

and Brazilian influences, for instance, were
simply stirred in together, in what could
either be a happy muddle or a groundbreaking fusion, according to one's allegiances.
Tjader's earlier groups were manned by relatively anonymous figures, but he later hired
Willie Bobo and Mongo Santamaria in the
percussion section. By the early 60s, he had
already made a large number of discs for
Fantasy, but his signature record was arguably one he made for Verve in 1963, *El
Sonido Nuevo*, considered by some to have
marked the start of *salsa* music. In fact, the
real force behind the record was pianist
Eddie Palmieri, who did the arrangements.
Tjader's own playing offered an unremarkable development of Milt Jackson's manner,
largely bluesless, and the cocktail-lounge
associations of the vibes helped to increase
his appeal to an audience that didn't really
care about jazz but enjoyed a mentholated
sort of West Coast sound (Tjader spent his
career in and around California). Two
decades after his death, most of his records
are still in print, and his unassuming presence – 'I'm not an innovator, I'm not a path-
finder, I'm a participant' – still abides in the
spread of Latin jazz.
**Cal Tjader's Greatest Hits** (Fantasy)

## Charles Tolliver
TRUMPET
*born* 6 March 1942

At one time Tolliver seemed set for a distinguished career, but little went his way after
a promising start. He first came to attention
as a sideman with Jackie McLean, recording
on the saxophonist's *It's Time* (Blue Note,
1964), before working with Gerald Wilson's
big band in California and then spending a
couple of years in Max Roach's small group.
An agile player with a clear, light-bodied
sound – Tolliver's horn brightened his surroundings and his unfussy style sounded
like a welcome alternative to that of some of
his contemporaries. He formed some associations in Europe before putting together a
band in 1969 called Music, Inc, which placed
himself in front of rhythm-section players
including John Hicks, Reggie Workman and
others. Together with Stanley Cowell, he
formed a record company called Strata-East
in 1971, but this was really the start of his
troubles: designed as a kind of cooperative

where artists had control of their own recordings, the financial side of it eventually went murky and a number of musicians reputedly wanted to ask Tolliver some hard questions about it. For the rest of the 70s and 80s the trumpeter enjoyed no more than a modest profile, and ever since he has only intermittently secured any prominence.

**Grand Max** (Black Lion)

## Radka Toneff

VOCAL
*born* 25 June 1952; *died* 21 October 1982

A fondly remembered singer from Norway, who didn't have time to establish an international career. She studied at the Oslo Conservatory in the early 70s while also singing with rock groups, but in 1975 she formed a small group with players such as Jon Balke and Arild Andersen, her own vocals setting the tone of the enterprise – beautifully crafted, quiet, but with a spare kind of intensity which still surprises on the surviving records. Latterly she worked in a duo with the expatriate American Steve Dobrogosz. Toneff's best work has the rigour and refinement of the poetry which she sometimes used for her lyrics, and her suicide was a cruel coda to her work.

**The Best Of Radka Toneff** (Universal)

## Pietro Tonolo

TENOR AND SOPRANO SAXOPHONES
*born* 30 May 1959

Tonolo began working on the Milan scene from the late 70s. He worked in Enrico Rava's groups for much of the 80s, but has otherwise mostly worked as his own leader, although he has also played in the US and in the rest of Europe with players of many backgrounds. Although his playing is couched mainly in the familiar post-bop tradition, Tonolo can sound lustily effective on tenor, while some recent sets for EGEA have seen him exploring his Italian heritage in a more chamberish setting.

**Tresse** (Splasc(h))

## Mel Tormé

VOCAL
*born* 13 September 1925; *died* 5 June 1999

Like his close friend and contemporary Buddy Rich, Tormé was a child star in vaudeville who sang and played drums. He performed in Chico Marx's band in the early 40s and then formed a vocal group, The Mel-Tones, which enjoyed success on radio and with records (where they worked with Artie Shaw). At this point, Tormé's voice had an almost wispy quality and lacked projection, which led to a disc jockey giving him the nickname 'The Velvet Fog'. Besides singing, Tormé grew into a considerable songwriter and arranger: his long pieces 'County Fair' and 'California Suite' became staples of their kind, and his celebrated 'The Christmas Song' (written in 40 minutes on a blazing hot day in Los Angeles) is the season's premier classic after 'White Christmas'. Though he was busy in films and television, his career on record and as a live performer didn't much accelerate until the later 50s. He had a major hit (especially in the UK) with a live version of 'Mountain Greenery', and then cut some oustanding sets for Verve with Marty Paich arrangements, particularly *Swings Shubert Alley* (1960). Despite another hit with 'Comin' Home Baby' (1964), Tormé had to go through the same struggles as other singers of his generation in the 60s as rock rose to prominence, but he endured, and came back stronger than ever in the 70s and 80s, latterly enjoying a long partnership with George Shearing ('I always feel better when I'm in the same *continent* as this man!'). Tormé's voice endured beautifully: it eventually settled down into a deceptive baritone which could float up to ethereal head notes in the top register, a feat which he still pulled off in his 70s. While he could swing and improvise on jazz material, he also doubled as a refined middle-of-the-road performer, and he loved entertaining on stages: if never quite a superstar, Mel had a loyal following, and he liked to characterize his audience as 'the vast minority' who appreciated finely made music.

**Mel Tormé Swings Shubert Alley** (Verve)

# Cy Touff
BASS TRUMPET
*born* 4 March 1927

Perhaps the only musician to specialize on an instrument which, in the end, doesn't sound too different to a trombone, Touff was busy and prominent for much of the 50s. Having previously played saxophone and trombone, he took up the bass trumpet in the late 40s and was with Woody Herman for three years from 1953, then working on the West Coast as a sessionman. From 1956 he was based principally in Chicago, where he made his featured albums, for Argo and Pacific Jazz. He was still playing there into the 80s.
**Havin' A Ball** (World Pacific)

# Dave Tough
DRUMS
*born* 26 April 1908; *died* 6 December 1948

Tough had a middle-class upbringing in Chicago and began drumming in his teens. A member of the celebrated Austin High School Gang, he played in and around the city until going to Europe with Danny Polo in 1927. He stayed two years and then went back to work in New York. But he was already having problems with alcohol, and it wasn't until later in the 30s that he was in good enough shape to play again. He joined Tommy Dorsey in 1936 and Benny Goodman in 1938, and in both bands he was superb, bringing a new subtlety and complexity to some aspects of swing drumming – particularly his use of the bass drum – without interrupting the flow of the music or failing to lift the orchestra. He also played with Bunny Berigan, Bud Freeman, Joe Marsala, Artie Shaw (who had to convince a disbelieving army doctor that Tough was fit, in order to get him into the clarinettist's forces band) and eventually Woody Herman's First Herd, which he joined in 1944 but found so combative an ensemble that he eventually left, even though Herman's bassist, Chubby Jackson, thought him masterful. Tough was still playing in New York small groups up until his death, but alcohol was still plaguing him: Herman thought he was an epileptic, but his seizures were more likely the simple consequence of his prodigious drinking. He died after fracturing his skull in a fall on the sidewalk.
**Bud Freeman, *1939–1940*** (Classics)

# Jean Toussaint
TENOR AND SOPRANO SAXOPHONES
*born* 27 July 1960

Toussaint was born in St Thomas in the Virgin Islands, learning saxophone in his teens and playing locally before going to Berklee for further study. He played in R&B bands before forming his own hard-bop group, and then joined Art Blakey's Jazz Messengers in 1982, staying four years. From there he shifted base to London, following a teaching appointment. Having a genuine Jazz Messenger in their midst was magnetic for many of London's younger players, and Toussaint has been an eminence there ever since, working on some of Julian Joseph's records and leading groups of his own which range from an orchestra to a fusion group. Unlike some of his illustrious Messenger predecessors, though, Toussaint is a solid rather than an exceptional saxophonist, and the few records under his own name have been poorly organized and thoroughly unremarkable.
**The Street Above The Underground** (All Tones)

# Ralph Towner
GUITAR, PIANO
*born* 1 March 1940

Towner has a dense musical background: his parents were both musicians, and he undertook long periods of formal study in Oregon and Vienna, going through most of the 60s. But by 1969 he was in New York, where among various gigs he formed a crucial alliance with the pioneer crossover figure Paul Winter. In 1971, he and three fellow Paul Winter Consort sidemen (Paul McCandless, Glen Moore and Collin Walcott) formed Oregon, whose calm mix of jazz, folk and classical forms offered a rural alternative to the metropolitanism of the new wave of jazz-rockers (even though, ironically enough, Towner had also performed with Weather Report for a spell in 1971). At the same time, the guitarist also began recording for ECM as a solo artist, beginning with *Trios/Solos* (1972). While the classical acoustic guitar remained his signature instrument, Towner is also a very good pianist – some judges even rate him a more interesting piano player than a guitarist – and there are a few projects from this period where he plays electric keyboards with the likes of Clive Barker and Horace Arnold. Perhaps his most striking music, though, has come from his unaccompanied twelve-string guitar playing, a mesmerizing sound which seemed like a completely new idiom as recorded by Eicher's ECM operation. Since then Towner has continued to record steadily for ECM, has kept the faith with Oregon, and worked occasionally as a duettist with fellow guitarist John Abercrombie. A handful of his tunes – 'Icarus', 'The Silence Of A Candle' and 'Spirit Lake' – are a perfect match of melodic hummability and formal compositional grace. If his records can sometimes sound like chamber-Muzak, there is usually a degree of earthiness – either real or cleverly contrived – which lifts them to a more engaging level.

*Diary* (ECM)

## Colin Towns

COMPOSER, ARRANGER
*born* 13 May 1948

Towns has prospered through a long musical career, but his jazz activities have only come front and centre relatively recently. He grew up in a tough east London community and played wedding gigs and other such work before spending a long period as the keyboard player with Ian Gillan's (rock) band, beginning in 1975. During that time he began writing soundtracks for film and television, a skill which he has parlayed into a very successful career. In the 90s, he put together the Mask Orchestra, an occasional ensemble convened to play his own jazz material, and he founded Provocateur Records to release their albums. Since then, Provocateur has gone on to become one of the leading British jazz independents, releasing records by such Mask alumni as Guy Barker, Alan Skidmore and Julian Arguëlles, although it is Towns's own work which the label is most closely identified with. His scores are hard, challenging and sometimes fantastical, mixing up genres with finesse and chutzpah, and generally flying dramatically free of the more sober British orchestral-jazz tradition. Because he comes across as such a risk-taker, the records have had their hit-and-miss qualities, but Towns is never one to take things too easy.

*Another Think Coming* (Provocateur)

## Clark Tracey

DRUMS
*born* 5 February 1961

Tracey's father Stan initially encouraged him to study piano and vibes, but Clark preferred the drums, and after a period of study with Bryan Spring he began playing in Tracey senior's small groups from around 1978. Since then, while continuing that association, he has also done a prodigious amount of sideman work all through the 80s and 90s and into the new century, as well as leading small groups of his own and composing for ensembles of every size. Since he has now been a busy professional for close on 30 years, Tracey's playing has sometimes been, like his father's, rather taken for granted, but his uncomplicated and direct style is superbly effective at lifting and driving a group.

*Full Speed Sideways* (33)

## Stan Tracey

PIANO
*born* 30 December 1926

A Londoner, Tracey began playing piano in wartime bands which were 'entertaining the troops', and from there he worked in dance bands. Besides this, he was involved in small-group jazz work by the middle 50s, and he spent two years in Ted Heath's band from 1957, here playing vibes as well as piano (he later gave up the former instrument because he got tired of carrying them around). He was already the inimitable Stan Tracey by the time he was with Heath: his feature on 'Limehouse Blues' from Heath's *Big Band Blues* (1959) is *sui generis*. Tracey's initial main influence was Duke Ellington, but so much in his style sounds akin to Thelonious Monk's piano playing that he has often been pigeonholed as a Monk disciple; both pianists probably arrived at their approaches separately, via Duke's example. He spent a long stint as the house pianist at Ronnie Scott's Club, between 1960 and 1967, backing most of the American visitors (and getting into some musically combative situations with some of them), and it was through the admiring opinions of the likes of Sonny Rollins that he built a wider reputation. He also embarked on a regimen of small- and large-group recording for Denis

Preston's Lansdowne operation, most of which has still not been reissued on CD, although at least his masterpiece of the period, a quartet date with Bobby Wellins inspired by Dylan Thomas's *Under Milk Wood* (1965), has been regularly available since. His music for the British film *Alfie* (1966) has sometimes been credited to the main soloist, Rollins, but the composing hand was Tracey's. Following the Scott's residency, he has been playing on the British pub and club circuit ever since, occasionally receiving commissions for large-scale music – his big-band work *Genesis* is one such – and recording mostly for independent labels, including his own operation Steam. While he has also worked with sextets and octets, the quartet has been his regular setting, with such saxophonists as Wellins, Peter King and Art Themen, and the drums handled by Bryan Spring or son Clark. Descriptions such as 'the grand old man of British modernism' are always likely to bring a wry remark to his lips in response, but Tracey has lived and worked through every rise and fall in British jazz's fortunes over the past 60 years and has contributed more creative music to its successive periods than any other figure, as both composer and performer. In the new century, he managed to open yet another chapter by making a record of improvised duets with Evan Parker.

***Under Milk Wood*** (Jazzizit/Columbia)

## Trad/traditional jazz

The idea of traditional jazz came about in the US at the end of the 30s, when some musicians and fans began to seek the re-establishment of what was then – at the height of the swing era of big bands – an older style of playing. Anything which pre-dated the swing idiom was seen as 'traditional', so Chicago Dixieland and New Orleans jazz alike were considered part of what was also known as 'revivalism'. In Europe and the UK, though, it was another ten years before such a movement got under way, and since the 'tradition' had been second-hand to start with and couldn't involve authentic American players, the notion of traditional jazz (or simply 'trad', as it became known) tended to be more about the letter than the spirit. By the middle 50s,

after skiffle had got under way and had managed to get into the popular charts, there was talk of a 'trad boom' in Britain. Its leaders were the men often characterized as 'The Three B's' – Chris Barber, Kenny Ball and Acker Bilk – all of whom shared the charts at some point with such pre-beat singers as Craig Douglas and Billy Fury. This also led to a raft of second-division trad outfits, many of whom subsequently gave the genre a bad name, although recorded evidence suggests that the groups were no worse than any other lusty amateurs hoping for a break. The two outsiders to all this were Ken Colyer, who only cared about the proper spirit of the music, and Humphrey Lyttelton, whose music had in any case moved more towards a mainstream style. The boom died out rapidly enough as soon as the beat era got under way, and ever since trad has been often sneered at as a relic of an era of duffel coats and CND marches. As an enduring part of British jazz, though, it deserves better than it customarily gets. The huge network of trad groups which still flourishes all over the UK has safeguarded jazz as a music of live performance even when it has been otherwise at its lowest ebb in terms of fashion and media awareness, and it is a tribute to these bands and their musicianship that they have nourished a 'local' jazz audience for decades. In an era when most pop stars want to be media personalities rather than musicians playing for people, these lusty amateurs, doing it for the love of it, are arguably more valuable than ever.

## Transcriptions

Notated copies of improvisations have been used as a helpmate for aspiring jazz players for many years. The act of transcribing a solo from a record might be laborious and fundamentally unrealistic – there is no real way to notate all the nuances of tone, timbre and attack which a soloist might use during the course of what they are spontaneously playing – but it is undeniably useful for nuts-and-bolts study, and many collections of solos by individual players have been published over the years.

'Transcription' was also used during the 30s and 40s for studio recordings which were made for broadcast purposes by one radio station, and thereafter disseminated to others in the same network. Many swing-era big bands in particular were engaged to provide transcriptions, which have subsequently been collected and commercially issued for the first time in the LP and CD eras.

## Theo Travis
TENOR AND SOPRANO SAXOPHONES, FLUTE
*born* 7 July 1964

Travis was born in Birmingham but studied in Manchester and settled in London in the late 80s. While he has perhaps been a typical journeyman on the British scene, he has sought to find some distinctive settings, with a considerable amount of success: a trio with guitarist Mark Wood and drummer John Marshall has been a fine exercise in full-on chopsmanship, his quartet works to a strong original book of tunes, and he has been investigating the possibilities of ambient and electronic music which doesn't lose the soloist in mere noodling indulgence. He could use more exposure of his work on more prominent labels.
*Heart Of The Sun* (33)

## Alphonso Trent
BANDLEADER, PIANO
*born* 24 August 1905; *died* 14 October 1959

Trent all but dominated southwestern jazz in the 20s. He worked with groups in Oklahoma and Arkansas before taking over another group, which was expanded to orchestral size and held a long residency at the Adolphus Hotel in Dallas from 1925, broadcasting regularly and subsequently touring. Four sides made in 1928 show how good the band was, but Trent refused offers to shift to New York, perhaps recognizing that it was a much tougher environment to lead the boss band in. There was a setback when a fire in Cleveland, where the band was playing a date, destroyed all their arrangements, but by 1933 Trent had family matters to deal with and the band passed into other hands: two final titles from that year show them still in fine form. Though he continued leading bands for a while, Trent subsequently pursued interests in real estate. Given that they made so few records

and worked away from where jazz history was being documented, Trent's band has slipped almost unnoticed into history.

## Lennie Tristano
PIANO
*born* 19 March 1919; *died* 18 November 1978

Tristano's problematical ghost still haunts modern jazz, many years after his death. The central paradox of his music – even though he never saw it that way – is that the most ingenious and cerebral of approaches was bound up in a delivery and concern for beauty which was profoundly exciting to experience. Born blind in Chicago, he was taught piano by his mother and then at Chicago's American Conservatory, before moving to New York in 1946. It was a fortuitous moment, since it coincided with the wildfire spread of bop, an idiom which Tristano was clearly in tune with even though he had arrived at quite different conclusions to those of either Monk or Powell. His Keynote sessions of 1946–7, although almost unknown in comparison to the 40s dates by Monk and Powell, set down an approach as striking as theirs. Tristano chose to work against rhythmical backgrounds which were foursquare, even bland, the better to emphasize his melodic and harmonic procedures. Actually, there is often as great a rhythmic variety in his playing as there is in that of the boppers, but it is often displayed so circumspectly that it asks for the listener's very best attention. More obvious are his seemingly endless melodies, articulated via sequences of eighth-notes that go on and on; his block-chording and polytonality; and an almost surgical precision, which in some ways cools off the impact of his more shocking playing, while ensuring that it continues to sound fresh and undated. Tristano assembled his own academy of musicians – Billy Bauer, Lee Konitz, Warne Marsh, Sal Mosca, Peter Ind – and founded his own jazz school in New York in 1951. But it took him away from public performance, and for the rest of his life he was more involved in teaching than in any kind of outgoing career. On record, he similarly managed only a miserly discography, although what survives – a few sessions for Atlantic, and various semi-private recordings which have been circulated via the Jazz label, curated by his daughter Carol – is enthralling. There were 1949 recordings with Konitz and Marsh which offered the first free, themeless jazz improvising on record, and sessions where he overdubbed piano parts and created almost fantastic extensions of his already demanding art.

After 1960, he made only a handful of public appearances, and his teachings secured a sort of notoriety, suggesting that pupils underwent a kind of brainwashing. It is more truthful to suggest that Tristano's approach had its face set against the world of jazz entertainment: his criticism of modern jazz, 'all emotion and no feeling', hints at his isolation. Of his two most famous disciples, Lee Konitz took what he wanted and moved on, and Warne Marsh remained a mature student while particularizing the Tristano idiom. Sal Mosca, though he also had few opportunities to record, was Tristano's real successor at the piano. A perfectionist in a lazy world, Tristano is hidden from most currents in jazz history, but his name is evoked every time something brainy and unsensational comes up in the music's progress: a strange legacy.

**Lennie Tristano/The New Tristano** (Rhino/Atlantic)

# Gianluigi Trovesi
ALTO SAXOPHONE, CLARINET
*born* 10 January 1944

Trovesi's music is almost indecently rich with contributing strains from many sources. He played brass-band music in his teens and studied in Bergamo and Piacenza before a long period working on compositional theory. In the 70s he worked with Giorgio Gaslini and in Andrea Centazzo's Mitteleuropa Orchestra before leading groups of his own and doing sideman gigs with Paolo Fresu. His work as a leader began to be documented in the 80s, and he has recorded for Splasc(h), Red, Soul Note (some of his best work), Enja and latterly ECM: a duo with the accordion player Gianni Coscia resulted in some almost painfully lovely music on *Radici* (Egea, 1995) and *In Cerca Di Cibo* (ECM, 1999), but more typical of his output are the extravagant works for medium-sized ensembles such as those on *From G To G* (Soul Note, 1992) and the marvellous *Fugace* (ECM, 2002), which mixes unusual instrumentations with music that blends any number of Italian folk and brass-band influences with Trovesi's own take on post-bop improvising. On record it can sometimes sound straitlaced, but in performance he can move quickly from heartbreaking melodies to rowdy and knockabout music.
*Fugace* (ECM)

# Frankie Trumbauer
C-MELODY SAXOPHONE
*born* 30 May 1901; *died* 11 June 1956

The peculiarity of Trumbauer's eminence was that it was based on an instrument – the C-melody saxophone – which hardly anybody has played since his heyday. Yet he was a major influence on black as well as white players of the alto and the tenor saxophone alike: Benny Carter and Lester Young both thought him wonderful. Born in Carbondale, Illinois, he was working with the technically irreproachable Benson Orchestra Of Chicago, one of the best white bands outside New York in the early 20s, before joining Jean Goldkette's band – along with his steady partner, Bix Beiderbecke, whom he had already played with in St Louis. Trumbauer often led the Goldkette band (its leader regularly contracted orchestras without actually fronting them), and by the time both he and Beiderbecke went on to join the Paul Whiteman group in 1927, they had already begun to set down some of the defining white jazz of the era together. After Bix's death, 'Tram' carried on with Whiteman well into the swing era: like Jack Teagarden, he was a star soloist with the band for years, although by 1937 Trumbauer had grown tired of the situation and moved out to California. He still led bands of his own, but became more involved in aviation – he had learned to fly early on, and often piloted his own plane to gigs – and left music altogether after 1948. Latterly he spent more time on the alto, but it was his C-melody playing which captivated other players: a light, fey, almost asexual sound masked a delivery so graceful and skilled that the most complicated phrases – and there were plenty of them – seemed effortless. As with so many, though, he really belonged to the 20s: the swing-era players developed his licks while he stood more or less still.
*Bix And Tram* (JSP)

# Bruce Turner

CLARINET, ALTO SAXOPHONE
*born* 5 July 1922; *died* 28 November 1993

The most famous anecdote in British jazz history surrounds a date where Bruce Turner played a Birmingham gig as the new member of Humphrey Lyttelton's group in 1953. It was at a moment when the audience felt obliged to show their colours in a war between ancient and modern, and diehards in the crowd unfurled a banner which read, 'Go Home Dirty Bopper!' Turner, a proud Yorkshireman who doubled on alto and clarinet, had by this time passed through various trad ensembles and had even taken lessons with Lennie Tristano and Lee Konitz; but with Lyttelton (he stayed until 1957) he blossomed into a chameleonic reed virtuoso who could sit comfortably in any style, Dixie to bebop. For the next ten years, he fronted his own Jump Band, which was only spottily documented: its smart revision of the small-group swing style remains mostly in the memories of those who heard it. But the group had no commercial appeal in its day, and Turner, a reluctant leader, disbanded and joined Acker Bilk before reuniting with Lyttelton in 1970. Humph made the most of his versatile reedsman: he could whisper 'Hodges!' in Bruce's ear while midway through a number, and the saxophonist would execute an impeccable and perfectly timed piece of suitable mimicry. Though he was fond of cream cakes but finally sworn off alcohol, his secret vice in his final years was a glass of milk. Humph and Acker cut the valedictory *Three In The Morning* in 1994, which Turner should have played on; but he had died a few months earlier.
*That's The Blues, Dad* (Lake)

# Joe Turner

PIANO, VOCAL
*born* 3 November 1907; *died* 21 July 1990

Sometimes confused with the blues and R&B singer of the same name, Turner arrived in New York from Baltimore in the mid-20s and was soon classed as a leading member of the Harlem piano aristocracy. But he didn't get many opportunities to record, and he went to Europe in 1931 and stayed for most of the decade. He returned home in 1939, working as a solo, but went back to Europe again at the end of the 40s and settled first in Switzerland and then in Paris. Most of his recording was done after 1950, and he was still busy making albums for Pablo and Black & Blue in the 70s and 80s. Turner performed in the grandest stride tradition: if he brought nothing strikingly original to the idiom, at least he could claim to have been around when it was coming into maturity, and his playing was as hard-swinging as the style has to be.
*Sweet And Lovely* (Vogue)

# Joe Turner

VOCAL
*born* 18 May 1911; *died* 24 November 1985

The owner of the biggest of all blues and jazz voices worked as a bartender in Kansas City from his teens, and while serving drinks he would sing along with the piano players. Although he sang with Count Basie and other bandleaders for a spell, small groups and solo players were his preferred accompaniment, and he appeared with his old friend Pete Johnson at the 1938 From Spirituals To Swing concert, making his debut on record not long afterwards. Turner continued to sing with the boogie pianists and in 1945 he opened his own club in Los Angeles, The Blue Room, in partnership with Johnson. He carried on touring all through the 50s, 60s and 70s. His jukebox records for Atlantic in the early 50s helped precipitate the rock'n'roll revolution: it was Bill Haley who had the big hit with 'Shake, Rattle And Roll', but it was Joe Turner who cut the monumental original. His huge voice would either shout off a line or cradle it in a cavernous baritone that had a thrilling sensuality to it, even if the singer – a 250-pound giant – was scarcely the purveyor of matinée-idol looks. His finest singing was often reserved for slow blues, sometimes taking a lyric through such a heartrending journey that it hardly seems like the work of the same jovial entertainer of the fast numbers. He did much festival work in his later years and made some enjoyable latter-day records for Norman Granz's Pablo, and although illness forced him to cut back in the 80s, he was still singing for the people in the last year of his life.
*The Boss Of The Blues* (Atlantic)

# Mark Turner

TENOR AND SOPRANO SAXOPHONES
*born* 10 November 1965

Turner's sound and style are a scintillating alternative to modern, mainstream saxophone. He was raised in southern California, started on alto and switched to tenor at 16. After a period studying art, he went to Berklee before joining the Delfeayo Marsalis group in 1991. From there he went to New York, and following a spell with Ellis Marsalis in New Orleans he became a notable presence on the New York scene, often playing in Kurt Rosenwinkel's groups, and making three oustanding records for Criss Cross. In 1995 he was signed to Warner Bros, for whom he made four further records before seemingly being dropped by the label. Turner's sound has an uninflected quality which has won many comparisons with Warne Marsh, a very rare influence these days, and Turner admits that he loves what he sees as 'such fury with such restraint' in Marsh's playing. He has a preference for very long, unspooling melody lines, and has a penchant for investigating the altissimo register of the tenor; coupled with his strikingly individual writing, these traits add up to a provocative spirit who demands a hearing. Besides Rosenwinkel, he has been a close associate of Ethan Iverson and Reid Anderson, and it's to be hoped that a man who sounds like an important figure will continue to be documented by a sympathetic company.
*In This World* (Warner Bros)

# Steve Turre

TROMBONE, SHELLS
*born* 12 September 1948

Turre was born in Omaha, Nebraska, and his early experience was in rock horn sections, but he performed with many stalwart leaders in the 70s, 80s and 90s, often leading big-band trombone sections and turning to the conch shell as a party piece (although Turre's efforts at turning this into a legitimate instrument have been extensive, culminating in a band called Sanctified Shells, it hasn't really developed beyond novelty status). One of his favourite leaders was Roland Kirk, to whom he has dedicated more than one recording, and he has been an important member of Lester Bowie's Brass Fantasy and McCoy Tyner's occasionally convened Big Band. By himself, Turre often seems a bit stuck for context, and his own-name recordings have tended towards jumbles of ideas.
*Steve Turre* (Verve)

# Stanley Turrentine

TENOR SAXOPHONE
*born* 5 April 1934; *died* 12 September 2000

Raised in Pittsburgh (his father was a member of the Savoy Sultans), Stan 'The Man' Turrentine took up saxophone at 11 and was already playing in blues and R&B bands in his teens. With his brother Tommy (1928–97), he joined Earl Bostic's group in 1953, and following army service was the tenor player with Max Roach in 1960. At the same time, he began a series of recordings for Blue Note, both under his own name and with Jimmy Smith: arguably, these remain his finest legacy. Turrentine was no great individualist but he brought out the bluesiest side of the hard-bop vocabulary and few could match him on the old form at a fierce mid-tempo. Blue Note entries such as *Blue Hour*, *Up At Minton's* and *ZT's Blues* are genre excursions which are as satisfying as any of their kind. He married the organist Shirley Scott and they appeared on many of each other's records, although they eventually divorced in 1971. Turrentine went the pop route early on – he was already covering The Beatles in 1964 – and in the 70s he buttered his bread handsomely with what were then easy-listening instrumental records, although they sound a bit tougher than most of today's smooth jazz. But his final years saw him going full circle, back to straight-ahead playing, even though much of the later music sounded either soft or thinly spread.
*Up At Minton's* (Blue Note)

# Richard Twardzik

PIANO
*born* 30 April 1931; *died* 21 October 1955

Twardzik was working on the Boston bebop scene at the start of the 50s, with Serge Chaloff, Charlie Parker and others. He then

toured with Lionel Hampton, cut a piano-trio set which was released as one half of an album shared with Russ Freeman, and then joined Chet Baker's quartet, recording with him in Paris. Twardzik's oddball tunes, including 'The Fable Of Mabel', which he recorded with Chaloff, and 'The Girl From Greenland', have a haunting quality to go with their Monk-like individuality, and what he might have gone on to do is yet another melancholy jazz what-might-have-been. His corpse was found in his Paris hotel, a hypodermic still allegedly stuck in his arm.
**Russ Freeman/Richard Twardzik,** *Trio* (Contemporary/OJC)

# 29th Street Saxophone Quartet
GROUP

New York, at the beginning of the 80s: Jim Hartog (baritone) and Ed Jackson (alto) started talking, they brought in Rich Rothenberg (tenor) and just before a tour to Europe was about to get under way, Bobby Watson (alto) also came on board (Marty Ehrlich and Kenny Garrett had been among his immediate predecessors). Hartog lived on 29th Street, and that provided the name. 29th Street might have been the most accomplished of the saxophone bands, at least in terms of the way they integrated different rhythms, counterpoint, melody and improvising: rather than providing solo vehicles or specific setpieces, their music had an almost classical precision and grace which was constantly offset by implied jazz, funk and Afro-Cuban rhythms. Watson's lubricious alto sound was often the lead voice, and it gave the group a sensuality which further oiled the joints of what is still a difficult instrumentation to swing. Despite making a couple of albums for Antilles (a part of Polygram), though, the group's recorded output was mostly confined to small labels and they were perceived, a little unfairly, as more of a band to go and hear than one to buy. Festival circuit favourites, they visited Europe many times but didn't muster the same applause at home. Perhaps their strongest suit was, surprisingly, their ballad playing: a piece such as 'New Moon' (1989) lingers long in the mind. They called it a day in 1996, although there have been thus far undocumented reunions in the new century.
*Live* (Red)

# Chris Tyle
CORNET, TRUMPET, VOCAL
*born* 1955

Tyle grew up in Portland, Oregon, and began playing in both swing-based bands and revivalist groups, although following a move to New Orleans in 1989 he based himself in the latter idiom. He is one of the key players – along with Hal Smith, John Gill and Steve Pistorius, all of whom play together in the Silver Leaf Jazz Band – in the modern revivalist axis which has done much to reinvigorate older styles of playing without making them sound like a museum-music. While this jazz hasn't won the kind of attention which has gone to the Lincoln Center programmes of similar music, it sounds both closer to the spirit and looser and more personal in its re-creation. Tyle has led important dedications to such as King Oliver and Freddie Keppard, and his own playing is sparkily faithful to those idols.
*Here Comes The Hot Tamale Man* (Stomp Off)

# Charles Tyler
ALTO AND BARITONE SAXOPHONES
*born* 20 July 1941; *died* 27 June 1992

Tyler played baritone sax in army bands before moving to New York in the early 60s. He had already befriended Albert Ayler, and was a regular in Ayler's groups between 1963 and 1966. His typically noisy and enjoyably chaotic ESP album *Charles Tyler Ensemble* gives some idea of what he was doing at that time. But after the 60s, he never came much to jazz prominence again. He taught in California, made some hit-and-miss albums for various labels during the 70s, and spent much of the 80s in Europe, eventually settling in France. He became ill towards the end of the 80s and had to give up the baritone. His sideman work on the record cited, pointed and powerful, suggests that in the right circumstances he was latterly still a fine artist.
**Billy Bang,** *Rainbow Gladiator* (Black Saint)

# McCoy Tyner

PIANO

*born* 11 December 1938

Tyner's close Philadelphia neighbours were Bud and Richie Powell, who would sometimes practise on the piano in his house, and McCoy led a high-school band which also featured Lee Morgan. He played locally with Benny Golson and others, and this led to his joining the Golson–Art Farmer Jazztet in 1959. But he had also previously worked with John Coltrane, and the following year Coltrane engaged him as the pianist in his new quartet, Tyner arriving in time to appear on the sessions for *My Favorite Things* (Atlantic, 1960). In the hothouse atmosphere of what would become the most intensely followed small group in jazz, Tyner's art didn't so much expand as coalesce into a method which exuded a tremendously strong, momentous discipline. Previously, he had played as if he were the pianist who had accompanied Coltrane in the saxophonist's previous group, Red Garland, but in the new environment he abandoned that kind of delicacy, backing the leader's marathon solos with one-chord vamps, developing solos as if he were carving out great blocks of sound, rippling with trills, huge pedal chords in the left hand and passages that suggested call-and-response figures played with a kind of benign fury. Oddly, his contemporaneous albums as a leader for Impulse! seem much more quiescent, as if he were simply taking a breather from his work with Coltrane. After leaving the group in 1965, he switched labels to Blue Note, started with a classic – *The Real McCoy* (1967) – but then faltered as the jazz record business went into decline. But a new contract for Milestone in the early 70s and the founding of a series of touring groups – with such sidemen as Sonny Fortune, Azar Lawrence and Alphonse Mouzon – revitalized his work, and at a time when fusion was becoming all the rage, his stoic perseverance with acoustic bands was almost a beacon for modal jazz playing. His 1973 Montreux Festival performance, with its tumultuous version of 'Walk Spirit, Talk Spirit', heard on *Enlightenment* (Milestone), typifies the power of his music of the 70s and early 80s.

He progressed his music further over the next ten years by going in two other direc-
tions, solo performance and big-band music. A trio of solo records for Blue Note documented some of his most personal and handsomely accomplished playing, while the big band which he first formed in 1984, and has convened since when the occasion and finances allow it, has been an exultant orchestra which has seemed to amplify and extend the ostinato forms which Tyner pursued in the Coltrane group. In his 60s, he has been recording for Telarc, a mixture of solo and all-star group records which suggest no new departures, just a grandmaster circling over familiar ground, renewing old familiarities. While often cited as one of the major influences on modern pianists, Tyner's mighty, inclusive manner is very hard to replicate, and unlike Hancock, Evans or Jarrett he does not really have a school of disciples. Some complain that he is not much of an improviser, which in a sense is true: his music depends, like that of many of the great beboppers, on a resource of familiar ideas which he turns over and over in his hands, reconstituting them as he pleases. But few if any other musicians have combined a fundamentally romantic approach with such thunderous executive power.

*Soliloquy* (Blue Note)

# Gebhard Ullmann

SAXOPHONES, CLARINETS

*born* 2 November 1957

Ullmann emerged on the German free-music scene in the middle 80s. He has since then worked a determined and often surprising course as a leader, with several groups to his name: Basement Research, a group of woodwind and accordion players which has reached ten in number, and Trad Corrosion, a trio, are two of them, but some of his most impressive music has been with The Clarinet Trio, where he plays bass clarinet alongside Jürgen Kupke (clarinet) and Theo Nabicht (bass clarinet). Its unique sonorities and dancing, serious, bubbling music have been beautifully caught on a series of CDs for the Leo label.

*Translucent Tones* (Leo)

# James 'Blood' Ulmer

GUITAR
*born* 2 February 1942

Ulmer came to attention with Ornette Coleman in the middle 70s, but he had many years in jazz and R&B behind him already. He took the guitar part in several organ combos in the 60s, with Jimmy Smith, Richard Holmes, Hank Marr and John Patton, with whom he recorded for Blue Note. But it was studying and playing with Coleman that brought him into the spotlight, and on *Tales Of Captain Black* (1978), where the saxophonist made a rare appearance as a sideman, Ulmer sounded in possession of a surprising new music. Coleman's 'harmolodics', a theory never satisfactorily explained by its creator, drove what was a complicated ensemble music where everyone seemed to be playing at right angles to everyone else, the whole engendering its own peculiar logic. Ulmer's twangy, scratched-out playing sounded both primeval and caustically modern. *Down Beat* called it 'harmolodic diatonic funk'. It won a Columbia contract for Ulmer, but they let him go again after three poor-selling records. Ulmer was right at the core of New York's new jazz in the early 80s, and his group Odyssey was thrilling to hear in person, but no musical revolution materialized and as the decade wore on the guitarist became angry if an interviewer even mentioned harmolodics. He often played with David Murray, usually under the heading of the Music Revelation Ensemble, and was frequently involved in Bill Laswell projects. But his own records took an almost formulaic turn, and by the end of the century he was playing in more or less straight blues situations (he has a suitably raw and often indecipherable singing voice). Some heart trouble has slowed him down.
***Odyssey*** (Columbia)

# United Jazz And Rock Ensemble

GROUP

Wolfgang Dauner organized this group initially to supply the music for a German television programme in 1975, but the results were considered so successful that it subsequently became a recording and touring band in its own right which has been occasionally convened ever since. Besides Dauner, among those involved have been Ian Carr, Jon Hiseman, Albert Mangelsdorff, Eberhard Weber, Barbara Thompson, Charlie Mariano and Christof Lauer. Basically, it's a chance for some old lags of the jazz-rock scene to get together and have some fun. The unpretentious results have been less than immortal, but enjoyable in their way. A 2002 tour was billed as their farewell, but with the way such goodbyes often are, one never knows.
***Live In Berlin*** (Mood)

# Massimo Urbani

ALTO SAXOPHONE
*born* 8 May 1957; *died* 24 June 1993

Scarcely known outside his native Italy, Urbani was an extraordinary player. He mastered the bebop idiom with such intensity that, at his finest, he made the most exhilarating music in the idiom since Parker. A Roman who studied early on with Giorgio Gaslini, he worked with various leaders through the 70s but led his own bands from 1979. He was a notorious wild man, and his appetites eventually killed him: he died of a heroin overdose. He seldom had the discipline needed to maintain a steady career as a leader. Marcello Piras called him a 'wastrel genius'. The surviving recordings are spotty, and Urbani is often let down by his playing company, but there are devastating moments on all of them, as well as hints of how he still had many further directions to explore: a set dedicated to Ayler and Coltrane suggested some of the ways he might have gone. *The Blessing* (1993), made only months before his death, with brother Maurizio on tenor and a good rhythm section, is perhaps his most fully achieved record, and his solo 'Blues For Bird', a breathtaking *tour de force*, is unforgettable once heard.
***The Blessing*** (Red)

## Michal Urbaniak
VIOLIN, TENOR SAXOPHONE
*born* 22 January 1943

Born in Warsaw, Urbaniak was a good enough classical student to win a scholarship to study under David Oistrakh, but he gave it up to play jazz. He liked the saxophone at least as much as the violin, and played both in various groups, in and around the Polish scene of the 60s. His wife, Urszula Dudziak, sang in some of them. In the 70s he was intrigued by jazz-rock, a genre which Polish musicians seem particularly fond of, and his groups Fusion and the later Urbanator made a noisy stab at contributing something to the style. Urbaniak has actually done rather better things in acoustic, straight-ahead music, where a presumably native sense of folkish melody lends touches of lyricism and poignancy to what would otherwise be skilful post-bop improvising of a conventional type. His records for Steeplechase, where he plays acoustic and electric instruments, have much to enjoy, though there is no real classic among them. Urbaniak may be leaving it a little late to set down a definitive statement on record.
***Songbird*** (Steeplechase)

## René Urtreger
PIANO
*born* 6 July 1934

France loves jazz more than any other country, yet French jazz musicians have made peculiarly little impact outside their borders. Urtreger is an excellent pianist grounded in the bebop manner, and he was a regular at Paris's Club Saint-Germain in the 50s (where Miles Davis and Lester Young were wont to turn up), and formed an association with Kenny Clarke during the drummer's Paris years. Though he spent some time accompanying singers outside the jazz sphere, he returned to the music as both soloist and group leader through the 80s and 90s. He has recorded regularly (and was on Davis's movie score for *Ascenseur pour l'échafaud*) but the albums haven't travelled much. His trio with Daniel Humair and Pierre Michelot, HUM, has seen some of his best work.
***Move*** (BB)

## Warren Vaché
CORNET
*born* 21 February 1951

Warren is the son of Warren Senior, a bassist, and older brother of Allan, a clarinettist, both of whom are adept players on their own horns. But the cornetist is the main reason why Vaché should be an honoured jazz name. His dad got him into playing the traditional end of the music, at a time when most young trumpeters (he switched to cornet later) wanted to play hard bop. Then he studied with Pee Wee Erwin, the swing-era veteran, while working in the circle of traditional-mainstreamers which grew up in the New York clubs of the 70s: Vaché and Scott Hamilton were an effective partnership, much recorded by Concord, which took the opportunity to play with those old-timers of previous generations who were then still active, such as Roy Eldridge and Benny Goodman. Vaché has since dipped into other styles, flirting every now and then with a more boppish text, but his inclinations are to play the American songbook and hot jazz tunes in a style which is melodious, mellowed, but still with enough rasp to cut through an ensemble. He is not a bad actor – he played a bandleader-cornetist in an excellent piece of jazz fiction, *The Gig*, made in 1985 – and an amusing note-writer. As a duet partner with a pianist he is never less than superb, and of his many recordings, the recent one with Bill Charlap listed below already has the feel of a timeless masterpiece, proving that the swing repertory still has much nourishment to offer if it's approached with their kind of imagination.
***2gether*** (Nagel Heyer)

## Chucho Valdés
PIANO
*born* 9 October 1941

Valdés is one of the three Cubans who, as émigrés or visitors, had an important impact on American jazz in the 80s (the others were Paquito D'Rivera and Arturo Sandoval, both of whom played alongside Valdés in the 60s). While the others defected to the US, Valdés, although touring regularly with his group Irakere, has remained based in Cuba, where he teaches and runs the

Havana Jazz Plaza festival. Whether playing solo or performing with Irakere and other groups, his style remains a constant: very fast, very flashy, and overloaded with the kind of technique that can generate astonishment and boredom in rapid succession. His music's appeal will depend to a large extent on the listener's sympathy for Latin pulses. The jazz content of any improvisation is often more decorative than substantial, and like much so-called Latin jazz, the real qualities in his idiom have more to do with native musics which have a genealogy and colour running as a complex parallel to jazz. Records have thus far come a poor second to the ebullience of Valdés in performance. In 1998, he retired from Irakere (his son leads the group) and now works with a different small group of his own choosing.
**Solo Piano** (Blue Note)

## Gary Valente
TROMBONE
*born* 26 June 1953

Valente's father also played trombone, and gave his son his first lessons. The younger Valente had some years of study and playing behind him when he arrived in New York in 1977. Since then, he has been a sideman with numerous leaders – George Russell, Joe Lovano, Andy Sheppard – but his main association has been with Carla Bley, who has used his braying, brassy sound with a sympathy worthy of Ellington. His signature setpiece is the tumultuous solo on her composition 'The Lord Is Listening To Ya, Hallelujah!' Although he has sometimes threatened to come to the fore as a leader – he can claim co-leadership of the four-'bone group Slideride, at least – Valente seems content with his lot as a rumbustious sideman.
**Carla Bley, *Live!*** (WATT)

## Kid Thomas Valentine
TRUMPET
*born* 3 February 1896; *died* 16 June 1987

One of the greatest of New Orleans trumpeters was actually born in Reserve, Louisiana, and didn't arrive in the city until 1922. He led bands from the 30s up until his death, and over the course of an extraordi-

narily long life he pared down an already taciturn style to its leanest and most meaningful essence. He played a tough, hard-bitten lead trumpet that treated melodies correctly but cut them up into jagged fistfuls of notes. There's an exaggerated drama in his treatment of tunes such as 'St James Infirmary', which speaks of an old-time showman, but Valentine never did anything more than he had to. Solos were rare, and little more than a twist out of some part of the melody. A master of mutes – plunger, derby and Harmon alike – that aspect of his playing was only rarely showcased on record. He didn't start recording until 1951, but was thereafter frequently in front of microphones, and with his doughty group The Algiers Stompers he left a big legacy on record. A slight, wiry little man with a mouth that seemed to stretch right round his face, he was surprised himself at how long his life had lasted. His jazz never varied, yet every set was different from every other. When offered a compliment, he would usually shrug and reply, 'Same old soupbone!'
**Kid Thomas–George Lewis Ragtime Stompers** (GHB)

## Hein Van de Geyn
BASS
*born* 18 July 1956

Van de Geyn's background is in classical violin, and study at the Tilburg Conservatory in the Netherlands, but in the late 70s he began playing stand-up jazz bass and he has stuck by it since. He went to the US on a tour in 1980 and stayed three years, forming an alliance with John Abercrombie among others, and back in Europe he worked with a variety of players, including a long stint with Dee Dee Bridgewater. His band Baseline, with Joe LaBarbera and Abercrombie, cut three fine records for the label which he set up in 1994, Challenge, which has since expanded into one of the leading Dutch independents.
**Baseline, *Baseline Returns*** (Challenge)

# Ken Vandermark

TENOR SAXOPHONE, BASS CLARINET
*born* 11 September 1964

Vandermark grew up in Boston but took up the saxophone while on a film studies course in Montreal. Back in Boston from the mid-80s, he played locally before shifting over to Chicago, where he has remained since, and quickly became one of the leading lights on the city's new jazz scene. His first association was with Hal Russell's NRG Ensemble, but after that he led bands of his own, and these grew into an extravagant span of groups and occasional tie-ups with international players – among the bands: Caffeine, Steelwool Trio, Cinghiale, Witches And Devils, Barrage Double Trio, Steam and the two groups he has put the majority of his time and focus into, The Vandermark 5 and DKV, the latter a trio with Kent Kessler and Hamid Drake. As the informal head of a group of players which includes bassists Kessler and Nate McBride, saxophonist Mars Williams, trombonist Jeb Bishop and drummer Tim Mulvenna, Vandermark has already set down a large body of work on record. He honours the work of Peter Brötzmann and has been a motivating force in the touring and recording work by Brötzmann's octet in recent times. Besides this, he often works with Mats Gustafsson and has regularly guested with the AALY Trio. Having grown up mainly with classical music and some jazz, Vandermark has steadily added to his listening and has done projects on such neglected jazz figures as Joe Harriott and Jimmy Giuffre, as well as playing comparatively neglected repertory by Don Cherry, Eric Dolphy and others. He can play with lung-busting ferocity on tenor as well as with chamberish quiet on clarinet, and it adds up to an exceptionally inclusive and absorbing outlook which has been compelling to follow. The Vandermark 5 records are the best place to start listening to him.
*Simpatico* (Atavistic)

# George Van Eps

GUITAR
*born* 7 August 1913; *died* 29 November 1998

George's dad was the great banjo virtuoso Fred Van Eps, who made countless records at the beginning of the 20th century, and the younger Van Eps began on banjo himself before switching to guitar at the beginning of the 30s. He was buried away in various dance orchestras before shifting into studio work, which basically took up the rest of his career until he started appearing at festivals in the 60s and 70s. Van Eps was an inveterate tinkerer and liked inventing things: he designed his own seven-string guitar, with an extra bass string, thereby creating a technique which has been used since by such players as Bucky Pizzarelli. Howard Alden started using it, too, after he made a record of duets with George in 1991. At the end of his long life, the often hidden-away Van Eps was an acknowledged master, and he kept playing up to the end. Three albums for Capitol and a solitary set for Columbia have never been reissued. Besides George, there were three other musical brothers in the Van Eps family: Johnny (sax), Fred (trumpet) and Bobby (piano).
*13 Strings* (Concord)

# Rudy Van Gelder

ENGINEER
*born* 2 November 1924

The saxophonist Gil Melle discovered an unassuming man, by profession an optometrist, who was a former radio ham and general technology nut and had set up what amounted to a little recording studio in his home in Hackensack, New Jersey. In 1952, Melle introduced him to Alfred Lion of Blue Note, who tried a record date there. From there, Rudy Van Gelder began to engineer jazz records on a regular basis, principally for Blue Note, but also for Prestige and other small labels – he disliked the big corporations and preferred to stick to people he knew he could work with. He finally abandoned optometry in 1959 and moved to a new home in Englewood Heights, New Jersey, where he had custom-designed new facilities, and he works from there to this day. Van Gelder had a magical ear and touch for finding the balance of a jazz group in the studio: drummers were given clear, spatial mixes, but he could equalize the differing styles of Art Blakey and Art Taylor without resorting to technical trickery, and he secured an especially clear and distinctive piano sound. In the 90s, the Japanese arm of Blue Note approached Van Gelder about having him remaster his old albums for the label, and the master engineer has since then worked on many of his classics, which the label has re-released in an 'RVG Edition'.

# Vanguard
RECORD COMPANY

Established in 1950, this independent was set up primarily for classical recordings, but John Hammond persuaded them to create a series called Vanguard Jazz Showcase, beginning in 1953, and the initial releases by such musicians as Vic Dickenson, Buck Clayton, Ruby Braff and others showcased what would be termed 'mainstream' jazz for the first time in the LP era. The jazz output fell away in the 60s but was later revitalized to some extent with albums by Oregon and Larry Coryell.

# Fred Van Hove
PIANO, ORGAN
*born* 19 February 1937

Van Hove grew up in Antwerp and became interested in bebop in the 50s, eventually playing in local festivals and forming an alliance with Peter Brötzmann, which led to his immersion in free playing. Van Hove's work in the trio with Brötzmann and Han Bennink resulted in some of the pioneering recordings of their kind for FMP at the end of the 60s (he somehow makes his way through the noise of *Machine Gun*, 1968), and from there he has moved on to work with most of Europe's leading improvisers at some point. His own groups, always with the prefix 'ML', have included MLA, MLB, MLBB and MLB III, all ensembles of different shapes and sizes, but a lot of his most distinctive playing has been done as a soloist: possessed of a classical virtuosity and a dense, thickly textured approach to even an improvised musical structure, his solo records can be hard but rewarding work. He is also one of the very few to try free improvisation on a church organ (*Church Organ*, SAJ 1979).
*Flux* (Potlatch)

# Willem Van Manen
TROMBONE
*born* 3 September 1940

Like many of his generation, Van Manen got his start in Dixieland bands in Amsterdam, but as the 60s went on he became drawn to modern and then free playing. He began an association with Willem Breuker around this time, and eventually became a full-time member of Breuker's Kollektief in 1974. He was one of the founding spirits in the contemporary music group De Volharding, created to play compositions for wind ensembles, and in 1985 created his own big band, Contraband, which has been a superbly colourful, swinging and musical orchestra: though much less well-known internationally than Breuker's group, and a generally more sober outfit, its handful of records are of comparable stature to that of the Kollektief.
*Pale Fire* (BVHaast)

# Ack Van Rooyen
TRUMPET, FLUGELHORN
*born* 1 January 1930

Van Rooyen studied in The Hague Conservatory and played symphonic music before playing in a small group with his brother Jerry, also a trumpeter. He then toured Europe in the brass section of various orchestras, and settled in Germany in 1960, where he stayed (in Berlin and Stuttgart) for the next 20 years, working in radio orchestras and as a sideman with Peter Herbolzheimer, Wolfgang Dauner and in the United Jazz And Rock Ensemble. Eventually, he moved back to Holland at the start of the 80s, and has worked there since in his own groups and with the Dutch Jazz Orchestra. Van Rooyen's Gillespie-like fluency and ebullience are probably to be heard on a huge number of records, but he has actually been featured very little as a leader on his own account. The record cited has him as the major soloist in front of a large orchestra, and he is typically skilful in his playing.
*Colores* (Koala)

# Jasper Van't Hof

KEYBOARDS
*born* 30 June 1947

Born in Enschede in the Netherlands, Van't Hof was already playing jazz in his teens, and he divided his time between straight-ahead and various kinds of fusion playing for much of the 70s, with bands such as Association PC (with Pierre Courbois) and his own band Pork Pie (including Charlie Mariano, a regular partner, and Philip Catherine). In the 80s he showed an interest in working with violin players, including Zbigniew Seifert and Jean-Luc Ponty, and formed a band called Eyeball, with Didier Lockwood and Bob Malach. Pili Pili, which involved African percussionists, was another venture of the period. Van't Hof's playing tends to mix strong ideas with passages of overcooked exuberance, and one feels that he has only rarely been caught at his best on record: a grandly presented solo recital (*At The Concertgebouw*, Challenge, 1993) is let down by a sense of hubris, and more interesting is his organ solo record, *Un Mondo Ilusorio* (Challenge, 1998). A lot of his work is, though, out of print and hard to find.
*Tomorrowland* (Challenge)

# Tom Varner

FRENCH HORN
*born* 17 June 1957

Varner grew up in New Jersey, taking up the french horn early on, and moving into jazz when he heard and later studied with Julius Watkins. He moved to New York in 1979 and besides sideman work with Dave Liebman, George Gruntz, John Zorn and Steve Lacy, he has mainly led his own groups, recording for Soul Note, New Note, New World and Omnitone. Varner's approach to an instrument which is rare in jazz has been thoughtful and careful to seek out areas where the instrument can make an individual mark, rather than just act as a trombone substitute: 'If you listen casually, people think, oh, that's a trombone. After a few more minutes, if you have a discerning ear, you know it's something different – it can sound like a saxophone or a flugelhorn too.' He has played straight bebop on the trombone ('Quasimodo' on *Jazz French Horn*, 1985, is a classic example), but his group records are

ambitious, beautifully detailed, and often cover surprising terrain: *The Window Up Above* (New World, 1998) covers American music from revivalist hymns to Bruce Springsteen, and the record cited is a dramatic variation on Don Cherry's *Complete Communion* album in a brilliant piece of revisionism.
*Second Communion* (Omnitone)

# John Varro

PIANO
*born* 11 January 1930

Varro grew up in New York and hung out at the Commodore Music Shop in his teens, where he got encouraging nods from the likes of Willie 'The Lion' Smith. He became part of the circle working at Nick's and Eddie Condon's in the 50s, and remained involved in Dixieland groups before moving first to Los Angeles in 1979, and latterly to Florida. Varro has been a journeyman without a great deal of honour on record until recently, but he is one of the several artists given a kind of rediscovery by the swing-orientated label Arbors, and a string of accomplished records for the company has given his playing – dyed-in-the-wool swing, with just a lick of bebop here and there – an overdue priority.
*Swing 7* (Arbors)

# Nana Vasconcelos

PERCUSSION
*born* 2 August 1944

Vasconcelos worked as a percussionist in local bands in Rio de Janeiro, and only left the country when he was hired by Gato Barbieri for his touring group in 1972. He then lived and worked in Paris and other parts of Europe, playing with Don Cherry and Collin Walcott in Codona, performing in Pat Metheny's touring bands in the early 80s, and doing other sideman work with Andy Sheppard, Jack DeJohnette and Arild Andersen. His own band Bushdance toured for a time. Vasconcelos could at times seem like the token 'Brazilian' element in some projects, but he did have a knack for hijacking concert stages, and audiences were always drawn to the spectacle of him playing an elaborate berimbau solo or one of his mischievous percussion features. Thus far, though, little has been heard from him in the new century.

**Codona,** *Codona* (ECM)

# Sarah Vaughan
VOCAL
*born* 27 March 1924; *died* 3 April 1990

'The Divine One' might be the greatest of all jazz singers, yet her popularity has never matched that of Fitzgerald, Holiday or Washington, her judgement could be strange, her manner unconvincing and her career on record inconsistent and sometimes misconceived in terms of its direction. She learned piano and sang in the choir of her local baptist church in Newark, but she was another of the jazz singers who won a contest in the more secular surroundings of the Apollo Theater in Harlem, in 1942. The following year she joined Earl Hines's band as the singer, sharing duties with Billy Eckstine, and Eckstine himself engaged Vaughan when he started his own big band a year later. After leaving in 1945 she worked as a solo. Her affiliations with her many friends among the bebop elite kept her jazz credibility high, but on record – at first with Musicraft, and then with Columbia, with whom she stayed for five years after signing in 1949 – she principally sang ballads, often weighted down with lavish orchestrations, and during her entire tenure with Columbia there was only a single date which had any hint of a jazz setting to it. This changed when she signed to Mercury, for the rest of the 50s, although only partially. Her Mercury albums continued to be in the slow orchestral vein, but for its subsidiary Emarcy she made small-group and much more jazz-orientated albums: *Sarah Vaughan* (1954), with superb solos in accompaniment by Clifford Brown, is one of the finest of all jazz vocal records, and *Swingin' Easy* (1954/7) and the live record *At Mister Kelly's* (1957) aren't far behind. By now, Vaughan's voice had matured and deepened into a huge, almost operatic contralto, with a luscious vibrato which she controlled to a nicety and a mastery of variation of timbre that allowed her to adopt different personas even within the course of a single tune. Even on her most middle-of-the-road records, it's hard not to enjoy the majesty and opulence of the voice. From the 60s she recorded for a variety of labels, including Roulette, which she made some fine albums for, and although there were some disastrous mistakes, such as a farcically wrong-headed Beatles collection, Vaughan's artistry remained intact. In concert, she worked mostly with small groups, sometimes played piano herself, and had a succession of fine accompanists: in person she was imperious and sometimes haughty, even when giving us her introductory joke ('For those of you who don't know me, my name is . . . Carmen McRae'), but there would always be at least something, in the midst of the most coolly professional set, where she could induce shivers, even on a well-worn ballad such as 'Misty'. Her last association on record was with Pablo, and her sequence of albums for the label had some sensitive and apposite settings for her to work in. Without the mystique of Holiday or the warmth of Fitzgerald, she has been almost neglected in terms of reputation since her death, yet she is, eternally, the Divine Sassy.

*Sarah Vaughan* (Emarcy)

# V-disc
RECORD LABEL

V-discs were an initiative designed to assist in entertaining the American troops during the Second World War. The records were a mix of music especially recorded for the imprint (often with messages of goodwill from the artists to the troops), broadcast material, and occasionally dubbings of commercially issued records. Established in 1943, it lasted some six years (even after the cessation of hostilities), with the discs being distributed to military personnel across the world, mainly for transmission via public-address systems and short-wave radio broadcasts. A large amount of jazz was recorded and distributed in this way, and the results are still eagerly collected by specialists around the world: because the discs were seldom maintained in fine condition, examples of V-discs in excellent condition are rare and sought-after.

# Reginald Veal

BASS
*born* 5 November 1963

Although born in Chicago, Veal grew up in New Orleans and became acquainted with Branford and Wynton Marsalis soon after his high-school years. He joined Wynton's band in 1987 and stayed until the middle 90s, thereafter working with Branford's groups as well as with other members of the Marsalis and Lincoln Center circle. An exponent of the 'woody' style which seems to have been a touchstone in the Marsalis approach to music, Veal is a strong and versatile bass man with failsafe hands.
**Wynton Marsalis, *Citi Movement*** (Columbia)

# Charlie Ventura

TENOR AND BARITONE SAXOPHONES
*born* 2 December 1916; *died* 17 January 1992

Ventura came out of his home Philadelphia scene to join Gene Krupa in 1942, the first of three spells with the drummer. He had a big band of his own in the middle 40s, then a septet, and finally a quartet with Buddy Rich in 1952. Ventura's sound was in the Hawkins–Berry tradition, big and blowsy, and with just enough of Illinois Jacquet's rabble-rousing to create a certain excitement. History hasn't dealt too kindly with him: the septet, which also included Kai Winding, went out under the unlikely banner of 'Bop For The People', ironic in that Ventura's own delivery had very little that was boppish about it; he was very popular for a while before almost completely disappearing from the jazz mainstream. Actually, many of his 40s and early-50s dates now emerge as surprisingly fresh and unpretentious, the playing unambitious but smart, and the singing of Jackie Cain and Roy Kral sounds hipper than ever. Ventura carried on into the 80s but jazz had long since left him behind.
**It's All Bop To Me** (RCA)

# Joe Venuti

VIOLIN
*born* 16 September 1903; *died* 14 August 1978

The facts of Venuti's early life have been difficult to sort out, mainly through his taste for tomfoolery, circulating stories about being born in steerage en route from Italy and so forth. He was, though, born in Philadelphia, where he studied classical violin for a time, although he preferred popular music and was soon collaborating with a fellow string player from the Italian community, guitarist Eddie Lang. They were still playing together in Jean Goldkette's band in 1925, and from there both moved to New York, where they became regulars in the studio community and with such contemporaries as Trumbauer, Beiderbecke, the Dorseys, Nichols and Mole. Venuti's duet records with Lang, and those credited to Joe Venuti's Blue Four, showcase the first great jazz violin stylist, hot, fluent, classical in his louche elegance but able to warm up the most conventional of dance-band settings. He and Lang were an indomitable partnership, but the guitarist's unexpected death in 1933 was a serious blow, and for many years Venuti worked comparatively quietly, leading a big band with only modest success and subsequently working as a studio musician. He turned up on Bing Crosby's radio show in the 50s but thereafter suffered with a drink problem and made no records in the 60s at all. But he began playing at Dick Gibson's Jazz Parties, had a warm welcome at the 1968 Newport Festival, and enjoyed a comeback which lasted up until his death. Venuti's penchant for practical joking left a fund of anecdotes which could fill several pages, but his playing style was, for all his ebullient humour, serious and entirely his own, and on his late records with such partners as Earl Hines and Dave McKenna fine music is bountiful: the final work of the last survivor of a school of players who once dominated white New York jazz.
***Violin Jazz*** (Yazoo)

# Verve

RECORD COMPANY

Norman Granz's label came into being in 1956, the immediate successor to his Clef and Norgan imprints, whose catalogues were subsumed into the new company and reissued in suitable form. Ella Fitzgerald's 'songbook' records were Verve's first great success, and thereafter the leading names of Granz's stable of artists – including Stan Getz, Oscar Peterson, Dizzy Gillespie, Roy

Eldridge and Anita O'Day – built on her commercial success. Creed Taylor arrived as a producer and A&R man in the 60s and brought in figures such as Wes Montgomery, but Granz sold the label to Polydor in 1967 and thereafter it went into a decline as far as 'new' records were concerned. As part of the Polygram group in the 80s and early 90s, the label was dramatically revitalized, and much of its old catalogue was reissued on CD; meanwhile, new records by Charlie Haden, Joe Henderson, Dee Dee Bridgewater, Abbey Lincoln, Stan Getz and others helped push the label towards a new eminence and relevance. When Polygram itself was subsumed into the new giant Universal Music Group, though, the label's identity all but disappeared: despite the integration of such successful acts as Diana Krall into what had once been 'Verve', it was really just a flag of convenience for a label which had become bloated with catalogues acquired by other parts of its parent group, and which had lost most of its stand-alone integrity via internal politicking and a dilution of any overall musical policy.

# Edward Vesala
DRUMS
born 15 February 1945; died 4 December 1999

Vesala was the great maverick spirit in Finnish jazz of the modern era. He studied percussion at the Sibelius Academy in Helsinki before working with Jan Garbarek (*Triptykon*, 1972, one of the finest early ECM albums) and working with his own groups. He founded the Leo label around 1978 (not the same as the one established by Leo Feigin in the UK), and thereafter led a group he called Sound And Fury, which also recorded for ECM. Vesala's music was an intense dramatization of his musical beliefs and practices. Unusual instrumentations, music as much directed by influences from outside jazz, so-called 'ethnic' strains and structures which owe little to any conventional post-bop practice – all this was fair game for Vesala's coolly articulated but raw and folk-like expression. The impressionism which seems to be cultivated in a record such as *Lumi* (1986) is to some extent civilized and rationalized by the impeccable ECM presentation, but Vesala's music had an almost brutal power in performance

which his records, for all their wintry beauty, perhaps never quite isolated. He toured with his ensemble as well as working with them in the remote environment of his country home, but his sudden early death deprived jazz of a singular spirit who surely had much else to impart.
*Lumi* (ECM)

# Harold Vick
TENOR SAXOPHONE
born 3 April 1936; died 13 November 1987

Vick's talent was largely wasted as far as recording opportunities were concerned. He took up the saxophone at 16 and while studying psychology began playing in R&B bands and with several organ/tenor combos. He made a single Blue Note session in 1962, *Steppin' Out!*, and also recorded with John Patton. Vick kept making eye-catching appearances, with Donald Byrd, Ray Charles and others, but his own-name career never really went anywhere, and in the end he made only five albums in total. For much of the 70s he worked in soul groups and eventually did most of his work as a studio musician. He could play with tremendous force, sometimes finding a spearing cry which could sound a little like Booker Ervin, and as a blues player he could distil a solo with a kind of immaculate calm. Sonny Rollins, for one, never forgot him: a track on Rollins's *This Is What I Do* (2000) is called 'Did You Hear Harold Vick?'
*Steppin' Out!* (Blue Note)

# Vienna Art Orchestra
GROUP

Founded by the composer Matthias Ruegg, the VAO was established in Austria in 1977 as an orchestral vehicle for the performance of Ruegg's music. Although at the time of its formation the ensemble had few players who were otherwise known in jazz circles, the likes of Bumi Fian (trumpet), Harry Sokal (saxes), Uli Scherer (piano) and Wolfgang Reisinger (drums) soon became familiar beyond their work in the ensemble. Besides Ruegg's own compositions, the Orchestra has built a repertory from such composers as Erik Satie, Anthony Braxton, Scott Joplin and Hans Koller, and it has recorded extensively for hat ART, Moers Music and Verve. Veering between big-band tradition, art-music and a dryly humorous delivery which almost has a taste of Spike-Jones-Goes-To-Vienna about it, the VAO has built a voluminous body of work which is energetic yet often curiously lacking in depth, and like much music from middle Europe, it has had little lasting impact on the broader perspective of contemporary jazz. Ruegg's great skill has been to keep the Orchestra intact and flourishing across some three decades of work: he is a master at finding subsidies and extracting sponsorships for what is, on the face of it, a decidedly 'uncommercial' vehicle.

**The Minimalism Of Erik Satie** (hat ART)

# Village Vanguard
JAZZ CLUB

The most enduring jazz venue in New York, and probably the most famous in the world. Max Gordon opened the original Village Vanguard on Charles Street and Greenwich Avenue in 1934, more as a hang-out for poets, who gathered to read their work. When he tried to put on music, he fell foul of the licensing laws, and had to move to another basement, at 178 Seventh Avenue. Music and poetry began to share time at the new venue, and it wasn't until the 50s that jazz finally took precedence. Under Gordon's watchful eye, hundreds of musicians played in the club's modest quarters over the course of decades, and many albums were recorded there, including masterpieces by Sonny Rollins and John Coltrane. As Max grew into a stately old age, everyone wondered what would happen to the old place when he was gone, but following his death in 1989 his widow Lorraine took over the running of the club, and she still takes care of business there. Virtually unchanged as time has gone on, the Vanguard continues to present the music in an honest and no-frills way: rather than any kind of fashionable place to be seen, the Vanguard is where jazz musicians play and jazz fans listen.

# Leroy Vinnegar
BASS
*born* 13 July 1928; *died* 3 August 1999

The titles of his three featured albums as a leader – *Leroy Walks* (Contemporary, 1957), *Leroy Walks Again* (1963) and *Walkin' The Basses* (1992) – offer a prominent clue as to Vinnegar's talent. While he was prepared to take bass solos, he preferred to play them in his normal four-to-the-bar, walking style, and it became his signature delivery. He played with Wes Montgomery in his home town of Indianapolis before moving to Chicago in 1952, where he worked as an accompanist to many major soloists. In 1954 he moved to Los Angeles and became a prolific sessionman there, a step which probably secured his leadership dates with Contemporary. This kind of freelancing lasted him through the 60s and 70s, when he worked with the likes of The Jazz Crusaders and Eddie Harris, but he began to suffer from heart and lung problems and eventually he moved to Oregon, in part because the LA smog was giving him trouble.

**Leroy Walks** (Contemporary)

# Eddie 'Cleanhead' Vinson
ALTO SAXOPHONE, VOCALS
*born* 18 December 1917; *died* 2 July 1988

Vinson was a hard musician to classify. Born in Houston, he took up the alto in his teens and played in local groups before touring the south with blues players such as Bill Broonzy. In 1942 he went to New York and became a star turn in the Cootie Williams band, singing a hit blues called 'Cherry Red' which gave him enough momentum to form his own big band, in 1946, recording the first version of his signature 'Mr Cleanhead Blues' that year. He slimmed the group down to a septet (and had John Coltrane as a sideman), and though he worked steadily enough, he was largely out of the public eye until the end of the 60s, when he toured Europe with Jay McShann and starred in roadshow packages with Johnny Otis and Count Basie. This led to a renewed career in both Europe and the US. Vinson was largely perceived as a blues man, but his saxophone playing was mostly formulated as a particularly terse kind of

bebop, and when dropped into the compacted context of a single blues chorus it could be devastatingly effective. His deadpan way with a ribald lyric won over audiences without any trouble – the 'Cleanhead' metaphor related to how his baldness had been induced by the hands of eager ladies – and he sang it night after night with no suspicion of boredom.
*Mr Cleanhead's Back In Town* (JSP)

## Miroslav Vitous

BASS
*born* 6 December 1947

Vitous was born in Prague and studied at the Conservatory there before winning a scholarship to Berklee in 1966. A year later, though, he was in New York, playing with Freddie Hubbard, Miles Davis and other leaders, and then spent two years in Herbie Mann's groups. In 1970 he was one of the founding trinity of Weather Report, along with Joe Zawinul and Wayne Shorter, but after three records he was already being sidelined and he moved on to other projects in 1973. After some years when he tinkered with the possibilities of the electric bass, he returned to the acoustic model, and while teaching at the New England Conservatory he continued performing and making records for ECM. In 1988 he returned to Germany, began working in a duo with his brother (where his brilliant virtuosity was given full rein), and turned up as a sideman on a variety of recordings. Vitous has sometimes seemed like a nearly man of fusion and the impressionist side of jazz-rock. A soloist rather than a timekeeper, he wasn't really what was required in Zawinul's Weather Report, and he does much better by his ECM albums and in more sympathetic sideman contexts. Much of his time in the 90s was taken up with creating music for commercial requirements, but Manfred Eicher persuaded him back with the triumphant *Universal Syncopations* in 2003, his best record for more than 20 years.
*Universal Syncopations* (ECM)

## Vocalese

A type of jazz singing where a text is set to the melody of a previously recorded jazz improvisation. The original pioneer of the idiom was Eddie Jefferson, who started doing it in the 40s, but he had some of his thunder stolen by his near contemporary King Pleasure, who had a hit version of 'Moody's Mood For Love' (1952), drawn from a James Moody solo, which was itself a Jefferson setpiece. Pleasure's treatment of 'Parker's Mood' (1953) was more his own. Latterly the master of the style was Jon Hendricks, who created vocalese settings both for Lambert, Hendricks and Ross and for his own subsequent solo work. More recent groups such as Manhattan Transfer and New York Voices have also created vocalese showcases. The idea that the texts of vocalese are spontaneously invented is mistaken: most of them come out of a lot of hard graft by the protagonist, much as modern rap has a great deal of work behind its apparently effortless rhymes.

## Nasheet Waits

DRUMS
*born* 15 June 1970

Waits's father Freddie (1943–89) played on Motown record dates, with Paul Winter, Gerald Wilson, Sonny Rollins, Freddie Hubbard, Max Roach's M'Boom, Johnny Hodges, Andrew Hill and Mulgrew Miller, among many others, which says much about his formidable versatility. His son Nasheet may turn out to be even more significant. He studied at Long Island University, and privately with Max Roach, and he was a regular in Antonio Hart's band from 1993. Since then he has been in continuous demand as a sideman, his brilliant style working from a base of knowledge and insight comparable to his father's while accommodating more free-ranging touches and a sense that the drummer has to be upfront and in direct dialogue with the rest of the group. In this respect, his work with Jason Moran's trio has been exceptional.
**Jason Moran, *The Bandwagon*** (Blue Note)

## Collin Walcott

TABLA, SITAR
*born* 24 April 1945; *died* 8 November 1984

Walcott only had a peripheral relationship with jazz, but his work with Oregon and

Codona was certainly influential. He studied percussion at Indiana University and was then a pupil of Ravi Shankar (sitar) and Alla Rakha (tabla). He worked with Tony Scott on the clarinettist's albums of 'yoga' and 'zen' music, and he played in the Paul Winter Consort and its successor, Oregon, and in Codona with Don Cherry and Nana Vasconcelos. His ECM albums *Cloud Dance* (1975) and *Grazing Dreams* (1977) set out a stall right at the start of the modern idea of 'world music', and did so in a satisfyingly unpretentious and not-too-serious way: Walcott's main purpose in his music always seemed to be the communication of joy. His death in a road accident while on tour brought a sad and abrupt end to his music-making.
*Grazing Dreams* (ECM)

## Mal Waldron
PIANO
*born* 16 August 1925; *died* 2 December 2002

Waldron set out to be a classical pianist, but he found work as a jazz player and began playing professionally in New York in 1950. He worked as a sideman with Charles Mingus and then led small groups of his own, recording regularly for Prestige from 1956 as both leader and sideman, and he worked as Billie Holiday's accompanist in the last two years of her life. In the next decade he did more sideman work with Max Roach and Eric Dolphy, but a nervous breakdown stalled his progress and he had to rebuild his style and method of working, and later in the decade he settled in Munich. Waldron remained a European resident for the rest of his life, moving to Brussels in the 90s, and from then on he was mostly recorded by European labels, including Enja, Soul Note and hatOLOGY. Thelonious Monk is the pianist usually said to be his principal influence, but Waldron doesn't sound much like Monk: he liked thundering left-hand vamps, and slow-moving improvisations which depended on motifs gradually gathering together into an implacable whole. Steve Lacy was one of his favourite partners, and the two men shared a liking for patiently worked-over details. He led trios and quintets in the 70s and 80s, as well as doing solo work, and he sometimes worked with the English baritone saxophonist George

Haslam, who produced some of his final recordings. While he left a large book of compositions, the only one which has really entered the jazz repertory is one of his first, 'Soul Eyes'.
*Impressions* (Prestige/OJC)

## Walking bass

The classic jazz bass line: a regular 4/4 meter marked out by the bassist, who 'walks' the rhythm without interrupting the line with any ornamentation. A pianist can also do a walking bass with the left hand, if playing a boogie-woogie rhythm.

## Bennie Wallace
TENOR SAXOPHONE
*born* 18 November 1946

Born in Chattanooga, Tennessee, Wallace played locally before graduating from the University of Tennessee, and he moved to New York in 1971, where he worked without gaining much attention until forming his own trio. His records were made for the German label Enja until he secured what turned out to be a brief affiliation with Blue Note, where he cut two records which mixed his usual style with his perceived roots in Southern and Louisiana music. Wallace's playing is an unusual mix of ancient and near-modern, even in a period where eclecticism is the norm. At one point he listened to nothing but swing-era music, which grafted the styles of older men such as Ben Webster on to an approach which was otherwise more in hock to Sonny Rollins, and Bennie sometimes sounds like a more humorous and slow-moving version of David Murray, with a lick of Southern soul as a twist. It is surely a refreshing switch from the orthodox approach of many of his contemporaries. He worked in Hollywood for a period in the 90s, writing a number of filmscores, but has since moved back East.
*Big Jim's Tango* (Enja)

# Byron Wallen
TRUMPET
*born* 17 July 1969

Born in London, Wallen took an ambitious path in his studies, going to New York to take lessons with Jon Faddis, going to Java to look into gamelan music and then studying Ugandan traditional music on its own turf. He has based his career in London from the mid-90s, although the recorded results – that often find him mixing all these worldly influences with the crushing overlay of funk, which tends to swamp all the delicacy he is presumably after – have been less than astonishing.

*Indigo* (Twilight Jaguar)

# Fats Waller
PIANO, ORGAN, VOCAL
*born* 21 May 1904; *died* 15 December 1943

Born Thomas Wright Waller in New York, he played the organ for his preacher father as a boy. By the early 20s he had begun to mix with some of the Harlem pianists, and was making piano rolls and his first records as early as 1922: 'as soon as I was old enough, I went right out and did all the things I'd been held back from doing', a philosophy which he followed relentlessly for the rest of his short life. He began accompanying blues singers on record dates, and started writing tunes with Clarence Williams and other collaborators, his principal lyricist being Andy Razaf: between them they wrote stage shows such as *Keep Shufflin'* (1928) and *Hot Chocolates* (1929), which often enjoyed Broadway success, although the always impecunious Waller often gave away rights to songs for the price of a plate of hamburgers. He became a regular on radio, singing and playing piano, and was signed to Victor in 1926, where he remained to make all of the rest of his records. While he occasionally turned up as a sideman or group leader, most of his early recordings are of piano and pipe-organ solos, some of which – 'Smashing Thirds', 'Numb Fumblin'', 'Valentine Stomp', 'Sweet Savannah Sue' – are among his best moments on record. Playing primarily in the stride tradition established by his mentor James P Johnson and others, Waller's extravagant gifts flow gracefully out of his fingers: charming,

perky melodies (too perky, thought Alec Wilder, who compared Waller's writing to the kind of ebullience associated with the 'Beer Barrel Polka'), which were bettered by his harmonic subtlety, passing tones, and a touch which seemed improbably light for such a big man.

He saw through the Depression with little or no loss of work and turned up as a guest sideman on record dates with Ted Lewis, Jack Teagarden and others, but in 1934 he formed a small group which appeared on his record labels as 'Fats Waller And His Rhythm'; this six-piece band – mostly with Herman Autrey, Gene Sedric and Al Casey as the regular sidemen – kept Waller busy for the rest of the decade, and he became one of Victor's best-selling artists. His humorous approach to much of his material was what sold the records, with his constant clowning through a lyric, and this resulted in Victor seemingly deliberately giving him poor material to send up: he became sick of it, but carried on none the less. As a result, many of his records are formulaic and have their best moments – from a jazz point of view – dispersed amid the general air of tomfoolery, and Waller often shouts over the solos by Sedric and Autrey. Nevertheless, even if Waller's humour grows tiresome, there are still gentler and less aggressively funny records to hear. When he wanted to, he could sing in a sonorous and beguiling tenor, and on some of his transcription material in particular a different Waller often emerges. He visited Europe in 1938, and recorded a six-part 'London Suite' in England: if it was an attempt to show his serious side as a composer, though, the flimsy results are disappointing. It is still Waller's enduring popular tunes – 'Ain't Misbehavin'', 'Honeysuckle Rose', 'Black And Blue', 'Keepin' Out Of Mischief Now', 'My Fate Is In Your Hands', 'I'm Going To Sit Right Down And Write Myself A Letter' – which define him best. He continued to tour and broadcast extensively into the 40s, going to Hollywood in 1943 to make *Stormy Weather*, but his health began to suffer: a huge appetite for alcohol had affected his constitution, and when travelling from Los Angeles to New York by train one evening in December, a respiratory infection which had suddenly turned into pneumonia caused his death.

*Fats Waller 1935* (Classics)

# Per-Henrik Wallin

PIANO
*born* 17 July 1946

Wallin's influence on a range of European jazz is wider than some think. He began playing as a soloist and duet partner of Sven-Åke Johansson, working in both his native Sweden and Germany in the early 70s, but formed a trio in 1978 which became one of the most significant groups of its time in Sweden, recording extensively for Dragon and Caprice: Wallin's tempestuous music worked a brilliant line between form and freedom, the group taking off into improvised flights from a starting position of something that might have been no more than a scrap of melody or a rhythmic motif. Wallin's own style, with monumental climaxes arriving from nowhere, keyboard hammering, cruel disfigurements of standards and Tatum-like virtuosity, personified the group's strange emotional climate. But the trio ended in 1988 when Wallin suffered an accident which has left him partly paralysed and in a wheelchair. His subsequent return to playing has been remarkable and resilient, and recent records have shown his imagination and interpretive powers to be undiminished.
***Dolphins Dolphins Dolphins*** (Dragon)

# George Wallington

PIANO
*born* 27 October 1924; *died* 15 February 1993

Born Giacinto Figlia – 'George Wallington' came from a nickname, Lord Wallington, bestowed by Stan Getz after he saw the pianist's natty style of dress – he studied classical piano and started playing on 52nd Street in the early 40s, in time to be caught up in the first wave of bebop. He played with the likes of Gillespie, Parker and Allen Eager and played sideman dates on record, although it was his composing as much as his neat bebop piano style which attracted attention: two of his tunes, 'Lemon Drop' and 'Godchild', the latter recorded by Miles Davis at the 'Birth Of The Cool' sessions, became virtual standards of the era. In the 50s he enjoyed some long residencies in the city, and recorded a number of group albums for Prestige, Norgran (including a little-known date with strings), New Jazz,

Savoy and Atlantic, but by the end of the decade he seemed to have lost interest in his career and went into his family's business, air-conditioning. He played some further engagements in the 80s and made a final album in 1984.
***Jazz For The Carriage Trade*** (Prestige/OJC)

# Bob Wallis

TRUMPET, VOCAL
*born* 3 June 1934; *died* 10 January 1991

Wallis and his Storyville Jazzmen were one of the bands who came in on the tide of popularity surrounding the British trad boom of the late 50s and early 60s. A Yorkshireman, he had played in Acker Bilk's band earlier in the decade, and his own band, doing a vigorous, unsubtle take on the staples of the idiom, with Wallis's own noisy trumpet to the fore, enjoyed a substantial following which largely died as the boom went bust. In the 70s he resettled in Switzerland and worked steadily there.
***The Pye Jazz Anthology*** (Castle)

# Jack Walrath

TRUMPET
*born* 5 May 1946

Walrath made his name as one of Charles Mingus's last characterful sidemen. He grew up in Montana and settled on the West Coast at the end of the 60s, working in Ray Charles's touring band for a time, before moving to New York in 1973 and joining Mingus a year later. He acted as, effectively, MD on some of Mingus's final projects and his crackling post-bop trumpet makes telling contributions to all the later works. Since then he has led small groups of his own, though none of them have really proved compelling, and he has inevitably been caught up in the Mingus industry which has grown up since the bassist's death, leading the Mingus Dynasty group for some years and taking a prominent role in the various editions of the Mingus Big Band.
**Charles Mingus,** ***Changes One & Two*** (Atlantic)

# Cedar Walton

PIANO

*born* 17 January 1934

Walton grew up in Dallas and studied in Denver, moving to New York in 1955 before being drafted, after which he played in army bands. He resumed his career in the late 50s in the city, where he held down important gigs with The Jazztet and Art Blakey's Jazz Messengers, staying with Blakey between 1961 and 1964 ('I think I might have left a little too soon, but I had the chance to take a gig right in New York City, and I thought I was tired of traveling all the time'). With club work and innumerable record dates, Walton has been busy in New York ever since, sitting out much of the fusion period and sticking with acoustic piano. He had long-standing associations with Bob Berg, Billy Higgins, Sam Jones, Milt Jackson, Clifford Jordan and others, some of which came together in a band called Eastern Rebellion. Cedar's breadth of experience has left him as one of the most distinguished figures in New York jazz. While never a startlingly original stylist, he plays satisfyingly orthodox post-bop piano that, when everything runs just right, can sound close to perfect, which is why his records can sometimes be either disappointingly ordinary or mysteriously compelling. As a composer, he has created a very good book of tunes, with 'Bolivia' one of the standards of the past 40 years.

*Manhattan Afternoon* (Criss Cross)

# Carlos Ward

TENOR AND ALTO SAXOPHONES

*born* 1 May 1940

A Panamanian by birth, Ward moved to Seattle in 1953 and played in rock'n'roll bands before being drafted, which took him to Germany, where he subsequently settled on his discharge, working in free-jazz circles, though without much impact. He went to New York in 1966, played with John Coltrane and Sam Rivers, and slowly built a reputation in playing free music. Abdullah Ibrahim, who had first played with him in Germany, took him on as a regular sideman in 1972, and in the 80s he worked in Carla Bley's groups and with Don Cherry's band Nu. He had a brief spell with Cecil Taylor before forming his own band and working with Don Pullen until the pianist's death. Ward's style has never quite settled down: his playing often sounds raw without seeming to be particularly expressive of anything, and he does best in a context where he has clear musical tasks to perform, which is perhaps why his best work is to be heard on Ibrahim's records.

**Abdullah Ibrahim,** *Water From An Ancient Well* (Tiptoe)

# David S Ware

TENOR SAXOPHONE

*born* 7 November 1949

Ware's stormy music sounds like the next stage on from Coltrane's final phase. He went to Berklee for a brief period in the late 60s but then settled in New York, where he started working with Cecil Taylor and became a sideman in Andrew Cyrille's regular band, which gave him his first serious exposure. In the 80s he found work very scarce and took to taxi driving in the city, but a couple of what were effectively comeback records for the Swedish label Silkheart got him noticed again at the end of the decade, and in the 90s he started working with what would become a long-standing quartet with Matthew Shipp, William Parker and a succession of drummers. Credited by some with sparking a free-jazz 'revival' – had it ever been away? – Ware's band played his version of energy music, dark and dense rhythms thickened by Shipp's blockbusting harmonic thunder and crested by the roar of Ware in full cry. It sounded like serious music and it was given a serious amount of attention, culminating in the rather amazing situation of Ware being signed to Columbia in the US, at the behest of the admiring Branford Marsalis – although the band only lasted two albums there. Since then, Ware has simply carried on at a different label, Thirsty Ear, and one recent project was his revision of Sonny Rollins's *The Freedom Suite*, rebuilt into a veritable firestorm. Ware's music has a rather wearying edge to it: as with some of the lesser free-jazz screamers, his music occasionally sounds to be sustained on momentum alone, and Shipp's piano can seem more like ballast than nourishment, but at their best the group do deliver music of rare as well as raw power.

*The Freedom Suite* (Thirsty Ear)

# Wilbur Ware

BASS

*born* 8 September 1923; *died* 9 September 1979

Ware grew up in Chicago and played in string bands at first, but he switched to jazz bass and went on to work with Johnny Griffin and other local players before moving to New York, where he worked steadily as one of the house regulars for Riverside Records, as well as gigging with Thelonious Monk, Sonny Rollins and others. While he was no virtuoso on the bass, his style turned out to be surprisingly forward-thinking: he couldn't attempt the Scott LaFaro kind of sound, and preferred to use the bottom notes of the chord, while he mixed a heavy tone with a quick articulation, and played rhythmically rather than in a legato manner. These paradoxical elements led him to be surprisingly influential, and even posed some ideas for the free-jazz bassists of the next generation to consider. He was still playing with the likes of Archie Shepp and Sun Ra into the 70s, but narcotics and alcohol problems affected his health and interrupted his career.

**Thelonious Monk, *With John Coltrane***
(Riverside/OJC)

# Tim Warfield

TENOR SAXOPHONE

*born* 2 July 1965

Warfield seemed like a potentially major force on saxophone, but his career has proceeded only slowly. He came to some attention in the early 90s, taking third place in the 1991 Monk Competition which Joshua Redman won (some thought it should have been Warfield), and then playing in groups led by Christian McBride and Nicholas Payton. In all of his work he suggests a dynamic, exciting player with a strong hand of fresh ideas on familiar principles, building on a Wayne Shorter model. At 40, he needs a significant career break.

***Gentle Warrior*** (Criss Cross)

# Earle Warren

ALTO SAXOPHONE, CLARINET

*born* 1 July 1914; *died* 4 June 1995

Warren joined Count Basie in 1937, and though he was often in and out of the band, he never shook the association off: he later ran a band of swing old-timers called The Countsmen. He only rarely took solos in a group which could boast Herschel Evans and Lester Young, and eventually he ran bands of his own, from the late 40s (though at first, 'I went to several publishing companies and they told me I looked too white and sang too white'). In the 50s, Warren worked with Johnny Otis and began managing R&B bands, including The Platters, for whom he sometimes played baritone. In between gigs, Earle ran a furniture store and became a Fuller Brush salesman, but then came The Countsmen. He spent his last years in Geneva.

***The Countsmen*** (RCA)

# Dinah Washington

VOCAL

*born* 29 August 1924; *died* 14 December 1963

Born Rutha (sic) Lee Jones, Washington grew up in Chicago and sang in a gospel choir as well as in nightclubs in her teens. Lionel Hampton hired her in 1943 and she spent three years with his band, mostly singing blues numbers with a mildly raunchy edge to them. From 1946, she worked as a solo, and steadily moved away from her more risqué earlier style and towards a middle-of-the-road act where her singing reached several kinds of audience. Washington was an amazing personality. She is often compared to Ray Charles, in that her gospel-derived style seemed to marry into every kind of popular idiom and be comfortable with all of them. Her straight 'jazz' records were comparatively rare: the disc cited is a memorable live session with Clifford Brown, Clark Terry and others, and she made a few other dates with jazz small groups, but much of her output for Mercury and Roulette was based around orchestral accompaniments and ballad singing. She sang lyrics very clearly and precisely, even as she could swoop between a cajoling whisper and a testifying shout, and she could be sexier than Vaughan, Holiday or Fitzgerald ever were.

There are times in her output where she seems curiously remote, as if it were all too easy for her, and often the material or the settings are unworthy, but surviving broadcast and live material shows how funny and warm she could be. She got through a large number of marriages and a lot of drinking, and her death came as a result of a seeming mix-up over sleeping pills.
*Dinah Jams* (Emarcy)

## Grover Washington Jr
TENOR AND SOPRANO SAXOPHONES
*born* 12 December 1943; *died* 17 December 1999

Washington might have remained as a journeyman saxophonist if it hadn't been for a lucky break. He grew up in Buffalo, New York, played in organ trios and army bands, and then moved to Philadelphia at the end of the 60s, where he became something of a sessionman for Prestige. He was due to play as support to Hank Crawford on a 1971 date, but when Crawford didn't show up, Grover took the lead on what became an unexpected hit record, *Inner City Blues*. From there, he began to score other hits, culminating at first in *Mister Magic* (1974), and then, following a switch of labels to Elektra, *Winelight* (1980). Smooth, mellow, but with a soupçon of tonal distinction, Washington's music was at once both the epitome of what would later become smooth jazz, and something individual enough to stand by itself – much as Bobby Hackett's music had done, a generation earlier. Washington spent the rest of his career vacillating between the soft stuff and something a little more interesting, and since he never entirely sold out to the easy option, there is at least something to listen to in all of his records. He died suddenly of a heart attack at 56.
*Winelight* (Elektra)

## Kenny Washington
DRUMS
*born* 29 May 1958

A Brooklynite, Washington began playing in and around New York in the late 70s and has become perhaps the most dependable of all the drummers to emerge on the New York scene of the past two decades: he dislikes touring and is entirely content to work

in the jazz capital of the world on a regular basis. This has inevitably led to a mass of sessionman duty for recordings, as well as high-profile live work in the city. There is little enough to say about his drumming from a stylistic point of view, except to suggest that his basic hard-bop approach is adaptable to most jazz situations.
**Mike LeDonne**, *The Feeling Of Jazz* (Criss Cross)

## Peter Washington
BASS
*born* 28 August 1964

Born in Los Angeles, Washington began playing in and around San Francisco in the early 80s, and moved to New York in 1986. Since then he has taken part in scores of record dates and live engagements of every kind. For the most part he is called on to do hard-bop and straight-ahead dates of the sort called by labels such as Criss Cross, but he seems perfectly able to handle whatever is required, as long as it's acoustic jazz: he seems to have no interest in playing fusion or anything involving the electric bass. He often works with Kenny Washington in a rhythm section, and sleevenote-writers always have to point out that they are not related in any way.
**David Hazeltine**, *The Classic Trio* (Sharp Nine)

## Sadao Watanabe
ALTO SAXOPHONE
*born* 1 February 1933

Japan's only jazz superstar of the post-bop era started on clarinet in his teens and changed to alto sax when he moved to Tokyo in 1951. He joined Toshiko Akiyoshi's band in 1953, and took it over when the pianist went to the US. He studied at Berklee in the 60s and on his return steadily built up a following for his small-group work, which mixed straight-ahead bebop with Brazilian music and a light kind of fusion. He has played at Montreux, Newport and the Bombay Jazz Yatra, and was the first Japanese musician to play in South Africa in the post-apartheid era. Sadao's music challenges no boundaries, and in a discography of close to 100 albums he has delivered plenty of lightly noodling work, but as an improviser and composer he isn't quite the

lightweight one expects: whatever there is in his playing that is 'Japanese' isn't clear, yet he doesn't sound like an American player of any sort, and he gets a lovely sound from both the alto and – surprisingly – the sopranino sax, which he has occasionally played since the 80s. He has also held his own on record with such heavyweights as Chick Corea, Nicholas Payton and Christian McBride.
*Remembrance* (Verve)

## Benny Waters
SAXOPHONES, CLARINET, VOCAL
*born* 23 January 1902; *died* 11 August 1998

Waters was a working jazzman longer than almost anybody else. He was playing with Clarence Williams and King Oliver on record while working in Charlie Johnson's orchestra in the late 20s, and he later turned up with Claude Hopkins and Jimmie Lunceford. He played R&B with Roy Milton and New Orleans jazz in Jimmy Archey's band, both in the 40s, and in the 60s, living in Paris and enjoying himself, he had a regular gig at the club La Cigale. He carried on touring in Europe through the 70s and 80s, although he finally went back to New York in 1991, and celebrated his 95th birthday with a stint at Birdland, before going on to join the Statesmen Of Jazz group. None of this resulted in any immortal music – Waters was basically a minor Hawkins disciple, even though he could play with ferocious energy, even into his 90s – but Benny loved being a living legend, and he never stopped entertaining his audiences even when virtually blind. He finally passed away a few months after celebrating yet another birthday with yet another gig.
*Benny Waters–Freddy Randall Jazz Band* (Jazzology)

## Ethel Waters
VOCAL
*born* 31 October 1896; *died* 1 September 1977

Older than Armstrong, Crosby and everyone else of that generation, Waters got a head start as arguably the original jazz singer. She grew up in Philadelphia and started out as a singer of coon songs, a vaudeville tradition which was different to the blues shows which would dominate black singing in the 20s, and she began making records in 1921. Never quite beholden to any one strain of popular music, she mixed up jazz and blues and vaudeville elements and came up with something strikingly her own. She didn't have a notably big voice and the early records don't seem so impressive now, but by the 30s she had matured into a more powerful singer and her later records with Benny Goodman and Duke Ellington mix theatricality with musicianship to make their impressive mark. Like every other black artist of her generation she had a difficult course through American entertainment, but she was able to punch her way out of trouble and in the end she had a long life and a sucessful career where many of her contemporaries fell by the wayside.
*Ethel Waters 1933–34* (Classics)

## Julius Watkins
FRENCH HORN
*born* 10 October 1921; *died* 4 April 1977

Watkins started on french horn as a boy, but he couldn't get any work with it at first and played trumpet with Milt Buckner in the late 40s. From the 50s, he was able to get gigs with the instrument, and he recorded with Sonny Rollins and Oscar Pettiford, as well as leading an occasional band, Les Jazz Modes, with Charlie Rouse. Session-work took up much of his time into the 60s and he also joined Charles Mingus's group on two occasions. Watkins made a perfectly plausible case for the french horn as a bopper's instrument, phrasing and articulating his lines with an unselfconscious immediacy that got his message straight across. In his final years he worked mainly as a teacher, and one of his last students was Tom Varner.
*The Jazz Modes* (Atlantic)

## Cleveland Watkiss
VOCAL
*born* 21 October 1959

Watkiss emerged on the London scene as a talented vocalist who touched several bases. He sang in funk and reggae groups – much as many of his later, instrumentalist collaborators did – before moving towards jazz, and he worked with the bandleader Simon Purcell in a Jazz Messengers-type outfit before taking the vocalist role in the Jazz Warriors. He then recorded two solo projects for Polydor, neither of which really established him: poorly produced and muddled in their conception, they obscured rather than highlighted his strengths. Since then he has worked in club music and has tried his hand at various projects in a number of idioms, never quite settling into anything: a third album finally emerged in 2003. The trend for artists to be as eclectic and barrier-crossing as possible hasn't done Cleveland's career many favours: he is a fine singer, and needs a framework which really celebrates his talent.

**Victory's Happy Song Book** (Touch Down)

## Bill Watrous
TROMBONE
*born* 8 June 1939

Born in Middletown, Connecticut, Watrous played traditional jazz in local bands and then joined Kai Winding's multi-trombone group in 1962. He subsequently played in groups such as Ten Wheel Drive, a fusion group, and fronted a big band called Manhattan Wildlife Refuge for much of the 70s. At the end of the decade he went to live in Los Angeles, where he mainly did studio work, although he is a frequent guest-star soloist in big bands both in the US and in Europe. Watrous might be the greatest trombone technician of the modern age. He plays so quickly and seemingly effortlessly, maintaining a smooth legato over the whole line while articulating notes with pinpoint clarity, that other trombonists tend to marvel at his chops. While such an approach could sound boring, he is inventive enough to keep listeners interested, even if the dexterity passes them by.

**Bone-ified** (GNP)

## Bobby Watson
ALTO SAXOPHONE
*born* 23 August 1953

Watson took up the alto in his teens and played in Kansas City and Miami before going to New York in 1976, joining Art Blakey's Jazz Messengers the following year

and remaining until 1981. From there, he went out as a leader himself, besides working in the 29th Street Saxophone Quartet, which he co-founded in 1983. He briefly ran a record label with Curtis Lundy, New Note, but later signed to first Blue Note and then Columbia. Watson's fierce, skirling sound is in the great alto tradition of Cannonball Adderley and Jackie McLean, and he can play bebop lines with head-spinning ease; but the title of one of his Blue Notes, *Post-Motown Bop* (1990), hints at how he would prefer to synthesize trends without giving up on jazz as his basic idiom. In a sense, Watson's progress has been disappointing: he is among the most sheerly enjoyable of musicians to hear in a live context, and his composing has many interesting traits that have yet to be fully explored. But his Columbia albums never found an audience, more recent records have been unambitious, and in his 50s he is unlikely to receive major-label patronage again. He has lately worked in education at the University of Missouri.

**Midwest Shuffle** (Columbia)

## Leo Watson
VOCAL
*born* 27 February 1898; *died* 2 May 1950

Although he played tiple in the Spirits Of Rhythm, and later the trombone, bass, drums and washboard, singing was Watson's real thing. He played in vaudeville before joining what would turn into the Spirits Of Rhythm around 1930, and from there he worked with John Kirby and Gene Krupa before rejoining the Spirits in 1939. By the middle of the 40s he was working as a solo, befriending beboppers such as Joe Albany and impressing Slim Gaillard (who surely stole some of his stuff) and Mel Tormé alike. Watson's nutty approach was grounded in a rare grasp of music. Good as many of them are, the records seem comparatively tame, but everyone who saw him remembered Watson's unquenchable invention, scatting and improvising words and melody lines, parading a gallery of voices and generally clowning around without losing sight of where the music was going for a second. Illness interrupted his playing later on and he eventually succumbed to pneumonia.

**The Spirits Of Rhythm, *1933–1945*** (Classics)

# Lu Watters

TRUMPET

*born* 19 December 1911; *died* 5 November 1990

Watters loved the sound of jazz from an early age, and he formed his own first band in San Francisco at the age of 15. He worked in a big band led by Carol Lofner, which fetched up in New Orleans for two months in the 30s, and Watters was so intrigued by the sound of the original New Orleans idiom that he resolved to follow that style instead. He began organizing jam sessions back in California, where the likes of Turk Murphy, Clancy Hayes and Bob Helm joined in. In 1939, he tried to get a swing band that also played New Orleans pieces off the ground, but they were sacked from their residency, and in the end he came back with a small group, the Yerba Buena Jazz Band, which opened at San Francisco's Dawn Club in December 1940. The first records were made a year later. Watters, Helm, Murphy and Bob Scobey were all involved. The band was a great hit, and though there was an interruption when Watters was drafted in 1942, he came back at the end of the war and re-formed the group. It lasted until 1950, still making records and playing in the two-beat style to roaring success, but then Scobey and Murphy went out on their own, and Watters suddenly lost interest, the New Orleans revival by now having a momentum of its own. He gave up playing, worked as a cook and in carpentry, and refused all offers of comebacks, although he finally accepted an award at the Santa Rosa Festival, not long before his death. His name and music are still revered by revivalist bands and fans across America.

*The Complete Good Time Jazz Recordings 1941–1950* (Good Time Jazz)

# Ernie Watts

TENOR AND SOPRANO SAXOPHONES

*born* 23 October 1945

Perpetually busy as a studio musician – he became a staffer for NBC as long ago as 1969 – Watts only established himself as a name leader somewhat belatedly. Having studied at Berklee, he was soon spending huge amounts of time in studio situations, and he might be one of the most recognized saxophonists of recent times, if his audience had any idea whom they were hearing: he is prominent on the soundtracks of such films as *Chariots Of Fire*, *Arthur* and *Ghostbusters*, and he turns in solo work on many rock engagements, such as the multiple alto parts on Steely Dan's 'Parker's Band'. His most distinctive jazz work of late came when he was engaged by Charlie Haden for the bassist's Quartet West project: Watts is, perhaps, no great individualist on the saxophone, and the role playing required in this gig suited him particularly well, casting him as a romantic though faceless saxophone narrator. But his own 90s albums for JVC (unfortunately not much publicized and indifferently distributed) have had a lot of admirable music, where his garrulous, muscular tenor work has found some proper definition.

*Reaching Up* (JVC)

# Jeff 'Tain' Watts

DRUMS

*born* 20 January 1960

Born in Pittsburgh, Watts undertook classical studies and went on to Berklee (where his first instrument was actually the vibraphone, which he doesn't seem to have touched since). His breakthrough came when he recorded with Wynton Marsalis in 1981: thereafter he was the trumpeter's regular drummer until 1988, and since then he has also been closely associated with Branford Marsalis, a gig which at one time saw them both working on television's *The Tonight Show*. Watts has been hired by many other leaders since but the Marsalis association is the one that defines him, and even his two solo records have featured the brothers from New Orleans. As a drummer, Tain takes the Elvin Jones style to something like its natural limit: furiously polyrhythmical, he seems to be all over the kit all of the time, and it must be fearsomely intimidating to a nervous soloist knowing that Watts is right behind you. Although there is nothing remotely subtle or tasteful about the drummer's playing, that doesn't mean he isn't supportive, or can't scale back when the music has to cool off. It is hard, though, to imagine him playing in any kind of cocktail lounge.

*Citizen Tain* (Columbia)

## Trevor Watts

ALTO AND SOPRANO SAXOPHONES
*born* 26 February 1939

Watts played in an RAF band during his national service, and on the London scene of the 60s he played with blues bands as well as forming an alliance with John Stevens and Paul Rutherford, which led to the formation of the Spontaneous Music Ensemble and the regular gigs at The Little Theatre, which became the focal point for London's new free-music scene. He formed the trio Amalgam in 1967, with Rutherford and Barry Guy: their *Prayer For Peace* (FMR, 1969) is one of the most important records of the era. In the 70s he expanded his range to encompass such groups as the String Ensemble and the Universal Music Group, and went further in the following decade with the Drum Orchestra and Moiré Music, groups which mixed his playing with percussion ensembles playing African rhythms. Watts built on the sound and innovations of Ornette Coleman with an Anglicized but strikingly personal effect. His free playing lasted into the 70s, and the final editions of SME: thereafter he seemed to move back towards a more orthodox kind of freebop, which his big-scale projects tended to settle him into, although these were just as idiosyncratic in their way. While the Moiré Music records have had rather mixed results, in performance the group was always more impressive. A recent partnership with pianist Veryan Weston has also drawn him back towards free playing.
*Trevor Watts And The Celebration Band* (Arc)

## Chuck Wayne

GUITAR
*born* 27 February 1923; *died* 29 July 1997

Wayne was a regular on 52nd Street in the 40s, first recording with Joe Marsala's group, but it was bop that interested him and he is on Dizzy Gillespie's 'Groovin' High' date for Guild. He was in Woody Herman's First Herd for a time and in 1949 joined George Shearing's quintet, staying three years and playing on several of the group's hits. He freelanced in the 50s before becoming a staffer at CBS, and he became a noted teacher in the 80s. Wayne's playing is scattered across many records, but he had a few

features of his own: *Morning Mist*, a 1965 date for Prestige, is a mix of ballads and light bebop, but his best record is a strong quintet session made with Brew Moore and Al Cohn in 1953, cut for Progressive and later reissued on Savoy.
*The Jazz Guitar Of Chuck Wayne* (Savoy)

## Teddy Weatherford

PIANO
*born* 11 October 1903; *died* 25 April 1945

Weatherford was long a mystery man whose few records intrigued early collectors. Born in Pocahontas, Virginia, he went to New Orleans when a boy and learned piano there. In 1922 he was in Chicago, where he cut a few sideman dates with Jimmy Wade and Erskine Tate, but in 1926 he went to the Far East and stayed eight years. After a brief return visit to the US, he began playing in Bombay and Ceylon, and in the 40s he settled in Calcutta, where he made some interesting small-group sides. Weatherford reputedly had a considerable impact on Earl Hines during his time in Chicago, but in some ways the records are rather disappointing, showing a conventional traditional-to-swing style. He died of cholera.

## Weather Report

GROUP

The first superstar group to emerge from the jazz-rock era, Weather Report originally seemed like an alliance between Joe Zawinul, Wayne Shorter and Miroslav Vitous. The group came together in 1970 and was almost immediately signed by Columbia (Miles Davis's label – both Zawinul and Shorter had been involved in Davis's then-recent records) Although the early records *Weather Report* (1971) and *I Sing The Body Electric* (1972) were comparatively tame mixes of modal playing, freeish passages and rockish vamps, by the time of *Sweetnighter* (1973) the band had suddenly gelled into a dramatic vehicle for Zawinul's personal fusions: he began using electric keyboards of all kinds to provide both the harmonic centre and sundry electronic exotica, hired rhythm sections that could play either fast jazz rhythms or (more consistently) rock and Latin beats and deployed Shorter as a kind

of jazz messenger, either soloing lustily against the barrage behind him or spelling out melodic curlicues which counterpointed the leader's structural thinking. Vitous departed early, and thereafter there was an almost continuous turnover in rhythm-section personnel, although bassist Jaco Pastorius was present throughout the group's commercial heyday (1976–81). The group's albums were beautifully tailored in their studio surroundings: Zawinul had a phenomenal ear for the contrast between electronic and acoustic sounds, and even as the technology of synthesizers was advancing in leaps and bounds, he was inventing new sound-palettes to accompany the progression. The group's albums were modelled and marketed like college-rock products, and won fans from several different camps, with the emphasis on group and groove-playing ('We always solo and we never solo,' said Zawinul, thereby allaying the fears of the non-jazz audience) providing a kind of universal appeal. The more jazz-inclined members of the audience were dismayed that Shorter seemed to be increasingly marginalized as the group went forward, but this was really Zawinul's band and their partnership only operated within WR's rules of engagement. *Mysterious Traveller* (1974), *Tale Spinnin'* (1975) and *Black Market* (1976) found Zawinul and his players at their creative peak, although it was the succeeding *Heavy Weather* (1976), with its huge hit 'Birdland', which really propelled the group into best-seller status – and actually marked the start of a slow but unarguable decline in the quality of the records. While they were an exhilarating live experience, their live album *8.30* (1979) was rather disappointing, and it was only the recent posthumous release *Live And Unreleased* (2002) which recalled how powerful they could be on stage. The albums from the 80s weren't so much poor as increasingly commonplace: WR's innovations had entered the mainstream, and with fusion itself preparing to turn towards the bland fields of smooth jazz, the group had run its course by 1985, when Shorter departed. Zawinul kept going under the name Weather Update for a while, but then settled into other projects under his own name. A handful of Weather Report records practically define the jazz-rock era of the middle 70s – very much of their time, yet still provocative and warmly entertain-ing well beyond the chopsmanship of the genre.
**Black Market** (Columbia)

# Chick Webb
DRUMS
*born* 10 February 1909; *died* 16 June 1939

Webb was a tiny man whose spine was deformed by the spread of tuberculosis at an early age. He grew up in Baltimore, started on the drums at the age of 12 and moved to New York in 1925, leading his own band a year later, although it didn't secure a record contract early on and Webb struggled to find regular work. He traded musicians with Fletcher Henderson and somehow kept going until 1932, when he toured in support of Louis Armstrong and finally won a long residency at the Savoy Ballroom. He may have been small, but Webb was a tough competitor: he loved battles of the bands on his home turf, which he almost always won, and he built his orchestra into a powerful ensemble, framed around Edgar Sampson's arrangements and his own zesty drumming, which quickly set a new standard among swing-era players. Using a special kit with a gigantic bass drum, he was a master of drum breaks and fills which directed the music, nudged at the next soloist, and gave the band a feel which seemed loose and tight at the same time: other drummers were jealous and amazed. Ella Fitzgerald joined as the band's girl singer in 1935 and gave Webb a further edge on his competition. Webb's records never quite display the range of his skills, in part because of the constricted medium, and owing to engineers never giving the drummer the recording range which would later become more of a standard. In 1938 he contracted pleurisy, which damaged his already frail constitution further, and it led to his death from uraemia and other complications: Ella Fitzgerald took over the band, but it never sounded the same.
**Chick Webb 1935–1938** (Classics)

# George Webb
PIANO
*born* 8 October 1917

The father of British trad. He formed his first group in London in 1942, the George

Webb Dixielanders, and their residency at a pub called the Red Barn in Barnehurst, Kent, is now the stuff of legend, and gave momentum to what would become a whole movement of Dixieland and revivalist bands, in a country which had never really had a traditional jazz to revive. Wally Fawkes was one of his first sidemen, and Humphrey Lyttelton joined in the fun after the war. It was a rough approximation of Armstrong's 20s music and its perceived rootsiness wasn't so much a simulation of anything as an eagerness to play something less smooth and sweet than the teatime swing of much British music of the day. Webb then shifted to Lyttelton's own band in 1948, but in the early 50s he went over to managing and booking bands. Webb led another band in the 70s, ran a pub, went to see his beloved Charlton FC whenever he could, and occasionally reassembled a group in the 80s and 90s.

*George Webb's Dixielanders* (Jazzology)

# Eberhard Weber

BASS, CELLO
*born* 22 January 1940

Weber grew up in Stuttgart and started on cello before switching to the upright bass in 1956. He played in semi-pro bands before meeting Wolfgang Dauner in 1961, and he played alongside the pianist for much of the rest of the decade, while also working in TV commercials and the theatre. Although he recorded with Dauner and others during the period, he still didn't become a full-time musician until 1972, when he formed a band called Spectrum, initially with Volker Kriegl. By now, Weber had begun experimenting with a kind of electric bass, and eventually he settled on a custom-made instrument which used five strings (he added a sixth later in the decade) with a small soundbox, which, together with a discreet effects unit, gave him a swimming, thickly resonant sound that sometimes had an almost speech-like quality. While Jaco Pastorius was about to bring a new fretless bass sound to American jazz, Weber did the same thing, from a different direction, in Europe. *The Colours Of Chloe* (1973), his debut on ECM, was a feat of extended group composition which sounded startlingly new, and Weber built on this with his subsequent records,

using Rainer Bruninghaus, Charlie Mariano and Jon Christensen in his group to superb effect. Less about solos and jazz interplay and focused on a carefully weighted ensemble approach, it sounded almost unique. Away from his Colours group, Weber also played in the United Jazz And Rock Ensemble, and has been a regular performer in Jan Garbarek's touring band for 20 years. Some of the juice ran out of his later group records, which occasionally stiffen up (John Marshall, a much less interesting drummer than Jon Christensen, took over that role in later years) and feel merely elegant, but an all-solo record, *Pendulum* (1993), was outstanding. And Weber did, in any case, slow down: there were 12 years between *Orchestra* (1988) and *Endless Days* (2000), for which he told his players, 'you can play anything, as long as it doesn't sound like jazz'.

*Yellow Fields* (ECM)

# Ben Webster

TENOR SAXOPHONE
*born* 7 March 1909

Webster was born in Kansas City and started on violin before he moved on to the piano. Budd Johnson got him started on the saxophone, and after playing in Lester Young's family band for a spell, he moved on to other groups before settling in the Bennie Moten band in 1931. From there he joined Andy Kirk, Fletcher Henderson, Benny Carter and Cab Calloway, as well as playing on record dates with Teddy Wilson and Billie Holiday. Wilson gave him a job in his new big band in 1939, but Webster was enticed away to join Duke Ellington within a year, and he helped bring a new style to the saxophone section, winning features such as 'Cotton Tail' (which he was never that fond of, since the tempo was too quick for him). He left in 1943 after a quarrel with Duke, and thereafter guested with small groups and worked as a solo in clubs in New York and Chicago. For two years he lived in a kind of retirement in Los Angeles, tending his mother, to whom he was devoted, but in 1952 he started going out with Jazz At The Philharmonic, and Norman Granz began recording him as a leader for Verve. These were Ben's greatest years: his tenor sound, grizzly and bad-tempered at a fast tempo, settled down at anything slower into a honeyed, luscious sound with a swooning vibrato, and sometimes all he needed to do was add the slightest ornamentation to a melody to fashion an absorbing solo. Granz set him up with strings, and with Oscar Peterson and Coleman Hawkins, and the results were magically beautiful; so was the session he made with Art Tatum (1956). He went back to New York in 1962, after his mother died, but in 1964 he went to Europe and settled permanently in Copenhagen. Webster had made many friends, but he could just as easily upset them: drink turned him into something of a monster (one of his nicknames was 'The Brute'), and one night at Ronnie Scott's patrons had to step over his insensible bulk as it lay on the floor. His playing began to retreat into shadows and corners, and occasionally he would hardly play notes at all, and instead just send the shivering column of air out through the horn. Somehow, it was all still worth hearing. He died in Amsterdam following a final engagement there in 1974.

*Soulville* (Verve)

# Freddie Webster

TRUMPET
*born* 7 October 1916; *died* 1 April 1947

Webster is known mainly as an influence on the young Miles Davis. He played in his native Cleveland in his teens and went to New York in 1938, playing in a stack of different bands without really settling into any of them. Davis loved his 'great big tone', which he used without much vibrato (another Davis trademark), and he was widely admired by other horn players too. But he left scarcely any solos on record, became drastically unreliable, and eventually died suddenly of a heart attack.

# Dave Weckl

DRUMS
*born* 8 January 1960

Weckl came to prominence on the New York session scene of the 80s, the natural successor to Steve Gadd as the master of drum chopsmanship in fusion circles. He played extensively in both the Akoustic and Elektric bands of Chick Corea, and since then has starred alongside such inevitable colleagues

as the Brecker brothers, Mike Stern and Dave Grusin. His own albums and work as a group leader showcase a level of executive skill which is both remarkable and fatiguingly tedious, and most of the records border on the unlistenable.

*Transition* (Stretch)

# George Wein

PIANO, IMPRESARIO
*born* 3 October 1925

Along with Norman Granz, Wein is probably the most successful of jazz businessmen – which hasn't stopped him from doing the music a lot of good, as he has built his personal fortune. He studied classical piano in his home town of Boston before forming his own band while still in his teens, and after graduating from Boston University he opened his own club, The Storyville, in 1950, subsequently starting a record label of the same name. But his most important initiative was to found the Newport Jazz Festival in 1954, which would grow into one of the most significant of the world's jazz events. Aside from his Newport activities, Wein continued to play alongside such musicians as Buck Clayton, Pee Wee Russell, Red Norvo and many others, often under a rubric such as the Newport All-Stars, and while continuing to diversify his festival business, he essentially kept his hand in as a performing musician, although his work in this regard has had a negligible impact on any part of the jazz discourse. One sometimes wonders what his fellow musicians thought of his abilities on the bandstand. He published a memoir of his activities in 2003.

*George Wein & The Newport All-Stars* (Impulse!)

# Don Weller

TENOR SAXOPHONE
*born* 19 December 1940

Born in Croydon, Weller played clarinet and tenor for fun until he was 30, when he finally turned professional. In the 70s he ran a mild kind of jazz-rock band called Major Surgery, and this gave way to a quartet with Bryan Spring in the 80s, although in the interim he also played with Stan Tracey as a regular sideman. Since then he has led a big band, whenever it can afford to work, and

other small groups. Weller is one of the most affectionately regarded of modern British jazz musicians. His big, comfortable sound masks a keen and probing style which resists clichéd phrases and can build epic solos of impressive cogency, something a bit like a meeting between Zoot Sims and Joe Henderson. He has been surprisingly under-recorded: there is almost nothing under his own leadership on CD, the record cited covering some of his big-band work, and someone should do a proper small-group session with him as soon as possible.
*Live* (33 Jazz)

## Bobby Wellins
TENOR SAXOPHONE
*born* 24 January 1936

A Glaswegian whose parents both worked as professional musicians, Wellins started on piano but then played alto, although by the time he moved to London in 1953 he was blowing the tenor. He worked under various leaders before forming a close relationship with pianist Stan Tracey, taking the saxophone role in Tracey's 1965 classic *Under Milk Wood*. A narcotics addiction restricted his activity for a long time, but by the end of the 70s he was back playing at full strength, and ever since he has worked on the British scene as a small-group leader, soloist in big bands and teacher. Wellins has a select group of recordings under his own name, and there is little to disappoint in most of them: even though it seems like comparatively little to show for 50 years of playing, his unsentimental but romantic and carefully self-aware approach speaks very directly to the listener, and there is nothing wasted or merely glib in any of his records. Wellins is held in very high regard by the British jazz audience, an enduring and respected spirit.
*Don't Worry 'Bout Me* (Cadillac)

## Dicky Wells
TROMBONE
*born* 10 June 1907; *died* 12 November 1985

Wells came from Kentucky, and went to New York in 1926, where he played in a string of bands, including those of Fletcher Henderson and Teddy Hill: while in Paris with the latter group, he cut some very fine sessions, including one of the classic trombone records, 'Dickie Wells' Blues' (1937). In 1938 he joined Count Basie and stayed, aside from one break, until 1950. Wells blossomed in Basie's ranks: his style continued to move on from Jimmy Harrison's smooth playing, but he also added humorous touches of his own which reminded listeners that the trombone was an instrument that could be expressive and amusing without losing its musicality. In the 50s he played more in small-group situations, but he never again found quite the same congenial setting that he enjoyed with Basie, and his playing in the LP era is often very mixed: a drink problem didn't help. After a period of inactivity he began playing again in the 70s, and worked in Earle Warren's group The Countsmen.
*Dicky Wells 1927–1943* (Classics)

## Dick Wellstood
PIANO
*born* 25 November 1927; *died* 24 July 1987

Wellstood picked up most of his skills working by himself at the piano, and in the late 40s he worked in semi-pro Dixieland bands, often with his friend Bob Wilber. He then studied law while moonlighting as a Dixieland player in several groups, and after qualifying (though he didn't practise until the 80s) he worked through much of the 60s in New York clubs such as Condon's, either as an ensemble player or as an intermission pianist. That work began to dry up, and he played in Gene Krupa's quartet and in bands with Kenny Davern, and in the 70s he worked either as a solo player or in a society band led by Paul Hoffman. He spent a long period as the house pianist at a club called Hanratty's, and was part of The Classic Jazz Quartet with Marty Grosz, Joe Muranyi and Dick Sudhalter: but his sudden death from a heart attack brought that group to an abrupt end. Wellstood was a great ironist, an imaginative jazz writer, an exemplary scholar of languages, an amusing raconteur, and a master of pretty much every kind of piano style from ragtime to boogie woogie and what one might call intelligent cocktail piano. Marty Grosz remembered that 'he was contrary. He loved to say, if you asked for a tune, I don't know it, or, I hate that tune. After a while I learned

not to say the name of the tune, I'd just say, oh, we're going to be in B flat. Because I knew he'd know it, anyway.'
**Live At The Sticky Wicket** (Arbors)

# Alex Welsh
CORNET
*born* 9 July 1929; *died* 25 June 1982

Edinburgh-born, Welsh worked locally before moving to London in 1954, where he put together one of the finest of the traditional British bands. Welsh stood to one side of the trad spectrum: fiercely true to a manner which was drawn entirely from the Chicago school, he didn't really play a part in the trad wars, and his only purism was in adhering to the highest playing standards. Archie Semple, Roy Crimmens, Lennie Hastings and Fred Hunt formed the nucleus of the band, and it stayed together in the same form for many years. Welsh himself played taut, heated lead horn, and the constituent sounds seemed to fall into place around him. The classics of the period include *Music Of The Mauve Decade* (1959) and *Echoes Of Chicago* (1962). But eventually there were line-up changes: John Barnes, Roy Williams and others spent time in Welsh's ranks, and the leader's book expanded to include a catholic choice of material. American visitors who worked with the Welsh group – Pee Wee Russell, Henry Allen, Earl Hines and above all Bud Freeman, who loved it – were surprised at its excellence. There were good records to come, when Black Lion recorded Welsh extensively in the early 70s; but eventually, Alex began to tire, and troubled by a bad leg and periods of illness he took to vodka drinking as a palliative. The more mainstream elements in his music departed with John Barnes in 1977, and the Welsh band spent its last years playing, again, terse Dixieland. Welsh's era was over when he died, at only 52.
**Music Of The Mauve Decade** (Lake)

# Scott Wendholt
TRUMPET
*born* 21 July 1965

Raised in Denver, Wendholt moved to New York in 1990, where he did what many aspiring jazz trumpeters do and found work in Latin bands. Since then he has patiently built a wider CV of work, in big bands and elsewhere, and has been recorded extensively as a leader by the Criss Cross and Double-Time labels. While he has the techniques and fluencies of post-bop trumpet down very well, his playing has an interesting, rather inward-looking cast to it, which can make his recordings seem a little passive but which particularize them well enough, although it's the kind of music which asks for an audience to pay attention and take their time.
**Beyond Thursday** (Double-Time)

# Kenny Werner
PIANO
*born* 19 November 1951

Werner studied classical piano in New York, and then did the jazz course at Berklee in the early 70s. Since then he has built up a number of long-lasting associations, including those with Joe Lovano, Archie Shepp, Bob Brookmeyer and Lee Konitz, and for many years he ran a trio with Tom Rainer and Ratzo Harris, although he has since worked with other bass/drums combinations. Werner has a questing approach to his work and idiom and doesn't settle for simple elaborations on standard material: this has sometimes led to his several records as a leader being overcrowded with ideas or procedures, and some early albums for Steeplechase were disappointing. At his best, though, Werner asks listeners to involve themselves in some intriguing ideas, particularly on the disc cited, which includes poetry and other stuff but which has some remarkable moments. He is also very good with singers and in duo situations.
**Beauty Secrets** (RCA)

## Fred Wesley
TROMBONE
*born* 4 July 1943

Wesley has bounced back and forth between
funk and jazz settings, which he seems to
enjoy equally. Born in Mobile, Alabama, he
played piano, drums (in his father's group)
and trombone as a youth, and after army service joined James Brown in 1967. In the 70s
he did time with both George Clinton and
Count Basie and in the 80s and 90s he has
been a stalwart associate of Maceo Parker,
the two of them more or less ruling the jazz-
funk axis as they please. Characteristically,
Wesley is less convincing as a soloist than
he is as a lead brass voice, but his best
records contrive to mix the perspiring
energy of funk with the cooler restraint of
jazz improvisation.
**Swing And Be Funky** (Minor Music)

## Frank Wess
TENOR SAXOPHONE, FLUTE
*born* 4 January 1922

Since he was born in Kansas City, it was perhaps no surprise when Wess eventually
joined the Count Basie band; but this wasn't
until 1953, when he already had ten years of
touring experience behind him in various
groups. He stayed with Basie until 1964,
forming an alliance with Frank Foster which
was rekindled in the 80s, when they shared
the front line of a quintet as 'The Two
Franks'. Next to Foster, Wess had a more
light-bodied sound on the tenor, but his
secret weapon was his ability to double on
flute, which he had taken the trouble to
study at some length: Basie featured him
regularly on flute, and his elegant solos
helped create a jazz position for the instrument. After the Basie years, Frank spent
much time in studio work, although he also
worked extensively with Clark Terry and in
several Basie-like situations: he co-fronted
a big band with Harry Edison at the end of
the 80s for a brief spell. In the 90s, he went
back to being an occasional star sideman, as
well as doing much work in jazz education.
Five albums for Prestige, made in the early
60s, aren't well-known, but they include
some of his best recorded playing.
**Touché** (New Jazz/Prestige)

## Bugge Wesseltoft
PIANO, KEYBOARDS
*born* 1 February 1964

Wesseltoft made his way through the
Norwegian scene of the 90s with energy and
aplomb. He did sideman work with the likes
of Arild Andersen and Jens Wendleboe, but
by the end of the decade he was asserting a
pivotal role in what some commentators
were starting to call 'the new Oslo underground'. Since he has his own studio and
label imprint – Jazzland, which is currently
distributed by Universal – many of the
younger players in this environment have
naturally graduated towards working with
him. As a pianist, Wesseltoft is able rather
than markedly individual, and his groups
revolve around what he has probably
unwisely tagged 'New Conception Of Jazz',
which is actually the old conception yoked
to electronic beats, sound effects and other
detritus. The results, though, are often melodious and inventive as well as propulsive,
and the cross-section of work on the live
record is engaging enough. Wesseltoft is also
fortunate to have the services of Ingebrigt
Flaten, a notably fine bassist.
**New Conception Of Jazz Live** (Jazzland)

## Kate Westbrook
VOCAL
*born* 18 September 1939

## Mike Westbrook
PIANO, TUBA, COMPOSER, BANDLEADER
*born* 21 March 1936

Mike Westbrook heard some jazz at school,
which got him interested: 'My generation
came out of art schools and the like, and we
were far less "professional musicians" than
the Ronnie Scott generation. We worked
through experimentation and trial and
error. We had a mission to play anywhere.'
Westbrook ran a workshop in Plymouth in
1960, and then moved to London two years
later and established a sextet including John
Surman. His Concert Band followed in 1967,
recording for Deram, and in the 70s these
ideas expanded to include Solid Gold
Cadillac, the Westbrook Brass Band, Cosmic
Circus, A Little Westbrook Music, Westbrook
Rossini, Les Deux Trios, Westbrook Dance
Band and the Westbrook Orchestra, all

ensembles of differing sizes, which bring together jazz, some mixed-media presentation, occasionally rock (Solid Gold Cadillac), and settings of librettos covering everything from Blake to J M W Turner. He has enlisted various musicians during this time: the 60s and early 70s records featured all-star (insofar as they were known at all) casts of modern British jazz players, while the later groups included his wife Kate, a singer and lyricist in her own right, and saxophonist Chris Biscoe, who might be Westbrook's Johnny Hodges. Westbrook's oeuvre is now a huge body of work stretching over nearly four decades, and while he has stoutly marched on, the impression that it is all massively sponsored work and that Westbrook is an arts establishment darling is mostly absurd: he has actually had relatively little support from British sources, and much of his recent work has had to be funded from Europe and has scarcely even been performed in the UK. He played tuba in his Brass Band, but his own piano playing is an interesting example of the species of 'composer's piano', even though he is modest about his abilities. Much of Kate's activity has been in connection with Mike's music, but the record cited features her in her own right and is a mostly remarkable piece of work.

**KW:** *Cuff Clout* (Voiceprint)
**MW:** *Chanson Irresponsable* (Enja)

## West Coast Jazz

The term came to represent the jazz which was played and recorded in California during the 50s, mostly by white musicians. The style was seen as a dilution of bebop into a sunny, lightweight kind of playing, where executive skill remained but the feeling was cool and repressed on an emotional level. Exemplars of the style included Shorty Rogers, the Lighthouse All Stars, stalwart professionals such as Bud Shank and Bob Cooper, and more or less everyone associated with the Stan Kenton Orchestra. Gerry Mulligan was seen as a good guy and an atypical West Coaster, but with hindsight the whole idea seems nonsensical: Rogers led a roaring big band, nobody in jazz played with as much painful feeling as Art Pepper, and 'West Coast jazz' also included such black musicians as Hampton Hawes,

Carl Perkins, Frank Morgan, Art Farmer and Curtis Counce.

## Randy Weston
PIANO
*born* 6 April 1926

Weston was a New Yorker who used to pay house visits to Thelonious Monk in the late 40s, to watch him playing piano. In the 50s he toured with R&B bands but began leading bands of his own, recording for Riverside (six albums, from 1956), United Artists (three), Dawn, Jubilee, Roulette and Jazzland (one apiece). He made several trips to Africa in the 60s and eventually settled in Morocco in 1968, returning to the US in 1972 but thereafter often spending time in Africa or Europe. He became much more visible again in the 90s, when he signed a new deal with Verve, and made a series of acclaimed records, some of which featured new arrangements by his friend Melba Liston, others including contributions by a trio of Gnawa musicians. Randy built on his Monk influence in his early writing – 'Hi Fly' and 'Little Niles' are oft-covered classics of their period – but later brought his interest in African music into a style which became more wide-ranging, whiile still recognizably the work of the same man. Weston is a gentle giant whose music has a great current of joy running through it, and it's a little surprising that his approach, which has elsewhere become so fashionable of late, hasn't brought him even more attention in recent times.

*Khepera* (Verve)

## George Wettling
DRUMS
*born* 28 November 1907; *died* 6 June 1968

Wettling began playing on the Chicago scene of the early 20s, eventually going to New York in the following decade and taking on big-band duties with Artie Shaw, Bunny Berigan, Benny Goodman and Red Norvo. He worked primarily as a studio musician in the 40s but was also playing in the Condon circle, and he recorded with many Dixieland small groups during the course of the decade. He also wrote journalism and did abstract paintings, but his drumming was his great talent: a session by George Wettling's Chicago Rhythm Kings in 1940 shows off all his skills, getting all over the kit with superb flair, taking imaginative breaks and getting the crispest sound out of the drums – even in a 1940 recording he sounds like crystal. He carried on working with such pals as Condon, Bud Freeman, Muggsy Spanier and others through the 50s and early 60s, but drink started to affect him in his final years of playing.

**Eddie Condon,** *Bixieland* (Columbia)

# Kenny Wheeler

TRUMPET, FLUGELHORN
*born* 14 January 1930

Although he was born in Toronto and studied at the Royal Conservatory there, Kenny Wheeler has been part of British jazz for more than 50 years. He moved to London in 1952 and was soon playing in dance bands and small jazz groups, eventually joining John Dankworth's orchestra (playing with them at their 1959 Newport Festival appearance) and from there working with numerous leaders on the British scene, including Tubby Hayes, Ronnie Scott, Alan Skidmore and John Surman. The burgeoning free-music scene also piqued his interest, and he played with the Spontaneous Music Ensemble, in Tony Oxley's sextet, and even with Anthony Braxton and the Globe Unity Orchestra – perhaps the only musician of his generation who was able to cross back and forth so easily between a mainstream modernism and complete freedom. His own work as a leader didn't truly get under way until the middle 70s, although there were a couple of earlier records, for Fontana and Incus. *Gnu High* (1975) and *Deer Wan* (1977) began a series of outstanding records for ECM, which continued, although at a very slow, steady pace, into the 90s, and he has also made very occasional records for Soul Note and, in the new century, for Evan Parker's label, psi. He remains in demand as a sideman, and his composing, once almost demurely offered for approval, has become a resource which many other musicians have looked to for material to work on. Wheeler's playing is the epitome of lyricism in post-bop jazz. Much of his improvising is cast in a carefully handled middle register, although he does like occasional high notes

as a kind of marker in a solo – one favourite device he uses is to play a note and then repeat it an octave higher, the second note almost squeezed out of the horn. He gets a notably songful timbre out of both the trumpet and the flugelhorn, yet his playing uses unusual harmonic thinking to keep it from merely being prettily decorative. Even when playing in free situations, he retains his constructive thinking, simply applying it to an open canvas rather than a preordained structure. His writing uses these touchstones to fashion a clever, amiable, gently amused sort of music. In his 70s, some of the lustre and sweetness has gone out of his tone, but he is still a considerable player, and a 75th birthday concert in 2005 was a predictably happy occasion.

*Gnu High* (ECM)

# Jiggs Whigham

TROMBONE
*born* 20 August 1943

Oliver Haydn Whigham III ('Jiggs' was a nickname derived from a comic book character) started on trombone in his teens and joined the Glenn Miller ghost band in 1961. He did section-work with Stan Kenton, Maynard Ferguson and others, and then settled in Cologne in 1965, where he worked in radio orchestras and with Peter Herbolzheimer's big band. He is still based there, a senior teacher in the city's music-education facilities and a regular at Stan Kenton conventions: a great trombone technician, rarely heard out front, although the record cited shows off his skills to fine effect.

*The Jiggs Up* (Capri)

# Andrew White

SAXOPHONES, BASS
*born* 6 September 1942

White was busy with his studies in Washington up until 1961, and that thoroughgoing apprenticeship served him well. He played locally with the JFK Quintet until 1964, then lived briefly in Paris before returning to his home base in the later 60s. He then worked in a variety of contexts – with touring soul revues, the American Ballet Theater and Weather Report (the latter as bassist) – before setting up his own

Andrew's Music label and publishing house back in Washington in the 70s. White produced literally scores of albums of his own playing on this label, including multi-volume sets from marathon gigs and homage records of saxophone solos, as well as transcribing and publishing hundreds of Parker and Coltrane solos and some hilariously scurrilous stories of life on the road, which all go to make up a larger-than-life persona which seems to be equally dedicated to the study of Coltrane and the female form. What tends to be obscured is the excellence of his own sax playing, cast in a personalized take on the hard bop–modal form. Despite his mass of self-documentation, the records are hard to get – you have to ask Andrew, and he will surely oblige.

**Seven Giant Steps For Coltrane** (Andrew's Music)

## Lenny White
DRUMS
*born* 19 December 1949

White was a young turk among fusion musicians, playing with Miles Davis in 1969, and eventually gaining prominence as part of Chick Corea's Return To Forever, which he joined in 1973, staying through their most bombastic fusion period. In the 80s he mostly played on big-ticket pop gigs and on all-star showcases, but after that his success waned a little and in the 90s he was back in more rootsy jazz contexts, playing with Geri Allen and touring with Stanley Clarke. White can play straight-ahead jazz grooves with real flair when he wants, but fusion has left a long-term mark on him and he tends to sound as if he's thinking about rock beats, whatever he happens to be playing.

**Return To Forever,** *Where Have I Known You Before* (Polydor)

## Michael White
CLARINET
*born* 29 November 1954

Despite the rise and rise of the Marsalis family in recent times, homegrown New Orleans jazz hasn't found much of a new audience in the past 20 years. White's work has been one of the most impressive of the few attempts to draw attention to the latest developments in the music's spiritual home. A professor of Spanish studies at Xavier University, he began playing in brass bands in 1975, joined the Young Tuxedo Brass Band, and in 1981 formed his own group with a mixture of old-timers, such as Louis Nelson, Chester Zardis and Danny Barker, and younger figures like himself. Wynton Marsalis has, perhaps inevitably, been a supporter and has sat in with White's band on occasion, especially when they make their occasional forays to New York. The senior members of White's group have passed away or retired by now, but it continues in a spirit of ancient-and-modern, addressing many of the old scriptures of New Orleans music while White tries to put something like a contemporary spin on them. His own playing is in the distinguished tradition of Dodds and Nicholas.

**Crescent City Serenade** (Antilles)

## Annie Whitehead
TROMBONE
*born* 16 July 1955

Whitehead moved south to London from her native Oldham at the start of the 80s, playing on pop sessions and mixing with free players and dance-music groups. While she has recorded a number of albums under her own name and has led several bands of her own, mostly under the heading of the Annie Whitehead Experience, she doesn't really command the kind of instrumental presence which would make these settings work for her: more an ensemble player than a soloist, she has tended to do her most effective work in other than straight-ahead groups.

**Naked** (EFZ)

## Paul Whiteman
BANDLEADER
*born* 28 March 1890; *died* 29 December 1967

This book would surely be incomplete without 'The King Of Jazz'. Yet Whiteman's curious contribution to jazz is hard to assess. He began his career as a viola player in the Denver Symphony Orchestra, led a navy band during the First World War, and on his discharge started organizing an ensemble which could play somewhat in the style of the new dance music, as it had filtered through to the West Coast, where he was then based. He moved to New York in 1920 and was soon recording for Victor, scoring a million-selling hit with 'Whispering' (1920), and leading a band which owed little or nothing to the Original Dixieland Jazz Band, yet which aimed to provide dance music to the same audience. Whiteman suffered (if that's the right word) from having few if any interesting potential soloists – his principal trumpet star, Henry 'Hot Lips' Busse, was close to useless from a jazz viewpoint, and only a few players such as Tommy Gott really suggested any kind of improvisational initiative – but his aim was to provide cleanly played, decent dance music in what was then the new style, and on that basis his orchestra became enormously influential – as much with black bands such as Fletcher Henderson's as with the straighter, 'society' dance bands. Whiteman also commissioned new works, the most notable being George Gershwin's *Rhapsody In Blue*, which was recorded with the composer at the piano in 1924. Within a few years, Whiteman's style had been squarely trumped in jazz terms by the advances sparked by Louis Armstrong, yet he remained immensely popular, and he had also begun hiring some significant soloists, including Bix Beiderbecke, Frankie Trumbauer and Jack Teagarden, all of them glad of the regular work. Being crowned 'The King Of Jazz', as he was for the 1930 talkie of the same name, was the final piece of hubris, yet Whiteman never had much more than a sidelong relationship with jazz: he sought the high polish of a quality dance orchestra, he aimed to put on packaged and value-for-money entertainment – a concept of a band 'show' which has been influential ever since – and he looked after his men. Whiteman stayed close to the top all through the 30s, though he never really competed with the big swing bands, and in 1944 he turned to music direction at ABC: he was still working in that capacity, and turning up on television, in the 60s.

**When Day Is Done** (Happy Days)

# Mark Whitfield
GUITAR
*born* 6 October 1966

Whitfield has made some poor career choices as a recording artist and he needs a fresh start. A Berklee graduate, he was recommended to Warners by George Benson, but his records for them were all duds in a light-fusion bag. While he then went on to make some worthwhile sets for Verve, the company clearly wanted a hit record when they obliged him to make the strings date *Forever Love* (1997), which flopped. Maybe his vocation is as a sideman: as a smart, lightly aggressive player basically in the Montgomery tradition, he can turn his talent to most contemporary situations. A new signing with MaxJazz has shown some promise.

**7th Avenue Stroll** (Verve)

# Tommy Whittle
TENOR SAXOPHONE
*born* 13 October 1926

A Scot who moved to the London dance-band scene in the 40s, Whittle is a ubiquitous and reliable mainstream stylist. He has played in numerous British bands as a freelance, more or less since he moved south, and though he has occasionally led small groups of his own (particularly in the 50s), Tommy is more likely to be heard taking a bright, amiable chorus of tenor on some otherwise anonymous studio date. A partial list of the bands he's graced would include the (posthumous) Ted Heath orchestra, the Jazz Journal All Stars and the Pizza Express All Stars. His wife, Barbara Jay, is a singer. He has led very few record dates himself.

**Warm Glow** (Tee Jay)

# Putte Wickman
CLARINET
*born* 10 September 1924

Sweden's Benny Goodman has hardly put a foot wrong in jazz playing over some six decades. He began touring in small groups in the middle 40s and eventually took over what had been Hasse Kahn's group in 1948, and the band carried on from there into the 60s, based in Nalen. While this inevitably attracted little international attention, Wickman did visit the US in 1959, playing a date at Carnegie Hall. He led a straight dance orchestra for the first half of the 60s and then ran his own club for a time in Stockholm. Since the early 70s he has played mainly as a freelance. Like Goodman, he has investigated the classical clarinet repertoire, but he has made a much better job out of addressing latter-day jazz developments than the American ever did. His playing has accrued a near-timeless quality which is unabashedly enjoyable.

*Mr Clarinet* (Four Leaf Clover)

## Gerry Wiggins
PIANO
*born* 12 May 1922

Wiggins grew up in New York but spent most of his jazz career on the West Coast. He took minor roles behind Louis Armstrong and Benny Carter in the early 40s before army service, and from 1947 he was based in Los Angeles, where he mostly worked as an accompanist to singers, Lena Horne, Kay Starr and Helen Humes among them. Besides these gigs, he also did studio work, recorded with such big bands as Gerald Wilson's orchestra, and played at festivals and jazz parties. His occasional records as a leader are charming but inconsequential: there isn't enough in his playing, agreeable though it is, to really hold the attention over the course of a full set, and his good-natured approach is best heard in the broader context of a more substantial group record.

*Live At Maybeck Recital Hall* (Concord)

## Johnny Wiggs
TRUMPET
*born* 25 July 1899; *died* 9 October 1977

Wiggs (born John Hyman) was inspired by King Oliver's playing to try and take up music in his native New Orleans, and he performed with minor groups until getting the chance to make his one early record, under the name John Hyman and his Bayou Stompers, in 1927. In the 30s and 40s he worked mostly as a teacher in the public school system, but the revival persuaded him to pick up his horn again, and he began playing as Johnny Wiggs (so as not to upset the disapproving school system). He helped sponsor concerts and generally became a prime mover in getting New Orleans jazz moving again, and after retiring from teaching in 1960 became a regular at Preservation Hall and elsewhere.

*Penn–Wiggs New Orleans All Stars Concert* (GHB)

## Bob Wilber
CLARINET, SOPRANO AND ALTO SAXOPHONES
*born* 15 March 1928

Born in New York, Wilber started on clarinet in his teens and managed to persuade Sidney Bechet to give him lessons in 1946. He led a band called The Wildcats in 1947, one of the first acts of revivalism in the New York area following the war, and after serving in an army band in the early 50s he began working with a variety of significant leaders, including Bechet, Benny Goodman and Jack Teagarden, as well as drifting into the Condon circle. This carried him through the 60s, when he was playing clarinet, tenor and a curved soprano sax, and he joined The World's Greatest Jazz Band in 1969, staying five years before starting up Soprano Summit, his two-sax band with Kenny Davern. Since the late 70s he has concerned himself mainly with jazz repertory, teaching, playing on soundtracks, and working through numerous concept albums dedicated to different aspects of the jazz past – Oliver, Goodman, Bechet, Morton, Ellington – of which two recent sets of 'unheard' Benny Goodman arrangements have been outstanding. Wilber's mastery of his subject hasn't always led to immediately enjoyable results, and some of these projects have sounded stiff and unrewarding, but at his best he inspires a band and his own playing has settled into a nicely personal distillation of his many jazz interests. His wife Joanne, usually called Pug, sometimes takes a vocal role in these situations. He announced his retirement in 1995, but that appears to have been a bit of leg-pulling.

*Dancing On A Rainbow* (Circle)

## Joe Wilder
DRUMS
*born* 22 February 1922

Wilder has quietly worked through a long and industrious sort of career. He studied in Philadelphia and worked in Lionel Hampton's band before serving in the Marine Corps, after which he served under a succession of bandleaders into the early 50s. He played in Broadway pit bands for much of the 50s, though he also did six months in Count Basie's orchestra, and he became a staffer at ABC in 1957, which lasted him 16 years. Since then he has worked mainly as a freelance, sometimes playing in theatre orchestras again, and occasionally turning up in all-star groups such as the Statesmen Of Jazz. On record, Joe has mostly been offered uncredited roles, but a ballad collection from 1959, *The Pretty Sound Of Joe Wilder* (Columbia), showed off his charming sound, and three recent albums for the independent Evening Star label have given the great professional a deserved showcase.
*Alone With Just My Dreams* (Evening Star)

## Barney Wilen
TENOR SAXOPHONE
*born* 4 March 1937; *died* 25 May 1996

Born in Nice, Wilen became a familiar face on the Paris scene of the middle 50s, and his star suddenly rose when Miles Davis had him appear with the trumpeter on the sessions for the soundtrack to *Ascenseur pour l'échafaud* (1957), even though, when working at the same club together, the thoughtful Davis had earlier asked Wilen, 'Man, why don't you stop playing those awful notes?' He joined Art Blakey's Jazz Messengers for a spell at the end of the 50s but he never had an opportunity for a career in the US. He spent several years living in Africa at the end of the 60s and latterly tried to create a music which mixed fusion leanings with African beats, although in the end he went back to a more straight-ahead bop delivery. Wilen had quite a following in Japan and did much of his later recording there, displaying a handsome, buffed sound which had very few awful notes in it.
*Sanctuary* (Ida)

## Lee Wiley
VOCAL
*born* 9 October 1908; *died* 11 December 1975

Wiley's seductive, grown-up sound brought a sense of real class to some otherwise down-at-heel jazz settings in the late 30s. She started as a band singer with Leo Reisman around 1930, got on to radio, and made the first 'concept albums' of songs by individual composers grouped as a sequence when she did some sessions for the Liberty Music Shop in 1939 (she was accompanied by a group of Condonites). Thereafter she often turned up on Condon's broadcasts, married Jess Stacy (although it didn't last), and thereafter led a rather interrupted career which resulted in only a handful of recordings in the LP era, a time which might have been expected to produce her best work. Wiley's smiling, knowing voice wasn't especially remarkable in itself and she was no vocal virtuoso, but her unaffected elegance still sounds very appealing.
*Night In Manhattan* (Columbia)

## Don Wilkerson
TENOR SAXOPHONE
*born* 6 July 1932; *died* 18 July 1986

Wilkerson grew up in Houston and started out playing rhythm and blues on alto sax, but he eventually changed to tenor, and spent long stints with T-Bone Walker and then Ray Charles, staying with him for most of the 50s. He made three rough but likeable albums for Blue Note in 1962–3, somewhat in a soul-jazz vein, but coloured by Wilkerson's Texas roots, which come through particularly effectively on 'Lone Star Shuffle' and Bob Wills's 'San Antonio Rose'. He then rejoined Charles for a few years before settling back in Texas, and continuing to play locally into the 80s.
*The Complete Blue Note Sessions* (Blue Note)

## Edward Wilkerson Jr
TENOR SAXOPHONE, CLARINET
*born* 1953

Wilkerson grew up near Cleveland and was inspired by a performance by the Art Ensemble Of Chicago to take up jazz seriously. He began playing in small groups on

the Chicago scene from the mid-70s, co-founded the Ethnic Heritage Ensemble with Kahil El'Zabar, and then led his own trio, Shadow Vignettes, which in the 80s grew into an unwieldy 25-piece band. This was succeeded by the much more successful octet, 8 Bold Souls, which has thus far only managed four albums in 19 years but has still served up some colourful, passionate, sometimes dazzling music which suggests Wilkerson is in the modern Chicago tradition of such player-composers as Mitchell, Abrams and Threadgill.
**Last Option** (Thrill Jockey)

# Ernie Wilkins
ARRANGER
*born* 20 July 1922; *died* 5 June 1999

Wilkins was raised in St Louis and, encouraged by childhood friend Jimmy Forrest, he took up saxophone at school. He played with local bands until serving in the navy, and thereafter worked with Earl Hines's last big band before getting an offer (via Clark Terry) to join Count Basie. Although he took the alto chair in the band, it was his burgeoning talents as an arranger and composer that proved crucial: along with Neal Hefti and Quincy Jones, he reshaped the Basie sound for the post-big-band era, and then went on to score for Dizzy Gillespie, Harry James, Sarah Vaughan and many others. But narcotics problems halted his progress and his career went into a serious downturn in the 60s. Emerging from rehabilitation in 1968, he was again assisted by Clark Terry, and then spent much of the rest of his life in Europe, writing and leading big bands and radio orchestras, although this was curtailed following a stroke in 1991. Ernie could easily have followed the path of bebop composers like Tadd Dameron ('I had to change my musical thinking to write for Basie's band'), but in the end his skills made him a great all-round pro and while his best-known work is enshrined in such Basie charts as 'Sixteen Men Swingin'' and 'Every Day I Have The Blues', he is one of the American jazzmen whose work left a profound mark on the development of post-bop orchestral jazz in Europe.
**Count Basie, *Count Basie Dance Session*** (Roulette)

# Baby Face Willette
ORGAN
*born* 11 September 1933

Roosevelt Willette was the son of a minister and first played the organ in church. He worked in gospel and R&B groups from the early 50s, and in 1961 he made two albums for Blue Note which, because of their scarcity and the style of music, have become, in their original form, among the most sought-after records in that catalogue by collectors. Both these and two later albums for Argo are really nothing special, but ah, the mystique! Willette was still apparently working in Chicago in the 70s, but then disappeared from jazz altogether. One wonders if Baby Face knows how prized his records have become.
**Face To Face** (Blue Note)

# Buster Williams
BASS
*born* 17 April 1942

Williams has only occasionally stepped out as a leader on record, even in an age when bassist-bosses are relatively commonplace, although only among audiences is he much taken for granted: he is one of the masters of his instrument. While he rose to gain some attention with Jimmy Heath in 1960, he was on the West Coast for much of the 60s, working with several singers and with The Jazz Crusaders. He went back to New York in 1969 and has remained there since, spending time alongside Herbie Hancock, Mary Lou Williams and Ron Carter in the 70s, with the Monk tribute band Sphere in the 80s, and subsequently as the most respected of freelances. In 1989 he formed a group of his own, Something More, which has only occasionally recorded but which has acted as another of the 'finishing school' units for up-and-coming talents. Buster has absorbed all the possibilities of the bass in post-bop modal jazz, which tends to make his every performance a matchless master-class: the record cited, made in 2000 with Geri Allen and Lenny White, is a blend of originals and Hancock and Shorter tunes, which emerges as a craftsman's essay on the acoustic idiom he has so thoroughly investigated.
**Houdini** (Sirocco)

## Clarence Williams

PIANO, VOCAL, JUG
*born* 8 October 1898; *died* 6 November 1965

Williams worked as a singer and dancer in minstrel shows in the early teens of the century and then played piano in New Orleans saloons, setting up a publishing company with A J Piron around 1915. A shrewd man, he parlayed this into a bigger publishing venture in New York, founding a number of music stores along the way, and in 1923 he was hired by OKeh as their principal jazz A&R man. Williams backed dozens of blues singers as well as leading his own groups, mostly under the rubric Clarence Williams And His Blue Five, a studio team which used stalwart players such as Ed Allen, Cecil Scott and Cyrus St Clair, as well as seniors including King Oliver and Lorenzo Tio and Young Turks like Louis Armstrong and Sidney Bechet. Williams's wife Eva Taylor sang on many of the sides, and when a jug or washboard kind of band was called for – as it was in many of his later sessions, for Vocalion and Victor in the 30s – Clarence cheerfully blew into the jug. All this added up to an enormously prolific output of hundreds of records, all of which are prized by early jazz collectors. For a less committed listener, they are rather less essential: Williams himself was no more than a workmanlike pianist, and many of the later records especially are saddled with routine material, although even there the dependable work of Allen in particular is usually worth following. In the end, Williams's music went dramatically out of style, and he sold his publishing business, which had included such hits as 'Royal Garden Blues' and 'Squeeze Me'. He retired to keep a store in Harlem, but died as a result of being injured in a street accident.
*Dreaming The Hours Away* (Frog)

## Claude Williams

VIOLIN, GUITAR
*born* 22 February 1908

Raised in Muskogee, Oklahoma, Williams first played in string bands and joined the Terrence Holder group before it became the Andy Kirk band. He then briefly worked in Chicago with Nat Cole before playing guitar in Count Basie's new band, although Freddie Green took over that spot soon enough.

Williams then mostly worked in out-of-the-way groups in Michigan and Kansas and wasn't really sighted again until Jay McShann brought him out of obscurity and worked with him at festivals in the 70s. Audiences heard a spirited and swinging fiddler, his style pitched somewhere between Joe Venuti and Stuff Smith, whose playing continued in much the same boisterous manner into the late 90s.
**With Jay McShann,** *The Man From Muskogee* (Sackville)

## Cootie Williams

TRUMPET
*born* 10 July 1911; *died* 14 September 1985

Williams tried out all sorts of instruments at school (in Mobile, Alabama) but eventually settled on trumpet. He arrived in New York in 1928, worked briefly with Fletcher Henderson, but was engaged by Duke Ellington to replace Bubber Miley – although not as a growl soloist in the Miley manner. In the end, Cootie ended up growling anyway, and he was soon one of the dominant soloists in the Ellington band, staying until the end of 1940 (news of his departure was so devastating that Raymond Scott recorded 'When Cootie Left The Duke' as a wake). Williams was a master of both muted and open playing: 'Concerto For Cootie' (1940) is the often-cited classic among his many Ellington features, but the author's favourite is his astonishing double-break on 'Harlem Air Shaft' (1939). Either way, he was, like Rex Stewart, a conversational brassman who could suggest both a heated intensity and a behind-the-hand remark. He joined Benny Goodman for a spell before running his own big band out of New York's Savoy Ballroom: curiously, since the leader was uninterested in the new developments, it managed to hire several of the coming boppers, including Powell, Monk and Parker (the first version of Monk's immortal 'Round Midnight' was made under Williams's name). Cootie began to fade from view as the swing era ended, and he was playing in rhythm-and-blues settings before a reunion with Rex Stewart in 1957 and then with Benny Goodman. In the end, and perhaps inevitably, he went back to Ellington in 1962, staying until after his leader's death and finally retiring around 1980. In his later years, something went a little sour in Cootie's tone, and the old surefootedness left him: in its place was an Armstrong-like implacability, which let him play over whatever beat was going through his head, rather than whatever one the band was playing.

**Duke Ellington, The Blanton–Webster Band** (Bluebird)

# Fess Williams
CLARINET
*born* 10 April 1894; *died* 17 December 1975

Williams came out of Danville, Kentucky, and from there made his way first to Cincinnati and then (1924) to New York. The Fess Williams Royal Flush Orchestra enjoyed a long spell at the Savoy Ballroom, and their records – 52 sides, for Gennett, Vocalion, Brunswick and Victor – show that the band could boast some exemplary players and were a tight and well-equipped outfit. The drawback is often Williams's own playing: while he could play respectable blues clarinet when he wanted, he could also come out with gargling novelty solos, not quite as ribald and ridiculous as Boyd Senter or Wilton Crawley, but discouraging all the same. When the Depression took hold, Williams drifted on the scene, and after the 40s played only occasionally.

**Fess Williams' Royal Flush Orchestra** (Retrieval)

# James Williams
PIANO
*born* 8 March 1951; *died* 20 July 2004

Williams was a gospel and R&B man in his native Memphis, and jazz came later, when he studied at the University. From there he taught at Berklee, from 1974, and played locally before spending four years in Art Blakey's Jazz Messengers (1977–81). Thereafter he worked mainly as a leader and occasional sideman in the New York area. Williams was a much-liked musician and a couple of his 90s records, *Meets The Saxophone Masters* (DIW, 1991) and *Talkin' Trash* (DIW, 1993) set him up with seniors such as George Coleman, Joe Henderson and Clark Terry, to fine effect. But the record cited, one of his last as a leader, sets him up in the grand company of Ray Brown and Elvin Jones, and the smiling, exuberant

results touch on his gospel background while remaining squarely in a modern jazz groove.

**Awesome!** (DIW)

# Jessica Williams
PIANO
*born* 17 March 1948

Williams was a local secret for much of her early career. Conservatory-trained in her native Baltimore, she quit her course when an obstinate teacher tried to steer her away from improvisation, and she spent the 70s in obscurity in Philadelphia and then San Francisco, where she gradually built up a following at venues, including Keystone Korner, in the 80s. She ran at least two record labels of her own, pouring out albums, including electronic-keyboard sessions and others where she overdubbed her own rhythm parts, but since 1985 she has been extensively recorded as an acoustic soloist and trio leader, in both Europe and America. Williams is an executant of high skill and forceful demeanour – her electric music doesn't seem to have steered her in any kind of new-age direction – and with Monk, Bill Evans and McCoy Tyner all figuring strongly in her work, she sometimes sounds like a synthesis of piano trends after bebop, and has won considerable popularity as a result. This tends to make her records impressive but an ounce short of anything individual.

**Jazz In The Afternoon** (Candid)

# Joe Williams
VOCAL
*born* 12 December 1918; *died* 30 March 1999

Williams and his singing prospered over a very long career. He didn't even become any kind of star until he was nearly 40. He grew up in Chicago, and sang with club groups and occasionally in Boston or New York, but he was still singing with the unremarkable Red Saunders band when Count Basie heard him in a Chicago club, and hired him in 1954. For seven years he was Basie's lead singer and a great ace in the hole for the leader: he brought hits such as 'Every Day I Have The Blues' into the book, and gave Basie a focal point at a time when singers were ruling the entertainment world. After leaving Basie in 1961, Williams worked the rest of his career as a solo, although he often participated in Basie reunions and toured with a Clark Terry group in 1977. He made many albums for Roulette (during and immediately after his Basie years) and RCA, and though he recorded little in the 70s, like many singers of his era he came back in the 80s and enjoyed an Indian summer with some attractive albums for Verve and Telarc. While he could sing blues with a suave, feelingful elegance, he was just as fine as a ballad and standards interpreter, his huge and avuncular voice settling gracefully between a bass and a baritone, and he was masterful at pleasing an audience while performing very much as a member of the band who were on stage with him.

*Count Basie Swings And Joe Williams Sings* (Verve)

# Martin Williams

WRITER

*born* 9 August 1924; *died* 12 April 1992

Williams began writing about jazz in the 50s, working more for the arts columns in the wider American press than specialist jazz titles, although he did write for *Down Beat* and co-founded the short-lived *Jazz Review* in 1960. He went on to be appointed to a directing post at the Smithsonian Institution, overseeing jazz concert programmes and jazz reissues sponsored by that body. A tough-minded, unsentimental critic of rare candour, Williams wrote without airs and was always concerned to get to the heart of his subject: in a frequently narcissistic area of musical criticism, he is often notable by his absence from his own writing. His taste more or less stopped at Coltrane, but he was respectful to every working jazz musician, and his patrician influence abides in the better American criticism.

# Mary Lou Williams

PIANO

*born* 8 May 1909; *died* 28 May 1981

Williams, born Mary Elfrieda Scruggs, was raised in Pittsburgh, where she began playing in vaudeville in the early 20s, eventually marrying the bandleader John Williams. She then played in New York and in 1929 became part of a new band led by Andy Kirk, working as both pianist and arranger. Her tunes were in the band's book from their first recording session onwards, and Kirk's musical success was based largely around Williams's work. She was a smart, engaging swing pianist, specializing in a rocking beat which was informed by both stride and boogie-woogie patterns, and her charts always sounded pointed and up to the minute, gifting hits such as 'Walkin' And Swingin'', 'In The Groove' and 'Mary's Idea' to Kirk's repertoire. Besides this, she began contributing to some of the other major swing bands, writing 'Roll 'Em' for Benny Goodman and several charts for the Earl Hines band, the pianist being one of her formative influences. She finally left Kirk in 1942 and married her second husband, Shorty Baker, although the marriage only lasted two years. She then worked as a solo pianist at Café Society for several years, in the meantime contributing arrangements for Dizzy Gillespie's big band – she was quickly in sympathy with the boppers, who also liked her style – and even writing a large-scale *Zodiac Suite*, which was given a partial performance by the New York Philharmonic. Trio work kept her busy until 1952, when she spent two years in Europe, and after a brief sabbatical from playing she returned to small-group work in New York, playing in clubs through the 60s and 70s. She latterly became involved in writing sacred works, including three masses and a cantata, yet her own pianism continued to develop, getting darker and more dissonant. This might account for why she decided to play in a duo concert with Cecil Taylor in 1977, a famously bizarre occasion. Her discography has been marked by only spottily available records, and a few strange sessions such as her Sue single 'Chuck-A-Lunk-Jug' (1964) are still hard to find, but more of her music is probably available now on CD than it has ever been, whch is only justice for a distinguished spirit of 20th-century black music.

*Free Spirits* (Steeplechase)

# Richard Williams

TRUMPET

*born* 4 May 1931; *died* 5 November 1985

Williams was an admirable trumpeter who had few breaks in what was finally an undistinguished career. Born in Galveston, Texas, he took up the trumpet in his teens and played in Texas bands before taking the lead trumpet chair in Lionel Hampton's touring band in 1956. In New York in the 60s he worked with Gigi Gryce, Charles Mingus, Slide Hampton and Duke Ellington, and thereafter, though he sometimes led small groups of his own, he mostly worked in such big bands as Clark Terry and the Jones–Lewis orchestra. His masters were Fats Navarro and Clifford Brown, working in their mould of a resilient attack married to a sometimes radiant lyricism, and though leaders such as Mingus made fine use of his talents, he never seemed to be a trumpeter much spoken of or feted by audiences. In his whole career he made only a single album as a leader, for Candid in 1961: *New Horn In Town* sounded like a major arrival, full of exemplary playing by a fine quintet, but nobody ever sponsored a follow-up.

*New Horn In Town* (Candid)

# Roy Williams

TROMBONE

*born* 7 March 1937

Williams took up the trombone at 18 and moved to London in 1960, joining in the late rumblings of the trad boom with Terry Lightfoot and then Alex Welsh, whom he joined in 1965 and stayed with some 13 years. He then switched to Humphrey Lyttelton's band and spent five years there before electing to spend his time as a freelance. Williams has always been a present-and-correct kind of player: his ensemble work locks in, his solos shine, and he always seems to know where he is and what he has to do. One could complain that this makes him too polished and unexciting, but he is more in the tradition of Teagarden, a musician who doesn't surprise but never plays below a formidably high level. He was never outplayed in the Welsh band, and since going out on his own he has performed as a guest soloist, which has often led him into situations where he easily out-

classes his surroundings but is too polite to make it too obvious. These have included gigs at home in the UK, in Europe and in the US. He has never shown much inclination to be a leader himself, but he has worked in a trio alongside his son Andrew, who plays guitar.

*Royal Trombone* (Phontastic)

# Rudy Williams

ALTO SAXOPHONE, CLARINET

Williams is almost forgotten, but his recorded solos suggest a significant and sophisticated musician. He was one of the main soloists in Al Cooper's Savoy Sultans (1937–43), and from there he worked with a variety of leaders as well as leading his own groups. While his work was basically in the swing idiom, he was outgoing enough to be working with Tadd Dameron and Dizzy Gillespie in the late 40s, and fragments of jam sessions with Hot Lips Page and Don Byas suggest a virile and harmonically adroit style on the alto. But he enjoyed less limelight in the 50s and never led a record date of his own: he died as a result of a swimming accident.

*Al Cooper's Savoy Sultans, 1938–1941* (Classics)

# Sandy Williams

TROMBONE

*born* 24 October 1906; *died* 25 March 1991

Williams was much in demand all through the 30s and 40s in New York jazz. He divided his time between the Horace and Fletcher Henderson bands in the early 30s, then spent seven years in the Chick Webb band. In the 40s he mixed big-band duties with Duke Ellington, Claude Hopkins and others with small-band work with Rex Stewart, Sidney Bechet and Art Hodes. He played with a bright and rather extravagant tone and his solos always have a lively edge to them. But he was another man more or less ruined by drink: his health began to suffer, and by the 50s he was working as an elevator man and playing only rarely thereafter.

*Sidney Bechet, Jazz Classics Vol 1* (Blue Note)

## Spencer Williams
COMPOSER
*born* 14 October 1889; *died* 14 July 1965

Williams had no real career as a performer: he played in Chicago in the teens of the century before settling in New York and joining forces with Clarence Williams in writing and publishing. He played a little as a pianist and cut some vocal duets later in the 20s, but mostly he was writing: 'Basin Street Blues', I've Found A New Baby', 'Careless Love' and 'Royal Garden Blues', among many others, were at least co-credited to him. He left for Europe in 1932, and thereafter lived in London and Sweden, although he finally came home as an invalid to New York.

## Tony Williams
DRUMS
*born* 12 December 1945; *died* 23 February 1997

Williams was the most exceptional of jazz prodigies. He was drumming as a child and was already working as a freelance in the Boston area by the time he was 15. Sam Rivers gave him much guidance early on, and in 1962 Jackie McLean hired him as his drummer, resulting in his moving to New York. Miles Davis heard him there and enticed him into joining his latest group, in May 1963, a brilliant piece of timing on Davis's part: Williams was a liberating player who introduced a supremely disciplined freedom into the trumpeter's music. Besides his work with Davis, which took him through to 1969, Williams played on such important record dates as Eric Dolphy's *Out To Lunch!* (Blue Note, 1964), Sam Rivers's *Fuchsia Swing Song* (1964) and Herbie Hancock's *Maiden Voyage* (1965), as well as recording his own albums *Lifetime* (1964) and *Spring* (1965) for Blue Note. Williams approached the drumkit as an assembly of different instruments, each requiring individual attention. His cymbals were used to accent the pulse in unusual ways, and he sometimes played patterns on them as if they might be drums themselves; he played quickly and lightly, slowing and accelerating pulses with an unprecedented deftness; he avoided metrical playing when left to himself and approached a solo as if it might be a composition. He was never as noisy as Elvin Jones, and was moving some of Jones's ideas

on a step even as their creator was perfecting them. In the Davis group, he left the conventional time playing of his predecessors far behind, and he was the ideal drummer for the inscrutable phase of the trumpeter's mid-60s music. After leaving Miles, he formed his own proto-fusion band, Lifetime, with Larry Young and John McLaughlin, and his playing suddenly became thicker and more bludgeoning, even as it demonstrated much of the same ingenuity. Lifetime largely failed, at least in comparison to the success which would be enjoyed by McLaughlin in the Mahavishnu Orchestra, and Williams eventually took a break from music, returning to the more quiescent surroundings of a trio with Hank Jones and the VSOP band, which was effectively a reunion of the Miles Davis quintet without Miles. In the 80s he formed a new quintet, which recorded a sequence of records for Blue Note, somewhat in his older acoustic style, although the group had a rather hard edge to it which suffered from a certain absence of flair. His final years were mixed: he went on a Miles Davis tribute tour, which communicated little between the players, cut a couple of records which mixed fusion with impressionism, and affirmed his old mastery in a trio record, with Mulgrew Miller and Ira Coleman, somewhat ironically entitled *Young At Heart* (Columbia, 1996). It was completed only months before his unexpected death following heart surgery.
*Lifetime* (Blue Note)

## Steve Williamson
TENOR AND SOPRANO SAXOPHONES
*born* 28 June 1964

Williamson is a brilliant talent whose missed opportunities have been frustrating. He emerged as one of the most interesting players in the brief boom of young performers who came out of the British scene of the mid-80s, a Coltrane acolyte with a big, somewhat severe sound and a fierce command of the horn. Like Courtney Pine, he had previous experience working in reggae bands, and he brought a strikingly new feel to the music as it was then being played in London. After he signed to the British wing of Verve in 1989, his debut, *A Waltz For Grace*, was made partly in London and

partly in New York, and was an exciting start. But Williamson's progress was poorly handled by his label, at that time managed by pop-oriented staff, and gradually his career fell to pieces. He tried an approach inspired by Steve Coleman's M-Base music but the resulting album was little more than a clutter, and after a string of managers and seemingly a new band at every gig, he drifted off the scene altogether. It was, however, heartening to find him back playing again in London in the new century. A shy man, Steve sometimes seems like a casualty of his times, but as a saxophone player he is still extraordinarily powerful.
*A Waltz For Grace* (Verve)

# Valerie Wilmer

AUTHOR, PHOTOGRAPHER
*born* 7 December 1941

Wilmer started writing about jazz in her teens and studied photography at the end of the 50s, eventually blending both occupations with an level of accomplishment which is unique. She has written extensively and candidly in the British music and national press for more than 40 years, publishing several important works such as *Jazz People* (1970), *As Serious As Your Life* (1977) and her own unsparing autobiography, *Mama Said There'd Be Days Like These* (1989). She has made a point of researching the contributions of black musicians to the British musical scene in the 20th century, although her definitive account of this issue in book form is still eagerly awaited. Her photographs are personal and revealing.

# Cassandra Wilson

VOCAL
*born* 4 December 1955

Wilson became the most successful jazz singer of the 90s. Born in Jackson, Mississippi, where her father was a bassist and music teacher, she began singing in soul bands while at college. She moved to New York (via New Orleans) in 1982, and fell in with the Steve Coleman circle of musicians that came to be called M-Base Collective: she is featured on several of Coleman's albums, and began making her own dates (for the German label JMT) in a similar style.

Although she cut one album of standards with a straight-ahead trio – the impeccable *Blue Skies* (1988) – she professed to dislike that direction. In 1992, she signed to Blue Note, and Bruce Lundvall persuaded her to move away from the M-Base music ('She'd sing a chorus, then turn it over to the band, and they'd drown her out') and towards a more mellifluous fusion of blues, folk, jazz and rock, where a wide mix of material – from Robert Johnson to The Monkees – was reinterpreted via Craig Street's surprising arrangements. The resulting debut, *Blue Light 'Til Dawn* (1993), was a huge hit and crossed her over to a rock audience. Since then, she has repeated the formula on subsequent discs, although *Traveling Miles* (2000) was an idiosyncratic homage to Miles Davis. Although she has a luscious contralto voice, it doesn't have great range, and much of her singing feels one-dimensional and even laden with artifice: she is a very self-conscious artist, and there is scarcely a glimmer of humour in anything that she does. While she is one of the few singers to build on Betty Carter's legacy, and creative approach to a melody line, she is at her best in simple settings where she lets the timbre of her voice tell the story: 'Darkness On The Delta', from *Belly Of The Sun* (2002), is a fine example. She might demur, but it is hard to see her ever surpassing the unpretentious excellence of *Blue Skies* at this point.
*Blue Skies* (JMT)

# Garland Wilson

PIANO
*born* 13 June 1909; *died* 31 May 1954

Wilson is one of the many maverick pianists that jazz seems full of, entering and departing the music and leaving little trace bar a few striking records. Born in Martinsburg, West Virginia, he was playing in New York clubs by 1931 (John Hammond sponsored his first record date) and two years later was touring Europe as the accompanist to singer Nina Mae McKinney. He liked London and Paris and divided his time between the two cities until the outbreak of war, when he returned to New York and again worked as an accompanist. In 1951, he moved back home to Europe and was still working a Paris residency when he died. Wilson played in a style which could sound like Art Tatum in a low gear: the delicacy of his fingering takes some of the steeliness out of his quickfire figures, double-time runs and bouncing syncopations, and he manages to skirt the sense of routine which even Tatum could fall prey to. The disc listed gathers in most of his important work of the 30s.

*Garland Wilson 1931–1938* (Classics)

# Gerald Wilson

TRUMPET, ARRANGER
*born* 4 September 1918

Wilson studied music at high school in Detroit before joining Jimmie Lunceford in 1939 as a staff arranger, contributing such pieces as 'Hi Spook' to the band's book. In 1942 he moved to Los Angeles, and has worked there ever since. He ran his own big bands during 1944–7 and went on to achieve the unique double of providing arrange-ments for both Count Basie and Duke Ellington. But he was getting so much work in film and TV writing that he rarely did any jazz scoring during the 50s. In 1961, though, he formed a new big band which recorded regularly for Pacific Jazz during the 60s and gave some profile work to some of the better soloists on the West Coast during the period, including Harold Land, Teddy Edwards and Carmell Jones. He taught exten-sively in California colleges during the 70s and 80s and still managed to keep an orches-tra going, recording for Discovery and MAMA and making occasional outside visits. In 2003, at the age of 85, he released a new record. Wilson might have a longer career than anyone else in jazz arranging, since it now extends well past 60 years (which beats even Benny Carter). If his Pacific Jazz albums had enjoyed a longer catalogue life and some CD reissues, he might be more acknowledged than he is. A capable trumpeter, he played in Lunceford's brass section and made some occasional side-man appearances in the 50s.

*State Street Swing* (MAMA)

# Phillip Wilson

DRUMS
*born* 8 September 1941; *died* 1 April 1992

Wilson grew up in St Louis and began work-ing in Chicago in the late 50s, eventually

touring with rock'n'roll shows and backing soul singers. He settled in Chicago in 1965 and joined the AACM, playing in Roscoe Mitchell's groups, but before the decade was out he was back on the road with Paul Butterfield's Blues Band. In the 70s he renewed his relationship with the avant-garde, playing with Anthony Braxton and regularly with David Murray. He also did session work for Stax records in Memphis. In the 80s he was often to be found in Lester Bowie's groups, including both From The Root To The Source and Brass Fantasy. Wilson was an unfussy, driving drummer with versatility enough to handle what was an often bewilderingly diverse history of associations. He was murdered in his own New York apartment during a robbery in 1992.

**Lester Bowie,** *The Great Pretender* (ECM)

# Steve Wilson

ALTO AND SOPRANO SAXOPHONES
*born* 9 February 1961

Wilson attracted a major amount of atten-tion in the late 80s, first as a member of the Out Of The Blue group, and some talked of him becoming the next major saxophone star. It didn't quite happen, although he's done much interesting work since. He has recorded very prolifically as a sideman, with Ralph Peterson, Don Braden, Don Byron, Bill Stewart and many others, and besides a stint in Dave Holland's working band has more recently been one of the principals in Chick Corea's Origin group. His own records as a leader, though, have been very mixed, sug-gesting a player who turns in a top-notch cameo role and can't quite sustain a leading part.

**Chick Corea,** *Origin Live At The Blue Note* (Stretch)

# Teddy Wilson

PIANO
*born* 24 November 1912; *died* 31 July 1986

Raised in Austin, Texas, by middle-class parents, the teenaged Wilson visited Chicago in 1928 and was sufficiently overwhelmed by the music scene there that he determined to join in himself. He was arranging for a band led by Speed Webb a year later, and in

1931 formed an alliance with his friend Art Tatum, playing in piano bars night after night from their base in Toledo, Ohio. He toured with Louis Armstrong in 1933 and was heard by John Hammond in Chicago, who brought him to New York, where he joined Willie Bryant. Wilson's breakthrough came with the recording sessions set up by Hammond, from 1935, where the pianist led a series of picked studio bands for both instrumental sides and sessions where they backed singer Billie Holiday. Between 1936 and 1939 he was also with Benny Goodman, playing in Goodman's trio and quartet. His style already fully mature, Wilson in this period was peerless: only Tatum and Earl Hines, from both of whom he drew elements of his style, could match him. His left hand was very strong, yet he subtly thinned or shifted the harmonies and adapted the rhythms of stride to his own ends: meanwhile, the right hand fragmented the melody in octaves without letting it slip too far from view. The impression was of a 'background' player determined to reward every listener who took the trouble to follow what he was doing. In a small-group setting he was virtually unrivalled, and his accompaniments and direction for Holiday resulted in many of the masterpieces of the day being set down (although, ironically, Wilson himself considered Holiday to be a lesser singer than several of her contemporaries – he liked to work with Ella Fitzgerald and Mildred Bailey).

Briefly, there was a Teddy Wilson big band, but it was a case of too much musicality and not enough crowd-pleasing and the venture was dead by the spring of 1940. He then worked with a sextet of varying personnel through the early 40s before rejoining Goodman and then working with a trio. It was typical of Wilson that he should also have been among the first jazz musicians to teach at Juilliard, which he did until 1952. Thereafter he spent his working life as a club and concert pianist, sometimes in reunions (with Goodman, and Benny Carter) but often going out as a solo or a guest. He was still visiting Europe almost up until his death. Towards the end, the sparkle in his playing took on a more brittle, professional quality, but that was the price of a prolific and uninterrupted career. Wilson almost defines the notion of elegance in jazz: he was as dapper and unflappable in person as his music, and the agreeable surfaces of his playing disguise the acute and tireless artistry (much as the man himself masked a sometimes suspicious and cautious nature behind good manners). Every lounge pianist would wish to sound like him; almost none of them do.
*Fine And Dandy* (Hep)

# Lem Winchester
VIBES
*born* 19 March 1928; *died* 13 January 1961

Winchester had a fleeting career. He took up the vibes while studying in Wilmington, Delaware, and mixed a haphazard career as a sideman with a regular job as a policeman. He played at the Newport festival of 1958 and made several modest records in a short space of time for Argo (with Ramsey Lewis), Moodsville and New Jazz. He gave up the police work to focus on his playing career, but was dead within a year, having apparently shot himself.
*Lem's Beat* (New Jazz)

# Kai Winding
TROMBONE
*born* 18 May 1922; *died* 7 May 1983

Like his frequent partner J J Johnson, Winding was in at the start of bebop trombone. He starred in the Stan Kenton band during 1946–7 and then went with Charlie Ventura's group, as well as turning up on one of the Miles Davis 'Birth Of The Cool' dates. During a long stint of session work in the 50s he formed a two-trombone front line with Johnson in what was a short-lived but popular quintet (1954–6). After that he went as far as leading a septet with four trombones in it, which lasted some five years until he slimmed back down to a four-piece group. Thereafter he was mostly a studio man until decamping for Spain in 1977, and in his last years he mostly played at festivals and in one-off tours. In the 40s, Winding played in a surprisingly gruff way, even though his phrasing was straight out of bop, but he was canny enough to smooth out his sound when playing with Johnson so that the two men worked together in an almost indistinguishable manner. His later solo records for Verve have some entertaining moments but often dawdle in novelty arrangements. For the record, his name was pronounced Kai (as in 'eye') Winding (as in 'blowing in the wind').

**The Great Kai And JJ** (Impulse!)

# Norma Winstone
VOCAL
*born* 23 September 1941

She grew up in east London with the voices of Frank Sinatra and Lena Horne, and began singing in the 50s, although it was mostly with dance bands, and it wasn't really until the middle 60s that she began performing in a jazz context. She soon found herself in situations which would tax any singer, performing with the New Jazz Orchestra and in Michael Garrick's group, eventually singing wordlessly and improvising lines, and she also worked with Mike Westbrook and her then husband, pianist John Taylor. She formed Azimuth with Taylor and Kenny Wheeler in 1977, which recorded three albums for ECM, and besides continuing to perform with Wheeler in his big band, Winstone has also worked with a solo vocal group, Vocal Summit, and with both players of her own generation and a younger set. Norma's clear, bright, immaculately pitched singing can seem at odds with the often tough musical surroundings she has dropped herself into, but she is the most self-aware of singers and always seems to find the soul of whatever kind of material she is performing. Her standards work has a beautiful lustre to it, and she sings English – 'It would sound silly, somebody from the East End of London singing "zwee-bop" and things like that' – rather than American. She has written lyrics to a number of modern jazz themes, including work by Steve Swallow and Jimmy Rowles, with whom she recorded his 'The Peacocks', with her lyric, 'The Timeless Place', in 1993. Although she considers herself to have 'an ordinary old voice', she sets a considerable standard for other jazz vocalists to aspire to.

**Well Kept Secret** (Koch)

# Jens Winther
TRUMPET
*born* 29 October 1960

Winther has been a great mainstay of Danish jazz since the late 70s. He played in a number of local small groups and big bands besides leading a quintet of his own, and he visited New York in 1989 and stayed two years. On his return he picked up where he had left off. The Stunt and Olufsen labels have recorded an ambitious musician who has settled his playing in small groups, in jazz orchestras, with choirs and with symphony orchestras. Little of his music has, though, travelled far outside Scandinavia.

**The Four Elements** (Stunt)

# Jimmy Witherspoon
VOCAL
*born* 18 August 1921; *died* 18 September 1997

Spoon crossed between jazz and blues singing better than anybody aside from Jimmy Rushing. He joined Jay McShann's band in 1944 and had a great R&B hit with 'Ain't Nobody's Business' (1947), a song he was happy to sing for the next 50 years. He led his own small groups and began to enjoy great success in the new R&B charts, but there was perhaps a shade too much blues and not enough rhythm in his singing for the emerging market for black pop, and a poor business sense led to his going bankrupt in 1953. A hit appearance at the 1959 Monterey Festival proved to be a grand comeback for the singer, and he began recording with the likes of Coleman Hawkins and Ben Webster, seeing out the 60s better than many of his R&B contemporaries and performing regularly into the 80s, never quite crossing over but staying busy enough. Cancer seemed set to put paid to his career early in the 80s, but he recovered, and was still singing and performing in the year of his death. His discography is stretched across some 20 labels in the LP era alone, and many of the records could stand a revival.

**Some Of My Best Friends Are The Blues** (Prestige)

# Mike Wofford

PIANO
*born 25 February 1938*

Wofford (although born in Texas) is one of several fine pianists on the Californian scene who have rather drifted out of sight in the CD era. In the 60s, he worked with such familiar leaders of the scene as Shelly Manne and led bands of his own, and in the 70s and 80s he built an interesting catalogue of records for Revelation and Discovery; the Jerome Kern collection, originally spread across three LPs, was a notable piece of repertory revision with Anthony Ortega also involved. Aside from a single CD in Concord's Maybeck Hall sequence, though, Wofford has been little heard of recently, and his best music is now long out of print. A new trio record did, however, emerge at the end of 2004.
**Plays Jerome Kern** (Discovery)

# Jimmy Woode

BASS
*born 23 September 1926; died 23 April 2005*

Woode (pronounced 'Wood-ee') is a Philadelphian who made his home in Europe for many years (following the example of his trumpet-playing father, whose second wife was Swedish). After working around Boston in the 40s, and then with Sarah Vaughan and Ella Fitzgerald, he spent five years as bassist in the Duke Ellington Orchestra from 1955. Thereafter he worked all across Europe in both studio and live situations, and often with the Clarke–Boland Big Band. Like most of Ellington's bassmen, Woode was a yeoman timekeeper rather than a dashing soloist, and his professionalism and no-nonsense acuity have lifted every band he's played in. He exemplifies the gentleman bassist, indispensable even though entirely out of the limelight.
**Duke Ellington, Ellington At Newport** (Columbia)

# Sam Wooding

PIANO, BANDLEADER
*born 17 June 1895; died 1 August 1985*

Sam Wooding was one of the first black bandleaders to make a significant impact on New York's nascent jazz scene, though his first group actually played in New Jersey in 1919. He had a capable rather than an outstanding orchestra, but when they went to Europe as the band for the touring revue Chocolate Kiddies (which included Adelaide Hall), they had a major impact on at least two important Europeans who heard them: Hugues Panassié, the noted discographer and Frenchman-about-jazz, and Alfred Lion, who later founded Blue Note Records. Wooding could boast Tommy Ladnier and Gene Sedric among his soloists, and the band undertook a second European jaunt in 1928; but at home the group had less success, Wooding's thunder on home turf having been stolen by the likes of Ellington and Henderson. The fact that the various editions of the orchestra never made any American records (bar one unreleased date for Columbia) helps explain their relative obscurity – their various European discs are much sought-after by collectors, but they're not particularly memorable and here and there are glimpses of the vaudevillian streak which Wooding was perhaps obliged to play up in his touring duties. The pianist forsook bandleading after 1935 in favour of teaching, and leading vocal groups, and he even ran his own record label in the 50s. He was interviewed on a number of occasions in the 60s, which brought his name back to brief prominence, but he seems likely to be a modest footnote in future jazz histories.
**Various, Americans In Paris Vol 1** (EMI Jazztime)

# Phil Woods

ALTO SAXOPHONE, CLARINET
*born 2 November 1931*

Perhaps the professor emeritus of bebop saxophone, as it has endured from one century to the next. He got his start in his early teens, even taking a lesson or two from Lennie Tristano, before going to Juilliard in 1948. When he came out, he had already mastered a fomidable bebop style on the alto saxophone: fast, lean, sweet-sour on ballads and with the blues always hovering in the backgound, it was a sound which soon drew parallels with Charlie Parker, although Woods's kind of emotion had nothing of Parker's tragic power. He began leading small groups in live work, but much of his time was spent as a studio man: he is on probably hundreds of records from the 50s

and 60s, besides numerous albums of his own for Prestige and New Jazz, some of them in tandem with fellow altoist Gene Quill. In 1968 he shifted base to France, where he ran his European Rhythm Machine – with George Gruntz, Gordon Beck, Henri Texier and Daniel Humair – for some four years. In 1972 he returned to the US, had the briefest flirtation with fusion, and then settled down into another sax-and-rhythm-section format, which has lasted some 30 years. Long-standing members of the Woods groups have included Steve Gilmore and Bill Goodwin, various pianists have taken the keyboard role, and Tom Harrell enjoyed a long stay with the group between 1983 and 1989, succeeded by Hal Crook and then Brian Lynch. Woods has kept up a vigorous recording regimen, for Concord, Chesky and other independents, and his number one fan, Paolo Piangiarelli, an Italian who is completely besotted with the saxophonist's playing, has recorded Woods at marathon length on dozens of sessions for his Philology label. A series of live sessions by the Harrell-era quintet has also been released by Mosaic in a boxed
set. Woods has sailed imperturbably on, although he was, after an earlier affiliation with RCA, never given the imprimatur of major-label support: some in the business thought him too consistent to really make a breakout record, and perhaps that reliability has been his long suit and his vulnerable spot, since many have more or less taken him for granted. The various quintet albums (there have been some strong big-band records too) are actually a fine store of original compositions as well as a textbook example of a band kept fresh by its sheer love of playing in a familiar idiom. Woods has, like many musicians, grown deeper on ballads, and remains adroit even if a little of the old failsafe velocity has been filed away now. For a long time, his group has attempted to play without any amplification, and it has sometimes made him testy with noisy audiences: 'I don't mind a little light chat at the bar, but that's all!' He has had problems with emphysema in the new century, but recent records suggest the indomitable spirit endures.

*Integrity* (Red)

# Sam Woodyard
DRUMS
*born* 7 January 1925; *died* 20 September 1988

Woodyard worked in Milt Buckner's trio in the early 50s, without drawing much attention to himself, but his major spell in the limelight came as a member of Duke Ellington's orchestra, which he joined in 1955 and where he stayed for 11 years. Of all Ellington's drummers, Woodyard is often the most exasperating – clumping and inappropriate on some music, deft and humorously swinging on other pieces, and on occasion so good that one hardly notices him. Depending on which Sam decided to turn up that day, Duke's band often thrived in his presence, which the leader must have settled for. After leaving the orchestra, Woodyard settled in Los Angeles but didn't do a great deal thereafter, bothered by spells of ill-health: he eventually settled in Paris, where Steve Lacy persuaded him to play on his RCA record *The Door* (1988), just a few weeks before Sam passed away. On the record cited, he hums and drums on 'Limbo Jazz' in a way which is pure Woodyard.

**Duke Ellington, *Duke Ellington Meets Coleman Hawkins* (Impulse!)**

# Reggie Workman
BASS
*born* 26 June 1937

Workman was an exception almost from his earliest days in the music: while he was as strong and solid a timekeeper as any of the hard-bop bassists of the late 50s, he became just as interested in playing the free music of a few years later, and he maintained that ambidexterity. He grew up in Philadelphia and was working with his fellow resident McCoy Tyner in a trio accompanying visiting players from around 1956. A year later he was in New York, and worked prolifically around the city, spending several important months with John Coltrane in 1961 and playing on *Live At The Village Vanguard* (Impulse!). While he also worked on records such as Archie Shepp's *Four For Trane* (1964), most of his 60s playing was done in more conventional hard-bop groups, including Art Blakey's Jazz Messengers and studio dates with Lee Morgan, Wayne Shorter, Freddie Hubbard and others. He has been involved in jazz education since the end of the 60s and has worked in theatre and dance projects with his wife, the choreographer Maya Milanovic. While carrying on long-term playing relationships with musicians such as Mal Waldron, in the 90s he reasserted his empathy with the avant-garde, working with Andrew Cyrille, Oliver Lake and Marilyn Crispell, and recording some outstanding sessions for the Postcards label.

*Summit Conference* (Postcards)

# World Saxophone Quartet
## GROUP

Perhaps the first supergroup to emerge from the loft jazz of the 70s, the World Saxophone Quartet was made up of David Murray, Oliver Lake, Hamiet Bluiett and Julius Hemphill, and they first came together as a performing group in 1976. While their early style was an informal and largely ad hoc mix of improvising and sketched-out structures, they soon settled down into a perhaps surprisingly formal outlook: Hemphill was one of their major writers, and the group mixed the feel of a vintage swing-era sax section with the bluster and bite of a free-music ensemble. They often appeared in evening dress and had their own kind of stage routines (such as Oliver Lake, a few minutes into the performance, asking the sound crew to shut off the amplification, always a crowd-pleaser). Arthur Blythe eventually replaced Hemphill after the latter became ill, and John Purcell became a regular dep for any member who wasn't able to take the stage (he eventually took over from Blythe full-time). Their many albums, some augmented by other musicians, include concept records devoted to the music of Ellington and others. What was once a radical band has settled, like most other such bands, into repertory, but it's still a good group.

*Steppin' With The World Saxophone Quartet* (Black Saint)

# World's Greatest Jazz Band
## GROUP

Yank Lawson and Bob Haggart had already been playing together for many years when, in 1968, they were urged by the jazz party organizer Dick Gibson to go full-time with a group of veteran Dixielanders who had been working on the same stage at Gibson's parties for a number of years. The line-up included Billy Butterfield, Bud Freeman, Ralph Sutton and Bob Wilber, and under Gibson's informal management The World's Greatest Jazz Band (a name which was also Gibson's idea) was born. Although there were high hopes for the group to stage a major revival in their kind of jazz, the end of the 60s was not the time or the place, and it existed mainly as a genial nostalgia band for anyone who was nostalgic enough to want to hear them. The personnel changed to accommodate many substitutions as the WGJB carried on, although Lawson and Haggart remained the linchpins, and in the end they abandoned their somewhat inaccurate title.

*Live At The Roosevelt Grill* (Atlantic)

# Frank Wright
## TENOR SAXOPHONE
*born* 9 July 1935; *died* 17 May 1990

Wright's blustering, almost chaotic tenor playing was inspired by Albert Ayler's example: previous to that he had played bass in R&B groups in Cleveland, where he first heard Ayler. He moved to New York in time to be part of the first wave of the new free players, where he performed in the usual circles and made the obligatory album for ESP, *Your Prayer*. He went over to Paris in 1969 and cut some recordings for BYG there, in company with Muhammad Ali, Bobby Few and Alan Silva. Thereafter he never seemed to stay in one place for long, working in Paris, New York, London and Berlin, and making desultory recordings as he went. Wright's playing eventually achieved a degree of expressive power, but a lot of the time he seemed to be playing almost in a crude parody of Ayler's idiom, and the results were rarely satisfying on any level.

*Adieu Little Man* (Center Of The World)

## Leo Wright
ALTO SAXOPHONE, FLUTE
*born* 14 December 1933; *died* 4 January 1991

Wright was a Texan who picked up saxophone tips from John Hardee before going on to study the flute at college. He joined Dizzy Gillespie's small group in 1959 and stayed for three years, after which he freelanced in New York as a sideman and led small groups of his own. But in 1963 he left for Europe and never returned. Settling at first in Scandinavia and then in Berlin, he became a familiar face at festivals and in studio big bands, eventually shifting base to Vienna, where he effectively retired in the early 80s although he returned to action a few times, notably in the Paris Reunion Band. Wright was very good on both alto and flute, a feelingful blues player in particular, which was nicely exploited on his two rather forgotten albums for Atlantic, *Blues Shout* (1960) and *Suddenly The Blues* (1962).
**Suddenly The Blues** (Atlantic)

## Richard Wyands
PIANO
*born* 2 July 1928

An evergreen musician whose authoritative but entirely orthodox musicianship has brought him only modest attention over the years. He grew up in California and worked as a member of the house rhythm section at San Francisco's Black Hawk club in the early 50s, before touring as an accompanist to both Ella Fitzgerald and Carmen McRae. The latter gig took him to New York in 1958, and he was notably busy as a sideman for the next few years on the New York scene. In 1965 he became the regular pianist for Kenny Burrell, touring with him over a ten-year period, and after that he could be seen accompanying another wide range of musicians, including Zoot Sims, Frank Wess, Frank Morgan, Benny Carter and Teddy Edwards. He has made a select handful of records under his own leadership, whose unassuming excellence probably says something abut his standing: there's nothing untoward in any of them, just honest, unfussy piano craftsmanship.
**Reunited** (Criss Cross)

## Xanadu
RECORD COMPANY

The experienced producer Don Schlitten founded this label in New York in 1975. At a time when bebop and hard bop were entirely out of jazz fashion, Schlitten saw to it that musicians such as Al Cohn, Jimmy Raney, Barry Harris, Dolo Coker and others were making records for a sympathetic label, and a fine catalogue of new releases was created in this idiom. At the same time, a parallel series reissued (or, in some cases, issued for the first time) rare and broadcast material from the 40s and 50s. Unfortunately, the label seemed to stop at the end of the vinyl era, and most of the catalogue is still awaited on CD, although some of the records have been licensed to a few territories for reissue in the newer format.

## Yosuke Yamashita
PIANO
*born* 26 February 1942

The Tokyo-born Yamashita began playing jazz in his teens, working with Sadao Watanabe and others, and playing in a reflective sort of bop idiom. By the end of the 60s he had taken a dramatic turn towards a more freely formed style, and he formed a long-standing trio with saxophonist Akira Sakata and drummer Shota Koyama, which could play in an explosive free manner as well as negotiating more structured music. They recorded numerous albums for the Japanese label Frasco, but word of Yamashita's eminence spread only slowly in a period when modern Japanese jazz was scarcely known outside its own territory. In the 80s he played more frequently at festivals, and was finally signed to the Japanese arm of Verve in the early 90s, when he commenced playing with his New York Trio, which featured Cecil McBee and Pheeroan akLaff. This was a more midstream post-bop band than his Japanese ensemble, but it was still a fine vehicle for his dense, exuberant and virtuosic playing, which can often sound like a meeting of the disparate methods of Paul Bley and Cecil Taylor: a crisp, decisive touch which picks at melodic structures with a flinty incisiveness. His solo work can be just as intense,

although it inevitably has a more musing quality to it too. Despite the Verve records being widely distributed, he remains comparatively and unjustly little-known.
***Kurdish Dance*** (Verve)

# Jimmy Yancey

PIANO

*born* 20 February 1898; *died* 17 September 1951

Yancey turned up at the height of the boogie-woogie piano boom of the late 30s and finally claimed some of the action which he had played a significant role in formulating. He had performed as a singer and dancer in vaudeville from the age of six and eventually settled in Chicago, where he learned to play piano and began working in that capacity around 1920. He was also a useful ball player, and eventually got a job at Comiskey Park, home of the Chicago White Sox, where he was the groundskeeper from 1925 for some 25 years. This took him away from becoming a more ubiquitous musician, but along with Meade Lux Lewis and others he began working out the details of the boogie-woogie piano style. Lewis's recording of 'Yancey Special' in 1936 got Jimmy some attention (and actually led to a court case over whose tune it was – Yancey won), and in 1939 he made his first records. Yancey was a very limited player: several of his originals are based on the same kind of material ('Midnight Stomp', 'Yancey Stomp' and 'Yancey Ltd', for instance, are all really the same tune), but he had a remarkable ability to differentiate the detail of each of his solos. He uses a greater range of bass figures than almost any of the other boogie masters, and he was ready to vary them in dialogue with his right hand as a solo progressed. This gave him even more expressivity when he was playing a blues, and when he also sang, as in his transfixing version of 'Death Letter Blues' (1940), it could be extraordinarily poignant. His wife Estella, usually known as Mama Yancey (1896–1986), sang on some of his records too, but by himself Yancey delivered his most personal work. His solo 'At The Window', part of his 1943 recordings for the Session label, is unforgettable once heard.
***Jimmy Yancey Vols 1–3*** (Document)

# Yellowjackets

GROUP

Among the most successful of all fusion bands, the Yellowjackets were formed in 1980 by Russell Ferrante (keyboards) and Jimmy Haslip (bass), who a year earlier had worked with the guitarist Robben Ford on an album: although Ford subsequently guested with the band and played on their first few records, he was never a full-time member. Saxophonist Marc Russo then became the solo voice in the group, and he was eventually replaced by Bob Mintzer in 1990, a move which at least gave the jazz content of their music a more rigorous feel. The band's output has tended to vacillate between jazz, rock and a bland kind of world music (one of their records is called *Samurai Samba*, 1984): they're not quite smooth enough for smooth jazz, but there's nothing abrasive or particularly challenging for listeners to feel unsettled by, and their records are cleverly produced to minimize any potential problems. Their audience tends to consist of the same people who support groups such as Mannheim Steamroller and Shadowfax, purveyors of busy and inconsequential music which, for all its hummability, vanishes from the mind as soon as it's over.
***Club Nocturne*** (Warner Bros)

# Yerba Buena Jazz Band

See LU WATTERS.

# John Young

PIANO

*born* 16 March 1922

Young hardly ventured outside his home base of Chicago, and as a result became something of a local legend. He started as a member of the Andy Kirk band in the early 40s, played behind R&B saxophonists in the 50s, and eventually established his own trio. Small-group work and backing visiting giants kept him busy thereafter, although he also formed a regular alliance with that other great Chicago homebody, Von Freeman. The record cited catches him on a typical 1959 trio session: catchy originals such as 'Cubana Chant' and the title track are very engaging, and his unfussy style

handles ballads and the blues with equal aplomb.
**Serenata** (Delmark)

## Larry Young
ORGAN, PIANO
*born* 7 October 1940; *died* 30 March 1978

Young studied piano but more or less taught himself the organ, and was playing in New Jersey R&B bands from the late 50s. He made his first album as a leader for Prestige but thereafter recorded for Blue Note, and took the almost unique step of using the organ in a dedicated hard-bop idiom rather than choosing the soul-jazz route. This led to records such as the very powerful *Unity* (1965), which featured Young with Joe Henderson, Woody Shaw and Elvin Jones, and has the piledriving intensity of the best post-Coltrane hard bop. Thereafter he drifted towards the unfolding medium of jazz-rock, worked in Lifetime with Tony Williams and John McLaughlin, jammed with Jimi Hendrix, and made it into the populous cast of Miles Davis's *Bitches Brew* (1970). But Young – sometimes known by his Muslim name, Khalid Yasin – never found his place in the music as it expanded in the 70s. His final albums were disappointing – feeble, in comparison with *Unity* – as, like many others, he struggled to mix music which was worthy of him with elements that seemed as if they might have audience appeal. He went into hospital with an infection early in 1978 and died as a result of contracting pneumonia while there.
**Unity** (Blue Note)

## Lee Young
DRUMS
*born* 7 March 1917

Lester's younger brother was born in New Orleans, and performed in the Young family band from his earliest years, having learned to play trumpet, trombone, soprano saxophone and piano. He eventually settled on the drums, and also worked as a singer in clubs on the West Coast. In the early 40s he played with Lionel Hampton and Nat Cole, before forming a group which Lester eventually joined at the end of 1941. The group split up when the Youngs' father died, and

thereafter Lee worked in various groups in and around Los Angeles, as well as doing studio work in Hollywood. From 1953 he was a regular member of Nat Cole's trio, and from the early 60s until his retirement around 1983 he worked as a record producer, often doing key work for Motown and other labels. Unobtrusive on the records he worked on as a performer, this shrewd, credible and failsafe professional was everything, basically, that Lester wasn't.
**Nat Cole, *After Midnight*** (Capitol)

## Lester Young
TENOR SAXOPHONE, CLARINET
*born* 27 August 1909; *died* 15 March 1959

Young's father raised his family near to New Orleans and taught them all music, which led to Lester and his brothers playing in a family band and appearing in carnival shows. Having tried several instruments, Lester took up the alto in his teens and played on that horn with a band called Art Bronson's Bostonians during 1928. Eventually, by now playing tenor, he joined Walter Page's Blue Devils and based himself in Kansas City from 1933. He was soon enough a local hero on the horn, and on a famous night in December 1933 he traded choruses with a visiting Coleman Hawkins for hours, tiring out all the piano players and obliging Ben Webster to go and wake up Mary Lou Williams so she could take over. The following year he joined Count Basie and began his most famous association, but at the start he was there for only a matter of weeks, subsequently moving to Fletcher Henderson's band, where he took over Coleman Hawkins's chair. His style was so unwelcome in the band, though, that he left within a few months and after playing with different groups rejoined Basie in Kansas City. He was with the Count when the band made their move to New York at the end of the year, stopping in Chicago to make Young's first records: 'Shoe Shine Boy' and 'Lady Be Good' mark perhaps the most extraordinary debut on record jazz has ever seen, Young's lithe, trippingly exuberant but almost singing delivery causing a sensation among musicians (although audiences, by now accustomed to the Hawkins tenor sound, were often divided). For four years, Young was one of the leading voices of

Basie's band, sparring with his friend Herschel Evans in the reed section and creating solos on records such as 'Lester Leaps In', 'Taxi War Dance', 'Tickle Toe' and (his own favourite) 'Clap Hands! Here Comes Charlie' which set a new style for tenor players. Instead of Hawkins, Young pointed to two surprise influences, Jimmy Dorsey and Frankie Trumbauer, whose light and clear playing and complete mastery of the architecture of a solo were paramount to him. Some of his best playing in the period comes on the session dates he did with Teddy Wilson, backing Billie Holiday's singing: she gave him his long-standing nickname, 'Pres', a reduction of 'President'.

Young left Basie in 1940 and led a sextet, and then a band with his brother Lee, which dispersed following the death of their father. He then freelanced in New York before rejoining Basie in 1943, appeared in Gjon Mili's film *Jamming The Blues*, and became a popular success with the public as well as with musicians: but it all came crashing down when he was drafted into the army in September 1944. An introvert with a language all his own and a curious kind of knowing naivety about him, Young could hardly have been less suited to army life, and he was court-martialled early in 1945, spending several months in detention (one army psychiatrist called him 'a constitutional psychopath'). On his release he began a round of touring with his own small groups, and playing regularly with Jazz At The Philharmonic. Many have suggested that Young's time in the army scarred him so badly that his playing never recovered, but that is scarcely borne out by his records: for much of the next few years he was still in wonderful form, and though his sound had begun to grow heavier and used a wider vibrato and more honking notes, many of his solos remain masterful. By 1950, though, a deterioration had started to set in, as his small-group records for Verve began to document. In this period, apologists for Young suggest that his musical thinking was growing ever more modern as bebop drifted around him, but what hurts about all of Young's post-1950 music is its constant stumbling. Often he will start a solo beautifully, only for it to fall apart somewhere in the middle, and on track after track there is something to spoil what he does. While never a hard-drug user – 'New Orleans ciga-

rettes' were about the worst he could tolerate in that line – Young had always been a drinker, and by the 50s he was a remorseless alcoholic.

He rejoined Basie on occasion during the decade, and he played with Billie Holiday on the celebrated 1957 telecast *The Sound Of Jazz*, but his solo sounded feeble. He was always something of a dandy, meticulous about his hair and cologne; his private language baffled many but was clear enough once you understood such phrases as 'Can Madam burn?' ('Can your wife cook?'), 'You rang the bell' ('You're right'), and so on. In January 1959, he played the start of an engagement at the Paris Blue Note club, but was too ill to complete it and returned home to New York, where he died a day later. His influence on a generation of tenor players – Stan Getz, Zoot Sims, Al Cohn and many more – was obvious enough, but his concern to play a flowing melodic line became itself a totemic part of modern jazz. In his memory, Charles Mingus wrote 'Goodbye Pork Pie Hat', a reference to Young's favourite headgear, and Wayne Shorter composed the even more poignant 'Lester Left Town'.

**Count Basie, *1936–1938*** (Classics)

# Snooky Young

TRUMPET
*born* 3 February 1919

Young toured the South as a boy with his family band, but his first important engagement was with Jimmie Lunceford's band, leading the trumpet section from 1939. In 1942 he joined Lionel Hampton, and from then on divided his time between that band and Count Basie's, although he eventually spent five years with Basie from 1957. In 1962 he took on a staffer's job at NBC, but also joined the Jones–Lewis orchestra in 1966, and played with them until leaving for the West Coast in 1972 to feature as part of the *Tonight Show* band. Since then he has been a regular in many West Coast institutions, including Frank Capp's Juggernaut big band, the Clayton–Hamilton Orchestra, and Jeannie and Jimmy Cheatham's group. Young was an impeccable lead-man for the duration of his long career, able to play the most demanding of parts, and as a result his skilful solos, often given a rascally, high-wire treatment, have been largely under-valued. The record cited is a very rare small-group date with his old friend and Basie bandmate Marshal Royal.

**Snooky's And Marshal's Album** (Concord)

# Trummy Young

TROMBONE

born 12 January 1912; died 10 September 1984

Having perfected an individual style on the trombone, Young found that all his working contexts were against him. He started on trumpet, changed to trombone when he began working in Washington DC in his teens, and joined Earl Hines's band in 1933, staying three years although he had little featured space on the band's records. In 1937 he joined Jimmie Lunceford and became a significant soloist with that talented ensemble: his 'trumpet' style is usually credited as a mix of Jimmy Harrison and Louis Armstrong, and Lunceford's outfit offered him some of his best solo opportunities. After leaving in 1943, though, Young searched without much success for a productive role. He worked under numerous leaders and turned up on a pioneer bebop session, playing on Dizzy Gillespie's 'Good Bait' (1945), where he sounds able if uncomprehending. By the end of the decade he was in Hawaii, and then came back to take a sideman role in Louis Armstrong's All Stars, a gig which lasted him until 1964. Like every other sideman in that band, Young was eventually worn down by the group's tiring schedules, and though he loved Pops, there was little enough of interest for him to do: some of his playing on surviving live records by the group is dispiriting. He was still playing at jazz parties and on occasional tours into the 80s.

**Jimmie Lunceford, 1939–1940** (Classics)

# Young Tuxedo Brass Band

GROUP

Established in New Orleans by the clarinettist John Casimir in 1938, the YTBB helped bring back the old brass-band tradition of the city in the post-war years, a useful counterweight to the kind of jazz which was otherwise being touted as 'central' to the New Orleans revival – even though many of the small-group jazz players, such as George Lewis, would also work in the brass bands when they were convened. The group – usually two trumpets, two trombones, two reeds, brass bass and two drummers – continued to be led by Casimir until his death in 1963, and made the seminal *Jazz Begins* for Atlantic in 1958, a document of what, to some, sounded like a raggedy old group trying to be deliberately primitive for anthropological microphones: actually, it was the way the Band sounded anyway. Several others led the ensemble as it continued into the 80s, and in 1983 it made another record – this time called *Jazz Continues* (504).

**Jazz Begins** (Atlantic)

# Rachel Z

KEYBOARDS

born 28 December 1962

Rachel Nicolazzo grew up in New York, attended the New England Conservatory and began following jazz, although her mother had hoped for a career in opera for her. She worked in the Boston area in the mid-80s before going back to New York and moving towards fusion-oriented music, touring with Najee and eventually joining Mike Mainieri's Steps Ahead. Perhaps her major association, though, has been with Wayne Shorter, and she took a significant hand in the playing and arranging on his *High Life* set (Verve, 1995). Her own solo records have suggested an idiosyncratic variety of approaches and influences, without making a memorable enough mark.

**Room Of One's Own** (NYC)

# Chester Zardis

BASS

born 27 May 1900; died 14 August 1990

The 'Little Bear' was perhaps the last of the old-time New Orleans bassists. He began playing in 1916 and worked for Buddy Petit, Chris Kelly, Kid Rena, Jack Carey, Fats Pichon – most of the great bandleaders of the day. He recorded with Bunk Johnson and George Lewis at the start of the revival in 1942, and then worked in Denver for a long spell before returning to New Orleans in 1951. But Zardis gave up music for farming three years later, and it wasn't until the establishment of Preservation Hall that he came back to the scene: he wrote a letter to Allan Jaffe which said: 'Tell George [Lewis] I want to join his band if he need a Dixie Bass man I am not doing anything' (sic). Thereafter he was busy both at the Hall and with bands such as the Legends Of Jazz and the Original Liberty Jazz Band, getting as far as Australia and having a documentary made about him in 1989. To the end he hung on to his fine bass tone – 'That comes before everything else' – and he played his last gig at the age of 90.

**Jim Robinson,** *Birthday Memorial Session* (GHB)

## Joe Zawinul
PIANO, KEYBOARDS
*born* 7 July 1932

Zawinul grew up in pre-war Vienna, with *Volksmusik* and *Zigeuner* songs in his ears, and he started on accordion before studying piano, later at the Vienna Conservatory. By the 50s he was playing in Austrian dance bands and doing club work with Hans Koller and Friedrich Gulda. He left for the US in 1959, playing as Dinah Washington's accompanist for two years, and then joined Cannonball Adderley's band in 1961: he remained with him until 1970, working all through the soul-jazz decade and writing such hits as 'Mercy Mercy Mercy'. If it didn't seem like a very radical band, Zawinul – 'I was more or less the quarterback and Cannonball was for me a security thing' – still began to contribute some surprising new ideas to what was otherwise a happy-go-lucky kind of band book, such as the mysterious '74 Miles Away' (1967), which seems to prefigure some of what he would do with Weather Report – 'I tell you, Cannonball's band at that time played more modern music than Miles'. But he went on to join the Miles Davis circle, on a somewhat informal basis (at this point Davis had a satellite group of musicians who would work on some of his innumerable studio sessions), and he gave Davis the music for 'In A Silent Way', as well as effectively setting up the electric keyboard axis which would settle the trumpeter's music for the next few years. At the end of 1970, he formed Weather Report, ostensibly with Wayne Shorter and Miroslav Vitous, although in

effect it was always really Zawinul's band. After Shorter left in 1985, Zawinul led first Weather Update and then the Zawinul Syndicate, which continued in a similar vein – although, with less for Zawinul to kick against in the later bands, they sound more like a one-man show. He has also done some quasi-classical projects, which have been largely disappointing. As the architect of much of what came to be called jazz-rock or fusion, Zawinul could arguably deserve as much opprobrium as praise, but the point that Weather Report at their best stood head and shoulders above their competitors underscores that the many bad fusion bands which came after them aren't really his fault. He helped formulate a whole playing vocabulary for the synthesizer, yet since those instruments have now acquired the ability to sound like anything, the individuality which he brought to them has been wholly dispersed, which may explain why his later music lacks much of his signature inventiveness. As a composer, he is surprisingly left alone by most other players: besides the inescapable 'Birdland' and 'Mercy Mercy Mercy', few of his tunes have ever been covered by other musicians.

**Weather Report,** *Black Market* (Columbia)

## Denny Zeitlin
PIANO
*born* 10 April 1938

Zeitlin has only rarely broken cover in the jazz field and gives the impression that he has a reluctance to commit to any one style. He was born in Chicago but moved West, having also qualified as a psychiatrist, a career which he has also practised, and for some years led an occasional trio in the San Francisco area with Charlie Haden on bass. He appeared to give up music altogether for a time in the 70s, but eventually began performing and recording again, although by the late 80s he was making prissy records for the new-age-orientated Windham Hill label. Albums in Concord's solo and duo series made at Maybeck Recital Hall were stronger meat, although Zeitlin's music does have the feel of a somewhat pointless cleverness to it. He might be better known as a writer than a performer, since Bill Evans made a popular piece out of his tune 'Quiet Now'.

*Live At Maybeck Recital Hall* (Concord)

## Si Zentner
TROMBONE, BANDLEADER
*born* 13 June 1917; *died* 21 January 2000

One of America's longest-serving band-leaders. He grew up in New York but spent most of his career based on the other coast, working for Les Brown and Harry James in the early 40s and then as a studio musician for MGM from 1949. In 1957, he swam against the tide by forming a new big band, playing primarily in the swing idiom, and against the odds kept it going, even into the 90s. While he was not an exceptional soloist himself, Zentner loved the sound of a big band and insisted on its primacy in American music. Remarkably, he recorded 20 albums for Liberty in the 60s (almost none of them have been reissued) and four for RCA. While some of them approach the material from a more middle-of-the-road perspective, Zentner wasn't concerned with jazz purism: he just cared about big-band music. He played his last engagement as a leader in Las Vegas when he was 83 years old.
*Waltz In Jazz Time* (Liberty)

## Monica Zetterlund
VOCAL
*born* 20 September 1938; *died* 12 May 2005

Zetterlund is a particularly European phenomenon, a singer grounded in jazz but whose work also touches on folk, pop and classical songs and who is familiar to Swedish audiences as an actress too. She began singing in her teens and by the time she was 20 she was one of Sweden's singing stars, working with Arne Domnérus and Lars Gullin and approaching her material with a cool restraint that has its own kind of charm: singing mostly in English, she delivered lines with a clarity which eschewed the breathy tendencies of many of her contemporaries. In the 60s, she cut a memorable session with Bill Evans's trio (*Waltz For Debby*, 1964), and dividing her time between singing and acting, she has released records regularly ever since, although some have more jazz-directed settings than others.
*Swedish Sensation!* (EMI)

## Attila Zoller
GUITAR
*born* 13 June 1927; *died* 26 January 1998

Zoller was a Hungarian who began playing in Budapest in the late 40s, then moved to Austria where he worked as an accompanist in Vienna. He played bop in Jutta Hipp's group in Germany and then worked with Hans Koller, before winning a scholarship to the Lenox School in 1959 and settling in the US. Zoller was catholic in his jazz tastes, and he worked for a range of leaders which included Herbie Mann, Red Norvo, Astrud Gilberto and Benny Goodman, as well as working in a trio with Lee Konitz and Albert Mangelsdorff. He played frequently as a soloist or small-group leader, and toured Europe on an almost annual basis while remaining resident in the US, and his gentle, romantically inclined playing was recorded many times, even though he never enjoyed the sponsorship of American labels. His records for Enja and L+R have perhaps the best of his work.
*Memories Of Pannonia* (Enja)

## John Zorn
ALTO SAXOPHONE
*born* 2 September 1953

Zorn's explosive evolution and mush-rooming output have been giddily entertaining to follow. Born in New York, he studied piano and other instruments and was a precocious absorber of music, getting stuck into the catalogue of 20th-century composers from an early age and writing (and recording) his first original works at 14. While at St Louis's Webster College he began listening to the jazz avant-garde, and after hearing Anthony Braxton's *For Alto*, he took up the saxophone himself. In 1975 he settled back in New York and became a focal point in an enclave of musicians who mixed free improvisation with organizational procedures which were their own variety of 'composing', and included Eugene Chadbourne, Tom Cora, Wayne Horvitz, Polly Bradfield and LaDonna Smith. This group steadily expanded until it encompassed what was effectively a movement characterized as the 'downtown' musicians. Zorn played alto and worked in both solo and group situations: he often delivered solo performances where he would dismantle the instrument, and use either just the mouthpiece or a set of game calls, occasionally blowing into a bucket of water. While this might have seemed like mere comedy, more in the Dutch tradition of Han Bennink than anything, Zorn approached it with a serious intensity which somehow made one believe that it was valid art. He also initiated a compositional procedure based around 'game theory', where – inspired by the wargames produced by the Avalon Hill company – the musical participants work via a series of commands chosen from cue cards and the gestural direction of the leader. *Lacrosse*, *Pool*, *Archery* and particularly *Cobra* were all examples of this idiom. By the early 80s, Zorn had attracted something of a cult media following as well as a local one, and he began receiving commissions from Europe and Japan in addition to his American work. The downtown movement gathered impetus from the establishment in 1987 of the club The Knitting Factory, which acted as the premier venue for the Zorn circle. Zorn himself had signed to the major label Nonesuch in 1984, and his albums *The Big Gundown* (1985), an homage to Ennio Morricone, and *Spillane* (1987) were major statements which set up the former duck-call blower as a premier American composer-arranger. His own work expanded to include a quartet convened to play the music of Sonny Clark; News For Lulu, a jazz-directed trio with George Lewis and Bill Frisell; a quintet sometimes called Spy Vs Spy, which performed Ornette Coleman's music, treating it much as a thrash-metal band might; and another quintet, Naked City, which featured Frisell, Horvitz, Fred Frith and Joey Baron, playing mostly wincingly brief but carefully scored outbursts of noise. By the 90s he was dividing his time between New York and Tokyo, where he received many commissions, particularly for filmscoring work. He then established his own record labels Tzadik and Avant, the first of which produces a series dedicated to Radical Jewish Culture, and – after a falling-out with The Knitting Factory – his own venue, Tonic. The most significant of his recent performing vehicles has been the group Masada, with Baron, Dave Douglas and Greg Cohen, which seemingly mixes various aspects of Jewish music with a performing aesthetic that displays a kinship with the old Ornette Coleman quartet: it has already created a large body of recorded work.

Zorn's relationship with jazz is at best side-long: while a dedicated improviser and someone who plays with many other 'jazz musicians', he deliberately resists category, and his huge consumption of other people's music has given his own work a hyperventilating quality. Zorn admirers often consider him a masterful bebop alto player, but when he does perform in something approaching that style his playing has little of the tension and none of the relaxation of the great beboppers, often sounding more strangulated than anything. His greatest skill is in assembling often unexpected groups of players and getting a startling, unrepeatable result, although lately, especially with his Masada work, he seems to have retreated into his own kind of repertory. The documentation of his music on Tzadik and Avant – there are something like 20 volumes of his film music alone, and at one time there was a report that a Japanese company would be issuing 150 CDs of Zorn music, although so far it hasn't happened – has become bloated, and at times Zorn reminds one of Frank Zappa: just as the endlessly prolific Zappa did his most original and inventive music in the 60s, so is Zorn's 70s work (collected in a boxed set called *The Parachute Years*) likely to be his most lasting or surprising. These days, the man who wrote a piece called 'The Perfume Of A Critic's Burning Flesh' rarely speaks to the media and reputedly forbids his musicians to as well – even though it was critical applause which set up his European commissions and thenceforth helped resource so much of his later work. But we don't mind.

**The Classic Guide To Strategy** (Tzadik)

# Bojan Zulfikarpasic
PIANO
*born* 2 February 1968

Born in Belgrade, Bojan Z (he regularly uses this abbreviated name to help out announcers and audiences) started playing jazz-rock in his teens and, given the scarcity of players in that place and time, was soon one of the top performers and a bit of a star in the city. And then, 'I went with these older guys, playing music that nobody likes, except a few alcoholics and a few prostitutes, which was more or less the steady audience in one jazz club in Belgrade – a hard decision but very good for me!' Since then he has settled in Paris (1988) and worked with Noël Akchoté, Henri Texier and others, and been a regular playing partner of saxophonist Julien Lourau. Zulfikarpasic is an expansive virtuoso with a notable inclination to use both hands to maximum effect, particularly when playing solo – 'That was my first shock when I did my first solo concert, my left hand felt paralysed. I was looking at it and going, come on!' His several records for Label Bleu – especially with trio partners Scott Colley and Nasheet Waits – highlight a clever and unpredictable imagination at work.

*Transpacifik* (Label Bleu)

## Bob Zurke

PIANO
*born* 17 January 1912; *died* 16 February 1944

Born in Detroit, Zurke got his start in the Philadelphia band of Oliver Naylor in the middle 20s, already a gifted player at an early age. After a period of club work in the Detroit area, he replaced Joe Sullivan in the 1936 Bob Crosby band and became one of the key players in the band, his skilful boogie-woogie playing helping the band to score some hits during that craze, particularly his rattling version of 'Honky Tonk Train Blues' (1938). In 1939 he went out on his own as a big-band leader, but despite cutting 29 titles for Victor over the course of a year, the group was nothing special and foundered in 1941. Thereafter Zurke worked as a solo, and it was during a long residency at Los Angeles' Hangover Club that he died suddenly, his health affected by a bad drinking problem.

**Bob Crosby,** *The Big Noise* (Halcyon)

## Mike Zwerin

WRITER, TROMBONE, BASS TRUMPET
*born* 18 May 1930

Zwerin was a New Yorker by birth, and his most famous hour on record was his association with the Miles Davis nonet, and he plays an ensemble role on airshot recordings of some of the 'Birth Of The Cool' material in 1948. He gave up music after graduating from college and went into the steel business, but resumed playing in 1957 and mixed freelancing with his day job for a number of years, performing with Orchestra USA in the early 60s and making a record of Kurt Weill tunes with a sextet drawn from the Orchestra. But writing was his real forte (he might dispute that), and he began working in journalism in 1964, writing for *The Village Voice* for five years before moving to London in 1969, and then settling in Paris, where he has long been a music correspondent for the *International Herald Tribune*. He has played more or less for fun since then (although he complains that French dentists ruined his teeth) and has written several entertaining books, two about his life, and another concerning the survival of jazz under Nazi regimes. A funny and perceptive writer and an entertaining man.

**Mack The Knife** (RCA)

## Axel Zwingenberger

PIANO
*born* 7 May 1955

Improbably enough, one of the leading and most prolific exponents of modern boogie-woogie piano is this Hamburger, whose many records on his own Vagabond label kept the music current through the 70s and 80s. He started playing the style in his teens and made his first records at 21, turning up regularly on German television and touring with trad leaders such as Max Collie and Monty Sunshine. He made a point of making contact with the music's roots, too, recording with Mama Yancey and Sippie Wallace during the 80s and also featuring alongside Joe Newman, Lionel Hampton and Jay McShann. But some of his best work on record has been with his brother Torsten (b 1959), a drummer. Zwingenberger's approach has all the hallmarks of the great boogie stylists and he makes sure that he has enough variety in his music to keep a limited form as fresh as it can be. Like Meade Lux Lewis, he has also tinkered with the celeste.

**Boogie Woogie Brothers** (Vagabond)